20

95bamz

Index to Festschriften in Librarianship

Index to Festschriften in Librarianship

J. PERIAM DANTON
with the assistance of OTTILIA C. ANDERSON

R. R. BOWKER COMPANY, New York & London 1970

Published by R. R. Bowker Company
(A XEROX COMPANY)
1180 Avenue of the Americas, New York, N.Y. 10036

Standard Book Number: 8352–0261–5
Library of Congress Catalog Card Number: 75–88796

MANUFACTURED IN THE UNITED STATES OF AMERICA

For JENNIFER and JAPY

who didn't interfere

at all this time

Contents

Preface ix

Introduction 1

Guide to the User 11

Guide de l'Usager 17

Anweisungen für den Benutzer 23

Code Abbreviations of Festschriften 29

Reviews of the Festschriften 53

Author and Subject Index to the Festschrift Articles 63

TABLES

I. Number of Festschriften by Country of Origin 9

II. Number of Festschriften by Date of Publication 10

Preface

THE INCEPTION OF THIS WORK goes back about a dozen years when Mrs. Kathryn G. Thayer, then Librarian of the School of Librarianship of the University of California, my colleague, Professor Fredric J. Mosher, and I chanced to discover that each of us, independently, was gathering titles of *Festschrift* publications in the field of librarianship with the idea of attempting some kind of bibliographical control of the articles in them. Out of generosity, or a sagacity greater than my own, they relinquished their interests in the project to me. I have since had occasion to regret this action, but I am glad to express my gratitude to them for letting me use the material they had collected.

A work such as this can hardly be begun, let alone brought to completion, without the aid of many institutions and individuals. For assistance and support I am greatly indebted to:

The Committee on Research, University of California, for continued support for typing, photocopying, supplies, and the like;

The Committee on Grants, Association of College and Research Libraries, for two grants-in-aid;

The Harvard College Library, for permission to use its extensive card file of *Festschrift* titles;

The editors of: *American Library Association Bulletin, Bulletin of Bibliography, Bibliographical Society of America Papers, College and Research Libraries, Library Journal, Libri, South African Library Association Newsletter, UNESCO Bulletin for Libraries, Wilson Library Bulletin, Zeitschrift für Bibliothekswesen und Bibliographie,* and *Zentralblatt für Bibliothekswesen,* for publishing notices about the project;

Mr. Howard Haycraft, President, the H. W. Wilson Company, for permission to use the subject heading list developed for *Library Literature*;

Mrs. Mario Cavaliere, Mrs. Harvard Holmes, Mr. Kenneth Lee Irby, Miss Jean Lyon, now Mrs. James R. Preer, Mr. Dennis Osmond, Miss Gloria Perry, Sister Margaret Redman, Mrs. Cornelia Shugart, now Mrs. Grant Skelley, and Mrs. F. W. Steinle, Jr., serving at various periods as part-time research assistants in the School of Librarianship, University of California, for a wide variety of bibliographical and biographical checking tasks, faithfully performed;

Miss Tyyne Ahman, Mr. Lionel Chiswell, Mrs. E. Hicks, Mrs. Oleg A.

Maslenikov, and Mr. Arthur M. Miyazaki, for translations, respectively, of Finnish, Hebrew, Dutch, Slavic, and Japanese works;

Mr. John Bebbington, City Librarian, Sheffield, England; Dr. Palle Birkelund, Director, the Royal Library, Copenhagen; Dr. T. Borov, Director, Bulgarian Bibliographical Institute, for Bulgarian titles; Dr. H. W. Brands, City and University Library, Frankfurt; Dr. Emanuele Casamassima, Director, National Central Library, Florence; Mr. Robert Collison, Librarian, University Research Library, University of California, Los Angeles; Dr. Vincent Duckles, Music Librarian, University of California; Mrs. Jacqueline W. Felter, Acting Director, Medical Library Center of New York; Mr. Isaac Goldberg, Van Nuys, California, for information on volumes honoring Jewish scholars; Mr. Pierre Gras, Librarian, Dijon Municipal Library; Dr. Halfmann, Deutsche Bücherei, Leipzig; Dr. Felix E. Hirsch, Librarian, Trenton State College, Trenton, New Jersey; Dr. Bengt Holmström, Director, Malmö City Library; Dr. Christian Hermann Jensen, The Royal Library, Copenhagen; Dr. Paul Kaegbein, Director of the Library, Technical University, Berlin; Mrs. Maria Kainarova, Sofia University; Dr. Tönnes Kleberg, Director Emeritus, University of Uppsala Library, for information concerning Swedish publications; Mr. Donald W. Krummel, Newberry Library, Chicago; Dr. Horst Kunze, Director, Deutsche Staatsbibliothek, Berlin; Mr. David Libbey, University of Connecticut; Mr. R. Liter, The National Library, Madrid; Dr. Hartwig Lohse, Director, University of Dortmund Library; Mr. Reuben Musiker, Rhodes University Library, for information on South African titles; Mrs. Lisbeth Ochsner, Librarian, Visby City Library; Dr. Gösta Ottervik, Librarian, Göteborg University Library; Miss Lisa-Christina Persson of *Biblioteksbladet;* Dr. C. Reedijk, Librarian, The Royal Library, The Hague; Mr. Hans Rothschild, Amsterdam; Mr. Y. Sakai, Division for Inter-library Services, National Diet Library, Tokyo, for information on Japanese imprints; Mr. Joseph W. Scott, Librarian, University College, London; Dr. Hristo Trenkow, The National Library, Sofia, for information on Bulgarian publications; Dr. J. Vallinkoski, Librarian, University of Helsinki, for Finnish titles; Dr. Hans-Oskar Weber, Hanover; and Dr. H. H. E. Wouters, Director, City Archive and Library, Maastricht;

Mrs. David J. Haykin, for permission to use the card file of homage volume titles, compiled by her late husband;

The British Museum, the Göteborg University Library, The National Diet Library, Tokyo, the New York Public Library, and the Royal Library, Copenhagen, for photocopies;

The libraries of the universities of: California at Los Angeles, Illinois, Iowa, Kansas, Michigan, Minnesota, Oregon, Pennsylvania and the Columbia, Cornell, Duke, Harvard, Princeton, and Yale university libraries; the California State Library, the Bergbau-Bücherei, Essen, the library of the Hebrew Union College, and the Library of Congress, for interlibrary loans;

Mrs. Hedwig Doehring, conscientious, meticulous, and long-suffering typist;

The Council on Library Resources and its first president, Verner Clapp, for a generous and indispensable grant which made possible completion of the final stages of the project, including preparation of the manuscript;

Mrs. Anne Marie Lasocki, for translations into French of the "Guide to the User";

And finally, Ottilia C. Anderson, to whose cataloging expertise, sound judgment, and tireless devotion this Index owes so much that I am honored to associate her with me on the title page.

In the "Prospectus" for his great *A Dictionary of Books Relating to America* (volume I, p. xi) Joseph Sabin included a paragraph which precisely expresses my sentiments as I conclude this work:

> "Had the magnitude and extreme difficulty of the undertaking been presented to my mind in full proportions at the outset, I should never have attempted it; and, indeed, I may remark, that I have more than once almost determined upon its abandonment; but a deep sense of its importance, however imperfectly it may be executed . . . [has] stimulated me to continue my labor, until the work has attained such a degree of completeness as to justify its publication, and render its conclusion a task of comparative ease . . ."

Introduction

THE VOLUME HONORING, on a significant anniversary, either a distinguished individual or an institution—university, museum, library, learned society—has for many years been a common genre in virtually every field of scholarship and learning. A wide variety of descriptive nouns characterizes works of this kind: *Festskrift* (Danish); *Festgabe, Festgruss, Festschrift* (German); *Homenaje* (Spanish); *Festskrift, Hyllningsskrift, Minnesskrift* (Swedish); *Festskrift* and *Minnesskrift* (Norwegian); *Mélanges* (French); *Opstellen* (Dutch); *Studi, Raccolta,* and *Miscellanea* (Italian); Studies or Essays (in honor of), among others. The most commonly known and used designation for the type is, however, the German word *Festschrift*. Even the *Library of Congress Catalog; Books: Subjects* uses the entries "Festschriften—Bibliography" and "Festschriften—Indexes." This probably results from the fact that the honor volume apparently originated in Germany; more works of the kind are still produced in German-speaking territory in general, and in Germany in particular, than elsewhere (See Table I). Individuals who would be unlikely to be accorded this recognition in other countries are there frequently honored with an homage volume; it is not uncommon for a single individual to be so honored two or even three times.

The Dimensions of *Festschrift* Publication

The precise origin of the *Festschrift* publication has not been determined. It is nonetheless clear that volumes honoring institutions and societies were published as early as the Renaissance. The volume honoring an individual, on the other hand, appears to date no earlier than the middle of the nineteenth century. Not surprisingly, the earliest publications were produced by and for classical scholars. A very early example, and the earliest covered in this bibliography, is the volume of 1864–1867 honoring Frederick Ritschl, Librarian of the University of Bonn. Ritschl was a classical philologist and, in accordance with the practice of the time—before the day of the professional librarian—held the librarianship as a post additional to his professorship. The volume obviously honors him as philologist rather than as librarian; none of the contributions has anything to do with libraries or librarianship.

Since the end of the nineteenth century, the rate of publication, except during war and depression years, has increased steadily (See Table II).[1] No one knows how many *Festschrift* volumes have been published, but information acquired during the compilation of this work suggests that the number cannot be far from 20,000, and may be more. Williams, for the relatively narrow field of medieval studies, examined about 500 volumes;[2] Dau's bibliography for law, limited to Germany, Switzerland, and Austria, has 148 titles;[3] Metzger, for the New Testament and Early Church, 650 volumes;[4] Rounds' *Articles on Antiquity in Festschriften* (through 1954) covers 1,178 volumes.[5] Between 1955 and 1964, 358 additional volumes "on Antiquity" have been published—again, a great increase in rate of publication.[6] Golden's and Simches's three bibliographies of homage volumes for modern French, modern Iberian, and modern Italian language and literature include 309, 424, and 474 titles, respectively.[7] One of the best known and most comprehensive indexes, covering over 2,600 titles, is the compilation of the Comité International des Sciences Historiques, *Bibliographie Internationale des Travaux Historiques Publiés dans les Volumes de "Mélanges,"* vol. I, 1880–1939; vol. II, 1940–1955 (Paris: Colin, 1955, 1965). The view of "historical works" here is exceedingly broad, but American publications are unfortunately not included. The above mentioned bibliographies list over 6,600 volumes although, clearly, there is some duplication of material indexed.

In addition to the foregoing illustrative indexes, Winchell and its supplements list a dozen further bibliographies covering nearly 11,000 publications with, however, considerable duplication of subject matter, and a good many titles which are probably better classified as histories than as *Festschriften.*[8] Nonetheless, it seems clear that there are no fewer than 15,000 *Festschrift* publications under at least some kind of bibliographical control, with many

---

[1] An increasing rate of publication appears to hold generally true. For example, Gurli Taube's *Svensk Festskriftbibliografi Åren 1891–1925* (Uppsala, 1954) lists 137 volumes for the thirty-five-year period, or an average of not quite four a year. Rosa Malmström's supplement, *Svensk Festskriftsbibliografi 1936–1960* (Göteborg, 1967) notes 348 volumes for the quarter century, an average of almost fourteen a year.

[2] Harry F. Williams, comp., *An Index of Mediaeval Studies Published in Festschriften, 1865–1946.* Berkeley and Los Angeles: University of California Press, 1951.

[3] Helmut Dau, *Bibliographie Juristischer Festschriften und Festschriftenbeiträge, 1945–1961.* Karlsruhe: Müller [1962].

[4] Bruce M. Metzger, *Index of Articles on the New Testament and Early Church Published in Festschriften.* Philadelphia: Society of Biblical Literature, 1951; (*Journal of Biblical Literature,* Monograph Series, V.) Supplement, 1955.

[5] Dorothy Rounds, comp., *Articles on Antiquity in Festschriften: An Index.* Cambridge: Harvard University Press, 1962.

[6] Letter, Dorothy Rounds, February 18, 1967.

[7] Herbert H. Golden and Seymour O. Simches, *Modern French Literature and Language: A Bibliography of Homage Studies.* [Cambridge: Harvard University Press, 1953.] The parallel volumes for Iberia and Italy were published in 1958 and 1959.

[8] Constance M. Winchell, *Guide to Reference Books.* 8th ed., Chicago: American Library Association, 1967. 7th ed., 1951, and Supplements, 1950–1952 (with Olive A. Johnson), 1953–1955, 1956–1958, and 1959–June, 1962.

large and important fields not covered. It is probably conservative to estimate a total of 20,000 homage volume titles in all fields.

It may be noted that Morley, implying the collection of all the titles he could locate, arrived at a total of only 130 for all subjects. This is certainly no more than one-one hundred fiftieth of the actual total today.[9]

Literature on the *Festschrift*

Considering the ubiquity of the honor volume, its century-long history, and the important position it has achieved in the world of scholarly publishing, it is surprising that so few serious studies have been made of it. Over half a century ago Colagrosso[10] wrote a small volume on the predecessors of the *Festschrift*, but hardly anything on the homage volume as we know it today appears before a brief inquiry by Morley.[11] This was supplemented by Gudeman whose article deals exclusively with classical and medieval *Festschriften*.[12]

R. Pick's article "Some Thoughts on Festschriften and a Projected Subject Index," notes the earliest honor volumes in several fields and countries, discusses the principal criticisms of the genre, and enters a strong plea for the analytical indexing of honor volumes in various subject fields.[13] Pick's assumption that the 1864–67 volume for Frederick Ritschl, referred to above, "was the first of its kind,"[14] appears to be incorrect; Rounds notes an 1863 publication for Frederick Haase.[15]

Preceding a review of the Williams bibliography, already cited, Father Ottokar Bonmann discusses briefly the nature of the homage volume and suggests, among other points, that a biography of the honoree is usually, and a bibliography of his works is always present.[16] In the field of librarianship, at least, there is a considerable number of works in which both are lacking. Indeed, in a few *Festschriften* there is no indication whatever, either on the title page, or in the preface, introduction, dedication, foreword, text, or appendix—of who the honoree is, where he was active, or in what field!

Apparently the most comprehensive, general article on the homage volume is that by Dow and Rounds. The article summarizes previous writings about *Festschriften*, lists "all the indexes thus far published of *Festschriften* in the humane fields," discusses the question of quality in contributions to

---

[9] S. Griswold Morley, "The Development of the Homage Volume," *Philological Quarterly*, VIII (January, 1929), pp. 61–68.

[10] Francesco Colagrosso, *Un'Usanza Letteraria in Gran Voga nel Settecento*. Florence: Le Monnier, 1908.

[11] *Op. cit.*

[12] Alfred Gudeman, "The Homage Volume Once More," *Philological Quarterly*, VIII (October, 1929), pp. 335–338.

[13] R. Pick, "Some Thoughts on Festschriften and a Projected Subject Index," *German Life and Letters*, N.S. XII (April, 1959), pp. 204–210.

[14] *Ibid.*, p. 205.

[15] *Op. cit.*, p. 202.

[16] "Eine Bibliographie der Festschriften," *Franziskanische Studien*, XXXVI (1954), p. 111.

honor volumes, gives statistics by period and country of such publications in the field of classics, and offers a series of detailed reasons for and against the publication of the homage volume.[17]

The Bibliographical Control of Articles in *Festschriften*

From the point of view of scholarship, and the scholarly libraries which serve it, the major problem of the homage volume is that of bibliographical control of its contents. The problem is especially acute because the titles of *Festschriften*, unlike those of most subject volumes, frequently provide no guide whatever to what they contain: *Studies in Honor of Richard Doe; Memorial Volume for John Smith;* or, even less helpful, such "literary" titles as *Ausfahrt und Landung; Ideer och Resultat; Nunquam Retrorsum;* and *Alere Flammam.* No more enlightening are volumes labeled *J. B.: From His Friends.* Many of the literally scores of thousands of individual contributions to homage volumes are lost to the potential user since, with the exceptions noted earlier and hereafter, they are not adequately indexed. They do not appear in the catalogs of libraries—Morley to the contrary notwithstanding[18]—in most standard subject bibliographies, in most abstracting journals, or, generally, in national bibliographies.[19]

This is one side of the coin. The other is that a *Festschrift,* honoring as it does a more or less distinguished individual, contains contributions by the honoree's friends and colleagues who are also usually prominent in their fields. It is certainly true that some contributions to homage volumes give evidence of having been written in haste and simply to discharge an unavoidable, not wholly welcome duty; some are derivative and present little or nothing that is new; some are suggestive, and not the result of intensive labor; and some, useful and interesting enough when written, have no value today except possibly a historical one. But a very large number of these contributions, and probably the majority, are solid, scholarly studies, often definitive in nature and not infrequently the only published writing on a topic. Herein lies the scholar's need and, by inference, his problem and his loss, if his field is one for which an index of homage volumes has not been produced. Unless he recalls that so-and-so contributed an article to a certain remembered *Festschrift,* or that an article on such and such a topic appeared in a particular *Festschrift,* he has, generally speaking, no way of locating the material of interest to him.

---

[17] Dorothy Rounds and Sterling Dow, "Festschriften," *Harvard Library Bulletin,* VIII (1954), pp. 283–298. The article is reprinted, with statistics brought up to date to 1960, in: Dorothy Rounds, comp., *Articles on Antiquity in Festschriften: An Index.* Cambridge: Harvard University Press, 1962, pp. 551–560.

[18] *Op. cit.,* p. 66.

[19] See, for example, Hermann Tiemann, "Die Frage der Literaturschliessung in Universitäts- und Hochschulbibliotheken," *Zeitschrift für Bibliothekswesen und Bibliographie,* VII (1960), p. 2; Joris Vorstius, "Zur Theorie der Primären Nationalbibliographie," *Zentralblatt für Bibliothekswesen* XLVII (July, 1930), pp. 338–339; Erich Küchenhoff and Karl S. Bader, "Festschriften-Titel," *Juristenzeitung,* XI (December 10, 1956), pp. 772–773.

"Inasmuch as the average article in *Festschriften* is of a high caliber (for every scholar, and particularly a disciple, is quite naturally eager to do honor to his teacher or colleague by producing a contribution of lasting significance), the lack of a comprehensive index constitutes a most serious lacuna among scholarly tools useful for research."[20]

In the homage volumes in librarianship there are hundreds of articles on manuscripts, incunabula, the history of scholarly libraries, and scores of other topics of like significance; the interested student or scholar has no way of locating them either through an author or a subject approach.

Since 1953 the *Deutsche Nationalbibliographie* has indexed the personal bibliographies which are frequently a part of homage volumes, as well as a selection of some of the longer contributions. The *Deutsche Bibliographie* (Frankfurt) also notes personal bibliographies but provides no other analytics. The same is true of the national bibliographies of Austria and Switzerland.

For some years the national bibliographies of Bulgaria, Hungary, Italy, Poland, Rumania, and the U.S.S.R. have included at least some analytics for *Festschrift* volumes. Subject analytics are not included in the *Bibliographie de la France;* the *Library of Congress Catalog* or the *Cumulative Book Index.*

A subject approach to some, but by no means all *Festschriften,* is provided in Dietrich's *Internationale Bibliographie der Zeitschriftenliteratur mit Einschluss von Sammelwerken und Zeitungen.*

Generally speaking, therefore, a considered judgment of forty years ago is still true:

> Memorial volumes ('Festschriften') and similar collections of works by many different authors have been the despair of librarians and bibliographers. Only the most exhaustive subject bibliographies have succeeded in gleaning from them all the articles pertinent. The name of the person or the occasion to which they are dedicated is only a very approximate guide to their content, and, as they appear with the utmost irregularity of time and place, no current index machinery has ever been set up. Some libraries make analytical entries for the most important articles—very few have attempted to do so completely—and there have been several projects (generally without result) of cooperative indexing by a group of libraries.[21]

About the same time, Merlino, in the preface to a bibliography of nineteen Italian homage volumes in the fields of literature and linguistics wrote:

> Nothing is more annoyingly elusive for research students, near or far as they may be from well-equipped libraries, than the so-called anniversary or homage-volumes.[22]

Twenty years earlier Paul Meyer had expressed the view that, "*Il faudra bientôt en faire une bibliographie spéciale.*"[23]

---

[20] Metzger, *op. cit.,* p. vii.

[21] Henry Bartlett Van Hoesen and Frank Keller Walter, *Bibliography: Practical, Enumerative, Historical.* New York: Scribner's, 1928, p. 201.

[22] Camillo P. Merlino, "A Bibliography of Italian Homage-Volumes," *Italica,* VII (March, 1930), p. 4.

[23] *Romania,* XXXVII (1908), p. 626.

Because of the now enormous and steadily increasing mass of individual contributions to *Festschriften,* it seems reasonably certain that we shall never have an adequate guide covering all fields and all countries. Attempts at control of the literature, especially in recent years, have consequently taken two forms: the special bibliography intended to cover all fields for a single country, and the subject bibliography intended to cover the publications of "all" countries for a single field. Instances of the first type are few and are typified by Gurli Taube's and Rosa Malmström's bibliographies for Sweden.[24] Although the main entries, by honoree, in these bibliographies contain full contents notes, the indexes are by broad subjects, rather than by topics. Examples of the second type are much more numerous. Several have been noted earlier. It is, of course, the purpose of the present work to provide a comparable guide, that is, in this case, both a detailed subject and an author approach, to the contributions in homage volumes in the field of librarianship. Such an approach is not now available through either of our principal bibliographical indexes, *Library Literature,* and *Library Science Abstracts.* The Index covers approximately 3,300 articles in 283 publications; twenty-two countries and sixteen languages are represented.

The bibliographer labors under a two-headed curse. On the one hand it is seldom possible for him to be certain, no matter how conscientious and careful his checking, that he has included every pertinent title. On the other hand, his work is "incomplete" not simply on the date of publication, but, more discouragingly, on the date he finishes correcting the last page of proof. The present compilation will be no exception. I have, of course, striven for completeness and in this effort I have had the assistance of a number of able co-workers. Among the very many sources checked have been the volumes of *Library Literature* and *Library Science Abstracts*; the *Dictionary Catalog of the Library of the School of Library Service, Columbia University* (Boston: Hall, 1962, 7 vols.); the *Catalogue of the Library,* [of] *The Library Association* (London: Chaucer House, 1958); the "Reviews" and "Books Received" sections of all volumes of the *Library Quarterly*; the similar sections of the *Zentralblatt für Bibliothekswesen* and of the *Zeitschrift für Bibliothekswesen und Bibliographie*; the very extensive file of cards for *Festschriften* maintained by the Harvard College Library—a file which, so far as I have been able to discover, is unique; the file of the *Internationale Bibliographie des Buch- und Bibliothekswesens* 1904–12, 1926–39; Gurli Taube's and Rosa Malmström's Swedish bibliographies, referred to above; the footnote references in the second edition of the *Handbuch der Bibliothekswissenschaft*; and the *Bibliographie Internationale des Travaux Historiques,* cited earlier. In addition, a number of leading library and bibliographical journals in the United States and abroad were kind enough to publish notices of the project and these notices produced numerous titles from a considerable number of generous persons. The journals

---

[24] *Op. cit.*

and the individuals are named in the list of acknowledgments in the Preface. Despite these and other measures I am resigned to the fact that some titles, particularly from South American countries, which are not at all represented, and from Eastern Europe, will have escaped my net. I regret the omissions more than any user of the volume can. (Those concerned with the resources of American libraries will not be heartened by the fact that, of the 283 publications covered in this Index, almost ten percent were not locatable through the National Union Catalog of the Library of Congress or through a circularization of sixty large scholarly libraries. Photocopies of most of these publications were secured and deposited in the Library School Library, University of California.)

"The bibliographer of this type of literature must be content with doing his best; and after exhausting the obvious works of reference and following up the obscurer clues, he must be willing to put his results into permanent form without waiting too long for mere windfalls."[25]

Distribution of *Festschriften* in Librarianship

Tables I and II show the distribution of *Festschrift* publications by country of origin and dates of publication, respectively. The data in both tables are classified by (a) items published separately and (b) those appearing as issues, or parts of issues of journals. These two rubrics are further subdivided by homage volumes for individuals and for institutions. In the half dozen cases where a *Festschrift* has been published with identical content, both as a journal issue and separately, it has been counted only once, as the separate. The tables are self-explanatory and several interesting facts are readily apparent from them.

From Table I it is evident that, in librarianship as in other fields, Germany is by far the largest producer of homage volumes both for individuals and for institutions. The United States is a poor second, with Denmark, Italy, Sweden, Switzerland, and Norway following. Germany has almost a third of the total and more than three times as many as second-place United States. Great Britain, again as in other fields, has very few and appears to take note of its distinguished citizens by honors and awards of different kinds.

Table II makes clear the almost uninterrupted increase in the total number of *Festschrift* publications. Only in the periods 1932–1936, during most of which there was a world-wide depression, 1942–1946, which included the last years of World War II, and 1962–1966 were the numbers of publications fewer than in the preceding periods. (Inasmuch as some late-1966 publications may not have been noted in the literature in time to be garnered for the Index, it is possible that the actual number of titles appearing in the 1962–1966 period is larger than shown in Table II. In any case, it would be unwise to assume that the small decrease from 1957–1961 to 1962–1966 is the beginning

[25] Metzger, *op. cit.*, p. xi.

of a decrease in the publication of homage volumes.) Well over half of all publications have appeared during the past two decades and nearly forty-five percent in the fifteen-year period, 1952–1966. Only about twelve percent of the total was published in the first sixty years, 1862–1921, of the 105-year period.

Also from Table II, publication in journal rather than in separate form has found somewhat increasing favor during the past twenty years. Very likely one explanation is that journal publication is less expensive. Another may be that editors and sponsors of homage publications know that the articles in a journal will be accessible to the scholar through periodical indexing and/or abstracting media.

TABLE I

Number of Festschriften by Country of Origin

COUNTRY	(A) SEPARATELY PUBLISHED			(B) JOURNALS			TOTAL
	INDIVIDUALS	INSTITUTIONS	SUBTOTAL	INDIVIDUALS	INSTITUTIONS	SUBTOTAL	
Austria	2	3	5	2	0	2	7
Belgium	3	0	3	0	0	0	3
Bulgaria	6	1	7	0	0	0	7
Canada	1	0	1	0	0	0	1
Czechoslovakia	2	0	2	0	0	0	2
Denmark	5	13	18	0	0	0	18
Finland	9	0	9	0	0	0	9
France	6	0	6	2	0	2	8
Germany	61	30	91	4	3	7	98
Great Britain	1	0	1	5	0	5	6
India	1	1	2	0	0	0	2
Italy	14	1	15	0	0	0	15
Japan	6	2	8	1	0	1	9
Netherlands	4	3	7	3	0	3	10
Norway	6	7	13	0	0	0	13
Poland	2	2	4	0	0	0	4
South Africa, Union of	1	0	1	3	0	3	4
Spain	2	0	2	1	0	1	3
Sweden	9	5	14	1	0	1	15
Switzerland	7	5	12	3	0	3	15
Union of Soviet Socialist Republics and Russia	2	0	2	0	0	0	2
United States	22	3	25	7	0	7	32
TOTALS	172	76	248	32	3	35	283

TABLE II

Number of Festschriften by Date of Publication

YEARS	(A) SEPARATELY PUBLISHED			(B) JOURNALS			TOTAL
	INDIVIDUALS	INSTITUTIONS	SUBTOTAL	INDIVIDUALS	INSTITUTIONS	SUBTOTAL	
1862–1866	1	0	1	0	0	0	1
1867–1871	0	0	0	0	0	0	0
1872–1876	0	0	0	0	0	0	0
1877–1881	0	0	0	0	0	0	0
1882–1886	1	0	1	0	0	0	1
1887–1891	1	1	2	0	0	0	2
1892–1896	2	1	3	0	0	0	3
1897–1901	1	0	1	0	1	1	2
1902–1906	2	2	4	0	0	0	4
1907–1911	4	2	6	0	0	0	6
1912–1916	4	0	4	2	0	2	6
1917–1921	8	1	9	1	0	1	10
1922–1926	9	5	14	1	0	1	15
1927–1931	15	10	25	2	1	3	28
1932–1936	9	3	12	2	0	2	14
1937–1941	15	8	23	0	0	0	23
1942–1946	8	6	14	1	0	1	15
1947–1951	18	6	24	2	0	2	26
1952–1956	24	6	30	5	0	5	35
1957–1961	28	12	40	6	1	7	47
1962–1966	22	13	35	10	0	10	45
TOTALS	172	76	248	32	3	35	283

Guide to the User

THE MAIN BODY of the work is a single alphabetical author and subject index, with cross references, to articles on libraries and closely related topics—publishing, printing, reading, etc.—appearing in *Festschriften* honoring librarians, libraries, and library associations. Editors and joint editors of the volumes are also included.

Definition, Scope, and Coverage

Webster's *New International Dictionary* (second edition) defines a *Festschrift* as "a collection of learned papers . . . issued by colleagues or admirers in honor of an anniversary celebration of a scholar or scientist." This definition provides the basic criterion upon which I have operated, except that I have extended its scope to include volumes honoring the anniversary of libraries and library associations, and have included, when designated a jubilee volume, collections of the writings of the honoree. Reports and histories, and volumes by a single author, even though of an anniversary nature, *e.g., The John Doe Library, 1850–1950: A History,* have been excluded not simply to conform to the specifics of the generally accepted definition, but rather on the justification that the contents of such works will be accessible to the scholar through the subject heading(s) of library catalogs. Some works of this nature, especially Scandinavian in origin, are specifically designated *Festgabe, Festskrift,* or *Minnesskrift* on the title page or elsewhere. These, yielding to the author's, editor's, or sponsor's view, I have included even though comparable accounts or histories not so designated have been ignored. I assume the resulting inconsistency will be sympathetically understood.

A considerable number of *Festschriften* appear as issues of journals. These have been included even though it is, of course, true that most major and many less important journals have been analyzed in *Library Literature* since 1921, and in *Library Science Abstracts* since 1950. But a number of *Festschriften* have appeared in journals which are not indexed, others appeared before the indexing of our professional literature was as satisfactory as it is now, and some have been published in non-library periodicals to which the searcher for information on librarianship would be unlikely to turn. It seemed preferable to include all journal *Festschriften* which could be located rather than to try to set up definitions and criteria which would exclude some and include others. The titles of journals are given in full, unabbreviated form in the list, Code Abbreviations of Festschriften.

I have been obliged to interpret "librarians, libraries, and library associations" strictly, and to exclude, therefore, the many works honoring publishers, printers, typographers, book binders, book dealers, archivists, and the like. I have done so with regret, realizing that much of the contents of such volumes is of interest to the library craft, but the time and means at my disposal did not permit what would have been a very substantial additional labor.

Articles dealing with manuscripts, special collections, bibliographical enterprises, and the like related to libraries in general or to particular libraries have been included. On the other hand, articles of a general bibliographical nature—points in the first editions of Mark Twain, early vulgate translations of Aristotle, or the literature of World War I—have been excluded. I have interpreted the distinction liberally and when in doubt, or in borderline cases, the article has been included.

Articles in the volumes indexed having nothing whatever to do with libraries, books, manuscripts, reading and so on have *not* been covered. The grounds for excluding this extraneous material are three: first, some of it has already been included in comparable guides in other fields, *e.g.*, Harry F. Williams's *An Index of Mediaeval Studies Published in Festschriften, 1865–1946* (Berkeley and Los Angeles: University of California Press, 1951); second, the researcher interested in types of German hayricks, the etymology of an Arabic word, the Greek sense of tragedy, early expressionistic painting, Jewish personality traits in literature, or Scarlatti's operas would not be likely to turn to this bibliography as a source; and third, the inclusion of these many articles, irrelevant to librarianship and its concerns, would have very greatly increased the size of the volume with a questionable increase in its utility since the few articles on, for example, the English ballad, would represent only a minute fraction of the literature on the subject.

Subject Headings, Arrangement of Entries, Code Designations, Search Method, Aids to the User

Subject Headings. Each article indexed has been entered under its author and under one or more assigned subject headings, the maximum for any article being eight, and the typical, or median, number being between three and four. The subject headings used are those which have been developed by the staff of the H. W. Wilson Co. for *Library Literature,* supplemented by those of the Library of Congress. In the surprising number of instances where a clearly desirable heading does not appear in either list, a new one has been invented.

Extensive cross references—"see" and "see also" entries—have been provided, *e.g.*,

"OSLO—College and university libraries," see "College and university libraries—Oslo";

"LEMBERG," see "L'vov";

"LIBRARIANS—Training," see "Education for librarianship."

"See also" references, serving as an aid to the user in directing him to other entries under which there may be articles of interest to him, will be found at the beginning of many subject headings, *e.g.*,

LIBRARY community relations
 see also, Library and the public
COOPERATION
 see also, Interlibrary relationships
INTERLIBRARY relationships
 see also, Cooperation

Arrangement of Entries. Entries are arranged in accordance with the *A.L.A. Rules for Filing Catalog Cards* (Chicago: American Library Association, 1942). Among the more important and relevant provisions are that all entries are arranged:

According to the order of the English alphabet;

Word by word, with letter by letter alphabetization to the end of each word;

With hyphenated words filed as though two words;

With ä, ö, ü, ø, å filed as though written ae, oe, ue, oe, aa;

With ć, č, ç, é, è, ł, ñ, š, ž, filed as c, c, c, e, e, l, n, s, z;

With disregard for initial articles—a, le, der, the, etc.;

With name prefixes M' and Mc filed as though spelled Mac;

As though abbreviations were spelled in full—*e.g.*, Dr.—Doctor, St, Ste—Saint, Sainte, N. Y.—New York.

Code Designations for the Festschriften. The code designation for each *Festschrift* is made up of the first four letters of the name of the honoree, whether a person or an institution, if the honoree has only one homage volume and there is no other honoree with the same four beginning letters. Thus, HARN for the volume honoring Adolf von Harnack, MUNT for the *Festschrift* for Wilhelm Munthe, etc. In cases where an individual or institution has been honored with two or more works, and in cases where the first four letters of the names of two honorees are the same (*e.g.*, Karl Schwarber and Paul Schwenke) an arbitrary fourth letter is used to distinguish between them. Institutional honorees are entered under, and their code designations derived from, the city of location. In the great majority of cases this is given in the title of the volume as in the *Festschriften* for the libraries of the cities of Aachen (AACH), and Göteborg (GÖTE), or the universities of Giessen (GIES), Königsberg (KÖNI), Uppsala (UPPS), and Utrecht (UTRE). In a few cases, most notably perhaps those of the national and royal libraries of Denmark and Holland, the Bavarian State Library, the Deutsche Bibliothek, the Deutsche Bücherei, and the present Deutsche Staatsbibliothek, formerly the Preussische Staatsbibliothek, the city of location does not appear in the title. These institutions are entered respectively under Copenhagen, The Hague, Munich, Frankfurt, Leipzig, and Berlin.

Search Method. Assume a researcher wishes to locate 1) an article by Sir Frederick Kenyon (or, alternatively, to discover what articles Sir Frederick contributed to *Festschriften* in librarianship), and 2) a historical account of the Prussian State Library in the early decades of this century. Under "Kenyon" in the Index he will find the reference, "Copyright Libraries," 248-254, PUTN; and under "BERLIN. Preussische Staatsbibliothek," he will find a cross reference to "BERLIN. Deutsche Staatsbibliothek," and there the subheading "History" with a reference, among others, to an article by Hugo A. Krüss, "'Zur Geschichte der Staatsbibliothek zu Berlin in den Letzten Dreissig Jahren," 263–274, PUTN. (As just indicated, author entries are in upper and lower case to distinguish them from the subject entries, in capitals, which refer to articles about the individual.) Turning to the alphabetical list of *Festschriften* and their code abbreviations, the researcher will find that PUTN refers to the following work: Bishop, William Warner and Andrew Keogh, eds., *Essays Offered to Herbert Putnam by His Colleagues and Friends on His Thirtieth Anniversary as Librarian of Congress 5 April 1929.* New Haven [Connecticut]: Yale University Press, 1929. (For the sake of simplicity, the same volume has been used for the examples of both the author and subject search; in actual practice, it is unlikely that such searches would lead to the same *Festschrift.*)

Aids to the User. At the conclusion of the bibliographical reference just cited appears the notation *"Who's Who in America, 1954/55."* For a few honorees a biographical directory reference could not be located.

Finally, there is a list of "Reviews of the Festschriften." The reviews (up to five) appear under the code letters of the *Festschrift.* Thus, in the list "Reviews of the Festschriften" there appears:

PUTN *American Historical Review,* XXXV (October, 1929), pp. 149–50
Minerva, VI (September/October, 1930), p. 170

which means that reviews of the homage volume to Herbert Putnam may be found in volume thirty-five, October, 1929, pages 149–50, of the *American Historical Review,* and in *Minerva,* volume six, September/October, 1930, page 170. No reviews are cited for *Festschriften* appearing as issues or part of issues of journals, and reviews could not be located for some monographs.

Had the search concerned S. R. Ranganathan and classification systems, two references would have led to the *Festschrift* DONK which proves to be:

Hommage à F. Donker Duyvis. [*Revue de la Documentation,* XXVII (November, 1960)], *Wie Is Dat?* 1956.

meaning that the entire issue of November, 1960, volume twenty-seven of the *Revue . . .* is an homage publication for F. Donker Duyvis, a biographical account of whom appears in *Wie Is Dat?* for 1956.

Festschriften appearing as a publication of a series are entered in the same way as journals, that is, the full series title is given in parentheses at the end of the citation. For series, however, place and date of publication are given, as for separate books, immediately following the volume title.

Editors and joint editors of the volumes are entered in the Index with the code designation of the edited work following their names, *e.g.*,

Bishop, William Warner, jt. ed.
  PUTN
  and
Keogh, Andrew, jt. ed.
  PUTN

All honorees, both individual and institutional, may be identified in the Index (irrespective of entries for them as authors or subjects), under their names, *below which appear the indented code designation(s),* for example:

LEYH, GEORG
  LEYG
  LEYH
  LEYV

which means that Georg Leyh is the honoree of the three indicated *Festschriften.*

The language in which an article is written will usually be evident from the language of its title. Cyrillic titles have been transliterated using the scheme employed by the Library of Congress and Japanese titles according to the modified Hepburn system.

Terminal Dates

Publication dates of the works included in the Index are 1864 through 1966.

Guide de l'Usager

Cet ouvrage est consacré aux articles traitant de bibliothèques, ou de sujets connexes tels que édition, impression, lecture, etc., qui auraient paru dans des *Festschriften* ou Mélanges offerts à des bibliothécaires, ou composés en l'honneur de bibliothèques ou d'associations de bibliothèques. Le gros du volume consiste en un simple répertoire alphabétique des auteurs et des matières, avec renvois d'orientation; le ou les noms des éditeurs ont également été inclus.

Définition, Portée et Etendue

Le nouveau dictionnaire Webster (Webster's *New International Dictionary,* deuxième édition) définit un *Festschrift* comme constituant "un recueil d'articles érudits . . . dédiés à la mémoire ou publiés en l'honneur d'un professeur ou d'un savant, composés par des collègues ou admirateurs." Cette définition m'a fourni le critère de base sur lequel j'ai opéré; j'en ai toutefois étendu la portée pour inclure des ouvrages commémorant des anniversaires de bibliothèques ou d'associations de bibliothèques, et, dans les cas d'ouvrages célébrant un jubilé, j'ai également inclu la liste des oeuvres et écrits de la personne ainsi honorée.

Les rapports, histoires et monographies, et les volumes à auteur unique ont été exclus—même lorsqu'il s'agissait de la commémoration d'un centenaire, comme par exemple dans le cas de: *The John Doe Library, 1850–1950: A History*—et ceci non seulement dans le but de se conformer aux spécifications de la définition généralement admise, mais surtout parce qu'on peut assumer que le contenu de ces ouvrages sera rendu accessible aux érudits grâce aux vedettes des matières des catalogues de bibliothèques. Certains des ouvrages de cette nature, tout particulièrement ceux d'origine scandinave, portent, en page de titre ou ailleurs, une notation spéciale: *Festgabe, Festskrift* ou *Minnesskrift*; cédant aux instances des auteurs, des éditeurs ou des organisateurs, j'ai inclus ces ouvrages dans mon répertoire d'articles, bien que j'en aie écarté d'autres qui étaient de nature semblable mais n'étaient point ainsi spécifiquement désignés. J'ose espérer que l'on voudra bien excuser le manque apparent de logique qui en résulte.

Un nombre considérable de *Festschriften* ont paru dans des revues, sous forme de numéros spéciaux; ils ont été inclus, bien que, naturellement, la plupart de ces publications ainsi que beaucoup d'autres de moindre importance aient déjà été analysées, depuis 1921 dans *Library Literature,* et depuis 1950 dans *Library Science Abstracts.* Mais un certain nombre de *Festschriften* ont également paru dans des publications qui ne sont pas cataloguées; d'autres ont paru avant que les catalogues ne fussent aussi satisfaisants qu'ils le sont devenus aujourd'hui; d'autres encore ont été publiés dans des périodiques non spécialisés en bibliothéconomie et ils risquaient donc de rester ignorés du chercheur. Il m'a semblé préférable d'insérer tous les *Festschriften* qui avaient pu être localisés, quel que fût le genre de périodique où ils avaient paru, plutôt que de m'en tenir à des définitions et à des critères qui m'auraient obligé à exclure les uns et à inclure les autres. Les titres des périodiques sont donnés au complet, sans abréviation aucune dans la liste, "Code Abbreviations of Festschriften."

Je me suis vu dans l'obligation d'interpréter les termes "bibliothécaires, bibliothèques et associations de bibliothèques" dans leur sens le plus strict, et donc d'exclure les innombrables volumes consacrés aux éditeurs, imprimeurs, typographes, relieurs, libraires, archivistes, etc. C'est avec regret que je m'y suis résigné, sachant l'intérêt que ces ouvrages représentent pour les bibliothécaires professionnels, mais le temps et les moyens dont je disposais ne me permettaient pas de m'atteler à ce qui eût représenté un fort surcroît de labeur.

Ont été inclus les articles ayant trait aux manuscrits, aux fonds spéciaux, aux entreprises bibliographiques, ainsi que tous ceux se rapportant de près ou de loin aux bibliothèques en général ou à certaines bibliothèques en particulier.

Par contre ont été exclus les articles présentant un intérêt bibliographique de caractère général, ceux rapportant par exemple des détails sur les premières éditions de Mark Twain, ou sur les premières traductions latines d'Aristote, ou encore les documents sur la Première Guerre Mondiale. Mais j'ai interprété cette distinction dans un sens libéral, et dans les cas douteux ou tangents les articles ont été inclus.

Il arrive que les volumes catalogués contiennent des articles n'ayant aucun rapport avec les bibliothèques, les livres, les manuscrits, la lecture, etc. De tels articles n'ont *point* été pris en considération, et ceci pour une triple raison; parce que: premièrement, certains d'entre eux avaient déjà été dépouillés dans des guides comparables consacrés à d'autres domains, par exemple *An Index of Mediaeval Studies Published in Festschriften, 1865–1946* d'Harry F. Williams (Berkeley and Los Angeles, University of California Press, 1951); deuxièmement, il est peu probable que se tourne vers la présente bibliographie en tant que possible source d'informations le chercheur qui s'intéresse aux types de râteliers d'écurie allemands, à l'étymologie d'un mot arabe, au sens grec du mot tragédie, aux traits de caractère juifs en littérature ou aux opéras de Scarlatti; et troisièmement, le fait d'inclure ces nombreux articles sans rapport avec l'art, le métier et les préoccupations de bibliothécaire, aurait grandement accru l'ampleur de cet ouvrage sans y apporter de bénéfice appréciable puisque les quelques articles sur, mettons, la ballade anglaise n'auraient guère représenté qu'une infime fraction de tout ce qui a été écrit à ce sujet.

Vedettes de Matières, Classement des Entrées, Code de Désignation, Méthode de Recherche, Moyens d'Aide pour l'Usager

Vedettes de Matières. Tous les articles catalogués ont été inscrits sous les noms d'auteurs et sous une ou plusieurs vedettes-matières, le maximum étant de huit, et la moyenne de trois ou quatre entrées pour un article. Les vedettes utilisées sont celles qui ont été établies par la maison d'édition H. W. Wilson Co. pour *Library Literature,* complétées par celles de la Bibliothèque du Congrès de Washington (Library of Congress). Une nouvelle vedette a été inventée dans les cas, étonnamment nombreux, où il n'en existait pas dans l'une ou l'autre des deux listes précitées.

On a prévu un système de renvois multiples—"see" et "see also" ("voir" et "voir aussi")—par exemple:

"OSLO—College and university libraries," voir "College and university libraries—Oslo";

"LEMBERG," voir "L'vov";

"LIBRARIANS—Training," voir "Education for librarianship" (Bibliothécaires—Stage, voir: Formation du personnel).

On trouvera également, au début de nombreuses vedettes-matières, des renvois "see also" ("voir aussi") destinés à aiguiller les recherches vers d'autres vedettes couvrant des articles susceptibles, peut-être, de présenter de l'intérêt pour le chercheur; par exemple:

LIBRARY community relations
    see also (voir aussi), Library and the public
COOPERATION
    see also (voir aussi), Interlibrary relationships
INTERLIBRARY relationships
    see also (voir aussi), Cooperation

Classement des Entrées. Les entrées ont été établies conformément aux instructions pour l'établissement des fiches de catalogues de l'Association des Bibliothèques des Etats-Unis, l'A.L.A. (*Rules for Filing Catalog Cards,* Chicago: American Library Association, 1942). Parmi les mentions les plus importantes, il convient de relever que toutes les entrées sont établies:

d'après l'ordre de l'alphabet anglais,

dans l'ordre des mots, chaque mot étant alphabétisé lettre par lettre sans aucune abréviation,

avec les mots comportant un trait d'union transcrits comme s'ils constituaient deux mots séparés,

avec les lettres ä, ö, ü, ø, å consignées comme si elles étaient écrites ae, oe, ue, oe, aa,

avec les lettres ć, č, ç, é, è, ł, ñ, š, ž transcrites c, c, c, e, e, l, n, s, z,

sans tenir compte des articles initiaux: a, le, der, the, etc.,
avec les noms comportant le préfixe M' ou Mc écrits Mac,
sans abréviations, les noms étant consignés en entier, par exemple: Dr.–Doctor, St, Ste—Saint, Sainte, N.Y.—New York.

Code de Désignation Spéciale pour les Festschriften. Chaque *Festschrift* est pourvu de son propre code spécial de désignation. Celui-ci est simplement formé des quatre premières lettres du nom du bénéficiaire des honneurs—qu'il s'agisse d'une personne ou d'une institution—lorsqu'un seul volume a été publié en son honneur et qu'il n'y a pas d'autre bénéficiaire d'hommage similaire dont le nom commence par les mêmes quatre lettres. Ainsi aura-t-on HARN pour le volume offert en hommage à Adolf von Harnack, MUNT pour le *Festschrift* offert à Wilhelm Munthe, etc. Dans les cas où une seule personne ou institution a pu recevoir l'hommage de deux ou trois ouvrages, dans les cas également où les quatre premières lettres du nom de deux bénéficiaires se trouvent être les mêmes (par exemple Karl Schwarber et Paul Schwenke), on s'est servi d'une quatrième lettre arbitraire pour distinguer entre eux (dans le cas précité SCHU et SCHW).

Lorsque les bénéficiares sont des institutions, celles-ci sont inscrites d'après la ville où elles sont situées, du nom de laquelle est tirée leur code de désignation, et que le titre même du volume indique dans la majorité des cas, comme par exemple dans les *Festschriften* en l'honneur des bibliothèques des villes d'Aachen (AACH), de Göteborg (GÖTE), ou des universités de Giessen (GIES), de Königsberg (KÖNI), d'Uppsala (UPPS) et d'Utrecht (UTRE). Dans quelques cas très rares,–et sans doute faut-il mentionner parmi les plus notoires ceux des bibliothèques nationales et royales du Danemark et de la Hollande, de la Bibliothèque d'État de Bavière, de la Deutsche Bibliothek, de la Deutsche Bücherei et de l'actuelle Deutsche Staatsbibliothek (autrefois Preussische Staatsbibliothek)–le nom de la ville où est située la bibliothèque n'apparaît pas dans le titre; ces institutions sont alors consignées sous les noms de leurs villes respectives: Copenhague, la Haye (The Hague), Munich, Francfort (Frankfurt), Leipzig et Berlin.

Méthode de Recherche. Supposons que l'on cherche à localiser: 1) un article de Sir Frederick Kenyon (ou, pour prendre une autre alternative, que l'on cherche à savoir si, et par quels articles, Sir Frederick a contribué à des *Festschriften* ayant trait à la bibliothéconomie) et 2) une étude historique sur la Bibliothèque d'État de Prusse (Prussian State Library) dans les premières décennies de ce siècle. Sous la rubrique "Kenyon" de l'Index, on trouvera un renvoi à "Copyright Libraries", 248–254, PUTN; et sous la rubrique "BERLIN. Preussische Staatsbibliothek", on trouvera un renvoi à "BERLIN. Deutsche Staatsbibliothek", et là la rubrique secondaire "History" avec, parmi d'autres, un renvoi à un article de Hugo A. Krüss, intitulé "Zur Geschichte der Staatsbibliothek zu Berlin in den Letzten Dreissig Jahren", 263–274, PUTN. (Comme il vient de l'être indiqué, les vedettes d'auteurs sont imprimées en lettres majuscules et minuscules afin de les distinguer des vedettes de matières, en majuscules, se référant aux articles sur l'individu.) En compulsant le répertoire alphabétique des *Festschriften* et leur code d'abréviations, on trouvera que PUTN se réfère à l'ouvrage suivant: Bishop, William Warner and Andrew Keogh, eds., *Essays Offered to Herbert Putnam by His Colleagues and Friends on His Thirtieth Anniversary as Librarian of Congress 5 April 1929.* New Haven [Connecticut]: Yale University Press, 1929. (Mélanges offerts à Herbert Putnam par ses collègues et amis, en commémoration de son trentième anniversaire en tant que bibliothécaire en chef de la Bibliothèque du Congrès.) (Par souci de simplification, le même volume a été utilisé pour donner l'exemple d'une recherche portant à la fois sur un auteur et sur une matière; dans la pratique courante, il est bien improbable que de telles recherches puissent conduire au même *Festschrift.*)

Moyens d'Aide pour l'Usager. A la fin de la référence bibliographique précédemment citée apparaît la notation "*Who's Who in America,* 1954/55." Dans des cas assez rares, il n'a pas été possible de trouver de données biographiques dans les répertoires consacrés à ce but.

Enfin, le présent ouvrage contient encore un répertoire des "Reviews of the Festschriften" (revues critiques des Mélanges offerts à...). Les revues critiques (cinq au maximum) sont inscrites sous le code de désignation du *Festschrift.* Ainsi, si dans le répertoire des "Reviews of the Festschriften" apparaît:

PUTN *American Historical Review,* XXXV (October, 1929), pp. 149–150
Minerva, VI (September/October, 1930), p. 170

cela signifie qu'on pourra trouver des revues critiques sur les Mélanges offerts à Herbert Putnam dans l'*American Historical Review,* trente-cinquième volume, numéro du mois d'octobre 1929, pages 149 et 150, et dans la revue *Minerva,* sixième volume, numéro des mois de septembre et octobre, 1930, page 170. Les numéros spéciaux de revues ou périodiques qui ont été partiellement ou même totalement consacrés à des hommages rendus à des personnes ou à des institutions n'ont pas été cités. Et il n'a pas été possible de localiser des revues critiques dans le cas de quelques rares monographies.

Si nous supposons, par exemple, que les recherches aient porté sur S. R. Ranganathan et sur les systèmes de classification, deux renvois conduiraient au code de quatre lettres du *Festschrift* DONK, qui se dévoilerait comme correspondant à:

Hommage à F. Donker Duyvis. [*Revue de la Documentation,*
XXVII (November, 1960)], *Wie Is Dat?* 1956.

c'est-à-dire que la *Revue de la Documentation* a publié, en novembre 1960, un numéro spécial, le vingt-septième volume, entièrement consacré à F. Donker Duyvis et qu'une notice biographique sur celui-ci avait auparavant paru dans le *Wie Is Dat* de l'année 1956.

Les *Festschriften* qui ont été publiés sous forme de séries d'articles sont consignés de la même façon que les revues, c'est-à-dire que le titre complet de la série est donné entre parenthèses à la fin de la notice. Il est à mentionner cependant que, pour les séries d'articles comme pour les ouvrages séparés, les lieu et date de publication sont cités immédiatement après le titre du volume.

Le ou les noms des éditeurs des volumes sont indiqués dans l'Index, et sont suivis du code de désignation de quatre lettres désignant l'ouvrage édité par eux, par exemple:

Bishop, William Warner, jt. ed.
PUTN
et
Keogh, Andrew, jt. ed.
PUTN

Toutes les personnes ou institutions honorées dans les *Festschriften* apparaissent dans l'Index sous leur propre nom, indépendamment de toute autre rubrique d'auteurs ou de matières, et sous leur nom sont inscrits le ou les codes de désignation de quatre lettres, par exemple:

LEYH, GEORG
LEYG
LEYH
LEYV

ce qui signifie que Georg Leyh a reçu l'hommage de trois *Festschriften* mentionnés dans l'Index.

La langue dans laquelle l'article est rédigé ressortira habituellement du titre. Les titres écrits en caractères cyrilliens ont été transposés d'après le modèle établi par la Bibliothèque du Congrès de Washington; et les titres japonais ont été transcrits selon le système modifié d'Hepburn.

Dates et Termes

Les dates de publications des ouvrages inclus dans cet Index couvrent la période 1864–1966.

Anweisungen für den Benutzer

Der hauptteil des Werkes besteht aus einem einzigen Autoren- und Sachregister für in Festschriften zu Ehren von Bibliothekaren, Bibliotheken und Bibliotheksvereinen erschienene Artikel über Bibliotheken und nahverwandte Themen wie Veröffentlichen, Drucken, Lesen usw. Herausgeber und gemeinsame Herausgeber sind ebenfalls einbezogen.

Begriffsbestimmung, Umfang und Reichweite

Webster's *New International Dictionary* (zweite Ausgabe) bezeichnet eine Festschrift als "eine Sammlung gelehrter Abhandlungen . . ., veröffentlicht von Kollegen oder Bewunderern zu Ehren des Jubiläums eines Gelehrten oder Wissenschaftlers." Von dieser Definition als Grundlage bin ich bei meiner Arbeit ausgegangen, habe jedoch den Rahmen erweitert und Werke zu Ehren von Jahresfeiern von Bibliotheken und Bibliotheksvereinen aufgenommen und auch gesammelte Schriften eines Jubilars eingereiht, wenn sie als Jubiläumsband bezeichnet waren. Berichte, geschichtliche Darstellungen und Werke eines einzelnen Autors, selbst wenn sie Jubiläumscharakter trugen (z.B. *The John Doe Library, 1850–1950: A History*) wurden ausgeschlossen, und zwar nicht einfach wegen Anpassung an die Eigenart der allgemein akzeptierten Definition, sondern eher mit der Rechtfertigung, dass der Inhalt solcher Werke dem Gelehrten durch die Sachtitel der Bibliothekskataloge zugänglich ist. Einige Arbeiten dieser Art, besonders solche skandinavischen Ursprungs, sind auf der Titelseite oder an anderer Stelle ausdrücklich als Festgabe, Festskrift oder Minnesskrift gekennzeichnet. Diese habe ich unter Berücksichtigung der Ansicht des Verfassers, Herausgebers oder Gönners eingeschlossen, nicht so bezeichnete vergleichbare Berichte und geschichtliche Darstellungen jedoch ausgeschieden. Die daraus entstandene Inkonsequenz wird wohl teilnahmsvolles Verständnis finden.

Eine beträchtliche Anzahl von Festschriften erscheinen als Zeitschriftenausgaben. Diese sind eingeschlossen, obwohl bekanntermassen die meisten bedeutenden und viele weniger wichtige Zeitschriften seit 1921 in *Library Literature* und seit 1950 in *Library Science Abstracts* analysiert worden sind. Aber eine Reihe von Festschriften sind in Journalen veröffentlicht, die nicht so analysiert sind, andere kamen heraus, bevor die Anlage von Verzeichnissen für unsere Fachliteratur so zufriedenstellend war, wie sie es heute ist, und wieder andere sind in Zeitschriften publiziert, die sich nicht auf Bibliothekswesen beziehen und in denen man wohl kaum Information darüber suchen würde. Es erschien wünschenswerter, alle auffindbaren Journal-Festschriften zu erfassen als zu versuchen, Definitionen und Kriterien zum Maßstab für Ein- oder Ausschluss zu machen. Die Titel der Zeitschriften erscheinen in voller, ungekürzter Form in der Liste, "Code Abbreviations of Festschriften."

Notwendigerweise musste ich "Bibliothekare, Bibliotheken und Bibliotheksvereine" genau interpretieren und konnte daher die vielen Werke zu Ehren von Verlegern, Druckern, Setzern, Buchbindern, Buchhändlern, Archivaren und ähnlichen Berufsgruppen nicht aufnehmen. Ich tat das mit Bedauern, da ich weiss, dass viel von dem Inhalt solcher Bände die Bibliothekswelt interessiert, aber die Zeit und die Mittel, die mir zur Verfügung standen, erlaubten diese beträchtliche zusätzliche Arbeit nicht.

Artikel, die sich mit Manuskripten, Spezialsammlungen, bibliographischen Unternehmungen und Ähnlichem in Bezug auf Bibliotheken im allgemeinen oder auf besondere Bibliotheken befassen, sind aufgeführt. Dagegen sind Abhandlungen allgemein bibliographischer Art (z.B. Einzelheiten über die ersten Ausgaben von Mark Twain, frühe lateinische Übersetzungen von Aristoteles oder Literatur über den Ersten Weltkrieg) nicht berücksichtigt worden. Die Unterscheidung ist grosszügig durchgeführt, und in Zweifels- oder Grenzfällen sind die Artikel aufgenommen worden.

In den verzeichneten Werken veröffentlichte Artikel, die mit Bibliotheken, Büchern, Manuskripten, Lesen usw. nicht das Geringste zu tun haben, wurden *nicht* erfasst, und zwar wurde dieses wesensfremde Material aus drei Gründen weggelassen: erstens ist Einiges davon bereits in vergleichbaren Verzeichnissen auf anderen Gebieten eingeschlossen, z.B. in Harry F. Williams' *An Index of Mediaeval Studies Published in Festschriften, 1865–1946* (Berkeley and Los Angeles: University of California Press, 1951); zweitens würden Forscher, die an Typen deutscher Heuschober, der Etymologie eines arabischen Wortes, dem Sinn der Tragödie bei den Griechen, frühexpressionistischer Malerei, jüdischen Persönlichkeitsmerkmalen in der Literatur oder Scarlattis Opern interessiert sind, diese Bibliographie wohl kaum als Quellennachweis zu Rate ziehen; und drittens hätte die Einbeziehung dieser vielen das Bibliothekswesen und seine Belange nicht betreffenden Abhandlungen den Umfang des Bandes bedeutend vergrössert und zugleich seine Nützlichkeit nur in fragwürdiger Weise vermehrt, da die wenigen Artikel, z.B. über die englische Ballade, nur einen winzigen Bruchteil der Literatur über diesen Gegenstand darstellen.

Sachtitel, Anordnung der Eintragungen, Kennworte, Suchmethode, Hilfen für den Benutzer

Sachtitel. Jeder verzeichnete Artikel ist unter dem Namen des Verfassers aufgeführt und ebenso unter einem oder mehreren Sachtiteln, deren Höchstzahl für einen Artikel acht ist, während die typische oder durchschnittliche

Anzahl zwischen drei und vier liegt. Benützt wurden die von dem Personal der H. W. Wilson Company für *Library Literature* ausgearbeiteten Sachtitel, ergänzt durch diejenigen der Library of Congress. In der erstaunlichen Reihe von Fällen, in denen keine der beiden Listen einen eindeutig wünschenswerten Sachtitel aufwies, wurde ein neuer ersonnen.

Zahlreiche Kreuzverweisungen ("see" und "see also"–Eintragungen) sind vorgesehen, z.B.
"OSLO—College and university libraries," see "College and university libraries—Oslo";
"LEMBERG," see "L'vov";
"LIBRARIANS—Training," see "Education for librarianship."

Am Anfang vieler Sachtitel stehen "see also"–Referenzen, um den Benutzer auf andere Eintragungen aufmerksam zu machen, unter denen er ihn interessierende Artikel finden mag, z.B.

LIBRARY community relations
    see also, Library and the public
COOPERATION
    see also, Interlibrary relationships
INTERLIBRARY relationships
    see also, Cooperation

Anordnung der Eintragungen. Die Eintragungen sind in Übereinstimmung mit den *A.L.A. Rules for Filing Catalog Cards* (Chicago, American Library Association, 1942) angeordnet. Zu den wichtigeren sachdienlichen Bestimmungen gehört, dass alle Eintragungen in folgender Weise aufgeführt sind:

gemäss der Reihenfolge des englischen Alphabets;
Wort für Wort mit buchstabenweiser Alphabetisierung bis zum Ende jedes Worts;
mit Bindestrich versehene Wörter sind als zwei Wörter behandelt;
ä, ö, ü, ø, å zählen als ae, oe, ue, oe, aa;
ć, č, ç, è, é, ł, ñ, š, ž zählen als c, c, c, e, e, l, n, s, z;
Anfangsartikel wie a, le, der, the usw. sind ausser acht gelassen;
die Präfixe M' und Mc vor Namen zählen als Mac;
Abkürzungen sind alphabetisiert, als ob sie voll ausbuchstabiert wären, z.B. Dr.—Doctor, St, Ste—Saint, Sainte, N. Y.—New York.

Kennworte für die Festschriften. Das Kennwort für jede Festschrift ist aus den ersten vier Buchstaben des Namens des Jubilars gebildet, gleichgültig ob es sich um eine Einzelperson oder um eine Institution handelt, wenn dem Jubilar nur ein Gedenkband gewidmet ist und kein anderer unter denselben vier Anfangsbuchstaben erscheint. So steht z.B. HARN für den Band zu Ehren Adolf von Harnacks, MUNT für die Wilhelm Munthe gewidmete Festschrift, usw. Wenn eine Einzelperson oder eine Institution durch mehrere

Werke geehrt wurde, und wenn die ersten vier Namensbuchstaben zweier Jubilare die gleichen sind (z.B. Karl Schwarber und Paul Schwenke), unterscheidet sie ein vierter willkürlich gewählter Buchstabe. Durch Festschriften geehrte Institutionen erscheinen unter ihren Ortsnamen, von denen auch die Kennworte abgeleitet sind. Meistens ist der Name der betreffenden Stadt im Titel erwähnt, wie z.B. in den Festschriften für die Bibliotheken von Aachen (AACH) und Göteborg (GÖTE) oder für die Universitäten von Giessen (GIES), Königsberg (KÖNI), Uppsala (UPPS) und Utrecht (UTRE). In einigen Fällen ist der Ortsname nicht aus dem Titel ersichtlich; hierher gehören als die bemerkenswertesten wohl die staatlichen und königlichen Bibliotheken von Dänemark und Holland, die Bayerische Staatsbibliothek, die Deutsche Bibliothek, die Deutsche Bücherei und die gegenwärtige Deutsche Staatsbibliothek, früher Preussische Staatsbibliothek). Diese Institutionen sind der Reihe nach unter Copenhagen (COPE), den Haag (HAGU), München (MUNI), Frankfurt (FRAD), Leipzig (LEIS, LEIZ) und Berlin (BERP, BERS) eingetragen.

Suchmethode. Angenommen, ein Forscher sucht 1) nach einem Artikel von Sir Frederick Kenyon (oder, zur Alternative, nach Artikel von Sir Frederick, die in Festschriften für Bibliothekswesen erschienen sind) und 2) nach einem historischen Bericht über die Preussische Staatsbibliothek in den ersten Jahrzehnten dieses Jahrhunderts. Unter "Kenyon" findet er in dem Index die Eintragung "Copyright Libraries," 248–254, PUTN, und unter "BERLIN. Preussische Staatsbibliothek" den Kreuzverweis auf "BERLIN. Deutsche Staatsbibliothek," wo ihn eine der Referenzen des Untertitels "History" auf einen Aufsatz von Hugo A. Krüss, "Zur Geschichte der Staatsbibliothek zu Berlin in den Letzten Dreissig Jahren," 263–274, PUTN, hinweist. (Wie eben gezeigt, sind die Verfassereintragungen mit grossen Anfangsbuchstaben gedruckt, um sie von den Sacheintragungen, die grossgeschrieben sind, und sich auf Artikel über die Einzelperson beziehen, zu unterscheiden. Schlägt er dann in der alphabetischen Liste der Festschriften mit ihren Kennworten nach, so bemerkt er, dass sich PUTN auf das folgende Werk bezieht: Bishop, William Warner and Andrew Keogh, eds., *Essays Offered to Herbert Putnam by His Colleagues and Friends on His Thirtieth Anniversary as Librarian of Congress 5 April 1929.* New Haven [Connecticut]: Yale University Press, 1929. (Der Einfachheit halber ist derselbe Band für die beiden Beispiele der Autoren- und Gegenstandssuche benützt worden; in der tatsächlichen Praxis würden solche Nachforschungen wohl kaum zu der gleichen Festschrift führen.)

Hilfen für den Benutzer. Am Ende der eben angeführten Referenz erscheint der Vermerk "*Who's Who in America,* 1954/55." Für einige Jubilare konnte keine Referenz in einem biographischen Nachschlagewerk gefunden werden.

Als zusätzliche Hilfe dient schliesslich die Liste "Reviews of the Festschriften". Die Besprechungen (bis zu fünf) erscheinen unter den Kennbuchstaben der Festschriften. So erscheint in der Liste "Reviews of the Festschriften":

PUTN *American Historical Review*, XXXV (October, 1929), pp. 149–50
Minerva, VI (September/October, 1930), p. 170

was besagt, dass Rezensionen der Festschrift zu Ehren Herbert Putnams in *American Historical Review*, Band XXXV, Oktober, 1929, Sn. 149–50, und in *Minerva*, Band VI, September/Oktober, 1930, S. 170, zu finden sind. Für ganz oder teilweise in Zeitschriften erschienene Jubiläumswerke sind keine Kritiken aufgeführt, und für einige der Einzelwerke konnten keine Besprechungen ermittelt werden.

Hätte sich die Suche auf S. R. Ranganathan und Klassifikationssysteme bezogen, so hätten zwei Referenzen auf die Festschrift DONK verwiesen, und zwar:

Hommage à F. Donker Duyvis. [*Revue de la Documentation*, XXVII (November, 1960)], *Wie Is Dat?* 1956.

das heisst, dass Nummer XXVII der *Revue* . . . von November 1960 ausschliesslich eine Ausgabe zu Ehren von F. Donker Duyvis ist, für den sich ein biographischer Vermerk in *Wie Is Dat* für 1956 findet.

In Serienform veröffentlichte Festschriften sind in derselben Weise verzeichnet wie Zeitschriften, d.h. der Titel der ganzen Serie ist am Ende jeder Eintragung in Klammern gegeben. Ort und Datum der Publikation von Serien stehen jedoch wie bei Einzelwerken direkt nach dem Titel des Bandes.

Herausgeber und gemeinsame Herausgeber erscheinen in dem Index; das Kennwort für das herausgegebene Werk folgt ihren Namen, z.B.

Bishop, William Warner, jt. ed.
PUTN
und
Keogh, Andrew, jt. ed.
PUTN

Alle Jubilare, sowohl Einzelpersonen als auch Institutionen, können in dem Index (ohne Rücksicht auf Eintragungen für sie unter Autoren- oder Sachtiteln) unter ihren Namen identifiziert werden, *worunter eingerückt die Kennworte gegeben sind*, z.B.

LEYH, GEORG
LEYG
LEYH
LEYV

was bedeutet, dass Georg Leyh der Jubilar der drei angeführten Festschriften ist.

Die Sprache, in der ein Artikel geschrieben ist, ergibt sich gewöhnlich aus dem Titel. Kyrillische Titel sind nach dem System der Library of Congress transkribiert, und japanische nach dem "modified Hepburn" system.

Zeitbegrenzung

Die Veröffentlichungsdaten der in dem Index erfassten Werke laufen von 1864 bis einschliesslich 1966.

Code Abbreviations of Festschriften*

AACH — Fromm, Emil, ed., *Festschrift aus Anlass der Eröffnung des Bibliotheksgebäudes der Stadt Aachen.* [*Zeitschrift des Aachener Geschichtsvereins,* XIX (1897.)]

AARH — Thomsen, Carl, *10 Aars Folkeligt Biblioteksarbejde i Aarhus By og Opland.* Aarhus: Aarhus Byraads Biblioteksudvalg, 1944.

AARU — *Statsbiblioteket i Aarhus 1902–1927.* Aarhus: Petersen, 1927.

ACCU — Donati, Lamberto, ed., *Miscellanea Bibliografica in Memoria di Don Tommaso Accurti.* Roma, Edizioni di "Storia e Letteratura," 1947. (*Storia e Letteratura,* No. 15.) *Enciclopedia Italiana di Scienze, Lettere, ed Arti.* (Appendix II, 1938–1948.)

ACKE — Rosin, Hans, ed., *Aus dem Volksbüchereiwesen der Gegenwart. Siebzehn Aufsätze zum Fünfzigsten Geburtstag von Dr. Erwin Ackerknecht.* Stettin: Verlag "Bücherei und Bildungspflege," 1930. *Who's Who in Germany,* 1960.

ACKR — *Büchereiplanung. Zehn Beiträge zum Volksbildungswesen der Gegenwart. Professor Dr. Erwin Ackerknecht zum 75. Geburtstag.* [Reutlingen]: Bücherei und Bildung, [1957.] *Who's Who in Germany,* 1960.

ALBA — Prete, Sesto, ed., *Didascaliae. Studies in Honor of Anselm M. Albareda. Presented by a Group of American Scholars.* New York: Rosenthal, [c. 1961.] *Who's Who in Italy,* 1957/58.

ALBB — *Collectanea Vaticana in Honorem Anselmi M. Card. Albareda a Biblioteca Apostolica Edita.* 2 vs. Città del Vaticano: Biblioteca Apostolica Vaticana, 1962. (*Studi e Testi,* 219, 220.) *Who's Who in Italy,* 1957/58.

ALTE — Schmidt, Franz Paul, ed., *Thüringische Studien. Festschrift zur Feier des 250Jährigen Bestehens der Thüringischen Landesbibliothek Altenburg.* Altenburg: Bonde, 1936.

---

* Titles preceded by an asterisk, among those not located in any library in the United States, are available in microfilm or photocopy in the Library of the University of California, Berkeley.

ANNE Nordisk Tidskrift för Bok- och Biblioteksväsen, *Bibliografiska Undersökningar Tillägnade Claes Annerstedt på Hans Sjuttiofemärsdag den 7 Juni 1914.* Upsala: Almqvist & Wilksell, 1914. *Svenskt Biografiskt Lexicon.*

ARTI Sociedad de Menéndez Pelayo, *Homenaje a Miguel Artigas. Estudios de Investigación.* 2 vs. Santander: Edición del Boletín de la Biblioteca de Menéndez Pelayo, 1931, 1932. *Diccionario Enciclopédico U.T.E.H.A.*

*BARA *Zum 100. Geburtstag von Karl August Barack.* [Oberndorf: Singer, 1927.] *Neue Deutsche Biographie.*

BASA *Festschrift zum 150-Jährigen Bestehen der Allgemeinen Lesegesellschaft in Basel, 1787–1937.* Basel: Helbing und Lichtenhahn, 1937.

BASE Heusler, Andreas, *Geschichte der Öffentlichen Bibliothek der Universität Basel.* (Festschrift zur Einweihung der Bibliothek in Basel.) Basel: Reinhardt, 1896.

BASL *Festschrift des Staatsarchivs Basel-Stadt 1899–1949.* Basel: Helbing und Lichtenhahn, 1949.

BAYJ *Hilsen til J. Christian Bay paa Firsaarsdagen 12. Oktober 1951.* København: Rosenkilde og Bagger, 1951. *Kraks blå Bog,* 1961.

BENZ *Festschrift für Josef Benzing zum Sechzigsten Geburtstag 4. Februar 1964.* Wiesbaden: Pressler, 1964. *Who's Who in Germany,* 1964.

BERL Magistrat von Gross-Berlin, Abt. Volksbildung, ed., *Festschrift der Stadt Berlin zum Hundertjährigen Bestehen der Volksbüchereien.* Berlin: Das Neue Berlin, 1950.

BERP Akademie der Künste. *Dreihundert Jahre Preußische Staatsbibliothek 1661–1961.* [Berlin: Akademie der Künste, 1962.] (*Anmerkungen zur Zeit,* no. 7.)

BERR [Weise-Standfest, Hilde and Adolf Weser, eds.], *Die Berliner Stadtbibliothek. Festgabe zur Eröffnung Ihres Neubaues im Oktober 1966.* [Berlin, 1966.]

BERS [Kunze, Horst, Werner Dube, and Günther Fröschner, eds.], *Deutsche Staatsbibliothek, 1661–1961.* I. *Geschichte und Gegenwart.* II. *Bibliographie.* Leipzig: VEB Verlag für Buch- und Bibliothekswesen, [1961.]

BERT Burgerbibliothek Bern, ed., *Schätze der Burgerbibliothek Bern.* Bern: Lang, 1953.

BERU *Fünfzig Jahre Schweizerische Landesbibliothek 1895–1945.* Bern: Schweizerische Landesbibliothek, 1945.

BICK Stummvoll, Josef, ed., *Die Österreichische Nationalbibliothek. Festschrift Herausgegeben zum 25Jährigen Dienstjubiläum des Generaldirektors Univ.-Prof. Dr. Josef Bick.* Wien: Bauer, 1948. *International Who's Who,* 1948.

BINZ *Festschrift Gustav Binz, Oberbibliothekar der Öffentlichen Bibliothek der Universität Basel, zum 70. Geburtstag am 16. Januar 1935 von Freunden und Fachgenossen Dargebracht.* Basel: Schwabe, 1935. *Who's Who in Central and East-Europe.*

BISH Lydenberg, Harry Miller and Andrew Keogh, eds., *William Warner Bishop: A Tribute.* New Haven: Yale University Press, 1941. *Who's Who in America,* 1954/55.

BLOC Berger, Abraham, Lawrence Marwick, and Isidore S. Meyer, eds., *The Joshua Bloch Memorial Volume.* New York: The New York Public Library, 1960. *Who's Who in World Jewry,* 1955.

BOCK [Kunze, Horst, ed.], *Buch und Papier. Buchkundliche und Papiergeschichtliche Arbeiten.* Leipzig: Harrassowitz, 1949. *Kürschners Deutscher Gelehrten-Kalender,* 1950.

BÖME [Degering, Hermann and Walter Menn, eds.], *Westfälische Studien. Beiträge zur Geschichte der Wissenschaft, Kunst und Literatur in Westfalen. Alois Bömer zum 60. Geburtstag Gewidmet.* Leipzig: Hiersemann, 1928. *Wer Ist's?* 1935.

BOLE [Hofmann, Hans, ed.], *Festschrift Martin Bollert zum Achtzigsten Geburtstag am 11. Oktober 1956.* Dresden: [Landesdruckerei Sachsen], 1956. *Kürschners Deutscher Gelehrten-Kalender,* 1950.

BOLL [Neubert, Hermann, ed.], *Festschrift Martin Bollert zum 60. Geburtstage.* Dresden, Jess, [1936.] *Kürschners Deutscher Gelehrten-Kalender,* 1950.

BONN *Mélanges d'Histoire Littéraire et de Bibliographie Offerts à Jean Bonnerot par Ses Amis et Ses Collègues.* Paris: Librairie Nizet, 1954. *Who's Who in France,* 1961/62.

BORO *Todor Borov za 60-Godishninata mu 30 Januari 1961.* Sofiîa, 1961. (Supplement to the *Yearbook* of the Bŭlgarski Bibliografski Institut, VII, 1958–60.) *Kleine Slavische Biographie.*

BORR [Clercx, Suzanne and Albert van der Linden, eds.], *Hommage à Charles van den Borren.* Anvers: N. V. de Nederlandsche Boekhandel, 1945. *Who's Who in Belgium,* 1957/58.

BORV [Van der Linden, Albert, ed.], *Liber Amicorum Charles van den Borren.* Anvers: Lloyd Anversois, 1964. *Who's Who in Belgium,* 1957/58.

BOUR *Sondernummer zum Rücktritt von Herrn Dr. Pierre Bourgeois als Direktor der Schweizerischen Landesbibliothek.* [Vereinigung Schweizerischer Bibliothekare. *Nachrichten,* XXXVIII, No. 6, (1962.)], pp. 167–188. *Who's Who in Switzerland,* 1960/61.

BRIE Stadtbibliothek Wuppertal, ed., *Ausfahrt und Landung. Festgabe für Bibliotheksdirektor Dr. Wolfgang van der Briele zum 65. Ge-*

burtstag am 16. Mai 1959. Wuppertal: Born, 1960. *Who's Who in Germany*, 1960.

BRUE Brummel, Leendert, *Miscellanea Libraria*. 's-Gravenhage: Nijhoff, 1957. *Wie Is Dat?* 1956.

BRUM *Opstellen op het Gebied van Bibliotheekwezen Aangeboden door Vakgenoten aan Prof. Dr. L. Brummel, bij Zijn Afscheid als Bibliothecaris van de Koninklijke Bibliotheek te 's-Gravenhage*. [*Bibliotheekleven*, XLVII (September, 1962.)] *Wie Is Dat?* 1956.

BULL Jena. Universität. Bibliothek. *Weite Welt und Breites Leben. Festschrift zum 80. Geburtstag von Prof. Dr. Karl Bulling am 24. Juli 1965*. (*Zentralblatt für Bibliothekswesen*, Beiheft 82, 1966.) *Kürschners Deutscher Gelehrten-Kalender*, 1966.

BURR Wenig, Otto, ed., *Freundesgabe für Viktor Burr*. Bonn: Bouvier, 1966. (*Bonner Beiträge zur Bibliotheks- und Bücherkunde*, v. 15.) *Who's Who in Germany*, 1964.

BYDG [Wiśniowski, Jerzy, *et al.*, eds.], Z *Życia i Pracy Bydgoskiej Książnicy: Księga Pamiątkowa Biblioteki Miejskiej w Bydgoszczy 1903–1963*. Bydgoszcz, 1965. (Towarzystwo Naukowe. Prace Popularnonaukowe, Nr. 1.)

CAIN *Hommage à Julien Cain*. [*Gazette des Beaux-Arts*, 6th series, LXVIII (July-August, 1966.)] *Who's Who in France*, 1967/68.

CALO *Mélanges d'Histoire du Livre et des Bibliothèques Offerts à Monsieur Frantz Calot*. Paris: Librairie d'Argences, 1960. (*Bibliothèque Elzévirienne, New series, Études et Documents*.) *Who's Who in France*, 1965/66.

CAST [Hasselblatt, Emil, *et al.*, eds.], *Festskrift Tillägnad Gunnar Castrén den 27 December 1938*. Helsingfors, 1938. (*Svenska Litteratursällskapet i Finland*, CCLXXI.) *Kuka Kukin On* (*Who's Who in Finland*), 1954.

CERI Milan. Biblioteca Ambrosiana, *Miscellanea Ceriani. Raccolta di Scritti Originali per Onorare la Memoria di Mr Antonio Maria Ceriani*. Milano, Hoepli, 1910. *Enciclopedia Cattolica*.

CHAT *Mélanges Offerts à M. Émile Chatelain par Ses Élèves et Ses Amis*. Paris: Champion, 1910. *Dictionnaire de Biographie Française*.

COET *University Library Problems, Dedicated to Dr. P. C. Coetzee, Chief Librarian of the University of Pretoria, on Occasion of His 50th Birthday*. [*Mousaion* Nr. 5 and 6, (1955.)] *Who's Who of Southern Africa*, 1966/67.

COLL *Bok- och Bibliotekshistoriska Studier Tillägnade Isak Collijn på Hans 50-Årsdag*. Uppsala: Almqvist & Wiksell, 1925. *Vem Är Det?* 1937.

COPA Dahl, Svend, *Universitetsbibliotekets Nye Bygning. Udgivet af Forening for Boghaandvaerk ved Foreningens 60 Aars Jubilaeum.* København: Fr. Bagges Kongelige Hofbogtrykkeri, 1938.

COPE Fabritius, Albert, *Det Kongelige Biblioteks Embedsmaend og Funktionaerer, 1653–1943.* København: Munksgaard, 1943.

DAAE *Historiske Skrifter Tilegnede og Overleverede Professor Dr. Ludvig Daae paa Hans Syttiende Fødseldag den Syvende December 1904 af Venner og Disciple.* Christiania: Aschehoug, 1904. *Norsk Biografisk Leksikon.*

DAHA *Svend Dahl [Nordisk Tidskrift för Bok- och Biblioteksväsen,* L (1963.)] (Also published separately as: *Nordiska Studier i Bok- och Biblioteksväsen Ägnade Minnet av Svend Dahl.* Uppsala: Almqvist & Wiksell, 1965.) *Kraks Blå Bog,* 1963.

DAHL [Lauri O. Th. Tudeer, *et al.*, eds.], *Ragnar Dahlberg A.D. MCMXLVII Septuagenario Dedicatum.* Helsinki, 1947. (*Miscellanea Bibliographica,* V. *Helsingfors Universitetsbiblioteks Skrifter,* XX.) *Vem Och Vad?* 1948.

DAVI Riggs, John Beverly, ed., *Charles Wendell David: Scholar, Teacher, Librarian.* Philadelphia, 1965. *Who's Who in America,* 1966/67.

DEGE *Mittelalterliche Handschriften. Festgabe zum 60. Geburtstage von Hermann Degering.* Leipzig: Hiersemann, 1926. *Wer Ist's?* 1935.

DEUD *Festschrift zum Zehnjährigen Bestehen der Deutschen Gesellschaft für Dokumentation e.V.* Köln, 1958.

DIAK *Sbornik Boris Diakovitch. Mélanges Boris Diakovitch; Izdanie na Narodnata Biblioteka v Plovdiv.* [Sofiia͡, Dŭrzhavna Pechatnitsa, 1927.]

DOEJ *Festschrift in Honor of Janet Doe. [Bulletin of the Medical Library Association,* XLV (July, 1957.)] *Who's Who of American Women,* 1961/62.

DØSS *Danske Folkebiblioteker. Arbejdets Opgaver og Vilkaar. Festskrift . . . Th. Døssing.* [København (?)]: Bibliotekar-Sammenslutningen for Folkebibliotekerne, 1937. *Dansk Biografisk Leksikon.*

DONK *Hommage à F. Donker Duyvis. [Revue de la Documentation,* XXVII (November, 1960.)] *Wie Is Dat?* 1956.

DONR Nederlands Instituut voor Documentie en Registratuur, *F. Donker Duyvis, His Life and Work.* The Hague: Netherlands Institute for Documentation and Filing, 1964. (NIDER publication series 2, no. 45.) *Wie Is Dat?* 1956.

DREL [Assmann, Karl, ed.], *Sächsische Landesbibliothek Dresden 1556–1956. Festschrift zum 400-Jährigen Bestehen.* Leipzig: Harrassowitz, 1956.

DRES *Festschrift Anläßlich des 50Jährigen Bestehens der Freien Öffentlichen Bibliothek Dresden-Plauen 1906–1956.* [Dresden], 1956.

EAME *Bibliographical Essays. A Tribute to Wilberforce Eames, June: MCMXXIV.* [Cambridge, Mass.: Harvard University Press], 1924. *Who's Who in America,* 1936/37.

EBRA *Festgabe für Friedrich Clemens Ebrard zur Vollendung Seines 70. Lebensjahres am 26. Juni 1920 Gewidmet von Seinen Freunden.* Frankfurt am Main: Baer, 1920. *Wer Ist's?* 1928.

EHRA *Scritti di Storia e Paleografia.* Vol. I. *Per la Storia della Teologia e della Filosofia.* Roma: Biblioteca Apostolica Vaticana, 1924. *Enciclopedia Italiana di Scienze, Lettere, ed Arti.*

EHRB Vol. II: *Per la Storia di Roma.*

EHRC Vol. III: *Per la Storia Ecclesiastica e Civile dell'Età di Mezzo.*

EHRD Vol. IV: *Paleografia e Diplomatica.*

EHRE Vol. V: *Biblioteca ed Archivio Vaticano Biblioteche Diverse.*

*ELBE *Festschrift zur Einweihung des Neubaues der Stadtbücherei* [Elberfeld.] [*Mitteilungen der Stadtbücherei Elberfeld,* II (February, 1929.)]

EMLE Bečka, Josef, Flora Kleinschnitzová and Jan Thon, eds., *Kapitoly Knihovědné a Knihovnické Janu Emlerovi k Šedesátce.* Praha, 1938. (*Slovanská Knihověda V.*) *International Who's Who,* 1938.

ENGE Reese, Gustave, ed., *A Birthday Offering to* [Carl Engel.] New York: Schirmer, 1943. *Who's Who in America,* 1945.

EPPE Köster, Kurt, ed. *Die Deutsche Bibliothek, 1945–1965. Festgabe für Hanns Wilhelm Eppelsheimer zum 75. Geburtstag.* [*Zeitschrift für Bibliothekswesen und Bibliographie,* Sonderheft 3 (1966.)] *Who's Who in Germany,* 1964.

EPST *Fritz T. Epstein zur Vollendung des 65. Lebensjahres Zugeeignet.* [*Jahrbücher für Geschichte Osteuropas.* New Series, XI (September, 1963.)] *Who's Who in Library Service,* 1955.

ESCH Escher, Hermann, *Ausgewählte Bibliothekswissenschaftliche Aufsätze von Dr. Hermann Escher.* Zürich: Rohr, 1937. *Wer Ist's?* 1935.

ESCK [Burckhardt, Felix, ed.], *Festgabe D. Dr. Hermann Escher zum 70. Geburtstage 27. August 1927 Dargebracht von Freunden und Kollegen.* [Zürich, 1927.] *Wer Ist's?* 1935.

ESCZ *Festgabe des Zwingli-Vereins zum 70. Geburtstage Seines Präsidenten Hermann Escher.* Zürich, 1927. *Wer Ist's?* 1935.

EVER *Opstellen bij Zijn Afscheid van de Bibliotheek der Rijksuniversiteit te Utrecht op 31 Mei 1940 Aangeboden aan G. A. Evers.* Utrecht: Oosthoek, 1940. *Wie Is Dat?* 1956.

FAVA *Omaggio a Domenico Fava nell'LXXX Compleanno, con l'Indice Cronologico dei Suoi Scritti.* Bologna, 1953. *Chi è?* 1948.

FEDO Heckmann, Harald and Wolfgang Rehm, eds., *Mélanges Offerts à Vladimir Fédorov à l'Occasion de Son Soixante-Cinquième Anniversaire 5 Août 1966.* [*Fontes Artis Musicae,* (1966, #1)] *Thompson's International Cyclopedia of Music and Musicians.*

FERR *Miscellanea di Scritti di Bibliografia ed Erudizione in Memoria di Luigi Ferrari.* Firenze: Olschki, 1952. *Chi è?* 1948.

FRAD *Bibliographie und Buchhandel. Festschrift zur Einweihung des Neubaus der Deutschen Bibliothek Frankfurt am Main.* [*Börsenblatt für den Deutschen Buchhandel,* Frankfurter Ausgabe, 15th year, No. 32a (22. April, 1959.)]

FRAN [Stevenson, L. G. *et al.,* eds.], *W. W. Francis: Tributes from His Friends on the Occasion of the Thirty-fifth Anniversary of the Osler Society of McGill University.* Montreal: The Osler Society, 1956. *Who's Who in Library Service,* 1955.

*FRED *Frederikshavn Folkebibliotek, 1912–1937.* Frederikshavn: Vogelius, 1937.

FREI [Ginzberg, Louis, *et al.,* eds.], *Studies in Jewish Bibliography and Related Subjects in Memeory of Abraham Solomon Freidus (1867–1923).* New York: The Alexander Kohut Memorial Foundation, 1929. *Universal Jewish Encyclopedia.*

FREN Marx, Alexander and Herrmann Meyer, eds., *Festschrift für Aron Freimann zum 60.Geburtstage.* Berlin. [Aldus Druck], 1935. *Universal Jewish Encyclopedia.*

FUCH Wagner, Ewald, ed., *Aktuelle Probleme der Bibliotheksverwaltung. Festgabe Hermann Fuchs.* Wiesbaden: Harrassowitz, 1966. *Who's Who in Germany,* 1964.

FULD Theele, Joseph, ed., *Aus Fuldas Geistesleben. Festschrift zum 150-Jährigen Jubiläum der Landesbibliothek Fulda.* Fulda: Verlag der Fuldaer Actiendruckerei, 1928.

GALL *Miscellanea di Scritti Vari in Memoria di Alfonso Gallo.* Firenze: Olschki, 1956. *Chi è?* 1948.

GARD [Nikula, Oscar and Olof Mustelin, eds.], *Böcker och Människor Hyllningsskrift till Carl-Rudolf Gardberg 9 September 1958.* [Åbo, 1958.] (Skrifter Utgivna Historiska Samfundet i Åbo VI.) *Kuka Kukin On* (*Who's Who in Finland*), 1954.

GIES [Schawe, Josef, ed.], *Universitätsbibliothek Giessen. Festgabe zur Weihe des Neuen Hauses am 1. Juli 1959.* [Giessen, Schmitz, 1959.]

GJEL Kaser, David, ed., *Books in America's Past. Essays Honoring Rudolph H. Gjelsness.* Charlottesville: University Press of Virginia, [1966.] *Who's Who in America,* 1966/67.

GLAU [Schreiber, Heinrich, ed.], *Otto Glauning zum 60. Geburtstag. Festgabe aus Wissenschaft und Bibliothek.* 2 vols. Leipzig: Hadl, 1936; 1938. *Wer Ist's?* 1935 (GLAU III is used to designate *Archiv für Buchgewerbe und Gebrauchsgraphik,* LXXIII (1936), Part 1, pp. 235–253, containing three articles which are part of the Glauning *Festschrift.*)

GLOS *Ein Wiener Stammbuch. Dem Director der Bibliothek und des Historischen Museums der Stadt Wien, Dr. Carl Glossy, zum 50. Geburtstage, 7. März 1898, Gewidmet von Freunden und Landsleuten.* Wien: Konegen, 1898. *Kürschners Deutscher Literatur-Kalender,* 1900.

GODE *Mélanges Offerts à M. Marcel Godet, Directeur de la Bibliothèque Nationale Suisse à Berne à l'Occasion de Son Soixantième Anniversaire, 8 Mai 1937.* [Neuchâtel, Attinger], 1937. *Who's Who in Central and East-Europe.*

GODM *Herrn Dr. Marcel Godet zum Rücktritt von der Leitung der Schweizerischen Landesbibliothek. Ueberreicht bei Anlass der Jahresversammlung der Vereinigung Schweizerischer Bibliothekare zu Fryburg am 7. und 8. September 1946.* [Vereinigung Schweizerischer Bibliothekare. *Nachrichten,* XXII (September, 1946.)] *Who's Who in Central and East-Europe.*

GÖTE *Göteborgs Stadsbibliotek 1891–1941, Minnesskrift.* Göteborg, 1941. (*Acta Bibliothecae Gotoburgensis,* I.)

GORI Gorizia. R. Biblioteca di Stato. Sezione Provinciale. *Studi Goriziani,* III. Gorizia, 1925.

GRAP *Donum Grapeanum. Festskrift Tillägnad Överbibliotekarien Anders Grape på Sextiofemårsdagen den 7 Mars 1945 . . .* Upsala: Almqvist & Wiksell, 1945. (*Acta Bibliothecae R. Universitatis Upsaliensis,* V.) *Vem Är Det?* 1945.

GRAS *Die Bayerische Staatsbibliothek in Bildern. Emil Gratzl zum Siebzigsten Geburtstag am 30. Dezember 1947 Gewidmet von der Bayerischen Staatsbibliothek.* München, 1947. *Who's Who in Germany,* 1956.

GRAT *Festgabe der Bayerischen Staatsbibliothek. Emil Gratzl zum 75. Geburtstag.* Wiesbaden: Harrassowitz, 1953. *Who's Who in Germany,* 1956.

GRAU Thorin, Ernest, ed., *Mélanges Graux. Recueil de Travaux d'Érudition Classique Dédié à la Mémoire de Charles Graux.* Paris: Thorin, 1884. *Universal Pronouncing Dictionary of Biography and Mythology* (*Lippincott's Pronouncing Biographical Dictionary*).

GREE Miner, Dorothy, ed., *Studies in Art and Literature for Belle da Costa Greene*. Princeton: Princeton University Press, 1954. *Publishers' Weekly*, June 10, 1950, p. 2560.

GREG [Arcamone, Guido, *et al.*, eds.] *Studi di Bibliografia e di Argomento Romano in Memoria di Luigi de Gregori*. Roma: Palombi, 1949. *Chi è?* 1940.

GRYC Biblioteka Narodowa. *Z Zagadnień Teorii i Praktyki Bibliotekarskiej. Studia Poświęcone Pamięci Józefa Grycza*. Wrocław-Warszawa-Kraków: Zakład Narodowy Imienia Ossolińskich-Wydawnictwo, 1961. *Przeglad Biblioteczny*, XXIII (January-March, 1955), pp. 3–40.

GÜST Wolff, Herbert, *Die Öffentlichen Bibliotheken des Kreises Güstrow. Ein Beitrag zur 75-Jahr-Feier der Stadt- und Kreisbibliothek Güstrow*. Güstrow, 1964.

HAEB Collijn, Isak, Ernst Crous, Hermann Degering, *et al.*, eds., *Wiegendrucke und Handschriften. Festgabe Konrad Haebler zum 60. Geburtstage*. Leipzig: Hiersemann, 1919. *Wer Ist's* 1935.

HAEK Schunke, Ilse, ed., *Beiträge zum Rollen- und Platten-einband im 16. Jahrhundert. Konrad Haebler zum 80. Geburtstage am 29. Oktober 1937 Gewidmet*. [(*Sammlung Bibliothekswissenschaftlicher Arbeiten*, XLVI (1937.)]*Wer Ist's?* 1935.

HAGU *Koninklijke Bibliotheek Gedenkboek 1798–1948*. 's-Gravenhage: Nijhoff, 1948.

HAKO *Hakodate Toshokan (Shiritsu): Kaikan Kinen Kōenshū*. (Municipal Hakodate Library, Lectures in Commemoration of the Opening of the Library.) Hakodate: Shiritsu Hakodate Toshokan, 1928. (*Hakodate Toshokan Sosho, Dai Ippen.*) (Hakodate Library Series No. 1.)

HALV Sommerfeldt, W. P., ed., *Minneskrift Utgitt i Anledning av Hundreårsdagen for J. B. Halvorsens Fødsel med Genealogisk Register til Norsk Forfatter-Lexikon 1814–1880*. Oslo: Tanum, 1945 (*Boken om Bøker*, VII.) *Norsk Biografisk Leksikon.*

HAMB *Hamburger Öffentliche Bücherhalle 1899–1949. Festschrift zum Fünfzigjährigen Bestehen*. [Hamburg: The Library, 1949 (?)]

HAMM *An Informal Record of George P. Hammond and His Era in the Bancroft Library*. Berkeley: The Friends of the Bancroft Library, University of California, 1965. *Who's Who in America*, 1960/61.

HANS *James Christian Meinich Hanson*. [*The Library Quarterly*, IV (April, 1934.)] *Who's Who in America*, 1934/35.

HARK Gunzburg, David von and Isaac Markon, eds., *Festschrift zu Ehren des Dr. A. Harkavy aus Anlass Seines am 20. November 1905 Vollendeten Siebzigsten Lebensjahres*. St. Petersburg: [Itzkowski Druck, Berlin], 1908. *Universal Jewish Encyclopedia.*

HARN *Fünfzehn Jahre Königliche und Staatsbibliothek. Dem Scheidenden Generaldirektor Exz. Adolf von Harnack zum 31. März 1921 Überreicht von den Wissenschaftlichen Beamten der Preußischen Staatsbibliothek.* Berlin: Preußische Staatsbibliothek, 1921. *Wer Ist's?* 1928.

HARV Walton, Clarence E., *The Three-Hundredth Anniversary of the Harvard College Library.* Cambridge: Massachusetts, Harvard College Library, 1939.

HASH *Hashimoto Takashi Sensei Koki Kinen Tokushūgō.* (Special Issue Dedicated to Professor Takashi Hashimoto on His 70th Birthday.) [*Mita Toshokan Gakkai* (1965.)] [Library Science, no. 3 (1965.)] *Who's Who in Japan,* 1950/51.

HAVE *Mélanges Julien Havet. Recueil de Travaux d'Érudition Dédiés à la Mémoire de Julien Havet (1853–1893).* Paris: Leroux, 1895. *Dictionnaire Universel des Contemporains (Vapereau).*

HEIN [Holmström, Bengt and Märta Sjögreen, eds.], *Idéer och Resultat. Nordiska Biblioteksuppsatser Tillägnade Ingeborg Heintze.* [Malmö]: Allhem, [1961.] (*Malmö Stadsbiblioteks Vänners Skriftserie* No. 7.) *Vem Är Det?* 1961.

HELD [Bauer, Andreas, ed.], *Festschrift für Hans Ludwig Held. Eine Gabe der Freundschaft und des Dankes. Zum 65. Geburtstag Dargebracht 1. August 1950.* München: Alber, 1950. *Wer Ist's?* 1935.

HEPD [Götze, Alfred and Georg Koch, eds.], *Volkskundliche Ernte. Hugo Hepding Dargebracht am 7. September 1938 von Seinen Freunden.* Gießen: Kindt, 1938. (*Gießener Beiträge zur Deutschen Philologie,* No. 60.) *Wer Ist's?* 1935.

HIRN [Castrén, Gunnar, K. S. Laurila, and Hans Ryin, eds.], *Festskrift Tillägnad Yrjö Hirn den 7 December 1930.* Helsingfors: Schildt, [1930.] *Vem Och Vad?* 1948.

HJEL *Bengt Hjelmquist 60 År den 28 Oktober . . .* [*Biblioteksbladet,* XLVIII (1963.)] *Vem Är Det?* 1967.

HOBO Schmidt-Görg, Joseph, ed., *Anthony van Hoboken. Festschrift zum 75. Geburtstag.* Mainz: Schott, [1962.] *Wie Is Dat?* 1956.

HOFF [Lissberger, Ewald, Theodor Pfizer, and Bernhard Zeller, eds.], *In Libro Humanitas. Festschrift für Wilhelm Hoffmann zum Sechzigsten Geburtstag 21. April 1961.* Stuttgart: Klett, 1962. *Who's Who in Germany,* 1964.

HOFM [Striedl, Hans and Joachim Wieder, eds.], *Buch und Welt. Festschrift für Gustav Hofmann zum 65. Geburtstag Dargebracht.* Wiesbaden: Harrassowitz, 1965. *Who's Who in Germany,* 1964.

*HOLS *Folkebogsamlingen i Holstebro. Centralbiblioteket 1903. 3 Oktober 1928.* Holstebro: Thomsen, 1928.

*HORS Jørgensen, Carl Th., *Fra en Favnfuld Bøger til Horsens Centralbibliotek. Traek af Oplysningsarbejdet i Horsens Gennem 75 Aar.* Horsens: Horsens Centralbibliotek, 1944.

HORT *Miscellanea di Studi in Onore di Attilio Hortis Trieste, Maggio, MCMIX.* 2 vols. Trieste: Caprin, 1910. *Enciclopedia Italiana di Scienze, Lettere, ed Arti.*

HULA *Studier Tillägnada Arvid Hultin på Hans Sextioårsdag den 3 Augusti 1915.* Helsingfors: [Arvingar], 1915. *Nordisk Familjebok.*

HULT *Bibliotekarien Dr. Arvid Hultin Tillägnas denna Skrift på Hans Sjuttioårsdag den 3 Augusti 1925.* Helsingfors: 1925. (*Miscellanea Bibliographica* I, *Helsingsfors Universitetsbiblioteks Skrifter* VIII.) *Nordisk Familjebok.*

HUTT *R. S. Hutton; On the Occasion of His Ninetieth Birthday. [The Journal of Documentation*, XXII (December, 1966), pp. 277–318.]

IMAI *Ōsaka Furitsu Toshokan Chō Imai, Kan'ichi-kun Zaishoku Nijūgonen Kinen Kōen Shū narabini Kinenkai Kiji.* (Collection of Lectures in Commemoration of the 25th Anniversary of the Appointment of Kan'ichi Imai, Director of the Ōsaka Prefectural Library, and the Record of the Celebration Ceremony.) Ōsaka: Ōsaka Furitsu Toshokan Chō Imai Kan'ichi-kun Kinenkai, 1928. *Who's Who in Japan,* 1938.

ISOM *Memorial Number Mary Frances Isom, Librarian 1902–1920. [Library Association of Portland Monthly Bulletin,* XV (May, 1920.)] *Who's Who in America,* 1920/21.

JENA Carl Zeiss-Stiftung, ed., *Buch und Volk. 60 Jahre Ernst-Abbe-Bücherei Jena.* Jena: Fischer, [(c.) 1956.]

JUCH Ohly, Kurt and Werner Krieg, eds., *Aus der Welt des Bibliothekars. Festschrift für Rudolf Juchhoff zum 65. Geburtstag.* Köln: Greven, [1961.] *Who's Who in Germany,* 1964.

JUCR Corsten, Hermann and Gerhart Lohse, eds., *Kölner Schule, Festgabe zum 60. Geburtstag von Rudolf Juchhoff.* Köln: Greven, 1955. (*Arbeiten aus dem Bibliothekar-Lehrinstitut des Landes Nordrhein-Westfalen,* No. 7.) *Who's Who in Germany,* 1964.

*KALU Møller, J. S. and S. Haugstrup, *Kalundborg Bibliotek 1901- 7. November- 1926.* Kalundborg: Vejløs, 1926.

KARA *Dr. Josef Ritter v. Karabacek zur Feier Seines 70. Geburtstages.* [*Wiener Zeitschrift für die Kunde des Morgenlandes,* XXIX (1915.)] *Wer Ist's?* 1914.

KASS Hopf, Wilhelm, ed., *Die Landesbibliothek Kassel 1580–1930.* 2 vols. Marburg: Elwert, 1930.

*KENN *Special Number in Honour of Mr. R. F. Kennedy.* [*The Cauldron,* VII (May, 1960.)] (The Official Staff Bulletin of the Johannesberg Public Library Africana and Geological Museums.) (Mimeo.) *Who's Who in Librarianship.*

KEOG [Withington, Mary C., *et al.*, eds.], *Papers in Honor of Andrew Keogh, Librarian of Yale University, by the Staff of the Library, 30 June 1938.* New Haven [Connecticut]: Privately Printed, 1938. *Who's Who in America,* 1948/49.

KILD *Kulturoptimisme og Folkeopplysning. Festskrift til Arne Kildal på 70-Års Dagen 10. Desember 1955.* Oslo: Aschehoug, 1956. *Hvem er Hvem?* 1964.

KINK [Seeger, Charles, ed.], *A Musicological Offering to Otto Kinkeldey on His 80th Anniversary.* [*Journal of the American Musicological Society,* XIII (1960).] *Who's Who in America,* 1950/51.

KINO *Otto Kinkeldey, in Honor of His Seventieth Birthday, November 27, 1948.* [*Notes,* second series, VI (December, 1948.)] *Who's Who in America,* 1950/51.

KISS Kisser, Alois, *see* STUM.

KJAE *Festskrift Tilegnet Førstebibliothekar A. Kjaer av Venner 26. September 1924.* Christiania: Dybwad and Grøndahl, 1924. *Norsk Biografisk Leksikon.*

*KLEM *Ur Några Antecknares Samlingar. Gärd af Tacksamhet och Vänskap till Mästaren i Svensk Bokkunskap G. E. Klemming.* Upsala: Berling, 1891. *Svensk Uppslagsbok.*

KÖNI *Königsberger Beiträge, Festgabe zur Vierhundertjährigen Jubelfeier der Staats- und Universitätsbibliothek zu Königsberg Pr.* Königsberg: Gräfe und Unzer, 1929.

KOSS [Brummel, Leendert, *et al.*, eds.], *Opstellen door Vrienden en Collega's Aangeboden aan Dr. F. K. H. Kossmann ter Gelegenheid van Zijn Vijf en Zestigste Verjaardag en van Zijn Afscheid als Bibliothecaris der Gemeente Rotterdam.* 's-Gravenhage: Nijhoff, 1958. *Who's Who in the Netherlands,* 1962/63.

KRAK [Tokarz-Wisłocka, Stanisława, *et al.*, eds.], *40 [Czterdzieści] lat Pracy. Pedagogicznej Biblioteki Wojewódzkiej w Krakowie 1922–1962; Praca Zbiorowa.* Warszawa: Stowarzyszenie Bibliotekarzy Polskich, 1963.

KRIS Edström, Wilhelm, *Arvet från Bildningscirkeln. Minnesskrift till Kristianstads Stadsbiblioteks 100-Årsjubileum den 2 Oktober 1961.* [Kristianstad, 1961.]

KRÜS Boeckler, Albert, *Heinrich von Veldeke "Eneide"; Die Bilder der Berliner Handschrift.* Leipzig: Harrassowitz, 1939. *Wer Ist's?* 1928.

KUHN Abb, Gustav, ed., *Von Büchern und Bibliotheken. Dem Ersten Direktor der Preussichen Staatsbibliothek Geheimen Regierungsrat Dr. phil. Ernst Kuhnert als Abschiedsgabe Dargebracht von Seinen Freunden und Mitarbeitern.* Berlin: Struppe & Winckler, 1928. *Wer Ist's?* 1935.

KYLE *Essays Presented to Barbara Kyle.* [*The Journal of Documentation,* XXI (December, 1965), pp. 227–295.]

KYOT *Toshokan no Gaku to Rekishi; Kyōto Toshokan Kyōkai Jisshūnen Kinen Ronshū.* (The Library, Its Science and History; a Collection of Articles Celebrating the Tenth Anniversary of the Kyoto Library Association.) Kyōto: Kyōto Toshokan Kyōkai, 1958.

*LAMB *J. P. Lamb, City Librarian, 1927–1956. [Spellbound* (Summer, 1956.)] (*Magazine of the Sheffield City Libraries Staff Association.*) *Librarian and Book World,* XXIII (July, 1934).

LANE Helweg-Larsen, P., ed., *H. O. Lange. En Mindebog.* København: Haase, 1955. *Dansk Biografisk Leksikon.*

LANF [Zifreund, Viktor, ed.], *Ziel und Wege Bibliothekarischer Bildung. Festgabe zum 65. Geburtstag von Johannes Langfeldt.* Köln: Greven, 1958. *Who's Who in Germany,* 1964.

LANJ Langfeldt, Johannes, *Volksbildung als Aufgabe. Beiträge zum Volks- und Schülerbüchereiwesen.* Köln: Schaffstein, [c. 1953.] *Who's Who in Germany,* 1964.

LASS [Jensen, E. Allerslev, ed.], *Oplands Arbejde. Utsendt som Festskrift til H. Hvenegaard Lassen på 70-Årsdagen 6. September 1956.* København: Dansk Bibliografisk Kontor, 1956. *Kraks Blå Bog,* 1956.

LEID [Hartmann, Albert, ed.], *Festschrift für Georg Leidinger zum 60. Geburtstag am 30. Dezember 1930.* München: Schmidt, [1930.] *Wer Ist's?* 1935.

LEIP Hofmann, Johannes, ed., *Die Bibliothek und ihre Kleinodien. Festschrift zum 250Jährigen Jubiläum der Leipziger Stadtbibliothek.* Leipzig: Hiersemann, 1927.

LEIS *Die Deutsche Bücherei nach dem Ersten Jahrzehnt Ihres Bestehens. Rückblicke und Ausblicke.* Leipzig: Deutsche Bücherei, 1925.

LEIZ *Deutsche Bücherei 1912–1962. Festschrift zum Fünfzigjährigen Bestehen der Deutschen Nationalbibliothek.* Leipzig: VEB Verlag für Buch- und Bibliothekswesen, 1962.

LEUN Vossnack, Lieselotte and Fritz Meyen, eds., *Festschrift zum Fünfundsechzigsten Geburtstag von Otto Leunenschloss, 2. Dezember 1948.* Hannover, 1958. *Kürschners Deutscher Gelehrten-Kalender,* 1954.

LEYG *Festschrift Georg Leyh. Aufsätze zum Bibliothekswesen und zur Forschungsgeschichte Dargebracht zum 60. Geburtstage am 6. Juni 1937 von Freunden und Fachgenossen.* Leipzig: Harrassowitz, 1937. *Who's Who in Germany*, 1964.

LEYH *Aus der Welt des Buches. Festgabe zum 70. Geburtstag von Georg Leyh Dargebracht von Freunden und Fachgenossen.* [(*Zentralblatt für Bibliothekswesen*, Beiheft 75, (1950.)] *Who's Who in Germany*, 1964.

LEYV Burr, Viktor, ed., *Georg Leyh. Verzeichnis Seiner Schriften. Zum 80. Geburtstag am 6. Juni 1957.* Wiesbaden: Harrassowitz, 1957. *Who's Who in Germany*, 1964.

LIND *Nordiska Namnstudier Tillägnade Erik Henrik Lind den 14 Augusti 1919.* Uppsala: Namn och Bygd, [1919–1920.] *Svensk Uppslagsbok.*

LOUB [Husung, Max Joseph, ed.], *Buch und Bucheinband. Aufsätze und Graphische Blätter zum 60. Geburtstage von Hans Loubier.* Leipzig: Hiersemann, 1923. *Wer Ist's?* 1928.

LÜBE Schneider, Heinrich, *Klaus Groth und Emanuel Geibel* [Festgabe zur Eröffnung des Geibelzimmers der Lübecker Stadtbibliothek . . .] Lübeck: Verlag der Lübecker Stadtbibliothek, 1930.

LÜLF *Festschrift zum 60. Geburtstag von Prof. Dr. Hans Lülfing am 24. November 1966.* (*Zentralblatt für Bibliothekswesen*, Beiheft 83, 1966.) *Kürschners Deutscher Gelehrten-Kalender*, 1966.

LÜTH *Karl J. Lüthi.* [*Zeitschrift für Buchdruk-, Bibliophilie- und Pressegeschichte*, XXII, No. 3, (1936.)] *Dictionnaire Historique et Biographique de la Suisse.*

LYDE [Fulton, Deoch, *et al.*, eds.], *Bookmen's Holiday. Notes and Studies Written and Gathered in Tribute to Harry Miller Lydenberg.* New York: The New York Public Library, 1943. *Who's Who in America*, 1942/43.

MAAS *Miscellanea Trajectensia. Bijdragen tot de Geschiedenis van Maastricht. Uitgegeven bij Gelegenheid van het 300-Jarig Bestaan van de Stadsbibliotheek van Maastricht 1662 · 31 Juli · 1962.* Maastricht, 1962. (Limburgs Geschieden Oudheidkundig Genootschap Gevestigd te Maastricht, Nr. 4.)

MADR Chandrasekharan, K., ed., *Library Science in India. Silver Jubilee Volume Presented to the Madras Library Association.* Madras: Madras Library Association; London: Blunt, 1953.

MAIN Busch, Jürgen, ed., *De Bibliotheca Moguntina. Festschrift der Stadtbibliothek Mainz zum Fünfzigjährigen Bestehen Ihres Gebäudes . . . am 7. November 1962.* Mainz: [Die Stadtbibliothek], 1963.

MAIZ [Eibel, Hermann and Hermann Sauter, eds.], *Gedenkschrift zur Einweihung der Neuen Universitätsbibliothek der Johannes Gutenberg-Universität Mainz.* [Mainz, 1966.]

MALE *Sertum Bibliologicum; v Čest' Presidenta Russkogo Bibliologicheskogo Obshchestva Prof. A. I. Malein.* Peterburg: Gosudarstvennoe Izdavatel'stvo, 1922.

MALU Bolay, Karl H., *Malungs Församlingsbibliotek 100 År, Bidrag till Malungs Bibliotekshistoria från 1860 till 1960.* [Malung: Abe, 1961.]

MANN Wendling, Willi, *Die Mannheimer Städtische Volks- und Musikbücherei,* 1895–1961. [Mannheim, 1961.].

MANO *Miscellanea di Studi Storici in Onore di Antonio Manno.* 2 vols. Torino: Officina Poligrafica Editrice Subalpina "O.P.E.S.," 1912. *Enciclopedia Italiana di Scienze, Lettere, ed Arti.*

MARX [Lieberman, Saul, ed.], *Alexander Marx Jubilee Volume. On the Occasion of His Seventieth Birthday. English Section.* New York: The Jewish Theological Seminary of America, 1950. (A second volume, Hebrew Section, has almost identical title page and imprint. See next title.) *Who's Who in America,* 1950/51.

MARY *Jubilee Volume in Honor of Alexander Marx on Completion of Seventy Years. Hebrew Section.* New York: The Jewish Theological Seminary of America, 1950. *Who's Who in America,* 1950/51.

MENE *Homenaje a Don Marcelino Menendez Pelayo. [Revista de Archivos Bibliotecas y Museos,* LXII (January-April, 1956.)] *Diccionario Cronológico Biográfico Universal.*

MENN [Gassen, Kurt, *et al.*, eds.], *Unbekannte Pommernbriefe aus der Universitätsbibliothek Greifswald: Walter Menn zum 50. Geburtstag.* Greifswald: Bamberg, 1940. (*Aus den Schätzen der Universitätsbibliothek zu Greifswald,* 15.) *Who's Who in Germany,* 1964.

MERC *Miscellanea Archivistica Angelo Mercati.* Città del Vaticano, Biblioteca Apostolica Vaticana, 1952. (*Studi e Testi,* 165.) *Chi è?* 1948.

MERG Donati, Lamberto, ed., *Studi e Ricerche nella Biblioteca e negli Archivi Vaticani in Memoria del Cardinale Giovanni Mercati (1866–1957).* Firenze: Olschki, 1959. *Chi è?* 1957.

MIKH *Sbornik v Čest na Akademik Nikola V. Mikhov po Slučaĭ Ocemdesetgodishninata mu.* Sofii͡a: Izdanie na Bulgarskata Akademiya na Naukite, 1959. *Kleine Slavische Biographie,* 1958.

MIKN Sofia. Bŭlgarski Bibliografski Institut, *Sbornik v Čest na Nikola V. Mikhov po Slučaĭ Negovata Sedemdesetgodishnina 18 Mart 1947.* Sofii͡a: 1948. (*Godishnik,* I, 1945–1946.) *Kleine Slavische Biographie,* 1958.

MILF [Leyh, Georg, ed.], *Aufsaetze Fritz Milkau Gewidmet.* Leipzig: Hiersemann, 1921. *Wer Ist's?* 1935.

MILK Abb, Gustav, ed., *Fritz Milkau zum Gedächtnis. Ansprachen, Vorträge und Verzeichnis Seiner Schriften.* Leipzig: Harrassowitz, 1934. *Wer Ist's?* 1928.

MIND *Alere Flammam. Georg Minde-Pouet zum Fünfzigsten Geburtstage Gewidmet von den Wissenschaftlichen Beamten der Deutschen Bücherei und der Gesellschaft der Freunde der Deutschen Bücherei.* Leipzig: Gesellschaft der Freunde der Deutschen Bücherei, 1921. *Kürschners Deutscher Literatur-Kalender,* 1949.

MOOR Spain, Frances Lander, ed., *Reading without Boundaries. Essays Presented to Anne Carroll Moore on the Occasion of the Fiftieth Anniversary of the Inauguration of Library Service to Children at the New York Public Library.* [*Bulletin of The New York Public Library,* Special Issue, LX (November-December, 1956.)] *Who's Who in America,* 1952/53.

MÜNS Münster. Universitäts-Bibliothek. *Aus dem Geistigen Leben und Schaffen in Westfalen. Festschrift zur Eröffnung des Neubaus der Königl. Universitäts-Bibliothek in Münster (Westfalen) am 3. November 1906.* Münster: Coppenrath, 1906.

MUNI [Munich. Bayerische Staatsbibliothek.] *400 Jahre Bayerische Staatsbibliothek.* München: Hirmer, [c. 1958.]

MUNT *Overbibliotekar Wilhelm Munthe på Femtiårsdagen 20. Oktober 1933 fra Fagfeller og Venner.* Oslo: Grøndahl, 1933. *Norsk Biografisk Leksikon.*

NASH *Silver Anniversary of the Joint University Libraries Serving Peabody College, Scarritt College, Vanderbilt University.* Nashville: Joint University Libraries, 1961. (*Miscellaneous Publications,* No. 3.) (Also in: *Peabody Reflector,* July-August, 1961.)

NEUB *Hermann Neubert zum 60. Geburtstage am 9. Dezember 1952.* Berlin: Bibliothek der Technischen Universität, 1952. *Who's Who in Germany,* 1960.

NORN [Ansteinsson, John, Arne Kildal, and Nancy Kobro, eds.], *Norsk Bibliotekforening Jubileumsskrift 1913–1938.* Oslo: Stenersen, 1938.

NORS [Wasberg, Gunnar Christie, ed.], *Bibliotek og Samfunn. Utgitt ved Norsk Bibliotekforenings 50-Årsjubileum.* Oslo, I Kommisjon Hos A/L Biblioteksentralen, 1963.

NYBE [Nivanka, Eino and Dolly Ölander, eds.], *Paul Nyberg A.D. MCMLIX Septuagenario Dedicatum.* Helsinki, 1959. *Miscellanea Bibliographica* VII, *Helsingfors Universitetsbiblioteks Skrifter,* XXVI. *Vem Och Vad?* 1948.

ÖREB [Wieslander, Henning, ed.], *Festskrift med Anledning av Örebro Stadsbiblioteks 75-Årsjubileum 1862–1937.* Örebro: Stadsbibliotek och Samfundet Örebro Stads- och Länsbiblioteks Vänner, [1937.]

OFFO *Essays in Honour of Dr. Offor.* [*The Journal of Documentation,* III (September, 1947), Continued in III (December, 1947.)] *Who's Who,* 1964.

OHAS *Ōhashi Shōun Ō Kiju Shukuga Chosaku Shū.* (A Collection of Articles in Commemoration of the 77th Anniversary of Shintaro Ohashi's Birth.) Tokyo: Ohashi Toshokan, 1939. *Japan Biographical Encyclopedia and Who's Who,* 1964/65.

OLDH *This Number of The Library is Presented to James Basil Oldham on the Occasion of His Eightieth Birthday (28 February 1962) by the Bibliographical Society.* [*The Library,* Fifth Series, XVII (March, 1962.)] *Who's Who,* 1962.

OLSS *Från Småland och Hellas. Studier Tillägnade Bror Olsson 19 6/8 59.* [Malmö]: Allhems Förlag, 1959. *Vem Är Det?* 1967.

OREL Federhofer, Hellmut, ed., *Festschrift Alfred Orel zum 70. Geburtstag Überreicht von Kollegen, Freunden und Schülern.* Wien-Wiesbaden: Rohrer, [1960.] *Who's Who in Germany,* 1960.

*OSLN Bull, Francis and Roar Tank, eds., *Festskrift til den Norske Avdeling ved Universitetsbiblioteket på Femti-årsdagen for Loven om Avgivelse av Trykksaker 1882 · Tyvende Juni · 1932.* Oslo: Steenske, [1932].

OSLO Oslo: Universitetsbiblioteket. *Norvegica. Minneskrift til Femti-årsdagen for Oprettelsen av Universitets Bibliotekets Norske Avdeling 1883 1. Januar 1933.* Oslo: Grøndahl, 1933.

OSLU Drolsum, A. C., *Universitets-Biblioteket 1811–1876. Festskrift i Anledning af 100-Aars Jubilaeet.* Kristiania: Bryde, 1911.

OTAT *Ōta Sensei Kinen Shoroku Kenki Hen.* (A Collection of Articles on Library Science in Commemoration of Tamesaburo Ōta.) Tokyo: Unsokai, 1934. *(Toshokan Kenkyū, Dai Jikkan.)* (Library Study, No. 10.) *Who's Who in Japan,* 1916.

*OURS *Autour d'une Bibliothèque. Pages Offertes à M. Charles Oursel, Conservateur de la Bibliothèque de Dijon de 1899 à 1942 à l'Occasion de Sa Retraite.* Dijon: Bernigaud & Privat, 1942. *Bulletin des Bibliothèques de France,* XII (June, 1967), pp. 239–241.

PARG Bluhm, Heinz, ed., *Essays in History and Literature. Presented by Fellows of the Newberry Library to Stanley Pargellis.* Chicago: The Newberry Library, 1965. *Who's Who in America,* 1960/61.

PELZ *Mélanges Auguste Pelzer. Études d'Histoire Littéraire et Doctrinale de la Scolastique Médiévale Offertes à Monseigneur Auguste Pelzer à l'Occasion de Son Soixante-dixième Anniversaire.* Louvain: 1947. (Université de Louvain. *Recueil de Travaux d'Histoire et de Philologie,* 3rd Series, 26th fasc.) *Speculum,* XXXIV (July, 1959), pp. 534–535.

PENN *Changing Patterns of Scholarship and the Future of Research Libraries. A Symposium in Celebration of the 200th Anniversary of the Establishment of the University of Pennsylvania Library.* Philadelphia: University of Pennsylvania Press, 1951.

PIEK *Studia Nad Książka Poświecone Pamięci Kazimierza Piekarskiego.* Wrocław: Wydawnictwo Zakładu Narodowego im. Ossolińskich, 1951. *Czy Wiesz?*

PUTN Bishop, William Warner and Andrew Keogh, eds., *Essays Offered to Herbert Putnam by His Colleagues and Friends on His Thirtieth Anniversary as Librarian of Congress 5 April 1929.* New Haven [Connecticut]: Yale University Press, 1929. *Who's Who in America,* 1954/55.

PUTP *Herbert Putnam, 1861–1955. A Memorial Tribute.* Washington: The Library of Congress, 1956.

*RAND Lehrmann, N. J., *Randers Folkebibliotek fra dets Oprettelse den 6. November 1862. Udarbejdet i Anledning af 50-Aars Jubilaeet den 6. November 1912.* Randers, 1962.

RANG Kaula, P[rithvi] N[ath], ed., *Library Science Today. Ranganathan Festschrift,* Volume 1, *Papers Contributed on the 71st Birthday of Dr. S. R. Ranganathan (12 August 1962).* Bombay: Asia Publishing House, [c. 1965]. (*Ranganathan Series in Library Science,* 14.) *International Who's Who,* 1966/67.

REDE Sinogowitz, Bernhard, ed., *Aus der Arbeit des Bibliothekars, Aufsätze und Abhandlungen Fritz Redenbacher zum 60. Geburtstag Dargebracht.* Erlangen: Universitäts-Bibliothek, 1960. (*Schriften der Universitäts-Bibliothek Erlangen,* 4.) *Who's Who in Germany,* 1964.

REFA [Ehinger, Hans and Ernst Mohr, eds.], *Edgar Refardt. Musik in der Schweiz. Ausgewählte Aufsätze.* Bern: Haupt, 1952. *Thompson's International Cyclopedia of Music and Musicians.*

RITS *Symbola Philologorum Bonnensium in Honoren Friderici Ritschelii.* Lipsiae: Teubner, 1864–1867. *Allgemeine Deutsche Biographie.*

RUBI *Homenatge a Antoni Rubió i Lluch. Miscellània d'Estudis Literaris Històrics i Lingüistics.* 3 vols. Barcelona: 1936. *Enciclopedia Universal Illustrada Europeo-Americana* (Appendix, Vol. IX).

RUPP Benzing, Josef and Helmut Presser, eds., *Fünfhundert Jahre Mainzer Buchdruck. Festgabe zum 70. Geburtstag von Aloys Ruppel.* Mainz: 1952. *Who's Who in Germany,* 1964.

SAXL Gordon, D. J., ed., *Fritz Saxl, 1890–1948. A Volume of Memorial Essays from His Friends in England.* London: Nelson, [1957.] *Dictionary of National Biography,* 1941/50.

SAYE Powell, Lawrence Clark, ed., *Come Hither! Papers on Children's Literature and Librarianship . . . Read at a Farewell Meeting for Frances Clarke Sayers upon Her Retirement from Library Service and Teaching Held at UCLA June 12, 1965.* Los Angeles: Yeasayers Press, 1966. *Who's Who in Library Service,* 1966.

SAYW Foskett, D. J. and B. I. Palmer, eds., *The Sayers Memorial Volume. Essays in Librarianship in Memory of William Charles Berwick Sayers.* London: The Library Association, 1961. *Who's Who,* 1961.

SCHA [Dahlberg, Ragnar, Holger Nohrström, and Paul Nyberg, eds.], *Festskrift Tillägnad Överbibliotekarien Dr. Georg Schauman på Hans Sextioårsdag den 14 September 1930.* Helsinki: 1930. (*Miscellanea Bibliographica* III, *Helsingfors Universitetsbiblioteks Skrifter* XV.) *Nordisk Familjebok.*

SCHL Gény, Joseph and Gustav C. Knod, *Die Stadtbibliothek zu Schlettstadt. Festschrift zur Einweihung des Neuen Bibliotheksgebäudes am 6. Juni 1889.* Strassburg: DuMont-Schauberg, 1889.

SCHO Geldner, Ferdinand, *Festgabe der Bayerischen Staatsbibliothek für Karl Schottenloher. Bamberger und Nürnberger Lederschnittbände.* München: Karl-Zink, 1953. *Who's Who in Germany,* 1956.

SCHR Stöwesand, Rudolf, ed., *Nunquam Retrorsum. Beiträge zur Schrift- und Buchkunde als Ehrengabe für Herrn Professor Dr. Albert Schramm Anläßlich Seines 50. Geburtstages am 5. August 1930.* [*Archiv für Schreib- und Buchwesen,* IV (August, 1930.)] *Der Grosse Brockhaus.*

SCHS Busch, Jürgen and Werner Jahrmann, eds., *Kleine Beiträge aus der Bibliothekarischen Arbeit. Wilhelm Schuster zum 70. Geburtstag am 10. Juni 1958 Gewidmet.* Berlin: [Amerika-Gedenkbibliothek], 1959. *Wer Ist's?* 1935.

SCHT Sutter, Berthold, ed., *Festschrift Julius Franz Schütz.* Graz-Köln: Hermann Böhlaus Nachf., 1954. *Wer Ist Wer?* 1955.

SCHU *Festschrift Karl Schwarber. Beiträge zur Schweizerischen Bibliotheks-, Buch- und Gelehrtengeschichte zum 60. Geburtstag am 22. November 1949 Dargebracht.* Basel: Schwabe, 1949. *Who's Who in Central and East-Europe.*

SCHV Arbeitsgemeinschaft Kirchlicher Archivare und Bibliothekare, *Archiv und Bibliothek im Kirchlichen Raum. Festschrift für D. Walter Schwarz.* [Kassel]: Kurhessen-Waldeck, 1959.

SCHW [Hortzschansky, Adalbert, ed.], *Beiträge zum Bibliotheks- und Buchwesen. Paul Schwenke zum 20. März 1913 Gewidmet.* Berlin, Breslauer, 1913. *Wer Ist's?* 1922.

*SKAG *Skagens Bibliothek Gennem 75 Aar. 1869–15. Martz–1944.* [Skagen: Skagens Bibliotek (?), 1944.]

SOFI Dobrev, Georgi Mihailov, *The National Library of Bulgaria Celebrates Its 80 Anniversary (1878–December 10–1958). Sofiia, 1958.* (Mimeo.)

SOME *J. F. van Someren, Bibliothecaris der Rijksuniversiteit te Utrecht 1889–1914.* Extra Nummer van "Het Boek." *Samengesteld door Zijne Ambtenaren.* Den Haag: Nijhoff, 1914. *Het Boek,* III (1914), pp. 113–115.

STAM *Miscellanea di Studi Critici in Onore di Ettore Stampini.* Torino-Genova: Lattes, 1920. *Chi è?* 1928.

STEI *Festschrift zum Achtzigsten Geburtstage Moritz Steinschneider's.* Leipzig: Harrassowitz, 1896. *Universal Jewish Encyclopedia.*

STOL Redenbacher, Fritz, ed., *Festschrift Eugen Stollreither zum 75. Geburtstage Gewidmet von Fachgenossen, Schülern und Freunden.* Erlangen: Universitätsbibliothek, 1950. *Who's Who in Germany,* 1956.

STUM Stickler, Michael, Bruno Zimmel, and Walter Krieg, eds. *Festschrift für Josef Stummvoll, Alois Kisser, Ernst Trenkler zum 50. Geburtstag.* [*Das Antiquariat,* VIII (15 August 1952.)] *Who's Who in Austria,* 1964.

SZAC Friedman, Philip, *et al.,* eds., *Jakób Szacki in Memoriam.* New York: Klub Żydów Polskich, 1957.

TEOB Sofiia. Bŭlgarski Bibliografski Institut. *V Čest ma Aleksandŭr Teodorov-Balan po Slučaĭ Negovata 95-Godishnina, 27 Oktomvri 1954.* Sofiia: 1956. (*Godishnik* IV, 1954.) *Kleine Slavische Biographie.*

TEOD *Sbornik v Čest na Akademik Aleksandŭr Teodorov-Balan, po Slučaĭ Devetdeset i Petata mu Godishnina.* Sofiia: Izdanie na Bŭlgarskata Akademiia na Naukite, 1955. *Kleine Slavische Biographie.*

THOM [Hansen, Robert L., ed.], *I Ideens Tjeneste. Udsendt Som Festskrift til Carl Thomsen ved Hans Afgang som Biblioteksleder 31. Oktober 1962.* København: Dansk Bibliografisk Kontor, 1962. *Kraks Blå Bog,* 1966.

TIEM *Libris et Litteris. Festschrift für Hermann Tiemann zum Sechzigsten Geburtstag am 9. Juli 1959.* Hamburg: Maximilian-Gesellschaft, [1959]. *Who's Who in Germany,* 1960.

TØND Skovrøy, P., *Tredive Aar i Tønder. Udgivet i Anledning af Tønder Biblioteks 25 Aars Jubilaeum.* [Tønder?]: Laursen, 1948.

TOKY *Gojūnen Kai: Toshokan no Hatten no Tame ni—Groshunen Kinen Ronbun Shū.* (For the Progress of Libraries—a Collection of Articles in Commemoration of the Fifth Anniversary of the Gojūnen Kai.) Tokyo: Gojūnen Kai, 1958.

TOMI *Tominaga Sensei Kakō Kinen Kohan Shoshi Ronso.* (A Collection of Studies on Ancient Bibliographies in Commemoration of the Sixty-First Anniversary of Makita Tominaga's Birth.) Tenri: Tenri Toshokan, 1962. *Jinji Kōshin.*, 1966.

*TORS *Torslev Sognebibliotek, 1893–1923.* [Torslev]: 1923.

TREN Trenkler, Ernst, *see* STUM.

TSUB *Tsuboya Sensei Kiju Kinen Chosakushū.* (A Collection of Articles in Commemoration of the 77th Anniversary of Zenshiro Tsuboya's Birth.) Tokyo: Ōhashi Toshokan, 1938. *Who's Who in Japan,* 1938.

TUDE *Lauri O. Th. Tudeer A.D. MCMXLIV Sexagenario Dedicatum.* Helsinki, 1944. (*Miscellanea Bibliographica,* IV, *Helsingfors Universitetsbiblioteks Skrifter,* XIX.) *Vem Och Vad?* 1948.

TUNK *Juhlajulkaisu Tohtori E. A. Tunkelon Täyttäessä 60 Vuotta 27. IV. 1930.* [*Suomi Kirjoituksia Isänmaallisista Aineista,* V, part 10, (1930.)] *Vem Och Vad?* 1931.

TVET *Med Boken som Bakgrunn. Festskrift til Harald L. Tveterås.* Oslo: Tanum, 1964. *Hvem er Hvem?* 1964.

UPPS *Uppsala Universitets Biblioteks Minnesskrift 1621–1921.* Uppsala: Almqvist & Wiksell, 1921. (*Acta Bibliothecae R. Universitatis Upsaliensis,* vol. 1.)

UTRE *Liber Libris Ditissimae Sacer. Opstellen Geschreven ter Herdenking van het 375-Jarig Bestaan van de Universiteitsbibliotheek te Utrecht 1584–1959.* 's-Gravenhage: Nijhoff, [c. 1961.] [Also in: *Het Boek,* XXXIV (1961), pp. 133–209.]

*VARL *D. H. Varley. [The Sapling* (October, 1961.)] (Staff News Sheet of the South African Library. Mimeo.) *Who's Who of Southern Africa,* 1966.

VERD Schulz, Erich, ed., *Festschrift zur 23. Versammlung Deutscher Bibliothekare in Dortmund.* Leipzig: Hiersemann, 1927.

VERE Eichler, Ferdinand, *Aus einer Österreichischen Bibliothek. Ein Festgruss der Sektion für Bibliothekswesen bei der 50. Versammlung Deutscher Philologen und Schulmänner in Graz.* Graz: im Selbstverlag des Verfassers, 1909.

VERP Focke, Rudolf, ed., *Festschrift zur Begrüssung der Sechsten Versammlung Deutscher Bibliothekare in Posen am 14. und 15. Juni 1905.* Posen: Jolowicz, 1905.

VERZ *Zeugnisse Fränkischer Kultur. Erinnerungsgabe der Universitätsbibliothek Erlangen zur 27. Versammlung Deutscher Bibliothekare 1931.* Nürnberg, Spindler, [1931.] [*Fränkische Halbjahrsschrift,* Heft 1, (1931.)]

*VIBO Aakjaer, Svend, *Tyllands Aeldste Offentlige Bibliotek. Viborg Stifts Bibliotek 1817–1942.* Viborg: Viborg Biblioteksforening, 1942.

VIEN *Festschrift der Nationalbibliothek in Wien. Herausgegeben zur Feier des 200Jährigen Bestehens des Gebäudes.* Wien: Druck und Verlag der Österreichischen Staatsdruckerei, 1926.

VIES *Festschrift zum Hundertjährigen Bestehen der Wiener Stadtbibliothek 1856–1956.* Wien: Verlag für Jugend und Volk, [c. 1956.].

VISB Sollerman, Pelle, ed. (?), *Visby Stadsbibliotek. Länsbibliotek för Gotland. Årsskrift 1965. Minnesskrift 1865–1965.* [Visby: Gotlands Allehandas Tryckeri, 1966.]

VLEE *Festschrift H. J. de Vleeschauwer.* Pretoria, 1960. (*Communications of the University of South Africa,* C Supplement 1.) *Who's Who of Southern Africa,* 1963.

VORS [Roloff, Heinrich, ed.], *Bibliothek · Bibliothekar · Bibliothekswissenschaft. Festschrift Joris Vorstius zum 60. Geburtstag Dargebracht.* Leipzig: Harrassowitz, 1954. *Kürschners Deutscher Gelehrten-Kalender,* 1961.

WAHL Hecker, Max, *et al.,* eds., *Funde und Forschungen. Eine Festgabe für Julius Wahle zum 15. Februar 1921.* Leipzig: Inselverlag, 1921. *Wer Ist's?* 1935.

WEHM [Joost, Siegfried, ed.], *Bibliotheca Docet. Festgabe für Carl Wehmer.* Amsterdam: Erasmus, 1963. *Wer Ist Wer?* 1962.

WEIM Blumenthal, Hermann, ed., *Aus der Geschichte der Landesbibliothek zu Weimar und Ihren Sammlungen. Festschrift zur Feier Ihres 250Jährigen Bestehens und zur 175Jährigen Wiederkehr Ihres Einzuges ins Grüne Schloss.* Jena: Fischer, 1941.

WHIT *Walter Muir Whitehill. A Record Compiled by His Friends.* Minot, Massachusetts [Anthoensen Press, Portland, Maine], 1958. *Who's Who in America,* 1966/67.

WIES Götting, Franz and Rupprecht Leppla, *Geschichte der Nassauischen Landesbibliothek zu Wiesbaden und der mit Ihr Verbundenen Anstalten 1813–1914. Festschrift zur 150-Jahrfeier der Bibliothek am 12. Oktober 1963.* Wiesbaden: Historische Kommission für Nassau, 1963. (*Veröffentlichungen der Historischen Kommission für Nassau,* XV.)

WILM *Beiträge zur Bücherkunde und Philologie. August Wilmanns zum 25. März 1903 Gewidmet.* Leipzig: Harrassowitz, 1903. *Kürschners Deutscher Literatur-Kalender,* 1917.

WILS *Louis Round Wilson. Papers in Recognition of a Distinguished Career in Librarianship.* Chicago: University of Chicago Press, [1942.] [Also in: *Library Quarterly,* XII (July, 1942)] *Who's Who in America,* 1952/53.

WOLF *Festschrift zu Ehren des Siebzigsten Geburtstages von Georg Wolfram mit Beiträgen Seiner Freunde und Fachgenossen.* Frankfurt a.M.: Selbstverlag des Elsaß-Lothringen-Instituts, 1929. (Elsaß-Lothringisches Jahrbuch, VIII.) *Wer Ist's?* 1928.

WOLJ Lott, Walter, Helmuth Osthoff, and Werner Wolffheim, eds., *Festschrift für Johannes Wolf zu Seinem Sechzigsten Geburtstage.* Berlin: Breslauer, 1929. *Wer Ist's?* 1922.

WRED *Festschrift Ferdinand Wrede zu Seinem Sechzigsten Geburtstage am 15. Juli 1923.* [*Zeitschrift für Deutsche Mundarten,* XVIII (1923), pp. 147–324.] *Wer Ist's?* 1928.

WROT [Goff, Frederick R., *et al.,* eds.], *Essays Honoring Lawrence C. Wroth.* Portland, Maine [Anthoensen Press,] 1951. *Who's Who in America,* 1950/51.

Wuppertal, *see* Elberfeld, ELBE.

ZIEG Zunker, Ernst, ed., *Ein Leben im Dienst der Bibliothek. Festgabe für Hans Ziegler zu Seinem 70. Geburtstag am 13. November 1957.* Greifswald: [Panzig'sche Buchdruckerei], 1957. (*Veröffentlichungen der Universitäts-Bibliothek Greifswald,* No. 2) *Zentralblatt für Bibliothekswesen,* LXXI (September-October, 1957), pp. 371–372.

ZIVN *Sborník Věnovaný Oslavě L. J. Živného.* Praze, 1935. *Who's Who in Central and East-Europe,* 1933/34.

Reviews of the Festschriften

AARU *Bogens Verden,* IX (January/February, 1927), 125–126.

ACKE *Zentralblatt für Bibliothekswesen,* XLVIII (December, 1931), 685–686.

ACKR *Bogens Verden,* XL (March, 1958), 105–106.
Biblioteksbladet, XLIII, n. 5 (1958), 352.
Zeitschrift für Bibliothekswesen und Bibliographie, V (1958), 222–223.

ALBA *Bibliographical Society of America Papers,* LVII (January, 1963), 104–106.

BASA *Schweizer Sammler. Le Collectionneur Suisse,* XII (1938), 154.

BASE *Zentralblatt für Bibliothekswesen,* XIV (May, 1897), 230.

BAYJ *Zentralblatt für Bibliothekswesen,* LXVI (November/December, 1952), 463.
Library Quarterly, XXIV (October, 1954), 407–408.

BENZ *Bulletin de Documentation Bibliographique,* IX (May, 1964), 249–251.
Bibliographical Society of America Papers, LVIII (October, 1964), 498–499.
Het Boek, XXXVII (1964/1965), 108.
Zeitschrift für Bibliothekswesen und Bibliographie, XII (1965), 245–248.

BERP *Zeitschrift für Bibliothekswesen und Bibliographie,* IX (1962), 189.

BERR *Bibliothekar,* XX (December, 1966), 1340–1341.
Zentralblatt für Bibliothekswesen, LXXXI (February, 1967), 113–114.

BERS *Zentralblatt für Bibliothekswesen,* LXXVII (April, 1963), 169–174.

BERU *Library Quarterly,* XVII (July, 1947), 236–238.

BICK *Zentralblatt für Bibliothekswesen,* LXIV (July/August, 1950), 308–310.
Nordisk Tidskrift för Bok-och-Biblioteksväsen, XXXVI, n. 2 (1949), 96–98.
Libri, I, n. 1 (1950), 91–93.
Journal of Documentation, VI (June, 1950), 108–112.

BINZ *Nordisk Tidskrift för Bok-och-Biblioteksväsen,* XXII (1935), 194–196.
Zentralblatt für Bibliothekswesen, LIV (April, 1937), 196–197.

BISH *Library World,* XLIV (December, 1941), 85.
Library Quarterly, XII (January, 1942), 112–114.
Library Journal, LXVI (1 October 1941), 834.
Library Association Record, XLIV (February, 1942), 22.

BLOC *Jewish Social Studies,* XXV (July, 1963), 232.
Reconstructionist, XXIX (December, 1963), 29–31.

BOCK *Zentralblatt für Bibliothekswesen,* LXVI (March /April, 1952), 139–143.

BÖME *Zentralblatt für Bibliothekswesen,* XLV (December, 1928), 747–748.
Revue des Bibliothèques, XL (January/July, 1930), 105–106.

BOLE *Zentralblatt für Bibliothekswesen,* LXXI (September/October, 1957), 382–384.

BOLL *Literarisches Zentralblatt für Deutschland,* LXXXVII (15 November 1936), 963.
Zentralblatt für Bibliothekswesen, LIV (August, 1937), 391–392.

BORO *Zentralblatt für Bibliothekswesen,* LVXXIII (January, 1964), 52–53.

BRIE *Bücherei und Bildung,* XIII (May, 1961), 212.
Verband der Bibliotheken des Landes Nordrhein-Westfalen Mitteilungsblatt, X (December, 1960), 171–172.

BRUE *Nachrichten Vereinigung Schweizerischer Bibliotheken,* XXXIV (March, 1958), 78.
Zeitschrift für Bibliothekswesen und Bibliographie, V (1958), 327–331.
Zentralblatt für Bibliothekswesen, LXXIII (March/April, 1959), 127–130.
Library Quarterly, XXVIII (October, 1958), 364–366.
Het Boek, XXXIII, n. 2 (1958), 127–128.

CALO *Bulletin de Documentation Bibliographique,* VI (February, 1961), 83–84.
Library (London), XVII (September, 1962), 260–262.

CERI *Philologische Wochenschrift,* XXX (1910), 585–590.

CHAT *Archiv für Stenographie,* LXII (January/March, 1911), 44–46.

COLL *Het Boek,* XV (January/March, 1926), 84–87.
Revue des Bibliothèques, XXXV (August/October, 1925), 474–475.
Historisk Tidskrift, XLVI (1926), 75.
Nordisk Tidskrift för Bok-och-Bibliotheksväsen, XII (1925), 241–244.

COPA	*Bogens Verden,* XX (October, 1938), 280.
COPE	*Bogens Verden,* XXVI (January/February, 1944), 10.
DAHA	*Bok og Bibliotek,* XXXIII (July, 1966), 229–230.
DAHL	*Nordisk Tidskrift för Bok-och-Biblioteksväsen,* XXXV, n. 1 (1948), 27–28.
DAVI	*Biblioteksbladet,* LI, n. 8 (1966), 577.
DEGE	*Deutsche Literaturzeitung,* XLVIII (31 December 1927), 2585–2590.
DØSS	*Bogens Verden,* XX (January/February, 1938), 7–10.
DONR	*Journal of Documentation,* XXI (September, 1965), 215–216. *Revue Internationale de la Documentation,* XXXII (May, 1965), 66. *Zentralblatt für Bibliothekswesen,* LXXX (June, 1966), 364.
DREL	*College and Research Libraries,* XVIII (November, 1957), 506–507. *Zentralblatt für Bibliothekswesen,* LXXII (March/June, 1958), 143–144. *Zeitschrift für Bibliothekswesen und Bibliographie,* IV (1957), 197–199.
DRES	*Bibliothekar,* X (November, 1956), 637–638. *Bogens Verden,* XXXVIII (September, 1957), 304–305. *Zentralblatt für Bibliothekswesen,* LXXI (November/December, 1957), 451–452.
EAME	*Zentralblatt für Bibliothekswesen,* XLIII (September/October, 1926), 500–502.
EBRA	*Kunstchronik und Kunstmarkt,* N.S. XXXIII (1921), 80. *Deutsche Literaturzeitung,* XLII (28 May 1921), 318. *Zeitschrift für Bücherfreunde,* S. 2, XIII (1921), 252–253. *Historische Zeitschrift,* CXXIV (1921), 484–485. *Zentralblatt für Bibliothekswesen,* XL (1923), 39–40.
EHRA	*Zentralblatt für Bibliothekswesen,* XLII (June, 1925), 273–276.
EHRB	*Zentralblatt für Bibliothekswesen,* XLII (June, 1925), 273–276.
EHRC	*Zentralblatt für Bibliothekswesen,* XLII (June, 1925), 273–276.
EHRD	*Zentralblatt für Bibliothekswesen,* XLII (June, 1925), 273–276.
EHRE	*Zentralblatt für Bibliothekswesen,* XLII (June, 1925), 273–276.
EPPE	*Het Boek,* XXXVII (1966), 245.
ESCH	*Bogens Verden,* XX (March, 1938), 73–74. *Library Quarterly,* VIII (April, 1938), 319–320. *Zentralblatt für Bibliothekswesen,* LIV (November, 1937), 569–571. *Het Boek,* XXV (1938/1939), 254.
EVER	*Zentralblatt für Bibliothekswesen,* LX (October/December, 1943), 285.

FRAD	*Bogens Verden,* XLI (October, 1959), 409–410. *Biblos,* IX, n. 1 (1960), 22–29. *Library Quarterly,* XXX (April, 1960), 148–149. *Zeitschrift für Bibliothekswesen und Bibliographie,* VI (1959), 257–258.
FRAN	*Library Association Record,* LIX (May, 1957), 184.
FREN	*Monatsschrift für Geschichte und Wissenschaft,* LXXXI (September/October, 1937), 449–452.
FUCH	*Zeitschrift für Bibliothekswesen und Bibliographie,* XIII (1966), 343. *Zentralblatt für Bibliothekswesen,* LXXXI (February, 1967), 105–107.
FULD	*Studien und Mitteilungen zur Geschichte des Benediktiner-Ordens und Seiner Zweige,* XLVII (1929), 406–407. *Revue des Bibilothèques,* XL (January/July, 1930), 105–107.
GALL	*Accademie e Biblioteche d'Italia,* XXIV (1956), 213.
GARD	*Bogens Verden,* XL (December, 1958), 562.
GIES	*Zentralblatt für Bibliothekswesen,* LXXIV (September, 1960), 293–294.
GJEL	*Library Journal,* XCII (15 March 1967), 1133. *College and Research Libraries,* XXVIII (March, 1967), 144–145.
GLAU	*Börsenbatt für den Deutschen Buchhandel,* CIII (December 12, 1936), 1091.
GODE	*Bibliotheekleven,* XXIII (February, 1938), 33–34. *Zentralblatt für Bibliothekswesen,* LV (June, 1938), 276–278. *Nordisk Tidskrift för Bok-och Biblioteksväsen,* XXIV, n. 3 (1937), 189–191. *Het Boek,* XXV (1938/1939), 254.
GÖTE	*Nordisk Tidskrift för Bok-och-Biblioteksväsen,* XXVIII, n. 3 (1941), 141–143. *Library Quarterly,* XII (April, 1942), 312–313. *Het Boek,* XXVIII (1944–1946), 90.
GRAP	*Library Quarterly,* XVI (April, 1946), 178–179. *Nordisk Tidskrift för Bok-och-Biblioteksväsen,* XXXII, n. 2 (1945), 95–98.
GRAS	*Zentralblatt für Bibliothekswesen,* LXII (September/December, 1948), 316–317.
GRAT	*Nachrichten für Wissenschaftliche Bibliotheken,* VI (February, 1953), 3–5.

GREE *American Journal of Archaeology,* LIX (April, 1955), 191.
Apollo, LXI (April, 1955), 127.
Burlington Magazine, XCVII (June, 1955), 185.
Speculum, XXX (April, 1955), 289–291.

GREG *Libri,* n. 1 (1950), 96.

HAEB *Deutsche Literaturzeitung,* XLI (3 January 1920), 7–10.
Zentralblatt für Bibliothekswesen, XXXVI (November/December, 1919), 279–280.

HAEK *Zentralblatt für Bibliothekswesen,* LV (December, 1938) 672–674.
Archiv für Buchgewerbe und Gebrauchsgraphik, LXXV (1938), 156–157.

HAGU *Bibliotheekleven,* XXXIV (March, 1949), 74.
Libri, I, n. 3 (1951), 289–290.
Library Quarterly, XIX (October, 1949), 297–298.

HAMB *Bücherei und Bildung,* II (January/February, 1950), 264–265.

HANS *Bogens Verden,* XVI (June, 1934), 133–134.

HARN *Zentralblatt für Bibliothekswesen,* XXXVIII (November/December, 1921), 298–302.

HEIN *Library Association Record,* LXIV (September, 1962), 326–328.
Bogens Verden, XLIV (March, 1962), 127–128.
Zentralblatt für Bibliothekswesen, LXXIX (January, 1965), 33–34.

HELD *Library Quarterly,* XXII (April, 1952), 151–152.

HOBO *Music and Letters,* XLVI (April, 1965), 163–165.

HOFF *Bücherei und Bildung,* XV (July/August, 1963), 364.
Library Quarterly, XXXIII (April, 1963), 213–214.
Zeitschrift für Bibliothekswesen und Bibliographie, X (1963), 172–174.

HOFM *Zentralblatt für Bibliothekswesen,* LXXX (July, 1966), 430–431.
Zeitschrift für Bibliothekswesen und Bibliographie, XII (1965), 333–337.

HORT *Giornale Storico della Letteratura Italiana,* LVII (1911), 139–140.
Philologische Wochenschrift, XXX (1910), 1253–1256.

HULA *Nordisk Tidskrift för Bok-och-Biblioteksväsen,* II (1915), 291–295.

HULT *Nordisk Tidskrift för Bok-och-Biblioteksväsen,* XIII (1926), 103–104.

JENA *Zentralblatt für Bibliothekswesen,* LXXI (November/December, 1957), 451–452.
Bücherei und Bildung, X (January, 1958), 26.
Bogens Verden, XXXIX, n. 2 (March, 1957), 119.

JUCH *Libri,* XIII, n. 1 (1963), 79–80.
Bulletin de Documentation Bibliographique, VII (April, 1962), 226.
Library (London), XVII (December, 1962), 318–320.
Zeitschrift für Bibliothekswesen und Bibliographie, IX (1962), 63–66.
Zentralblatt für Bibliothekswesen, LXXVII (July, 1963), 320–323.

JUCR *Zentralblatt für Bibliothekswesen,* LXX (September/October, 1956), 375–378.
Het Boek, XXXII, n. 3 (1956), 282–283.
Library Quarterly, XXVI (April, 1956), 140.

KASS *Minerva Zeitschrift,* VII (July/August, 1931), 129.
Deutsche Literaturzeitung, LII (20 September 1931), 1777–1780.

KEOG *Nordisk Tidskrift för Bok-och-Biblioteksväsen,* XVI, n. 1 (1939), 46–47.
Library Quarterly, IX (January, 1939), 101–102.

KILD *Bogens Verden,* XXXVIII (December, 1956), 416–417.
Bok og Bibliotek, XXIII (September, 1956), 260–263.

KJAE *Zentralblatt für Bibliothekswesen,* XLII (February, 1925), 88–89.

KÖNI *Zeitschrift für Geschichte und Altertumskunde Ermlands,* XXIV (1931), 252.

KOSS *Het Boek,* XXXIV, n. 2 (1960), 115–117.

KRIS *Biblioteksbladet,* XLVII (January, 1962), 38.
Bogens Verden, XLIII (December, 1961), 524–525.

KRÜS *Zentralblatt für Bibliothekswesen,* LVII (August/September, 1940), 428–430.

KUHN *Göttingische Gelehrte Anzeigen,* CXCI (June, 1929), 280–286.

LANE *Bogens Verden,* XXXVII (December, 1955), 486.

LANF *Bogens Verden,* XLI (May, 1959), 159–160.

LANJ *Bogens Verden,* XXXV (September, 1953), 269.

LASS *Bok og Bibliotek,* XXIII (November, 1956), 301–302.

LEID *Archiv für Buchgewerbe und Gebrauchsgraphik,* LXVIII (1931), 179–180.
Historische Zeitschrift, CXLV (February, 1932), 611.
Mitteilungen aus der Historischen Literatur, XX (1932), 65–66.
Minerva Zeitschrift, VII (July/August, 1931), 128.

LEIP *Zentralblatt für Bibliothekswesen,* XLV (April, 1928), 198–200.
Zeitschrift für Bücherfreunde (Beiblatt), S.2, XX (May/June, 1928), 105–106.

LEIZ *Australian Library Journal,* XII (June, 1963), 94.
Zeitschrift für Bibliothekswesen und Bibliographie, X (1963), 228–234.

Bibliothekar, XVII (January, 1963), 60–65.
Biblos, XII, n. 2 (1963), 74–75.

LEYG *Zentralblatt für Bibliothekswesen,* LV (December, 1938), 664–668.
Deutsche Literaturzeitung, LIX (10 April 1938), 505–508.
Nordisk Tidskrift för Bok-och-Biblioteksväsen, XXV, n. 1 (1938), 44–51.

LOUB *Nordisk Tidskrift för Bok-och-Biblioteksväsen,* XI (1924), 68–70.

LYDE *Bibliographical Society of America Papers,* XXXVII (October/December, 1943), 316–319.
Library Quarterly, XIV (January, 1944), 62–63.
Library Journal, LXVIII (1 December 1943), 1011.

MADR *Library Association Record,* LVI (January, 1954), 31–32.
Libri, IV, n. 3 (1954), 265–270.

MAIN *Zentralblatt für Bibliothekswesen,* LXXX (June, 1966), 370.

MALU *Nordisk Tidskrift för Bok-och-Biblioteksväsen,* L, n. 3 (1963), 113–114.

MANO *Archives Belges,* XV (July 25, 1913), 227.
Archivio Storico Italiano, LXXI, n. 1 (1913), 380–387.
Giornale Storico della Letteratura Italiana, LXI (1913), 436–439.

MARX *Biblica,* XXXV, n. 3 (1954), 390–391.

MARY *Biblica,* XXXV, n. 3 (1954), 390–391.

MIKH *Zentralblatt für Bibliothekswesen,* LXXV (December, 1961), 548–552.

MILF *Zentralblatt für Bibliothekswesen,* XXXVIII (November/December, 1921), 298–302.

MILK *Zeitschrift des Veriens für die Geschichte Mahrens und Schlesiens,* LXVIII (1935), 381.

MÜNS *Literarisches Zentralblatt für Deutschland,* LVIII (April, 1907), 445–446.
Deutsche Literaturzeitung, XXVII (December, 1907), 3143–3146.
Literarische Rundschau für das Katholische Deutschland, XXXIII (October, 1907), 471.

MUNI *Zeitschrift für Bibliothekswesen und Bibliographie,* V (1958), 338.

MUNT *Nordisk Tidskrift för Bok-och-Biblioteksväsen,* XXI (1934), 138–141.
Zentralblatt für Bibliothekswesen, LI (March, 1934), 177–178.

NORN *Bogens Verden,* XX (December, 1938), 357–361.

NORS *Bok og Bibliotek,* XXX (November, 1963), 343–344.

NYBE *Nordisk Tidskrift för Bok-och-Biblioteksväsen,* LVII (1960), 72–73.
Biblioteksbladet, XLIV (1959), 681.

ÖREB *Zentralblatt für Bibliothekswesen,* LVI (April, 1939), 200–201.
Bibliotheksbladet, XXII, n. 6 (1937), 234–237.

OLSS *Nordisk Tidskrift för Bok-och-Biblioteksväsen,* XLVII (1960), 155–156.

OREL *Bücherei und Bildung,* XIII (March, 1961), 135–136.

OSLN *Bibliographical Society of America Papers,* VII, n. 1/2 (1912/1913), 51–68.

OSLO *Bogens Verden,* XV (April/May, 1933), 77–78.
Nordisk Tidskrift för Vetenskap, IX (1933), 239.
Zentralblatt für Bibliothekswesen, LI (April, 1934), 225–226.

PARG *Library Quarterly,* XXXVI (April, 1966), 175–177.

PENN *Library Association Record,* LIV (May, 1952), 184.
South African Libraries, XX (July, 1952), 23.
College and Research Libraries, XIII (October, 1952), 393–395.
Library Review, n. 109 (Spring, 1954), 310–312.
Library Journal, LXXVII (1 May 1952), 776.

PIEK *Bibliotekarz,* XIX (July/August, 1952), 119–120.

PUTN *American Historical Review,* XXXV (October, 1929), 149–150.
Minerva, VI (September/October, 1930), 170.

RANG *Indian Librarian,* XX (June, 1965), 32.
Library Quarterly, XXXV (October, 1965), 388.
Biblioteksbladet, LI, n. 7 (1966), 473–474.

REDE *Bücherei und Bildung,* XIII (October, 1961), 416–417.
Bulletin de Documentation Bibliographique, VII (January, 1962), 21–22.

RUBI *Byzantinisch-Neugriechische Jahrbücher,* XIII (1937), 123.
Neophilologus, XXIII, n. 1, (1937), 62–63.

RUPP *Library Quarterly,* XXIII (October, 1953), 311.
Nordisk Tidskrift för Bok-och-Biblioteksväsen, XL, n. 4 (1953), 166–167.

SAYW *Libri,* XII, n. 2 (1962), 162–163.
Library Quarterly, XXXII (July, 1962), 239–240.
Reol, I (December, 1962), 283.
Bulletin de Documentation Bibliographique, VII (September, 1962), 605–607.
Revue Internationale de la Documentation, XXIX (August, 1962), 108.

SCHA *Nordisk Tidskrift för Bok-och-Biblioteksväsen,* XVIII (1931), 33–35.

SCHL *Zentralblatt für Bibliothekswesen,* VII (May, 1890), 207–208.

SCHO *Nachrichten für Wissenschaftliche Bibliotheken,* VI (February, 1953), 1–2.
Zeitschrift für Bibliothekswesen und Bibliographie, I (1954), 147–148.

SCHR *Literarisches Zentralblatt für Deutschland,* LXXXI (15 October 1930), 1314.

SCHS *Bulletin de Documentation Bibliographique,* VI (April, 1961), 178.
Library Quarterly, XXX (April, 1960), 153–154.

SCHT *Zentralblatt für Bibliothekswesen,* LXX (November/December, 1956), 465–466.

SCHU *Library Association Record,* LII (April, 1950), 138–139.
Nordisk Tidskrift för Bok-och-Biblioteksväsen, XXXVII, n. 2 (1950), 91–93.
Library Quarterly, XXI (January, 1951), 69–71.
Libri, I, n. 1 (1950), 93–95.
Het Boek, XXX, n. 3 (1949/1951), 318–319.

SCHW *Zentralblatt für Bibliothekswesen,* XXX (April, 1913), 185–186.

STEI *Zentralblatt für Bibliothekswesen,* XIV (August, 1897), 365–372.

STOL *Library Quarterly,* XXIII (January, 1953), 53–54.
Bibliographical Society of America Papers, XLVII (January/March, 1953), 89–93.
Libri, I, n. 4 (1951), 393–394.
Zentralblatt für Bibliothekswesen, LXVI (January/February, 1952), 50–55.
Bibliotheekgids, XXVIII (March/April, 1952), 41.

THOM *Bogens Verden,* XLIV (December, 1962), 528–530.
Reol, II (December, 1963), 240.

TIEM *Library Quarterly,* XXXI (January, 1961), 121–124.

TUDE *Nordisk Tidskrift för Bok-och-Bibliotheksväsen,* XXXII, n. 2 (1945), 88–90.

TVET *Libri,* XV, n. 1 (1965), 124.
Nordisk Tidskrift för Bok-och-Biblioteksväsen, LIII, n. 1 (1966), 25–26.
College and Research Libraries, XXVI (November, 1965), 527–528.
Zentralblatt für Bibliothekswesen, LXXX (October, 1966), 619–622.
Reol, III (December, 1964), 247–248.

UPPS *Nordisk Tidskrift för Bok-och-Biblioteksväsen,* IX (1922), 51–53.
Het Boek, XI (1922), 312–316.

VERD *Die Heimat,* IX (1927), 356.
Revue des Bibliothèques, XXXVIII (July/October, 1928), 329–335.
Zentralblatt für Bibliothekswesen, XLV (April, 1928), 201–202.

VERE *Deutsche Literaturzeitung*, XXXI (20 August 1910), 2122–2125.

VERP *Görris-Gesellschaft zur Pflege der Wissenschaft im Katholischen Deutschland*, XXVII (1906), 236–237.

VERZ *Zentralblatt für Bibliothekswesen*, XLIX (1932), 91–94.

VIEN *Zentralblatt für Bibliothekswesen*, XLIII (November, 1926), 564–568.

VIES *Das Antiquariat*, XII (April, 1956), 95.

VORS *Accademie e Biblioteche d'Italia*, XXIII (January/February, 1955), 65–67.
Australian Library Journal, IV (October, 1955), 155–156.
Bibliotekar (Belgrade), IX, n. 1/2 (1957), 101–102.
Journal of Documentation, XI (September, 1955), 149–151.
Library Quarterly, XXV (April, 1955), 195–197.

WAHL *Göttingische Gelehrte Anzeigen*, CLXXXIV (July/September, 1922), 237–240.
Literarisches Zentralblatt für Deutschland, LXXII (5 November 1921), 876.

WIES *Zentralblatt für Bibliothekswesen*, LXXX (June, 1966), 368.
Zeitschrift für Bibliothekswesen und Bibliographie, XII (1965), 116–119.

WILM *Mitteilungen des Österreichischen Vereins für Bibliothekswesen*, VII (18 July, 1903), 133–134.

WILS *Library Association Record*, XLIV (November, 1942), 175–176.

WOLJ *Die Musik*, XXII, n. 1 (October, 1929), 55.

WROT *Bibliographical Society of America Papers*, XLVI (January/March, 1952), 78–82.

ZIEG *Zentralblatt für Bibliothekswesen*, LXXI (September/October, 1957), 371–372.

ZIVN *Library Quarterly*, VIII (January, 1938), 146–147.

Author and Subject Index to the Festschrift Articles

Åberg, Åke.
Visby Stadsbibliotek. Förhistoria och Begynnelseår. 5-30, VISB

ÅBO, Finland
see Turku, Finland

AACHEN - Architecture and building - Public libraries
see Architecture and building - Public libraries - Aachen

AACHEN - Astrological literature - Collections
see Astrological literature - Collections - Aachen

AACHEN - Gifts, contributions, etc.
see Gifts, contributions, etc. - Aachen

AACHEN - Public libraries
see Public libraries - Aachen

AACHEN. Rathshandbibliothek
see also Aachen. Stadtbibliothek; Public libraries - Aachen

AACHEN. Rathshandbibliothek - Hist.

Fromm, Emil. Geschichte der Stadtbibliothek. I. Die Rathshandbibliothek im 17. und 18. Jahrhundert. II. Die Dautzenbergsche Schenkung. III. Die Stadtbibliothek von Ihrer Eröffnung (1831) bis zum J. 1889. IV. Die Verwaltung der Stadtbibliothek seit dem J. 1889. 21-48, (pt. 1), AACH

AACHEN. Roerdepartement. Archiv

Pauls, E. Zur Geschichte des Archivs des Roerdepartements in Aachen. 72-92, (pt. 2), AACH

AACHEN. Stadtarchiv

Laurent, J. Das Neu Errichtete Archiv- und Bibliothek-Gebäude der Stadt Aachen. 1-20, (pt. 1), AACH

AACHEN. Stadtbibliothek

AACH

Ågren, Sven.
Om Nordinska Handskriftssamlingen i Uppsala Universitetsbibliotek. Några Anteckningar. 468-497, UPPS
Till Arkivleveransernas Historia. Några Anteckningar. 338-349, GRAP

Aakjaer, Svend
VIBO

AARHUS, Denmark - Architecture and building - State libraries
see Architecture and building - State libraries - Aarhus, Denmark

AARHUS, Denmark - Catalogs
see Catalogs - Aarhus, Denmark

AARHUS, Denmark - Catalogs - Classed
see Catalogs - Classed - Aarhus, Denmark

AARHUS, Denmark - Catalogs - Subject
see Catalogs - Subject - Aarhus, Denmark

AARHUS, Denmark - Interlibrary loans
see Interlibrary loans - Aarhus, Denmark

AARHUS, Denmark. Kommunens Biblioteker

AARH

Bredsted, Åge. Oplandsarbejdets Okonomi. 37-47, LASS

AARHUS, Denmark - Legal deposit (of books, etc.)
see Legal deposit (of books, etc.) - Aarhus, Denmark

AARHUS, Denmark - Newspaper libraries and collections
see Newspaper libraries and collections - Aarhus, Denmark

AARHUS, Denmark - Personnel
see Personnel - Aarhus, Denmark

AARHUS, Denmark - Public libraries
see Public libraries - Aarhus, Denmark

AARHUS, Denmark - Rural libraries - Finance
see Rural libraries - Finance - Aarhus, Denmark

AARHUS, Denmark - Special collections
see Special collections - Aarhus, Denmark

AARHUS, Denmark - State and provincial library agencies - Public library services
see State and provincial library agencies - Public library services - Aarhus, Denmark

AARHUS, Denmark - State libraries
see State libraries - Aarhus, Denmark

AARHUS, Denmark - State libraries - Acquisitions
see State libraries - Acquisitions - Aarhus, Denmark

AARHUS, Denmark - State libraries - Finance
see State libraries - Finance - Aarhus, Denmark

AARHUS, Denmark. Statsbibliotek

AARU

Sejr, Emanuel. Statsbiblioteket og Centralbibliotekerne. 96-102, LASS

AARHUS, Denmark. Statsbibliotek - Bibl.

Christensen, Tagea Egede. Bibliografi. 181-188, AARU

AARHUS, Denmark. Statsbibliotek - Hist.

Sejr, Emanuel. En Udlånsindskraenkning. Statsbibliotekets Krise 1912. 71-89, DAHA

AARHUS, Denmark - Use studies - State libraries
see Use studies - State libraries - Aarhus, Denmark

Abb, Gustav, ed.
KUHN; MILK

Abb, Gustav.
Eine Denkschrift Philipp Buttmanns über Katalogfragen vom Jahre 1791. 177-181, KUHN
Die Einführung der Täglichen Ausleihe in der Berliner Kgl. Bibliothek. 179-185, GODE
Milkaus Literarisches Lebenswerk. 39-45, MILK
Von der Kollegialverfassung zum Führerprinzip. Ein Beitrag zur Verfassungsgeschichte der Preußischen Staatsbibliothek. 245-256, LEYG
Von der Verschollenen Bibliothek des Klosters Lehnin. 1-14, DEGE

ABBE, ERNST CARL

Jobst, Rudolf. Einleitende Bemerkungen: Ernst Abbe, die Carl-Zeiss-Stiftung und die "Jenaer Lesehalle." 11-16, JENA

ABBREVIATIONS

Schaible, Eduard. Abkürzung in Schrift und Sprache. 73-81, SCHR

ABDINGHOF (MONASTERY) PADERBORN
see Paderborn. Abdinghof (Monastery)

ABERDEEN - Bookbinding - Fine bindings - Collections
see Bookbinding - Fine bindings - Collections - Aberdeen

ABERDEEN. University. Library

Mitchell, Wm. S. German Bindings in Aberdeen University Library: Iconographic Index, and Indices of Initials, Binders and Dates. 46-55, OLDH

ABINU, ISRAEL BEN ABRAHAM

Bamberger, S. Wandsbeker Druckperiode des Israel ben Abraham 1726 bis 1733. 101-108, FREN

Abitz, Oluf.
Foellesbogsamlinger. 48-56, LASS

Abrahams, I.
The Bodleian Mss. Entitled "The Fear of Sin." 72-75, STEI

ABSTRACTING

Loosjes, Th. P. Documentanalyse. 521-526, BRUM

ABSTRACTS
see Indexes and abstracts

ACADEMIA DE LA HISTORIA, Madrid. Mss. (Casas)

Hanke, Lewis. The Historia de las Indias of Bartolomé de las Casas. 143-150, WROT

ACADÉMIE DES SCIENCES, ARTS ET BELLES-LETTRES DE DIJON

Tisserand, Roger. L'Académie de Dijon et Denis Diderot. 152-162, OURS

ACADEMY OF SCIENCES OF THE USSR. Library. Slavic Division

Shafranovskij, K. I. and G. F. Podozerskaia. Iz Istorii Organizatsii v XIX Veke Slavianskogo Otdeleniia Biblioteki Akademii Nauk v Peterburge. 351-362, MIKH

ACCESS TO SHELVES

Becker, Henrik. Schaubüchereien auch Heute? 43-46, BULL
Koopman, Harry Lyman. The Open-Shelf Library. 257-262, PUTN
Lemaître, Henry. Le Libre Accès au Rayon. 343-349, LEYG

Schmidt, Wieland. Offene Buchbestände in Universalbibliotheken. 125-142, FUCH
Vleeschauwer, H. J. de. Le Libre Accès aux Livres dans la Bibliothèque Universitaire. 70-87, COET

ACCESSIONING

Battisti, Carlo. Registro d'Ingresso e Inventario Topografico. 56-80, GORI

ACCREDITATION OF LIBRARIANS
see Certification of librarians

ACCURTI, TOMMASO

ACCU

Ackerknecht, Erwin.
Aus der Frühzeit der Ernst-Abbe-Bücherei. 46-48, JENA
Erinnerungen an die Anfänge der Berliner Büchereischule. 7-12, LANF
Lieber Johannes Langfeldt. 7-8, LANJ
Stadtbüchereibauten. 194-204, LEYH

ACKERKNECHT, ERWIN

ACKE

ACKR

Beer, J. Pädagogische Menschenkunde. 9-14, ACKE
Schiller, Karl-Heinz. Das Ludwigsburger Beispiel. 49-60, ACKR

ACKERKNECHT, ERWIN - Bibl.

Endell, F. and H. Messin. Schriften von Dr. Erwin Ackerknecht. Eine Bibliographische Zusammenstellung. 167-178, ACKE

ACQUISITIONS
see also Book selection; Books - Prices; College and university libraries - Acquisitions; Exchange of books, periodicals, etc.; Gifts, contributions, etc.; Importation and exportation of books; Inexpensive editions; Library resources; National libraries - Acquisitions; Public libraries - Acquisitions; Rare books - Acquisitions; Reprints; Second-hand books; Technical services

ACQUISITIONS

Lifka, Bohumír. Radosti a Strasti Knižní Akvisice. 120-124, EMLE

ACQUISITIONS, COOPERATIVE

Busse, Gisela von. Warum Gemeinschaftliche Erwerbungspläne? 137-150, HOFM

ACQUISITIONS, COOPERATIVE
see also Farmington plan

ACQUISITIONS, COOPERATIVE - Pakistan

Khan, M. Siddiq. A Farmington Plan for Pakistan. 428-433, RANG

ACQUISITIONS - Czechoslovakia

Van Toch, Jeannie. Styky L. J. Živného s Knihovnictvím Anglickým a Americkým. 25-64, ŽIVN

ACQUISITIONS - Germany (Federal Republic, 1949-)

Tiemann, Hermann. Materialien zur Bedarfsberechnung für ein Etatmodell. 9-20, REDE

ACQUISITIONS - Order processes

Bauhuis, Walter. Arbeitsmethoden der Erwerbungsabteilung. 37-41, REDE

ACQUISITIONS - Order processes - Germany

Jürgens, Adolf. Der Suchdienst der Reichstauschstelle. I, 105-111, GLAU

ACQUISITIONS - Order processes - Uppsala

Henriksson, Karl-Erik. Notes on the Acquisition Work in the Uppsala University Library. 228-236, DAHL

ACQUISITIONS - Vatican - 1579

Berra, Luigi. Due Listi di Libri per la Biblioteca Vaticana. 19-27, MERG

ADALBERT VON SACHSEN

Arens, Fritz. Das Brevier des Administrators Adalbert von Sachsen in der Mainzer Universitätsbibliothek. 67-89, MAIZ

Adam, Paul.
Der Einfluß der Klosterarbeit auf die Einbandkunst. 148-169, LOUB

Adamczak, Helena.
Rozwój i Charakterystyka Pedagogicznej Biblioteki Powiatowej w Wadowicach. 89-97, KRAK

ADAMNAN, SAINT. Mss. Vita S. Columbae.

Frauenfelder, Reinhard. Die Älteste Handschrift in der Stadtbibliothek Schaffhausen. 155-160, LÜTH

Adamovich, Ludwig.
Zur Frage des Rechtsschutzes für Private Bibliotheken. 203-207, BICK

Adams, Marion W. and Jeannette D. Black.
A List of Published Writings of Lawrence C. Wroth to December 31, 1950. 485-504, WROT

Adams, Percy G.
The Case of Swaine Versus Drage: An Eighteenth-Century Publishing Mystery Solved. 157-168, PARG

Adams, Randolph G.
A Goodly Company of American Book Collectors. 29-32, LYDE
A Translation of the Rosetta Stone. 227-241, EAME

ADAPTATIONS OF LIBRARY BUILDINGS (from houses, churches, etc.)
see Architecture and building - Remodeled buildings and additions

Adde, Gustaf.
Äldre Finskspråkiga Skrifter i Svenska Bibliotek. 269-294, COLL
Förteckning öfver Bibliotekarien Claes Annerstedts Utgifna Skrifter. 1-10, ANNE

Adhémar, Jean.
Julien Cain et le Cabinet des Estampes. 76-82, CAIN

Adler, Elkan N.
A Bibliography of the Writings of Adolf Neubauer (1832-1907). 31-54, FREI

Adlerová, Eliška.
Několik Uměleckohistorických Poznámek k Výstavě Francouzské Ilustrované Knihy v Praž. Národní a Universitni Knihovně. 80-83, EMLE

ADMINISTRATION
see Libraries - Administration; Personnel - Administration

ADMINISTRATION - Manuscripts
see Manuscripts - Administration

ADOLESCENTS, Services to
see Young adults' library services

ADREMA MACHINE
Kragemo, Helge Bergh. Zur Frage der Rationalisierung des Tauschverkehrs einer Wissenschaftlichen Bibliothek. 377-381, MUNT
Lund, Hanna. Der Adrema-Betrieb in der Katalogisierung. 404-409, MUNT
Predeek, A. Fortschritte im Katalogdruck nach dem Adrema-System. 197-210, MUNT

ADULT EDUCATION
see also Books and reading

ADULT EDUCATION - Library participation
see also Public libraries - Services to groups; Reader guidance

ADULT EDUCATION - Library participation
Möhring, Werner. Vom Volksbildnerischen Bemühen des Bibliothekars. 61-74, LANF

ADULT EDUCATION - Library participation - Denmark
Pihl, Bent. Bogen i det Frie Oplysningsarbejde. 35-44, THOM
Thomsen, Carl. Bibliotekerne og det Øvrige Oplysningsarbejde. 85-93, DØSS

ADULT EDUCATION - Library participation - Germany
LANJ

ADULT EDUCATION - Library participation - Norway
Bakken, Asbjørn. Små Bemerkninger om Store Saker. 177-186, NORS
Zachariassen, Aksel. Bibliotekene og Opplysningsorganisasjonene. 161-167, NORS

ÄLF, SAMUEL - Library
Lagerborg, Rolf. Ur Hecatompolis Suionum. 112-125, HULA

AESOPUS. Mss.
Branca, Vittore. Un Esopo Volgare Veneto. 105-115, FERR

AESCHYLUS. Choephori
Krause, Heinrich. De Aeschyli Choephororum Versibus 261-297 Kirchh. 229-242, WILM

AFRICANUS, SEXTUS JULIUS
Harnack, Adolf von. Julius Afrikanus, der Bibliothekar des Kaisers Alexander Severus. 142-146, MILF

AGAPITO
Tocci, Luigi Michelini. Agapito, Bibliotecario "Docto, Acorto et Diligente" della Biblioteca Urbinata alla Fine del Quattrocento. II, 245-280, ALBB

AGRICOLA, MICHAEL OLAVI, Bp. - Library
Carlsson, A. B. Rester av Michael Agricolas Boksamling i Svenska Bibliotek. 335-353, COLL
Dahlberg, Ragnar. En Volym ur Michael Agricolas Boksamling. 57-70, SCHA

AGRICOLA, MICHAEL OLAVI, Bp. - Manuscripts - Collections - Uppsala
Carlsson, A. B. Fragment av en Ordspråkssamling av Michael Agricola i Uppsala Universitetsbibliotek. 142-146, GRAP

AGRICULTURAL LIBRARIES - Japan
Sawamoto, Takahisa. Agricultural Sci-

ence Libraries in Japan. 107-119, HASH

AGRIPPINAS, HEILRICUS ZEELL
see Zell, Heinrich

Aguilera, Ignacio.
En Torno al Concepto de la Estética en Menéndez Pelayo. 115-128, MENE

AHMEDABAD - Classification
see Classification - Ahmedabad

AIMS OF LIBRARIANSHIP
see Librarianship - Aims and objectives

Aizawa, Toyokatsu.
Beikoku Giin Toshokan Insatsu Kādo ni tsuite. (On the Printed Cards of the Library of Congress.) 83-104, TSUB
Yōsho Mokurokuhō Nyumon. (An Introduction to the Cataloguing of Foreign Books.) 33-73, (part 1), OHAS

AKADEMIIA NAUK SSSR. Biblioteka. Slavianskii Otdel
see Academy of Sciences of the USSR. Library. Slavic Division.

AKADEMISKA BOKTRYCKERIET - Uppsala
see Uppsala Akademiska Boktryckeriet

Alarcos, Emilio.
El Toledano y los Poetas Clásicos Latinos. II, 325-335, ARTI

Alba, Duke of.
En Tributo de la Memoria de Belle da Costa Greene. 3, GREE

ALBANI COLLECTION, Catholic University of America
see Catholic University of America. Library. Albani Collection

ALBANI, GIANFRANCESCO
see Clemens XI, Pope, 1649-1721

Albareda, Anselmo M., Cardinal.
Un Incunabulo Sconosciuto dello Stampatore J. Luschner. 29-50, ACCU
Il Vescovo di Barcellona Pietro Garsias Bibliotecario della Vaticana sotto Alessandro VI. 1-18, MERG

ALBAREDA, ANSELMO M., Cardinal

ALBA

ALBB

Alberts, W. Jappe.
De Maastrichtse Raadsverdragen uit de Middeleeuwen. 169-178, MAAS

Albion, Robert G.
Mentor at Mystic. 61-68, DAVI

Alblas, J.
De Nederlandsche Incunabelen der Universiteitsbibliotheek. 33-36, SOME

ALBRECHT, DUKE OF PRUSSIA - Library

Diesch, Carl. Crotus Rubeanus im Dienste des Herzogs Albrecht. 45-61, KÖNI
Kuhnert, Ernst. Die Nova Bibliotheca des Herzogs Albrecht. 209-219, MILF
Warda, Arthur. Die Exlibris des Herzogs Albrecht von Preussen. 349-354, KÖNI

ALBRECHT VON BRANDENBURG, DUKE
see Albrecht, Duke of Prussia

ALBRECHTSON, H. C. - Library

Christiansen, Reidar Th. Albrechtsons Visesamling. 106-130, OSLN

ALBUMS, POMMERANIAN - Collections - Greifswald

Ziegler, Hans. Pommersche Stammbücher. 19-30, ZIEG

Alcalde, Lesmes.
El "Liber Anniversariorum" del Antiguo Convento de Santa Catalina de Barcelona. II, 519-539, RUBI

ALCUIN

Wallach, Luitpold. The Unknown Author of the _Libri Carolini_: Patristic Exegesis, Mozarabic Antiphons, and the _Vetus Latina_. 469-515, ALBA

ALDERSBACH (CISTERCIAN MONASTERY) BIBLIOTECA. Mss.

Hörmann, Wolfgang. Probleme einer Aldersbacher Handschrift (Clm. 2599). 335-389, HOFM

Alexander, Gerhard.
Ein Prachteinband aus Gräflich Oldenburgischem Besitz in der Staats- und Universitätsbibliothek Hamburg. 167-176, TIEM

ALEXANDER KOHUT MEMORIAL FOUNDATION

Kohut, Rebekah. Prof. Alexander Marx. xi-xxiii, MARX

ALEXANDER KOHUT STIFTUNG
see Alexander Kohut Memorial Foundation

ALEXANDER OF APHRODISIAS. _De Anima_

Bruns, Ivo. Un Chapitre d'Alexandre d'Aphrodisias sur l'Âme. 567-572, GRAU

ALEXANDER SEVERUS, Emperor of Rome
see Severus Alexander, Emperor of Rome

ALEXANDER THE GREAT (Romances, etc.) Mss.
Pietschmann, Richard. Zu den Überbleibseln des Koptischen Alexanderbuches. 301-312, WILM
Yarmolinsky, Avrahm. A Seventeenth-Century Russian Manuscript in the New York Public Library. 323-334, LYDE

ALEXANDER TURNBULL LIBRARY, Wellington, N.Z.
Tautz, Kurt. Die Turnbull Library in Wellington - ein Spiegel des Pazifischen Raumes. 263-270, JUCH

ALEXANDRE DE VILLEDIEU. Doctrinale. 1485
Keyman, Johanna M. Enkele Opmerkingen over een Merkwaardige Incunabel der Utrechtsche Universiteitsbibliotheek. 204-216, EVER

ALFONSO V, EL MAGNANIMO, King of Aragon - Library
D'Alós, Ramon. Documenti per la Storia della Biblioteca d'Alfonso il Magnanimo. 390-422, EHRE

ALFONSO X, EL SABIO, King of Castile and Leon. Mss. Cantigas de Santa Maria
Pousa, Ramón Fernández. Menéndez Pelayo y el Códice Florentino de las Cantigas de Santa Maria de Alfonso X el Sabio. 235-255, MENE

Aliprandi, Giuseppe.
Aspetti Particolari della Grafia. 39-46, GALL

Alker, Hugo.
Geschichte der Sachkatalogisierung an der Universitätsbibliothek Wien 1774-1954. 118-132, VORS

Allen, Th. W.
Three Greek Scribes. 22-33, EHRD

ALLGEMEINE LESEGESELLSCHAFT, Basel
see Basel. Allgemeine Lesegesellschaft

ALLOCATION OF FUNDS
see Budgets

ALL-UNION LIBRARY OF FOREIGN LITERATURE, Moscow
see Moscow. All-Union Library of Foreign Literature

Almagià, Roberto.
Alcune Preziose Carte Geografiche di Recente Acquisite alle Collezioni Vaticane. I, 1-22, ALBB

ALMANACS - Hist.
Schottenloher, Karl. Tagebuch-Aufzeichnungen in Immerwährenden Kalendern der Frühdruckzeit. II, 88-96, GLAU

Alonso, B. Sánchez.
Epistolario de Menéndez Pelayo con Bibliotecarios y Bibliófilos. 183-190, MENE

Alonso, Dámaso.
Góngora y la Literatura Contemporánea. 246-284, ARTI

ALPHABETING
see Filing

Alphen, G. van.
Anthony Smets, Bibliothecaris van Drie Prinsen van Oranje (1636-1689). 119-160, HAGU

ALSACE - Monastic libraries
see Monastic libraries - Alsace

Alschner, Christian and Marie Bundesmann.
Bibliographie zur Geschichte der Sächsischen Landesbibliothek. 209-279, DREL

ALTENBURG, Ger. - Cards - Collections
see Cards - Collections - Altenburg, Ger.

ALTENBURG, Ger. Spielkartenmuseum
Reisig, Otto. Die Kartenrückseiten in Ihrer Bedeutung für die Zeitliche Festlegung der Spielkarten. 123-133, ALTE

ALTENBURG, Ger. Thüringische Landesbibliothek
ALTE

Altermatt, Leo.
Die von Staalsche Historienbibel der Zentralbibliothek Solothurn. 35-71, SCHU

Altmann, Ursula.
Die Inkunabelsammlung. I, 381-403, BERS

Altmann, Wilhelm.
Die Entwicklung der Musikabteilung. 211-217, HARN
Die Königliche Bibliothek in Berlin in Ihren Beziehungen zum Königlichen Opernhaus (1788-1843). 51-66, WILM
Zur Aufstellung und Katalogisierung der Bücher. 310-315, KUHN

ALTZELLE (CISTERCIAN ABBEY) - Bookbinding
Glauning, Otto. Drei Lederschnittbände von der Wende des XIV. Jahrhunderts aus Altzelle. 188-195, BOLL

ALXINGER, J. B. - Collections - Halle
Prokert, Heinz. Fünf Briefe J. B. Alxingers an Ch. F. Blankenburg. 221-233, BULL

AMALIA, DUCHESS OF SAXE-WEIMAR-EISENACH
Münnich, Richard. Aus der Musikaliensammlung der Weimarer Landesbibliothek, besonders dem Nachlass der Anna Amalia. 168-184, WEIM
Wahl, Hans. Die Weimarische Bibliothek als Erbin der Herzogin Anna Amalia. 158-167, WEIM

Amano, Keitarō.
Sakuin ni tsuite. (On Indexes.) 142-147, KYOT

Amatya, P. P.
Salute to Dr. Ranganathan. 723-724, RANG

AMBRAS, Austria. Schloss Ambras. Bibliothek. Mss.
Menhardt, Hermann. Die Altdeutschen Ambrasiani der Österreichischen Nationalbibliothek. 56-57, STUM

Ameisenowa, Zofia.
Nieznany Wzór Złotniczy z XV w. w Bibliotece Jagiellońskiej. 365-369, PIEK

AMERBACH FAMILY (Basel)
Roth, Carl. Conrad Pfister, Basilius Iselin und die Amerbachsche Bibliothek. 179-200, BINZ

AMERICA - Hist. - Collections - Providence, R.I.
Wagner, Henry R. Hispanic Americana in the John Carter Brown Library. 423-455, WROT

AMERICA - Maps - 1600-1850 - Bibl.
Stevens, Henry and Roland Tree. Comparative Cartography Exemplified in an Analytical & Bibliographical Description of Nearly One Hundred Maps and Charts of the American Continent Published in Great Britain during the Years 1600-1850. 305-363, WROT

AMERICAN LIBRARY ASSOCIATION. Reading with a Purpose
Milam, Carl H. Reading Courses: An Experiment in Adult Education. 356-364, PUTN

AMERICAN LIBRARY ASSOCIATION - War Service
Utley, George B. The Library War Service and Its General Director. 474-491, PUTN

AMERICAN LITERATURE - 18th cent. - Collections - New Haven, Conn.
Johnson, Margaret L. American Imprints and Their Donors in the Yale College Library of 1742. 355-371, KEOG

AMERICAN PERIODICALS
see Periodicals, American

AMERIKA-GEDENKBIBLIOTHEK, Berlin
see Berlin. Amerika-Gedenkbibliothek

Amezúa, Agustin González.
Un Escritor Olvidado. El Doctor Don Juan Enriquez de Zúñiga. II, 189-218, ARTI

Ammundsen, Vibeke.
De Videnskabelige Biblioteker Som Dokumentationscentraler. 159-173, TVET

AMPLONIUS DE BERKA, fl. 1400 - Library
Schmidt, Adolf. Kölnische Einbände des Vierzehnten Jahrhunderts in der Amploniana zu Erfurt. 401-409, COLL

AMSTERDAM - Belinfante, Isaac Ha-Cohen - Collections
see Belinfante, Isaac Ha-Cohen - Collections - Amsterdam

AMSTERDAM. Bibliotheca Rosenthaliana
Enelow, H. G. Isaac Belinfante, an Eighteenth Century Bibliophile. 5-30, FREI

AMSTERDAM - Montezinos Library
Enelow, H. G. Isaac Belinfante, an Eighteenth Century Bibliophile. 5-30, FREI

Amundsen, Inger.
Genealogisk Register til J. B. Halvorsens Norsk Forfatter-Lexikon 1814-1880. 69-202, HALV

Amundsen, Leiv.
Bokauksjoner i Christiania på 1700-Tallet. 227-238, OSLO
Hjalmar Pettersen. 57-67, OSLN

ANABAPTISTS - Germany
Schottenloher, Karl. Buchdrucker und Buchführer im Kampf der Schwärmer

und Wiedertäufer, 1524-1568. 90-113, BOCK

ANALYTICAL BIBLIOGRAPHY
see Bibliography, Analytical

ANCIENT LIBRARIES
see Libraries and librarianship - History

ANCIENT PRIVATE LIBRARIES - Greece
see Private libraries - Greece, Ancient

Anders, Georg.
[An Address.] 8-10, BERP

Andersen, S. B.
Centralbiblioteket - Set fra en Sognebibliotekars Side. 103-106, LASS

Anderson, Eduard.
Vom Kneiphöfschen Rathaus zum Stadtgeschichtlichen Museum. 1-10, KÖNI

Andersson, Aksel.
Bibliographia Klemmingiana 1844-1889. [v]-[vi], 1-40, KLEM
Några Rangfrågor vid Uppsala Universitet vid Tiden för Erik Benzelius d. y:s Utnämning till Bibliotekarie. 373-390, UPPS

ANDREA DI CRETA. Mss. Canon.

Follieri, Enrica. Un Canone Inedito di S. Andrea di Creta per l'Annunciazione (Vat. gr. 2008 e Crypt. Δ. a. VII). I, 337-357, ALBB

Andreassen, Anders.
Fragmenter av Min Svenske Dagbok. 23-31, HEIN
Hva Vil det Kreves av Fremtidens Folkebibliotekarer? 113-122, NORS

Andrews, Charles McLean.
The Story of the Transcripts. 47-56, PUTN

Andrieu, Michel.
Le Missel de la Chapelle Papale à la Fin du XIIIe Siècle. 348-376, EHRB

Andronicus, Livius
see Livius Andronicus

Anesaki, Masaharu.
Some Unrecorded Japanese Martyrdoms of the Catholic Church in the Second Half of the Seventeenth Century. A Study on Newly Disclosed Documents from the Prefectural Library of Nagasaki. 343-384, EHRC

Anglés, Higinio.
Relations Epistolaires entre César Cui et Philippe Pedrell. 15-21, FEDO
El Tesoro Musical de la Biblioteca Vaticana. I, 23-55, ALBB

ANGLIA
see Utrecht. Rijksuniversiteit. Anglistische Bibliotheek Anglia

ANGLISTISCHE BIBLIOTHEEK ANGLIA. Utrecht. Rijksuniversiteit
see Utrecht. Rijksuniversiteit. Anglistische Bibliotheek Anglia

Anker, Øyvind.
Bibliotekaren og Publikum. 86-91, KILD
Fire Akvareller av Henrik Ibsen. 3-22, TVET

Ankwicz-Kleehoven, Hans.
Die Bibliothek des Dr. Johann Cuspinian. 208-227, BICK

ANN ARBOR, Mich. - Catalogs
see Catalogs - Ann Arbor, Mich.

ANN ARBOR, Mich. - Classification
see Classification - Ann Arbor, Mich.

ANNA AMALIA, DUCHESS OF SAXE-WEIMAR-EISENACH
see Amalia, Duchess of Saxe-Weimar-Eisenach

Annaeus, Seneca, Lucius
see Seneca, Lucius Annaeus

Annan, Gertrude L.
Outstanding Acquisitions of Rare Books in Medical Libraries of the United States in the Last Decade. 291-300, DOEJ

Annerstedt, Claes.
Förteckning å Upsala Universitetsbiblioteks Ledare Jämte Korta Upplysningar Rörande deras Verksamhet. 1-39, UPPS

ANNERSTEDT, CLAES
ANNE

ANNERSTEDT, CLAES - Bibl.

Adde, Gustaf. Förteckning öfver Bibliotekarien Claes Annerstedts Utgifna Skrifter. 1-10, ANNE

ANNOTATIONS
see also Book reviews

ANNOTATIONS

Reichardt, Günther. Die Bedeutung der Annotation für Bibliographie und Katalog. 86-109, VORS
Vallinkoski, J. Poimintoja Kirjojen Kansimerkinnöistä Helsingin Yliopiston Kirjastossa. 9-23, TUDE

ANNUITY RECEIPTS - Collections - Dortmund

Winterfeld, Luise von. Vier Leibrentenquittungen von 1456-1478 aus dem Dortmunder Stadtarchiv. 27-28, VERD

ANONYMOUS BOOKS

Medina, Jose Toribio. Quienes Fueron los Autores, hasta ahora Ignorados, de Dos Libros Ingleses que Interesan a America. 79-84, EAME

ANONYMOUS CLASSICS - Cataloging

MacPherson, Harriet D. The Anonymous Classic and Some Problems of Its Cataloging. 274-281, HANS

ANONYMS AND PSEUDONYMS - Collections - Vienna

Krawiec, Ferdinand. Die Anonymen Handschriften der Stadtbibliothek. 70-81, VIES

ANSBACH, Ger. (City) SANKT GUMBERT (BENEDICTINE MONASTERY). Mss.

Redenbacher, Fritz. Adoratio Magorum. Die Heiligen Drei Könige in der Bibel von St. Gumbertus, Gesehen im Rahmen der Ikonographischen Überlieferung. 305-334, HOFM

ANSBACH, Ger. Schloss. Bibliothek

Redenbacher, Fritz. Adoratio Magorum. Die Heiligen Drei Könige in der Bibel von St. Gumbertus, Gesehen im Rahmen der Ikonographischen Überlieferung. 305-334, HOFM

Ansteinsson, John, jt. ed., NORN

Ansteinsson, John.
Dilemmas of Classification. 136-147, HANS
Norsk Bibliotekforening Gjennem 25 År. 5-25, NORN
"Samkjøring." 1-12, MUNT

ANTIPHONARIES (Music)

Pietzsch, Gerhard. Mscr. Dresd. A 52. 167-174, BOLL

ANTIQUARIANS

Räuber, Friedrich. Der Begriff des Antiquariats nach der Verkaufsordnung. 286-299, MILF
Schroers, Paul. Antiquar und Bibliographie. 133-137, FRAD

ANTIQUARIANS - Germany

Wendt, Bernhard. Antiquariatskataloge als Bibliographische Hilfsmittel für Reformationsdrucke. 476-491, BENZ

ANTIQUARIANS - Paris

Nivanka, Eino. Seinen Rantojen Kirjakauppiaat. 78-88, NYBE

ANTIQUARIANS - Rome (City)

Kleberg, Tönnes. Om Romersk Antikvariatbokhandel. 84-94, TVET

ANTOINE, ANNY - Library

Roelofs, Sjoerdtje. La "Collection Anny Antoine - Louis Koopman" à la Bibliothèque Royale de la Haye. 577-580, BRUM

ANTWERP. Hoofdbibliotheek

Schmook, Ger. Dringende Bibliotheekproblemen te Antwerpen. 581-589, BRUM

ANTWERP - Libraries
see Libraries - Antwerp

ANTWERP - Manuscripts, German - 14th cent. - Fragments
see Manuscripts, German - 14th cent. - Fragments - Antwerp

ANTWERP. Musée Plantin-Moretus

Heitjan, Isabel. Die Korrespondenz des Kölner Buchhändlers Hermann Demen mit dem Hause Plantin-Moretus zu Antwerpen 1673-1706. 187-207, BENZ

ANTWERP. Plantin-Moretus firm
see Plantin-Moretus, firm, Antwerp

ANTWERP. Stadsbibliotheek
see Antwerp. Hoofdbibliotheek

Anzai, Ikuo.
Shuyō Ippan Bunruihō ni okeru Bunka-Jinruigaku no Ichi. (The Position of Cultural Anthropology in Major General Classification.) 181-190, HASH

APOLLINARIS. Sidonius, C. Sollius Modestus
see Sidonius, C. Sollius Modestus Apollinaris

Apollonj, Ettore.
Problemi Estetici nella Ricostruzione di Biblioteche Sinistrate dalla Guerra. 79-85, GALL

APPOINTMENTS AND TENURE OF OFFICE
see College and university librarians - Status

ARABIC LITERATURE - 16th-17th cent. - Collections - Uppsala

Lewin, Bernhard. Uppsala Universitetsbiblioteks Samling av Arabiska 1500- och 1600-Talstryck. 577-604, GRAP

ARABIC MANUSCRIPTS
see Manuscripts, Arabic

Arai, Toshi.
Kirishitan-ban no Shuppan to Sono Shū-

hen, I. (Publication of the Jesuit Printings in Japan and Related Problems, 16th-17th Centuries, Part I.) 45-59, TOMI

Araki, Toyosaburō.
Ōsaka Hōmen no Fudazukai to Ginsatsu Hangi no Kosho. (Circulation of Bank Notes in the Osaka Area and the Wood-Blocks Used for Printing Them in the Edo Period.) 211-220, TOMI

ARAUJO, JOAQUIM DE - Library
Mariutti De Sánchez Rivero, Angela. Il Carteggio Inedito del Legato Araujo. 369-382, FERR

ARAUJO, JOAQUIM DE - Mss. - Collections - Venice
Mariutti De Sánchez Rivero, Angela. Il Carteggio Inedito del Legato Araujo. 369-382, FERR

Arbesmann, Rudolph.
The Three Earliest Vitae of St. Galganus. 1-37, ALBA

Arcamone, Guido, ed.
GREG

Arcamone, Guido.
Premessa. 11-13, FAVA

ARCHITECTURAL PLANS - Collections - Basel
Hui, Franz. Die Bau- und Häuserpläne des Staatsarchivs. 34-36, BASL

ARCHITECTURE AND BUILDING
Bauhuis, Walter. Alte und Neue Ideen im Bibliotheksbau. 72-82, HOFF
Macdonald, Angus Snead. A Library of the Future. 168-184, MUNT
Schirrmeister, Georg. Über den Stand beim Bau Wissenschaftlicher Bibliotheken. 103-116, BULL
Thomsen, Carl. Bygherren, Bygmesteren og Bibliotekaren. 237-247, HEIN

ARCHITECTURE AND BUILDING - College and university libraries
Munthe, Wilhelm. Vom Lesesaal ins Magazin Zurück. 350-357, LEYG
Towne, Jackson E. University Library Building Planning. 461-471, RANG

ARCHITECTURE AND BUILDING - College and university libraries - Copenhagen
Dahl, Svend. 9-85, COPA

ARCHITECTURE AND BUILDING - College and university libraries - Erlangen
Petz-Gebauer, Hannelore. Zur Baugeschichte der Erlanger Universitätsbibliothek. 149-162, REDE
Redenbacher, Fritz. Das Gebäude der Universitätsbibliothek Erlangen. 232-251, VORS

ARCHITECTURE AND BUILDING - College and university libraries - Frankfurt a.M.
Köttelwesch, Clemens. Zum Neubau der Stadt- und Universitätsbibliothek Frankfurt am Main. 125-136, HOFM

ARCHITECTURE AND BUILDING - College and university libraries - Giessen
Kohler, Hans. Neubau der Universitätsbibliothek in Giessen 1959. 11-14, GIES
Schawe, Josef. Die Früheren Unterkünfte der Universitätsbibliothek Giessen. 15-25, GIES

ARCHITECTURE AND BUILDING - College and university libraries - Mainz
Fuchs, Hermann. Der Neubau der Universitätsbibliothek Mainz. 39-63, MAIZ

ARCHITECTURE AND BUILDING - College and university libraries - Münster
Molitor, Karl. Das Neue Bibliotheks-Gebäude in Münster i.W. V-VIII, MÜNS

ARCHITECTURE AND BUILDING - College and university libraries - Uppsala
Samzelius, Jonas L:Son. Om- och Tillbyggnaden av Carolina Rediviva Åren 1934-1945. 293-337, GRAP

ARCHITECTURE AND BUILDING - College and university libraries - Utrecht
Evers, Garrit Albert. Het Paleis van Koning Lodewijk Napoleon te Utrecht en Zijne Inrichting tot Universiteitsbibliotheek. 42-62, SOME

ARCHITECTURE AND BUILDING - Color, decoration, etc.
Masson, André. Montesquieu, le Président de Brosses et le Décor des Bibliothèques. 317-324, CALO

ARCHITECTURE AND BUILDING - Color, decoration, etc. - Leipzig
Baer, Karl Julius. Das Gebäude und Sein Künstlerischer Schmuck. 36-57, LEIS

ARCHITECTURE AND BUILDING - Furniture
see Furniture

ARCHITECTURE AND BUILDING - Hist.
Koch, Theodore Wesley. New Light on Old Libraries. 244-252, HANS

Leyh, Georg. Vom Büchersaal zum Magazin. 160-167, MUNT
———— Zur Geschichte des Neueren Bibliotheksbaues. 156-162, KUHN
Pescheck, Paul. Die Entwicklung des Neueren Bibliotheksbaues. 264-280, MILF

ARCHITECTURE AND BUILDING - Lighting

Lemaître, Henri. Magasins de Livres et Lumière Naturelle. 23-31, GODE

ARCHITECTURE AND BUILDING - Maintenance - Italy

Bonaventura, Gustavo. La Minaccia delle Termiti e di Altri Insetti al Nostro Patrimonio Artistico e Culturale. 205-234, GALL

ARCHITECTURE AND BUILDING - Nashville

Nashville Libraries House over 2,000,000 Volumes. 12-13, NASH

ARCHITECTURE AND BUILDING - National libraries - Berlin

BERS

ARCHITECTURE AND BUILDING - National libraries - Berlin - Hist.

Pick, Hermann. Der Unvollendet Gebliebene Bibliotheksbau des Großen Kurfürsten. 211-215, SCHW

ARCHITECTURE AND BUILDING - National libraries - Copenhagen

Dahl, Svend. Det Kongelige Biblioteks Bygning. Traek af dens Forhistorie. 39-56, BAYJ

ARCHITECTURE AND BUILDING - National libraries - Leipzig

Baer, Karl Julius. Das Gebäude und Sein Künstlerischer Schmuck. 36-57, LEIS
Krieger, Waldemar and Gottfried Rost. Das Gebäude der Deutschen Bücherei und Seine Technischen Einrichtungen. 259-270, LEIZ

ARCHITECTURE AND BUILDING - National libraries - Paris

Hautecoeur, Louis. Les Travaux d'Architecture de Julien Cain à la Bibliothèque Nationale. 27-33, CAIN

ARCHITECTURE AND BUILDING - National libraries - Vienna

Bick, Josef. Der Unveröffentlichte Zweite Teil der Dilucida Repraesentatio Bibliothecae Caesareae des S. Kleiner und J. J. Sedelmayr. 75-86, VIEN

ARCHITECTURE AND BUILDING - Proprietary libraries - Basel

Grütter, Wilhelm. Das Ehemalige Bauhaus des Basler Münsters und Seine Nachbarhäuser. 47-86, BASA

ARCHITECTURE AND BUILDING - Public libraries

Bredsted, Aage. Biblioteksbygninger og deres Indretning. 38-55, DØSS

ARCHITECTURE AND BUILDING - Public libraries - Aachen

Laurent, J. Das Neu Errichtete Archiv- und Bibliothek-Gebäude der Stadt Aachen. 1-20, (pt. 1), AACH

ARCHITECTURE AND BUILDING - Public libraries - Berlin

Mehlan, Heinz. Der Architekt zum Neubau der Berliner Stadtbibliothek. 52-55, BERR

ARCHITECTURE AND BUILDING - Public libraries - Copenhagen

Thomsen, Carl. Bygherren, Bygmesteren og Bibliotekaren. 237-247, HEIN

ARCHITECTURE AND BUILDING - Public libraries - Frankfurt a.M.

Köster, Kurt. Der Neubau der Deutschen Bibliothek. Vorgeschichte, Planungen, Wirklichkeit. 29-52, FRAD
Köttelwesch, Clemens. Zum Neubau der Stadt- und Universitätsbibliothek Frankfurt am Main. 125-136, HOFM

ARCHITECTURE AND BUILDING - Public libraries - Germany

Ackerknecht, Erwin. Stadtbüchereibauten. 194-204, LEYH

ARCHITECTURE AND BUILDING - Public libraries - Gothenburg, Sweden

Noreen, Ärland. Plan till Nybyggnad för Göteborgs Stadsbibliotek. Ritningar med Beskrivning. 1-23, (second paper), GÖTE

ARCHITECTURE AND BUILDING - Public libraries - Kristianstad, Norway

Liljeroth, Erik. Bibliotekets Vardag. 137-154, KRIS

ARCHITECTURE AND BUILDING - Public libraries - Mainz

Wermter, Ernst Manfred. Die Raumverteilung im Gebäude der Stadtbibliothek seit 1912. 31-34, MAIN

ARCHITECTURE AND BUILDING - Public libraries - Malmö, Sweden

Mark, Jan. Några Bilder från Malmö Stadsbibliotek. [272]ff, HEIN

ARCHITECTURE AND BUILDING - Public libraries - Mannheim

MANN

ARCHITECTURE AND BUILDING - Remodeled buildings and additions - Paris

Kleindienst, Thérèse. M. Julien Cain et les Transformations de la Bibliothèque Nationale. 51-59, CAIN

ARCHITECTURE AND BUILDING - Remodeled buildings and additions - Prague

Emler, Jan. Das Neue im Alten. 297-308, LEYG

ARCHITECTURE AND BUILDING - Remodeled buildings and additions - Uppsala

Samzelius, Jonas L:Son. Om- och Tillbyggnaden av Carolina Rediviva Åren 1934-1945. 293-337, GRAP

ARCHITECTURE AND BUILDING - Remodeled buildings and additions - Utrecht

Evers, Gerrit Albert. Het Paleis van Koning Lodewijk Napoleon te Utrecht en Zijne Inrichting tot Universiteitsbibliotheek. 42-62, SOME

ARCHITECTURE AND BUILDING - Research libraries - Trondheim

Landmark, Joh. D. Videnskabers Selskabs Bibliotek i Trondheim og Dets Bygningshistorie 1855-1867. 148-159, MUNT

ARCHITECTURE AND BUILDING - State libraries - Aarhus, Denmark

Grundtvig, Vilh. Andre Forhold. 159-165, AARU

ARCHITECTURE AND BUILDING - State libraries - Berlin - Pictorial works - Bibl.

Otto, Paul. Ikonographie der Königlichen Bibliothek zu Berlin. 43-50, WILM

ARCHITECTURE AND BUILDING - State libraries - Munich

GRAS

ARCHITECTURE AND BUILDING - State libraries - Munich - Hist.

Buttmann, Rudolf. Beiträge zur Baugeschichte der Bayerischen Staatsbibliothek. 193-215, LEYG

ARCHITECTURE AND BUILDING - State libraries - Weimar

Scheidig, Walther. Zur Baugeschichte der Weimarischen Bibliothek. 1-32, WEIM

<u>ARCHIV FÜR GESCHICHTE DES BUCHWESENS</u>

Hack, Bertold. Vor- und Frühgeschichte des "Archivs für Geschichte des Buchwesens." 157-169, BENZ

<u>DAS ARCHIV UNGEDRUCKTER WISSENSCHAFTLICHER SCHRIFTEN</u>

Eppelsheimer, Hanns Wilhelm. Das Archiv Ungedruckter Wissenschaftlicher Schriften. 90-91, FRAD

ARCHIVES

Gini, Corrado. Gli Archivi e il Progresso delle Scienze Sociali. 15-19, MERC

ARCHIVES - Administration

Samaran, Charles. Problèmes Archivistiques d'Aujourd'hui et de Demain. 1-13, MERC

ARCHIVES, AUTHORS'
see Archives, Literary

ARCHIVES - Basel

BASL

ARCHIVES - Business - Bergen

Munthe, Gerhard. Firma-Arkivene i Universitetsbiblioteket i Bergen. 216-231, TVET

ARCHIVES - Care and restoration
see also Manuscripts - Care and restoration; Paper

ARCHIVES - Care and restoration

Blaas, Richard. Cellon und Pergamin in der Archivalienrestaurierung. 187-197, GALL
Grill, Erik. The Barrow Method in Sweden. 489-492, GALL
Lodolini, Armando. Origine e Attività del Laboratorio di Restauro Presso L'Archivio Centrale dello Stato. 519-534, GALL

ARCHIVES - Church - Germany

SCHV

ARCHIVES - Church - Gt. Brit. - Hist. - 1925-1950

Jenkinson, Hilary. Archive Developments in England 1925-1950. 337-361, MERC

ARCHIVES - Church - Inventories, calendars, etc. - Rome (City)

Göller, Emil. Untersuchungen über das Inventar des Finanzarchivs der Renaissancepäpste (1447-1521). 227-272, EHRE

ARCHIVES - Church - Italy

Cenci, Pio. L'Archivio della Cancelleria della Nunziatura Veneta. 273-330, EHRE

ARCHIVES - Church - Italy - Hist.

Panella, Antonio. Per Una "Guida Storica degli Archivi Ecclesiastici." 375-382, MERC

ARCHIVES - College and university - U.S. - Hist.

Posner, Ernst. The College and University Archives in the United States. 363-374, MERC

ARCHIVES, CONTENTS
see Research materials

ARCHIVES, DISPOSAL OF
see Archives - Retention

ARCHIVES, GOVERNMENT - U.S.

Ford, Worthington Chauncey. A Division of Manuscripts. 156-161, PUTN

ARCHIVES - Gt. Brit. - Hist. - 1925-1950

Jenkinson, Hilary. Archive Developments in England 1925-1950. 337-361, MERC

ARCHIVES - Holland

Sevensma, Tietse Pieter. Eine Bibliothekarische Kriegserfahrung. 591-596, BICK

ARCHIVES - Inventories, calenders, etc. - 1440

Bååth, L. M. L'Inventaire de la Chambre Apostolique de 1440. 135-157, MERC

ARCHIVES - Italy

Lodolini, Armando. Origine e Attività del Laboratorio di Restauro Presso L'Archivio Centrale dello Stato. 519-534, GALL

ARCHIVES - Literary - Swabia

Hoffmann, Wilhelm. Vom Sammeln und Bewahren. Gedanken über Dichter-Archive in Schwaben. 287-294, WEHM

ARCHIVES - Mainz

Falck, Ludwig. Die Bestände des Mainzer Stadtarchivs und Ihre Findmittel. 75-88, MAIN

——— Die Sammlung Mittelalterlicher Quellen zur Geschichte der Stadt Mainz. 71-73, MAIN

ARCHIVES - Monte Cassino

Leccisotti, Tommaso. La Tradizione Archivistica di Montecassino. 227-261, MERC

ARCHIVES - Naples

Filangieri di Candida, Riccardo. Perdita e Ricuperi del Diplomatico Farnesiano. 269-279, MERC

ARCHIVES - Reggio Emilia

Tondelli, Leone. Cenni sull'Archivio Capitolare di Reggio Emilia. 263-267, MERC

ARCHIVES - Retention

Kandler, Gottfried. Verbesserung der Archive bei Verminderung Ihrer Bestände. 69-81, SCHV

ARCHIVES - Sheffield, Eng.

Walton, Mary. J. P. Lamb and the Archives. 17-18, LAMB

ARCHIVES - Spain

Pou y Marti, José M. Los Archivos de la Embajada de España cerca de la Santa Sede. 297-311, MERC

ARCHIVES - Use studies
see Use studies - Archives

ARCHIVES - Vatican

Renouard, Yves. Intérêt et Importance des Archives Vaticanes pour L'Histoire Économique du Moyen Âge Spécialement du XIVe Siècle. 21-41, MERC

ARCHIVES - Vienna

Santifaller, Leo. Das Oesterreichische Staatsarchiv. 313-336, MERC

ARCHIVISTS

Febvre, Lucien. Le Bibliothécaire, la Bibliothèque et L'Histoire. 106-114, OURS

ARCHYTAS, OF TARENTUM. <u>Fragmenta</u>

Blass, Frédéric. De Archytae Tarentini Fragmentis Mathematicis. 573-584, GRAU

Arenas, Manuel Núñez de.
Páginas Románticas: Una Carta Inédita de Trueba y Cosío. I, 56-61, ARTI

Arens, Fritz.
Das Brevier des Administrators Adalbert von Sachsen in der Mainzer Universitätsbibliothek. 67-89, MAIZ

ARETIN, JOHANN CHRISTOPH, FREIHERR VON. Über den gegenwärtigen Zustand . . .

Hilsenbeck, Adolf. Eine Denkschrift Aretins über die Bayerischen Provinzialbibliotheken. 153-161, MILF

ARGENSON, MARC ANTOINE RENÉ DE VOYER, Marquis de Paulmy d'

Kraemer, Erik von. En Bibliofiliens Storman. Antoine-René de Voyer d'Argenson, Markis av Paulmy. 182-196, DAHL

ARGENSON, MARC ANTOINE RENÉ DE VOYER, Marquis de Paulmy d'. Mélanges Tirés d'une Grande Bibliothèque

Le Gal, Simonne. La Bibliothèque des Dames au XVe Siècle, Vue par le Marquis de Paulmy. 55-63, CALO

ARISTOPHANES. Mss.

Holzinger, Charles. Sur la Date de Quelques Manuscrits d'Aristophane. 204-218, CHAT

ARISTOPHANES. Pax

Nicole, Jules. Le Poète Tragique Carcinus et Ses Fils dans la Parabase de la Paix d'Aristophane. 163-167, GRAU

ARISTOTELES - Collections - Trentino-Alto Adige, Italy

Franceschini, Ezio. Le Versioni Latine Medievali di Aristotele e dei Suoi Commentatori Greci ed Arabi nelle Biblioteche delle Tre Venezie. 313-326, FERR

ARISTOTELES. Physica

Ermatinger, Charles J. Additional Questions on Aristotle's Physics, by Siger of Brabant or His School. 97-120, ALBA

ARISTOTELES. Rhetorica

Susemihl, François. De Rhetoricorum Aristoteleorum Libro Primo Quaestiones Criticae. 87-96, GRAU

ARMED FORCES LIBRARIES - Germany - 1914-1918

Paalzow, Hans. Die Kriegsbücherei. 285, HARN

ARMED FORCES LIBRARIES - Norway

Tveito, Dagfinn. Soldater og Kulturfront. 74-85, KILD

ARMED FORCES LIBRARIES - Switzerland

Wild, H. Hermann Escher und die Schweizerischen Volksbibliotheken. 22-34, ESCK

ARMENIAN PALEOGRAPHY
see Paleography, Armenian

ARNALDUS DE MONTE. Mss. Liber S. Jacobi

Hämel, Adalbert. Arnaldus de Monte und der "Liber S. Jacobi." I, 147-159, RUBI

Arnesen, Arne.
How Norway Became the Focus of American Library Methods in Europe. 148-155, HANS
Vare Bybiblioteker 1913-1938. 39-52, NORN

AROUK DE NATHAN BAR YEHIEL. Mss. - Bibl.

Blondheim, D. S. Liste des Manuscrits de L'Arouk de Nathan Bar Yehiel. 24-30, FREN

ARRANGEMENT OF BOOKS ON SHELVES
see Shelf Arrangement

Arrighi, Marie.
La Bibliothèque de L'Empereur Napoléon à Sainte-Hélène. 55-65, BONN

ARS SCRIPTURARUM

Jacobs, Emil. Ars Scripturarum. 177-186, MILF

ART LIBRARIES AND COLLECTIONS

Olivieri-Sangiocomo, Laura. La Nuova Sistemazione della Biblioteca di Archeologia e Storia dell'Arte (Problemi di una Moderna Biblioteca Specializzata). 333-346, GREG

ART LIBRARIES AND COLLECTIONS - Berlin

Weise-Standfest, Hilde. Musikbibliothek und Diskothek, Kunstblätter-Sammlung, Musik- und Literaturveranstaltungen. 36-41, BERR

ART LIBRARIES AND COLLECTIONS - Erlangen

Hampe, Theodor. Der Sog. Ferdinand Neuberger-Codex in der Erlanger Universitätsbibliothek. 32-39, VERZ

ART LIBRARIES AND COLLECTIONS - Germany

Oettingen, Wolfgang von. Über Goethes Kunstsammlungen. 72-78, WAHL

ART LIBRARIES AND COLLECTIONS - Innsbruck
Hochenegg, Hans. Die Roschmannsche Kupferstichsammlung. 400-414, BICK

ART LIBRARIES AND COLLECTIONS - Uppsala
Ekholm, Gunnar. Om Uppsala Universitetsbiblioteks Handteckningssamling. 575-585, UPPS
———. Upsala Universitetsbiblioteks Gravyrsamling. 125-138, ANNE

ART LIBRARIES AND COLLECTIONS - Vienna
Freiberg, Siegfried. Die Bibliothek der Akademie der Bildenden Künste in Wien. 32-33, STUM
Hadamowsky, Franz. Das Hoftheater Leopolds I. und das Kostümwerk des L. O. Burnacini. 384-398, BICK
Pauer, Hans. Ein Staatsarchiv der Bildenden Künste. 516-522, BICK

ART OBJECTS - Collections - Leipzig
Funke, Fritz. Originales Sammelgut im Deutschen Buch- und Schriftmuseum. 219-241, LEIZ

ART OBJECTS - Collections - New York (City)
GREE

ART OBJECTS - Collections - Paris
Le Rider, Georges. Julien Cain et le Cabinet des Médailles. 72-75, CAIN

ARTEGNA, GUARNERIO d'
see Guarnerio d'Artegna

ARTIGAS Y FERRANDO, MIGUEL
ARTI
Escalante, Luis de. Prólogo. I, v-xii, ARTI

ARTIGAS Y FERRANDO, MIGUEL - Bibl.
Publicaciones de Miguel Artigas. I, xiii-xvi, ARTI

ARTISTIC BOOKS
see Limited edition books

ASBJØRNSEN, PETER CHRISTEN
Bakken, Hallvard Sand. P. Chr. Asbjørnsen og Universitetsbiblioteket. 299-324, MUNT

ASCANIUS
Berger, Philippe. Ascagne. 611-619, GRAU

ASCOLI, CECCO d'
see Cecco d'Ascoli

Asen, Johannes.
Die Universitätsbibliothek Greifswald zur Zeit des Übergangs an Preussen. 271-277, KUHN

Ashley, Frederick W.
Three Eras in the Library of Congress. 57-67, PUTN

ASLIB
see Association of Special Libraries

ASSISI. San Francesco (Monastery). Biblioteca. Mss.
Mercati, Giovanni. Codici del Convento di S. Francesco in Assisi nella Biblioteca Vaticana. 83-127, EHRE

Assmann, Karl, ed.
DREL
Assmann, Karl.
Die Anfänge der Sächsischen Landesbibliothek. 15-25, DREL
Die Sächsische Landesbibliothek von 1945 bis 1955. Zerstörung, Wiederaufbau und Gegenwärtiger Stand der Arbeit. 29-85, DREL

ASSOCIATION DES BIBLIOTHÉCAIRES SUISSES
see Vereinigung Schweizerischer Bibliothekare

ASSOCIATION INTERNATIONALE DE BIBLIOPHILIE
Guignard, Jacques. M. Julien Cain et L'Association Internationale de Bibliophilie. 34-36, CAIN

ASSOCIATION LIBRARIES
see Public libraries

ASSOCIATION OF SPECIAL LIBRARIES - Hist.
Patrick, L. G., et al. R. S. Hutton; on the Occasion of His Ninetieth Birthday. 277-286, HUTT

ASSOCIATION SUISSE DE DOCUMENTATION
see Schweizerische Vereinigung für Dokumentation

ASSOCIATION SUIZZERA DI DOCUMENTAZIONE
see Schweizerische Vereinigung für Dokumentation

ASSOCIATIONS
Breycha-Vauthier, A. C. La Collaboration Internationale des Bibliothèques dans la Fédération Internationale des Associations des Bibliothécaires. 7-11, EMLE

Guignard, Jacques. M. Julien Cain et L'Association Internationale de Bibliophilie. 34-36, CAIN

ASSOCIATIONS - Gt. Brit.

Patrick, L. G., et al. R. S. Hutton; on the Occasion of His Ninetieth Birthday. 277-286, HUTT

ASSOCIATIONS - Norway

Fiskaa, H. M. Norsk Bibliotekforenings Virke. Resultater og Oppgaver. 58-73, NORS
Kildal, Arne. Da Norsk Bibliotekforening Ble Til. 43-57, NORS
Klemp, Helene L. Norsk Bibliotekforenings Jubileumsskrift. 9-15, NORS

ASSOCIATIONS - Scandinavia

Tveterås, Harald L. A Federation for Library Co-operation across the Frontiers: Nordisk Vitenskapelig Bibliotekarforbund. 601-602, BRUM

ASSOCIATIONS - Switzerland

Godet, Marcel. Hermann Escher et les Bibliothèques Suisses. 8-19, ESCK

ASSOCIATIONS - Württemberg

Maier, Walter. Anfänge, Werden und Wirken der Württembergischen Bibliotheksgesellschaft, 276-288, HOFF

ASSURBANIPAL, KING OF ASSYRIA - Library

Meissner, Bruno. Wie Hat Assurbanipal Seine Bibliothek Zusammengebracht? 244-248, MILF

ASSYRIA - Private libraries
see Private libraries - Assyria

ASTI. Seminario. Biblioteca

Dervieux, Ermanno. Incunabuli della Biblioteca del Seminario di Asti. II, 451-480, MANO

ASTOR LIBRARY, New York

Lydenberg, Harry Miller. A Forgotten Trail Blazer. 302-314, PUTN

ASTROLOGICAL LITERATURE - Bibl.

Richel, Arthur. Astrologische Volksschriften der Aachener Stadtbibliothek. 49-93, (pt. 1), AACH

ASTROLOGICAL LITERATURE - Collections - Aachen

Richel, Arthur. Astrologische Volksschriften der Aachener Stadtbibliothek. 49-93, (pt. 1), AACH

Atherton, Percy Lee.
Boston Days (1909-1922): Some Engeliana. 27-34, ENGE

ATHOS (MONASTERIES) VATOPEDI. Biblioteca. Mss. (180)

Mras, Karl. Eine Neuentdeckte Handschrift des Eusebius. 485-487, BICK

ATLANTA UNIVERSITY. School of Library Service

Gleason, Eliza Atkins. The Atlanta University School of Library Service—Its Aims and Objectives. 504-510, WILS

ATLASES
see Maps

ATTENDORN, PETER

Voullième, Ernst. Peter Attendorn, ein Buchhändler und Drucker in Straßburg um 1490. 344-353, MILF

AUCTION SALES - Åbo, Finland - 18th cent.

Grönroos, Henrik. Då Böckerna Bytte Ägare. Bokauktioner i Åbo under "Hertiginnans av Finland" tid. 92-108, GARD

AUCTION SALES - Netherlands - 16th-17th cent.

Lange, H. O. De Hollandske Bogauktioner i Deres Første Halve Aarhundrede. 179-194, ANNE

AUCTION SALES - Oslo - 18th cent. - Catalogs - Bibl.

Amundsen, Leiv. Bokauksjoner i Christiania på 1700-Tallet. 227-238, OSLO

Audollent, Aug.
Bandeau de Plomb avec Inscription Trouvé à Haïdra (Tunisie). 545-556, CHAT

Auerbach, Erich.
Die Randglossen des Cod. Hamilton 203 zum Ersten und Zweiten Gesang der Göttlichen Komödie. 45-50, KUHN

Augapfel, Julius.
Das سب im Qurân. 384-393, KARA

AUGSBURG - Bookbinders
see Bookbinders - Augsburg

AUGSBURG. Staats-, Kreis- und Stadtbibliothek

Geissler, Paul. Ein Seltener Augsburger Wiegendruck. Das Älteste Gedruckte Buch über Altötting. 316-322, VORS

AUGSBURG. Staats-, Kreis- und Stadtbibliothek. Mss. (Woodcut)
Schmidbauer, Richard. Ein Unbekanntes Augsburger Pestblatt des 15. Jahrhunderts. 229-231, LEID

AUGUST, ELECTOR OF SAXONY, 1526-1586
Schunke, Ilse. Die Pariser Büchersendung des Hubert Languet an Kurfürst August von Sachsen 1566. 49-66, BOLL

AUGUST, ELECTOR OF SAXONY, 1526-1586 - Library
Assmann, Karl. Die Anfänge der Sächsischen Landesbibliothek. 15-25, DREL

AUGUSTINUS AURELIUS, SAINT, Bp. of Hippo. Mss. De Concensu Evangelistarum
Lowe, E. A. Greek Symptoms in a Sixth-Century Manuscript of St. Augustine and in a Group of Latin Legal Manuscripts. 277-289, ALBA

Augustyniak, Jan.
Nieznane Fragmenty z Historii Biblioteki Publicznej w Łodzi. 330-337, GRYC

AUNGERVILLE, RICHARD, known as Richard de Bury, Bp. of Durham (1287-1345)
Nelson, Axel. Richard de Bury och Thomas à Kempis. 59-70, COLL

AURAS, Lower Silesia
see Uraz, Poland under specific subject headings, e.g., Printing - Uraz, Poland

AURIFABER, ANDREAS - Library
Dahlberg, Ragnar. Två Böcker med Märklig Proveniens i Helsingfors Universitetsbibliotek. 127-136, SCHA

AUSKUNFTSBUREAU DER DEUTSCHEN BIBLIOTHEKEN, Berlin
see Prussia. Auskunftsbureau der Deutschen Bibliotheken

Ausserer, Karl.
Die Heraldischen Handschriften der Wiener Nationalbibliothek. 7-36, VIEN
Die Jagdtagebücher der Österreichischen Nationalbibliothek. 228-238, BICK

Auster, Guido.
Die Orientalische Abteilung. I, 275-317, BERS

AUSTRALIA AND MADRAS LIBRARY ASSOCIATION
Koranne, T. N. Australia and Madras Library Association. 127-129, MADR

AUSTRIA. Archivio di Stato, Innsbruck
see Innsbruck, Archivio di Stato

AUSTRIA - Bookbinding
see Bookbinding - Austria

AUSTRIA. Bücherkommission
Richter, Günter. Die Sammlung von Drucker-, Verleger- und Buchführerkatalogen in den Akten der Kaiserlichen Bücherkommission. 317-372, BENZ

AUSTRIA - Education for librarianship
see Education for librarianship - Austria

AUSTRIA - Government publications
see Government publications - Austria

AUSTRIA - Legends - Collections
see Legends - Collections - Austria

AUSTRIA - Librarianship
see Librarianship - Austria

AUSTRIA - Libraries
see Libraries - Austria

AUSTRIA - Library legislation
see Library legislation - Austria

AUSTRIA - Officials and employees
Loehr, August. Josef Bick und die Organisation des Wissenschaftlichen Dienstes. 45-50, BICK

AUSTRIA - Private libraries
see Private libraries - Austria

AUSTRIA. Staatsarchiv
Santifaller, Leo. Die Älteste Originalurkunde des Österreichischen Staatsarchivs. 538-575, BICK
——————. Das Oesterreichische Staatsarchiv. 313-336, MERC

AUSTRIA. Staatsdruckerei
Haiböck, Lambert. Nationalbibliothek und Staatsdruckerei. 39, STUM

Autenrieth, Johanne.
Ältere und Neuere Handschriftenkataloge aus dem Umkreis der Stuttgarter Handschriftensammlung. 165-188, HOFF

AUTHOR NAMES
see Book numbers

AUTHOR-TITLE CATALOGS
see Catalogs - Author

AUTHORS AND LIBRARIES
Bakken, Hallvard Sand. P. Chr. Asbjørn-

sen og Universitetsbiblioteket. 299-324, MUNT
Dahl, Svend. P. A. Munch i Vatikanets Arkiv. 30-48, MUNT
Holtzmann, Walter. Paolo Kehr e le Ricerche Archivistiche per L'Italia Pontificia. 43-49, MERC
Ritzler, Remigius. Die Archivalischen Quellen der "Hierarchia Catholica." 51-74, MERC

AUTHORS AND LIBRARIES - Denmark

Jepsen, Hans Lyngby. Biblioteksafgiften —Vederlag for Hvad og Hvordan? 87-94, THOM

AUTHORS AND LIBRARIES - Dijon

Drouot, Henri. Un Familier de la Bibliothèque: Henri Chabeuf. 92-105, OURS
Hauser, Henri. Souvenirs d'un Vieux Rat de Bibliothèque. 120-124, OURS

AUTHORS AND LIBRARIES - Dresden

Büscher, Alfred. Skandinavier, Dresden und die Landesbibliothek. 99-104, BOLL

AUTHORS AND LIBRARIES - Oslo

Bakken, Hallvard Sand. P. Chr. Asbjørnsen og Universitetsbiblioteket. 299-324, MUNT

AUTHORS AND LIBRARIES - Sweden

Palmaer, Margit. Mina Bibliotek. 63-70, ÖREB
Wistrand, Pär. Mina Bibliotek. 539-547, HJEL

AUTHORS AND LIBRARIES - Zürich

Hirzel, B. Conrad Ferdinand Meyer und die Zürcher Stadtbibliothek. [45]-60, ESCK

AUTHORS AS LIBRARIANS
see Librarians as authors

AUTHORS AS READERS
see Authors and libraries

AUTHORS - INCUNABULA
see Incunabula - Authors

AUTHORS, Norwegian

Amundsen, Inger. Genealogisk Register til J. B. Halvorsens Norsk Forfatter-Lexikon 1814-1880. 69-202, HALV

AUTHORS, Swedish

Lundgren, Hj. Diktare Bland Svenska Bibliotheksmän. 499-505, COLL

AUTOGRAPHS - Collections - Mönchengladbach, Ger.

Dreimüller, Karl. Musikerbriefe an einen Rheinischen Musikliebhaber. Aus der Sammlung Ludwig Bisschopinck in Mönchengladbach. 29-49, HOBO

AUTOMATION
see Mechanization of library processes

Auvray, Lucien.
Notices sur Quelques Cartulaires et Obituaires Français Conservés à la Bibliothèque du Vatican. 381-409, HAVE

AUXERRE. Saint-Étienne (Cathedral) Mss.

Schapiro, Meyer. Two Romanesque Drawings in Auxerre and Some Iconographic Problems. 331-349, GREE

Avanzi, Giannetto.
Bibliografia Cronologica e Analitica degli Scritti a Stampa del Prof. Alfonso Gallo, Pubblicati dal 1912 al 1953. 1-38, GALL
Gli Scritti sulla Catalogazione e Classificazione Speciale e Specializzata. 87-186, GALL

AVENARIUS, JOANNES
see Habermann, Johann

AVIGNON. Bibliothèque Municipale. Mss. (100)

Andrieu, Michel. Le Missel de la Chapelle Papale à la Fin du XIIIe Siècle. 348-376, EHRB

AVIGNON - Book industry and trade
see Book industry and trade - Avignon

Avilés, A. Fernández de.
Menéndez Pelayo en la "Historia de la Cultura" de Francisco Esteve Barba. 271-281, MENE

AWARDS, CITATIONS AND PRIZES - Bydgoszcz

Podgóreczny, Józef. Zasłużeni są Wśród Nas. 139-144, BYDG

AZZOLINI FAMILY - Correspondence - Collections - Forli

Servolini, Luigi. Le Carte Azzolini nella Biblioteca Comunale di Forlì. 615-701, GALL

BGK
see Berlin. Gesamtkatalog

Baader, Peter.
Kirchen und Liturgien im Alphabetischen Katalog. Probleme Ihrer Einordnung. 24-40, FUCH

BÅNG, PETRUS. Chronologia Sacra
Nohrström, Holger. En Variant av Petrus Bångs Chronologia Sacra. 82-87, HULT

Bååth, L. M.
L'Inventaire de la Chambre Apostolique de 1440. 135-157, MERC

Baba, Shigenori.
An Aspect Regarding Quantification Method for Selection of Bibliographical Vessels. 283-292, RANG

BABYLONIA - Stylus
see Stylus - Babylonia

BACH, JOHANN SEBASTIAN. Mss. Canon
Nowak, Leopold. Ein Bach-Fund. 95-98, FEDO

Bach, Ursula.
Zur Fachbibliographie der Musikwissenschaft. 17-19, VORS

Bacher, W.
Die Zweite Version von Saadja's Abschnitt über die Wiederbelebung der Todten. 219-226, STEI

Bachmair, Heinrich F. S.
Über "Luxusausgaben." 161-163, HELD

BACON, FRANCIS - Collections - Yale
Livingston, Dorothy Flower, Mollie Marjorie Patton, et al. Contribution to a Bibliography of Francis Bacon. Editions before 1700 in Yale Libraries. 95-143, KEOG

BAD OEYNHAUSEN, Ger. Intelligence Library
see Germany (Territory under Allied Occupation, 1945- British Zone) Control Commission. Intelligence Library

Badalić, Josip.
Die Deutschen Offizinen in den Wiegendrucksammlungen Jugoslawiens. 31-37, SCHT
Inkunabelforschungen in Jugoslawien. 13-15, STUM

Badecki, Karol.
Bartłomieja Zimorowicza "Żywot Kozaków Lisowskich." 351-364, PIEK

BADEN. Generallandesarchiv, Karlsruhe. Mss. (Schirmbriefe)
Molitor, Karl. Zur Druckergeschichte des XV. Jahrhunderts. 205-209, SCHW

BADEN-WÜRTTEMBERG - Catalogs - Union
see Catalogs - Union - Baden-Württemberg

BADIER FAMILY (Bookbinders)
Husung, Max Joseph. Ein Neuer Signierter und Datierter Badier, Gefunden in der Preussischen Staatsbibliothek. 435-442, COLL

BADISCHE LANDESBIBLIOTHEK, Karlsruhe
see Karlsruhe. Badische Landesbibliothek

Bäckman, Edvin.
Lagstiftningen Angående Pliktexemplar i Sovjetunionen. 118-129, TUDE

Baer, Karl Julius.
Das Gebäude und Sein Künstlerischer Schmuck. 36-57, LEIS

Bärmann, Johannes.
Ansprache. 11-13, MAIZ

Baeumker, Clemens.
Zur Frage nach Abfassungszeit und Verfasser des Irrtümlich Witelo Zugeschriebenen Liber de Intelligentiis. 87-102, EHRA

Bago, Mercedes A. de.
Una Versión Desconocida del Soneto "Al Sol" de Tassara. I, 68-69, ARTI

Bahlmann, P.
Die Königliche Universitäts-Bibliothek zu Münster. 1-56, MÜNS

Baillet, Lina.
Le Premier Manuel de Grec Paru à Strasbourg. 25-36, BENZ

Baker, Augusta.
Once upon a Time. 9-14, SAYE

Bakken, Asbjørn.
Små Bemerkninger om Store Saker. 177-186, NORS

Bakken, Hallvard Sand.
Asbjørnsen i Grøtstrid. 23-29, TVET
P. Chr. Asbjørnsen og Universitetsbiblioteket. 299-324, MUNT

BALBI, GIOVANNI, d. 1298. Catholicon
Geldner, Ferdinand. Das "Catholicon" des Johannes Balbus im Ältesten Buchdruck. 90-98, JUCH
——————. Der Verkaufspreis des Günther Zainer'schen Catholicon von 1469 (GW 3183). 37-42, STOL

Balboni, Dante.
Il Rito della Benedizione delle Palme (Vat. lat. 4770). I, 55-74, ALBB

Balcke, Curt.
Heinrich Friedrich von Diez und Sein Vermächtnis in der Preussischen Staatsbibliothek. 187-200, KUHN

Verzeichnis der Schriften Milkaus. 48-55, MILK

BALDENSHEYM, ADOLAR, bookbinder
Schreiber, Heinrich. Adolar Baldensheym, ein Leipziger Renaissance-buchbinder. 176-200, HAEK

Baldini, Antonio.
La Bibbia di Borso. 41-45, GREG

Balke, Siegfried.
[On the Deutsche Gesellschaft für Dokumentation.] 3, DEUD

BALLARD, ROBERT, printer
Hofer, Philip. Adrian Le Roy and Robert Ballard: Printers of the Late Renaissance. 475-482, LYDE

BALTIMORE. WALTERS ART GALLERY
see Walters Art Gallery, Baltimore

BALZAC, HONORÉ DE. Gambara
Pierrot, R. La Véritable Édition Originale de "Gambara." 175-179, CALO

BAMBERG - Bookbinding
see Bookbinding - Bamberg

BAMBERG - Printing
see Printing - Bamberg

BAMBERG. Staatliche Bibliothek
Müller, Max. Der Älteste Bisher Bekannte Buchumschlag. 195-197, LEID

BAMBERGER FÜRSTBISCHÖFE, Druckerei der
see Druckerei der Bamberger Fürstbischöfe

Bamberger, S.
Trennungsstrich, Fragezeichen und Ausrufungszeichen im Hebräischen Buchdruck. 109-110, FREN
Wandsbeker Druckperiode des Israel ben Abraham 1726 bis 1733. 101-108, FREN

BANCROFT LIBRARY. California. University, Berkeley
see California. University, Berkeley. Bancroft Library

Baneth, D. Z.
Geniza Documents on Jewish Communal Affairs in Egypt. 75-93, MARY

BANK NOTES - Collections - Tenri, Japan
Iwamuro, Shinobu. Tenri Toshokan Zō Shigen Tsukoho Sho. (On the Bank Note of the Chin-yüan Era in the Yüan Dynasty in the Tenri Central Library.) 339-343, TOMI

BANNED BOOKS
see Prohibited books and publications

Bannier, W. A. F.
G. A. Evers als Medebestuurslid. 28-32, EVER

Bannister, Henry Marriott.
Signs in Kalendarial Tables. 141-149, CHAT

BARACK, KARL AUGUST
BARA

BARACK, KARL AUGUST - Bibl.
BARA

Barberi, Francesco.
Le Edizioni Romane di Francesco Minizio Calvo. 57-98, FERR
Luigi de Gregori. 17-31, GREG

BARCELONA. Archivo Condal
see Spain. Archivo General de la Corona de Aragón.

BARCELONA. Biblioteca Central. Fonds Pedrell
Anglés, Higinio. Relations Épistolaires entre César Cui et Philippe Pedrell. 15-21, FEDO

BARCELONA. Biblioteca Central. Fonds Pedrell - Mss. (C. Cui)
Anglés, Higinio. Relations Épistolaires entre César Cui et Philippe Pedrell. 15-21, FEDO

BARCELONA. Biblioteca Central. Fonds Pedrell - Mss. (Cod. 548)
Vilar, Joan. L' "Expositio Remigii Super Matheum" en el Còd. 548 de la Biblioteca de Catalunya. III, 263-281, RUBI

BARCELONA. Biblioteca de Catalunya
see Barcelona. Biblioteca Central

BARCELONA - Cui, César. Lettres - Collections
see Cui, César - Correspondence - Collections - Barcelona

BARCELONA (DIOCESE) MUSEO. Mss. (Cassianus)
Rius i Serra, Josep. Un Full Visigòtic del Segle IX. II, 441-450, RUBI

BARCELONA - Musicians - Correspondence - Collections
see Musicians - Correspondence - Collections - Barcelona

BARCELONA. Santa Catalina (Dominican convent). Mss. (Liber Anniversariorum)
Alcalde, Lesmes. El "Liber Anni-

versariorum'' del Antiguo Convento de Santa Catalina de Barcelona. II, 519-539, RUBI

BARCELONA. Seminario Conciliare Biblioteca
Albareda, Anselmo. Un Incunabulo Sconosciuto dello Stampatore J. Luschner. 29-50, ACCU

BARCELONA. Universidad. Biblioteca. Mss. (Liber Anniversariorum)
Alcalde, Lesmes. El ''Liber Anniversariorum'' del Antiguo Convento de Santa Catalina de Barcelona. II, 519-539, RUBI

Bardet, Bernard.
Oeuvres de Vladimir Fédorov. 150-152, FEDO

Barker, Tommie Dora.
Library Progress in the South, 1936-42. 353-362, WILS

Barnett, Claribel R.
The Size Factor in Library Problems. 68-79, PUTN

Baron, Hans.
A Forgotten Chronicle of Early Fifteenth-Century Venice. 19-36, PARG

Baron, Salo W.
Moritz Steinschneider's Contribution to Jewish Historiography. 83-148, MARX

Barot, C. P.
Problems of Reorganisation in India. 130-134, MADR
Colon Classification in Gujarat. 102-104, RANG

Barrau-Dihigo, L.
À Propos d'un Manuscript Hispanique de Leyde (XIIIe Siècle). 332-340, CHAT

Barreda, Fernando.
Aportaciones a la Biografía de d. Telesforo Trueba y Cosío. I, 32-55, ARTI

Barroux, Robert.
Recueil Historique en Français Composé, Transcrit et Enluminé à Saint-Denis, vers 1280. 15-34, CALO

BARROW, W. J.
Grill, Erik. The Barrow Method in Sweden. 489-492, GALL

BARTAS, GUILLAUME DE SALLUST DU
see Du Bartas, Guillaume de Sallust

BARTLETT, ROGER, binder
Nixon, Howard M. Roger Bartlett's Bookbindings. 56-65, OLDH

BARTOLUS DE SAXOFFERATO. Opera. 1482
Rath, Erich von. Der Drucker von Buyers Ausgabe der Werke des Bartolus von 1482. Ein Beitrag zur Buchdruckergeschichte Lyons. 217-225, SCHW

Bartoš, F. M.
Bible Kněze Jakuba, Faráře u. Sv. Mikuláše na Starém Městě v Praze. 83-86, EMLE

BASEL. Allgemeine Lesegesellschaft
BASA

BASEL - Architectural plans - Collections
see Architectural plans - Collections - Basel

BASEL - Architecture and building - Proprietary libraries
see Architecture and building - Proprietary libraries - Basel

BASEL - Archives
see Archives - Basel

BASEL - Archives - Use studies
see Archives - Use studies - Basel

BASEL - Correspondence - Collections
see Correspondence - Collections - Basel

BASEL - Genealogical libraries and Collections
see Genealogical libraries and Collections - Basel

BASEL - Legal deposit (of books, etc.)
see Legal deposit (of books, etc.) - Basel

BASEL MISSAL
see Missale Basiliense

BASEL - Music literature and scores, Swiss - Manuscripts - Collections
see Music literature and scores, Swiss - Manuscripts - Collections - Basel

BASEL - Music printing
see Music printing - Basel

BASEL - Musicians - Correspondence - Collections
see Musicians - Correspondence - Collections - Basel

BASEL - Printing
see Printing - Basel

BASEL - Proprietary libraries
see Proprietary libraries - Basel

BASEL - Research materials - Collections
see Research materials - Collections - Basel

BASEL - Seals (Numismatics) - Collections
see Seals (Numismatics) - Collections - Basel

BASEL. Universität. Bibliothek

BASE

Godet, Marcel. Au Temps de la "Respublica Litterarum." Jacob Christophe Iselin et Louis Bourguet. 117-127, SCHU

Husner, Fritz. Die Editio Princeps des "Corpus Historiae Byzantinae." Johannes Oporin, Hieronymus Wolf und die Fugger. 143-162, SCHU

Nidecker, Heinrich. Wilhelm Wackernagel. Bücher and Freunde. Ein Streifzug durch Seine Bibliothek. 177-191, SCHU

Salfinger, Theodor. Zur Sprachkunst des Germanisten Andreas Heusler. 193-205, SCHU

Schwarber, Karl. Das Basler Pflichtexemplar. 145-163, GODE

Vischer, Christoph. Die Stammbücher der Universitätsbibliothek Basel. Ein Beschreibendes Verzeichnis. 247-264, SCHU

BASEL. Universität. Bibliothek. Amerbach-Iselin Collection

Roth, Carl. Conrad Pfister, Basilius Iselin und die Amerbachische Bibliothek. 179-200, BINZ

BASEL. Universität. Bibliothek - Hist.

BASE

BASEL. Universität. Bibliothek. Mss.

Zehntner, Hans. Die Handschriftlichen Nachlässe von Schweizer Komponisten in der Universitätsbibliothek Basel. 297-315, SCHU

BASEL. Universität. Bibliothek. Mss. (A, IX)

Husner, Fritz. Die Handschrift der Scholien des Erasmus von Rotterdam zu den Hieronymusbriefen. 132-146, BINZ

BASEL. Universität. Bibliothek. Mss. (F. III. 15a)

Macé, Alcide. Le Basiliensis F III 15a (VIIIe Siècle). 383-395, CHAT

BASEL. Universität. Bibliothek. Mss. (Gothaer Sammlung)

Straub, Hans. Christoph Martin Wieland and Johann III Bernoulli. Ein Unveröffentlichter Brief aus der "Gothaer Sammlung" der Basler Universitätsbibliothek. 233-245, SCHU

BASEL. Universität. Bibliothek. Mss. (Liudprand)

Meyer, Gustav. Ein Neues Bruchstück zu Liudprand von Cremona. 163-175, SCHU

BASEL. Universität. Bibliothek. Mss. (Music correspondence)

Zehntner, Hans. Musikerbriefe in der Universitätsbibliothek Basel. 140-149, FEDO

BASEL-STADT (CANTON) STAATSARCHIV

BASL

Bashiruddin, S.
Ranganathan: An Inventive Genius. 645-646, RANG

BASKERVILLE, JOHN

Bockwitz, Hans H. Baskerville im Urteil Deutscher Zeitgenossen. III, 250-253, GLAU

BASKERVILLE, JOHN - Collections - Yale

Townsend, Rebecca Dutton, Margaret Currier, et al. A Selection of Baskerville Imprints in the Yale University Library. 285-297, KEOG

BASSANI, SAMUEL HAYIM - Library

Roth, Cecil. A Seventeenth Century Library and Trousseau. 160-169, FREI

Bassi, D.
φιλοδήμου ΠΕρί ᾿Επικούρου(A ?.) B. 511-529, CERI

Bates, Albert Carlos.
The Work of Hartford's First Printer. List of Thomas Green's Hartford Imprints, 1764-1768. 345-361, EAME

Bathia, Sant Ram.
Contribution of the Punjab to the Indian Library Movement. 379-383, RANG

Batiffol, Abbé Pierre.
Note sur un Bréviaire Cassinésien du XIe Siècle. 201-209, HAVE

Batllori, Miquel.
El Pare Ehrle, Prefecte de la Vaticana, en la Seva Correspondència amb el Card. Rampolla. I, 75-117, ALBB

BATOPEDI (MONASTERY) MT. ATHOS
see Athos (Monasteries) Vatopedi

BATTIFERRI, MATTEO

Husung, Max Joseph. Aus der Zeit des Übergangs von der Handschrift zum Druck. Nach einem Band der Preussischen Staatsbibliothek. 155-159, DEGE

Battisti, Carlo.
Il Centenario della Biblioteca Governativa di Gorizia. 9-24, GORI
Registro d'Ingresso e Inventario Topografico. 56-80, GORI

Bauer, Andreas, ed.
HELD

Bauer, Hanns.
Aus dem Ersten Jahrhundert des Elbinger Gymnasiums und Seiner Bibliothek. 19-34, KÖNI

Bauer, Johannes.
Schleiermacherbildnisse. 86-89, KUHN

Bauermann, Johannes.
Die Gründungsurkunde des Klosters Abdinghof in Paderborn. Ein Beitrag zur Frage der Abdinghofer Fälschungen. 16-36, BÖME

Bauhuis, Walter.
Alte und Neue Ideen im Bibliotheksbau. 72-82, HOFF
Arbeitsmethoden der Erwerbungsabteilung. 37-41, REDE
Vereinfachungen beim Gang des Buches durch die Bibliothek. 133-142, VORS
Warnung vor Publikumskatalogen. 386-392, JUCH

Baumgart, Jan.
Struktura Organizacyjna Bibliotek Naukowych. 131-154, GRYC

BAVARIA - Catalogs - Union
see Catalogs - Union - Bavaria

BAVARIA. Hauptstaatsarchiv. Mss. (Bible O.T. Glossary)
Hartl, Eduard. Ein Neues Althochdeutsches Glossenfragment. 95-101, LEID

BAVARIA - Legal deposit (of books, etc.)
see Legal deposit (of books, etc.) - Bavaria

BAVARIA - Libraries
see Libraries - Bavaria

BAVARIA - State libraries
see State libraries - Bavaria

Bay, Jens Christian.
Private Book Collectors of the Chicago Area: A Brief Review. 363-374, WILS

Bay, Jens Christian.
Letter [to Topsøe-Jensen] in Topsøe-Jensen, H. Om et Eksemplar af H. Steffens: "Was Ich Erlebte" i Universitetsbibliotekets 1. Afd., København. 95-100, DAHA

BAY, JENS CHRISTIAN
BAYJ

Bayer, Wilhelm.
Gedanken zum Bibliothekarischen Berufsbild. 49-60, LANF

BAYERISCHE STAATSBIBLIOTHEK, Munich
see Munich. Bayerische Staatsbibliothek

BAYERISCHER ZENTRALKATALOG
see Munich. Bayerischer Zentralkatalog

Beaulieux, Ch.
Manuscrits et Imprimés en France XVe et XVIe Siècles. 417-428, CHAT

Bechyňová, Věnceslava.
Bibliografická Spolupráce Ivana V. Šopova s P. J. Šafaříkem. 41-50, MIKH

Beck, Helmut.
Das Schlagwortregister zum Systematischen Katalog. 23-42, BULL

Beck, Marcel.
Die Ausländischen Bestände. 77-80, BERU
Begegnungen mit Marcel Godet. 13-16, GODM
Das Bibliographische Bulletin. 144-147, BERU
Die Handbibliothek im Lesesaal und der Bibliographische Apparat im Katalogsaal. 84-87, BERU

Bečka, Josef, jt. ed.
EMLE

Becker, Henrik.
Schaubüchereien auch Heute? 43-46, BULL

Becker, Josef.
Die Bibliothek des Zacharias Konrad von Uffenbach. 129-148, LEYG

Becker, Robert H.
A Time of Adventure. 31-39, HAMM

Beckwith, Frank.
The Eighteenth-Century Proprietary Library in England. 81-98, OFFO

Beer, J.
Pädagogische Menschenkunde. 9-14, ACKE

Beeson, Charles H.
The Ars Grammatica of Julian of Toledo. 50-70, EHRA

Beetz, Wilhelm.
Zur Geschichte der Porträtsammlung der Nationalbibliothek in Wien. 59-74, VIEN

BEHAM, HANS SEBALD - Collections - Erlangen
Zimmermann, Hildegard. Hans Sebald Beham und Sein Werkanteil an der Holzschnittsammlung der Erlanger Universitätsbibliothek. 105-114, VERZ

Behrend, Fritz.
Höxter-Corvey in Geschichte, Sage und Dichtung. 277-286, BÖME

Belden, Charles F. D.
The Library Service of Herbert Putnam in Boston. 10-14, PUTN

BELGIUM - Illumination of books and manuscripts
see Illumination of books and manuscripts - Belgium

BELGIUM - Monastic libraries
see Monastic libraries - Belgium

BELINFANTE, ISAAC HA-COHEN - Collections - Amsterdam
Enelow, H. G. Isaac Belinfante, an Eighteenth Century Bibliophile. 5-30, FREI

BELLES-LETTRES
see Literature of the humanities

Below, Erich.
Merwürdige Bücherbestellungen. 316-321, KUHN
Das Schlagwortregister zum Fachkatalog. 113-119, HARN

Bémont, Ch.
La Date de la Composition du Modus Tenendi Parliamentum in Anglia. 465-480, HAVE

Bendtsen, F. M.
Systematisering. Trykte Kataloger. 114-122, AARU

Benedetti, Luigi De.
I Regesti dei Romani Pontefici per l'Abbazia di Casamari. 325-356, GALL

BENEDIKTBEUERN (BENEDICTINE ABBEY)
Ruf, Paul. Ausgaben des Klosters Benediktbeuern für Bücher und Schreibzeug von 1495-1510. 219-227, LEID

Beneš, K. J.
Emler—Člověk a Budovatel. 46-49, EMLE

BENEVENTAN PALEOGRAPHY
see Paleography, Italian (Beneventan)

BENEVENTO. San Pietro (Church) Biblioteca
Mottironi, Sergio. La Chiesa di S. Pietro di Benevento e la Sua Biblioteca nel Sec. XIII. 559-562, GALL

BENEVENTO. S. Sofia (Benedictine monastery). Liber Preceptorum Ms.
Bertolini, Ottorino. La Collezione Canonica Beneventana del Vat. lat. 4939. I, 119-137, ALBB

Bengtsson, Bent.
Boktryckets "Gamla" och "Nya" Metoder på 1700-talet. 33-44, GARD

Benn, T. V.
Bibliographical Sources for Contemporary French Literature. 69-80, OFFO

Benndorf, Gottfried and Hans Hofmann.
Die Sächsische Landesbibliothek 1920-36. 1-14, BOLL

Benton, Rita.
Ignace Pleyel, Disputant. 21-24, FEDO

BENZELIUS, ERIK, d.y.
Andersson, Aksel. Några Rangfrågor vid Uppsala Universitet vid Tiden för Erik Benzelius d. y:s Utnämning till Bibliotekarie. 373-390, UPPS
Holmgren, Gustaf. Om Cronstedtska Samlingen i Uppsala Universitetsbibliotek och dess Tillkomst. Några Anteckningar. 519-560, GRAP

BENZELIUS, ERIK, d.y. Itineris Eruditi Album
Gobom, Nils. Eric Benzelius d. y:s Itineris Eruditi Album i Linköpings Stiftsbibliotek. 385-394, COLL

Benzing, Josef, jt. ed.
RUPP

Benzing, Josef.
Buchgeschichtliche Beiträge zu einigen Frühdrucken der UB Mainz. 103-128, MAIZ
Der Kupferstecher, Kunstdrucker and Verleger Johann Bussemacher zu Köln (1580? bis 1616?). 129-146, JUCH

Benzing, Josef and Helmut Presser, eds.
Fünfhundert Jahre Mainzer Buchdruck. 1-317, (whole volume), RUPP

BENZING, JOSEF
BENZ

BENZING, JOSEF - Bibl.
Geck, Elisabeth. Verzeichnis der

Veröffentlichungen von Josef Benzing in den Jahren 1928-1963. 13-24, BENZ

BEQUESTS
see Gifts, contributions, etc.

BER, LUDWIG - Library

Kimmenauer, Alfred. Colmarer Beriana. Zu Ludwig Ber's Bibliothek und Papieren. 244-251, BENZ

Berchem, V. van.
Hermann Escher Historien. 35-43, ESCK

Berend, Eduard.
Jean Pauls Handschriftlicher Nachlass. 336-346, HOFF

Berg, Gösta and Kurt Jonson.
Bouppteckningar från Borgarhem i Stormaktstidens Örebro. 186-240, ÖREB

BERGEN - Archives, Business
see Archives, Business - Bergen

BERGEN - Book collecting
see Book collecting - Bergen

BERGEN - Business literature - Collections
see Business literature - Collections - Bergen

BERGEN - Manuscripts - Collections
see Manuscripts - Collections - Bergen

BERGEN, Norway. Universitetet. Biblioteket

Munthe, Gerhard. Firma-Arkivene i Universitetsbiblioteket i Bergen. 216-231, TVET

BERGEN, Norway. Universitetet. Biblioteket. Mss. (Frederik III. Brev [till Rosenkrantz])

Munthe, Gerhard. Ludvig Rosenkrantz og Gjenerobringen av Trondhjems Len. Et Dokument i Universitetsbiblioteket i Bergen. 90-94, DAHA

Berger, Abraham, jt. ed.
BLOC

Berger, Elie.
Bulle de Clément V en Faveur de Guillaume de Nogaret. 268-270, CHAT

BERGER, JÖRG - Correspondence - Collections - Zürich

Muralt, Leonhard von. Jörg Berger. 98-126, ESCZ

Berger, Philippe.
Ascagne. 611-619, GRAU

Berger, Samuel.
De Quelques Anciens Textes Latins des Actes des Apôtres. 9-14, HAVE

Berghoeffer, Christian Wilhelm.
Die Wissenschaftliche Arbeit des Bibliothekars. 97-103, EBRA

Bergmann, Werner and Heinz Kleeberg.
Der Beitrag der Deutschen Bücherei zur Lösung Volkswirtschaftlicher Aufgaben. 91-103, LEIZ

BERKELEY, California - Picture collections
see Picture collections - Berkeley, California

BERKELEY, GEORGE, Bp. of Cloyne

Keogh, Andrew. Bishop Berkeley's Gift of Books to Yale in 1733. 128-147, MUNT

Berkov, P. N.
Tragediia A. P. Shopova "Smurt'ta na Kniaza Potemkina" i ee Russkii Istochnik (Bibliograficheskoe Razyskanie). 19-30, MIKH

BERLIN. Ärztebibliothek
see Berlin. Stadtbibliothek. Ärztebibliothek

BERLIN. Amerika-Gedenkbibliothek

Busch, Jürgen. Der Berliner Leihverkehr in den Jahren 1956-1958. 205-213, SCHS
Sauer, Bruno. Die Literarischen Sammlungen der Amerika-Gedenkbibliothek. 191-204, SCHS

BERLIN - Architecture and building - National libraries
see Architecture and building - National Libraries - Berlin

BERLIN - Architecture and building - Public libraries
see Architecture and building - Public libraries - Berlin

BERLIN - Art libraries and collections
see Art libraries and collections - Berlin

BERLIN. Auskunftsbureau der Deutschen Bibliotheken
see Prussia. Auskunftsbureau der Deutschen Bibliotheken

BERLIN. Berliner Bibliothekarschule

Otto, Hanna. Berliner Bibliothekarschule seit 1949. 173-181, SCHS

BERLIN. Berliner Büchereischule

Ackerknecht, Erwin. Erinnerungen an

die Anfänge der Berliner Büchereischule. 7-12. LANF

BERLIN. Berliner Gesamtkatalog

Lullies, Hildegard. Der Berliner Gesamtkatalog. 131-157, SCHS

BERLIN. Berliner Zentralbibliothek
see Berlin. Amerika-Gedenkbibliothek

BERLIN. Bibliothek des Grossen Kurfürsten
See Berlin. Deutsche Staatsbibliothek

BERLIN - Bookbinding
see Bookbinding - Berlin

BERLIN - Bookbinding - Fine bindings - Collections
see Bookbinding - Fine bindings - Collections - Berlin

BERLIN - Books - Owners' marks
see Books - Owners' marks - Berlin

BERLIN - Büchereischule
see Berlin. Berliner Büchereischule

BERLIN - Cataloging
see Cataloging - Berlin

BERLIN - Catalogs
see Catalogs - Berlin

BERLIN - Catalogs - Author
see Catalogs - Author - Berlin

BERLIN - Catalogs - Classed
see Catalogs - Classed - Berlin

BERLIN - Catalogs - Subject
see Catalogs - Subject - Berlin

BERLIN - Catalogs - Union
see Catalogs - Union - Berlin

BERLIN - Children's library services
see Children's library services - Berlin

BERLIN - Circulation procedures
see Circulation procedures - Berlin

BERLIN - Classification
see Classification - Berlin

BERLIN - College and university libraries. Departmental and divisional libraries
see College and university libraries. Departmental and divisional libraries - Berlin

BERLIN. Deutsche Staatsbibliothek [honoree]

BERP

BERS

BERLIN. Deutsche Staatsbibliothek [subject]

HARN

WILM

Altmann, Wilhelm. Die Königliche Bibliothek in Berlin in Ihren Beziehungen zum Königlichen Opernhaus (1788-1843). 51-66, WILM

Fick, Richard. Der Ankauf der Celler Kirchenministerialbibliothek durch den Preussischen Staat. 149-158, LEYG

Hortzschansky, Adalbert. Heinrich Pertz' Berufung zum Oberbibliothekar der Königlichen Bibliothek in Berlin. 115-126, SCHW

Husung, Max Joseph. Aus der Zeit des Übergangs von der Handschrift zum Druck. Nach einem Band der Preussischen Staatsbibliothek. 155-159, DEGE

——— Ein Neuer Signierter und Datierter Badier, Gefunden in der Preussischen Staatsbibliothek. 435-442, COLL

Lindau, Hans. Aus der Berliner Dienststelle der Universitätsschriften. 238-244, KUHN

Moeltzner, August. Zwanzig Jahre Maskierte Druckerarbeit. Pierre du Marteaus Drucke aus den Jahren 1660-1680 in der Königl. Bibliothek zu Berlin. 197-204, SCHW

Pick, Herman. Der Unvollendet Gebliebene Bibliotheksbau des Großen Kurfürsten. 211-215, SCHW

Schultze, Walther. Die Zukunft Unserer Realkataloge. 224-237, KUHN

Spanier, Arthur. Über Umfang und Herkunft der Sammlung Hebräischer Handschriften in der Kurfürstlichen Bibliothek zu Berlin. 245-253, KUHN

Transfeldt, Walter. Preussische Staatsbibliothek und Familienforschung. 261-270, KUHN

BERLIN. Deutsche Staatsbibliothek. Auskunftsabteilung

Gittig, Heinz. Das Auskunftsbüro der Deutschen Bibliotheken. I, 223-240, BERS

BERLIN. Deutsche Staatsbibliothek. Benutzungsabteilung

Unger, Willy. Benutzungseinrichtungen, Benutzungspolitik und Gebrauchsöffentlichkeit. I, 175-221, BERS

BERLIN. Deutsche Staatsbibliothek - Bibl.

Kittel, Peter. Bibliographie. II, 1-123, BERS

Otto, Paul. Ikonographie der Königlichen Bibliothek zu Berlin. 43-50, WILM

BERLIN. Deutsche Staatsbibliothek - Catalogs

Below, Erich. Das Schlagwortregister zum Fachkatalog. 113-119, HARN
Fick, Richard. Die Kataloge der Druckschriftenabteilung. 92-99, HARN
Kaiser, Rudolf. Der Alphabetische Zettelkatalog. 99-109, HARN
Pfennig, Richard. Unser Realkatalog. 109-113, HARN

BERLIN. Deutsche Staatsbibliothek. Gesellschaftswissenschaftliche Beratungsstelle

Gittig, Heinz. Die Gesellschaftswissenschaftliche Beratungsstelle. I, 425-432, BERS

BERLIN. Deutsche Staatsbibliothek. Handschriftenabteilung

Haebler, Konrad. Die Handschriftenabteilung. 126-131, HARN
Lülfing, Hans. Die Handschriftenabteilung. I, 319-380, BERS
Schmidt, Wieland. Hermann Degering, Erinnerungen aus der Staatsbibliothek. 126-129, LEUN

BERLIN. Deutsche Staatsbibliothek - Hist.

Abb, Gustav. Eine Denkschrift Philipp Buttmanns über Katalogfragen vom Jahre 1791. 177-181, KUHN
———— Die Einführung der Täglichen Ausleihe in der Berliner Kgl. Bibliothek. 179-185, GODE
———— Von der Kollegialverfassung zum Führerprinzip. Ein Beitrag zur Verfassungsgeschichte der Preussischen Staatsbibliothek. 245-256, LEYG
Balcke, Curt. Heinrich Friedrich von Diez und Sein Vermächtnis in der Preußischen Staatsbibliothek. 187-200, KUHN
Juchhoff, Rudolf. Die Büchersammlung des Generalpostmeisters von Nagler in der Preussischen Staatsbibliothek. 201-208, KUHN
Krieg, Werner. Die Revision der Preussischen Staatsbibliothek im Sommer 1939. 404-421, JUCH
Krüss, Hugo Andres. Zur Geschichte der Staatsbibliothek zu Berlin in den Letzten Dreissig Jahren. 263-274, PUTN
Kunze, Horst. Demokratisierung und Sozialistische Umgestaltung. I, 49-76, BERS
Kunze, Horst and Werner Dube. Zur Vorgeschichte der Deutschen Staatsbibliothek. I, 1-47, BERS
Schwenke, Paul. Zur Älteren Geschichte der Berliner Königlichen Bibliothek (1687-1698). 1-14, WILM
Tyszko, Oskar. Die Bestandsvermehrung der Hauptabteilung und Ihre Organisation. I, 89-129, BERS

BERLIN. Deutsche Staatsbibliothek. Inkunabelsammlung

Altmann, Ursula. Die Inkunabelsammlung. I, 381-403, BERS

BERLIN. Deutsche Staatsbibliothek. Kartenabteilung

Klemp, Egon. Die Kartenabteilung. I, 405-423, BERS

BERLIN. Deutsche Staatsbibliothek. Kinder- und Jugendbuchabteilung

Meyer, Hanna. Die Kinder- und Jugendbuchabteilung. I, 433-441, BERS

BERLIN. Deutsche Staatsbibliothek. Kriegssammlung

Hirsch, Paul. Die "Kriegssammlung" der Königlichen Bibliothek zu Berlin. 97-106, WILM

BERLIN. Deutsche Staatsbibliothek. Lautabteilung

Doegen, Wilhelm. Die Lautabteilung. 253-258, HARN

BERLIN. Deutsche Staatsbibliothek- Mss. (Bible. Latin)

Günther, Otto. Der Neapolitaner Johannes Bernardinus Bonifacius, Marchese von Oria, und die Anfänge der Danziger Stadtbibliothek. 107-128, WILM

BERLIN. Deutsche Staatsbibliothek - Mss. (Cod. Ham. 253)

Kirchner, Joachim. Das Staveloter Evangeliar der Preussischen Staatsbibliothek. 160-171, DEGE

BERLIN. Deutsche Staatsbibliothek - Mss. [Nr. 77 (Cod. Ham. 407)]

Schuster, Julius. Secreta Salernitana und Gart der Gesundheit. Eine Studie zur Geschichte der Naturwissenschaften und Medizin des Mittelalters. 203-237, DEGE

BERLIN. Deutsche Staatsbibliothek - Mss. (Germ. fol. 282)

KRÜS

BERLIN. Deutsche Staatsbibliothek - Mss. (Germ. fol. 1394)

Rosenfeld, Hans-Friedrich. Die Berliner Parzivalfragmente. 192-202, DEGE

BERLIN. Deutsche Staatsbibliothek - Mss. (Germ. oct. 87)

Wegener, Hans. Das Gebetbuch der Johanna von Bocholt. 228-232, BÖME

BERLIN. Deutsche Staatsbibliothek - Mss. (Germ. 4° 1532)

Kirchner, Joachim. Die Berliner Gregoriusfragmente. 148-156, HARN

BERLIN. Deutsche Staatsbibliothek - Mss. (Hamilton-Sammlung)

Schunke, Ilse. Die Italienischen Einbände aus der Hamilton-Sammlung in Berlin. 17-32, LÜLF

BERLIN. Deutsche Staatsbibliothek - Mss. (Jean Paul)

Berend, Eduard. Jean Pauls Handschriftlicher Nachlass. 336-346, HOFF

BERLIN. Deutsche Staatsbibliothek - Mss. [Lat. fol. 60 and 88 (Rose no. 909, 908)]

Lehmann, Paul. Aus einer Münchner Büchersammlung des Ausgehenden Mittelalters. 157-164, LEID

BERLIN. Deutsche Staatsbibliothek - Mss. (Lat. oct. 188)

Degering, Hermann. Ein Calendarium Pugillare mit Computus aus dem Jahre 1294. 79-88, LOUB

BERLIN. Deutsche Staatsbibliothek - Mss. (Lat. qu. 736)

Freitag, Albert. Ein Band aus Luthers Erfurter Klosterbibliothek. 93-110, DEGE

BERLIN. Deutsche Staatsbibliothek - Mss. (Lat. theol. fol. 733)

Degering, Hermann. Das Prümer Evangeliar (Ms. lat. theol. Fol. 733) in Berlin. 132-148, HARN

BERLIN. Deutsche Staatsbibliothek - Mss. (Mus. ms. 40580)

Wolf, Johannes. Zwei Tagelieder des 14. Jahrhunderts. 325-327, DEGE

BERLIN. Deutsche Staatsbibliothek - Mss. (Willems)

Vreese, Willem de. Briefwisseling van Jan Frans Willems en Jakob Grimm. 264-295, DEGE

BERLIN. Deutsche Staatsbibliothek. Musikabteilung

Altmann, Wilhelm. Die Entwicklung der Musikabteilung. 211-217, HARN
Köhler, Karl-Heinz. Die Musikabteilung. I, 241-274, BERS

BERLIN. Deutsche Staatsbibliothek. Orientalische Abteilung

Auster, Guido. Die Orientalische Abteilung. I, 275-317, BERS
Weil, Gotthold. Die Orientalische Abteilung. 180-186, HARN

BERLIN. Deutsche Staatsbibliothek. Stimmensammlung

Doegen, Wilhelm. Die Stimmensammlung zur Dokumentensammlung Darmstädter.

BERLIN - Dissertations, Academic - Collections
see Dissertations, Academic - Collections - Berlin

BERLIN - Documents - Collections
see Documents - Collections - Berlin

BERLIN - Duplicates
see Duplicates - Berlin

BERLIN - Genealogical libraries and collections
see Genealogical libraries and collections - Berlin

BERLIN. Gesamtkatalog der Preussischen Wissenschaftlichen Bibliotheken
see Gesamtkatalog der Preussischen Wissenschaftlichen Bibliotheken Berlin

BERLIN - Gifts, contributions, etc.
see Gifts, contributions, etc. - Berlin

BERLIN. Grosse Kurfürsten Bibliothek
see Berlin. Deutsche Staatsbibliothek

BERLIN. Humboldt-Universität. Bibliothek

Göber, Willi. Das Bibliothekswesen einer Universität als Einheit. 154-171, VORS

BERLIN - Incunabula - Collections
see Incunabula - Collections - Berlin

BERLIN - Information services
see Information services - Berlin

BERLIN - Interlibrary loans
see Interlibrary loans - Berlin

BERLIN - Inventories of books
see Inventories of books - Berlin

BERLIN. Joachimsthalisches Gymnasium
see Templin, Ger. Joachimsthalisches Gymnasium

BERLIN. Königliche Bibliothek
see Berlin. Deutsche Staatsbibliothek

BERLIN. Kurfürstliche Bibliothek
see Berlin. Deutsche Staatsbibliothek

BERLIN- Learned institutions and societies
Faden, Eberhard. Aus der Geschichte Gelehrter Gesellschaften und Ihrer Bibliotheken in Berlin. 17-40, SCHS

BERLIN - Librarians
see Librarians - Berlin

BERLIN - Librarians - Memoirs, reminiscences, etc.
see Librarians - Memoirs, reminiscences, etc. - Berlin

BERLIN - Libraries
see Libraries - Berlin

BERLIN - Library and the state
see Library and the state - Berlin

BERLIN - Library legislation
see Library legislation - Berlin

BERLIN - Library resources
see Library resources - Berlin

BERLIN - Library schools
see Library schools - Berlin

BERLIN - Literature of the humanities - Collections
see Literature of the humanities - Collections - Berlin

BERLIN - Luther, Martin - Collections
see Luther, Martin - Collections - Berlin

BERLIN - Manuscripts - Cataloging
see Manuscripts - Cataloging - Berlin

BERLIN - Manuscripts - Collections
see Manuscripts - Collections - Berlin

BERLIN - Manuscripts, Hebrew - Collections
see Manuscripts, Hebrew - Collections - Berlin

BERLIN - Manuscripts, Indic - Collections
see Manuscripts, Indic - Collections - Berlin

BERLIN - Manuscripts, Oriental - Collections
see Manuscripts, Oriental - Collections - Berlin

BERLIN - Maps - Collections
see Maps - Collections - Berlin

BERLIN - Medical libraries
see Medical libraries - Berlin

BERLIN - Municipal reference libraries
see Municipal reference libraries - Berlin

BERLIN - Music libraries and collections
see Music libraries and collections - Berlin

BERLIN - Music libraries and collections - Programs
see Music libraries and collections - Programs - Berlin

BERLIN - National libraries
see National libraries - Berlin

BERLIN - National libraries - Acquisitions
see National libraries - Acquisitions - Berlin

BERLIN - National libraries - Administration
see National libraries - Administration - Berlin

BERLIN - National libraries - Reference services
see National libraries - Reference services - Berlin

BERLIN. Öffentliche Wissenschaftliche Bibliothek
see Berlin. Deutsche Staatsbibliothek

BERLIN. Opernhaus
Altmann, Wilhelm. Die Königliche Bibliothek zu Berlin in Ihren Beziehungen zum Königlichen Opernhaus (1788-1843). 51-66, WILM

BERLIN - Oriental literature - Collections
see Oriental literature - Collections - Berlin

BERLIN - Periodicals - Collections
see Periodicals - Collections - Berlin

BERLIN. Preussische Staatsbibliothek
see Berlin. Deutsche Staatsbibliothek

BERLIN - Propaganda and the library
see Propaganda and the library - Berlin

BERLIN - Public libraries
see Public libraries - Berlin

BERLIN - Public libraries - Reference services
see Public libraries - Reference services - Berlin

BERLIN - Public libraries - Statistics
see Public libraries - Statistics - Berlin

BERLIN. Ratsbibliothek
see Berlin. Stadtbibliothek. Ratsbibliothek

BERLIN - Reader services
see Reader services - Berlin

BERLIN - Recordings - Collections
see Recordings - Collections - Berlin

BERLIN - Revolutionary literature - Collections
see Revolutionary literature - Collections - Berlin

BERLIN - Social science literature - Collections
see Social science literature - Collections - Berlin

BERLIN - Special collections
see Special collections - Berlin

BERLIN - Special libraries
see Special libraries - Berlin

BERLIN. Staatsbibliothek
see Berlin. Deutsche Staatsbibliothek

BERLIN. Stadtbibliothek

BERR

BERLIN. Stadtbibliothek. Abteilung Allgemeinbildende Bibliotheken

Woita, Irene. Abteilung Allgemeinbildende Bibliotheken. 48-51, BERR

BERLIN. Stadtbibliothek. Ärztebibliothek

Rohrbach, Peter P. Fachabteilungen und Sondersammlungen. 42-47, BERR

BERLIN. Stadtbibliothek. Benutzungsabteilung

Sabotke, Alice. Benutzungsabteilung - Ausleihe, Lesesäle, Freihandabteilung. 28-32, BERR

BERLIN. Stadtbibliothek. Ratsbibliothek

Rohrbach, Peter P. Fachabteilungen und Sondersammlungen. 42-47, BERR

BERLIN - Technical literature - Collections
see Technical literature - Collections - Berlin

BERLIN - Use studies - National libraries
see Use studies - National libraries - Berlin

BERLIN. Volksbüchereien

BERL

BERLIN - War and the library
see War and the library - Berlin

BERLIN - War records - Collections
see War records - Collections - Berlin

BERLIN - War records (1870-71 War) - Collections
see War records (1870-71 War) - Collections - Berlin

BERLIN. Weltkriegsbücherei
see Stuttgart. Bibliothek für Zeitgeschichte

BERLIN. Wissenschaftliche Bibliothek
see Berlin. Deutsche Staatsbibliothek

BERLIN. Wissenschaftliche Zentralbibliothek

Krohn, Gerhard. Wie die Wissenschaftliche Zentralbibliothek (WZB) Entstand. 159-171, SCHS

BERLIN - Young adults' library services
see Young adults' library services - Berlin

BERLIN. Zentralbibliothek
see Berlin. Amerika-Gedenkbibliothek

BERLINER BÜCHEREISCHULE, Berlin
see Berlin. Berliner Büchereischule

BERLINER GESAMTKATALOG
see Berlin. Berliner Gesamtkatalog

BERLINER ZENTRALBIBLIOTHEK, Berlin
see Berlin. Amerika-Gedenkbibliothek

Berlstein, Alfred.
Bibliotekarz i Pracownik Naukowy. 41-46, SZAC

BERN - Bible collections
see Bible collections - Bern

BERN - Bibliography
see Bibliography - Bern

BERN. Bibliothèque Nationale Suisse
see Bern. Schweizerische Landesbibliothek

BERN. Burgerbibliothek

BERT

BERN - Catalogs
see Catalogs - Bern

BERN - Catalogs - Printed book
see Catalogs - Printed book - Bern

BERN - Catalogs - Subject
see Catalogs - Subject - Bern

BERN - Depository libraries
see Depository libraries - Bern

BERN - Foreign language books - Collections
see Foreign language books - Collections - Bern

BERN - Government publications - Collections
see Government publications - Collections - Bern

BERN - Italian literature - Collections
see Italian literature - Collections - Bern

BERN. Landesbibliothek
see Bern. Schweizerische Landesbibliothek

BERN - Library resources
see Library resources - Bern

BERN - Manuscripts - Collections
see Manuscripts - Collections - Bern

BERN - Maps - Collections
see Maps - Collections - Bern

BERN - Music libraries and collections
see Music libraries and collections - Bern

BERN - National libraries
see National libraries - Bern

BERN - National libraries - Acquisitions
see National libraries - Acquisitions - Bern

BERN - Newspaper libraries and collections
see Newspaper libraries and collections - Bern

BERN - Ott, Arnold - Mss. - Collections
see Ott, Arnold - Mss - Collections - Bern

BERN - Photographic reproduction services
see Photographic reproduction services - Bern

BERN - Picture collections
see Picture collections - Bern

BERN - Printing
see Printing - Bern

BERN - Prohibited books and publications - Collections
see Prohibited books and publications - Collections - Bern

BERN - Public libraries
see Public libraries - Bern

BERN - Raeto-Romance literature - Collections
see Raeto-Romance literature - Collections - Bern

BERN - Rare books - Collections
see Rare books - Collections - Bern

BERN - Reader services
see Reader services - Bern

BERN - Reference books - Collections
see Reference books - Collections - Bern

BERN - Russian literature - Collections
see Russian literature - Collections - Bern

BERN. Schweizerische Landesbibliothek [honoree]

BERU

BERN. Schweizerische Landesbibliothek [subject]

GODM

Bourgeois, P. Le Dépôt Gratuit et Volontaire en Suisse. 397-401, BRUM

Escher, Hermann. Die Schweizerische Landesbibliothek (1911). 123-130, ESCH

Godet, Marcel. M. Gustave Binz et la Bibliothèque Nationale Suisse. 30-32, BINZ

——— Monsieur K. J. Lüthi et la Bibliothèque Nationale Suisse. 147-149, LÜTH

Schazmann, Paul-Emile. La Bulle d'Excommunication de Georges de Superşaxo. Un Imprimé Officiel de 1519 Émanant de la Chancellerie Épiscopale de Bâle. 207-212, SCHU

Vontobel, Willy. Dr. Pierre Bourgeois als Direktor der Schweizerischen Landesbibliothek. 168-177, BOUR

BERN. Schweizerische Landesbibliothek. <u>Bibliographisches Bulletin</u>

Beck, Marcel. Das Bibliographische Bulletin. 144-147, BERU

BERN. Schweizerische Landesbibliothek - Schweizerischer Gesamtkatalog

Grosser, Hermann. Der Gesamtkatalog der Schweizerischen Bibliotheken. 157-162, BERU

——— Marcel Godet und der Schweizerische Gesamtkatalog. 16-19, GODM

——— Die Zusammenarbeit der Schweizerischen Bibliotheken. Rückblick und Ausschau. 129-142, SCHU

BERN. Schweizerische Volksbibliothek

Burckhardt, Felix. Marcel Godet und die Schweizerische Volksbibliothek. 24-27, GODM

Schwarber, Karl. Marcel Godet und die Vereinigung Schweizerischer Bibliothekare. 3-8, GODM

BERN. Schweizerisches Gutenbergmuseum

Lüthi, Karl Jakob. Die Depositen des Schweizerischen Gutenbergmuseums. 120-123, BERU

BERN - Serial publications - Collections
see Serial publications - Collections - Bern

BERN - Society publications - Collections
see Society publications - Collections - Bern

BERN - Special collections
see Special collections - Bern

BERN. Stadtbibliothek

Bloesch, Hans. Ein Englischer Gönner der Berner Stadtbibliothek im 18. Jahrhundert. 112-118, BINZ
Refardt, Edgar. Die Musiktexte J. V. Widmanns. 134-139, REFA

BERN. Stadtbibliothek - Hist.

Bloesch, Hans. Albrecht Haller als Bibliothekar. 165-178, GODE

BERN - Theatrical libraries and collections
see Theatrical libraries and collections - Bern

BERN - Widmann, J. V. - Collections
see Widmann, J. V. - Collections - Bern

BERNARD DE CLAIRVAUX, SAINT. Mss.

Schulze, Alfred. Zu den Altfranzösischen Bernhardhandschriften. 389-404, WILM

BERNHARD VON BREYDENBACH
see Breydenbach, Bernhard von

BERNHARD VON KRAIBURG, Bp. of Chiemsee - Library

Ruf, Paul. Eine Altbayerische Gelehrtenbibliothek des 15. Jahrhunderts und Ihr Stifter Bernhard von Kraiburg. 219-239, STOL

Bernhardt, Børge.
Litt om Gjenfinning fra Brukersynspunkt. 174-182, TVET

BERNHART, JOHANN BAPTIST

Freys, Ernst. Johann Baptist Bernharts "Gesammelte Schriften." Ein Vorläufer von Haeblers Typenrepertorium. 145-174, HAEB

Bernhart, Joseph.
Selbstauffindung auf der Reise. 121-123, HELD

Bernheimer, Carlo.
The Library of the Talmud Torah at Leghorn. 1-4, FREI

Bernoulli, Rudolf.
Das Weltallbild in Hartmann Schedels Weltchronik. 48-58, LOUB
Das Werk. 3-10, LOUB

BERNOULLI FAMILY - Mss. - Collections - Basel

Straub, Hans. Christoph Martin Wieland an Johann III Bernoulli. Ein Unveröffentlichter Brief aus der "Gothaer Sammlung" der Basler Universitätsbibliothek. 233-245, SCHU

Berntsen, Bernhard.
Biblioteksentralen - en Tjener i Bibliotekenes Opplysningsarbeid. 98-103, NORS

Bernus, Alexander von.
Das aber Bindet. 36, HELD

BEROUN, Czechoslovakia - Public libraries
see Public libraries - Beroun, Czechoslovakia

Berra, Luigi.
Due Listi di Libri per la Biblioteca Vaticana. 19-27, MERG

BERSEN, JOHANN VON
see Johann von Bersen

Berthold, Werner.
Die Sondersammlung Exil-Literatur 1933-1945. 136-148, EPPE

Bertolini, Ottorino.
La Collezione Canonica Beneventana del Vat. Lat. 4939. I, 119-137, ALBB

Bertoni, Giulio.
Sulla Composizione del Codice Estense 232 delle Egloghe del Petrarca e sull'Autenticità dei così Detti Argomenti. II, 719-725, HORT

Bertout, Marie.
Une Visite à Madame de Noailles. 217-223, CALO

BESANÇON, France. Bibliothèque Municipale

Piquard, Maurice. La Bibliothèque d'un Homme d'État au XVIe Siècle. 227-235, CALO

BESANÇON, France. Bibliothèque Municipale - Mss.

Strittmatter, Anselm. The Pentecost Exultet of Reims and Besançon. 384-400, GREE

BESANÇON, France. Bibliothèque Municipale - Mss. (no. 1167)

Piquard, Maurice. Le Mémorial du Recteur de l'Université d'Ingolstadt Bénigne de Chaffoy (1555). Ms. 1167 de la Bibliothèque Municipale de Besançon. 219-232, HOFM

Beschorner, Hans.
Johannes Nienborg. 67-77, BOLL

BESKOW, BERNHARD VON - Library

Kleberg, Tönnes. Zwei Stammbuchblätter von Grillparzer in der Universitätsbibliothek Uppsala. 51, STUM

Besterman, Theodore.
Notes on the Development of Bibliographic Technique. 37-40, MIKH

BETRIEBSBÜCHEREI (ZEISS), Jena
see Zeiss (Carl) Jena, VEB. Betriebsbücherei

Bevilacqua, Mario.
Una "Quaestio" di Niccolò Matarelli (Vat. lat. 10726). I, 139-157, ALBB

BEYLE, MARIE HENRI. Lucien Leurven

Wagner, R. L. Les Valeurs de l'Italique. Notes de Lecture sur Lucien Leurven de Stendhal. 381-390, BONN

Bianchini, Bianca.
Muhammed och Berget. Redogörelse för en Experimentverksamhet i Sundbyberg. 33-50, HEIN

Biber, Arthur.
Gelegenheitsschriften, Familienkunde und Bibliotheken. 1-9, MILF

BIBLE COLLECTIONS - Bern

Lüthi, Karl Jakob. Die Bibelsammlung. 80-83, BERU

BIBLE COLLECTIONS - Münster

Zimmermann, Hildegard. Luther-Bibeln des 16. Jahrhunderts in der Universitätsbibliothek zu Münster i.W. 153-159, BÖME

BIBLE COLLECTIONS - Solothurn

Altermatt, Leo. Die von Staalsche Historienbibel der Zentralbibliothek Solothurn. 35-71, SCHU

BIBLE. Dutch. 1710-1712. (Pentapla)

Vogel, Paul Heinz. Ein "Kuriosum" des 18. Jahrhunderts. Die Biblia Pentapla. 445-455, BENZ

BIBLE. German. ca. 1475-76 - Hist.

Dold, Alban. Ein Unbekanntes Spezimen einer "Günther-Zainer"-Bibel. 105-110, LEYG

BIBLE. German. 1710-1712. (Pentapla)

Vogel, Paul Heinz. Ein "Kuriosum" des 18. Jahrhunderts. Die Biblia Pentapla. 445-455, BENZ

BIBLE. Hebrew

Zafren, Herbert C. Elias Hutter's Hebrew Bible. 29-39, BLOC

BIBLE - Illustrations
see Bible - Pictures, illustrations, etc.

BIBLE. Mss.

Durrieu, Comte Paul. Ingobert: un Grand Calligraphe du IXe Siècle. 1-14, CHAT
Redenbacher, Fritz. Adoratio Magorum. Die Heiligen Drei Könige in der Bibel von St. Gumbertus, Gesehen im Rahmen der Ikonographischen Überlieferung. 305-334, HOFM

BIBLE. Mss. - Ethiopic. N.T. Gospels

Skehan, Patrick W. An Illuminated Gospel Book in Ethiopic. 350-357, GREE

BIBLE. Mss. - German (Old High German). N.T. Gospels. Matthew

Sonnleithner, Rudolf. Die Mondseer Bruchstücke der Ältesten Hochdeutschen Evangelienübersetzung. 795-804, VIEN

BIBLE. Mss. - Gothic and Latin. N.T. Romans.

Dold, Alban. Die Provenienz der Altlateinischen Römerbrieftexte in den Gotisch-Lateinischen Fragmenten des Codex Carolinus von Wolfenbüttel. 13-29, LEYH

BIBLE. Mss. - Greek

Mercati, Giovanni, Cardinal. Un'Oscura Nota del Codice Alessandrino. 79-82, CHAT

BIBLE. Mss. - Greek. N.T.

Hannemann, Kurt. Antwerpener Fragmente einer Deutschen Geistlichen Prosahandschrift des 14. Jahrhunderts. 55-64, LEYH

BIBLE. Mss. - Greek. O.T.

Wessely, Charles. Un Nouveau Fragment de la Version Grecque du Vieux Testament par Aquila. 224-229, CHAT

BIBLE. Mss. - Greek. O.T. - Genesis

Kemke, Johannes. Die Geschichte einer Handschriften-Versendung. 489-498, WILM

BIBLE. Mss. - Latin

Baldini, Antonio. La Bibbia di Borso. 41-45, GREG
Bartoš, F. M. Bible Kněze Jakuba, Faráře u. Sv. Mikuláše na Starém Městě v Praze. 83-86, EMLE
Souter, Alexander. A Fragment of an Unpublished Latin Text of the Epistle to the Hebrews, with a Brief Exposition. 39-49, EHRA

Van der Briele, Wolfgang. Eine Bibelhandschrift des 13. Jahrhunderts in der Dortmunder Stadtbibliothek. 7-11, VERD

BIBLE. Mss. - Latin. N.T. Acts

Berger, Samuel. De Quelques Anciens Textes Latins des Actes des Apôtres. 9-14, HAVE

BIBLE. Mss. - Latin. N.T. Gospels

Campana, Augusto. Per il "Textus Evangelii" Donato da Enrico II a Montecassino (Vat. Ottobon. lat. 74). 34-47, MERG

Koehler, Wilhelm. The Fragments of an Eighth-Century Gospel Book in the Morgan Library (M. 564): A Contribution to the History of the Vulgate. 238-265, GREE

Lowe, Elias Avery. The Morgan Golden Gospels: The Date and Origin of the Manuscript. 266-279, GREE

Rand, Edward Kennard. A Carolingian Gospel-Book in the Pierpont Morgan Library in New York. 89-104, EHRD

BIBLE. Mss. - N.T. Apocryphal books. Protevangelium Jacobi

Schöne, Hermann. Palimpsestblätter des Protevangelium Jacobi in Cesena. 263-276, BÖME

BIBLE. Mss. - N.T. Mark

Haseloff, Arthur. Der Einband der Hs. des Marcusevangeliums des Harderadus. 507-528, EHRE

BIBLE. New Testament. Mss.
see Bible. Mss.

BIBLE. Old Testament. Mss.
see Bible. Mss.

BIBLE - Pictures, illustrations, etc.

Redenbacher, Fritz. Einzelbild und Zyklus in der Bibelillustration des Frühen Mittelalters. 110-118, TIEM

Schmidt, Philipp. Die Bibelillustration als Laienexegese. 228-239, BINZ

BIBLE - Publication and distribution

Wegelin, Oscar. Mills Day's Proposed Hebrew Bible. 221-226, EAME

<u>BIBLIA PENTAPLA</u>

Vogel, Paul Heinz. Ein "Kuriosum" des 18. Jahrhunderts. Die Biblia Pentapla. 445-455, BENZ

BIBLIOGRAFIA del Prof. Antoni Rubió i Lluch. I, ix-xv, RUBI

BIBLIOGRAFIA di Antonio Manno. I, xiii-xxv, MANO

BIBLIOGRAFIA o Pedagogiczna Biblioteka Wojewódzka w Krakowie. 125-127, KRAK

BIBLIOGRAPHERS
see also Special librarians

BIBLIOGRAPHERS

Trenkov, Khristo. Za Bibliografskata Profesiia. 313-322, MIKH

<u>BIBLIOGRAPHIA MEDICA HELVETICA</u>

Graf, Lucia. Bibliographia Medica Helvetica. 152-153, BERU

BIBLIOGRAPHICAL CITATIONS

Baba, Shigenori. An Aspect Regarding Quantification Method for Selection of Bibliographical Vessels. 283-292, RANG

BIBLIOGRAPHICAL CONTROL
see also Bibliography, International; Bibliography, National; Cataloging; Indexes and abstracts; Information retrieval

BIBLIOGRAPHICAL CONTROL

Berghoeffer, Christian Wilhelm. Die Wissenschaftliche Arbeit des Bibliothekars. 97-103, EBRA

Schneider, Georg. Die Bibliographie an den Wissenschaftlichen Bibliotheken. 322-326, KUHN

BIBLIOGRAPHICAL COOPERATION
see Catalogs - Union

BIBLIOGRAPHICAL ENTITY
see Bibliography

BIBLIOGRAPHICAL PRESS, Yale University
see Yale University, Bibliographical Press

BIBLIOGRAPHIE de Monseigneur Pelzer. 17-21, PEIZ

BIBLIOGRAPHIE der Arbeiten Josef Bicks. 61-69, BICK

BIBLIOGRAPHIE der Gedruckten Arbeiten von Johannes Wolf. 1-5, WOLJ

BIBLIOGRAPHIE der Schriften W. van der Brieles. 153-156, BRIE

<u>BIBLIOGRAPHIE DER SCHWEIZER-GESCHICHTE</u>

Vontobel, Willy. Bibliographie der Schweizergeschichte. 153-154, BERU

<u>BIBLIOGRAPHIE DER SCHWEIZERISCHEN LANDESKUNDE</u>

Wernly, Julia. Bibliographie der

Schweizerischen Landeskunde. 149-150, BERU

BIBLIOGRAPHIE DER SCHWEIZERISCHEN NATURWISSENSCHAFTLICHEN LITERATUR

Rytz, Walter. Bibliographie der Schweizerischen Naturwissenschaftlichen Literatur. 151-152, BERU

BIBLIOGRAPHIE der Wissenschaftlichen Veröffentlichungen von Alfred Orel. 9-19, OREL

BIBLIOGRAPHIE FÉMININE SUISSE

Muriset, Annie. Bibliographie Féminine Suisse. 154-157, BERU

BIBLIOGRAPHIE zur Geschichte der Deutschen Bücherei. 197-211, LEIS

BIBLIOGRAPHIE zur Geschichte der Stadtbibliothek. 15-16, MAIN

BIBLIOGRAPHISCHES BULLETIN (Bern)

Beck, Marcel. Das Bibliographische Bulletin. 144-147, BERU

BIBLIOGRAPHY

Collison, R. L. The Future of Bibliography. 215-218, MIKH
Dembowska, Maria. Bibliotekarstwo i Bibliografia a Dokumentacja. 169-182, GRYC
Fleischhack, Curt. Zur Rationalisierung der Bibliographischen Arbeit. 323-328, MIKH
Ferrari, Giorgio E. La Metodologia Bibliografica, Verso una Definizione del Suo Svolgimento. 287-311, FERR
Gode, M. Dokumentat͡siia͡, Biblioteki i Bibliografiia͡. 327-333, MIKN
Leyh, Georg. Bibliographisches. 78-85, VORS
Reichardt, Günther. Die Bedeutung der Annotation für Bibliographie und Katalog. 86-109, VORS
Schmidt, Wieland. Wissenschaft und Bibliographie. 127-129, FRAD
Sevensma, Tietse Pieter. Bibliographie ou Documentation? 45-51, GODE
Stein, Ernst. Die Herstellung von Fachbibliographien, Dargestellt an einem Beispiel aus der Arbeit der Technisch-Wissenschaftlichen Auskunftsstelle der Universitätsbibliothek Jena an der Bibliographischen Erfassung der Internationalen Laser-Literatur. 117-129, BULL
Trenkov, Khr. Za Otboro na Materiala v Obshtata Tekushta Registratsionna Bibliografiia͡. 375-379, TEOD
Weber, Hans-Oskar. Bibliographisch Selbständig / Bibliographisch Unselbständig. Ein Diskussionsbeitrag. 143-151, FUCH

BIBLIOGRAPHY ANALYSIS
see Bibliography

BIBLIOGRAPHY, Analytical

Danton, J. Periam. William Cartwright and His Comedies, Tragi-Comedies, with Other Poems ....1651. 438-456, WILS
Juchhoff, Rudolf. Aus der Werkstatt der Frühdruckforschung. 119-129, TIEM
Kaiser, Rudolf. Zur Unterscheidung Anscheinend Identischer Drucke. 127-129, SCHW

BIBLIOGRAPHY, Analytical - Examples

Adams, Percy G. The Case of Swaine Versus Drage: An Eighteenth-Century Publishing Mystery Solved. 157-168, PARG
Clapp, Clifford Blake. Analytical Methods in Bibliography Applied to Daniel Webster's Speech at Worcester in 1832. 211-219, EAME
Geissler, Paul. Zwei Unbekannte Holzschnittprobedrucke zum Theuerdank und Konrad Peutinger. 118-128, JUCH
Ilchester, the Earl of. Some Pages Torn from the Last Journals of Horace Walpole. 449-458, GREE
Polain, M.-Louis. Notes pour la Çollation des Deux Tirages de L'Édition du Speculum Doctrinale, s. ind. typ. [Strasbourg, Adolphe Rusch]. 111-120, COLL
Zafren, Herbert C. Elias Hutter's Hebrew Bible. 29-39, BLOC

BIBLIOGRAPHY - Berlin

Weser, Adolf. Erschliessung der Bestände durch Kataloge und Bibliographien. 22-27, BERR

BIBLIOGRAPHY - Bern

Wissler, Gustav. Marcel Godet als Direktor der Schweizerischen Landesbibliothek. 8-12, GODM

BIBLIOGRAPHY - Bibl.

Ferrari, Giorgio E. La Metodologia Bibliografica, Verso una Definizione del Suo Svolgimento. 287-311, FERR
Homeyer, Fritz. Versuch eines Bibliographen-Lexikons. 141-163, FRAD
Pregled na Disertatsii po Bibliotekoznanie i Bibliografiia͡ v SSSR. 381-391, MIKN
Schmitt, Franz Anselm. Stoff und Motiv in der Deutschen Literatur. Gedanken zu einer Neuen Bibliographie. 110-117, VORS
Totok, Wilhelm. Die Nationalbibliographien. Versuch einer Analyse. 107-123, FRAD

Trajkov, Veselin. Nesamostoiatelnite bibliografii i Vkliuchvaneto im v Tekushchata Bibliografiia na Bibliografiite. 307-312, MIKH

BIBLIOGRAPHY - Bibl. - Bulgarian literature

Borov, Todor. Die Primäre Nationalbibliographie Bulgariens. 20-44, VORS

BIBLIOGRAPHY - Bibl. - Chinese literature

Schubert, Johannes. Chinesische Bucherverzeichnisse. I, 176-184, GLAU

BIBLIOGRAPHY - Bibl. - Collections
see Bibliography - Collections

BIBLIOGRAPHY - Bibl. - French literature

Benn, T. V. Bibliographical Sources for Contemporary French Literature. 69-80, OFFO

BIBLIOGRAPHY - Bibl. - German literature

Blum, Rudolf. Die Deutsche Bibliographie. 59, FRAD
——— Das Mehrjahres-Verzeichnis der Bücher und Karten. 68-72, FRAD
Büttner, Liselotte. Das Halbjahres-Verzeichnis. 64-67, FRAD
Fleischhack, Curt. Die Bibliographische Tätigkeit der Deutschen Bücherei. 105-140, LEIZ
Frels, Wilhelm. Die Bibliographischen Arbeiten und Aufgaben. 120-136, LEIS
Friesenhahn, Heinz. Das Wöchentliche Verzeichnis. 60-63, FRAD
Fuchs, Hermann. Die Deutschen Nationalbibliographien im Rahmen der Ausländischen Nationalbibliographien 103-106, FRAD
Schäfer, Rosa Maria. Das Deutsche Buch. 76-77, FRAD

BIBLIOGRAPHY - Bibl. - German periodicals

Jaeger, Friedrich. Das Mehrjahres-Verzeichnis der Zeitschriften. 73-75, FRAD

BIBLIOGRAPHY - Bibl. - Hebrew literature

Schwarz, Arthur Zacharias. Ein Vorschlag. 144, FREN

BIBLIOGRAPHY - Bibl. - Maps

Blum, Rudolf. Das Mehrjahres-Verzeichnis der Bücher und Karten. 68-72, FRAD

BIBLIOGRAPHY - Bibl. - Music

Bach, Ursula. Zur Fachbibliographie der Musikwissenschaft. 17-19, VORS
Plesske, Hans-Martin. Musikbibliographie und Deutsche Bücherei. 141-156, LEIZ

BIBLIOGRAPHY - Bibl. - Natural history

Zirkle, Conway. Patterns of Research and Changing Library Needs from the Viewpoint of the Natural Sciences. 12-18, PENN

BIBLIOGRAPHY - Bibl. - Rare books

Schroers, Paul. Antiquar und Bibliographie. 133-137, FRAD

BIBLIOGRAPHY - Bibl. - Reformation

Wendt, Bernhard. Antiquariatskataloge als Bibliographische Hilfsmittel für Reformationsdrucke. 476-491, BENZ

BIBLIOGRAPHY - Bibl. - Saxony

Jatzwauk, Jacob. Kurzer Abriss einer Geschichte der Sächsischen Bibliographie. 38-48, BOLL

BIBLIOGRAPHY - Bibl. - South African literature

Holdsworth, H. Bibliography in South Africa. 151-159, OFFO

BIBLIOGRAPHY - Bulgaria

Vŭzharova, M. Aleksandŭr Teodorov-Balan kato Bibliograf. 9-41, TEOB

BIBLIOGRAPHY - Bulgaria - Hist.

Borov, Todor. Bŭlgarska Bibliografiia. 99-110, MIKH

BIBLIOGRAPHY - China

Fen Chzhun-I͡Un. Bibliografskoto Delo v Kitaĭskata Narodnata Republika. 134-140, TEOB

BIBLIOGRAPHY - Classification
see Classification - Special subjects - Bibliography

BIBLIOGRAPHY - Collections - Leipzig

Fleischhack, Curt. Die Bibliographische Tätigkeit der Deutschen Bücherei. 105-140, LEIZ
Frels, Wilhelm. Die Bibliographischen Arbeiten und Aufgaben. 120-136, LEIS

BIBLIOGRAPHY - Early printed books - 16th cent.
see Rare books - 16th cent. - Bibl.

BIBLIOGRAPHY - France

Cain, Julien. Bibliothécaires et Bibliographes. L'Enseignement Bibliographique en France. 151-157, HOFM

BIBLIOGRAPHY - Hist.

Besterman, Theodore. Notes on the Development of Bibliographic Technique. 37-40, MIKH
Simon, K. R. Rannie Bibliografii po Istorii. 247-255, MIKH
Taylor, Archer. The History of Bibliography. 193-199, PARG

BIBLIOGRAPHY - Hist. - 15th-16th cent.

Schottenloher, Karl. Die Anfänge der Neueren Bibliographie. 233-239, LEID

BIBLIOGRAPHY - Indexes

Ikonomova, Diana and Dimitŭr Boshnakov. Imenniîat Pokazalets v Registratsionnata Bibliografiîa. 163-185, TEOB

BIBLIOGRAPHY - International

Brummel, Leendert. National and International Organization of Bibliography. 17-19, STUM
Selbmann, Ehrhard. Zur Melanchthonbibliographie. Ein Werk Internationaler Bibliothekarischer Gemeinschaftsarbeit. 245-250, BULL
Whitrow, Magda. Some Aspects of Descriptive Cataloguing in International Bibliography. 291-295, KYLE

BIBLIOGRAPHY - Italy

Moneti, Elena Amico. Giacomo Sardini, Patrizio Lucchese, Erudito e Bibliografo. 47-48, GALL

BIBLIOGRAPHY - National

Brummel, Leendert. National and International Organization of Bibliography. 17-19, STUM
Fuchs, Hermann. Die Deutschen Nationalbibliographien im Rahmen der Ausländischen Nationalbibliographien. 103-106, FRAD
Hleb-Koszańska, Helena. De la Coordination Bibliographique à L'Échelle Nationale. 329-334, MIKH
Ivanchev, Dimitur P. Po Vŭprosa za Otbora na Materiala v Obshchata Natsionalna Bibliografiîa. 171-181, MIKH

BIBLIOGRAPHY - National - Bibl.

Homeyer, Fritz. Versuch eines Bibliographen-Lexikons. 141-163, FRAD
Totok, Wilhelm. Die Nationalbibliographien. Versuch einer Analyse. 107-123, FRAD

BIBLIOGRAPHY - National - Bulgaria

Borov, Todor. Bŭlgarskata Pŭrvichna Natsionalna Bibliografiîa. 113-130, TEOD
———— Die Primäre Nationalbibliographie Bulgariens. 20-44, VORS
Ivanchev, Dimitur and Stefan Stanchev. Bibliografiîa na Statiite v Bulgarskiîa Periodichen Pechat s Ogled na Praktikata na "Bŭlgarski Knigopis" za 1930 i 1931 g. 404-408, MIKN
Masanov, ÎU. I. Za Nîakoi Zadachi na Dŭrzhavnata Bibliografiîa v SSSR. 127-133, TEOB
Nikolaev, N. N. "Bŭlgarski Knigopis" na K. Irechek. (Po Sluchaĭ Sto Godini ot Rozhdenieto na Irechek.) 98-112, TEOB
Teodorov-Balan, A. Rozhdenie i Otrechenie na Edin Stoletnik. 9-15, MIKN
Traĭkov, Nikola. Khŭrvatska Bibliografiîa na Bŭlgarskata Knizhnina. 189-204, MIKN
Traĭkov, Veselin N. Bulgarica; Literatura na Chuzhdi Ezitsi Vŭrkhu Bŭlgariîa i Bŭlgarskiîa Narod. 43-66, TEOB

BIBLIOGRAPHY, National - Bulgaria - Hist.

Borov, Todor. Bŭlgarska Bibliografiîa. 99-110, MIKH

BIBLIOGRAPHY, National - China

Fen Chzhun-ÎUn. Bibliografskoto Delo v Kitaĭskata Narodna Republika. 134-140, TEOB

BIBLIOGRAPHY, National - Croatia

Rojnić, Matko. Überblick über die Bibliographische Tätigkeit in Kroatien. 70-73, STUM

BIBLIOGRAPHY, National - Czechoslovakia - Hist.

Nosovský, Karel. Snahy Spolku Československých Knihkupeckých Účetních o Zřízení Bibliografické Kanceláře. 185-192, ŽIVN
Schmitt, Jan. Pokus o Českosl. Bibliografický Katalog 4, Třídy Desetinného Třídení. 171-173, ŽIVN

BIBLIOGRAPHY, National - Denmark

Dancke, Per. Claus Lydersen Fasting og Hans Bokfortegnelse. 5-24, HALV

BIBLIOGRAPHY, National - Finland

Sallander, Hans. Om Anders Anton von Stiernman Som Bibliografisk Författare. 561-576, GRAP

BIBLIOGRAPHY, National - France

Malclès, Louise-Noëlle. Le Fondateur de la Bibliographie Nationale en

France: le R. P. Louis Jacob de Saint-Charles. 243-255, CALO

BIBLIOGRAPHY, National - Germany

Blum, Rudolf. Die Deutsche Bibliographie. 59, FRAD
——— Die Deutsche Bibliographie. Rückblick und Ausblick. 91-116, EPPE
——— Das Mehrjahres-Verzeichnis der Bücher und Karten. 68-72, FRAD
Büttner, Liselotte. Das Halbjahres-Verzeichnis. 64-67, FRAD
Fleischhack, Curt. Die Bibliographische Tätigkeit der Deutschen Bücherei. 105-140, LEIZ
——— Zur Rationalisierung der Bibliographischen Arbeit. 323-328, MIKH
Frels, Wilhelm. Die Bibliographischen Arbeiten und Aufgaben. 120-136, LEIS
Friesenhahn, Heinz. Das Wöchentliche Verzeichnis. 60-63, FRAD
Fuchs, Hermann. Die Deutschen Nationalbibliographien im Rahmen der Ausländischen Nationalbibliographien. 103-106, FRAD
Jaeger, Friedrich. Das Mehrjahres-Verzeichnis der Zeitschriften. 73-75, FRAD
Praesent, Hans. Karten und Atlanten in den Bibliographien des Deutschen Buchhandels. 79-90, MIND
Schäfer, Rosa Maria. Das Deutsche Buch. 76-77, FRAD
Schulz, Hans Ferdinand. Buchhandel und Bibliographie. 130-132, FRAD
Uhlendahl, Heinrich. Leipziger Zetteldruck. 53-61, GODE

BIBLIOGRAPHY, National - Germany - Hist.

Drews, Erich. Zur Entwicklung der Nationalen Deutschen Bibliographien seit 1945. 110-117, JENA

BIBLIOGRAPHY, National - Germany - Indexes - Hist.

Drews, Erich. Zur Entwicklung der Register in den Deutschen Allgemeinbibliographien. 48-53, SCHT

BIBLIOGRAPHY, National - India - Madras (State)

Thillainayagam, V. The Madras State Bibliography. 506-507, RANG

BIBLIOGRAPHY, National - Norway

Amundsen, Inger. Genealogisk Register til J. B. Halvorsens Norsk Forfatter-Lexikon 1814-1880. 69-202, HALV
Bull, Francis. Norske Avdeling og Norsk Bibliografi. 68-73, OSLN
Dancke, Per. Claus Lydersen Fasting og Hans Bokfortegnelse. 5-24, HALV
Haukaas, Kaare. Norsk Litteraert Registreringsarbeid. 25-68, HALV

BIBLIOGRAPHY, National - Poland

Jolowicz, J. Die Polnische Bibliographie in Ihrer Entwicklung und Ihrem Gegenwärtigen Stande. 75-88, VERP
Mikulski, Tadeusz. Historia Literatury Wobec Zagadnień Księgoznawstwa. 65-77, PIEK

BIBLIOGRAPHY, National - Rumania - Hist.

Tomescu, Mircea. Sur L'Évolution de la Bibliographie dans la République Populaire Roumaine. 293-306, MIKH

BIBLIOGRAPHY, National - South Africa

Holdsworth, H. Bibliography in South Africa. 151-159, OFFO
Robinson, A. M. L. Mr. Varley's Contribution to Bibliography. 18-19, VARL

BIBLIOGRAPHY, National - Sweden

Sallander, Hans. Om Anders Anton von Stiernman Som Bibliografisk Författare. 561-576, GRAP

BIBLIOGRAPHY, National - U.S. - Hist.

Krummel, Donald W. The Library World of Norton's Literary Gazette. 237-266, GJEL

BIBLIOGRAPHY of James C. M. Hanson. 131-135, HANS

BIBLIOGRAPHY of the Writings of D. H. Varley. 59-66, VARL

BIBLIOGRAPHY - Russia

Toropov, A. D. Moskovskiĭ Bibliograficheskiĭ Kruzhok; Stranichka Vospominaniĭ. 275-276, MALE

BIBLIOGRAPHY - Russia - Hist.

Zamkov, Nikolaĭ K. "Uleĭ," Zhurnal V. G. Anastasevicha (1811-1812 g.g.); Bibliograficheskoe Opisanie. 39-57, MALE

BIBLIOGRAPHY - Scandinavia

Qvigstad, J. Bibliografiens Betydning for Forskningen. 1-4, HALV

BIBLIOGRAPHY - Terminology

Shamurin, E. I. Nekotorye Voprosy Bibliograficheskoj Terminologii. (V Sviazi s Razgranicheniem Otraslej i Vidov Bibliografii.) 335-350, MIKH

BIBLIOGRAPHY - U.S. - Hist.

Shera, Jesse H. The Beginnings of Systematic Bibliography in America, 1642-1799. 263-278, WROT

BIBLIOMANIA
see Book collecting

BIBLIOPHILE'S BOOKS
see Limited edition books

BIBLIOTECA AMBROSIANA, Milan
see Milan. Biblioteca Ambrosiana

BIBLIOTECA ANGELICA, Rome (city)
see Rome (city) Biblioteca Angelica.

BIBLIOTECA CASANATENSE, Rome (city)
see Rome (city) Biblioteca Casanatense

BIBLIOTECA DI ARCHEOLOGIA E STORIA DELL'ARTE
see Istituto di Archeologia e Storia dell'Arte. Biblioteca

BIBLIOTECA ERCOLANESE
see Herculaneum. Biblioteca

BIBLIOTECA LANDAU-FINALY
see Florence. Biblioteca Nazionale Centrale. Biblioteca Landau-Finaly

BIBLIOTECA MARCIANA
see Venice. Biblioteca Nazionale Marciana

BIBLIOTECA MEDICEO-LAURENZIANA, Florence
see Florence. Biblioteca Mediceo-Laurenziana

BIBLIOTECA QUERINIANA, Brescia
see Brescia. Biblioteca Civica Queriniana

BIBLIOTECA ROMANA SARTI, Rome (city)
see Rome (city) Biblioteca Romana Sarti

BIBLIOTECA VALLICELLIANA, Rome (city)
see Rome (city) Biblioteca Vallicelliana

BIBLIOTHECA ALBANA URBINAS
see Catholic University of America. Library. Albani Collection

BIBLIOTHECA AMERICANA VETUSTISSIMA

Goldschmidt, E. P. Not in Harrisse. 129-141, WROT

BIBLIOTHECA BERNARDINA, Bydgoszcz
see Monastic libraries - Poland

BIBLIOTHECA MEMMIANA

Blum, Rudolf. Bibliotheca Memmiana. Untersuchungen zu Gabriel Naudés "Advis pour Dresser une Bibliothèque." 209-232, WEHM

BIBLIOTHECA MOGUNTINA
see Mainz. Stadtbibliothek

BIBLIOTHECA NEERLANDICA MANUSCRIPTA DE VREESE

Sevensma, Tietse Pieter. De Bibliotheca Neerlandica Manuscripta De Vreese in Leiden. 167-175, BISH

BIBLIOTHECA PALATINA, Heidelberg
see Heidelberg. Bibliotheca Palatina

BIBLIOTHECA ROSENTHALIANA, Amsterdam
see Amsterdam. Bibliotheca Rosenthaliana

BIBLIOTHECARIUS (Word)

Mooy, A. J. de. De Benaming "Bibliothecaris." 544-547, BRUM

BIBLIOTHEK DES GROSSEN KÜRFURSTEN, Berlin
See Berlin. Deutsche Staatsbibliothek

BIBLIOTHEK DRESDEN-PLAUEN
see Dresden. Bibliothek Dresden-Plauen

BIBLIOTHEKAR-LEHRINSTITUT DES LANDES NORDRHEIN-WESTFALEN. Cologne
see Cologne. Bibliothekar-Lehrinstitut des Landes Nordrhein-Westfalen

BIBLIOTHEKWESEN ODER BIBLIOTHEKSWESEN?

Milkau, Fritz. Bibliothekwesen oder Bibliothekswesen? 443-474, COLL

BIBLIOTHÈQUE BOURGOGNE, Brussels
see Brussels. Bibliothèque Royale de Belgique

BIBLIOTHÈQUE DE L'ARSENAL, Paris
see Paris. Bibliothèque de l'Arsenal

BIBLIOTHÈQUE DE SAINT-MARC, Venice
see Venice. Biblioteca Nazionale Marciana

"BIBLIOTHÈQUE DES DAMES"

Le Gal, Simonne. La Bibliothèque des Dames au XVe Siècle, Vue par le Marquis de Paulmy. 55-63, CALO

BIBLIOTHÈQUE NATIONALE, Paris
see Paris. Bibliothèque Nationale

BIBLIOTHÈQUE NATIONALE SUISSE, Bern
see Bern. Schweizerische Landesbibliothek

BIBLIOTHÈQUE PUBLIQUE ET UNIVERSITAIRE, Geneva
see Geneva. Bibliothèque Publique et Universitaire

BIBLIOTHÈQUE ROYALE DE BELGIQUE, Brussels
see Brussels. Bibliothèque Royale de Belgique

BIBLIOTHÈQUE SAINTE-GENEVIÈVE, Paris
see Paris. Bibliothèque Sainte-Geneviève

Bick, Josef.
Der Unveröffentlichte Zweite Teil der Dilucida Repraesentatio Bibliothecae Caesareae des S. Kleiner und J. J. Sedelmayr. 75-86, VIEN

BICK, JOSEF
BICK
Godet, Marcel. Les Éminents Mérites de M. Bick. Ein Brief. 44, BICK
Gregor, Joseph. Josef Bick. Die Persönlichkeit und das Wirken als Bibliothekar. 22-43, BICK
Loehr, August. Josef Bick und die Organisation des Wissenschaftlichen Dienstes. 45-50, BICK

BICK, JOSEF - Bibl.
Bibliographie der Arbeiten Josef Bicks. 61-69, BICK

BIDDING SYSTEMS
see Acquisitions - Order processes

Bidlack, Russell E.
The Early Handling of Books at the University of Michigan. 149-164, GJEL

Bieber, Hedwig.
Die Öffentliche Bücherei als Ausbildungsstätte. Erfahrungen und Anregungen. 75-87, LANF

BIELKE, HOGENSKILD - Library
Walde, O. En Svensk Boksamlare från Vasatiden. Hogenskild Bielke och Hans Bibliotek. 193-267, UPPS

Biernat, Barbara.
Organizacja i Skład Osobowy. 63-68, BYDG

BIESTER, JOHANN ERICH
Abb, Gustav. Eine Denkschrift Philipp Buttmanns über Katalogfragen vom Jahre 1791. 177-181, KUHN

Billanovich, Giuseppe.
Un Amico e un Libro del Petrarca. 99-104, FERR

Billington, Ray Allen.
Stanley Pargellis: Newberry Librarian, 1942-1962. 3-18, PARG

BINDERIES
see Bookbinders

Bing, Gertrud.
Fritz Saxl (1890-1948): A Memoir. 1-46, SAXL

Binwal, J. C.
Scientific Method. 312-320, RANG

Binz, Gustav.
Ein Bisher Unbekannter Katalog der Bibliothek des Klosters Fulda. 97-108, GODE

BINZ, GUSTAV
BINZ
Diepenbach, Wilhelm. Gustav Binz als Direktor der Mainzer Stadtbibliothek. 23-29, BINZ
Godet, Marcel. M. Gustave [sic!] Binz et la Bibliothèque Nationale Suisse. 30-32, BINZ

BIOGRAPHY - Dresden - Subject headings - Special subjects
see Subject headings - Special subjects - Biography - Dresden

Bird, Jack.
The Education of Librarians and Information Officers: General Review. 312-318, HUTT

BIRGITTA, SAINT, of Sweden
Jörgensen, Arne. En Birgitta-Handskrift i Helsingfors Universitetsbibliotek. 19-68, HULT

BIRGITTA SIGFUSDATTER
Collijn, Isak Gustav Alfred. Kalendarium Munkalivense. Ein Schwedisch-Norwegisches Birgittinerkalendarium. 82-92, DEGE

BIRGITTINES. Mss.
Collijn, Isak Gustaf Alfred. En Birgitta-Handskrift från Klostret Maria Maihingen. 8-14, GRAP

Birkelund, Palle.
Det Kongelige Bibliotek og dets Publikum. 119-132, DAHA
Nordmaend i Det Kgl. Biblioteks Tjeneste. 30-51, TVET
Svend Dahl. iii-ix, DAHA

Birkenmajer, Aleksander.
Die Wiegendrucke der Physischen Werke Johannes Versors. 121-135, COLL
Rodowód Krakowskiego Plateana. 211-221. PIEK
W Sprawie Rejestracji i Katalogowania Opraw Zabytkowych. 105-121, PIEK

BIRMINGHAM, Eng. - Printing
see Printing - Birmingham, Eng.

BIRTHON, MATHIAS
Vekené, Emil van der. Die Anfänge der Buchdruckerkunst in Luxemburg. Mathias Birthon (1598-1604). 434-444, BENZ

Bischoff, Bernhard.
Hadoardus and the Manuscripts of Classical Authors from Corbie. 39-57, ALBA
Kreuz und Buch im Frühmittelalter und in den Ersten Jahrhunderten der Spanischen Reconquista. 19-34, WEHM
Eine Sammelhandschrift Walahfrid Strabos (Cod. Sangall. 878). 30-48, LEYH

Bischoff, Johannes.
Erlangens Buchbinder als Handwerk und Universitätszunft. 11-26, STOL

Bishop, Olga Bernice.
The First Printing Press in Canada, 1751-1800. 129-148, GJEL

Bishop, W. J.
Medical Book Societies in England in the Eighteenth and Nineteenth Centuries. 337-350, DOEJ

Bishop, William Warner, jt. ed.
PUTN

Bishop, William Warner.
Centralized Purchasing for American College Libraries. 1-6, GODE
J. C. M. Hanson and International Cataloging. 165-168, HANS
One Problem for 1950—Woodpulp Paper in Books. 407-415, LYDE
Rare Book Rooms in Libraries. 375-385, WILS
Research Libraries in America. 13-19, MUNT
Thirty Years of the Library of Congress, 1899 to 1929. 24-34, PUTN

BISHOP, WILLIAM WARNER
BISH
Godet, Marcel. Monsieur William Warner Bishop et la Fédération Internationale des Associations de Bibliothécaires. 56-62, BISH
Keppel, Frederick Paul. William Warner Bishop. 1-4, BISH
Lydenberg, Harry Miller. William Warner Bishop. 11-17, BISH
Putnam, Herbert. Reflections from Ingonish. 5-10, BISH

BISSCHOPINCK, LUDWIG - Library
Dreimüller, Karl. Musikerbriefe an einen Rheinischen Musikliebhaber. Aus der Sammlung Ludwig Bisschopinck in Mönchengladbach. 29-49, HOBO

Björkbom, Carl.
Bokvalsproblem vid ett Tekniskt Centralbibliotek. 51-61, DAHA
Om Ordnandet av Grafiska Porträttsamlingar. 20-22, MUNT

Bjørnstad, Per.
Norsk Faglitteratur og Norsk Bibliotektjeneste i Vår Tékniske Tidsalder. 141-146, NORS

Blaas, Richard.
Cellon und Pergamin in der Archivalienrestaurierung. 187-197, GALL

Black, Jeannette D., jt. author
Adams, Marion W. and Jeannette D. Black. A List of Published Writings of Lawrence C. Wroth to December 31, 1950. 485-504, WROT

Bladergroen, Susanna H.
Het Ontstaan van het Museum van het Boek. 387-390, BRUM

BLADH, PETER JOHAN
Lunelund-Grönroos, Birgit. Peter Johan Bladhs "Räkning öfwer Böcker til 1771. Års slut." 85-100, TUDE

Blakiston, J. M. G.
Winchester College Library in the Eighteenth and Early Nineteenth Centuries. 23-45, OLDH

Blamowska, Krystyna.
Zagadnienia Metodyczne Urządzania Wystaw. 72-80, KRAK

Blanchard, J. R.
Development and Mechanization of Libraries of the University of California. 1-7, HASH

BLANKET ORDERS
see Acquisitions - Order processes

Blaser, Fritz.
Die Luzerner Buchbinder-Handwerksordnung von 1658. 37-49, BENZ
Eine Projektierte Papiermühle. 11-17, BOCK

Blass, Frédéric.
De Archytae Tarentini Fragmentis Mathematicis. 573-584, GRAU

BLAUBIRER, JOHANN. Kalender von 1483
Schmid, Helmut H. Ein Nürnberger Kalender von 1430 und Johann Blaubirer's Kalender von 1483. 247-253, STOL

BLIND IMPRESSIONS - Printing
see Printing - Blind impressions

BLISS, HENRY. The Organization of Knowledge in Libraries

Farrell, Colman J. The Classification of Books in Libraries. 207-222, HANS

Bloch, Herbert.
The Structure of Sallust's Historiae: The Evidence of the Fleury Manuscript. 59-76, ALBA

Bloch, Joshua.
The Classification of Jewish Literature in the New York Public Library. L-LXXVII, FREI
The People and the Book. 275-315, LYDE

BLOCH, JOSHUA

BLOC

Lebeson, Anita Libman. Joshua Bloch: An Appreciation. ix-xix, BLOC

BLOCH, JOSHUA - Bibl.

Steinglass, Dora. A Bibliography of the Writings of Joshua Bloch. 180-219, BLOC

BLOCK-BOOKS

Nohrström, Holger. Några Anteckningar Kring den s. k. Pälkäne-Abcboken. 341-354, HIRN

BLOCK-BOOKS - China - Hist.

Kanda, Kiichiro. Chugoku no Meika no Te ni Natta Shakokubon. (Chinese Books Printed from Wood-Blocks Written by Noted Calligraphers.) 367-373, TOMI

BLOCK-BOOKS - Japan - Hist.

Yuda, Yoshio, Hajime Uetani and Minoru Imanishi. Tenri Toshokan Zō Jōruri Hangi Mokuroku. (Catalogue of the Wood-Blocks of Jōruri Texts in the Tenri Central Library.) 259-294, TOMI

BLOEMENDAAL, Netherlands - Incunabula
see Incunabula - Bloemendaal, Netherlands

BLOEMENDAAL, Netherlands. Nieuwlicht (Carthusian monastery)
see Bloemendaal, Netherlands. Nova lux (Carthusian monastery)

BLOEMENDAAL, Netherlands. Nova lux (Carthusian monastery)

Hulshof, Abraham. Uitgaven voor de Boekerij van het Karthuizerklooster te Utrecht in de Jaren 1466-1470. 170-175, LOUB

Bloesch, Hans.
Albrecht Haller als Bibliothekar. 165-178, GODE
Ein Englischer Gönner der Berner Stadtbibliothek im 18. Jahrhundert. 112-118, BINZ

Blondheim, D. S.
Liste des Manuscrits de L'Arouk de Nathan Bar Yehiel. 24-30, FREN

BLOTIUS, HUGO

Brummel, Leendert. Hugo Blotius in Straßburg. 211-217, HOFM
Smital, Ottokar. Miszellen zur Geschichte der Wiener Palatina. 771-794, VIEN

Bluhm, Heinz, ed.
PARG

Blum, Rudolf.
Bibliotheca Memmiana. Untersuchungen zu Gabriel Naudés "Advis pour Dresser une Bibliothèque." 209-232, WEHM
Die Deutsche Bibliographie. 59, FRAD
Die Deutsche Bibliographie. Rückblick und Ausblick. 91-116, EPPE
Das Mehrjahres-Verzeichnis der Bücher und Karten. 68-72, FRAD

Blum, Rudolf, jt. author

Friesenhahn, Heinz and Rudolf Blum. Die Bibliothekarische Arbeit der Deutschen Bibliothek. 55-58, FRAD

Blume, Friedrich.
An Vladimir Fédorov. 5-8, FEDO

BLUMENSCHEIN, ADALBERT

Teichl, Robert. Ein Europäischer Bibliothekenführer um das Jahr 1780. Die Handschrift des Pfarrverwalters von Maria-Taferl Adalbert Blumenschein. 172-179, LEYG

Blumenthal, Hermann, ed.
WEIM

Blumenthal, Hermann.
Älteste Verwaltungsgeschichte der Landesbibliothek Weimar (1691-1750). 46-86, WEIM

BOARDS
see Trustees and boards

BOBBIO, Italy (Benedictine monastery). Mss.

Ratti, Achille. Reliquie di Antico Codice Bobbiese Ritrovate. 789-810, CERI
Steffens, Franz. Über die Abkürzungsmethoden der Schreibschule von Bobbio. 244-254, CHAT

BOCCACCIO, GIOVANNI. Il Ninfale Fiesolano

Wiese, Berthold. Zu einer Kritischen Ausgabe des "Ninfale Fiesolano" Boccaccios. 347-361, HORT

BOCHOLT, JOHANNA VON. Mss.

Wegener, Hans. Das Gebetbuch der Johanna von Bocholt. 228-232, BÖME

Bock, Friedrich.
Aus der Geschichte der Nürnberger Stadtbibliothek. 9-15, VERZ
Ein Nürnberger Lederschnittband mit Accipies-Bild. 15-17, LEID
Splitter zur Älteren Geschichte des Schlagwortkatalogs. 27-30, STOL

Bockel, W. J. van.
Iets over de "Binnendienst" der Utrechtsche Universiteitsbibliotheek. 63-69, SOME

Bockwitz, Hans H.
Baskerville im Urteil Deutscher Zeitgenossen. III, 250-253, GLAU

BOCKWITZ, HANS H.

BOCK

Boden, Charlotte.
Der Biographische Katalog und das Personalrepertorium der Sächsischen Landesbibliothek. 21-37, BOLL
Das Buchmuseum in den Semper-Räumen des Japanischen Palais. 46-51, BOLE

BODLEIAN LIBRARY, Oxford. University
see Oxford. University. Bodleian Library

Böck, Karl.
Zum Geleit. xxiii-xxvi, HOFM

Boeckler, Albert
KRÜS

Boeckler, Albert.
Beiträge zur Romanischen Kölner Buchmalerei. 15-28, DEGE
Corveyer Buchmalerei unter Einwirkung Wibalds von Stablo. 133-147, BÖME
Das Erhardbild im Utacodex. 219-230, GREE

Boehm, Peter.
Die Anfänge der Landesbibliothek Fulda. 59-88, FULD

BOEHM, PETER

Theele, Joseph. Aus der Geschichte der Landesbibliothek Fulda. 289-292, LEID

BOEHME, JOHANN GOTTLOB - Library

Leskien, Elfriede. Johann Gottlob Böhme, ein Leipziger Bücherfreund des 18. Jahrhunderts. 69-79, LEIP

Böhme, Rudolf.
Volksbüchereiarbeit in Dresden. 31-40, DRES

Bömer, Aloys (= Alois).
Die Fünf Frühdrucke der Epistolae Obscurorum Virorum. 17-29, SCHW

Bömer, Alois.
Ein Gotisches Prachtmissale Utrechtscher Herkunft in der Universitäts-Bibliothek Münster. 29-41, DEGE
Das Literarische Leben in Münster bis zur Endgültigen Rezeption des Humanismus. 57-136, MÜNS

Bömer, Aloys (= Alois).
Die Schlussschrift des Mainzer Catholicon-Druckes von 1460. 51-55, KUHN
Eine Volkstümliche Deutsche Enzyklopädie eines Werdener Bibliothekars aus dem Jahre 1527. 38-53, LEYG

BÖMER, ALOIS

BÖME

Boerlin, E.
Dr. Pierre Bourgeois und die UNESCO. 186-188, BOUR

BÖRSENVEREIN DER DEUTSCHEN BUCHHÄNDLER

Rötzsch, Helmut. Der Börsenverein der Deutschen Buchhändler zu Leipzig und die Deutsche Bücherei. 47-66, LEIZ

BÖRSENVEREIN DER DEUTSCHEN BUCHHÄNDLER - Bibliothek

Debes, Martha and Lieselotte Reuschel. Die Ehemalige Bibliothek des Börsenvereins der Deutschen Buchhändler zu Leipzig. 243-257, LEIZ

BÖRSENVEREIN DER DEUTSCHEN BUCHHÄNDLER - Historische Kommission

Hack, Bertold. Vor- und Frühgeschichte des "Archivs für Geschichte des Buchwesens." 157-169, BENZ

Boese, Helmut.
Ein Mittelalterliches Bücherverzeichnis von Croyland Abbey. 286-295, VORS

BOETHIUS. De Consolatione Philosophiae

Huet, Gédéon. La Première Édition de la Consolation de Boèce en Néerlandais. 561-569, HAVE

BOETHIUS. Mss. De Institutione Musica.

Bragard, R. Boethiana—Études sur le "De Institutione Musica" de Boèce. 84-139, BORR

Bogdanovaîa, Nadezhda G.
Knizhnye Bogatstva Stroganovykh v 1578 g. 277-284, MALE

Bogeng, Gustav Adolf Erich.
Einbandkunst und Einbandliebhaberei. 206-212, LOUB
Über Zacharias Conrad von Uffenbachs Erfahrungen und Erlebnisse bei der Benutzung Deutscher, Englischer, Holländischer Öffentlicher Büchersammlungen in den Jahren 1709-1711. 30-46, SCHW

BOGUSLAV RADZIWILL, PRINCE - Library
Diesch, Carl. Fürst Boguslav Radziwill und Seine Bücherschenkung an die Königsberger Schloßbibliothek. 117-128, LEYG

BOILEAU-DESPRÉAUX, NICOLAS. Oeuvres.
Marchand, Jean. Une Édition de Boileau Inconnue. 115-118, CALO

Bojer, Johan.
Hilsen til Yrjö Hirn. 43, HIRN

Bolay, Karl H.
MALU

Bollert, Martin.
Epistel von der Festschrift. 107, BOLE
Johann Joachim Winckelmann als Bibliothekar des Grafen Bünau. 19-24, LEID
Joh. Joach. Winckelmann und Joh. Mich. Francke. I, 11-17, GLAU
Ein Kastenband mit Lederschnitt in der Sächsischen Landesbibliothek zu Dresden. 95-104, LOUB
Ein Neuer Lederschnittband aus dem 14. Jahrhundert. 80-82, LEIP

BOLLERT, MARTIN
BOLE
BOLL
Hofmann, Hans. Facit. 71-75, BOLE
Müller-Graupa, Edw. Epistola Iocosa. 92-96, BOLE
Neubert, Hermann. Martin Bollerts Wirken für Gegenwart und Zukunft. 23-28, BOLE

BOLOGNA. Biblioteca Comunale dell'Archiginnasio
Sorbelli, Albano. Un Nuovo Codice della "Vita C. J. Caesaris" di Francesco Petrarca. II, 677-682, HORT

BOLOGNA - Copyists
see Copyists - Bologna

BOLOGNA. Università. Biblioteca. Mss. (182)
Frati, Lodovico. Una Miscellanea Umanistica della R. Biblioteca Universitaria di Bologna. I, 321-329, HORT

BOLOGNA. Università. Biblioteca. Mss. (2221)
Lenchantin de Gubernatis, M. De Codice Bononiensi quo Copa et Moretum Continentur. 199-201, STAM

BOMBAY (State) - Library legislation
see Library legislation - Bombay (State)

Bonasera, Francesco.
Un'Antica Pianta della Città di Rimini Conservata nella Biblioteca Fredericiana di Fano. 199-203, GALL

Bonaventura, Gustavo.
La Minaccia delle Termiti e di Altri Insetti al Nostro Patrimonio Artistico e Culturale. 205-234, GALL

Bonelli, Giuseppe.
Una Soscrizione in Metro. 174-179, CHAT

BONET, HONORÉ. Mss. Somnium Prioris de Sallono super Materia Scismatis
Ouy, Gilbert. Une Maquette de Manuscrit à Peintures. 43-51, CALO

Bonet, Paul.
La Reliure Originale et la B. N. 37-40, CAIN

BONGARS, JACQUES - Library
Müller, Konrad. Jacques Bongars und Seine Handschriftensammlung. 79-106, BERT

Bongertman, W.
De Centrale Duitsche Bibliotheek. 33-37, EVER
Hoe de Utrechtsche Akademie-Boekerij in de St. Janskerk Gehuisvest Was. 37-41, SOME

BONIFAZIO, GIOVANNI BERNARDINO, MARCHESE D'ORIA
Günther, Otto. Der Neapolitaner Johannes Bernardinus Bonifacius, Marchese von Oria, und die Anfänge der Danziger Stadtbibliothek. 107-128, WILM

BONIFAZIO, GIOVANNI BERNARDINO, MARCHESE D'ORIA - Library
Schwarz, F. Analyse eines Kataloges. 326-338, KÖNI

Bonk, W. J.
Periodical Publishing in the Michigan Territory. 85-104, GJEL

Bonn, George S.
Some Thoughts on the Education of Science Documentalists. 9-17, HASH

BONN. Universität. Bibliothek

Rath, Erich von. Karl Schaarschmidt. 283-296, LEYG

Bonnerot, Jean.

En Marge du Manuscrit Français 147 de la B. N. 644-661, CHAT

Sainte-Beuve Bibliophile. 369-374, CALO

BONNEROT, JEAN

BONN

Cain, Julien. Jean Bonnerot. 15-20, BONN

Malclès, Louise-Noëlle. Jean Bonnerot et la Bibliographie. 21-23, BONN

BONNEROT, JEAN - Bio-Bibl.

Malclès, Jean. Bio-Bibliographie de Jean Bonnerot. 25-49, BONN

BONONIA
see Bologna

BONSIGNORI, FRANCESCO, printer - Bio-Bibl.

Moneti, Elena Amico. L'Attività di una Tipografia Lucchese nel Settecento. 27-55, FERR

BOOK BINDING
see Bookbinding

BOOK BUDGETS
see Budgets

BOOK BUYING
see also Acquisitions; Book selection; College and university libraries - Acquisitions; Importation and Exportation of books; National libraries - Acquisitions; Public libraries - Acquisitions; Rare books - Acquisitions; Second-hand books; Technical services

BOOK BUYING (Libraries) - Yale, 1805-1806

Keogh, Andrew. Benjamin Silliman's Trip to Europe in 1805. 416-422, LYDE

BOOK BUYING (Libraries) - Yale, 1845

Powers, Zara Jones. A Yale Bibliophile in European Book Shops. 373-422, KEOG

BOOK COLLECTING
see also Private libraries

BOOK COLLECTING

Chiavacci, V. Ein Fossiler Bibliophage. Aus einem Vortrage, Gehalten in der Akademie der Wissenschaften im Jahre 10,000 nach Christi Geburt. 400-403, GLOS

Kästner, Erhart. Über das Bibliothekarische Mißvergnügen und noch ein Zweiter Traktat. 295-302, WEHM

Lehmann, Paul. Bücherliebe und Bücherpflege bei den Karthäusern. 364-389, EHRE

Lewis, Wilmarth S. Introduction, xix-xxi, WROT

Stefl, Max. Von Büchern und Büchermenschen. 20-23, HELD

Stevens, Henry Newton. The DeBry Collector's Painefull Peregrination along the Pleasant Pathway to Perfection. 269-276, EAME

BOOK COLLECTING - Bergen

Wiesener, A. M. Bergenske Boksamlere. 254-286, MUNT

BOOK COLLECTING - Chicago region

Bay, Jens Christian. Private Book Collectors of the Chicago Area: A Brief Review. 363-374, WILS

BOOK COLLECTING - Jews

Bloch, Joshua. The People and the Book. 275-315, LYDE

BOOK COLLECTING - Norway - Hist.

Munthe, Wilhelm. Norske Boksamlere i Eldre Tid. 249-263, COLL

BOOK COLLECTING - U.S.

Adams, Randolph G. A Goodly Company of American Book Collectors. 29-32, LYDE

Kubler, George. John Carter Brown and America. 203-207, WROT

BOOK COSTS
see Books - Prices

BOOK DEALERS
see Book industry and trade

BOOK DISCOUNTS
see Books - Prices

BOOK FAIRS - Germany - Catalogs

Müller, Hans von. Die Messkataloge als Quelle für die Literaturgeschichte. An dem Beispiel E. T. A. Hoffmann Dargelegt. 97-102, KUHN

BOOK FAIRS - U.S.

Nichols, Charles. The Literary Fair in the United States. 85-92, EAME

BOOK ILLUSTRATION
see also Illumination of books and manuscripts

BOOK ILLUSTRATION

Daugherty, James. Illustrating for Children. 569-572, MOOR

Geissler, Paul. Zwei Unbekannte Holzschnittprobedrucke zum Theuerdank und Konrad Peutinger. 118-128, JUCH
Oldenbourg, M. Consuelo. Die Holzschnitte des Vrs Graf zur Passion und die des Johann Wechtlin zum Leben Jesu. Ein Bibliographisches Verzeichnis Ihrer Verwendungen. 291-310, BENZ
Rästner, Erhart. Scherenschnitt-Illustration. 196-219, BOLL
Rosenfeld, Hellmut. Die Titelholzschnitte der Bauernpraktik von 1508-1600 als Soziologische Selbstinterpretation. 373-389, BENZ
Wille, Hans. Dürer-Erinnerungen in Josef Führichs Illustrationen zu "Der Wilde Jäger" von G. A. Bürger. 60-74, BRIE

BOOK ILLUSTRATION - France - Hist.

Adlerova, Eliška. Několik Umělecko-historických Poznámek k Výstavě Francouzské Ilustrované Knihy v Praž. Národní a Universitní Knihovně. 80-83, EMLE

BOOK ILLUSTRATION - Germany

Luther, Arthur. Russische Dichter in Deutschen Künstlerischen Drucken. 75-79, BOCK

BOOK ILLUSTRATION - Germany - Hist. - 16th cent.

Rosenfeld, Hellmut. Die Titelholzschnitte der Bauernpraktik von 1508-1600 als Soziologische Selbstinterpretation. 373-389, BENZ

BOOK ILLUSTRATION - Gt. Brit. - Hist. - 18th cent.

Wieder, Joachim. Bickham's "Musical Entertainer" in der Englischen Buchkunst des 18. Jahrhunderts. 147-158, JUCH

BOOK ILLUSTRATION - Hist.

Donati, Lamberto. Note Empiriche sul Libro Illustrato. 61-102, ACCU
———— Note Inedite di Alfred Cartier su Giorgio Reverdino, Illustratore di Libri. 379-401, GALL
Husung, Max Joseph. Über die Entwicklung der Monatsbilder in Kalendern. 13-32, LOUB
Tiemann, Hermann. Wort und Bild in der Fabeltradition bis zu La Fontaine. 237-260, HOFM
Weitenkampf, Frank. Influences and Trends in Nineteenth-century Illustration. 345-350, LYDE

BOOK ILLUSTRATION - Hist. - 15th cent.

Bernoulli, Rudolf. Das Weltallbild in Hartmann Schedel's Weltchronik. 48-58, LOUB
Rath, Erich von. Die Kupferstichillustration im Wiegendruckzeitalter. 58-68, LEIP
Schmidbauer, Richard. Ein Unbekanntes Augsburger Pestblatt des 15. Jahrhunderts. 229-231, LEID

BOOK ILLUSTRATION - Hist. - 15th-16th cent.

Donati, Lamberto. Leonardo da Vinci ed il Libro Illustrato. 117-138, WEHM

BOOK ILLUSTRATION - Hist. - 16th cent.

Ficker, Johannes. Hortulus Animae. 59-68, LOUB

BOOK ILLUSTRATION - Italy

Donati, Lamberto. Appunti di Biblioiconologia. 243-262, FERR

BOOK ILLUSTRATION - Poznań - Hist. - 16th cent.

Chyczewska, Alina. Zasób Drzeworytów Ilustracyjnych i Herbowych w XVI-Wiecznych Oficynach Poznańskich. 354-382, GRYC

BOOK ILLUSTRATION - U.S. - Hist.

Lewis, Benjamin M. Engravings in Early American Magazines, 1741-1810. 203-218, GJEL

BOOK INDUSTRY AND TRADE
see also Publishers and Publishing

BOOK INDUSTRY AND TRADE - Avignon

Lelièvre, Pierre. Livres et Libraires en Avignon à L'Époque Romantique. 269-275, BONN

BOOK INDUSTRY AND TRADE - Benediktbeuern - Hist. - 15th-16th cent.

Ruf, Paul. Ausgaben des Klosters Benediktbeuern für Bücher und Schreibzeug von 1495-1510. 219-227, LEID

BOOK INDUSTRY AND TRADE - Borgå, Finland

Lunelund-Grönroos, Birgit. Gymnasister och Böcker i det Gamla Borgå. 51-58, NYBE

BOOK INDUSTRY AND TRADE - Boston - Hist. - 1790-1799

Silver, Rollo G. The Boston Book Trade, 1790-1799. 279-303, WROT

BOOK INDUSTRY AND TRADE - Cologne - Hist. - 17th cent.

Benzing, Josef. Der Kupferstecher, Kunstdrucker und Verleger Johann Bussemacher zu Köln (1580? bis 1616?). 129-146, JUCH

BOOK INDUSTRY AND TRADE - Europe

Powers, Zara Jones. A Yale Bibliophile in European Book Shops. 373-422, KEOG

BOOK INDUSTRY AND TRADE - Germany

Debes, Martha and Lieselotte Reuschel. Die Ehemalige Bibliothek des Börsenvereins der Deutschen Buchhändler zu Leipzig. 243-257, LEIZ
Praesent, Hans. Karten und Atlanten in den Bibliographien des Deutschen Buchhandels. 79-90, MIND
Rosin, Hans. Buchwirtschaftliche Konzentrationsbestrebungen im Volksbüchereiwesen. 93-102, ACKE
Schroers, Paul. Antiquar und Bibliographie. 133-137, FRAD
Schulz, Hans Ferdinand. Buchhandel und Bibliographie. 130-132, FRAD

BOOK INDUSTRY AND TRADE - Germany - Hist.

Knaus, Hermann. Fischer von Waldheim als Handschriften- und Inkunabelhändler. 255-280, BENZ

BOOK INDUSTRY AND TRADE - Hist.

Lange, Wilhelm H. Buchhandel, Buchverlag, Buchvertrieb. Bëitrage zur Wirtschaftlichen und Geistigen Situation des 15. und 16. Jahrhunderts. 55-74, BOCK
Lunelund-Grönroos, Birgit. Peter Johan Bladhs "Räkning öfwer Böcker til 1771. Års slut." 85-100, TUDE
Schottenloher, Karl. Buchdrucker und Buchführer im Kampf der Schwärmer und Wiedertäufer, 1524-1568. 90-113, BOCK

BOOK INDUSTRY AND TRADE - Hist. - Ancient

Kleberg, Tönnes. Om Romersk Antikvariatbokhandel. 84-94, TVET

BOOK INDUSTRY AND TRADE - Hist. - 15th cent.

Rhodes, Dennis E. Konrad Stepeck of Nuremberg (c. 1424-c.1495). 311-316, BENZ

BOOK INDUSTRY AND TRADE - Incunabula - 15th cent.

Schmidt, Adolf. Baron Hüpsch in Köln als Inkunabelnsammler und Händler. 45-63, HAEB

BOOK INDUSTRY AND TRADE - Incunabula - 18th cent.

Jacobs, Emil. Zur Kenntnis Maugérards. 64-73, HAEB

BOOK INDUSTRY AND TRADE - Italy

Lippi, Silvio. La Libreria di Monserrato Rossellò Giureconsulto e Bibliografo Sardo del Sec. XVI. II, 319-332, MANO

BOOK INDUSTRY AND TRADE - Laws, regulations, etc.

Räuber, Friedrich. Der Begriff des Antiquariats nach der Verkaufsordnung. 286-299, MILF

BOOK INDUSTRY AND TRADE - Leipzig - Hist.

Brauer, Adalbert. Beziehungen der Vorfahren von Gottfried Wilhelm Leibniz zu Buchdruck und Buchhandel. 50-67, BENZ

BOOK INDUSTRY AND TRADE - Leyden

Sevensma, Tietse Pieter. Der Salomons-Tempel in Leiden. 80-81, STUM

BOOK INDUSTRY AND TRADE - Lübeck - Hist.

Paulli, R. Bogfører-Dokumenter fra det 16. Aarhundrede. 215-223, COLL

BOOK INDUSTRY AND TRADE - Music

Refardt, Edgar. Vom Musikhändler Nägeli. 24-27, REFA

BOOK INDUSTRY AND TRADE - New York (City) - Hist.

Granniss, Ruth Shepard. The New York Printers and the Celebration of the French Revolution of 1830. 193-202, EAME
Hewlett, Leroy. James Rivington, Tory Printer. 165-194, GJEL

BOOK INDUSTRY AND TRADE - Paris

Jacobsen, R. La Cité des Livres. 59-68, KOSS

BOOK INDUSTRY AND TRADE - Philadelphia, Pa. - Hist.

Harlan, Robert D. David Hall's Bookshop and Its British Sources of Supply. 1-24, GJEL

BOOK INDUSTRY AND TRADE - Philadelphia, Pa. - Hist. - 17th cent.

McDonald, Gerald D. William Bradford's Book Trade and John Bowne, Long Island Quaker, as His Book Agent, 1686-1691. 209-222, WROT

BOOK INDUSTRY AND TRADE - Rotterdam - Hist. - 18th cent.

Hazewinkel, H. C. Rotterdamse Boekverkopers uit de Patriottentijd. 35-58, KOSS

BOOK INDUSTRY AND TRADE - Strasbourg - Hist.

Voulliéme, Ernst. Peter Attendorn, ein

Buchhändler und Drucker in Straßburg um 1490. 344-353, MILF

BOOK INDUSTRY AND TRADE - Switzerland
Brouty, Barth. Statistique de la Production Littéraire. 130-131, BERU

BOOK INDUSTRY AND TRADE - U.S. - Hist.
Kaser, David. Bernard Dornin, America's First Catholic Bookseller. 105-128, GJEL
Nichols, Charles. The Literary Fair in the United States. 85-92, EAME
Winship, George Parker. The Eliot Indian Tracts. 179-192, EAME

BOOK LISTS
see also Library publications

BOOK MUSEUMS
see Literary museums

BOOK NUMBERS
Takeuchi, Zensaku. Tosho Bunrui to Tosho Kigo ni Kansuru Ichi Kosatsu. (An Observation Relating to Classification of Books and Book Numbers.) 1-24, (part 1), OHAS

BOOK NUMBERS - Copenhagen
Drachmann, A. G. Call Numbers. 198-206, HANS

BOOK NUMBERS - Japan
Takeuchi, Zensaku. Genkō no Nihon Chosha Kigo no Shujuso. (Various Aspects of Author Marks Used in Japan at Present.) 3-21, TSUB

BOOK ORNAMENTATION
Schreiber, Heinrich. Von der Goldschnittlyrik zum Schmetterlingsbuch. Orientalische Literatur in Deutscher Ausstattung. 82-92, SCHR

BOOK ORNAMENTATION - German
Claus, Helmut. Migration von Bildstöcken bei den Leipziger Buchdruckern in der Frühen Reformationszeit. 63-81, LÜLF
Kistner, Erwin. Studien an Teigdrucken aus dem Besitz des Germanischen Nationalmuseums in Nürnberg. 65-97, STOL

BOOK ORNAMENTATION - Hist.
Gardberg, Carl-Rudolf. Ur Paradsidornas Historia. Från Barock till Nyklassicism. 31-41, DAHA
Luther, Johannes. Die Anfänge des Klischee. 181-192, WILM
Pächt, Otto. Notes and Observations on the Origin of Humanistic Book-Decoration. 184-194, SAXL

BOOK ORNAMENTATION - Jewish
Reider, Joseph. The New Ornament of Jewish Books. 10-18, BLOC
———— Non-Jewish Motives in the Ornament of Early Hebrew Books. 150-159, FREI

BOOK PRICES
see Books - Prices

BOOK PRODUCTION
see also Publishers and publishing

BOOK REPAIRING
see Books - Care and restoration

BOOK REVIEWS
Nuiver, J. A. Centrale Boekbespreking voor de Openbare Bibliotheken. 552-558, BRUM

BOOK SELECTION
see also College and university libraries - Book selection; Public libraries - Book selection; Technical libraries - Book selection; Technical services

BOOK SELECTION
Bauhuis, Walter. Arbeitsmethoden der Erwerbungsabteilung. 37-41, REDE

BOOK SELECTION - Standards
Bramsen, Bo. Den Praktiske Bog. 77-85, THOM

BOOK SELECTION - Standards - Japan
Ogata, Yoshihiko. Dokushozai Sentaku no Ketteiin - Sono Kigōronteki Apurōchi. (The Definite Factor in the Selection of Reading Matter—an Approach from the Theory of Language as a Symbol.) 76-101, TOKY

BOOK SELECTION - Visby, Sweden - Hist.
Åberg, Åke. Visby Stadsbibliotek. Förhistoria och Begynnelseår. 5-30, VISB

BOOK SHELVES AND STACKS
see Access to shelves; Shelves and shelving

BOOK TRADE
see Book industry and trade

BOOK (Word) - Synonyms
Loebeling, Isolde. Buch und Synonyma im Tatian, Heliand und bei Otfrid. 59-69, JUCR

BOOKBINDERS
Michon, Louis-Marie. Notes sur les Reliures de L'Atelier des Monnier. 509-513, BONN

BOOKBINDERS - Åbo, Finland

Vallinkoski, J. Turun Kirjansitojat Vapauden ajan Alkupuoliskolla. 197-227, DAHL

BOOKBINDERS - Augsburg - 16th cent.

Kyriss, Ernst. Beiträge zu Augsburger Buchbindern. 134-164, HAEK

BOOKBINDERS - Brunswick (City) - 16th cent.

Herbst, Hermann. Braunschweigische Buchbinder des 16. Jahrhunderts. 274-310, HAEK

THE BOOKBINDERS CASE UNFOLDED

Middleton, Bernard C. The Bookbinders Case Unfolded. 66-76, OLDH

BOOKBINDERS - Erlangen

Bischoff, Johannes. Erlangens Buchbinder als Handwerk und Universitätszunft. 11-26, STOL

BOOKBINDERS - Germany - 15th cent.

Schwenke, Paul. Die Buchbinder mit dem Lautenspieler und dem Knoten. 122-144, HAEB

BOOKBINDERS - Germany - 16th cent.

Schmidt, Adolf. Zur Geschichte Deutscher Buchbinder im 16. Jahrhundert. 1-109, HAEK

BOOKBINDERS - Jena - 16th cent.

Helwig, Hellmuth. Jenaer Buchbinder des 16. Jahrhunderts. 225-241, HAEK

BOOKBINDERS - Lucerne - Laws, regulations, etc., 1658

Blaser, Fritz. Die Luzerner Buchbinder-Handwerksordnung von 1658. 37-49, BENZ

BOOKBINDERS - Mecklenburg-Schwerin - 16th-17th cent.

Floerke, Anna Marie. Die Ersten Buchbinder in Mecklenburg-Schwerin. 242-273, HAEK

BOOKBINDING
see also Bookbinders; Technical services

BOOKBINDING

Schreiber, Heinrich. Von der Goldschnittlyrik zum Schmetterlingsbuch. Orientalische Literatur in Deutscher Ausstattung. 82-92, SCHR

BOOKBINDING - Austria

Eichler, Ferdinand. Lederschnittbände in Österreich. 86-94, MILF

BOOKBINDING - Austria - Hist.

Laurin, Gertraut. Blindgedruckte Einzelstempelbände des XV. und XVI. Jahrhunderts im Zisterzienserstift Rein bei Graz. 10-30, SCHT

BOOKBINDING - Bamberg - Hist. - 15th cent.

Geldner, Ferdinand. Bamberger und Nürnberger Lederschnittbände der Zweiten Hälfte des 15. Jahrhunderts. 7-46, SCHO

BOOKBINDING - Berlin

Paalzow, Hans. Die Buchbinderei. 21-22, HARN

BOOKBINDING - Care and preservation

Birkenmajer, Aleksander. W Sprawie Rejestracji i Katalogowania Opraw Zabytkowych. 105-121, PIEK
Fischer, Anton. Ersatzmöglichkeiten für Verlorene und Nicht Mehr Restaurable Einbände. 441-453, GALL
Procházka, Jan Sv. Jak Konservovat Kožené Vazby. 218-223, ŽIVN

BOOKBINDING - Cologne - Hist.

Schunke, Ilse. Der Kölner Rollen- und Platteneinband im 16. Jahrhundert. 311-397, HAEK

BOOKBINDING - Dresden - Hist.

Schunke, Ilse. Beiträge zur Dresdner Bibliotheksgeschichte auf Grund von Einbandstudien. 397-414, VORS

BOOKBINDING - Erfurt - Hist. - 15th cent.

Endres, Heinrich. Meister Ulrich Frenckel aus Hirschau. 176-182, LOUB

BOOKBINDING - Fine bindings

HAEK

Alexander, Gerhard. Ein Prachteinband aus Gräflich Oldenburgischem Besitz in der Staats- und Universitätsbibliothek Hamburg. 167-176, TIEM
Bischoff, Bernhard. Kreuz und Buch im Frühmittelalter und in den Ersten Jahrhunderten der Spanischen Reconquista. 19-34, WEHM
Bock, Friedrich. Ein Nürnberger Lederschnittband mit Accipies-Bild. 15-17, LEID
Bogeng, Gustav Adolf Erich. Einbandkunst und Einbandliebhaberei. 206-212, LOUB
Bollert, Martin. Ein Kastenband mit Lederschnitt in der Sächsischen Landesbibliothek zu Dresden. 95-104, LOUB
———— Ein Neuer Lederschnittband

aus dem 14. Jahrhundert. 80-82, LEIP
Brun, Robert. Sept Nouvelles Reliures de Grolier. 183-190, CALO
Collijn, Isak Gustaf Alfred. Zwei Widmungsexemplare eines Werkes des Valentinus Erythraeus (1574). 111-116, LEYG
Dahlberg, Ragnar. Två Böcker med Märklig Proveniens i Helsingfors Universitetsbibliotek. 127-136, SCHA
Eichler, Ferdinand. Ausgewählte Bucheinbände des 15. und 16. Jahrhunderts aus der Universitätsbibliothek Graz. 110-124, HAEK
——— Eine Bucheinbandverzierung aus dem Formenschatz Hans Holbeins d. J. 63-66, LEID
——— Lederschnittbände des 15. Jahrhunderts in der Steiermark. 77-102, SCHW
——— Lederschnittbände in Österreich. 86-94, MILF
Endres, Heinrich. Meister Ulrich Frenckel aus Hirschau. 176-182, LOUB
Ettinghausen, Richard. The Covers of the Morgan Manâfi' Manuscript and Other Early Persian Bookbindings. 459-473, GREE
Frisch, Ernst von. Einbände des 16. Jahrhunderts in und aus Salzburg. 125-133, HAEK
Glauning, Otto. Drei Lederschnittbände von der Wende des XIV. Jahrhunderts aus Altzelle. 188-195, BOLL
Gratzl, Emil. Islamische Handschriftenbände der Bayerischen Staatsbibliothek. 118-147, LOUB
Guignard, Jacques. A propos d'un Grolier Inédit. La Date des Reliures à Plaquettes: Étienne ou Jean Grolier? 191-216, CALO
Haebler, Konrad. Die Bucheinbände des Petrus Leßl. 103-110, SCHW
Hannover, Emil. Von Bozérian bis Trautz. 199-205, LOUB
Haseloff, Arthur. Der Einband der Hs. des Marcusevangeliums des Harderadus. 507-528, EHRE
Helwig, Hellmuth. Jenaer Buchbinder des 16. Jahrhunderts. 225-241, HAEK
Herbst, Hermann. Braunschweigische Buchbinder des 16. Jahrhunderts. 274-310, HAEK
——— Nürnberger Lederschnittbände. 83-94, LEIP
Husung, Max Joseph. Aus der Zeit des Übergangs von der Handschrift zum Druck. Nach einem Band der Preussischen Staatsbibliothek. 155-159, DEGE
——— Dreimal das Gleiche Lederschnittmotiv. 123-126, LEID
——— Der Löwener Renaissance-Buchbinder mit der Gesprungenen Einbandplatte. II, 29-35, GLAU
——— Ein Neuer Signierter und Datierter Badier, Gefunden in der Preussischen Staatsbibliothek. 435-442, COLL
Italiener, Bruno. Isak B. Secharjah, ein Jüdischer Lederschnittkünstler des 15. Jahrhunderts. 159-161, FREN
Juntke, Fritz. Georg Rumler, ein Hallischer Buchbinder aus der Zweiten Hälfte des 16. Jahrhunderts. 201-224, HAEK
Kilpi, Volter. Suomalainen Virsikirja [Manuale-nide] v:lta 1630 Teuven Kirkonarkistossa. 122-126, SCHA
Kyriss, Ernst. Beiträge zu Augsburger Buchbindern. 134-164, HAEK
——— Einbände mit Hoheitszeichen Herzog Carl Eugens. 232-243, HOFF
——— Johannes Zoll, ein Tübinger Buchbinder des 15. Jahrhunderts. 84-93, LEYH
——— Nördlinger Bucheinbände eines Zeit- und Kunstgenossen Johann Richenbachs. I, 119-139, GLAU
Laurin, Gertraut. Blindgedruckte Einzelstempelbände des XV. und XVI. Jahrhunderts im Zisterzienserstift Rein bei Graz. 10-30, SCHT
Loubier, Hans. Versuch einer Klassifizierung der Einbände für Jean Grolier. 421-434, COLL
Meyer, Wilhelm Josef. Einbände. 119-120, BERU
Michon, Louis-Marie. Notes sur les Reliures de L'Atelier des Monnier. 509-513, BONN
Nixon, Howard M. Roger Bartlett's Bookbindings. 56-65, OLDH
Rudbeck, Johannes. Några Italienska Bokband från 1500-Talet. 411-420, COLL
——— Über die Herkunft der Grolier-Einbände. 183-190, LOUB
Schmidbauer, Richard. "Nachlese": Ein Unbekannter Maioliband.—Eine Spielkarte und ein Kartenspiel. 255-259, STOL
Schmidt, Adolf. Der Einband der Goldenen Bulle von 1356 in der Landesbibliothek zu Darmstadt. 105-117, LOUB
——— Kölnische Einbände des Vierzehnten Jahrhunderts in der Amploniana zu Erfurt. 401-409, COLL
——— Zur Geschichte Deutscher Buchbinder im 16. Jahrhundert. 1-109, HAEK
Schmidt, Christel. Aus der Sammlung Olga Hirsch: Ein Kreisrunder Einband von Caspar Meuser. 194-198, LOUB
——— Jakob Krause-Forschung: Ein Beitrag zur Methodik der Bucheinbandkunde. 191-193, LOUB
Schmidt, Wieland. Bemerkungen zum

Einband des Karlsruher Skizzenbuches von Hans Baldung Grien. 505-523, HOFM
———— In einem Kopert Gebunden. 59-82, REDE
Schmidt-Herrling, Eleonore. Einbände von Thomas Krüger in der Universitätsbibliothek Erlangen. 285-293, STOL
Schreiber, Heinrich. Adolar Baldensheym, ein Leipziger Renaissancebuchbinder. 176-200, HAEK
Schunke, Ilse. Der Kölner Rollen- und Platteneinband im 16. Jahrhundert. 311-397, HAEK
———— Der Lederschnitt im Mittleren Deutschen Gebiet. 57-63, BOLE
———— Die Pariser Büchersendung des Hubert Languet an Kurfürst August von Sachsen 1566. 49-66, BOLL
———— Signet-Einbände. II, 104-112, GLAU
Schwenke, Paul. Die Buchbinder mit dem Lautenspieler und dem Knoten. 122-144, HAEB
Sillib, Rudolf. Ein Nachkömmling der Heidelberger Hofbuchbinderei des Kurfürsten Karl Ludwig von der Pfalz. 249-251, LEID
Strübing, Eduard. Zwei Einbände Jakob Krauses in der Weimarer Landesbibliothek. 153-157, WEIM
Theele, Joseph. Fuldaer Bucheinbände des 16. Jahrhunderts. 165-175, HAEK
Thomas, Sir Henry. Diego Hurtado de Mendoza and his Plaquette Bindings. 474-480, GREE
Wieser, Hans. Ein Tiroler Lederschnittband. 662-665, BICK

BOOKBINDING - Fine bindings - Bibl.

Bruchet, Andrée. Quelques Reliures Estampées Signées de la Fin du XVe et du Début du XVIe Siècle de la Bibliothèque Municipale de Lille. 81-91, BONN
Glauning, Otto. Ein Beitrag zur Kenntnis der Einbände Johann Richenbachs. 95-112, LEIP
Kyriss, Ernst. Spätgotische Einbände des Benediktinerklosters Schuttern. 147-152, WEHM
Mitchell, Wm. S. German Bindings in Aberdeen University Library: Iconographic Index, and Indices of Initials, Binders, and Dates. 46-55, OLDH

BOOKBINDING - Fine bindings - Box

Bollert, Martin. Ein Kastenband mit Lederschnitt in der Sächsischen Landesbibliothek zu Dresden. 95-104, LOUB

BOOKBINDING - Fine bindings - Collections - Aberdeen

Mitchell, Wm. S. German Bindings in Aberdeen University Library: Iconographic Index, and Indices of Initials, Binders, and Dates. 46-55, OLDH

BOOKBINDING - Fine bindings - Collections - Berlin

Schunke, Ilse. Die Italienischen Einbände aus der Hamilton-Sammlung in Berlin. 17-32, LÜLF

BOOKBINDING - Fine bindings - Collections - Dresden

Schunke, Ilse. Beiträge zur Dresdner Bibliotheksgeschichte auf Grund von Einbandstudien. 397-414, VORS

BOOKBINDING - Fine bindings - Collections - Germany

Geldner, Ferdinand. Bamberger und Nürnberger Lederschnittbände der Zweiten Hälfte des 15. Jahrhunderts. 7-46, SCHO

BOOKBINDING - Fine bindings - Collections - Hague

Verwey, Eleonore de la Fontaine. Boekbanden uit de Oranje Nassau-Bibliotheek. 161-179, HAGU

BOOKBINDING - Fine bindings - Collections - Königsberg

Husung, Max Josef. Über den Plattenstempelschnitt in Königsberg. 283-287, KUHN

BOOKBINDING - Fine bindings - Collections - Lille

Bruchet, Andrée. Quelques Reliures Estampées Signées de la Fin du XVe et du Début du XVIe Siècle de la Bibliothèque Municipale de Lille. 81-91, BONN

BOOKBINDING - Fine bindings - Collections - Munich

Glauning, Otto. Die Einbandsammlung der Bayerischen Staatsbibliothek zu München. 111-122, MILF

BOOKBINDING - Fine bindings - Collections - Nuremberg

Bock, Friedrich. Ein Nürnberger Lederschnittband mit Accipies-Bild. 15-17, LEID

BOOKBINDING - Fine bindings - Collections - Paris

Bonet, Paul. La Reliure Originale et la B. N. 37-40, CAIN

BOOKBINDING - Fine bindings - Collections - Vatican

Schunke, Ilse. Die Entwicklung der Päpstlichen Einbände vom 16. zum 17. Jahrhundert. II, 331-354, ALBB

BOOKBINDING - Fine bindings - Collective

Nielsen, L. Et Sjaeldent Danicum. 225-229, COLL

BOOKBINDING - Fine bindings - Paper

Leuze, Otto. Mit Holzschnitten Verzierte Buchumschläge des 15. Jahrhunderts in der Württembergischen Landesbibliothek in Stuttgart. 165-169, LEID
Müller, Max. Der Älteste Bekannte Buchumschlag. 195-197, LEID

BOOKBINDING - Fine bindings - Purse

Klauser, Renate. Ein Beutelbuch aus Isny. 139-145, WEHM

BOOKBINDING - Fine bindings - Silver

Waetzoldt, Stephan. Ein Silbereinband von Jörg Seld. 53-57, REDE

BOOKBINDING - France - Hist.

Hannover, Emil. Von Bozérian bis Trautz. 199-205, LOUB

BOOKBINDING - Fulda - Hist.

Theele, Joseph. Fuldaer Bucheinbände des 16. Jahrhunderts. 165-175, HAEK

BOOKBINDING - Germany - Bibl.

Mitchell, Wm. S. German Bindings in Aberdeen University Library: Iconographic Index, and Indices of Initials, Binders, and Dates. 46-55, OLDH

BOOKBINDING - Gt. Brit. - Hist.

Jackson, William A. Notes on English "Publishers' Bindings" of the Sixteenth and Seventeenth Centuries. 483-488, LYDE
Middleton, Bernard C. The Bookbinders Case Unfolded. 66-76, OLDH
Pollard, Graham. The Construction of English Twelfth-Century Bindings. 1-22, OLDH

BOOKBINDING - Halle - Hist.

Juntke, Fritz. Georg Rumler, ein Hallischer Buchbinder aus der Zweiten Hälfte des 16. Jahrhunderts. 201-224, HAEK

BOOKBINDING - Hist.

Adam, Paul. Der Einfluß der Klosterarbeit auf die Einbandkunst. 148-169, LOUB
Loubier, Jean. Methodische Erforschung des Bucheinbands. 175-184, SCHW

BOOKBINDING - Holy Roman Empire - Hist. - 800-1000

Christ, Karl. Karolingische Bibliothekseinbände. 82-104, LEYG

BOOKBINDING - Hungary - Hist.

Scheiber, Alexander. Medieval Hebrew Manuscripts as Bindings in the Libraries and Archives of Hungary. 19-28, BLOC

BOOKBINDING - Italy

Schunke, Ilse. Die Italienischen Einbände aus der Hamilton-Sammlung in Berlin. 17-32, LÜLF

BOOKBINDING - Königsberg - Hist.

Husung, Max Joseph. Über den Plattenstempelschnitt in Königsberg. 283-287, KUHN

BOOKBINDING - Leipzig - Hist.

Schreiber, Heinrich. Adolar Baldensheym, ein Leipziger Renaissancebuchbinder. 176-200, HAEK

BOOKBINDING - Louvain - Hist.

Husung, Max Joseph. Der Löwener Renaissance-Buchbinder mit der Gesprungenen Einbandplatte. II, 29-35, GLAU

BOOKBINDING - Materials

Schmidt, Wieland. In einem Kopert Gebunden. 59-82, REDE

BOOKBINDING - Early filling paper

Dold, Alban. Ein Fragment eines Collectars, d. i. eines Horen-Orationenbuches. 31-36, STOL
Lewicka-Kamińska, Anna. Neues Donatfragment in der Type der 42zeiligen Bibel in der Jagiellonischen Bibliothek. 13-16, LÜLF
Tudeer, Lauri O. Th. En Mainzer Gratulation från 1604-1605. 250-253, MUNT
Vallinkoski, J. Ett Danskt Bokfynd i Finland. 15-19, DAHA

BOOKBINDING - Hist. - 15th cent.

Eichler, Ferdinand. Lederschnitt und Hornverzierung beim Bucheinband. 89-94, LOUB

BOOKBINDING - Mohammedan countries - Hist.

Gratzl, Emil. Islamische Handschriftenbände der Bayerischen Staatsbibliothek. 118-147, LOUB

BOOKBINDING - Nördlingen, Ger. - Hist

Kyriss, Ernst. Nördlinger Bucheinbände eines Zeit- und Kunstgenossen Johann Richenbachs. I, 119-139, GLAU

BOOKBINDING - Norway - Hist.

Paulli, R. Gregorius Middelthun. Bogbinder i Bergen, Stempelskaerer på Kongsberg. 140-148, TVET

BOOKBINDING - Nuremberg - Hist.

Herbst, Hermann. Nürnberger Lederschnittbände. 83-94, LEIP

BOOKBINDING - Nuremberg - Hist. - 15th cent.

Geldner, Ferdinand. Bamberger und Nürnberger Lederschnittbände der Zweiten Hälfte des 15. Jahrhunderts. 7-46, SCHO

BOOKBINDING - Oslo - Hist.

Kleppa, Peter. Universitetsbibliotekets Bokbindere og Innbinding. 255-257, OSLO

BOOKBINDING - Paris - Hist.

Schunke, Ilse. Die Pariser Büchersendung des Hubert Languet an Kurfürst August von Sachsen 1566. 49-66, BOLL

BOOKBINDING - Persia

Ettinghausen, Richard. The Covers of the Morgan Manâfi' Manuscript and Other Early Persian Bookbindings. 459-473, GREE

BOOKBINDING - Rome (City) - Hist.

Schunke, Ilse. Die Entwicklung der Päpstlichen Einbände vom 16. zum 17. Jahrhundert. II, 331-354, ALBB

BOOKBINDING - Salzburg - Hist.

Frisch, Ernst von. Einbände des 16. Jahrhunderts in und aus Salzburg. 125-133, HAEK

BOOKBINDING - Styria - Hist. - 15th cent.

Eichler, Ferdinand. Lederschnittbände des 15. Jahrhunderts in der Steiermark. 77-102, SCHW

BOOKBINDING - Tübingen - Hist. - 15th cent.

Kyriss, Ernst. Johannes Zoll, ein Tübinger Buchbinder des 15. Jahrhunderts. 84-93, LEYH

BOOKMAKING - Collections - Frankfurt a.M.

Schauer, Georg Kurt. Die Sammlung Buchkunst. 149-161, EPPE

BOOKMAKING - Germany - Hist. - 16th-18th cent.

Crous, Ernst. Schrift und Satz im Berliner Buchdruck von der Mitte des 16. bis zur Mitte des 18. Jahrhunderts. Ein Beitrag zur Geschichte des Deutschen Buchstils in Wenig Bekannter Zeit. 37-45, LEID

BOOKMENDING
see Books - Care and restoration

BOOKMOBILE SERVICES - Hawaii

Gray, Margaret. Bookmobile Service in Hawaii. 408-419, RANG

BOOKMOBILE SERVICES - Public libraries
see also Branch libraries

BOOKMOBILE SERVICES - Public libraries - Norway

Rongen, Bjørn. Bøker Langs Landeveien. 120-130, KILD

BOOKMOBILE SERVICES - Public libraries - Sweden

Nyman, Gunborg. Bibliotek på Hjul. Sommarsamhällets Bokförsörjning. 215-223, HEIN

BOOKMOBILE SERVICES - Regional libraries - Switzerland

Escher, Hermann. Die Schweizerische Volksbibliothek (1922). 131-137, ESCH

BOOKPLATES

Dahlberg, Ragnar. Ätten Reuterholms Exlibris. 108-114, HULT
Kawasaki, Misao. Zōshoin ka Zōshohyō ka. (Bookstamp or Bookplate?) 57-65, OTAT

BOOKPLATES - Berlin

Crous, Ernst. Die Bücherzeichen (Exlibris) in den Wiegendrucken der Staatsbibliothek. 240-253, HARN

BOOKPLATES - Königsberg

Warda, Arthur. Die Exlibris des Herzogs Albrecht von Preussen. 349-354, KÖNI

BOOKPLATES - Nashville

Morrissey, Eleanor Fleming. Reading Bookplates. 14-16, NASH

BOOKPLATES - New Haven, Conn.

Troxell, Gilbert McCoy. Bookplates of the Yale Libraries, 1780-1846. 145-156, KEOG

BOOKPLATES - Uppsala

Rudbeck, Gustaf. Uppsala Universitetsbiblioteks Exlibris. 391-397, UPPS

BOOKS
see also Bookmaking

BOOKS

Heber, Lilly. Boken. 115-121, HIRN
Hertz, Aleksander. Jakób Szacki - Człowiek Książki. 47-51, SZAC
Liermann, Hans. Buch und Recht. 33-35, REDE
——— Das Buch im Deutschen Rechtsgang. 137-146, STOL
Meier, Franz Joseph, [trans.] Der Artikel Tosho "Buch" im Nihon-Bungaku-Daijiten. [Translation of Japanese Article by Shinkichi Hashimoto and Yasushi Uematsu.] 205-216, LEYH
Muszkowski, Jan. Książka Jako Zjawisko Społeczne. 79-104, PIEK
Neuscheler, Eugen. Buch und Leben. 381-387, LEYG
Stefl, Max. Von Büchern und Büchermenschen. 20-23, HELD
Stevens, David H. Islands of Influence. 679-684, WILS
Stöwesand, Rudolf. Buch und Buchstabe. Prinzipielles und Persönliches als Einführung. 7-17, SCHR
Teodorov-Balan, Aleksandŭr. Komu Shto e Knigata? 7-8, TEOB
Vesaas, Halldis Moren. Bøkenes Rike. 7-8, NORS

BOOKS AND READING
see also Reading; Reading interests

BOOKS AND READING

Busse, Gisela von. Vom Rechten Bücherlesen. Gedanken zur Herder-Interpretation. 244-257, TIEM
Freiberg, Siegfried. Begegnungen mit Büchern. 348-357, BICK
Koch, Herbert. ICH—der Leser! 106-108, JENA
Putnam, Herbert. Reflections from Ingonish. 5-10, BISH
Tanaka, Takashi. Tosho no Chikara. (The Utility of Books.) 13-21, HAKO
Wieselgren, O. Några Anteckningar om Våra Dagars Folklitteratur. 251-265, ANNE
Zweig, Arnold. Pforten der Zukunft. 7-9, JENA

BOOKS AND READING - Russia - Hist. - 19th cent.

Feyl, Othmar. Bücher, Bibliotheken und Leser in der Russischen Gesellschaft des 19. Jahrhunderts. 97-133, LÜLF

BOOKS - Annotations
see Annotations

BOOKS AS CARRIERS OF DISEASE
see also Disinfection of books

BOOKS AS CARRIERS OF DISEASE

Fiskaa, Haakon M. Bøker Som Smittebaerere og Bokdesinfeksjon. 325-338, MUNT

BOOKS AS FIGURES OF SPEECH

Pipping, Rolf. Metaforer ur Böckernas Värld. 168-177, GARD

BOOKS - Care and restoration
see also Manuscripts - Care and restoration

BOOKS - Care and restoration

Bishop, William Warner. One Problem for 1950—Woodpulp Paper in Books. 407-415, LYDE
Blaas, Richard. Cellon und Pergamin in der Archivalienrestaurierung. 187-197, GALL
Bravi, Lamberto. Le Materie Plastiche nella Rilegatura dei Libri. 235-238, GALL
Lemaître, Henri. Magasins de Livres et Lumière Naturelle. 23-31, GODE
Luyn, J. L. van. Schimmel op Boeken in de Utrechtsche Universitetsbibliotheek. 237-241, EVER
Procházka, Jan Sv. Jak Konşervovat Kožené Vazby. 218-223, ŽIVN
Takeda, Goichi. Tosho no Hozon ni tsuite. (On the Conservation of Books.) 16-28, IMAI
Tisserant, Eugène. On the Use of Ultraviolet Rays for Detecting Repairs in Printed Books, Especially Incunabula. 341-343, HANS

BOOKS - Care and restoration - Hist.

Hosius, Carl. Bibliotheksfeinde und -funde. 150-155, KUHN

BOOKS - Disinfection
see Disinfection of books

BOOKS - Exportation
see Importation and exportation of books

BOOKS - Finland - Hist. - 18th cent.

Grönroos, Henrik. Om Böcker och Bokägare i Finland för 200 År Sedan. 1-15, NYBE

BOOKS - Format

Dalgliesh, Alice and Margaret B. Evans. Designing Children's Books. 573-577, MOOR
Kunze, Horst. Bemerkungen zur Buchform. 54-55, STUM
Van Hoesen, Henry B. and Norman Kilpatrick. Heights of Books in Relation to Height of Stack Tiers. 352-357, HANS

BOOKS - Format - Germany - Hist. - 16th-18th cent.

Crous, Ernst. Schrift und Satz im Berliner Buchdruck von der Mitte des 16. bis zur Mitte des 18. Jahrhunderts. Ein Beitrag zur Geschichte des Deutschen Buchstils in Wenig Bekannter Zeit. 37-45, LEID

BOOKS - Format - Hist.

Rodenberg, Julius. Zur Architektonik des Buches. 91-102, MIND

BOOKS - Hist.

Eichler, Ferdinand. Die Renaissance des Buches im 15. Jahrhundert und Ihre Nachwirkung. 1-10, LEYG
Kufaev, M. N. Problemy Filosofii Knigi; Opyt Vvedeniia v Istoriiu Knigi. 22-38, MALE
Liermann, Hans. Das Buch im Deutschen Rechtsgang. 137-146, STOL
Rajbee, M. Ranganathan: My Benefactor: A Book's Appreciation of Dr. Ranganathan. 305-311, RANG

BOOKS - HIST. - Poland

Simonsen, D. Zur Bücherkunde. 164-168, STEI

BOOKS - Importation
see Importation and exportation of books

BOOKS IN ART

Schmook, Ger. Wat Met de Rug op de Plank, in Het Rek? 29-50, JUCH

BOOKS - Legal aspects
see Libraries - Legal aspects

BOOKS - Obsolescence
see Obsolescence of books

BOOKS OF HOURS
see Hours, Books of

BOOKS - Orient - Hist.

Meier, Franz Joseph, [trans.] Der Artikel Tosho "Buch" im Nihon-Bungaku-Daijiten. [Translation of Japanese Article by Shinkichi Hashimoto and Yasushi Uematsu.] 205-216, LEYH

BOOKS - Owners' marks

Croix, Jean Tremblot de la. Marques de la Bibliothèque Capitulaire de Noyon. 237-242, CALO
Flury, Hans. Die Rechtliche Natur des Bibliotheksbuches. 99-115, SCHU
Josserand, Pierre and Jean Bruno. Les Estampilles du Département des Imprimés de la Bibliothèque Nationale. 261-298, CALO
Kawasaki, Misao. Zōshoin ka Zōshohyō ka. (Bookstamp or Bookplate?) 57-65, OTAT
Pipping, Hugo E. Två Bokägarmärken Anbragta Som Rygg- och Pärmstämpel. 1-11, DAHL

BOOKS - Owners' marks - Berlin

Crous, Ernst. Die Bücherzeichen (Exlibris) in den Wiegendrucken der Staatsbibliothek. 240-253, HARN

BOOKS - Owners' marks - Sweden

Dahlberg, Ragnar. Några Okända Svenska Kungliga Pärmstämplar. 42-50, TUDE

BOOKS - Preservation
see Books - Care and restoration

BOOKS - Prices

Paulli, R. Bogfører-Dokumenter fra det 16. Aarhundrede. 215-223, COLL

BOOKS - Prices - 18th cent.

Lunelund-Grönroos, Birgit. Peter Johan Bladhs "Räkning öfwer Böcker til 1771. Års slut." 85-100, TUDE

BOOKS - Prices - Scania - 17th cent.

Carlquist, Gunnar. Skåneprästen Albert Raffn och Finansieringen av Hans Bok "Den Himmelske Herredag" (1633). 42-50, DAHA

BOOKS - Prices - 1601

Kernkamp, J. H. De Bibliotheek van den Koopman Daniel van der Meulen onder den Hamer. 187-203, EVER

BOOKS - Privately printed
see Privately printed books

BOOKS - Repair
see Books - Care and restoration

BOOKS - Reviews
see Book reviews

BOOKS, Sacred
see Sacred books

BOOKS - Sizes
see Books - Format

BOOKS THAT OUGHT TO BE WRITTEN

Couch, W. T. Books That Ought to Be Written. 429-437, WILS

BOOKSELLERS AND BOOKSELLING
see Book industry and trade

BOOKSELLERS AND LIBRARIES - Denmark

Madsen, Viggo. Boghandelen og Bibliotekerne. 45-53, THOM

BOOKSELLERS AND LIBRARIES - Leipzig

Rötzsch, Helmut. Der Börsenverein der

Deutschen Buchhändler zu Leipzig und die Deutsche Bücherei. 47-66, LEIZ

BOOKSELLERS AND LIBRARIES - Norway

Thommessen, Olaf. Bibliotek og Bokhandel. 156-160, NORS

BOOKSELLERS AND LIBRARIES - U.S.

Melcher, Frederic G. Working Together: Publisher, Bookseller, and Librarian. 619-621, MOOR

BOOKSELLERS' CATALOGS

Lippi, Silvio. La Libreria di Monserrato Rossellò Giureconsulto e Bibliografo Sardo del Sec. XVI. II, 319-332, MANO

BOOKSELLERS' CATALOGS - 15th cent.

Voulliéme, Ernst. Nachträge zu den Buchhändleranzeigen des 15. Jahrhunderts in Getreuen Nachbildungen Hrsg. von K. Burger. 18-44, HAEB

——— Eine Neue Bücheranzeige des Anton Sorg in Augsburg. 43-47, LOUB

BOOKSELLERS' CATALOGS - Germany - Bibl.

Wendt, Bernhard. Antiquariatskataloge als Bibliographische Hilfsmittel für Reformationsdrucke. 476-491, BENZ

BOOKSELLERS' CATALOGS - U.S. - Bibl.

Brigham, Clarence Saunders. American Booksellers' Catalogues, 1734-1800. 31-67, WROT

BOOKWORMS
see Books - Care and restoration

Borchard, Edwin Montefiore.
The Law Division of the Library of Congress. 89-96, PUTN

BORGÅ, Finland. Gymnasium

Lunelund-Grönroos, Birgit. Gymnasister och Böcker i det Gamla Borgå. 51-58, NYBE

Borgeaud, Marc-Auguste.
Le Rôle de M. Pierre Bourgeois à L'ABS. 177-180, BOUR

Borghezio, Gino.
Inventarii e Notizie della Biblioteca Capitolare d'Ivrea nel Secolo XV. 423-454, EHRE

Borov, Todor.
Bibliotechna Nauka. 304-320, MIKN
Bŭlgarska Bibliografiia͡. 99-110, MIKH
Bŭlgarskata Pŭrvichna Natsionalna Bibliografiia͡. 113-130, TEOD
Die Primäre Nationalbibliographie Bulgariens. 20-44, VORS

BOROV, TODOR

BORO

Ivanov, D. D. Professor T. Borov i Ego Trudy po Bibliotekovedeniu͡e i Bibliografii. 13-19, BORO

BOROV, TODOR - Bibl.

Trajkov, Veselin and Bozhana Troi͡anova. Literaturna i Nauchna Dejnost Bibliografii͡a na Po-Znachitelnite Publikatsii 1920-1960. 20-43, BORO

Borowy, Wacław.
Wspomnienie. 13-31, PIEK

BORREN, CHARLES VAN DEN

BORR

BORV

Clercx, Suzanne. Charles van den Borren. 1-18, BORR
Wangermée, R. Les Oeuvres de Charles van den Borren. 19-53, BORR

Borromeo, Giberto.
Lettere in Gallavresi, G. Alcune Lettere del Barone Custodi Riguardanti le Relazioni del Munifico Bibliofilo coll'Ambrosiana e colla Famiglia Borromeo. 403-412, CERI

BORROWERS
see Registration of borrowers

BORSO D'ESTE, DUKE OF FERRARA, MODENA AND REGGIO - Library

Baldini, Antonio. La Bibbia di Borso. 41-45, GREG

Bosch, J. F.
Classificatie en Kennisleer. 391-396, BRUM

Boschot, Adolphe.
Saint-Saëns et Sa "Correspondance Générale." 399-402, BONN

Boshnakov, Dimitŭr, jt. author

Ikonomova, Diana and Dimitŭr Boshnakov. Imenniia͡t Pokazalets v Registratsionnata Bibliografiia͡. 163-185, TEOB

BOSSE, Elise Hofmann-
see Hofmann-Bosse, Elise

BOSTON ATHENAEUM

Roden, Carl B. The Boston Years of Dr. W. F. Poole. 388-394, PUTN

BOSTON - Book industry and trade
see Book industry and trade- Boston

BOSTON BURIENSIS
see Boston, John, of Bury

BOSTON, JOHN, of Bury. Cathologus de Libris Autenticis et Apocrisis

Mynors, R. A. B. The Latin Classics Known to Boston of Bury. 199-217, SAXL

BOSTON. Public Library

Belden, Charles F. D. The Library Service of Herbert Putnam in Boston. 10-14, PUTN
Roden, Carl B. The Boston Years of Dr. W. F. Poole. 388-394, PUTN

Bostwick, Arthur Elmore.
Nomads. 97-102, PUTN

Bourgeois, Pierre.
Le Dépôt Gratuit et Volontaire en Suisse. 397-401, BRUM
Quelques Considerations sur les Bibliothèques Suisses dans la Vie Internationale. 73-80, SCHU
Zweck und Aufbau der Gesamtkataloge. 16-17, STUM

BOURGEOIS, PIERRE

BOUR

BOURGUET, LOUIS

Godet, Marcel. Au Temps de la "Respublica Litterarum." Jacob Christophe Iselin et Louis Bourguet. 117-127, SCHU

Boussard, Jacques.
L'Évangéliaire d'Or, Manuscrit 599 de la Bibliothèque de L'Arsenal. 3-14, CALO

BOUVET, HONORÉ
see Bonet, Honoré

Bowerman, George F.
Some Library Personnel Problems. 103-112, PUTN

Bowker, Richard R.
The Appointment of Herbert Putnam as Librarian of Congress. 15-21, PUTN

BOWNE, JOHN

McDonald, Gerald D. William Bradford's Book Trade and John Bowne, Long Island Quaker, as His Book Agen 1686-1691. 209-222, WROT

BOWRING, SIR JOHN. Brev.

Hirn, Yrjö. Utländsk Välgörenhet mot Universitetsbiblioteket. 9-18, HULT

Boysen, Karl.
Die Handschriftliche Überlieferung der Lateinischen Josephus-Übersetzung in der Ersten Hälfte der Antiquitates Judaicae. 277-292, WILM
Systematischer oder Schlagwortkatalog? 19-36, MILF

BOYSEN, KARL

Fick, Richard. Karl Boysen und Seine Stellung zum Gesamtkatalogproblem. I, 36-42, GLAU

BOZÉRIAN FAMILY (bookbinders)

Hannover, Emil. Von Bozérian bis Trautz. 199-205, LOUB

Bozhinov, Liuben Al.
Dokumentite na Sŭrbokhŭrvatski Ezik v Bŭlgarskiia Istoricheski Arkhiv. 51-59, MIKH

Bozhinova, Bozhana.
Anketa za Sŭstoianieto na Bibliotekite i na Bibliotechniia Personal v Bulgariia v Kraia na 1945 Godina. 392-404, MIKN

Bozhinova, Bozhana and Dimitŭr P. Ivanchev.
Opit za Razgranichavane Poniatiiata "Spisanie" i "Vestnik"; Doklad. 411-417, MIKN

Bozhinova-Troianova, B.
Chitalishtnite Biblioteki. 266-280, MIKN
Profilirane na Nauchnite Biblioteki u Nas. 61-72, MIKH

Bozhinova-Troianova, B. and Dora Ganchev.
D-r Nikola V. Mikhov: Bibliografiia Izrabotena v Bŭlgarskiia Bibliografski Institut. IX-XIV, MIKN

BRABANT, SIGER DE
see Siger de Brabant

BRACCIOLINI, POGGIO-
see Poggio-Bracciolini

Brachvogel, Eugen, Monsignore.
Die Bibliotheken der Geistlichen Residenzen des Ermlandes. 35-44, KÖNI

BRADFORD, WILLIAM, printer

McDonald, Gerald D. William Bradford's Book Trade and John Bowne, Long Island Quaker, as His Book Agent, 1686-1691. 209-222, WROT

Bradlow, F. R.
Douglas Varley and the Quarterly Bulletin, the Friends of the S. A. Library and Africana. 19-21, VARL

Bradshaw, S.
D. H. Varley: a Tribute. 10-12, VARL

Bragard, R.
Boethiana—Études sur le "De Institutione Musica" de Boèce. 84-139, BORR

Brahmer, Mieczysław.
O Bibliotece Pinoccich. 251-265, PIEK

BRAKEL, JOHANNES VON
see Johannes Braclensis

BRAMBACH, WILHELM - Correspondence - Collections - Göttingen

Weber, Ulrich. Vier Unveröffentlichte Briefe Wilhelm Brambachs an Carl Dziatzko aus dem Besitz der Universitätsbibliothek Göttingen oder: Scherz- und Schimpfspiel zwischen Gelehrten. 171-178, JUCR

Bramsen, Bo.
Den Praktiske Bog. 77-85, THOM

Branca, Vittore.
Un Esopo Volgare Veneto. 105-115, FERR

BRANCH LIBRARIES - Sheffield, Eng.

Walker, J. M. The Branches—Some Recollections. 21-23, LAMB

Brandenburg, Hans.
Held von Schwabing Gesehen. 15-17, HELD

Brandenstein, Wilhelm.
Die Reichsgründersage des Makedonischen Herrscherhauses. 54-58, SCHT

Branscomb, Harvie.
Some Characteristics of Southern Libraries. 386-398, WILS

Brauer, Adalbert.
Beziehungen der Vorfahren von Gottfried Wilhelm Leibniz zu Buchdruck und Buchhandel. 50-67, BENZ

Braun, Hellmut.
Der Hamburger Koran von 1694. 149-166, TIEM
Verfasser und Urheber. 41-51, FUCH

Braun, W.
Die Stüdienbücherei. 15-24, ACKE

BRAUNSBERG, Ger. - Libraries
see Libraries - Braunsberg, Ger.

Braunsberger, Otto, S.J.
Ein Freund der Bibliotheken und Ihrer Handschriften. 455-472, EHRE

BRAUNSCHWEIG
see Brunswick (City) as subdivision under specific subjects, e.g., Bookbinders - Brunswick (City)

Bravi, Lamberto.
Le Materie Plastiche nella Rilegatura dei Libri. 235-238, GALL

Bréal, Michel.
Fortu, Gratu. 500, CHAT

Brechler, Otto.
Die Handschriftensammlung. 105-118, BICK
Handschriftensammlungen als Kunstsammlungen. 252-263, BICK

Breddin, Hans Harold.
Die Bibliothekarische Arbeitsgemeinschaft der Hamburger Öffentlichen Bücherhallen. 110-114, HAMB

Bredsted, Aage [=Åge].
Biblioteksbygninger og deres Indretning. 38-55, DØSS
Oplandsarbejdets Okonomi. 37-47, LASS

BREITENBACH, BERNHARD VON
see Breydenbach, Bernhard von

BREITKOPF, JOHANN GOTTLOB IMMANUEL - Library

Schmieder, Wolfgang. Johann Gottlob Immanuel Breitkopfs Privatbibliothek. Werden und Vergehen. II, 73-87, GLAU

BREITKOPF UND HÄRTEL

Volkmann, Ludwig. Nachricht von dem Drucke einer Poetischen Bilderbibel. III, 235-242, GLAU

BREMEN. Staatsbibliothek. Mss. (a 233)

Wegener, Hans. Eine Hamburger Großgärtherei des 18. Jahrhunderts und Ihr Katalog. 177-181, TIEM

Brenn, Franz.
Die Sequenzen des Graduale von St. Katharinenthal. 23-42, OREL

BRENTA, NICOLÒ, da Varenna

Campana, Augusto. Osservazione sullo Stampatore Nicolò Brenta da Varenna. 57-64, GREG

BRERA (BRAIDENSE) MILAN
see Milan. Biblioteca Nazionale Braidense

BRESCIA. Biblioteca Civica Queriniana. Mss.

Muñoz, Antonio. Miniature Bizantine nella Biblioteca Queriniana di Brescia. 169-179, CERI

Bresha-Botie, A. S.
Biblioteka Ob̆edinennykh Natsij v Zheneve i Mezhdunarodnoe Mezhbibliotechnoe Sotrudnichestvo. 121-126, MIKH

BRESLAU-REGIS, Gottlob. Mss. - Collections
see Regis, Gottlob. Mss. - Collections - Breslau

BRESLAU. Staats- und Universitäts-Bibliothek

Molsdorf, Wilhelm. Zwei Unbekannte Holzschnitte des Formschneiders Casper in der Breslauer Staats- und Universitäts-Bibliothek. 249-254, MILF -

Oehler, Richard. Milkau als Kommissar für die Belgischen Bibliotheken und als Bibliotheksdirektor in Breslau. 30-35, MILK

BRESLAU. Staats- und Universitäts-Bibliothek - Mss. (Regis)

Schneider, Alfred. Aus Johann Gottlob Regis' Breslauer Tagen. 321-338, MILF

BRESLAU. - Stadtbibliothek - Hist.

Hippe, Max. Zur Vorgeschichte der Breslauer Stadtbibliothek. 162-176, MILF

Breuning, P. S.

Over de Plaatsing der Boeken in de Universiteitsbibliotheek te Utrecht. 38-48, EVER

BREVIARIES

Arens, Fritz. Das Brevier des Administrators Adalbert von Sachsen in der Mainzer Universitätsbibliothek. 67-89, MAIZ

Batiffol, Abbé Pierre. Note sur un Bréviaire Cassinésien du XIe Siècle. 201-209, HAVE

Reifenberg, Hermann. Die Liturgische Bedeutung der Mainzer Brevierhandschrift MS $4^{\circ}33$ des Jahres 1482. 90-102, MAIZ

BREVIARIES - Collections - Gotha

Roob, Helmut. Schöne Breviere in der Gothaer Bibliothek. 55-61, LÜLF

Breycha-Vauthier, Arthur C. de.

La Collaboration Internationale des Bibliothèques dans la Fédération Internationale des Associations des Bibliothécaires. 7-11, EMLE

The Federation of Library Associations. A Study of the Mechanism of an International Organisation. 34-49, BISH

International Libraries and Their Problems. 102-107, MADR

Internationale Bibliotheken und Ihre Probleme. 20-21, STUM

Marcel Godet Bibliothécaire "International." 27-30, GODM

Österreichs Bibliotheken und die Welt. 264-270, BICK

Le Rôle des Publications Gouvernementales et des Publications d'Organisations Internationales. 7-14, GODE

Role of the United Nations Libraries in the World of Librarianship. 488-491, RANG

Vital Problems of International Libraries. 248-251, KYLE

BREYDENBACH, BERNHARD VON. Peregrinationes in Terram Sanctam, 1486

Oehme, Ruthardt. Die Palästinakarte aus Bernhard von Breidenbachs Reise in das Heilige Land 1486. 70-83, LEYH

Bridgman, Nanie.

La Typographie Musicale Italienne (1475-1630) dans les Collections de la Bibliothèque Nationale de Paris. 24-27, FEDO

Bridgwater, Dorothy Wildes.

President Stiles's Letter to Ebeling. 307-316, KEOG

Briele, Wolfgang van der.

Aufbau und Aufgaben Unserer Stadtbücherei. 2-7, ELBE

Bibliothekarische Ausbildungsfragen im Wandel der Jahrzehnte. 17-33, LANF

Die Wissenschaftliche Stadtbibliothek Heute. Probleme und Erfahrungen. 308-324, JUCH

BRIELE, WOLFGANG VAN DER

BRIE

Springmann, Wolfgang. W. van der Briele und die Geschichtliche Entwicklung der Wuppertaler Bibliotheken. 7-40, BRIE

BRIELE, WOLFGANG VAN DER - Bibl.

Bibliographie der Schriften W. van der Brieles. 153-156, BRIE

Briet, Suzanne.

Note sur Quelques Projets de Translation de la Bibliothèque Royale sous la Monarchie de Juillet. 22-23, STUM

Situation de la Bibliographie Rimbaldienne. 403-408, BONN

Brigham, Clarence Saunders.

American Booksellers' Catalogues, 1734-1800. 31-67, WROT

Wall-Paper Newspapers of the Civil War. Checklist of Issues. 203-209, EAME

Brilling, Bernhard.

Die Jüdische Buchdruckerei in Auras (Niederschlesien). 97-100, FREN

Brin, Erwana.

Du Bartas, La Semaine ou Création du Monde. Une Édition Inconnue? 111-114, CALO

Bring, Samuel E.
Från Tempeltornet till Carolina? 199-213, GRAP

Uppsala Universitetsbiblioteks Bytesförbindelser. Några Anteckningar om deras Uppkomst och Utveckling. 425-460, UPPS

Brinkmann, Donald.
Der Mensch im Zeitalter der Automation. 96-113, VLEE

Brinton, Crane.
Patterns of Research and Changing Library Needs from the Viewpoint of the Humanities and Social Sciences. 7-12, PENN

BRITISH COLUMBIA. University. Library

Smith, Anne M. Social Sciences Journals Frequently Cited. 127-134, HASH

BRITISH COLUMBIA - Use studies - College and university libraries
see Use studies - College and university libraries - British Columbia

BRITISH LIBRARY ASSOCIATION
see Library Association

BRITISH MUSEUM

Francis, Sir Frank. The Large General Library in the Mid-Twentieth Century. 427-430, BRUM
——— The National Library as the Basis of a National Library. 244-247, KYLE
Kenyon, Sir Frederic G. Copyright Libraries. 248-254, PUTN
——— A Tribute from the British Museum. 4-5, GREE
Scholderer, Victor. Hans Ringer zu Wimbschpach. 417-420, BENZ
Wharton, Leonard C. Brief Notes of Prague Printed Books in the British Museum. 42-45, EMLE

BRITISH MUSEUM - Catalogs

Predeek, Albert. Antonio Panizzi und der Alphabetische Katalog des Britischen Museums. 257-282, LEYG

BRITISH MUSEUM - Hist.

Lomer, Gerhard Richard. Sir Henry Ellis in France. A Chapter in the History of the British Museum. 116-144, BISH

BRITISH MUSEUM - Mss. (Add. 5463)

Mottironi, Sergio. La Chiesa di S. Pietro di Benevento e la Sua Biblioteca nel Sec. XIII. 559-562, GALL

BRITISH MUSEUM - Mss. (Add. 38023)

Branca, Vittore. Un Esopo Volgare Veneto. 105-115, FERR

BRITISH MUSEUM - Mss. (Add. 46487)

Wormald, Francis. The Sherborne "Chartulary." 101-119, SAXL

BRITISH MUSEUM - Mss. (Arundel 277)

Goldschmidt, E. Ph. Lucian's Calumnia. 228-244, SAXL

BRITISH MUSEUM - Mss. (Cotton Ms., Otho B. VI)

Kemke, Johannes. Die Geschichte einer Handschriften-Versendung. 489-498, WILM

BRITISH MUSEUM - Mss. (Cotton: Tiberius C. VII and Claudius E. III)

Galbraith, V. H. The Chronicle of Henry Knighton. 136-145. Appendix by R. A. B. Mynors. 146-148, SAXL SAXL

BRITISH MUSEUM - Mss. (Cottonian Nero A. ii)

Legg, J. Wickham. Ratio Decursus Qui Fuerunt ex Auctores. 149-167, CERI

BRITISH MUSEUM - Mss. (Kabbala)

Scholem, Gerhard. Einige Kabbalistische Handschriften im Britischen Museum. 51-69, FREN

BRITISH MUSEUM - Mss. (Qirqisâni)

Poznański, S. Die Qirqisâni-Handschriften im British Museum. 195-218, STEI

BRITISH MUSEUM - Mss. (Royal App. 58)

Ward, John. The Lute Music of MS Royal Appendix 58. 117-125, KINK

THE BRITISH NATIONAL BIBLIOGRAPHY

Wells, A. J. Our Debt to India. 57-63, MADR

BRITISH PRINTERS
see Printers, British

BRITTEN, THOMAS - Library

Granniss, Ruth Shepard. Thomas Britton. 196-202, LYDE

Broberg, Sven Grén.
Några Minnen och Anteckningar. 1-10, (third paper), GÖTE

Broch, Mathilde Oftedal.
Kulturoptimisme. 23-36, KILD

Brodman, Estelle and Chester R. Gough.
Computers in Medical and University Libraries; Review of the Situation in the U.S. in 1964. 19-39, HASH

BROEKE, BEREND TEN
see Paludanus, Bernardus

Brom, A., Jr.
Afbeeldingen van Orgels in het Utrechtsche Psalterium. 29-32, SOME
De Universiteitsbibliotheek te Utrecht en de Gestichtsarbeid. 49-54, EVER

Brotanek, Rudolf.
Beschreibung der Handschrift 14090 (Suppl. 1776) der Nationalbibliothek in Wien. 145-162, VIEN

Brouty, Barth.
Le Service des Entrées. 127-129, BERU
Statistique de la Production Littéraire. 130-131, BERU

Brown, Charles Harvey.
Some Similarities and Differences in the Administration of University Libraries in the United States and Germany. 329-342, LEYG

BROWN FAMILY (Providence, R.I.)
Roelker, William Greene. The Browns and Brown University. 235-246, WROT

BROWN, JOHN CARTER
Kubler, George. John Carter Brown and America. 203-207, WROT

Brown, Ruth.
George Catlin's Portraits of North American Indians. 157-162, KEOG

BROWN UNIVERSITY. John Carter Brown Library
Roelker, William Greene. The Browns and Brown University. 235-246, WROT
Wagner, Henry R. Hispanic Americana in the John Carter Brown Library. 423-455, WROT

Brownson, Helen L.
Evaluation of Document Searching Systems and Procedures. 261-266, KYLE

BROWSING ROOMS
see Dormitory libraries; Reading rooms

Bruchet, Andrée.
Quelques Reliures Estampées Signées de la Fin du XVe et du Début du XVIe Siècle de la Bibliothèque Municipale de Lille. 81-91, BONN

Bruckner, Albert.
Die Anfänge des St. Galler Stiftsarchivs. 119-131, BINZ

BRÜLL, NEHEMIAH - Bio-bibl.
Cohen, Boaz. Nehemiah Brüll (1843-1891). 219-246, FREI

Brumati, Antonio.
L'"Atlas Mayor" della Biblioteca Civica di Trieste. II, 665-675, HORT

Brummel, Leendert, ed.
KOSS

Brummel, Leendert
BRUE

Brummel, Leendert
Bibliotheekproblemen in Amerika. 48-63, BRUE
De Boeken van Tongerloo in de Koninklijke Bibliotheek te 's-Gravenhage. 151-168, BRUE
Confrontation of Libraries and Documentation. 9-16, DONR
Dr. Ludwig Tross en de Koninklijke Bibliotheek. 169-177, BRUE
The Fagel Library in Trinity College, Dublin. 204-233, BRUE
Hugo Blotius in Straßburg. 211-217, HOFM
De Koninklijke Bibliotheek 1948-1957. 123-150, BRUE
The Librarian as a Scholar. 100-122, BRUE
Literatuur als Museumobjekt. 81-99, BRUE
National and International Organization of Bibliography. 17-19, STUM
The Netherlands and the International Exchange of Publications. 1-47, BRUE
Een Stiefkind der Geschiedenis: Bibliotheekgeschiedenis. 64-80, BRUE
Tien Jaren Koninklijke Bibliotheek (1938-1947). 1-34, HAGU

BRUMMEL, LEENDERT
BRUE
BRUM
Verwey, H. de la Fontaine. Bij het Afscheid van Prof. Dr. L. Brummel als Bibliothecaris van de Koninklijke Bibliotheek. 379-386, BRUM

Brun, Robert.
Sept Nouvelles Reliures de Grolier. 183-190, CALO

Bruneau, Charles.
Une Création de Sainte-Beuve: La Phrase "Molle" de Volupté. 189-196, BONN

Bruno, Jean, jt. author
Josserand, Pierre and Jean Bruno. Les Estampilles du Département des Imprimés de la Bibliothèque Nationale. 261-298, CALO

Bruns, Ivo.
Un Chapitre d'Alexandre d'Aphrodisias sur l'Âme. 567-572, GRAU

BRUNSHAUSEN (Benedictine abbey)
Höfner, Curt. Zur Geschichte der

Gandersheimer Büchersammlungen. Ein Beitrag aus Coburg. 197-210, HOFM

BRUNSWICK (City) - Bookbinders
see Bookbinders - Brunswick (City)

BRUSSELS. Bibliothèque de Bourgogne
see Brussels. Bibliothèque Royale de Belgique

BRUSSELS. Bibliothèque Royale de Belgique

Liebaers, Herman. De Koninklijke Bibliotheek van België na 125 Jaar. 514-520, BRUM

BRUSSELS. Bibliothèque Royale de Belgique - Mss. (Bibliothèque de Bourgogne, 5348-5352)

Thomas, Émile. Note sur un Gemblacensis Aujourd'hui à Bruxelles n° 5348-5352, XIIe Siècle. 47-48, GRAU

BRUSSELS. Bibliothèque Royale de Belgique - Mss. (Bibliothèque de Bourgogne, 10057)

Thomas, Paul. Un Commentaire du Moyen Âge sur la Rhétorique de Cicéron. 41-45, GRAU

BRUSSELS. Koninklijke Bibliotheek van België
see Brussels. Bibliothèque Royale de Belgique

BRUSSELS - Music libraries and collections
see Music libraries and collections - Brussels

BRUSSELS. Muziekconservatorium. Bibliotheek

Mertens, C. Proeve eener Documentatie over Onze Belgische Toonkunstenaars, Musicologen en Instrumentenbouwers. 216-239, BORR

BRY, DE
see De Bry

Bryant, Louise May and Mary Patterson.
The List of Books Sent by Jeremiah Dummer. 423-492, KEOG

Buchwald, Reinhard.
Die Jenaer "Lesehalle" vor 50 Jahren: Aus den Ungedruckten Lebenserinnerungen von Walter Hofmann. 50-68, JENA

Budach, Anneliese.
Amtliche Druckschriften. 78-85, FRAD

BUDAPEST. Hungarian Academy of Sciences
see Hungarian Academy of Sciences. Budapest

BUDAPEST - Piyutim - Collections
see Piyutim - Collections - Budapest

BUDDHIST LIBRARIES - Japan

Taira, Shunsei. Meiji no Ichi Zasshi ni Arawareta Bukkyo Toshokan Kensetsuron. (A Proposal for Establishing a Buddhist Library in Japan.) 95-98, KYOT

BUDGETS
Coney, Donald. An Experimental Index for Apportioning Departmental Book Funds for a University Library. 422-428, WILS
Ellsworth, Ralph E. Some Aspects of the Problem of Allocating Book Funds among Departments in Universities. 486-494, WILS

BUDGETS - Germany (Federal Republic, 1949-)

Tiemann, Hermann. Materialien zur Bedarfsberechnung für ein Etatmodell. 9-20, REDE

BUDGETS - Munich - 1932-1936

Gratzl, Emil. Bedarfsberechnung an der Bayerischen Staatsbibliothek 1932-1936. 369-372, LEYG

Budka, Włodzimierz.
Papiernia w Młodziejowicach. 199-210, PIEK
Papiernia w Poczesnej. 408-413, GRYC

DER BÜCHERWURM

Schmekel, Ruth. Der Bücherwurm. 14, ZIEG

BÜCKEN, ERNST - Library

Kahl, Willi. Musikhandschriften aus dem Nachlass Ernst Bückens in der Kölner Universitäts- und Stadtbibliothek. 159-171, JUCH

Bühler, Curt F.
Authors and Incunabula. 401-406, GREE
Novello Cattanio: Un Viaggio Fatto alli Paesi del Continente Nuovo. 85-99, WROT
Roman Types and Roman Printing in the Fifteenth Century 101-110, WEHM
Variants in English Incunabula. 459-474, LYDE

BUELNA, PEDRO NIÑO, CONDE DE.

Palencia, Angel González. Don Pedro Niño y el Condado de Buelna. II, 105-146, ARTI

BÜNAU, HEINRICH, GRAF VON - Library

Bollert, Martin. Joh. Joach. Winckelmann und Joh. Mich. Francke. I, 11-17, GLAU
———— Johann Joachim Winckel-

mann als Bibliothekar des Grafen Bünau. 19-24, LEID
Leyh, Georg. Ein Brief Johann Michael Franckes von 1748. 78-81, BOLL

BÜRGER, GOTTFRIED A.

Wille, Hans. Dürer-Erinnerungen in Josef Führichs Illustrationen zu "Der Wilde Jäger" von G. A. Bürger. 60-74, BRIE

Büscher, Alfred.
Skandinavier, Dresden und die Landesbibliothek. 99-104, BOLL

Büttner, Liselotte.
Das Halbjahres-Verzeichnis. 64-67, FRAD

BUILDING CAMPAIGNS
see Public libraries - Finance

BUILDINGS
see Architecture and building

BULGARIA - Bibliography
see Bibliography - Bulgaria

BULGARIA - Bibliography, National
see Bibliography, National - Bulgaria

BULGARIA - Education for librarianship
see Education for librarianship - Bulgaria

BULGARIA - Librarians
see Librarians - Bulgaria

BULGARIA - Libraries
see Libraries - Bulgaria

BULGARIA. National Library
see Sofia. National Library

BULGARIA - Printing
see Printing - Bulgaria

BULGARIA - Public libraries
see Public libraries - Bulgaria

BULGARIA - Scientific libraries
see Scientific libraries - Bulgaria

BULGARIAN BIBLIOGRAPHICAL INSTITUTE. Sofia
see Sofia. Bulgarian Bibliographical Institute

BULGARIAN HISTORICAL ARCHIVE. Sofia. National Library
see Sofia. National Library. Bulgarian Historical Archive

BULGARIAN PERIODICALS
see Periodicals, Bulgarian

Bull, Francis, jt. ed.
OSLN

Bull, Francis.
Norske Avdeling og Norsk Bibliografi. 68-73, OSLN

BULLETIN BOARDS
see also Exhibits and displays

BULLETIN BOARDS - Japan

Miyake, Takashi. Kōkyō Toshokan no Keiji ni tsuite. (On the Notices Put up in Public Libraries.) 25-32, (part 1), OHAS

Bulling, Karl.
Aus der Jenaer Bibliothekarischen Tätigkeit Johann Samuel Erschs. Ein Beitrag zu Goethes Plan eines Gesamtkatalogs der Weimarischen Bibliotheken. 296-315, VORS
Zur Jenaer Tätigkeit des Weimarer Bibliothekars Christian August Vulpius während der Jahre 1802-1817. 102-116, WEIM

BULLING, KARL

BULL

Kunze, Horst. Zum Geleit. 21-22, BULL

BULLING, KARL - Bibl.

Veröffentlichungen von Prof. Dr. Karl Bulling. 9-11, BULL

Bulling, Klaus.
Zur Anlage Biographischer Schlüssel innerhalb Systematischer Kataloge. 47-62, BULL

BULLS, PAPAL - Collections - Einsiedeln

Henggeler, Rudolf. Die Mittelalterlichen Papsturkunden im Stiftsarchiv Einsiedeln. 201-225, MERC

BUMA BIBLIOTHEEK, Leeuwarden
see Leeuwarden. Buma Bibliotheek

Bundesmann, Marie, jt. author
Alschner, Christian and Marie Bundesmann. Bibliographie zur Geschichte der Sächsischen Landesbibliothek. 209-279, DREL

BUNDESVERFASSUNGSGERICHT. Germany
see Germany (Federal Republic, 1949-). Bundesverfassungsgericht

Buonanno-Schellembrid, Maria.
Di Due Recenti Acquisti della Biblioteca Nazionale Braidense di Milano. 46-56, GREG

Burauen, Theo.
[On the Deutsche Gesellschaft für Dokumentation.] 4, DEUD

Burckhardt, August.
Feststellungen und Gedanken über die Benützung des Archivs. 29-33, BASL

Burckhardt, Felix.
Marcel Godet und die Schweizerische Volksbibliothek. 24-27, GODM
Die Schweizer Bücherhilfe für das Kriegsgeschädigte Ausland. 271-277, BICK

Burgemeister, Burghard.
Der Dresdner Fachkatalog. 95-116, DREL

Burger, K., ed.
Voulliéme, Ernst. Nachträge zu den Buchhändleranzeigen des XV. Jahrhunderts in Getreuen Nachbildungen Hrsg. von K. Burger. 18-44, HAEB

BURGERBIBLIOTHEK, Bern
see Bern. Burgerbibliothek

BURGERSDIJK & NIERMANS, firm, booksellers, Leyden
Sevensma, Tietse Pieter. Der Salomons-Tempel in Leiden. 80-81, STUM

BURKE, EDMUND - Correspondence - Collections - Sheffield, Eng.
Copeland, Thomas. The Opening of the Burke Papers. 24-25, LAMB

Burke, Robert E.
History Before It Cools. 41-45, HAMM

Burnam, John M.
Un Fragment en Écriture Onciale. 135-140, CHAT

Bŭrov, D.
N. V. Mikhov. 1-4, MIKN
Trudovete na Nikola Mikhov Kato Neobkhodimi Iztochnitsi za Nauchno-izsledovatelski Raboti v Oblastta na Stopanskata Istoriia. 127-130, MIKH

Burr, Viktor, ed.
LEYV

Burr, Viktor.
Aus dem Ersten Jahr nach der Zerstörung der Universitätsbibliothek Jena (1945/46). 63-81, BULL
Buch und Bibliothek bei Plinius d. J. 94-100, LEYH
[Georg Leyh] Verzeichnis der Schriften. 7-40, LEYV

BURR, VIKTOR
BURR

BURTENBACH, SEBASTIAN SCHERTLIN VON, RITTER
see Schertlin von Burtenbach, Sebastian, Ritter

Burton, Theodore E.
Herbert Putnam. 2-3, PUTN

BURY, Boston of
see Boston, John, of Bury

BURY, RICHARD DE
see Aungerville, Richard, known as Richard de Bury, Bp. of Durham (1287-1345)

Busch, August.
Statistische Forschung in Frankfurt a.M. 161-168, EBRA

Busch, Friedrich.
Alltagssorgen, die Immer Zeitgemäss Bleiben (aus Friedrich Adolf Eberts Freundeskreis). 136-139, LEUN

Busch, Jürgen, ed.
MAIN

Busch, Jürgen, jt. ed.
SCHS

Busch, Jürgen.
Der Berliner Leihverkehr in den Jahren 1956-1958. 205-213, SCHS
Die Stadtbibliothek und Ihre Aufgaben. 9-13, MAIN

Bush, Helen E. and David Judson Haykin.
Music Subject Headings. 39-45, KINO

BUSHELL, JOHN
Bishop, Olga Bernice. The First Printing Press in Canada, 1751-1800. 129-148, GJEL

BUSINESS LITERATURE - Collections - Bergen
Munthe, Gerhard. Firma-Arkivene i Universitetsbiblioteket i Bergen. 216-231, TVET

BUSINESSMAN AND THE LIBRARY
see Public libraries - Services to business and industry

Busse, Gisela von.
Vom Rechten Bücherlesen. Gedanken zur Herder-Interpretation. 244-257, TIEM
Warum Gemeinschaftliche Erwerbungspläne? 137-150, HOFM
Zur Entstehung der Tausch- und Beschaffungsstelle für Ausländische Literatur im Jahre 1949. 83-93, HOFF

Bussels, C. M.
Over de Bibliotheek en de Kunstwerken van Charles Clement Roemers. 557-566, MAAS

BUSSEMACHER, JOHANN - Bibl.
Benzing, Josef. Der Kupferstecher, Kunstdrucker und Verleger Johann Bussemacher zu Köln (1580? bis 1616?). 129-146, JUCH

Bustamante, Ciriaco Pérez.
Un Juicio Inédito Sobre Felipe II. II, 336-349, ARTI

BUSUTTIL, SALVATORE - Collections - Rome (City)
Garinei-Canori, Costanza. La Collezione Busuttil della Biblioteca Romana Sarti. 177-182, GREG

Butenschøn, Barthold A.
Forleggeren og Biblioteket. 149-155, NORS

Butler, Pierce.
James Christian Meinich Hanson. 127-130, HANS
A Possible Field for Book Conservation. 399-403, WILS

Buttmann, Philipp.
Brief [an Biester] 1791 in Abb, Gustav. Eine Denkschrift Philipp Buttmanns über Katalogfragen vom Jahre 1791. 177-181, KUHN

Buttmann, Rudolf.
Beiträge zur Baugeschichte der Bayerischen Staatsbibliothek. 193-215, LEYG

Butzmann, Hans.
Vom Schmuck der Heidelberger Otfrid-Handschrift. 35-44, WEHM

BUYER, BARTHÉLÉMY
Rath, Erich von. Der Drucker von Buyers Ausgabe der Werke des Bartolus von 1482. Ein Beitrag zur Buchdruckergeschichte Lyons. 217-225, SCHW

BYDGOSZCZ - Awards, citations and prizes
see Awards, citations and prizes - Bydgoszcz

BYDGOSZCZ. Biblioteca Miejska
see Bydgoszcz. Municipal Library

BYDGOSZCZ - Exhibits and displays
see Exhibits and displays - Bydgoszcz

BYDGOSZCZ - Library and the public
see Library and the public - Bydgoszcz

BYDGOSZCZ - Maps - Collections
see Maps - Collections - Bydgoszcz

BYDGOSZCZ - Memorial collections and shelves
see Memorial collections and shelves - Bydgoszcz

BYDGOSZCZ. Municipal Library
BYDG

BYDGOSZCZ. Municipal Library. Bernardine Library
Sarnowska, Klara. Bibliotheca Bernardina. 69-79, BYDG

BYDGOSZCZ. Municipal Library - Bibl.
Sarnowska, Klara. Źródła i Opracowania Dotyczące Dziejów i Działalności Biblioteki Miejskiej w Bydgoszczy. 169-171, BYDG

BYDGOSZCZ. Municipal Library. Reference Division
Makowski, Jerzy. Służba Informacyjno-Bibliograficzna. 124-130, BYDG

BYDGOSZCZ - Periodicals, Polish - Collections
see Periodicals, Polish - Collections - Bydgoszcz

BYDGOSZCZ - Personnel
see Personnel - Bydgoszcz

BYDGOSZCZ - Public libraries
see Public libraries - Bydgoszcz

BYDGOSZCZ - Public libraries - Reference services
see Public libraries - Reference services - Bydgoszcz

BYDGOSZCZ - Publicity
see Publicity - Bydgoszcz

Bykowski, Lev.
L. J. Živný w Polskiem Bibljotekarstwie i Bibljografji. 18-22, ŽIVN

Byvanck, A. W.
Een Nieuwe Aanwinst van de Koninklijke Bibliotheek. 35-43, HAGU

BYZANCE
see Istanbul

BYZANTINE HYMNS
see Hymns, Greek

Cagin, Paul.
L'Observation Paléographique dans L'Étude du "Sacramentarium Triplex" de Saint-Gall. 92-112, CHAT

CAGLIARI, LUCIFER, Bp. of
see Lucifer, Bp. of Cagliari

Cain, Julien.
Bibliothécaires et Bibliographes. L'Enseignement Bibliographique en France. 151-157, HOFM
Jean Bonnerot. 15-20, BONN

CAIN, JULIEN
CAIN

CAIRO. Bibliothèque Égyptienne
see Cairo. Egyptian Library

CAIRO. Bibliothèque Khédiviale
see Cairo. Egyptian Library

CAIRO. Dār al-Kutub al-Misrīyah
see Cairo. Egyptian Library

CAIRO. Egyptian Library

Littmann, Enno. Ein Arabisches Lied über die Ägyptische Bibliothek in Kairo. 309-311, LEYG

CAIRO. Khedivial Library
see Cairo. Egyptian Library

CAIRO - Printing
see Printing - Cairo

CALENDAR, Assyro-Babylonian

König, Friedrich Wilhelm. Ein Festkalendarium aus dem Armenischen Alpenland im 9. bis 7. Jahrhundert v. Chr. 59-68, SCHT

CALENDAR - German

Schmid, Helmut H. Ein Nürnberger Kalender von 1430 and Johann Blaubirer's Kalender von 1483. 247-253, STOL

CALENDAR - Hist.

Krusch, Bruno. Das Älteste Fränkische Lehrbuch der Dionysianischen Zeitrechnung. 232-242, CHAT

CALENDAR - 1294. Mss.

Degering, Hermann. Ein Calendarium Pugillare mit Computus aus dem Jahre 1294. 79-88, LOUB

CALENDARS - Hist.

Schottenloher, Karl. Tagebuch-Aufzeichnungen in Immerwährenden Kalendern der Frühdruckzeit. II, 88-96, GLAU

CALIFORNIA - College and university libraries
see College and university libraries - California

CALIFORNIA - Mechanization of library processes
see Mechanization of library processes - California

CALIFORNIA. University, Berkeley. Bancroft Library

Becker, Robert H. A Time of Adventure. 31-39, HAMM
Camp, Charles L. Bancroft, Old and Ever New. 21-29, HAMM
Dakin, Susanna Bryant. "His Mild and Magnificent Eye." 55-61, HAMM

CALIFORNIA - University. Libraries - Hist.

Blanchard, J. R. Development and Mechanization of Libraries of the University of California. 1-7, HASH

CALISTO III
see Calixtus III, Pope, c. 1378-1458

CALIXTUS III, POPE - Library

Martorell, Francesco. Un Inventario della Biblioteca di Calisto III. 166-191, EHRE

CALL NUMBERS
see Book numbers

CALLIGRAPHY

Shigehiro, Torao. Sho Wa Geijutsu Nariya. (Is Calligraphy a Fine Art?) 116-127, (part 1), OHAS

CALLIGRAPHY - China

Kanda, Kiichiro. Chugoku no Meika no Te ni Natta Shakokubon. (Chinese Books Printed from Wood-Blocks Written by Noted Calligraphers.) 367-373, TOMI

CALLIGRAPHY - Hist.

Jacob, Alfred. La Miniscule Grecque Penchée et L'Âge du Parisinus Grec 1741. 52-56, CHAT

CALLIGRAPHY - Japan

Kanai, Toranosuke. Saikaku Okimiyage no Hanshita. (Study of the Calligraphy of the Wood-Blocks of Saikaku's Okimiyage.) 97-112, TOMI

CALLINIQUE, Nicolas La Pinte de Livry, Bp. of
see La Pinte de Livry, Nicolas, Bp. of Callinique

Calmette, Joseph.
Souvenirs de Bourgogne. 55-65, OURS

CALOT, FRANTZ

CALO

CALOT, FRANTZ - Bibl.

Le Gal, Simonne. Bibliographie des Travaux de Frantz Calot. xiii-xviii, CALO

CALVO, FRANCESCO MINIZIO, printer - Bio-Bibl.

Barberi, Francesco. Le Edizioni Romane di Francesco Minizio Calvo. 57-98, FERR

CAMBRIDGE, Eng. - Music libraries and collections
see Music libraries and collections - Cambridge, Eng.

CAMBRIDGE, Eng. University. Fitzwilliam Museum. Library

Cudworth, Charles. Richard, Viscount Fitzwilliam, and the French Baroque Music in the Fitzwilliam Museum, Cambridge. 27-31, FEDO

CAMBRIDGE, Mass. - Printing
see Printing - Cambridge, Mass.

Cameron, Donald F.
The Library Builder. 42-45, DAVI

Camino Y Aguirre, Fernando González.
Bibliotecas Medievales Montañesas. II, 14-50, ARTI

Camino Y Aguirre, Francisco González.
Nuevos Datos para la Biografía del Pintor Don José de Madrazo. II, 538-557, ARTI

Camp, Charles L.
Bancroft, Old and Ever New. 21-29, HAMM

CAMPAIGNS, Tax
see Public libraries - Finance

Campana, Augusto.
Osservazioni sullo Stampatore Nicolò Brenta da Varenna. 57-64, GREG
Per il "Textus Evangelii" Donato da Enrico II a Montecassino (Vat. Ottobon. lat. 74). 34-47, MERG

Campion, Eleanor Este.
The Union Library Catalogue. 19-24, DAVI

CANADA - Government publications
see Government publications - Canada

CANADA - Printing
see Printing - Canada

CANADA - Private libraries
see Private libraries - Canada

CANISIUS, PETRUS, SAINT. Mss.

Braunsberger, Otto, S.J. Ein Freund der Bibliotheken und Ihrer Handschriften. 455-472, EHRE

CANON LAW - Collections - Vatican

Bertolini, Ottorino. La Collezione Canonica Beneventana del Vat. lat. 4939. I, 119-137, ALBB

CAPE OF GOOD HOPE - Research libraries
see Research libraries - Cape of Good Hope

CAPETOWN. South African Public Library
see South African Public Library, Capetown

Caputo, Ada Moricca.
Frammenti dello "Speculum Perfectionis" (in un Manoscritto Casatanense). 549-558, GALL

CARACCIOLI, LUIGI ANTONIO, supposed author. L'Europe Française

Muñoz, Antonio. L'Europa Francese e il Marchese Caraccioli. 317-322, GREG

CARCANO, ANTONIO, printer - Bio-Bibl.

Leporace, Tullia Gasparrini. Notizie e Documenti Inediti sul Tipografo Antonio Carcano (1475-1525). 327-356, FERR

CARD CATALOGS
see Catalogs

CARDS

Schmidbauer, Richard. "Nachlese": Ein Unbekannter Maioliband.—Eine Spielkarte und ein Kartenspiel. 255-259, STOL

CARDS - Collections - Altenburg, Ger.

Reisig, Otto. Die Kartenrückseiten in Ihrer Bedeutung für die Zeitliche Festlegung der Spielkarten. 123-133, ALTE

CARDS - Collections - Geneva

Gagnebin, Bernard. Un Maniaque de L'Introspection Révélé par 35.000 Cartes à Jouer: Georges-Louis Le Sage. 145-157, CALO

CARE OF BOOKS
see Books - Care and restoration

Carini-Dainotti, Virginia.
Biblioteche Generali e Biblioteche Speciali nelle Discussioni Parlamentari. 117-167, FERR

CARINTHIA. Sankt Paul (Benedictine Abbey)
see Sankt Paul (Benedictine Abbey)

CARL EUGEN, DUKE OF WÜRTTEMBERG

Kyriss, Ernst. Einbände mit Hoheitszeichen Herzog Carl Eugens. 232-243, HOFF

CARL-ZEISS-STIFTUNG

Jobst, Rudolf. Einleitende Bemerkungen: Ernst Abbe, die Carl-Zeiss-Stiftung und die "Jenaer Lesehalle." 11-16, JENA

Carlquist, Gunnar.
Skåneprästen Albert Raffn och Finansieringen av Hans Bok "Den Himmelske Herredag" (1633). 42-50, DAHA

Carlsson, A. B.
Fragment av en Ordspråkssammling av Michael Agricola i Uppsala Universitetsbibliotek. 142-146, GRAP
Jonas Hallenbergs Anteckningar och Samlingar till Gustaf II Adolfs Historia i Uppsala Universitetsbibliotek. 498-525, UPPS
Rester av Michael Agricolas Boksamling i Svenska Bibliotek. 335-353, COLL
En Supplik af Gjörwell 1772. Ett Stycke Svensk Lärdomshistoria i Kanslikollegiet. 67-73, ANNE

CARLYLE, THOMAS - Collections - Yale
Hall, Emily Hardy. Carlyle, Neuberg, and Frederick the Great. 89-94, KEOG

CARMEN (Mss.) de Pascha
see De Pascha. Mss. Carmen

CARNEGIE CORPORATION OF NEW YORK
Keppel, Frederick Paul. William Warner Bishop. 1-4, BISH

CARNEGIE CORPORATION OF NEW YORK - Advisory Group on College Libraries
Bishop, William Warner. Centralized Purchasing for American College Libraries. 1-6, GODE

Carnovsky, Leon.
Preparation for the Librarian's Profession. 404-411, WILS

CAROLINA REDIVIVA
see Uppsala. Universitet. Bibliotek

CAROLSFELD, HANS SCHNORR VON
see Schnorr von Carolsfeld, Hans

Carossa, Hans.
Miniatur. 12, HELD

CARRELS - Uppsala
Lundberg, Oskar. Frågan om Forskarplatser och Forskarrum vid Uppsala Universitetsbibliotek. 59-76, GRAP

Cartault, A.
Encore les Causes de la Rélégation d'Ovide. 42-51, CHAT

Carter, Edward.
The Birth of Unesco's Library Programmes. 183-196, TVET

CARTHAGE - Inscriptions, Latin
see Inscriptions, Latin - Carthage

CARTHUSIANS - Libraries
Lehmann, Paul. Bücherliebe und Bücherpflege bei den Karthäusern. 364-389, EHRE

CARTIER, ALFRED
Donati, Lamberto. Note Inedite di Alfred Cartier su Giorgio Reverdino, Illustratore di Libri. 379-401, GALL

CARTULARIES. Mss.
Wormald, Francis. The Sherborne "Chartulary." 101-119, SAXL

CARTWRIGHT, WILLIAM
Danton, J. Periam. William Cartwright and His Comedies, Tragi-Comedies, with Other Poems .... 1651. 438-456, WILS

CARUS, FRIEDRICH AUGUST
Joachim, Johannes. Aus Briefen Christian Gottlob Heynes an Friedrich August Carus. 187-208, MILF

CASALE MONFERRATO. Seminario. Biblioteca
Guarnaschelli, Teresa. Alfonso Fernandez da Cordova e la Prima Stampa di Murcia. 125-132, ACCU

CASAMARI (Benedictine-Cistercian Abbey)
Benedetti, Luigi De. I Regesti dei Ro~~mani~~ mani Pontefici per l'Abbazia di Casamari. 325-356, GALL

CASAS, BARTOLOMÉ DE LAS. Mss. Historia de las Indias.
Hanke, Lewis. The Historia de las Indias of Bartolomé de las Casas. 143-150, WROT

Caspar, Erich.
Paläographisches zum Kanon des Eusebius. 42-56, DEGE

CASPER, MEISTER - Collections - Breslau
Molsdorf, Wilhelm. Zwei Unbekannte Holzschnitte des Formschneiders Casper in der Breslauer Staats- und Universitäts-Bibliothek. 249-254, MILF

CASSIANUS, JOANNES. Mss. Collationes
Rius i Serra, Josep. Un Full Visigòtic del Segle IX. II, 441-450, RUBI

CASSIODORUS SENATOR, Flavius Magnus Aurelius. Mss.
Milkau, Fritz. Zu Cassiodor. 23-44, KUHN

Cassuto, Umberto.
Manoscritti Ebraici della R. Biblioteca Laurenziana in Firenze. 17-23, FREN

Castella, Gaston.
Comment Fut Composée L'Histoire du Sonderbund de Crétineau-Joly (1850). 201-216, GODE

Castrén, Gunnar, jt. ed.
HIRN

CASTRÉN, GUNNAR
CAST

Castrén, Lisa.
Bibliografi över Ragnar Dahlbergs Tryckta Skrifter 1900-1947. 351-360, DAHL

CASUS SYNODALES
Müller, Max. Casus synodales. Ein Bisher Unbekannter Bamberger Incunabeldruck. 40-44, VERZ

CATALOG CARDS - Reproduction
Lund, Hanna. Der Adrema-Betrieb in der Katalogisierung. 404-409, MUNT
Predeek, Albert. Fortschritte im Katalogdruck nach dem Adrema-System. 197-210, MUNT

CATALOGERS
Horiuchi, Ikuko. Gendai no Toshokan Mokuroku to Katarogā no Kyōiku ni tsuite. (Trends of the Library Catalog and Training of Catalogers.) 229-237, HASH

CATALOGING
see also Classification; Documents - Cataloging; Foreign language books - Cataloging; Indexing; Manuscripts - Cataloging; Maps - Cataloging; Medical literature - Cataloging; Music literature and scores - Cataloging; Oriental literature - Cataloging; Public libraries - Cataloging; Religious literature - Cataloging; Subject headings; Technical services

CATALOGING
Altmann, Wilhelm. Zur Aufstellung und Katalogisierung der Bücher. 310-315, KUHN
De Gregori, Giorgio. Appunti di Tecnica Catalografica (la Scheda d'Autore per i Cataloghi di Musei e Gallerie). 215-226, FERR
Dieserud, Juul. The Abbreviation of Imprints. 179-184, HANS
Mills, J. Using Classification in Teaching Indexing. 279-286, KYLE
Pflug, Günther. Der Einfluss der Elektronischen Datenverarbeitung auf die Katalogisierungspraxis. 111-124, FUCH
Schmidt-Phiseldeck, Kay. Notes sur les Buts du Catalogage des Livres et de la Musique. 117-121, FEDO
Strout, Ruth French. An Enquiry into the Role of the Cataloger. 135-141, HASH

CATALOGING - Author entry
see also Cataloging - Corporate entry

CATALOGING - Author entry
Braun, Hellmut. Verfasser und Urheber. 41-51, FUCH

CATALOGING - Berlin - Hist.
Abb, Gustav. Eine Denkschrift Philipp Buttmanns über Katalogfragen vom Jahre 1791. 177-181, KUHN

CATALOGING - Bibl.
Avanzi, Giannetto. Gli Scritte sulla Catalogazione e Classificazione Speciale e Specializzata. 87-186, GALL

CATALOGING - Centralized
Roloff, Heinrich. Zur Theorie des Zentralkatalogs. 252-273, VORS
Semrau, Eberhard. Aufgaben und Probleme beim Aufbau eines Zentralkatalogs. 377-385, JUCH

CATALOGING - Centralized - Germany
Fleischhack, Curt. Deutsche Bücherei und Zentralkatalogisierung. 143-150, VORS

CATALOGING CODES
see Cataloging - Rules

CATALOGING, Cooperative
see also Catalogs - Union

CATALOGING, Cooperative
Tauber, Maurice F. Dr. Ranganathan and Proposals for Co-operative Cataloguing. 171-174, RANG

CATALOGING, Cooperative - U.S.
Hastings, Charles Harris. Reminiscences and Observations on the Card Distribution Work of the Library of Congress. 195-206, PUTN
Mearns, David C. Herbert Putnam and His Responsible Eye—A Memorial Tribute. 1-52, PUTP

CATALOGING - Corporate entry
Childs, James B. Corporate Author Entry as Regards the German Federal Republic. 151-162, RANG
Kaul, M. L. Cataloguer's Puzzle: Corporate Authorship. 147-150, RANG
Pierson, Harriet Wheeler. The Forest of Pencils. 306-313, HANS

CATALOGING - Cost and economies
see Technical services - Cost and economies

CATALOGING - Czechoslovakia
Smetana, Robert and Bedřich Václavek. Jak Katalogisovati Kramářské Písně. 137-143, EMLE

CATALOGING - Folk-songs, Czechoslovakian
see Folk-songs, Czechoslovakian - Cataloging

CATALOGING - Hist.
see also Catalogs - Hist.

CATALOGING - Hist. - 16th cent.
Escher, Hermann. Konrad Gessner über Aufstellung und Katalogisierung von Bibliotheken. 119-127, GODE
Also appears in: 163-168, ESCH

CATALOGING - Hungarian literature
see Hungarian literature - Cataloging

CATALOGING - Japan
Hattori, Kintaro. Cataloguing in the Prefectural Libraries and Five City Libraries. 190-201, RANG
Kato, Shuko. Cataloguing and Classification. 209-214, RANG

Nakamura, Hatsuo. Problems in Search of Common Basis in Cataloguing. 181-189, RANG
Suzuka, Osamu. Kinyū ni okeru Hompō Kosho no Toriatsukai ni tsuite. (A Guide for Cataloging Old Japanese Books.) 115-130, KYOT

CATALOGING - Japanese literature
see Japanese literature - Cataloging

CATALOGING - Medical literature
see Medical literature - Cataloging

CATALOGING - Museum publications
see Museum publications - Cataloging

CATALOGING - Music literature and scores
see Music literature and scores - Cataloging

CATALOGING - Music literature and scores scores - Manuscripts
see Music literature and scores - Manuscripts - Cataloging

CATALOGING - Recataloging - Washington, D.C.
Hanson, James Christian Meinich. The Library of Congress and Its New Catalogue: Some Unwritten History. 178-194, PUTN

CATALOGING - Religious literature
see Religious literature - Cataloging

CATALOGING - Rules
Bishop, William Warner. J. C. M. Hanson and International Cataloging. 165-168, HANS
Braun, Hellmut. Verfasser und Urheber. 41-51, FUCH
Coblans, Herbert. A Note on Cataloguing at the International Level. 197-202, TVET
Frauendorfer, Sigmund v. Internationale Einheitskatalogisierung? Hemmnisse und Möglichkeiten. 335-347, BICK
Goyal, R. S. Library Catalogue. 64-67, MADR
Schmidt-Phiseldeck, Kay. Notes sur les Buts du Catalogage des Livres et de la Musique. 117-121, FEDO
Tyaganatarajan, T. Universal Cataloguing Code: Ifla's Initiative. 141-146, RANG
Whitrow, Magda. Some Aspects of Descriptive Cataloguing in International Bibliography. 291-295, KYLE

CATALOGING - Rules - Europe
Escher, Hermann. Die Stellung der Schweizerischen Bibliotheken zur Frage einer Einheitlichen Regelung der Katalogisierung (1912). 33-44, ESCH

CATALOGING - Simplified - Japan
Mori, Koichi T. Simplified Practice of Cataloguing. 202-208, RANG

CATALOGING - Teaching
Horiuchi, Ikuko. Gendai no Toshokan Mokuroku to Katarogā no Kyōiku ni tsuite. (Trends of the Library Catalog and Training of Catalogers.) 229-237, HASH
Sickmann, Ludwig. Der Katalogisierungsunterricht für Anfänger. Bericht über Erfahrungen im Bibliothekar-Lehrinstitut. 448-457, JUCH

CATALOGS
see also Private libraries - Catalogs

CATALOGS
Battisti, Carlo. Registro d'Ingresso e Inventario Topografico. 56-80, GORI
Binz, Gustav. Ein Bisher Unbekannter Katalog der Bibliothek des Klosters Fulda. 97-108, GODE
Boese, Helmut. Ein Mittelalterliches Bücherverzeichnis von Croyland Abbey. 286-295, VORS
Degering, Hermann. Der Katalog der Bibliothek des Klosters Marienfeld vom Jahre 1185. 53-64, SCHW
Horiuchi, Ikuko. Gendai no Toshokan Mokuroku to Katarogā no Kyōiku ni tsuite. (Trends of the Library Catalog and Training of Catalogers.) 229-237, HASH
Meyer, Hermann H. B. Cards and Common Sense. 351-355, PUTN
Molitor, Karl. Ein Westfälischer Bi-

bliotheks-Katalog von 1353. 301-314, MÜNS
Reichardt, Günther. Die Bedeutung der Annotation für Bibliographie und Katalog. 86-109, VORS
Schawe, Josef. D. Steuberi Catalogi und Nachrichten von der Marpurger und Giesser Bibliothec. Giessener Hs. 30. 204-214, JUCH
Schmidt, Franz Paul. Der Katalog der Klosterbibliothek Nienburg a.S. 31-79, ALTE

CATALOGS - Aarhus, Denmark

Stensgård, Erling. Katalogiseringen. 95-114, AARU

CATALOGS - Ann Arbor, Mich. - Hist.

Bidlack, Russell E. The Early Handling of Books at the University of Michigan. 149-164, GJEL

CATALOGS - Author

Mullerott, Martin. Author-Title Catalogue as a Sequence of Quasi-Classes and Its Legitimate Subject Functions. 239-242, RANG

CATALOGS - Author - Berlin

Kaiser, Rudolf. Der Alphabetische Zettelkatalog. 99-109, HARN

CATALOGS - Author - Kutná Hora, Czechoslovakia (1850)

Siegl, Jaromír. Seznam Knih Městské Knihovny Kutnohorské z r. 1850. 199-207, ŽIVN

CATALOGS - Author - Leipzig

Ruppert, Hans. Der Alphabetische Katalog. 91-102, LEIS

CATALOGS - Author - Vienna

Stummvoll, Josef. Die Druckschriftenbestände der Österreichischen Nationalbibliothek und die Abschreibung des Alphabetischen Kataloges 1501 bis 1929. 105-118, HOFM

CATALOGS - Berlin

Auster, Guido. Die Orientalische Abteilung. I, 275-317, BERS
Fick, Richard. Die Kataloge der Druckschriftenabteilung. 92-99, HARN
Lülfing, Hans. Die Handschriftenabteilung. I, 319-380, BERS
Meyer, Hanna. Die Kinder- und Jugendbuchabteilung. I, 433-441, BERS
Weser, Adolf. Erschliessung der Bestände durch Kataloge und Bibliographien. 22-27, BERR

CATALOGS - Berlin - Hist.

Roloff, Heinrich. Aufstellung und Katalogisierung der Bestände. I, 131-174, BERS

CATALOGS - Bern

Wissler, Gustav. Die Kataloge. 133-139, BERU
——— Marcel Godet als Direktor der Schweizerischen Landesbibliothek. 8-12, GODM

CATALOGS, Booksellers'
see Booksellers' catalogs

CATALOGS - Classed

Beck, Helmut. Das Schlagwortregister zum Systematischen Katalog. 23-42, BULL
Boysen, Karl. Systematischer oder Schlagwortkatalog? 19-36, MILF
Bulling, Klaus. Zur Anlage Biographischer Schlüssel innerhalb Systematischer Kataloge. 47-62, BULL
Fischer, Klaus. Freiheit und Bindung in Geisteswissenschaftlichen Teilen von Realkatalogen. Beobachtungen Ausländischer Bibliotheksbenutzer in Pakistan und Indien. 21-41, JUCR
Fock, Johannes. "Katalog der Wissenschaften" und "Katalog der Sachen." 93-109, TIEM
Focke, Rudolf. Allgemeine Theorie der Klassifikation und Kurzer Entwurf einer Instruktion für den Realkatalog. 5-18, VERP
Garde, R. K. Ranganathan's Contribution to Subject Cataloguing. 217-221, RANG
Mogk, Helmut. Die Abfolge der Ortsbegriffe in Systematischen Katalogen. I, 150-159, GLAU
——— System und Schlagwort. Erfahrungen am Fachkatalog der Universitätsbibliothek Leipzig. 214-224, VORS
Parkhi, G. R. Symbiosis between Classification and Catalogue. 222-227, RANG
Passi, N. N. Subject Indexing and Dr. Ranganathan. 228-238, RANG
Rasmussen, Detlef. Andreas Schleiermacher und das Prinzip der Schlüsselung. 163-175, REDE

CATALOGS - Classed - Aarhus, Denmark

Bendtsen, F. M. Systematisering. Trykte Kataloger. 114-122, AARU

CATALOGS - Classed - Berlin

Pfennig, Richard. Unser Realkatalog. 109-113, HARN
Schultze, Walther. Die Zukunft Unserer Realkataloge. 224-237, KUHN

CATALOGS - Classed - Dresden

Burgemeister, Burghard. Der Dresdner Fachkatalog. 95-116, DREL

CATALOGS - Classed - Erlangen

Stählin, Agnes. Zur Geschichte der Systematischen Kataloge der Univeristätsbibliothek Erlangen. 137-147, REDE

CATALOGS - Classed - Germany

Fick, Richard. Gesamt-Realkataloge. 95-110, MILF

CATALOGS - Classed - Hist.

Meyer, Adolf. Realkataloge in Geistesgeschichtlicher Beleuchtung. I, 145-149, GLAU

CATALOGS - Classed - Leeuwarden

Douma, S. Over een Systematisch Trefwoordenregister. 408-413, BRUM

CATALOGS - Classed - Posen

Schultheiss, Fr. G. Zur Fortbildung des Halleschen Schemas. 43-56, VERP

Wenzel, B. Die Abteilung Bücherkunde im Realkatalog der Kaiser-Wilhelm-Bibliothek. 19-42, VERP

CATALOGS - Classed - Utrecht

Gras, Elisabeth J. De Systematische Catalogus der Utrechtse Universiteitsbibliotheek. 107-115, EVER

Grolman, Hermina C. A. Hoe de Centrale Systematische Catalogus aan het Volkenkundig Instituut te Utrecht tot Stand Kwam. 116-122, EVER

CATALOGS - Copenhagen

Drachmann, A. G. Call Numbers. 198-206, HANS

Prytz, Johansen J. Den Gamle Medicinske Katalog på Universitetsbiblioteket, København. 1-7, DAHA

CATALOGS - Danzig - 1443

Ziesemer, Walther. Zur Kenntnis des Bibliothekswesens Preussens im 15. Jahrhundert. 393-400, KÖNI

CATALOGS - Danzig - 16th cent.

Schwarz, F. Analyse eines Kataloges. 326-338, KÖNI

CATALOGS - Dictionary

Fuchs, Hermann. Der Alphabetische Katalog und Seine Leute. 84-92, TIEM

Neubert, Hermann. Alphabetischer Katalog—Formalkatalog? 126-132, BOLL

Schwidetzky, Georg. Die Unpersönlichen Drucksachen im Alphabetischen Katalog. 123-133, MIND

CATALOGS - Dictionary - London

Predeek, Albert. Antonio Panizzi und der Alphabetische Katalog des Britischen Museums. 257-282, LEYG

CATALOGS - Dresden

Assmann, Karl. Die Sächsische Landesbibliothek von 1945 bis 1955. Zerstörung, Wiederaufbau und Gegenwärtiger Stand der Arbeit. 29-85, DREL

Bollert, Martin. Johann Joachim Winckelmann als Bibliothekar des Grafen Bünau. 19-24, LEID

CATALOGS - Germany

Altmann, Wilhelm. Zur Aufstellung und Katalogisierung der Bücher. 310-315, KUHN

Bauhuis, Walter. Warnung vor Publikumskatalogen. 386-392, JUCH

Schriewer, F. Die Zentralbücherei als Büchereityp. 103-111, ACKE

CATALOGS - Gorizia (City)

Battisti, Carlo. Il Centenario della Biblioteca Governativa di Gorizia. 9-24, GORI

CATALOGS - Gothenburg, Sweden

Hallberg, S. and O. von Feilitzen. Göteborgs Stadsbibliotek. Det Första Halvseklet 1891-1940. 1-142, (first paper), GÖTE

CATALOGS - Hist.
see also Cataloging - Hist.

CATALOGS - Hist.

Leyh, Georg. Aus der Älteren Bibliothekspraxis. 159-174, SCHW

CATALOGS - Hist. - Early

Binz, Gustav. Ein Bisher Unbekannter Katalog der Bibliothek des Klosters Fulda. 97-108, GODE

Mercati, Giovanni, Cardinal. I. Uno Scambio Strano di Qualche Interesse per Tre Grandi Biblioteche. II. Amici Innominati del Savile in Roma? 17-26, FERR

CATALOGS - Hist. - Middle Ages

De Ghellinck, Joseph. En Marge des Catalogues des Bibliothèques Médiévales. 331-363, EHRE

CATALOGS - Japan

Yayoshi, Mitsunaga. Kokusho Mokuroku ni okeru Bunrui Shisō no Hattatsu. (Progress of the Idea of Classification in the Catalogues of Japanese Books.) 66-83, OTAT

CATALOGS - Lucca - 1447

Corsi, Domenico. La Biblioteca dei Frati Domenicani di S. Romano di Lucca nel Sec. XV. 295-310, GALL

CATALOGS - Mainz

Nissen, Claus. Die Kataloge der Stadtbibliothek. Geschichte und Überblick. 39-46, MAIN

CATALOGS - Marienfeld - 1185

Degering, Hermann. Der Katalog der Bibliothek des Klosters Marienfeld vom Jahre 1185. 53-64, SCHW

CATALOGS - Münster

Bahlmann, P. Die Königliche Universitäts-Bibliothek zu Münster. 1-56, MÜNS

CATALOGS - Munich

Ruf, Paul. Schmeller als Bibliothekar. 9-95, GRAT

CATALOGS - New Haven, Conn.

Monrad, Anna Marie, et al. Historical Notes on the Catalogues and Classifications of the Yale University Library. 251-284, KEOG

CATALOGS - Nienburg a. Saale (Benedictine Abbey) - 1473

Schmidt, Franz Paul. Der Katalog der Klosterbibliothek Nienburg a.S. 31-79, ALTE

CATALOGS - Nuremberg - Hist.

Bock, Friedrich. Aus der Geschichte der Nürnberger Stadtbibliothek. 9-15, VERZ

CATALOGS - Printed book - Aarhus, Denmark

Bendtsen, F. M. Systematisering. Trykte Kataloger. 114-122, AARU

CATALOGS - Printed Book - Bern

Wissler, Gustav. Das Systematische Verzeichnis. 148-149, BERU

CATALOGS - Printed book - China

Suzuki, Ryūchi. Ryūkō Fushi no Gakujutsu Mokuroku. (On the First Chinese Book Catalog by Ryūkō [father and son].) 104-114, KYOT

CATALOGS - Printed Book - Japan

Nishimura, Suteya. Shina Chihoshi Mokuroku Groshu to Hōshi Henmoku no Jūyosei. (On the Importance of Catalogues of the Books on Local History of China, with Special Reference to Five of Them Recently Published.) 46-53, OTAT

CATALOGS - Printed book - Jena

Gemmel, Ursula. Druckkataloge der Ernst-Abbe-Bücherei und Lesehalle. 140-143, JENA

CATALOGS - Printed book - Karlsruhe

Längin, Theodor. Fünfundfünfzig Jahre Katalogdruck. 145-156, LEID

CATALOGS - Printed book - U.S. - Hist.

Shera, Jesse H. The Beginnings of Systematic Bibliography in America, 1642-1799. 263-278, WROT

CATALOGS - Printed book - Washington, D.C.

Dewton, Johannes L. Die Kataloge der Kongressbibliothek in Buchform. 27-28, STUM

CATALOGS - Rome (City) - 1440

Bååth, L. M. L'Inventaire de la Chambre Apostolique de 1440. 135-157, MERC

CATALOGS - Rome (City) - 15th cent.

Meersseman, G. La Bibliothèque des Frères Prêcheurs de la Minerve à la Fin du XVe Siècle. 605-634, PELZ

CATALOGS - Subject

Beck, Helmut. Das Schlagwortregister zum Systematischen Katalog. 23-42, BULL
Boysen, Karl. Systematischer oder Schlagwortkatalog? 19-36, MILF
Fischer, Klaus. Freiheit und Bindung in Geisteswissenschaftlichen Teilen von Realkatalogen. Beobachtungen Ausländischer Bibliotheksbenutzer in Pakistan und Indien. 21-41, JUCR
Fischer, Walther. Zum Thema "Sachkataloge." 41-45, BOLE
Fock, Johannes. "Katalog der Wissenschaften" und "Katalog der Sachen." 93-109, TIEM
Focke, Rudolf. Allgemeine Theorie der Klassifikation und Kurzer Entwurf einer Instruktion für den Realkatalog. 5-18, VERP
Merrill, William Stetson. Order of Books by Date under Subjects. 282-284, HANS
Meyer-Abich, Adolf. Bibliotheken als Forschungsinstitute für Wissenschaftsgeschichte. 77-83, TIEM
Mogk, Helmut. System und Schlagwort. Erfahrungen am Fachkatalog der Universitätsbibliothek Leipzig. 214-224, VORS
Neubert, Hermann. Alphabetischer

Katalog—Formalkatalog? 126-132, BOLL
Ruckert, Ernest. An Intermediate Form of Catalogue between the Classified and Subject Catalogue. 243-247, RANG
Skwarnicka, Zofia. Jak Przygotować i Przeprowadzić Omówienie Nowości Pedagogicznych. 67-72, KRAK

CATALOGS - Subject - Aarhus, Denmark

Bendtsen, F. M. Systematisering. Trykte Kataloger. 114-122, AARU

CATALOGS - Subject - Berlin

Below, Erich. Das Schlagwortregister zum Fachkatalog. 113-119, HARN
Pfennig, Richard. Unser Realkatalog. 109-113, HARN
Schultze, Walther. Die Zukunft Unserer Realkataloge. 224-237, KUHN
Weser, Adolf. Erschliessung der Bestände durch Kataloge und Bibliographien. 22-27, BERR

CATALOGS - Subject - Bern

Wissler, Gustav. Der Sachkatalog. 139-143, BERU

CATALOGS - Subject - Dresden

Boden, Charlotte. Der Biographische Katalog und das Personalrepertorium der Sächsischen Landesbibliothek. 21-37, BOLL
Trepte, Heinz. Die Richtlinien für den Schlagwortkatalog der Sächsischen Landesbibliothek. 117-135, DREL

CATALOGS - Subject - Frankfurt a.M.

Lohse, Hartwig. Zum Aufbau eines Neuen Sachkatalogs nach dem "System Eppelsheimer" an der Senckenbergischen Bibliothek unter Besonderer Berücksichtigung der Medizin. 102-110, FUCH

CATALOGS - Subject - Germany

Fick, Richard. Gesamt-Realkataloge. 95-110, MILF
Stählin, Agnes. Kleine Sprachlehre des Schlagwortkatalogs. 333-345, STOL

CATALOGS - Subject - Hist.

Bock, Friedrich. Splitter zur Älteren Geschichte des Schlagwortkatalogs. 27-30, STOL
Meyer, Adolf. Realkataloge in Geistesgeschichtlicher Beleuchtung. I, 145-149, GLAU

CATALOGS - Subject - Jena

Gemmel, Ursula. Druckkataloge der Ernst-Abbe-Bücherei und Lesehalle. 140-143, JENA

CATALOGS - Subject - Kiel

Seyffert, Hans. Über den Schlagwortkatalog der Universitätsbibliothek Kiel. 129-139, JUCR

CATALOGS - Subject - Kraków

Skwarnicka, Zofia. Jak Przygotować i Przeprowadzić Omowienie Nowości Pedagogicznych. 67-72, KRAK
———— Katalog Rzeczowy: Metodyka i Wykorzystanie. 56-61, KRAK

CATALOGS - Subject - Leeuwarden

Douma, S. Over een Systematisch Trefwoordenregister. 408-413, BRUM

CATALOGS - Subject - Leipzig

Luther, Arthur. Der Sachkatalog. 103-119, LEIS
Rückert, Ernst and Rudi Franz. Geschichte, Problematik und Gegenwärtiger Stand des Gruppenschlagwortkatalogs der Deutschen Bücherei. 175-196, LEIZ

CATALOGS - Subject - Posen

Wenzel, B. Die Abteilung Bücherkunde im Realkatalog der Kaiser-Wilhelm-Bibliothek. 19-42, VERP

CATALOGS - Subject - Utrecht

Snoek, Johs. De Trefwoordencatalogus van de Bibliotheek der Psychiatrisch-Neurologische Kliniek. 261-277, EVER

CATALOGS - Subject - Vatican

Fraschetti-Santinelli, Italia. L'Ordinamento della Voce "Roma" nel Catalogo per Soggetti. 151-163, GREG

CATALOGS - Subject - Vienna

Alker, Hugo. Geschichte der Sachkatalogisierung an der Universitätsbibliothek Wien 1774-1954. 118-132, VORS

CATALOGS - Subject - Zürich

Escher, Hermann. Der Schlagwortkatalog der Stadtbibliothek Zürich (1890-1897). 59-70, ESCH

CATALOGS - Union
see also Incunabula - Union catalogs; under names of cities

CATALOGS - Union

Bourgeois, Pierre. Zweck und Aufbau der Gesamtkataloge. 16-17, STUM
Escher, Hermann. Die Stellung der Schweizerischen Bibliotheken zur Frage einer Einheitlichen Regelung

der Katalogisierung (1912). 33-44, ESCH
Hellmér, Sven-Ola. Samkatalogen i Ny Gestalt. Ett Förslag. 109-115, HEIN
Roloff, Heinrich. Zur Theorie des Zentralkatalogs. 252-273, VORS
Semrau, Eberhard. Aufgaben und Probleme beim Aufbau eines Zentralkatalogs. 377-385, JUCH
Zunker, Ernst. Die Bedeutung Regionaler Zentralkataloge für das Erfassungsgebiet. 151-164. HOFF

CATALOGS - Union - Baden-Württemberg

Zunker, Ernst. Die Bedeutung Regionaler Zentralkataloge für das Erfassungsgebiet. 151-164, HOFF

CATALOGS - Union - Bavaria

Hofmann, Gustav. Der Bayerische Zentralkatalog in München. 473-477, BRUM
Middendorf, Heinrich. Die Bayerische Staatsbibliothek 1945-1964. 7-61, HOFM

CATALOGS - Union - Berlin

Lullies, Hildegard. Der Berliner Gesamtkatalog. 131-157, SCHS

CATALOGS - Union - Germany

Fick, Richard. Gesamt-Realkataloge. 95-110, MILF
Fuchs, Hermann. Aus den Anfängen des Preussischen Gesamtkatalogs. 355-362, JUCH
——— Der Gesamtkatalog der Preußischen Bibliotheken und Sein Ausbau zu einem Deutschen Gesamtkatalog. 209-216, KUHN
Gittig, Heinz. Das Auskunftsbüro der Deutschen Bibliotheken. I, 223-240, BERS
Haebler, Konrad. Der Gesamtkatalog der Wiegendrucke. 278-284, HARN
Iwand, Käthe. Der Zentralkatalog der Ausländischen Literatur. 369-376, JUCH
Weber, Christoph. Der Gesamtkatalog der Preussischen Wissenschaftlichen Bibliotheken. 259-272, HARN

CATALOGS - Union - Germany - Hist.

Fick, Richard. Karl Boysen und Seine Stellung zum Gesamtkatalogproblem. I, 36-42, GLAU
Lehmann, Paul. Alte Vorläufer des Gesamtkatalogs. 69-81, LEYG

CATALOGS - Union - Hesse

Köttelwesch, Clemens. Vom Frankfurter Sammelkatalog zum Hessischen Zentralkatalog. 92-101, FUCH

CATALOGS - Union - Netherlands

Soeters, P. C. Hoe de Nederlandse Centrale Catalogus Begon. 590-593, BRUM

CATALOGS - Union - North Rhine-Westphalia

Iwand, Käthe. Der Zentralkatalog der Ausländischen Literatur. 369-376, JUCH

CATALOGS - Union - Philadelphia

Campion, Eleanor Este. The Union Library Catalogue. 19-24, DAVI

CATALOGS - Union - Saxony, Lower

Kiefert, Hans-Joachim. Der Niedersächsische Zentralkatalog 1956-1966. 82-91, FUCH

CATALOGS - Union - Switzerland

Escher, Hermann. Ein Schweizerisches Gesamtzuwachsverzeichnis (1926). 45-58, ESCH
Grosser, Hermann. Der Gesamtkatalog der Schweizerischen Bibliotheken. 157-162, BERU
——— Marcel Godet und der Schweizerische Gesamtkatalog. 16-19, GODM
——— Die Zusammenarbeit der Schweizerischen Bibliotheken. Rückblick und Ausschau. 129-142, SCHU
Schwarber, Karl. Marcel Godet und die Vereinigung Schweizerischer Bibliothekare. 3-8, GODM

CATALOGS - Union - Thuringia

Pomassl, Gerhard. Zehn Jahre Thüringer Zentralkatalog. 87-102, BULL

CATALOGS - Union - Weimar

Bulling, Karl. Aus der Jenaer Bibliothekarischen Tätigkeit Johann Samuel Erschs. Ein Beitrag zu Goethes Plan eines Gesamtkatalogs der Weimarischen Bibliotheken. 296-315, VORS

CATALOGS - Use studies
see Use studies - Catalogs

CATALOGS - Vienna

Doublier, Othmar. Ein Vierteljahrhundert aus der Geschichte der Hofbibliothek 1891-1916. 163-210, VIEN
Stummvoll, Josef. Die Abschreibung des Alphabetischen Kataloges der Österreichischen Nationalbibliothek. 594-600, BRUM
Stummvoll, Josef and Laurenz Strebl. Copying of the Old Catalogue of the Austrian National Library. 175-178, RANG

CATALOGS - Washington, D.C.

Hanson, James Christian Meinich. The Library of Congress and Its New Catalogue: Some Unwritten History. 178-194, PUTN

CATALOGS - Weimar

Blumenthal, Hermann. Älteste Verwaltungsgeschichte der Landesbibliothek Weimar (1691-1750). 46-86, WEIM

CATALOGS - (Wolgast)-Greifswald

Deutsch, Josef. Ebers Calendarium Historicum mit Handschriftlichen Eintragungen aus Wolgast. 71-78, KUHN

CATALOGS - Zürich

Wyss, W. von. Erinnerungen an Alte Zeiten auf der Stadtbibliothek Zürich. 1-7, ESCK

CATALONIA - Manuscripts, Hebrew
see Manuscripts, Hebrew - Catalonia

CATCHWORD CATALOGS
see Catalogs - Subject

Cate, Chester March.
The First California Laws Printed in English. 331-336, EAME

CATHOLIC CHURCH. Camera Apostolica - Catalogs - 1440

Bååth, L. M. L'Inventaire de la Chambre Apostolique de 1440. 135-157, MERC

CATHOLIC CHURCH - Hist. - Collections - Einsiedeln

Henggeler, Rudolf. Die Mittelalterlichen Papsturkunden im Stiftsarchiv Einsiedeln. 201-225, MERC

CATHOLIC LIBRARIES
see also Church libraries

CATHOLIC LIBRARIES - Hist. - Collections - Mainz

Wermter, Ernst Manfred. Studien und Quellen zur Geschichte der Jesuitenbibliotheken in Mainz 1561-1773. 51-70, MAIN

CATHOLIC LIBRARIES - Ivrea, Italy

Borghezio, Gino. Inventarii e Notizie della Biblioteca Capitolare d'Ivrea nel Secolo XV. 423-454, EHRE

CATHOLIC LIBRARIES - Latin America - Hist. - 16th-19th cent.

Thompson, Lawrence S. The Libraries of Colonial Spanish America. 257-266, WEHM

CATHOLIC LIBRARIES - Sweden

Collijn, Isak Gustav Alfred. Bibliotheca "Collegii Societatis Jesu in Suetia." Några Bidrag till Kännedomen om Jesuiternas Boksamling på Gråmunkeholmen. 75-91, ANNE

CATHOLIC LITERATURE - Collections - Mainz

Wermter, Ernst Manfred. Studien und Quellen zur Geschichte der Jesuitenbibliotheken in Mainz 1561-1773. 51-70, MAIN

CATHOLIC UNIVERSITY OF AMERICA. Library. Albani Collection

Peebles, Bernard M. The _Bibliotheca Albana Urbinas_ as Represented in the Library of the Catholic University of America. 327-352, ALBA

Witty, Francis J. Four Music Books at Washington from the Pontificate of Benedict XIII. 517-[533], ALBA

CATHOLICON

Geldner, Ferdinand. Das "Catholicon" des Johannes Balbus im Ältesten Buchdruck. 90-98, JUCH

———— Der Verkaufspreis des Günther Zainer'schen Catholicon von 1469 (GW 3183). 37-42, STOL

CATHOLICON - Mainz, 1460

Bömer, Aloys. Die Schlußschrift des Mainzer Catholicon-Druckes von 1460. 51-55, KUHN

CATLIN, GEORGE - Collections - Yale

Brown, Ruth. George Catlin's Portraits of North American Indians. 157-162, KEOG

CATTANIO, NOVELLO. _Mss. Un Viaggio Fatto alli Paesi del Continente Nuovo._

Bühler, Curt F. Novello Cattanio: _Un Viaggio Fatto alli Paesi del Continente Nuovo._ 85-99, WROT

Cecchini, Giovanni.
La Quattrocentesca Biblioteca del Convento di S. Domenico di Perugia. 249-254, GALL

CECCO D'ASCOLI. _Mss. L'Acerba_

Buonanno-Schellembrid, Maria. Di Due Recenti Acquisti della Biblioteca Nazionale Braidense di Milano. 46-56, GREG

CELLE, Ger. - Church libraries
see Church libraries - Celle, Ger.

CELLE, Ger. Kirchen-Ministerial-Bibliothek - Hist.

Fick, Richard. Der Ankauf der Celler

Kirchenministerialbibliothek durch den Preussischen Staat. 149-158, LEYG

Cenci, Pio.
L'Archivio della Cancelleria della Nunziatura Veneta. 273-330, EHRE

CENSORSHIP
see also Prohibited books and publications; Propaganda and the library

CENSORSHIP - Heidelberg - Hist.
Dyroff, Hans-Dieter. Die Bücherzensur der Universität Heidelberg 1652-1693. 98-119, BENZ

CENSORSHIP - Hist.
Schottenloher, Karl. Buchdrucker und Buchführer im Kampf der Schwärmer und Wiedertäufer, 1524-1568. 90-113, BOCK

CENSORSHIP - Norway - Hist.
Sollied, P. R. Relationer fra Christiania, Bergen og Trondhjem om Smaae Piecers Censur. 91-105, OSLN

CENSORSHIP - Nuremberg
Jegel, August. Altnürnberger Zensur, vor Allem des 16. Jahrhunderts. 55-64, STOL

CENSORSHIP - Russia - Hist. - 19th cent.
Poliakov, A. S. Epizod iz Istorii Goneniia na Knigu. 306-345, MALE

EL CENTENARIO de Menéndez Pelayo en la Prensa Española.
285-322, MENE

CENTRAL CATALOGS
see Catalogs - Union

CENTRAL EUROPE - Incunabula
see Incunabula - Central Europe

CENTRAL EUROPE - Printing
see Printing - Central Europe

CENTRALIZATION - Libraries
see Public libraries - Centralization

CENTRALIZED CATALOGING
see Cataloging, Centralized

CENTRALNA BIBLIOTEKA NAUCZYCIELSKA KOSK, Kraków
see Kraków. Pedagogical Library

CERIANI, ANTONIO MARIA
CERI
Ratti, Achille. Reliquie di Antico Codice Bobbieso Ritrovate. 789-810, CERI

Černá, Marie L.
Emlerovo Působení v Bratislavě. 50-59, EMLE

CERTIFICATION OF LIBRARIANS - Gt. Brit.
Minto, John. The Library Association Examinations. 285-295, HANS

Cerulli, Enrico.
Gli Atti di Zēnā Mārqos, Monaco Etiope del Sec. XIV. I, 191-212, ALBB

CERVINI DEGLI SPANNOCHI, Marcello
see Marcellus II, Pope

CERVINI, MARCELLO
see Marcellus II, Pope

CESNA. Biblioteca Malatestiana. Mss. (Cod. gr. Caecen. lat. dextr. plut. XXVIII, 2 et 3)
Schöne, Hermann. Palimpsestblätter des Protevangelium Jacobi in Cesena. 263-276, BÖME

ČESKÁ SKALICE. Městská Školní Knihovna
see Česká Skalice. Municipal School Library

ČESKÁ SKALICE. Municipal School Library
Krtička, Jan. Josef Arnošt Kolisko. 208-212, ŽIVN

Ceva Valla, Elena.
Nota su Alcuni Incunaboli Posseduti dalla Biblioteca Braidense di Milano. 51-59, ACCU

CHABEUF, HENRI
Drouot, Henri. Un Familier de la Bibliothèque: Henri Chabeuf. 92-105, OURS

Chacón Y Calvo, José María.
El Consejo de Indias y la Historia de América. II, 285-324, ARTI

CHAIN INDEXING
see Indexing - Systems

Chand, Gian.
Implications of the Five Laws of Library Science, 326-330, RANG

Chandrasekharan, K., ed.
MADR

Chandrasekharan, K.
Ranganathan as I Know Him. 711-714, RANG

CHANTILLY. Musée Condé. Bibliothèque. Mss. (1688)
Sturel, René. A Propos d'un Manuscrit du Musée Condé, 575-583, CHAT

Chapin, Howard Millar.
Ann Franklin of Newport, Printer, 1736-1763. 337-344, EAME

CHARGING SYSTEMS
see Circulation procedures

Charpentier, Jarl.
Die Hāthigumphā-Inschrift des Khāravea. 208-230, KARA

Chatelain, Émile.
Notes Tironiennes d'un Manuscrit de Genève. 81-86, HAVE
Recherches sur un Manuscrit Célèbre de Sidoine Apollinaire. 321-327, GRAU

CHATELAIN, ÉMILE
CHAT

Chaume, Maurice.
Quelques Souvenirs. 66-77, OURS

CHEAP REPRINTS
see Inexpensive editions

Cheney, Frances Neel.
Reference Service in English and American Literature. 41-47, HASH

Chevrier, Georges.
La Littérature Juridique Bourguignonne et les Collections Manuscrites de la Bibliothèque Publique de Dijon. 78-86, OURS

Chew, Samuel C.
Spenser's Pageant of the Seven Deadly Sins. 37-54, GREE

Chiavacci, V.
Ein Fossiler Bibliophage. Aus einem Vortrage, Gehalten in der Akademie der Wissenschaften im Jahre 10.000 nach Christi Geburt. 400-403, GLOS

CHICAGO. Newberry Library
see Newberry Library, Chicago

CHICAGO REGION - Book collecting
see Book collecting - Chicago region

CHICAGO. University. Graduate Library School
Randall, William M. Louis R. Wilson and the Graduate Library School. 645-650, WILS
Roden, Carl B. An Essay in Retrospection. 659-665, WILS

CHICAGO. University. Graduate Library School - Hist.
Howe, Harriet E. Two Decades in Education for Librarianship. 557-570, WILS

CHICAGO - University. Library
Dorf, A. Th. The University of Chicago Libraries. 185-197, HANS

CHICAGO - University. Library - Hist.
Hanson, James Christian Meinich. Organization and Reorganization of Libraries. 519-532, WILS

CHILDREN'S LIBRARIANS
Cory, John Mackenzie. The Relative Theory of Specialization. 611-617, MOOR

CHILDREN'S LIBRARIANS - Education - U.S. - Hist.
Nesbitt, Elizabeth. Training of Children's Librarians—History and Implications. 605-610, MOOR

CHILDREN'S LIBRARY SERVICES
see also Public libraries - Services to schools; School and public library relationship; School libraries; Story hour and story telling; Young adults' library services

CHILDREN'S LIBRARY SERVICES - Berlin
Krimmer, Therese. Schattentheater. 93-98, SCHS
Meyer, Hanna. Die Kinder- und Jugendbuchabteilung. I, 433-441, BERS

CHILDREN'S LIBRARY SERVICES - Denmark
Plovgaard, Sven. Børnebiblioteksarbejdet. 65-86, LASS
Sørensen, Eleonora. Børne- og Skolebiblioteksarbejde. 94-104, DØSS
Thomsen, Carl. Die Zusammenarbeit zwischen Kinderbüchereien und Schülerbüchereien in Dänemark. 61-66, ACKR

CHILDREN'S LIBRARY SERVICES - Germany
LANJ
Jahrmann, Werner. Bücherei und Schule. Gedanken zur Jugendbüchereiarbeit. 215-231, SCHS

CHILDREN'S LIBRARY SERVICES - Gt. Brit.
Colwell, Eileen. W. C. Berwick Sayers and Children's Libraries. 18-21, SAYW

CHILDREN'S LIBRARY SERVICES - Hamburg
Wulf, Ursel. Die Jugendbüchereien der Hamburger Öffentlichen Bücherhallen. 63-67, HAMB

CHILDREN'S LIBRARY SERVICES - Jena
Schuhmann, Ursula. Aus der Arbeit der Kinder- und Jugendbibliothek Jena. 135-139, JENA

CHILDREN'S LIBRARY SERVICES - Kalundborg, Denmark
Haugstrup, S. Kalundborg Bibliotek 1920-1926. 22-36, KALU

CHILDREN'S LIBRARY SERVICES - New York (City)
Masten, Helen Adams. The Central Children's Room. 551-560, MOOR
Strang, Mary. Good Labour of Old Days. 537-550, MOOR

CHILDREN'S LIBRARY SERVICES - Norway
Wiig, Hanna. Barnearbeide i Norske Byer og Ladesteder. 66-72, NORN

CHILDREN'S LIBRARY SERVICES - U.S. - Hist.
Massee, May. Children's Books on Demand. 579-584, MOOR

CHILDREN'S LIBRARY SERVICES - Uppsala-Hist.
Hanninger, Vivica. Barn- och Ungdomsbibliotek: Tre Decennier med Barn och Böcker. 555-562, HJEL

CHILDREN'S LITERATURE
see also Young adults' literature

CHILDREN'S LITERATURE
SAYE
Dalgliesh, Alice and Margaret B. Evans. Designing Children's Books. 573-577, MOOR

CHILDREN'S LITERATURE - Authors and illustrators
see also Book illustration

CHILDREN'S LITERATURE - Authors and illustrators
Langfeldt, Johannes. Kinderausgaben der Grimmschen Märchen. Eine Bibliothekarische Besinnung auf Deren Grundsätze. 49-59, BRIE

CHILDREN'S LITERATURE - Germany (Democratic Republic, 1949-)
Kunze, Horst. Books for Children and Youth. 523-527, RANG

CHILDREN'S LITERATURE - History and criticism
Eaton, Anne Thaxter. Reviewing and Criticism of Children's Books. 589-592, MOOR
Sayers, Frances Clarke. Big Walking Day. 561-568, MOOR

CHILDREN'S LITERATURE - Illustration
see Book illustration

CHILDREN'S LITERATURE - Japan - Hist.
Watanabe, Shigeo. Post-war Children's Literature in Japan. 151-158, HASH

CHILDREN'S LITERATURE - Sheffield, Eng.
Scott, E. "There's Nothing Like a Good Book." 15-16, LAMB

CHILDREN'S LITERATURE - U.S. - Hist.
Darling, Richard L. Children's Books Following the Civil War. 63-84, GJEL
Massee, May. Children's Books on Demand. 579-584, MOOR

CHILDREN'S PERIODICALS
Jordan, Alice M. Magazines for Children. 599-604, MOOR

CHILDREN'S WORK
see Children's library services

Childs, James B.
Author Entries for Canadian Government Publications. 169-174, HANS
Corporate Author Entry as Regards the German Federal Republic. 151-162, RANG
French Government Document Bibliography. 85-97, MADR
Government and Official Publications in a People's Democracy. 163-170, RANG

Chill, Gertrud.
Ausgewählte Statistische Angaben. 133-139, HAMB

CHINA - Bibliography
see Bibliography - China

CHINA - Bibliography, National
see Bibliography, National - China

CHINA - Block-books
see Block-books - China

CHINA - Calligraphy
see Calligraphy - China

CHINA - Catalogs - Printed book
see Catalogs - Printed book - China

CHINA - Printing
see Printing - China

CHINESE LITERATURE - Cataloging
see Oriental literature - Cataloging

CHINESE LITERATURE - Collections - Gothenburg, Sweden

Peterson, John. Kina i Göteborgs Stadsbibliotek. 1-21, (ninth paper), GÖTE

CHINESE LITERATURE - Collections - Helsinki

Mustonen, Aarne. Kaukoidän Kirjatietoa. 66-77, NYBE

CHINESE LITERATURE - Collections - Washington, D.C.

Swingle, Walter T. Chinese Books: Their Character and Value and Their Place in the Western Library. 429-444, PUTN

Uematsu, Yasushi. Beikoku Giin Toshokan no Kanseki ni tsuite. (On the Chinese Collections in the Library of Congress, U.S.A.) 9-12, HAKO

CHINESE MANUSCRIPTS
see Manuscripts, Chinese

CHOKUHAN (Imperial editions)

Kumura, Miyogo and Kazumasa Kaneko. Chokuhan Ko, 1, Kobun Kokyo 1. (Study of the Chokuhan, or the Imperial Editions, 16th Century, Part 1, Kobun Kokyo 1.) 61-86, TOMI

Christ, Karl.
Ältere Drucke Volkstümlicher Italienischer Dichtung in der Preussischen Staatsbibliothek. 61-69, HARN
Die Handschriftenverzeichnisse der Fuldaer Klosterbibliothek aus dem 16. Jahrhundert. 24-39, FULD
Karolingische Bibliothekseinbände. 82-104, LEYG
Eine Unbekannte Handschrift der Ersten Fassung der Dionysiana und der Capitula e Canonibus Excerpta A.813. 25-36, LEID

Christensen, Chr. A. R.
Presse og Bibliotek. 168-176, NORS

Christensen, Tagea Egede.
Bibliografi. 181-188, AARU

CHRISTIAN ART AND SYMBOLISM - Collections - New York (City)

GREE

CHRISTIANIA
see Oslo

Christiansen, Reidar Th.
Albrechtsons Visesamling. 106-130, OSLN

CHRISTINA, queen of Sweden
see Kristina, queen of Sweden

CHRONICLES. Mss. ca. 1450

Baron, Hans. A Forgotten Chronicle of Early Fifteenth-Century Venice. 19-36, PARG

CHURCH AND THE LIBRARY
see Catholic libraries

CHURCH ARCHIVES
see Archives, Church

CHURCH LIBRARIES
see also Religious libraries; Sunday school libraries

CHURCH LIBRARIES - Celle, Ger.

Fick, Richard. Der Ankauf der Celler Kirchenministerialbibliothek durch den Preußischen Staat. 149-158, LEYG

CHURCH LIBRARIES - Germany

SCHV

Brachvogel, Eugen, Monsignore. Die Bibliotheken der Geistlichen Residenzen des Ermlandes. 35-44, KÖNI
Polthier, Wilhelm. Die Ehemalige Domstiftsbibliothek in Havelberg. 163-176, KUHN

CHURCH LIBRARIES - Gt. Brit. - Hist.

Langfeldt, Johannes. Ein Kapitel aus der Vorgeschichte der "Public Library" in Grossbritannien. 281-292, JUCH

CHURCH LIBRARIES - Hist. - Early

Wieland, Franz. Früheste Vorläufer der Vaticana. 159-168, LEYG

CHURCH LIBRARIES - Hof, Ger.

Dumrath, Karlheinrich. "Gott zu Ehren und Unsern Nachkommen zum-Besten." 2-15, SCHV

CHURCH LIBRARIES - Ivrea, Italy

Borghezio, Gino. Inventarii e Notizie della Biblioteca Capitolare d'Ivrea nel Secolo XV. 423-454, EHRE

CHURCH LIBRARIES - Lüben, Ger.

Stern, Ludwig. Mitteilungen aus der Lübener Kirchenbibliothek. 67-96, WILM

CHURCH LIBRARIES, Medieval
see Monastic libraries

CHURCH LIBRARIES - U.S. (Colonial period)

Langfeldt, Johannes. Ein Kapitel aus der Vorgeschichte der "Public Library" in Grossbritannien. 281-292, JUCH

CHURCH LIBRARIES - Växjö, Sweden (Diocese)

Johansson, Herbert. Biblar och Andra Böcker i Kyrkor Inom Växjö Stift 1650-85. 207-220, OLSS

Chwalewik, Edward. Jan Filipowicz Rytownik i Drukarz. 223-239, PIEK

Chyczewska, Alina.
Zasób Drzeworytów Ilustracyjnych i Herbowych w XVI-Wiecznych Oficynach Poznańskich. 354-382, GRYC

Ciceri, Angelo.
Un Precursore ed un Amico di Alfonso Gallo: Mons. Achille Ratti (Papa Pio XI). 279-294, GALL

CICERO, MARCUS TULLIUS. Mss.

Clark, Albert C. A Bodleian Fragment of Cicero Tusc. Quaest. 169-173, CHAT

Ricci, Seymour de. Un Fragment en Onciale du "Pro Plancio" de Cicéron. 442-447, CHAT

Thomas, Émile. Note sur un Gemblacensis Aujourd'hui à Bruxelles, n° 5348-5352, XIIe Siècle. 47-48, GRAU

CICERO, MARCUS TULLIUS. Mss. Epistulae

Mendelssohn, Louis. De Ciceronis Epistularum Codice Turonensi. 169-173, GRAU

CICERO, MARCUS TULLIUS. Pro Flacco

Dareste, Rodolphe. Cicéron, Pro Flacco, XXIX-XXXII. 7-12, GRAU

CICERO, MARCUS TULLIUS. Rhetorica

Thomas, Paul. Un Commentaire du Moyen Âge sur la Rhétorique de Cicéron. 41-45, GRAU

CICERONIAN NOTES
see Tironian notes

Cimino, Maria.
The Picture Books of Bruno Munari. 585-588, MOOR

CINGOLI, Italy. Archivio del Comune

Galeazzi, A. G. L'Archivio del Comune di Cingoli. 455-460, GALL

Cipolla, C.
La Tachygraphie Ligurienne au XIe Siècle. 87-96, HAVE

CIRCULATION ANALYSIS - Hamburg

Volbehr, Lilli. Eine Tagesausleihe in der Bücherhalle Mönckebergstrasse. 83-96, HAMB

CURCULATION ANALYSIS - Mainz - Hist.

Darapsky, Elisabeth. Ein Altes Ausleihebuch. 47-50, MAIN

CIRCULATION PROCEDURES
see also Reader services; Registration of borrowers

CIRCULATION PROCEDURES - Borrowers
see Registration of borrowers

CIRCULATION PROCEDURES - Copenhagen

Drachmann, A. G. Call Numbers. 198-206, HANS

CIRCULATION PROCEDURES - Germany

Abb, Gustav. Die Einführung der Täglichen Ausleihe in der Berliner Kgl. Bibliothek. 179-185, GODE

Hofmann, Walter. Die Behandlung der Organisation der Ausleihe in der Modernen Deutschen Bildungsbibliothek. 17-29, DRES

CIRCULATION PROCEDURES - Hours of opening

Unger, Willy. Benutzungseinrichtungen, Benutzungspolitik und Gebrauchsöffentlichkeit. I, 175-221, BERS

CIRCULATION PROCEDURES - Japan

Itakura, Yoshikazu. Suitōshu no Shido ni tsuite. (On the Training of Circulation-Desk Attendants.) 105-115, (part 1), OHAS

CIRCULATION PROCEDURES - Krakow

Głodek, Stefania. Wypożyczalnia. 29-34, KRAK

CIRCULATION PROCEDURES - Randers, Denmark

RAND

CIRCULATION PROCEDURES - Viborg, Denmark - Hist.

VIBO

CIRCULATION - Statistics - Hamburg

Volbehr, Lilli. Eine Tagesausleihe in der Bücherhalle Mönckebergstrasse. 83-96, HAMB

CIRCULATION - Statistics - Stockholm

Hjelmqvist, Fredrik. Utlandets Författere och Allmänheten i Stockholm. Några Siffror ur Stockholms Stadsbiblioteks Utlåning. 88-96, MUNT

CIRIACO DE' PIZZICOLLI, of Ancona. Mss. Kyriaci Anconitani Itinerarium

Sabbadini, R. Ciriaco d'Ancona e la Sua Descrizione Autografa del Peloponneso Trasmessa da Leonardo Botta. 181-247, CERI

Clapp, Clifford Blake.
Analytical Methods in Bibliography

Applied to Daniel Webster's Speech at Worcester in 1832. 211-219, EAME

Clapp, Verner W.
The Balance of Conflicting Interests in the Building of Collections: Comprehensiveness Versus Selectivity. 65-72, PENN
Bibliographical Vision. 35-41, DAVI

Clark, Albert C.
A Bodleian Fragment of Cicero Tusc. Quaest. 169-173, CHAT

Clason, W. E.
The Life of Frits Donker Duyvis. 5-8, DONR

CLASSED CATALOGS
see Catalogs - Classed

CLASSIFICATION

Ansteinsson, John. Dilemmas of Classification. 136-147, HANS
Farradane, J. Fundamental Fallacies and New Needs in Classification. 120-135, SAYW
Farrell, Colman J. The Classification of Books in Libraries. 207-222, HANS
Feyl, Othmar. Die Klassifikation für die Bibliographien der Buchkammer der Sowjetunion. Bemerkungen zur Gleichnamigen Publikation. 50-60, VORS
Focke, R. Allgemeine Theorie der Klassifikation und Kurzer Entwurf einer Instruktion für den Realkatalog. 5-18, VERP
Foskett, D. J. Classification and Integrative Levels. 136-150, SAYW
———— Language and Classification. 275-278, KYLE
Groeneveld, C. Analyse van Bibliotheekstukken. 441-449, BRUM
Kaula, P. N. Library Classification. 51-56, MADR
Mills, J. Using Classification in Teaching Indexing. 279-286, KYLE
Palmer, B. I. Classification as a Foundation Study for Librarians. 202-212, SAYW
Rasmussen, Detlef. Andreas Schleiermacher und das Prinzip der Schlüsselung. 163-175, REDE
Rusk, George Yeisley. Techniques for the Resolution of Cultural Conflicts. 14-31, MADR
Shaw, Ralph R. Classification. 63-67, RANG
Shera, Jesse H. and James W. Perry. Changing Concepts of Classification, Philosophical and Educational Implications. 37-48, RANG
Takeuchi, Zensaku. Tosho Bunrui to Tosho Kigo ni Kansuru Ichi Kosatsu. (An Observation Relating to Classification of Books and Book Numbers.) 1-24, (part 1), OHAS
Vengerov, S. A. Nasha Zadacha. 1-4, MALE
Vickery, B. C. Ranganathan's Work on Classification. 108-110, RANG
Zeltner, Hermann. Philosophie als Bibliographischer Begriff. 177-194, REDE

CLASSIFICATION - Ahmedabad

Barot, G. P. Colon Classification in Gujarat. 102-104, RANG

CLASSIFICATION - Ann Arbor, Mich. - Hist.

Bidlack, Russell E. The Early Handling of Books at the University of Michigan. 149-164, GJEL

CLASSIFICATION - Berlin

Schultze, Walther. Die Zukunft Unserer Realkataloge. 224-237, KUHN

CLASSIFICATION - Chemistry - Hist.

Vickery, B. C. The Classification of Chemical Substances: An Historical Survey. 151-167, SAYW

CLASSIFICATION DÉCIMALE UNIVERSELLE
see Classification - Systems - Universal decimal

CLASSIFICATION - Fulda - Hist.

Boehm, P. Peter. Die Anfänge der Landesbibliothek Fulda. 59-88, FULD

CLASSIFICATION - Hist.

Grolier, Eric de. Points de Vue Retrospectif et Prospectif dans la Classification. 96-119, SAYW

CLASSIFICATION - Hist. - 16th cent.

Escher, Hermann. Konrad Gessner über Aufstellung und Katalogisierung von Bibliotheken. 119-127, GODE

CLASSIFICATION - Hist. - 1876-1960

Ranganathan, S. R. Library Classification on the March. 72-95, SAYW

CLASSIFICATION - India

Parkhi, R. S. Colon Classification: The National Scheme of Classification for India. 94-98, RANG

CLASSIFICATION - Japan

Kato, Shuko. Cataloguing and Classification. 209-214, RANG
Yayoshi, Mitsunaga. Kokusho Mokuroku ni okero Bunrui Shisō no Hattatsu. (Progress of the Idea of Classification in the Catalogues of Japanese Books.) 66-83, OTAT

CLASSIFICATION - Munich - Hist.

Striedl, Hans. 150 Jahre Münchener Aufstellungsschema. 73-103, HOFM

CLASSIFICATION - New Haven, Conn.

Monrad, Anna Marie, et al. Historical Notes on the Catalogues and Classifications of the Yale University Library. 251-284, KEOG

CLASSIFICATION - Philosophy

Shera, J. H. The Changing Philosophy of Bibliographic Classification. 139-140, DONK

CLASSIFICATION - Reclassification - Washington, D.C.

Hanson, James Christian Meinich. The Library of Congress and Its New Catalogue: Some Unwritten History. 178-194, PUTN

CLASSIFICATION RESEARCH GROUP

Crossley, Charles A. New Schemes of Classification: Principles and Practice. 113-129, RANG

CLASSIFICATION - Special subjects

Zeltner, Hermann. Philosophie als Bibliographischer Begriff. 177-194, REDE

CLASSIFICATION - Special subjects - Agriculture

Frauendorfer, Sigmund von. Classification Problems in an International Special Library. 223-233, HANS

CLASSIFICATION - Special subjects - Anthropology

Anzai, Ikuo. Shuyō Ippan Bunruihō ni okeru Bunka-Jinruigaku no Ichi. (The Position of Cultural Anthropology in Major General Classification.) 181-190, HASH

CLASSIFICATION - Special subjects - Bibl.

Avanzi, Giannetto. Gli Scritti sulla Catalogazione e Specializzata. 87-186, GALL

CLASSIFICATION - Special subjects - Bibliography

Wenzel, B. Die Abteilung Bücherkunde im Realkatalog der Kaiser-Wilhelm-Bibliothek. 19-42, VERP

CLASSIFICATION - Special subjects - Bibliography - Russia

Feyl, Othmar. Die Klassifikation für die Bibliographien der Buchkammer der Sowjetunion. Bemerkungen zur Gleichnamigen Publikation. 50-60, VORS

CLASSIFICATION - Special subjects - Biography

Bulling, Klaus. Zur Anlage Biographischer Schlüssel innerhalb Systematischer Kataloge. 47-62, BULL

CLASSIFICATION - Special subjects - Civilization

Anzai, Ikuo. Shuyō Ippan Bunruihō ni okeru Bunka-Jinruigaku no Ichi. (The Position of Cultural Anthropology in Major General Classification.) 181-190, HASH

CLASSIFICATION - Special subjects - Expeditions

Kojima, Fumiyasu. Tokushu Shiryō no Bunrui, Ōtani Tankentai Shōraihin. (Classification of the Material Found in Central Asia by the Ōtani Expedition.) 131-141, KYOT

CLASSIFICATION - Special subjects - Geography

Mogk, Helmut. Die Abfolge der Ortsbegriffe in Systematischen Katalogen. I, 150-159, GLAU

CLASSIFICATION - Special subjects - Hist.

Schultheiss, Fr. G. Zur Fortbildung des Halleschen Schemas. 43-56, VERP

CLASSIFICATION - Special subjects - Jewish literature

Bloch, Joshua. The Classification of Jewish Literature in the New York Public Library. L-LXXVII, FREI

Freimann, A. Das Einteilungssystem der Judaica in der Stadtbibliothek Frankfurt a.M. 55-64, FREI

CLASSIFICATION - Special subjects - Medicine

Lohse, Hartwig. Zum Aufbau eines Neuen Sachkatalogs nach dem "System Eppelsheimer" an der Senckenbergischen Bibliothek unter Besonderer Berücksichtigung der Medizin. 102-110, FUCH

CLASSIFICATION - Special subjects - Medicine - Hist. - 19th cent.

Prytz, Johansen J. Den Gamle Medicinske Katalog på Universitetsbiblioteket, København. 1-7, DAHA

CLASSIFICATION - Special subjects - Music

Coates, E. J. Classification Scheme of the British Catalogue of Music. 135-138, RANG

CLASSIFICATION - Special subjects - Philology

Rother, Karl. Die Philologie in den

Realkatalogsystemen seit 1600 mit Besonderer Berücksichtigung der Klassischen Altertumswissenschaft. 300-320, MILF

CLASSIFICATION - Special subjects - Philosophy

Bosch, J. F. Classificatie en Kennisleer. 391-396, BRUM

CLASSIFICATION - Special subjects - Picture collections

Pauer, Hans. Grosser Entschluss. Ein Neues Ordnungssystem in der Porträtsammlung der Österreichischen Nationalbibliothek. 62-64, STUM

CLASSIFICATION - Special subjects - Science

Lancaster-Jones, Joyce. The UDC and the Science Museum Library. 163-164, DONK

CLASSIFICATION - Special subjects - Social science literature

Ranganathan, S. R. Barbara Kyle and the Classification of Sociology. 271-274, KYLE

Wesseling, J. C. G. La CDU et les Sciences Sociales. 157-159, DONK

CLASSIFICATION - Special subjects - Technical Literature

Moulijn, E. The Development of the UDC from an Electrotechnical Point of View. 165-166, DONK

CLASSIFICATION - Systems
see also Information retrieval - Systems

CLASSIFICATION - Systems

Donker, Duyvis Frits. The Jubilee of the Creator of Colon Classification. 31-35, RANG

——— On the Future Work for the Comparison of Classifications. 32-37, MADR

Mills, J. Dr. Ranganathan and the Study of Classification. 38-41, MADR

Palmer, Bernard I. The Wider Uses of Library Classification. 42-50, MADR

CLASSIFICATION - Systems - Colon

Barot, G. P. Colon Classification in Gujarat. 102-104, RANG

Eaton, Thelma. Effect of Colon Classification on the Teachings of Classification in American Library Schools. 588-592, RANG

Kaula, P. N. Colon Classification: Genesis and Development. 73-93, RANG

——— Library Classification. 51-56, MADR

Melton, Jessica. Compatibility of Two Information Systems, Colon Classification and Western Reserve University. 49-62, RANG

Misra, Jatadhari. My Thoughts on Colon. 99-101, RANG

Nadejde, Florence. Philosophy of Colon Classification. 105-107, RANG

Parkhi, R. S. Colon Classification: The National Scheme of Classification for India. 94-98, RANG

Ranganathan, S. R. Telescoping of Facets and Mixed Notation. 154-156, DONK

CLASSIFICATION - Systems - Dewey Decimal

Kotani, Seiichi. D C no Junansei (The Flexibility of the Dewey Decimal Classification.) 128-141, (part 1) OHAS

Sustrac, Charles. Quelques Observations sur la Classification Décimale. 37-38, EMLE

CLASSIFICATION - Systems - Dewey Decimal - Prague - Hist.

Koutníková, Ludmila. L. J. Živný a Desetinné Třídění u Nás. 73-130, ŽIVN

CLASSIFICATION - Systems - Eppelsheimer

Lohse, Hartwig. Zum Aufbau eines Neuen Sachkatalogs nach dem "System Eppelsheimer" an der Senckenbergischen Bibliothek unter Besonderer Berücksichtigung der Medizin. 102-110, FUCH

CLASSIFICATION - Systems - Expansive

Lamb, Eliza. The Expansive Classification in Use. 265-269, HANS

CLASSIFICATION - Systems - Faceted

Coates, E. J. Classification Scheme of the British Catalogue of Music. 135-138, RANG

Crossley, Charles A. New Schemes of Classification: Principles and Practice. 113-129, RANG

Foskett, D. J. Comments on Fundamental Categories in Document Classification. 130-134, RANG

CLASSIFICATION - Systems - Halle. Universität

Schultheiss, Fr. G. Zur Fortbildung des Halleschen Schemas. 43-56, VERP

CLASSIFICATION - Systems - Library of Congress

Martel, Charles. The Library of Congress Classification. 327-332, PUTN

Mueller, Theodore A. A Seldom Used Device. 68-69, RANG

CLASSIFICATION - Systems - Universal decimal

Frank, Otto. Über die Zukünftige Entwicklung der Internationalen Dezimalklassifikation. 141-144, DONK
Lancaster-Jones, Joyce. The UDC and the Science Museum Library. 163-164, DONK
Lasso de la Vega, Javier. La CDU como Medio para Hacer Sistemáticas las Listas de Epígrafes de los Catálogos de Asuntos. 169-170, DONK
Lloyd, G. A. A "New Deal" for Universal Classification? 149-153, DONK
Lorphèvre, Georges. Donker Duyvis et la Classification Décimale Universelle. 17-24, DONR
Michailov, A. I. Donker Duyvis' Contribution to the Progress of Scientific Information and Documentation. 30-38, DONR
Moulijn, E. The Development of the UDC from an Electrotechnical Point of View. 165-166, DONK
Ranganathan, S. R. Telescoping of Facets and Mixed Notation. 154-156, DONK
Wellisch, H. New Publication Methods for the UDC, a Proposal. 145-148, DONK
Wesseling, J. C. G. La CDU et les Sciences Sociales. 157-159, DONK

CLASSIFICATION - Systems - Universal decimal - Germany

Walther, Carl and Karl Fill. Die Deutsche Gesamtausgabe der Dezimalklassifikation. 167-168, DONK

CLASSIFICATION - Systems - Universal decimal - Switzerland

Mathys, E. Der Anteil der Schweiz an der Dezimalklassifikation. 160-162, DONK

CLASSIFICATION - Teaching

Kyle, Barbara. Classification in the School Curriculum. 194-201, SAYW

CLASSIFICATION - Teaching - U.S.

Eaton, Thelma. Effect of Colon Classification on the Teachings of Classification of American Library Schools. 588-592, RANG

Claus, Helmut.
Migration von Bildstöcken bei den Leipziger Buchdruckern in der Frühen Reformationszeit. 63-81, LÜLF

CLAY TABLETS
see Tablets (Paleography)

CLÉMENCE, ABEL

Verwey, H. de la Fontaine. Une Presse Secrète du XVe Siècle Abel Clémence, Imprimeur à Rouen. 81-89, CALO

CLEMENS XI, Pope, 1649-1721 - Library

Peebles, Bernard M. The Bibliotheca Albana Urbinas as Represented in the Library of the Catholic University of America. 327-352, ALBA

Clercx, Suzanne, jt. ed.

Clercx, Suzanne.
Charles van den Borren. 1-18, BORR

CLERICAL ASSISTANTS
see Non-professional assistants

THE CLERK OF BREUKELYN

Koopman, Harry L. The Clerk of Breukelyn. v-vi, EAME

CLEVELAND. Public Library

Eastman, Linda A. Library Service to a City. 128-139, PUTN

CLOSED SHELVES
see Access to shelves

Cluzel, Étienne.
De Quelques Livres Scientifiques à Vignettes, des XVIIe et XVIIIe Siècles. 127-143, CALO

Coates, E. J.
Classification Scheme of the British Catalogue of Music. 135-138, RANG

Cobet, Charles-Gabriel.
In Memoriam Optimi Viri Charles Graux (sur Quelques Passages Corrompus et Interpolés d'Hérodote). 1-5, GRAU

Coblans, Herbert.
Barbara Kyle: an Annotated Bibliography. 229-235, KYLE
F. Donker Duyvis: a Bibliography. 65-80, DONR
A Note on Cataloguing at the International Level. 197-202, TVET
Some Thoughts on Machines. 279-282, RANG

COBURG (City) Landesbibliothek

Höfner, Curt. Zur Geschichte der Gandersheimer Büchersammlungen. Ein Beitrag aus Coburg. 197-210, HOFM

CODES, Cataloging
see Cataloging - Rules

CODEX ALEXANDRINUS

Mercati, Giovanni, Cardinal. Un'Oscura Nota del Codice Alessandrino. 79-82, CHAT

CODEX AUGIENSIS LVII, Karlsruhe
see Karlsruhe. Badische Landesbibliothek. Mss. (LVII)

CODEX CAROLINUS

Dold, Alban. Die Provenienz der Altlateinischen Römerbrieftexte in den Gotisch-Lateinischen Fragmenten des Codex Carolinus von Wolfenbüttel. 13-29, LEYH

CODEX MARCIANUS 246

Ruelle, Charles-Émile. Nitice du Codex Marcianus 246, Contenant le Traité du Philosophe Damascius sur les Premiers Principes. 547-552, GRAU

CODEX SANGALLENSIS 878

Bischoff, Bernhard. Eine Sammelhandschrift Walahfrid Strabos (Cod. Sangall. 878). 30-48, LEYH

CODEX THEODOSIANUS (Vatican Reg. 886)
see Vatican. Biblioteca Vaticana. Mss. (Reg. 886)

CODEX TRECENSIS

Thewrewk de Ponor, Émile. Codex Festi Breviati Trecensis. 659-669, GRAU

CODEX VENETUS 246

Ruelle, Charles-Émile. Notice du Codex Marcianus 246, Contenant le Traité du Philosophe Damascius sur les Premiers Principes. 547-552, GRAU

CODEX VOSSIANUS LATINUS III

Prete, Sesto. The Vossianus Latinus III and the Arrangement of the Works of Ausonius. 353-366, ALBA

CODICES
see Manuscripts

CODING SYSTEMS
see Information retrieval - Systems

Coen-Pirani, Emma.
Il Contributo di Eruditi Veneti alla Pubblicazione dei "Rerum Italicarum Scriptores." 169-190, FERR

Coetzee, P. C.
Die Voorgeskiedenis van die Openbare Biblioteek. Kultuur-Historiese Beskouing. 221-233, VLEE

COETZEE, P. C.

COET

Le Mousaion à Monsieur P. C. Coetzee. 6-13, COET

COGSWELL, JOSEPH GREEN

Lydenberg, Harry Miller. A Forgotten Trail Blazer. 302-314, PUTN

Mackall, Leonard L. Goethe's Letter to Joseph Green Cogswell. 315-326, PUTN

Cohen, Boaz.
Bibliography of the Writings of Prof. Alexander Marx. 35-59, MARX
Nehemiah Brüll (1843-1891). 219-246, FREI

COINS - Collections - Erlangen

Schwabacher, Willy. Ein Fränkischer Gnadenpfennig aus der Voit von Salzburg'schen Münzsammlung in der Erlanger Universitätsbibliothek. 68-74, VERZ

COINS - Oriental - Collections - Erlangen

Zambaur, Eduard von. Die Orientalischen Münzen der Sammlung Will in der Universitätsbibliothek Erlangen. 94-104, VERZ

Cole, George Watson.
Elizabethan Americana. 161-177, EAME
The Ideally Perfect Library. 113-127, PUTN

Colehan, Philip.
A Difficult but Agreeable Task. 26-27, LAMB

Colinese, P. E.
The Education of Librarians and Information Officers: Industrial Information Departments. 305-311, HUTT

COLLECTARIUMS - Fragments - 11th or 12th cent.

Dold, Alban. Ein Fragment eines Collectars, d. i. eines Horen-Orationenbuches. 31-36, STOL

COLLECTIO BRUGENSIS

Holtzmann, Walther. Über die Vatikanische Handschrift der "Collectio Brugensis" (Ottob. lat. 3027). I, 391-414, ALBB

COLLECTOR'S BOOKS
see Limited edition books

COLLEGE AND UNIVERSITY ARCHIVES
see Archives, College and university

COLLEGE AND UNIVERSITY LIBRARIANS
see also Rare book librarians

COLLEGE AND UNIVERSITY LIBRARIANS

Gebhardt, Walther. Gedanken zum Personalbedarf einer Wissenschaftlichen Bibliothek. 55-65, HOFF
McDiarmid, E. W. The Place of Experience in Developing College and University Librarians. 614-621, WILS

Perry, J. W. The University Library as a Capital Asset. 46-53, COET

COLLEGE AND UNIVERSITY LIBRARIANS - Education - Sweden

Ottervik, Gösta. Kompetenskrav och Utbildning vid de Svenska Universitetsbiblioteken. 225-236, HEIN

COLLEGE AND UNIVERSITY LIBRARIANS - Finland - Hist.

Henriksson, Karl-Erik. Oppihistoriasta. 130-148, TUDE

COLLEGE AND UNIVERSITY LIBRARIANS - Gt. Brit.

Richnell, D. T. The Education of Librarians and Information Officers: University Libraries. 291-300, HUTT

COLLEGE AND UNIVERSITY LIBRARIANS - Oslo

OSLU

COLLEGE AND UNIVERSITY LIBRARIANS - Oslo - Hist.

Prytz, Lizzie. Universitetsbibliotekets Personale 1813-1932. 258-276, OSLO

COLLEGE AND UNIVERSITY LIBRARIANS - Status - Finland - Hist.

Henriksson, Karl-Erik. Oppihistoriasta. 130-148, TUDE

COLLEGE AND UNIVERSITY LIBRARIES see also Research libraries

COLLEGE AND UNIVERSITY LIBRARIES

Ansteinsson, John. "Samkjøring." 1-12, MUNT
Downs, Robert B. The Future of University Libraries. 451-456, RANG
Robinson, M. U. School and College Libraries and the Teacher in Training. 147-150, OFFO
Subramaniam, D. Ideal of University Education. 443-450, RANG

COLLEGE AND UNIVERSITY LIBRARIES - Acquisitions - Germany - Hist.

Menn, Walter. Aus der Geschichte der Universitätsbibliothek Greifswald in den Letzten Jahren der Preussischen Zeit. 230-255, JUCH

COLLEGE AND UNIVERSITY LIBRARIES - Acquisitions - New Haven, Conn.

Bryant, Louise May and Mary Patterson. The List of Books Sent by Jeremiah Dummer. 423-492, KEOG
Keogh, Andrew. Benjamin Silliman's Trip to Europe in 1805. 416-422, LYDE
Pratt, Anne Stokely. The Books Sent from England by Jeremiah Dummer to Yale College. 7-44, KEOG

COLLEGE AND UNIVERSITY LIBRARIES - Acquisitions - U.S.

Bishop, William Warner. Centralized Purchasing for American College Libraries. 1-6, GODE

COLLEGE AND UNIVERSITY LIBRARIES - Acquisitions - Uppsala

Henriksson, Karl-Erik. Notes on the Acquisition Work in the Uppsala University Library. 228-236, DAHL

COLLEGE AND UNIVERSITY LIBRARIES - Administration

Perry, J. W. The University Library as a Capital Asset. 46-53, COET
Sivaraman, K. M. Team Work, Staff Council and Renaissance in Library Science. 475-485, RANG

COLLEGE AND UNIVERSITY LIBRARIES - Administration - Geneva

Gardy, Fréd. La Réorganisation de Genève au Début du XVIIIe Siècle. 133-143, GODE

COLLEGE AND UNIVERSITY LIBRARIES - Administration - Germany

Brown, Charles Harvey. Some Similarities and Differences in the Administration of University Libraries in the United States and Germany. 329-342, LEYG

COLLEGE AND UNIVERSITY LIBRARIES - Administration - Halle

Juntke, Fritz. Das Reglement für die Bibliothek der Universität zu Halle vom 20. Mai 1823. 323-342, VORS

COLLEGE AND UNIVERSITY LIBRARIES - Administration - Sweden

Kleberg, Tönnes. Das Bibliothekssystem einer Universität als Einheit. Reflexionen über einen Organisationsvorschlag an der Universität Uppsala. 119-124, HOFM

COLLEGE AND UNIVERSITY LIBRARIES - Administration - U.S.

Brown, Charles Harvey. Some Similarities and Differences in the Administration of University Libraries in the United States and Germany. 329-342, LEYG

COLLEGE AND UNIVERSITY LIBRARIES - Administration - Utrecht

Bockel, W. J. van. Iets over de "Binnendienst'' der Utrechtsche Universiteitsbibliotheek. 63-69, SOME

COLLEGE AND UNIVERSITY LIBRARIES - Aims and objectives

Isaac, K. A. My Ideal College Library. 139-144, MADR
Nagasawa, Masao. Daigaku Toshokan Kindaika no Kijiku to shite no Refarensu Wāku. (Reference Work as the Axis for the Modernization of the University Library.) 267-279, HASH

COLLEGE AND UNIVERSITY LIBRARIES - Architecture and building
see Architecture and building - College and university libraries

COLLEGE AND UNIVERSITY LIBRARIES - Book collections
see also Library resources

COLLEGE AND UNIVERSITY LIBRARIES - Book collections - Nashville

Copeland, J. Isaac. Developing the Peabody Book Collection. 10-11, NASH
Robison, Dan M. The Library Books of Nashville. 5-7, NASH

COLLEGE AND UNIVERSITY LIBRARIES - Book selection

Pafford, J. H. P. Book Selection in the University Library. 422-426, JUCH

COLLEGE AND UNIVERSITY LIBRARIES - Branch systems
see College and university libraries - Departmental and divisional libraries

COLLEGE AND UNIVERSITY LIBRARIES - California - Hist.

Blanchard, J. R. Development and Mechanization of Libraries of the University of California. 1-7, HASH

COLLEGE AND UNIVERSITY LIBRARIES - Classification

Lamb, Eliza. The Expansive Classification in Use. 265-269, HANS

COLLEGE AND UNIVERSITY LIBRARIES - Classification - Hist.

Tauber, Maurice F. Classification of Books in College and University Libraries: Historical Aspects. 706-724, WILS

COLLEGE AND UNIVERSITY LIBRARIES - Decorah, Iowa

Jacobsen, Karl T. The Reorganization of the Library of a Small College. 234-243, HANS

COLLEGE AND UNIVERSITY LIBRARIES - Departmental and divisional libraries

Ansteinsson, John. "Samkjøring." 1-12, MUNT
Coney, Donald. An Experimental Index for Apportioning Departmental Book Funds for a University Library. 422-428, WILS
Ellsworth, Ralph E. Some Aspects of the Problem of Allocating Book Funds among Departments in Universities. 486-494, WILS

COLLEGE AND UNIVERSITY LIBRARIES - Departmental and divisional libraries - Berlin

Göber, Willi. Das Bibliothekswesen einer Universität als Einheit. 154-171, VORS

COLLEGE AND UNIVERSITY LIBRARIES - Departmental and divisional libraries - Germany - Hist.

Widmann, Hans. Johann Jakob Moser und die Bibliotheken. Zugleich trag zur Geschichte des Verhältnisses zwischen Zentralbibliothek und Institutsbibliotheken. 125-146, LEYH

COLLEGE AND UNIVERSITY LIBRARIES - Departmental and divisional libraries - Nashville

New Libraries for the University Center. 20, NASH

COLLEGE AND UNIVERSITY LIBRARIES - Departmental and Divisional libraries - Sweden

Kleberg, Tönnes. Das Bibliothekssystem einer Universität als Einheit. Reflexionen über einen Organisationsvorschlag an der Universität Uppsala. 119-124, HOFM

COLLEGE AND UNIVERSITY LIBRARIES - Erlangen

VERZ

Strollreither, Eugen. Die Universitätsbibliothek Erlangen zur Zeit der Praktikantentätigkeit August von Platens. 216-229, LEYG

COLLEGE AND UNIVERSITY LIBRARIES - Evaluation
see also Surveys - College and university libraries

COLLEGE AND UNIVERSITY LIBRARIES - Evaluation

Purdy, G. Flint. The Evaluation of University Library Service. 638-644, WILS

COLLEGE AND UNIVERSITY LIBRARIES - Germany

Handwerker, Otto. Bibliothekare und Universitäten, mit Belegen aus der

Geschichte der Würzburger Universitätsbibliothek. 85-94, LEID
Meyen, Fritz. Die Technisch-Wissenschaftlichen Bibliotheken, Ihre Entwicklung und Ihre Stellung im Rahmen des Deutschen Bibliothekswesens. 102-125, LEUN

COLLEGE AND UNIVERSITY LIBRARIES - Hamburg

Voigt, Christian. Die Staats- und Universitäts-Bibliothek Hamburg. Ihr Weg von der Gelehrtenbibliothek zur Wissenschaftlichen Gebrauchsbibliothek. 23-39, TIEM

COLLEGE AND UNIVERSITY LIBRARIES - India - Hist.

Dutta, Bimal Kumer. An Ancient Indian University Library. 457-460, RANG

COLLEGE AND UNIVERSITY LIBRARIES - Königsberg

KÖNI

COLLEGE AND UNIVERSITY LIBRARIES - Nashville

NASH

COLLEGE AND UNIVERSITY LIBRARIES - Netherlands

Woude, S. van der. Uit de Prille Jeugd van de Nederlandse Stads-Universiteitsbibliotheken. 618-625, BRUM

COLLEGE AND UNIVERSITY LIBRARIES - New Haven, Conn.

KEOG

COLLEGE AND UNIVERSITY LIBRARIES - Norway

Munthe, Wilhelm. De Videnskapelige Biblioteker. 97-108, NORN

COLLEGE AND UNIVERSITY LIBRARIES - Oslo

OSLU

COLLEGE AND UNIVERSITY LIBRARIES - Professional school libraries
see College and university libraries - Departmental and divisional libraries

COLLEGE AND UNIVERSITY LIBRARIES - Reference services

Noé, A. C. The University Library and Research. 300-305, HANS

COLLEGE AND UNIVERSITY LIBRARIES - Reference services - Utrecht

Prins, A. A. De Behandeling der Postaanvragen. 250-253, EVER

COLLEGE AND UNIVERSITY LIBRARIES - Relations with faculty and curriculum - Nashville

Teaching with the Joint University Libraries (Symposium). 7-9, NASH

COLLEGE AND UNIVERSITY LIBRARIES - Relations with public libraries
see Public libraries - Services to colleges and universities

COLLEGE AND UNIVERSITY LIBRARIES - Required reading materials - Germany

Kehr, Wolfgang. Studentenbücherei und Hochschulbibliothek. Zur Frage der "Core Collections" in Deutschen Studentenbüchereien und Hochschulbibliotheken. 62-81, FUCH

COLLEGE AND UNIVERSITY LIBRARIES - Southern States

Lyle, Guy R. The University Library in the Self Survey Program of the Southern Association of Colleges and Secondary Schools, Inc. 91-96, HASH

COLLEGE AND UNIVERSITY LIBRARIES - Statistics - Münster

Bahlmann, P. Die Königliche Universitäts-Bibliothek zu Münster. 1-56, MÜNS

COLLEGE AND UNIVERSITY LIBRARIES - Statistics - Utrecht

Rije, To van. Statistische Gegevens van de Utrechtsche Universiteitsbibliotheek over de Laatste 25 Jaren. 70-75, SOME
Weelderen, C. P. A. A. Buyen van. Statistische Gegevens van de Bibliotheek der Rijksuniversiteit te Utrecht over 1914-1939. 55-59, EVER

COLLEGE AND UNIVERSITY LIBRARIES - Surveys
see Surveys - College and university libraries

COLLEGE AND UNIVERSITY LIBRARIES - Technical services - Utrecht

Bockel, W. J. van. Iets over de "Binnendienst" der Utrechtsche Universiteitsbibliotheek. 63-69, SOME

COLLEGE AND UNIVERSITY LIBRARIES - Tübingen- Hist.

Widmann, Hans. Die Zugänglichkeit der Universitätsbibliothek Tübingen bis zur Mitte des 19. Jahrhunderts. 215-229, JUCH

COLLEGE AND UNIVERSITY LIBRARIES - Undergraduate libraries and collections

Koopman, Harry Lyman. The Open-Shelf Library. 257-262, PUTN

COLLEGE AND UNIVERSITY LIBRARIES - Undergraduate libraries and collections - Germany

Kehr, Wolfgang. Studentenbücherei und Hochschulbibliothek. Zur Frage der "Core Collections" in Deutschen Studentenbüchereien und Hochschulbibliotheken. 62-81, FUCH

COLLEGE AND UNIVERSITY LIBRARIES - Undergraduate libraries and collections - U.S.

Schulz, Werner. Die Amerikanischen Studentenbüchereien. 115-126, JUCR

COLLEGE AND UNIVERSITY LIBRARIES - U.S.

Brodman, Estelle and Chester R. Gough. Computers in Medical and University Libraries; A Review of the Situation in the U.S. in 1964. 19-39, HASH
Hirsch, Felix E. Die Amerikanische College-Bibliothek. Gedanken über einen Hauptpfeiler des Wissenschaftlichen Bibliothekswesens in den Vereinigten Staaten. 267-278, WEHM

COLLEGE AND UNIVERSITY LIBRARIES - U.S. - Hist.

Moore, Everett T. A Revolution in American University Libraries. 97-105, HASH
Rouse, Roscoe. The Libraries of Nineteenth-Century College Societies. 25-42, GJEL

COLLEGE AND UNIVERSITY LIBRARIES - Use studies
see Use studies - College and university libraries

COLLEGE AND UNIVERSITY LIBRARIES - Utrecht

EVER

SOME

COLLEGE AND UNIVERSITY LIBRARIES - Winchester, Eng.

Blakiston, J. M. G. Winchester College Library in the Eighteenth and Early Nineteenth Centuries. 23-45, OLDH

COLLEGE OF ARMS, London
see Gt. Brit. College of Arms. Library. Mss. (Arundel no. 9)

COLLEGIUM SOCIETATIS JESU IN SUETIA. Bibliotheca. Stockholm
see Stockholm. Collegium Societatis Jesu in Suetia. Bibliotheca

Colliander, Elof.
Die Niederdeutschen Drucke der Universitätsbibliothek zu Uppsala aus dem 16., 17. und 18. Jahrhundert. 147-170, GRAP

Collijn, Isak Gustav Alfred.
Biblioteca "Collegii Societatis Jesu in Suetia." Några Bidrag till Kännedomen om Jesuiternas Boksamling på Gramunkeholmen. 75-91, ANNE
En Birgitta-Handskrift från Klostret Maria Maihingen. 8-14, GRAP
Journal de Voyage en Scandinavie d'un Bibliophile Français. 187-199, GODE
Kalendarium Munkalivense. Ein Schwedisch-Norwegisches Birgittinerkalendarium. 82-92, DEGE
Några ord om Böcker Tryckta på Svenska i Utlandet under 1500-Talet. Med Anledning av ett till Universitetsbiblioteket i Oslo Gjort Nyförvärv. 23-29, MUNT
Paul Grijs, Uppsalas Förste Boktryckare 1510-1519. 97-138, UPPS
Schwedische Donate. 47-52, SCHW
Some Rare Americana. 50-55, BISH
Über den Verfasser des Cod. Vindob. 14105. 286-290, BICK
Die Wanderung eines Druckerzeichens. Zu GfT 785-786. 74-79, HAEB
Zwei Widmungsexemplare eines Werkes des Valentinus Erythraeus (1574). 111-116, LEYG

Collijn, Isak Gustav Alfred, jt. ed.
HAEB

COLLIJN, ISAK GUSTAV ALFRED

COLL

COLLIJN, ISAK GUSTAV ALFRED - Bibl.

Nelson, Axel. Förteckning över Isak Collijns intill den 17 Juli 1925 Utgivna Skrifter. 1-45, COLL

Collin, Torborg.
Bibliografi over Harald L. Tveterås' Trykte Arbeider. 255-263, TVET

Collison, R. L.
The Future of Bibliography. 215-218, MIKH

Collmann, O.
Einige Mitteilungen über die Raczyńskische Bibliothek. 57-65, VERP

COLMAR. Stadtbibliothek

Kimmenauer, Alfred. Colmarer Beriana. Zu Ludwig Ber's Bibliothek und Papieren. 244-251, BENZ

Colmi, Elsbet.
Thomas Kees Wesaliensis. Aus der Werkstatt eines Weseler Druckers in Paris 1507-1515/16. 68-97, BENZ

COLOGNE. Bibliothekar-Lehrinstitut des Landes Nordrhein-Westfalen

Sickmann, Ludwig. Der Katalogisierungsunterricht für Anfänger. Bericht über Erfahrungen im Bibliothekar-Lehrinstitut. 448-457, JUCH

COLOGNE - Book industry and trade
see Book industry and trade - Cologne

COLOGNE - Bookbinding
see Bookbinding - Cologne

COLOGNE - Illumination of books and manuscripts
see Illumination of books and manuscripts - Cologne

COLOGNE - Incunabula
see Incunabula - Cologne

COLOGNE. Klarissenkloster. Mss.

Galley, Eberhard. Miniaturen aus dem Kölner Klarissenkloster. Ein Kapitel Rheinischer Buchmalerei des 14. Jahrhunderts. 15-28, JUCH

COLOGNE. Kreuzbrüderkloster. Bibliothek

Theele, Joseph. Aus der Bibliothek des Kölner Kreuzbrüderklosters. 253-263, DEGE

COLOGNE - Library schools
see Library schools - Cologne

COLOGNE - Music libraries and collections
see Music libraries and collections - Cologne

COLOGNE - Music literature and scores - Manuscripts - Collections
see Music literature and scores - Manuscripts - Collections - Cologne

COLOGNE - Printers
see Printers - Cologne

COLOGNE - Printing
see Printing - Cologne

COLOGNE. Universitäts- und Stadtbibliothek. Mss. (Music)

Kahl, Willi. Musikhandschriften aus dem Nachlass Ernst Bückens in der Kölner Universitäts- und Stadtbibliothek. 159-171, JUCH

COLOGNE. Zentralkatalog der Wissenschaftlichen Bibliotheken des Landes Nordrhein-Westfalen

Iwand, Käthe. Der Zentralkatalog der Ausländischen Literatur. 369-376, JUCH

COLON CLASSIFICATION
see Classification - Systems - Colon

COLOPHONS

Garitte, Gérard. Sur une Formule des Colophons de Manuscrits Grecs (η μὲτ χει ρ η γράΨαδα).I, 359-390, ALBB

COLOR IN LIBRARIES
see Architecture and building - Color, decoration, etc.

Colwell, Eileen.
W. C. Berwick Sayers and Children's Libraries. 18-21, SAYW

COMESTOR, PETRUS
see Petrus Comestor

COMMUNIST COUNTRIES - Government publications
see Government publications - Communist countries

COMMUNITY AND THE LIBRARY
see Library and the public

Comparetti, Dominique.
La Bibliothèque de Philodème. 118-129, CHAT
Sur une Inscription d'Halicarnasse. 175-185, GRAU

Compton, Charles H.
An Unfinished Chapter in Missouri Library Legislation. 412-421, WILS

COMPUTERS

Pflug, Günther. Der Einfluss der Elektronischen Datenverarbeitung auf die Katalogisierungspraxis. 111-124, FUCH

COMPUTERS - U.S.

Brodman, Estelle and Chester R. Gough. Computers in Medical and University Libraries; A Review of the Situation in the U.S. in 1964. 19-39, HASH

Coney, Donald.
An Experimental Index for Apportioning Departmental Book Funds for a University Library. 422-428, WILS

CONFERENCES, meetings, etc. - Poland

Grycz, Józef. Po Czwartym Zjeździe Bibliotekarzy Polskich w Warszawie 30. Maja—2. Czerwca 1936 r. 24-28, EMLE

CONGRESO DE COOPERACIÓN INTELECTUAL. 2d, Santander, 1956

El II Congreso de Cooperación Intelectual y Menéndez Pelayo. 283-284, MENE

CONNECTICUT - Libraries
see Libraries - Connecticut

CONNECTICUT. State Library, Hartford

Godard, George Seymour. A Brief Summary of the Activities of the Connecticut State Library, Hartford. 172-177, PUTN

CONSTANCE. Von Wessenbergische Stadtbibliothek

Reinhard, Ewald. I. H. von Wessenberg als Freund der Schönen Künste. 59-63, VERD

CONSTANTINOPLE
see Istanbul

COOPERATION
see also Interlibrary loans; Interlibrary relationships; School and public library relationship; Storage and deposit libraries

COOPERATION - Gt. Brit.

Filon, S. P. L. W. C. Berwick Sayers: His Connection with the National Central Library and His Contribution to Library Co-operation. 22-25, SAYW
Walford, A. J. Documentation Services and Library Co-operation in the Social Sciences. 256-260, KYLE

COOPERATION, International
see also Research materials

COOPERATION, International

Bresha-Botie, A. S. Biblioteka Obŭedinennykh Natsij v Zheneve i Mezhdunarodnoe Mezhbibliotechnoe Sotrudnichestvo. 121-126, MIKH
Coblans, Herbert. A Note on Cataloguing at the International Level. 197-202, TVET
Frauendorfer, Sigmund v. Internationale Einheitskatalogisierung? Hemmnisse und Möglichkeiten. 335-347, BICK
Lydenberg, Harry Miller. Some Thoughts on the Part the Printed Book May Play in the International Field. 463-471, BICK
Sevensma, Tietse Pieter. Le Dr. Jan Emler et la Collaboration Internationale des Bibliothèques. 34-37, EMLE
Thompson, Anthony. Verden er Én (The World is One). 248-254, TVET

COOPERATION, International - Pakistan and India

Huq, A. M. Abdul. Co-operation in Indo-Pakistan Librarianship. 425-427, RANG

COOPERATION, International - Scandinavia

Schauman, Henrik. Samarbetet Mellan de Nordiska Parlamentsbiblioteken. 232-237, TVET

COOPERATION - Public libraries

Geldenblom, Gertrud. Co-operation in Public Libraries. 420-424, RANG

COOPERATION - Scandinavia

Tveterås, Harold L. A Federation for Library Co-operation across the Frontiers: Nordisk Vitenskapelig Bibliotekarforbund. 601-602, BRUM

COOPERATION - Sweden

Hjelmqvist, Bengt. Interessenkreise und Zentralmagazine: Über einen Neuen Schwedischen Organisationsplan. 15-18, ACKR
Silow, Alvar. Bibliotekens Samarbete. 214-220, GRAP

COOPERATION - Switzerland

Grosser, Hermann. Die Zusammenarbeit der Schweizerischen Bibliotheken. Rückblick und Ausschau. 129-142, SCHU

COOPERATIVE CATALOGING
see Cataloging, Cooperative

COOPERATIVE COMMITTEE ON LIBRARY BUILDING PLANS

Cameron, Donald F. The Library Builder. 42-45, DAVI

COOPERATIVE LIBRARY SYSTEMS - Denmark

Abitz, Oluf. Foellesbogsamlinger. 48-56, LASS

COOPERATIVE LIBRARY SYSTEMS - Nashville

NASH

COOPERATIVE LIBRARY SYSTEMS - Norway

Berntsen, Bernhard. Biblioteksentralen - en Tjener i Bibliotekenes Opplysningsarbeid. 98-103, NORS

COORDINATE INDEXING (Uniterm system)
see Indexing - Systems

Copeland, J. Isaac.
Developing the Peabody Book Collection. 10-11, NASH

Copeland, Thomas.
The Opening of the Burke Papers. 24-25, LAMB

COPENHAGEN - Architecture and building - College and university libraries
see Architecture and building - College and university libraries - Copenhagen

COPENHAGEN - Architecture and building - National libraries
see Architecture and building - National libraries - Copenhagen

COPENHAGEN - Architecture and building - Public libraries
see Architecture and building - Public libraries - Copenhagen

COPENHAGEN - Book numbers
see Book numbers - Copenhagen

COPENHAGEN - Catalogs
see Catalogs - Copenhagen

COPENHAGEN - Circulation procedures
see Circulation procedures - Copenhagen

COPENHAGEN. Kommunebibliotekerne

Thomsen, Carl. Bygherren, Bygmesteren og Bibliotekaren. 237-247, HEIN

COPENHAGEN - Kongelige Bibliotek

COPE

Dahl, Svend. Det Kongelige Biblioteks Bygning. Traek af dens Forhistorie. 39-56, BAYJ
———— H. O. Lange og de Videnskabelige Biblioteker. 322-340, LANE
Lange, Hans Ostenfeldt. Tale ved Det Kongelige Bibliotheks Nye Bygnings Indvielse d. 27. November 1906. 57-67, BAYJ
Madsen, Victor. Pergamenttryk i det Kongelige Bibliotek i København. Et Supplement. 199-214, COLL

COPENHAGEN - Kongelige Bibliotek - Hist.

Birkelund, Palle. Det Kongelige Bibliotek og dets Publikum. 119-132, DAHA

————. Nordmænd i Det Kgl. Biblioteks Tjeneste. 30-51, TVET

COPENHAGEN - Kongelige Bibliotek - Mss. (Ingrids Helgenproces)

Jørgensen, Ellen. Et Brudstykke af den Hellige Ingrid af Skenninges Helgenproces. 71-73, COLL

COPENHAGEN - Librarians
see Librarians - Copenhagen

COPENHAGEN - Medical literature - Cataloging
see Medical literature - Cataloging - Copenhagen

COPENHAGEN - National libraries
see National libraries - Copenhagen

COPENHAGEN - Personnel
see Personnel - Copenhagen

COPENHAGEN - Questionnaires
see Questionnaires - Copenhagen

COPENHAGEN. Universitet. Bibliotek

COPA

Drachmann, A. G. Call Numbers. 198-206, HANS
Prytz, Johansen J. Den Gamle Medicinske Katalog på Universitetsbiblioteket, København. 1-7, DAHA
Topsøe-Jensen, H. Om et Eksemplar af H. Steffens: "Was Ich Erlebte" i Universitetsbibliotekets 1. Afd., København. 95-100, DAHA

COPENHAGEN. Universitet. Bibliotek - Hist.

Birkelund, Palle. Svend Dahl. iii-ix, DAHA

COPERNICUS, NICOLAUS. <u>De Revolutionibus Orbium Caelestium</u>

Rosen, Edward. Copernicus' Quotation from Sophocles. 367-379, ALBA

COPTIC MANUSCRIPTS
see Manuscripts, Coptic

COPTIC PALEOGRAPHY
see Paleography, Coptic

COPYING METHODS
see also Duplicating processes; Photographic reproduction

COPYING METHODS

Kragemo, Helge Bergh. Zur Frage der Rationalisierung des Tauschverkehrs einer Wissenschaftlichen Bibliothek. 377-381, MUNT
Lund, Hanna. Der Adrema-Betrieb in der Katalogisierung. 404-409, MUNT
Predeek, A. Fortschritte im Katalogdruck nach dem Adrema-System. 197-210, MUNT

COPYING SERVICES
see Photographic reproduction services

COPYISTS

Martin, Henry. Notes sur les Écrivains au Travail. 535-544, CHAT

COPYISTS - Bologna - Hist. - 13th cent.

Leicht, Pier Silverio. Scrittori e Miniatori di Codici nei Loro Rapporti cogli Scolari Bolognesi nella Seconda Metà del Sec. XIII. 227-233, GREG

COPYISTS - Ferrara

Fava, Domenico. Scrittorii Conventuali Ferraresi del Quattrocento. 129-135, GREG

COPYISTS - Jewish

Freimann, Aaron. Jewish Scribes in Medieval Italy. 231-342, MARX

COPYISTS - Westphalia

Pfannmüller, Gustav. Westfälische Schreiberverse aus dem Jahre 1238. 71-72, SCHR

COPYRIGHT

Solberg, Thorvald. Copyright and Librarians. 315-328, HANS

COPYRIGHT - Germany

Stois, Max. Bibliothek und Editio Princeps. 283-288, LEID

COPYRIGHT - Gt. Brit.

Colehan, Philip. A Difficult but Agreeable Task. 26-27, LAMB

COPYRIGHT - International

Gilbert, Francis. Two Conflicting Theories of International Copyright Protection. 106-114, ENGE
Solberg, Thorvald. The United States and International Copyright. 410-422, PUTN

COPYRIGHT LIBRARIES
see Depository libraries

COPYRIGHT - Royalties - Denmark

Jepsen, Hans Lyngby. Biblioteksafgiften—Vederlag for Hvad og Hvordan? 87-94, THOM

COPYRIGHT - Unauthorized reprints
see Reprints, Unauthorized

COPYRIGHT - U.S. - Hist. - 1790-1800

Goff, Frederick R. The First Decade of the Federal Act for Copyright, 1790-1800. 101-128, WROT

CORBIE. Abbaïe de Saint Pierre. Mss.

Bischoff, Bernhard. Hadoardus and the Manuscripts of Classical Authors from Corbie. 39-57, ALBA

CORNELIUS VAN ZIERICKZEE

Corsten, Severin. Zur Person des Kölner Druckers Cornelius von Zierickzee. 9-17, JUCR

CORPORATE ENTRY
see Cataloging - Corporate entry

CORRESPONDENCE - Administration

Schmieder, Wolfgang. Ein Beitrag zur Verwaltung von Briefautographen. 133-140, BOLL

CORRESPONDENCE - Collections - Basel

Husner, Fritz. Die Editio Princeps des "Corpus Historiae Byzantinae." Johannes Oporin, Hieronymus Wolf und die Fugger. 143-162, SCHU
Zehntner, Hans. Musikerbriefe in der Universitätsbibliothek Basel. 140-149, FEDO

CORRESPONDENCE - Collections - Greifswald

MENN

CORRESPONDENCE - Collections - Innsbruck

Galante, Andrea. L'Epistolario del Cardinale Cristoforo Madruzzo presso L'Archivio di Stato di Innsbruck. II, 787-805, HORT

CORRESPONDENCE - Collections - Königsberg

Goldstein, Ludwig. Karl Rosenkranz und Alexander Jung. Mit Vierzehn Unveröffentlichten Rosenkranz-Briefen. 132-158, KÖNI

CORRESPONDENCE - Collections - Neuchâtel

Godet, Marcel. Au Temps de la "Respublica Litterarum." Jacob Christophe Iselin et Louis Bourguet. 117-127, SCHU

CORRESPONDENCE - Collections - New York (City)

Davidson, Israel. A Collection of Letters from Sages of Israel only Found in the Jewish Theological Seminary. 1-14, (Hebrew section), FREI
Rivkind, Isaac. Correspondence of Elijah Morpugo. 138-159, (Hebrew section), FREI

CORRESPONDENCE - Collections - Sheffield

Copeland, Thomas. The Opening of the Burke Papers. 24-25, LAMB

CORRESPONDENCE - Collections - Uppsala

Lewenhaupt, Eugène. Upsala Universitetsbiblioteks Brefsamlingar. Försök till Historik. 195-207, ANNE

CORRESPONDENCE - Preservation

Dormoy, Marie. Du Droit de Détruire. 489-492, BONN
Hamilton, J. G. de Roulhac. On the Importance of Unimportant Documents. 511-518, WILS

CORRESPONDENCE - Scandinavian - Collections - Helsinki

Hasselblatt, Emil. Brev av Nordiska

Författare i Helsingfors Universitetsbibliotek. 71-97, HULA

CORRESPONDENCE - Serbo-Croatian - Collections - Sofia

Bozhinov, Liuben Al. Dokumentite na Sŭrbokhŭrvatski ezik v Bŭlgarskiia Istoricheski Arkhiv. 51-59, MIKH

CORRESPONDENCE - Swedish - Bibl.

Lewenhaupt, Eugène. Upsala Universitetsbibliotek Brefsamlingar. Försök till Historik. 195-207, ANNE

Corrodi-Sulzer, A.
Neues aus dem Leben des Bürgermeisters Jörg Müller. 212-238, ESCZ

Corsi, Domenico.
La Biblioteca dei Frati Domenicani di S. Romano di Lucca nel Sec. XV. 295-310, GALL

Corsten, Hermann, jt. ed.
JUCR

Corsten, Severin.
Zur Person des Kölner Druckers Cornelius von Zierickzee. 9-17, JUCR

Cortés, Narciso Alonso.
Un Cómico Hidalgo. I, 62-67, ARTI

Cortissoz, Royal.
Lydenberg as a Friend. 455, LYDE

CORVEY (Benedictine abbey)

Behrend, Fritz. Höxter-Corvey in Geschichte, Sage und Dichtung. 277-286, BÖME
Boeckler, Albert. Corveyer Buchmalerei unter Einwirkung Wibalds von Stablo. 133-147, BÖME

CORVEY (Castle). Bibliothek.

Löffler, Klemens. Die Corveyer Schlossbibliothek. 287-296, BÖME

Cory, John Mackenzie.
The Relative Theory of Specialization. 611-617, MOOR

COSIO, JOAQUIN TELESFORO TRUEBA y
see Trueba y Cosio, Joaquin Telesforo

Cossío, José María de.
Noticia de Don Manuel de la Cuesta y Sus Versos. II, 446-498, ARTI

Costantini, Guido.
L'Opera Letteraria di Attilio Hortis. I, 7-112, HORT

Couch, W. T.
Books That Ought to Be Written. 429-437, WILS

Couderc, C.
Essai de Classement des Manuscrits des Annales de Flodoard. 719-731, HAVE

Coudres, Hans-Peter des.
Die Bibliothek des Max-Planck-Instituts für Ausländisches und Internationales Privatrecht in Hamburg. Ihr Werden und Ihre Stellung Innerhalb Verwandter Sammlungen. 50-60, TIEM

Countryman, Gratia A.
Mr. Putnam and the Minneapolis Public Library. 5-9, PUTN

COUNTY LIBRARIES
see also Cooperative library systems; Package libraries

COUNTY LIBRARIES - Gt. Brit.

Jensen, Erik Allerslev. Engelsk Oplandsarbejde. 123-134, LASS

COUNTY LIBRARIES - Multi-county libraries
see Regional libraries

COUNTY LIBRARIES - Services to schools
see School libraries (Rural schools)

Courbaud, Edmond.
Sur L'Épitre I,l d'Horace. 354-366, CHAT

Cowley, A. E.
Ein Soncino-Druck aus Kairo 1566. 89-90, FREN

Cowley, John D.
The English Librarian. 15-22, GODE
What Shall We Teach the Librarian? 18-23, EMLE

Coyecque, Ern.
Guillaume Larcher, Bibliothécaire du Cabinet Henri IV. 129-132, GODE

CRACOW
see Kraków

Crane, Verner W.
The Promotion Literature of Georgia. 281-298, EAME

Cranshaw, J.
Between the Wars. 10-12, LAMB

Craster, Herbert Henry Edmund.
A Note on the Early History of Libraries in Oxford. 169-171, LEYG

Cristofari, Maria.
La Tipografia Vicentina nel Secolo XVI. 191-214, FERR

CROATIA - Bibliography, National
see Bibliography, National - Croatia

CROATIA - Libraries
see Libraries - Croatia

Croiset, Alfred.
Essai de Restitution d'un Passage de L'Éloge d'Hélène Attribué à Gorgias. 127-132, GRAU

Croix, Jean Tremblot de la.
Deux Vrais Bibliophiles. 525-534, BONN
Marques de la Bibliothèque Capitulaire de Noyon. 237-242, CALO

CRONSTEDSKA SAMLINGEN. Uppsala. Universitet. Biblioteket
see Uppsala. Universitet. Biblioteket. Cronstedska Samlingen

CRONSTEDT, JACOB, greve - Library
Holmgren, Gustaf. Om Cronstedtska Samlingen i Uppsala Universitets-bibliotek och dess Tillkomst. Några Anteckningar. 519-560, GRAP

Crossley, Charles A.
New Schemes of Classification: Principles and Practice. 113-129, RANG

CROTUS, JOHANNES
see Crotus Rubeanus, Johannes

CROTUS RUBEANUS, JOHANNES
Diesch, Carl. Crotus Rubeanus im Dienste des Herzogs Albrecht. 45-61, KÖNI
Kuhnert, Ernst. Die Nova Bibliotheca des Herzogs Albrecht. 209-219, MILF

Crous, Ernst, jt. ed.
HAEB

Crous, Ernst.
Die Anfänge des Antiquadrucks in Deutschland und Seinen Nachbarländern. 33-42, LOUB
Die Bücherzeichen (Exlibris) in den Wiegendrucken der Staatsbibliothek. 240-253, HARN
Münster i.W. und der Wiegendruck. 107-121, HAEB
Schrift und Satz im Berliner Buchdruck von der Mitte des 16. bis zur Mitte des 18. Jahrhunderts. Ein Beitrag zur Geschichte des Deutschen Buchstils in Wenig Bekannter Zeit. 37-45, LEID

CROWLAND ABBEY. Library - Catalog
Boese, Helmut. Ein Mittelalterliches Bücherverzeichnis von Croyland Abbey. 286-295, VORS

CROWLAND, Eng. - Manuscripts - Collections
see Manuscripts - Collections - Crowland, Eng.

CROYLAND ABBEY
see Crowland Abbey

CRUGERUS, LAURENTIUS JOHANNIS - Library
Dahlberg, Ragnar. En Volym ur Michael Agricolas Boksamling. 57-70, SCHA

CRYPTOGRAPHY - Hist. - Ancient
Piccoli, Giuseppe. Metodi Steganografici e Sistemi Crittografici Antichi. 597-605, GALL

CUBICLES, Study
see Carrels

Cudworth, Charles.
Richard, Viscount Fitzwilliam, and the French Baroque Music in the Fitzwilliam Museum, Cambridge. 27-31, FEDO

CUERPO FACULTATIVO DE ARCHIVEROS, BIBLIOTECARIOS Y ARQUEÓLOGOS, Spain
see Spain. Cuerpo Facultativo de Archiveros, Bibliotecarios y Arqueólogos

CUI, CÉSAR - Correspondence - Collections - Barcelona
Anglés, Higinio. Relations Épistolaires entre César Cui et Philippe Pedrell. 15-21, FEDO

CUJAS, decipherer of papyrus
Delisle, Léopold Victor. Cujas Déchiffreur de Papyrus. 486-491, CHAT

Cunningham, Eileen-R.
Some Items of Americana Medica Published Southwest of the Alleghenies and Their Authors. 25-26, STUM

CURRICULUM VITAE DEL PROF. DOMENICO FAVA. 39-40, FAVA

CURRICULUM VITAE DI MONS. ANGELO MERCATI. VII-VIII, MERC

Currier, Margaret, jt. author
Townsend, Rebecca Dutton, Margaret Currier, et al. A Selection of Baskerville Imprints in the Yale University Library. 285-297, KEOG

Currier, Thomas Franklin.
The Whittier Leaflet "Pericles." 175-178 178, HANS

CUSPINIANUS, JOANNES - Library
Ankwicz-Kleehoven, Hans. Die Bibliothek des Dr. Johann Cuspinian. 208-227, BICK

Custodi, Pietro, Barone.
Lettere in: Gallavresi, G. Alcune Lettere del Barone Custodi Riguardanti le Re-

lazioni del Munifico Bibliofilo coll'Ambrosiana e colla Famiglia Borromeo. 403-412, CERI

Cutolo, Alessandro.
Due Momenti Essenziali nella Storia del Libro in Italia. 311-323, GALL

CUT-OUTS, Paper
see Paper work

CUTTER EXPANSIVE CLASSIFICATION
see Classification - Systems - Expansive

CUTTER NUMBERS
see Book numbers

CYRIACUS ANCONITANUS
see Ciriaco de' Pizzicolli, of Ancona

CYRIAQUE D'ANCONA
see Ciriaco de' Pizzicolli, of Ancona

CZECHOSLOVAK BIBLIOGRAPHICAL INSTITUTE
Emler, Jan. L. J. Živného Úsilí o Českou Bibliografii. 69-73, ŽIVN

CZECHOSLOVAKIA - Acquisitions
see Acquisitions - Czechoslovakia

CZECHOSLOVAKIA - Bibliography, National
see Bibliography, National - Czechoslovakia

CZECHOSLOVAKIA - Cataloging
see Cataloging - Czechoslovakia

CZECHOSLOVAKIA - Depository libraries
see Depository libraries - Czechoslovakia

CZECHOSLOVAKIA - Education for librarianship
see Education for librarianship - Czechoslovakia

CZECHOSLOVAKIA - Legal deposit (of books, etc.)
see Legal deposit (of books, etc.) - Czechoslovakia

CZECHOSLOVAKIA - Libraries
see Libraries - Czechoslovakia

CZECHOSLOVAKIA - Libraries and librarianship
see Libraries and librarianship - Czechoslovakia

CZECHOSLOVAKIA - Library legislation
see Library legislation - Czechoslovakia

CZECHOSLOVAKIA - Printing
see Printing - Czechoslovakia

CZECHOSLOVAKIA - Research libraries
see Research libraries - Czechoslovakia

CZECHOSLOVAKIAN ACADEMY OF SCIENCES. Library
Horák, František. Die Bibliothek der Tschechoslowakischen Akademie der Wissenschaften. 192-202, VORS

CZECHOSLOVAKIAN INCUNABULA
see Incunabula, Czechoslovakian

CZECHOSLOVAKIAN LITERATURE - Collections - London
Wharton, Leonard C. Brief Notes of Prague Printed Books in the British Museum. 42-45, EMLE

CZECHOSLOVAKIAN MANUSCRIPTS
see Manuscripts, Czechoslovakian

CZEEL, HEINRICUS
see Zell, Heinrich

Czumpelik, Rudolf.
Kardinal Passionei und Seine Beziehungen zu Prinz Eugen. 23-24, STUM

CZYTELNICY O BIBLIOTECE. 149-157, BYDG

CZYTELNICY O NAS. 114-122, KRAK

D. H. VARLEY. 5-7, VARL

Daae, Ludvig Ludvigsen.
Professor Georg Sverdrup. 1-42, (pt. 2), OSLU
Universitets-Bibliothekar F. W. Keyser. 43-55, (pt. 2), OSLU

DAAE, LUDVIG LUDVIGSEN
DAAE
Halvorsen, Jens Braage. Professor Ludvig Daae. Supplement af K. V. Hammer. 61-63, (pt. 2), OSLU
Nielsen, Yngvar. Professor Ludvig Daae: Mindetale. 63-71, (pt. 2), OSLU

DAAE, LUDVIG LUDVIGSEN - Library
Schaanning, Maja. Litt om Professor Ludvig Daaes Boksamling. 214-225, MUNT

DAG HAMMERSKJOLD LIBRARY. United Nations
see United Nations. Dag Hammerskjold Library

Dahl, Svend
COPA

Dahl, Svend.
Friedrich Münter und Seine Bibliothek. 291-305, BICK
H. O. Lange og de Videnskabelige Biblioteker. 322-340, LANE
Det Kongelige Biblioteks Bygning. Traek af dens Forhistorie. 39-56, BAYJ
P. A. Munch i Vatikanets Arkiv. 30-48, MUNT

DAHL, SVEND
DAHA
Birkelund, Palle. Svend Dahl. iii-ix, DAHA

DAHL, SVEND - Bibl.
Møller, Gerda. Svend Dahl-Bibliografi 1948-1963. x-xii, DAHA

Dahlberg, Ragnar, jt. ed.
SCHA

Dahlberg, Ragnar.
Åtten Reuterholms Exlibris. 108-114, HULT
Bidrag till den Svenska Reformationstidens Bibliografi. 58-70, HULA
Gutterwitziana. 295-301, COLL
Helsingfors Universitetsbiblioteks Exemplar af Psalterium Dauidis 1510. 140-144, HULA
Några Okända Svenska Kungliga Pärmstämplar. 42-50, TUDE
Två Böcker med Märklig Proveniens i Helsingfors Universitetsbibliotek. 127-136, SCHA
En Volym ur Michael Agricolas Boksamling. 57-70, SCHA

DAHLBERG, RAGNAR
DAHL

DAHLBERG, RAGNAR - Bibl.
Castrén, Lisa. Bibliografi över Ragnar Dahlbergs Tryckta Skrifter 1900-1947. 351-360, DAHL

Dahlgren, E. W.
Gamla Tyska Kartor i Kungl. Biblioteket. 93-123, ANNE

Dainotti, Virginia Carini.
Domenico Fava - Profilo. 15-38, FAVA

Dakin, Susanna Bryant.
"His Mild and Magnificent Eye." 55-61, HAMM

Dalgliesh, Alice and Margaret B. Evans.
Designing Children's Books. 573-577, MOOR

D'Alós, Ramon.
Documenti per la Storia della Biblioteca di Alfonso il Magnanimo. 390-422, EHRE

DAMASCIUS, the Syrian. Ms.
Ruelle, Charles-Émile. Notice du Codex Marcianus 246, Contenant le Traité du Philosophe Damascius sur les Premiers Principes. 547-552, GRAU

Dancke, Per.
Claus Lydersen Fasting og Hans Bokfortegnelse. 5-24, HALV

DANMARKS BIBLIOTEKSFORENING.
Optryksudvalg
see Nyt Dansk Litteraturselskab

Danner, H. W.
Het Gebouw Drift 31. 60-63, EVER

DANTE ALIGHIERI - Collections - Aachen
Fromm, Emil. Die Dante-Sammlung der Alfred von Reumont'schen Bibliothek. 94-141, (pt. 1), AACH

DANTE ALIGHIERI - De Vulgari Eloquentia
Rajna, Pio. Il Primo Capitolo del Trattato De Vulgari Eloquentia Tradotto e Commentato. 113-128, HORT

DANTE ALIGHIERI - Divina Commedia
Zingarelli, N. La Processione nell'Eden Dantesco. 363-369, HORT

DANTE ALIGHIERI - Divina Commedia - Inferno: V: 70-142
Schulz, Erich. Immermanns Übersetzung aus Dante. 297-301, BÖME

DANTE ALIGHIERI - Mss. Divina Commedia
Auerbach, Erich. Die Randglossen des Cod. Hamilton 203 zum Ersten und Zweiten Gesang der Göttlichen Komödie. 45-50, KUHN

Danton, J. Periam.
William Cartwright and His Comedies, Tragi-Comedies, with Other Poems . . . . 1651. 438-456, WILS

DANZIG. Biblioteka Miejska
see Danzig. City Library

DANZIG - Catalogs
see Catalogs - Danzig

DANZIG. City Library
Günther, Otto. Mittelalterliches aus den Handschriften der Marienkirche in Danzig. 123-141, MILF
——— Der Neapolitaner Johannes Bernardinus Bonifacius, Marchese von Oria, und die Anfänge der Danziger Stadtbibliothek. 107-128, WILM

Schwarz, F. Analyse eines Kataloges. 326-338, KÖNI

DANZIG. Elisabeth-Hospital

Ziesemer, Walther. Zur Kenntnis des Bibliothekswesens Preussens im 15. Jahrhundert. 393-400, KÖNI

DANZIG. Hospitalis Sancte Elisabeth
see Danzig. Elisabeth-Hospital

DANZIG - Manuscripts - Collections
see Manuscripts - Collections - Danzig

DANZIG. Marienbibliothek
see Danzig. Marienkirche. Bibliothek

DANZIG. Marienkirche. Bibliothek. Mss.

Günther, Otto. Mittelalterliches aus den Handschriften der Marienkirche in Danzig. 123-141, MILF

DANZIG. Oberpfarrkirche von St. Marien
see Danzig. Marienkirche. Bibliothek

DANZIG. Stadtbibliothek
see Danzig. City Library

Darapsky, Elisabeth.
Ein Altes Ausleihebuch. 47-50, MAIN
Bibliothekare der Stadtbibliothek Mainz. 17-30, MAIN

Dareste, Rodolphe.
Cicéron, Pro Flacco, XXIX-XXXII. 7-12, GRAU

Darling, Richard L.
Children's Books Following the Civil War. 63-84, GJEL

DARMSTADT. Hof- und Landesbibliothek
see Darmstadt. Landesbibliothek

DARMSTADT - Incunabula - Collections
see Incunabula - Collections - Darmstadt

DARMSTADT. Landesbibliothek

Schmidt, Adolf. Baron Hüpsch in Köln als Inkunabelnsammler und Händler. 45-63, HAEB

DARMSTADT. Landesbibliothek - Mss. (3065)

Schmidt, Adolf. Der Einband der Goldenen Bulle von 1356 in der Landesbibliothek zu Darmstadt. 105-117, LOUB

Darmstaedter, Ludwig.
Die Dokumentensammlung Darmstaedter und Ihr Übergang an die Preussische Staatsbibliothek. 167-169, HARN

DARMSTAEDTER, LUDWIG

Doegen, Wilhelm. Die Stimmensammlung zur Dokumentensammlung Darmstaedter. 258-259, HARN

DARMSTAEDTER, LUDWIG - Library

Darmstaedter, Ludwig. Die Dokumentensammlung Darmstaedter und Ihr Übergang an die Preussische Staatsbibliothek. 167-169, HARN

DATA PROCESSING, Electronic
see Electronic data processing

DATING OF MUSIC SCORES
see Music literature and scores - Dating

Datta, B. K.
Acharya Ranganathan. 753-754, RANG

Datta, S., jt. author

Farradane, J., R. K. Poulton, and Mrs. S. Datta. Problems in Analysis and Terminology for Information Retrieval. 287-290, KYLE

Daugherty, James.
Illustrating for Children. 569-572, MOOR

DAUTZENBERG, P. J. F.

Fromm, Emil. Geschichte der Stadtbibliothek. I. Die Rathshandbibliothek im 17. und 18. Jahrhundert. II. Die Dautzenbergsche Schenkung. III. Die Stadtbibliothek von Ihrer Eröffnung (1831) bis zum J. 1889. IV. Die Verwaltung der Stadtbibliothek seit dem J. 1889. 21-48, (pt. 1), AACH

DAVID, CHARLES WENDELL

DAVI

David, Henri.
À la Bibliothèque. 87-91, OURS

Davidson, Israel.
A Collection of Letters from Sages of Israel only Found in the Jewish Theological Seminary. 1-14, (Hebrew section), FREI

Davidsson, Åke.
Smaländska Bilder i Uppsala Universitetsbibliotek. 75-85, OLSS

Davis, Herbert.
The Manuscripts of Swift's "Directions to Servants." 433-444, GREE

DAY, MILLS. <u>Proposals for Publishing . . . the Hebrew Bible</u>

Wegelin, Oscar. Mills Day's Proposed Hebrew Bible. 221-226, EAME

<u>DE ARTE VENANDI CUM AVIBUS</u>

Unterkircher, Franz. "De Arte Venandi cum Avibus." 653-661, BICK

"DE BRY" - Collections
Stevens, Henry Newton. The DeBry Collector's Painefull Peregrination along the Pleasant Pathway to Perfection. 269-276, EAME

DE BRY FAMILY (Theodore de Bry), publishers
Stevens, Henry Newton. The DeBry Collector's Painefull Peregrination along the Pleasant Pathway to Perfection. 269-276, EAME

D'Ewes, D. R.
Douglas Varley and the Cape Tercentenary Foundation. 27, VARL

DE FREESKA LANDRIUCHT-DRUKKERIJ
Kruitwagen, Bonaventura. De Freeska Landriucht-Drukkerij. 45-69, HAGU

De Ghellinck, Joseph.
En Marge des Catalogues des Bibliothèques Médiévales. 331-363, EHRE

De Gregori, Giorgio.
Appunti di Tenica Catalografica (la Scheda d'Autore per i Cataloghi di Musei e Gallerie). 215-226, FERR
Sulla Legislazione Italiana Relativa al Deposito degli Stampati. 75-87, GREG

DE LUXE BOOKS
see Limited edition books

De Maio, Romeo.
La Biblioteca Apostolica Vaticana sotto Paolo IV e Pio IV (1555-1565). I, 265-313, ALBB

De Marchi, A.
Vesti, Armi, Riti e Costumi nel Codice Omerico Illustrato dell'Ambrosiana. 1-35, CERI

De Marinis, Tammaro.
Nota su Angelo Catone di Benevento. 227-232, FERR

"DE PASCHA." Mss. Carmen
Rasi, P. Nuove Osservazioni sul Carmen de Pascha. 577-604, CERI

Debes, Dietmar.
Das Sequestrationsverzeichnis der Bibliothek des Thomasklosters zu Leipzig. 83-95, LÜLF
Zur Erwerbung des Papyrus Ebers. 139-141, BULL

Debes, Martha and Lieselotte Reuschel.
Die Ehemalige Bibliothek des Börsenvereins der Deutschen Buchhändler zu Leipzig. 243-257, LEIZ

Deckert, Helmut.
Karl Marx und Seine Kommilitonen als Hörer Schlegels in Bonn. 33-53, LÜLF
Die Übrigen Sondersammlungen. 166-171, DREL
Wider die Legende von den Bücherfriedhöfen. 36-40, BOLE

Deckert, Helmut, Marita Kremer, Hans Pfeifer and Lieselotte Willi.
Das Neue Buchmuseum der Sächsischen Landesbibliothek. 175-205, DREL

DECORAH, Iowa. Luther College
see Luther College, Decorah, Iowa

DEDICATIONS (in books)
Nyberg, Paul. Dedikationerna i Zachris Topelii Bibliotek. 145-163, HULA

Dedo, Richard.
Dichter unter den Deutschen Bibliothekaren. 37-47, MILF

Deetjen, Werner.
Die Weimarische Bibliothek unter Ernst August und Ernst August Constantin. 87-101, WEIM
Wielands Bibliothek. 1-10, WAHL

DEFENSE AND THE LIBRARY
see War and the library

Degering, Hermann, jt. ed.
BÖME; HAEB

Degering, Hermann.
Ein Calendarium Pugillare mit Computus aus dem Jahre 1294. 79-88, LOUB
Gottfried von Raesfeld. Sein Geschlecht, Sein Leben und Sein Testament. 137-250, MÜNS
Handschriften aus Echternach und Orval in Paris. 48-85, MILF
Der Katalog der Bibliothek des Klosters Marienfeld vom Jahre 1185. 53-64, SCHW
Nachträgliches zur Vitruvausgabe vom Jahre 1487 in der Leipziger Stadtbibliothek. 54-57, LEIP
Das Prümer Evangeliar (Ms. lat. theol. Fol. 733) in Berlin. 132-148, HARN
Wer War der Drucker der Erstausgabe des Vitruv? Ein Beitrag zur Geschichte des Römischen Buchdrucks. 175-202, HAEB

DEGERING, HERMANN
DEGE
Schmidt, Wieland. Hermann Degering, Erinnerungen aus der Staatsbibliothek. 126-129, LEUN

Deinboll, Rikka Bjølgerud.
Samarbeide Mellem Skole og Bibliotek. 73-82, NORN

Dekker, Annie F.
In de Spiegel der Horatiana. 402-407, BRUM

Del Re, Niccolò.
Il "Consilium pro Urbano VI" di Bartolomeo da Saliceto (Vat. lat. 5608). I, 213-263, ALBB

Delaborde, Comte François.
Note sur le Carolinus de Gilles de Paris. 195-203, CHAT

Delisle, Léopold Victor.
Cujas Déchiffreur de Papyrus. 486-491, CHAT
Discours. v-ix, HAVE
Notes sur les Anciennes Impressions des Classiques Latins et d'Autres Auteurs Conservées au XVe Siècle dans la Librairie Royale de Naples. 245-296, GRAU
Un Nouveau Manuscrit des Livres des Miracles de Grègoire de Tours. 1-8, HAVE

DELISLE, LÉOPOLD VICTOR
Klaiber, Ludwig. Léopold Delisle und die Reform der Bibliothèque Nationale. 156-168, LEYH

DELITSCH, HERMANN. Geschichte der Abendländischen Schreibformen
Löffler, Karl. Zur Geschichte der Abendländischen Schreibformen. Eine Würdigung des Gleichbetitelten Buches von Hermann Delitsch. 61-66, SCHR

Della Bona, Giuseppe Domenico.
Il Regesto delle Pergamene Goriziane e Friulane della Biblioteca Civica. 25-55, GORI

Della Vida, Levi.
Manoscritti Arabi di Origine Spagnola nella Biblioteca Vaticana. II, 133-189, ALBB

Dembowska, Maria.
Bibliotekarstwo i Bibliografia a Dokumentacja. 169-182, GRYC

DEMEN, HERMANN
Heitjan, Isabel. Die Korrespondenz des Kölner Buchhändlers Hermann Demen mit dem Hause Plantin-Moretus zu Antwerpen 1673-1706. 187-207, BENZ

DEMOSTHENES. Ms. In Midiam
Weil, Henri. D'un Signe Critique dans le Meilleur Mansucrit de Démosthène. 13-20, GRAU

Denecke, Dorothee.
Schnitzelbank, 1920-1937. [110]-[114], Sonderbeilage. BOLE

Denkinger, Marc.
Sainte-Beuve et L'Imprimeur Marc Ducloux. 209-219, BONN

DENMARK - Adult education - Library participation
see Adult education - Library participation - Denmark

DENMARK - Authors and libraries
see Authors and libraries - Denmark

DENMARK - Bibliography, National
see Bibliography, National - Denmark

DENMARK - Booksellers and libraries
see Booksellers and libraries - Denmark

DENMARK - Children's library services
see Children's library services - Denmark

DENMARK - Cooperative library systems
see Cooperative library systems - Denmark

DENMARK - Copyright - Royalties
see Copyright - Royalties - Denmark

DENMARK - Education for librarianship
see Education for librarianship - Denmark

DENMARK - Fines, fees, etc.
see Fines, fees, etc. - Denmark

DENMARK - Handicapped, Library services for
see Handicapped, Library services for - Denmark

DENMARK - Inexpensive editions
see Inexpensive editions - Denmark

DENMARK - In-service training
see In-service training - Denmark

DENMARK - Interlibrary loans
see Interlibrary loans - Denmark

DENMARK - Libraries
see Libraries - Denmark

DENMARK - Library legislation
see Library legislation - Denmark

DENMARK - Library schools
see Library schools - Denmark

DENMARK - Literary societies
see Literary societies - Denmark

DENMARK - Parish libraries
see Parish libraries - Denmark

DENMARK - Private libraries
see Private libraries - Denmark

DENMARK - Public libraries
see Public libraries - Denmark

DENMARK - Public libraries - Book selection -
see Public libraries - Book selection - Denmark

DENMARK - Public libraries - Centralization
see Public libraries - Centralization - Denmark

DENMARK - Public libraries - Services to groups
see Public libraries - Services to groups - Denmark

DENMARK - Public libraries - Services to hospitals
see Public libraries - Services to Hospitals - Denmark

DENMARK - Recruitung for librarianship
see Recruiting for librarianship - Denmark

DENMARK - Rules and regulations
see Rules and regulations - Denmark

DENMARK - Rural libraries
see Rural libraries - Denmark

DENMARK - Rural libraries - Book selection
see Rural libraries - Book selection - Denmark

DENMARK - School and public library relationship
see School and public library relationship - Denmark

DENMARK - School libraries
see School libraries - Denmark

DENMARK - Special libraries
see Special libraries - Denmark

DENTAL LIBRARIES

Lage, Louise C., Lois B. Miller, and Donald Washburn. Dental, Nursing, and Pharmaceutical Libraries, 1947-1957. 371-377, DOEJ

DENTAL LIBRARIES - Utrecht

Hulshoff, Margaretha H. De Bibliotheek van het Tandheelkundig Instituut. 160-163, EVER

DEPARTMENTALIZATION
see College and university libraries - Departmental and divisional libraries

DEPOSIT LIBRARIES
see Storage and deposit libraries

DEPOSITORY LIBRARIES - Acquisitions - Frankfurt a.M.

Günther, Eberhard. Die Sammlung des Deutschsprachigen Schrifttums durch die Deutsche Bibliothek. Probleme und Methoden. 78-90, EPPE

DEPOSITORY LIBRARIES - Bern

Bourgeois, Pierre. Le Dépôt Gratuit et Volontaire en Suisse. 397-401, BRUM

Brouty, Barth. Le Service des Entrées. 127-129, BERU

DEPOSITORY LIBRARIES - Czechoslovakia

Hrozný, Jindřich. Povinné Výtisky. 64-68, EMLE

DEPOSITORY LIBRARIES - Frankfurt a.M.

FRAD

DEPOSITORY LIBRARIES - Gothenburg, Sweden

Marklund, E. "Svenstrycket." 21-34, (fifth paper), GÖTE

DEPOSITORY LIBRARIES - Gt. Brit.

Kenyon, Sir Frederic G. Copyright Libraries. 248-254, PUTN

DEPOSITORY LIBRARIES - Oslo

OSLN

DEPOSITORY LIBRARIES - Russia

Bäckman, Edvin. LagstiftningenAngående Pliktexemplar i Sovjetunionen. 118-129, TUDE

DEPOSITORY LIBRARIES - Scandinavia

Munthe, Wilhelm. National Departments in Scandinavian Libraries. 296-299, HANS

DEPOSITORY LIBRARIES - Stockholm

Sundström, Einar. Om Tillkomsten av Kungl. Bibliotekets Svenska Tryckavdelning. 507-516, COLL

DEPOSITORY LIBRARIES - Sweden - Hist.

Ågren, Sven. Till Arkivleveransernas Historia. Några Anteckningar. 338-349, GRAP

Der Nersessian, Sirarpie.
An Armenian Lectionary of the Fourteenth Century. 231-237, GREE

Dervieux, Ermanno.
Incunabuli della Biblioteca del Seminario di Asti. II, 451-480, MANO

DESCRIPTIVE CATALOGING
see Cataloging

DETMOLD - Indulgences - Collections
see Indulgences - Collections - Detmold

DETMOLD-LIPPE, House of - Collections
see Lippe, House of - Collections - Detmold

Deuerlein, Ernst.
Die Erlanger Universitätsbibliothek im Spiegel der Reise- und Briefliteratur der Aufklärungszeit. 16-23, VERZ

Deutsch, Josef.
Ebers Calendarium Historicum mit Handschriftlichen Eintragungen aus Wolgast. 71-78, KUHN
Die Handschrift des Weseler Stadtrechts in der Abteilung für Niederdeutsche Literatur bei der Universitätsbibliothek in Greifswald. 233-247, BÖME

DEUTSCHE AKADEMIE DER DICHTER UND KÜNSTLER

Uhde-Bernays, Hermann. Eine Deutsche Akademie. 24-25, HELD

DEUTSCHE BIBLIOGRAPHIE
see Frankfurt a.M. Deutsche Bibliothek. Deutsche Bibliographie

DEUTSCHE BIBLIOTHEK, Frankfurt a.M.
see Frankfurt a.M. Deutsche Bibliothek

DIE DEUTSCHE BIBLIOTHEK IN ZAHLEN. 175-192, EPPE

DAS DEUTSCHE BUCH
see Frankfurt a.M. Deutsche Bibliothek. Deutsche Bibliographie; Deutsches Buch

DEUTSCHE BÜCHEREI, Leipzig
see Leipzig. Deutsche Bücherei

DEUTSCHE GESELLSCHAFT FÜR DOKUMENTATION

DEUD

DEUTSCHE MUSIKBIBLIOGRAPHIE

Franz, Rudi. Die Titeldrucke der Deutschen Bücherei. 157-173, LEIZ

DEUTSCHE NATIONALBIBLIOGRAPHIE

Franz, Rudi. Die Titeldrucke der Deutschen Bücherei. 157-173, LEIZ

DEUTSCHE NATIONALVERSAMMLUNG, Frankfurt a.M., 1848-1849. Bibliothek

Uhlendahl, Heinrich. Die Bibliothek der Deutschen Nationalversammlung von 1848/49. Eine Vorläuferin der Deutschen Bücherei. 147-155, LEYH

DEUTSCHER GESAMTKATALOG

Fick, Richard. Gesamt-Realkataloge. 95-110, MILF
Fuchs, Hermann. Der Gesamtkatalog der Preußischen Bibliotheken und Sein Ausbau zu einem Deutschen Gesamtkatalog. 209-216, KUHN
Kaiser, Rudolf. Die Behandlung der Ungarica im Preussischen Gesamtkatalog. 217-223, KUHN
Lehmann, Paul. Alte Vorläufer des Gesamtkatalogs. 69-81, LEYG
Vorstius, Joris. Vergangenheit, Gegenwart und Zukunft des Deutschen Gesamtkatalogs. 312-328, LEYG
Weber, Christoph. Der Gesamtkatalog der Preussischen Wissenschaftlichen Bibliotheken. 259-272, HARN

DEUTSCHER GESAMTKATALOG - Hist.

Fuchs, Hermann. Aus den Anfängen des Preussischen Gesamtkatalogs. 355-362, JUCH

DEUTSCHES ARCHÄOLOGISCHES INSTITUT. Römische Abteilung. Bibliothek

Harnack, Axel von. Einige Beobachtungen an den Deutschen Bibliotheken in Rom. 304-309, KUHN

DEUTSCHES BUCH- UND SCHRIFTMUSEUM, Leipzig
see Leipzig. Deutsches Buch- und Schriftmuseum

DEUTSCHES HISTORISCHES INSTITUT, Rome (City)

Harnack, Axel von. Einige Beobachtungen an den Deutschen Bibliotheken in Rom. 304-309, KUHN

DEUTSCHES MUSEUM FÜR BUCH UND SCHRIFT, Leipzig.
see Leipzig. Deutsches Buch- und Schriftmuseum

Devreesse, Robert.
Pour L'Histoire des Manuscrits du Fonds Vatican Grec. I, 315-336, ALBB

Dewey, Melvil.
Herbert Putnam. 22-23, PUTN

Dewton, Johannes L.
Die Kataloge der Kongressbibliothek in Buchform. 27-28, STUM

DI͡AKOVICH, BORIS

DIAK

Di͡akovich, Vl. Semeĭstvoto Ivan i Evdokii͡a Di͡akovich; po Sluchaĭ 25 Godishnii͡a Īubilei na B. Di͡akovich. [79]-102, DIAK
Pīeev, Aleksandr K. Nauchna deĭnost'. 30-34, DIAK
——— Proslaven Den' na Boris Di͡akovich. [5]-68, DIAK

——— Reformirane na Plovdivskata Narodna Biblioteka. 26-29, DIAK

DI͡AKOVICH, BORIS - Bibl.

Pi͡eev, Aleksandr K. Nauchna deĭmost'. 30-34, DIAK

DI͡AKOVICH FAMILY

Di͡akovich, Vl. Semeĭstvoto Ivan i Evdokii͡a Di͡akovich; po Sluchaĭ 25 Godishnii͡a Iubilei na B. Di͡akovi [79]-102, DIAK

DIBDIN, THOMAS F.
Kisser, Alois. Th. F. Dibdin (1776-1847). 435-445, BICK

DICTIONARY CATALOGS
see Catalogs - Dictionary

DIDEROT, DENIS

Tisserand, Roger. L'Académie de Dijon et Denis Diderot. 152-162, OURS

DIDOT, FRANÇOIS AMBROISE

Veyrin-Forrer, Jeanne. Les Premiers Caractères de François-Ambroise Didot (1781-1785). 159-173, CALO

Diepenbach, Wilhelm.
Gustav Binz als Direktor der Mainzer Stadtbibliothek. 23-29, BINZ

Diesch, Carl.
Crotus Rubeanus im Dienste des Herzogs Albrecht. 45-61, KÖNI
Fürst Boguslav Radziwill und Seine Bücherschenkung an die Königsberger Schloßbibliothek. 117-128, LEYG

Dieserud, Juul.
The Abbreviation of Imprints. 179-184, HANS

DIESSENHOFEN, Ger. Sankt Katharinenthal (Dominican monastery)
see Sankt Katharinenthal (Dominican monastery)

DIETRICHSTEIN'SCHE FIDEICOMMISS-BIBLIOTHEK
see Mikulov, Moravia. Fürstlich Dietrichstein'sche Fideicommiss-Bibliothek

Dietzel, Armin.
Ein Altkirchlicher Christushymnus. Der Papyrus Erlangensis 1 im Vergleich mit den Abendhymnen (Ms. Erlg. 1234). 83-93, REDE

DIEZ, HEINRICH FRIEDRICH VON - Library

Balcke, Curt. Heinrich Friedrich von Diez und Sein Vermächtnis in der Preußischen Staatsbibliothek. 187-200, KUHN

Diez, Ortwin.
Otto, Abgeordneter für Trier. Ein Beitrag zur Preussischen Verfassungsgeschichte. 136-169, MAIZ

DIJON. Académie des Sciences, Arts et Belles-Lettres
see Académie des Sciences, Arts et Belles-Lettres de Dijon

DIJON. Archives Municipales

Grémaud, Gabriel. Aux Archives de Dijon. Quelques Documents Portant la Signature des Rois de France. 115-119, OURS
Lebel, Paul. Les Registres d'Échevinage aux Archives de Dijon. 137-146, OURS

DIJON - Authors and libraries
see Authors and libraries - Dijon

DIJON. Bibliothèque Municipale

Chaume, Maurice. Quelques Souvenirs. 66-77, OURS
Chevrier, Georges. La Littérature Juridique Bourguignonne et les Collections Manuscrites de la Bibliothèque Publique de Dijon. 78-86, OURS
David, Henri. À la Bibliothèque. 87-91, OURS
Drouot, Henri. Un Familier de la Bibliothèque: Henri Chabeuf. 92-105, OURS
Hauser, Henri. Souvenirs d'un Vieux Rat de Bibliothèque. 120-124, OURS
Laurent, Jacques. Charles Oursel, Esquisse Biographique. 9-36, OURS
——— L'Oeuvre de P.-C. Marillier à la Bibliothèque de Dijon. 125-136, OURS

DIJON - Legal literature (Bourgogne) - Collections
see Legal literature (Bourgogne) - Collections - Dijon

DIJON - Letters patent - Collections
see Letters patent - Collections - Dijon

DIJON - Marillier, P. C. - Collections
see Marillier, P. C. - Collections - Dijon

Dinekov, Petŭr.
Akademik Aleksandŭr Teodorov-Balan i Bŭlgarskata Literatura. 31-37, TEOD
Pŭrviiat Bŭlgarski Prevod iz Proizvedeniiata na Adam Mitskevich. 151-156, MIKH

DIOCESAN ARCHIVES
see Archives, Church

DIODORUS SICULUS. Mss.

Jacob, Alfred. Le Classement des Manuscrits de Diodore de Sicile. 525-531, GRAU

DIONYSIUS EXIGUUS. Ms.

Christ, Karl. Eine Unbekannte Handschrift der Ersten Fassung der Dionysiana und der Capitula e Canonibus Excerpta A. 813. 25-36, LEID

DIONYSIUS, THE TRACIAN. Mss. Ars Grammatica

Göber, Willi. Ein Spätantiker Pergamentkodex des Dionysius Thrax. P. Hal. 55a. 111-118, DEGE

DIPLOMATICS. Mss.

Santifaller, Leo. Die Älteste Originalurkunde des Österreichischen Staatsarchivs. 538-575, BICK

DIRECTORIES
see Publishers and publishing - Directories

DISCARDING BOOKS
see Obsolescence of books

DISCOUNTS ON BOOKS
see Books - Prices

DISEASE, Transmission of
see Books as carrier of disease

DISINFECTION OF BOOKS
see also Books - Care and restoration

DISINFECTION OF BOOKS

Fiskaa, Haakon. Bøker Som Smittebærere og Bokdesinfeksjon. 325-338, MUNT

DISPLAYS
see Exhibits and displays

DISSERTATIONS, Academic - Collections - Berlin

Lindau, Hans. Aus der Berliner Dienststelle der Universitätsschriften. 238-244, KUHN

DISSERTATIONS, Academic - Collections - Leipzig

Kern, Anton. Die Promotionsschriften der Jesuitenuniversitäten in der Zeit des Barocks. Eine Bibliothekarische Studie. 38-47, SCHT

DISSERTATIONS, Academic - Collections - Uppsala

Stjernberg, C. W. Domkapitelsavhandlingar efter 1890. Jämte Tillägg och Rättelser till Aks. Josephson, Avhandlingar ock Program (1855-1890). Bibliografi. 608-620, UPPS

DIURNUS PONTIFICUM
see Liber Diurnus

DIVISIONAL PLAN
see College and university libraries - Departmental and divisional libraries

Dmochowska, Maria.
Cymelia Kartograficzne. 80-88, BYDG

DOBREV, GEORGI MIHAILOV

SOFI

DOCUMENTALISTS

Pietsch, Erich. Zur Frage der Ausbildung von Dokumentaren. 458-470, JUCH
Saha, J. Professional Training in Documentation. 293-302, RANG

DOCUMENTATION
see also Bibliographical control; Bibliography; Indexing; Information retrieval; Research materials

DOCUMENTATION

Bernhardt, Børge. Litt om Gjenfinning fra Brukersynspunkt. 174-182, TVET
Brummel, Leendert. Confrontation of Libraries and Documentation. 9-16, DONR
Dembowska, Maria. Bibliotekarstwo i Bibliografia a Dokumentacja. 169-182, GRYC
Ferrari, Giorgio E. La Metodologia Bibliografica, Verso una Definizione del Suo Svolgimento. 287-311, FERR
Frauendorfer, Sigmund von. Was Ist Dokumentation? 32, STUM
Gode, M. Dokumentat͡siia, Biblioteki i Bibliografii͡a. 327-333, MIKN
King, Alexander. International Trends in Librarianship and Documentation. 489-491, BRUM
Michailov, A. I. Donker Duyvis' Contribution to the Progress of Scientific Information and Documentation. 30-38, DONR
Sevensma, Tietse Pieter. Bibliographie ou Documentation? 45-51, GODE
Voorhoeve, N. A. J. F. Donker Duyvis and Standardization. 39-50, DONR
Zuuren, P. van. Donker Duyvis and the NIVE. 51-64, DONR

DOCUMENTATION CENTERS

Ammundsen, Vibeke. De Videnskabelige Biblioteker Som Dokumentationscentraler. 159-173, TVET

DOCUMENTATION - Germany

DEUD

Kunze, Horst. Bemerkungen zum Thema "Wissenschaftliche Bibliotheken und Dokumentation." 203-213, VORS

DOCUMENTATION - Germany - Hist.

Krüss, Hugo Andres. Die Entwicklung der Dokumentationsarbeit in Deutschland vor dem Wirken Unserer Gesellschaft. 8-9, DEUD

DOCUMENTATION - Indexes and abstracts - Vienna

Kaliba, Hans. Gesellschaft und Kultur im Spiegel der Zeitung. Eine Dokumentationsstelle der Stadtbibliothek. 154-165, VIES

DOCUMENTATION - Netherlands

Laan, A. van der. Het Karakter van de Overheidsdocumentatie. 501-504, BRUM

Michailov, A. I. Donker Duyvis' Contribution to the Progress of Scientific Information and Documentation. 30-38, DONR

DOCUMENTATION - Special subjects - Antibiotics

Neelameghan, A. Indexing Physical Chemical Properties of Antibiotic Substances. 248-254, RANG

DOCUMENTATION - Special Subjects - Law - France

Dubuc, R. La Documentation de L'Avocat Français. 171-174, DONK

DOCUMENTATION - Special Subjects - Literature of the humanities

Ferrari, Giorgio E. Fondamenti Attuali al Problema della Documentazione Umanistica. 403-425, GALL

DOCUMENTATION - Special subjects - Science

Bonn, George S. Some Thoughts on the Education of Science Documentalists. 9-17, HASH

King, Alexander. Scientific Information and the Economy. 203-208, TVET

Maltha, D. J. Speelse Gedachten. 537-543, BRUM

DOCUMENTATION - Special Subjects - Social sciences - Gt. Brit.

Walford, A. J. Documentation Services and Library Co-operation in the Social Sciences. 256-260, KYLE

DOCUMENTATION - Standards - India

Kaul, Jainath and Gurcharan Singh. Dr. Ranganathan and Standards for Documentation. 271-278, RANG

DOCUMENTATION - Teaching

Bonn, George S. Some Thoughts on the Education of Science Documentalists. 9-17, HASH

Focke, Helen M. Education in Documentation at Western Reserve University; Yesterday, Today and (Tomorrow?), 49-57, HASH

DOCUMENTATION - Terminology

Farradane, J., R. K. Poulton, and Mrs. S. Datta. Problems in Analysis and Terminology for Information Retrieval. 287-290, KYLE

Foskett, D. J. Language and Classification. 275-278, KYLE

Fujikawa, Masanobu. Bunken Tansaku ni okeru Imi no Mondai. (Problems of "Meaning" in Documentation.) 191-220, HASH

DOCUMENTS
see also Government publications

DOCUMENTS

Hamilton, J. G. de Roulhac. On the Importance of Unimportant Documents. 511-518, WILS

DOCUMENTS - Care and restoration
see also Archives - Care and restoration

DOCUMENTS - Care and restoration

Grill, Erik. The Barrow Method in Sweden. 489-492, GALL

DOCUMENTS - Cataloging

Childs, James B. Author Entries for Canadian Government Publications. 169-174, HANS

——— Corporate Author Entry as Regards the German Federal Republic. 151-162, RANG

Živný, Ladislav Jan. Znaky Literárních a Grafických Dokumentů a Jejich Funkca v Soupisné Praxi. 152-157, EMLE

DOCUMENTS - Collections - Berlin

Darmstaedter, Ludwig. Die Dokumentensammlung und Ihr Übergang an die Preussische Staatsbibliothek. 167-169, HARN

DOCUMENTS - Collections - Washington, D.C.

Andrews, Charles McLean. The Story of the Transcripts. 47-56, PUTN

DOCUMENTS, Public
see Government publications

DOE, JANET

DOEJ

Janet Doe: Portrait, Biographical Sketch, Bibliography. 280-284, DOEJ

Döbeln, Ernst von.
Björkholms-Samlingen i Uppsala Universitetsbibliotek. Några ord om von Döbelnska Släktarkivet. 398-406, UPPS

DÖBELN FAMILY (of Björkholm) - Collections - Uppsala

Döbeln, Ernst von. Björkholms-Samlingen i Uppsala Universitetsbibliotek. Några ord om von Döbelnska Släktarkivet. 398-406, UPPS

Doegen, Wilhelm.
Die Lautabteilung. 253-258, HARN
Die Stimmensammlung zur Dokumentensammlung Darmstaedter. 258-259, HARN

DÖLL, JOHANN CHRISTOPH

Weinacht, Paul. Johann Christoph Döll als Vorstand der Karlsruher Hofbibliothek 1843-1872. II, 150-157, GLAU

Doelle, Ferdinand.
Ein Fragment der Verlorengegangenen Prager Universitätsmatrikel aus dem 14. Jahrhundert. 88-102, EHRC

DØSSING, THOMAS

DØSS

Dold, Alban.
Ein Fragment eines Collectars, d. i. eines Horen-Orationenbuches. 31-36, STOL
Klassische Dichter-Bruchstücke nebst einem Bericht über die Palimpsestphotographische Aufnahme des Plinius-Codex von St. Paul in Kaernten. 369-377, GALL
Die Provenienz der Altlateinischen Römerbrieftexte in den Gotisch-Lateinischen Fragmenten des Codex Carolinus von Wolfenbüttel. 13-29, LEYH
Ein Unbekanntes Spezimen einer "Günther-Zainer"-Bibel. 105-110, LEYG

D'Olwer, L. Nicolau.
La "Crònica" de Ramon Muntaner. Filiació dels Seus Textos. I, 69-76, RUBI

Donati, Lamberto, ed.
MERG

Donati, Lamberto.
Appunti di Biblioiconologia. 243-262, FERR
Le Fonti Iconografiche di Alcuni Manoscritti Urbinati della Biblioteca Vaticana—Osservazioni Intorno ai Cosiddetti "Tarocchi del Mantegna." 48-129, MERG
Leonardo da Vinci ed il Libro Illustrato. 117-138, WEHM
Meditationes Johannis de Turrecremata. 99-128, GREG
Note Empiriche sul Libro Illustrato. 61-102, ACCU
Note Inedite di Alfred Cartier su Giorgio Reverdino, Illustratore di Libri. 379-401, GALL
Proemio. VII-VIII, MERG

DONAUESCHINGEN. Fürstenbergische Bibliothek

Singer, F. X., BARA

Donker Duyvis, Frits.
Die Internationale Bedeutung des Index Bibliographicus. 45-49, VORS
The Jubilee of the Creator of Colon Classification. 31-35, RANG
On the Future Work for the Comparison of Classifications. 32-37, MADR

DONKER DUYVIS, FRITS

DONK

DONR

DONKER DUYVIS, FRITS - Bibl.

Coblans, Herbert. F. Donker Duyvis: a Bibliography. 65-80, DONR

Donner, Kai.
Tryckalster från Storstrejken. 164-169, HULA

Dorez, Léon. Evangéliaire Exécuté à L'Abbaye de Schuttern (VIIIe-IXe Siècle). 293-299, CHAT

Dorf, A. Th.
The University of Chicago Libraries. 185-197, HANS

Dorfmüller, Kurt.
Gustav-Mahler-Dokumente in München. 33-39, FEDO

DORMITORY LIBRARIES - U.S.

Schulz, Werner. Die Amerikanischen Studentenbüchereien. 115-126, JUCR

Dormoy, Marie.
Du Droit de Détruire. 489-492, BONN

DORNIN, BERNARD

Kaser, David. Bernard Dornin, America's First Catholic Bookseller. 105-128, GJEL

DORTMUND - Annuity receipts - Collections
see Annuity receipts - Collections - Dortmund

DORTMUND - Immermann, Karl Leberecht - Correspondence - Collections
see Immermann, Karl Leberecht - Correspondence - Collections - Dortmund

DORTMUND - Libraries
see Libraries - Dortmund

DORTMUND. Stadt- und Landesbibliothek - Hist.

Wand, Albert. Zur Geschichte der Dortmunder Bibliotheken. 29-58, VERD

DORTMUND. Stadt- und Landesbibliothek - Mss. (Immermann)

Risse, Joseph. Ein Neuer Immermann-Fund, die Urhandschrift des "Alexis." 89-117, VERD
Schulz, Erich. Immermanns Briefe an Ferdinand Gessert. Ein Vorbericht. 119-133, VERD

DORTMUND. Stadt- und Landesbibliothek - Mss. (77-8°)

Van der Briele, Wolfgang. Eine Bibelhandschrift des 13. Jahrhunderts in der Dortmunder Stadtbibliothek. 7-11, VERD

DORTMUND - Stadtarchiv. Mss. (Annuity receipts)

Winterfeld, Luise von. Vier Leibrentenquittungen von 1456-1478 aus dem Dortmunder Stadtarchiv. 27-28, VERD

Doublier, Othmar.
Ein Vierteljahrhundert aus der Geschichte der Hofbibliothek 1891-1916. 163-210, VIEN

Douma, S.
Over een Systematisch Trefwoordenregister. 408-413, BRUM

Downs, Robert B.
The Future of University Libraries. 451-456, RANG
Leading American Library Collections. 457-473, WILS

Draat, P. Fijn van.
Anglia. 69-73, EVER

Drachmann, A. G.
Call Numbers. 198-206, HANS

DRAGE, THEODORUS SWAINE

Adams, Percy G. The Case of Swaine Versus Drage: An Eighteenth-Century Publishing Mystery Solved. 157-168, PARG

DRAKE FAMILY (Magnus Knutsson Drake) - Collections - Uppsala

Heyman, Harald J. Något om Drakeska Arkivet i Uppsala Universitetsbibliotek. 249-256, GRAP

DRAMA AND THE LIBRARY
see Theatrical libraries and collections

Drawert, Ernst Arno.
Schriftenverzeichnis Rudolf Juchhoff 1923-1954. 221-227, JUCR
Verzeichnis der Schriften von Rudolf Juchhoff, 1923-1960. 471-478, JUCH

DRAWINGS - Collections - Rome (City)

Garinei-Canori, Costanza. La Collezione Busuttil della Biblioteca Romana Sarti. 177-182, GREG

DRAWINGS - Collections - Uppsala

Ekholm, Gunnar. Om Uppsala Universitetsbiblioteks Handteckningssamling. 575-585, UPPS

DRAWINGS - Collections - Vienna

Gregor, Joseph. Die Handzeichnungen der Sammlung Perera in der Wiener Nationalbibliothek. 407-420, VIEN

DRAWINGS IN LIBRARIES
see Art libraries and collections

Dreimüller, Karl.
Musikerbriefe an einen Rheinischen Musikliebhaber. Aus der Sammlung Ludwig Bisschopinck in Mönchengladbach. 29-49, HOBO

DRESDEN - Authors and libraries
see Authors and libraries - Dresden

DRESDEN. Bibliothek Dresden-Plauen

DRES

Günnel, Peter. Walter Hofmann und das Deutsche Volksbüchereiwesen. 7-16, DRES

DRESDEN - Bookbinding - Fine bindings - Collections
see Bookbinding - Fine bindings - Collections - Dresden

DRESDEN. Buchmuseum
see Dresden. Sächsische Landesbibliothek. Buchmuseum

DRESDEN - Catalogs
see Catalogs - Dresden

DRESDEN - Catalogs - Subject
see Catalogs - Subject - Dresden

DRESDEN - Exhibits and displays
see Exhibits and displays - Dresden

DRESDEN. Freie Öffentliche Bibliothek Dresden-Plauen
see Dresden. Bibliothek Dresden-Plauen

DRESDEN. Japanisches Palais

Ermisch, Hubert Georg. Landesbibliothek, Japanisches Palais und Denkmalpflege. 15-20, BOLL

DRESDEN. Japanisches Palais. Buchmuseum
see Dresden. Sächsische Landesbibliothek. Buchmuseum

DRESDEN. Kurfürstliche Bibliothek (after 1787)
see Dresden. Sächsische Landesbibliothek

DRESDEN - Library resources
see Library resources - Dresden

DRESDEN. Lingnersche Lesehalle
see Dresden. Städtische Bücherei

DRESDEN - Literary museums
see Literary museums - Dresden

DRESDEN - Manuscripts - Collections
see Manuscripts - Collections - Dresden

DRESDEN - Maps - Collections
see Maps - Collections - Dresden

DRESDEN - Music libraries and collections
see Music libraries and collections - Dresden

DRESDEN. Öffentliche Bibliothek
see Dresden. Sächsische Landesbibliothek

DRESDEN - Public libraries
see Public libraries - Dresden

DRESDEN - Reader services
see Reader services - Dresden

DRESDEN. Sächsische Landesbibliothek

DREL

Boden, Charlotte. Der Biographische Katalog und das Personalrepertorium der Sächsischen Landesbibliothek. 21-37, BOLL
Bollert, Martin. Johann Joachim Winckelmann als Bibliothekar des Grafen Bünau. 19-24, LEID
Büscher, Alfred. Skandinavier, Dresden und die Landesbibliothek. 99-104, BOLL
Ermisch, Hubert Georg. Landesbibliothek, Japanisches Palais und Denkmalpflege. 15-20, BOLL
Hofmann, Hans. Auskunft. 97-104, BOLE
———— Facit. 71-75, BOLE
Kleinstück, Hans. Erinnerung. 81-83, BOLE
Leyh, Georg. Über die Sächsische Landesbibliothek in Dresden. 69-70, BOLE
Lülfing, Hans. Zur Sächsischen Bibliotheksgeschichte im 19. Jahrhundert. 343-356, VORS
Schunke, Ilse. Beiträge zur Dresdner Bibliotheksgeschichte auf Grund von Einbandstudien. 397-414, VORS
Zaunick, Rudolph. Erinnerungen und Glückwunsch. 84-87, BOLE

DRESDEN. Sächsische Landesbibliothek - Bibl.

Alschner, Christian and Marie Bundesmann. Bibliographie zur Geschichte der Sächsischen Landesbibliothek. 209-279, DREL

DRESDEN. Sächsische Landesbibliothek. Buchmuseum

Boden, Charlotte. Das Buchmuseum in den Semper-Räumen des Japanischen Palais. 46-51, BOLE
Deckert, Helmut, Marita Kremer, Hans Pfeifer, and Liselotte Willi. Das Neue Buchmuseum der Sächsischen Landesbibliothek. 175-205, DREL
Kremer, Marita. Blick in das Buchmuseum der Sächsischen Landesbibliothek 1956. 52-56, BOLE

DRESDEN. Sächsische Landesbibliothek. Handschriftenabteilung

Kremer, Marita. Die Handschriftenabteilung. 139-146, DREL

DRESDEN. Sächsische Landesbibliothek - Hist.

Benndorf, Gottfried and Hans Hofmann. Die Sächsische Landesbibliothek 1920-36. 1-14, BOLL
Neubert, Hermann. Der Ruf Christian Gottlob Heynes nach Dresden. II, 43-52, GLAU

DRESDEN. Sächsische Landesbibliothek. Kartenabteilung

Pfeifer, Hans. Die Kartenabteilung. 147-155, DREL

DRESDEN. Sächsische Landesbibliothek. Mss. (A 52)

Pietzsch, Gerhard. Mscr. Dresd. A 52. 167-174, BOLL

DRESDEN. Sächsische Landesbibliothek. Mss. (Bible. Hebrew and Aramaic)

Bollert, Martin. Ein Kastenband mit Lederschnitt in der Sächsischen Landesbibliothek zu Dresden. 95-104, LOUB

DRESDEN. Sächsische Landesbibliothek. Mss. (Fuero Hds.)

Häbler, Konrad. Die Fuero-Handschrift der Sächsischen Landesbibliothek. 146-155, BOLL

DRESDEN. Sächsische Landesbibliothek. Mss. (Marx)
Deckert, Helmut. Karl Marx und Seine Kommilitonen als Hörer Schlegels in Bonn. 33-53, LÜLF

DRESDEN. Sächsische Landesbibliothek. Musikabteilung
Schnoor, Hans. Rechts und Links der Elbe. 88-91, BOLE
Willi, Liselotte. Die Musikabteilung. 156-165, DREL

DRESDEN - Special collections
see Special collections - Dresden

DRESDEN. Städtische Bücherei
Böhme, Rudolf. Volksbüchereiarbeit in Dresden. 31-40, DRES

DRESDEN. Städtische Zentralbibliothek
see Dresden. Städtische Bücherei

DRESDEN - State libraries
see State libraries - Dresden

DRESDEN - State libraries - Reference services
see State libraries - Reference services - Dresden

DRESDEN - State libraries - Statistics
see State libraries - Statistics - Dresden

DRESDEN - Use studies - State libraries
see Use studies - State libraries - Dresden

DRESDEN - War and the library
see War and the library - Dresden

Drews, Erich.
Zur Entwicklung der Nationalen Deutschen Bibliographien seit 1945. 110-117, JENA
Zur Entwicklung der Register in den Deutschen Allgemeinbibliographien. 48-53, SCHT

Drolsum, Axel Charlot
OSLU
Universitets-Biblioteket 1811-1911. 1-118, (pt. 1), OSLU

DROLSUM, AXEL CHARLOT
Halvorsen, Jens Braage. Overbibliothekar A. C. Drolsum. Supplement av K. V. Hammer. 72-73, (pt. 2), OSLU
Kjaer, A. Overbibliothekar A. C. Drolsum. 74-79, (pt. 2), OSLU
Nyhuus, Haakon. Overbibliothekar A. C. Drolsum. 79, (pt. 2), OSLU

Drouot, Henri.
Un Familier de la Bibliothèque: Henri Chabeuf. 92-105, OURS

DRUCKEREI DER BAMBERGER FÜRSTBISCHÖFE - Hist.
Wirth, Georg. Die Druckerei der Bamberger Fürstbischöfe—die Erste "Staatsdruckerei." 383-389, STOL

DRUCKEREI "ZUM FÄRBEFASS," Erfurt
Luther, Johannes. Ludwig Trutebul und die Druckerei "Zum Färbefaß" in Erfurt. 185-195, SCHW

DU BARTAS, GUILLAUME DE SALLUST, SEIGNEUR. La Semaine, ou Création du Monde
Brin, Erwana. Du Bartas, La Semaine ou Création du Monde. Une Édition Inconnue? 111-114, CALO

DU MARTEAU, PIERRE, imaginary printer
see Marteau, Pierre du, imaginary printer

Dube, Werner, jt. ed.
BERS

Dube, Werner, jt. author
Kunze, Horst and Werner Dube. Zur Vorgeschichte der Deutschen Staatsbibliothek. I, 1-47, BERS

DUBLIN. University. Trinity College. Library. Fagel Collection
Brummel, Leendert. The Fagel Library in Trinity College, Dublin. 204-233, BRUE

Dubuc, R.
La Documentation de L'Avocat Français. 171-174, DONK

DUCLOUX, MARC
Denkinger, Marc. Sainte-Beuve et L'Imprimeur Marc Ducloux. 209-219, BONN

DÜRER, ALBRECHT
Wille, Hans. Dürer-Erinnerungen in Josef Führichs Illustrationen zu "Der Wilde Jäger" von G. A. Bürger. 60-74, BRIE

Dumaitre, Paule, jt. author
Hahn, André, Paule Dumaitre, J. Samion-Contet. Le "De Humani Corporis Fabrica" d'André Vésale (1543). 91-97, CALO

DUMMER, JEREMIAH
Bryant, Louise May and Mary Patterson. The List of Books Sent by Jeremiah Dummer. 423-492, KEOG
Pratt, Anne Stokely. The Books Sent from England by Jeremiah Dummer to Yale College. 7-44, KEOG

Dumrath, Karlheinrich.
"Gott zu Ehren und Unsern Nachkommen zum Besten." 2-15, SCHV

DUPLICATES

Hamel, G. A. Wat te Doen met Doubletten? 463-472, BRUM

DUPLICATES - Berlin

Perlbach, Max. Die Berliner Doubletten von 1697 in Halle. 15-42, WILM

DUPLICATES - Germany

Jürgens, Adolf. Der Suchdienst der Reichstauschstelle. I, 105-111, GLAU

DUPLICATING PROCESSES
see Catalog cards - Reproduction; Copying methods

Durand, René.
L'Élection de C. Scribonius Curio au Tribunat de la Plèbe en 51. 557-575, CHAT

Durham, Mae J.
"Dream Possessed and Young." 15-22, SAYE

Durrieu, Comte Paul.
Ingobert: un Grand Calligraphe du IXe Siècle. 1-14, CHAT
L'Origine du Manuscrit Célèbre, Dit le Psautier d'Utrecht. 639-657, HAVE

DUTCH MANUSCRIPTS
see Manuscripts, Dutch

DUTIES OF LIBRARIANS

Berghoeffer, Christian Wilhelm. Die Wissenschaftliche Arbeit des Bibliothekars. 97-103, EBRA
Escher, Hermann. Was Es in einer Bibliothek zu Tun Gibt (Zentralbibliothek Zürich 1928). 105-122, ESCH
Möhlenbrock, Sigurd. Om Arbets- och Ansvarsfördelning. 203-214, HEIN

DUTIES OF LIBRARIANS - Utrecht

Brom, A., Jr. De Universiteitsbibliotheek te Utrecht en de Gestichtsarbeid. 49-54, EVER

Dutta, Bimal Kumer.
An Ancient Indian University Library. 457-460, RANG

Dyczkowska, Ludwika.
W spółpraca Pedagogicznej Biblioteki Powiatowej w Żywcu z Ośrodkami Metodycznymi. 99-103, KRAK

Dyroff, Hans-Dieter.
Die Bücherzensur der Universität Heidelberg 1652-1693. 98-119, BENZ

DZIATZKO, KARL

Weber, Ulrich. Vier Unveröffentlichte Briefe Wilhelm Brambachs an Carl Dziatzko aus dem Besitz der Universitätsbibliothek Göttingen oder: Scherz- und Schimpf-spiel zwischen Gelehrten. 171-178, JUCR

Eames, Wilberforce.
On the Use of Hebrew Types in English America before 1735. 481-502, FREI

EAMES, WILBERFORCE

EAME

Koopman, Harry Lyman. The Clerk of Breukelyn. v-vi, EAME
Lydenberg, Harry Miller. Two Bookmen. 1-9, BLOC

EAMES, WILBERFORCE - Bio-bibl.

Paltsits, Victor Hugo. Wilberforce Eames, A Bio-Bibliographical Narrative. Works and Contributions. 1-26, EAME

EARLY PRINTED BOOKS - 16th cent. - Bibl.
see Rare books - 16th cent. - Bibl.

EAST INDIA COMPANY (Swedish)
see Svenska Ostindiska Companiet

Eastman, Linda A.
Library Service to a City. 128-139, PUTN

Eaton, Anne Thaxter.
Reviewing and Criticism of Children's Books. 589-592, MOOR

Eaton, Thelma.
Effect of Colon Classification on the Teachings of Classification in American Library Schools. 588-592, RANG

EBER, PAUL. Calendarium Historicum. 1551

Deutsch, Josef. Ebers Calendarium Historicum mit Handschriftlichen Eintragungen aus Wolgast. 71-78, KUHN

Ebers, Georg.
[Brief an Karl von Gerber] in: Debes, Deitmar. Zur Erwerbung des Papyrus Ebers. 139-141, BULL

EBERT, FRIEDRICH ADOLF

Schreiber, Heinrich. Friedrich Adolf Ebert und die Monumenta Germaniae. 82-98, BOLL

EBERT, FRIEDRICH ADOLF - Collections - Wolfenbüttel

Busch, Friedrich. Alltagssorgen, die Immer Zeitgemäss Bleiben (aus Friedrich Adolf Eberts Freundeskreis). 136-139, LEUN

Ebert, Otto Erich.
Aus der Werkstatt von Poeschel & Trepte. Ein Beitrag zur Bibliographie des Deutschen Privatdrucks. 7-37, MIND
Die Privatdrucke und Ihre Pflege in der Deutschen Bücherei. 177-187, LEIS

EBRARD, FRIEDRICH CLEMENS
EBRA

Ebstrup, E.
Biblioteksmuligheder paa Landet. Forsøg paa en Nyorientering. 70-84, DØSS

ECCLESIASTICAL ARCHIVES
see Archives, Church

ECHTERNACH (Abbey) Mss.
Degering, Hermann. Handschriften aus Echternach und Orval in Paris. 48-85, MILF

Ecker, Karl.
Die Sammlung Stefan Zweig. 321-330, BICK

ECONOMICS - Collections - Leipzig
Bergmann, Werner and Heinz Kleeberg. Der Beitrag der Deutschen Bücherei zur Lösung Volkswirtschaftlicher Aufgaben. 91-103, LEIZ

EDDY, ISAAC - Bio-bibl.
Rugg, Harold Goddard. Isaac Eddy, Printer-Engraver. Bibliography of Eddy Publications. 313-329, EAME

EDICIÓN NACIONAL DE LAS OBRAS COMPLETAS DE MENENDEZ PELAYO. 337-341, MENE

EDITIONS
see also Inexpensive editions

EDITIONS
Vendryes, J. Réflexions sur les Éditions de Textes. 539-547, BONN

EDITIONS - Bibliography - Incunabula
Zedler, Gottfried. Über die Preise und Auflagenhöhe Unserer Ältesten Drucke. 267-288, SCHW

EDITIONS, Inexpensive
see Inexpensive editions

EDITORIAL WORK
Vendryes, J. Réflexions sur les Éditions de Textes. 539-547, BONN

Edström, Wilhelm
KRIS

EDUCATION FOR LIBRARIANSHIP
see also Children's librarians - Education; College and university librarians; In-service training; Library schools; Negro librarians - Education; Recruiting for librarianship

EDUCATION FOR LIBRARIANSHIP
Carnovsky, Leon. Preparation for the Librarian's Profession. 404-411, WILS
Cory, John Mackenzie. The Relative Theory of Specialization. 611-617, MOOR
Cowley, J. D. What Shall We Teach the Librarian? 18-23, EMLE
Juchhoff, Rudolf. Ziel und Wege Bibliothekarischer Bildung. 34-48, LANF
Kaula, Prithvi Nath. Library Education in Perspective. 541-552, RANG
Leyh, Georg. Bildung und Ausbildung des Bibliothekars. 55-56, STUM
Lichtenstein, Walter. Library Education. 270-273, HANS
Pietsch, Erich. Zur Frage der Ausbildung von Dokumentaren. 458-470, JUCH
Schuder, Werner. Der Bibliothekar und die Universitas Litterarum. 59-81, SCHS
Schulz, Kurd. Zur Literaturpädagogischen Schulung der Nebenamtlichen Volksbibliothekare. 113-120, ACKE
Schuster, Wilhelm. Ein Studium Generale der Bibliothekare? 427-447, JUCH
Staveley, Ronald. Student and Tutor. 56-71, SAYW
Stokes, Roy. "... Not for Trafficking Alone..." 48-55, SAYW

EDUCATION FOR LIBRARIANSHIP - Austria
Gans, Johann. Bibliothekarausbildung in Verbindung mit Hochschulstudium. 151-153, VORS

EDUCATION FOR LIBRARIANSHIP - Bulgaria
Kirova, Elena. Kŭm Vŭprosa za Podgotovka na Bibliotekari s Vische Obrazovanie. 205-214, MIKH

EDUCATION FOR LIBRARIANSHIP - Czechoslovakia
Gillarová, Vlasta. L. J. Živný v Knihovnickém Školstvi. 146-164, ŽIVN

EDUCATION FOR LIBRARIANSHIP - Denmark
Hansen, Robert L. Om Uddannelse af

Bibliotekarer ved Folkebibliotekerne. 17-37, DØSS

EDUCATION FOR LIBRARIANSHIP - France

Cain, Julien. Bibliothécaires et Bibliographes. L'Enseignement Bibliographique en France. 151-157, HOFM

EDUCATION FOR LIBRARIANSHIP - Germany

Handwerker, Otto. Bibliothekare und Universitäten, mit Belegen aus der Geschichte der Würzburger Universitätsbibliothek. 85-94, LEID
Heinrich, Gisela. Heutige Probleme der Katalogarbeit und Annotierung in der Öffentlichen Bücherei und deren Bedeutung für die Ausbildung. 88-112, LANF
Pawlack, Erna. Zur Frage der Ausbildung Nebenamtlicher Büchereileiter im Rahmen des Ländlichen Büchereiwesens. 124-134, LANF
Reuter, Rudolf. Berufsausbildung des Volksbibliothekars in Deutschland. II, 60-63, GLAU
Troost, Karl. Zur Volksbibliothekarischen Ausbildung an der Büchereischule. 135-156, LANF

EDUCATION FOR LIBRARIANSHIP - Germany (Democratic Republic, 1949-)

Kunze, Horst. Das Fach Wissenschaftskunde in der Ausbildung von Wissenschaftlichen Bibliothekaren und Bibliothekaren. 219-224, MIKH

EDUCATION FOR LIBRARIANSHIP - Germany - Hist.

Briele, Wolfgang van der. Bibliothekarische Ausbildungsfragen im Wandel der Jahrzehnte. 17-33, LANF

EDUCATION FOR LIBRARIANSHIP - Gt. Brit.

HUTT

Minto, John. The Library Association Examinations. 285-295, HANS

EDUCATION FOR LIBRARIANSHIP - Hamburg - Hist.

Propach, Elisabeth. Die Ausbildung des Nachwuchses in Hamburg. 97-109, HAMB

EDUCATION FOR LIBRARIANSHIP - India

Guha, B. Dr. Ranganathan as a Teacher of Library Science. 578-584, RANG
Kaula, Asha. Dr. Ranganathan and Library Education. 553-557, RANG
Parthasarathy, S. Training of Library Personnel in India. 158-162, MADR

EDUCATION FOR LIBRARIANSHIP - Japan

Nakamura, Hatsuo. Shiryō Soshiki Kyōjuho no Hensen; Amerika no Toshokan Gakko o Chūshin to Shite. (On Teaching the Organization of Materials for Use. Based on Courses in American Library Schools.) 281-296, HASH

EDUCATION FOR LIBRARIANSHIP - Kraków

Popiel, Jadwiga. Dział Instrukcyjno-Metodyczny. 36-38, KRAK

EDUCATION FOR LIBRARIANSHIP - Netherlands

Waal, Anna de. De Opleiding. 610-617, BRUM

EDUCATION FOR LIBRARIANSHIP - Pretoria

Friis, Th. Education for Librarianship in South Africa at the Crossroads. 14-24, COET
Le Mousaion à Monsieur P. C. Coetzee. 6-13, COET

EDUCATION FOR LIBRARIANSHIP - Southern States

Wilson, Louis Round. Optima in Library Service for the South by 1950. 186-204, BISH

EDUCATION FOR LIBRARIANSHIP - Switzerland

Schwarber, Karl. Marcel Godet und die Vereinigung Schweizerischer Bibliothekare. 3-8, GODM

EDUCATION FOR LIBRARIANSHIP - U.S. - Hist.

Howe, Harriet E. Two Decades in Education for Librarianship. 557-570, WILS

EDUCATION LIBRARIES - Acquisitions - Kraków

Ślusarczyk, Jadwiga. Gromadzenie i Opracowanie Księgozbioru. 17-21, KRAK

EDUCATION LIBRARIES - Kraków

KRAK

Madrjas, Halina. Rozwój i Działalność Pedagogicznych Bibliotek Powiatowych w Województwie Krakowskim w Latach: 1951, 1961. 38-49, KRAK

EDUCATION LIBRARIES - Poland

Jarosik, Emilia. Praca Pedagogicznych Bibliotek Powiatowych a Reforma Oświaty i Wychowania. 97-99, KRAK

Ocena Pracy Bibliotek Pedagogicznych Przez Instytucje Oświatowe i ZNP. 110-113, KRAK
Rekowa, Stanisława. Formy Współpracy Pedagogicznej Biblioteki z Nauczycielem. 103-106, KRAK

EDUCATION LIBRARIES - Reference services

Kondolewicz, Wanda. Dział Informacyjnobibliograficzny. 34-36, KRAK
———— Dział Informacyjnobibliograficzny Jako Warsztat Pracy Nauczyciela. 61-66, KRAK

EDUCATION LIBRARIES - Żywiec, Poland

Dyczkowska, Ludwika. Współpraca Pedagogicznej Biblioteki Powiatowych w Żywcu z Ośrodkami Metodycznymi. 99-103, KRAK

Eells, Walter Crosby.
Periodicals Read by Junior College Students. 474-485, WILS
Eggebrecht, W.
Bücherei und Volkshochschule. 25-28, ACKE

EGYPT - Inscriptions, Greek
see Inscriptions, Greek - Egypt

EGYPTIAN LIBRARY, Cairo
see Cairo. Egyptian Library

Ehinger, Hans, jt. ed.
REFA

Ehlers, D. L.
Adventures in Africana. 22-23, VARL

Ehrle, Francesco, Cardinal.
Die Frangipani und der Untergang des Archivs und der Bibliothek der Päpste am Anfang des 13. Jahrhunderts. 448-485, CHAT

EHRLE, FRANCESCO, Cardinal

EHRA

EHRB

EHRC

EHRD

EHRE

Batllori, Miquel. El Pare Ehrle, Prefecte de la Vaticana, en la Seva Correspondència amb el Card. Rampolla. I, 75-117, ALBB
Ehwald, Rudolf. Über eine Französische Missalhandschrift des XIV. Jahrhunderts. 65-75, SCHW

Eichholz, Fritz.
Ansprache. 26-28, MAIZ

Eichler, Ferdinand
VERE
Eichler, Ferdinand.
Ausgewählte Bucheinbände des 15. und 16. Jahrhunderts aus der Universitatsbibliothek Graz. 110-124, HAEK
Eine Bucheinbandverzierung aus dem Formenschatz Hans Holbeins d. J. 63-66, LEID
Lederschnitt und Hornverzierung beim Bucheinband. 89-94, LOUB
Lederschnittbände des 15. Jahrhunderts in der Steiermark. 77-102, SCHW
Lederschnittbände in Österreich. 86-94, MILF
Die Renaissance des Buches im 15. Jahrhundert und Ihre Nachwirkung. 1-10, LEYG

EINSIEDELN - Catholic Church - Hist. - Middle Ages - Sources - Collections
see Catholic Church - Hist. - Collections - Einsiedeln

EINSIEDELN, Switzerland (Benedictine abbey). Archiv

Henggeler, Rudolf. Die Mittelalterlichen Papsturkunden im Stiftsarchiv Einsiedeln. 201-225, MERC

EINSIEDELN, Switzerland (Benedictine abbey). Biblioteca. Mss. (281)

Piper, Paul. Supersitiones et Paganiae Einsidlenses. 300-311, CHAT

EITNER, ROBERT. Bibliographisch-bibliographisches Quellen-Lexikon. [Supplement]

Schenk, Erich. Die Österreichische Musiküberlieferung der Züricher Zentralbibliothek. 576-581, BICK

Ekholm, Gunnar.
Om Uppsala Universitetsbiblioteks Handteckningssamling. 575-585, UPPS
Upsala Universitetsbiblioteks Gravyrsamling. 125-138, ANNE

EKKEHARDUS I, Dean of St. Gall. Mss. Waltharius

Lebègue, Henri. Le Waltharius du Parisinus 8488a. 584-587, CHAT

Elahi, Nur.
Importance of a Library in a Developing Country. 341-345, RANG

ELBERFELD, Ger. Stadtbücherei
see Wuppertal. Stadtbibliothek

ELBERFELD, Ger. Volksbücherei
see Wuppertal. Stadtbibliothek

ELBING
see Elbląg

ELBLĄG. Gymnasium - Hist.
Bauer, Hanna. Aus dem Ersten Jahrhundert des Elbinger Gymnasiums und Seiner Bibliothek. 19-34, KÖNI

ELECTRONIC DATA PROCESSING
Pflug, Günther. Der Einfluss der Elektronischen Datenverarbeitung auf die Katalogisierungspraxis. 111-124, FUCH

ELEMENTALE INTRODUCTORIUM IN NOMINUM & VERBORUM DECLINATIONES GRAECAS, 1512
Baillet, Lina. Le Premier Manuel de Grec Paru à Strasbourg. 25-36, BENZ

ELEUTHERIAN MILLS HISTORICAL LIBRARY, Greenville, Del.
Williams, Richmond D. The Longwood Achievement. 46-53, DAVI

ELIOT INDIAN TRACTS
Winship, George Parker. The Eliot Indian Tracts. 179-192, EAME

ELISABETH-HOSPITAL, Danzig
see Danzig. Elisabeth-Hospital

ELLIS, SIR HENRY
Lomer, Gerhard Richard. Sir Henry Ellis in France. A Chapter in the History of the British Museum. 116-144, BISH

Ellsworth, Ralph E.
The Balance of Conflicting Interests in the Building of Collections: Comprehensiveness Versus Selectivity. 73-79, PENN
Some Aspects of the Problem of Allocating Book Funds Among Departments in Universities. 486-494, WILS

ELSASS
see Alsace

EMBLEMS - Collections (Imaginary) - Spain
Selig, Karl-Ludwig. Three Spanish Libraries of Emblem Books and Compendia. 81-90, PARG

EMBLEMS, Library
see Library emblems, inscriptions, etc.

Emler, Jan.
L. J. Živného Úsilí o Českou Bibliografii. 69-73, ZIVN
Das Neue im Alten. 297-308, LEYG

EMLER, JAN
EMLE

ÉMLER, JAN - Bibl.
Emlerová, Marie. Bibliografie Prací Dr. Jana Emlera. 159-164, EMLE

Emlerová, Marie.
Bibliografie Prací Dr. Jana Emlera. 159-164, EMLE

Emmrich, Hanna.
Aron Freimann-Bibliographie. 5-16, FREN

Emrich, Duncan B.
Folklore Section of the Library of Congress. 331-334, BICK

ENCYCLOPEDIAS AND DICTIONARIES
Shores, Louis. Encyclopedists Beware. 495-505, RANG

Endell, F. and H. Messin.
Schriften von Dr. Erwin Ackerknecht. Eine Bibliographische Zusammenstellung. 167-178, ACKE

Endlicher, Otto.
Der Tschechische Dramatiker V. Kl. Klicpera und das Wiener Theater (Zwei Briefe in der Handschriftensammlung). 82-97, VIES

ENDOWMENTS
see Gifts, contributions, etc.

Endres, Heinrich.
Meister Ulrich Frenckel aus Hirschau. 176-182, LOUB

Enelow, H. G.
Isaac Belinfante, an Eighteenth Century Bibliophile. 5-30, FREI

ENEMAN, MICHAEL - Library
Gren, Erik. Bidrag till Michael Enemans Biografi. Studier och Bokförvärv. 445-494, GRAP

Engel, Carl.
Concert, A.D. 2025, in the Library of Congress. 140-145, PUTN

ENGEL, CARL
ENGE

ENGEL, CARL - Bibl.
Selected List of Works by Carl Engel. 23-26, ENGE

Engl, Hans.
Zur Geschichte der Münchener Stadtbibliothek. 49-51, HELD

ENGLAND
see Gt. Brit.

ENGLISH INCUNABULA
see Incunabula, English

ENGRAVERS, German - Cologne

Wehmer, Carl. Zur Echtheitskritik der Metallschnittplatten Schreiber 2746a und Schreiber 2865. 143-157, BOCK

ENGRAVINGS - Collections - Paris

Adhémar, Jean. Julien Cain et le Cabinet des Estampes. 76-82, CAIN
Noailles, Duc de. Lecteur aux Estampes. 83, CAIN
Vieillard, Roger. M. Julien Cain et les Estampes. 20-21, CAIN

ENGRAVINGS - Collections - Rome (City)

Garinei-Canori, Costanza. La Collezione Busuttil della Biblioteca Romana Sarti. 177-182, GREG
Moricca, Luciano. Le Stampe del Goltzius nella Biblioteca Casanatense di Roma. 286-303, GREG

ENGRAVINGS - Collections - Uppsala

Ekholm, Gunnar. Upsala Universitets-biblioteks Gravyrsamling. 125-138, ANNE

ENGRAVINGS IN LIBRARIES
see Art libraries and collections

EPHEMERAL MATERIALS
see also Pamphlets; Picture collections

EPHEMERAL MATERIALS

Karanova, L. Mîastoto na Drebnite Izdaniîa v Bibliotekite. 408-411, MIKN
Wall, Alexander J. Ephemeral Library Material, Its Preservation, Care and Value. 423-430, LYDE

EPHEMERAL MATERIALS - Collections - Hague

Timmer, E. M. A. Pamfletten en Perikelen. 199-218, HAGU

<u>EPISTEL VON DER FESTSCHRIFT</u>

Bollert, Martin. Epistel von der Festschrift. 107, BOLE

EPPELSHEIMER CLASSIFICATION
see Classification - Systems - Eppelsheimer

Eppelsheimer, Hanns Wilhelm.
Das Archiv Ungedruckter Wissenschaftlicher Schriften. 90-91, FRAD
Die Bibliothek der Emigration. 89, FRAD
Die Deutsche Bibliothek. Erinnerungen an eine Gründung. 13-28, FRAD

EPPELSHEIMER, HANNS WILHELM

EPPE

Schneider, Lambert. Dank an Hanns W. Eppelsheimer. 165-166, FRAD

EPPELSHEIMER, HANNS WILHELM - Bibl.

Tiedemann, Eva. Hanns Wilhelm Eppelsheimer, Curriculum Vitae und Bibliographischer Bericht. 9-19, EPPE

Epstein, A.
Der Gerschom Meor ha-Golah Zugeschriebene Talmud-Commentar. 115-143, STEI

EPSTEIN, FRITZ

EPST

EQUIPMENT AND SUPPLIES
see Catalog cards— Reproduction; Copying methods; Furniture; Printing - Presses; Shelves and shelving

ERASMUS, DESIDERIUS - Collections - Hague

Kronenberg, M. E. Erasmus-Uitgaven A°. 1531 in het Bezit van Kanunnik Mr. Jan Dircsz. van der Haer te Gorkum. 99-117, KOSS

ERASMUS, DESIDERIUS. <u>Institutio Principis Christiani</u> - Bibl.

Vincent, Auguste. Les Premières Éditions de <u>L'Institutio Principis Christiani</u> d'Erasme. 91-96, GODE

ERASMUS, DESIDERIUS. <u>Mss. Scholia</u>

Husner, Fritz. Die Handschrift der Scholien des Erasmus von Rotterdam zu den Hieronymusbriefen. 132-146, BINZ

ERASMUS OF ROTTERDAM
see Erasmus, Desiderius

Erbacher, Hermann.
Bibliographie des Wissenschaftlichen Schrifttums in einer Landeskirche. 16-24, SCHV

ERFURT. Augustinerkloster. Bibliothek

Freitag, Albert. Ein Band aus Luthers Erfurter Klosterbibliothek. 93-110, DEGE

ERFURT - Bookbinding
see Bookbinding - Erfurt

ERFURT - Printing
see Printing - Erfurt

ERFURT. Stadtbibliothek. Mss. (Amplon. Q 12 and Q 345)
Walther, Hans. Kleine Mittellateinische Dichtungen aus Zwei Erfurter Handschriften. 296-315, DEGE

ERFURT. Stadtbücherei
Schmidt, Adolf. Kölnische Einbände des Vierzehnten Jahrunderts in der Amploniana zu Erfurt. 401-409, COLL

ERFURT - Type and type-founding
see Type and type-founding - Erfurt

Erichsen, Finn.
Overbibliotekar Wilhelm Munthes Trykte Arbeider. 493-502, MUNT

Erichsen, W.
H. O. Lange som Aegyptolog. 356-373, LANE

ERIK HENRIK LIND—70 ÅR.
[v]-viii, LIND

ERITREO, GIANO NICIO, pseud.
see Rossi, Giovanni Vittorio

ERLANGEN - Architecture and building - College and university libraries
see Architecture and building - College and university libraries - Erlangen

ERLANGEN - Art libraries and collections
see Art libraries and collections - Erlangen

ERLANGEN - Beham, Hans Sebald - Collections
see Beham, Hans Sebald - Collections - Erlangen

ERLANGEN - Bookbinders
see Bookbinders - Erlangen

ERLANGEN - Catalogs - Classed
see Catalogs - Classed - Erlangen

ERLANGEN - Coins - Collections
see Coins - Collections - Erlangen

ERLANGEN - Coins, Oriental - Collections
see Coins, Oriental - Collections - Erlangen

ERLANGEN - College and university libraries
see College and university libraries - Erlangen

ERLANGEN - Gifts, contributions, etc.
see Gifts, contributions, etc. - Erlangen

ERLANGEN - Manuscripts, French - Collections
see Manuscripts, French - Collections - Erlangen

ERLANGEN - Manuscripts, Italian - Collections
see Manuscripts, Italian - Collections - Erlangen

ERLANGEN - Rare Books - Collections
see Rare books - Collections - Erlangen

ERLANGEN - Songs - Collections
see Songs - Collections - Erlangen

ERLANGEN. Universität. Bibliothek
VERZ
Schmidt-Herrling, Eleonora. Einbände von Thomas Krüger in der Universitätsbibliothek Erlangen. 285-293, STOL

ERLANGEN. Universität. Bibliothek - Bibl.
Veröffentlichungen der Universitätsbibliothek Erlangen. 115-118, VERZ

ERLANGEN. Universität. Bibliothek - Catalogs
Stählin, Agnes. Zur Geschichte der Systematischen Kataloge der Universitätsbibliothek Erlangen. 137-147, REDE

ERLANGEN. Universität. Bibliothek - Hist.
Petz-Gebauer, Hannelore. Zur Baugeschichte der Erlanger Universitätsbibliothek. 149-162, REDE
Redenbacher, Fritz. Das Gebäude der Universitätsbibliothek Erlangen. 232-251, VORS
Stollreither, Eugen. Die Universitätsbibliothek Erlangen zur Zeit der Praktikantentätigkeit August von Platens. 216-229, LEYG

ERLANGEN. Universität. Bibliothek - Mss.
Pirson, Julius. Aus Französischen und Italienischen Handschriften der Erlanger Universitätsbibliothek. 185-195, STOL

ERLANGEN. Universität. Bibliothek - Mss. (Ant. III, 399)
Hampe, Theodor. Der Sog. Ferdinand Neuberger-Codex in der Erlanger Universitätsbibliothek. 32-39, VERZ

ERLANGEN. Universität. Bibliothek - Mss. no. 1, (Bible)
Redenbacher, Fritz. Adoratio Magorum. Die Heiligen Drei Könige in der Bibel von St. Gumbertus, Gesehen im Rahmen der Ikonographischen Überlieferung. 305-334, HOFM

ERLANGEN. Universität. Bibliothek - Mss. (1620)
Lutze, Eberhard. Eine Augsburger

Bilderhandschrift aus dem Besitz des Sebastian Schertlin von Burtenbach (Ms. 1620 der UB Erlangen). 147-156, STOL

ERLANGEN. Universität. Bibliothek - Mss. (Papyrus 1 and Ms. 1234)
Dietzel, Armin. Ein Altkirchlicher Christushymnus. Der Papyrus Erlangensis 1 im Vergleich mit den Abendhymnen (Ms. Erlg. 1234). 83-93, REDE

ERLANGEN. Universität. Bibliothek - Sammlung Will
Zambaur, Eduard von. Die Orientalischen Münzen der Sammlung Will in der Universitätsbibliothek Erlangen. 94-104, VERZ

ERLANGEN - Wood-engravings - Collections
see Wood-engravings - Collections - Erlangen

Ermatinger, Charles J.
Additional Questions on Aristotle's Physics, by Siger of Brabant or His School. 97-120, ALBA

Ermisch, Hubert Georg.
Landesbibliothek, Japanisches Palais und Denkmalpflege. 15-20, BOLL

ERMLAND - Church libraries
see Church libraries - Germany

ERMLAND - Private libraries
see Private libraries - Ermland

ERMLAND - Religious libraries
see Religious libraries - Germany

Ernout, A.
Codex Trecensis, n° 504. 83-91, CHAT

ERNST-ABBE-BÜCHEREI UND LESEHALLE JENA

ERNST AUGUST, DUKE
Deetjen, Werner. Die Weimarische Bibliothek unter Ernst August und Ernst August Constantin. 87-101, WEIM

ERNST AUGUST CONSTANTIN, DUKE
Deetjen, Werner. Die Weimarische Bibliothek unter Ernst August und Ernst August Constantin. 87-101, WEIM

ERRATA (in books)
Wilmerding, Lucius. Le Prince, by Jean Louis Guez de Balzac: Note on a Paris Printing, 1631. 489-497, LYDE

ERSCH, JOHANN SAMUEL
Bulling, Karl. Aus der Jenaer Bibliothekarischen Tätigkeit Johann Samuel Erschs. Ein Beitrag zu Goethes Plan eines Gesamtkatalogs der Weimarischen Bibliotheken. 296-315, VORS

Erskine, John.
Portrait of Carl Engel. 5-12, ENGE

ERUDITION
see Learning and scholarship

ERYTHRAEUS, JANUS NICIUS, pseud.
see Rossi, Giovanni Vittorio

Esben-Petersen, O.
Bogvalget i Oplandsarbejdet. 87-95, LASS

Escalante, Luis de.
Prólogo. I, v-xii, ARTI

ESCHENBACH, WOLFRAM VON
see Wolfram von Eschenbach

Escher, Hermann.
Ein Amtlicher Bericht über die Schweizerischen Bibliotheken aus der Zeit der Helvetik. 84-111, BINZ (Also appears in pp. 208-230, ESCH.)
Die Bibliotheca Universalis Konrad Gessners (1934). 145-162, ESCH
Der Bibliothecarius Quadripartitus des Joh. Heinrich Hottinger (1664). 169-184, ESCH
Die Errichtung der Zentralbibliothek in Zürich (1915). 86-104, ESCH
Konrad Gessner über Aufstellung und Katalogisierung von Bibliotheken. 119-127, GODE (Also appears in pp. 163-168, ESCH.)
Moderne Bibliotheksbestrebungen und Bibliotheksaufgaben mit Besonderer Rücksicht auf die Geplante Zürcherische Zentralbibliothek (1912). 71-85, 85, ESCH
Das Neue Pestalozzihaus in Zürich (1933). 138-142, ESCH
Der Schlagwortkatalog der Stadtbibliothek Zürich (1890-1897). 59-70, ESCH
Die Schweizerische Landesbibliothek (1911). 123-130, ESCH
Die Schweizerische Volksbibliothek (1922). 131-137, ESCH
Die Schweizerischen Bibliotheken in der Zeit der Helvetik, 1798-1803 (1936). 185-207, ESCH
Schweizerisches Bibliothekswesen (1929). 3-32, ESCH
Ein Schweizerisches Gesamtzuwachsverzeichnis (1926). 45-58, ESCH
Die Stellung der Schweizerischen Bibliotheken zur Frage einer Einheitlichen Regelung der Katalogisierung (1912). 33-44, ESCH
Was Es in einer Bibliothek zu Tun Gibt (Zentralbibliothek Zürich 1928). 105-122, ESCH

ESCHER, HERMANN
ESCH
ESCK
ESCZ
Wild, Helen. Hermann Escher und der Zwingli-Verein; mit Liste der Historischen Publikationen Hermann Eschers. 1-5, ESCZ

ESCHER, HERMANN - Bibl.
Gutknecht, E. Bibliothekswissenschaftliche Arbeiten von Dr. Hermann Escher. 19-21, ESCK

ESCORIAL. Biblioteca. Mss. (Spanish, F II, 19)
Werner, Mulertt. La Fecha del Manuscrito Escurialense del "Paso Honroso." II, 242-245, ARTI

ESKILSTUNA, Sweden. Centralbibliotek
Nyman, Gunborg. Bibliotek på Hjul. Sommarsamhällets Bokförsörjning. 215-223, HEIN

ESSEN. Essener Büchereischule - Hist.
Sulz, Eugen. Die Büchereischule der Stadt Essen 1921-1933. 13-16, LANF

ESSEN - Library schools
see Library schools - Essen

ESSEN. Volksbücherei-Fachschule
see Essen. Essener Büchereischule

ESTAÇO, AQUILES
Ullman, B. L. Achilles Statius' Manuscripts of Tibullus. 449-468, ALBA

ETHICS
Sasaki, Kanzō. Toshokan Rinri. (Ethical Standards for Library and Librarian.) 15-20, KYOT

ETHIOPIC MANUSCRIPTS
see Manuscripts, Ethiopic

Ettinghausen, Richard.
The Covers of the Morgan Manâfi' Manuscript and Other Early Persian Bookbinding. 459-473, GREE

EUGEN, CARL, Duke of Württemberg
see Carl Eugen, Duke of Württemberg

EUGÈNE, Prince of Savoi-Carignan - Library
Czumpelik, Rudolf. Kardinal Passionei und Seine Beziehungen zu Prinz Eugen. 23-24, STUM

EURIPIDES. Andromache
Schwartz, Édouard. De Quibusdam Scholiis in Euripidis Andromachen. 651-657, GRAU

EURIPIDES. Hippolitus
Vitelli, Jérôme. Ad Euripide e Sofocle (Eur. Hipp. 115. 441 Soph. Frgm. 609 Dnd.). 97-102, GRAU

EUROPE - Book industry and trade
see Book industry and trade - Europe

EUROPE - CATALOGING - Rules
see Cataloging - Rules - Europe

L'EUROPE FRANÇAISE
Munoz, Antonio. L'Europa Francese e il Marchese Caraccioli. 317-322, GREG

EUROPE - Legal deposit (of books, etc.)
see Legal deposit (of books, etc.) - Europe

EUROPE - Libraries
see Libraries - Europe

EUROPE - Libraries and librarianship
see Libraries and librarianship - Europe

EUROPE - Printing
see Printing - Europe

EUROPE - Private libraries
see Private libraries - Europe

EUROPE - Publishers' catalogs
see Publishers' catalogs - Europe

EUROPEAN PERIODICALS
see Periodicals, European

EUSEBIUS PAMPHILI, Bp. of Caesarea. Mss. Eusebius Pamphili Chronici Canones . . .
Caspar, Erich. Paläographisches zum Kanon des Eusebius. 42-56, DEGE

EUSEBIUS PAMPHILI, Bp. of Caesarea. Mss. Preparatio Evangelica
Mras, Karl. Eine Neuentdeckte Handschrift des Eusebius. 485-487, BICK

EVANGELIARIES
Boeckler, Albert. Das Erhardbild im Utacodex. 219-230, GREE
Boussard, Jacques. L'Évangéliaire d'Or, Manuscrit 599 de la Bibliothèque de L'Arsenal. 3-14, CALO
Degering, Hermann. Das Prümer Evangeliar (Ms. lat. theol. Fol. 733) in Berlin. 132-148, HARN
Dorez, Léon. Évangéliaire Exécuté à L'Abbaye de Schuttern (VIIIe-IXe Siècle). 293-299, CHAT
Kirchner, Joachim. Das Staveloter

Evangeliar der Preussischen Staatsbibliothek. 160-171, DEGE

EVANGELISCHE LANDESKIRCHE IN BADEN

Erbacher, Hermann. Bibliographie des Wissenschaftlichen Schrifttums in einer Landeskirche. 16-24, SCHV

Evans, D. Wyn.
John Francis Campbell, of Islay, (1822-1885) and Norway. 52-64, TVET

Evans, Luther H.
Current Microfilm Projects at the Library of Congress. 31, STUM

Evans, Margaret B., jt. author

Dalgliesh, Alice and Margaret B. Evans. Designing Children's Books. 573-577, MOOR

Evers, Gerrit Albert.
Jan Frederik van Someren. 5-6, EVER
Het Paleis van Koning Lodewijk Napoleon te Utrecht en Zijne Inrichting tot Universiteitsbibliotheek. 42-62, SOME

EVERS, GERRIT ALBERT

EVER

Bannier, W. A. F. G. A. Evers als Medebestuurslid. 28-32, EVER
Hulshof, A. Een Woord Vooraf. 1-4, EVER
Reynvann, Marie J. Lijst van de Geschriften van G. A. Evers 1907-1 Jan. 1940. 7-25, EVER

EVERS, GERRIT ALBERT. Lijst van Gedrukte Geschriften over de Rijksuniversiteit te Utrecht

Hamel, A. G. van. Boekbespreking. 26-27, EVER

EVERSHAM, Belgium (Augustine monastery)

Hannemann, Kurt. Antwerpener Fragmente einer Deutschen Geistlichen Prosahandschrift des 14. Jahrhunderts. 55-64, LEYH

EXAMINATIONS - Personnel
see Personnel - Qualifications and selection

EXCHANGE OF BOOKS, PERIODICALS, ETC.
see also Duplicates

EXCHANGE OF BOOKS, PERIODICALS, ETC.

Brummel, Leendert. The Netherlands and the International Exchange of Publications. 1-47, BRUE
Kleberg, Tönnes. Some Facts about the International Exchange Relations of the Uppsala University Library. 98-101, MADR
Sevensma, Tietse Pieter. Eine Bibliothekarische Kriegserfahrung. 591-596, BICK

EXCHANGE OF BOOKS, PERIODICALS, ETC. - Administration

Kragemo, Helge Bergh. Zur Frage der Rationalisierung des Tauschverkehrs einer Wissenschaftlichen Bibliothek. 377-381, MUNT

EXCHANGE OF BOOKS, PERIODICALS, ETC. - Centers - Germany

Busse, Gisela von. Zur Entstehung der Tausch- und Beschaffungsstelle für Ausländische Literatur im Jahre 1949. 83-93, HOFF

EXCHANGE OF BOOKS, PERIODICALS, ETC. - Germany

Jürgens, Adolf. Der Suchdienst der Reichstauschstelle. I, 105-111, GLAU

EXCHANGE OF BOOKS, PERIODICALS, ETC. - Gothenburg, Sweden

Kleberg, Tönnes. De Internationella Bytesförbindelserna. 35-48, (sixth paper), GÖTE

EXCHANGE OF BOOKS, PERIODICALS, ETC. - Hague

Mooy, A. J. de. Het Ruilbureau. 235-240, HAGU

EXCHANGE OF BOOKS, PERIODICALS, ETC. - U.S.

Butler, Pierce. A Possible Field for Book Conservation. 399-403, WILS

EXCHANGE OF BOOKS, PERIODICALS, ETC. - Uppsala

Bring, Samuel E. Uppsala Universitetsbiblioteks Bytesförbindelser. Några Anteckningar om deras Uppkomst och Utveckling. 425-460, UPPS
Kleberg, Tönnes. Gli Scambi Internazionali della Reale Biblioteca Universitaria di Upsala. 505-510, GALL

EXHIBITS AND DISPLAYS
see also Bulletin boards

EXHIBITS AND DISPLAYS

Brummel, Leendert. Literatuur als Museumobjekt. 81-99, BRUE
Liebaers, Herman. Des Expositions dans les Bibliothèques. 159-168, HOFM

EXHIBITS AND DISPLAYS - Bydgoszcz

Skudlarska, Danuta. Wrażenia z Wystaw. 165-167, BYDG

EXHIBITS AND DISPLAYS - Dresden
Boden, Charlotte. Das Buchmuseum in den Semper-Räumen des Japanischen Palais. 46-51, BOLE
Kremer, Marita. Blick in das Buchmuseum der Sächsischen Landesbibliothek 1956. 52-56, BOLE

EXHIBITS AND DISPLAYS - Germany
Wahl, Gustav. Statistisches über Bibliotheksausstellungen. 141-145, BOLL

EXHIBITS AND DISPLAYS - Kraków
Blamowska, Krystyna. Zagadnienia Metodyczne Urządzania Wystaw. 72-80, KRAK

EXHIBITS AND DISPLAYS - Special subjects - Book illustration - Prague
Adlerová, Eliška. Několik Umělecko-historických Poznámek k Výstavě Francouzské Ilustrované Knihy v Praž. Národní a Universitní Knihovně. 80-83, EMLE

EXHIBITS AND DISPLAYS - Special subjects - Manuscripts - Munich - Catalogs
MUNI

EXHIBITS AND DISPLAYS - Vienna
Doublier, Othmar. Ein Vierteljahrhundert aus der Geschichte der Hofbibliothek 1891-1916. 163-210, VIEN

EXPANSIVE CLASSIFICATION
see Classification - Systems - Expansive

EXPORTATION OF BOOKS
see Importation and exportation of books

EXULTET (Pentecost hymn) Mss.
Strittmatter, Anselm. The Pentecost Exultet of Reims and Besançon. 384-400, GREE

Fabritius, Albert
COPE

Faden, Eberhard.
Aus der Geschichte Gelehrter Gesellschaften und Ihrer Bibliotheken in Berlin. 17-40, SCHS

Fage, Jean.
M. Julien Cain et la Photographie. 41-43, CAIN

FAGEL FAMILY (Netherlands) - Library
Brummel, Leendert. The Fagel Library in Trinity College, Dublin. 204-233, BRUE

FAIRS, Book
see Book fairs

Fairthorne, Robert A.
Some Basic Comments on Retrieval Testing. 267-270, KYLE

FAIRY TALES - Classification - Three brothers theme
Brandenstein, Wilhelm. Die Reichsgründersage des Makedonischen Herrscherhauses. 54-58, SCHT

Falck, Ludwig.
Die Bestände des Mainzer Stadtarchivs und Ihre Findmittel. 75-88, MAIN
Die Sammlung Mittelalterlicher Quellen zur Geschichte der Stadt Mainz. 71-73, MAIN

FANO, Italy. Biblioteca Comunale Federiciana
Bonasera, Francesco. Un'Antica Pianta della Città di Rimini Conservata nella Biblioteca Fredericiana di Fano. 199-203, GALL

FANO, Italy - Maps - Collections
see Maps - Collections - Fano, Italy

Fantini, Bianca Saraceni.
Prime Indagini sulla Stampa Padovana del Cinquecento. 415-485, FERR

FAR EASTERN LITERATURE
see Oriental literature

FARBENFABRIKEN BAYER. AKTIENGESELLSCHAFT - Kekulé-Bibliothek
Stoetzer, Walter. Die Kekulé-Bibliothek als Hilfsmittel der Dokumentation in der Chemischen Industrie. 130-135, LEUN

FARMINGTON PLAN
Busse, Gisela von. Warum Gemeinschaftliche Erwerbungspläne? 137-150, HOFM
Metcalf, Keyes de Witt. The Farmington Plan with Particular Reference to Austria. 57-59, STUM

Farquhar, Francis P.
George P. Hammond's Publications. 83-106, HAMM

Farradane, J.
Fundamental Fallacies and New Needs in Classification. 120-135, SAYW

Farradane, J., R. K. Poulton, and Mrs. S. Datta.

Problems in Analysis and Terminology for Information Retrieval. 287-290, KYLE

Farrand, Max.
William H. Whitmore and the Early Printed Laws of Massachusetts. 146-150, PUTN

Farrell, Colman J.
The Classification of Books in Libraries. 207-222, HANS

FARWELL, ARTHUR
Waters, Edward N. The Wa-Wan Press: An Adventure in Musical Idealism. 214-233, ENGE

FASCICULUS TEMPORUM
Stillwell, Margaret Bingham. The Fasciculus Temporum, a Genealogical Survey of Editions before 1480. 409-440, EAME

FASTING, CLAUS LYDERSEN
Dancke, Per. Claus Lydersen Fasting og Hans Bokfortegnelse. 5-24, HALV

Fava, Domenico.
I Corali degli Olivetani di Bologna. 277-286, FERR
Scrittorii Conventuali Ferraresi del Quattrocento. 129-135, GREG

FAVA, DOMENICO
FAVA

FAVA, DOMENICO - Bibl.
Toschi, Antonio. Elenco delle Pubblicazioni del Prof. Domenico Fava. 41-62, FAVA

Febvre, Lucien.
Le Bibliothécaire, la Bibliothèque et L'Histoire. 106-114, OURS

Feder, Georg.
Zur Datierung Haydnscher Werke. 50-54, HOBO

FEDERAL LIBRARIES
see Government libraries

FÉDÉRATION INTERNATIONALE DE DOCUMENTATION
see International Federation for Documentation

FÉDÉRATION INTERNATIONALE DES ASSOCIATIONS DE BIBLIOTHÉCAIRES
see International Federation of Library Associations

FEDERATION OF LIBRARY ASSOCIATIONS, International
see International Federation of Library Associations

Federhofer, Hellmut, ed.
OREL

Fédorov, Vladimir.
V. V. Stasov chez L'Abb. F. Santini à Rome. 55-62, HOBO

FÉDOROV, VLADIMIR
FEDO
Blume, Friedrich. An Vladimir Fédorov. 5-8, FEDO

FÉDOROV, VLADIMIR - Bibl.
Bardet, Bernard. Oeuvres de Vladimir Fédorov. 150-152, FEDO

Feilitzen, O. Von.
Litteratur om Göteborgs Stadsbibliotek in: Hallberg, S. Göteborgs Stadsbibliotek. Det Första Halvseklet 1891-1940. 113-142, (first paper), GÖTE

Fen Chzhun-i͡un.
Bibliografskoto Delo v Kitaĭskata Narodna Republika. 134-140, TEOB

Fendt, Franz.
Glückwunsch. 9-10, HELD

Fenske, Herbert.
Soziologische Zusammensetzung der Leserschaft. 75-82, HAMB

Ferguson, Milton J.
South African Libraries. 151-155, PUTN

FERNANDEZ DE CORDOVA Y AGUILAR, GONZALVO, called El Gran Capitan. Ms.
Werner, Mulertt. La Fecha del Manuscrito Escurialense del "Paso Honroso." II, 242-245, ARTI

FERRANDO, MIGUEL ARTIGAS Y
see Artigas y Ferrando, Miguel

FERRARA - Copyists
see Copyists - Ferrara

Ferrari, Giorgio E.
Fondamenti Attuali al Problema della Documentazione Umanistica. 403-425, GALL
La Metodologia Bibliografica, Verso una Definizione del Suo Svolgimento. 287-311, FERR

FERRARI, LUIGI
FERR
Pintor, Fortunato. Luigi Ferrari—Primi Studi e Uffici. 1-15, FERR

Fess, Simeon D.
The Library of Congress. 1, PUTN

Festa, N.
Nota Sui Versiculi in Vitia et Virtutes. 568-576, CERI

FESTSCHRIFTEN - Bibl.

Schauman, Henrik. Festskrifter och Festnummer Tillägnade Lärare och Tjänstemän vid Universiteten i Helsingfors och Åbo. 319-350, DAHL

FESTUS, SEXTUS POMPEIUS. Mss. (Codex Trecensis)

Thewrewk de Ponor, Émile. Codex Festi Breviati Trecensis. 659-669, GRAU

Feyl, Othmar.
Aus der Jenaer Aufklärung. 179-188, BULL
Bücher, Bibliotheken und Leser in der Russischen Gesellschaft des 19. Jahrhunderts. 97-133, LÜLF
Die Klassifikation für die Bibliographien der Buchkammer der Sowjetunion. Bemerkungen zur Gleichnamigen Publikation. 50-60, VORS

Fick, Richard.
Der Ankauf der Celler Kirchenministerialbibliothek durch den Preußischen Staat. 149-158, LEYG
Das Auskunftsbureau der Deutschen Bibliotheken. 272-277, HARN
Gesamt-Realkataloge. 95-110, MILF
Karl Boysen und Seine Stellung zum Gesamtkatalogproblem. I, 36-42, GLAU
Die Kataloge der Druckschriftenabteilung. 92-99, HARN

Ficker, Johannes.
Handschriftliches der Alten Strassburger Universitätsbibliothek. 44-65, ESCZ
Hortulus Animae. 59-68, LOUB
Ein Straßburger Akademisches Gedenkbuch aus dem Reformationszeitalter. 211-229, WOLF

FICTION
see also Science fiction

FICTION

Wieselgren, O. Några Anteckningar om Våra Dagars Folklitteratur. 251-265, ANNE

Filangieri Di Candida, Riccardo.
Perdita e Ricuperi del Diplomatico Farnesiano. 269-279, MERC

FILING

Merrill, William Stetson. Order of Books by Date under Subjects. 282-284, HANS
Meyer, Hermann H. B. Cards and Common Sense. 351-355, PUTN

FILING - Chinese characters

Schubert, Johannes. Chinesische Bücherverzeichnisse. I, 176-184, GLAU

FILIPOWICZ, JAN

Chwalewik, Edward. Jan Filipowicz Rytownik i Drukarz. 223-239, PIEK

Fill, Karl, jt. author

Walther, Carl and Karl Fill. Die Deutsche Gesamtausgabe der Dezimalklassifikation. 167-168, DONK

FILODEMO DI GADARA. Mss.

Bassi, D. Φιλοδημον πεξι 'Επικονξον (A?) B. 511-529, CERI

Filon, S. P. L.
W. C. Berwick Sayers: His Connection with the National Central Library and His Contribution to Library Co-operation. 22-25, SAYW

FINANCE
see Budgets

FINANCE OF LIBRARIES
see Public libraries - Finance

FINE BINDINGS
see Bookbinding - Fine bindings

FINE BOOKS
see Limited edition books

FINES, FEES, etc. - Denmark

Krogh-Jensen, G. Om Adgangen til Folkebibliotekerne Betragtninger over Bibliotekernes Reglementer. 105-131, DØSS

FINES, FEES, etc. - Japan

Okuda, Katsumasa. Toshokan no Seisai Kitei no Iroiro. (On the Various Rules of Punishment in Libraries.) 63-74, TSUB

Fink, Karl August.
Poggio-Autographen Kurialer Herkunft. 129-133, MERC

FINLAND - Bibliography, National
see Bibliography, National - Finland

FINLAND - Books
see Books - Finland

FINLAND - College and university librarians
see College and university librarians - Finland

FINLAND - College and university librarians - Status
see College and university librarians - Status - Finland

FINLAND - Germany - Descr. and trav. - Collections
see Germany - Descr. and trav. - Collections - Finland

FINLAND - Government publications
see Government publications - Finland

FINLAND - Maps, Early - Collections - Helsingfors
Nyberg, Paul. Finlands Kuster i 1600-Talets Kartografi. 88-107, HULT

FINLAND - Political parties
see Political parties - Finland

FINLAND - Printing
see Printing - Finland

FINLAND - Private libraries
see Private libraries - Finland

FINLAND - Public libraries
see Public libraries - Finland

FINLAND. Riksdagen. Biblioteket. Arkivet
Schauman, Henrik. Monarkisternas och Republikanernas Arkiv. 97-100, NYBE

FINNISH LITERATURE - Bibl. - Collections - Finland
Schauman, Henrik. Festskrifter och Festnummer Tillägnade Lärare och Tjänstemän vid Universiteten i Helsingfors och Abo. 319-350, DAHL

FINNISH LITERATURE - Collections - Sweden
Adde, Gustaf. Aldre Finskspråkiga Skrifter i Svenska Bibliotek. 269-294, COLL

FIRENZE
see Florence

Fischer, Anton.
Ersatzmöglichkeiten für Verlorene und Nicht Mehr Restaurable Einbände. 441-453, GALL

Fischer, Bonifaz.
Zur Textüberlieferung des Lucifer von Cagliari. 49-54, LEYH

Fischer, H. Th.
De Bibliotheek van het Fonds ten Behoeve van Indologische Studiën aan de Rijksuniversiteit te Utrecht. 64-68, EVER

Fischer, Karl, [Germany.]
Margarete Karteuserin, eine Nürnberger Klosterschreiberin des 15. Jahrhunderts. 24-31, VERZ

Fischer, Karl, [Norway.]
Biblioteksakens Utvikling i Norge 1836-1937. 26-38, NORN

Fischer, Klaus.
Freiheit und Bindung in Geisteswissenschaftlichen Teilen von Realkatalogen. Beobachtungen Ausländischer Bibliotheksbenutzer in Pakistan und Indien. 21-41, JUCR

Fischer, Luise and Lieselotte Henopp.
Schriftenverzeichnis Hermann Fuchs. 11-23, FUCH

Fischer, Norbert.
Milkau als Lehrer. 36-38, MILK

Fischer, Rudolf von.
Die Handschriften der Burgerbibliothek als Spiegel der Älteren Bernischen Vergangenheit. 9-49, BERT

FISCHER VON WALDHEIM, GOTTHELF
Knaus, Hermann. Fischer von Waldheim als Handschriften- und Inkunabelhändler. 255-280, BENZ

Fischer, Walther.
Zum Thema "Sachkataloge." 41-45, BOLE

Fiskaa, Haakon.
Bøker Som Smittebærere og Bokdesinfeksjon. 325-338, MUNT
Norsk Bibliotekforenings Virke. Resultater og Oppgaver. 58-73, NORS

Fitzgerald, William A.
American Librarianship. 7-13, MADR

FITZWILLIAM MUSEUM. Library, Cambridge, Eng. University
see Cambridge, Eng. University. Fitzwilliam Museum. Library

FITZWILLIAM, RICHARD, VISCOUNT - Library
Cudworth, Charles. Richard, Viscount Fitzwilliam, and the French Baroque Music in the Fitzwilliam Museum, Cambridge. 27-31, FEDO

Flach, Willy.
Beiträge zur Vorgeschichte der Landesbibliothek Weimar. 33-45, WEIM

FLAMENT, AUGUSTE JEAN. Catalogus der Stadsbibliotheek van Maastricht
Vermeeren, P. J. H. Handschriften van het Kapittel van Sint Servaas ter Koninklijke Bibliotheek in 's-Gravenhage. 179-193, MAAS

Fleischhack, Curt.
Die Bibliographische Tätigkeit der Deutschen Bücherei. 105-140, LEIZ
Deutsche Bücherei und Zentralkatalogisierung. 143-150, VORS
Frau Dr. Snimščikova. 83-85, BULL
Zur Rationalisierung der Bibliographischen Arbeit. 323-328, MIKH

FLEURY-ST. BENOÎT, France (Benedictine abbey)
see St. Benoît-sur-Loire, France (Benedictine abbey)

FLODOARD, of Reims. Mss. Annales

Couderc, C. Essai de Classement des Manuscrits des Annales de Flodoard. 719-731, HAVE

Floerke, Anna Marie.
Die Ersten Buchbinder in Mecklenburg-Schwerin. 242-273, HAEK

FLOIRE AND BLANCHEFLOR. Ms.

Nordling, Arnold. Helsingfors Universitetsbiblioteks Fragment av Flores och Blanzeflor. 129-142, HULT

FLORENCE. Biblioteca Mediceo-Laurenziana

Lodi, Teresa. La Vera Storia di un Presunto Cimelio Cinquecentesco (Il Cosiddetto Torchio della Biblioteca Medicea Orientale). 234-253, GREG

FLORENCE. Biblioteca Mediceo-Laurenziana - Mss.

Cassuto, Umberto. Manoscritti Ebraici della R. Biblioteca Laurenziana in Firenze. 17-23, FREN

FLORENCE. Biblioteca Mediceo-Laurenziana - Mss. (Palat. 7)

Haydon, Glen. The Dedication of Francesco Corteccia's Hinnario. 112-116, KINK

FLORENCE. Biblioteca Mediceo-Laurenziana - Mss. (San Marco 350)

Rühl, Franz. Sur un Manuscrit Négligé de Justinus. 412-416, CHAT

FLORENCE. Biblioteca Mediceo-Laurenziana - Mss. (XXXII.9)

Wendel, Carl. Aus der Vorgeschichte des Laurentianus XXXII.9. 16-22, KUHN

FLORENCE. Biblioteca Nazionale Centrale. Biblioteca Landau-Finaly

Mondolfo, Anita. La Biblioteca Landau-Finaly. 265-285, GREG

FLORENCE. Biblioteca Nazionale Centrale. Mss. (II.I.213; B.R.20; y Cl.xxxv, 259 bis)

Pousa, Ramón Fernández. Menéndez Pelayo y el Códice Florentino de las Cantigas de Santa María de Alfonso X el Sabio. 235-255, MENE

FLORENCE - Manuscripts, Hebrew - Collections
see Manuscripts, Hebrew - Collections - Florence

FLORES OCH BLANZEFLOR
see Floire and Blancheflor

Flury, Hans.
Die Rechtliche Natur des Bibliotheksbuches. 99-115, SCHU

Fock, Johannes
"Katalog der Wissenschaften" und "Katalog der Sachen." 93-109, TIEM

Focke, Helen M.
Education in Documentation at Western Reserve University; Yesterday, Today, and (Tomorrow?). 49-57, HASH

Focke, Rudolf, ed.
VERP

Focke, Rudolf.
Allgemeine Theorie der Klassifikation und Kurzer Entwurf einer Instruktion für den Realkatalog. 5-18, VERP

FÖRTECKNING ÖVER UPPSATSER OCH SKRIFTER AV INGEBORG HEINTZE. 273-278, HEIN

FOLK COLLEGES

Möhring, Werner. Volkshochschule und Volksbücherei. 95-124, ACKR

FOLK COLLEGES - Germany

Eggebrecht, W. Bücherei und Volkshochschule. 25-28, ACKR

FOLK LITERATURE

Wieselgren, O. Några Anteckningar om Våra Dagars Folklitteratur. 251-265, ANNE

FOLK LITERATURE - Italian - Collections - Berlin

Christ, Karl. Ältere Drucke Volkstümlicher Italienischer Dichtung in der Preussischen Staatsbibliothek. 61-69, HARN

FOLK MANUSCRIPTS
see Manuscripts

FOLK-SONGS, Czechoslovakian - Cataloging

Smetana, Robert and Bedřich Václavek. Jak Katalogisovati Kramářské Písně. 137-143, EMLE

FOLK-SONGS - German - Collections - Berlin

Kopp, Arthur. Das Liederbuch der Berliner Bibliothek vom Jahre 1582 und Verwandte Sammlungen. 445-454, WILM

FOLK-SONGS - Norwegian - Collections - Oslo

Christiansen, Reidar Th. Albrechtsons Visesamling. 106-130, OSLN

FOLK TALES
see Folk literature

FOLKLORE - Collections - Washington, D.C.

Emrich, Duncan B. Folklore Section of the Library of Congress. 331-334, BICK

Follieri, Enrica.
Un Canone Inedito di S. Andrea di Greta per L'Annunciazione (Vat. gr. 2008 e Crypt.Δ. a. VII). I, 337-357, ALBB

FONAGER, JENS

Hesselaa, Peder. Fonager og Folkebogsamlingen. 22-24, HOLS

Foncin, Myriem.
L'Histoire d'une Collection de Cartes Réunies pour Louis XIV. 119-126, CALO

FONDS TEN BEHOEVE VAN INDOLOGISCHE STUDIËN. Bibliotheek. Utrecht. Rijksuniversiteit
see Utrecht. Rijksuniversiteit. Fonds ten Behoeve van Indologische Studiën. Bibliotheek

Ford, Worthington Chauncey.
A Division of Manuscripts. 156-161, PUTN
The New England Primer. 61-65, EAME

FOREIGN LANGUAGE BOOKS - Acquisitions - Germany - Hist.

Busse, Gisela von. Zur Entstehung der Tausch- und Beschaffungsstelle für Ausländische Literatur im Jahre 1949. 83-93, HOFF

FOREIGN LANGUAGE BOOKS - Cataloging - Japan

Aizawa, Toyokatsu. Yōsho Mokurokuhō Nyumon. (An Introduction to the Cataloguing of Foreign Books.) 33-73, (part 1), OHAS

FOREIGN LANGUAGE BOOKS - Collections - Bern

Beck, Marcel. Die Ausländischen Bestände. 77-80, BERU

FOREIGN LANGUAGE BOOKS - Collections - Moscow

Rudomino, M. Die Staatliche Allunionsbibliothek für Ausländische Literatur zu Moskau - Heute und Morgen. 175-181, HOFM

FOREIGN LANGUAGE BOOKS - Collections - Stockholm

Hjelmqvist, Fredrik. Utlandets Författere och Allmänheten i Stockholm. Några Siffror ur Stockholms Stadsbiblioteks Utlåning. 88-96, MUNT

FOREIGN LITERATURE
see Foreign language books

FORLÌ - Azzolini family - Correspondence - Collections
see Azzolini family - Correspondence - Collections - Forlì

FORLÌ. Biblioteca Comunale. Mss. (Carte)

Servolini, Luigi. Le Carte Azzolini nella Biblioteca Comunale di Forli. 615-701, GALL

FORMAT
see Books - Format

FORMÉ, NICOLAS. Mss. Cantique

Launay, Denise. À propos de Deux Manuscrits Musicaux aux Armes de Louis XIII. 63-67, FEDO

FORMULARIES (Diplomatics). Mss.

Haskins, Charles Homer. Two Roman Formularies in Philadelphia. 275-286, EHRD

Forrer, L., ed.
Die Sog. Waldmannschen Spruchbriefe. [61]-[112], ESCK

FORSCHUNGSSTELLE PAPIERGESCHICHTE. Mainz
see Mainz. Gutenberg-Museum. Forschungsstelle Papiergeschichte

FORTEGNELSE OVER A. KJAERS TRYKTE ARBEIDER. 125-126, KJAE

FORTEGNELSE OVER ARTIKLER OG BØGER AF CARL THOMSEN; 105-112, THOM

FOSDIC
see Computers

Foskett, D. J., jt. ed.
SAYW

Foskett, D. J.
Classification and Integrative Levels. 136-150, SAYW
Comments on Fundamental Categories in Document Classification. 130-134, RANG
Language and Classification. 275-278, KYLE
Technique of Reference Service. 68-72, MADR

FOUCHER, ADÈLE
see Hugo, Adèle (Foucher)

FOXING
see Books - Care and restoration

FRANCE - Bibliography, National
see Bibliography, National - France

FRANCE - Book illustration
see Book illustration - France

FRANCE - Documentation - Special subjects - Law
see Documentation - Special subjects - Law - France

FRANCE - Education for librarianship
see Education for librarianship - France

FRANCE - Government publications
see Government publications - France

FRANCE - Liberty of the Press
see Liberty of the Press - France

FRANCE - Library inspection
see Library inspection - France

FRANCE - Maps - Collections
see Maps - Collections - France

FRANCE - Monastic libraries
see Monastic libraries - France

FRANCE - Private libraries
see Private libraries - France

FRANCE - Public libraries - Centralization
see Public libraries - Centralization - France

Franceschini, Ezio.
Le Versioni Latine Medievali di Aristotele e dei Suoi Commentatori Greci ed Arabi nelle Biblioteche delle Tre Venezie. 313-326, FERR

FRANCESCO D'ASSISI, SAINT. Legend. Speculum Perfectionis. Mss.

Caputo, Ada Moricca. Frammenti dello "Speculum Perfectionis" (in un Manoscritto Casatanense). 549-558, GALL

Francis, Sir Frank.
Dr. Hofmann, President of IFLA 1958-1963. 187-189, HOFM
The Large General Library in the Mid-Twentieth Century. 427-430, BRUM
The National Library as the Basis of a National Library. 244-247, KYLE

FRANCIS, WILLIAM WILLOUGHBY

FRAN

FRANCISCUS DE PLATEA
see Plateanus, Franciscus

FRANCKE, JOHANN MICHAEL

Bollert, Martin. Joh. Joach. Winckelmann und Joh. Mich. Francke. I, 11-17, GLAU
Leyh, Georg. Ein Brief Johann Michael Franckes von 1748. 78-81, BOLL

FRANGIPANI FAMILY (Rome)

Ehrle, Francesco, Cardinal. Die Frangipani und der Untergang des Archivs und der Bibliothek der Päpste am Anfang des 13. Jahrhunderts. 448-485, CHAT

Frank, Leonhard.
Grussbotschaft. 105, JENA

Frank, Otto.
Über die Zukünftige Entwicklung der Internationalen Dezimalklassifikation. 141-144, DONK

FRANKFURT a.M. - Architecture and building - College and university libraries
see Architecture and building - College and university libraries - Frankfurt a.M.

FRANKFURT a.M. - Architecture and building - Public libraries
see Architecture and building - Public libraries - Frankfurt a.M.

FRANKFURT a.M. - Bookmaking - Collections
see Bookmaking - Collections - Frankfurt a.M.

FRANKFURT a.M. - Catalogs - Subject
see Catalogs - Subject - Frankfurt a.M.

FRANKFURT a.M. - Depository libraries
see Depository libraries - Frankfurt a.M.

FRANKFURT a.M. Deutsche Bibliothek [honoree]

FRAD

FRANKFURT a.M. Deutsche Bibliothek [subject]

EPPE

Günther, Eberhard. Die Sammlung des Deutschsprachigen Schrifttums durch die Deutsche Bibliothek. Probleme und Methoden. 78-90, EPPE

FRANKFURT a.M. Deutsche Bibliothek. Bibl.

Die Veröffentlichungen der Deutschen Bibliothek. 165-171, EPPE
Veröffentlichungen über die Deutsche Bibliothek. 172-174, EPPE

FRANKFURT a.M. Deutsche Bibliothek Deutsche Bibliographie

Blum, Rudolf. Die Deutsche Bibliographie. 59, FRAD
——— Die Deutsche Bibliographie. Rückblick und Ausblick. 91-116, EPPE
Fuchs, Hermann. Die Deutschen Nationalbibliographien im Rahmen der Ausländischen Nationalbibliographien. 103-106, FRAD

FRANKFURT a.M. Deutsche Bibliothek. Deutsche Bibliographie - Bücher und Karten

Blum, Rudolf. Das Mehrjahres-Verzeichnis der Bücher und Karten. 68-72, FRAD

FRANKFURT a.M. Deutsche Bibliothek. Deutsche Bibliographie - Das Deutsche Buch

Schäfer, Rosa Maria. Das Deutsche Buch. 76-77, FRAD

FRANKFURT a.M. Deutsche Bibliothek. Deutsche Bibliographie - Halbjahres-Verzeichnis

Büttner, Liselotte. Das Halbjahres - Verzeichnis. 64-67, FRAD

FRANKFURT a.M. Deutsche Bibliothek. Deutsche Bibliographie - Wöchentliches Verzeichnis

Friesenhahn, Heinz. Das Wöchentliche Verzeichnis. 60-63, FRAD

FRANKFURT a.M. Deutsche Bibliothek. Deutsche Bibliographie - Zeitschriften

Jaeger, Friedrich. Das Mehrjahres-Verzeichnis der Zeitschriften. 73-75, FRAD

FRANKFURT a.M. Deutsche Bibliothek. Zeitschriftenverzeichnisse

Jaeger, Friedrich. Die Zeitschriftenverzeichnisse der Deutschen Bibliothek. 117-135, EPPE

FRANKFURT a.M. - German literature - Collections
see German literature - Collections - Frankfurt a.M.

FRANKFURT a.M. - Government publications - Collections
see Government publications - Collections - Frankfurt a.M.

FRANKFURT a.M. Hessischer Zentralkatalog

Köttelwesch, Clemens. Vom Frankfurter Sammelkatalog zum Hessischen Zentralkatalog. 92-101, FUCH

FRANKFURT a.M. - Incunabula - Collections
see Incunabula - Collections - Frankfurt a.M.

FRANKFURT a.M. - Manuscripts - Collections
see Manuscripts - Collections - Frankfurt a.M.

FRANKFURT a.M. - National libraries
see National libraries - Frankfurt a.M.

FRANKFURT a.M. - National libraries - Statistics
see National libraries - Statistics - Frankfurt a.M.

FRANKFURT a.M. - Public libraries
see Public libraries - Frankfurt a.M.

FRANKFURT a.M. - Public libraries - Reference services
see Public libraries - Reference services - Frankfurt a.M.

FRANKFURT a.M. - Public libraries - Statistics
see Public libraries - Statistics - Frankfurt a.M.

FRANKFURT a.M. Senckenbergische Bibliothek

Lohse, Hartwig. Zum Aufbau eines Neuen Sachkatalogs nach dem "System Eppelsheimer" an der Senckenbergischen Bibliothek unter Besonderer Berücksichtigung der Medizin. 102-110, FUCH

FRANKFURT a.M. Stadt- und Universitätsbibliothek

Köttelwesch, Clemens. Zum Neubau der Stadt- und Universitätsbibliothek Frankfurt am Main. 125-136, HOFM

FRANKFURT a.M. Stadtbibliothek

Freimann, A. Das Einteilungssystem der Judaica in der Stadtbibliothek Frankfurt a.M. 55-64, FREI
——— Die Hebräischen Inkunabeln der Stadtbibliothek zu Frankfurt a.M. 129-144, EBRA
Müller, Bernard. Pompeo Marchesi's Goethe-Statue in der Frankfurter Stadtbibliothek. 191-210, EBRA
Richel, Arthur. Ein Frankfurter Theater-Programm vom Jahre 1668. 117-127, EBRA

FRANKFURT a.M. - Statistical research
see Statistical research - Frankfurt a.M.

FRANKFURT a.M. - Trustees and boards
see Trustees and boards - Frankfurt a.M.

FRANKFURT a.M. - Unpublished works - Collections
see Manuscripts - Collections - Frankfurt a.M.

FRANKLIN, ANN, printer

Chapin, Howard Millar. Ann Franklin of Newport, Printer, 1736-1763. 337-344, EAME

Franklin, Benjamin.
Letters in: Reid, Winnifred Reynolds.

Beginnings of Printing in New Haven. From Letters of Benjamin Franklin and James Parker. 67-88, KEOG

Franz, Günther.
Die Bibliothek der Landwirtschaftlichen Hochschule Hohenheim. 139-150, HOFF

Franz, Rudi.
Die Titeldrucke der Deutschen Bücherei. 157-173, LEIZ

Franz, Rudi, joint author
Rückert, Ernst and Rudi Franz. Geschichte, Problematik und Gegenwärtiger Stand des Gruppenschlagwortkatalogs der Deutschen Bücherei. 175-196, LEIZ

Fraschetti-Santinelli, Italia.
L'Ordinamento della Voce "Roma" nel Catalogo per Soggetti. 151-163, GREG

FRATERNITY HOUSE LIBRARIES
see Dormitory libraries

Frati, Lodovico.
Una Miscellanea Umanistica della R. Biblioteca Universitaria di Bologna. I, 321-329, HORT

FRAUDS, Literary
see Literary forgeries and mystifications

Frauendorfer, Sigmund von.
Classification Problems in an International Special Library. 223-233, HANS
Internationale Einheitskatalogisierung? Hemmnisse und Möglichkeiten. 335-347, BICK
Was Ist Dokumentation? 32, STUM

Frauenfelder, Reinhard.
Die Älteste Handschrift in der Stadtbibliothek Schaffhausen. 155-160, LÜTH

FREDENHEIM, CARL FREDERIC - Library
Johansson, Cari. Carl Frederic Fredenheim and His Collection of Eighteenth-Century Music. 46-49, FEDO

FREDERIKSBERG, Denmark. Kommunebibliotekerne
Laursen, Johs. Lehm. Biblioteksbenyttelsens Intensivering og Dens Følger. 169-182, HEIN

FREDERIKSBERG, Denmark - Use studies - Public libraries
see Use studies - Public libraries - Frederiksberg, Denmark

FREDERIKSHAVN, Denmark. Folkebibliotek
FRED

FREDERIKSHAVN, Denmark - Public libraries - Statistics
see Public libraries - Statistics - Frederikshavn, Denmark

FREEDOM OF THE PRESS
see Liberty of the Press

Freiberg, Siegfried.
Begegnungen mit Büchern. 348-357, BICK
Die Bibliothek der Akademie der Bildenden Künste in Wien. 32-33, STUM

FREIBURG i. Br. Universität. Bibliothek
Will, Erich. Die Wiegendrucke des Gratianischen Dekretes und Ihr Bestand in der Universitätsbibliothek Freiburg i. Br. 191-217, JUCR

FREIDUS, ABRAHAM SOLOMON
FREI
Kohut, George Alexander. Steinschneideriana. 65-127, FREI
Kohut, Rebekah. Freidus—A Personal Reminiscence. XL-XLIII, FREI
Lydenberg, Harry Miller. Freidus the Bookman. XLIV-XLIX, FREI
Wiernik, Peter. Abraham Solomon Freidus (1867-1923). XXIII-XXX, FREI

FREIDUS, ABRAHAM SOLOMON - Bibl.
Freidusiana. A List of Writings by and about A. S. Freidus. XI-XXII, FREI

FREIDUSIANA
A List of Writings by and about A. S. Freidus. XI-XXII, FREI

Freimann, Aaron.
Das Einteilungssystem der Judaica in der Stadtbibliothek Frankfurt a.M. 55-64, FREI
Die Hebräischen Inkunabeln der Stadtbibliothek zu Frankfurt a.M. 129-144, EBRA
Jewish Scribes in Medieval Italy. 231-342, MARX

FREIMANN, ARON [=Aaron]
FREN

FREIMANN, ARON [=Aaron] - Bibl.
Emmrich, Hanna. Aron Freimann-Bibliographie. 5-16, FREN

Freitag, Albert.
Ein Band aus Luthers Erfurter Klosterbibliothek. 93-110, DEGE

Frels, Wilhelm.
Die Bibliographischen Arbeiten und Aufgaben. 120-136, LEIS

Das Deutsche Drama 1913-1920. Statistisches aus der Deutschen Bücherei. 38-50, MIND

FRENCH LITERATURE - Collections - Hague

Roelofs, Sjoerdtje. La "Collection Anny Antoine - Louis Koopman" à la Bibliothèque Royale de la Haye. 577-580, BRUM

FRENCH LITERATURE - Collections - Utrecht

Valkhoff, P. Het Franse Boek in de Utrechtse Universiteitsbibliotheek. 278-281, EVER

FRENCKEL, ULRICH, bookbinder

Endres, Heinrich. Meister Ulrich Frenckel aus Hirschau. 176-182, LOUB

FREUD, SIGMUND - Library

Berlstein, Alfred. Bibliotekarz i Pracownik Naukowy. 41-46, SZAC

FREUNDE DER DEUTSCHEN BÜCHEREI, GESELLSCHAFT DER
see Gesellschaft der Freunde der Deutschen Bücherei

Frewer, Louis B.
Samuel Johnson and Oxford. 65-76, TVET

Frey, Jaroslav.
Pozorování a Experiment v Pedagogice Čtenáře. 97-102, EMLE

Frey, Theophil.
Nicolaus Ochsenbach, der Kunstliebende und -Sammelnde Schloßhauptmann auf Hohen-Tübingen (1562-1626). 407-427, LEYG

Freys, Ernst.
Johann Baptist Bernharts "Gesammelte Schriften." Ein Vorläufer von Haeblers Typenrepertorium. 145-174, HAEB

FRIBOURG. Bibliothèque Cantonale et Universitaire. Mss. (Fonds Fournier)

Castella, Gaston. Comment Fut Composée L'Histoire du Sonderbund de Crétineau-Joly (1850). 201-216, GODE

Frieberger, Kurt.
Habent Sua Fata Libelli. 34, STUM

Friedrich, Marie.
Daten aus der Geschichte der Hamburger Öffentlichen Bücherhallen. 128-131, HAMB

FRIEDRICH II, Emperor of Germany. De Arte Venandi cum Avibus

Unterkircher, Franz. "De Arte Venandi cum Avibus." 653-661, BICK

FRIENDS OF THE LIBRARY - Leipzig

Linnemann, Richard. Die Gesellschaft der Freunde der Deutschen Bücherei. 188-196, LEIS

FRIENDS OF THE LIBRARY - Public libraries - Denmark - Hist.

SKAG

FRIENDS OF THE LIBRARY - Public libraries - Randers, Denmark

RAND

Friesenhahn, Heinz.
Das Wöchentliche Verzeichnis. 60-63, FRAD

Friesenhahn, Heinz and Rudolf Blum.
Die Bibliothekarische Arbeit der Deutschen Bibliothek. 55-58, FRAD

FRIESLAND, East - Scientific libraries
see Scientific libraries - Friesland, East

FRIESLAND - Printing
see Printing - Friesland

FRIESLAND - Type and type-founding
see Type and type-founding - Friesland

Friis, Th.
Education for Librarianship in South Africa at the Crossroads. 14-24, COET

Frisch, Ernst von.
Einbände des 16. Jahrhunderts in und aus Salzburg. 125-133, HAEK
Über die Salzburger Handschrift von Hugo von St. Victors Opusculum de Fructu Carnis et Spiritus. 67-71, LEID

Fritzsche, Hans-Joachim.
Erweiterter Benutzungsdienst und Beratungsstelle für Technische und Naturwissenschaftliche Literatur. 33-35, BERR

Fröschner, Günther, jt. ed.
BERS

Fromm, Emil, ed.
AACH

Fromm, Emil.
Die Dante-Sammlung der Alfred von Reumont'schen Bibliothek. 94-141, (pt. 1), AACH
Geschichte der Stadtbibliothek. I. Die Rathshandbibliothek im 17. und 18.

Jahrhundert. II. Die Dautzenbergsche Schenkung. III. Die Stadtbibliothek von Ihrer Eröffnung (1831) bis zum J. 1889. IV. Die Verwaltung der Stadtbibliothek seit dem J. 1889. 21-48, (pt. 1), AACH

FRULOVISI, TITO LIVIO DEI

Weiss, Roberto. Humphrey Duke of Gloucester and Tito Livio Frulovisi. 218-227, SAXL

Fryček, Václav M.
Veřejné Knihovny a Veřejné Mínění. 192-199, ŽIVN

Fuchs, Hermann.
Der Alphabetische Katalog und Seine Leute. 84-92, TIEM
Aus den Anfängen des Preussischen Gesamtkatalogs. 355-362, JUCH
Die Deutschen Nationalbibliographien im Rahmen der Ausländischen Nationalbibliographien. 103-106, FRAD
Der Gesamtkatalog der Preussischen Bibliotheken und Sein Ausbau zu einem Deutschen Gesamtkatalog. 209-216, KUHN
Der Neubau der Universitätsbibliothek Mainz. 39-63, MAIZ

FUCHS, HERMANN

FUCH

Wagner, Ewald. Grusswort. 5-8, FUCH

FUCHS, HERMANN - Bibl.

Fischer, Luise and Lieselotte Henopp. Schriftenverzeichnis Hermann Fuchs. 11-23, FUCH

FÜHRICH, JOSEF

Wille, Hans. Dürer-Erinnerungen in Josef Führichs Illustrationen zu "Der Wilde Jäger" von G. A. Bürger. 60-74, BRIE

DIE FUERO-HANDSCHRIFT

Häbler, Konrad. Die Fuero-Handschrift der Sächsischen Landesbibliothek. 146-155, BOLL

FÜRSTENSTEIN, Silesia. Hochbergsche Majoratsbibliothek

Nentwig, Heinrich. Zwei Schlesische Majoratsbibliotheken. 129-138, WILM

FÜRSTLICH DIETRICHSTEIN'SCHE FIDEICOMMISS-BIBLIOTHEK, Mikulov, Moravia
see Mikulov, Moravia. Fürstlich Dietrichstein'sche Fideicommiss-Bibliothek

FÜRTH, HERMANN ARIOVIST, FREIHERR VON - Library

Fromm, Emil. Geschichte der Stadtbibliothek. I. Die Rathshandbibliothek im 17. und 18. Jahrhundert. II. Die Dautzenbergsche Schenkung. III. Die Stadtbibliothek von Ihrer Eröffnung (1831) bis zum J. 1889. IV. Die Verwaltung der Stadtbibliothek seit dem J. 1889. 21-48, (pt. 1), AACH

FUGGER FAMILY (Anton Fugger) - Library

Husner, Fritz. Die Editio Princeps des "Corpus Historiae Byzantinae." Johannes Oporin, Hieronymus Wolf und die Fugger. 143-162, SCHU

FUGGER FAMILY (Augsburg) - Library

Nowak, Leopold. Die Musikhandschriften aus Fuggerschem Besitz in der Österreichischen Nationalbibliothek. 505-515, BICK

Fujikawa, Masanobu.
Bunken Tansaku ni okeru Imi no Mondai. (Problems of "Meaning" in Documentation.) 191-220, HASH

FULDA, Ger. (Benedictine monastery)

Lehmann, Paul. Quot et Quorum Libri Fuerint in Libraria Fuldensi. 47-57, COLL

FULDA, Ger. (Benedictine monastery). Biblioteca. Mss.

Lehmann, Paul. Eine Fuldaer Handschrift. I, 140-144, GLAU

FULDA, Ger. (Benedictine monastery). Bibliothek - Catalogs

Binz, Gustav. Ein Bisher Unbekannter Katalog der Bibliothek des Klosters Fulda. 97-108, GODE

FULDA, Ger. (Benedictine monastery) - Mss.

Christ, Karl. Die Handschriftenverzeichnisse der Fuldaer Klosterbibliothek aus dem 16. Jahrhundert. 24-39, FULD
———— Eine Unbekannte Handschrift der Ersten Fassung der Dionysiana und der Capitula e Canonibus Excerpta A. 813. 25-36, LEID

FULDA, Ger. - Bookbinding
see Bookbinding - Fulda, Ger.

FULDA, Ger. Landesbibliothek

FULD

Lehmann, Paul. Fulda und die Antike Literatur. 9-23, FULD

FULDA, Ger. Landesbibliothek - Hist.

Boehm, P. Peter. Die Anfänge der Landesbibliothek Fulda. 59-88, FULD

Theele, Joseph. Aus der Geschichte der Landesbibliothek Fulda. 289-292, LEID

——— Beiträge zur Geschichte der Landesbibliothek Fulda. 89-96, FULD

FULDA, Ger. Landesbibliothek. Mss. (1993)

Pfannmüller, Gustav. Westfälische Schreiberverse aus dem Jahre 1238. 71-72, SCHR

FULDA, Ger. - Manuscripts - Collections
see Manuscripts - Collections - Fulda, Ger.

Fuller, Henry.
The Philosophical Apparatus of Yale College. 163-180, KEOG

Fulton, Deoch, ed.
LYDE

Funke, Fritz.
Originales Sammelgut im Deutschen Buch- und Schriftmuseum. 219-241, LEIZ

FURNITURE
see also Shelves and shelving

FURNITURE - Hist.

Koch, Theodore Wesley. New Light on Old Libraries. 244-252, HANS

FURTMEYR, BERTHOLD, illustrator

Rosenthal, Erwin. Eine Neuaufgefundene Arbeit Berthold Furtmeyrs. 213-217, LEID

GADARA, FILODEMO DI
see Filodemo di Gadara

Gagnebin, Bernard.
Un Maniaque de L'Introspection Révélé par 35.000 Cartes à Jouer: Georges-Louis Le Sage. 145-157, CALO

Galante, Andrea.
L'Epistolario del Cardinale Cristoforo Madruzzo presso L'Archivio di Stato di Innsbruck. II, 787-805, HORT

Galassi-Paluzzi, Carlo.
Il Volume di L. de Gregori sulle Piante di Roma. 164-176, GREG

Galbraith, V. H.
The Chronicle of Henry Knighton. 136-145.
Appendix by R. A. B. Mynors. 146-148, SAXL

Galbreath, D. L.
Ausgewählte Siegel des Basler Staatsarchivs. 90-94, BASL

Galeazzi, A. G.
L'Archivio del Comune di Cingoli. 455-460, GALL

GALICIA - Public libraries
see Public libraries - Galicia

Gallavresi, G.
Alcune Lettere del Barone Custodi Riguardanti le Relazioni del Munifico Bibliofilo coll'Ambrosiana e colla Famiglia Borromeo. 403-412, CERI

GALLERY PUBLICATIONS
see Museum publications

Galley, Eberhard.
Miniaturen aus dem Kölner Klarissenkloster. Ein Kapitel Rheinischer Buchmalerei des 14. Jahrhunderts. 15-28, JUCH

GALLO, ALFONSO

GALL

Vigilucci, P. D. Alfonso Gallo e Camaldoli. 703-706, GALL

GALLO, ALFONSO - Bibl.

Avanzi, Giannetto. Bibliografia Cronologica e Analitica degli Scritti a Stampa del Prof. Alfonso Gallo, Pubblicati dal 1912 al 1953. 1-38, GALL

Gallo, Gratiniano Nieto.
La Arquitectura en las "Ideas Estéticas" de Menéndez Pelayo. 129-157, MENE
El Monumento Funerario de Menéndez Pelayo, Obra de Victorio Macho. 257-261, MENE

Ganchev, Dora, jt. author

Bozhinova-Troi͡anova, B. and Dora Ganchev. D-r Nikola V. Mikhov: Bibliografii͡a Izrabotena v Bŭlgarskii͡a Bibliografski Institut. IX-XIV, MIKN

GANDERSHEIM (Benedictine abbey)

Höfner, Curt. Zur Geschichte der Gandersheimer Büchersammlungen. Ein Beitrag aus Coburg. 197-210, HOFM

Ganovsky, Sava and Todor Borov.
Nikola Mikhov. 1-13, MIKH

Gans, Johann.
Bibliothekarausbildung in Verbindung mit Hochschulstudium. 151-153, VORS
Die Universitätsbibliothek in Wien im und nach dem Kriege. 358-367, BICK

GARCIA Y TASSARA, GABRIEL

Bago, Mercedes A. de. Una Versión Desconocida del Soneto "Al Sol" de Tassara. I, 68-69, ARTI

Gardberg, Carl-Rudolf.
Ur Paradsidornas Historia. Från Barock till Nyklassicism. 31-41, DAHA

GARDBERG, CARL-RUDOLF

GARD

GARDBERG, CARL-RUDOLF - Bibl.

Holmberg, Marianne. Förteckning över Carl-Rudolf Gardbergs Tryckta Skrifter intill 9.9.1958. 202-229, GARD

Garde, R. K. Ranganathan's Contribution to Subject Cataloguing. 217-221, RANG

Gardner, Frank.
Humanity and Vision. 536-538, HJEL

Gardthausen, V.
Amtliche Citate in den Beschlüssen des Römischen Senates. 15-25, CHAT
Différences Provinciales de la Minuscule Grecque. 731-736, GRAU

Gardy, Fréd.
La Réorganisation de la Bibliothèque de Genève au Début du XVIIIe Siècle. 133-143, GODE

Garinei-Canori, Costanza.
La Collezione Busuttil della Biblioteca Romana Sarti. 177-182, GREG

Garitte, Gérard.
Sur une Formule des Colophons de Manuscrits Grecs (ἥμὲν χεὶρ ἥ γράψασα). I, 359-390, ALBB

Garrison, Fielding Hudson.
The Medical Library in Relation to the University Library. 162-171, PUTN

GARSIAS, PIETRO, Bp. of Barcelona

Albareda, Anselmo M. Il Vescovo di Barcellona Pietro Garsias Bibliotecario della Vaticana sotto Alessandro VI. 1-18, MERG

Garside, Kenneth.
An Intelligence Library in Germany. 99-106, OFFO

Gartland, Henry J.
The Veterans Administration Library Program, 1946-1956. 389-398, DOEJ

Gassen, Kurt, ed.
MENN

Gautier, Léon.
À Julien Havet. x, HAVE

GDANSK
see Danzig

Gebhard, Annie C.
Inlichtingendiensten in Openbare Bibliotheken. 431-435, BRUM

Gebhardt, Oskar von.
Eine Verlorene und eine Wiedergefundene Stobaeus-Handschrift. 243-264, WILM

Gebhardt, Walther.
Gedanken zum Personalbedarf einer Wissenschaftlichen Bibliothek. 55-65, HOFF

Geck, Elisabeth.
Verzeichnis der Veröffentlichungen von Josef Benzing in den Jahren 1928-1963. 13-24, BENZ

Geel, Jacob.
Brieven - Collections in: Verwey, Eleonore de la Fontaine. Jacob Geel en de Koninklijke Bibliotheek. 414-426, BRUM

GEIBEL, EMANUEL - Collections - Lübeck

LÜBE

Geisberg, Max.
Der Ingenieur J. L. M. Gröninger. 9-15, BÖME

Geissler, Paul.
Ein Seltener Augsburger Wiegendruck. Das Älteste Gedruckte Buch über Altötting. 316-322, VORS
Ein Unbekannter Reuchlin-Wiegendruck. 120-126, BENZ
Zwei Unbekannte Holzschnittprobedrucke zum Theuerdank und Konrad Peutinger. 118-128, JUCH

Geldenblom, Gertrud.
Co-operation in Public Libraries. 420-424, RANG

Geldner, Ferdinand
SCHO

Geldner, Ferdinand.
Bamberger und Nürnberger Lederschnittbände der Zweiten Hälfte des 15. Jahrhunderts. 7-46, SCHO
Das "Catholicon" des Johannes Balbus im Ältesten Buchdruck. 90-98, JUCH

Handschriftliche Einträge in Wiegendrucken und Ihre Druckgeschichtliche Bedeutung. 127-131, BENZ
Der Verkaufspreis des Günther Zainer'schen Catholicon von 1469 (GW 3183). 37-42, STOL

GEMBLACENSE
see Gembloux, Belgium

GEMBLOUX, Belgium. Benedictine Abbey. Mss.
Thomas, Émile. Note sur un Gemblacensis Aujourd'hui à Bruxelles, n° 5348-5352, XIIe Siècle. 47-48, GRAU

GEMINIACUM
see Gembloux, Belgium

Gemmel, Ursula.
Druckkataloge der Ernst-Abbe-Bücherei und Lesehalle. 140-143, JENA

GENEALOGICAL LIBRARIES AND COLLECTIONS
Biber, Arthur. Gelegenheitsschriften, Familienkunde und Bibliotheken. 1-9, MILF

GENEALOGICAL LIBRARIES AND COLLECTIONS - Basel
Vischer, Christoph. Die Stammbücher der Universitätsbibliothek Basel. Ein Beschreibendes Verzeichnis. 247-264, SCHU

GENEALOGICAL LIBRARIES AND COLLECTIONS - Berlin
Transfeldt, Walter. Preussische Staatsbibliothek und Familienforschung. 261-270, KUHN

GENEALOGICAL RESEARCH - Berlin
Transfeldt, Walter. Preussische Staatsbibliothek und Familienforschung. 261-270, KUHN

GENEVA. Bibliothèque Publique et Universitaire - Hist.
Gardy, Fréd. La Réorganisation de la Bibliothèque de Genève au Début du XVIIIe Siècle. 133-143, GODE

GENEVA. Bibliothèque Publique et Universitaire. Mss.
Gagnebin, Bernard. Un Maniaque de L'Introspection Révélé par 35.000 Cartes à Jouer: Georges-Louis Le Sage. 145-157, CALO

GENEVA. Bibliothèque Publique et Universitaire. Mss. (no. 84)
Chatelain, E. Notes Tironiennes d'un Manuscrit de Genève. 81-86, HAVE

GENEVA - Cards - Collections
see Cards - Collections - Geneva

GENIZA COLLECTION (KAUFMANN)
see Hungarian Academy of Sciences, Budapest

Gény, Joseph.
Geschichte der Stadtbibliothek zu Schlettstadt. First Book, 1-75, SCHL

GEOGRAPHICAL LIBRARIES AND COLLECTIONS - Netherlands
Nieuwenkamp, J. L. M. Kits. Op Nieuwe Leest. 492-495, BRUM

GEORGE PEABODY COLLEGE FOR TEACHERS, Nashville. Library
Copeland, J. Isaac. Developing the Peabody Book Collection. 10-11, NASH

Gerhard, Karl.
Die Ungarische Nationalbibliothek der Universität Halle-Wittenberg. 139-158, WILM

GERMAN BOOK ORNAMENTATION
see Book ornamentation, German

GERMAN ENGRAVERS
see Engravers, German

GERMAN FOLK-SONGS
see Folk-songs, German

GERMAN LIBRARIANS
see Librarians, German

GERMAN LITERATURE - Bibliography - Bibl.
see Bibliography - Bibl. - German literature

GERMAN LITERATURE - Collections - Frankfurt a.M.
Berthold, Werner. Die Sondersammlung Exil-Literatur 1933-1945. 136-148, EPPE
Eppelsheimer, Hanns W. Die Bibliothek der Emigration. 89, FRAD
Günther, Eberhard. Die Sammlung des Deutschsprachigen Schrifttums durch die Deutsche Bibliothek. Probleme und Methoden. 78-90, EPPE

GERMAN LITERATURE - Collections - Leipzig
Halfmann, Horst. Das Schrifttum der Emigration in der Deutschen Bücherei. 197-217, LEIZ

GERMAN LITERATURE - Collections - Utrecht
Bongertman, W. De Centrale Duitsche Bibliotheek. 33-37, EVER

GERMAN MANUSCRIPTS
see Manuscripts, German

GERMAN MAPS
see Maps, German

GERMAN PERIODICALS
see Periodicals, German

GERMANIC PHILOLOGY - Collections - Basel

Salfinger, Theodor. Zur Sprachkunst des Germanisten Andreas Heusler. 193-205, SCHU

GERMANY - Acquisitions - Order processes
see Acquisitions - Order processes - Germany

GERMANY - Adult education - Library participation
see Adult education - Library participation - Germany

GERMANY - Anabaptists
see Anabaptists - Germany

GERMANY AND SWITZERLAND - Manuscripts - Collections
see Manuscripts - Collections - Germany and Switzerland

GERMANY - Antiquarians
see Antiquarians - Germany

GERMANY - Architecture and building - Public libraries
see Architecture and building - Public libraries - Germany

GERMANY - Armed forces libraries
see Armed forces libraries - Germany

GERMANY - Bibliography, National
see Bibliography, National - Germany

GERMANY - Book fairs
see Book fairs - Germany

GERMANY - Book industry and trade
see Book industry and trade - Germany

GERMANY - Bookbinders
see Bookbinders - Germany

GERMANY - Bookbinding
see Bookbinding - Germany

GERMANY - Bookbinding - Fine bindings - Collections
see Bookbinding - Fine bindings - Collections - Germany

GERMANY - Bookmaking
see Bookmaking - Germany

GERMANY - Books - Format
see Books - Format - Germany

GERMANY - Bookseller's catalogs
see Bookseller's catalogs - Germany

GERMANY - Cataloging, Centralized
see Cataloging, Centralized - Germany

GERMANY - Catalogs
see Catalogs - Germany

GERMANY - Catalogs - Classed
see Catalogs - Classed - Germany

GERMANY - Catalogs - Subject
see Catalogs - Subject - Germany

GERMANY - Catalogs - Union
see Catalogs - Union - Germany

GERMANY - Children's library services
see Children's library services - Germany

GERMANY - Children's literature
see Children's literature - Germany

GERMANY - Circulation procedures
see Circulation procedures - Germany

GERMANY - College and university libraries
see College and university libraries - Germany

GERMANY - College and university libraries - Acquisitions
see College and university libraries - Acquisitions - Germany

GERMANY - College and university libraries - Administration
see College and university libraries - Administration - Germany

GERMANY - College and university libraries - Required reading materials
see College and university libraries - Required reading materials - Germany

GERMANY - College and university libraries - Undergraduate libraries and collections
see College and university libraries - Undergraduate libraries and collections - Germany

GERMANY - Copyright
see Copyright - Germany

GERMANY - Descr. and travel - Collections - Finland

Grönroos, Henrik. Mitä Kirjat Kertoivat Saksasta ja Venäjästä 1700-Luvun Suomalaisille. 62-84, TUDE

GERMANY - Documentation
see Documentation - Germany

GERMANY - Duplicates
see Duplicates - Germany

GERMANY - Education for librarianship
see Education for librarianship - Germany

GERMANY - Exchange of books, periodicals, etc.
see Exchange of books, periodicals, etc. - Germany

GERMANY (Federal Republic, 1949-). Bundesverfassungsgericht. Bibliothek

Mackert, Josef. Die Bibliothek des Bundesverfassungsgerichts. Ein Bericht. 87-111, JUCR

GERMANY - Folk colleges
see Folk colleges - Germany

GERMANY - Government publications
see Government publications - Germany

GERMANY - Hist. Sources - Collections

Ihme, Heinrich. Landesbibliothek und Landesgeschichte. 94-111, HOFF

GERMANY - Illustration of books
see Illustration of books - Germany

GERMANY - Incunabula
see Incunabula - Germany

GERMANY - Information services
see Information services - Germany

GERMANY - In-service training
see In-service training - Germany

GERMANY - Interlibrary loans
see Interlibrary loans - Germany

GERMANY - Librarians as authors
see Librarians as authors - Germany

GERMANY - Librarianship
see Librarianship - Germany

GERMANY - Libraries
see Libraries - Germany

GERMANY - Library and the public
see Library and the public - Germany

GERMANY - Library legislation
see Library legislation - Germany

GERMANY - Library science
see Library science - Germany

GERMANY - Manuscripts
see Manuscripts - Germany

GERMANY - Manuscripts - Cataloging
see Manuscripts - Cataloging - Germany

GERMANY - Monastic libraries
see Monastic libraries - Germany

GERMANY - National libraries
see National libraries - Germany

GERMANY - National libraries - Reference services
see National libraries - Reference services - Germany

GERMANY - Newspaper libraries and collections
see Newspaper libraries and collections - Germany

GERMANY - Newspapers
see Newspapers - Germany

GERMANY - Printers marks
see Printers marks - Germany

GERMANY - Printing
see Printing - Germany

GERMANY - Private libraries
see Private libraries - Germany

GERMANY - Privately printed books
see Privately printed books - Germany

GERMANY - Public librarians
see Public librarians - Germanv

GERMANY - Public libraries - Administration
see Public libraries - Administration - Germany

GERMANY - Public libraries (small)
see Public libraries (small) - Germany

GERMANY - Public libraries - Book selection
see Public libraries - Book selection - Germany

GERMANY - Public libraries - Cataloging
see Public libraries - Cataloging - Germany

GERMANY - Public libraries - Services to students
see Public libraries - Services to students - Germany

GERMANY - Reader guidance
see Reader guidance - Germany

GERMANY - Reading - Educational aspects
see Reading - Educational aspects - Germany

GERMANY - Research libraries
see Research libraries - Germany

GERMANY - Scandinavian literature - Collections
see Scandinavian literature - Collections - Germany

GERMANY, Scandinavians in
see Scandinavians in Germany

GERMANY - School and public library relationship
see School and public library relationship - Germany

GERMANY - School libraries
see School libraries - Germany

GERMANY - Secularization
see Secularization - Germany

GERMANY - Special collections
see Special collections - Germany

GERMANY - State libraries
see State libraries - Germany

GERMANY - Subject Headings
see Subject Headings - Germany

GERMANY - Technical libraries
see Technical libraries - Germany

GERMANY - Technical literature
see Technical literature - Germany

GERMANY - Technical literature - Collections
see Technical literature - Collections - Germany

GERMANY - Technical services - Teaching
see Technical services - Teaching - Germany

GERMANY (Territory under Allied occupation, 1945- British Zone) Control Commission. Intelligence Library

Garside, Kenneth. An Intelligence Library in Germany. 99-106, OFFO

GERMANY - Type and Type-founding
see Type and type-founding - Germany

GERMANY - Type and type-founding - Gothic type
see Type and type-founding - Gothic type - Germany

GERMANY, WEST
see Germany (Federal Republic, 1949-)

GERMANY - Young adults' library services
see Young adults' library services - Germany

GERMANY - Young adults' literature
see Young adults' literature - Germany

GERSDORF, KARL GOTTHELF

Lülfing, Hans. Zur Sächsischen Bibliotheksgeschichte im 19. Jahrhundert. 343-356, VORS

Gerstinger, Hans.
Aus dem "Tagebuche" des Kaiserl. Hofhistoriographen Johannes Sambucus (1531-1584). Cod. Vindob. Latin. 9039, Fol. 1 und 5. 373-383, BICK
Ein Bisher Unbeachtetes Verzeichnis Griechischer Handschriften der Vaticana aus dem Jahre 1553. 11-19, LEYG
Johannes Sambucus als Handschriftensammler. 251-400, VIEN

Gertz, Martin-Clarence.
Emendationes Annaeanae. 353-379, GRAU

GESAMTKATALOG. Berlin
see Berlin. Gesamtkatalog

GESAMTKATALOG DER DEUTSCHEN PRESSE

Jessen, Hans. Aus der Werkstatt des Gesamtkatalogs der Deutschen Presse. 363-368, JUCH

GESAMTKATALOG DER PREUSSISCHEN BIBLIOTHEKEN
see Deutscher Gesamtkatalog

<u>GESAMTKATALOG DER PREUSSISCHEN WISSENSCHAFTLICHEN BIBLIOTHEKEN</u>

Fuchs, Hermann. Aus den Anfängen des Preussischen Gesamtkatalogs. 355-362, JUCH
——— Der Gesamtkatalog der Preußischen Bibliotheken und Sein Ausbau zu einem Deutschen Gesamtkatalog. 209-216, KUHN
Lehmann, Paul. Alte Vorläufer des Gesamtkatalogs. 69-81, LEYG
Weber, Christoph. Der Gesamtkatalog der Preussischen Wissenschaftlichen Bibliotheken. 259-272, HARN

GESAMTKATALOG DER SCHWEIZERISCHEN BIBLIOTHEKEN
see Bern. Schweizerische Landesbibliothek. Schweizerischer Gesamtkatalog

<u>GESAMTKATALOG DER WIEGENDRUCKE</u>

Altmann, Ursula. Die Inkunabelsammlung. I, 381-403, BERS
Haebler, Konrad. Der Gesamtkatalog der Wiegendrucke. 278-284, HARN

GESAMTKATALOG, Deutscher
see Deutscher Gesamtkatalog

GESELLSCHAFT DER BIBLIOPHILEN, Bern
see Schweizerische Bibliophilen Gesellschaft

GESELLSCHAFT DER FREUNDE DER DEUTSCHEN BÜCHEREI

Linnemann, Richard. Die Gesellschaft der Freunde der Deutschen Bücherei. 188-196, LEIS

GESELLSCHAFTSWISSENSCHAFTLICHE BERATUNGSSTELLE
see Berlin. Deutsche Staatsbibliothek

GESNER, KONRAD

Escher, Hermann. Konrad Gessner über Aufstellung und Katalogisierung von Bibliotheken. 119-127, GODE
Also appears in: 163-168, ESCH
Lutz, Hans. Konrad Gesners Beziehungen zu den Verlegern Seiner Zeit nach Seinen Pandekten von 1548. 109-117, GODE

GESNER, KONRAD. Die Bibliotheca Universalis

Escher, Hermann. Die Bibliotheca Universalis Konrad Gessners (1934). 145-162, ESCH

GESSNER, KONRAD
see Gesner, Konrad

Ghatak, B. N.
Dr. Ranganathan in Banaras. 725-728, RANG

GHENT. Universiteit. Bibliotheek. Mss. (Grimm)

Vreese, Willem de. Briefwisseling van Jan Frans Willems en Jakob Grimm. 264-295, DEGE

GHOTAN, BARTHOLOMAEUS

Collijn, Isak. Die Wanderung eines Druckerzeichens. Zu GfT 785-786. 74-79, HAEB

Gichtel, Paul.
Die Bilder der Münchener Tristan-Handschrift (Cod. Germ. 51). 391-457, HOFM

Gierow, Krister.
Biblioteksmannen Peter Wieselgren. 127-155, OLSS
Den Förste Universitetsbibliotekarien i Lund och "Bibliotheca Rostiana." 76-91, GARD
Henrik Reuterdahl Som Biblioteksman. 51-76, HEIN
Lundaprofessorn Arvid Moller Som Tillfällighetsdiktare. 133-143, DAHA

GIESSEN - Architecture and building - College and university libraries
see Architecture and building - College and university libraries - Giessen

GIESSEN - Librarians
see Librarians - Giessen

GIESSEN - Papyrus collections
see Papyrus collections - Giessen

GIESSEN. Universität. Bibliothek

GIES

GIESSEN. Universität. Bibliothek - Catalogs - 1631

Schawe, Josef. D. Steuberi Catalogi und Nachrichten von der Marpurger und Giesser Bibliothec. Giessener Hs. 30. 204-214, JUCH

GIFTS, CONTRIBUTIONS, etc.
see also Memorial collections and shelves

GIFTS, CONTRIBUTIONS, etc.

ELBE

Burckhardt, Felix. Die Schweizer Bücherhilfe für das Kriegsgeschädigte Ausland. 271-277, BICK
Usher, Robert James. The Place of the Endowed Reference Library in the Community. 467-473, PUTN

GIFTS, CONTRIBUTIONS, etc. - Aachen

Fromm, Emil. Geschichte der Stadtbibliothek. I. Die Rathshandbibliothek im 17. und 18. Jahrhundert. II. Die Dautzenbergsche Schenkung. III. Die Stadtbibliothek von Ihrer Eröffnung (1831) bis zum J. 1889. IV. Die Verwaltung der Stadtbibliothek seit dem J. 1889. 21-48, (pt. 1), AACH

GIFTS, CONTRIBUTIONS, etc. - Basel

Nidecker, Heinrich. Wilhelm Wackernagel. Bücher und Freunde. Ein Streifzug durch Seine Bibliothek. 177-191, SCHU

GIFTS, CONTRIBUTIONS, etc. - Berlin

Balcke, Curt. Heinrich Friedrich von Diez und Sein Vermächtnis in der Preussischen Staatsbibliothek. 187-200, KUHN

GIFTS, CONTRIBUTIONS, etc. - Bydgoszcz

Michałkiewicz, Kazimiera. Ofiarodawcy i ich Dary. 105-114, BYDG

GIFTS, CONTRIBUTIONS, etc. - Erlangen

Schmidt-Herrling, Eleonore. Zwei Geschenkbände von Heinrich Rantzau in der Universitätsbibliothek Erlangen. 57-61, VERZ

GIFTS, CONTRIBUTIONS, etc. - Gothenburg, Sweden

Hallberg, S. and O. von Feilitzen. Göteborgs Stadsbibliotek. Det Första Halvseklet 1891-1940. 1-142, (first paper), GÖTE

GIFTS, CONTRIBUTIONS, etc. - Halle

Perlbach, Max. Die Berliner Doubletten von 1697 in Halle. 15-42, WILM

GIFTS, CONTRIBUTIONS, etc. - Hamburg

Sierks, Ruth. Hilfe des Auslandes. 115-127, HAMB

GIFTS, CONTRIBUTIONS, etc. - Helsingfors

Hirn, Yrjo. Utländsk Välgörenhet mot Universitetsbiblioteket. 9-18, HULT

GIFTS, CONTRIBUTIONS, etc. - Mainz

Nissen, Claus. Stiftungen und Nachlässe in der Stadtbibliothek. 35-38, MAIN

GIFTS, CONTRIBUTIONS, etc. - McGill University

FRAN

GIFTS, CONTRIBUTIONS, etc. - Nashville

Morrissey, Eleanor Fleming. Reading Bookplates. 14-16, NASH

GIFTS, CONTRIBUTIONS, etc. - Tokyo (Ohashi)

Ishii, Munetsugu. Ōhashi Toshokan ni Kisō Seraretaru Nidai Seijika no Iaisho ni tsuite. (On the Collections Prized by the Late Two Statesmen Which Were Donated to the Ohashi Library.) 90-104, (part 1), OHAS

GIFTS, CONTRIBUTIONS, etc. - Uppsala

Kleberg, Tönnes. Ett Decennium av Gåvor. Kring en Utställning i Uppsala Universitetsbibliothek. 149-167, HEIN

Lundgren, Hjalmar. En Uppsala-Biblioteks Donator och dennes Biblioteksplaner. Några Randanmärkningar till ett par Ritningar. 461-467, UPPS

GIFTS, CONTRIBUTIONS, etc. - Vienna

Gladt, Karl. Hundert Jahre Stadtbibliothek. 18-45, VIES

GIFTS, CONTRIBUTIONS, etc. - Weimar

Blumenthal, Hermann. Älteste Verwaltungsgeschichte der Landesbibliothek Weimar (1691-1750). 46-86, WEIM

Wahl, Hans. Die Weimarische Bibliothek als Erbin der Herzogin Anna Amalia. 158-167, WEIM

GIFTS, CONTRIBUTIONS, etc. - Yale

Bryant, Louise May and Mary Patterson. The List of Books Sent by Jeremiah Dummer. 423-492, KEOG

Keogh, Andrew. Bishop Berkeley's Gift of Books to Yale in 1733. 128-147, MUNT

Pratt, Anne Stokely. The Books Sent from England by Jeremiah Dummer to Yale College. 7-44, KEOG

Gilbert, Francis.
Two Conflicting Theories of International Copyright Protection. 106-114, ENGE

Gillarová, Vlasta.
L. J. Živný v Knihovnickém Školstvi. 146-164, ŽIVN

Gillett, Frederick H.
Herbert Putnam. 4, PUTN

Gimpera, Pedro Bosch.
El Problema de los Cántabros y Su Origen. II, 429-445, ARTI

Gini, Corrado.
Gli Archivi e il Progresso delle Scienze Sociali. 15-19, MERC

Ginzberg, Louis, ed.
FREI

Gioever, Hanna.
Skoleboksamlinger på Landet. 83-96, NORN

Giordani, Igino.
La Scuola Vaticana di Biblioteconomia. 495-503, WILS

Giraud, Jeanne.
Notes de Lectures Romantiques: Encore les Strophes Supprimées du Lac. 253-259, BONN

Girnus, Wilhelm.
Staatssekretär für das Hoch- und Fachschulwesen. XIII-XV, LEIZ
Vorwort. I, ix-xii, BERS

Gitler, Robert L.
Toshokangaku Kyōiku no Kijun to Nintei. (Accreditation in Library Science Education.) 159-165, HASH

Gittig, Heinz.
Das Auskunftsbüro der Deutschen Bibliotheken. I, 223-240, BERS
Die Gesellschaftswissenschaftliche Beratungsstelle. I, 425-432, BERS

Gjeldaker, Ivar.
Folkeskolen Trenger Gode Skoleboksamlinger. 104-112, NORS

GJELSNESS, RUDOLPH H.

GJEL

GJÖRWELL, CARL CHRISTOFFER

Carlsson, A. B. En Supplik af Gjörwell 1772. Ett Stycke Svensk Lärdomshistoria i Kanslikollegiet. 67-73, ANNE

Gladt, Karl.
Hundert Jahre Stadtbibliothek. 18-45, VIES

GLAUBURG, ADOLF VON - Library
Traut, Hermann. Dr. Adolf von Glauburg und Seine Bibliothek. 1-34, EBRA

Glauning, Otto.
Ein Beitrag zur Kenntnis der Einbände Johann Richenbachs. 95-112, LEIP
Drei Lederschnittbände von der Wende des XIV. Jahrhunderts aus Altzelle. 188-195, BOLL
Die Einbandsammlung der Bayerischen Staatsbibliothek zu München. 111-122, MILF

GLAUNING, OTTO
GLAU

GLAUNING, OTTO - Bibl.
Schreiber, Heinrich. Die Veröffentlichungen Otto Glaunings. I, 1-9, GLAU

Gleason, Eliza Atkins.
The Atlanta University School of Library Service—Its Aims and Objectives. 504-510, WILS

GLEIWITZ, Ger.
see Gliwice, Upper Silesia (City)

Gleixner, Paul.
Bibliographie Bayerische Staatsbibliothek 1945-1964. 63-71, HOFM
Verzeichnis der Schriften von Gustav Hofmann, 1930-1964. 1-5, HOFM

GLIWICE, Upper Silesia (City) Library
Horstmann, H. Altersaufbau und Lesestetigkeit in einer Volksbücherei. 47-54, ACKE

GLIWICE, Upper Silesia (City) - Use studies - Public libraries
see Use studies - Public libraries - Gliwice, Upper Silesia (City)

Głodek, Stefania.
Wypożyczalnia. 29-34, KRAK

GLOSSY, CARL
GLOS

GLOUCESTER, HUMPHREY, DUKE OF
Weiss, Roberto. Humphrey Duke of Gloucester and Tito Livio Frulovisi. 218-227, SAXL

Gluth, Oskar.
Epistel der Freundschaft. 18-19, HELD

Gnoli, Tomaso.
Giggi Zanazzo e le Sue Opere Edite ed Inedite alla Biblioteca Angelica. 183-191, GREG

GOBIUS, JOHANNES. Scala Coeli
Juchhoff, Rudolf. Verwertung einer Restauflage um 1500. 478-481, BRUM

Gobom, Nils.
Eric Benzelius d. y:s Itineris Eruditi Album i Linköpings Stiftsbibliotek. 385-394, COLL
Gustaf Odencrants' E. T. A. Hoffmann-Samling i Linköpings Stifts- och Landsbibliotek. 262-279, GRAP

Godard, George Seymour.
A Brief Summary of the Activities of the Connecticut State Library, Hartford. 172-177, PUTN

GODDARD, WILLIAM
Swan, Bradford F. The First Printing in Providence. 365-369, WROT

Gode, M.
Dokumentat͡sii͡a, Biblioteki i Bibliografii͡a. 327-333, MIKN

Godet, Marcel.
Au Temps de la "Respublica Litterarum." Jacob Christophe Iselin et Louis Bourguet. 117-127, SCHU
La Bibliothèque Nationale Suisse et Son Oeuvre, 1895-1945. 1-31, BERU
Les Éminents Mérites de M. Bick. Ein Brief. 44, BICK
Hermann Escher et les Bibliothèques Suisses. 8-19, ESCK
Une Lettre Amicale au Rédacteur. 23-24, EMLE
M. Gustave Binz et la Bibliothèque Nationale Suisse. 30-32, BINZ
Monsieur K. J. Lüthi et la Bibliothèque Nationale Suisse. 147-149, LÜTH
Monsieur William Warner Bishop, et la Fédération Internationale des Associations de Bibliothécaires. 56-62, BISH

GODET, MARCEL
GODE
GODM
Brummel, Leendert. Confrontation of Libraries and Documentation. 9-16, DONR
Schmidt, Charles. Des Vivres et des Livres. 41-44, GODE

Göber, Willi.
Das Bibliothekswesen einer Universität als Einheit. 154-171, VORS
Ein Spätantiker Pergamentkodex des Dionysius Thrax. P. Hal. 55a. 111-118, DEGE

Gödel, Vilhelm.
Erik Sparre. Till Historien om Hans Litterära Samlingar. 171-178, ANNE

Göller, Emil.
Untersuchungen über das Inventar des Finanzarchivs der Renaissancepäpste (1447-1521). 227-272, EHRE

Goelzer, Henri.
Ovide et Saint Avit. 275-280, CHAT

Goes, Rudolf.
Ein Unfirmierter Lutherdruck aus Köln vom Jahre 1526. 132-139, BENZ

Goethe, Johann Wolfgang Von.
Brief [an Diez] in: Weil, Gotthold. Goethes Brief an H. F. von Diez vom 15. November 1815. 182-186, KUHN

GOETHE, JOHANN WOLFGANG VON

Bulling, Karl. Aus der Jenaer Bibliothekarischen Tätigkeit Johann Samuel Erschs. Ein Beitrag zu Goethes Plan eines Gesamtkatalogs der Weimarischen Bibliotheken. 296-315, VORS
Mackall, Leonard L. Goethe's Letter to Joseph Green Cogswell. 315-326, PUTN
Oettingen, Wolfgang von. Über Goethes Kunstsammlungen. 72-78, WAHL
Paszkowski, Wilhelm. Goethes Verhältnis zum Bibliothekswesen. 159-172, WILM

GOETHE, JOHANN WOLFGANG VON. Mss. - Collections - Jena

Karpe, Georg. Handschriften von Johann Wolfgang Goethe im Autographenbestand der Universitätsbibliothek Jena. 189-197, BULL

Götting, Franz.
Die Öffentliche Bibliothek zu Wiesbaden, die Übrigen Nassauischen Bibliotheken und die Museen. 1-231, WIES

GÖTTINGEN - Incunabula - Music - Collections
see Incunabula - Music - Collections - Göttingen

GÖTTINGEN - Interlibrary loans
see Interlibrary loans - Göttingen

GÖTTINGEN. Niedersächsische Staats- und Universitäts-Bibliothek

Weber, Hans-Oskar. Die Beanspruchung der Staats- und Universitätsbibliothek Göttingen durch den Deutschen Leihverkehr. 161-168, JUCR

GÖTTINGEN. Niedersächsischer Zentralkatalog

Kiefert, Hans-Joachim. Der Niedersächsische Zentralkatalog 1956-1966. 82-91, FUCH

GÖTTINGEN. Staats- und Universitätsbibliothek
see Göttingen. Niedersächsische Staats- und Universitätsbibliothek

GÖTTINGEN. Universität. Bibliothek

Fick, Richard. Der Ankauf der Celler Kirchenministerialbibliothek durch den Preussischen Staat. 149-158, LEYG
Leyh, Georg. Chr. G. Heynes Eintritt in die Göttinger Bibliothek. 220-228, MILF
Luther, Wilhelm Martin. Die Accessisten der Göttinger Universitätsbibliothek. 527-536, BRUM
———— Die Nichtliturgischen Musikinkunabeln der Göttinger Bibliothek. 130-148, TIEM

GÖTTINGEN. Universität. Bibliothek - Hist.

Leyh, Georg. Bibliothekshistorisches aus dem J. D. Reuss-Briefwechsel. 1-9, SCHT
Nelson, Axel. Aus J. H. Lidéns Tagebuch über Seinen Aufenthalt in Göttingen in den Jahren 1768-1769. 255-263, MILF

GÖTTINGEN. Universität. Bibliothek. Mss. (Brambach Briefe)

Weber, Ulrich. Vier Unveröffentlichte Briefe Wilhelm Brambachs an Carl Dziatzko aus dem Besitz der Universitätsbibliothek Göttingen oder: Scherz- und Schimpf-spiel zwischen Gelehrten. 171-178, JUCR

GÖTTWEIG (Benedictine abbey). Biblioteca

Riedel, Friedrich W. Die Libretto-Sammlung im Benediktinerstift Göttweig. 105-111, FEDO

GÖTTWEIG (Benedictine abbey). Biblioteca. Mss. (75)

Bollert, Martin. Ein Neuer Lederschnittband aus dem 14. Jahrhundert. 80-82, LEIP

GÖTTWEIG - Librettos - Collections
see Librettos - Collections - Göttweig

Götze, Alfred, jt. ed.
HEPD

Goetzee, P. C.
Grand Old Man of Librarianship. 643-644, RANG

Gøtzsche, E.
Folkebibliotekernes Laan fra de Videnskabelige og Faglige Biblioteker. 153-168, DØSS

Goff, Frederick R., ed.
WROT

Goff, Frederick R.
Early Music Books in the Rare Books Division of the Library of Congress. 58-74, KINO
The First Decade of the Federal Act for Copyright, 1790-1800. 101-128, WROT

GOJU-NEN KAI
see Tokyo. Library Staff Training Institute. Students

GOLDEN GOSPELS
see Bible. Mss., Latin. N.T. Gospels

Goldman, Solomon.
The Man of the Book. 1-34, MARX

GOLDSCHMID, ANDREAS
see Aurifaber, Andreas

Goldschmidt, E. P.
Not in Harrisse. 129-141, WROT
Lucian's Calumnia. 228-244, SAXL
An Obituary Rotulus from York, 1405. 379-383, GREE

Goldschmidt, Günther.
Ein Beitrag zur Ältesten Geschichte der Handschriftensammlung der Staats- und Universitäts-Bibliothek. 125-131, KÖNI

Goldstein, Ludwig.
Karl Rosenkranz und Alexander Jung. Mit Vierzehn Unveröffentlichten Rosenkranz-Briefen. 132-158. KÖNI

Gollub, H.
Die Beiden Buchdrucker und Erzpriester Maletius. 159-180, KÖNI

GOLTZIUS, HENDRIK - Collections - Rome (City)

Moricca, Luciano. Le Stampe del Goltzius nella Biblioteca Casanatense di Roma. 286-303, GREG

Golub, I'lja.
Informačně-bibliografické Funkce Vědecké Knihovny. 102-107, EMLE

Gordon, D. J., ed.
SAXL

Gordon, R. J.
A Long Look Back. 8-9, LAMB

GORGIAS, of Leontini. Oratio in Helenam

Croiset, Alfred. Essai de Restitution d'un Passage de L'Éloge d'Hélène Attribué à Gorgias. 127-132, GRAU

GORIZIA. Biblioteca Civica
see Gorizia (City) Biblioteca Governativa

GORIZIA (City) BIBLIOTECA

GORI

GORIZIA (City) BIBLIOTECA GOVERNATIVA

Della Bona, Giuseppe Domenico. Il Regesto delle Pergamene Goriziane e Friulane della Biblioteca Civica. 25-55, GORI

GORIZIA (City) BIBLIOTECA GOVERNATIVA - Hist.

Battisti, Carlo. Il Centenario della Biblioteca Governativa di Gorizia. 9-24, GORI

GORIZIA (City) - Catalogs
see Catalogs - Gorizia (City)

GORIZIA (City) - Hist. - Sources - Collections - Gorizia (City)

Della Bona, Giuseppe Domenico. Il Regesto delle Pergamene Goriziane e Friulane della Biblioteca Civica. 25-55, GORI

GORIZIA (City) - Library resources
see Library resources - Gorizia (City)

GORIZIA (City) - Manuscripts - Collections
see Manuscripts - Collections - Gorizia (City)

Gorter, A.
Het Nut van Tijdschriftenlijsten. 436-440, BRUM

GOSPELS
see Bible. Mss., Latin. N.T. Gospels

GOTHA - Breviaries - Collections
see Breviaries - Collections - Gotha

GOTHA (City) Herzogliche Bibliothek
see Gotha (City) Landesbibliothek

GOTHA (City). Landesbibliothek

Weil, Gotthold. Goethes Brief an H. F. von Diez vom 15. November 1815. 182-186, KUHN

GOTHA (City). Landesbibliothek. Mss.

Roob, Helmut. Schöne Breviere in der Gothaer Bibliothek. 55-61, LÜLF

GOTHA (City). Landesbibliothek. Mss. (Chart. B 237)

Schenk zu Schweinsberg, Eberhard, Frhr. Margarete von Rodemachern, eine Deutsche Bücherfreundin in Lothringen. 117-152, WEIM

GOTHA (City). Landesbibliothek. Mss. (I, 122)

Ehwald, Rudolf. Über eine Französische

Missalhandschrift des XIV. Jahrhunderts. 65-75, SCHW

GOTHA - Miniature painting - Collections
see Miniature painting - Collections - Gotha

GOTHA (City) Öffentliche Bibliothek
see Gotha (City) Landesbibliothek

GOTHAER SAMMLUNG, Basel
see Basel. Universität. Bibliothek. Mss. (Gothaer Sammlung)

GOTHENBURG, Sweden - Architecture and building - Public libraries
see Architecture and building - Public libraries - Gothenburg, Sweden

GOTHENBURG, Sweden - Chinese literature Collections
see Chinese literature - Collections - Gothenburg, Sweden

GOTHENBURG, Sweden - Depository libraries
see Depository libraries - Gothenburg, Sweden

GOTHENBURG, Sweden - Exchange of books, periodicals, etc.
see Exchange of books, periodicals, etc. - Gothenburg, Sweden

GOTHENBURG, Sweden - Manuscripts - Collections
see Manuscripts - Collections - Gothenburg, Sweden

GOTHENBURG, Sweden. Museum. Bibliothek

Hallberg, S. and O. von Feilitzen. Göteborgs Stadsbibliotek. Det Första Halvseklet 1891-1940. 1-142, (first paper), GÖTE

GOTHENBURG, Sweden - Public libraries
see Public libraries - Gothenburg, Sweden

GOTHENBURG, Sweden - Public libraries - Statistics
see Public libraries - Statistics - Gothenburg, Sweden

GOTHENBURG, Sweden - Public libraries - Technical services
see Public libraries - Technical services - Gothenburg, Sweden

GOTHENBURG, Sweden - School libraries
see School libraries - Gothenburg, Sweden

GOTHENBURG, Sweden. Stadsbibliotek

GÖTE

Möhlenbrock, Sigurd. Om Arbets- och Ansvarsfördelning. 203-214, HEIN

GOTHENBURG, Sweden. Stadsbibliotek - Bibl.

Hallberg, S. and O. von Feilitzen. Göteborgs Stadsbibliotek. Det Första Halvseklet 1891-1940. 1-142, (first paper), GÖTE

GOTHENBURG, Sweden - Swedish literature - Collections
see Swedish literature - Collections - Gothenburg, Sweden

GOTLAND, Sweden. Länsbiblioteket
see Visby, Sweden. Länsbiblioteket.

GOTTFRIED VON STRASSBURG. Mss. Tristan

Gichtel, Paul. Die Bilder der Münchener Tristan-Handschrift (Cod. Germ. 51). 391-457, HOFM

GOTTHOLD, FRIEDRICH AUGUST - Library

Killer, Hermann. Zur Musik des Deutschen Ostens im 18. Jahrhundert. 228-243, KÖNI
Wermke, Ernst. Friedrich August Gotthold und Seine Bibliothek. 354-373, KÖNI

GOTZKIRCHER, SIGMUND - Library

Lehmann, Paul. Aus einer Münchner Büchersammlung des Ausgehenden Mittelalters. 157-164, LEID

GOUDA - Manuscripts
see Manuscripts - Gouda

GOUDA. Sint Margareta (Franciscan monastery) Bibliotheek. Mss.

Lieftinck, G. I. Enige Problemen met Betrekking tot Gedateerde Goudse Handschriften. 139-154, KOSS

Gough, Chester R., jt. author
Brodman, Estelle and Chester R. Gough. Computers in Medical and University Libraries; A Review of the Situation in the U.S. in 1964. 19-39, HASH

GOVERNING AUTHORITIES OF LIBRARIES
see also Trustees and boards

GOVERNING AUTHORITIES OF LIBRARIES - Geneva

Gardy, Fréd. La Réorganisation de la Bibliothèque de Genève au Début du XVIIIe Siècle. 133-143, GODE

GOVERNMENT LIBRARIES
see also State libraries

GOVERNMENT LIBRARIES

Prinzhorn, Fritz. Eigenart und Be-

deutung der Parlaments- und Behördenbibliotheken. 293-307, JUCH
Tobolka, Zdeněk V. De Quelques Problèmes Relatifs aux Bibliothèques Parlementaires. 144-148, EMLE

GOVERNMENT LIBRARIES - Gt. Brit.

Mallaber, K. A. The Education of Librarians and Information Officers: Government Libraries. 301-304, HUTT

GOVERNMENT LIBRARIES - Scandinavia

Schauman, Henrik. Samarbetet Mellan de Nordiska Parlamentsbiblioteken. 232-237, TVET

GOVERNMENT PUBLICATIONS
see also
Archives, Government; Documents; Serial publications

GOVERNMENT PUBLICATIONS

Breycha-Vauthier, A. C. de. Le Rôle des Publications Gouvernementales et des Publications d'Organisations Internationales. 7-14, GODE

GOVERNMENT PUBLICATIONS - Austria

Haiböck, Lambert. Nationalbibliothek und Staatsdruckerei. 39, STUM

GOVERNMENT PUBLICATIONS - Canada

Childs, James B. Author Entries for Canadian Government Publications. 169-174, HANS

GOVERNMENT PUBLICATIONS - Cataloging
see Documents - Cataloging

GOVERNMENT PUBLICATIONS - Collections - Bern

Schazmann, Paul-Emile. Les Périodiques Officiels. 48-50, BERU

GOVERNMENT PUBLICATIONS - Collections - Frankfurt a.M.

Budach, Anneliese. Amtliche Druckschriften. 78-85, FRAD

GOVERNMENT PUBLICATIONS - Communist countries

Childs, James B. Government and Official Publications in a People's Democracy. 163-170, RANG

GOVERNMENT PUBLICATIONS - Finland - Bibl.

Melander, Toini. Bibliografisia Lisiä Suomenkielisiin Virallisiin Julkaisuihin Ruotsin Vallan Aikana. 89-109, DAHL

GOVERNMENT PUBLICATIONS - France - Bibl.

Childs, James B. French Government Document Bibliography. 85-97, MADR

GOVERNMENT PUBLICATIONS - Germany

Childs, James B. Corporate Author Entry as Regards the German Federal Republic. 151-162, RANG

GOVERNMENT PUBLICATIONS - Hist.

Kaspers, Heinz. Zur Älteren Geschichte der Deutschen Amtsdrucksachen. 45-55, JUCR

Goyal, R. S.
Library Catalogue. 64-67, MADR

Graafland, H. J. P. Hooft.
De Tijdschriften en de Reekswerken der Universiteitsbibliotheek. 146-149, EVER

Grabmann, Martin.
Mitteilungen aus Münchner Handschriften über Bisher Unbekannte Philosophen der Artistenfakultät (Codd. Lat. 14246 und 14383). 73-83, LEID
Neuaufgefundene "Quaestionen" Sigers von Brabant zu den Werken des Aristoteles (Clm. 9559). 103-147, EHRA

GRADUALS (Music)

Brenn, Franz. Die Sequenzen des Graduale von St. Katharinenthal. 23-42, OREL

Graf, Lucia.
Bibliographia Medica Helvetica. 152-153, BERU

GRAF, URS

Oldenbourg, M. Consuelo. Die Holzschnitte des Vrs Graf zur Passion und die des Johann Wechtlin zum Leben Jesu. Ein Bibliographisches Verzeichnis Ihrer Verwendungen. 291-310, BENZ

Graft, C. Cath. van de.
Bibliografie Betreffende de Camera Obscura. 74-106, EVER

Granniss, Ruth Shepard.
The New York Printers and the Celebration of the French Revolution of 1830. 193-202, EAME

Thomas Britton. 196-202, LYDE

GRANVELLE, ANTOINE PERRENOT DE, CARDINAL - Library

Piquard, Maurice. La Bibliothèque d'un

Homme d'État au XVIe Siècle. 227-235, CALO

Grape, Anders.
Om Bröderna Salan och Deras Handskriftssamling. 139-170, ANNE

GRAPE, ANDERS
GRAPE

GRAPHOLOGY
Aliprandi, Giuseppe. Aspetti Particolari della Grafia. 39-46, GALL

Gras, Elisabeth J.
De Systematische Catalogus der Utrechtsche Universiteitsbibliotheek. 107-115, EVER

Grasberger, Franz.
Katalogisierungsprobleme einer Musikbibliothek. 172-181, VORS

Grasberger, Hans.
Der Antiquar. Eine Gedankliche Geschichte. 7-13, GLOS

Gratzl, Emil.
Bedarfsberechnung an der Bayerischen Staatsbibliothek 1932-1936. 369-372, LEYG
Islamische Handschriftenbände der Bayerischen Staatsbibliothek. 118-147, LOUB

GRATZL, EMIL
GRAS
GRAT

GRAUX, CHARLES
GRAU

GRAUX, CHARLES.
Lavisse, Ernest. Charles Graux. xi-1, GRAU

GRAUX, CHARLES. Bibl.
Graux, Henri. Notice Bibliographique des Publications de Charles Graux. li-lvi, GRAU

Graux, Henri.
Notice Bibliographique des Publications de Charles Graux. li-lvi, GRAU

Gray, Margaret.
Bookmobile Service in Hawaii. 408-419, RANG

GRAY, THOMAS. Elegy Written in a Country Church Yard
Rothkrug, Michael. An Apparently Unrecorded Appearance of Gray's Elegy, 1751: An Appendix to Stokes. 343-353, KEOG

GRAZ - Manuscripts
see Manuscripts - Graz

GRAZ. Universität. Bibliothek
VERE
Eichler, Ferdinand. Ausgewählte Bucheinbände des 15. und 16. Jahrhunderts aus der Universitätsbibliothek Graz. 110-124, HAEK
———— Eine Bucheinbandverzierung aus dem Formenschatz Hans Holbeins d. J. 63-66, LEID

Grazie, M. E. delle.
Der Blaue Vogel. 15-21, GLOS

GT. BRIT. - Archives
see Archives - Gt. Brit.

GT. BRIT. - Archives, Church
see Archives, Church - Gt. Brit.

GT. BRIT. ARMY. 21 Army group
Garside, Kenneth. An Intelligence Library in Germany. 99-106, OFFO

GT. BRIT. - Associations
see Associations - Gt. Brit.

GT. BRIT. - Book illustration
see Book illustration - Gt. Brit.

GT. BRIT. - Bookbinding
see Bookbinding - Gt. Brit.

GT. BRIT. - Certification of librarians
see Certification of librarians - Gt. Brit.

GT. BRIT. - Children's library services
see Children's library services - Gt. Brit.

GT. BRIT. College of Arms. Library. Mss. (Arundel no. 9)
James, M. R. A Graeco-Latin Lexicon of the Thirteenth Century. 396-411, CHAT

GT. BRIT. - Cooperation
see Cooperation - Gt. Brit.

GT. BRIT. - Copyright
see Copyright - Gt. Brit.

GT. BRIT. - County libraries
see County libraries - Gt. Brit.

GT. BRIT. - Depository libraries
see Depository libraries - Gt. Brit.

GT. BRIT. Government libraries
see Government libraries - Gt. Brit.

GT. BRIT. - Illumination of books and manuscripts
see Illumination of books and manuscripts - Gt. Brit.

GT. BRIT. - Industrial libraries
see Industrial libraries - Gt. Brit.

GT. BRIT. - Medical libraries
see Medical libraries - Gt. Brit.

GT. BRIT. - Monastic libraries
see Monastic libraries - Gt. Brit.

GT. BRIT. - Personnel - Qualifications and selection
see Personnel - Qualifications and selection - Gt. Brit.

GT. BRIT. - Private libraries
see Private libraries - Gt. Brit.

GT. BRIT. - Proprietary libraries
see Proprietary libraries - Gt. Brit.

GT. BRIT. - Reader guidance
see Reader guidance - Gt. Brit.

GT. BRIT. - Rural libraries
see Rural libraries - Gt. Brit.

GT. BRIT. - Special librarianship
see Special librarianship - Gt. Brit.

GREEK HYMNS
see Hymns, Greek

GREEK INSCRIPTIONS
see Inscriptions, Greek

GREEK LANGUAGE - Writing

Gardthausen, V. Différences Provinciales de la Minuscule Grecque. 731-736, GRAU

GREEK PALEOGRAPHY
see Paleography, Greek

GREEK SHORTHAND
see Shorthand, Greek

GREEN, THOMAS, printer - Bio-bibl.

Bates, Albert Carlos. The Work of Hartford's First Printer. List of Thomas Green's Hartford Imprints, 1764-1768 345-361, EAME

Greenberg, Solomon.
Midrash Koheleth Zuta. 103-114, MARY

GREENE, BELLE DA COSTA

GREE

Alba, the Duke of. En Tributo de la Memoria de Belle da Costa Greene. 3, GREE
Kenyon, Sir Fredrick G. A Tribute from the British Museum. 4-5, GREE
Lydenberg, Harry Miller. The Ecology of the Pierpont Morgan Library and Its First Director. 6-9, GREE

Gregor, Joseph.
Die Handzeichnungen der Sammlung Perera in der Wiener Nationalbibliothek. 407-420, VIEN
Josef Bick. Die Persönlichkeit und das Wirken als Bibliothekar. 22-43, BICK

Gregor, Joseph and Karl Ecker.
Die Theatersammlung. 180-199, BICK

GREGORI, LUIGI DE

GREG

Barberi, Francesco. Luigi de Gregori. 17-31, GREG
Galassi-Paluzzi, Carlo. Il Volume di L. de Gregori sulle Piante di Roma. 164-176, GREG

GREGORI, LUIGI DE - Bibl.

Pubblicazioni di Luigi de Gregori. 32-39, GREG

GREGORIUS, Saint, Bp. of Nyssa. Commentarius in Canticum Canticorum

Musurillo, Herbert. A Note on Gregory of Nyssa's Commentary on the Song of Solomon, Homily IV. 321-326, ALBA

GREGORIUS, Saint, Bp. of Tours. Miracula

Delisle, M. L. Un Nouveau Manuscrit des Livres des Miracles de Grégoire de Tours. 1-8, HAVE

GREGORIUS I, the Great, Saint, Pope. Mss. Fragmentum

Kirchner, Joachim. Die Berliner Gregoriusfragmente. 148-156, HARN

GREGORIUS I, the Great, Saint, Pope. Mss. Regulae Pastoralis Liber

Schmitz, Wilhelm. Tironianum. 77-80, HAVE

GREGORIUS XII, Pope - Library

Mercati, Angelo. La Biblioteca Privata e gli Arredi di Cappella di Gregorio XII. 128-165, EHRE

GREIFSWALD - Albums, Pommeranian - Collections
see Albums, Pommeranian - Collections - Greifswald

GREIFSWALD - Correspondence - Collections
see Correspondence - Collections - Greifswald

GREIFSWALD - Manuscripts, German
see German manuscripts - Greifswald

GREIFSWALD - Medical literature - Collections
see Medical literature - Collections - Greifswald

GREIFSWALD - Rare books - Collections
see Rare books - Collections - Greifswald

GREIFSWALD. Universität. Bibliothek,

MENN

GREIFSWALD. Universität. Bibliothek

Deutsch, Josef. Ebers Calendarium Historicum mit Handschriftlichen Eintragungen aus Wolgast. 71-78, KUHN

GREIFSWALD. Universität. Bibliothek - Hist.

Asen, Johannes. Die Universitätsbibliothek Greifswald zur Zeit des Übergangs an Preussen. 271-277, KUHN
Menn, Walter. Aus der Geschichte der Universitätsbibliothek Greifswald in den Letzten Jahren der Preussischen Zeit. 230-255, JUCH
Zunker, Ernst. Der Greifswalder "Medizinische Lesezirkel" vom Jahre 1802. Ein Randkapitel der Greifswalder Bibliotheksgeschichte. 415-431, VORS

GREIFSWALD. Universität. Bibliothek. Mss.

Ziegler, Hans. Pommersche Stammbücher. 19-30, ZIEG

GREIFSWALD. Universität. Bibliothek. Mss. (Niederd. Abt. 1927. 242)
Deutsch, Josef. Die Handschrift des Weseler Stadtrechts in der Abteilung für Niederdeutsche Literatur bei der Universitätsbibliothek in Greifswald. 233-247, BÖME

Grémaud, Gabriel.
Aux Archives de Dijon. Quelques Documents Portant la Signature des Rois de France. 115-119, OURS

Gren, Erik.
Bidrag till Michael Enemans Biografi Studier och Bokförvärv. 445-494, GRAP

Grenier, A.
Quelques Fautes des Manuscrits et des Textes Latins Touchant les Mots Composés. 180-192, CHAT

GRIJS, PAUL

Collijn, Isak. Paul Grijs, Uppsalas Förste Boktryckare 1510-1519. 97-138, UPPS

Grill, Erik.
The Barrow Method in Sweden. 489-492, GALL

GRILLPARZER, FRANZ

Paunel, Eugen. Grillparzer als Bibliothekar. Meinungen, Hoffnungen, Enttäuschungen. 357-383, VORS

GRILLPARZER, FRANZ - Collections - Uppsala

Kleberg, Tönnes. Zwei Stammbuchblätter von Grillparzer in der Universitätsbibliothek Uppsala. 51, STUM

GRILLPARZER, FRANZ. <u>Ein Bruderzwist in Habsburg</u>

Sauer, August, ed. "Ein Bruderzwist in Habsburg." Bruchstücke Früherer Fassungen. 321-342, GLOS

GRILLPARZER, FRANZ. <u>König Ottokars Glück und Ende</u>

Zeidler, Jakob. Ein Censurexemplar von Grillparzer's: "König Ottokar's Glück und Ende." 287-311, GLOS

GRIMANI, DOMENICO, CARDINAL. <u>Questio de Intensione et Remissione Qualitatis</u>

Kibre, Pearl. Cardinal Domenico Grimani, <u>Questio de Intensione et Remissione Qualitatis</u>: A Commentary on the Tractate of that Title by Richard Suiseth (Calculator). 147-203, ALBA

Grimm, Heinrich.
Ulrichs von Hutten Persönliche Beziehungen zu den Druckern Johannes Schöffer in Mainz, Johannes Schott in Strassburg und Jakob Köbel zu Oppenheim. 140-156, BENZ

GRIMM, JACOB

Langfeldt, Johannes. Kinderausgaben der Grimmschen Märchen. Eine Bibliothekarische Besinnung auf Deren Grundsätze. 49-59, BRIE

GRIMM, JACOB - Correspondence - Collections - Ghent

Vreese, Willem de. Briefwisseling van Jan Frans Willems en Jakob Grimm. 264-295, DEGE

GRIMM, WILHELM. <u>Märchen</u>

Langfeldt, Johannes. Kinderausgaben der Grimmschen Märchen. Eine Bibliothekarische Besinnung auf Deren Grundsätze. 49-59, BRIE

Grisar, Hartmann, S. J.
Die Stationen und Ihre Perikopen im

Römischen Missale. Liturgiegeschichtliche Studien aus der Römischen Stadtgeschichte. 101-140, EHRB

Groag, Edmund.
Zur Geschichte des Bücherankaufes in der Hofbibliothek. 421-430, VIEN

Groeneveld, C.
Analyse van Bibliotheekstukken. 441-449, BRUM

Grönroos, Henrik.
Då Böckerna Bytte Ägare. Bokauktioner i Åbo under "Hertiginnans av Finland" Tid. 92-108, GARD
Mitä Kirjat Kertoivat Saksasta ja Venäjästä 1700-Luvun Suomalaisille. 62-84, TUDE
Om Böcker och Bokägare i Finland för 200 År Sedan. 1-15, NYBE

Grönroos, Henrik and Birgit Lunelund-Grönroos.
Förteckning över Skrifter Rörande Helsingfors Universitetsbibliotek, dess Samlingar och Enskilda Bokverk. 256-318, DAHL

Grohmann, Adolf.
Bibliotheken und Bibliophilen im Islamischen Orient. 431-442, VIEN

Grolier, Eric de.
Points de Vue Rétrospectif et Prospectif dans la Classification. 96-119, SAYW

GROLIER, ÉTIENNE

Guignard, Jacques. À propos d'un Grolier Inédit. La Date des Reliures à Plaquettes: Étienne ou Jean Grolier? 191-216, CALO

GROLIER, JEAN

Brun, Robert. Sept Nouvelles Reliures de Grolier. 183-190, CALO
Guignard, Jacques. À propos d'un Grolier Inédit. La Date des Reliures à Plaquettes: Étienne ou Jean Grolier? 191-216, CALO
Loubier, Hans. Versuch einer Klassifizierung der Einbände für Jean Grolier. 421-434, COLL
Rudbeck, Johannes. Über die Herkunft der Grolier-Einbände. 183-190, LOUB

Grolman, Hermina C. A.
Hoe de Centrale Systematische Catalogus aan het Volkenkundig Instituut te Utrecht tot Stand Kwam. 116-122, EVER

Groot, J. R. de.
Thorbecke en de Leidse Bibliothecaris Van Voorst. 450-455, BRUM

Grosheide, D.
Aankondiging van Nieuwe Uitgaven in de Zeventiende Eeuw. 456-462, BRUM

Grosser, Hermann.
Der Auskunftsdienst. 168-173, BERU
Der Gesamtkatalog der Schweizerischen Bibliotheken. 157-162, BERU
Marcel Godet und der Schweizerische Gesamtkatalog. 16-19, GODM
Die Zusammenarbeit der Schweizerischen Bibliotheken. Rückblick und Ausschau. 129-142, SCHU

GROT, JACOB

Widnäs, Maria. Jacob Grot och Universitets Ryska Bibliotek. 144-163, DAHL

Grotewohl, Otto.
Geleitwort. I, vii, BERS

GRUDZINSKI, SIGISMUND

Warschauer, A. Über Einige Seltene Gelegenheitsdrucke aus der Provinz Posen. 67-74, VERP

Grün, Hugo.
Die Pfarrarchive im Dienste der Kirchlichen Heimatforschung. 25-41, SCHV

Grütter, Wilhelm.
Das Ehemalige Bauhaus des Basler Münsters und Seine Nachbarhäuser. 47-86, BASA

Grundtvig, Vilh.
Almindelig Historie. 11-51, AARU
Andre Forhold. 159-165, AARU
Forbindelse med Andre Institutioner. 155-158, AARU
Statens Avissamling i Aarhus. 166-174, AARU

Grunwald, Wilhelm.
Der Spezialbibliothekar. Aufgaben, Auswahl, Ausbildungsvorschläge. 182-191, VORS
Zur Sacherschliessung im Bereiche der Chemie. 393-403, JUCH

Grycz, Józef.
Po Czwartym Zjeździe Bibliotekarzy Polskich w Warszawie 30. Maja—2. Czerwca 1936 r. 24-28, EMLE
Polska Polityka Biblioteczna w Latach Powojennych. 71-88, GRYC

GRYCZA, JÓZEF

GRYC

Horodyski, Bogdan. Józef Grycz. 22-54, GRYC

GRYCZA, JÓZEF - Bibl.

Kurdybacha, Emilia. Bibliografia Drukowanych Prac, Artykulów i Notatek J. Grycza. 55-68, GRYC

Gryczowa, Alodia.
Dzie*l*o Kazimierza Piekarskiego. 39-61, PIEK

Guarnaschelli, Teresa.
Alfonso Fernandez da Cordova e la Prima Stampa di Murcia. 125-132, ACCU

GUARNERIO D'ARTEGNA - Library
Leicht, Pier Silverio. La Biblioteca d'un Umanista. 77-81, GODE

GUAZZELLI, PIETRO DEMETRIO
Guidi, Pietro. Pietro Demetrio Guazzelli da Lucca il Primo Custode della Biblioteca Vaticana (1481-1511) e L'Inventario dei Suoi Libri. 192-218, EHRE

Günnel, Peter.
Walter Hofmann und das Deutsche Volksbüchereiwesen. 7-16, DRES

Günther, Eberhard.
Die Sammlung des Deutschsprachigen Schrifttums durch die Deutsche Bibliothek. Probleme und Methoden. 78-90, EPPE

Günther, Otto.
Mittelalterliches aus den Handschriften der Marienkirche in Danzig. 123-141, MILF
Der Neapolitaner Johannes Bernardinus Bonifacius, Marchese von Oria, und die Anfänge der Danziger Stadtbibliothek. 107-128, WILM

Guerrieri, Guerriera.
Note sulla Raccolta dei Manoscritti della Biblioteca Nazionale di Napoli. 192-200, GREG

GÜSTROW - Public libraries
see Public libraries - Güstrow

GÜSTROW. Stadt- und Kreisbibliothek - Bibl.
GÜST

GÜSTROW. Stadt- und Kreisbibliothek - Hist.
GÜST

Güttler, Hermann.
Die Gelegenheitskompositionen Georg Riedels. 181-195, KÖNI

Guha, B.
Dr. Ranganathan as a Teacher of Library Science. 578-584, RANG

Guidi, Pietro.
Pietro Demetrio Guazzelli da Lucca il Primo Custode della Biblioteca Vaticana (1481-1511) e L'Inventario dei Suoi Libri. 192-218, EHRE

Guignard, Jacques.
À propos d'un Grolier Inédit. La Date des Reliures à Plaquettes: Étienne ou Jean Grolier? 191-216, CALO
M. Julien Cain et L'Association Internationale de Bibliophilie. 34-36, CAIN

Guilland, R.
La Basilique, la Bibliothèque et L'Octogone de Byzance. 97-107, BONN

Gundel, Hans Georg.
Giessener Papyrus-Sammlungen im Neuen Raum. 51-55, GIES

Gunzburg, David von, jt. ed.
HARK

Gupta, K. Balasundara.
A Tribute to Dr. Ranganathan. 767-768, RANG

GUSTAF II ADOLF, King of Sweden - Collections - Uppsala
Carlsson, A. B. Jonas Hallenbergs Anteckningar och Samlingar till Gustaf II Adolfs Historia i Uppsala Universitetsbibliotek. 498-525, UPPS

GUSTAV VASA FÖRSAMLINGSBIBLIOTEK, Stockholm
see Stockholm. Gustav Vasa Församlingsbibliotek

GUTBERLET, KONSTANTIN
Hartmann, Eduard. Constantin Gutberlet. 53-56, FULD

GUTENBERG, JOHANN
Bömer, Aloys. Die Schlußschrift des Mainzer Catholicon-Druckes von 1460. 51-55, KUHN
Menn, Walter. Ein Neues Dogma um Gutenberg? 65-69, LEYH
———— Unsichere Kriterien in der Gutenbergforschung. 181-184, STOL
Munthe, Wilhelm. Gutenberg og Hans Verk. 19-35, NORS

GUTENBERG, JOHANNES - Monuments, etc.
Ruppel, Aloys. Früheste Planung eines Gutenbergdenkmals. 241-246, STOL

GUTENBERGMUSEUM, Bern
see Bern. Schweizerisches Gutenbergmuseum

GUTENBERGMUSEUM, Mainz
see Mainz. Gutenbergmuseum

Gutknecht, E.
Bibliothekswissenschaftliche Arbeiten

von Dr. Hermann Escher. 19-21, ESCK

GUTTERWITZ, ANDREAS

Dahlberg, Ragnar. Gutterwitziana. 295-301, COLL

Gyde-Pedersen, Mette.
Kulturelle og Sociale Særopgaver. 132-152, DØSS

Gysi, Klaus.
Vorsteher des Börsenvereins der Deutschen Buchhändler zu Leipzig. XVIII-XX, LEIZ

HABERMANN, JOHANN - Collections - Uppsala

Sallander, Hans. Några Sällsynta, Delvis Okända Lågtyska, Danska och Svenska Upplagor av Johannes Avernarius' Christliche Gebete i Uppsala Universitetsbibliotek. 8-14, DAHA

Hack, Bertold.
Vor- und Frühgeschichte des "Archivs für Geschichte des Buchwesens." 157-169, BENZ

Hadamowsky, Franz.
Das Hoftheater Leopolds I. und das Kostümwerk des L. O. Burnacini. 384-398, BICK
Wiener Theater-Periodica. 35-38, STUM

HADOARDUS, PRESBYTER

Bischoff, Bernhard. Hadoardus and the Manuscripts of Classical Authors from Corbie. 39-57, ALBA

Haeberli, Hans.
Die Handschriftensammlungen Gottlieb Emanuel von Hallers und der Familie von Mülinen. 51-78, BERT

Haebler, Konrad.
Die Bucheinbände des Petrus Leßl. 103-110, SCHW
Die Fuero-Handschrift der Sächsischen Landesbibliothek. 146-155, BOLL
Der Gesamtkatalog der Wiegendrucke. 278-284, HARN
Die Handschriftenabteilung. 126-131, HARN
Ramon Lull und Seine Schule. Aus Anlass einer Neu Erworbenen Inkunabel. 36-47, HARN
Zwei Nürnberger Tonformen. 103-110, COLL

HAEBLER, KONRAD

HAEB

HAEK

Freys, Ernst. Johann Baptist Bernharts "Gesammelte Schriften." Ein Vorläufer von Haeblers Typenrepertorium. 145-174, HAEB

HAEBLER, KONRAD - Bibl.

Rath, Erich von. Die Schriften Konrad Haeblers. 1-17, HAEB

HAEBLER, KONRAD. Rollen- und Plattenstempel des XVI. Jahrhunderts

HAEK

Haeckel, Ilse.
Schrettinger und die Säkularisation des Klosters Weißenohe. 117-120, REDE

Hämel, Adalbert.
Arnaldus de Monte und der "Liber S. Jacobi." I, 147-159, RUBI

Haenisch, Wolf.
Die Kanazawa Bunko, eine Japanische Bibliotheksgründung des 13. Jahrhunderts. 271-280, JUCH

HAER, JAN VAN DER
see Van der Haer, Jan

Häuser, Helmut.
Zum Kartographischen Werk des Mainzer Kupferstechers und Ingenieurs Nikolaus Person. 170-186, BENZ

Hafftka, Alexander.
Życie i Twórczość Dr. Jakóba Szackiego. 13-23, SZAC

Hagemann, Sonja.
Det Var i Tredveårene. 74-85, NORS

HAGUE - Ephemeral materials - Collections
see Ephemeral materials - Collections - Hague

HAGUE - Exchange of books, periodicals, etc.
see Exchange of books, periodicals, etc. - Hague

HAGUE. Hof van Holland. Bibliotheek

Kronenberg, M. E. Erasmus-Uitgaven A°. 1531 in het Bezit van Kanunnik Mr. Jan Dircsz. van der Haer te Gorkum. 99-117, KOSS

HAGUE - Incunabula
see Incunabula - Hague

HAGUE. Koninklijke Bibliotheek

HAGU

Brummel, Leendert. De Boeken van Tongerloo in de Koninklijke Bibliotheek te 's-Gravenhage. 151-168, BRUE
———— Dr. Ludwig Tross en de Koninklijke Bibliotheek. 169-177, BRUE

———— De Koninklijke Bibliotheek 1948-1957. 123-150, BRUE
Dekker, Annie F. In de Spiegel der Horatiana. 402-407, BRUM
Nieuwenkamp, J. L. M. Kits. Op Nieuwe Leest. 492-495, BRUM
Roelofs, Sjoerdtje. La "Collection Anny Antoine—Louis Koopman" à la Bibliothèque Royale de la Haye. 577-580, BRUM
Verwey, Eleonore de la Fontaine. Jacob Geel en de Koninklijke Bibliotheek. 414-426, BRUM
Verwey, H. de la Fontaine. Bij het Afscheid van Prof. Dr. L. Brummel als Bibliothecaris van de Koninklijke Bibliotheek. 379-386, BRUM

HAGUE. Koninklijke Bibliotheek. Exchange Bureau
See Hague. Koninklijke Bibliotheek. Ruilbureau

HAGUE. Koninklijke Bibliotheek - Hist.
Brummel, Leendert. Tien Jaren Koninklijke Bibliotheek (1938-1947). 1-34, HAGU

HAGUE. Koninklijke Bibliotheek. Mss.
Vermeeren, P. J. H. Handschriften van het Kapittel van Sint Servaas ter Koninklijke Bibliotheek in 's-Gravenhage. 179-193, MAAS

HAGUE. Koninklijke Bibliotheek. Nederlandse Centrale Catalogus
Soeters, P. C. Hoe de Nederlandse Centrale Catalogus Begon. 590-593, BRUM

HAGUE. Koninklijke Bibliotheek. Oranje Nassau-Verzameling
Alphen, G. van. Anthony Smets, Bibliothecaris van Drie Prinsen van Oranje (1636-1689). 119-160, HAGU
Verwey, Eleonore de la Fontaine. Boekbanden uit de Oranje Nassau-Bibliotheek. 161-179, HAGU

HAGUE. Koninklijke Bibliotheek. Ruilbureau
Brummel, Leendert. The Netherlands and the International Exchange of Publications. 1-47, BRUE
Mooy, A. J. de. Het Ruilbureau. 235-240, HAGU

HAGUE - Manuscripts - Collections
see Manuscripts - Collections - Hague

HAGUE. Museum Meermanno-Westreenianum
Vermeeren, P. J. H. W. H. J. Baron van Westreenen van Tiellandt als Handschriftenverzamelaar. 603-609, BRUM

HAGUE. Museum Meermanno-Westreenianum. Museum van het Boek
Bladergroen, Susana H. Het Ontstaan van het Museum van het Boek. 387-390, BRUM

HAGUE. Museum van het Boek
see Hague. Museum Meermanno-Westreenianum. Museum van het Boek

HAGUE - National libraries
see National libraries - Hague

HAGUE. Nederlands Letterkundig Museum en Documentatiecentrum
Brummel, Leendert. Literatuur als Museumobjekt. 81-99, BRUE

HAGUE - Rare books - Collections
see Rare books - Collections - Hague

HAGUE - Rijksmuseum Meermanno-Westreenianum
see Hague. Museum Meermanno-Westreenianum

Hahn, André, Paule Dumaitre, and J. Samion-Contet.
Le "De Humani Corporis Fabrica" d'André Vésale (1543). 91-97, CALO

Haiböck, Lambert.
Nationalbibliothek und Staatsdruckerei. 39, STUM

HAIN, LUDWIG
Rath, Erich von. Zur Biographie Ludwig Hains. 161-182, COLL

HAKODATE, Japan. Library
HAKO

HAKUBUNKAN, publisher - Bibl.
Kotani, Genzō. Ōhashi Toshokan Shozō Hakubunkan Hakkō Tosho Mokuroku. (A Catalogue of the Books Published by Hakubunkan in the Collection of the Ōhashi Library.) 105-132, TSUB
————. Ōhashi Toshokan Shozō Hakubunkan Hakkō Tosho Mokuroku—Showa Juyonen Gogatsu Matsujitsu Genzai. (The List of Books Published by Hakubunkan Which Are in the Collections of the Ōhashi Library—as of the End of March, 1939.) 1-157, (part 2), OHAS

HAKUBUNKAN, publisher - Collections - Tokyo
Kotani, Genzō. Ōhashi Toshokan Shozō Hakubunkan Hakkō Tosho Mokuroku. (A Catalogue of the Books Published by Hakubunkan in the Collections of the Ōhashi Library.) 105-132, TSUB
————. Ōhashi Toshokan Shozō

Hakubunkan Hakkō Tosho Mokuroku—Showa Juyonen Gogatsu Matsujitsu Genzai. (The List of Books Published by Hakubunkan Which Are in the Collections of the Ohashi Library—as of the End of March, 1939.) 1-157, (part 2), OHAS

HALBERSTADT. Dom. Bibliothek. Mss.

Haseloff, Arthur. Der Einband der Hs. des Marcuseevangeliums des Harderadus. 507-528, EHRE

HALBERSTADT. Dom-Gymnasium. Bibliothek
see Halberstadt. Dombibliothek

DAS HALBJAHRES-VERZEICHNIS
see Frankfurt a.M. Deutsche Bibliothek. Deutsche Bibliographie; Halbjahres-Verzeichnis

Hald, H. A.
Frederikshavn Folkebibliotek i 25 Aar. 3-14, FRED

Halfmann, Horst.
Das Schrifttum der Emigration in der Deutschen Bücherei. 197-217, LEIZ

HALF-UNCIAL MANUSCRIPTS

Lowe, Elias Avery. A Hand-List of Half-Uncial Manuscripts. 34-61, EHRD

HALICARNASSUS - Inscriptions, Greek
see Inscriptions, Greek - Halicarnassus

HALIFAX, Nova Scotia - Printing
see Printing - Halifax, Nova Scotia

HALL, DAVID

Harlan, Robert D. David Hall's Bookshop and Its British Sources of Supply. 1-24, GJEL

Hall, Emily Hardy.
Carlyle, Neuberg, and Frederick the Great. 89-94, KEOG

Hallberg, S. and O. von Feilitzen.
Göteborgs Stadsbibliotek. Det Första Halvseklet 1891-1940. 1-142, (first paper), GÖTE

HALLE - Alxinger, J. B. - Collections
see Alxinger, J. B. - Collections - Halle

HALLE - Bookbinding
see Bookbinding - Halle

HALLE - College and university libraries - Administration
see College and university libraries - Administration - Halle

HALLE - Gifts, contributions, etc.
see Gifts, contributions, etc. - Halle

HALLE. Universität. Bibliothek - Hist.

Gerhard, Karl. Die Ungarische Nationalbibliothek der Universität Halle-Wittenberg. 139-158, WILM
Juntke, Fritz. Das Reglement für die Bibliothek der Universität zu Halle vom 20. Mai 1823. 323-342, VORS
Perlbach, Max. Die Berliner Doubletten von 1697 in Halle. 15-42, WILM

HALLE. Universität. Philologisches Seminar. Mss. (55a)

Göber, Willi. Ein Spätantiker Pergamentkodex des Dionysius Thrax. P. Hal. 55a. 111-118, DEGE

HALLE. Universitäts- und Landesbibliothek Sachsen-Anhalt. Mss. (Alxinger)

Prokert, Heinz. Fünf Briefe J. B. Alxingers an Ch. F. Blankenburg. 221-233, BULL

HALLENBERG, JONAS - Collections - Uppsala

Carlsson, A. B. Jonas Hallenbergs Anteckningar och Samlingar till Gustaf II Adolfs Historia i Uppsala Universitetsbibliotek. 498-525, UPPS

HALLER, ALBRECHT

Bloesch, Hans. Albrecht Haller als Bibliothekar. 165-178, GODE

HALLER, GOTTLIEB EMANUEL VON - Library

Haeberli, Hans. Die Handschriftensammlungen Gottlieb Emanuel von Hallers und der Familie von Mülinen. 51-78, BERT

Hallvik, Bengt.
Svensk Biblioteksdebatt Omkring År 1860. Ur en Tidningsläsares Citatsamling. 77-95, HEIN

Halm, Hans.
Eine Unbekannte Handschrift der "Kinder-Symphonie." 101-102, HOBO

HALM, KARL

Pauer, Max. Anton Ruland und Karl Halm. Ein Bibliothekarischer Streit um Dublettenverkäufe vor Hundert Jahren. 121-135, REDE

Halvorsen, Jens Braage.
Overbibliothekar A. C. Drolsum. Supplement av K. V. Hammer. 72-73, (pt. 2), OSLU
Professor Ludvig Daae. Supplement av K. V. Hammer. 61-63, (pt. 2), OSLU
Universitets-Bibliothekar P. Botten Hansen. 56-60, (pt. 2), OSLU

HALVORSEN, JENS BRAAGE
HALV
Nygård-Nilssen, Arne. J. B. Halvorsen. 33-56, OSLN

HALVORSEN, JENS BRAAGE. Norsk Forfatterlexikon, 1814-1900
Amundsen, Inger. Genealogisk Register til J. B. Halvorsens Norsk Forfatter-Lexikon 1814-1880. 69-202, HALV

Hamada, Toshio.
Kenmei Kosei no Ichishian; Senpaku no Shuruimei o to Chūsin to shite. (A Trial Method of Constructing a Subject Index Using Names Indicating Kinds of Ships.) 221-227, HASH

HAMANN, JOHANN GEORG. Gedanken über Meinen Lebenslauf
Bernhart, Joseph. Selbstauffindung auf der Reise. 121-123, HELD

Hamannová, Pavlína.
Hrst Podnětů Dr. J. Emlera. 59-64, EMLE

HAMBURG - Children's library services
see Children's library services - Hamburg

HAMBURG - Circulation analysis
see Circulation analysis - Hamburg

HAMBURG - Circulation - Statistics
see Circulation - Statistics - Hamburg

HAMBURG - Education for librarianship
see Education for librarianship - Hamburg

HAMBURG - Gifts, contributions, etc.
see Gifts, contributions, etc. - Hamburg

HAMBURG - In-service training
see In-service training - Hamburg

HAMBURG - Law libraries
see Law libraries - Hamburg

HAMBURG - Libraries - Sociological aspects
see Libraries - Sociological aspects - Hamburg

HAMBURG. Max-Planck-Institut für Ausländisches und Internationales Privatrecht. Bibliothek
Coudres, Hans-Peter des. Die Bibliothek des Max-Planck-Instituts für Ausländisches und Internationales Privatrecht in Hamburg. Ihr Werden und Ihre Stellung Innerhalb Verwandter Sammlungen. 50-60, TIEM

HAMBURG. Öffentliche Bücherhalle
HAMB

HAMBURG. Öffentliche Bücherhallen - Hist.
Friedrich, Marie. Daten aus der Geschichte der Hamburger Öffentlichen Bücherhallen. 128-131, HAMB

HAMBURG - Personnel
see Personnel - Hamburg

HAMBURG - Public libraries
see Public libraries - Hamburg

HAMBURG - Public libraries - Statistics
see Public libraries - Statistics - Hamburg

HAMBURG REGION - Public libraries (Small)
see Public libraries (Small) - Hamburg region

HAMBURG. Staats- und Universitäts-Bibliothek
Alexander, Gerhard. Ein Prachteinband aus Gräflich Oldenburgischem Besitz in der Staats- und Universitätsbibliothek Hamburg. 167-176, TIEM
Braun, Hellmut. Der Hamburger Koran von 1694. 149-166, TIEM

HAMBURG. Staats- und Universitäts-Bibliothek - Hist.
Voigt, Christian. Die Staats- und Universitäts-Bibliothek Hamburg. Ihr Weg von der Gelehrtenbibliothek zur Wissenschaftlichen Gebrauchsbibliothek. 23-39, TIEM
Zimmermann, Erich. Hinrich Murmester und die Älteste Hamburger Stadtbibliothek (1479/81). 40-49, TIEM

HAMBURG. Stadtbibliothek
see Hamburg. Staats- und Universitäts-Bibliothek

HAMBURG - Use studies - Public libraries
see Use studies - Public libraries - Hamburg

HAMBURG - Volunteer assistants
see Volunteer assistants - Hamburg

HAMBURG - War and the library
see War and the library - Hamburg

HAMBURG - Young adults' library services
see Young adults' library services - Hamburg

Hamel, A. G. van.
Boekbespreking. 26-27, EVER
De Studie der Ierse Handschriften. 123-145, EVER

Hamel, G. A.
Wat te Doen met Doubletten? 463-472, BRUM

HAMILTON, ALEXANDER HAMILTON DOUGLAS, 10th Duke of - Library

Schunke, Ilse. Die Italienischen Einbände aus der Hamilton-Sammlung in Berlin. 17-32, LÜLF

Hamilton, J. G. de Roulhac.
On the Importance of Unimportant Documents. 511-518, WILS

HAMILTON-SAMMLUNG
see Berlin. Deutsche Staatsbibliothek. Mss. (Hamilton-Sammlung)

HAMMARSKJÖLD LIBRARY
see United Nations. Dag Hammarskjöld Library

HAMMER, K. V., Supplement

Halvorsen, J. B. Oberbibliothekar A. C. Drolsum. Supplement av K. V. Hammer. 72-73, (pt. 2), OSLU
———— Professor Ludvig Daae. Supplement av K. V. Hammer. 61-63, (pt. 2), OSLU

Hammond, George P.
GPH's First Appearance in Print: Impressions of Spain in 1923. 107-119, HAMM
Response to the Academy of American Franciscan History. 77-81, HAMM

HAMMOND, GEORGE P.

HAMM

Farquhar, Francis P. George P. Hammond's Publications. 83-106, HAMM

Hampe, Theodor.
Der Sog. Ferdinand Neuberger-Codex in der Erlanger Universitätsbibliothek. 32-39, VERZ

HANDICAPPED, Library services for - Denmark

Gyde-Pedersen, Mette. Kulturelle og Sociale Særopgaver. 132-152, DØSS

Handwerker, Otto.
Bibliothekare und Universitäten, mit Belegen aus der Geschichte der Würzburger Universitätsbibliothek. 85-94, LEID

HANDWRITING
see Graphology

Hanke, Lewis.
The Historia de las Indias of Bartolomé de las Casas. 143-150, WROT

Hannemann, Kurt.
Antwerpener Fragmente einer Deutschen Geistlichen Prosahandschrift des 14. Jahrhunderts. 55-64, LEYH

Hanninger, Vivica.
Barn- och Ungdomsbibliotek: Tre Decennier med Barn och Böcker. 555-562, HJEL

Hannover, Emil.
Von Bozérian bis Trautz. 199-205, LOUB

HANOVER. Königliche und Provinzialbibliothek
see Hanover. Niedersächsische Landesbibliothek

HANOVER - Libraries
see Libraries - Hanover

HANOVER. Niedersächsische Landesbibliothek. Mss. (186)

Lehmann, Paul. Eine Fuldaer Handschrift. I, 140-144, GLAU

HANOVER - Public libraries - Centralization
see Public libraries - Centralization - Hanover

HANOVER - Regional libraries
see Regional libraries - Hanover

HANOVER. Technische Hochschule. Bibliothek. Sammlung Haupt. Mss. (XX e 1)

Vossnack, Lieselotte. Ein Vorentwurf zu Berninis Johannespredigt (Bibliothek der Tech. Hochschule Hannover, Sammlung Haupt XX e 1). 55-65, LEUN

HANSEN, PAUL BOTTEN

Halvorsen, J. B. Universitets-Bibliothekar P. Botten Hansen. 56-60, (pt. 2), OSLU

Hansen, Robert L., ed.
THOM

Hansen, Robert L.
Centralbibliotekets Udvikling og Administration under Biblioteksloven. 17-36, LASS
Franske Centralbiblioteker. 97-107, HEIN
H. O. Lange og Folkebibliotekerne. 341-355, LANE
Nyt Danske Litteraturselskab. 95-103, THOM
Om Uddannelse af Bibliotekarer ved Folkebibliotekerne. 17-37, DØSS

Hanson, James Christian Meinich.
Amerikansk og Europeisk Biblioteks-

vesen. Streiflys og Sammenligninger. 287-292, MUNT
The Library of Congress and Its New Catalogue: Some Unwritten History. 178-194, PUTN
Organization and Reorganization of Libraries. 519-532, WILS

HANSON, JAMES CHRISTIAN MEINICH

HANS

Bishop, William Warner. J. C. M. Hanson and International Cataloging. 165-168, HANS
Butler, Pierce. James Christian Meinich Hanson. 127-130, HANS
Dorf, A. Th. The University of Chicago Libraries. 185-197, HANS
Putnam, Herbert. Letter to Mr. Hanson. 314, HANS
Starr, Helen K. Mr. Hanson and His Friends. 329-333, HANS

HANSON, JAMES CHRISTIAN MEINICH - Bibl.

Bibliography of James C. M. Hanson. 131-135, HANS

HARDERADUS

Haseloff, Arthur. Der Einband der Hs. des Marcusevangeliums des Harderadus. 507-528, EHRE

HARDRADUS
see Harderadus

HARIUS, JAN
see Van der Haer, Jan

HARKAVY, ABRAHAM XIYAHU

HARK

HARKAVY, ABRAHAM XIYAHU - Bibl.

Maggid, David. Bibliographie der Schriften und Aufsätze A. Harkavy's. IX-LII, (Hebrew section), HARK

Harlan, Robert D.
David Hall's Bookshop and Its British Sources of Supply. 1-24, GJEL

Harnack, Adolf von.
Die Älteste Inschrift über einer Öffentlichen Kirchen-Bibliothek. 111-114, SCHW
Julius Afrikanus, der Bibliothekar des Kaisers Alexander Severus. 142-146, MILF

HARNACK, ADOLF VON

HARN

Harnack, Axel von.
Einige Beobachtungen an den Deutschen Bibliotheken in Rom. 304-309, KUHN

Harrie, Ivar.
Bokväsendets PR-man. 532-533, HJEL

HARRIET G. STILLMAN LIBRARY, Mystic, Conn.
see Marine Historical Association. Library

HARRISSE, HENRY. Bibliotheca Americana Vetustissima . . .

Goldschmidt, E. P. Not in Harrisse. 129-141, WROT

Harrsen Meta.
Figural Grisaille Ornament on a Historiated Initial of about 1400, and the Derivation of this Style from the Indulgences of Avignon. 316-322, LYDE

HARTEL, WILHELM VON

Doublier, Othmar. Ein Vierteljahrhundert aus der Geschichte der Hofbibliothek 1891-1916. 163-210, VIEN

HARTFORD, Conn. State Library
see Connecticut. State Library, Hartford

Hartl, Eduard.
Ein Neues Althochdeutsches Glossenfragment. 95-101, LEID

Hartmann, Albert, ed.
LEID

Hartmann, Albert.
Eine Federzeichnung auf einem Münchener Papyrus. 103-108, LEID
Die Schriften Georg Leidingers 1891-1930. 307-320, LEID

Hartmann, Eduard.
Constantin Gutberlet. 53-56, FULD

Hartmann, Karl.
Ein Medizingeschichtlicher Besitz der Staats- und Universitätsbibliothek zu Königsberg. 196-209, KÖNI

HARTWIG, OTTO

Weber, Ulrich. Vier Unveröffentlichte Briefe Wilhelm Brambachs an Carl Dziatzko aus dem Besitz der Universitätsbibliothek Göttingen oder: Scherz- und Schimpf-spiel zwischen Gelehrten. 171-178, JUCR

HARVARD COLLEGE
see Harvard University

HARVARD UNIVERSITY. Library

HARV

Mackall, Leonard L. Goethe's Letter to Joseph Green Cogswell. 315-326, PUTN

HARVARD UNIVERSITY. Library - Hist.

Lane, William Coolidge. The Sojourn of the Harvard Library in Concord, Massachusetts, 1775-1776. 275-287, PUTN

Hase, Martin von.
Zwei Drucke des Temporals des Johannes Regiomontanus von Wolfgang Stürmer in Erfurt. I, 61-66, GLAU

Haseloff, Arthur.
Der Einband der Hs. des Marcusevangeliums des Harderadus. 507-528, EHRE

Hashimoto, Shinkichi, jt. author

Meier, Franz Joseph, [trans.] Der Artikel Tosho "Buch" im Nihon-Bungaku-Daijiten. [Translation of a Japanese Article by Shinkichi Hashimoto and Yasushi Uematsu.] 205-216, LEYH

Hashimoto, Takashi.
Toshokangakka no Jittai to Sono Tembō. Japan Library School, Yesterday, Today, and Tomorrow. (In both English and Japanese.) 1-11, (3rd section), HASH

HASHIMOTO, TAKASHI

HASH

Hayashi, T. Hashimoto Takashi Sensei Ryakureki. Biographical Sketch of Prof. Takashi Hashimoto. (In both English and Japanese.) iii-iv, HASH

Hashimoto, Tatsuki.
Kōtogakko Toshokan ni okeru Dokusho Shidō. (A Guide for Reading in High School Library.) 177-191, KYOT

Haskins, Charles Homer.
Two Roman Formularies in Philadelphia. 275-286, EHRD

Hasselblatt, Emil, ed.
CAST

Hasselblatt, Emil.
Brev av Nordiska Författare i Helsingfors Universitetsbibliotek. 71-97, HULA

Hastings, Charles Harris.
Reminiscences and Observations on the Card Distribution Work of the Library of Congress. 195-206, PUTN

Hatano, Ken'ichi.
Meiji Shonen ni okeru Kanritsu Toshokan Hakubutsukan no Hassei to Sono Hensen—Fu, Toshokan Kankei Horei, Shuppanho. (The Establishment of National Libraries and Museums in the Early Period of the Meiji Era and Their Progress—Appendix: Laws Relating to Libraries and Laws on Publication.) 85-160, OTAT

Hatch, Benton.
Thoreau's Plan of a Farm. 317-324, KEOG

Hattori, Kintaro.
Cataloguing in the Prefectural Libraries and Five City Libraries. 190-201, RANG

Hattum, M. A. C. M. van.
Van een Oud Boekblad. 87-96, HAGU

Haugh, W. S.
The Education of Librarians and Information Officers: Public Libraries. 287-290, HUTT

Haugsted, Ejler.
Ordning, Opstilling, Bogbestand. 53-80, AARU

Haugstrup, S.
Kalundborg Bibliotek 1920-1926. 22-36, KALU

Haukaas, Kaare.
Norsk Litteraert Registreringsarbeid. 25-68, HALV

Hauke, Walter.
Die Entwicklung der Berliner Volksbüchereien von 1945 bis 1950. 27-48, BERL

Hauler, Edmond.
Fronto über Klassische Ausgaben Lateinischer Schriftsteller. 622-627, CHAT

Hauptmann, Hansheinz.
Über die Unentbehrlichkeit Geistiger Voraussetzungen für die Bestandsauswahl der Schönen Literatur. 9-13, ACKR

Hauser, Henri.
Souvenirs d'un Vieux Rat de Bibliothèque. 120-124, OURS

Haussoullier, B.
Lettre de Ptolémée à Diodora. 281-283, CHAT

Hautecoeur, Louis.
Les Travaux d'Architecture de Julien Cain à la Bibliothèque Nationale. 27-33, CAIN

HAVELBERG (Diöcese) Bibliothek

Polthier, Wilhelm. Die Ehemalige Domstiftsbibliothek in Havelberg. 163-176, KUHN

HAVET, JULIEN

HAVE

Delisle, L. Discours. x-ix, HAVE
Gautier, Léon. À Julien Havet. x, HAVE

HAVET, JULIEN - Bibl.

Bibliographie des Travaux de Julien Havet. xi-xvi, HAVE

Havet, Louis.
Les Fautes Issues de Corrections dans les Manuscrits de Nonius. 803-814, GRAU
La Lacune des "Captifs." 26-32, CHAT

HAWAII - Bookmobile services
see Bookmobile services - Hawaii

Hayashi, T.
Hashimoto Takashi Sensei Ryakureki. Biographical Sketch of Prof. Takashi Hashimoto. (In both English and Japanese.) iii-iv, HASH

HAYDN, JOSEPH. Mss. <u>Sinfonia</u> [Kinder-symphonie]

Halm, Hans. Eine Unbekannte Handschrift der "Kinder-Symphonie." 101-102, HOBO

Haydon, Glen.
The Dedication of Francesco Corteccia's <u>Hinnario</u>. 112-116, KINK

Haykin, David Judson, jt. author
Bush, Helen E. and David Judson Haykin. Music Subject Headings. 39-45, KINO

Hazewinkel, H. C.
Rotterdamse Boekverkopers uit de Patriottentijd. 35-58, KOSS

Hebbelynck, Ad.
Inventaire Sommaire des Manuscrits Coptes de la Bibliothèque Vaticane. 35-82, EHRE

Heber, Lilly.
Boken. 115-121, HIRN

HEBREW INCUNABULA
see Incunabula, Hebrew

HEBREW MANUSCRIPTS
see Manuscripts, Hebrew

HEBREW type - Type and type-founding
see Type and type-founding - Hebrew type

Heckel, Rudolf von.
Eine Kanzleianweisung über die Schriftmässige Ausstattung der Papsturkunden aus dem 13. Jahrhundert in Durantis Speculum Iudiciale. 109-118, LEID

Hecker, Max, ed.
WAHL

Hecker, Max, ed.
Ein "Weimarischer Kunstfreund" in der Gemäldesammlung der Brüder Boisserée. Zwei Briefe Heinrich Meyers an die Erbgrossherzogin Maria Paulowna. 185-200, WEIM

Heckmann, Harald, jt. ed.
FEDO

HEIDELBERG. Bibliotheca Palatina. Mss.

Preisendanz, Karl. Handschriftenausleihe in der Bibliotheca Palatina. 54-68, LEYG

HEIDELBERG - CENSORSHIP
see Censorship - Heidelberg

Heidelberg - Manuscripts - Circulation procedures
see Manuscripts - Circulation procedures - Heidelberg

HEIDELBERG - Manuscripts - Collections
see Manuscripts - Collections - Heidelberg

HEIDELBERG - Presses, University
see Presses, University - Heidelberg

HEIDELBERG. Universität. Bibliothek. Mss.

Jammers, Ewald. Die Salemer Handschriftensammlung. 45-64, WEHM

HEIDELBERG. Universität. Bibliothek. Mss. (Orient. 63)

Rudnitzky, Günter. Ein Sermon aus dem Schatzkästlein Unseres Vaters Apa Schenute. 12-18, WEHM

HEIDENSTAM, VERNER VON - Collections - Örebro

Waldén, Bertil. Verner von Heidenstam Som Målare. 71-106, ÖREB

HEILSBRONN (Cistercian abbey) Bibliothek

Stollreither, Eugen. Die Auflösung der Heilsbronner Universitätsbibliothek. 75-84, VERZ

HEINRICH II, Emperor of Germany

Campana, Augusto. Per il "Textus Evangelii" Donato da Enrico II a Montecassino (Vat. Ottobon. Lat. 74). 34-47, MERG

Heinrich, Gisela.
Heutige Probleme der Katalogarbeit und Annotierung in der Öffentlichen Bücherei und deren Bedeutung für die Ausbildung. 88-112, LANF

HEINRICH, VON DEM TÜRLIN. Mss. Crone
Nörrenberg, Constantin. Kieler Bruchstücke aus Heinrichs von dem Türlin Crone. 405-418, WILM

HEINRICH VON VELDEKE. Mss. Eneide
KRÜS

HEINTZE, INGEBORG
HEIN

HEINTZE, INGEBORG - Bibl.
Förteckning över Uppsatser och Skrifter av Ingeborg Heintze. 273-278, HEIN

Heitjan, Isabel.
Die Korrespondenz des Kölner Buchhändlers Hermann Demen mit dem Hause Plantin-Moretus zu Antwerpen 1673-1706. 187-207, BENZ

HELD, HANS LUDWIG
HELD
Bernus, Alexander von. Das aber Bindet. 36, HELD
Brandenburg, Hans. Held von Schwabing Gesehen. 15-17, HELD
Carossa, Hans. Miniatur. 12, HELD
Fendt, Franz. Glückwunsch. 9-10, HELD
Gluth, Oskar. Epistel der Freundschaft. 18-19, HELD
Heldt, Andreas. Der Besuch im Rathaus. 26-27, HELD
Ott, Alfons. Musikalisches Portrait. 28-30, HELD
Ullmann, Regina. Ein Sich in der Erinnerung Spiegelndes Bild. 13-14, HELD

Heldt, Andreas.
Der Besuch im Rathaus. 26-27, HELD

HELIAND
Loebeling, Isolde. Buch und Synonyma im Tatian, Heliand und bei Otfrid. 59-69, JUCR

Helimér, Sven-Ola.
Samkatalogen i Ny Gestalt. Ett Förslag. 109-115, HEIN

HELSINGFORS
see Helsinki

HELSINKI - Chinese literature - Collections
see Chinese literature - Collections - Helsinki

HELSINKI - Correspondence, Scandinavian - Collections
see Correspondence, Scandinavian - Collections - Helsinki

HELSINKI - Japanese literature - Collections
see Japanese literature - Collections - Helsinki

HELSINKI - Oriental literature - Collections
see Oriental literature - Collections - Helsinki

HELSINKI - Rare books - 16th cent. - Collections
see Rare books - 16th cent. - Collections - Helsinki

HELSINKI - Russian literature - Collections
see Russian literature - Collections - Helsinki

HELSINKI. Universitet. Bibliotek
HULT
Dahlberg, Ragnar. Helsingfors Universitetsbiblioteks Exemplar af Psalterium Dauidis 1510. 140-144, HULA
__________ Två Böcker med Märklig Proveniens i Helsingfors Universitetsbibliotek. 127-136, SCHA
Donner, Kai. Tryckalster från Storstrejken. 164-169, HULA
Mickwitz, Ann-Mari. Kejsaren och den Gamla Kartan. 59-65, NYBE
Mustonen, Aarne. Kaukoidän Kirjatietoa. 164-181, DAHL
__________. Kaukoidän Kirjatietoa. 66-77, NYBE
Nivanka, Eino. Amsterdamilainen Fr. Mullerin Antikvariaatti Nordenskiöldin Kirjakokoelman Päähankkijana. 122-133, DAHL
Nohrström, Holger. Några Krigsbytesböcker från Åbo Akademibiblioteks Grundläggningstid i Helsingfors Universitetsbibliotek. 69-81, HULT
Nyberg, Paul. En Kartografisk Kuriositet. 115-121, HULT
Pipping, Hugo E. Två Bokägarmärken Anbragta Som Rygg- och Pärmstämpel. 1-11, DAHL
Seppälä, Arvo. Eräitä Kansi- Ja Reunamerkintöjä Helsingin Yliopiston Kirjaston Kaksoiskappalekokoelmissa. 237-255, DAHL
Vallinkoski, J. Ett Danskt Bokfynd i Finland. 15-19, DAHA

HELSINKI. Universitet. Bibliotek - Bibl.
Grönroos, Henrik and Birgit Lunelund-Grönroos. Förteckning över Skrifter Rörande Helsingfors Universitetsbibliotek, dess Samlingar och Enskilda Bokverk. 256-318, DAHL

HELSINKI. Universitet. Bibliotek - Hist.
Jörgensen, Arne. Anteckningar om Universitetsbiblioteket under Första Året efter Åbo Brand. 17-42, HULA

HELSINKI. Universitet. Bibliotek. Mss. (Correspondence)
Hasselblatt, Emil. Brev av Nordiska Författare i Helsingfors Universitetsbibliotek. 71-97, HULA

HELSINKI. Universitet. Bibliotek. Mss. (Map)

Nyberg, Paul. En Missuppfattad Rågångsurkund från 1500-Talet i Nordenskiöldska Samlingen. 92-104, SCHA

HELSINKI. Universitet. Bibliotek. Ryska Biblioteket

Widnäs, Maria. Jacob Grot och Universitetets Ryska Bibliotek. 144-163, DAHL

HELSINKI. Universitet. Employees

Schauman, Henrik. Festskrifter och Festnummer Tillägnade Lärare och Tjänstemän vid Universiteten i Helsingfors och Åbo. 319-350, DAHL

Helweg-Larsen, P., ed.
LANE

Helweg-Larsen, P.
Af H. O. Langes Breve til Hjemmet. 9-303, LANE
Hans Ostenfeldt Lange. 304-321, LANE

Helwig, Hellmuth.
Jenaer Buchbinder des 16. Jahrhunderts. 225-241, HAEK

Henggeler, Rudolf.
Die Mittelalterlichen Papsturkunden im Stiftsarchiv Einsiedeln. 201-225, MERC

Henne, Frances and Mildred Hawksworth Lowell.
The Preparation of Secondary-School Teachers in the Use of Library Materials. 533-556, WILS

Henopp, Lieselotte, jt. author
Fischer, Luise and Lieselotte Henopp. Schriftenverzeichnis Hermann Fuchs. 11-23, FUCH

HENRI DE MESMES
see Mesmes, Henri de

HENRI IV, King of France - Library

Coyecque, Ern. Guillaume Larcher, Bibliothécaire du Cabinet Henri IV. 129-132, GODE

Henriksson, Karl-Erik.
Notes on the Acquisition Work in the Uppsala University Library. 228-236, DAHL
Oppihistoriasta. 130-148, TUDE

HENRY, ANTHONY

Bishop, Olga Bernice. The First Printing Press in Canada, 1751-1800. 129-148, GJEL

HENRY E. HUNTINGTON LIBRARY AND ART GALLERY, San Marino, Calif.

Wagner, Henry R. The Portolan Atlases of American Interest in the Henry E. Huntington Library and Art Gallery. 498-509, PUTN

HENRY VIII, King of England. <u>Assertio Septem Sacramentorum</u> . . .

Vian, Nello. La Presentazione e gli Esemplari Vaticani della "Assertio Septem Sacramentorum" di Enrico VIII. II, 355-375, ALBB

HEPDING, HUGO

HEPD

HEPDING, HUGO - Bibl.

Lehnert, Georg. Verzeichnis der Schriften von Hugo Hepding. 261-273, HEPD

Herbst, Hermann.
Braunschweigische Buchbinder des 16. Jahrhunderts. 274-310, HAEK
Johannes von Brakel. Ein Beitrag zur Bibliotheksgeschichte des Benediktinerklosters Klus bei Gandersheim. 31-46, SCHR
Nürnberger Lederschnittbände. 83-94, LEIP

HERCULANEUM. Biblioteca.

Comparetti, D. La Bibliothèque de Philodème. 118-129, CHAT

HERCULANEUM. Biblioteca. Mss. (Papiri 1232 e 1289)

Bassi, D. Øiλσήμδν περi 'Eπiκδύρδν (A?.) B. 511-529, CERI

HERDER, JOHANN GOTTFRIED VON

Busse, Gisela von. Vom Rechten Bücherlesen. Gedanken zur Herder-Interpretation. 244-257, TIEM

HERDER, JOHANN GOTTFRIED VON. <u>Journal Meiner Reise im Jahre 1769</u>

Bernhart, Joseph. Selbstauffindung auf der Reise. 121-123, HELD

Herrman, L.
Mr. Varley's Contribution to the English Association. 26, VARL

Hertz, Aleksander.
Jakób Szacki—Człowiek Książki. 47-51, SZAC

HERZOG-AUGUST-BIBLIOTHEK. Wolfenbüttel
see Wolfenbüttel. Herzog-August-Bibliothek

HESS, JOHANNES - Library
Lehmann, Paul. Aus der Bibliothek des Reformators Johannes Hessius. 101-124, LEYH

HESSE - Catalogs - Union
see Catalogs - Union - Hesse

Hesse, Gerhard.
Gesellschaftliche Faktoren bei der Gründung und in der Entwicklung der Deutschen Bücherei bis zum Jahre 1923. 19-46, LEIZ

HESSE. Landesbibliothek
see Fulda, Ger. Landesbibliothek

Hessel, Alfred.
Mabillons Musterbibliothek. 119-122, DEGE

Hesselaa, Peder.
Fonager og Folkebogsamlingen. 22-24, HOLS

HESSISCHER ZENTRALKATALOG
see Frankfurt a.M. Hessischer Zentralkatalog

HESSIUS, JOHANNES
see Hess, Johannes

Heusler, Andreas.
Geschichte der Öffentlichen Bibliothek der Universität Basel. 2-83, (whole volume), BASE

HEUSLER, ANDREAS. Mss. - Collections - Basel
Salfinger, Theodor. Zur Sprachkunst des Germanisten Andreas Heusler. 193-205, SCHU

Hewlett, Leroy.
James Rivington, Tory Printer. 165-194, GJEL

Heyman, Harald J.
Något om Drakeska Arkivet i Uppsala Universitetsbibliotek. 249-256, GRAP

Heyne, Christian Gottlob.
Briefe in: Joachim, Johannes. Aus Briefen Christian Gottlob Heynes an Friedrich August Carus. 187-208, MILF

HEYNE, CHRISTIAN GOTTLOB
Leyh, Georg. Chr. G. Heynes Eintritt in die Göttinger Bibliothek. 220-228, MILF
Neubert, Hermann. Der Ruf Christian Gottlob Heynes nach Dresden. II, 43-52, GLAU

Heyst, M. G. M. A. van.
Proeve ener Genealogie van het Maastrichtse Kooplieden- en Magistraatsgeslacht Nootstock. 227-261, MAAS

Hicks, Frederick C.
Thirty Years Ago. 207-210, PUTN

HIERONYMUS, SAINT. Epistolae. Ms.
Husner, Fritz. Die Handschrift der Scholien des Erasmus von Rotterdam zu den Hieronymusbriefen. 132-146, BINZ

Higger, Michael.
Sefer Amarkol. The Halakhoth of Passover. 143-173, MARY

HILDUIN, supposed author. Annales Einhardi
Monod, M. G. Hilduin et les Annales Einhardi. 57-65, HAVE

Hilka, Alfons.
Zur Konstantinlegende. 147-152, MILF

Hilsenbeck, Adolf.
Eine Denkschrift Aretins über die Bayerischen Provinzialbibliotheken. 153-161, MILF
Die Universitätsbibliothek Landshut-München und die Säkularisation (1803). 180-192, LEYG

Hingwe, H. S.
Dr. Ranganathan's Contribution to the Library World. 632-635, RANG

Hippe, Max.
Zur Vorgeschichte der Breslauer Stadtbibliothek. 162-176, MILF

Hirn, Yrjö.
Utländsk Välgörenhet mot Universitetsbiblioteket. 9-18, HULT

HIRN, YRJÖ
HIRN
Bojer, Johan. Hilsen til Yrjö Hirn. 43, HIRN

Hirsch, Felix E.
Die Amerikanische College-Bibliothek. Gedanken über einen Hauptpfeiler des Wissenschaftlichen Bibliothekswesens in den Vereinigten Staaten. 267-278, WEHM

HIRSCH, OLGA - Library
Schmidt, Christel. Aus der Sammlung Olga Hirsch: Ein Kreisrunder Einband von Caspar Meuser. 194-198, LOUB

Hirsch, Paul.
Die "Kriegssammlung" der Königlichen Bibliothek zu Berlin. 97-106, WILM

Hirsch, Rudolf and Margaret C. Nolan.
The Peaceful Revolution. 25-34, DAVI

HIRSCHING, FRIEDRICH KARL GOTTLOB

Schreiber, Heinrich. Ein Erlanger Bibliothekenkenner des 18. Jahrhunderts: Friedrich Karl Gottlob Hirsching. 62-67, VERZ

Hirzel, B.
Conrad Ferdinand Meyer und die Zürcher Stadtbibliothek. [45]-69, ESCK

HISTORICAL LITERATURE - Collections - Germany

Ihme, Heinrich. Landesbibliothek und Landesgeschichte. 94-111, HOFF

Hjelmqvist, Bengt.
Interessenkreise und Zentralmagazine: Über einen Neuen Schwedischen Organisationsplan. 15-18, ACKR
Lika Möjligheter till Lån. Fragment av Liktal över Betankande. 117-126, HEIN

HJELMQVIST, BENGT

HJEL

Gardner, Frank. Humanity and Vision. 536-538, HJEL
Harrie, Ivar. Bokväsendets PR-man. 532-533, HJEL

Hjelmqvist, Fredrik.
Die Stockholmer Stadtbücherei als Einheitsbücherei. 43-46, ACKE
Utlandets Författere och Allmänheten i Stockholm. Några Siffror ur Stockholms Stadsbiblioteks Utlåning. 88-96, MUNT

Hleb-Koszańska, Helena.
De la Coordination Bibliographique à L'Échelle Nationale. 329-334, MIKH

HOBOKEN, ANTHONY VAN

HOBO

Schmidt-Görg, Joseph. Anthony van Hoboken zum 75. Geburtstag. 7-9, HOBO

HOCHBERGSCHE MAJORATSBIBLIOTHEK, FÜRSTENSTEIN, SILESIA
see Fürstenstein, Silesia. Hochbergsche Majoratsbibliothek

Hochenegg, Hans.
Die Roschmannsche Kupferstichsammlung. 400-414, BICK

Höfner, Curt.
Zur Geschichte der Gandersheimer Büchersammlungen. Ein Beitrag aus Coburg. 197-210, HOFM

Högberg, Paul.
Une Édition Rarissime du Roman de la Rose dans la Bibliothèque de L'Université Royale d'Uppsala. 268-291, UPPS

HÖLDERLIN, FRIEDRICH - Collections - Stuttgart

Lohrer, Liselotte. Hölderlin-Ausgabe und Hölderlin-Archiv. Entstehung und Geschichte. 289-314, HOFF

HÖLTZEL, HIERONYMUS

Schottenloher, Karl. Hans Sachs und Hieronymus Höltzel. Ein Beitrag zur Geschichte der Nürnberger Flugschriften vom Jahre 1524. 235-255, SCHW

Hörmann, Wolfgang.
Probleme einer Aldersbacher Handschrift (Clm. 2599). 355-389, HOFM

HÖXTER-CORVEY (Benedictine Abbey)
see Corvey (Benedictine Abbey)

Høydal, Reinh.
Folkebogsamlingane og Vår Tid. 89-97, NORS

HOF, GER. - Church libraries
see Church libraries - Hof, Ger.

HOF, GER. - Manuscripts - Collections
see Manuscripts - Collections - Hof, Ger.

HOF, GER. - Monastic libraries
see Monastic libraries - Hof, Ger.

HOF, GER. Stadtbibliothek

Hommel, Hildebrecht. Die Handschriften der Stadtbibliothek Hof. 47-60, SCHR

HOF VAN HOLLAND
see Hague. Hof van Holland

Hofer, Philip.
Adrian Le Roy and Robert Ballard: Printers of the Late Renaissance. 475-482, LYDE

HOFFMANN, ERNST THEODOR AMADEUS - Collections - Linköping, Sweden

Gobom, Nils. Gustaf Odencrants' E.T.A. Hoffmann-Samling i Linköpings Stifts- och Landsbibliotek. 262-279, GRAP

Hoffmann, Wilhelm.
Einige Gedanken zum Wiederaufbau Kriegsgeschädigter Bibliotheken. 39-41, STUM
Vom Sammeln und Bewahren. Gedanken über Dichter-Archive in Schwaben. 287-294, WEHM

HOFFMANN, WILHELM
HOFF

Hofinger, Josef.
Die Öffentlichen Studienbibliotheken Österreichs. 415-422, BICK

Hofmann, Gustav.
Der Bayerische Zentralkatalog in München. 473-477, BRUM
Gedanken zur Verwaltung von Handschriften in Öffentlichen Wissenschaftlichen Bibliotheken. 52-61, FUCH
Karl Schottenloher zum 75. Geburtstag. 1-6, SCHO
Musikpflege und Wissenschaftliche Universitätsbibliothek. 41-43, STUM
Pierre Bourgeois und die IFLA. 182-186, BOUR
Die Rolle des Gehobenen Mittleren Dienstes in den Deutschen Öffentlicher Wissenschaftlichen Bibliotheken. 43-54, STOL

HOFMANN, GUSTAV
HOFM
Böck, Karl. Zum Geleit. xxiii-xxvi, HOFM
Francis, Sir Frank. Dr. Hofmann, President of IFLA 1958-1963. 187-189, HOFM
Ranganathan, Shiyali Ramamrita. International Library Scene. 191-196, HOFM

HOFMANN, GUSTAV - Bibl.
Gleixner, Paul. Verzeichnis der Schriften von Gustav Hofmann, 1930-1964. 1-5, HOFM

Hofmann, Hans E., ed.
BOLE

Hofmann, Hans E.
Auskunft. 97-104, BOLE
Bibliographie Walter Hofmann/Elise Hofmann-Bosse. 41-67, DRES
Facit. 71-75, BOLE

Hofmann, Hans E., jt. author
Benndorf, Gottfried and Hans Hofmann. Die Sächsische Landesbibliothek 1920-36. 1-14, BOLL

Hofmann, Johannes, ed.
LEIP

Hofmann, Johannes.
Die Leipziger Stadtbibliothek 1677-1927. 9-21, LEIP

Hofmann, Walter.
Die Behandlung der Organisation der Ausleihe in der Modernen Deutschen Bildungsbibliothek. 17-29, DRES
Die Leseordnung in der Volksbücherei. I, 71-79, GLAU

HOFMANN, WALTER
Buchwald, Reinhard. Die Jenaer "Lesehalle" vor 50 Jahren: Aus den Ungedruckten Lebenserinnerungen von Walter Hofmann. 50-68, JENA
Günnel, Peter. Walter Hofmann und das Deutsche Volksbüchereiwesen. 7-16, DRES

HOFMANN, WALTER - Bibl.
Hofmann, Hans E. Bibliographie Walter Hofmann/Elise Hofmann-Bosse. 41-67, DRES

HOFMANN-BOSSE, ELISE - Bibl.
Hofmann, Hans E. Bibliographie Walter Hofmann/Elise Hofmann-Bosse. 41-67, DRES

HOFMANNSTHAL, HUGO HOFMANN VON. Mss. Werke. Nachlass.
Steiner, Herbert. Zur Hofmannsthal-Ausgabe. 347-348, HOFF

HOHENHEIM. Landwirtschaftliche Hochschule. Bibliothek
Franz, Günther. Die Bibliothek der Landwirtschaftlichen Hochschule Hohenheim. 139-150, HOFF

HOHENTÜBINGEN, SCHLOSS. Tübingen see Tübingen. Schloss Hohentübingen

Hohmann, Georg.
Erinnerungen. 37-40, HELD

HOLBACH, PAUL HENRI THIRY, BARON D' - Bibl.
Sauter, Hermann. Bibliographie der Holbach-Drucke in Deutschen und Österreichischen Bibliotheken. 390-416, BENZ

HOLBEIN, HANS, d. J.
Eichler, Ferdinand. Eine Bucheinbandverzierung aus dem Formenschatz Hans Holbeins d. J. 63-66, LEID

Holder, Alfred.
Der Isidorus-Codex Augiensis LVII der Gr. Hof- und Landesbibliothek in Karlsruhe. 634-643, CHAT

Holdsworth, H.
Bibliography in South Africa. 151-159, OFFO

Holenstein, J.
Geleitwort der Redaktion. 167, BOUR

HOLKAM HALL. Mss. (no. 17)
Dorez, Léon. Évangéliaire Exécuté à L'Abbaye de Schuttern (VIIIe-IXe Siècle). 293-299, CHAT

Hollaender, Albert E. J.
Ein Unveröffentlichter Augenzeugenbericht über Napoleon I. an Bord des "Bellerophon" im Kriegshafen von Plymouth, Juli-August 1815. 44-45, STUM

HOLLAND
see Netherlands

HOLLAND - Archives
see Archives - Holland

HOLLAND - War and the library
see War and the library - Holland

Holliday, J. S.
Remarks on the Occasion of the Wagner Award. 63-68, HAMM

HOLLIS, SIR THOMAS
Bloesch, Hans. Ein Englischer Gönner der Berner Stadtbibliothek im 18. Jahrhundert. 112-118, BINZ

Holmberg, Marianne.
Förteckning över Carl-Rudolf Gardbergs Tryckta Skrifter intill 9.9.1958 202-229, GARD

Holmes, Thomas J.
The Surreptitious Printing of One of Cotton Mather's Manuscripts. 149-160, EAME

Holmgren, Gustaf.
Om Cronstedtska Samlingen i Uppsala Universitetsbibliotek och dess Tillkomst. Några Anteckningar. 519-560, GRAP

Holmström, Bengt, jt. ed.
HEIN

HOLSTEBRO, Denmark. Centralbibliotek
HOLS

HOLSTEBRO, Denmark - Librarians
see Librarians - Holstebro, Denmark

HOLSTEBRO, Denmark - Public libraries
see Public libraries - Holstebro, Denmark

HOLSTEBRO, Denmark - Public libraries - Centralization
see Public libraries - Centralization - Holstebro, Denmark

Holstein Rathlou, V. J. v.
Pligtafleveringen. 81-85, AARU

HOLSTENIUS, LUCAS
Mogenet, Joseph. Holstenius et L'Horoscope de Proclus. II, 281-308, ALBB

HOLT, JOHN - Bibl.
Vail, R. W. G. A Patriotic Pair of Peripatetic Printers, the Up-State Imprints of John Holt and Samuel Loudon, 1776-1783. 391-422, WROT

HOLTROP, JAN WILLEM
Verwey, Eleonore de la Fontaine. Jacob Geel en de Koninklijke Bibliotheek. 414-426, BRUM

Holtsmark, Anne.
En Side av Norsk Bokhistorie. 74-90, OSLN

Holtzmann, Walther.
Paolo Kehr e le Ricerche Archivistiche per L'Italia Pontificia. 43-49, MERC
Über die Vatikanische Handschrift der "Collectio Brugensis" (Ottob. Lat. 3027). I, 391-414, ALBB

HOLY ROMAN EMPIRE - Bookbinding
see Bookbinding - Holy Roman Empire

Holzinger, Charles.
Sur la Date de Quelques Manuscrits d'Aristophane. 204-218, CHAT

Homburger, Otto.
Über die Kunstgeschichtliche Bedeutung der Handschriften der Burgerbibliothek. 107-131, BERT

HOME LIBRARIES
see Private libraries

HOMENAJE A MENÉNDEZ PELAYO. 5, MENE

HOMERUS. Mss. Iliad
De Marchi, A. Vesti, Armi, Riti e Costumi nel Codice Omerico Illustrato dell'Ambrosiana. 1-35, CERI

Homeyer, Fritz.
Versuch eines Bibliographen-Lexikons. 141-163, FRAD

Hommel, Hildebrecht.
Die Handschriften der Stadtbibliothek Hof. 47-60, SCHR

Hopf, Wilhelm, ed.
KASS

Hopf, Wilhelm.
Die Landesbibliothek Kassel, in Ihrer Geschichtlichen Entwicklung 1580-1930. 1-108, (part 1), KASS

Horák, František.
Die Bibliothek der Tschechoslowakischen Akademie der Wissenschaften. 192-202, VORS

HORATIUS FLACCUS, QUINTUS - Collections - Hague

Dekker, Annie F. In de Spiegel der Horatiana. 402-407, BRUM

HORATIUS FLACCUS, QUINTUS - Mss.

Keller, Otto. Über einen Verbrannten Codex des Horaz. 531-534, CHAT
Lejay, Paul. Les Recensions Antiques d'Horace. 59-74, CHAT

Horiuchi, Ikuko.
Gendai no Toshokan Mokuroku to Katarogā no Kyōiku ni tsuite. (Trends of the Library Catalog and Training of Catalogers.) 229-237, HASH

Horner, G. W.
The Answer?--That is the Question. 252-255, KYLE

Hornwall, Gert.
Ett Föregångsbibliotek i Stockholm. Gustav Vasa Församlingsbibliotek 1909-1927. 127-135, HEIN

Horodisch, Abraham.
Ein Abenteuer im Geiste: Die Soncino-Gesellschaft der Freunde des Jüdischen Buches. 181-208, WEHM
Die Anfänge des Buchdrucks in Moskau. 208-225, BENZ

Horodyski, Bogdan.
Józef Grycz. 22-54, GRYC
Zarys Dziejów Biblioteki Ord. Zamojskiej. 295-341, PIEK

Horovitz, Jakob.
Aus der Oxforder Handschrift des Josif Omez. 35-50, FREN

HORSENS, Denmark. Centralbibliotek

HORS

HORSENS, Denmark - Librarians
see Librarians - Horsens, Denmark

HORSENS, Denmark - Public libraries - Centralization
see Public libraries - Centralization - Horsens, Denmark

HORSENS, Denmark - Public libraries - Statistics
see Public libraries - Statistics - Horsens, Denmark

Horstmann, H.
Altersaufbau und Lesestetigkeit in einer Volksbücherei. 47-54, ACKE

HORTIS, ATTILIO

HORT

Costantini, Guido. L'Opera Letteraria di Attilio Hortis. I, 7-112, HORT

Hortzschansky, Adalbert, ed.
SCHW

Hortzschansky, Adalbert.
Heinrich Pertz' Berufung zum Oberbibliothekar der Königlichen Bibliothek in Berlin. 115-126, SCHW

Hosius, Carl.
Bibliotheksfeinde und -Funde. 150-155, KUHN

HOSPITAL LIBRARIES
see Medical libraries; Public libraries-Services to hospitals

HOTTINGER, JOHANN HEINRICH. Der Bibliothecarius Quadripartitus

Escher, Hermann. Der Bibliothecarius Quadripartitus des Joh. Heinrich Hottinger (1664) (1934). 169-184, ESCH

HOURS, Book of

Trenkler, Ernst. Ein Unbekanntes "Livre d'Heures" der Österreichischen Nationalbibliothek. 639-645, BICK

HOURS, Books of

Köster, Kurt. Religiöse Medaillen und Wallfahrts-Devotionalien in der Flämischen Buchmalerei des 15. und Frühen 16. Jahrhunderts. Zur Kenntnis Gemalter und Wirklicher Kollektionen in Spätmittelalterlichen Gebetbuch-Handschriften. 459-504, HOFM

Howe, Harriet.
Two Decades in Education for Librarianship. 557-570, WILS

Howell, N.
A Great Loss. 13, VARL

Howell, Warren R.
A Thorough Bibliophile. 47-54, HAMM

Hrozný, Jindřich.
Povinné Výtisky. 64-68, EMLE

Hülle, Hermann.
Die Fortschritte der Ostasiatischen Sammlungen. 190-211, HARN
Über Alphabetische Anordnung Chinesischer und Japanischer Titelaufnahmen. 254-260, KUHN

HÜPSCH-LONTZEN, JOHANN WILHELM CARL ADOLPH VON HORVLEZ-ARDENN, Freiherr von, 1726-1805
Schmidt, Adolf. Baron Hüpsch in Köln als Inkunabelnsammler und Händler. 45-63, HAEB

Huet, Gédéon.
La Première Édition de la Consolation de Boèce en Néerlandais. 561-569, HAVE

HUGO, ADÈLE (Foucher). Lettres
Dormoy, Marie. Du Droit de Détruire. 489-492, BONN

HUGO, MME. VICTOR
see Hugo, Adèle (Foucher)

HUGO OF SAINT VICTOR. Mss. De Fructu Carnis et Spiritus.
Frisch, Ernst von. Über die Salzburger Handschrift von Hugo von St. Victors Opusculum de Fructu Carnis et Spiritus. 67-71, LEID

Hui, Franz.
Die Bau- und Häuserpläne des Staatsarchivs. 34-36, BASL

Hulewicz, Janem.
O Centralnej Bibliotece Nauczycielskiej KOSK. 14-16, KRAK

Hulshof, Abraham.
De Handschriften en de Incunabulen der Utrechtsche Universiteitsbibliotheek en de Moderne Reproductietechniek. 150-159, EVER
Uitgaven voor de Boekerij van het Karthuizerklooster te Utrecht in de Jaren 1466-1470. 170-175, LOUB
Het Utrechtsche Psalterium. 4-28, SOME
Een Woord Vooraf. 1-4, EVER

Hulshoff, Margaretha H.
De Bibliotheek van het Tandheelkundig Instituut. 160-163, EVER

Hulth, J. M.
Studenten Carolus Linnaeus' Bibliotek 395-400, COLL
Uppsala Universitetsbiblioteks Förvärv av Linneanska Originalmanuskript. 407-424, UPPS

Hultin, Arvid.
Sånger av Runeberg och Topelius i Vårt Skillingstryck. 9-24, SCHA

HULTIN, ARVID
HULA
HULT

HUMANITIES
see Literature of the humanities

HUMBOLDT, ALEXANDER VON - Collections - Leipzig
Wustmann, Felix. Drei Unbekannte Briefe Alexander v. Humboldts in der Universitätsbibliothek Leipzig. 265-269, BULL

HUMBOLDT-UNIVERSITÄT. Bibliothek, Berlin
see Berlin. Humboldt-Universität. Bibliothek

HUMPHREY, DUKE OF GLOUCESTER
see Gloucester, Humphrey, Duke of

HUNGARIAN ACADEMY OF SCIENCES, Budapest. Geniza Collection (Kaufmann)
Scheiber, Alexander. Piyyutim from the Geniza Collection of David Kaufmann. 537-546, MARX

HUNGARIAN LITERATURE - Cataloging
Kaiser, Rudolf. Die Behandlung der Ungarica im Preußischen Gesamtkatalog. 217-223, KUHN

HUNGARY - Bookbinding
see Bookbinding - Hungary

HUNGARY - Manuscripts, Hebrew
see Manuscripts, Hebrew - Hungary

HUNGARY - Private libraries
see Private libraries - Hungary

Hunger, Herbert.
Die Druckvorlage der Editio Princeps des Anonymus Neobarii. 46, STUM

Hunt, Hannah.
Young Adults and Libraries: Crisis or Challenge? 59-69, HASH

HUNTING DIARIES - Collections - Vienna
Ausserer, Karl. Die Jagdtagebücher der Österreichischen Nationalbibliothek. 228-238, BICK

HUNTINGTON LIBRARY, San Marino, Calif.
see Henry E. Huntington Library and Art Gallery, San Marino, Calif.

Huq, A. M. Abdul.
Co-operation in Indo-Pakistan Librarianship. 425-427, RANG

Huri, Nelly.
Quatre Lettres d'Albert Stapfer. 499-507, BONN

HURTADO DE MENDOZA, DIEGO
Thomas, Sir Henry. Diego Hurtado de Mendoza and His Plaquette Bindings. 474-480, GREE

Husner, Fritz.
Die Editio Princeps des "Corpus Historiae Byzantinae." Johannes Oporin, Hieronymus Wolf und die Fugger. 143-162, SCHU
Die Handschrift der Scholien des Erasmus von Rotterdam zu den Hieronymusbriefen. 132-146, BINZ

Husung, Max Joseph, ed.
LOUB

Husung, Max Joseph.
Aus der Zeit des Übergangs von der Handschrift zum Druck. Nach einem Band der Preussischen Staatsbibliothek. 155-159, DEGE
Dreimal das Gleiche Lederschnittmotiv. 123-126, LEID
Joseph Niesert. Aus dem Leben eines Gelehrten Westfälischen Büchersammlers. 119-124, BÖME
Der Löwener Renaissance-Buchbinder mit der Gesprungenen Einbandplatte. II, 29-35, GLAU
Ein Neuer Signierter und Datierter Badier, Gefunden in der Preussischen Staatsbibliothek. 435-442, COLL
Über die Entwicklung der Monatsbilder in Kalendern. 13-32, LOUB
Über den Plattenstempelschnitt in Königsberg. 283-287, KUHN

Hutchings, F. G. B.
J. P. Lamb. 4-5, LAMB

HUTTEN, ULRICH VON

Grimm, Heinrich. Ulrichs von Hutten Persönliche Beziehungen zu den Druckern Johannes Schöffer in Mainz, Johannes Schott in Strassburg und Jakob Köbel zu Oppenheim. 140-156, BENZ

HUTTER, ELIAS

Zafren, Herbert C. Elias Hutter's Hebrew Bible. 29-39, BLOC

HUTTON, R. S.

HUTT

Patrick, L. G., et al. R. S. Hutton; on the Occasion of His Ninetieth Birthday. 277-286, HUTT

HUYGENS, CONSTANTIJN, Heer van Zuilichem - Library

Alphen, G. van. Anthony Smets, Bibliothecaris van Drie Prinsen van Oranje (1636-1689). 119-160, HAGU

HYMNS, Byzantine
see Hymns, Greek

HYMNS, Greek. Ms.

Dietzel, Armin. Ein Altkirchlicher Christushymnus. Der Papyrus Erlangensis 1 im Vergleich mit den Abendhymnen (Ms. Erlg. 1234). 83-93, REDE

IFLA
see International Federation of Library Associations

Iben, Icko.
Die Zeitung im Archiv- und Bibliothekswesen. 47-50, STUM

IBN SHAPRUT, SHEM-TOB. Eben Bohan. Ms.

Marx, Alexander. The Polemical Manuscripts in the Library of the Jewish Theological Seminary of America. 247-278, FREI

Ibrovac, Miodrog.
Francis Jammes en Yougoslavie. 439-447, BONN

ICELANDIC LITERATURE (Modern) - Collections - Uppsala

Uggla, Arvid HJ. Uppsala Universitetsbiblioteks Samling av Nyisländsk Litteratur. Några Meddelanden. 537-574, UPPS

ICHIHASHI, SHIMOSA - Library

Naito, Torajiro. Kansei Jidai no Zōshoka Ichihashi Shimosa no Kami. (On Lord Ichihashi Shimosa, a Book Collector of the Kansei Period.) 42-69, IMAI

Ihme, Heinrich.
Landesbibliothek und Landesgeschichte. 94-111, HOFF

Ikonomova, Diana and Dimitŭr Boshnakov.
Imenniiat Pokazalets v Registratsionnata Bibliografiia. 163-185, TEOB

IL ZIBALDONE. Ms.

Frati, Lodovico. Una Miscellanea Umanistica della R. Biblioteca Universitaria di Bologna. I, 321-329, HORT

Ilchester, the Earl of.
Some Pages Torn from the Last Journals of Horace Walpole. 449-458, GREE

Il'inskiĭ, L. K.
Biblioteka Iv. Mikh. Khvostova; k Istorii Bibliotek XVIII Veka. 346-374, MALE

ILLUMINATION OF BOOKS AND MANUSCRIPTS

KRÜS

MUNI

Arens, Fritz. Das Brevier des Ad-

ministrators Adalbert von Sachsen in der Mainzer Universitätsbibliothek. 67-89, MAIZ
Aus den Schätzen der Landesbibliothek. [Plates 5-12], FULD
Baldini, Antonio. La Bibbia di Borso. 41-45, GREG
Barroux, Robert. Recueil Historique en Français Composé, Transcrit et Enluminé à Saint-Denis, vers 1280. 15-34, CALO
Bischoff, Bernhard. Kreuz und Buch im Frühmittelalter und in den Ersten Jahrhunderten der Spanischen Reconquista. 19-34, WEHM
Boeckler, Albert. Corveyer Buchmalerei unter Einwirkung Wibalds von Stablo. 133-147, BÖME
Bömer, Alois. Ein Gotisches Prachtmissale Utrechtscher Herkunft in der Universitäts-Bibliothek Münster. 29-41, DEGE
Bonnerot, Jean. En Marge du Manuscrit Français 147 de la B. N. 644-661, CHAT
Boussard, Jacques. L'Évangéliaire d'Or, Manuscrit 599 de la Bibliothèque de L'Arsenal. 3-14, CALO
Brechler, Otto. Handschriftensammlungen als Kunstsammlungen. 252-263, BICK
Briele, Wolfgang van der. Eine Bibelhandschrift des 13. Jahrhunderts in der Dortmunder Stadtbibliothek. 7-11, VERD
Butzmann, Hans. Vom Schmuck der Heidelberger Otfrid-Handschrift. 35-44, WEHM
Byvanck, A. W. Een Nieuwe Aanwinst van de Koninklijke Bibliotheek. 35-43, HAGU
De Marchi, A. Vesti, Armi, Riti e Costumi nel Codice Omerico Illustrato dell'Ambrosiana. 1-35, CERI
Der Nersessian, Sirarpie. An Armenian Lectionary of the Fourteenth Century. 231-237, GREE
Donati, Lamberto. Le Fonti Iconografiche di Alcuni Manoscritti Urbinati della Biblioteca Vaticana—Osservazioni Intorno ai Cosiddetti "Tarocchi del Mantegna." 48-129, MERG
Ehwald, Rudolf. Über eine Französische Missalhandschrift des XIV. Jahrhunderts. 65-75, SCHW
Fava, Domenico. I Corali degli Olivetani di Bologna. 277-286, FERR
Fischer, Karl. Margarete Karteuserin, eine Nürnberger Klosterschreiberin des 15. Jahrhunderts. 24-31, VERZ
Galley, Eberhard. Miniaturen aus dem Kölner Klarissenkloster. Ein Kapitel Rheinischer Buchmalerei des 14. Jahrhunderts. 15-28, JUCH
Gichtel, Paul. Die Bilder der Münchener Tristan-Handschrift (Cod. Germ. 51). 391-457, HOFM
Harrsen, Meta. Figural Grisaille Ornament on a Historiated Initial of about 1400, and the Derivation of This Style from the Indulgences of Avignon. 316-322, LYDE
Homburger, Otto. Über die Kunstgeschichtliche Bedeutung der Handschriften der Burgerbibliothek. 107-131, BERT
Hulshof, A. Het Utrechtsche Psalterium. 4-28, SOME
Kirchner, Joachim. Das Staveloter Evangeliar der Preussischen Staatsbibliothek. 160-171, DEGE
Launay, Denise. À Propos de Deux Manuscrits Musicaux aux Armes de Louis XIII. 63-67, FEDO
Leporini, Heinrich. Simon von Niederaltaich und Martin v. Senging. 575-590, VIEN
Lutze, Eberhard. Eine Augsburger Bilderhandschrift aus dem Besitz des Sebastian Schertlin von Burtenbach (Ms. 1620 der UB Erlangen). 147-156, STOL
Martin, Henry. Notes sur les Écrivains au Travail. 535-544, CHAT
Muñoz, Antonio. Miniature Bizantine nella Biblioteca Queriniana di Brescia. 169-179, CERI
Ouy, Gilbert. Une Maquette de Manuscrit à Peintures. 43-51, CALO
Pächt, Otto. Notes and Observations on the Origin of Humanistic Book-Decoration. 184-194, SAXL
Petersen, Theodore. The Paragraph Mark in Coptic Illuminated Ornament. 295-330, GREE
Priest, Alan. An Illuminated Buddhist Scroll in the Metropolitan Museum of Art. 122-128, GREE
Redenbacher, Fritz. Einzelbild und Zyklus in der Bibelillustration des Frühen Mittelalters. 110-118, TIEM
Reider, Joseph. Non-Jewish Motives in the Ornament of Early Hebrew Books. 150-159, FREI
Roob, Helmut. Schöne Breviere in der Gothaer Bibliothek. 55-61, LÜLF
Rosenthal, Erwin. Eine Neuaufgefundene Arbeit Berthold Furtmeyrs. 213-217, LEID
Santoro, Enza Fioroni. Dell'Origine e degli Autori di Alcune Stampe Attribuite ad "Ignoto." 427-439, GALL
Sawicka, Stanisława M. Czeski Rękopis Iluminowany w Książnicy Miejskiej im. Kopernika w Toruniu. 28-34, EMLE
Schapiro, Meyer. Two Romanesque Drawings in Auxerre and Some Iconographic Problems. 331-349, GREE
Skehan, Patrick W. An Illuminated Gospel Book in Ethiopic. 350-357, GREE
Söderhjelm, Werner. Un Manuscrit du Roman de la Rose à la Bibliothèque Royale de Stockholm. 75-90, COLL
Struck, Gustav. Handschriftenschätze der Landesbibliothek Kassel. 1-127, (part 2), KASS

Trenkler, Ernst. Ein Unbekanntes "Livre d'Heures" der Österreichischen Nationalbibliothek. 639-645, BICK
Vilar, Joan. L'"Expositio Remigii Super Matheum" en el Còd. 548 de la Biblioteca de Catalunya. III, 263-281, RUBI
Wegener, Hans. Die Deutschen Volkshandschriften des Späten Mittelalters. 316-324, DEGE
——— Das Gebetbuch der Johanna von Bocholt. 228-232, BÖME
Weitzmann, Kurt. The Constantinopolitan Lectionary, Morgan 639. 358-373, GREE
Wieselgren, O. Två i Kungl. Biblioteket Befintliga Miniatyrhandskrifter ur den Gent-Brüggeska Skolan. 91-101, COLL
Wischnitzer-Bernstein, Rahel. Der Siddur der Altstädtischen Synagoge in Rzeszów. 77-80, FREN

ILLUMINATION OF BOOKS AND MANUSCRIPTS - Belgium
Köster, Kurt. Religiöse Medaillen und Wallfahrts-Devotionalien in der Flämischen Buchmalerei des 15. und Frühen 16. Jahrhunderts. Zur Kenntnis Gemalter und Wirklicher Kollektionen in Spätmittelalterlichen Gebetbuch-Handschriften. 459-504, HOFM

ILLUMINATION OF BOOKS AND MANUSCRIPTS - Cologne
Boeckler, Albert. Beiträge zur Romanischen Kölner Buchmalerei. 15-28, DEGE

ILLUMINATION OF BOOKS AND MANUSCRIPTS - Germany
Schenk zu Schweinsberg, Eberhard, Frhr. Margarete von Rodemachern, eine Deutsche Bücherfreundin in Lothringen. 117-152, WEIM

ILLUMINATION OF BOOKS AND MANUSCRIPTS - Gt. Brit.
Millar, Eric G. Fresh Materials for the Study of English Illumination. 286-294, GREE

ILLUMINATION OF BOOKS AND MANUSCRIPTS - Hist.
Redenbacher, Fritz. Die Buchmalerei des Frühen Mittelalters im Urteil der Deutschen Romantik. 203-217, STOL

ILLUMINATION OF BOOKS AND MANUSCRIPTS - Hist. - 9th cent.
Durrieu, Comte Paul. Ingobert: un Grand Calligraphe du IXe Siècle. 1-14, CHAT

ILLUMINATION OF BOOKS AND MANUSCRIPTS - Italy
Cutolo, Alessandro. Due Momenti Essenziali nella Storia del Libro in Italia. 311-323, GALL

ILLUMINATION OF BOOKS AND MANUSCRIPTS - Kaisheim
Stange, Alfred. Beiträge zur Kaisheimer Buchmalerei. 277-281, LEID

ILLUMINATION OF BOOKS AND MANUSCRIPTS - Vatican - Hist.
Llorens, José Maria. Los Codices Musicales de la "Capella Sixtina" en la Historia del Arte. II, 191-209, ALBB

ILLUSTRATED BOOKS - 17th-18th cent.
Cluzel, Étienne. De Quelques Livres Scientifiques à Vignettes, des XVIIe et XVIIIe Siècles. 127-143, CALO

ILLUSTRATION OF BOOKS
see Book illustration

ILLUSTRATION OF PERIODICALS
see Book illustration

ILLUSTRATORS, Jewish - Bio-bibl.
Reider, Joseph. The New Ornament of Jewish Books. 10-18, BLOC

IMAI, KAN'ICHI
IMAI

Imanishi, Minoru, jt. author
Yuda, Yoshio, Hajime Uetani and Minoru Imanishi. Tenri Toshokan Zō Jōruri Hangi Mokuroku. (Catalogue of the Wood-Blocks of Jōruri Texts in the Tenri Central Library.) 259-294, TOMI

Immelman, R. F. M.
A Contribution to the History of Scholarly Libraries in the Cape Province (before 1920). 25-44, COET
D. H. Varley—Outside the S.A.P.L. 14-17, VARL

IMMERMANN, KARL LEBERECHT - Correspondence - Collections - Dortmund
Schulz, Erich. Immermanns Briefe an Ferdinand Gessert. Ein Vorbericht. 119-133, VERD

IMMERMANN, KARL LEBERECHT. Mss. Alexis.
Risse, Joseph. Ein Neuer Immermann-Fund, die Urhandschrift des "Alexis." 89-117, VERD

IMMERMANN, KARL LEBERECHT. tr.

Schulz, Erich. Immermanns Übersetzung aus Dante. 297-301, BOME

IMPERIAL EDITIONS
see Chokuhan (Imperial editions)

IMPORTATION AND EXPORTATION OF BOOKS

Lydenberg, Harry Miller. Some Thoughts on the Part the Printed Book May Play in the International Field. 463-471, BICK

IMPORTATION AND EXPORTATION OF BOOKS - Hist.

Paulli, R. Bogfører-Dokumenter fra det 16. Aarhundrede. 215-223, COLL

IMPRINTS (in books)

Dieserud, Juul. The Abbreviation of Imprints. 179-184, HANS

Incisa Della Rocchetta, Giovanni. Osservazioni sugli Autografi delle "Epistolae ed Thyrrenum" di Giano Nicio Eritreo. 215-226, GREG

INCUNABULA
see also Colophons

INCUNABULA

RUPP

Albareda, Anselmo. Un Incunabulo Sconosciuto dello Stampatore J. Luschner. 29-50, ACCU

Beaulieux, Ch. Manuscrits et Imprimés en France XVe et XVIe Siècles. 417-428, CHAT

Bernoulli, Rudolf. Das Weltallbild in Hartmann Schedels Weltchronik. 48-58, LOUB

Birkenmajer, Alexander. Die Wiegendrucke der Phvsischen Werke Johannes Versors. 121-135, COLL

Bömer, Aloys. Die Schlußschrift des Mainzer Catholicon-Druckes von 1460. 51-55, KUHN

Collijn, Isak. Schwedische Donate. 47-52, SCHW

Degering, Hermann. Nachträgliches zur Vitruvausgabe vom Jahre 1487 in der Leipziger Stadtbibliothek. 54-57, LEIP

———— Wer War der Drucker der Erstausgabe des Vitruv? Ein Beitrag zur Geschichte des Römischen Buchdrucks. 175-202, HAEB

Dervieux, Ermanno. Incunabuli della Biblioteca del Seminario di Asti. II, 451-480, MANO

Dold, Alban. Ein Unbekanntes Spezimen einer "Günther-Zainer"-Bibel. 105-110, LEYG

Eichler, Ferdinand. Die Renaissance des Buches im 15. Jahrhundert und Ihre Nachwirkung. 1-10, LEYG

Geissler, Paul. Ein Seltener Augsburger Wiegendruck. Das Älteste Gedruckte Buck über Altötting. 316-322, VORS

Geldner, Ferdinand. Das "Catholicon" des Johannes Balbus im Ältesten Buchdruck. 90-98, JUCH

Goldschmidt, E. Ph. Lucian's Calumnia. 228-244, SAXL

Guarnaschelli, Teresa. Alfonso Fernandez da Cordova e la Prima Stampa di Murcia. 125-132, ACCU

Högberg, Paul. Une Édition Rarissime du Roman de la Rose dans la Bibliothèque de L'Université Royale d'Uppsala. 268-291, UPPS

Hulshof, Abraham. Uitgaven voor de Boekerij van het Karthuizerklooster te Utrecht in de Jaren 1466-1470. 170-175, LOUB

Husung, Max Joseph. Über die Entwicklung der Monatsbilder in Kalendern. 13-32, LOUB

Juchhoff, Rudolf. Johann und Konrad von Paderborn. Die Anfänge Ihrer Druckertätigkeit in Venedig und Strassburg. 211-227, BÖME

Keyman, Johanna M. Enkele Opmerkingen over een Merkwaardige Incunabel der Utrechtsche Universiteitsbibliotheek. 204-216, EVER

Kruitwagen, Bonaventura. De Freeska Landriucht-Drukkerij. 45-69, HAGU

Larsen, Sofus. To Danske Palaeotyper Trykte i Paris. 183-197, COLL

Lewicka-Kamińska, Anna. Neues Donatfragment in der Type der 42zeiligen Bibel in der Jagiellonischen Bibliothek. 13-16, LULF

Lydenberg, Harry Miller. More Blind Impressions: With Light Therefrom? 601-613, WILS

Mercati, Giovanni, Cardinal. Da Incunaboli a Codici. 3-28, ACCU

Meyer, Wilhelm Joseph. Die Ersten für das Wallis Gedruckten Bücher im 15. Jahrhundert. 83-90, GODE

Müller, Max. Der Älteste Bisher Bekannte Buchumschlag. 195-197, LEID

———— Casus Synodales. Ein Bisher Unbekannter Bamberger Incunabeldruck. 40-44, VERZ

Oehme, Ruthardt. Die Palästinakarte aus Bernhard von Breidenbachs Reise in das Heilige Land 1486. 70-83, LEYH

Omont, H. Deux Incunables Imprimés à Tours le 7 Mai 1496. 153-160, COLL

Pons, Abelardo Palanca. Incunable Valenciano Poco Conocido. 589-596, GALL

Rath, Erich von. Der Drucker von Buyers Ausgabe der Werke des Bartolus von 1482. Ein Beitrag zur Buchdruckergeschichte Lyons. 217-225, SCHW

——— Die Kupferstichillustration im Wiegendruckzeitalter. 58-68, LEIP
Scaccia-Scarafoni, Camillo. La Grammatica di Sulpizio Verolano in un Incunabulo Ignoto ai Bibliografi. 378-384, GREG
Schmidt-Künsemüller, Friedrich Adolf. Ein Früher Typenmethodologischer Versuch in der Inkunabelkunde. 69-75, WEHM
Schottenloher, Karl. Tagebuch-Aufzeichnungen in Immerwährenden Kalendern der Frühdruckzeit. II, 88-96, GLAU
Sorbelli, Albano. Lo "Specchio della Prudenza" di Frate Beltrame da Ferrara (GW 3807) Presunto Incunabulo. 205-213, ACCU
Stillwell, Margaret Bingham. The Fasciculus Temporum, a Genealogical Survey of Editions before 1480. 409-440, EAME
Tominaga, Makita. Inkyunabura—Insatsu Moji o Meguru Kaisetsu to Shōkai. (Incunabula—an Introduction Centering on the Problem of the Types.) 1-23, TOMI
Voulliéme, Ernst. Zur Bibliographie Heinrich Knoblochtzers in Heidelberg. Der Totentanz. 137-151, COLL
Will, Erich. Die Wiegendrucke des Gratianischen Dekretes und Ihr Bestand in der Universitätsbibliothek Freiburg i. Br. 191-217, JUCR

INCUNABULA - Authors

Bühler, Curt F. Authors and Incunabula. 401-406, GREE

INCUNABULA - Bibl.

Alblas, J. De Nederlandsche Incunabelen der Universiteitsbibliotheek. 33-36, SOME
Benzing, Josef. Buchgeschichtliche Beiträge zu Einigen Frühdrucken der UB Mainz. 103-128, MAIZ
Birkenmajer, Alexander. Die Wiegendrucke der Physischen Werke Johannes Versors. 121-135, COLL
Ceva Valla, Elena. Nota su Alcuni Incunaboli Posseduti dalla Biblioteca Braidense di Milano. 51-59, ACCU
Crous, Ernst. Die Bücherzeichen (Exlibris) in den Wiegendrucken der Staatsbibliothek. 240-253, HARN
Deckert, Helmut, Marita Kremer, Hans Pfeifer, and Liselotte Willi. Das Neue Buchmuseum der Sächsischen Landesbibliothek. 175-205, DREL
Inguanez, Mauro. A Hand-List of the Incunabula of the Royal Malta Library. 407-411, GREE
Leporace, Tullia Gasparrini. Notizie e Documenti Inediti sul Tipografo Antonio Carcano (1475-1525). 327-356, FERR
Moricca-Caputi, Ada. Appunti Su Alcuni Incunaboli Casanatensi. 304-316, GREG
Ohly, Kurt. Das Inkunabelverzeichnis Bernhards von Mallinckrodt. (Handschrift des Staatsarchivs Münster I 261.) 37-62, BÖME
Voulliéme, Ernst. Die Inkunabelsammlung. 22-31, HARN

INCUNABULA (Block-books)
see Block-books

INCUNABULA - Bloemendaal, Netherlands

Hulshof, Abraham. Uitgaven voor de Boekerij van het Karthuizerklooster te Utrecht in de Jaren 1466-1470. 170-175, LOUB

INCUNABULA - Buying and selling
see Book industry and trade - Incunabula

INCUNABULA - Care and restoration
see Books - Care and restoration

INCUNABULA - Cataloging
see Manuscripts - Cataloging

INCUNABULA - Central Europe - Hist.

Crous, Ernst. Die Anfänge des Antiquadrucks in Deutschland und Seinen Nachbarländern. 33-42, LOUB

INCUNABULA - Collections - Berlin

Altmann, Ursula. Die Inkunabelsammlung. I, 381-403, BERS
Crous, Ernst. Die Bücherzeichen (Exlibris) in den Wiegendrucken der Staatsbibliothek. 240-253, HARN
Schwenke, Paul. Die Mainzer Donatdrucke der Staatsbibliothek. 31-36, HARN
Voulliéme, Ernst. Die Inkunabelsammlung. 22-31, HARN

INCUNABULA - Collections - Darmstadt

Schmidt, Adolf. Baron Hüpsch in Köln als Inkunabelnsammler und Händler. 45-63, HAEB

INCUNABULA - Collections - Frankfurt a.M.

Freimann, A. Die Hebräischen Inkunabeln der Stadtbibliothek zu Frankfurt a.M. 129-144, EBRA

INCUNABULA - Collections - Mainz

Benzing, Josef. Buchgeschichtliche Beiträge zu Einigen Frühdrucken der UB Mainz. 103-128, MAIZ

INCUNABULA - Collections - Malta

Inguanez, Mauro. A Hand-List of the Incunabula of the Royal Malta Library. 407-411, GREE

INCUNABULA - Collections - Milan

Ceva Valla, Elena. Nota su Alcuni Incunaboli Posseduti dalla Biblioteca Braidense di Milano. 51-59, ACCU

INCUNABULA - Collections - Münster

Küster, A. Die Juristische Abteilung der Königlichen Universitäts-Bibliothek zu Münster. 268-300, MÜNS

INCUNABULA - Collections - Naples

Delisle, Léopold. Notes sur les Anciennes Impressions des Classiques Latins et d'Autres Auteurs Conservées au XVe Siècle dans la Librairie Royale de Naples. 245-296, GRAU

INCUNABULA - Collections - Paris

Le Gal, Simonne. La Bibliothèque des Dames au XVe Siècle, Vue par le Marquis de Paulmy. 55-63, CALO

INCUNABULA - Collections - Rome (City)

Moricca-Caputi, Ada. Appunti Su Alcuni Incunaboli Casanatensi. 304-316, GREG

———— Di Alcuni Opuscoli Rari nella Biblioteca Casanatense. 153-165, ACCU

INCUNABULA - Collections - Stuttgart

Leuze, Otto. Mit Holzschnitten Verzierte Buchumschläge des 15. Jahrhunderts in der Württembergischen Landesbibliothek in Stuttgart. 165-169, LEID

INCUNABULA - Collections - Utrecht

Alblas, J. De Nederlandsche Incunabelen der Universiteitsbibliotheek. 33-36, SOME

Hulshof, A. De Handschriften en de Incunabelen der Utrechtsche Universiteitsbibliotheek en de Moderne Reproductietechniek. 150-159, EVER

INCUNABULA - Collections - Yugoslavia

Badalić, Josip. Die Deutschen Offizinen in den Wiegendrucksammlungen Jugoslawiens. 31-37, SCHT

———— Inkunabelforschungen in Jugoslawien. 13-15, STUM

INCUNABULA - Cologne

Juchhoff, Rudolf. Die Universität Köln und die Frühen Typographen. 233-243, BENZ

INCUNABULA - Czechoslovakian - Collections - Prague

Volf, Josef. Jak Získalo Národní Museum Své České Prvotisky. 148-152, EMLE

INCUNABULA - Dutch

Vooys, C. G. N. de. Heeft de Utrechtse Kunstenaar Erhard Reeuwich ook Letterkundige Verdiensten? 284-288, EVER

INCUNABULA - Editions - Bibliography
see Editions - Bibliography - Incunabula

INCUNABULA, English

Bühler, Curt F. Variants in English Incunabula. 459-474, LYDE

INCUNABULA - Facsimiles

RUPP

Voulliéme, Ernst. Nachträge zu den Buchhändleranzeigen des 15. Jahrhunderts in Getreuen Nachbildungen Herausg. von K. Burger. 18-44, HAEB

———— Eine Neue Bücheranzeige des Anton Sorg in Augsburg. 43-47, LOUB

INCUNABULA - French - Bibl.

Le Gal, Simonne. La Bibliothèque des Dames au XVe Siècle, Vue par le Marquis de Paulmy. 55-63, CALO

INCUNABULA - German

Geissler, Paul. Ein Seltener Augsburger Wiegendruck. Das Älteste Gedruckte Buch über Altötting. 316-322, VORS

Oehme, Ruthardt. Die Palästinakarte aus Bernhard von Breidenbachs Reise in das Heilige Land 1486. 70-83, LEYH

Schmid, Helmut H. Ein Nürnberger Kalender von 1430 und Johann Blaubirer's Kalender von 1483. 247-253, STOL

Schmidt, Adolf. Lippische Ablaßbriefe. 227-233, SCHW

INCUNABULA - Germany - Hist.

Crous, Ernst. Die Anfänge des Antiquadrucks in Deutschland und Seinen Nachbarländern. 33-42, LOUB

INCUNABULA - Hague

Pennink, R. Petrarca, Teghen die Strael der Minnen. 71-85, HAGU

INCUNABULA - Hebrew

Marx, Moses. On the Date of Appearance of the First Printed Hebrew Books. 481-501, MARX

INCUNABULA - Hebrew - Bibl.

Freimann, A. Die Hebräischen Inkunabeln der Stadtbibliothek zu Frankfurt a.M. 129-144, EBRA

INCUNABULA - Hist. - Map

Teichl, Robert. Der Wiegendruck im Kartenbild. 805-806, VIEN

INCUNABULA - Latin

Geissler, Paul. Ein Unbekannter Reuchlin-Wiegendruck. 120-126, BENZ
Haebler, Konrad. Ramon Lull und Seine Schule. Aus Anlass einer Neu Erworbenen Inkunabel. 36-47, HARN
Scaccia-Scarafoni, Camillo. La Grammatica di Sulpizio Verolano in un Incunabulo Ignoto ai Bibliografi. 378-384, GREG

INCUNABULA - Latin - Bibl.

Delisle, Léopold. Notes sur les Anciennes Impressions des Classiques Latins et d'Autres Auteurs Conservées au XVe Siècle dans la Librairie Royale de Naples. 245-296, GRAU

INCUNABULA - Manuscript inserts

Geldner, Ferdinand. Handschriftliche Einträge in Wiegendrucken und Ihre Druckgeschichtliche Bedeutung. 127-131, BENZ

INCUNABULA - Münster

Crous, Ernst. Münster i.W. und der Wiegendruck. 107-121, HAEB

INCUNABULA - Music

Goff, Frederick R. Early Music Books in the Rare Books Division of the Library of Congress. 58-74, KINO
Springer, Hermann. Zur Musiktypographie in der Inkunabelzeit. 173-180, WILM

INCUNABULA - Music - Collections - Göttingen

Luther, Wilhelm Martin. Die Nichtliturgischen Musikinkunabeln der Göttinger Bibliothek. 130-148, TIEM

INCUNABULA - Prices - 15th cent.

Geldner, Ferdinand. Der Verkaufspreis des Günther Zainer'schen Catholicon von 1469 (GW 3183). 37-42, STOL
Zedler, Gottfried. Über die Preise und Auflagenhöhe Unserer Ältesten Drucke. 267-288, SCHW

INCUNABULA - Prices - 18th cent.

Schmidt, Adolf. Baron Hüpsch in Köln als Inkunabelnsammler und Händler. 45-63, HAEB

INCUNABULA - Strasbourg

Geissler, Paul. Ein Unbekannter Reuchlin-Wiegendruck. 120-126, BENZ

INCUNABULA - Union catalogs - Germany

Haebler, Konrad. Der Gesamtkatalog der Wiegendrucke. 278-284, HARN

INDEX BIBLIOGRAPHICUS

Donker Duyvis, Frits. Die Internationale Bedeutung des Index Bibliographicus. 45-49, VORS

INDEXES AND ABSTRACTS
see also Documentation - Indexes and abstracts; Periodicals - Indexes and abstracts

INDEXES AND ABSTRACTS
Amano, Keitarō. Sakuin ni tsuite. (On Indexes.) 142-147, KYOT
Kunze, Horst. Über das Registermachen. 18-34, BOCK

INDEXING

Langridge, Derek. Classification and Book-Indexing. 182-193, SAYW
Mills, J. Using Classification in Teaching Indexing. 279-286, KYLE
Takada, Sadakichi. Sakuin no Kōsatsu. (Consideration on Indexing.) 14-19, OTAT

INDEXING - Systems

Garde, R. K. Ranganathan's Contribution to Subject Cataloguing. 217-221, RANG
Neelameghan, A. Indexing Physical Chemical Properties of Antibiotic Substances. 248-254, RANG
Parkhi, G. R. Symbiosis between Classification and Catalogue. 222-227, RANG
Passi, N. N. Subject Indexing and Dr. Ranganathan. 228-238, RANG

INDIA AND PAKISTAN - Cooperation, International
see Cooperation, International - India and Pakistan

INDIA - Classification
see Classification - India

INDIA - Documentation - Standards
see Documentation - Standards - India

INDIA - Education for Librarianship
see Education for Librarianship - India

INDIA - Librarians - Memoirs, reminiscences, etc.
see Librarians - Memoirs, reminiscences, etc. - India

INDIA - Librarians - Status
see Librarians - Status - India

INDIA - Libraries
see Libraries - India

INDIA - Libraries - Administration
see Libraries - Administration - India

INDIA - Libraries and librarianship
see Libraries and librarianship - India

INDIA - Library schools
see Library schools - India

INDIA - Library science
see Library science - India

INDIAN STANDARDS INSTITUTION, Delhi. Documentation Sectional Committee

Kaul, Jainath and Gurcharan Singh. Dr. Ranganathan and Standards for Documentation. 271-278, RANG

INDIANS OF NORTH AMERICA - Portraits - Collections - New Haven, Conn.

Brown, Ruth. George Catlin's Portraits of North American Indians. 157-162, KEOG

INDIC MANUSCRIPTS
see Manuscripts, Indic

INDULGENCES - Collections - Detmold

Schmidt, Adolf. Lippische Ablaßbriefe. 227-233, SCHW

INDUSTRIAL LIBRARIES - Gt. Brit.

Colinese, P. E. The Education of Librarians and Information Officers: Industrial Information Departments. 305-311, HUTT

INDUSTRIAL LIBRARIES - Japan

Uemura, Chōzaburō. Sangyō Toshokan. (Industrial Libraries.) 1-13, OTAT

INDUSTRIAL LIBRARIES - Leverkusen

Stoetzer, Walter. Die Kekulé-Bibliothek als Hilfsmittel der Dokumentation in der Chemischen Industrie. 130-135, LEUN

INEXPENSIVE EDITIONS
see also Paperback books; Reprints

INEXPENSIVE EDITIONS

Hultin, Arvid. Sånger av Runeberg och Topelius i Vårt Skillingstryck. 9-24, SCHA
Räuber, Friedrich. Der Begriff des Antiquariats nach der Verkaufsordnung. 286-299, MILF

INEXPENSIVE EDITIONS - Denmark

Olsen, Lars M. Billigbogens Betydning og Udbredelse. 55-63, THOM

INFORMATION CENTERS
see Documentation centers

INFORMATION RETRIEVAL
see also Indexing - Systems

INFORMATION RETRIEVAL

Fairthorne, Robert A. Some Basic Comments on Retrieval Testing. 267-270, KYLE
Farradane, J., R. K. Poulton, and Mrs. S. Datta. Problems in Analysis and Terminology for Information Retrieval. 287-290, KYLE
Foskett, D. J. Language and Classification. 275-278, KYLE
Loosjes, Th. P. Documentanalyse. 521-526, BRUM

INFORMATION RETRIEVAL - Machines
see also Computers

INFORMATION RETRIEVAL - Machines

Coblans, Herbert. Some Thoughts on Machines. 279-282, RANG
Ferrari, Giorgio E. Fondamenti Attuali al Problema della Documentazione Umanistica. 403-425, GALL

INFORMATION RETRIEVAL - Monterey, Calif. (U.S. Naval)

Larson, Edgar R. Technical Reports Retrieval by Computer at the U.S. Naval Postgraduate School Library. 71-80, HASH

INFORMATION RETRIEVAL - Systems

Brownson, Helen L. Evaluation of Document Searching Systems and Procedures. 261-266, KYLE
Melton, Jessica. Compatibility of Two Information Systems, Colon Classification and Western Reserve University. 49-62, RANG

INFORMATION SERVICES
see also Reference services; Research and the library; Research materials; Special libraries

INFORMATION SERVICES

Bernhardt, Børge. Litt om Gjenfinning fra Brukersynspunkt. 174-182, TVET
Horner, G. W. The Answer?—That is the Question. 252-255, KYLE

INFORMATION SERVICES - Berlin

Gittig, Heinz. Das Auskunftsbüro der Deutschen Bibliotheken. I, 223-240, BERS

INFORMATION SERVICES - Germany

Rückert, Ernst. Die Auskunftserteilung, eine der Hauptaufgaben der Deutschen Bücherei. 274-285, VORS

INFORMATION SERVICES - Norway

Zachariassen, Aksel. Bibliotekene og Opplysningsorganisasjonene. 161-167, NORS

INGOBERT, calligrapher

Durrieu, Comte Paul. Ingobert: un Grand Calligraphe du IXe Siécle. 1-14, CHAT

INGRID OF SKENNINGE, Saint. Mss.

Jørgensen, Ellen. Et Brudstykke af den Hellige Ingrid af Skenninges Helgenproces. 71-73, COLL

Inguanez, Mauro.
A Hand-List of the Incunabula of the Royal Malta Library. 407-411, GREE

INITIALS

Harrsen, Meta. Figural Grisaille Ornament on a Historiated Initial of about 1400, and the Derivation of This Style from the Indulgences of Avignon. 316-322, LYDE

INJURIES TO BOOKS
see Books - Care and restoration

INNOCENZO A PRATO

Oberziner, Ludovico. La Libreria di un Patrizio Trentino del Secolo XVI. I, 371-412, HORT

INNSBRUCK. Archivio di Stato. Mss.

Galante, Andrea. L'Epistolario del Cardinale Cristoforo Madruzzo presso L'Archivio di Stato di Innsbruck. II, 787-805, HORT

INNSBRUCK - Art libraries and collections
see Art libraries and collections - Innsbruck

INNSBRUCK. Universität. Bibliothek

Hochenegg, Hans. Die Roschmannsche Kupferstichsammlung. 400-414, BICK

INSCRIPTIONS - Collections - Leipzig

Funke, Fritz. Originales Sammelgut im Deutschen Buch- und Schriftmuseum. 219-241, LEIZ

INSCRIPTIONS - Greek

Audollent, Aug. Bandeau de Plomb avec Inscription Trouvé à Haïdra (Tunisie). 545-556, CHAT
Lambros, Spyridion P. Notes Épigraphiques et Paléographiques. 621-628, GRAU
Wilhelm, Adolf. Inscriptiones Graecae I^{2} 945. 666-672, BICK

INSCRIPTIONS - Greek - Egypt

Robiou, Félix. De Quelques Monuments Gréco-Égyptiens du Louvre. 601-609, GRAU

INSCRIPTIONS - Greek - Halicarnassus

Comparetti, Dominique. Sur une Inscription d'Halicarnasse. 175-185, GRAU

INSCRIPTIONS - Indic - Hāthigumphā cave, India

Charpentier, Jarl. Die Hāthigumphā-Inschrift des Khāravela. 208-230, KARA

INSCRIPTIONS - Latin - Carthage

Mommsen, Théodore. Officialium et Militum Romanorum Sepulcretum Carthaginiense. 505-513, GRAU

INSCRIPTIONS - Latin - Kaysersberg, Ger.

Knörich, Gerhard. Detmar Mülhers Römische Inschriften vom Kaisberg. 1-6, VERD

INSCRIPTIONS - Latin - Moselle, France (Dept.)

Robert, Pierre-Charles. Inscriptions Laissés dans une Carrière de la Haute Moselle par des Légions Romaines. 329-340, GRAU

INSCRIPTIONS - Latin - Salamanca

Reyes, Enrique Sánchez. Lenguas de Piedra: Sobre los Enigmas del Claustro Universitario Salmantino. I, 261-295, ARTI

INSCRIPTIONS - Latin - Taranto

Thédenat, Henri. Sur une Inscription Inédite Conservée au Municipe de Tarante. 515-524, GRAU

INSCRIPTIONS, Library
see Library emblems, inscriptions, etc.

INSECT PESTS
see Books - Care and restoration

IN-SERVICE TRAINING
see also Education for librarianship

IN-SERVICE TRAINING - Denmark

Hansen, Robert L. Om Uddannelse af Bibliotekarer ved Folkebibliotekerne. 17-37, DØSS

IN-SERVICE TRAINING - Germany

Bieber, Hedwig. Die Öffentliche Bücherei als Ausbildungsstätte.

Erfahrungen und Anregungen. 75-87, LANF
Wallraf, Karlheinz. Zur Besprechungsarbeit mit Praktikanten. 113-123, LANF

IN-SERVICE TRAINING - Hamburg
Propach, Elisabeth. Die Ausbildung des Nachwuchses in Hamburg. 97-109, HAMB

IN-SERVICE TRAINING - Japan
Itakura, Yoshikazu. Suitōshu no Shido ni tsuite. (On the Training of Circulation-Desk Attendants.) 105-115, (part 1), OHAS

IN-SERVICE TRAINING - Kraków
Wisłocka, Stanisława. Szkolenie Zawodowe. 83-88, KRAK

INSPECTION OF PUBLIC LIBRARIES
see Public libraries - Standards

INSTITUTE LIBRARIES
see College and university libraries - Departmental and divisional libraries

INSTRUCTION IN LIBRARY USE - Kraków
Popiel, Jadwiga. Udział Pedagogicnej Biblioteki Wojewódzkiej w Realizacji Działu Programu Języka Polskiego: Podstawowe Wiadomości o Książce. 80-83, KRAK

INSTRUCTION IN LIBRARY USE - Teachers and administrators - U.S.
Henne, Frances and Mildred Hawksworth Lowell. The Preparation of Secondary-School Teachers in the Use of Library Materials. 533-556, WILS

INTELLECTUAL FREEDOM
see Censorship

INTELLIGENCE LIBRARY, Bad Oeynhausen, Ger.
see Germany (Territory under Allied occupation, 1945- British Zone) Control Commission. Intelligence Library

INTERLIBRARY LOANS
Bostwick, Arthur Elmore. Nomads. 97-102, PUTN

INTERLIBRARY LOANS - Aarhus, Denmark
Sejr, Emanuel. Benyttelse. 123-154, AARU

INTERLIBRARY LOANS - Berlin
Busch, Jürgen. Der Berliner Leihverkehr in den Jahren 1956-1958. 205-213, SCHS

INTERLIBRARY LOANS - Denmark
Gøtzsche, E. Folkebibliotekernes Laan fra de Videnskabelige og Faglige Biblioteker. 153-168, DØSS

INTERLIBRARY LOANS - Denmark - Hist.
Sejr, Emanuel. En Udlånsindskraenkning, Statsbibliotekets Krise 1912. 71-89, DAHA

INTERLIBRARY LOANS - Germany
Walter, Kurt. Zur Gegenwärtigen Lage des Auswärtigen Leihverkehrs der Wissenschaftlichen Bibliotheken. 143-157, JUCR

INTERLIBRARY LOANS - Göttingen
Weber, Hans-Oskar. Die Beanspruchung der Staats- und Universitätsbibliothek Göttingen durch den Deutschen Leihverkehr. 161-168, JUCR

INTERLIBRARY LOANS - Malmö, Sweden
Paulsson, Egon. Lånecentralen i Malmö. 548-551, HJEL

INTERLIBRARY LOANS - Scandinavia
Schauman, Henrik. Samarbetet Mellan de Nordiska Parlamentsbiblioteken. 232-237, TVET

INTERLIBRARY RELATIONSHIPS
see also Cooperation

INTERLIBRARY RELATIONSHIPS
Bourgeois, Pierre. Quelques Considérations sur les Bibliothèques Suisses dans la Vie Internationale. 73-80, SCHU

INTERLIBRARY RELATIONSHIPS - Denmark
Grundtvig, Vilh. Forbindelse med Andre Institutioner. 155-158, AARU

INTERNATIONAL AGENCIES
Breycha-Vauthier, Arthur C. de. Le Rôle des Publications Gouvernementales et des Publications d'Organisations Internationales. 7-14, GODE

INTERNATIONAL CATALOGING RULES
see Cataloging - Rules

INTERNATIONAL COOPERATION
see Cooperation, International

INTERNATIONAL COPYRIGHT
see Copyright, International

INTERNATIONAL EXCHANGE
see Exchange of books, periodicals, etc.

INTERNATIONAL FEDERATION FOR DOCUMENTATION

Michailov, A. I. Donker Duyvis' Contribution to the Progress of Scientific Information and Documentation. 30-38, DONR

Rajagopalan, T. S. India's Contribution to the International Federation for Documentation. 257-267, RANG

INTERNATIONAL FEDERATION FOR DOCUMENTATION - Decimal Classification

Walther, Carl and Karl Fill. Die Deutsche Gesamtausgabe der Dezimalklassifikation. 167-168, DONK

Wellisch, H. New Publication Methods for the UDC, a Proposal. 145-148, DONK

INTERNATIONAL FEDERATION OF LIBRARY ASSOCIATIONS

Breycha-Vauthier, Arthur C. de. La Collaboration Internationale des Bibliothèques dans la Fédération Internationale des Associations de Bibliothécaires. 7-11, EMLE

———— The Federation of Library Associations. A Study of the Mechanism of an International Organisation. 34-49, BISH

———— Marcel Godet Bibliothécaire "International." 27-30, GODM

Francis, Sir Frank. Dr. Hofmann, President of IFLA 1958-1963. 187-189, HOFM

Godet, Marcel. Monsieur William Warner Bishop et la Fédération Internationale des Associations de Bibliothécaires. 56-62, BISH

Hofmann, G. Pierre Bourgeois und die IFLA. 182-186, BOUR

Tyaganatarajan, T. Universal Cataloguing Code: Ifla's Initiative. 141-146, RANG

INTERNATIONAL INSTITUTE OF AGRICULTURE, Rome (City)

Frauendorfer, Sigmund von. Classification Problems in an International Special Library. 223-233, HANS

INTERNATIONAL LIBRARIES

Breycha-Vauthier, Arthur C. de. International Libraries and Their Problems. 102-107, MADR

———— Internationale Bibliotheken und Ihre Probleme. 20-21, STUM

———— Role of the United Nations Libraries in the World of Librarianship. 488-491, RANG

———— Vital Problems of International Libraries. 248-251, KYLE

Landheer, B. De Bibliotheek van de Verenigde Naties en Andere Internationale Bibliotheken. 505-513, BRUM

INTERNATIONALER VERBAND DER BIBLIOTHEKAR-VEREINE
see International Federation of Library Associations

INVENTORIES OF BOOKS

Battisti, Carlo. Registro d'Ingresso e Inventario Topografico. 56-80, GORI

INVENTORIES OF BOOKS - Berlin - 1939

Krieg, Werner. Die Revision der Preussischen Staatsbibliothek im Sommer 1939. 404-421, JUCH

INVENTORIES OF ESTATES - Örebro, Sweden, 17th cent.

Berg, Gösta and Kurt Johnson. Bouppteckningar från Borgarhem i Stormaktstidens Örebro 186-240, ÖREB

IRISH MANUSCRIPTS
see Manuscripts - Irish

Irtenkauf, Wolfgang.
Zur Liturgischen Seite des Eberhardgebetbuches. 189-203, HOFF

ISAAC BEN SECHARJAH

Italiener, Bruno. Isak B. Secharjah, ein Jüdischer Lederschnittkünstler des 15. Jahrhunderts. 159-161, FREN

Isaac, K. A.
My Ideal College Library. 139-144, MADR

ISELIN, BASILIUS

Roth, Carl. Conrad Pfister, Basilius Iselin und die Amerbachische Bibliothek. 179-200, BINZ

ISELIN, JACOB CHRISTOPH

Godet, Marcel. Au Temps de la "Respublica Litterarum." Jacob Christophe Iselin et Louis Bourguet. 117-127, SCHU

Ishii, Atsushi.
Shoki ni okeru Paionia no Katsuyaku—Wagakuni Junkai Bunko no Taihaika no Rekishi, I. (Activities of the Pioneers in the Early Period—a History of Circulating Libraries in Japan, I.) 34-49, TOKY

Ishii, Munetsugu.
Ohashi Toshokan ni Kisō Seraretaru Nidai Seijika no Iaisho ni tsuite. (On the Collections Prized by the Late Two Statesmen Which Were Donated to the Ōhashi Library.) 90-104, (part 1), OHAS

Tsuboya Sensei to Toshokan Jigyō. (Mr. Tsuboya and His Library Activities.) 73-82, TSUB

Ishizu, Teruzi.
Tenri Toshokan Zō Kierukegoru Zencho-saku no Shohanbon. (The First Editions of all Kierkegaard's Works in the Tenri Central Library.) 477-484, TOMI

ISIDORUS, SAINT, Bp. of Seville. Mss.
Holder, Alfred. Der Isidorus-Codex Augiensis LVII der Gr. Hof- und Landesbibliothek in Karlsruhe. 634-643, CHAT
Macé, Alcide. Le Basiliensis F III 15a (VIIIe Siècle). 383-395, CHAT

ISNY, Württemberg. Heilig-Geist-Spital. Urbar
Klauser, Renate. Ein Beutelbuch aus Isny. 139-145, WEHM

ISNY, Württemberg. Nikolauskirche. Bibliothek
Klauser, Renate. Ein Beutelbuch aus Isny. 139-145, WEHM

ISOCRATES. Ms. Ad Nicoclem
Schoene, Alfred. De Isocratis Papyro Massiliensi (Isocr. or. II ad Nicoclem, paragr. 1-30). 481-504, GRAU

ISOM, MARY FRANCES
ISOM

Isono, Kōzaburo.
Jimu Kokorooboe Issoku. (Memoranda on Library Works.) 74-78, (part 1), OHAS

ISRAEL BEN ABRAHAM
see Abinu, Israel ben Abraham

ISRAEL GER
see Abinu, Israel ben Abraham

ISTANBUL. Bibliothèque du Métogne du Saint-Sépulcre au Phanar. Mss. (no. 462)
Psichari, Jean. L'Arbre Chantant. 628-633, CHAT

ISTANBUL. Library
Guilland, R. La Basilique, la Bibliothèque et L'Octogone de Byzance. 97-107, BONN

ISTANBUL - Printing
see Printing - Istanbul

ISTITUTO DI ARCHEOLOGIA E STORIA DELL'ARTE. Biblioteca
Olivieri-Sangiacomo, Laura. La Nuova Sistemazione della Biblioteca di Archeologia e Storia dell'Arte (Problemi di una Moderna Biblioteca Specializzata). 333-346, GREG

Itakura, Yoshikazu.
Suitōshu no Shido ni tsuite. (On the Training of Circulation-Desk Attendants.) 105-115, (part 1), OHAS

ITALIAN FOLK LITERATURE
see Folk literature, Italian

ITALIAN LITERATURE - Collections - Bern
Wissler, Gustav. Pubblicazioni in Lingua Italiana. 59-64, BERU

ITALIAN POETRY - Collections - Berlin
Christ, Karl. Ältere Drucke Volkstümlicher Italienischer Dichtung in der Preussischen Staatsbibliothek. 61-69, HARN

ITALIAN STATUTES
see Statutes, Italian

ITALICS
Wagner, R. L. Les Valeurs de L'Italique. Notes de Lecture sur Lucien Leurven de Stendhal. 381-390, BONN

Italiener, Bruno.
Isak B. Secharjah, ein Jüdischer Lederschnittkünstler des 15. Jahrhunderts. 159-161, FREN

ITALY - Architecture and building - Maintenance
see Architecture and building - Maintenance - Italy

ITALY - Archives
see Archives - Italy

ITALY - Archives, Church
see Archives, Church - Italy

ITALY. Archivio di Stato, Naples
see Naples. Archivio di Stato.

ITALY. Biblioteca Nazionale, Naples
see Naples. Biblioteca Nazionale

ITALY - Book illustration
see Book illustration - Italy

ITALY - Book industry and trade
see Book industry and trade - Italy

ITALY - Bookbinding
see Bookbinding - Italy

ITALY - Legal deposit (of books, etc.)
see Legal deposit (of books, etc.) - Italy

ITALY - Libraries
see Libraries - Italy

ITALY - Library legislation
see Library legislation - Italy

ITALY - Manuscripts
see Manuscripts - Italy

ITALY - Monastic libraries
see Monastic libraries - Italy

ITALY - Music printing
see Music printing - Italy

ITALY - National libraries
see National libraries - Italy

ITALY - Printing
see Printing - Italy

ITALY - Private libraries
see Private libraries - Italy

ITALY - Termite damage
see Termite damage - Italy

ITALY - War and the library
see War and the library - Italy

Iuchi, Ryūzō.
Kyoto no Gakko Toshokan Junen no Ayumi. (Ten Years of School Libraries in Kyoto.) 153-167, KYOT

Ivanchev, Dimitŭr P.
Po Vŭprosa za Otbora na Materiala v Obshchata Natsionalna Bibliografiia. 171-182, MIKH
Pouki ot Stogodishninata na Bulgarskiia Periodichen Pechat. 298-303, MIKN

Ivanchev, Dimitŭr P. and Stefan Stanchev.
Bibliografiia na Statiite v Bulgarskiia Periodichen Pechat s Ogled na Praktikata na "Bulgarski Knigopis" za 1930 i 1931 g. 404-408, MIKN

Ivanchev, Dimitŭr P., jt. author
Bozhinova, Bozhana and Dimitŭr P. Ivanchev. Opit za Razgranichavane Poniatiiata "Spisanie" i "Vestnik"; Doklad. 411-417, MIKN

Ivanov, D. D.
Professor T. Borov i Ego Trudy po Bibliotekovedeniiu i Bibliografii. 13-19, BORO

IVANOV, IURDAN
Neikov, Stoian. IUrdan Ivanov. 281-297, MIKN

Ivey, D. L.
An Ex-Sapling's View of Salisbury. 29-31, VARL

IVREA, Italy. Biblioteca Capitolare
Borghezio, Gino. Inventarii e Notizie della Biblioteca Capitolare d'Ivrea nel Secolo XV. 423-454, EHRE

IVREA, Italy - Catholic libraries
see Catholic libraries - Ivrea, Italy

IVREA, Italy - Church libraries
see Church libraries - Ivrea, Italy

Iwamura, Shinobu.
Tenri Toshokan Zō Shigen Tsukoho Sho. (On the Bank Note of the Chin-yüan Era in the Yüan Dynasty in the Tenri Central Library.) 339-343, TOMI

Iwand, Käthe.
Der Zentralkatalog der Ausländischen Literatur. 369-376, JUCH

Iwasaru, Toshio.
Toshokangaku ni okeru Hikakuhō ni tsuite. (Comparative Method in Library Science.) 1-6, KYOT

J. F. VAN SOMEREN, 1889-1914. 1-3, SOME

J. P.
Más Datos Sobre el Nombramiento de Menéndez Pelayo como Director de la Biblioteca Nacional. 69-72, MENE

Jackson, William A.
Notes on English "Publishers' Bindings" of the Sixteenth and Seventeenth Centuries. 483-488, LYDE
Tunc et Nunc: or the Pepys and Taylor Collections of Early English Books on Navigation. 195-201, WROT

Jacob, Alfred.
Le Classement des Manuscrits de Diodore de Sicile. 525-531, GRAU
La Miniscule Grecque Penchée et L'Âge du Parisinus Grec 1741. 52-56, CHAT
Notes sur les Manuscrits Grecs Palimpsestes de la Bibliothèque Nationale. 759-770, HAVE

JACOB, LOUIS, in religion Louis de Saint-Charles
Malclès, Louise-Noëlle. Le Fondateur de la Bibliographie Nationale en France: le R. P. Louis Jacob de Saint-Charles. 243-255, CALO

Jacobs, Emil.
Ars Scripturarum. 177-186, MILF
Büchergeschenke für Sultan Mehemmed II. 20-26, LEYG
Zur Kenntnis Maugérards. 64-73, HAEB

JACOBS, EMIL
Leyh, Georg. August Wilmanns und Emil Jacobs. 125-136, STOL

Jacobsen, Karl T.
The Reorganization of the Library of a Small College. 234-243, HANS

Jacobsen, R.
La Cité des Livres. 59-68, KOSS

Jacot, L. Réminiscences Typographiques. 152-155, LÜTH

Jaeger, Friedrich.
Das Mehrjahres-Verzeichnis der Zeitschriften. 73-75, FRAD
Die Zeitschriftenverzeichnisse der Deutschen Bibliothek. 117-135, EPPE

JAFFE, MEIR, bookbinder

Husung, Max Joseph. Dreimal das Gleiche Lederschnittmotiv. 123-126, LEID

JAGIELLONIAN UNIVERSITY
see Kraków. Jagiellonian University

Jahier, Enrico.
Note di Tecnica e Specializzazione Bibliotecaria. 209-214, GREG

JAHRESVERZEICHNIS DER DEUTSCHEN HOCHSCHULSCHRIFTEN

Franz, Rudi. Die Titeldrucke der Deutschen Bücherei. 157-173, LEIZ

Jahrmann, Werner, jt. ed.
SCHS

Jahrmann, Werner.
Bücherei und Schule. Gedanken zur Jugendbüchereiarbeit. 215-231, SCHS

Jallut, Marguerite.
Les Bibliothèques de Marie-Antoinette. 325-332, CALO

James, M. R.
A Graeco-Latin Lexicon of the Thirteenth Century. 396-411, CHAT

Jammers, Ewald.
Neumen im Lateinunterricht. 64-68, BOLE
Die Salemer Handschriftensammlung. 45-64, WEHM
Zur Entwicklung der Neumenschrift im Karolingerreich. I, 89-98, GLAU

JAMMES, FRANCIS. Lettres

Ibrovac, Miodrag. Francis Jammes en Yougoslavie. 439-448, BONN

JAN Z SĄCZA
see Sandecki, Jan

JANET DOE: PORTRAIT, BIOGRAPHICAL SKETCH, BIBLIOGRAPHY. 280-284, DOEJ

JANSSONIUS VAN WAESBERGHE, firm
see Waesberghe, Janssonius van, firm

JAPAN - Agricultural libraries
see Agricultural libraries - Japan

JAPAN - Block-books
see Block-books - Japan

JAPAN- Book numbers
see Book numbers - Japan

JAPAN - Book selection - Standards
see Book selection - Standards - Japan

JAPAN - Buddhist libraries
see Buddhist libraries - Japan

JAPAN - Bulletin boards
see Bulletin boards - Japan

JAPAN - Calligraphy
see Calligraphy - Japan

JAPAN - Cataloging
see Cataloging - Japan

JAPAN - Cataloging, Simplified
see Cataloging, Simplified - Japan

JAPAN - Catalogs
see Catalogs - Japan

JAPAN - Catalogs - Printed book
see Catalogs - Printed book - Japan

JAPAN - Children's literature
see Children's literature - Japan

JAPAN - Circulation procedures
see Circulation procedures - Japan

JAPAN - Classification
see Classification - Japan

JAPAN - Education for librarianship
see Education for librarianship - Japan

JAPAN - Fines, fees, etc.
see Fines, fees, etc. - Japan

JAPAN - Foreign language books - Cataloging
see Foreign language books - Cataloging - Japan

JAPAN - Industrial libraries
see Industrial libraries - Japan

JAPAN - In-service training
see In-service training - Japan

JAPAN - Libraries
see Libraries - Japan

JAPAN - Library and the public
see Library and the public - Japan

JAPAN - Library legislation
see Library legislation - Japan

JAPAN - Library publications
see Library publications - Japan

JAPAN - Library schools
see Library schools - Japan

JAPAN LIBRARY SCHOOL, Tokyo. Keio University
see Tokyo. Keio University. Japan Library School

JAPAN - Library science literature
see Library science literature - Japan

JAPAN - National libraries
see National libraries - Japan

JAPAN - Printing
see Printing - Japan

JAPAN - Private libraries
see Private libraries - Japan

JAPAN - Publishers and publishing
see Publishers and publishing - Japan

JAPAN - Rental libraries
see Rental libraries - Japan

JAPAN - Rules and regulations
see Rules and regulations - Japan

JAPAN - School libraries
see School libraries - Japan

JAPAN - School libraries - Cataloging
see School libraries - Cataloging - Japan

JAPAN - School libraries (High School) - Guidance activities
see School libraries (High School) - Guidance activities - Japan

JAPAN - Technical services
see Technical services - Japan

JAPANESE LITERATURE - Cataloging
see Oriental literature - Cataloging

JAPANESE LITERATURE - Collections - Helsinki

Mustonen, Aarne. Kaukoidän Kirjatietoa. 66-77, NYBE

JAPANISCHES PALAIS, Dresden
see Dresden. Japanisches Palais

Jarosik, Emilia.
Praca Pedagogicznych Bibliotek Powiatowych a Reforma Oświaty i Wychowania. 97-99, KRAK

Jasińska, Stanisława.
Czy Jan z Sącza Mógł Być Drukarzem Poznańskim? 341-353, GRYC

Jatzwauk, Jacob.
Kurzer Abriss einer Geschichte der Sächsischen Bibliographie. 38-48, BOLL

Jegel, August.
Altnürnberger Zensur, vor Allem des 16. Jahrhunderts. 55-64, STOL

JENA - Bookbinders
see Bookbinders - Jena

JENA - Catalogs - Printed book
see Catalogs - Printed book - Jena

JENA - Catalogs - Subject
see Catalogs - Subject - Jena

JENA - Children's library services
see Children's library services - Jena

JENA. Ernst-Abbe Bücherei und Lesehalle

JENA

JENA - Goethe, Johann Wolfgang von. Mss. - Collections
see Goethe, Johann Wolfgang von. Mss. - Collections - Jena

JENA. Herzogliche Bibliothek
see Jena. Universität. Bibliothek

JENA. Herzogliche Schlossbibliothek
see Jena. Universität. Bibliothek

JENA - Public libraries
see Public libraries - Jena

JENA - Public libraries - Aims and objectives
see Public libraries - Aims and objectives - Jena

JENA - Public libraries - Services to colleges and universities
see Public libraries - Services to colleges and universities - Jena

JENA - Public libraries - Statistics
see Public libraries - Statistics - Jena

JENA - Technical literature - Collections
see Technical literature - Collections - Jena

JENA. Thüringer Zentralkatalog

Pomassl, Gerhard. Zehn Jahre Thüringer Zentralkatalog. 87-102, BULL

JENA. Universität. Bibliothek

JENA

Bulling, Karl. Zur Jenaer Tätigkeit des Weimarer Bibliothekars Christian August Vulpius während der Jahre 1802-1817. 102-116, WEIM
Paszkowski, Wilhelm. Goethes Verhältnis zum Bibliothekswesen. 159-172, WILM

Ronneberger, Werner. Die Schlossbibliothek zu Jena. II, 64-72, GLAU
Stössel, Waldemar. Ernst-Abbe-Bücherei und Universitätsbibliothek Jena. 118-119, JENA

JENA. Universität. Bibliothek - Hist.
Bulling, Karl. Aus der Jenaer Bibliothekarischen Tätigkeit Johann Samuel Erschs. Ein Beitrag zu Goethes Plan eines Gesamtkatalogs der Weimarischen Bibliotheken. 296-315, VORS

JENA. Universität. Bibliothek - Hist. - 1945-46
Burr, Viktor. Aus dem Ersten Jahr nach der Zerstörung der Universitätsbibliothek Jena (1945/46). 63-81, BULL

JENA. Universität. Bibliothek. Mss. (Goethe)
Karpe, Georg. Handschriften von Johann Wolfgang Goethe im Autographenbestand der Universitätsbibliothek Jena. 189-197, BULL

JENA. Universität. Bibliothek. Mss. (Scherer)
Feyl, Othmar. Aus der Jenaer Aufklärung. 179-188, BULL

JENA. Universität. Bibliothek. Technisch-Wissenschaftliche Auskunftsstelle
Stein, Ernst. Die Herstellung von Fachbibliographien, Dargestellt an einem Beispiel aus der Arbeit der Technisch-Wissenschaftlichen Auskunftsstelle der Universitätsbibliothek Jena an der Bibliographischen Erfassung der Internationalen Laser-Literatur. 117-129, BULL

JENA - War and the library
see War and the library - Jena

JENA - Young adults' library services
see Young adults' library services - Jena

Jenkins, Frances B.
Medical Reference Sources—A Backward Glance. 361-370, DOEJ

Jenkinson, Hilary.
Archive Developments in England 1925-1950. 337-361, MERC

Jensen, Erik Allerslev, ed.
LASS

Jensen, Erik Allerslev.
Engelsk Oplandsarbejde. 123-134, LASS
Forudsaetningerne for en Ny Dansk Bibliotekslov. 13-22, HEIN

Jensen, Wilhelm.
Die Anfänge der Evangelischen Pfarrbibliothek im Niederdeutschen Raum. 63-68, SCHV

Jepsen, Hans Lyngby.
Biblioteksafgiften—Vederlag for Hvad og Hvordan? 87-94, THOM

JEROME, SAINT
see Hieronymus, Saint

JERUSALEM. Jewish National and University Library
Wormann, C. The Jewish National and University Library in Jerusalem since the Establishment of the State of Israel. 116-117, MADR

JERUSALEM - National libraries
see National libraries - Jerusalem

Jessen, Hans.
Aus der Werkstatt des Gesamtkatalogs der Deutschen Presse. 363-368, JUCH

Jessen, Peter.
Der Mann. 1-2, LOUB

JESUIT LIBRARIES
see Catholic libraries

JESUIT LITERATURE
see Catholic literature

JESUITS - Education - Collections - Leipzig
Kern, Anton. Die Promotionsschriften der Jesuitenuniversitäten in der Zeit des Barocks. Eine Bibliothekarische Studie. 38-47, SCHT

JEWISH BOOK ORNAMENTATION
see Book ornamentation - Jewish

JEWISH COPYISTS
see Copyists, Jewish

JEWISH ILLUSTRATORS
see Illustrators, Jewish

JEWISH LIBRARIES AND COLLECTIONS - Leghorn
Bernheimer, Carlo. The Library of the Talmud Torah at Leghorn. 1-4, FREI

JEWISH LITERATURE - Classification
see Classification - Special subjects - Jewish literature

JEWISH NATIONAL AND UNIVERSITY LIBRARY, Jerusalem
see Jerusalem. Jewish National and University Library

JEWISH PRINTERS
see Printers, Jewish

JEWISH THEOLOGICAL SEMINARY OF AMERICA. Library. Mss.

Davidson, Israel. A Collection of Letters from Sages of Israel only Found in the Jewish Theological Seminary. 1-14, (Hebrew section), FREI
Marx, Alexander. The Polemical Manuscripts in the Library of the Jewish Theological Seminary of America. 247-278, FREI

JEWISH THEOLOGICAL SEMINARY OF AMERICA. Library. Mss. (Adler no. 726)

Schwartz, Benjamin. A Judaeo-Greek Lament. 107-114, BLOC

JEWS - Book collecting
see Book collecting - Jews

JEWS - Printing
see Printing - Jews

JIREČEK, KONSTANTIN. Knigopis na Novobŭlgarskata Knizhnina

Nikolaev, N. N. "Bŭlgarski Knigopis" na K. Irechek. (Po Sluchaĭ Sto Godini ot Rozhdenieto na Irechek.) 98-112, TEOB

JOACHIM FRIEDRICH, Elector of Brandenburg - Library

Joost, Siegfried. Bibliotheca Joachimica. Werden und Vergehen einer Deutschen Schulbibliothek. 233-256, WEHM

Joachim, Johannes.
Aus Briefen Christian Gottlob Heynes an Friedrich August Carus. 187-208, MILF

JOACHIMSTHAL, Ger. Joachimsthalisches Gymnasium
see Templin, Ger. Joachimsthalisches Gymnasium

JOACHIMSTHALISCHES GYMNASIUM, Templin, Ger.
see Templin, Ger. Joachimsthalisches Gymnasium

Jobst, Rudolf.
Einleitende Bemerkungen: Ernst Abbe, die Carl-Zeiss-Stiftung und die "Jenaer Lesehalle." 11-16, JENA

Joeckel, Carleton B.
Design for a Regional Library Service Unit. 571-582, WILS

Joerden, Rudolf.
Einige Richtlinien für die Aufbauplanung im Großstädtischen Büchereiwesen. 19-25, ACKR
Die Entwicklung der Bücherhallen seit 1945. 9-24, HAMB
Gefährdetenpädagogik und Volksbücherei. 55-64, ACKE

Jörgensen, Arne.
Anteckningar om Universitetsbiblioteket under Första Året efter Åbo Brand. 17-42, HULA
Ett Bidrag till Swedenborgs Bibliografi. 105-107, SCHA
En Birgitta-handskrift i Helsingfors Universitetsbibliotek. 19-68, HULT

Jørgensen, Carl Th.
HORS

Jørgensen, Ellen.
Et Brudstykke af den Hellige Ingrid af Skenninges Helgenproces. 71-73, COLL

JOHANN VON BERSEN - Library

Molitor, Karl. Ein Westfälischer Bibliotheks-Katalog von 1353. 301-314, MÜNS

JOHANN VON PADERBORN

Juchhoff, Rudolf. Johann und Konrad von Paderborn. Die Anfänge Ihrer Druckertätigkeit in Venedig und Strassburg. 211-227, BÖME

JOHANN VON PADERBORN, printer

Juchhoff, Rudolf. Verwertung einer Restauflage um 1500. 478-481, BRUM

JOHANNA VON BOCHOLT
see Bocholt, Johanna von

JOHANNES AFFLIGEMENSIS. Mss. De Musica

Hörmann, Wolfgang. Probleme einer Aldersbacher Handschrift (Clm. 2599). 335-389, HOFM

JOHANNES BRACLENSIS

Herbst, Hermann. Johannes von Brakel. Ein Beitrag zur Bibliotheksgeschichte des Benediktinerklosters Klus bei Gandersheim. 31-46, SCHR

JOHANNES DE BRACLIS
see Johannes Braclensis

JOHANNES GOBIUS
see Gobius, Johannes

JOHANNES OF WESTPHALIA
see Johann von Paderborn

JOHANNESBURG. Public Library,
KENN

Johansson, Cari.
Carl Frederic Fredenheim and His Collection of Eighteenth-Century Music. 46-49, FEDO

Johansson, Herbert.
Biblar och Andra Böcker i Kyrkor Inom Växjö Stift 1650-85. 207-220, OLSS

Johansson, J. Viktor.
Göteborgs Stadsbibliotek Handskrifts-samling. En Översikt. 1-99, (seventh paper), GÖTE

JOHN CARTER BROWN LIBRARY, Brown University
see Brown University. John Carter Library

JOHN JACOB ASTOR LIBRARY, New York
see Astor Library, New York

JOHN RYLANDS LIBRARY, Manchester, Eng. Mss. (Coptic)

Till, Walter. Die Nicht-Katalogisierten Coptica der John Rylands Library. 89-90, STUM

Johnson, Alfred F.
Notes on Some German Types Used in the Reformation Period. 226-232, BENZ

Johnson, Allen.
The Library of Congress: A Depository of American Biography. 224-225, PUTN

Johnson, Margaret L.
American Imprints and Their Donors in the Yale College Library of 1742. 355-371, KEOG

THE JOINT UNIVERSITY LIBRARIES IN PRINT. 22-23, NASH

Jolowicz, J.
Die Polnische Bibliographie in Ihrer Entwicklung und Ihrem Gegenwärtigen Stande. 75-88, VERP

Jonas, Franz.
Zum Geleit. 5, VIES

Jonas, Oswald.
Musikalische Meisterhandschriften. 103-109, HOBO

Jones, Helen Dudenbostel.
Writings and Addresses of Herbert Putnam and Books and Articles about Him. 53-80, PUTP

Jonson, Kurt, jt. author

Berg, Gösta and Kurt Jonson. Bouppteckningar från Borgarhem i Stormaktstidens Örebro. 186-240, ÖREB

Joost, Siegfried, ed.
WEHM

Joost, Siegfried.
Bibliotheca Joachimica. Werden und Vergehen einer Deutschen Schulbibliothek. 233-256, WEHM

Jordan, Alice M.
Magazines for Children. 599-604, MOOR

Jordan, Mildred.
Events in the Development of Education for Medical Librarianship in the Last Decade. 351-360, DOEJ

JORDAN, PASCUAL. <u>Verdrängung und Komplementarität</u>

Sommerfeld, Arnold. Zu Pascual Jordans "Verdrängung und Komplementarität." 128, HELD

<u>JŌRURI</u> TEXTS - Collections - Tenri, Japan

Yuda, Yoshio, Hajime Uetani, and Minoru Imanishi. Tenri Toshokan Zō Jōruri Hangi Mokuroku. (Catalogue of the Wood-Blocks of <u>Jōruri</u> Texts in the Tenri Central Library.) 259-294, TOMI

JOSEPHUS, FLAVIUS Mss. <u>Antiquitates Judaicae</u>

Boysen, Karl. Die Handschriftliche Überlieferung der Lateinischen Josephus-Übersetzung in der Ersten Hälfte der Antiquitates Judaicae. 277-292, WILM

Josserand, Pierre.
L'Œuvre de Julien Cain au Département des Imprimés. 60-64, CAIN

Josserand, Pierre and Jean Bruno.
Les Estampilles du Département des Imprimés de la Bibliothèque Nationale. 261-298, CALO

<u>JOSUAROLLE</u>

Lietzmann, Hans. Zur Datierung der Josuarolle. 181-185, DEGE

Juchhoff, Rudolf.
Aus der Werkstatt der Frühdruckforschung. 119-129, TIEM
Die Büchersammlung des Generalpostmeisters von Nagler in der Preußischen Staatsbibliothek. 201-208, KUHN
Johann und Konrad von Paderborn. Die Anfänge Ihrer Druckertätigkeit in Venedig und Strassburg. 211-227, BÖME
Die Literarische Fälschung des Thomas J. Wise. 41-48, BRIE
Die Universität Köln und die Frühen Typographen. 233-243, BENZ

Verwertung einer Restauflage um 1500. 478-481, BRUM
Ziel und Wege Bibliothekarischer Bildung. 34-48, LANF

JUCHHOFF, RUDOLF
JUCH
JUCR
Krieg, Werner. [Introduction.] 7-9, JUCH

JUCHHOFF, RUDOLF - Bibl.
Drawert, Ernst Arno. Schriftenverzeichnis Rudolf Juchhoff 1923-1954. 221-227, JUCR
———— Verzeichnis der Schriften von Rudolf Juchhoff, 1923-1960. 471-478, JUCH

Jürgens, Adolf.
Die Skandinavischen Studien und die Bibliotheken in Deutschland im Letzten Menschenalter. 97-127, MUNT
Der Suchdienst der Reichstauschstelle. I, 105-111, GLAU

JUGOSLAVIA
see Yugoslavia

JULIANUS, SAINT, Bp. of Toledo. Ars Grammatica.
Beeson, Charles H. The Ars Grammatica of Julian of Toledo. 50-70, EHRA

JULIUS AFRICANUS
see Africanus, Sextus Julius

JUNIOR COLLEGE STUDENTS' READING
see Reading - Special groups of readers - Junior college students

Juntke, Fritz.
Georg Rumler, ein Hallischer Buchbinder aus der Zweiten Hälfte des 16. Jahrhunderts. 201-224, HAEK
Die Öffentlichen Bibliotheken in Königsberg in Preussen im 17. Jahrhundert. 288-293, KUHN
Das Reglement für die Bibliothek der Universität zu Halle vom 20. Mai 1823. 323-342, VORS

Jusselin, Maurice.
La Garde et L'Usage du Sceau dans les Chancelleries Carolingiennes d'après les Notes Tironiennes. 35-41, CHAT

Kabát, Karel.
Typologické Badání. 115-117, EMLE

Kabutogi, Shokyo.
Heian Jidai no Kaihan. (Buddhist Sutras Printed during the Heian Period, 11th-13th Centuries.) 35-43, TOMI

Kachler, Karl G.
Die Schweizerische Theatersammlung. 125, BERU

Kaegbein, Paul.
Hermann Neuberts Schriften. 9-15, NEUB
Veröffentlichungen von Joris Vorstius 1917-1953. 1-16, VORS

KAERNTEN
see Carinthia

Kästner, Erhart.
Über das Bibliothekarische Mißvergnügen und noch ein Zweiter Traktat. 295-302, WEHM

Kahl, Willi.
Musikhandschriften aus dem Nachlass Ernst Bückens in der Kölner Universitäts- und Stadtbibliothek. 159-171, JUCH

KAISBERG
see Kaysersberg

Kaiser, Rudolf.
Der Alphabetische Zettelkatalog. 99-109, HARN
Die Behandlung der Ungarica im Preußischen Gesamtkatalog. 217-223, KUHN
Zur Unterscheidung Anscheinend Identischer Drucke. 127-129, SCHW

KAISER-WILHELM-BIBLIOTHEK, Posen
see Posen. Kaiser-Wilhelm-Bibliothek

KAISHEIM (Cistercian abbey) Biblioteca. Mss.
Stange, Alfred. Beiträge zur Kaisheimer Buchmalerei. 277-281, LEID

Kaliba, Hans.
Gesellschaft und Kultur im Spiegel der Zeitung. Eine Dokumentationsstelle der Stadtbibliothek. 154-165, VIES

KALUNDBORG, Denmark. Bibliotek
KALU

KALUNDBORG, Denmark. Bibliotek
Haugstrup, S. Kalundborg Bibliotek 1920-1926. 22-36, KALU
Møller, J. S. Kalundborg Folkebogsamling 1901-1920. 5-21, KALU

KALUNDBORG, Denmark - Public libraries - Centralization
see Public libraries - Centralization - Kalundborg, Denmark

KALUNDBORG, Denmark - Public libraries - Finances
see Public libraries - Finances - Kalundborg, Denmark

Kammel, Karl.
Dr. Ernst Trenkler, Oberstaatsbibliothekar, Direktor der Druckschriftensammlung der Österreichischen Nationalbibliothek. 11-12, STUM
Die Prüfungen des Wissenschaftlichen Bibliotheksdienstes in Österreich. 423-428, BICK

Kamo, Hiroshi.
Gakko Toshokan Yo Kemmei Hyomoku Hyo. (Subject Headings for School Library.) 206-217, KYOT

Kanai, Toranosuke.
Saikaku Okimiyage no Hanshita. (Study of the Calligraphy of the Wood-Blocks of Saikaku's Okimiyage.) 97-112, TOMI

KANAZAWA BUNKO
Haenisch, Wolf. Die Kanazawa Bunko, eine Japanische Bibliotheksgründung des 13. Jahrhunderts. 271-280, JUCH

Kanda, Kiichiro.
Chugoku no Meika no Te ni Natta Shakokubon. (Chinese Books Printed from Wood-Blocks Written by Noted Calligraphers.) 367-373, TOMI

Kandler, Gottfried.
Verbesserung der Archive bei Verminderung Ihrer Bestände. 69-81, SCHV

Kaneko, Kazumasa.
Kintei Bueiden Shuchin-ban Teishiki. (Japanese translation of: Ching-tin Wu-ying-tien chü-ch'en-pan Ch'eng-shih: "Brief Explanation of the Printing Process by Movable Types in the Wu-ying-tien Editions.") 409-434, TOMI

Kaneko, Kazumasa, jt. author
Kumura, Miyogo and Kazumasa Kaneko. Chokuhan Ko, 1, Kobun Kokyo 1. (Study of the Chokuhan, or the Imperial Editions, 16th Century, Part 1, Kobun Kokyo 1.) 61-86, TOMI

Kannila, Helle.
Två Pionjärer för Folkbiblioteksidén i Finland. 137-147, HEIN

KANSAI BUNKO KYŌKAI
Takebayashi, Kumahiko. Kansai Bunko Kyōkai, Sono Rekishiteki Igi. (Kansai Bunko Kyōkai, Its Historical Significance.) 37-52, KYOT

Kapelrud, Arvid S.
Et Fønikisk Bibliotek fra det 14. Århundre før Kr. 77-83, TVET

KARABACEK, JOSEF Ritter von
KARA

Doublier, Othmar. Ein Vierteljahrhundert aus der Geschichte der Hofbibliothek 1891-1916. 163-210, VIEN
Klos, Herbert. Papyrologen-Bibliothekare. 51-53, STUM

Karanova, L.
Mi͡astoto na Drebnite Izdanii͡a v Bibliotekite. 408-411, MIKN

KARL LUDWIG, Elector Palatine
Sillib, Rudolf. Ein Nachkömmling der Heidelberger Hofbuchbinderei des Kurfürsten Karl Ludwig von der Pfalz. 249-251, LEID

KARL THEODOR, Abp. and Elector of Mainz. Mss. Brief
Mühl, Werner. Ein Brief von C. Th. Dalberg. 129-135, MAIZ

KARLSRUHE. Badische Landesbibliothek
Schmitt, Franz Anselm. Der Stand der Handschriften-Katalogisierung bei der Badischen Landesbibliothek in Karlsruhe. 216-231, HOFF

KARLSRUHE. Badische Landesbibliothek - Hist.
Längin, Theodor. Fünfundfünfzig Jahre Katalogdruck. 145-156, LEID
Weinacht, Paul. Johann Christoph Döll als Vorstand der Karlsruher Hofbibliothek 1843-1872. II, 150-157, GLAU

KARLSRUHE. Badische Landesbibliothek - Mss. (LVII)
Holder, Alfred. Der Isidorus-Codex Augiensis LVII der Gr. Hof- und Landesbibliothek in Karlsruhe. 634-643, CHAT

KARLSRUHE - Catalogs - Printed book
see Catalogs - Printed book - Karlsruhe

KARLSRUHE. Generallandesarchiv
see Baden. Generallandesarchiv, Karlsruhe.

KARLSRUHE. Grossherzogliche Hofbibliothek
see Karlsruhe. Badische Landesbibliothek

KARLSRUHE. Hofbibliothek
see Karlsruhe. Badische Landesbibliothek

KARLSRUHE - Manuscripts -
see Manuscripts - Karlsruhe

KARLSRUHE - Manuscripts - Cataloging
see Manuscripts - Cataloging - Karlsruhe

Karpe, Georg.
Handschriften von Johann Wolfgang Goethe im Autographenbestand der Universitätsbibliothek Jena. 189-197, BULL

Karpinski, Louis C.
Colonial American Arithmetics. List of Arithmetics Published in America up to 1775. 243-248, EAME

Karstedt, Peter.
Zur Soziologie der Bibliothekstypen. 61-76, TIEM

KARTEUSERIN, MARGARETE
see Margarete Karteuserin

Kaser, David, ed.
GJEL

Kaser, David.
Bernard Dornin, America's First Catholic Bookseller. 105-128, GJEL
How Big Is a Research Library? 17-19, NASH

Kaspers, Heinz.
Zur Älteren Geschichte der Deutschen Amtsdrucksachen. 45-55, JUCR

KASSEL. Landesbibliothek
KASS

KASSEL. Landesbibliothek. Mss. (Cod. Theol. Q. 1)
Christ, Karl. Eine Unbekannte Handschrift der Ersten Fassung der Dionysiana und der Capitula e Canonibus Excerpta A. 813. 25-36, LEID

KASSEL - Librarians
see Librarians - Kassel

KASSEL - Manuscripts - Collections
see Manuscripts - Collections - Kassel

KASSEL - State libraries
see State libraries - Kassel

Kato, Shuko.
Cataloguing and Classification. 209-214, RANG

Katterbach, Bruno and Wilhelm Maria Peitz, S. J.
Unterschriften der Päpste und Kardinäle in den Bullae Maiores vom 11. bis 14. Jhdt. 177-274, EHRD

KAUFMANN, DAVID - Library
Scheiber, Alexander. Piyyutim from the Geniza Collection of David Kaufmann. 537-546, MARX

Kaul, Jainath and Gurcharan Singh.
Dr. Ranganathan and Standards for Documentation. 271-278, RANG

Kaul, M. L.
Cataloguer's Puzzle: Corporate Authorship. 147-150, RANG

Kaula, Asha.
Dr. Ranganathan and Library Education. 553-557, RANG

Kaula, Prithvi Nath., ed.
RANG

Kaula, Prithvi Nath.
Colon Classification: Genesis and Development. 73-93, RANG
Conspectus. 26-28, RANG
Introduction. 17-25, RANG
Library Classification. 51-56, MADR
Library Education in Perspective. 541-552, RANG
Ranganathan: A Study. 649-676, RANG

Kaulfuss-Diesch, Carl.
Die Neuerwerbungen der Luthersammlung. 47-60, HARN

Kawai, Tadanobu.
Yoroppa ni okeru Printing Equipment ni tsuite. (On the Printing Equipment Used in Europe, 17th-19th Centuries.) 497-502, TOMI

Kawasaki, Misao.
Zōshoin ka Zoshoyō ka. (Bookstamp or Bookplate?) 57-65, OTAT

Kayser, Werner.
Verzeichnis der Veröffentlichungen, Vorlesungen, Vorträge und Referate Hermann Tiemanns, 1923-1959. 350-360, TIEM

KAYSERSBERG, Ger. - Inscriptions, Latin
see Inscriptions, Latin - Kaysersberg, Ger.

<u>KAZANIA ŚWIĘTOKRZYSKIE</u>
Krzyżanowski, Julian. O Artyźmie "Kazań Świętokrzyskich." 345-350, PIEK

KEES, THOMAS, printer - Bibl.
Colmi, Elsbet. Thomas Kees Wesaliensis. Aus der Werkstatt eines Weseler Druckers in Paris 1507-1515/16. 68-97, BENZ

KEESE, THOMAS
see Kees, Thomas, printer

Kehr, Wolfgang.
Studentenbücherei und Hochschulbibliothek. Zur Frage der "Core Collections" in Deutschen Studentenbüchereien und Hochschulbibliotheken. 62-81, FUCH

Kehrli, J. O.
Äthiopisch in der Schweiz. 202-203, LÜTH

Der Kämmerer aus dem Mohrenland. 201-202, LÜTH
Vom Setzer zum Ehrendoktor. 145-147, LÜTH

KEIO UNIVERSITY, Tokyo
see Tokyo. Keio University

KEKULÉ-Bibliothek. Leverkusen
see Farbenfabriken Bayer Aktiengesellschaft. Kekulé-Bibliothek

KEKULÉ VON STRADONITZ, August - Library
Stoetzer, Walter. Die Kekulé-Bibliothek als Hilfsmittel der Dokumentation in der Chemischen Industrie. 130-135, LEUN

Keller, Otto.
Über einen Verbrannten Codex des Horaz. 531-534, CHAT

Kemke, Johannes.
Die Geschichte einer Handschriften-Versendung. 489-498, WILM

KENNEDY, R. F.
KENN

Kent, Henry W.
Chez Moreau de St-Méry, Philadelphie. Publications of Moreau de St-Méry. 67-78, EAME
Encore Moreau de Saint-Méry. 239-247, LYDE

KENTUCKY - Printing
see Printing - Kentucky

KENTUCKY - Printing - Specimens - Collections
see Printing - Specimens - Collections - Kentucky

Kenyon, Sir Frederic George.
Book Divisions in Greek and Latin Literature. 63-75, BISH
Copyright Libraries. 248-254, PUTN
A Tribute from the British Museum. 4-5, GREE

Keogh, Andrew, jt. ed.
BISH; PUTN

Keogh, Andrew.
Benjamin Silliman's Trip to Europe in 1805. 416-422, LYDE
Bishop Berkeley's Gift of Books to Yale in 1733. 128-147, MUNT
The Yale Library of 1742. 76-87, BISH

KEOGH, ANDREW
KEOG
Rush, Charles Everett.
There is Honor in One's Own Country. 1-5, KEOG

Kephart, John E.
Antislavery Publishing in Michigan. 219-236, GJEL

Keppel, Frederick Paul.
Herbert Putnam. 255-256, PUTN
Louis Round Wilson. 583-584, WILS
A Whole Man. 147, LYDE
William Warner Bishop. 1-4, BISH

Kern, Anton.
Magnum Legendarium Austriacum. 429-434, BICK
Die Promotionsschriften der Jesuitenuniversitäten in der Zeit des Barocks. Eine Bibliothekarische Studie. 38-47, SCHT

Kernkamp, J. H.
De Bibliotheek van den Koopman Daniel van der Meulen onder den Hamer. 187-203, EVER

Keyman, Johanna M.
Enkele Opmerkingen over een Merkwaardige Incunabel der Utrechtsche Universiteitsbibliotheek. 204-216, EVER

Keynes, Geoffrey L.
Blake's Vision of the Circle of the Life of Man. 202-208, GREE

Keys, Thomas E.
Some American Medical Imprints of the Nineteenth Century. 309-318, DOEJ

KEYSER, F. W.
Daae, Ludvig. Universitets-Bibliothekar F. W. Keyser. 43-55, (pt. 2), OSLU

Khan, M. Siddig.
A Farmington Plan for Pakistan. 428-433, RANG

Khanna, Jang Bahadur.
Philosophy of Librarianship. 346-347, RANG

KHEDIVIAL LIBRARY, Cairo
see Cairo. Egyptian Library

Khurshid, Anis.
Public Library and the Development of Its Purpose. 434-440, RANG

KHVOSTOV, IVAN MIKHAILOVICH - Library
Il'inskiĭ, L. K. Biblioteka Iv. Mikh. Khvostova; k Istorii Bibliotek XVIII Veka. 346-374, MALE

Kibre, Pearl.
Cardinal Domenico Grimani, Questio de Intensione et Remissione Qualitatis: A Commentary on the Tractate of that Title by Richard Suiseth (Calculator). 147-203, ALBA

Kiefert, Hans-Joachim.
Der Niedersächsische Zentralkatalog 1956-1966. 82-91, FUCH

KIEL - Catalogs - Subject
see Catalogs - Subject - Kiel

KIEL. Universität. Bibliothek - Catalogs
Seyffert, Hans. Über den Schlagwortkatalog der Universitätsbibliothek Kiel. 129-139, JUCR

KIEL. Universität. Bibliothek. Mss. (K. B. 481)
Nörrenberg, Constantin. Kieler Bruchstücke aus Heinrichs von dem Türlin Crone. 405-418, WILM

KIERKEGAARD, SØREN AABYE - Collections - Tenri, Japan
Ishizu, Teruzi. Tenri Toshokan Zō Kierukegoru Zenchosaku no Shohanbon. (The First Editions of all Kierkegaard's Works in the Tenri Central Library.) 477-484, TOMI

KIEV. Pecherskaia Lavra
Zelenka, Ignác. Edizioni Liturgiche della Pečerskaja Lavra di Kiev nella Biblioteca Vaticana. II, 377-414, ALBB

Kievits, A. P. M.
Het Bibliotheekvak. 482-488, BRUM

Kildal, Arne, jt. ed.
NORN

Kildal, Arne.
Books for Norwegian Seamen. 401-407, RANG
Da Norsk Bibliotekforening Ble Til. 43-57, NORS
Fremditslinjer i Norsk Folkebibliotekvesen. 119-128, NORN
Reminiscences and Felicitations. 747-748, RANG

KILDAL, ARNE
KILD
Broch, Mathilde Oftedal. Kulturoptimisme. 23-36, KILD
Skancke, Mally. Fra Arbeidet "Ute i Marken." 37-50, KILD
Stoltz, G. Arne Kildals Første Bedrift som Biblioteksmann. 18-22, KILD

Killer, Hermann.
Zur Musik des Deutschen Ostens im 18. Jahrhundert. 228-243, KÖNI

Kilpatrick, Norman, jt. author
Van Hoesen, Henry B. and Norman Kilpatrick. Heights of Books in Relation to Height of Stack Tiers. 352-357, HANS

Kilpi, Volter.
Suomalainen Virsikirja [Manuale-nide] v:lta 1630 Teuvan Kirkonarkistossa. 122-126, SCHA

Kimmenauer, Alfred.
Colmarer Beriana. Zu Ludwig Ber's Bibliothek und Papieren. 244-251, BENZ

Kindervater, Josef.
Nachrichten von einer Bibliotheksreise vor 100 Jahren. 230-244, LEYG

King, A. Hyatt.
C. G. Röder's Music-Printing Business in 1885. 53-59, FEDO

King, Alexander.
International Trends in Librarianship and Documentation. 489-491, BRUM
Scientific Information and the Economy. 203-208, TVET

Kingsley, James Luce.
Letters in: Powers, Zara Jones. A Yale Bibliophile in European Book Shops. 373-422, KEOG

Kinkeldey, Otto.
Palm Leaf Books. 88-115, BISH

KINKELDEY, OTTO
KINK
KINO
Smith, Carleton Sprague. Otto Kinkeldey. 27-37, KINO

Kirchner, Joachim.
Die Berliner Gregoriusfragmente. 148-156, HARN
Gedanken zur Wissenschaftsgeschichtlichen Forschung. 325-332, JUCH
Sammlung, Bekanntmachung und Katalogisierung Altdeutscher Handschriften im 17. und 18. Jahrhundert. 127-134, LEID
Das Staveloter Evangeliar der Preussischen Staatsbibliothek. 160-171, DEGE

KIRISHITAN EDITIONS
Moriguchi, Ryuji. Sunpo-ho ni Yoru Kirishitan-ban no Shishitsu Chosa. (Research by the "Sumpu" Method on the Quality of Paper Used in the Kirishitan Editions.) 503-510, TOMI

Kirkegaard, Preben.
Amerikansk Oplandsarbejde. 135-146, LASS

Kirkova, Tatiana E.
Doktorskata Disertatsiia na d-r Atanas Bogoridi. 191-203, MIKH

Kirova, Elena.
Kŭm Vŭprosa za Podgotovka na Bibliotekari s Vische Obrazovanie. 205-214, MIKH

Kisser, Alois.
Die Druckschriftensammlung. 73-104, BICK
Th. F. Dibdin (1776-1847). 435-445, BICK

KISSER, ALOIS
STUM
Stickler, Michael. Dr. Alois Kisser, Generaldirektor-Stellvertreter der Österreichischen Nationalbibliothek. 9-10, STUM

Kistner, Erwin.
Studien an Teigdrucken aus dem Besitz des Germanischen Nationalmuseums in Nürnberg. 65-97, STOL

KITASATO MEMORIAL MEDICAL LIBRARY. Tokyo. Keio University
see Tokyo. Keio University. Kitasato Memorial Medical Library

Kittel, Peter.
Bibliographie. II, 1-123, BERS

Kjaer, A.
Overbibliothekar A. C. Drolsum. 74-79, (pt. 2), OSLU

KJAER, A.
KJAE

KJAER, A. - Bibl.
Fortegnelse over A. Kjaers Trykte Arbeider. 125-126, KJAE

Kjørvik, M. A.
Folkebogsamlingane på Landsbygda og Vilkåra for Dei. 53-61, NORN

Klaiber, Ludwig.
Léopold Delisle und die Reform der Bibliothèque Nationale. 156-168, LEYH

KLARISSENKLOSTER. Cologne
see Cologne. Klarissenkloster

Klauser, Renate.
Ein Beutelbuch aus Isny. 139-145, WEHM

Kleberg, Tönnes.
Das Bibliothekssystem einer Universität als Einheit. Reflexionen über einen Organisationsvorschlag an der Universität Uppsala. 119-124, HOFM
Catalogus Codicum Graecorum et Latinorum Bibliothecae Gotoburgensis. 1-48, (eighth paper), GÖTE
Ett Decennium av Gåvor. Kring en Utställning i Uppsala Universitetsbibliotek. 149-167, HEIN
De Internationella Bytesförbindelserna. 35-48, (sixth paper), GÖTE
Om Romersk Antikvariatbokhandel. 84-94, TVET
Gli Scambi Internazionali della Reale Biblioteca Universitaria di Upsala. 505-510, GALL
Some Facts about the International Exchange Relations of the Uppsala University Library. 98-101, MADR
Zwei Stammbuchblätter von Grillparzer in der Universitätsbibliothek Uppsala. 51, STUM

Kleeberg, Heinz, jt. author
Bergmann, Werner and Heinz Kleeberg. Der Beitrag der Deutschen Bücherei zur Lösung Volkswirtschaftlicher Aufgaben. 91-103, LEIZ

Kleindienst, Thérèse.
M. Julien Cain et les Transformations de la Bibliothèque Nationale. 51-59, CAIN

KLEINER, SALOMON. Dilucida Repraesentatio
Bick, Josef. Der Unveröffentlichte Zweite Teil der Dilucida Repraesentatio Bibliothecae Caesareae des S. Kleiner und J. J. Sedelmayr. 75-86, VIEN

Kleinschnitzová, Flora, jt. ed.
EMLE

Kleinstück, Hans.
Erinnerung. 81-83, BOLE

KLEMMING, GUSTAV EDVARD
KLEM

KLEMMING, GUSTAV EDVARD - Bibl.
Andersson, Aksel. Bibliographia Klemmingiana 1844-1889. [v] - [vi], 1-40, KLEM

Klemp, Egon.
Die Kartenabteilung. I, 405-423, BERS

Klemp, Helene L.
Norsk Bibliotekforenings Jubileumsskrift. 9-15, NORS

Kleppa, Peter.
Universitetsbibliotekets Bokbindere og Innbinding. 255-257, OSLO

Kleve, Knut.
Forskerens Ønskebibliotek. 138-140, NORS

Kliemann, Horst.
Über Einige Versuche, sich gegen Nachdruck zu Wehren. 252-254, BENZ

Klos, Herbert.
Papyrologen-Bibliothekare. 51-53, STUM

Klose, Olaf.
Die Privatbibliotheken in Schleswig-Holstein. 256-262, JUCH

KLOSTERLASSE
see Laurentius Nicolai

Klotz, Alfred.
M/2: Ein Palaeographisches Problem. 99-104, STOL

KLUS, Ger. (Benedictine abbey)

Herbst, Hermann. Johannes von Brakel. Ein Beitrag zur Bibliotheksgeschichte des Benediktinerklosters Klus bei Gandersheim. 31-46, SCHR

Knaus, Hermann.
Fischer von Waldheim als Handschriften- und Inkunabelhändler. 255-280, BENZ

KNIAŹNIN, FRANCISZEK DIONIZY

Mikulski, Tadeusz. Kniaźnin w Bibliotece Załuskich. 267-281, PIEK

KNIGHTON, HENRY. Mss. Chronicle

Galbraith, V. H. The Chronicle of Henry Knighton. 136-145. Appendix by R. A. B. Mynors. 146-148, SAXL

KNOBLOCHTZER, HEINRICH - Bibl.

Voulliéme, Ernst. Zur Bibliographie Heinrich Knoblochtzers in Heidelberg. Der Totentanz. 137-151, COLL

Knod, Gustav C.
Aus der Bibliothek des Beatus Rhenanus. Second Book, 1-109, SCHL

Knörich, Gerhard.
Detmar Mülhers Römische Inschriften vom Kaisberg. 1-6, VERD

Knorr, Friedrich.
Der Beruf des Wissenschaftlichen Bibliothekars in Unserer Zeit. I, 112-118, GLAU

KOBERGER, ANTON, printer

Bernoulli, Rudolf. Das Weltallbild in Hartmann Schedels Weltchronik. 48-58, LOUB

Kobro, Nancy, jt. ed.
NORN

Kobro, Nancy.
Nye Strømninger i Bibliotekarbeidet på Landsbygden. 62-65, NORN

Koch, Georg, jt. ed.
HEPD

Koch, Herbert.
ICH—der Leser! 106-108, JENA

Koch, Theodore Wesley.
New Light on Old Libraries. 244-252, HANS
Notes on Trends in Library Planning. 358-368, LEYG

Kochowa, Róża.
Z Ksiąg Pamiątkowych Biblioteki i z Prasy Miejscowej—Uwagi, Opinie. 158-164, BYDG

Kock, R.
Zur Frage der Auswertung Statistischer Erhebungen Kleinstädtischer und Dörflicher Büchereien. 65-74, ACKE

KÖBEL, JAKOB, printer

Grimm, Heinrich. Ulrichs von Hutten Persönliche Beziehungen zu den Druckern Johannes Schöffer in Mainz, Johannes Schott in Strassburg und Jakob Köbel zu Oppenheim. 140-156, BENZ

Köhler, Karl-Heinz.
Die Musikabteilung. I, 241-274, BERS

Koehler, Wilhelm.
The Fragments of an Eighth-Century Gospel Book in the Morgan Library (M. 564): A Contribution to the History of the Vulgate. 238-265, GREE
Turonische Handschriften aus der Zeit Alkuins. 172-180, DEGE

KÖLN
see Cologne

König, Friedrich Wilhelm.
Ein Festkalendarium aus dem Armenischen Alpenland im 9. bis 7. Jahrhundert v. Chr. 59-68, SCHT

KÖNIGSBERG - Bookplates
see Bookplates - Königsberg

KÖNIGSBERG - College and university libraries
see College and university libraries - Königsberg

KÖNIGSBERG - Manuscripts - Collections
see Manuscripts - Collections - Königsberg

KÖNIGSBERG - Music libraries and collections
see Music libraries and collections - Königsberg

KÖNIGSBERG - Public libraries
see Public libraries - Königsberg

KÖNIGSBERG. Schloss-Bibliothek

Diesch, Carl. Fürst Boguslav Radziwill und Seine Bücherschenkung an die Königsberger Schlossbibliothek. 117-128, LEYG

KÖNIGSBERG - Shelf lists
see Shelf lists - Königsberg

KÖNIGSBERG. Staats- und Universitätsbibliothek

KÖNI

Husung, Max Joseph. Über den Plattenstempelschnitt in Königsberg. 283-287, KUHN

KÖNIGSBERG. Staats- und Universitätsbibliothek - Catalogs

Kuhnert, Ernst. Heinrich Zell. 137-147, SCHW

KÖNIGSBERG. Staats- und Universitätsbibliothek. Handschriftensammlung-Hist.

Goldschmidt, Günther. Ein Beitrag zur Ältesten Geschichte der Handschriftensammlung der Staats- und Universitäts-Bibliothek. 125-131, KÖNI

KÖNIGSBERG. Staats- und Universitätsbibliothek - Hist.

Diesch, Carl. Fürst Boguslav Radziwill und Seine Bücherschenkung an die Königsberger Schlossbibliothek. 117-128, LEYG

KÖNIGSBERG. Staats- und Universitätsbibliothek. Sammlung Gotthold

Killer, Hermann. Zur Musik des Deutschen Ostens im 18. Jahrhundert. 228-243, KÖNI

KÖNIGSBERG. Stadtbibliothek. Mss. (Stammbuch)

Meyer, William. Nachklänge von der Dordrechter Nationalsynode. 272-283, KÖNI

KÖNIGSBERG - State libraries
see State libraries - Königsberg

KÖRNING, JOANNES

Collijn, Isak. Über den Verfasser des Cod. Vindob. 14105. 286-290, BICK

Köster, Kurt, ed.
EPPE

Köster, Kurt.
Die Deutsche Bibliothek 1945-1965. Weg und Auftrag. 21-77, EPPE
Der Neubau der Deutschen Bibliothek. Vorgeschichte, Planungen, Wirklichkeit. 29-52, FRAD
Religiöse Medaillen und Wallfahrts-Devotionalien in der Flämischen Buchmalerei des 15. und Frühen 16. Jahrhunderts. Zur Kenntnis Gemalter und Wirklicher Kollektionen in Spätmittelalterlichen Gebetbuch-Handschriften. 459-504, HOFM

Köttelwesch, Clemens.
Vom Frankfurter Sammelkatalog zum Hessischen Zentralkatalog. 92-101, FUCH
Zum Neubau der Stadt- und Universitätsbibliothek Frankfurt am Main. 125-136, HOFM

KOHLBRUGGE, HERMANN FRIEDRICH

Kohlbrugge, J. H. F. Dr. H. F. Kohlbrugge en Zijn Archief in de Universiteitsbibliotheek. 217-236, EVER

Kohlbrugge, J. H. F.
Dr. H. F. Kohlbrugge en Zijn Archief in de Universiteitsbibliotheek. 217-236, EVER

Kohler, Hans.
Neubau der Universitätsbibliothek in Giessen 1959. 11-14, GIES

Kohut, George Alexander.
Bibliography of the Writings of Prof. Dr. M. Steinschneider. V-XXXIX, STEI
Steinschneideriana. 65-127, FREI

KOHUT, GEORGE ALEXANDER

Kohut, Rebekah. Prof. Alexander Marx. xi-xxiii, MARX

Kohut, Rebekah.
Freidus—A Personal Reminiscence. XL-XLIII, FREI
Prof. Alexander Marx. xi-xxiii, MARX

Kojima, Fumiyasu.
Tokoshu Shiryō no Bunrui, Ōtani Tanken-tai Shōraihin. (Classification of the Material Found in Central Asia by the Ōtani Expedition.) 131-141, KYOT

Kolhatker, V. P.
The Reference Librarian and His Tools. 80-84, MADR

KOLISKO, JOSEF ARNOŠT

Krtička, Jan. Josef Arnošt Kolisko. 208-212, ZIVN

Kolmodin, Torsten.
Om Personalredovisning. 257-261, GRAP

KOMMISSION DER ÖFFENTLICHEN BIBLIOTHEK DER UNIVERSITÄT
SCHU

Kondolewicz, Wanda.
Dział Informacyjno-bibliograficzny. 34-36, KRAK
Dział Informacyjno-bibliograficzny Jako Warsztat Pracy Nauczyciela. 61-66, KRAK

KONGELIGE BIBLIOTEK, Copenhagen
see Copenhagen. Kongelige Bibliotek

KONINKLIJKE BIBLIOTHEEK, Hague
see Hague. Koninklijke Bibliotheek

KONINKLIJKE BIBLIOTHEEK VAN BELGIË, Brussels
see Brussels. Bibliothèque Royale de Belgique

Konrad, Joachim.
Das Fachbuch im Buchhandel und in den Bibliotheken. 120-126, JENA

KONRAD OF WESTPHALIA
see Konrad von Paderborn

KONRAD VON PADERBORN
Juchhoff, Rudolf. Johann und Konrad von Paderborn. Die Anfänge Ihrer Druckertätigkeit in Venedig und Strassburg. 211-227, BÖME

Koopman, Harry Lyman.
The Clerk of Breukelyn. v-vi, EAME
The Open-Shelf Library. 257-262, PUTN

KOOPMAN, LOUIS
Roelofs, Sjoerdtje. La "Collection Anny Antoine-Louis Koopman" à la Bibliothèque Royale de la Haye. 577-580, BRUM

Kopp, Arthur.
Das Liederbuch der Berliner Bibliothek vom Jahre 1582 und Verwandte Sammlungen. 445-454, WILM

Koranne, T. N.
Australia and Madras Library Association. 127-129, MADR

KOREA - Printing
see Printing - Korea

Korpała Józef.
Z Dziejów Miejskich Bibliotek Publicznych w Galicji. 307-329, GRYC

Kossmann, F. K. H.
Rotterdam en de "Bijzondere" O. B. 496-500, BRUM

KOSSMANN, F. K. H.
KOSS

KOSSMANN, F. K. H. - Bibl.
Mazure, J. C. Overzicht der Geschriften van Dr. F. K. H. Kossmann. 260-264, KOSS

Kotani, Genzō.
Ōhashi Toshokan Shozō Hakubunkan Hakkō Tosho Mokuroku. (A Catalogue of the Books Published by Hakubunkan in the Collections of the Ōhashi Library.) 105-132, TSUB
Ōhashi Toshokan Shozō Hakubunkan Hakkō Tosho Mokuroku—Showa Juyonen Gogatsu Matsujitsu Genzai. (The List of Books Published by Hakubunkan Which Are in the Collections of the Ōhashi Library—as of the End of March, 1939.) 1-157, (part 2), OHAS

Kotani, Seiichi.
D C no Jūnansei. (The Flexibility of the Dewey Decimal Classification.) 128-141, (part 1), OHAS
Kankai Jinbutsushi. (Contemporary Men in the Library World.) 22-32, TSUB

Koul, Doroti Etlin.
Tezi, Prieti ot Bibliotekarskite Uchilishta v Sŭedinenite Shtati ot Ĭuli 1938 do Ĭuni 1945 g. 346-380, MIKN

Koutník, Bohuslav.
K Základům Knihovědy a Knihovnictví. 174-185, ŽIVN

Koutníková, Lidmila.
L. J. Živný a Desetinné Tříděni u Nás. 73-130, ŽIVN

Krabbe, Wilhelm.
Die Revolutionssammlung. 90-91, HARN

Kraemer, Erik von.
En Bibliofiliens Storman. Antoine-René de Voyer d'Argenson, Markis av Paulmy. 182-196, DAHL

Kragemo, Helge Bergh.
Zur Frage der Rationalisierung des Tauschverkehrs einer Wissenschaftlichen Bibliothek. 377-381, MUNT

KRAIBURG, BERNHARD VON, Bp. of Chiemsee
see Bernhard von Kraiburg, Bp. of Chiemsee

KRAKÓW - Catalogs - Subject
see Catalogs - Subject - Kraków

KRAKÓW. Centralna Biblioteka Nauczycielska KOSK
see Kraków. Pedagogical Library

KRAKÓW - Circulation procedures
see Circulation procedures - Kraków

KRAKÓW - Education for librarianship
see Education for librarianship - Kraków

KRAKÓW - Education libraries
see Education libraries - Kraków

KRAKÓW - Education libraries - Acquisitions
see Education libraries - Acquisitions - Kraków

KRAKÓW - Exhibits and displays
see Exhibits and displays - Kraków

KRAKÓW - In-service training
see In-service training - Kraków

KRAKÓW - Instruction in library use
see Instruction in library use - Kraków

KRAKÓW. Jagiellonion University. Library

Ameisenowa, Zofia. Nieznany Wzór Złotniczy z XV w. w Bibliotece Jagiellońskiej. 365-369, PIEK

KRAKÓW. Jagiellonion University. Library. Mss. (Nr. 1944)

Lewicka-Kamińska, Anna. Neues Donatfragment in der Type der 42zeiligen Bibel in der Jagiellonischen Bibliothek. 13-16, LÜLF

KRAKÓW. Jagiellonion University. Library. Pinocci Collection

Brahmer, Mieczysław. O Bibliotece Pinoccich. 251-265, PIEK

KRAKÓW. Kuratorium Okregu Szkolnego. Centralna Biblioteka Nauczycielska
see Kraków. Pedagogical Library

KRAKÓW - Library and the public
see Library and the public - Kraków

KRAKÓW. Pedagogical Library

KRAK

KRAKÓW. Pedagogical Library - Bibl.

Bibliografia o Pedagogiczna Biblioteka Wojewódzka w Krakowie. 125-127, KRAK

KRAKÓW. Pedagogical Library. Division of Instruction

Popiel, Jadwiga. Dział Instrukcyjno-Metodyczny. 36-38, KRAK

KRAKÓW. Pedagogical Library. Loan Hall

Głodek, Stefania. Wypożyczalnia. 29-34, KRAK

KRAKÓW. Pedagogical Library. Reading Room

Ponińska, Irena. Czytelnia. 24-29, KRAK

KRAKÓW. Pedagogical Library. Reference Division

Kondolewicz, Wanda. Dział Informacyjno-Bibliograficzny. 34-36, KRAK

———— Dział Informacyjno-Bibliograficzny Jako Warsztat Pracy Nauczyciela. 61-66, KRAK

KRAKÓW - Periodicals - Collections
see Periodicals - Collections - Kraków

KRAKÓW. Polish Academy of Art
see Polish Academy of Art, Kraków

KRAKOW. Polska Akademia Umiejetności
see Polish Academy of Art, Kraków

KRAKÓW - Rare books - Collections
see Rare books - Collections - Kraków

KRAKÓW. Uniwersytet Jagielloński. Biblioteca
see Kraków. Jagiellonian University. Library

KRAKÓW. Uniwersytet Jagielloński. Biblioteka dei Pinocci
see Kraków. Jagiellonian University. Library. Pinocci Collection

Kramp, Joseph, S. J.
Chronologisches zu Peters des Ehrwürdigen Epistola Adversus Petrobrusianos. 71-79, EHRA

Krause, Heinrich.
Die Bibliotheksbenutzung von 1905-1920. 119-125, HARN
De Aeschyli Choephororum Versibus 261-297 Kirchh. 229-242, WILM
Die Drucklegung der Andriaausgabe Joh. Agricolas. 131-136, SCHW

KRAUSE, JAKOB

Schunke, Ilse. Beiträge zur Dresdner Bibliotheksgeschichte auf Grund von Einbandstudien. 397-414, VORS

KRAUSE, JAKOB, bookbinder

Schmidt, Christel. Jakob Krause-Forschung: Ein Beitrag zur Methodik der Bucheinbandkunde. 191-193, LOUB
Strübing, Eduard. Zwei Einbände Jakob Krauses in der Weimarer Landesbibliothek. 153-157, WEIM

Krawiec, Ferdinand.
Die Anonymen Handschriften der Stadtbibliothek. 70-81, VIES

Kreft, Friedrich.
Papst Pius XI. als Bibliothekar. 105-116, STOL

Krefting, Achim.
Briefe eines Gefallenen Wuppertaler Bibliothekars. 147-152, BRIE

Kremer, Marita.
Blick in das Buchmuseum der Sächsischen Landesbibliothek 1956. 52-56, BOLE
Die Handschriftenabteilung. 139-146, DREL

Kremer, Marita, jt. author
Deckert, Helmut, Marita Kremer, Hans Pfeifer, and Liselotte Willi. Das Neue Buchmuseum der Sächsischen Landesbibliothek. 175-205, DREL

Kresse, Walter.
Oberbürgermeister der Stadt Leipzig. XVI-XVII, LEIZ

Kreuziger, Max.
Zur Neuorientierung Unserer Kulturarbeit. 5-6, BERL

Kreyenborg, Hermann.
Proben einer Ungedruckten Übertragung Arabischer Sprüche und Sinngedichte von Friedrich Rückert, aus dem in der Universitätsbibliothek zu Münster i. W. Aufbewahrten Teilnachlasse des Dichters zum Erstenmal Mitgeteilt. 125-129, BÖME

Krieg, Walter, jt. ed.
STUM

Krieg, Werner, jt. ed.
JUCH

Krieg, Werner.
[Introduction.] 7-9, JUCH
Die Revision der Preussischen Staatsbibliothek im Sommer 1939. 404-421, JUCH

Krieger, Waldemar and Gottfried Rost.
Das Gebäude der Deutschen Bücherei und seine Technischen Einrichtungen. 259-270, LEIZ

Krimmer, Therese.
Schattentheater. 93-98, SCHS

Krishna Rao, D. B.
Research in Library Science. 150-154, MADR

Krishnan, A.
Dr. Ranganathan's Humanisation of Teaching Technique. 558-567, RANG

Krishnayya, D.
Librarianship in Me. 751-752, RANG

KRISTIANSTAD, Norway - Public libraries
see Public libraries - Kristianstad, Norway

KRISTIANSTAD, Norway. Stadsbibliotek
KRIS

KRISTINA, Queen of Sweden - Library
Odier, J. Bignami. Le Fonds de la Reine à la Bibliothèque Vaticane. I, 159-189, ALBB

Kristoffersen, Magn. K.
Folkebogsamling til Centralbibliotek. 7-21, HOLS

Křížek, O.
Logická Struktura Knihovnické Práce. 117-120, EMLE

Krogh-Jensen, G.
Om Adgangen til Folkebibliotekerne Betragtninger over Bibliotekernes Reglementer. 105-131, DØSS

Krohn, Gerhard.
Wie die Wissenschaftliche Zentralbibliothek (WZB) Entstand. 159-171, SCHS

Kroker, Ernst.
Bruchstücke einer Handschrift des Jüngeren Titurel in der Leipziger Stadtbibliothek. 42-48, LEIP

Kronenberg, M. E.
Erasmus-Uitgaven A°. 1531 in het Bezit van Kanunnik Mr. Jan Dircsz. van der Haer te Gorkum. 99-117, KOSS

Krtička, Jan.
Josef Arnošt Kolisko. 208-212, ŽIVN

KRÜGER, THOMAS, bookbinder
Schmidt-Herrling, Eleonore. Einbände von Thomas Krüger in der Universitätsbibliothek Erlangen. 285-293, STOL

Krüss, Hugo Andres.
Ansprache bei der Trauerfeier am 29. Januar 1934 im Krematorium Wilmersdorf. 15-16, MILK
Einleitende Worte. 21, MILK
Die Entwicklung der Dokumentationsarbeit in Deutschland vor dem Wirken Unserer Gesellschaft. 8-9, DEUD
Geleitwort. v-vi, KUHN
Zur Geschichte der Staatsbibliothek zu Berlin in den Letzten Dreissig Jahren. 263-274, PUTN

KRÜSS, HUGO ANDRES
KRÜS

Kruitwagen, Bonaventura.
Das Antidotarium Animae von Fr. Serva-

sanctus O. F. M. (Lovanii, Joh. de Westfalia, c. 1485). 80-106, HAEB
De Freeska Landriucht-Drukkerij. 45-69, HAGU

Krummel, Donald W.
The Library World of Norton's Literary Gazette. 237-266, GJEL
The Writings of Stanley Pargellis. 221-231, PARG

Krusch, Bruno.
Das Älteste Fränkische Lehrbuch der Dionysianischen Zeitrechnung. 232-242, CHAT

Krzyżanowski, Julian.
O Artyźmie "Kazań Świętokrzyskich." 345-350, PIEK

Kubler, George.
John Carter Brown and America. 203-207, WROT

Kuczewski-Poray, Kasimir.
Ein Joseph Marx-Autograph der Österreichischen Nationalbibliothek. 446-449, BICK

Küntzel, Georg.
Niebuhrs Römische Geschichte und Ihr Zeitgenössischer Politischer Gehalt. 175-190, EBRA

Küster, A.
Die Juristische Abteilung der Königlichen Universitäts-Bibliothek zu Münster. 268-300, MÜNS

Kufaev, M. N.
Problemy Filosofii Knigi; Opyt Vvedenii͡a v Istorii͡u Knigi. 22-38, MALE

Kuhlman, A. F.
A Quarter Century of Service. 2-4, NASH
Wanted: A New Policy for the Organization and Development of Library Resources for Research. 585-600, WILS

Kuhnert, Ernst.
Heinrich Zell. 137-147, SCHW
Milkau als Mensch und Bibliothekar. 25-29, MILK
Die Nova Bibliotheca des Herzogs Albrecht. 209-219, MILF

KUHNERT, ERNST

KUHN

Krüss, Hugo Andres. Geleitwort. v-vi, KUHN

Kumar, Girja.
Dr. Ranganathan: A Brief Appraisal. 604-608, RANG
The Librarian and the Community. 135-138, MADR

Kumura, Miyogo and Kazumasa Kaneko.
Chokuhan Ko, 1, Kobun Kokyo 1. (Study of the Chokuhan, or the Imperial Editions, 16th Century, Part 1, Kobun Kokyo 1.) 61-86, TOMI

Kunze, Horst, ed.
BOCK

Kunze, Horst, jt. ed.
BERS

Kunze, Horst.
Bemerkungen zum Thema "Wissenschaftliche Bibliotheken und Dokumentation." 203-213, VORS
Bemerkungen zur Buchform. 54-55, STUM
Books for Children and Youth. 523-527, RANG
Demokratisierung und Sozialistische Umgestaltung. I, 49-76, BERS
Das Fach Wissenschaftskunde in der Ausbildung von Wissenschaftlichen Bibliothekaren und Bibliothekaren. 219-224, MIKH
Glückwünsche. 9-11, LÜLF
Die Landesbibliotheken Gestern, Heute und Morgen. 1-14, DREL
Über den Motorisierten Bibliothekar. 29-35, BOLE
Über das Registermachen. 18-34, BOCK
Zum Geleit. 21-22, BULL

Kunze, Horst and Werner Dube.
Zur Vorgeschichte der Deutschen Staatsbibliothek. I, 1-47, BERS

KURATORIUM UND BEIRAT DER DEUTSCHEN BIBLIOTHEK. 162-164, EPPE

Kurdybacha, Emilia.
Bibliografia Drukowanych Prac, Artykułów i Notatek J. Grycza. 55-68, GRYC

KUTNÁ HORA, Czechoslovakia (1850) - Catalogs - Author
see Catalogs - Author - Kutná Hora, Czechoslovakia (1850)

Kuttner, Stephan.
Analecta Iuridica Vaticana (Vat. Lat. 2343). I, 415-452, ALBB

Kyle, Barbara.
Classification in the School Curriculum. 194-201, SAYW
A Few Ideas on Dr. Ranganathan's Personality. 693-695, RANG

KYLE, BARBARA

KYLE

Ranganathan, S. R. Barbara Kyle and the Classification of Sociology. 271-274, KYLE
Wilson, Leslie. Barbara Kyle. 227-228, KYLE

KYLE, BARBARA - Bibl.
Coblans, Herbert. Barbara Kyle: an Annotated Bibliography. 229-235, KYLE

KYODO KENKYU. TOSHOKAN NO HATTEN O HABAMU MONO. (A Joint Study. Obstacles to the Progress of Libraries.) 1-32, TOKY

KYOTO - Librarians
see Librarians - Kyoto

KYOTO LIBRARY ASSOCIATION
KYOT

KYOTO LIBRARY ASSOCIATION - Hist.
Kyōto Toshokan Kyōkai Nempyō. (Chronology of Kyoto Toshokan Kyōkai, 1947-1957.) 230-234, KYOT

KYOTO LIBRARY ASSOCIATION - Young Men's Research Group
Nakama, Zukuri. Kyōto Toshokan Kyōkai Seinen Kenkyū Gurūpu no Rei. (Organizing Librarians in the Region—the Case of the Young Men's Research Group of the Kyoto Library Association.) 50-75, TOKY

KYOTO - School libraries
see School libraries - Kyoto

KYOTO TOSHOKAN KYOKAI
see Kyoto Library Association

KYOTO TOSHOKAN KYOKAI NEMPYO. (Chronology of Kyoto Toshokan Kyokai, 1947-1957.) 230-234, KYOT

KYRIACE ANCONITANI
see Ciriaco de' Pizzicolli, of Ancona

Kyriss, Ernst.
Der Altdorfer Professor Georg Siegel als Büchersammler. 117-124, STOL
Beiträge zu Augsburger Buchbindern. 134-164, HAEK
Einbände mit Hoheitszeichen Herzog Carl Eugens. 232-243, HOFF
Johannes Zoll, ein Tübinger Buchbinder des 15. Jahrhunderts. 84-93, LEYH
Nördlinger Bucheinbände eines Zeit- und Kunstgenossen Johann Richenbachs. I, 119-139, GLAU
Spätgotische Einbände des Benediktinerklosters Schuttern. 147-152, WEHM

LA PINTE DE LIVRY, NICOLAS, Bp. of Callinique
Croix, Jean Tremblot de la. Deux Vrais Bibliophiles. 525-534, BONN

La Rue, Jan.
Classification of Watermarks for Musicological Purposes. 59-63, FEDO

Laan, A. van der.
Het Karakter van de Overheidsdocumentatie. 501-504, BRUM

Labarre, E. J.
The Sizes of Paper, Their Names, Origin and History. 35-54, BOCK

Laceulle, J. W. R.
Enige Opmerkingen inzake de Toekomst van het Wettelijk Dépôt in Nederland. 219-233, HAGU

Lach, Robert.
Aus dem Handschriftenschatze der Musikaliensammlung der Wiener Nationalbibliothek. 553-574, VIEN

Längin, Theodor.
Fündundfünfzig Jahre Katalogdruck. 145-156, LEID

Lafaye, Georges.
Lucilius, Iter Siculum (Sat. III, Vers 98-109, [Marx]). 75-78, CHAT

Lafuma, Louis.
À Propos d'un Petit Écrit de Pascal. 109-114, BONN

Lage, Louise C., Lois B. Miller, and Donald Washburn.
Dental, Nursing, and Pharmaceutical Libraries, 1947-1957. 371-377, DOEJ

Lagerborg, Rolf.
Ur Hecatompolis Suionum. 112-125, HULA

Lallier, Roger.
Note sur la Tragédie de Livius Andronicus Intitulée Equox Troianus. 103-109, GRAU

LAMARTINE, ALPHONSE MARIE LOUIS DE. Le Lac
Giraud, Jeanne. Notes de Lectures Romantiques: Encore les Strophes Supprimées du Lac. 253-260, BONN

Lamb, Eliza.
The Expansive Classification in Use. 265-269, HANS

LAMB, J. P.
LAMB

LAMB, J. P. - Bibl.
Olle, James G. The Professional Writings of J. P. Lamb, A Check List. 27-30, LAMB

Lambert, Mayer.
Die Hebräischen Erklärungen im Hebräisch-Französischen Glossar der Pariser Nationalbibliothek. 368-390, (Hebrew section), HARK

Lambros, Spyridion P.
Notes Épigraphiques et Paléographiques. 621-628, GRAU

Lampe, Walther.
Über das Erste Inventar der Evangelischen Kirche in Deutschland vor 100 Jahren... 82-85, SCHV

Lancaster-Jones, Joyce.
The UDC and the Science Museum Library. 163-164, DONK

Landahl, Heinrich.
[An Address.] 24-33, BERP

LANDAU, HORACE, Barone - Library

Mondolfo, Anita. La Biblioteca Landau-Finaly. 265-285, GREG

LANDESBIBLIOTHEKEN (Germany)
see State libraries - Germany

Landheer, B.
De Bibliotheek van de Verenigde Naties en Andere Internationale Bibliotheken. 505-513, BRUM

Landmark, Joh. D.
Bibliotekarer og Assistenter ved Det Kgl. Norske Videnskabers Selskab Bibliotek i Trondhjem 1766-1858. 131-149, OSLN
Videnskabers Selskabs Bibliotek i Trondheim og Dets Bygningshistorie 1855-1867. 148-159, MUNT

LANDRIUCHT-DRUKKERIJ, DE FREESKA
see De Freeska Landriucht-Drukkerij

LANDSHUT. Universität. Bibliothek - Hist.

Hilsenbeck, Adolf. Die Universitätsbibliothek Landshut-München und die Säkularisation (1803). 180-192, LEYG

Lane, William Coolidge.
The Sojourn of the Harvard Library in Concord, Massachusetts, 1775-1776. 275-287, PUTN

Lange, Eugenie.
Schweizer Drucke in Russischer Sprache. 68-76, BERU

Lange, Hans Ostenfeldt.
De Hollandske Bogauktioner i Deres Første Halve Aarhundrede. 179-194, ANNE
Tale ved Det Kongelige Bibliotheks Nye Bygnings Indvielse d. 27. November 1906. 57-67, BAYJ

Lange, Hans Ostenfeldt.
Breve in: Helweg-Larsen, P. Af H. O. Langes Breve til Hjemmet. 9-303, LANE

LANGE, HANS OSTENFELDT

LANE

Lange, Wilhelm H.
Buchhandel, Buchverlag, Buchvertrieb. Beiträge zur Wirtschaftlichen und Geistigen Situation des 15. und 16. Jahrhunderts. 55-74, BOCK

Langfeldt, Johannes
LANJ

Langfeldt, Johannes.
Das Buch, die Bücherei und der Jugendliche. 105-112, LANJ
Die Buchauswahl in Grossen Büchereien: Ein Beitrag zur Nationalisierung Unserer Arbeit. 27-28, ACKR
Fragen des Ländlichen Büchereiwesens. 50-58, LANJ
Gehört die Kinderbüchereiarbeit zum Aufgabenkreis der Schule oder der Bücherei? 91-104, LANJ
Ein Kapitel aus der Vorgeschichte der "Public Library" in Grossbritannien. 281-292, JUCH
Kinderausgaben der Grimmschen Märchen. Eine Bibliothekarische Besinnung auf deren Grundsätze. 49-59, BRIE
Märchen und Pädagogik. 113-129, LANJ
Möglichkeiten der Zusammenarbeit zwischen Schule und Bücherei. 59-81, LANJ
Die Organisation des Schulbüchereiwesens in Gotenburg. 75-86, ACKE
Über den Schlagwortkatalog der Belehrenden Literatur. 152-172, LANJ
Ein Volk von Bücherlesern? 43-49, LANJ
Vom Wissenschaftlichen Lesen. 130-151, LANJ
Von den Grundlagen Unserer Volksbildungsarbeit. 33-42, LANJ
Welche Wege Kann die Schule in Ihrer Büchereiarbeit Gehen? 82-90, LANJ
Zur Büchereipolitischen Lage. 9-32, LANJ

LANGFELDT, JOHANNES

LANF

LANJ

Ackerknecht, Erwin. Lieber Johannes Langfeldt. 7-8, LANJ

LANGFELDT, JOHANNES - Bibl.

Schriftenverzeichnis Johannes Langfeldt 1923-1957. 157-166, LANF

Langridge, Derek.
Classification and Book-Indexing. 182-193, SAYW

LANGUET, HUBERT
Schunke, Ilse. Die Pariser Büchersendung des Hubert Languet an Kurfürst August von Sachsen 1566. 49-66, BOLL

Lantschoot, Arnold van.
Inventaire Sommaire des Manuscrits Vaticans Éthiopiens. I, 453-[514], ALBB

Lanzara, M. Giuseppina Castellano.
La Casa del Salvatore in Napoli. 239-247, GALL

LARCHER, GUILLAUME
Coyecque, Ern. Guillaume Larcher, Bibliothécaire du Cabinet Henri IV. 129-132, GODE

Larsen, Hans Christian.
Et År i et Sognebibliotek. 57-64, LASS

Larsen, Sofus.
To Danske Palaeotyper Trykte i Paris. 183-197, COLL

Larson, Edgar R.
Technical Reports Retrieval by Computer at the U.S. Naval Postgraduate School Library. 71-80, HASH

LASCARIS, GIANO
see Lascaris, Janus

LASCARIS, JANUS
Mercati, Giovanni, Cardinal. Cenni di A. del Monte e G. Lascaris sulle Perdite della Biblioteca Vaticana nel Sacco del 1527. 605-632, CERI

LASCARY, JEAN
see Lascaris, Janus

Lassen, Harald Hvenegaard.
Carl Thomsen. 27-33, THOM
Centralbibliotekerne og deres Arbejdsvilkaar. 56-69, DØSS

LASSEN, HARALD HVENEGAARD
LASS
Thomsen, Carl. Harald Hvenegaard Lassen. 9-16, LASS

Lasso de La Vega, Javier.
La CDU como Medio para Hacer Sistemáticas las Listas de Epígrafes de los Catálogos de Asuntos. 169-170, DONK

LATHERON, MATTHIEU
Omont, H. Deux Incunables Imprimés à Tours le 7 Mai 1496. 153-160, COLL

LATIN AMERICA - Catholic libraries
see Catholic libraries - Latin America

LATIN AMERICA - Libraries
see Libraries - Latin America

LATIN INCUNABULA
see Incunabula, Latin

LATIN INSCRIPTIONS
see Inscriptions, Latin

LATIN LITERATURE - Collections - Danzig - 15th cent.
Ziesemer, Walther. Zur Kenntnis des Bibliothekswesens Preussens im 15. Jahrhundert. 393-400, KÖNI

LATIN MANUSCRIPTS
see Manuscripts, Latin

LATIN PALEOGRAPHY
see Paleography, Latin

LATIN POETRY - Collections - Erfurt
Walther, Hans. Kleine Mittellateinische Dichtungen aus Zwei Erfurter Handschriften. 296-315, DEGE

LATIN POETRY - Collections - Linköping, Sweden
Lagerborg, Rolf. Ur Hecatompolis Suionum. 112-125, HULA

LATIN SHORTHAND
see Shorthand, Latin

Laue, Max.
Zeitschriftenkuriosa. 149-158, SCHW
Der Zeitschriftensaal. 14-20, HARN

Launay, Denise.
À propos de Deux Manuscrits Musicaux aux Armes de Louis XIII. 63-67, FEDO

Laurent, J.
Das Neu Errichtete Archiv- und Bibliothek-Gebäude der Stadt Aachen. 1-20, (pt. 1), AACH

Laurent, Jacques.
Charles Oursel, Esquisse Biographique. 9-36, OURS
L'Oeuvre de P.-C. Marillier à la Bibliothèque de Dijon. 125-136, OURS

Laurent, M.-H.
L'Abbé Paul Liebaert, Scriptor Honoraire Adj. de la Vaticane. Sa Vie et Ses Oeuvres (1883-1915). II, 1-132, ALBB
Guillaume des Rosières et la Bibliotheque Pontificale à L'Époque de Clément VI. 579-603, PELZ
Les Sources Hagiographiques de S. Catherine de Sienne et le Ms. Marciano Ital. CL. V. 26. 521-531, FERR

LAURENTIUS, NICOLAI
Collijn, Isak. Biblioteca "Collegii So-

cietatis Jesu in Suetia." Några Bidrag till Kännedomen om Jesuiternas Boksamling på Gråmunkeholmen. 75-91, ANNE

LAURENTIUS NORVEGUS
see Laurentius Nicolai

Laurila, K. S., jt. ed.
HIRN

Laurin, Gertraut.
Blindgedruckte Einzelstempelbände des XV. und XVI. Jahrhunderts im Zisterzienserstift Rein bei Graz. 10-30, SCHT

Lauritzen, V.
Hilsen fra Bibliotekets Første Bibliotekar. 21-22, FRED

Laursen, Johs. Lehm.
Biblioteksbenyttelsens Intensivering og dens Følger. 169-182, HEIN

Lausten-Thomsen, H.
Inledning. 7-14, TØND

LAVERDE RUIZ, GUMERSINDO

Solana, Marcial. Colaboración de Laverde en la Ciencia Española de Menéndez y Pelayo. II, 51-104, ARTI

Lavisse, Ernest.
Charles Graux. xi-1, GRAU

LAW - Codification - Germany - Hist.

Liermann, Hans. Das Buch im Deutschen Rechtsgang. 137-146, STOL

LAW - Codification - Hist.

Liermann, Hans. Buch und Recht. 33-35, REDE

LAW LIBRARIES - Hamburg

Coudres, Hans-Peter des. Die Bibliothek des Max-Planck-Instituts für Ausländisches und Internationales Privatrecht in Hamburg. Ihr Werden und Ihre Stellung Innerhalb Verwandter Sammlungen. 50-60, TIEM

LAW LIBRARY, U. S. Library of Congress
see U. S. Library of Congress. Law Library

Le Gal, Simonne.
Bibliographie des Travaux de Frantz Calot. xiii-xviii, CALO
La Bibliothèque des Dames au XVe Siècle, Vue par le Marquis de Paulmy. 55-63, CALO

LE MONNIER FAMILY (Bookbinders)

Michon, Louis-Marie. Notes sur les Reliures de L'Atélier des Monnier. 509-513, BONN

Le Rider, Georges.
Julien Cain et le Cabinet des Médailles. 72-75, CAIN

Le ROY, ADRIAN, printer

Hofer, Philip. Adrian Le Roy and Robert Ballard: Printers of the Late Renaissance. 475-482, LYDE

LE SAGE, GEORGES LOUIS. Mss.

Gagnebin, Bernard. Un Maniaque de L'Introspection Révélé par 35.000 Cartes à Jouer: Georges-Louis Le Sage. 145-157, CALO

LEAGUE OF NATIONS
see United Nations

LEAGUE OF NATIONS. Library

Sevensma, Tietse Pieter. The Library of the League of Nations. 399-408, PUTN

LEARNING AND SCHOLARSHIP

Morison, Stanley. The Learned Press as an Institution. 153-179, WEHM
Schmidt, Wieland. Wissenschaft und Bibliographie. 127-129, FRAD

LEATHER
see Bookbinding - Materials; Books - Care and restoration

LEATHER - Fine bindings
see Bookbinding - Fine bindings

Lebeau, Elisabeth.
Les Catalogues de Vente de Tableaux et d'Objets d'Art, Source de Documentation Musicale. 67-72, FEDO

Lebègue, Henri.
Le Waltharius du Parisinus 8488^{a}. 584-587, CHAT

Lebel, Paul.
Les Registres d'Échevinage aux Archives de Dijon. 137-146, OURS

Lebeson, Anita Libman.
Joshua Bloch ז"ל : An Appreciation. ix-xix, BLOC

Leccisotti, Tommaso.
La Tradizione Archivistica di Montecassino. 227-261, MERC

Lecourt, Marcel.
Antoine de La Sale et Simon de Hesdin. Une Restitution Littéraire. 341-353, CHAT

LECTIONARIES

Der Nersessian, Sirarpie. An Armenian Lectionary of the Fourteenth Century. 231-237, GREE
Schmidt, Adolf. Das Reichenauer Evan-

gelistar. Handschrift CXC der Stadtbibliothek zu Leipzig. 22-41, LEIP
Waetzoldt, Stephan. Ein Silbereinband von Jörg Seld. 53-57, REDE
Weitzmann, Kurt. The Constantinopolitan Lectionary, Morgan 639. 358-373, GREE

LEEUWARDEN. Buma Bibliotheek
Douma, S. Over een Systematisch Trefwoordenregister. 408-413, BRUM

LEEUWARDEN - Catalogs - Classed
see Catalogs - Classed - Leeuwarden

LEEUWARDEN - Catalogs - Subject
see Catalogs - Subject - Leeuwarden

LEGACIES
see Gifts, contributions, etc.

LEGAL DEPOSIT (of books, etc.)
Munthe, Wilhelm. Einforderungsrecht eine Selektive Pflichtablieferung. 33-39, GODE

LEGAL DEPOSIT (of books, etc.) - Aarhus, Denmark
Holstein, Rathlou, V. J. v. Pligtafleveringen. 81-85, AARU

LEGAL DEPOSIT (of books, etc.) - Basel
Schwarber, Karl. Das Basler Pflichtexemplar. 145-163, GODE

LEGAL DEPOSIT (of books, etc.) - Bavaria
Sinogowitz, Bernhard. Gedanken zum Bayerischen Pflichtexemplarrecht. 195-202, REDE

LEGAL DEPOSIT (of books, etc.) - Czechoslovakia
Hrozný, Jindřich. Povinné Výtisky. 64-68, EMLE

LEGAL DEPOSIT (of books, etc.) - Europe
Munthe, Wilhelm. Norske Avdelings Forhistorie. 1-44, OSLO

LEGAL DEPOSIT (of books, etc.) - Italy
De Gregori, Giorgio. Sulla Legislazione Italiana Relativa al Deposito degli Stampati. 75-87, GREG

LEGAL DEPOSIT (of books, etc.) - Netherlands
Laceulle, J. W. R. Enige Opmerkingen inzake de Toekomst van het Wettelijk Dépôt in Nederland. 219-233, HAGU

LEGAL DEPOSIT (of books, etc.) - Norway
Haukaas, Kaare. Norsk Litterært Registreringsarbeid. 25-68, HALV
Munthe, Wilhelm. Norske Avdelings Forhistorie. 1-44, OSLO
Tank, Roar. De Femti År. 9-32, OSLN

LEGAL DEPOSIT (of books, etc.) - Russia
Bäckman, Edvin. Lagstiftningen Angående Pliktexemplar i Sovjetunionen. 118-129, TUDE

LEGAL DEPOSIT (of books, etc.) - Thuringia
Pflaume, Heinz. Zur Geschichte des Pflichtexemplars in Thüringen. 225-231, VORS

LEGAL LITERATURE (Bourgogne) - Collections - Dijon
Chevrier, Georges. La Littérature Juridique Bourguignonne et les Collections Manuscrites de la Bibliothèque Publique de Dijon. 78-86, OURS

LEGAL LITERATURE - Collections - Münster
Küster, A. Die Juristische Abteilung der Königlichen Universitäts-Bibliothek zu Münster. 268-300, MÜNS

Legendre, Paul.
Notes Tironiennes du Vatic. Lat. Reg. 846. 312-331, CHAT

LEGENDS - Collections - Austria
Kern, Anton. Magnum Legendarium Austriacum. 429-434, BICK

Legg, J. Wickham.
Ratio Decursus Qui Fuerunt ex Auctores. 149-167, CERI

LEGHORN - Jewish libraries and collections
see Jewish libraries and collections - Leghorn

LEGHORN. Talmud Tora. Biblioteca
Bernheimer, Carlo. The Library of the Talmud Torah at Leghorn. 1-4, FREI

LEGIBILITY
Zachrisson, Bror. Probleme des Studiums der Lesbarkeit von Gedrucktem Text. 158-164, BOCK

LEGISLATION - Libraries
see Library legislation

Lehmann, Paul.
Alte Vorläufer des Gesamtkatalogs. 69-81, LEYG
Aus der Bibliothek des Reformators Johannes Hessius. 101-124, LEYH
Aus einer Münchner Büchersammlung

des Ausgehenden Mittelalters. 157-164, LEID
Bücherliebe und Bücherpflege bei den Karthäusern. 364-389, EHRE
Fulda und die Antike Literatur. 9-23, FULD
Eine Fuldaer Handschrift. I, 140-144, GLAU
Quot et Quorum Libri Fuerint in Libraria Fuldensi. 47-57, COLL

Lehnert, Georg.
Verzeichnis der Schriften von Hugo Hepding. 261-273, HEPD

LEHNIN, Ger. (Cistercian monastery). Biblioteca

Abb, Gustav. Von der Verschollenen Bibliothek des Klosters Lehnin. 1-14, DEGE

Lehrmann, N. J.
RAND

LEIBNIZ FAMILY (Ambrosius Leibniz)

Brauer, Adalbert. Beziehungen der Vorfahren von Gottfried Wilhelm Leibniz zu Buchdruck und Buchhandel. 50-67, BENZ

LEIBNIZ, GOTTFRIED WILHELM, Freiherr von

Brauer, Adalbert. Beziehungen der Vorfahren von Gottfried Wilhelm Leibniz zu Buchdruck und Buchhandel. 50-67, BENZ

Leicht, Pier Silverio.
La Biblioteca d'un Umanista. 77-81, GODE
L'Editore Veneziano Michele Tramezino ed i Suoi Privilegi. 357-367, FERR
Scrittori e Miniatori di Codici nei Loro Rapporti cogli Scolari Bolognesi nella Seconda Metà del Sec. XIII. 227-233, GREG

LEIDEN
see Leyden

LEIDINGER, GEORG

Handwerker, Otto. Bibliothekare und Universitäten, mit Belegen aus der Geschichte der Würzburger Universitätsbibliothek. 85-94, LEID

LEIDINGER, GEORG - Bibl.

Hartmann, Albert. Die Schriften Georg Leidingers 1891-1930. 307-320, LEID

LEIPZIG - Architecture and building - Color, decoration, etc.
see Architecture and building - Color, decoration, etc. - Leipzig

LEIPZIG - Architecture and building - National libraries
see Architecture and building - National libraries - Leipzig

LEIPZIG - Bibliography - Collections
see Bibliography - Collections - Leipzig

LEIPZIG - Book industry and trade
see Book industry and trade - Leipzig

LEIPZIG - Bookbinding
see Bookbinding - Leipzig

LEIPZIG - Booksellers and libraries
see Booksellers and libraries - Leipzig

LEIPZIG - Catalogs - Author
see Catalogs - Author - Leipzig

LEIPZIG - Catalogs - Subject
see Catalogs - Subject - Leipzig

LEIPZIG. Deutsche Bücherei

LEIS

LEIZ

Fleischhack, Curt. Deutsche Bücherei und Zentralkatalogisierung. 143-150, VORS
Frels, Wilhelm. Das Deutsche Drama 1913-1920. Statistisches aus der Deutschen Bücherei. 38-50, MIND
Paust, Albert. Johann Heinrich Plath, ein Wegbereiter der Deutschen Bücherei. 64-67, STUM
Rückert, Ernst. Die Auskunftserteilung, eine der Hauptaufgaben der Deutschen Bücherei. 274-285, VORS
Seemann, Artur. Alere Flammam. 3-6, MIND

LEIPZIG. Deutsche Bücherei, Auskunftsstelle

Uhlendahl, Heinrich. Ernstes und Heiteres aus der Auskunftsstelle der Deutschen Bücherei. 90-91, STUM

LEIPZIG. Deutsche Bücherei - Bibl.

Bibliographie zur Geschichte der Deutschen Bücherei. 197-211, LEIS
Paust, Albert, et al. Bibliographie zur Geschichte der Deutschen Bücherei. 287-367, LEIZ

LEIPZIG. Deutsche Bücherei. Deutsche Musikbibliographie
see Deutsche Musikbibliographie

LEIPZIG. Deutsche Bücherei. Deutsche Nationalbibliographie
see Deutsche Nationalbibliographie

LEIPZIG. Deutsche Bücherei - Hist. - 1945-49

Fleischhack, Curt. Frau Dr. Snimščikova. 83-85, BULL

LEIPZIG. Deutsche Bücherei. Jahresverzeichnis der Deutschen Hochschulschriften
see Jahresverzeichnis der Deutschen Hochschulschriften

LEIPZIG. Deutsche Bücherei. Leipziger Zetteldruck

Uhlendahl, Heinrich. Leipziger Zetteldruck. 53-61, GODE

LEIPZIG. Deutsches Buch- und Schriftmuseum

Funke, Fritz. Originales Sammelgut im Deutschen Buch- und Schriftmuseum. 219-241, LEIZ

LEIPZIG. Deutsches Museum für Buch und Schrift
see Leipzig. Deutsches Buch- und Schriftmuseum

LEIPZIG - Friends of the library
see Friends of the library - Leipzig

LEIPZIG - German literature - Collections
see German literature - Collections - Leipzig

LEIPZIG - Humboldt, Alexander von - Collections
see Humboldt, Alexander von - Collections - Leipzig

LEIPZIG - Inscriptions - Collections
see Inscriptions - Collections - Leipzig

LEIPZIG - Library resources
see Library resources - Leipzig

LEIPZIG - Manuscripts, Latin - Collections
see Manuscripts, Latin - Collections - Leipzig

LEIPZIG - Maps - Collections
see Maps - Collections - Leipzig

LEIPZIG - Music printing
see Music printing - Leipzig

LEIPZIG - National libraries
see National libraries - Leipzig

LEIPZIG - National libraries - Acquisitions
see National libraries - Acquisitions - Leipzig

LEIPZIG - Paleography - Collections
see Paleography - Collections - Leipzig

LEIPZIG - Printing
see Printing - Leipzig

LEIPZIG - Public libraries
see Public libraries - Leipzig

LEIPZIG - Publishers and libraries
see Publishers and libraries - Leipzig

LEIPZIG - Publishers and publishing
see Publishers and publishing - Leipzig

LEIPZIG - Reader services
see Reader services - Leipzig

LEIPZIG. Sankt Thomas (Abbey) Biblioteca

Debes, Dietmar. Das Sequestrationsverzeichnis der Bibliothek des Thomasklosters zu Leipzig. 83-95, LÜLF

LEIPZIG. Stadtbibliothek

LEIP

Degering, Hermann. Nachträgliches zur Vitruvausgabe vom Jahre 1487 in der Leipziger Stadtbibliothek. 54-57, LEIP

LEIPZIG. Stadtbibliothek - Hist.

Hofmann, Johannes. Die Leipziger Stadtbibliothek 1677-1927. 9-21, LEIP

LEIPZIG. Stadtbibliothek, Mss. (CXC)

Schmidt, Adolf. Das Reichenauer Evangelistar. Handschrift CXC der Stadtbibliothek zu Leipzig. 22-41, LEIP

LEIPZIG. Stadtbibliothek. Mss. (Rep. II, fol. 21a)

Kroker, Ernst. Bruchstücke einer Handschrift des Jüngeren Titurel in der Leipziger Stadtbibliothek. 42-48, LEIP

LEIPZIG. Thomaskloster
see Leipzig. Sankt Thomas (Abbey) Biblioteca

LEIPZIG. Universität. Bibliothek

Kern, Anton. Die Promotionsschriften der Jesuitenuniversitäten in der Zeit des Barocks. Eine Bibliothekarische Studie. 38-47, SCHT
Mogk, Helmut. System und Schlagwort. Erfahrungen am Fachkatalog der Universitätsbibliothek Leipzig. 214-224, VORS
Schreiber, Heinrich. Von der Goldschnittlyrik zum Schmetterlingsbuch. Orientalische Literatur in Deutscher Ausstattung. 82-92, SCHR

LEIPZIG. Universität. Bibliothek - Hist. - 15th-16th cent.

Debes, Dietmar. Das Sequestrationsverzeichnis der Bibliothek des Thomasklosters zu Leipzig. 83-95, LÜLF

LEIPZIG. Universität. Bibliothek - Hist. - 16th cent.

Müller, Johannes. Gegenseitige Beziehungen der Universitäten Leipzig und Krakau, Insbesondere in den Ersten Jahrhunderten des Bestehens dieser Universitäten. 209-211, BULL

LEIPZIG. Universität. Bibliothek. Mss.

Glauning, Otto. Drei Lederschnittbände von der Wende des XIV. Jahrhunderts aus Altzelle. 188-195, BOLL

LEIPZIG. Universität. Bibliothek. Mss. (Cod. ms. 305)

Frisch, Ernst von. Über die Salzburger Handschrift von Hugo von St. Victors Opusculum de Fructu Carnis et Spiritus. 67-71, LEID

LEIPZIG. Universität. Bibliothek. Mss. (Humboldt)

Wustmann, Felix. Drei Unbekannte Briefe Alexander v. Humboldts in der Universitätsbibliothek Leipzig. 265-269, BULL

LEIPZIG. Universität. Bibliothek. Mss. (Papyrus Ebers)

Debes, Dietmar. Zur Erwerbung des Papyrus Ebers. 139-141, BULL

LEIPZIGER TITELDRUCKE

Franz, Rudi. Die Titeldrucke der Deutschen Bücherei. 157-173, LEIZ

LEIPZIGER ZETTELDRUCK
see Leipzig. Deutsche Bücherei. Leipziger Zetteldruck

Lejay, Paul.
Les Recensions Antiques d'Horace. 59-74, CHAT

Lelièvre, Pierre.
La Bibliothèque de Richard Mique, Architecte de la Reine Marie-Antoinette. 333-336, CALO
Livres et Libraires en Avignon à L'Epoque Romantique. 269-275, BONN

Lemaître, Henri [=Henry].
Le Libre Accès au Rayon. 343-349, LEYG
Magasins de Livres et Lumière Naturelle. 23-31, GODE

LEMBERG
see L'vov

Lenchantin de Gubernatis, M.
De Codice Bononiensi quo Copa et Moretum Continentur. 199-201, STAM

Lengstorf, Ewald.
Die Musiksammlung Liebeskind. 94-96, BERU

LENINGRAD. Academy of Sciences of the USSR
see Academy of Sciences of the USSR

LENINGRAD. Library

Schmitz-Kallenberg, Ludwig. Ein in Vergessenheit Geratener Druck einer Papsturkundenlehre aus dem 18. Jahrhundert. 130-132, BÖME

LENINGRAD. Public Library. Firkowitz Collection. Mss. (127, Qu.)

Bacher, W. Die Zweite Version von Saadja's Abschnitt über die Wiederbelebung der Todten. 219-226, STEI

LENINGRAD. Publichnaîa Biblioteka
see Leningrad. Library

LEONARDO DA VINCI

Donati, Lamberto. Leonardo da Vinci ed il Libro Illustrato. 117-138, WEHM

Leporace, Tullia Gasparrini.
Notizie e Documenti Inediti sul Tipografo Antonio Carcano (1475-1525). 327-366, FERR

Leporini, Heinrich.
Simon von Niederaltaich und Martin v. Senging. 575-590, VIEN

Leppla, Rupprecht.
Die Landesbibliothek von 1866 bis zum Weltkrieg 1914. 233-365, WIES
Die Landesbibliotheken als Gattung. 116-125, BOLL

Lerch, Alice Hollister.
Aids to the Identification of American Imprints. 27-34, EAME
Who Was the Printer of Jefferson's Notes? 44-56, LYDE

LEROY, GUILIELMUS REGIS, printer

Rath, Erich von. Der Drucker von Buyers Ausgabe der Werke des Bartolus von 1482. Ein Beitrag zur Buchdruckergeschichte Lyons. 217-225, SCHW

Leskien, Elfriede.
Johann Gottlob Böhme, ein Leipziger Bücherfreund des 18. Jahrhunderts. 69-79, LEIP

Leslie, Sir Shane.
The Swift Manuscripts in the Morgan Library. 445-448, GREE

LESSL, PETRUS, bookbinder

Haebler, Konrad. Die Bucheinbände des Petrus Leßl. 103-110, SCHW

LETTERS
see Correspondence

LETTERS PATENT - Collections - Dijon
Grémaud, Gabriel. Aux Archives de Dijon. Quelques Documents Portant la Signature des Rois de France. 115-119, OURS

LEUNENSCHLOSS, OTTO
LEUN

LEUTHOLF, HIOB
see Ludolf, Hiob

Leuze, Otto.
Mit Holzschnitten Verzierte Buchumschläge des 15. Jahrhunderts in der Württembergischen Landesbibliothek in Stuttgart. 165-169, LEID

Levaillant, Maurice.
Le "Pline-le-Jeune" de Sainte-Beuve. 285-292, BONN

LEVERKUSEN - Industrial libraries
see Industrial libraries - Leverkusen

LEVERKUSEN. Kekulé-Bibliothek
see Farbenfabriken Bayer Aktiengesellschaft. Kekulé-Bibliothek

Levi, A.
Tracce di Bassa Latinità nei Cognomi Piemontesi. 131-141, STAM

Levyns, J. E. P.
Mr. D. H. Varley and the Institute of Citizenship. 25, VARL

Lewenhaupt, Eugène.
Rosenhaneska Handskriftssamlingen i Uppsala Universitetsbibliotek. 292-316, UPPS
Upsala Universitetsbiblioteks Brefsamlingar. Försök till Historik. 195-207, ANNE

Lewicka-Kamińska, Anna.
Neues Donatfragment in der Type der 42zeiligen Bibel in der Jagiellonischen Bibliothek. 13-16, LÜLF

Lewin, Bernhard.
Uppsala Universitetsbiblioteks Samling av Arabiska 1500- och 1600-Talstryck. 577-604, GRAP

Lewis, Benjamin M.
Engravings in Early American Magazines, 1741-1810. 203-218, GJEL

Lewis, John F., Jr.
Introduction. 7-9, DAVI

Lewis, Wilmarth S.
Introduction. xix-xxi, WROT

LEYDEN - Book industry and trade
see Book industry and trade - Leyden

LEYDEN. Rijksuniversiteit. Bibliotheek
Sevensma, Tietse Pieter. De Bibliotheca Neerlandica Manuscripta De Vreese in Leiden. 167-175, BISH

LEYDEN. Rijksuniversiteit. Bibliotheek. Mss. (Vossius 0 91)
Barrau-Dihigo, L. À Propos d'un Manuscrit Hispanique de Leyde (XIIIe Siècle). 332-340, CHAT

Leyh, Georg, ed.
MILF

Leyh, Georg.
Ansprache bei der Trauerfeier am 29. Januar 1934 im Krematorium Wilmersdorf. 17, MILK
August Wilmanns und Emil Jacobs. 125-136, STOL
Aus der Älteren Bibliothekspraxis. 159-174, SCHW
Bibliographisches. 78-85, VORS
Bibliothekshistorisches aus dem J. D. Reuss-Briefwechsel. 1-9, SCHT
Bildung und Ausbildung des Bibliothekars. 55-56, STUM
Ein Brief Johann Michael Franckes von 1748. 78-81, BOLL
Die Camera della Segnatura—ein Bibliotheksraum? 171-177, LEID
Chr. G. Heynes Eintritt in die Göttinger Bibliothek. 220-228, MILF
Nachwort. 41-47, LEYV
Über die Sächsische Landesbibliothek in Dresden. 69-70, BOLE
Vom Büchersaal zum Magazin. 160-167, MUNT
Zur Geschichte des Neueren Bibliotheksbaues. 156-162, KUHN
Zur Vorgeschichte des Bibliothekarischen Berufes. 475-498, COLL

LEYH, GEORG
LEYG
LEYH
LEYV
L[eyh], G[eorg]. Nachwort. 41-47, LEYV

LEYH, GEORG - Bibl.
Burr, Victor. [Georg Leyh] Verzeichnis der Schriften. 7-40, LEYV
Raff, Hermann. Verzeichnis der Schriften von Georg Leyh. XIII-XXVI, LEYG
Schmid, Paul. Verzeichnis der Schriften von Georg Leyh seit Juni 1937. 7-12, LEYH

Lhotsky, Alphons.
Die Wiener Palatina und die Geschichtsforschung unter Sebastian Tengnagel. 450-462, BICK

LIBELLUS VARIARUM MEDICINARUM

Wieser, Hans. Ein Tiroler Lederschnittband. 662-665, BICK

LIBER DE INTELLIGENTIIS

Baeumker, Clemens. Zur Frage nach Abfassungszeit und Verfasser des Irrtümlich Witelo Zugeschriebenen Liber de Intelligentiis. 87-102, EHRA

LIBER DIURNUS

Sickel, Th. von. Nouveaux Éclaircissements sur la Première Édition du Diurnus. 15-30, HAVE

LIBER DIURNUS. Mss.

Steinacker, Harold. Zum Liber Diurnus und zur Frage nach dem Ursprung der Frühminuskel. 105-176, EHRD

LIBERTY OF THE PRESS

Trenkov, Khristo. Svobodata na Pechata; Sushtina i Ogranichena. 255-265, MIKN

LIBERTY OF THE PRESS - France - Hist.

Granniss, Ruth Shepard. The New York Printers and the Celebration of the French Revolution of 1830. 193-202, EAME

LIBRARIAN (Word)

Mooy, A. J. de. De Benaming "Bibliothecaris." 544-547, BRUM

LIBRARIANS
see also Children's librarians; College and university librarians; Special librarians

LIBRARIANS

Febvre, Lucien. Le Bibliothécaire, la Bibliothèque et L'Histoire. 106-114, OURS
Kotani, Seiichi. Kankai Jinbutsushi. (Contemporary Men in the Library World.) 22-32, TSUB
Schuster, Wilhelm. Ein Studium Generale der Bibliothekare? 427-447, JUCH
Wilson, Louis Round. What Type Research Librarian? 112-122, PENN

LIBRARIANS - Anecdotes, Facetiae, Satire, etc.

Cowley, John D. The English Librarian. 15-22, GODE

LIBRARIANS AS AUTHORS

Lundgren, Hjalmar. Diktare Bland Svenska Biblioteksmän. 499-505, COLL
Paunel, Eugen. Grillparzer als Bibliothekar. Meinungen, Hoffnungen, Enttäuschungen. 357-383, VORS
Postell, William Dosite. Research and Medical Librarianship. 399-403, DOEJ

LIBRARIANS AS AUTHORS - Germany

Abb, Gustav. Milkaus Literarisches Lebenswerk. 39-45, MILK
Dedo, Richard. Dichter unter den Deutschen Bibliothekaren. 37-47, MILF
Ruppert, Hans. Deutsche Bibliothekare in Selbstdarstellungen. 76-78, STUM

LIBRARIANS AS RESEARCH WORKERS

Henriksson, Karl-Erik. Oppihistoriasta. 130-148, TUDE

LIBRARIANS AS TEACHERS (Univ.)

Henriksson, Karl-Erik. Oppihistoriasta. 130-148, TUDE

LIBRARIANS - Berlin

BERS

Kunze, Horst and Werner Dube. Zur Vorgeschichte der Deutschen Staatsbibliothek. I, 1-47, BERS

LIBRARIANS - Bulgaria

Bozhinova, Bozhana. Anketa za Sŭstoi͡anieto na Bibliotekite i na Bibliotechnii͡a Personal v Bŭlgarii͡a v Krai͡a na 1945 Godina. 392-404, MIKN

LIBRARIANS - Certification
see Certification of librarians

LIBRARIANS - Copenhagen

Birkelund, Palle. Nordmænd i det Kgl. Biblioteks Tjeneste. 30-51, TVET
Fabritius, Albert, COPE

LIBRARIANS - Duties
see Duties of librarians

LIBRARIANS - Education
see Education for librarianship

LIBRARIANS, English

Cowley, John D. The English Librarian. 15-22, GODE

LIBRARIANS, German

Dedo, Richard. Dichter unter den Deutschen Bibliothekaren. 37-47, MILF
Rückert, Ernst. Bedeutende Deutsche Bibliothekare der Neueren Zeit. 73-76, STUM
Ruppert, Hans. Deutsche Bibliothekare in Selbstdarstellungen. 76-78, STUM

LIBRARIANS - Giessen

Schmidt, Erwin. Giessener Bibliothekare. 26-50, GIES

LIBRARIANS - Holstebro, Denmark

HOLS

LIBRARIANS - Horsens, Denmark

HORS

LIBRARIANS - Kassel

KASS

LIBRARIANS - Kyoto

Nakama, Zukuri. Kyōto Toshokan Kyōkai Seinen Kenkyū Gurūpu no Rei. (Organizing Librarians in the Region—the Case of the Young Men's Research Group of the Kyoto Library Association.) 50-75, TOKY

LIBRARIANS - Mainz

Darapsky, Elisabeth. Bibliothekare der Stadtbibliothek Mainz. 17-30, MAIN

Ruppel, Aloys. Bemerkenswerte und Merkwürdige Mainzer Bibliothekare. 187-203, JUCH

LIBRARIANS - Marburg

Rohde, Fritz. Verzeichnis der Bibliothekare an der Universitätsbibliothek in Marburg. 294-303, KUHN

LIBRARIANS - Memoirs, Reminiscences, etc. - Berlin

Löffler, Carl. Bibliothekarische Erinnerungen aus den Zwanziger Jahren. 83-91, SCHS

LIBRARIANS - Memoirs, Reminiscences, etc. - India

Rao, C. V. Subba. Diary Leaves Afloat. 639-642, RANG

LIBRARIANS - Memoirs, Reminiscences, etc. - Sheffield, Eng.

LAMB

LIBRARIANS - Qualifications and selection
see Personnel - Qualifications and selection

LIBRARIANS - Rome (City)

Harnack, Adolf von. Julius Afrikanus, der Bibliothekar des Kaisers Alexander Severus. 142-146, MILF

LIBRARIANS - Southern States

Branscomb, Harvie. Some Characteristics of Southern Libraries. 386-398, WILS

LIBRARIANS - Status - India

Kumar, Girija. The Librarian and the Community. 135-138, MADR

LIBRARIANS - Status - Uppsala - Hist. - 17th-18th cent.

Andersson, Aksel. Några Rangfrågor vid Uppsala Universitet vid Tiden för Erik Benzelius d. y:s Utnämning till Bibliotekarie. 373-390, UPPS

LIBRARIANS - Swedish

Lundgren, Hjalmar. Diktare Bland Svenska Biblioteksmän. 499-505, COLL

LIBRARIANS - Training
see Education for librarianship

LIBRARIANS - Trondheim

Landmark, Joh. D. Bibliotekarer og Assistenter ved det Kgl. Norske Videnskabers Selskabs Bibliotek i Trondhjem 1766-1858. 131-149, OSLN

LIBRARIANS - Uppsala

Annerstedt, Claes. Förteckning å Upsala Universitetsbiblioteks Ledare Jämte Korta Upplysningar Rörande deras Verksamhet. 1-39, UPPS

LIBRARIANS - Vienna

Stummvoll, Josef. Die Präfekten der Bibliotheca Palatina Vindobonensis, der Früheren Kaiserl. Königl. Hof- und Jetzigen Österreichischen Nationalbibliothek bis zur Gegenwart. 3-21, BICK

LIBRARIANS - Weimar - Hist.

WEIM

LIBRARIANSHIP

Bayer, Wilhelm. Gedanken zum Bibliothekarischen Berufsbild. 49-60, LANF
Jahier, Enrico. Note di Tecnica e Specializzazione Bibliotecaria. 209-214, GREG
Lifka, Bohumír. Radosti a Strasti Knižní Akvisice. 120-124, EMLE
Majumdar, H. K. Librarianship: A Science or an Art? 348-350, RANG
Schnorr von Carolsfeld, Ludwig. Über den Bibliothekar, von dem Sohne eines Solchen. 295-299, STOL
Sevensma, Tietse Pieter. Modern Librarianship. 235-240, MUNT
Shera, Jesse H. and James W. Perry. Changing Concepts of Classification, Philosophical and Education Implications. 37-48, RANG
Vajpayee, S. B. Ranganathan: The Teacher. 593, RANG

LIBRARIANSHIP - Aims and objectives

Solomon, A. G. What Is a Library? 333-340, RANG

LIBRARIANSHIP AS A CAREER
see also Recruiting for librarianship

LIBRARIANSHIP AS A CAREER

Brummel, Leendert. The Librarian as a Scholar. 100-122, BRUE
Knorr, Friedrich. Der Beruf des Wissenschaftlichen Bibliothekars in Unserer Zeit. I, 112-118, GLAU

LIBRARIANSHIP - Austria

Kammel, Karl. Die Prüfungen des Wissenschaftlichen Bibliotheksdienstes in Österreich. 423-428, BICK

LIBRARIANSHIP - Educational aspects

Joerden, R. Gefährdetenpädagogik und Volksbücherei. 55-64, ACKE
Schuder, Werner. Der Bibliothekar und die Universitas Litterarum. 59-81, SCHS

LIBRARIANSHIP - Germany - Hist. - 1941

Schmidt-Künsemüller, Friedrich Adolf. Hermann Tiemann und das Deutsche Bibliothekswesen der Gegenwart. 11-22, TIEM

LIBRARIANSHIP - Hist.
see Libraries and librarianship - Hist.

LIBRARIANSHIP - International aspects

Arnesen, Arne. How Norway Became the Focus of American Library Methods in Europe. 148-155, HANS
Bishop, William Warner. J. C. M. Hanson and International Cataloging. 165-168, HANS
Breycha-Vauthier, A.-C. Marcel Godet Bibliothécaire "International." 27-30, GODM
Brummel, Leendert. Confrontation of Libraries and Documentation. 9-16, DONR
King, Alexander. International Trends in Librarianship and Documentation. 489-491, BRUM
Michailov, A. I. Donker Duyvis' Contribution to the Progress of Scientific Information and Documentation. 30-38, DONR
Ranganathan, Shiyali Ramamrita. International Library Scene. 191-196, HOFM
Voorhoeve, N. A. J. F. Donker Duyvis and Standardization. 39-50, DONR

LIBRARIANSHIP - Norway

Klemp, Helene L. Norsk Bibliotekforenings Jubileumsskrift. 9-15, NORS

LIBRARIANSHIP - Norway - Hist.

Fiskaa, H. M. Norsk Bibliotekforenings Virke. Resultater og Oppgaver. 58-73, NORS

LIBRARIANSHIP - Philosophical aspects

Khanna, Jang Bahadur. Philosophy of Librarianship. 346-347, RANG
Kievits, A. P. M. Het Bibliotheekvak. 482-488, BRUM
Koutník, Bohuslav. K Základům Knihovědy a Knihovnictví. 174-185, ŽIVN
Müller, Gerhard H. Epistel eines Bibliothekarischen Laien. 66-71, HOFF
Prinzhorn, Fritz. Rationalisierung im Bibliotheks-, Buch- und Zeitschriftenwesen. 327-332, KUHN
Scherrer, Paul. Sub Aeternitatis Specie. 163-165, MADR
——————. Die Zeit im Bibliothekarischen Beruf. 169-173, HOFM
Shaw, Ralph R. The Form and the Substance. 238-247, TVET

LIBRARIANSHIP - Psychological aspects

Kästner, Erhart. Über das Bibliothekarische Mißvergnügen und noch ein Zweiter Traktat. 295-302, WEHM
Sekino, Shinkichi. Toshokan'in no Seikatsu Taido ni tsuite. (On the Attitude of Life of Librarians.) 37-40, OTAT

LIBRARIANSHIP - Research
see Research in librarianship

LIBRARIANSHIP - Social aspects

Joerden, R. Gefährdetenpädagogik und Volksbücherei. 55-64, ACKE

LIBRARIANSHIP - Study and teaching
see Education for librarianship

LIBRARIANSHIP - U.S.

Fitzgerald, William A. American Librarianship. 7-13, MADR

LIBRARIES

Francis, Sir Frank. The Large General Library in the Mid-Twentieth Century. 427-430, BRUM
Gode, M. Dokumentat͡siia, Biblioteki i Bibliografii͡a. 327-333, MIKN

LIBRARIES - Acquisitions
see Acquisitions

LIBRARIES - Administration

Abb, Gustav. Von der Kollegialverfas-

sung zum Führerprinzip. Ein Beitrag zur Verfassungsgeschichte der Preußischen Staatsbibliothek. 245-256, LEYG
Escher, Hermann. Moderne Bibliotheksbestrebungen und Bibliotheksaufgaben mit Besonderer Rücksicht auf die Geplante Zürcherische Zentralbibliothek (1912). 71-85, ESCH
Hanson, J. C. M. Organization and Reorganization of Libraries. 519-532, WILS
Nakamura, Hatsuo. Shiryō Soshiki Kyōjuho no Hensen; Amerika no Toshokan Gakko o Chūshin to Shite. (On Teaching the Organization of Materials for Use. Based on Courses in American Library Schools.) 281-296, HASH
Rogers, Frank B. Management Improvement in the Library. 404-409, DOEJ
Shukla, D. N. Scientific Management of Libraries. 486-487, RANG

LIBRARIES - Administration - Hist.

Ramabhadran, S. Development of Library Administration. 155-157, MADR

LIBRARIES - Administration - Hist. - 1627

Blum, Rudolf. Bibliotheca Memmiana. Untersuchungen zu Gabriel Naudés "Advis pour Dresser une Bibliothèque." 209-232, WEHM

LIBRARIES - Administration - India

Barot, C. P. Problems of Reorganisation in India. 130-134, MADR

LIBRARIES - Administration - Poland

Grycz, Józef. Polska Polityka Biblioteczna w Latach Powojennych. 71-88, GRYC

LIBRARIES - Administration - Warsaw

Skwarnicki, Marek. Zarys Rozwoju Koncepcji i Organizacji Biblioteki Narodowej w Warszawie (1918-1954). 89-130, GRYC

LIBRARIES - Aims and objectives

Cole, George Watson. The Ideally Perfect Library. 113-127, PUTN
Elahi, Nur. Importance of a Library in a Developing Country. 341-345, RANG
Shaw, Ralph R. The Form and the Substance. 238-247, TVET
Shera, Jesse H. The Library as an Agency of Social Communication. 241-243, KYLE
Tazawa, Kyōji. Toshokan Wa Doko e Ikuka. (Future of the Library.) 7-14, KYOT
Togashi, Shigehiro. Toshokanjin no Negoto. (Function of the Library.) 223-227, KYOT

LIBRARIES, Ancient
see Libraries and librarianship - Hist.

LIBRARIES AND BOOKSELLERS
see Booksellers and libraries

LIBRARIES AND LIBRARIANS - Hist.

Burr, Viktor. Buch und Bibliothek bei Plinius d. J. 94-100, LEYH
Comparetti, D. La Bibliothèque de Philodème. 118-129, CHAT

LIBRARIES AND LIBRARIANSHIP
see also Library science literature

LIBRARIES AND LIBRARIANSHIP

Křížek, O. Logická Struktura Knihovnické Práce. 117-120, EMLE
Tazawa, Kyōji. Toshokan Wa Doko e Ikuka. (Future of the Library.) 7-14, KYOT

LIBRARIES AND LIBRARIANSHIP - Europe

Hanson, J. C. M. Amerikansk og Europeisk Biblioteksvesen. Streiflys og Sammenligninger. 287-292, MUNT

LIBRARIES AND LIBRARIANSHIP - Hist.
see also
Cataloging - Hist.; Catalogs - Hist.; Monastic libraries

LIBRARIES AND LIBRARIANSHIP - Hist.

Brummel, Leendert. Een Stiefkind der Geschiedenis: Bibliotheekgeschiedenis. 64-80, BRUE
Harnack, Adolf. Die Älteste Inschrift über einer Öffentlichen Kirchen-Bibliothek. 111-114, SCHW
Kapelrud, Arvid S. Et Fønikisk Bibliotek fra det 14. Århundre før Kr. 77-83, TVET
Koch, Theodore Wesley. New Light on Old Libraries. 244-252, HANS
Leyh, Georg. Zur Vorgeschichte des Bibliothekarischen Berufes. 475-498, COLL
Meissner, Bruno. Wie Hat Assurbanipal Seine Bibliothek Zusammengebracht? 244-248, MILF
Naidu, R. Janardhanam. The Library Movement. 118-122, MADR
Schirrmeister, Georg. Über den Stand beim Bau Wissenschaftlicher Bibliotheken. 103-116, BULL

LIBRARIES AND LIBRARIANSHIP - Hist. - Middle Ages

De Ghellinck, Joseph. En Marge des Catalogues des Bibliothèques Médiévales. 331-363, EHRE

LIBRARIES AND LIBRARIANSHIP - India

Rastogi, V. S. Indian Librarianship and Dr. Ranganathan. 362-373, RANG

LIBRARIES AND LIBRARIANSHIP - Madhya Pradesh, India

Moghe, V. S. Dr. Ranganathan and Madhya Pradesh. 374-378, RANG

LIBRARIES AND LIBRARIANSHIP - Punjab

Bathia, Sant Ram. Contribution of the Punjab to the Indian Library Movement. 379-383, RANG

LIBRARIES AND LIBRARIANSHIP - South Africa - Hist.

S[mith], A[nna] H[ester]. First in South Africa—as Far as We Know! 61-63, KENN

LIBRARIES AND LIBRARIANSHIP - U.S.

Hanson, J. C. M. Amerikansk og Europeisk Biblioteksvesen. Streiflys og Sammenligninger. 287-292, MUNT

LIBRARIES AND PUBLISHERS
see Publishers and libraries

LIBRARIES AND SCHOOLS
see Public libraries - Services to Schools; School and public library relationship

LIBRARIES - Antwerp

Schmook, Ger. Dringende Bibliotheekproblemen te Antwerpen. 581-589, BRUM

LIBRARIES - Austria

Breycha-Vauthier, A. C. Österreichs Bibliotheken und die Welt. 264-270, BICK

Hofinger, Josef. Die Öffentlichen Studienbibliotheken Österreichs. 415-422, BICK

LIBRARIES - Austria - Hist. - 1830

Kindervater, Josef. Nachrichten von einer Bibliotheksreise vor 100 Jahren. 230-244, LEYG

LIBRARIES - Bavaria - Hist.

Hilsenbeck, Adolf. Eine Denkschrift Aretins über die Bayerischen Provinzialbibliotheken. 153-161, MILF

LIBRARIES - Berlin - Hist. - 1920-1930

Löffler, Carl. Bibliothekarische Erinnerungen aus den Zwanziger Jahren. 83-91, SCHS

LIBRARIES - Braunsberg, Ger. - Hist.

Will, Edmund. Zur Geschichte der Braunsberger Bibliotheken bis zum Beginn des Neunzehnten Jahrhunderts. 374-388, KÖNI

LIBRARIES, Buddhist
see Buddhist libraries

LIBRARIES - Bulgaria

Bozhinova, Bozhana. Anketa za Sŭstoi͡anieto na Bibliotekite i na Bibliotechnii͡a Personal v Bŭlgarii͡a v Krai͡a na 1945 Godina. 392-404, MIKN

LIBRARIES - Collections
see Library resources; Acquisitions

LIBRARIES - Connecticut - Hist.

Sills, R. Malcolm and Eleanor Stuart Upton. The "Trumbull Manuscript Collections" and Early Connecticut Libraries. 325-342, KEOG

LIBRARIES - Croatia

Rojnič, Matko. Überblick über die Bibliographische Tätigkeit in Kroatien. 70-73, STUM

LIBRARIES - Czechoslovakia

Breycha-Vauthier, A. C. La Collaboration Internationale des Bibliothèques dans la Fédération Internationale des Associations des Bibliothécaires. 7-11, EMLE

LIBRARIES - Denmark

Jensen, Erik Allerslev. Forudsætningerne for en Ny Dansk Biblioteksslov. 13-22, HEIN

LIBRARIES, Depository
see Depository libraries

LIBRARIES, Dormitory
see Dormitory libraries

LIBRARIES - Dortmund - Hist.

Wand, Albert. Zur Geschichte der Dortmunder Bibliotheken. 29-58, VERD

LIBRARIES - Europe - Hist. - 16th-18th cent.

Kunze, Horst and Werner Dube. Zur Vorgeschichte der Deutschen Staatsbibliothek. I, 1-47, BERS

LIBRARIES - Europe - Hist. - 1709-1711

Bogeng, G. A. E. Über Zacharias Conrad von Uffenbachs Erfahrungen und Erlebnisse bei der Benutzung

Deutscher, Englischer, Holländischer Öffentlicher Büchersammlungen in den Jahren 1709-1711. 30-46, SCHW

LIBRARIES - Europe - Hist. - 18th cent.

Teichl, Robert. Ein Europäischer Bibliothekenführer um das Jahr 1780. Die Handschrift des Pfarrverwalters von Maria-Taferl Adalbert Blumenschein. 172-179, LEYG
Theele, Joseph. Bibliothekskundliche Nachrichten aus dem 18. Jahrhundert. II, 144-149, GLAU

LIBRARIES - Exhibits and displays
see Exhibits and displays

LIBRARIES - Germany

Uhlendahl, Heinrich. Die Deutsche Bücherei im Rahmen der Deutschen Bibliotheken. 1-35, LEIS

LIBRARIES - Germany - Hist.

Paust, Albert. Johann Heinrich Plath, ein Wegbereiter der Deutschen Bücherei. 64-67, STUM

LIBRARIES - Germany - Hist. - 1830

Kindervater, Josef. Nachrichten von einer Bibliotheksreise vor 100 Jahren. 230-244, LEYG

LIBRARIES - Germany - Hist. - 15th cent.

Jacobs, Emil. Ars Scripturarum. 177-186, MILF

LIBRARIES - Germany - Hist. - Sources

Leyh, Georg. Bibliothekshistorisches aus dem J. D. Reuss-Briefwechsel. 1-9, SCHT

LIBRARIES - Germany - Hist. - 20th cent.

Hoffmann, Wilhelm. Einige Gedanken zum Wiederaufbau Kriegsgeschädigter Bibliotheken. 39-41, STUM

LIBRARIES - Gifts, contributions, etc.
see Gifts, contributions, etc.

LIBRARIES - Gothenburg, Sweden

Hallberg, S. and O. von Feilitzen. Göteborgs Stadsbibliotek. Det Första Halvseklet 1891-1940. 1-142, (first paper), GÖTE

LIBRARIES - Hanover

May, Otto Heinrich. Bibliothekswesen in Hannover. 88-101, LEUN

LIBRARIES - Hist.
see Libraries and librarianship - Hist.

LIBRARIES - India - Hist.

Swaminathan, S. Libraries in India: Yesterday and Today. 353-361, RANG

LIBRARIES, International
see International libraries

LIBRARIES - Italy

Carini-Dainotti, Virginia. Biblioteche Generali e Biblioteche Speciali nelle Discussioni Parlamentari. 117-167, FERR

LIBRARIES - Italy - Hist. - 1945

Apollonj, Ettore. Problemi Estetici nella Ricostruzione di Biblioteche Sinistrate dalla Guerra. 79-85, GALL

LIBRARIES - Japan

Kyōdō Kenkyū. (A Joint Study.) Toshokan no Hatten o Habamu Mono. (Obstacles to the Progress of Libraries.) 1-32, TOKY

LIBRARIES - Latin America - Hist. - 16th-19th cent.

Thompson, Lawrence S. The Libraries of Colonial Spanish America. 257-266, WEHM

LIBRARIES - Legal aspects

Flury, Hans. Die Rechtliche Natur des Bibliotheksbuches. 99-115, SCHU

LIBRARIES - Mainz - Hist.

Ruppel, Aloys. Bemerkenswerte und Merkwürdige Mainzer Bibliothekare. 187-203, JUCH

LIBRARIES - Mechanical aids
see Mechanization of library processes

LIBRARIES - Mohammedan countries

Grohmann, Adolf. Bibliotheken und Bibliophilen im Islamischen Orient. 431-442, VIEN

LIBRARIES - Nashville

Nashville Libraries House over 2,000,000 Volumes. 12-13, NASH

LIBRARIES - Nassau (Duchy) - Hist.

WIES

LIBRARIES - Norway

Arnesen, Arne. How Norway Became the Focus of American Library Methods in Europe. 148-155, HANS
Klemp, Helene L. Norsk Bibliotekforenings Jubileumsskrift. 9-15, NORS

LIBRARIES - Norway - Hist.

Fischer, Karl. Biblioteksakens Utvikling i Norge 1836-1937. 26-38, NORN

LIBRARIES - Organization
see Libraries - Administration

LIBRARIES - Oxford - Hist. - Early

Craster, Herbert Henry Edmund. A Note on the Early History of Libraries in Oxford. 169-171, LEYG

LIBRARIES - Personnel
see Personnel

LIBRARIES - Ras Shamra

Kapelrud, Arvid S. Et Fønikisk Bibliotek fra det 14. Århundre før Kr. 77-83, TVET

LIBRARIES - Registration of borrowers
see Registration of borrowers

LIBRARIES - Relations with publishers
see Publishers and libraries

LIBRARIES, Research
see Research libraries

LIBRARIES - Rome (City)

Harnack, Axel von. Einige Beobachtungen an den Deutschen Bibliotheken in Rom. 304-309, KUHN

LIBRARIES - Russia - Hist. - 18th cent.

Il'inskiĭ, L. K. Biblioteka Iv. Mikh. Khvostova; k Istorii Bibliotek XVIII Veka. 346-374, MALE

LIBRARIES - Russia - Hist. - 19th cent.

Feyl, Othmar. Bücher, Bibliotheken und Leser in der Russischen Gesellschaft des 19. Jahrhunderts. 97-133, LÜLF

LIBRARIES - Salisbury, Rhodesia

Ivey, D. L. An Ex-Sapling's View of Salisbury. 29-31, VARL

LIBRARIES - Saxony - Hist.

Schmidt, Ludwig. Die Sächsischen Bibliotheken im Mittelalter. 105-115, BOLL

LIBRARIES - Scandinavia

Mookerjee, S. Libraries of Scandinavia. 108-115, MADR

LIBRARIES - 17th cent.

Escher, Hermann. Der Bibliothecarius Quadripartitus des Joh. Heinrich Hottinger (1664) (1934). 169-184, ESCH

LIBRARIES - Size

Barnett, Claribel R. The Size Factor in Library Problems. 68-79, PUTN

LIBRARIES - Sociological aspects

Karstedt, Peter. Zur Soziologie der Bibliothekstypen. 61-76, TIEM
Ranck, Samuel H. Social Service of the Public Library. 365-377, PUTN

LIBRARIES - Sociological aspects - Hamburg

Fenske, Herbert. Soziologische Zusammensetzung der Leserschaft. 75-82, HAMB

LIBRARIES - South Africa

Ferguson, Milton J. South African Libraries. 151-155, PUTN
Holdsworth, H. Bibliography in South Africa. 151-159, OFFO

LIBRARIES - Southern States

Branscomb, Harvie. Some Characteristics of Southern Libraries. 386-398, WILS
Wilson, Louis Round. Library Conditions and Objectives in the South. 528-538, PUTN

LIBRARIES - Southern States - Hist.

Barker, Tommie Dora. Library Progress in the South, 1936-42. 353-362, WILS

LIBRARIES - Spain

Vega, Javier Lasso de la. El Cuerpo Facultativo de Archiveros, Bibliotecarios y Arqueólogos de España. 183-186, HOFM

LIBRARIES - Special collections
see Special collections

LIBRARIES - Sweden - Hist.

Silow, Alvar. Bibliotekens Samarbete. 214-220, GRAP

LIBRARIES - Switzerland

Bourgeois, Pierre. Quelques Considérations sur les Bibliothèques Suisses dans la Vie Internationale. 73-80, SCHU
Escher, Hermann. Die Stellung der Schweizerischen Bibliotheken zur Frage einer Einheitlichen Regelung der Katalogisierung (1912). 33-44, ESCH
Godet, M. Hermann Escher et les Bibliothèques Suisses. 8-19, ESCK
Grosser, Hermann. Die Zusammenarbeit der Schweizerischen Bibliotheken. Rückblick und Ausschau. 129-142, SCHU

LIBRARIES - Switzerland - Hist.

Escher, Hermann. Ein Amtlicher Bericht über die Schweizerischen

Bibliotheken aus der Zeit der Helvetik. 84-111, BINZ (Also appears pp. 208-230, ESCH)
——— Die Schweizerischen Bibliotheken in der Zeit der Helvetik, 1798-1803 (1936). 185-207, ESCH
——— Schweizerisches Bibliothekswesen (1929). 3-32, ESCH

LIBRARIES - Trentino-Alto Adige, Italy

Franceschini, Ezio. Le Versioni Latine Medievali di Aristotele e dei Suoi Commentatori Greci ed Arabi nelle Biblioteche delle Tre Venezie. 313-326, FERR

LIBRARIES - Turkey

Thompson, Lawrence S. Das Moderne Türkische Bibliothekswesen. 86-89, STUM

LIBRARIES - U.S. - Foreign impressions

Brummel, Leendert. Bibliotheekproblemen in Amerika. 48-63, BRUE
Tisserant, Eugène, Cardinal. Notes et Impressions sur les Bibliothèques d'Amérique. 445-457, PUTN
Wild, Helen. Hermann Escher und die Schweizerischen Volksbibliotheken. 22-34, ESCK

LIBRARIES - U.S. - Hist.

Krummel, Donald W. The Library World of Norton's Literary Gazette. 237-266, GJEL

LIBRARY AIDE
see Non-professional assistants

LIBRARY AND THE PUBLIC
see also Library community relations

LIBRARY AND THE PUBLIC

Anker, Øyvind. Bibliotekaren og Publikum. 86-91, KILD
Birkelund, Palle. Det Kongelige Bibliotek og dets Publikum. 119-132, DAHA
Fryček, Václav M. Veřejné Knihovny a Veřejné Mínění. 192-199, ŽIVN
Müller, Gerhard H. Epistel eines Bibliothekarischen Laien. 66-71, HOFF
Sealoff, Georgia. Anyone Can Make a Library Materials Center. It's What Happens There That Counts. 121-126, HASH
Skudlarska, Danuta. Działalność Oświatowa i Kulturalna w Środowisku. 115-123, BYDG

LIBRARY AND THE PUBLIC - Bydgoszcz

Czytelnicy o Bibliotece. 149-157, BYDG

LIBRARY AND THE PUBLIC - Germany

Hesse, Gerhard. Gesellschaftliche Faktoren bei der Gründung und in der Entwicklung der Deutschen Bücherei bis zum Jahre 1923. 19-46, LEIZ

LIBRARY AND THE PUBLIC - Germany - Hist.

Unger, Willy. Benutzungseinrichtungen, Benutzungspolitik und Gebrauchsöffentlichkeit. I, 175-221, BERS

LIBRARY AND THE PUBLIC - Japan - Hist.

Ono, Noriaki. Edo-ki ni okeru Kokugakusha no Toshokan Undo. (Library Activities of Japanese Scholars in the Edo Period.) 53-94, KYOT

LIBRARY AND THE PUBLIC - Kraków

Czytelnicy o Nas. 114-122, KRAK

LIBRARY AND THE STATE
see also Propaganda and the library

LIBRARY AND THE STATE - Berlin - Hist.

Kunze, Horst. Demokratisierung und Sozialistische Umgestaltung. I, 49-76, BERS

LIBRARY AND THE STATE - Weimar

Deetjen, Werner. Die Weimarische Bibliothek unter Ernst August und Ernst August Constantin. 87-101, WEIM

LIBRARY ASSOCIATION

Minto, John. The Library Association Examinations. 285-295, HANS

LIBRARY ASSOCIATION - County Libraries Section. Readers' Guides

Wright, A. Shaw. The Series, "Readers' Guides." 73-79, MADR

LIBRARY ASSOCIATION - Hist. - 20th cent.

Munford, W. A. The Library Association in the Twentieth Century: Selected Aspects. 26-47, SAYW

LIBRARY ASSOCIATIONS
see Associations

LIBRARY BUILDINGS
see Architecture and building

LIBRARY COMMUNITY RELATIONS
see also Library and the public

LIBRARY COMMUNITY RELATIONS

Shera, J. H. The Library as an Agency of Social Communication. 241-243, KYLE

LIBRARY COOPERATION
see Cooperation

LIBRARY COPYING SERVICES
see Photographic reproduction services

LIBRARY COUNCILS
see Governing authorities of libraries

LIBRARY DEVELOPMENT - Regional plans
see Public libraries - State and regional development plans

LIBRARY EMBLEMS, INSCRIPTIONS, etc.

Harnack, Adolf. Die Älteste Inschrift über einer Öffentlichen Kirchen-Bibliothek. 111-114, SCHW
Odelstierna, Ingrid. ΨΥΧΗΣ Iatpeion. 376-407, GRAP
Teichl, Robert. Bibliotheksinschriften. 81-83, STUM

LIBRARY EXTENSION
see also Bookmobile services; County libraries; Package libraries; Rural libraries

LIBRARY EXTENSION - U.S.

Tyler, Alice S. Library-Extension: A Basic Factor in Adequate Book Service. 458-466, PUTN

LIBRARY FIRSTS
see Libraries and librarianship - History

LIBRARY INSPECTION - France

Schmidt, Charles. Des Vivres et des Livres. 41-44, GODE

LIBRARY LEGISLATION - Austria

Adamovich, Ludwig. Zur Frage des Rechtsschutzes für Private Bibliotheken. 203-207, BICK

LIBRARY LEGISLATION - Austria - Hist.

Poch, Josef. Snahy L. J. Živného o Knihovní Zákonodárstvi. 130-144, ŽIVN

LIBRARY LEGISLATION - Berlin - Hist. - 1955

Stremlau, Willi and Martin Thilo. Berliner Büchereigesetz und Büchereibau. 183-189, SCHS

LIBRARY LEGISLATION - Bohemia - Hist.

Poch, Josef. Snahy L. J. Živného o Knihovní Zákonodárstvi. 130-144, ŽIVN

LIBRARY LEGISLATION - Bombay (State)

Parkhi, R. S. Dr. Ranganathan's Plan for Library Development in Bombay. 397-400, RANG

LIBRARY LEGISLATION - Czechoslovakia - Hist.

Poch, Josef. Snahy L. J. Živného o Knihovní Zákonodárstvi. 130-144, ŽIVN
Velemínský, Karel. L. J. Živný a Jeho Účast na Vzniku Našeho Zákona o Veřejných Knihovnách Obecních. 144-146, ŽIVN

LIBRARY LEGISLATION - Denmark

Hansen, Robert L. Centralbibliotekets Udvikling og Administration under Biblioteksloven. 17-36, LASS
Haugstrup, S. Kalundborg Bibliotek 1920-1926. 22-36, KALU
Jensen, Erik Allerslev. Forudsætningerne for en Ny Dansk Bibliotekslov. 13-22, HEIN
Møller, J. S. Kalundborg Folkebogsamling 1901-1920. 5-21, KALU

LIBRARY LEGISLATION - Germany

Rottacker, Gustav. Zur Büchereigesetzgebung in der Bundesrepublik. 39-47, ACKR
Wolff, Hans J. Grundsätze des Bibliotheksverwaltungsrechts. 279-286, WEHM

LIBRARY LEGISLATION - Italy

Carini-Dainotti, Virginia. Biblioteche Generali e Biblioteche Speciali nelle Discussioni Parlamentari. 117-167, FERR

LIBRARY LEGISLATION - Japan

Hatano, Ken'ichi. Meiji Shonen ni okeru Kanritsu Toshokan Hakubutsukan no Hassei to Sono Hensen—Fu, Toshokan Kankei Horei, Shuppanho. (The Establishment of National Libraries and Museums in the Early Period of the Meiji Era and Their Progress—Appendix: Laws Relating to Libraries and Laws on Publication.) 85-160, OTAT

LIBRARY LEGISLATION - Madras (State)

Ranganathan, Shiyali Ramarita. Then, Now and Hereafter. 1-6, MADR
Sivaraman, K. M. March of Library Legislation in Madras. 387-396, RANG

LIBRARY LEGISLATION - Missouri

Compton, Charles H. An Unfinished Chapter in Missouri Library Legislation. 412-421, WILS

LIBRARY LITERATURE
see Library science literature

LIBRARY OF CONGRESS CLASSIFICATION
see Classification - Systems - Library of Congress

LIBRARY PHOTOGRAPHIC REPRODUCTION SERVICES
see Photographic reproduction services

LIBRARY PLANNING
see Planning, Library

LIBRARY PUBLICATIONS - Japan

Isono, Kōzaburo. Jimu Kokorooboe Issoku. (Memoranda on Library Works.) 74-78, (part 1), OHAS

LIBRARY RESOURCES
see also College and university libraries - Book collections

LIBRARY RESOURCES - Berlin

Tyszko, Oskar. Die Bestandsvermehrung der Hauptabteilung und Ihre Organisation. I, 89-129, BERS

LIBRARY RESOURCES - Berlin - Hist. - 1940-1959

Schmidt, Werner. Die Verlagerung der Bestände im Zweiten Weltkrieg und Ihre Rückführung. I, 77-86, BERS

LIBRARY RESOURCES - Bern

BERU

Grosser, Hermann. Der Auskunftsdienst. 168-173, BERU

LIBRARY RESOURCES - Dresden

Pepino, Jan. Aus der Täglichen Arbeit der Sächsischen Landesbibliothek. 86-91, DREL

LIBRARY RESOURCES - Gorizia (C[illegible])

Battisti, Carlo. Il Centenario della Biblioteca Governativa di Gorizia. 9-24, GORI

LIBRARY RESOURCES - Leipzig

Bergmann, Werner und Heinz Kleeberg. Der Beitrag der Deutschen Bücherei zur Lösung Volkswirtschaftlicher Aufgaben. 91-103, LEIZ
Rückert, Ernst. Das Wachsen und Werden der Bestände. 75-90, LEIS
Schwidetzky, Georg. Der Benutzungsdienst. 137-147, LEIS

LIBRARY RESOURCES - Maastricht

Wouters, H. H. E. "Een Bibliotheque voor den Meesten Luyster van de Stadt." 9-28, MAAS

LIBRARY RESOURCES - Southern States

Branscomb, Harvie. Some Characteristics of Southern Libraries. 386-398, WILS

LIBRARY RESOURCES - U.S.

Downs, Robert B. Leading American Library Collections. 457-473, WILS
Kuhlman, A. F. Wanted: A New Policy for the Organization and Development of Library Resources for Research. 585-600, WILS

LIBRARY RESOURCES - Vienna

BICK

Stummvoll, Josef. Die Druckschriftenbestände der Österreichischen Nationalbibliothek und die Abschreibung des Alphabetischen Kataloges 1501 bis 1929. 105-118, HOFM

LIBRARY SCHOOLS
see also Education for librarianship

LIBRARY SCHOOLS - Accreditation and standards - U.S.

Gitler, Robert L. Toshokangaku Kyōiku no Kijun to Nintei. (Accreditation in Library Science Education.) 159-165, HASH

LIBRARY SCHOOLS - Atlanta

Gleason, Eliza Atkins. The Atlanta University School of Library Service—Its Aims and Objectives. 504-510, WILS

LIBRARY SCHOOLS - Berlin

Ackerknecht, Erwin. Erinnerungen an die Anfänge der Berliner Büchereischule. 7-12, LANF
Otto, Hanna. Berliner Bibliothekarschule seit 1949. 173-181, SCHS

LIBRARY SCHOOLS - Cologne

Sickmann, Ludwig. Der Katalogisierungsunterricht für Anfänger. Bericht über Erfahrungen im Bibliothekar-Lehrinstitut. 448-457, JUCH

LIBRARY SCHOOLS - Denmark

Hansen, Robert L. Om Uddannelse af Bibliotekarer ved Folkebibliotekerne. 17-37, DØSS

LIBRARY SCHOOLS - Essen

Sulz, Eugen. Die Büchereischule der Stadt Essen 1921-1933. 13-16, LANF

LIBRARY SCHOOLS - India

Kaula, P. N. Library Education in Perspective. 541-552, RANG

LIBRARY SCHOOLS - Japan - Hist.

Hashimoto, Takashi. Toshokangakka no Jittai to Sono Tembō. Japan Library School, Yesterday, Today, and Tomorrow. (In both English and Japanese.) 1-11, (3rd section), HASH

LIBRARY SCHOOLS - Theses - Russia - Bibl.

Pregled na Disertatsii po Bibliotekoznanie i Bibliografii͡a v SSSR. 381-391, MIKN

LIBRARY SCHOOLS - Theses - U.S. - Bibl.

Koul, Doroti Etlin. Tezi, Prieti ot Bibliotekarskite Uchilishta v Sŭidinenite Shtati ot I͡uli 1938 do I͡uni 1945 g. 346-380, MIKN

LIBRARY SCIENCE

Binwal, J. C. Scientific Method. 312-320, RANG
Borov, T. Bibliotechna Nauka. 304-320, MIKN
Chand, Gian. Implications of the Five Laws of Library Science. 326-330, RANG
Dimchevska, Margarita. Bibliotechna Ratsionalizatsii͡a. 148-151, MIKN
Iwasaru, Toshio. Toshokangaku ni okeru Hikakuhō ni tsuite. (Comparative Method in Library Science.) 1-6, KYOT
Lisovskiĭ, N. M. Knigovedenie, Ego Predmet i Zadacha. 5-21, MALE
Predeek, Albert. Die Bibliothekswissenschaft als Disziplin und Universitätslehrfach. 169-184, LEYH
Prinzhorn, Fritz. Rationalisierung im Bibliotheks-, Buch- und Zeitschriftenwesen. 327-332, KUHN
Puranik, K. D. Emergence of the Laws of Library Science. 145-149, MADR
Schauman, Georg. Biblioteksväsendets Organisation. 1-16, HULA
Singh, Hakam. Dr. Ranganathan and Library Science. 614-621, RANG
Thirumalaimuthuswamy, A. Five Laws of Library Science. 321-325, RANG

LIBRARY SCIENCE - Germany

Handwerker, Otto. Bibliothekare und Universitäten, mit Belegen aus der Geschichte der Würzburger Universitätsbibliothek. 85-94, LEID

LIBRARY SCIENCE - India

Saxena, R. S. India's Contribution to Library Science. 625-631, RANG

LIBRARY SCIENCE LITERATURE - Japan

Isono, Kōzaburo. Jimu Kokorooboe Issoku. (Memoranda on Library Works.) 74-78, (part 1), OHAS

LIBRARY SCIENCE - Research
see Research in librarianship

LIBRARY SCIENCE - Russia - Bibl.

Pregled na Disertatsii po Bibliotekoznanie i Bibliografii͡a v SSSR. 381-391, MIKN

LIBRARY SCIENCE - Teaching

Predeek, Albert. Die Bibliothekswissenschaft als Disziplin und Universitätslehrfach. 169-184, LEYH

LIBRARY SERVICE
see also Library and the public; Reader services

LIBRARY SERVICE

Shaw, Ralph R. The Form and the Substance. 238-247, TVET

LIBRARY SERVICE - Southern States

Wilson, Louis Round. Optima in Library Service for the South by 1950. 186-204, BISH

LIBRARY SERVICES ACT - State and regional development plans
see Public libraries - State and regional development plans

LIBRARY SYSTEMS
see Libraries - Aims and objectives; Public libraries - Centralization

LIBRARY TRAINING
see Education for librarianship

LIBRARY WORK
see Duties of librarians

LIBRETTOS - Collections - Göttweig

Riedel, Friedrich W. Die Libretto-Sammlung im Benediktinerstift Göttweig. 105-111, FEDO

LIBRI CAROLINI

Wallach, Luitpold. The Unknown Author of the *Libri Carolini*: Patristic Exegesis, Mozarabic Antiphons, and the *Vetus Latina*. 469-515, ALBA

Lichtenstein, Walter.
Library Education. 270-273, HANS

LIDÉN, JOHAN HENRIK

Lundgren, Hjalmar. En Uppsala-Biblioteks Donator och dennes Biblioteksplaner. Några Randanmärkningar till ett par Ritningar. 461-467, UPPS

LIDÉN, JOHAN HENRIK. Mss. *Dagbok*

Nelson, Axel. Aus J. H. Lidéns Tagebuch über Seinen Aufenthalt in Göttingen in den Jahren 1768-1769. 255-263, MILF

Liebaers, Herman.
Des Expositions dans les Bibliothèques. 159-168, HOFM
De Koninklijke Bibliotheek van België na 125 Jaar. 514-520, BRUM

LIEBAERT, PAUL
Laurent, M.-H. L'Abbé Paul Liebaert, Scriptor Honoraire Adj. de la Vaticane. Sa Vie et Ses Oeuvres (1883-1915). II, 1-132, ALBB

Lieberman, Saul, ed.
MARX

Lieberman, Saul.
Commentary on the Palestinian Talmud. 313-315, MARY
The New Fragments from the Yerushalmi. 284-286, MARY

LIEBESKIND, JOSEF - Library
Lengstorf, Ewald. Die Musiksammlung Liebeskind. 94-96, BERU

Lieftinck, G. I.
Enige Problemen met Betrekking tot Gedaterrde Goudse Handschriften. 139-154, KOSS

LIÈGE. Université. Bibliothèque. Mss. (no. 3460)
Stiennon, J. Un Fragment Inédit d'un Obituaire de Saint-Servais de Maestricht (XIVe et XVe Siècles). 131-167, MAAS

Liermann, Hans.
Das Buch im Deutschen Rechtsgang. 137-146, STOL
Buch und Recht. 33-35, REDE

Lietzmann, Hans.
Handschriftliches zur Rekonstruktion des Sacramentarium Gregorianum. 141-158, EHRB
Zur Datierung der Josuarolle. 181-185, DEGE

Lifka, Bohumír.
Radosti a Strasti Knižní Akvisice. 120-124, EMLE

LIGURIA - Shorthand, Italian
see Shorthand, Italian - Liguria

Likhatscheff, Nicolas.
Une Lettre de Nicolas Eymerici. 130-134, CHAT

Liliev, Nikolaĭ.
Edno Pismo. 45-48, MIKN

Liljeroth, Erik.
Bibliotekets Vardag. 137-154, KRIS

LILLE. Bibliothèque Municipale
Bruchet, Andrée. Quelques Reliures Estampées Signées de la Fin du XVe et du Début du XVIe Siècle de la Bibliothèque Municipale de Lille. 81-91, BONN

LILLE - Bookbinding - Fine bindings - Collections
see Bookbinding - Fine bindings - Collections - Lille

LIMITED EDITION BOOKS
Bachmair, Heinrich F. S. Über "Luxusausgaben." 161-163, HELD

LIMITED EDITION BOOKS - Acquisitions
Semrau, Eberhard. Die Erwerbund Moderner Bibliophiler Werke. 43-52, REDE

LIMITED EDITION BOOKS - Collections - Leipzig
Rodenberg, Julius. Die Sammlung der Künstlerischen Drucke. 165-176, LEIS

LIND, ERIK HENRIK
LIND
Erik Henrik Lind—70 År. [v]-viii, LIND

Lindau, Hans.
Aus der Berliner Dienststelle der Universitätsschriften. 238-244, KUHN

Lindberg, Folke.
Broadcasting Libraries and Archives as Music Research Centres. 76-79, FEDO

Linder, Greta.
När Vi Började. Minnen från Bibliotekskonsulenternas Tidiga År. 183-201, HEIN

Lindqvist, J. C. Sune.
Hiob Ludolf och Sverige. 605-625, GRAP

Lindsay, W.-M.
The Notae Iuris of Vat. Reg. 886. 155-162, CHAT

LINKÖPING, Sweden. Stifts- och Landsbiblioteket
Gobom, Nils. Gustaf Odencrants' E. T. A. Hoffmann-Samling i Linköpings Stifts- och Landsbibliotek. 262-279, GRAP
Lagerborg, Rolf. Ur Hecatompolis Suionum. 112-125, HULA

LINKÖPING, Sweden. Stifts- och Landsbiblioteket. Mss. (B 59)

Gobom, Nils. Eric Benzelius d. y:s Itineris Eruditi Album i Linköpings Stiftsbibliotek. 385-394, COLL

LINNÉ, CARL VON. Förteckning över Johan Moraeus' Boksamling

Uggla, Arvid HJ. Ett Läkarebibliotek från Början av 1700-Talet. 221-248, GRAP

LINNÉ, CARL VON. Library

Hulth, J. M. Studenten Carolus Linnaeus' Bibliotek. 395-400, COLL

LINNÉ, CARL VON. Mss.

Hulth, J. M. Uppsala Universitetsbiblioteks Förvärv av Linneanska Originalmanuskript. 407-424, UPPS

Linnemann, Richard.
Die Gesellschaft der Freunde der Deutschen Bücherei. 188-196, LEIS

LIPPE, House of - Collections - Detmold

Schmidt, Adolf. Lippische Ablaßbriefe. 227-233, SCHW

Lippi, Silvio.
La Libreria di Monserrato Rossellò Giureconsulto e Bibliografo Sardo del Sec. XVI. II, 319-332, MANO

Lipš, František.
První Soustavná Práce Knihovnická v Písku. 164-166, ZIVN

Lipska, Helena.
Bibliografia Prac Kazimierza Piekarskiego. 377-393, PIEK

Lisovskiĭ, N. M.
Knigovedenie, Ego Predmet i Zadacha. 5-21, MALE

Lisowski, Stanisław.
Do Dziejów Biblioteki Zygmunta Augusta. 241-249, PIEK

Lissberger, Ewald, jt. ed.
HOFF

LISTE DES TRAVAUX PUBLIÉS PAR M. CH. OURSEL. 37-47, OURS

LITERARY FAIRS
see Book fairs

LITERARY FORGERIES AND MYSTIFICATIONS

Currier, Thomas Franklin. The Whittier Leaflet "Pericles." 175-178, HANS
Juchhoff, Rudolf. Aus der Werkstatt der Frühdruckforschung. 119-129, TIEM
———— Die Literarische Fälschung des Thomas J. Wise. 41-48, BRIE

LITERARY FRAUDS
see Literary forgeries and mystifications

LITERARY GAZETTE, NORTON'S
see Norton's Literary Gazette

LITERARY MUSEUMS

Brummel, Leendert. Literatuur als Museumobjekt. 81-99, BRUE

LITERARY MUSEUMS - Dresden

Boden, Charlotte. Das Buchmuseum in den Semper-Räumen des Japanischen Palais. 46-51, BOLE
Deckert, Helmut, Marita Kremer, Hans Pfeifer, and Liselotte Willi. Das Neue Buchmuseum der Sächsischen Landesbibliothek. 175-205, DREL
Kremer, Marita. Blick in das Buchmuseum der Sächsischen Landesbibliothek 1956. 52-56, BOLE

LITERARY MUSEUMS - Marbach

Zeller, Bernhard. Fünf Jahre Deutsches Literaturarchiv in Marbach. Ergebnisse, Erfahrungen, Planungen. 349-384, HOFF

LITERARY MUSEUMS - Zürich

Wild, Helen. Hermann Escher und der Zwingli-Verein; mit Liste der Historischen Publikationen Hermann Eschers. 1-5, ESCZ

LITERARY SOCIETIES - Denmark

Hansen, Robert L. Nyt Danske Litteraturselskab. 95-103, THOM

LITERATURE - Museums
see Literary Museums

LITERATURE OF THE HUMANITIES

Cheney, Frances Neel. Reference Service in English and American Literature. 41-47, HASH

LITERATURE OF THE HUMANITIES - Collections - Berlin

Sauer, Bruno. Die Literarischen Sammlungen der Amerika-Gedenkbibliothek. 191-204, SCHS

LITERATURE OF THE HUMANITIES, foreign
see Foreign language books

LITERATURE OF THE HUMANITIES - Selection

Hauptmann, Hansheinz. Über die Unentbehrlichkeit Geistiger Voraussetzungen für die Bestandsauswahl der Schönen Literatur. 9-13, ACKR

LITERATURE SEARCHING
see Information retrieval

Littmann, Enno.
Ein Arabisches Lied über die Ägyptische Bibliothek in Kairo. 309-311, LEYG

LITURGIES - Collections - Vatican

Zelenka, Ignác. Edizioni Liturgiche della Pečerskaja Lavra di Kiev nella Biblioteca Vaticana. II, 377-414, ALBB

LIU, HSIANG

Suzuki, Ryūichi. Ryūkō Fushi no Gakujutsu Mokuroku. (On the First Chinese Book Catalog by Ryūkō [father and son].) 104-114, KYOT

LIUDPRANDUS, Bp. of Cremona. Mss. Antapodosis

Meyer, Gustav. Ein Neues Bruchstück zu Liudprand von Cremona. 163-175, SCHU

Livingston, Dorothy Flower and Mollie Marjorie Patton, et al.
Contribution to a Bibliography of Francis Bacon. Editions before 1700 in Yale Libraries. 95-143, KEOG

LIVIUS ANDRONICUS. Equox Troianus

Lallier, Roger. Note sur la Tragédie de Livius Andronicus Intitulée Equox Troianus. 103-109, GRAU

LIVRY, NICOLAS LA PINTE DE
see La Pinte de Livry, Nicolas, Bp. of Callinique

Livsey, Rosemary E.
Fiction, a Way of Life. 23-28, SAYE

Ljunggren, Evald.
Fragment av en Katolsk Andaktsbok på Svenska från 1525 (?). 265-267, COLL

Llorens, José Maria.
Los Codices Musicales de la "Capella Sixtina" en la Historia del Arte. II, 191-209, ALBB

Lloyd, G. A.
A "New Deal" for Universal Classification? 149-153, DONK

LLUCH, ANTONIO RUBIÓ Y
see Rubió y Lluch, Antonio

LOAN WORK
see Circulation procedures

LOCAL HISTORY AND RECORDS
see Research materials

LOCKE, JOHN. Essay Concerning Human Understanding

Meyer, A. M. T. Enkele Opmerkings oor die Doel van Locke se Essay. 207-210, VLEE

Lodi, Teresa.
La Vera Storia di un Presunto Cimelio Cinquecentesco (Il Cosiddetto Torchio della Biblioteca Medicea Orientale). 234-253, GREG

Lodolini, Armando.
Origine e Attività del Laboratorio di Restauro Presso L'Archivio Centrale dello Stato. 519-534, GALL

ŁÓDŹ, Poland. Biblioteca Publiczna
see Łódź, Poland. Public Library

ŁÓDŹ, Poland. Miejska Biblioteka Publiczna
see Łódź, Poland. Public Library

ŁÓDŹ, Poland. Public Library - Hist.

Augustyniak, Jan. Nieznane Fragmenty z Historii Biblioteki Publicznej w Łodzi. 330-337, GRYC

ŁÓDŹ, Poland - Reading
see Reading - Łódź, Poland

ŁÓDŹ, Poland. Regional Lending Library

Nagórska, Izabela. Portrety Czytelników-Robotników w Łodzkiej Dzielnicy Chojny. 155-168, GRYC

ŁÓDŹ, Poland. Rejonowa Wypozyczalna Książek
see Łódź, Poland. Regional Lending Library

ŁÓDŹ, Poland - Use Studies - Public libraries
see Use studies - Public libraries - Łódź, Poland

Loebeling, Isolde.
Buch und Synonyma im Tatian, Heliand und bei Otfrid. 59-69, JUCR

Löffler, Carl.
Bibliothekarische Erinnerungen aus den Zwanziger Jahren. 83-91, SCHS

Löffler, Karl.
Zur Geschichte der Abendländischen Schreibformen. Eine Würdigung des Gleichbetitelten Buches von Hermann Delitsch. 61-66, SCHR

Löffler, Klemens.
Die Corveyer Schlossbibliothek. 287-296, BÖME

Loehr, August.
Josef Bick und die Organisation des Wis-

senschaftlichen Dienstes. 45-50, BICK

Loewinger, D. S.
New Fragments from the Yerushalmi Pesaḥim ch. 5-7, 237-283, MARY

Lohikoski, Inga and Dolly Ölander.
Förteckning över Paul Nybergs Tryckta Skrifter 1910-1958. 133-146, NYBE

Lohrer, Alice.
School Libraries in the U.S. Meet the Challenges of Today. 81-90, HASH

Lohrer, Liselotte.
Hölderlin-Ausgabe und Hölderlin-Archiv. Entstehung und Geschichte. 289-314, HOFF

Lohse, Gerhart, jt. ed.
JUCR

Lohse, Gerhart.
Gedanken zur Auswahl des Nachwuchses für die Wissenschaftliche Bibliothekarische Laufbahn. 73-84, JUCR

Lohse, Hartwig.
Zum Aufbau eines Neuen Sachkatalogs nach dem "System Eppelsheimer" an der Senckenbergischen Bibliothek unter Besonderer Berücksichtigung der Medizin. 102-110, FUCH

Lomba y Pedraja, José Ramón.
Un Libro de Don José Somoza o si Se Quiere un Articulito. II, 229-241, ARTI

Lomer, Gerhard Richard.
Sir Henry Ellis in France. A Chapter in the History of the British Museum. 116-144, BISH

LOMPA, JÓZEF (1797-1863) - Library

Rudnicka, Jadwiga. Fragment Biblioteki Lompy. 281-306, GRYC

LONDON. British Museum
see British Museum

LONDON - Catalogs - Dictionary
see Catalogs - Dictionary - London

LONDON. College of Arms
see Gt. Brit. College of Arms. Library - Mss. (Arundel no. 9)

LONDON - Czechoslovakian literature - Collections
see Czechoslovakian literature - Collections - London

LONDON. Guildhall Library. Noble Collection

Hollaender, Albert E. J. Ein Unveröffentlichter Augenzeugenbericht über Napoleon I. an Bord des "Bellerophon" im Kriegshafen von Plymouth, Juli-August 1815. 44-45, STUM

LONDON - Manuscripts, Hebrew - Collections
see Manuscripts, Hebrew - Collections - London

LONDON. National Central Library

Filon, S. P. L. W. C. Berwick Sayers: His Connection with the National Central Library and His Contribution to Library Co-operation. 22-25, SAYW

Longo, Luigi.
Nuovo Materiale per la Produzione di Fotografie Inalterabili di Documenti: Vetro Fotosensibile. 535-537, GALL

LONGWOOD LIBRARY
see Eleutherian Mills Historical Library, Greenville, Del.

Loosjes, Th. P.
Documentanalyse. 521-526, BRUM

Lorphèvre, Georges.
Donker Duyvis et la Classification Décimale Universelle. 17-24, DONR

Lott, Walter, jt. ed.
WOLJ

Loubier, Hans.
Versuch einer Klassifizierung der Einbände für Jean Grolier. 421-434, COLL

LOUBIER, HANS

LOUB

Jessen, Peter. Der Mann. 1-2, LOUB

LOUBIER, HANS - Bibl.

Bernoulli, Rudolf. Das Werk. 3-10, LOUB

Loubier, Jean.
Methodische Erforschung des Bucheinbands. 175-184, SCHW

LOUDON, SAMUEL - Bibl.

Vail, R. W. G. A Patriotic Pair of Peripatetic Printers, the Up-State Imprints of John Holt and Samuel Loudon, 1776-1783. 391-422, WROT

LOUIS BONAPARTE, King of Holland

Oudendijk, Johanna K. De Universiteitsbibliotheek te Utrecht als Koninklijk Paleis en als Voorwerp van Koninklijke Belangstelling. 244-249, EVER

LOUIS XVI, King of France - Imprisonment - Library

Bring, Samuel E. Från Tempeltornet till Carolina? 199-213, GRAP

LOUIS XIV, King of France - Library

Foncin, Myriem. L'Histoire d'une Collection de Cartes Réunies pour Louis XIV. 119-126, CALO

Louis-Lucas, Pierre.
Voisinage. 147-151, OURS

LOUVAIN - Bookbinding
see Bookbinding - Louvain

LOW GERMAN LITERATURE - 16th-18th cent. - Collections

Colliander, Elof. Die Niederdeutschen Drucke der Universitätsbibliothek zu Uppsala aus dem 16., 17. und 18. Jahrhundert. 147-170, GRAP

Lowe, Elias Avery.
Greek Symptoms in a Sixth-Century Manuscript of St. Augustine and in a Group of Latin Legal Manuscripts. 277-289, ALBA
A Hand-List of Half-Uncial Manuscripts. 34-61, EHRD
The Morgan Golden Gospels: The Date and Origin of the Manuscript. 266-279, GREE
A New List of Beneventan Manuscripts. II, 211-244, ALBB

LOWE, ELIAS AVERY. The Beneventan Script. Suppl.

Lowe, Elias Avery. A New List of Beneventan Manuscripts. II, 211-244, ALBB

Lowell, Mildred Hawksworth, jt. author

Henne, Frances and Mildred Hawksworth Lowell. The Preparation of Secondary-School Teachers in the Use of Library Materials. 533-556, WILS

Lowinsky, Edward E.
Early Scores in Manuscript. 126-173, KINK

LUCCA - Catalogs
see Catalogs - Lucca

LUCCA - Printing
see Printing - Lucca

LUCCA. San Romano (Dominican convent) Biblioteca - Catalogs

Corsi, Domenico. La Biblioteca dei Frati Domenicani di S. Romano di Lucca nel Sec. XV. 295-310, GALL

LUCERNE - Bookbinders
see Bookbinders - Lucerne

LUCERNE. Bürgerbibliothek

Schnellmann, Meinrad. Die Innerschweizerischen Handschriften der Bürgerbibliothek Luzern. 223-232, SCHU

LUCERNE (Canton) - Paper making and trade
see Paper making and trade - Lucerne (Canton)

LUCERNE - Manuscripts, Swiss - Collections
see Manuscripts, Swiss - Collections - Lucerne

LUCIAN OF SAMOSATA
see Lucianus Samosatensis

LUCIANUS SAMOSATENSIS. Calumnia. Mss.

Goldschmidt, E. Ph. Lucian's Calumnia. 228-244, SAXL

LUCIEN LEURVEN

Wagner, R. L. Les Valeurs de L'Italique. Notes de Lecture sur Lucien Leurven de Stendhal. 381-390, BONN

LUCIFER, Bp. of Cagliari. Mss.

Fischer, P. Bonifaz. Zur Textüberlieferung des Lucifer von Cagliari. 49-54, LEYH

LUDOLF, HIOB

Lindqvist, J. C. Sune. Hiob Ludolf och Sverige. 605-625, GRAP

LUDWIG, KARL, Elector Palatine
see Karl Ludwig, Elector Palatine

LUDVIG XVI
see Louis XVI, King of France

LÜBECK. Stadtbibliothek

LÜBE

LÜBECK. Stadtbibliothek. Geibelzimmer

LÜBE

LÜBEN, Ger. - Church libraries
see Church libraries - Lüben, Ger.

LÜBEN, Ger. Evangelische Gemeinde. Kirchenbibliothek. Mss.

Stern, Ludwig. Mitteilungen aus der Lübener Kirchenbibliothek. 67-96, WILM

LÜBEN, Ger. - Manuscripts - Collections
see Manuscripts - Collections - Lüben, Ger.

Lülfing, Hans.
Die Handschriftenabteilung. I, 319-380, BERS
Zur Sächsischen Bibliotheksgeschichte im 19. Jahrhundert. 343-356, VORS

LÜLFING, HANS

LÜLF

Kunze, Horst. Glückwünsche. 9-11, LÜLF

LÜLFING, HANS - Bibl.

Veröffentlichungen von Hans Lülfing. 7-8, LÜLF

LÜNEBURG. Stadtbibliothek. Mss. (Prag. Univ.-Matrikel)

Doelle, Ferdinand. Ein Fragment der Verlorengegangenen Prager Universitätsmatrikel aus dem 14. Jahrhundert. 88-102, EHRC

Lüthi, Karl Jakob.
Die Abteilung V (Vereine, Gesellschaften und Anstalten). 45-47, BERU
Die Bibelsammlung. 80-83, BERU
Die Depositen des Schweizerischen Gutenbergmuseums. 120-123, BERU
Meine Selbstbibliographie. 180-200, LÜTH
Die Zeitschriften und Serienwerke. 51-55, BERU
Die Zeitungen. 56-59, BERU

LÜTHI, KARL JAKOB

LÜTH

Godet, Marcel. Monsieur K. J. Lüthi et la Bibliothèque Nationale Suisse. 147-149, LÜTH
Kehrli, J. O. Der Kämmerer aus dem Mohrenland. 201-202, LÜTH
———— Vom Setzer zum Ehrendoktor. 145-147, LÜTH
Schwerz, F. Karl J. Lüthi und das Buch. 150-152, LÜTH

LÜTHI, KARL JAKOB. Äthiopisch in der Schweiz

Kehrli, J. O. Äthiopisch in der Schweiz. 202-203, LÜTH

LÜTHI, KARL JAKOB - Bibl.

Lüthi, Karl Jakob. Meine Selbstbibliographie. 180-200, LÜTH

LULL, RAMÓN - Collections - Palma, Majorca

Pons, Antoni. Fra Mario de Passa, Lul-Lista i Bibliòfil. III, 317-337, RUBI

Lullies, Hildegard.
Der Berliner Gesamtkatalog. 131-157, SCHS

Lund, Hanna.
Der Adrema-Betrieb in der Katalogisierung. 404-409, MUNT

LUND. Universitet. Biblioteket

Gierow, Krister. Biblioteksmannen Peter Wieselgren. 127-155, OLSS
Ljunggren, Evald. Fragment av en Katolsk Andaktsbok på Svenska från 1525 (?). 265-267, COLL

LUND. Universitet. Biblioteket - Hist.

Gierow, Krister. Den Förste Universitetsbibliotekarien i Lund och "Bibliotheca Rostiana." 76-91, GARD

LUND. Universitet. Biblioteket. Mss. (Moller)

Gierow, Krister. Lundaprofessorn Arvid Moller Som Tillfällighetsdiktare. 133-143, DAHA

Lundberg, Oskar.
Frågan om Forskarplatser och Forskarrum vid Uppsala Universitetsbibliotek. 59-76, GRAP

Lundgren, Hjalmar.
Carl Bernhard Wadströms Bibliotek. 95-106, GRAP
Diktare Bland Svenska Biblioteksmän. 499-505, COLL
En Uppsala-Biblioteks Donator och dennes Biblioteksplaner. Några Randanmärkningar till ett par Ritningar. 461-467, UPPS

Lundström, Herman.
Det Äldsta Tryckta Svenska Synodalcirkuläret. Ett Nyupptäckt Upsalatryck från 1513. 215-225, ANNE

Lunelund-Grönroos, Birgit.
Gymnasister och Böcker i det Gamla Borgå. 51-58, NYBE
Peter Johan Bladhs "Räkning öfwer Böcker til 1771. Års slut." 85-100, TUDE

Lunelund-Grönroos, Birgit, jt. author

Grönroos, Henrik and Birgit Lunelund-Grönroos. Förteckning över Skrifter Rörande Helsingfors Universitetsbibliotek, dess Samlingar och Enskilda Bokverk. 256-318, DAHL

Luther, Arthur.
Russische Dichter in Deutschen Künstlerischen Drucken. 75-79, BOCK
Der Sachkatalog. 103-119, LEIS

LUTHER COLLEGE, Decorah, Iowa. Library

Jacobsen, Karl T. The Reorganization of the Library of a Small College. 234-243, HANS

Luther, Johannes.
Die Anfänge des Klischee. 181-192, WILM
Drucker- und Verlegernöte in Wittenberg zur Zeit des Schmalkaldischen Krieges. 229-243, MILF
Ludwig Trutebul und die Druckerei "Zum Färbefaß" in Erfurt. 185-195, SCHW

LUTHER, MARTIN

Freitag, Albert. Ein Band aus Luthers Erfurter Klosterbibliothek. 93-110, DEGE

LUTHER, MARTIN - Collections - Berlin

Kaulfuss-Diesch, Carl. Die Neuerwerbungen der Luthersammlung. 47-60, HARN

LUTHER, MARTIN, supposed author. De Servo Arbitrio. 1526

Goes, Rudolf. Ein Unfirmierter Lutherdruck aus Köln vom Jahre 1526. 132-139, BENZ

Luther, Wilhelm Martin.
Die Accessisten der Göttinger Universitätsbibliothek. 527-536, BRUM
Der Komponist und Seine Eigenschrift. 172-186, JUCH
Die Nichtliturgischen Musikinkunabeln der Göttinger Bibliothek. 130-148, TIEM

Lutz, Hans.
Konrad Gesners Beziehungen zu den Verlegern Seiner Zeit nach Seinen Pandekten von 1548. 109-117, GODE

Lutze, Eberhard.
Eine Augsburger Bilderhandschrift aus dem Besitz des Sebastian Schertlin von Burtenbach (Ms. 1620 der UB Erlangen). 147-156, STOL

LUXEMBURG - Printing
see Printing - Luxemburg

LUXUSAUSGABE
see Limited edition books

Luyn, J. L. van.
Schimmel op Boeken in de Utrechtsche Universiteitsbibliotheek. 237-241, EVER

L'VOV - Reformation
see Reformation - L'vov

Lydenberg, Harry Miller, jt. ed.
BISH

Lydenberg, Harry Miller.
Anne Carroll Moore. An Appreciation. 535-536, MOOR
The Ecology of the Pierpont Morgan Library and Its First Director. 6-9, GREE
A Forgotten Trail Blazer. 302-314, PUTN
Freidus the Bookman. XLIV-XLIX, FREI
Libraries and Scholarship: Should Libraries Be Passive Instruments of, or Active Participants in, Research? 90-98, PENN
More Blind Impressions: With Light Therefrom? 601-613, WILS
Some Thoughts on the Part the Printed Book May Play in the International Field. 463-471, BICK
Two Bookmen. 1-9, BLOC
William Warner Bishop. 11-17, BISH

LYDENBERG, HARRY MILLER

LYDE

Cortissoz, Royal. Lydenberg as a Friend. 455, LYDE
MacLeish, Archibald. No Man in Our Time. 335, LYDE
Mather, Frank Jewett, Jr. A Great Administrator. 351, LYDE
Melcher, Frederic G. Harry Lydenberg—Bookman. 437-439, LYDE
Metcalf, Keyes DeWitt. A Builder of Library Research Collections. 399-404, LYDE
Updike, Daniel Berkeley. Amicus Amico. 525, LYDE
Winship, George Parker. Lydenberg in Cambridge and New York. 269-272, LYDE

LYDENBERG, HARRY MILLER - Bibl.

McKay, George L. A Bibliography of the Published Writings of Harry Miller Lydenberg. 5-26, LYDE

Lyle, Guy R.
The University Library in the Self Survey Program of the Southern Association of Colleges and Secondary Schools, Inc. 91-96, HASH

LYON - Printing
see Printing - Lyon

M'

For all names beginning M'
see Mac

M. C.
Zur Geschichte des Hebräischen Buchdruckes in Russland und Polen. 91-96, FREN

Maass, Ernest.
Observationes Palaeographicae. 749-766, GRAU

MAASTRICHT - Hist., Medieval - Collections
Alberts, W. Jappe. De Maastrichtse Raadsverdragen uit de Middeleeuwen. 169-178, MAAS

MAASTRICHT - Library resources
see Library resources - Maastricht

MAASTRICHT - Public libraries
see Public libraries - Maastricht

MAASTRICHT. Sint Servaas (Cathedral). Mss.
Vermeeren, P. J. H. Handschriften van het Kapittel van Sint Servaas ter Koninklijke Bibliotheek in 's-Gravenhage. 179-193, MAAS

MAASTRICHT. Sint Servaas (Cathedral). Mss. (Obituaries)
Stiennon, J. Un Fragment Inédit d'un Obituaire de Saint-Servais de Maestricht (XIVe et XVe Siècles). 131-167, MAAS

MAASTRICHT. Stadsarchief en Bibliotheek
Alberts, W. Jappe. De Maastrichtse Raadsverdragen uit de Middeleeuwen. 169-178, MAAS
Heyst, M. G. M. A. van. Proeve ener Genealogie van het Maastrichtse Kooplieden- en Magistraatsgeslacht Nootstock. 227-261, MAAS

MAASTRICHT. Stadsarchief en Bibliotheek - Hist.
Wouters, H. H. E. "Een Bibliotheque voor den Meesten Luyster van de Stadt." 9-28, MAAS

MAASTRICHT. Stadsbibliotheek
see also Maastricht. Stadsarchief en Bibliotheek

MAASTRICHT. Stadsbibliotheek
MAAS

MABILLON, JEAN
Hessel, Alfred. Mabillons Musterbibliothek. 119-122, DEGE

McDaniel, W. B., 2d.
Snapshot of the Medical Librarian as Historian and Bibliographer, to 1947. 301-308, DOEJ

McDiarmid, E. W.
The Place of Experience in Developing College and University Librarians. 614-621, WILS

MacDonald, Angus Snead.
A Library of the Future. 168-184, MUNT

McDonald, Gerald D.
William Bradford's Book Trade and John Bowne, Long Island Quaker, as His Book Agent, 1686-1691. 209-222, WROT

Macé, Alcide.
Le Basiliensis F III 15a (VIIIe Siècle). 383-395, CHAT

McGILL UNIVERSITY. Montreal. Osler Library
FRAN

MACHINES AND THE LIBRARY
see Mechanization of library processes

MacKall, Leonard L.
Goethe's Letter to Joseph Green Cogswell. 315-326, PUTN

McKay, George L.
A Bibliography of the Published Writings of Harry Miller Lydenberg. 5-26, LYDE

Mackert, Josef.
Die Bibliothek des Bundesverfassungsgerichts. Ein Bericht. 87-111, JUCR

Macleish, Archibald.
No Man in Our Time. 335, LYDE

Macpherson, Harriet D.
The Anonymous Classic and Some Problems of Its Cataloging. 274-281, HANS

Macray, W. D., ed.
A Letter from Isaac Abendana. 89-90, STEI

MADHYA PRADESH, India - Libraries and Librarianship
see Libraries and librarianship - Madhya Pradesh, India

MADRAS LIBRARY ASSOCIATION
MADR
Koranne, T. N. Australia and Madras Library Association. 127-129, MADR
Parthasarathy, K. S. The Madras Library Association. 123-126, MADR
Ranganathan, S. R. Then, Now and Hereafter. 1-6, MADR

MADRAS STATE BIBLIOGRAPHY
Thillainayagam, V. The Madras State Bibliography. 506-507, RANG

MADRAS (State) - Bibliography, National - India
see Bibliography, National - India - Madras (State)

MADRAS (State) - Library legislation
see Library legislation - Madras (State)

MADRAS. University. Library

Sivaraman, K. M. Team Work, Staff Council and Renaissance in Library Science. 475-485, RANG

MADRAZO, JOSÉ DE

Camino y Aguirre, Francisco González. Nuevos Datos para la Biografiía del Pintor Don José de Madrazo. II, 538-557, ARTI

MADRID. Biblioteca Nacional

J. P. Más Datos Sobre el Nombramiento de Menéndez Pelayo como Director de la Biblioteca Nacional. 69-72, MENE

Reyes, Enrique Sánchez. Menéndez Pelayo, Director de la Biblioteca Nacional. 27-67, MENE

Madrjas, Halina.
Rozwój i Działalność Pedagogicznych Bibliotek Powiatowych w Województwie Krakowskim w Latach: 1951, 1961. 38-49, KRAK
Starodruki Pedagogicznej Biblioteki Wojewódzkiej w Krakowie. 50-55, KRAK

MADRUZZO, CRISTOFORO DE, Cardinal. Mss. Correspondence - Collections - Innsbruck

Galante, Andrea. L'Epistolario del Cardinale Cristoforo Madruzzo presso L'Archivio di Stato di Innsbruck. II, 787-805, HORT

Madsen, Victor.
Pergamenttryk i det Kongelige Bibliotek i København. Et Supplement. 199-214, COLL

Madsen, Viggo.
Boghandelen og Bibliotekerne. 45-53, THOM

Madshus, Sigrid.
Fag- og Forskningsbibliotekene i Siste Decennium. 125-130, NORS

MAFFEI FAMILIES (Rome) - Libraries

Ruysschaert, José. Recherche des Deux Bibliothèques Romaines Maffei des XVe et XVIe Siècles. 306-355, MERG

Maggid, David.
Bibliographie der Schriften und Aufsätze A. Harkavy's. IX-LII, (Hebrew section), HARK

MAGIC - Collections - New York (City)

Mulholland, John. Magic in the Library. 446-453, LYDE

MAGYAR TUDOMÁNYOS AKADÉMIA, Budapest
see Hungarian Academy of Sciences, Budapest

MAHLER, GUSTAV - Collections - Munich

Dorfmüller, Kurt. Gustav-Mahler-Dokumente in München. 33-39, FEDO

MAI, ANGELO, Cardinal

Santoro, Enza Fioroni. Dell'Origine e degli Autori di Alcune Stampe Attribuite ad "Ignoto." 427-439, GALL

Maier, Walter.
Anfänge, Werden und Wirken der Württembergischen Bibliotheksgesellschaft. 276-288, HOFF

MAINZ - Architecture and building - Public libraries
see Architecture and building - Public libraries - Mainz

MAINZ - Archives
see Archives - Mainz

MAINZ - Catalogs
see Catalogs - Mainz

MAINZ - Catholic libraries - Hist. - Collections
see Catholic libraries - Hist. - Collections - Mainz

MAINZ - Catholic literature - Collections
see Catholic literature - Collections - Mainz

MAINZ - Circulation analysis
see Circulation analysis - Mainz

MAINZ. Forschungsstelle Papiergeschichte
see Mainz. Gutenberg-Museum. Forschungsstelle Papiergeschichte

MAINZ. Gutenberg-Museum

RUPP

MAINZ. Gutenberg-Museum. Forschungsstelle Papiergeschichte

Renker Armin, Die Forschungsstelle Papiergeschichte im Gutenberg-Museum zu Mainz. 80-89, BOCK

MAINZ - Librarians
see Librarians - Mainz

MAINZ - Libraries
see Libraries - Mainz

MAINZ - Manuscripts - Collections
see Manuscripts - Collections - Mainz

MAINZ - Music printing
see Music printing - Mainz

MAINZ - Personnel
see Personnel - Mainz

MAINZ - Printers
see Printers - Mainz

MAINZ - Printing
see Printing - Mainz

MAINZ - Public libraries
see Public libraries - Mainz

MAINZ - Publishers and publishing
see Publishers and publishing - Mainz

MAINZ. Stadtarchiv

Falck, Ludwig. Die Bestände des Mainzer Stadtarchivs und Ihre Findmittel. 75-88, MAIN

MAINZ. Stadtbibliothek

MAIN

Diepenbach, Wilhelm. Gustav Binz als Direktor der Mainzer Stadtbibliothek. 23-29, BINZ

MAINZ. Stadtbibliothek - Bibl.

Bibliographie zur Geschichte der Stadtbibliothek. 15-16, MAIN

MAINZ. Universität. Bibliothek

MAIZ

MAINZ. Universität. Bibliothek - Hist.

Ruppel, Aloys. Bemerkenswerte und Merkwürdige Mainzer Bibliothekare. 187-203, JUCH

MAINZ. Universität. Bibliothek. Mss.

Arens, Fritz. Das Brevier des Administrators Adalbert von Sachsen in der Mainzer Universitätsbibliothek. 67-89, MAIZ

MAINZ. Universität. Bibliothek. Mss. (Album)

Diez, Ortwin. Otto, Abgeordneter für Trier. Ein Beitrag zur Preussischen Verfassungsgeschichte. 136-169, MAIZ

MAINZ. Universität. Bibliothek. Mss. (Dalberg)

Mühl, Werner. Ein Brief von C. Th. Dalberg. 129-135, MAIZ

MAINZ. Universität. Bibliothek. Mss. (4033)

Reifenberg, Hermann. Die Liturgische Bedeutung der Mainzer Brevierhandschrift MS 4033 des Jahres 1482. 90-102, MAIZ

MAIOLUS, THOMAS, bookbinder

Schmidbauer, Richard. "Nachlese": Ein Unbekannter Maioliband.—Eine Spielkarte und ein Kartenspiel. 255-259, STOL

Majors, O. Cort.
Foreword. ix-xiii, HAMM

Majumdar, H. K.
Librarianship: A Science or an Art? 348-350, RANG

Makowski, Jerzy.
Służba Informacyjnobibliograficzna. 124-130, BYDG

MALA
see Madras Library Association

Malclès, Jean.
Bio-Bibliographie de Jean Bonnerot. 25-47, BONN

Malclès, Louise-Noëlle.
Le Fondateur de la Bibliographie Nationale en France: le R. P. Louis Jacob de Saint-Charles. 243-255, CALO
Jean Bonnerot et la Bibliographie. 21-23, BONN

MALECKI, HIERONYMUS

Gollub, H. Die Beiden Buchdrucker und Erzpriester Maletius. 159-180, KÖNI

MALECKI, JAN

Gollub, H. Die Beiden Buchdrucker und Erzpriester Maletius. 159-180, KÖNI

MALEIN, ALEKSANDR IUSTINOVICH

MALE

Poliakov, A. Predislovie Redaktora. [xi]-xix, MALE

MALEIN, ALEKSANDR IUSTINOVICH - Bibl.

Spisok Trudov Professora Aleksandra Iustinovicha Maleina. [xx]-xxxii, MALE

MALETIUS
see Malecki

Mallaber, K. A.
The Education of Librarians and Information Officers: Government Libraries. 301-304, HUTT

MALLARMÉ, STÉPHANE. Symphonie Littéraire

Mondor, Henri. Sur la Symphonie Littéraire de Mallarmé. 461-467, BONN

MALLINCKRODT, BERNHARD VON. Mss.

Ohly, Kurt. Das Inkunabelverzeichnis Bernhards von Mallinckrodt. (Handschrift des Staatsarchivs Münster I 261.) 37-62, BÖME

MALMÖ, Sweden - Architecture and building - Public libraries
see Architecture and building - Public libraries - Malmö, Sweden

MALMÖ, Sweden - Interlibrary loans
see Interlibrary loans - Malmö, Sweden

MALMÖ, Sweden. Lånecentralen
see Malmö, Sweden. Stadsbiblioteket. Lånecentralen

MALMÖ, Sweden. Stadsbiblioteket

Mark, Jan. Några Bilder från Malmö Stadsbibliotek. [272]ff., HEIN

MALMÖ, Sweden. Stadsbiblioteket. Lånecentralen

Paulsson, Egon. Lånecentralen i Malmö. 548-551, HJEL

MALTA - Incunabula - Collections
see Incunabula - Collections - Malta

MALTA. Royal Library
see Valleta, Malta. Royal Public Library

Maltha, D. J.
Speelse Gedachten. 537-543, BRUM

MALUNG, Sweden. Församlingsbiblioteket.

MALU

MALUNG, Sweden - Parish libraries
see Parish libraries - Malung, Sweden

MALVEZZI, FLORIANO. Lettere - Collections - Modena

Mischiati, Oscar. Un'Inedita Testimonianza su Bartolomeo Ramis de Pareia. 84-86, FEDO

Malý, Jaromír.
Pro Bibliografii Česko-amerického Tisku. 167-171, ŽIVN

MANÂFI'-I ḤAYAVÂN (Mss.)

Ettinghausen, Richard. The Covers of the Morgan Manafi' Manuscript and Other Early Persian Bookbindings. 459-473, GREE

MANCHESTER, Eng. John Rylands Library
see John Rylands Library, Manchester, Eng.

MANCHESTER, Eng. - Manuscripts, Coptic - Collections
see Manuscripts, Coptic - Collections - Manchester, Eng.

MANCHESTER, Eng. - Papyrus collections
see Papyrus collections - Manchester, Eng.

Manders, Johanna H. M.
Donker Duyvis and the Patent Office. 25-29, DONR

Mandl, Hans.
Vorwort. 7-8, VIES

MANNHEIM - Architecture and building - Public libraries
see Architecture and building - Public libraries - Mannheim

MANNHEIM - Music libraries and collections
see Music libraries and collections - Mannheim

MANNHEIM. Städtische Volks- und Musikbücherei

MANN

MANNHEIM. Städtische Volks- und Musikbücherei - Hist.

MANN

MANNO, ANTONIO

MANO

MANNO, ANTONIO - Bibl.

Bibliografia di Antonio Manno. I, xiii-xxv, MANO

Mansion, A.
Le Texte du "De Intellectu" de Philopon Corrigé à L'Aide de la Collation de Monseigneur Pelzer. 325-346, PELZ

MANUSCRIPTS - Administration

Hofmann, Gustav. Gedanken zur Verwaltung von Handschriften in Öffentlichen Wissenschaftlichen Bibliotheken. 52-61, FUCH
Omang, Reidar. Samarbeide Mellem Håndskriftsamlinger. 418-422, MUNT
Schmieder, Wolfgang. Ein Beitrag zur Verwaltung von Briefautographen. 133-140, BOLL

MANUSCRIPTS, Arabic

STEI

MANUSCRIPTS, Arabic - Bibl.

Della Vida, G. Levi. Manoscritti Arabi di Origine Spagnola nella Biblioteca Vaticana. II, 133-189, ALBB

Tisserant, Eugène, Cardinal. Inventaire Sommaire des Manuscrits Arabes du Fonds Borgia à la Bibliothèque Vaticane. 1-34, EHRE

MANUSCRIPTS, Arabic - Collections - London

Poznański, S. Die Qirqisâni-Handschriften im British Museum. 195-218, STEI

MANUSCRIPTS, Arabic - Collections - New Haven

Nemoy, Leon. Notes on Some Arabic Manuscripts on Curious Subjects in the Yale University Library. 45-66, KEOG

MANUSCRIPTS, Arabic - Collections - Vatican

Della Vida, G. Levi. Manoscritti Arabi di Origine Spagnola nella Biblioteca Vaticana. II, 133-189, ALBB

Tisserant, Eugène, Cardinal. Inventaire Sommaire des Manuscrits Arabes du Fonds Borgia à la Bibliothèque Vaticane. 1-34, EHRE

MANUSCRIPTS, Arabic - Hist. and crit.

Nemoy, Leon. Notes on Some Arabic Manuscripts on Curious Subjects in the Yale University Library. 45-66, KEOG

MANUSCRIPTS - Bibl.

Della Bona, Giuseppe Domenico. Il Regesto delle Pergamene Goriziane e Friulane della Biblioteca Civica. 25-55, GORI

Gerstinger, Hans. Johannes Sambucus als Handschriftensammler. 251-400, VIEN

Marx, Alexander. The Polemical Manuscripts in the Library of the Jewish Theological Seminary of America. 247-278, FREI

Unterkircher, Franz. "De Arte Venandi cum Avibus." 653-661, BICK

MANUSCRIPTS - Binding
see Bookbinding

MANUSCRIPTS - Binding - Fine bindings
see Bookbinding - Fine bindings

MANUSCRIPTS - Buying and selling
see Book industry and trade

MANUSCRIPTS - Care and restoration
see also Archives - Care and restoration

MANUSCRIPTS - Care and restoration

Birkenmajer, Aleksander. W Sprawie Rejestracji i Katalogowania Opraw Zabytkowych. 105-121, PIEK

Blaas, Richard. Cellon und Pergamin in der Archivalienrestaurierung. 187-197, GALL

Ciceri, Angelo. Un Precursore ed un Amico di Alfonso Gallo: Mons. Achille Ratti (Papa Pio XI). 279-294, GALL

MANUSCRIPTS - Cataloging - Berlin - Hist.

Lülfing, Hans. Die Handschriftenabteilung. I, 319-380, BERS

MANUSCRIPTS - Cataloging - Germany

Schmidt, Wieland. Zur Frage der Handschriftenkatalogisierung in Deutschland. 185-193, LEYH

MANUSCRIPTS - Cataloging - Karlsruhe

Schmitt, Franz Anselm. Der Stand der Handschriften-Katalogisierung bei der Badischen Landesbibliothek in Karlsruhe. 216-231, HOFF

MANUSCRIPTS, Chinese

Priest, Alan. An Illuminated Buddhist Scroll in the Metropolitan Museum of Art. 122-128, GREE

MANUSCRIPTS, Chinese - Tun-Huang, China

Taam, Cheuk-Woon. The Discovery of the Tun-Huang Library and Its Effect on Chinese Studies. 686-705, WILS

MANUSCRIPTS - Circulation procedures - Heidelberg

Preisendanz, Karl. Handschriftenausleihe in der Bibliotheca Palatina. 54-68, LEYG

MANUSCRIPTS - Collections

Brechler, Otto. Handschriftensammlungen als Kunstsammlungen. 252-263, BICK

MANUSCRIPTS - Collections - Benediktbeuern

Ruf, Paul. Ausgaben des Klosters Benediktbeuern für Bücher und Schreibzeug von 1495-1510. 219-227, LEID

MANUSCRIPTS - Collections - Bergen

Munthe, Gerhard. Ludvig Rosenkrantz og Gjenerobringen av Trondhjems Len. Et Dokument i Universitetsbiblioteket i Bergen. 90-94, DAHA

MANUSCRIPTS - Collections - Berlin

Balcke, Curt. Heinrich Friedrich von Diez und Sein Vermächtnis in der Preussischen Staatsbibliothek. 187-200, KUHN

Darmstaedter, Ludwig. Die Dokumentensammlung Darmstaedter und Ihr Übergang an die Preussische Staatsbibliothek. 167-169, HARN
Haebler, Konrad. Die Handschriftenabteilung. 126-131, HARN
Lülfing, Hans. Die Handschriftenabteilung. I, 319-380, BERS
Schunke, Ilse. Die Italienischen Einbände aus der Hamilton-Sammlung in Berlin. 17-32, LÜLF

MANUSCRIPTS - Collections - Bern

BERT

Meyer, Wilhelm Joseph. Die Handschriftensammlung. 111-118, BERU

MANUSCRIPTS - Collections - Crowland, Eng.

Boese, Helmut. Ein Mittelalterliches Bücherverzeichnis von Croyland Abbey. 286-295, VORS

MANUSCRIPTS - Collections - Danzig

Günther, Otto. Mittelalterliches aus den Handschriften der Marienkirche in Danzig. 123-141, MILF

MANUSCRIPTS - Collections - Dresden

Kremer, Marita. Die Handschriftenabteilung. 139-146, DREL

MANUSCRIPTS - Collections - Frankfurt a.M.

Eppelsheimer, Hanns Wilhelm. Das Archiv Ungedruckter Wissenschaftlicher Schriften. 90-91, FRAD

MANUSCRIPTS - Collections - Fulda, Ger.

Aus den Schätzen der Landesbibliothek. [Plates 5-12], FULD

MANUSCRIPTS - Collections - Fulda, Ger. - Catalogs

Christ, Karl. Die Handschriftenverzeichnisse der Fuldaer Klosterbibliothek aus dem 16. Jahrhundert. 24-39, FULD

MANUSCRIPTS - Collections - Germany

Lehmann, Paul. Aus einer Münchner Büchersammlung des Ausgehenden Mittelalters. 157-164, LEID

MANUSCRIPTS - Collections - Germany and Switzerland

Christ, Karl. Karolingische Bibliothekseinbände. 82-104, LEYG

MANUSCRIPTS - Collections - Gorizia (City)

Della Bona, Giuseppe Domenico. Il Regesto delle Pergamene Goriziane e Friulane della Biblioteca Civica. 25-55, GORI

MANUSCRIPTS - Collections - Gothenburg, Sweden

Johansson, J. Viktor. Göteborgs Stadsbiblioteks Handskriftssamling. En Översikt. 1-99, (seventh paper), GÖTE

MANUSCRIPTS - Collections - Hague

Byvanck, A. W. Een Nieuwe Aanwinst van de Koninklijke Bibliotheek. 35-43, HAGU
Vermeeren, P. J. H. W. H. J. Baron van Westreenen van Tiellandt als Handschriftenverzamelaar. 603-609, BRUM

MANUSCRIPTS - Collections - Heidelberg

Jammers, Ewald. Die Salemer Handschriftensammlung. 45-64, WEHM

MANUSCRIPTS - Collections - Hof, Ger. - Catalogs

Hommel, Hildebrecht. Die Handschriften der Stadtbibliothek Hof. 47-60, SCHR

MANUSCRIPTS - Collections - Kassel

Struck, Gustav. Handschriftenschätze der Landesbibliothek Kassel. 1-127, (part 2), KASS

MANUSCRIPTS - Collections - Königsberg

Goldschmidt, Günther. Ein Beitrag zur Ältesten Geschichte der Handschriftensammlung der Staats- und Universitäts-Bibliothek. 125-131, KÖNI

MANUSCRIPTS - Collections - Lüben, Ger.

Stern, Ludwig. Mitteilungen aus der Lübener Kirchenbibliothek. 67-96, WILM

MANUSCRIPTS - Collections - Mainz

Darapsky, Elisabeth. Ein Altes Ausleihebuch. 47-50, MAIN

MANUSCRIPTS - Collections - Munich

Glauning, Otto. Die Einbandsammlung der Bayerischen Staatsbibliothek zu München. 111-122, MILF

MANUSCRIPTS - Collections - Naples

Guerrieri, Guerriera. Note sulla Raccolta dei Manoscritti della Biblioteca Nazionale di Napoli. 192-200, GREG

MANUSCRIPTS - Collections - New York (City)

GREE

Marx, Alexander. The Polemical Manuscripts in the Library of the Jewish Theological Seminary of America. 247-278, FREI
Wroth, Lawrence C. The Pierpont Morgan Library and the Historian. 10-22, GREE

MANUSCRIPTS - Collections - Norway

Omang, Reidar. Samarbeide Mellem Håndskriftsamlinger. 418-422, MUNT

MANUSCRIPTS - Collections - Paris

Degering, Hermann. Handschriften aus Echternach und Orval in Paris. 48-85, MILF
Thomas, Marcel. L'Œuvre de Julien Cain au Cabinet des Manuscrits. 65-71, CAIN

MANUSCRIPTS - Collections - Rome (City)

Mercati, Giovanni, Cardinal. Codici del Convento di S. Francesco in Assisi nella Biblioteca Vaticana. 83-127, EHRE

MANUSCRIPTS - Collections - Strasbourg

Ficker, Johannes. Handschriftliches der Alten Strassburger Universitätsbibliothek. 44-65, ESCZ

MANUSCRIPTS - Collections - Sweden

Grape, Anders. Om Bröderna Salan och Deras Handskriftssamling. 139-170, ANNE

MANUSCRIPTS - Collections - Tours

Köhler, Wilhelm. Turonische Handschriften aus der Zeit Alkuins. 172-180, DEGE

MANUSCRIPTS - Collections - U.S.

Ford, Worthington Chauncey. A Division of Manuscripts. 156-161, PUTN

MANUSCRIPTS - Collections - Uppsala

Ågren, Sven. Om Nordinska Handskriftssamlingen i Uppsala Universitetsbibliotek. Några Anteckningar. 468-497, UPPS

MANUSCRIPTS - Collections - Utrecht

Hulshof, A. De Handschriften en de Incunabelen der Utrechtsche Universiteitsbibliotheek en de Moderne Reproductietechniek. 150-159, EVER

MANUSCRIPTS - Collections - Vatican

ALBB

Donati, Lamberto. Le Fonti Iconografiche di Alcuni Manoscritti Urbinati della Biblioteca Vaticana—Osservazioni Intorno ai Cosiddetti "Tarocchi del Mantegna." 48-129, MERG

MANUSCRIPTS - Collections - Vienna

Ausserer, Karl. Die Heraldischen Handschriften der Wiener Nationalbibliothek. 7-36, VIEN
Brechler, Otto. Die Handschriftensammlung. 105-118, BICK
Ecker, Karl. Die Sammlung Stefan Zweig. 321-330, BICK
Endlicher, Otto. Der Tschechische Dramatiker V. Kl. Klipcera und das Wiener Theater (Zwei Briefe in der Handschriftensammlung). 82-97, VIES
Gerstinger, Hans. Johannes Sambucus als Handschriftensammler. 251-400, VIEN
Gladt, Karl. Hundert Jahre Stadtbibliothek. 18-45, VIES
Krawiec, Ferdinand. Die Anonymen Handschriften der Stadtbibliothek. 70-81, VIES

MANUSCRIPTS, Coptic

Pietschmann, Richard. Zu den Überbleibseln des Koptischen Alexanderbuches. 301-312, WILM
Rudnitzky, Günter. Ein Sermon aus dem Schatzkästlein Unseres Vaters Apa Schenute. 12-18, WEHM
Till, Walter. Die Koptischen Eheverträge. 627-638, BICK

MANUSCRIPTS, Coptic - Bibl.

Hebbelynck, Ad. Inventaire Sommaire des Manuscrits Coptes de la Bibliothèque Vaticane. 35-82, EHRE

MANUSCRIPTS, Coptic - Collections - Manchester, Eng.

Till, Walter. Die Nicht-Katalogisierten Coptica der John Rylands Library. 89-90, STUM

MANUSCRIPTS, Coptic - Collections - Vatican

Hebbelynck, Ad. Inventaire Sommaire des Manuscrits Coptes de la Bibliothèque Vaticane. 35-82, EHRE

MANUSCRIPTS, Czechoslovakian

Sawicka, Stanisława M. Czeski Rękopis Iluminwany w Książnicy Miejskiej im. Kopernika w Toruniu. 28-34, EMLE

MANUSCRIPTS - Dating

Bannister, Henry Marriott. Signs in Kalendarial Tables. 141-149, CHAT
Holzinger, Charles. Sur la Date de Quelques Manuscrits d'Aristophane. 204-218, CHAT

MANUSCRIPTS, Dutch

Sevensma, Tietse Pieter. De Bibliotheca Neerlandica Manuscripta De Vreese in Leiden. 167-175, BISH

MANUSCRIPTS, Dutch (Early)

Strauch, Philipp. Rigaer Handschriftenfragmente. 238-243, DEGE

MANUSCRIPTS, English

Brotanek, Rudolf. Beschreibung der Handschrift 14090 (Suppl. 1776) der Nationalbibliothek in Wien. 145-162, VIEN

MANUSCRIPTS, Ethiopian

Skehan, Patrick W. An Illuminated Gospel Book in Ethiopic. 350-357, GREE

MANUSCRIPTS, Ethiopian - Bibl.

Lantschoot, Arnold van. Inventaire Sommaire des Manuscrits Vaticans Éthiopiens. I, 453-[514], ALBB

MANUSCRIPTS, Ethiopian - Collections - Vatican

Cerulli, Enrico. Gli Atti di Zēnā Mārqos, Monaco Etiope del Sec. XIV. I, 191-212, ALBB
Lantschoot, Arnold van. Inventaire Sommaire des Manuscrits Vaticans Éthiopiens. I, 453-[514], ALBB

MANUSCRIPTS - Europe

CHAT

MANUSCRIPTS - Facsimiles

ALBB

Millar, Eric G. Fresh Materials for the Study of English Illumination. 286-294, GREE

MANUSCRIPTS - France

Beaulieux, Ch. Manuscrits et Imprimés en France XVe et XVIe Siècles. 417-428, CHAT

MANUSCRIPTS, French - Collections - Erlangen

Pirson, Julius. Aus Französischen und Italienischen Handschriften der Erlanger Universitätsbibliothek. 185-195, STOL

MANUSCRIPTS, German

Ruhland, Wilhelm. Kunz von Kauffungen als Vogt des Amtes Altenburg. Eine Amtsrechnung vom Jahre 1445/46. 9-30, ALTE
Wegener, Hans. Die Deutschen Volkshandschriften des Späten Mittelalters. 316-324, DEGE

MANUSCRIPTS, German - Bibl.

Ausserer, Karl. Die Jagdtagebücher der Österreichischen Nationalbibliothek. 228-238, BICK
Rooth, Erik. Die Mittelalterlichen Deutschen Handschriften Einschliesslich der Lateinischen mit Deutschen Bestandteilen der Universitätsbibliothek zu Uppsala. 40-96, UPPS

MANUSCRIPTS, German - Collections - Uppsala

Rooth, Erik. Die Mittelalterlichen Deutschen Handschriften Einschliesslich der Lateinischen mit Deutschen Bestandteilen der Universitätsbibliothek zu Uppsala. 40-96, UPPS

MANUSCRIPTS, German - Collections - Vienna

Ausserer, Karl. Die Jagdtagebücher der Österreichischen Nationalbibliothek. 228-238, BICK

MANUSCRIPTS, German - 15th cent. - Bibl.

Schmidt, Wieland. Christus und die Sieben Laden. Betrachtungen zur Spätmittelalterlichen Deutschen Literaturgeschichte. 261-284, STOL

MANUSCRIPTS, German - 14th cent. - Fragments - Antwerp

Hannemann, Kurt. Antwerpener Fragmente einer Deutschen Geistlichen Prosahandschrift des 14. Jahrhunderts. 55-64, LEYH

MANUSCRIPTS, German - Greifswald

MENN

MANUSCRIPTS, German (Middle High German)

Strauch, Philipp. Rigaer Handschriftenfragmente. 238-243, DEGE

MANUSCRIPTS, German - Old High German - Collections - Germany

Kirchner, Joachim. Sammlung, Bekanntmachung und Katalogisierung Altdeutscher Handschriften im 17. und 18. Jahrhundert. 127-134, LEID

MANUSCRIPTS, German - Old High German - Collections - Vienna

Menhardt, Hermann. Die Altdeutschen Ambrasiani der Österreichischen Nationalbibliothek. 56-57, STUM

MANUSCRIPTS - Germany

Husung, Max Joseph. Aus der Zeit des Übergangs von der Handschrift zum Druck. Nach einem Band der

Preussischen Staatsbibliothek. 155-159, DEGE

MANUSCRIPTS - Germany - Catalogs

Kirchner, Joachim. Sammlung, Bekanntmachung und Katalogisierung Altdeutscher Handschriften im 17. und 18. Jahrhundert. 127-134, LEID
Schmidt, Wieland. Hermann Degering, Erinnerungen aus der Staatsbibliothek. 126-129, LEUN

MANUSCRIPTS - Germany - Catalogs - Hist.

Autenrieth, Johanne. Ältere und Neuere Handschriftenkataloge aus dem Umkreis der Stuttgarter Handschriftensammlung. 165-188, HOFF

MANUSCRIPTS - Gouda

Lieftinck, G. I. Enige Problemen met Betrekking tot Gedateerde Goudse Handschriften. 139-154, KOSS

MANUSCRIPTS - Graz - Bibl.

VERE

MANUSCRIPTS, Greek

Weitzmann, Kurt. The Constantinopolitan Lectionary, Morgan 639. 358-373, GREE
Wendel, Carl. Aus der Vorgeschichte des Laurentianus XXXII.9. 16-22, KUHN

MANUSCRIPTS, Greek - Bibl.

Garitte, Gérard. Sur une Formule des Colophons de Manuscrits Grecs (ἡμὲν χεὶρ ἡ γράψασα). I, 359-390, ALBB
Gerstinger, Hans. Ein Bisher Unbeachtetes Verzeichnis Griechischer Handschriften der Vaticana aus dem Jahre 1553. 11-19, LEYG
Kleberg, Tönnes. Catalogus Codicum Graecorum et Latinorum Bibliothecae Gotoburgensis. 1-48, (eighth paper), GÖTE
Omont, Henry. Inventaire Sommaire des Manuscrits Grecs des Bibliothèques Mazarine, de L'Arsenal et Sainte-Geneviève, à Paris. 305-320, GRAU
Wendel, Carl. Die Griechischen Handschriften der Provinz Sachsen. 354-378, MILF

MANUSCRIPTS, Greek - Collections - Brescia

Muñoz, Antonio. Miniature Bizantine nella Biblioteca Queriniana di Brescia. 169-179, CERI

MANUSCRIPTS, Greek - Collections - Gothenburg, Sweden

Kleberg, Tönnes. Catalogus Codicum Graecorum et Latinorum Bibliothecae Gotoburgensis. 1-48, (eighth paper), GÖTE

MANUSCRIPTS, Greek - Collections - Paris

Omont, Henry. Inventaire Sommaire des Manuscrits Grecs des Bibliothèques Mazarine, de L'Arsenal et Sainte-Geneviève, à Paris. 305-320, GRAU

MANUSCRIPTS, Greek - Collections - Ravenna

Martin, Albert. Notice sur les Manuscrits Grecs de la Bibliothèque Classense, à Ravenne. 553-556, GRAU

MANUSCRIPTS, Greek - Collections - Saxony

Wendel, Carl. Die Griechischen Handschriften der Provinz Sachsen. 354-378, MILF

MANUSCRIPTS, Greek - Collections - Vatican

Devreese, Robert. Pour L'Histoire des Manuscrits du Fonds Vatican Grec. I, 315-336, ALBB
Garitte, Gérard. Sur une Formule des Colophons de Manuscrits Grecs (ἡμὲν χεὶρ ἡ γράψασα). I, 359-390, ALBB

MANUSCRIPTS, Greek - Collections - Vatican - Catalogs

Gerstinger, Hans. Ein Bisher Unbeachtetes Verzeichnis Griechischer Handschriften der Vaticana aus dem Jahre 1553. 11-19, LEYG

MANUSCRIPTS, Greek - Facsimiles

Serruys, Daniel. Contribution à L'Étude des "Canons" de L'Onciale Grecque. 492-499, CHAT

MANUSCRIPTS, Greek - Hist. and crit.

Premerstein, Anton v. Griechisch-Heidnische Weissagungen über die Christliche Lehre in Handschriften und Kirchenmalereien. 647-666, VIEN

MANUSCRIPTS, Hebraic - Collections - London

Poznański, S. Die Qirqisâni-Handschriften im British Museum. 195-218, STEI

MANUSCRIPTS, Hebrew

FREN

MARY

STEI

Epstein, A. Der Gerschom Meor ha-Golah Zugeschriebene Talmud-Commentar. 115-143, STEI

MANUSCRIPTS, Hebrew - Catalogs

Roth, Cecil. Catalogue of Manuscripts in the Roth Collection. 503-535, MARX

MANUSCRIPTS, Hebrew - Catalonia

Millàs i Vallicrosa, Josep M.[a]. Manuscrits Hebraics d'Origen Català a la Biblioteca Vaticana. I, 97-109, RUBI

MANUSCRIPTS, Hebrew - Collections - Berlin

Spanier, Arthur. Über Umfang und Herkunft der Sammlung Hebräischer Handschriften in der Kurfürstlichen Bibliothek zu Berlin. 245-253, KUHN

MANUSCRIPTS, Hebrew - Collections - Florence

Cassuto, Umberto. Manoscritti Ebraici della R. Biblioteca Laurenziana in Firenze. 17-23, FREN

MANUSCRIPTS, Hebrew - Collections - London

Scholem, Gerhard. Einige Kabbalistische Handschriften im Britischen Museum. 51-69, FREN

MANUSCRIPTS, Hebrew - Collections - Mikulov, Moravia

Schwarz, Arthur Zacharias. Nikolsburger Hebräische Handschriften. 170-181, FREI

MANUSCRIPTS, Hebrew - Collections - New York (City)

Davidson, Israel. A Collection of Letters from Sages of Israel only Found in the Jewish Theological Seminary. 1-14, (Hebrew section), FREI

Rivkind, Isaac. Correspondence of Elijah Morpugo. 138-159, (Hebrew section), FREI

MANUSCRIPTS, Hebrew - Collections - Oxford

Roth, Cecil. Catalogue of Manuscripts in the Roth Collection. 503-535, MARX

MANUSCRIPTS, Hebrew - Hungary - Bibl.

Scheiber, Alexander. Medieval Hebrew Manuscripts as Bindings in the Libraries and Archives of Hungary. 19-28, BLOC

MANUSCRIPTS - Hist.

Burr, Viktor. Buch und Bibliothek bei Plinius d. J. 94-100, LEYH

MANUSCRIPTS, Icelandic and old Norse

Holtsmark, Anne. En Side av Norsk Bokhistorie. 74-90, OSLN

MANUSCRIPTS - Illumination

see Illumination of books and manuscripts

MANUSCRIPTS - Indexes

Tisserant, Eugène, Cardinal. The Preparation of a Main Index for the Vatican Library Manuscripts. 176-185, BISH

MANUSCRIPTS, Indic - Collections - Berlin

Nobel, Johannes. Die Śārada-Handschrift des Rāmāyaṇa. 186-190, HARN

MANUSCRIPTS, Irish

Hamel, A. G. van. De Studie der Ierse Handschriften. 123-145, EVER

MANUSCRIPTS, Italian - Collections - Erlangen

Pirson, Julius. Aus Französischen und Italienischen Handschriften der Erlanger Universitätsbibliothek. 185-195, STOL

MANUSCRIPTS - Italy

Mercati, Giovanni, Cardinal. Da Incunaboli a Codici. 3-28, ACCU

MANUSCRIPTS, Judo-Arabic

STEI

MANUSCRIPTS - Karlsruhe - Catalogs

Schmitt, Franz Anselm. Der Stand der Handschriften-Katalogisierung bei der Badischen Landesbibliothek in Karlsruhe. 216-231, HOFF

MANUSCRIPTS, Latin

Grabmann, Martin. Mitteilungen aus Münchner Handschriften über Bisher Unbekannte Philosophen der Artistenfakultät (Codd. Lat. 14246 und 14383). 73-83, LEID

Lowe, E. A. Greek Symptoms in a Sixth-Century Manuscript of St. Augustine and in a Group of Latin Legal Manuscripts. 277-289, ALBA

MANUSCRIPTS, Latin - Bibl.

Bischoff, Bernhard. Hadoardus and the Manuscripts of Classical Authors from Corbie. 39-57, ALBA

Debes, Dietmar. Das Sequestrationsverzeichnis der Bibliothek des Thomasklosters zu Leipzig. 83-95, LÜLF

Kleberg, Tönnes. Catalogus Codicum

Graecorum et Latinorum Bibliothecae Gotoburgensis. 1-48, (eighth paper), GÖTE
Lowe, E. A. A Hand-List of Half-Uncial Manuscripts. 34-61, EHRD
——— A New List of Beneventan Manuscripts. II, 211-244, ALBB
Rooth, Erik. Die Mittelalterlichen Deutschen Handschriften Einschliesslich der Lateinischen mit Deutschen Bestandteilen der Universitätsbibliothek zu Uppsala. 40-96, UPPS
Schmidt, Franz Paul. Der Katalog der Klosterbibliothek Nienburg a.S. 31-79, ALTE

MANUSCRIPTS, Latin - Collections

Laurent, M.-H. Guillaume des Rosières et la Bibliothèque Pontificale à L'Époque de Clément VI. 579-603, PELZ

MANUSCRIPTS, Latin - Collections - Carinthia

Dold, Alban. Klassische Dichter-Bruchstücke nebst einem Bericht über die Palimpsestphotographische Aufnahme des Plinius-Codex von St. Paul in Kaernten. 369-377, GALL

MANUSCRIPTS, Latin - Collections - Göttweig

Bollert, Martin. Ein Neuer Lederschnittband aus dem 14. Jahrhundert. 80-82, LEIP

MANUSCRIPTS, Latin - Collections - Gothenburg, Sweden

Kleberg, Tönnes. Catalogus Codicum Graecorum et Latinorum Bibliothecae Gotoburgensis. 1-48, (eighth paper), GÖTE

MANUSCRIPTS, Latin - Collections - Leipzig

Debes, Dietmar. Das Sequestrationsverzeichnis der Bibliothek des Thomasklosters zu Leipzig. 83-95, LÜLF

MANUSCRIPTS, Latin - Collections - Nienburg a.S. (Benedictine abbey)

Schmidt, Franz Paul. Der Katalog der Klosterbibliothek Nienburg a.S. 31-79, ALTE

MANUSCRIPTS, Latin - Collections - Rome

Meersseman, G. La Bibliothèque des Frères Prêcheurs de la Minerve à la Fin du XVe Siècle. 605-634, PELZ

MANUSCRIPTS, Latin - Collections - Uppsala

Rooth, Erik. Die Mittelalterlichen Deutschen Handschriften Einschliesslich der Lateinischen mit Deutschen Bestandteilen der Universitätsbibliothek zu Uppsala. 40-96, UPPS

MANUSCRIPTS, Latin - Facsimiles

Degering, Hermann. Ein Calendarium Pugillare mit Computus aus dem Jahre 1294. 79-88, LOUB

MANUSCRIPTS, Latin - 15th cent.

Baron, Hans. A Forgotten Chronicle of Early Fifteenth-Century Venice. 19-36, PARG

MANUSCRIPTS, Latin - Rome (City)

Muzzioli, Giovanni. Il Più Antico Codice della Biblioteca Casanatense. 323-332, GREG

MANUSCRIPTS - Music
see Music literature and scores - Manuscripts

MANUSCRIPTS, Oriental - Collections - Berlin

Auster, Guido. Die Orientalische Abteilung. I, 275-317, BERS

MANUSCRIPTS, Oriental - Collections - Munich

Gratzl, Emil. Islamische Handschriftenbände der Bayerischen Staatsbibliothek. 118-147, LOUB

MANUSCRIPTS, Oriental - Tun-Huang, China

Taam, Cheuk-Woon. The Discovery of the Tun-Huang Library and Its Effect on Chinese Studies. 686-705, WILS

MANUSCRIPTS (Palimpsests), Greek - Collections - Paris

Jacob, Alfred. Notes sur les Manuscrits Grecs Palimpsestes de la Bibliothèque Nationale. 759-770, HAVE

MANUSCRIPTS (Papyri)
see Papyrus

MANUSCRIPTS - Publication rights

Stois, Max. Bibliothek und Editio Princeps. 283-288, LEID

MANUSCRIPTS - Reichenau, Ger. - Catalogs

Preisendanz, Karl. Der Reichenauer Handschriftenkatalog von 1724. 199-206, LEID

MANUSCRIPTS, Russian - Collections

Bogdanovaîa, Nadezhda G. Knizhnye Bogatstva Stroganovykh v 1578 g. 277-284, MALE

MANUSCRIPTS - Spain - Bibl.

Camino y Aguirre, Fernando González. Bibliotecas Medievales Montañesas. II, 14-50, ARTI

MANUSCRIPTS, Spanish

Barrau-Dihigo, L. À Propos d'un Manuscrit Hispanique de Leyde (XIIIe Siècle). 332-340, CHAT

MANUSCRIPTS, Swedish - Bibl.

Johansson, J. Viktor. Göteborgs Stadsbiblioteks Handskriftssamling. En Översikt. 1-99, (seventh paper), GÖTE

MANUSCRIPTS, Swedish - Collections - Gothenburg, Sweden

Johansson, J. Viktor. Göteborgs Stadsbiblioteks Handsskriftssamling. En Översikt. 1-99, (seventh paper), GÖTE

MANUSCRIPTS, Swiss - Collections - Lucerne

Schnellmann, Meinrad. Die Innerschweizerischen Handschriften der Bürgerbibliothek Luzern. 223-232, SCHU

MANUZIO, ALDO PIO

Scaccia Scarafoni, Camillo. La Più Antica Edizione della Grammatica Latina di Aldo Manuzio Finora Sconosciuta ai Bibliografi. 193-203, ACCU

MAPS - Bibliography - Bibl.
see Bibliography - Bibl. - Maps

MAPS - Cataloging

Vartdal, Hroar. Über Kartenkatalogisierung. Die Kartensammlung der Universitätsbibliothek zu Oslo. 481-492, MUNT

MAPS - Collections - Berlin

Klemp, Egon. Die Kartenabteilung. I, 405-423, BERS
Pretzsch, Karl. Die Kartensammlung. 232-239, HARN

MAPS - Collections - Bern

Muriset, Annie. La Collection de Cartes Géographiques. 108-111, BERU

MAPS - Collections - Bydgoszcz

Dmochowska, Maria. Cymelia Kartograficzne. 80-88, BYDG

MAPS - Collections - Dresden

Pfeifer, Hans. Die Kartenabteilung. 147-155, DREL

MAPS - Collections - Fano, Italy

Bonasera, Francesco. Un'Antica Pianta della Città di Rimini Conservata nella Biblioteca Fredericiana di Fano. 199-203, GALL

MAPS - Collections - France

Foncin, Myriem. L'Histoire d'une Collection de Cartes Réunies pour Louis XIV. 119-126, CALO

MAPS - Collections - Leipzig

Praesent, Hans. Die Kartensammlung. 148-164, LEIS

MAPS - Collections - Oslo

Nissen, Kristian. Den Werlauffske Gave. En Innholdsrik Kartbunke i Universitetsbibliotekets Kartsamling. 150-167, OSLN
Vartdal, Hroar. Über Kartenkatalogisierung. Die Kartensammlung der Universitätsbibliothek zu Oslo. 481-492, MUNT

MAPS - Collections - San Marino, Calif.

Wagner, Henry R. The Portolan Atlases of American Interest in the Henry E. Huntington Library and Art Gallery. 498-509, PUTN

MAPS - Collections - Trieste

Brumati, Antonio. L'"Atlas Mayor" della Biblioteca Civica di Trieste. II, 665-675, HORT

MAPS - Collections - Uppsala

Taube, N. E. Några Ord om Utländska Kartor i Uppsala Universitetsbibliotek. 526-536, UPPS

MAPS - Collections - Vatican

Almagià, Roberto. Alcune Preziose Carte Geografiche di Recente Acquisite alle Collezioni Vaticane. I, 1-22, ALBB

MAPS - Collections - Vienna

Trenkler, Ernst. Die Kartensammlung. 139-148, BICK

MAPS - German - Collections - Stockholm

Dahlgren, E. W. Gamla Tyska Kartor i Kungl. Biblioteket. 93-123, ANNE

MAQUETTES - Facsimiles

Ouy, Gilbert. Une Maquette de Manuscrit à Peintures. 43-51, CALO

MARBACH - Literary museums
see Literary museums - Marbach

MARBACH. Schiller-Nationalmuseum
Zeller, Bernhard. Fünf Jahre Deutsches Literaturarchiv in Marbach. Ergebnisse, Erfahrungen, Planungen. 349-384, HOFF

MARBURG - Librarians
see Librarians - Marburg

MARBURG. Universität. Bibliothek - Catalogs - 1631
Schawe, Josef. D. Steuberi Catalogi und Nachrichten von der Marpurger und Giesser Bibliothec. Giessener Hs. 30. 204-214, JUCH

MARBURG. Universität. Bibliothek - Hist.
Rohde, Fritz. Verzeichnis der Bibliothekare an der Universitätsbibliothek in Marburg. 294-303, KUHN

MARCELLUS II, Pope
Paschini, Pio. Un Cardinale Editore: Marcello Cervini. 383-413, FERR

Marchand, Jean.
Une Édition de Boileau Inconnue. 115-118, CALO

Marchut, Maria.
Czasopisma. 21-24, KRAK

MARCIANO
see Venice. Biblioteca Nazionale Marciana

MARGARETE KARTEUSERIN
Fischer, Karl. Margarete Karteuserin, eine Nürnberger Klosterschreiberin des 15. Jahrhunderts. 24-31, VERZ

MARGINALIA
Seppälä, Arvo. Eräitä Kansi- Ja Reunamerkintöjä Helsingin Yliopiston Kirjaston Kaksoiskappalekokoelmissa. 237-255, DAHL
Vallinkoski, J. Poimintoja Kirjojen Kansimerkinnöistä Helsingin Yliopiston Kirjastossa. 9-23, TUDE

MARIA MAIHINGEN (Birgittine monastery). Ries, Ger.
see Ries, Ger. Maria Maihingen (Birgittine monastery)

MARIA-TAFERL. Blumenscheinsche Bibliothek
Teichl, Robert. Ein Europäischer Bibliothekenführer um das Jahr 1780. Die Handschrift des Pfarrverwalters von Maria-Taferl Adalbert Blumenschein. 172-179, LEYG

MARIA-TAFERL. Kirchenbibliothek
Teichl, Robert. Ein Europäischer Bibliothekenführer um das Jahr 1780. Die Handschrift des Pfarrverwalters von Maria-Taferl Adalbert Blumenschein. 172-179, LEYG

MARIA-TAFERL. Pfarrbibliothek
Teichl, Robert. Ein Europäischer Bibliothekenführer um das Jahr 1780. Die Handschrift des Pfarrverwalters von Maria-Taferl Adalbert Blumenschein. 172-179, LEYG

MARIE-ANTOINETTE, Queen Consort of Louis XVI, King of France - Library
Jallut, Marguerite. Les Bibliothèques de Marie-Antoinette. 325-332, CALO

MARIENBIBLIOTHEK, Danzig
see Danzig. Marienkirche. Bibliothek

MARIENFELD, Ger. (Cistercian monastery). Library - Catalog
Degering, Hermann. Der Katalog der Bibliothek des Klosters Marienfeld vom Jahre 1185. 53-64, SCHW

MARIENKIRCHE. Bibliothek. Danzig
see Danzig. Marienkirche. Bibliothek

MARILLIER, P.-C. - Collections - Dijon
Laurent, Jacques. L'Oeuvre de P.-C. Marillier à la Bibliothèque de Dijon. 125-136, OURS

MARINE HISTORICAL ASSOCIATION. Library
Albion, Robert G. Mentor at Mystic. 61-68, DAVI

Marino, Samuel J.
French-Language Printing in the United States, 1711-1825. 43-62, GJEL

MARINUS, of Flavia Neapolis. Mss. Vita Procli.
Mogenet, Joseph. Holstenius et L'Horoscope de Proclus. II, 281-308, ALBB

MARIO DE PASSA, Monk - Library
Pons, Antoni. Fra Mario de Passa, Lul-Lista i Bibliòfil. III, 317-337, RUBI

Mariutti de Sánchez Rivero, Angela.
Il Carteggio Inedito del Legato Araujo. 369-382, FERR

Mark, Jan.
Några Bilder från Malmö Stadsbibliotek. [272]ff, HEIN

Marklund, E.
"Svensktrycket." 21-34, (fifth paper), GÖTE

Markon, Isaac, jt. ed.
HARK

Marouzeau, J.
La Graphie ei = ï dans le Palimpseste de Plaute. 150-154, CHAT

MĀRQOS, ZĒNĀ
see Zēnā Mārqos

MARTEAU, PIERRE DU, imaginary printer - Bibl.

Moeltzner, August. Zwanzig Jahre Maskierte Druckerarbeit. Pierre du Marteaus Drucke aus den Jahren 1660-1680 in der Königl. Bibliothek zu Berlin. 197-204, SCHW

Martel, Charles.
The Library of Congress Classification. 327-332, PUTN

Martha, Jules.
Sur un Passage de la Consolatio ad Marciam de Sénèque. 219-223, CHAT

Martin, Albert.
Notice sur les Manuscrits Grecs de la Bibliothèque Classense à Ravenne. 553-556, GRAU

Martin, Henry.
Notes sur les Écrivains au Travail. 535-544, CHAT

MARTIN VON SENGING

Leporini, Heinrich. Simon von Niederaltaich und Martin v. Senging. 575-590, VIEN

Martineau, Henri.
La Publication du "Mariage de Don Quichotte" de Paul-Jean Toulet. 457-460, BONN

Martini, E.
Una Lettera del Retore Teodulo (Thomas Magistros) al Monaco Ieroteo. 433-447, CERI

Martorell, Francesco.
Un Inventario della Biblioteca di Calisto III. 166-191, EHRE

Marwick, Lawrence, jt. ed.
BLOC

Marx, Alexander, jt. ed.
FREN

Marx, Alexander.
The Polemical Manuscripts in the Library of the Jewish Theological Seminary of America. 247-278, FREI

Some Notes on the Use of Hebrew Type in Non-Hebrew Books, 1475-1520. 381-408, EAME

MARX, ALEXANDER

MARX

MARY

Goldman, Solomon. The Man of the Book. 1-34, MARX

Kohut, Rebekah. Prof. Alexander Marx. xi-xxiii, MARX

MARX, ALEXANDER - Bibl.

Cohen, Boaz. Bibliography of the Writings of Prof. Alexander Marx. 35-59, MARX

MARX, JOSEPH. Mss.

Kuczewski-Poray, Kasimir. Ein Joseph Marx-Autograph der Österreichischen Nationalbibliothek. 446-449, BICK

MARX, KARL. Mss. [Autograph]

Deckert, Helmut. Karl Marx und Seine Kommilitonen als Hörer Schlegels in Bonn. 33-53, LÜLF

Marx, Moses.
On the Date of Appearance of the First Printed Hebrew Books. 481-501, MARX

Masanov, I͡u. I.
Za Ni͡akoi Zadachi na Dŭrzhavnata Bibliografii͡a v SSSR. 127-133, TEOB

MASETTI, TOMMASO

Taurisano, Innocenzo. Il Padre Tommaso Masetti Ultimo Prefetto della Casanatense. 385-389, GREG

MASON CITY, Ia., region - Public libraries
see Public libraries - Mason City, Ia., region

Massee, May.
Children's Books on Demand. 579-584, MOOR

Masson, André.
Montesquieu, le Président de Brosses et le Décor des Bibliothèques. 317-324, CALO

Masten, Helen Adams.
The Central Children's Room. 551-560, MOOR

MASTER CASPER
see Casper, Meister

"MASTER D", 15th cent. engraver

Wehmer, Carl. Zur Echtheitskritik der Metallschnittplatten Schreiber 2746a und Schreiber 2865. 143-157, BOCK

Masuyama, Takehiko.
Tokkyo Bunken to Yunitāmu no Riyō. (Patent Literature and the Feasibility of Employing Uniterm System.) 239-266, HASH

MATARELLI, NICCOLÒ. Mss. Questio Notabilis . . .
Bevilacqua, Mario. Una "Quaestio" di Niccolò Matarelli (Vat. Lat. 10726). I, 139-157, ALBB

MATERIALS CENTERS
see School libraries

Mather, Frank Jewett, Jr.
A Great Administrator. 351, LYDE

Mathur, V. S.
Dr. S. R. Ranganathan. 536-538, RANG

Mathys, E.
Der Anteil der Schweiz an der Dezimalklassifikation. 160-162, DONK

MATTEO BATTIFERRI
see Battiferri, Mateo

MAUGÉRARD, JEAN BAPTISTE
Jacobs, Emil. Zur Kenntnis Maugérards. 64-73, HAEB

Maurenbrecher, Rolf.
Berliner Volksbüchereien 1945-1955. 119-130, SCHS

MAXILLUS, GEORGIUS
see Uebelin, Georg

MAXIMILIAN I, Emperor
Wehmer, Carl. Mit Gemäl und Schrift. Kaiser Maximilian I. und der Buchdruck. 244-275, HOFF

May, Otto Heinrich.
Bibliothekswesen in Hannover. 88-101, LEUN

Mayer, Georg.
Rektor der Karl-Marx-Universität Leipzig. XXI-XXII, LEIZ

Mazure, J. C.
Overzicht der Geschriften van Dr. F. K. H. Kossmann. 260-264, KOSS

Mazzoleni, Iole.
Note Paleografiche e Diplomatiche su Alcune Carte Ravellesi dei Sec. XII-XIV. 539-547, GALL

Mc
For all names beginning Mc
see Mac

Mearns, David C.
A Chronology. 81-94, PUTP
Herbert Putnam and His Responsible Eye—A Memorial Tribute. 1-52, PUTP

MECHANIZATION OF LIBRARY PROCESSES
see also Computers; Information retrieval - Machines

MECHANIZATION OF LIBRARY PROCESSES
Kragemo, Helge Bergh. Zur Frage der Rationalisierung des Tauschverkehrs einer Wissenschaftlichen Bibliothek. 377-381, MUNT
Krieger, Waldemar and Gottfried Rost. Das Gebäude der Deutschen Bücherei und Seine Technischen Einrichtungen. 259-270, LEIZ
Kunze, Horst. Über den Motorisierten Bibliothekar. 29-35, BOLE
Lund, Hanna. Der Adrema-Betrieb in der Katalogisierung. 404-409, MUNT
Mumford, L. Quincy. Automation in Research Libraries. 548-551, BRUM
Pflug, Günther. Der Einfluss der Elektronischen Datenverarbeitung auf die Katalogisierungspraxis. 111-124, FUCH
Predeek, Albert. Fortschritte im Katalogdruck nach dem Adrema-System. 197-210, MUNT
Shera, Jesse H. Automation Without Fear. 168-181, SAYW

MECHANIZATION OF LIBRARY PROCESSES - California
Blanchard, J. R. Development and Mechanization of Libraries of the University of California. 1-7, HASH

MECKLENBURG-SCHWERIN - Bookbinders
see Bookbinders - Mecklenburg-Schwerin

MEDICAL LIBRARIANS
McDaniel, W. B., 2d. Snapshot of the Medical Librarian as Historian and Bibliographer, to 1947. 301-308, DOEJ
Postell, William Dosite. Research and Medical Librarianship. 399-403, DOEJ
Robinson, Ida Marian. Personnel Trends of a Decade in Medical Libraries. 386-388, DOEJ

MEDICAL LIBRARIANS - Education
Jordan, Mildred. Events in the Development of Education for Medical Librarianship in the Last Decade. 351-360, DOEJ

MEDICAL LIBRARIES
see also Dental libraries; Pharmaceutical libraries

MEDICAL LIBRARIES
Garrison, Fielding Hudson. The Medical

Library in Relation to the University Library. 162-171, PUTN

MEDICAL LIBRARIES - Acquisitions - U.S.

Annan, Gertrude L. Outstanding Acquisitions of Rare Books in Medical Libraries of the United States in the Last Decade. 291-300, DOEJ

MEDICAL LIBRARIES - Berlin

Rohrbach, Peter P. Fachabteilungen und Sondersammlungen. 42-47, BERR

MEDICAL LIBRARIES - Gt. Brit.

Bishop, W. J. Medical Book Societies in England in the Eighteenth and Nineteenth Centuries. 337-350, DOEJ

MEDICAL LIBRARIES - Montreal

FRAN

MEDICAL LIBRARIES - New York (City)

Berlstein, Alfred. Bibliotekarz i Pracownik Naukowy. 41-46, SZAC

MEDICAL LIBRARIES - U.S.

Brodman, Estelle and Chester R. Gough. Computers in Medical and University Libraries; A Review of the Situation in the U.S. in 1964. 19-39, HASH

MEDICAL LIBRARIES - Use studies
see Use studies - Medical libraries

MEDICAL LIBRARY ASSOCIATION

Troxel, Wilma. The Medical Library Association, 1947-1957. 378-385, DOEJ

MEDICAL LITERATURE - Cataloging - Copenhagen

Prytz, Johansen J. Den Gamle Medicinske Katalog på Universitetsbiblioteket, København. 1-7, DAHA

MEDICAL LITERATURE - Collections

Garrison, Fielding Hudson. The Medical Library in Relation to the University Library. 162-171, PUTN

MEDICAL LITERATURE - Collections - Greifswald

Zunker, Ernst. Der Greifswalder "Medizinische Lesezirkel" vom Jahre 1802. Ein Randkapitel der Greifswalder Bibliotheksgeschichte. 415-431, VORS

MEDICAL LITERATURE - Collections - Nashville

Cunningham, Eileen-R. Some Items of Americana Medica Published Southwest of the Alleghenies and Their Authors. 25-26, STUM

MEDICAL PERIODICALS
see Periodicals, Medical

MEDICAL REFERENCE BOOKS
see Reference books - Special subjects - Medicine

MEDIEVAL CHURCH LIBRARIES
see Monastic libraries

Medina, José Toribio.
Quienes Fueron los Autores, hasta ahora Ignorados, de Dos Libros Ingleses que Interesan a America. 79-84, EAME

MEDINA, JOSÉ TORIBIO. La Imprenta en Mexico. [Supplement]

Wagner, Henry R. Sixteenth-Century Mexican Imprints. Location Table of Mexican Sixteenth-Century Books. 249-268, EAME

Meersseman, G.
La Bibliothèque des Frères Prêcheurs de la Minerve à la Fin du XVe Siècle. 605-634, PELZ

MEHEMMED
see Mehmet II, the Great, Sultan of the Turks

Mehlan, Heinz.
Der Architekt zum Neubau der Berliner Stadtbibliothek. 52-55, BERR

MEHMET II, THE GREAT, Sultan of the Turks - Library

Jacobs, Emil. Büchergeschenke für Sultan Mehemmed II. 20-26, LEYG

DAS MEHRJAHRES-VERZEICHNIS DER BÜCHER UND KARTEN
see Frankfurt a.M. Deutsche Bibliothek. Deutsche Bibliographie; Bücher und Karten

DAS MEHRJAHRES-VERZEICHNIS DER ZEITSCHRIFTEN
see Frankfurt a.M. Deutsche Bibliothek. Deutsche Bibliographie; Zeitschriften

Meier, Franz Joseph, [trans.]
Der Artikel Tosho "Buch" im Nihon-Bungaku-Daijiten. [Translation of Japanese Article by Shinkichi Hashimoto and Yasushi Uematsu.] 205-216, LEYH

Meier, Franz Joseph.
Ein Bibliophiles Gedicht von Wang An-Shi (1019-86). 121-123, GRAT

Meillet, Antoine.
Le Groupe -VV-. 33-34, CHAT

Meinhardt, Walter.
Betriebsbücherei des VEB Carl Zeiss, Jena. 128-134, JENA

MEIR JAFFE
see Jaffe, Meir

Meiss, Millard.
Ovum Struthionis, Symbol and Allusion in Piero della Francesca's Montefeltro Altarpiece. 92-101, GREE

Meissner, Bruno.
Wie Hat Assurbanipal Seine Bibliothek Zusammengebracht? 244-248, MILF

MEISTER CASPER
see Casper, Meister

MELANCHTHON-BIBLIOGRAPHIE

Selbmann, Ehrhard. Zur Melanchthonbibliographie. Ein Werk Internationaler Bibliothekarischer Gemeinschaftsarbeit. 245-250, BULL

Melander, Toini.
Bibliografisia Lisiä Suomenkielisiin Virallisiin Julkaisuihin Ruotsin Vallan Aikana. 89-109, DAHL

Melcher, Frederic G.
Harry Lydenberg—Bookman. 437-439, LYDE
Working Together: Publisher, Bookseller, and Librarian. 619-621, MOOR

MELK, SIMON VON
see Simon von Melk

Melton, Jessica.
Compatibility of Two Information Systems, Colon Classification and Western Reserve University. 49-62, RANG

MEMORIAL COLLECTIONS AND SHELVES - Bydgoszcz

Podóreczny, Józef. Ciekawe Zbiory Zabytkowe. 97-104, BYDG

Mendelssohn, Louis.
De Ciceronis Epistularum Codice Turonensi. 169-173, GRAU

MENDING OF BOOKS
see Books - Care and restoration

MENDOZA, HURTADO DE, DIEGO
see Hurtado de Mendoza, Diego

MENÉNDEZ, PELAYO, MARCELINO
see Menéndez y Pelayo, Marcelino

MENÉNDEZ Y PELAYO, MARCELINO

MENE

Solano, Tomás Maza. La Sociedad de Bibliófilos Cántabros que Intentó Formar Menéndez Pelayo. II, 147-188, ARTI

MENÉNDEZ Y PELAYO, MARCELINO - Anniversaries, etc.

El Centenario de Menéndez Pelayo en la Prensa Española. 285-322, MENE
Serna, Gaspar Gómez de la. El Centenario de Menéndez Pelayo en Italia. Dos Articulos del Padre Mondrone en "La Civiltá Cattolica." 263-270, MENE

MENÉNDEZ Y PELAYO, MARCELINO - Bibl.

Notas Bibliográficas. 325-335, MENE

MENÉNDEZ Y PELAYO, MARCELINO. La Ciencia Española

Solana, Marcial. Colaboración de Laverde en la Ciencia Española de Menéndez y Pelayo. II, 51-104, ARTI

MENÉNDEZ Y PELAYO, MARCELINO. Edición Nacional de las Obras Completas

Edición Nacional de las Obras Completas de Menéndez Pelayo. 337-341, MENE

MENÉNDEZ Y PELAYO, MARCELINO. Epistolario

Alonso, B. Sánchez. Epistolario de Menéndez Pelayo con Bibliotecarios y Bibliófilos. 183-190, MENE

MENÉNDEZ Y PELAYO, MARCELINO - Monuments, etc.

Gallo, Gratiniano Nieto. El Monumento Funerario de Menéndez Pelayo, Obra de Victorio Macho. 257-261, MENE

Menhardt, Hermann.
Die Altdeutschen Ambrasiani der Österreichischen Nationalbibliothek. 56-57, STUM

Menn, Walter, jt. ed.
BÖME

Menn, Walter.
Aus der Geschichte der Universitätsbibliothek Greifswald in den Letzten Jahren der Preussischen Zeit. 230-255, JUCH
Ein Neues Dogma um Gutenberg? 65-69, LEYH
Der Oberpräsident von Vincke und die Aufhebung der Universität Münster. 160-178, BÖME
Unsichere Kriterien in der Gutenbergforschung. 181-184, STOL

MENN, WALTER

MENN

MENNANDER, C. F., Bp. - Library
Nohrström, Holger. Några Anteckningar Kring den s. k. Pälkäne-Abcboken. 341-354, HIRN

Mentz, Arthur.
Die Anfügung in den Tironischen Noten. 501-507, CHAT
Römische und Griechische Stenographie. 67-70, SCHR

Mercati, Angelo.
La Biblioteca Privata e gli Arredi di Cappella di Gregorio XII. 128-165, EHRE

MERCATI, ANGELO
MERC
Curriculum Vitae di Mons. Angelo Mercati. VII-VIII, MERC

MERCATI, ANGELO - Bibl.
Scritti di Mons. Angelo Mercati. IX-XXVII, MERC

Mercati, Giovanni, Cardinal.
Cenni di A. del Monte e G. Lascaris sulle Perdite della Biblioteca Vaticana nel Sacco del 1527. 605-632, CERI
Codici del Convento di S. Francesco in Assisi nella Biblioteca Vaticana. 83-127, EHRE
Due Supposte Spogliazioni della Biblioteca di Monte Cassino. II, 967-984, HORT
Da Incunabuli a Codici. 3-28, ACCU
Un'Oscura Nota del Codice Alessandrino. 79-82, CHAT
A Proposito dei Codici Naniani Greci 32 e 37. 280-285, GREE
I. Uno Scambio Strano di Qualche Interesse per Tre Grandi Biblioteche. II. Amici Innominati del Savile in Roma? 17-26, FERR

MERCATI, GIOVANNI, Cardinal
MERG
Donati, Lamberto. Proemio. VII-VIII, MERG

Merk, August, S. J.
Armenische und Griechische Palaeographie. 1-21, EHRD

Merrill, William Stetson.
Order of Books by Date under Subjects. 282-284, HANS

Merritt, Percival.
The Royal Primer. Check List of Royal Primers. 35-60, EAME

Mertens, C.
Proeve eener Documentatie over Onze Belgische Toonkunstenaars, Musicologen en Instrumentenbouwers. 216-239, BORR

Merz, Otto.
Die Schweizerische Vereinigung für Dokumentation Dankt. 180-181, BOUR

MESMES, HENRI DE - Library
Blum, Rudolf. Bibliotheca Memmiana. Untersuchungen zu Gabriel Naudés "Advis pour Dresser une Bibliothèque." 209-232, WEHM

Messin, H., jt. author
Endell, F. and H. Messin. Schriften von Dr. Erwin Ackerknecht. Eine Bibliographische Zusammenstellung. 167-178, ACKE

METAL ENGRAVERS
see Engravers

Metcalf, Keyes DeWitt.
A Builder of Library Research Collections. 399-404, LYDE
The Ever Expanding Demand for Materials and the Threatened Decline for Support: How Shall the Gap Be Filled? 27-36, PENN
The Farmington Plan with Particular Reference to Austria. 57-59, STUM
The New England Deposit Library. 622-628, WILS
Some Trends in Research Libraries. 145-166, BISH

METROPOLITAN MUSEUM OF ART, New York (City)
see New York (City). Metropolitan Museum of Art

MEULEN, DANIEL VAN DER - Library
Kernkamp, J. H. De Bibliotheek van den Koopman Daniel van der Meulen onder den Hamer. 187-203, EVER

MEURER, IGNATIUS, printer
Kilpi, Volter. Suomalainen Virsikirja [Manuele-nide] v:lta 1630 Teuvan Kirkonarkistossa. 122-126, SCHA

MEUSER, CASPAR
Schmidt, Christel. Aus der Sammlung Olga Hirsch: Ein Kreisrunder Einband von Caspar Meuser. 194-198, LOUB
——— Jakob Krause-Forschung: Ein Beitrag zur Methodik der Bucheinbandkunde. 191-193, LOUB

MEXICAN LITERATURE - 16th cent. - Collections
Wagner, Henry R. Sixteenth-Century Mexican Imprints. Location Table

of Mexican Sixteenth-Century Books. 249-268, EAME

Meyen, Fritz, jt. ed.
LEUN

Meyen, Fritz.
Konrad Arnold Schmid (1716-1789), Professor am Collegium Carolinum zu Braunschweig. Ein Freund und Mitarbeiter Lessings. 333-354, JUCH
Die Technisch-Wissenschaftlichen Bibliotheken, Ihre Entwicklung und Ihre Stellung im Rahmen des Deutschen Bibliothekswesens. 102-125, LEUN

Meyer, A. M. T.
Enkele Opmerkings oor die Doel van Locke se Essay. 207-210, VLEE

Meyer, Adolf.
Realkataloge in Geistesgeschichtlicher Beleuchtung. I, 145-149, GLAU

MEYER, CONRAD FERDINAND
Hirzel, B. Conrad Ferdinand Meyer und die Zürcher Stadtbibliothek. [45]-60, ESCK

Meyer, Gustav.
Ein Neues Bruchstück zu Liudprand von Cremona. 163-175, SCHU

Meyer, Hanna.
Die Kinder- und Jugendbuchabteilung. I, 433-441, BERS

Meyer, Heinrich.
Briefe in: Hecker, Max, ed. Ein "Weimarischer Kunstfreund" in der Gemäldesammlung der Brüder Boisserée. Zwei Briefe Heinrich Meyers an die Erbgrossherzogin Maria Paulowna. 185-200, WEIM

Meyer, Herbert.
Über die Namen Wissenschaftlicher Bibliotheken. 46-54, HOFF

Meyer, Herman H. B.
Cards and Common Sense. 351-355, PUTN

Meyer, Herrmann, jt. ed.
FREN

Meyer, Isidore S., jt. ed.
BLOC

Meyer, Wilhelm Joseph.
Der Benützungsdienst. 163-168, BERU
Die Bibliothek der Schweizer Bibliophiler Gesellschaft. 123-124, BERU
Die Bibliothek der Schweizerischen Gesellschaft für Familienforschung. 124-125, BERU
Direktor Godet Erwirbt den Nachlass des Dichters Arnold Ott. 19-22, GODM
Einbände. 119-120, BERU
Die Ersten für das Wallis Gedruckten Bücher im 15. Jahrhundert. 83-90, GODE
Die Handschriftensammlung. 111-118, BERU
Der Photographische Dienst. 168, BERU

Meyer, William.
Nachklänge von der Dordrechter Nationalsynode. 272-283, KÖNI

Meyer-Abich, Adolf.
Bibliotheken als Forschungsinstitute für Wissenschaftsgeschichte. 77-83, TIEM

Michailov, A. I.
Donker Duyvis' Contribution to the Progress of Scientific Information and Documentation. 30-38, DONR

Michałkiewicz, Kazimiera.
Ofiarodawcy i ich Dary. 105-114, BYDG

Michelini, Tocci Luigi.
I Due Manoscritti Urbinati dei Privilegi dei Montefeltro. 206-257, MERG

MICHIGAN - Periodicals, American
see Periodicals, American - Michigan

MICHIGAN - Publishers and Publishing
see Publishers and publishing - Michigan

MICHIGAN. University. Library - Hist.
Bidlack, Russell E. The Early Handling of Books at the University of Michigan. 149-164, GJEL

Michon, Louis-Marie.
Notes sur les Reliures de L'Atelier des Monnier. 509-513, BONN

MICKIEWICZ, ADAM, 1798-1855
Dinekov, Petŭr. Pŭrviiat Bŭlgarski Prevod iz Proizvedeniiata na Adam Mitskevich. 151-155, MIKH

Mickwitz, Ann-Mari.
Kejsaren och den Gamla Kartan. 59-65, NYBE

MICROFILMS
see also Microforms

MICROFILMS - Collections - Washington, D.C.
Evans, Luther H. Current Microfilm Projects at the Library of Congress. 31, STUM

MICROFORMS - Collections - Nashville
Research Materials in Microform. 21, NASH

MICROPHOTOGRAPHY
see Copying methods; Microforms; Photographic reproduction

MIDDELTHUN, GREGORIUS, bookbinder

Paulli, R. Gregorius Middelthun. Bogbinder i Bergen, Stempelskærer på Kongsberg. 140-148, TVET

Middendorf, Heinrich.
Die Bayerische Staatsbibliothek 1945-1964. 7-61, HOFM

Middleton, Bernard C.
The Bookbinders Case Unfolded. 66-76, OLDH

MIEJSKA BIBLIOTEKA PUBLICZNA, Łódź, Poland
see Łódź, Poland. Public Library

MIKHOV, NIKOLA VASILEV

MIKH

MIKN

Bŭrov, D. N. V. Mikhov. 1-4, MIKN
——— Trudovete na Nikola Mikhov Kato Neobkhodimi Iztochnitsi za Nauchno-izsledovatelski Raboti v Oblastta na Stopanskata Istoriîa. 127-130, MIKH
Ganovski, Sava and Todor Borov. Nikola Mikhov. 1-13, MIKH
Rusenov, M. V. D-r Nikola Mikhov v Svishchov. 243-246, MIKH
Stoilov, Vasil. Spomeni za D-r Nikola V. Mikhov. 273-282, MIKH

MIKHOV, NIKOLA VASILEV - Bibl.

Bozhinova-Troianova, B. and Dora Ganchev. D-r Nikola V. Mikhov: Bibliografiîa Izrabotenaa v Bulgarskiîa Bibliografski Institut. IX-XIV, MIKN
Spisŭk na po-Znachitelnite Trudove na Nikola V. Mikhov. 15-16, MIKH

Mikkelsen, Skov.
Forberedelserne. 5-6, HOLS

MIKULOV, MORAVIA. Fürstlich Dietrichstein'sche Fideicommissbibliothek
see Fürstlich Dietrichstein'sche Fideicommissbibliothek, Mikulov

MIKULOV, MORAVIA. Fürstlich Dietrichstein'sche Fideicommiss-Bibliothek

Schwarz, Arthur Zacharias. Nikolsburger Hebräische Handschriften. 170-181, FREI

MIKULOV, MORAVIA - Manuscripts - Hebrew - Collections
see Manuscripts - Hebrew - Collections - Mikulov, Moravia.

Mikulski, Tadeusz.
Historia Literatury Wobec Zagadnień Księgoznawstwa. 65-77, PIEK
Kniaźnin w Bibliotece Załuskich. 267-281, PIEK

Milam, Carl H.
Reading Courses: An Experiment in Adult Education. 356-364, PUTN

MILAN. Biblioteca Ambrosiana - Hist.

Ciceri, Angelo. Un Precursore ed un Amico di Alfonso Gallo: Mons. Achille Ratti (Papa Pio XI). 279-294, GALL
Gallavresi, G. Alcune Lettere del Barone Custodi Riguardanti le Relazioni del Munifico Bibliofilo coll'Ambrosiana e colla Famiglia Borromeo. 403-412, CERI

MILAN. Biblioteca Ambrosiana. Mss.

Ratti, Achille. Manoscritti di Provenienza Francese nella Bibliotheca Ambrosiana di Milano. 588-597, CHAT
——— Reliquie di Antico Codice Bobbiese Ritrovate. 789-810, CERI

MILAN. Biblioteca Ambrosiana. Mss. (Cod. Omerico)

De Marchi, A. Vesti, Armi, Riti e Costumi nel Codice Omerico Illustrato dell'Ambrosiana. 1-35, CERI

MILAN. Biblioteca Ambrosiana. Mss. (Trotti)

Sabbadini, R. Ciriaco d'Ancona e la Sua Descrizione Autografa del Peloponneso Trasmessa da Leonardo Botta. 181-247, CERI

MILAN. Biblioteca Nazionale Braidense

Buonanno-Schellembrid, Maria. Di Due Recenti Acquisti della Biblioteca Nazionale Braidense di Milano. 46-56, GREG
Ceva Valla, Elena. Nota su Alcuni Incunaboli Posseduti dalla Biblioteca Braidense di Milano. 51-59, ACCU
Meiss, Millard. Ovum Struthionis, Symbol and Allusion in Piero della Francesca's Montefeltro Altarpiece. 92-101, GREE

MILAN. Biblioteca Nazionale Braidense. Mss. (Ms. Boncompagni)

Buonanno-Schellembrid, Maria. Di Due Recenti Acquisti della Biblioteca Nazionale Braidense di Milano. 46-56, GREG

MILAN. Biblioteca Nazionale di Brera (Braidense)
see Milan. Biblioteca Nazionale Braidense

MILAN. Brera (Braidense)
see Milan. Biblioteca Nazionale Braidense

MILAN. Duomo. Archivio - Hist.

Ciceri, Angelo. Un Precursore ed un Amico di Alfonso Gallo: Mons. Achille Ratti (Papa Pio XI). 279-294, GALL

MILAN - Incunabula - Collections
see Incunabula - Collections - Milan

MILAN - Printing
see Printing - Milan

MILDEW
see Books - Care and restoration

MILITARY INTELLIGENCE LIBRARIES

Garside, Kenneth. An Intelligence Library in Germany. 99-106,OFFO

Milkau, Fritz.
Bibliothekwesen oder Bibliothekswesen? 443-474, COLL
Zu Cassiodor. 23-44, KUHN

MILKAU, FRITZ

MILF

MILK

MILKAU, FRITZ - Bibl.

Balcke, Curt. Verzeichnis der Schriften Milkaus. 48-55, MILK

Millàs I Vallicrosa, Joseph M.a.
Manuscrits Hebraics d'Origen Català a la Biblioteca Vaticana. I, 97-109, RUBI

Miller, Eric G.
Fresh Materials for the Study of English Illumination. 286-294, GREE

Miller, Lois B., jt. author

Lage, Louise C., Lois B. Miller, and Donald Washburn. Dental, Nursing, and Pharmaceutical Libraries, 1947-1957. 371-377, DOEJ

Miller, Robert A.
On the Use of the Card Catalog. 629-637, WILS

Mills, J.
Dr. Ranganathan and the Study of Classification. 38-41, MADR
Using Classification in Teaching Indexing. 279-286, KYLE

MINDEN, Ger. St. Martin (Benedictine abbey) Bibliotheca - Catalogs

Molitor, Karl. Ein Westfälischer Bibliotheks-Katalog von 1353. 301-314, MÜNS

MINDE-POUET, GEORG

MIND

Miner, Dorothy, ed.
GREE

MINERVA (Church) Rome
see Rome (City). Santa Maria sopra Minerva (Church) Biblioteca

MINIATURE EDITIONS
see Bookmaking

MINIATURE PAINTING (in books and manuscripts)
see Illumination of books and manuscripts

MINNEAPOLIS. Public Library

Countryman, Gratia A. Mr. Putnam and the Minneapolis Public Library. 5-9, PUTN

MINNESOTA. University. Library - Hist.

Walter, Frank Keller. Notes on the Beginning of a Mid-West University Library. 510-519, PUTN

Minto, John.
The Library Association Examinations. 285-295, HANS

MIQUE, RICHARD - Library

Lelièvre, Pierre. La Bibliothèque de Richard Mique, Architecte de la Reine Marie-Antoinette. 333-336, CALO

Mischiati, Oscar.
Un'Inedita Testimonianza su Bartolomeo Ramis de Pareia. 84-86, FEDO

Misiewicz, Danuta.
Zainteresowania Czytelnicze Nauczycieli. 107-109, KRAK

MISPRINTS
see Errata (in books)

Misra, Jatadhari.
My Thoughts on Colon. 99-101, RANG

MISSALE BASILIENSE

Pfister, Arnold. Vom Frühsten Musikdruck in der Schweiz. 160-178, BINZ

MISSALE SPECIALE CONSTANTIENSE

Schmidt-Künsemüller, Friedrich-Adolf. Der Streit um das Missale Speciale. 51-89, JUCH

MISSALS

Andrieu, Michel. Le Missel de la Chapelle Papale à la Fin du XIIIe Siècle. 348-376, EHRB
Balboni, Dante. Il Rito della Benedi-

zione delle Palme (Vat. Lat. 4770). I, 55-74, ALBB
Bömer, Alois. Ein Gotisches Prachtmissale Utrechtscher Herkunft in der Universitäts-Bibliothek Münster. 29-41, DEGE
Ehwald, Rudolf. Über eine Französische Missalhandschrift des XIV. Jahrhunderts. 65-75, SCHW
Hattum, M. A. C. M. van. Van een Oud Boekblad. 87-96, HAGU
Pfister, Arnold. Vom Frühsten Musikdruck in der Schweiz. 160-178, BINZ
Rest, Josef. Das Basler Missale vom Jahre 1586. 207-212, LEID
Schmidt-Künsemüller, Friedrich-Adolf. Der Streit um das Missale Speciale. 51-89, JUCH

MISSALS - Hist.

Grisar, Hartmann, S. J. Die Stationen und Ihre Perikopen im Römischen Missale. Liturgiegeschichtliche Studien aus der Römischen Stadtgeschichte. 101-140, EHRB

MISSOURI - Library Legislation
see Library legislation - Missouri

Mitchell, Wm. S.
German Bindings in Aberdeen University Library: Iconographic Index, and Indices of Initials, Binders, and Dates. 46-55, OLDH

Mitringer, Albert.
Struktur und Programm der Wissenschaftlichen Bibliothek der Stadt Wien. 9-17, VIES

Mittal, R. L.
Study of Dr. Ranganathan as an Author and a Teacher. 574-577, RANG

Mittler, Max.
P. Bourgeois und der SBVV. 181-182, BOUR

Miyake, Takashi, ed.
Zaidan Hōjin Ōhashi Toshokan Nenpyō. (A Chronological Table of the Ōhashi Library, a Private Library.) 33-61, TSUB

Miyake, Takashi.
Kōkyō Toshokan no Keiji ni tsuite. (On the Notices Put up in Public Libraries.) 25-32, (part 1), OHAS

Miyanaka, Ichiko.
Zasshi Towa Nani ka. (Definition of Periodicals.) 148-152, KYOT

MŁADZIEJOWICE, Poland - Paper making and trade
see Paper making and trade - Mładziejowice, Poland

MŁADZIEJOWICE, Poland - Printing
see Printing - Mładziejowice, Poland

Mocquereau, A.
De la Clivis Épisématique dans les Manuscrits de Saint-Gall. 508-530, CHAT

MODENA. Archivio di Stato. Mss. (F. Malvezzi)

Mischiati, Oscar. Un'Inedita Testimonianza su Bartolomeo Ramis de Pareia. 84-86, FEDO

MODENA - Malvezzi, Floriano. <u>Lettere</u>. - Collections
see Malvezzi, Floriano. <u>Lettere</u>. - Collections - Modena

<u>MODUS TENENDI PARLIAMENTUM IN ANGLIA</u>

Bémont, Ch. La Date de la Composition du <u>Modus Tenendi Parliamentum in Anglia</u>. 465-480, HAVE

Møballe, E.
Maj 1920 til November 1926. 25-32, HOLS

Möhlenbrock, Sigurd.
Om Arbets- och Ansvarsfördelning. 203-214, HEIN

Möhlmann, Günther.
Die Wissenschaftlichen Bibliotheken Ostfrieslands. 140-144, LEUN

Möhring, Werner.
Volkshochschule und Volksbücherei. 95-124, ACKR
Vom Volksbildnerischen Bemühen des Bibliothekars. 61-74, LANF

Møller, Gerda.
Svend Dahl-Bibliografi 1948-1963. x-xii, DAHA

Møller, J. S.
Kalundborg Folkebogsamling 1901-1920. 5-21, KALU

Møller, P.
Skagens Bibliotek. Gennem 75 Aar. 3-6, (whole volume), SKAG

Moeltzner, August.
Zwanzig Jahre Maskierte Druckerarbeit. Pierre du Marteaus Drucke aus den Jahren 1660-1680 in der Königl. Bibliothek zu Berlin. 197-204, SCHW

MÖNCHENGLADBACH, Ger. - Autographs - Collections
see Autographs - Collections - Mönchengladbach, Ger.

MÖNCHENGLADBACH, Ger. - Music libraries and collections
see Music libraries and collections - Mönchengladbach, Ger.

MÖNCHENGLADBACH, Ger. - Musicians - Correspondence - Collections
see Musicians - Correspondence - Collections - Mönchengladbach, Ger.

Mogenet, Joseph.
Holstenius et L'Horoscope de Proclus. II, 281-308, ALBB

Moghe, V. S.
Dr. Ranganathan and Madhya Pradesh. 374-378, RANG

Mogk, Helmut.
Die Abfolge der Ortsbegriffe in Systematischen Katalogen. I, 150-159, GLAU
System und Schlagwort. Erfahrungen am Fachkatalog der Universitätsbibliothek Leipzig. 214-224, VORS

MOHAMMEDAN COUNTRIES - Bookbinding
see Bookbinding - Mohammedan countries

MOHAMMEDAN COUNTRIES - Libraries
see Libraries - Mohammedan countries

MOHAMMEDAN COUNTRIES - Private libraries
see Private libraries - Mohammedan countries

Mohr, Ernst, jt. ed.
REFA

MOLD
see Books - Care and restoration

MOLDENHAUER, HANS - Library
Nettl, Paul. Hans Moldenhauer, Pionier der Musikwissenschaft. 133-137, OREL

Molin, Nils.
Från Låneexpeditionen. 11-20, (fourth paper), GÖTE

Molitor, Karl.
Das Neue Bibliotheks-Gebäude in Münster i.W. V-VIII, MÜNS
Ein Westfälischer Bibliotheks-Katalog von 1353. 301-314, MÜNS
Zur Druckergeschichte des XV. Jahrhunderts. 205-209, SCHW

MOLLER, ARVID. Mss. Skaldestycken
Gierow, Krister. Lundaprofessorn Arvid Moller Som Tillfällighetsdiktare. 133-143, DAHA

Molsdorf, Wilhelm.
Zwei Unbekannte Holzschnitte des Formschneiders Casper in der Breslauer Staats- und Universitäts-Bibliothek. 249-254, MILF

MOLZA, FRANCESCO MARIA. Mss. - Collections - Rome
Vattasso, M. I Codici Molziani della Biblioteca Vaticana con un'Appendice di Carmi Inediti o Rari. 531-555, CERI

Mommsen, Théodore.
Officialium et Militum Romanorum Sepulcretum Carthaginiense. 505-513, GRAU

Monaci, Ernesto.
Un Rotolo Miniato d'Arte Francese a Velletri. 440-441, CHAT

MONASTIC LIBRARIES
Adam, Paul. Der Einfluss der Klosterarbeit auf die Einbandkunst. 148-169, LOUB
Braunsberger, Otto, S. J. Ein Freund der Bibliotheken und Ihrer Handschriften. 455-472, EHRE
De Ghellinck, Joseph. En Marge des Catalogues des Bibliothèques Medievales. 331-363, EHRE

MONASTIC LIBRARIES - Alsace
Gény, Joseph. Geschichte der Stadtbibliothek zu Schlettstadt. First Book, 1-75, SCHL

MONASTIC LIBRARIES - Belgium
Brummel, Leendert. De Boeken van Tongerloo in de Koninklijke Bibliotheek te 's-Gravenhage. 151-168, BRUE

MONASTIC LIBRARIES - Book lists
Hessel, Alfred. Mabillons Musterbibliothek. 119-122, DEGE

MONASTIC LIBRARIES - Catalogs
Binz, Gustav. Ein Bisher Unbekannter Katalog der Bibliothek des Klosters Fulda. 97-108, GODE

MONASTIC LIBRARIES - Europe
Christ, Karl. Karolingische Bibliothekseinbände. 82-104, LEYG

MONASTIC LIBRARIES - France
Croix, Jean Tremblot de la. Marques de la Bibliothèque Capitulaire de Noyon. 237-242, CALO

MONASTIC LIBRARIES - Germany
Abb, Gustav. Von der Verschollenen Bibliothek des Klosters Lehnin. 1-14, DEGE
Bock, Friedrich. Aus der Geschichte der Nürnberger Stadtbibliothek. 9-15, VERZ

Bömer, Alois. Das Literarische Leben in Münster bis zur Endgültigen Rezeption des Humanismus. 57-136, MÜNS
Debes, Dietmar. Das Sequestrationsverzeichnis der Bibliothek des Thomasklosters zu Leipzig. 83-95, LÜLF
Degering, Hermann. Der Katalog der Bibliothek des Klosters Marienfeld vom Jahre 1185. 53-64, SCHW
Fischer, Karl. Margarete Karteuserin, eine Nürnberger Klosterschreiberin des 15. Jahrhunderts. 24-31, VERZ
Herbst, Hermann. Johannes von Brakel. Ein Beitrag zur Bibliotheksgeschichte des Benediktinerklosters Klus bei Gandersheim. 31-46, SCHR
Höfner, Curt. Zur Geschichte der Gandersheimer Büchersammlungen. Ein Beitrag aus Coburg. 197-210, HOFM
Lehmann, Paul. Quot et Quorum Libri Fuerint in Libraria Fuldensi. 47-57, COLL
Stollreither, Eugen. Die Auflösung der Heilsbronner Universitätsbibliothek. 75-84, VERZ
Theele, Joseph. Aus der Bibliothek des Kölner Kreuzbrüderklosters. 253-263, DEGE
Wand, Albert. Zur Geschichte der Dortmunder Bibliotheken. 29-58, VERD

MONASTIC LIBRARIES - Gt. Brit.

Boese, Helmut. Ein Mittelalterliches Bücherverzeichnis von Croyland Abbey. 286-295, VORS
Mynors, R. A. B. The Latin Classics Known to Boston of Bury. 199-217, SAXL

MONASTIC LIBRARIES - Hof, Ger.

Dumrath, Karlheinrich. "Gott zu Ehren und Unsern Nachkommen zum Besten." 2-15, SCHV

MONASTIC LIBRARIES - Italy

Benedetti, Luigi de. I Regesti dei Romani Pontefici per L'Abbazia di Casamari. 325-356, GALL
Cecchini, Giovanni. La Quattrocentesca Biblioteca del Convento di S. Domenico di Perugia. 249-254, GALL
Corsi, Domenico. La Biblioteca dei Frati Domenicani di S. Romano di Lucca nel Sec. XV. 295-310, GALL
Mottironi, Sergio. La Chiesa di S. Pietro di Benevento e la Sua Biblioteca nel Sec. XIII. 559-562, GALL

MONASTIC LIBRARIES - Nassau (Duchy) - Hist.

WIES

MONASTIC LIBRARIES - Netherlands

Woude, S. van der. Uit de Prille Jeugd van de Nederlandse Stads-Universiteitsbibliotheken. 618-625, BRUM

MONASTIC LIBRARIES - Poland

Sarnowska, Klara. Biblioteca Bernardina. 69-79, BYDG

MONASTIC LIBRARIES - Rome (City)

Meersseman, G. La Bibliothèque des Frères Prêcheurs de la Minerve à la Fin du XVe Siècle. 605-634, PELZ

MONASTIC LIBRARIES - Saxony

Schmidt, Ludwig. Die Sächsischen Bibliotheken im Mittelalter. 105-115, BOLL

MONASTIC LIBRARIES - Spain

Camino y Aguirre, Fernando González. Bibliotecas Medievales Montañesas. II, 14-50, ARTI

MONASTIC LIBRARIES - Sweden

Silfverstolpe, C. En Blick i Vadstena Klosters Arkiv och Bibliotek. [89]-[115], KLEM

MONASTIC LIBRARIES - Westphalia

Küster, A. Die Juristische Abteilung der Königlichen Universitäts-Bibliothek zu Münster. 268-300, MÜNS

Mondolfo, Anita.
La Biblioteca Landau-Finaly. 265-285, GREG

Mondor, Henri.
Sur la Symphonie Littéraire de Mallarmé. 461-467, BONN

MONDSEE, Austria (Benedictine monastery). Ms. (Gospels)

Sonnleithner, Rudolf. Die Mondseer Bruchstücke der Ältesten Hochdeutschen Evangelienübersetzung. 795-804, VIEN

Moneti, Elena Amico.
L'Attività di una Tipografia Lucchese nel Settecento. 27-55, FERR
Giacomo Sardini, Patrizio Lucchese, Erudito e Bibliografo. 47-78, GALL

MONNIER FAMILY (Bookbinders)
see Le Monnier Family (Bookbinders)

Monod, M. G.
Hilduin et les Annales Einhardi. 57-65, HAVE

Monrad, Anna Marie, et al.
Historical Notes on the Catalogues and Classifications of the Yale University Library. 251-284, KEOG

MONTE, ANTONIO DEL, Cardinal

Mercati, G. Cenni di A. del Monte e G. Lascaris sulle Perdite della Biblioteca Vaticana nel Sacco del 1527. 605-632, CERI

MONTE, ARNALDUS DE
see Arnaldus de Monte

MONTE CASSINO - Archives
see Archives - Monte Cassino

MONTE CASSINO (Benedictine monastery). Archivio - Hist.

Leccisotti, Tommaso. La Tradizione Archivistica di Montecassino. 227-261, MERC

MONTE CASSINO (Benedictine monastery). Biblioteca. Mss. (Bible. N.T. Gospels)

Campana, Augusto. Per il "Textus Evangelii" Donato da Enrico II a Montecassino (Vat. Ottobon. Lat. 74). 34-47, MERG

MONTE CASSINO (Benedictine monastery). Mss. (Breviary)

Batiffol, Abbé Pierre. Note sur un Bréviaire Cassinésien du XIe Siècle. 201-209, HAVE

MONTE OLIVETO (Benedictine abbey). Mss

Fava, Domenico. I Corali degli Olivetan di Bologna. 277-286, FERR

Montebaur, Josef.
Vinricus, Episcopus Placentinus, Scholasticus Trevirensis. 186-191, DEGE

MONTESQUIEU, CHARLES LOUIS DE SECONDAT, BARON DE LA BRÈDE ET DE

Masson, André. Montesquieu, le Président de Brosses et le Décor des Bibliothèques. 317-324, CALO

MONTEZINOS LIBRARY, Amsterdam
see Amsterdam. Montezinos Library

MONTREAL - Medical libraries
see Medical libraries - Montreal

MONUMENTA GERMANIAE HISTORICA

Schreiber, Heinrich. Friedrich Adolf Ebert und die Monumenta Germaniae. 82-98, BOLL

Mookerjee, S.
Libraries of Scandinavia. 108-115, MADR

MOORE, ANNE CARROLL

MOOR

MOORE, ANNE CARROLL - Bibl.

Weeks, Elizabeth Harriet and Frances Lander Spain. Anne Carroll Moore—A Contribution Toward a Bibliography. 629-636, MOOR

Moore, Everett T.
A Revolution in American University Libraries. 97-105, HASH

Mooy, A. J. de.
De Benaming "Bibliothecaris." 544-547, BRUM
Het Ruilbureau. 235-240, HAGU

MORAEUS, JOHAN - Library

Uggla, Arvid HJ. Ett Läkarebibliotek från Början av 1700-Talet. 221-248, GRAP

MOREAU DE SAINT-MÉRY, MÉDÉRIC LOUIS ÉLIE

Kent, Henry W. Chez Moreau de St-Méry, Philadelphie. Publications of Moreau de St-Méry. 67-78, EAME
———— Encore Moreau de Saint-Méry. 239-247, LYDE

MOREL, EUGÈNE

Raux, Henri F. Un Initiateur de la Lecture Publique en France: Eugène Morel (1869-1934). 197-202, STOL

MORETUS-PLANTIN, firm, Antwerp
see Plantin-Moretus, firm, Antwerp

Morgan, Dale L.
GHP. 1-12, HAMM

Mori, Koichi T.
Simplified Practice of Cataloguing. 202-208, RANG

MORIAU, ANTOINE

Croix, Jean Tremblot de la. Deux Vrais Bibliophiles. 525-534, BONN

Moricca, Luciano.
Le Stampe del Goltzius nella Biblioteca Casanatense di Roma. 286-303, GREG

Moricca, Umberto.
Cenni Biografici. ix-xvi, STAM

Moricca-Caputi, Ada.
Appunti su Alcuni Incunaboli Casanatensi. 304-316, GREG
Di Alcuni Opuscol Rari nella Biblioteca Casanatense. 153-165, ACCU

Moriguchi, Ryuji.
Sunpo-ho ni Yoru Kirishitan-ban no Shishitsu Chosa. (Research by the "Sumpu" Method on the Quality of Paper Used in the Kirishitan Editions.) 503-510, TOMI

Morison, Stanley.
The Learned Press as an Institution. 153-179, WEHM

MORPUGO, ELIJAH. Correspondence
Rivkind, Isaac. Correspondence of Elijah Morpugo. 138-159, (Hebrew section), FREI

Morpugo, J. E.
The Publishing Problem—a Kite for Policy Makers. 236-240, KYLE

Morrissey, Eleanor Fleming.
Reading Bookplates. 14-16, NASH

Mortet, Victor.
La Mesure de la Figure Humaine et le Canon des Proportions d'après les Dessins de Villard de Honnecourt, d'Albert Durer et de Léonard de Vinci. 367-382, CHAT

Mortimer, R. S.
Biographical Notices of Printers and Publishers of Friends' Books up to 1750. 107-125, OFFO

MORTON, HENRY, 1836-1902
Adams, Randolph G. A Translation of the Rosetta Stone. 227-241, EAME

MOSCOW. All-Union Library of Foreign Literature
Rudomino, M. Die Staatliche Allunionsbibliothek für Ausländische Literatur zu Moskau—Heute und Morgen. 175-181, HOFM

MOSCOW - Foreign language books - Collections
see Foreign language books - Collections - Moscow

MOSCOW - Printing
see Printing - Moscow

MOSELLE, France - Inscriptions, Latin
see Inscriptions, Latin - Moselle, France

MOSER, JOHANN JAKOB
Widmann, Hans. Johann Jakob Moser und die Bibliotheken. Zugleich ein Beitrag zur Geschichte des Verhältnisses zwischen Zentralbibliothek und Institutsbibliotheken. 125-146, LEYH

MOSKOVSKIĬ BIBLIOGRAFICHESKIĬ KRUZHOK
Toropov, A. D. Moskovskiĭ Bibliograficheskiĭ Kruzhok; Stranichka Vospominaniĭ. 275-276, MALE

MOSO PICTURE-WRITING
see Picture-writing, Moso

Mottironi, Sergio.
La Chiesa di S. Pietro di Benevento e la Sua Biblioteca nel Sec. XIII. 559-562, GALL

MOTTOES, Library
see Library emblems, inscriptions, etc.

Moulijn, E.
The Development of the UDC from an Electrotechnical Point of View. 165-166, DONK

MT. ATHOS
see Athos

LE MOUSAION À MONSIEUR P. C. COETZEE. 6-13, COET

Mras, Karl.
Eine Neuentdeckte Handschrift des Eusebius. 485-487, BICK

Mühl, Werner.
Ein Brief von C. Th. Dalberg. 129-135, MAIZ

MÜLHER, DETMAR
Knörich, Gerhard. Detmar Mülhers Römische Inschriften vom Kaisberg. 1-6, VERD

Müller, Bernard.
Pompeo Marchesi's Goethe-Statue in der Frankfurter Stadtbibliothek. 191-210, EBRA

Müller, C. A.
Wie ein Geschichtsfreund aus dem Volk das Basler Staatsarchiv Benützen Kann. 37-43, BASL

Mueller, Charles-Conrad.
Sur les Manuscrits de Polyen. 723-729, GRAU

MÜLLER, FRANZ, bookbinder
Sillib, Rudolf. Ein Nachkömmling der Heidelberger Hofbuchbinderei des Kurfürsten Karl Ludwig von der Pfalz. 249-251, LEID

MUELLER (Fr.) & Co., firm, Amsterdam
Nivanka, Eino. Amsterdamilainen Fr. Mullerin Antikvariaatti Nordenskiöldin Kirjakokoelman Päähankkijana. 122-133, DAHL

Müller, Gerhard H.
Epistel eines Bibliothekarischen Laien. 66-71, HOFF

Müller, Hans von.
Die Meβkataloge als Quelle für die Literaturgeschichte. An dem Beispiel E. T. A. Hoffmann Dargelegt. 97-102, KUHN

MÜLLER, JÖRG - Mss. Correspondence - Collections - Zürich

Corrodi-Sulzer, A. Neues aus dem Leben des Bürgermeisters Jörg Müller. 212-238, ESCZ

Müller, Johannes.
Gegenseitige Beziehungen der Universitäten Leipzig und Krakau, Insbesondere in den Ersten Jahrhunderten des Bestehens dieser Universitäten. 209-211, BULL

Müller, Konrad.
Jacques Bongars und Seine Handschriftensammlung. 79-106, BERT

Müller, Max.
Der Älteste Bisher Bekannte Buchumschlag. 195-197, LEID
Casus Synodales. Ein Bisher Unbekannter Bamberger Incunabeldruck. 40-44, VERZ

Mueller, Theodore A.
A Seldom Used Device. 68-69, RANG

Müller-Blattau, Joseph.
Die Pflege der Örtlichen Musikgeschichtlichen Überlieferung durch die Staats- und Universitäts-Bibliothek Königsberg Pr. 283-292, KÖNI

Müller-Graupa, Edw.
Epistola Iocosa. 92-96, BOLE

Münnich, Richard.
Aus der Musikaliensammlung der Weimarer Landesbibliothek, Besonders dem Nachlass der Anna Amalia. 168-184, WEIM

MÜNSTER - Architecture and building - College and university libraries
see Architecture and building - College and university libraries - Münster

MÜNSTER - Bible collections
see Bible collections - Münster

MÜNSTER - Catalogs
see Catalogs - Münster

MÜNSTER - College and university libraries - Statistics
see College and university libraries - Statistics - Münster

MÜNSTER. Dom. Bibliothek

Bahlmann, P. Die Königliche Universitäts-Bibliothek zu Münster. 1-56, MÜNS
Bömer, Alois. Das Literarische Leben in Münster bis zur Endgültigen Rezeption des Humanismus. 57-136, MÜNS
Degering, Hermann. Gottfried von Raesfeld. Sein Geschlecht, Sein Leben und Sein Testament. 137-250, MÜNS
Küster, A. Die Juristische Abteilung der Königlichen Universitäts-Bibliothek zu Münster. 268-300, MÜNS

Münster, Hans A.
Zeitungswissenschaft und Deutsche Bibliotheken. Aufgaben der Zeitungswissenschaft und der Bibliothekswissenschaft zur 500-Jahrfeier 1940. II, 40-42, GLAU

MÜNSTER— Incunabula
see Incunabula - Münster

MÜNSTER. Jesuitenkolleg. Bibliothek

Degering, Hermann. Gottfried von Raesfeld. Sein Geschlecht, Sein Leben und Sein Testament. 137-250, MÜNS

MÜNSTER - Legal literature - Collections
see Legal literature - Collections - Münster

MÜNSTER - Monastic libraries
see Monastic libraries - Germany

MÜNSTER - Music libraries and collections
see Music libraries and collections - Münster

MÜNSTER. Paulinische Bibliothek
see Münster. Universität. Bibliothek

MÜNSTER - Printing
see Printing - Münster

MÜNSTER. Staatsarchiv
see Westphalia. Staatsarchiv

MÜNSTER. Universität

Menn, Walter. Der Oberpräsident von Vincke und die Aufhebung der Universität Münster. 160-178, BÖME

MÜNSTER. Universität. Bibliothek

MÜNS

Bahlmann, P. Die Königliche Universitäts-Bibliothek zu Münster. 1-56, MÜNS
Molitor, Karl. Das Neue Bibliotheks-Gebäude in Münster i.W. V-VIII, MÜNS
Zimmermann, Hildegard. Luther-Bibeln des 16. Jahrhunderts in der Universitätsbibliothek zu Münster i.W. 153-159, BÖME

MÜNSTER. Universitat. Bibliothek - Hist.

Bahlmann, P. Die Königliche Universitäts-Bibliothek zu Münster. 1-56, MÜNS

Degering, Hermann. Gottfried von Raesfeld. Sein Geschlecht, Sein Leben und Sein Testament. 137-250, MÜNS

MÜNSTER. Universität. Bibliothek. Juristische Abteilung

Küster, A. Die Juristische Abteilung der Königlichen Universitäts-Bibliothek zu Münster. 268-300, MÜNS

MÜNSTER. Universität. Bibliothek. Mss. (Missal)

Bömer, Alois. Ein Gotisches Prachtmissale Utrechtscher Herkunft in der Universitäts-Bibliothek Münster. 29-41, DEGE

MÜNSTER. Universität. Bibliothek. Mss. (Rückert)

Kreyenborg, Hermann. Proben einer Ungedruckten Übertragung Arabischer Sprüche und Sinngedichte von Friedrich Rückert, aus dem in der Universitätsbibliothek zu Münster i.W. Aufbewahrten Teilnachlasse des Dichters zum Erstenmal Mitgeteilt. 125-129, BÖME

MÜNSTER. Universität. Bibliothek. Mss. (25 bzw. 1299)

Geisberg, Max. Der Ingenieur J. L. M. Gröninger. 9-15, BÖME

MÜNSTER. Universität. Bibliothek. Niesert Collection

Husung, Max Joseph. Joseph Niesert. Aus dem Leben eines Gelehrten Westfälischen Büchersammlers. 119-124, BÖME

MÜNSTER. Universität. Bibliothek. Santini Collection

Smend, Friedrich. Zur Kenntnis des Musikers Fortunato Santini. 90-98, BÖME

MÜNTER, FRIEDRICH, Bp. - Library

Dahl, Svend. Friedrich Münter und Seine Bibliothek. 291-305, BICK

Müntz, Eugène.
La Bibliothèque de Vatican pendant la Révolution Française. 579-591, HAVE

MUḪAMMAD AL-HIRRĀWĪ

Littmann, Enno. Ein Arabisches Lied über die Ägyptische Bibliothek in Kairo. 309-311, LEYG

Mulholland, John.
Magic in the Library. 446-453, LYDE

Mullerott, Martin.
Author-Title Catalogue as a Sequence of Quasi-Classes and Its Legitimate Subject Functions. 239-242, RANG

MULTIPLE-AUTHORSHIP - Cataloging
see Cataloging - Author entry

Mumford, L. Quincy.
Automation in Research Libraries. 548-551, BRUM
The National Union Catalog of the Library of Congress—Its Past and Its Prospects. 209-215, TVET

MUNARI, BRUNO

Cimino, Maria. The Picture Books of Bruno Munari. 585-588, MOOR

Munck, Peter Andreas.
Brev in: Dahl, Svend. P. A. Munch i Vatikanets Arkiv. 30-48, MUNT

Munford, W. A.
The Library Association in the Twentieth Century: Selected Aspects. 26-47, SAYW

MUNICH - Architecture and building - State Libraries
see Architecture and building - State libraries - Munich

MUNICH. Bayerische Staatsbibliothek

MUNI

Glauning, Otto. Die Einbandsammlung der Bayerischen Staatsbibliothek zu München. 111-122, MILF
Gratzl, Emil. Bedarfsberechnung an der Bayerischen Staatsbibliothek 1932-1936. 369-372, LEYG
Pauer, Max. Anton Ruland und Karl Halm. Ein Bibliothekarischer Streit um Dublettenverkäufe vor Hundert Jahren. 121-135, REDE

MUNICH. Bayerische Staatsbibliothek - Bibl.

Gleixner, Paul. Bibliographie Bayerische Staatsbibliothek 1945-1964. 63-71, HOFM

MUNICH. Bayerische Staatsbibliothek. Bibliotheksschule

Middendorf, Heinrich. Die Bayerische Staatsbibliothek 1945-1964. 7-61, HOFM

MUNICH. Bayerische Staatsbibliothek - Catalogs

Ruf, Paul. Schmeller als Bibliothekar. 9-95, GRAT

MUNICH. Bayerische Staatsbibliothek. Exhibitions

MUNI

MUNICH. Bayerische Staatsbibliothek - Hist.

Buttmann, Rudolf. Beiträge zur Baugeschichte der Bayerischen Staatsbibliothek. 193-215, LEYG

MUNICH. Bayerische Staatsbibliothek - Hist. - 1945-1964

Middendorf, Heinrich. Die Bayerische Staatsbibliothek 1945-1964. 7-61, HOFM

MUNICH. Bayerische Staatsbibliothek. Mss.

Gratzl, Emil. Islamische Handschriftenbände der Bayerischen Staatsbibliothek. 118-147, LOUB

MUNICH. Bayerische Staatsbibliothek. Mss. (Clm. 2599)

Hörmann, Wolfgang. Probleme einer Aldersbacher Handschrift (Clm. 2599). 335-389, HOFM

MUNICH. Bayerische Staatsbibliothek. Mss. (Clm. 9559)

Grabmann, Martin. Neuaufgefundene "Quaestionen" Sigers von Brabant zu den Werken des Aristoteles (Clm. 9559). 103-147, EHRA

MUNICH. Bayerische Staatsbibliothek. Mss. (Cod. Germ. 51)

Gichtel, Paul. Die Bilder der Münchener Tristan-Handschrift (Cod. Germ. 51). 391-457, HOFM

MUNICH. Bayerische Staatsbibliothek. Mss. (Codd. Lat. 14246 and 14383)

Grabmann, Martin. Mitteilungen aus Münchner Handschriften über Bisher Unbekannte Philosophen der Artistenfakultät (Codd. Lat. 14246 und 14383). 73-83, LEID

MUNICH. Bayerische Staatsbibliothek. Mss. (Lat. 19544)

Hilka, Alfons. Zur Konstantinlegende. 147-152, MILF

MUNICH. Bayerische Staatsbibliothek. Mss. (Mahler)

Dorfmüller, Kurt. Gustav-Mahler-Dokumente in München. 33-39, FEDO

MUNICH. Bayerische Staatsbibliothek. Mss. (Mus. Ms. 5369)

Halm, Hans. Eine Unbekannte Handschrift der "Kinder-Symphonie." 101-102, HOBO

MUNICH. Bayerische Staatsbibliothek. Mss. (Pap. gr. mon. 128)

Hartmann, Albert. Eine Federzeichnung auf einem Münchener Papyrus. 103-108, LEID

MUNICH. Bayerische Staatsbibliothek. Mss. (Utacodex)

Boeckler, Albert. Das Erhardbild im Utacodex. 219-230, GREE

MUNICH. Bayerische Staatsbibliothek - Pictorial works

GRAS

MUNICH. Bayerischer Zentralkatalog

Hofmann, G. Der Bayerische Zentralkatalog in München. 473-477, BRUM
Middendorf, Heinrich. Die Bayerische Staatsbibliothek 1945-1964. 7-61, HOFM

MUNICH - Bookbinding - Fine bindings - Collections
see Bookbinding - Fine bindings - Collections - Munich

MUNICH - Budgets
see Budgets - Munich

MUNICH - Classification
see Classification - Munich

MUNICH - Exhibits and displays - Special subjects - Manuscripts
see Exhibits and displays - Special subjects - Manuscripts - Munich

MUNICH. Hauptstaatsarchiv
see Bavaria. Hauptstaatsarchiv

MUNICH - Mahler, Gustav - Collections
see Mahler, Gustav - Collections - Munich

MUNICH - Manuscripts - Collections
see Manuscripts - Collections - Munich

MUNICH - Manuscripts, Oriental - Collections
see Manuscripts, Oriental - Collections - Munich

MUNICH - Music libraries and collections
see Music libraries and collections - Munich

MUNICH - Special collections
see Special collections - Munich

MUNICH. Stadtbibliothek - Hist.

Engl, Hans. Zur Geschichte der Münchener Stadtbibliothek. 49-51, HELD

MUNICH - State libraries - Statistics
see State libraries - Statistics - Munich

MUNICH. Universität. Bibliothek - Hist.

Hilsenbeck, Adolf. Die Universitätsbibliothek Landshut-München und die Säkularisation (1803). 180-192, LEYG

MUNICH. Universität. Bibliothek. Mss. (Q 808)

Lehmann, Paul. Aus einer Münchner Büchersammlung des Ausgehenden Mittelalters. 157-164, LEID

MUNICIPAL REFERENCE LIBRARIES - Berlin

Rohrbach, Peter P. Fachabteilungen und Sondersammlungen. 42-47, BERR

MUNKALIV, Norway (Birgittine monastery)

Collijn, Isak Gustaf Alfred. Kalendarium Munkalivense. Ein Schwedisch-Norwegisches Birgittinerkalendarium. 82-92, DEGE

Muñoz, Antonio.
L'Europa Francese e il Marchese Caraccioli. 317-322, GREG
Miniature Bizantine nella Biblioteca Queriniana di Brescia. 169-179, CERI

MUNTAMER, RAMÓN. Mss. Crònica

D'Olwer, L. Nicolau. La "Crònica" de Ramón Muntaner. Filiació dels Seus Textos. I, 69-76, RUBI

Munthe, Gerhard.
Firma-Arkivene i Universitetsbiblioteket i Bergen. 216-231, TVET
Ludvig Rosenkrantz og Gjenerobringen av Trondhjems Len. Et Dokument i Universitetsbiblioteket i Bergen. 90-94, DAHA

Munthe, Wilhelm.
Einforderungsrecht, eine Selektive Pflichtablieferung. 33-39, GODE
Gutenberg og Hans Verk. 19-35, NORS
National Departments in Scandinavian Libraries. 296-299, HANS
Norske Avdelings Forhistorie. 1-44, OSLO
Norske Boksamlere i Eldre Tid. 249-263, COLL
De Videnskapelige Biblioteker. 97-108, NORN
Vom Lesesaal ins Magazin Zurück. 350-357, LEYG

MUNTHE, WILHELM

MUNT

MUNTHE, WILHELM - Bibl.

Erichsen, Finn. Overbibliotekar Wilhelm Munthes Trykte Arbeider. 493-502, MUNT

Muralt, Leonhard von.
Jörg Berger. 98-126, ESCZ

MURATORI, LODOVICO ANTONIO. Rerum Italicarum Scriptores

Coen-Pirani, Emma. Il Contributo di Eruditi Veneti alla Pubblicazione dei "Rerum Italicarum Scriptores." 169-190, FERR

MURCIA - Printing
see Printing - Murcia

MURET, MARC ANTOINE. Lettres

Nolhac, Pierre de. Lettres Inédites de Muret. 381-403, GRAU

Muriset, Annie.
Bibliographie Féminine Suisse. 154-157, BERU
La Collection de Cartes Géographiques. 108-111, BERU
La Division N (Nouvelles Publications). 39-44, BERU

MURMESTER, HINRICH

Zimmermann, Erich. Hinrich Murmester und die Älteste Hamburger Stadtbibliothek (1479/81). 40-49, TIEM

Murray, I. M.
Mr. and Mrs. Varley's Work for the V.R.S. 24, VARL

MUSÉE PLANTIN-MORETUS, Antwerp
see Antwerp. Musée Plantin-Moretus

MUSEUM MEERMANNO-WESTREENIANUM, Hague
see Hague. Museum Meermanno-Westreenianum

MUSEUM PUBLICATIONS - Cataloging

De Gregori, Giorgio. Appunti di Tecnica Catalografica (la Scheda d'Autore per i Cataloghi di Musei e Gallerie). 215-226, FERR

MUSEUM VAN HET BOEK, Hague
see Hague. Museum Meermanno-Westreenianum. Museum van het Boek

MUSEUMS, Book
see Literary museums

MUSEUMS, Literary
see Literary museums

MUSIC AND THE LIBRARY

Engel, Carl. Concert, A.D. 2025, in the Library of Congress. 140-145, PUTN

MUSIC - Bibliography - Bibl.
see Bibliography - Bibl. - Music

MUSIC LIBRARIES AND COLLECTIONS

Christiansen, Reidar Th. Albrechtsons Visesamling. 106-130, OSLN

Grasberger, Franz. Katalogisierungsprobleme einer Musikbibliothek. 172-181, VORS
Hofmann, Gustav. Musikpflege und Wissenschaftliche Universitätsbibliothek. 41-43, STUM
Lindberg, Folke. Broadcasting Libraries and Archives as Music Research Centres. 76-79, FEDO

MUSIC LIBRARIES AND COLLECTIONS - Berlin

Altmann, Wilhelm. Die Entwicklung der Musikabteilung. 211-217, HARN
Köhler, Karl-Heinz. Die Musikabteilung. I, 241-274, BERS
Weise-Standfest, Hilde. Musikbibliothek und Diskothek, Kunstblätter-Sammlung, Musik- und Literaturveranstaltungen. 36-41, BERR

MUSIC LIBRARIES AND COLLECTIONS - Berlin - Hist.

Schermall, Herbert. Die Berliner Musikbibliotheken im Rückblick und in der Gegenwart. 99-117, SCHS

MUSIC LIBRARIES AND COLLECTIONS - Bern

Lengstorf, Ewald. Die Musiksammlung Liebeskind. 94-96, BERU
Wissler, Gustav. Die Musikalien. 87-94, BERU

MUSIC LIBRARIES AND COLLECTIONS - Brussels

Mertens, C. Proeve eener Documentatie over Onze Belgische Toonkunstenaars, Musicologen en Instrumentenbouwers. 216-239, BORR

MUSIC LIBRARIES AND COLLECTIONS - Cambridge, Eng.

Cudworth, Charles. Richard, Viscount Fitzwilliam, and the French Baroque Music in the Fitzwilliam Museum, Cambridge. 27-31, FEDO

MUSIC LIBRARIES AND COLLECTIONS - Classification
see Classification - Special subjects - Music

MUSIC LIBRARIES AND COLLECTIONS - Cologne

Kahl, Willi. Musikhandschriften aus dem Nachlass Ernst Bückens in der Kölner Universitäts- und Stadtbibliothek. 159-171, JUCH

MUSIC LIBRARIES AND COLLECTIONS - Dresden

Schnoor, Hans. Rechts und Links der Elbe. 88-91, BOLE
Willi, Liselotte. Die Musikabteilung. 156-165, DREL

MUSIC LIBRARIES AND COLLECTIONS - Königsberg

Killer, Hermann. Zur Musik des Deutschen Ostens im 18. Jahrhundert. 228-243, KÖNI

MUSIC LIBRARIES AND COLLECTIONS - Mannheim

MANN

MUSIC LIBRARIES AND COLLECTIONS - Mönchengladbach, Ger.

Dreimüller, Karl. Musikerbriefe an einen Rheinischen Musikliebhaber. Aus der Sammlung Ludwig Bischopinck in Mönchengladbach. 29-49, HOBO

MUSIC LIBRARIES AND COLLECTIONS - Münster
Smend, Friedrich. Zur Kenntnis des Musikers Fortunato Santini. 90-98, BÖME

MUSIC LIBRARIES AND COLLECTIONS - Munich

Dorfmüller, Kurt. Gustav-Mahler-Dokumente in München. 33-39, FEDO

MUSIC LIBRARIES AND COLLECTIONS - Paris

Bridgman, Nanie. La Typographie Musicale Italienne (1475-1630) dans les Collections de la Bibliothèque Nationale de Paris. 24-27, FEDO
Lebeau, Elisabeth. Les Catalogues de Vente de Tableaux et d'Objets d'Art, Source de Documentation Musicale. 67-72, FEDO

MUSIC LIBRARIES AND COLLECTIONS - Programs - Berlin

Weise-Standfest, Hilde. Musikbibliothek und Diskothek, Kunstblätter-Sammlung, Musik- und Literaturveranstaltungen. 36-41, BERR

MUSIC LIBRARIES AND COLLECTIONS - Rome (City)

Fédorov, Vladimir. V. V. Stasov chez L'Abb. F. Santini à Rome. 55-62, HOBO

MUSIC LIBRARIES AND COLLECTIONS - Spain

Querol, Miguel. Lista de los Catálogos Musicales Publicados en España. 103-105, FEDO

MUSIC LIBRARIES AND COLLECTIONS - Spokane

Nettl, Paul. Hans Moldenhauer, Pionier der Musikwissenschaft. 133-137, OREL

MUSIC LIBRARIES AND COLLECTIONS - Sweden

Johansson, Cari. Carl Frederic Fredenheim and His Collection of Eighteenth-Century Music. 46-49, FEDO

MUSIC LIBRARIES AND COLLECTIONS - Vatican

Anglés, Higinio. El Tesoro Musical de la Biblioteca Vaticana. I, 23-53, ALBB

MUSIC LIBRARIES AND COLLECTIONS - Vienna

Gladt, Karl. Hundert Jahre Stadtbibliothek. 18-45, VIES

Nowak, Leopold. Die Musikhandschriften aus Fuggerschem Besitz in der Österreichischen Nationalbibliothek. 505-515, BICK

——— Die Musiksammlung. 119-138, BICK

MUSIC LIBRARIES AND COLLECTIONS - Washington, D.C.

Goff, Frederick R. Early Music Books in the Rare Books Division of the Library of Congress. 58-74, KINO

MUSIC LIBRARIES AND COLLECTIONS - Weimar

Münnich, Richard. Aus der Musikaliensammlung der Weimarer Landesbibliothek, Besonders dem Nachlass der Anna Amalia. 168-184, WEIM

MUSIC LIBRARIES AND COLLECTIONS - Zürich

Schenk, Erich. Die Österreichische Musiküberlieferung der Züricher Zentralbibliothek. 576-581, BICK

MUSIC LITERATURE AND SCORES - Bibl. - Bibl.
see Bibliography - Bibl. - Music

MUSIC LITERATURE AND SCORES - Buying and selling
see Book industry and trade - Music

MUSIC LITERATURE AND SCORES - Cataloging

Grasberger, Franz. Katalogisierungsprobleme einer Musikbibliothek. 172-181, VORS

Schmidt-Phiseldeck, Kay. Notes sur les Buts du Catalogage des Livres et de la Musique. 117-121, FEDO

MUSIC LITERATURE AND SCORES - Catalogs - Bibl.

Querol, Miguel. Lista de los Catálogos Musicales Publicados en España. 103-105, FEDO

MUSIC LITERATURE AND SCORES - Classification
see Music libraries and collections

MUSIC LITERATURE AND SCORES - Dating

Feder, Georg. Zur Datierung Haydnscher Werke. 50-54. HOBO

Weinhold, Liesbeth. Musiktitel und Datierung. 136-140, FEDO

MUSIC LITERATURE AND SCORES - Incunabula
see Incunabula - Music

MUSIC LITERATURE AND SCORES - Manuscripts

Fava, Domenico. I Corali degli Olivetani di Bologna. 277-286, FERR

Haydon, Glen. The Dedication of Francesco Corteccia's Hinnario. 112-116, KINK

Jonas, Oswald. Musikalische Meisterhandschriften. 103-109, HOBO

Launay, Denise. À Propos de Deux Manuscrits Musicaux aux Armes de Louis XIII. 63-67, FEDO

Lowinsky, Edward E. Early Scores in Manuscript. 126-173, KINK

Luther, Wilhelm Martin. Der Komponist und Seine Eigenschrift. 172-186, JUCH

Mocquereau, A. De la Clivis Épisématique dans les Manuscrits de Saint-Gall. 508-530, CHAT

Nowak, Leopold. Die Musiksammlung. 119-138, BICK

Pietzsch, Gerhard. Mscr. Dresd. A 52. 167-174, BOLL

Ward, John. The Lute Music of MS Royal Appendix 58. 117-125, KINK

MUSIC LITERATURE AND SCORES - Manuscripts - Bibl.

Goff, Frederick R. Early Music Books in the Rare Books Division of the Library of Congress. 58-74, KINO

Nowak, Leopold. Die Musikhandschriften aus Fuggerschem Besitz in der Österreichischen Nationalbibliothek. 505-515, BICK

Witty, Francis J. Four Music Books at Washington from the Pontificate of Benedict XIII. 517-[533], ALBA

MUSIC LITERATURE AND SCORES - Manuscripts - Cataloging

Schmieder, Wolfgang. Werkstatt-Erfahrungen beim Katalogisieren von Musikhandschriften. 121-125, FEDO

MUSIC LITERATURE AND SCORES - Manuscripts - Collections - Cologne

Kahl, Willi. Musikhandschriften aus dem Nachlass Ernst Bückens in der Kölner Universitäts- und Stadtbibliothek. 159-171, JUCH

MUSIC LITERATURE AND SCORES - Manuscripts - Collections - Spokane

Nettl, Paul. Hans Moldenhauer, Pionier der Musikwissenschaft. 133-137, OREL

MUSIC LITERATURE AND SCORES - Manuscripts - Collections - Vatican

Llorens, José Maria. Los Codices Musicales de la "Capella Sixtina" en la Historia del Arte. II, 191-209, ALBB

MUSIC LITERATURE AND SCORES - Manuscripts - Collections - Vienna

Lach, Robert. Aus dem Handschriftenschatze der Musikaliensammlung der Wiener Nationalbibliothek. 553-574, VIEN

Racek, Fritz. Von den Schuberthandschriften der Stadtbibliothek. 98-124, VIES

MUSIC LITERATURE AND SCORES - Manuscripts - Facsimiles

Kuczewski-Poray, Kasimir. Ein Joseph Marx-Autograph der Österreichischen Nationalbibliothek. 446-449, BICK

Wolf, Johannes. Zwei Tagelieder des 14. Jahrhunderts. 325-327, DEGE

MUSIC LITERATURE AND SCORES, Swiss - Manuscripts - Collections - Basel

Zehntner, Hans. Die Handschriftlichen Nachlässe von Schweizer Komponisten in der Universitätsbibliothek Basel. 297-315, SCHU

MUSIC PRINTING - Basel - Hist.

Pfister, Arnold. Vom Frühsten Musikdruck in der Schweiz. 160-178, BINZ

MUSIC PRINTING - Germany

Benton, Rita. Ignace Pleyel, Disputant. 21-24, FEDO

MUSIC PRINTING - Hist.

Springer, Hermann. Zur Musiktypographie in der Inkunabelzeit. 173-180, WILM

MUSIC PRINTING - Italy - Hist.

Bridgman, Nanie. La Typographie Musicale Italienne (1475-1630) dans les Collections de la Bibliothèque Nationale de Paris. 24-27, FEDO

Sartori, Claudio. Un Catalogo di Guiseppe Sala del 1715. 112-116, FEDO

MUSIC PRINTING - Leipzig - Hist. - 19th cent.

King, A. Hyatt. C. G. Röder's Music-Printing Business in 1885. 53-59, FEDO

MUSIC PRINTING - Mainz - Hist.

Ziegler, Benno. Zur Geschichte des Privilegium Exclusivum des Mainzer Musikstechers Bernhard Schott. 293-305, LEID

MUSIC PRINTING - U.S. - Hist.

Waters, Edward N. The Wa-Wan Press: An Adventure in Musical Idealism. 214-233, ENGE

MUSIC PUBLISHING
see Music printing

MUSICIANS - Correspondence - Collections - Barcelona

Anglés, Higinio. Relations Épistolaires entre César Cui et Philippe Pedrell. 15-21, FEDO

MUSICIANS - Correspondence - Collections - Basel

Zehntner, Hans. Musikerbriefe in der Universitätsbibliothek Basel. 140-149, FEDO

MUSICIANS - Correspondence - Collections - Mönchengladbach, Ger.

Dreimüller, Karl. Musikerbriefe an einen Rheinischen Musikliebhaber. Aus der Sammlung Ludwig Bisschopinck in Mönchengladbach. 29-49, HOBO

Mustelin, Olof, jt. ed.
GARD

Mustonen, Aarne.
Kaukoidän Kirjatietoa. 164-181, DAHL
Kaukoidän Kirjatietoa. 66-77, NYBE

Musurillo, Herbert.
A Note on Gregory of Nyssa's Commentary on the Song of Solomon, Homily IV. 321-326, ALBA

Muszkowski, Jan.
Książka Jako Zjawisko Społeczne. 79-104, PIEK

Muthiah, V. S. and A. N. Rajamoni.
Dr. Ranganathan as a Public Speaker. 732-733, RANG

MUTILATION OF BOOKS AND PERIODICALS
see Books - Care and restoration

Muzzioli, Giovanni.
Il Più Antico Codice della Biblioteca Casanatense. 323-332, GREG

Mynors, R. A. B.
The Latin Classics Known to Boston of Bury. 199-217, SAXL

MYNORS, R. A. B., appendix

Galbraith, V. H. The Chronicle of Henry

Knighton. 136-145. Appendix by R. A. B. Mynors. 146-148, SAXL

MYRÉEN, DANIEL

Pipping, Hugo E. Tva Bokägarmärken Anbragta Som Rygg- och Pärmstämpel. 1-11, DAHL

MYSTIC, Conn. Marine Historical Association Library
see Marine Historical Association. Library

NA-KHI PICTURE-WRITING
see Picture-writing, Moso

NACHWORT. I, 443-446, BERS

Nadejde, Florence.
Philosophy of Colon Classification. 105-107, RANG

NÄGELI, HANS GEORG

Refardt, Edgar. Vom Musikhändler Nägeli. 24-27, REFA

NAGASAKI. Prefectural Library. Mss.

Anesaki, Masaharu. Some Unrecorded Japanese Martyrdoms of the Catholic Church in the Second Half of the Seventeenth Century. A Study on Newly Disclosed Documents from the Prefectural Library of Nagasaki. 343-384, EHRC

Nagasawa, Masao.
Daigaku Toshokan Kindaika no Kijiku toshite no Refarensu Wāku. (Reference Work as the Axis for the Modernization of the University Library.) 267-279, HASH

NAGLER, KARL FERDINAND FRIEDRICH - Library

Juchhoff, Rudolf. Die Büchersammlung des Generalpostmeisters von Nagler in der Preussischen Staatsbibliothek. 201-208, KUHN

Nagórska, Izabela.
Portrety Czytelników-Robotników w Łodzkiej Dzielnicy Chojny. 155-168, GRYC

Naidu, R. Janardhanam.
The Library Movement. 118-122, MADR

Naito, Torajiro.
Kansei Jidai no Zōshoka Ichihashi Shimosa no Kami. (On Lord Ichihashi Shimosa, a Book Collector of the Kansei Period.) 42-69, IMAI

Nakama, Zukuri.
Kyōto Toshokan Kyōkai Seinen Kenkyū Gurūpu no Rei. (Organizing Librarians in the Region—the Case of the Young Men's Research Group of the Kyōto Library Association.) 50-75, TOKY

Nakamura, Hatsuo.
Problems in Search of Common Basis in Cataloguing. 181-189, RANG
Shiryō Soshiki Kyōjuho no Hensen; Amerika no Toshokan Gakko o Chūshin to shite. (On Teaching the Organization of Materials for Use. Based on Courses in American Library Schools.) 281-296, HASH

Nakamura, Hidetaka.
Chosen-ban Kohan Insatsu ni tsuite. (On Early Korean Printed Books.) 375-386, TOMI

Nakamura, Yukihiko.
Kogidō no Zōhan ni Kansuru Monjo ni tsuite. (Documents concerning the Arrangements for the Publication of Works of the Kogidō Masters of the Ito Family.) 113-151, TOMI

NALANDA UNIVERSITY. Library

Dutta, Bimal Kumer. An Ancient Indian University Library. 457-460, RANG

NANI FAMILY - Library

Mercati, Giovanni, Cardinal. A Proposito dei Codici Naniani Greci 32 e 37. 280-285, GREE

NAPLES - Archives
see Archives - Naples

NAPLES. Archivio di Stato

Filangieri di Candida, Riccardo. Perdita e Ricuperi del Diplomatico Farnesiano. 269-279, MERC

NAPLES. Archivio di Stato. Mss.

Mazzoleni, Iole. Note Paleografiche e Diplomatiche su Alcune Carte Ravellesi dei Secc. XII-XIV. 539-547, GALL

NAPLES. Biblioteca Nazionale

Delisle, Léopold. Notes sur les Anciennes Impressions des Classiques Latins et d'Autres Auteurs Conservées au XVe Siècle dans la Librairie Royale de Naples. 245-296, GRAU

NAPLES. Biblioteca Nazionale. Mss.

Guerrieri, Guerriera. Note sulla Raccolta dei Manoscritti della Biblioteca Nazionale di Napoli. 192-200, GREG

NAPLES. Biblioteca Universitaria
see Naples. Università. Biblioteca

NAPLES - Incunabula - Collections
see Incunabula - Collections - Naples

NAPLES - Manuscripts - Collections
see Manuscripts - Collections - Naples

NAPLES. Università. Biblioteca

Lanzara, M. Giuseppina Castellano. La Casa del Salvatore in Napoli. 239-247, GALL

NAPOLÉON I - Library, St. Helena

Arrighi, Marie. La Bibliothèque de L'Empereur Napoléon à Sainte-Hélène. 55-65, BONN

Narciss, G. A.
Zum Problem der Kritik. 87-92, ACKE

NASHVILLE - Architecture and building
see Architecture and building - Nashville

NASHVILLE - Bookplates
see Bookplates - Nashville

NASHVILLE - College and university libraries
see College and university libraries - Nashville

NASHVILLE - College and university libraries - Book collections
see College and university libraries - Book collections - Nashville

NASHVILLE - College and university libraries - Departmental and divisional libraries
see College and university libraries - Departmental and divisional libraries - Nashville

NASHVILLE - College and university libraries - Relations with faculty and curriculum
see College and university libraries - Relations with faculty and curriculum - Nashville

NASHVILLE - Cooperative library systems
see Cooperative library systems - Nashville

NASHVILLE - Gifts, contributions, etc.
see Gifts, contributions, etc. - Nashville

NASHVILLE. Joint University Libraries

NASH

NASHVILLE. Joint University Libraries - Bibl.

The Joint University Libraries in Print. 22-23, NASH

NASHVILLE. Joint University Libraries - Hist.

Kuhlman, A. F. A Quarter Century of Service. 2-4, NASH

NASHVILLE - Libraries
see Libraries - Nashville

NASHVILLE LIBRARIES HOUSE OVER 2,000,000 VOLUMES. 12-13, NASH

NASHVILLE - Medical literature - Collections
see Medical literature - Collections - Nashville

NASHVILLE - Microforms - Collections
see Microforms - Collections - Nashville

NASHVILLE - Research materials - Collections
see Research materials - Collections - Nashville

NASSAU (Duchy) - Libraries
see Libraries - Nassau (Duchy)

NASSAU (Duchy) - Monastic libraries
see Monastic libraries - Nassau (Duchy)

NATIONAL BIBLIOGRAPHY
see Bibliography - National

NATIONAL FEDERATION OF ECONOMIC RESEARCH ORGANIZATIONS

Tamai, Tōkichi. Zenkoku Keizai Chōsa Kikan Rengōkai Seitei Gaikoku Zasshi-mei Ryakugo Shokitei ni tsuite. (On the Rules of Abbreviation of the Titles of Foreign Periodicals, Established by the National Federation of Economic Research Organizations.) 20-36, OTAT

NATIONAL LIBRARIES - Acquisitions - Berlin

Hülle, Hermann. Die Fortschritte der Ostasiatischen Sammlungen. 190-211, HARN
Nickel, Wilhelm. Die Vermehrung der Druckschriftenabteilung. 10-14, HARN
Tyszko, Oskar. Die Bestandsvermehrung der Hauptabteilung und Ihre Organisation. I, 89-129, BERS

NATIONAL LIBRARIES - Acquisitions - Berlin - Hist.

Tyszko, Oskar. Die Bestandsvermehrung der Hauptabteilung und Ihre Organisation. I, 89-129, BERS

NATIONAL LIBRARIES - Acquisitions - Bern

Brouty, Barth. Le Service des Entrées. 127-129, BERU

NATIONAL LIBRARIES - Acquisitions - Leipzig
Paust, Albert. Sammelgebiet und Werbung. 58-74, LEIS
Rückert, Ernst. Das Wachsen und Werden der Bestände. 75-90, LEIS

NATIONAL LIBRARIES - Acquisitions - Vienna
Kisser, Alois. Die Druckschriftensammlung. 73-104, BICK

NATIONAL LIBRARIES - Acquisitions - Vienna - Hist.
Groag, Edmund. Zur Geschichte des Bücherankaufes in der Hofbibliothek. 421-430, VIEN

NATIONAL LIBRARIES - Administration - Berlin
Kunze, Horst. Demokratisierung und Sozialistische Umgestaltung. I, 49-76, BERS

NATIONAL LIBRARIES - Architecture and building
see Architecture and building - National libraries

NATIONAL LIBRARIES - Berlin
BERP
BERS
HARN

NATIONAL LIBRARIES - Bern
BERU
GODM

NATIONAL LIBRARIES - Copenhagen
Birkelund, Palle. Det Kongelige Bibliotek og dets Publikum. 119-132, DAHA

NATIONAL LIBRARIES - Frankfurt a.M.
EPPE
Günther, Eberhard. Die Sammlung des Deutschsprachigen Schrifttums durch die Deutsche Bibliothek. Probleme und Methoden. 78-90, EPPE

NATIONAL LIBRARIES - Germany
Paust, Albert. Johann Heinrich Plath, ein Wegbereiter der Deutschen Bücherei. 64-67, STUM

NATIONAL LIBRARIES - Germany - Hist.
Paust, Albert. Die Reichsbibliothek von 1848, ein Denkmal der Deutschen Einheit. 384-396, VORS

NATIONAL LIBRARIES - Gt. Brit.
Francis, Sir Frank. The National Library as the Basis of a National Library. 244-247, KYLE

NATIONAL LIBRARIES - Hague
HAGU

NATIONAL LIBRARIES - Italy
Carini-Dainotti, Virginia. Biblioteche Generali e Biblioteche Speciali nelle Discussioni Parlamentari. 117-167, FERR

NATIONAL LIBRARIES - Japan - Hist.
Hatano, Ken'ichi. Meiji Shonen ni okeru Kanritsu Toshokan Hakubutsukan no Hassei to Sono Hensen—Fu, Toshokan Kankei Horei, Shuppanho. (The Establishment of National Libraries and Museums in the Early Period of the Meiji Era and Their Progress—Appendix: Laws Relating to Libraries and Laws on Publication.) 85-160, OTAT

NATIONAL LIBRARIES - Jerusalem
Wormann, C. The Jewish National and University Library in Jerusalem since the Establishment of the State of Israel. 116-117, MADR

NATIONAL LIBRARIES - Leipzig
LEIS
LEIZ
Fleischhack, Curt. Deutsche Bücherei und Zentralkatalogisierung. 143-150, VORS

NATIONAL LIBRARIES - Madrid
J. P. Más Datos Sobre el Nombramiento de Menéndez Pelayo como Director de la Biblioteca Nacional. 69-72, MENE
Reyes, Enrique Sánchez. Menéndez Pelayo, Director de la Biblioteca Nacional. 27-67, MENE

NATIONAL LIBRARIES - Paris
CAIN

NATIONAL LIBRARIES - Plovdiv, Bulgaria
Pi͡eev, Aleksandr K. Reformirane na Plovdivskata Narodna Biblioteka. 26-29, DIAK

NATIONAL LIBRARIES - Reference services - Berlin
Gittig, Heinz. Das Auskunftsbüro der Deutschen Bibliotheken. I, 223-240, BERS

NATIONAL LIBRARIES - Reference services - Germany
Rückert, Ernst. Die Auskunftserteilung,

eine der Hauptaufgaben der Deutschen Bücherei. 274-285, VORS

Uhlendahl, Heinrich. Ernetes und Heiteres aus der Auskunftsstelle der Deutschen Bücherei. 90-91, STUM

NATIONAL LIBRARIES - Sofia

SOFI

NATIONAL LIBRARIES - Statistics - Frankfurt a.M.

Die Deutsche Bibliothek in Zahlen. 175-192, EPPE

NATIONAL LIBRARIES - Vienna

BICK

Doublier, Othmar. Ein Vierteljahrhundert aus der Geschichte der Hofbibliothek 1891-1916. 163-210, VIEN

NATIONAL LIBRARIES - Washington, D.C.

Mearns, David C. Herbert Putnam and His Responsible Eye—A Memorial Tribute. 1-52, PUTP

NATIONAL LIBRARIES - Wellington, N.Z.

Tautz, Kurt. Die Turnbull Library in Wellington—ein Spiegel des Pazifischen Raumes. 263-270, JUCH

THE NATIONAL LIBRARY

Slade, William Adams. The National Library: A Sonnet. 409, PUTN

NATIONAL MUSIC - Prussia, East - Collections - Königsberg

Müller-Blattau, Joseph. Die Pflege der Örtlichen Musikgeschichtlichen Überlieferung durch die Staats- und Universitäts-Bibliothek Königsberg Pr. 283-292, KÖNI

NATIONAL UNION CATALOG, U.S. Library of Congress
see U.S. Library of Congress. National Union Catalog

NATURAL HISTORY AND SCIENCE
see Documentation - Special subjects - Science

NATURWISSENSCHAFTLICHE GESELLSCHAFT ISIS, Dresden. Bibliothek

Zaunick, Rudolph. Erinnerungen und Glückwunsch. 84-87, BOLE

NAUDÉ, GABRIEL. Advis pour Dresser une Bibliothèque

Blum, Rudolf. Bibliotheca Memmiana. Untersuchungen zu Gabriel Naudés "Advis pour Dresser une Bibliothèque." 209-232, WEHM

NAUMANN, JOHANN ANDREAS

Thomsen, Peter. Die Erste Ausgabe von Johann Friedrich Naumanns Naturgeschichte der Vögel Deutschlands. 220-239, BOLL

NAUMANN, JOHANN FR.

Thomsen, Peter. Die Erste Ausgabe von Johann Friedrich Naumanns Naturgeschichte der Vögel Deutschlands. 220-239, BOLL

NAVARRA (Kingdom). Laws, statutes, etc. Fueros. Mss.

Häbler, Konrad. Die Fuero-Handschrift der Sächsischen Landesbibliothek. 146-155, BOLL

NEDERLANDS LETTERKUNDIG MUSEUM EN DOCUMENTATIECENTRUM, Hague

see Hague. Nederlands Letterkundig Museum en Documentatiecentrum

NEDERLANDSE CENTRALE CATALOGUS
see Hague. Koninklijke Bibliotheek. Nederlandse Centrale Catalogus

Nedkov, Boris.
Orientalistikata v Sofiiskata Narodna Biblioteka. 226-239, MIKN

Neelameghan, A.
Indexing Physical Chemical Properties of Antibiotic Substances. 248-254, RANG

NEGRO LIBRARIANS - Education - U.S.

Gleason, Eliza Atkins. The Atlanta University School of Library Service—Its Aims and Objectives. 504-510, WILS

Neĭkov, Stoi͡an.
Ĭurdan Ivanov. 281-297, MIKN

Nelson, Axel.
Aus J. H. Lidéns Tagebuch über Seinen Aufenthalt in Göttingen in den Jahren 1768-1769. 255-263, MILF
Förteckning över Isak Collijns intill den 17 Juli 1925 Uitgivna Skrifter. 1-45, COLL
Richard de Bury och Thomas à Kempis. 59-70, COLL
Zum Wimpfeling-Codex der Universitätsbibliothek zu Uppsala. 27-37, LEYG

Nemoy, Leon.
Notes on Some Arabic Manuscripts on Curious Subjects in the Yale University Library. 45-66, KEOG

Nentwig, Heinrich.
Zwei Schlesische Majoratsbibliotheken. 129-138, WILM

NEOBARIUS, KONRAD, printer

Hunger, Herbert. Die Druckvorlage der Editio Princeps des Anonymus Neobarii. 46, STUM

Nesbitt, Elizabeth.
Training of Children's Librarians—History and Implications. 605-610, MOOR

NETHERLANDS - Auction sales
see Auction sales - Netherlands

NETHERLANDS - Catalogs - Union
see Catalogs - Union - Netherlands

NETHERLANDS - College and university libraries
see College and university libraries - Netherlands

NETHERLANDS - Documentation
see Documentation - Netherlands

NETHERLANDS - Education for librarianship
see Education for librarianship - Netherlands

NETHERLANDS EXCHANGE BUREAU
see Hague. Koninklijke Bibliotheek. Ruilbureau

NETHERLANDS - Geographical libraries and collections
see Geographical libraries and collections - Netherlands

NETHERLANDS - Legal deposit (of books, etc.)
see Legal deposit (of books, etc.) - Netherlands

NETHERLANDS - Monastic libraries
see Monastic libraries - Netherlands

NETHERLANDS - Printing
see Printing - Netherlands

NETHERLANDS - Private libraries
see Private libraries - Netherlands

NETHERLANDS - Public libraries
see Public libraries - Netherlands

NETHERLANDS - Public libraries - Standards
see Public libraries - Standards - Netherlands

NETHERLANDS - Registration of borrowers
see Registration of borrowers - Netherlands

Nettl, Paul.
Hans Moldenhauer, Pionier der Musikwissenschaft. 133-137, OREL

Neubauer, Adolf.
Zakkuth's Non-Jewish Chronicle According to Ms. Hebr. d. 16, Recently Acquired by the Bodleian Library. 243-244, STEI

NEUBAUER, ADOLF - Bibl.

Adler, Elkan N. A Bibliography of the Writings of Adolf Neubauer (1832-1907). 31-54, FREI

NEUBERGER, FERDINAND. Mss.

Hampe, Theodor. Der Sog. Ferdinand Neuberger-Codex in der Erlanger Universitätsbibliothek. 32-39, VERZ

Neubert, Hermann, ed.
BOLL

Neubert, Hermann.
Alphabetischer Katalog—Formalkatalog? 126-132, BOLL
Martin Bollerts Wirken für Gegenwart und Zukunft. 23-28, BOLE
Der Ruf Christian Gottlob Heynes nach Dresden. II, 43-52, GLAU

NEUBERT, HERMANN

NEUB

Schmidt, Wieland. Hermann Neubert zum 60. Geburtstag am 9. Dezember 1952. 5-8, NEUB

NEUBERT, HERMANN - Bibl.

Kaegbein, Paul. Hermann Neuberts Schriften. 9-15, NEUB

NEUCHÂTEL. Bibliothèque. Mss. (Fonds Bourguet)

Godet, Marcel. Au Temps de la "Respublica Litterarum." Jacob Christophe Iselin et Louis Bourguet. 117-127, SCHU

NEUMES

Jammers, Ewald. Neumen im Lateinunterricht. 64-68, BOLE
Mocquereau, A. De la Clivis Épisématique dans les Manuscrits de Saint-Gall. 508-530, CHAT

NEUMES - Hist.

Jammers, Ewald. Zur Entwicklung der Neumenschrift im Karolingerreich. I, 89-98, GLAU

Neuscheler, Eugen.
Buch und Leben. 381-387, LEYG

NEW ENGLAND DEPOSIT LIBRARY

Metcalf, Keyes DeWitt. The New England Deposit Library. 622-628, WILS

THE NEW ENGLAND PRIMER

Ford, Worthington Chauncey. The New England Primer. 61-65, EAME

NEW HAVEN, Conn. - American literature, 18th cent. - Collections
see American literature, 18th cent. - Collections - New Haven, Conn.

NEW HAVEN, Conn. - Catalogs
see Catalogs - New Haven, Conn.

NEW HAVEN, Conn. - Classification
see Classification - New Haven, Conn.

NEW HAVEN, Conn. - College and university libraries
see College and university libraries - New Haven, Conn.

NEW HAVEN, Conn. - College and university libraries - Acquisitions
see College and university libraries - Acquisitions - New Haven, Conn.

NEW HAVEN, Conn. - Indians of North America - Portraits - Collections
see Indians of North America - Portraits - Collections - New Haven, Conn.

NEW HAVEN, Conn. - Presses, University
see Presses, University - New Haven, Conn.

NEW HAVEN, Conn. - Printing - Presses
see Printing - Presses - New Haven, Conn.

NEW LIBRARIES FOR THE UNIVERSITY CENTER. 20, NASH

NEW YORK (City) - Art objects - Collections
see Art objects - Collections - New York (City)

NEW YORK (City) Astor Library
see Astor Library, New York (City)

NEW YORK (City) - Book industry and trade
see Book industry and trade - New York (City)

NEW YORK (City) - Children's library services
see Children's library services - New York (City)

NEW YORK (City) - Correspondence - Collections
see Correspondence - Collections - New York (City)

NEW YORK (City) Jewish Theological Seminary of America
see Jewish Theological Seminary of America

NEW YORK (City) - Magic - Collections
see Magic - Collections - New York (City)

NEW YORK (City) - Manuscripts - Collections
see Manuscripts - Collections - New York (City)

NEW YORK (City) - Manuscripts, Hebrew - Collections
see Manuscripts, Hebrew - Collections - New York (City)

NEW YORK (City) - Medical libraries
see Medical libraries - New York (City)

NEW YORK (City) Metropolitan Museum of Art. Mss.

Priest, Alan. An Illuminated Buddhist Scroll in the Metropolitan Museum of Art. 122-128, GREE

NEW YORK (City) - Printers
see Printers - New York (City)

NEW YORK (City) - Printing
see Printing - New York (City)

NEW YORK (City) Public Library

Bloch, Joshua. The Classification of Jewish Literature in the New York Public Library. L-LXXVII, FREI
Lydenberg, Harry Miller. Two Bookmen. 1-9, BLOC
Mulholland, John. Magic in the Library. 446-453, LYDE

NEW YORK (City) Public Library. Children's Room

Masten, Helen Adams. The Central Children's Room. 551-560, MOOR

NEW YORK (City) Public Library. Mss.

Yarmolinsky, Avraham. A Seventeenth-Century Russian Manuscript in the New York Public Library. 323-334, LYDE

NEW YORK (City) Public Library. Office of Work with Children

Strang, Mary. Good Labour of Old Days. 537-550, MOOR

NEW YORK (City) Public Library. Reference Dept.

Wright, Wyllis E. Subject Headings in the Reference Department of the New York Public Library. 431-436, LYDE

NEW YORK (City) State Psychiatric Institute. Library

Hafftka, Alexander. Życie i Twórczość Dr. Jakóba Szackiego. 13-23, SZAC

NEW YORK (City) State Psychiatric Institute. Library - Hist.

Berlstein, Alfred. Bibliotekarz i Pracownik Naukowy. 41-46, SZAC

NEW YORK (City) United Nations Library see United Nations. Library

NEW YORK (State) - Printing see Printing - New York (State)

NEWBERRY LIBRARY, Chicago

Billington, Ray Allen. Stanley Pargellis: Newberry Librarian, 1942-1962. 3-18, PARG

NEWBERRY LIBRARY, Chicago - Hist.

Hanson, J. C. M. Organization and Reorganization of Libraries. 519-532, WILS

NEWBERRY LIBRARY, Chicago. Mss. (F.87.1)

Baron, Hans. A Forgotten Chronicle of Early Fifteenth-Century Venice. 19-36, PARG

NEWBERRY, WALTER LOOMIS

Utley, George B. An Early "Friend" of Libraries. 725-730, WILS

NEWSPAPER LIBRARIES AND COLLECTIONS

Iben, Icko. Die Zeitung im Archiv- und Bibliothekswesen. 47-50, STUM

NEWSPAPER LIBRARIES AND COLLECTIONS - Aarhus, Denmark

Grundtvig, Vilh. Statens Avissamling i Aarhus. 166-174, AARU

NEWSPAPER LIBRARIES AND COLLECTIONS - Bern

Lüthi, Karl Jakob. Die Zeitungen. 56-59, BERU

NEWSPAPER LIBRARIES AND COLLECTIONS - Germany

Münster, Hans A. Zeitungswissenschaft und Deutsche Bibliotheken. Aufgaben der Zeitungswissenschaft und der Bibliothekswissenschaft zur 500-Jahrfeier 1940. II, 40-42, GLAU

Schöne, Walter. Zeitungswissenschaft und Deutsche Bibliotheken. Inkunabeln der Periodischen Presse. II, 36-39, GLAU

NEWSPAPERS - Bibl.

Jaeger, Friedrich. Die Zeitschriftenverzeichnisse der Deutschen Bibliothek. 117-135, EPPE

NEWSPAPERS - Collections see Newspaper libraries and collections

NEWSPAPERS - Germany - Hist. - 16th-17th cent.

Münster, Hans A. Zeitungswissenschaft und Deutsche Bibliotheken. Aufgaben der Zeitungswissenschaft und der Bibliothekswissenschaft zur 500-Jahrfeier 1940. II, 40-42, GLAU

Schöne, Walter. Zeitungswissenschaft und Deutsche Bibliotheken. Inkunabeln der Periodischen Presse. II, 36-39, GLAU

NEWSPAPERS ON WALLPAPER

Brigham, Clarence Saunders. Wall-Paper Newspapers of the Civil War. Checklist of Issues. 203-209, EAME

NEWSPAPERS - Printing

Rodenberg, Julius. Über Zeitungs- und Zeitschriftentypographie. 373-380, LEYG

NEWSPAPERS - U.S. - Bibl.

Brigham, Clarence Saunders. Wall-Paper Newspapers of the Civil War. Checklist of Issues. 203-209, EAME

Nichols, Charles.
The Literary Fair in the United States. 85-92, EAME

Nickel, Wilhelm.
Die Vermehrung der Druckschriftenabteilung. 10-14, HARN

Nicolai, Karl.
Danksagung. 69-70, JENA

Nicole, Jules.
Le Poète Tragique Carcinus et Ses Fils dans la Parabase de la Paix d'Aristophane. 163-167, GRAU

Nidecker, Heinrich.
Wilhelm Wackernagel. Bücher und Freunde. Ein Streifzug durch Seine Bibliothek. 177-191, SCHU

NIEBUHR, BARTHOLD GEORG. Römische Geschichte

Küntzel, Georg. Niebuhrs Römische Geschichte und Ihr Zeitgenössischer Politischer Gehalt. 175-190, EBRA

NIEDERMÜNSTER (abbey) Ratisbon see Ratisbon. Niedermünster (abbey)

NIEDERSÄCHSISCHER ZENTRALKATALOG, Göttingen see Göttingen. Niedersächsischer Zentralkatalog

Nielsen, L.
Et Sjaeldent Danicum. 225-229, COLL

Nielsen, Yngvar.
Professor Ludvig Daae: Mindetale. 63-71, (pt. 2), OSLU

NIENBORG, JOHANNES
Beschorner, Hans. Johannes Nienborg. 67-77, BOLL

NIENBURG a.S. (Benedictine abbey) Biblioteca - Catalog
Schmidt, Franz Paul. Der Katalog der Klosterbibliothek Nienburg a.S. 31-79, ALTE

NIENBURG a.S. (Benedictine abbey) - Catalogs
see Catalogs - Nienburg a.S. (Benedictine abbey)

NIENBURG a.S. (Benedictine abbey) - Manuscripts, Latin - Collections
see Manuscripts, Latin - Collections - Nienburg a.S. (Benedictine abbey)

NIESERT, JOSEPH - Library
Husung, Max Joseph. Joseph Niesert. Aus dem Leben eines Gelehrten Westfälischen Büchersammlers. 119-124, BÖME

Nieuwenkamp, J. L. M. Kits.
Op Nieuwe Leest. 492-495, BRUM

NIEUWLICHT (Carthusian monastery) Bloemendaal, Netherlands
see Bloemendaal, Netherlands. Nova Lux (Carthusian monastery)

NIGRAVALLE, JOHANNES DE, fictitious librarian of the Vatican
Twemlow, J. A. John de Nigravalle a Fictitious Librarian of the Vatican. 219-226, EHRE

NIHON-BUNGAKU-DAIJITEN (Fujimura Saku)
Meier, Franz Joseph, trans. Der Artikel Tosho "Buch" im Nihon-Bungaku-Daijiten. [Trans. of Japanese Article by Shinkichi Hashimoto and Yasushi Uematsu.] 205-216, LEYH

Nikolaev, N. N.
"Bŭlgarski Knigopis" na K. Irechek. (Po Sluchaĭ Sto Godini ot Rozhdenieto na Irechek.) 98-112, TEOB

NIKOLSBURG, MORAVIA
see Mikulov, Moravia

Nikula, Oscar, jt. ed.
GARD

NIÑO, PEDRO, Conde de Buelna
see Buelna, Pedro Niño, Conde de

Nishida, Tatsuo.
Tenri Toshokan Zō Seikabun Muryojushu Yokyo ni tsuite. (The Hsi-hsia Version of Wu-liang-shou-tsung yao-ching in the Tenri Central Library.) 357-366, TOMI

Nishimura, Suteya.
Shina Chihoshi Mokuroku Groshu to Hōshi Henmoku no Jūyosei. (On the Importance of Catalogues of the Books on Local History of China, with Special Reference to Five of Them Recently Published.) 46-53, OTAT

Nissen, Claus.
Die Kataloge der Stadtbibliothek. Geschichte und Überblick. 39-46, MAIN
Naturhistorische Bilderbücher des 16. Jahrhunderts. 281-290, BENZ
Stiftungen und Nachlässe in der Stadtbibliothek. 35-38, MAIN

Nissen, Kristian.
Den Werlauffske Gave. En Innholdsrik Kartbunke i Universitetsbibliotekets Kartsamling. 150-167, OSLN

Nivanka, Eino, jt. ed.
NYBE

Nivanka, Eino.
Amsterdamilainen Fr. Mullerin Antikvariaatti Nordenskiöldin Kirjakokoelman Päähankkijana. 122-133, DAHL
Seinen Rantojen Kirjakauppiaat. 78-88, NYBE

Nixon, Howard M.
Roger Bartlett's Bookbindings. 56-65, OLDH

Noailles, Duc de.
Lecteur aux Estampes. 83, CAIN

Nobel, Johannes.
Die Śārada-Handschrift des Rāmāyaṇa. 186-190, HARN

NOBLE, THEOPHILUS CHARLES - Library
Hollaender, Albert E. J. Ein Unveröffentlichter Augenzeugenbericht über Napoleon I. an Bord des "Bellerophon" im Kriegshafen von Plymouth, Juli-August 1815. 44-45, STUM

NODIER, CHARLES. Mss. La Fée aux Miettes
Richer, Jean. Le Manuscrit et les Premières Éditions de "La Fée aux Miettes" de Charles Nodier. 365-371, BONN

Noé, A. C.
The University Library and Research. 300-305, HANS

Noël, L.
Hommage à Monseigneur Pelzer. 1-6, PELZ

NÖRDLINGEN, Ger. - Bookbinding
see Bookbinding - Nördlingen, Ger.

Nörrenberg, Constantin.
Kieler Bruchstücke aus Heinrichs von dem Türlin Crone. 405-418, WILM

Nogami, Mamoru.
Toshokan Kino no Bunseki to Ruien Kikan. Kokyo Toshokan no Refarensu Waku no Tachiba Kara. (On the Function of the Library from the Standpoint of Reference Work.) 21-36, KYOT

Nogara, B.
Di Alcune Vite e Commenti Medioevali di Ovidio. 413-431, CERI

Noguer I Mosqueras, Tomàs.
Un Text Litúrgic en Català. II, 451-462, RUBI

Nohrström, Holger, jt. ed.
SCHA

Nohrström, Holger.
Några Anteckningar Kring den s. k. Pälkäne-Abcboken. 341-354, HIRN
Några Krigsbytesböcker från Åbo Akademibiblioteks Grundläggningstid i Helsingfors Universitetsbibliotek. 69-81, HULT
En Variant av Petrus Bångs Chronologia Sacra. 82-87, HULT

Nolan, Margaret C., jt. author
Hirsch, Rudolf and Margaret C. Nolan. The Peaceful Revolution. 25-34, DAVI

Nolhac, Pierre de.
Une Lettre Inédite de Mabillon à Ciampini. 13, CHAT
Lettres Inédites de Muret. 381-403, GRAU
Vers Inédits de Pétrarque. 481-486, HAVE

NONIUS MARCELLUS. Ms.
Chatelain, E. Notes Tironiennes d'un Manuscrit de Genève. 81-86, HAVE

NONIUS MARCELLUS. Mss.
Havet, Louis. Les Fautes Issues de Corrections dans les Manuscrits de Nonius. 803-814, GRAU

NON-PROFESSIONAL ASSISTANTS
Luther, Wilhelm Martin. Die Accessisten der Göttinger Universitätsbibliothek. 527-536, BRUM

NON-PROFESSIONAL ASSISTANTS - Training
see In-service training

NON-RESIDENT BORROWERS
see Registration of borrowers

NORDENSKIÖLD, NILS ADOLF ERIK, Friherre - Library
Mickwitz, Ann-Mari. Kejsaren och den Gamla Kartan. 59-65, NYBE
Nivanka, Eino. Amsterdamilainen Fr. Mullerin Antikvariaatti Nordenskiöldin Kirjakokoelman Päähankkijana. 122-133, DAHL

NORDIN, CARL GUSTAF, Bp. - Library
Ågren, Sven. Om Nordinska Handskriftssamlingen i Uppsala Universitetsbibliotek. Några Anteckningar. 468-497, UPPS

NORDISK VIDENSKABELIGT BIBLIOTEKARFORBUND
Tveterås, Harald L. A Federation for Library Co-operation across the Frontiers: Nordisk Vitenskapelig Bibliotekarforbund. 601-602, BRUM

NORDISKA VETENSKAPLIGA BIBLIOTEKARIEFÖRBUNDET
see Nordisk Videnskabeligt Bibliotekarforbund

Nordling, Arnold.
Helsingfors Universitetsbiblioteks Fragment av Flores och Blanzeflor. 129-142, HULT

Noreen, Ärland.
Plan till Nybyggnad för Göteborgs Stadsbibliotek. Ritningar med Beskrivning. 1-23, (second paper), GÖTE

NORRKÖPING, Sweden. Stadsbiblioteket
Lundgren, Hjalmar. Carl Bernhard Wadströms Bibliotek. 95-106, GRAP

NORSK BIBLIOTEKFORENING
NORN
NORS
Fiskaa, H. M. Norsk Bibliotekforenings Virke. Resultater og Oppgaver. 58-73, NORS
Klemp, Helene L. Norsk Bibliotekforenings Jubileumsskrift. 9-15, NORS

NORSK BIBLIOTEKFORENING - Hist.
Ansteinsson, John. Norsk Bibliotekforening Gjennem 25 År. 5-25, NORN
Kildal, Arne. Da Norsk Bibliotekforening Ble Til. 43-57, NORS

NORSKE VIDENSKABERS SELSKAB, Trondheim. Bibliotek

Landmark, Joh. D. Bibliotekarer og Assistenter ved Det Kgl. Norske Videnskabers Selskabs Bibliotek i Trondhjem 1766-1858. 131-149, OSLN

NORSKE VIDENSKABERS SELSKAB, Trondheim. Bibliotek - Hist.

Landmark, Joh. D. Videnskabers Selskabs Bibliotek i Trondheim og Dets Bygningshistorie 1855-1867. 148-159, MUNT

NORTON, CHARLES BENJAMIN

Krummel, Donald W. The Library World of Norton's Literary Gazette. 237-266, GJEL

NORTON'S LITERARY GAZETTE

Krummel, Donald W. The Library World of Norton's Literary Gazette. 237-266, GJEL

NORWAY - Adult education - Library participation
see Adult education - Library participation - Norway

NORWAY - Associations
see Associations - Norway

NORWAY - Bibliography, National
see Bibliography, National - Norway

NORWAY. Biblioteksentralen

Berntsen, Bernhard. Biblioteksentralen—en Tjener i Bibliotekenes Opplysningsarbeid. 98-103, NORS

NORWAY - Book collecting
see Book collecting - Norway

NORWAY - Bookbinding
see Bookbinding - Norway

NORWAY - Bookmobile services - Public libraries
see Bookmobile services - Public libraries - Norway

NORWAY - Booksellers and libraries
see Booksellers and libraries - Norway

NORWAY - Censorship
see Censorship - Norway

NORWAY - Children's library services
see Children's library services - Norway

NORWAY - College and university libraries
see College and university libraries - Norway

NORWAY - Cooperative library systems
see Cooperative library systems - Norway

NORWAY - Information services
see Information services - Norway

NORWAY - Legal deposit (of books, etc.)
see Legal deposit (of books, etc.) - Norway

NORWAY - Librarianship
see Librarianship - Norway

NORWAY - Libraries
see Libraries - Norway

NORWAY - Manuscripts - Collections
see Manuscripts - Collections - Norway

NORWAY - Personnel - Qualifications and selection
see Personnel - Qualifications and selection - Norway

NORWAY - Printing
see Printing - Norway

NORWAY - Private libraries
see Private libraries - Norway

NORWAY - Professional libraries
see Professional libraries - Norway

NORWAY - Public libraries
see Public libraries - Norway

NORWAY - Public libraries - Aims and objectives
see Public libraries - Aims and objectives - Norway

NORWAY - Public libraries - Centralization
see Public libraries - Centralization - Norway

NORWAY - Public libraries (small)
see Public libraries (small) - Norway

NORWAY - Publishers and libraries
see Publishers and libraries - Norway

NORWAY - Reading - Special groups of readers - Journalists
see Reading - Special groups of readers - Journalists - Norway

NORWAY - Research libraries
see Research libraries - Norway

NORWAY - Research libraries - Aims and objectives
see Research libraries - Aims and objectives - Norway

NORWAY - Rural libraries
see Rural libraries - Norway

NORWAY - School and public library relationship
see School and public library relationship - Norway

NORWAY - School libraries
see School libraries - Norway

NORWAY - School libraries (Rural school)
see School libraries (Rural school) - Norway

NORWAY - Special libraries
see Special libraries - Norway

NORWAY - Technical libraries
see Technical libraries - Norway

NORWAY - War and the library
see War and the library - Norway

NORWAY - Writing
see Writing - Norway

NORWEGIAN AUTHORS
see Authors, Norwegian

NORWEGIAN LITERATURE - Collections - Oslo

Munthe, Wilhelm. Norske Avdelings Forhistorie. 1-44, OSLO

NORWEGIAN SHIP LIBRARIES
see Ship libraries, Norwegian

Nosovský, Karel.
Snahy Spolku Československých Knihkupeckých Učetních o Zřízení Bibliografické Kanceláře. 185-192, ŽIVN

NOTA BIOGRAFICZNA. 11-12, PIEK

NOTAS BIBLIOGRÁFICAS. 325-335, MENE

Nougaret, F.
Juvénal, Omission du Fragment Windstedt. 255-267, CHAT

NOVA LUX (Carthusian monastery) Bloemendaal, Netherlands
see Bloemendaal, Netherlands. Nova Lux (Carthusian monastery)

Novati, Francesco.
Dagoberto I Re d'Austrasia e la Val Bregaglia, per la Storia d'una Falsificazionne. 598-613, CHAT

Nowak, Leopold.
Ein Bach-Fund. 95-98, FEDO
Ein Druck mit Melodien für Theophilanthropen. 61, STUM
Die Musikhandschriften aus Fuggerschem Besitz in der Österreichischen Nationalbibliothek. 505-515, BICK
Die Musiksammlung. 119-138, BICK

Nowakowska, Izabela.
Czasopisma Rzadkie i Cenne. 89-96, BYDG

NOYON, France. Notre-Dame (Cathedral) Chapitre. Bibliothèque

Croix, Jean Tremblot de la. Marques de la Bibliothèque Capitulaire de Noyon. 237-242, CALO

Nuiver, J. A.
Centrale Boekbespreking voor de Openbare Bibliotheken. 552-558, BRUM

NUREMBERG - Bookbinding
see Bookbinding - Nuremberg

NUREMBERG - Bookbinding - Fine bindings - Collections
see Bookbinding - Fine bindings - Collections - Nuremberg

NUREMBERG - Catalogs
see Catalogs - Nuremberg

NUREMBERG - Censorship
see Censorship - Nuremberg

NUREMBERG. Germanisches Nationalmuseum

Kistner, Erwin. Studien an Teigdrucken aus dem Besitz des Germanischen Nationalmuseums in Nürnberg. 65-97, STOL

NUREMBERG. Germanisches Nationalmuseum. Mss. (3155 b)

Waetzoldt, Stephan. Ein Silbereinband von Jörg Seld. 53-57, REDE

NUREMBERG. Katharinenkloster

Fischer, Karl. Margarete Karteuserin, eine Nürnberger Klosterschreiberin des 15. Jahrhunderts. 24-31, VERZ

NUREMBERG - Printing
see Printing - Nuremberg

NUREMBERG. Rat

Jegel, August. Altnürnberger Zensur, vor Allem des 16. Jahrhunderts. 55-64, STOL

NUREMBERG. Ste. Catharine (Monastery)
see Nuremberg. Katharinenkloster

NUREMBERG. Stadtbibliothek

Haebler, Konrad. Zwei Nürnberger Tonformen. 103-110, COLL

NUREMBERG. Stadtbibliothek - Hist.

Bock, Friedrich. Aus der Geschichte der Nürnberger Stadtbibliothek. 9-15, VERZ

NURSING SCHOOL LIBRARIES
Lage, Louise C., Lois B. Miller, and Donald Washburn. Dental, Nursing, and Pharmaceutical Libraries, 1947-1957. 371-377, DOEJ

NYBERG, HENRIK - Library
Grönroos, Henrik. Om Böcker och Bokägare i Finland för 200 År Sedan. 1-15, NYBE

Nyberg, Paul, jt. ed.
SCHA

Nyberg, Paul.
Dedikationerna i Zachris Topelii Bibliotek. 145-163, HULA
Finlands Kuster i 1600-Talets Kartografi. 88-107, HULT
En Kartografisk Kuriositet. 115-121, HULT
En Missuppfattad Rågångsurkund från 1500-Talet i Nordenskiöldska Samlingen. 92-104, SCHA
Några Anmärkningsvärda Böcker i Z. Topelius' Boksamling. 101-117, TUDE

NYBERG, PAUL
NYBE

NYBERG, PAUL - Bibl.
Lohikoski, Inga and Dolly Ölander. Förteckning över Paul Nybergs Tryckta Skrifter 1910-1958. 133-146, NYBE

Nygård-Nilssen, Arne.
J. B. Halvorsen. 33-56, OSLN

Nyhuus, Haakon.
De Norske Statsunderstøttede Folkebogsamlinger. 36-42, NORS
Overbibliothekar A. C. Drolsum. 79, (pt. 2), OSLU

NYHUUS, HAAKON
Arnesen, Arne. How Norway Became the Focus of American Library Methods in Europe. 148-155, HANS

Nyman, Gunborg.
Bibliotek på Hjul. Sommarsamhällets Bokförsörjning. 215-223, HEIN

NYT DANSK LITTERATURSELSKAB
Hansen, Robert L. Nyt Danske Litteraturselskab. 95-103, THOM

Oberdorffer, Kurt.
Von einem Cancionale und dem Stadtschreiber Andreas von Ochsenstein. 65-67, WEHM

Oberziner, Ludovico.
La Libreria di un Patrizio Trentino del Secolo XVI. I, 371-412, HORT

OBSOLESCENCE OF BOOKS
Deckert, Helmut. Wider die Legende von den Bücherfriedhöfen. 36-40, BOLE
Maltha, D. J. Speelse Gedachten. 537-543, BRUM
Vanselow, Otto. Veraltete Literatur. 339-348, KÖNI

Očadlík, Mirko.
Diskotéka. 124-128, EMLE

OCCASIONAL WRITINGS - Collections
Biber, Arthur. Gelegenheitsschriften, Familienkunde und Bibliotheken. 1-9, MILF

OCENA PRACY BIBLIOTEK PEDAGOGICZNYCH PRZEZ INSTYTUCJE OŚWIATOWE I ZNP. 110-113, KRAK

OCHSENBACH, NICOLAUS - Library
Frey, Theophil. Nicolaus Ochsenbach, der Kunstliebende und -Sammelnde Schloßhauptmann auf Hohen-Tübingen (1562-1626). 407-427, LEYG

Oda, Takeo.
Tenri Toshokan Zō Vopell ni Chikyugi ni tsuite. (Vopell's Terrestrial Globe, Printed with Wood-Blocks, Dated 1536.) 449-462, TOMI

Odelstierna, Ingrid.
ΨΥΧΗΣ ΙΑΤΡΕΙΟΝ. 376-407, GRAP

ODENCRANTS, GUSTAF - Library
Gobom, Nils. Gustaf Odencrants' E. T. A. Hoffmann-Samling i Linköpings Stifts- och Landsbibliotek. 262-279, GRAP

Odier, J. Bignami.
Le Fonds de la Reine à la Bibliothèque Vaticane. I, 159-189, ALBB

Oehler, Richard.
Milkau als Kommissar für die Belgischen Bibliotheken und als Bibliotheksdirektor in Breslau. 30-35, MILK

Oehme, Ruthardt.
Der Ämteratlas des Herzogtums Württemberg 1575 (WLB Cod. Hist. Q 102). 204-215, HOFF
Die Palästinakarte aus Bernhard von Breidenbachs Reise in das Heilige Land 1486. 70-83, LEYH

Ölander, Dolly, jt. ed.
NYBE

Ölander, Dolly, jt. author
Lohikoski, Inga and Dolly Ölander.

Förteckning över Paul Nybergs Tryckta Skrifter 1910-1958. 133-146, NYBE

ÖREBRO, Sweden - Inventories of estates
see Inventories of estates - Örebro, Sweden

ÖREBRO, Sweden - Public libraries
see Public libraries - Örebro, Sweden

ÖREBRO, Sweden. Stadsbibliotek

ÖREB

Waldén, Bertil. Verner von Heidenstam Som Målare. 71-106, ÖREB

ÖREBRO, Sweden. Stadsbibliotek - Hist.

Wieslander, Henning. Hundra Års Bibliotekskrönika från Örebro. 7-48, ÖREB

ÖSTERREICHISCHE NATIONALBIBLIOTHEK, Vienna
see Vienna. Nationalbibliothek

Östling, Gösta.
Stimulera Individens Strävan. Om Bibliotekens Uppgift i Samhället. 257-269, HEIN

Oettingen, Wolfgang von.
Über Goethes Kunstsammlungen. 72-78, WAHL

OFFICIAL PUBLICATIONS
see Government publications

OFFOR, RICHARD

OFFO

Woledge, G. Richard Offor. 63-65, OFFO

OFFOR, RICHARD - Bibl.

Scott, J. W. Richard Offor: A Bibliography of His Printed Works. 66-68, OFFO

Ogata, Yoshihiko.
Dokushozai Sentaku no Ketteiin—Sono Kigōronteki Apurōchi. (The Definite Factor in the Selection of Reading Matter—an Approach from the Theory of Language as a Symbol.) 76-101, TOKY

ŌHASHI LIBRARY, Tokyo
see Tokyo. Ōhashi Library

OHASHI, SHINTARO

OHAS

Tsuboya, Zenshirō. Jushi. (Words of Congratulation.) [prelim.], OHAS

Ohly, Kurt, jt. ed.
JUCH

Ohly, Kurt.
Das Inkunabelverzeichnis Bernhards von Mallinckrodt. (Handschrift des Staatsarchivs Münster I 261). 37-62, BÖME

Okuda, Katsumasa.
Toshokan no Seisai Kitei no Iroiro. (On the Various Rules of Punishment in Libraries.) 63-74, TSUB
Toshokan Tōkei Omoumama. (Occasional Thoughts on Library Statistics.) 79-89, (part 1), OHAS

Oldenbourg, M. Consuelo.
Die Holzschnitte des Vrs Graf zur Passion und die des Johann Wechtlin zum Leben Jesu. Ein Bibliographisches Verzeichnis Ihrer Verwendungen. 291-310, BENZ

OLDHAM, JAMES BASIL

OLDH

Oliger, Livario.
Intorno alla Bibliografia Francescana. 167-184, ACCU

OLIVETANI
see Monte Oliveto (Benedictine abbey)

Olivieri-Sangiacomo, Laura.
La Nuova Sistemazione della Biblioteca di Archeologia e Storia dell'Arte (Problemi di una Moderna Biblioteca Specializzata). 333-346, GREG

Olle, James G.
The Professional Writings of J. P. Lamb, A Check List. 27-30, LAMB

Olsen, Lars M.
Billigbogens Betydning og Udbredelse. 55-63, THOM

OLSSON, BROR

OLSS

Olszewicz, Bolesław.
Wzmianki o Mapach Bernarda Wapowskiego w Listach z r. 1529. 371-376, PIEK

Omang, Reidar.
Overgangen fra Gotisk til Latinsk Skrift. 239-254, OSLO
Samarbeide Mellem Håndskriftsamlinger. 418-422, MUNT

Omont, Henry.
Deux Incunables Imprimés à Tours le 7 Mai 1496. 153-160, COLL
Inventaire Sommaire des Manuscrits Grecs des Bibliothèques Mazarine, de L'Arsenal et Sainte-Geneviève, à Paris. 305-320, GRAU

Ono, Noriaki.
Edo-ki ni okeru Kokugakusha no Tosho-kan Undo. (Library Activities of Japanese Scholars in the Edo Period.) 53-94, KYOT

OPEN SHELVES
see Access to shelves

OPORINUS, JOANNES
Husner, Fritz. Die Editio Princeps des "Corpus Historiae Byzantinae." Johannes Oporin, Hieronymus Wolf und die Fugger. 143-162, SCHU

Oppermann, O.
De Verzameling Photo's van het Instituut voor Middeleeuwsche Geschiedenis. 242-243, EVER

ORANGE-NASSAU, House of - Library
Alphen, G. van. Anthony Smets, Bibliothecaris van Drie Prinsen van Oranje (1636-1689). 119-160, HAGU
Verwey, Eleonore de la Fontaine. Boekbanden uit de Oranje Nassau-Bibliotheek. 161-179, HAGU

ORAZIO
see Horatius Flaccus, Quintus

ORDER PROCESSES
see Acquisitions - Order processes

ORDER WORK
see Acquisitions

OREL, ALFRED
OREL
Alfred Orel—Siebzig Jahre. 5-7, OREL

OREL, ALFRED - Bibl.
Bibliographie der Wissenschaftlichen Veröffentlichungen von Alfred Orel. 9-19, OREL

ORIA, BONIFAZIO, GIOVANNI BERNARDINO, Marchese von
see Bonifazio, Giovanni Bernardino, Marchese von Oria

ORIENT - Books
see Books - Orient

ORIENT, Islamic
see Mohammedan countries

ORIENTAL LANGUAGES - Transliteration
Hülle, Hermann. Über Alphabetische Anordnung Chinesischer und Japanischer Titelaufnahmen. 254-260, KUHN

ORIENTAL LITERATURE - Cataloging
Hülle, Hermann. Über Alphabetische Anordnung Chinesischer und Japanischer Titelaufnahmen. 254-260, KUHN
Suzuka, Osamu. Kinyū ni okeru Hompō Kosho no Toriatsukai ni tsuite. (A Guide for Cataloging Old Japanese Books.) 115-130, KYOT

ORIENTAL LITERATURE - Collections - Berlin
Auster, Guido. Die Orientalische Abteilung. I, 275-317, BERS
Hülle, Hermann. Die Fortschritte der Ostasiatischen Sammlungen. 190-211, HARN
Weil, Gotthold. Die Orientalische Abteilung. 180-186, HARN

ORIENTAL LITERATURE - Collections - Helsinki
Mustonen, Aarne. Kaukoidän Kirjatietoa. 164-181, DAHL

ORIENTAL LITERATURE - Collections - Poland - 18th cent.
Reychman, Jan. Zbiory Orientaliów w Polsce XVIII w. 283-294, PIEK

ORIENTAL LITERATURE - Collections - Sofia
Nedkov, Boris. Orientalistikata v Sofiiskata Narodna Biblioteka. 226-239, MIKN

ORIENTAL LITERATURE - Translations into German - Collections - Leipzig
Schreiber, Heinrich. Von der Goldschnittlyrik zum Schmetterlingsbuch. Orientalische Literatur in Deutscher Ausstattung. 82-92, SCHR

ORIENTAL MANUSCRIPTS
see Manuscripts, Oriental

ORTHODOX EASTERN CHURCH, Russian - Liturgy and ritual - Collections - Vatican
Zelenka, Ignác. Edizioni Liturgiche della Pečerskaja Lavra di Kiev nella Biblioteca Vaticana. II, 377-414, ALBB

ORVAL, Belgium (Abbey). Mss.
Degering, Hermann. Handschriften aus Echternach und Orval in Paris. 48-85, MILF

OSBORN, T. E.
Osborn, T. E. Retrospect. 6-7, LAMB

OSLER LIBRARY
see McGill University, Montreal. Osler Library

OSLER, SIR WILLIAM, Bart. - Library
FRAN

OSLO - Auction sales
see Auction sales - Oslo

OSLO - Bookbinding
see Bookbinding - Oslo

OSLO - College and university libraries
see College and university libraries - Oslo

OSLO - Depository libraries
see Depository libraries - Oslo

OSLO - Folk-songs, Norwegian - Collections
see Folk-songs, Norwegian - Collections - Oslo

OSLO. K. Fredericks Universitet
see Oslo. Universitet. Bibliotek

OSLO - Maps - Collections
see Maps - Collections - Oslo

OSLO - Norwegian literature - Collections
see Norwegian literature - Collections - Oslo

OSLO - Personnel
see Personnel - Oslo

OSLO. Universitet. Bibliotek

OSLN

OSLO

OSLU

Bakken, Hallvard Sand. P. Chr. Asbjørnsen og Universitetsbiblioteket. 299-324, MUNT

Collijn, Isak Gustaf Alfred. Några Ord om Böcker Tryckta på Svenska i Utlandet under 1500-Talet. Med Anledning av ett till Universitetsbiblioteket i Oslo Gjort Nyförvärv. 23-29, MUNT

Kleve, Knut. Forskerens Ønskebibliotek. 138-140, NORS

Kragemo, Helge Bergh. Zur Frage der Rationalisierung des Tauschverkehrs einer Wissenschaftlichen Bibliothek. 377-381, MUNT

Nissen, Kristian. Den Werlauffske Gave. En Innholdsrik Kartbunke i Universitetsbibliotekets Kartsamling. 150-167, OSLN

Vartdal, Hroar. Über Kartenkatalogisierung. Die Kartensammlung der Universitätsbibliothek zu Oslo. 481-492, MUNT

OSLO. Universitet. Bibliotek - Hist.

OSLU

Kleppa, Peter. Universitetsbibliotekets Bokbindere og Innbinding. 255-257, OSLO

Tellefsen, Th. Fra det Gamle Bibliotek. 423-448, MUNT

OSLO. Universitet. Bibliotek. Norske Avdeling

OSLN

Haukaas, Kaare. Norsk Litterært Registreringsarbeid. 25-68, HALV

OSLO. Universitet. Bibliotek. Norske Avdeling - Hist.

Munthe, Wilhelm. Norske Avdelings Forhistorie. 1-44, OSLO

Osthoff, Helmuth, jt. ed.
WOLJ

OSTI, HEINRICH FERDINAND FRIEDRICH - Collections - Uppsala

Taube, Gurli. Fotografen Osti och den Ostiska Plåtsamlingen på Carolina Rediviva. 280-292, GRAP

ŌTA, TAMESABURŌ

OTAT

OTFRIED VON WEISSENBURG. Mss. Evangelienbuch

Butzmann, Hans. Vom Schmuck der Heidelberger Otfrid-Handschrift. 35-44, WEHM

OTGOVOR NA PRIVETSTVIIA OT AKADEMIK ALEKSANDŬR TEODOROV-BALAN. 49-52, TEOD

Ott, Alfons.
Musikalisches Portrait. 28-30, HELD

OTT, ARNOLD. Mss. - Collections - Bern

Meyer, Wilhelm Joseph. Direktor Godet Erwirbt den Nachlass des Dichters Arnold Ott. 19-22, GODM

Ottervik, Gösta.
Kompetenskrav och Utbildning vid de Svenska Universitetsbiblioteken. 225-236, HEIN

Otto, Hanna.
Berliner Bibliothekarschule seit 1949. 173-181, SCHS

Otto, Paul.
Ikonographie der Königlichen Bibliothek zu Berlin. 43-50, WILM

Ouchida, Sadao.
Tenri Toshokan Zō Moku-Katsuji Ban Shomoku Kō. (Check List of Japanese Printed Books in Movable Types of the Late Edo Period in the Tenri Central Library.) 295-305, TOMI

Oudendijk, Johanna K.
De Universiteitsbibliotheek te Utrecht als Koninglijk Paleis en als Voorwerp van Koninklijke Belangstelling. 244-249, EVER

OURSEL, CHARLES
OURS
Calmette, Joseph. Souvenirs de Bourgogne. 55-65, OURS
Laurent, Jacques. Charles Oursel, Esquisse Biographique. 9-36, OURS
Louis-Lucas, Pierre. Voisinage. 147-151, OURS

OURSEL, CHARLES - Bibl.
Liste des Travaux Publiés par M. Ch. Oursel. 37-47, OURS

OUT-OF-PRINT BOOKS
see Reprints

Ouy, Gilbert.
Une Maquette de Manuscrit à Peintures. 43-51, CALO

OVIDIUS NASO, PUBLIUS. Mss.
Nogara, B. Di Alcune Vite e Commenti Medioevali di Ovidio. 413-431, CERI

OWNERSHIP MARKS - Books
see Books - Owners' marks

OXFORD - Libraries
see Libraries - Oxford

OXFORD - Manuscripts, Hebrew - Collections
see Manuscripts, Hebrew - Collections - Oxford

OXFORD. University. Bodleian Library - Hist.
Craster, Herbert Henry Edmund. A Note on the Early History of Libraries in Oxford. 169-171, LEYG

OXFORD. University. Bodleian Library. Mss. (Cat. Neubauer 120 and 380)
Abrahams, I. The Bodleian MSS. Entitled "The Fear of Sin." 72-75, STEI

OXFORD. University. Bodleian Library. Mss. (Cod. Bodl. 29)
Ranke, Friedrich. Eine Neue Handschrift des Gereimten Passionals. 301-316, KÖNI

OXFORD. University. Bodleian Library. Mss. (D'Orville 144)
Porcher, Jean. Un Amateur de Peinture sous Charles VI: Jean Lebègue. 35-41, CALO

OXFORD. University. Bodleian Library. Mss. (Hebr. d. 16)
Neubauer, A. Zakkuth's Non-Jewish Chronicle According to Ms. Hebr. d. 16, Recently Acquired by the Bodleian Library. 243-244, STEI

OXFORD. University. Bodleian Library. Mss. (Laud. Lat. 29)
Clark, Albert C. A Bodleian Fragment of Cicero Tusc. Quaest. 169-173, CHAT

OXFORD. University. Bodleian Library. Mss. (Misc. 127)
Mercati, Giovanni, Cardinal. I. Uno Scambio Strano di Qualche Interesse per Tre Grandi Biblioteche. II. Amici Innominati del Savile in Roma? 17-26, FERR

OXFORD. University. Bodleian Library. Mss. (Neubauer. Cat. Hebr. 908)
Horovitz, Jakob. Aus der Oxforder Handschrift des Josif Omez. 35-50, FREN

OXFORD. University. Bodleian Library. Mss. (Sam. Johnson)
Frewer, Louis B. Samuel Johnson and Oxford. 65-76, TVET

OXFORD. University. Bodleian Library. Mss. (Smith 8)
Macray, W. D., ed. A Letter from Isaac Abendana. 89-90, STEI

Paalzow, Hans.
Die Buchbinderei. 21-22, HARN
Einiges über die Italienischen Stadtrechte. 371-388, WILM
Die Kriegsbücherei. 285, HARN

PACCASSI, NICOLAS VON
Teichl, Robert. Die Rettung des Prunksaales der Wiener Hofbibliothek durch Nicolas v. Paccassi (1760-1769). 615-626, BICK

PACKAGE LIBRARIES - Switzerland
Wild, Helen. Hermann Escher und die Schweizerischen Volksbibliotheken. 22-34, ESCK

PADERBORN. Abdinghof (Monastery)
Bauermann, Johannes. Die Gründungsurkunde des Klosters Abdinghof in Paderborn. Ein Beitrag zur Frage der Abdinghofer Fälschungen. 16-36, BÖME

PADERBORN, JOHANN VON
see Johann von Paderborn

PADERBORN, KONRAD VON
see Konrad von Paderborn

PADUA - Printing
see Printing - Padua

PADUA - Publishers and publishing
see Publishers and publishing - Padua

Pächt, Otto.
Notes and Observations on the Origin of Humanistic Book-Decoration. 184-194, SAXL

Pafford, J. H. P.
Book Selection in the University Library. 422-426, JUCH

PAKISTAN - Acquisitions, Cooperative
see Acquisitions, Cooperative - Pakistan

PAKISTAN AND INDIA - Cooperation, International
see Cooperation, International - Pakistan and India

PALEIS VAN LODEWIJK NAPOLEON, Utrecht
see Utrecht. Paleis van Lodewijk Napoleon

Palencia, Angel González.
Don Pedro Niño y el Condado de Buelna. II, 105-146, ARTI

PALEOGRAPHY
see also Calligraphy; Writing - History

PALEOGRAPHY

CHAT

Löffler, Karl. Zur Geschichte der Abendländischen Schreibformen. Eine Würdigung des Gleichbetitelten Buches von Hermann Delitsch. 61-66, SCHR
Lowe, E. A. A Hand-List of Half-Uncial Manuscripts. 34-61, EHRD
Mentz, Arthur. Die Anfügung in den Tironischen Noten. 501-507, CHAT
Pietschmann, Richard. Paläographisches. 281-285, MILF
Robert, Ulysse. Note sur L'Origine de L'Ę Cédillé dans les Manuscrits. 633-637, HAVE
Schaible, Eduard. Abkürzung in Schrift und Sprache. 73-81, SCHR
Schreiber, Heinrich. Cavilla—ein Spätmittelalterliches Lesezeichen? II, 97-103, GLAU
Van den Gheyn, J., S. J. Rectifications Paléographiques. 163-168, CHAT

PALEOGRAPHY, Armenian

Merk, August, S. J. Armenische und Griechische Palaeographie. 1-21, EHRD

PALEOGRAPHY - Collections - Leipzig

Funke, Fritz. Originales Sammelgut im Deutschen Buch- und Schriftmuseum. 219-241, LEIZ

PALEOGRAPHY, Coptic

Petersen, Theodore. The Paragraph Mark in Coptic Illuminated Ornament. 295-330, GREE

PALEOGRAPHY, Greek

Allen, Th. W. Three Greek Scribes. 22-33, EHRD
Cagin, Paul. L'Observation Paléographique dans L'Étude du "Sacramentarium Triplex" de Saint-Gall. 92-112, CHAT
Gardthausen, V. Différences Provinciales de la Minuscule Grecque. 731-736, GRAU
Garitte, Gérard. Sur une Formule des Colophons de Manuscrits Grecs (ἡμὲν χεὶρ ἡ γράψασα). I, 359-390, ALBB
Holzinger, Charles. Sur la Date de Quelques Manuscrits d'Aristophane. 204-218, CHAT
Lambros, Spyridion P. Notes Épigraphiques et Paléographiques. 621-628, GRAU
Lowe, E. A. Greek Symptoms in a Sixth-Century Manuscript of St. Augustine and in a Group of Latin Legal Manuscripts. 277-289, ALBA
Maass, Ernest. Observationes Palaeographicae. 749-766, GRAU
Marouzeau, J. La Graphie ei = ï dans le Palimpseste de Plaute. 150-154, CHAT
Merk, August, S. J. Armenische und Griechische Palaeographie. 1-21, EHRD
Serruys, Daniel. Contribution à L'Étude des "Canons" de L'Onciale Grecque. 492-499, CHAT
Weil, Henri. D'un Signe Critique dans le Meilleur Manuscrit de Démosthène. 13-20, GRAU
Wendel, Carl. Aus der Vorgeschichte des Laurentianus XXXII.9. 16-22, KUHN
Wessely, Charles. Un Nouveau Fragment de la Version Grecque du Vieux Testament par Aquila. 224-229, CHAT
Zeretelli, G. Zwei Unedierte Griechische Schultafeln. 113-117, CHAT

PALEOGRAPHY, Italian (Beneventan)

Lowe, E. A. A New List of Beneventan Manuscripts. II, 211-244, ALBB

PALEOGRAPHY, Latin

Bannister, Henry Marriott. Signs in Kalendarial Tables. 141-149, CHAT
Bischoff, Bernhard. Eine Sammelhandschrift Walahfrid Strabos (Cod. Sangall. 878). 30-48, LEYH
Caspar, Erich. Paläographisches zum Kanon des Eusebius. 42-56, DEGE
Dold, Alban. Die Provenienz der Altlateinischen Römerbrieftexte in den Gotisch-Lateinischen Fragmenten des Codex Carolinus von Wolfenbüttel. 13-29, LEYH
Fischer, P. Bonifaz. Zur Textüberlieferung des Lucifer von Cagliari. 49-54, LEYH

Grenier, A. Quelques Fautes des Manuscrits et des Textes Latins Touchant les Mots Composés. 180-192, CHAT
Heckel, Rudolf von. Eine Kanzleianweisung über die Schriftmässige Ausstattung der Papsturkunden aus dem 13. Jahrhundert in Durantis Speculum Judiciale. 109-118, LEID
Katterbach, Bruno and Wilhelm Maria Peitz, S. J. Die Unterschriften der Päpste und Kardinäle in den Bullae Maiores vom 11. bis 14. Jhdt. 177-274, EHRD
Klotz, Alfred. $\frac{M}{2}$: Ein Palaeographisches Problem. 99-104, STOL
Lietzmann, Hans. Handschriftliches zur Rekonstruktion des Sacramentarium Gregorianum. 141-158, EHRB
Lindsay, W.-M. The Notae Iuris of Vat. Reg. 886. 155-162, CHAT
Lowe, E. A. A Hand-List of Half-Uncial Manuscripts. 34-61, EHRD
——— The Morgan Golden Gospels: The Date and Origin of the Manuscript. 266-279, GREE
Macé, Alcide. Le Basiliensis F III 15ª (VIIIᵉ Siècle). 383-395, CHAT
Mazzoleni, Iole. Note Paleografiche e Diplomatiche su Alcune Carte Ravellesi dei Sec. XII-XIV. 539-547, GALL
Muzzioli, Giovanni. Il Più Antico Codice della Biblioteca Casanatense. 323-332, GREG
Poupardin, René. Un Fragment en Écriture Onciale de Julianus Antecessor. 221-223, CHAT
Rand, Edward Kennard. A Carolingian Gospel-Book in the Pierpont Morgan Library in New York. 89-104, EHRD
Steffens, Franz. Über die Abkürzungsmethoden der Schreibschule von Bobbio. 244-254, CHAT
Turner, C. H. The Nomina Sacra in Early Latin Christian Mss. 62-74, EHRD
Weinburger, Wilhelm. Handschriften von Vivarium. 75-88, EHRD

PALEOGRAPHY, Latin. Mss.

Steinacker, Harold. Zum Liber Diurnus und zur Frage nach dem Ursprung der Frühminuskel. 105-176, EHRD

PALEOGRAPHY, Musical

Mocquereau, A. De la Clivis Episématique dans les Manuscrits de Saint-Gall. 508-530, CHAT

PALIMPSESTS
see Manuscripts (Palimpsests)

PALM LEAF BOOKS

Kinkeldey, Otto. Palm Leaf Books. 88-115, BISH

PALMA, MAJORCA - Lull, Ramón - Collections
see Lull, Ramón - Collections - Palma, Majorca

PALMA, MAJORCA. Universidad. Biblioteca

Pons, Antoni. Fra Mario de Passa, Lul-Lista i Bibliòfil. III, 317-337, RUBI

Palmaer, Margit.
Mina Bibliotek. 63-70, ÖREB

Palmer, Bernard I., jt. ed.
SAYW

Palmer, Bernard I.
Classification as a Foundation Study for Librarians. 202-212, SAYW
A Problem in Communication. 597-603, RANG
The Wider Uses of Library Classification. 42-50, MADR

Paltsits, Victor Hugo.
Wilberforce Eames, A Bio-Bibliographical Narrative. Works and Contributions. 1-26, EAME

PALUDANUS, BERNARDUS. [Album Amicorum]

Wijk, Louise E. van. Het Album Amicorum van Bernardus Paludanus (Berend ten Broeke). 97-118, HAGU

PAMPHLETS

Karanova, L. Mi͡astoto na Drebnite Izdanii͡a v Bibliotekite. 408-411, MIKN

Panella, Antonio.
Per Una "Guida Storica degli Archivi Ecclesiastici." 375-382, MERC

PANIZZI, SIR ANTHONY

Predeek, Albert. Antonio Panizzi und der Alphabetische Katalog des Britischen Museums. 257-282, LEYG

PAPAL BULLS
see Bulls, Papal

PAPAL LIBRARIES
see Private Libraries

PAPAL LIBRARY
see Vatican. Biblioteca Vaticana - Hist.

PAPER
see also Bookbinding - Materials; Books - Care and restoration

PAPER

Bishop, William Warner. One Problem for 1950—Woodpulp Paper in Books. 407-415, LYDE

Moriguchi, Ryuji. Sunpo-ho ni Yoru Kirishitan-ban no Shishitsu Chosa. (Research by the "Sumpu" Method on the Quality of Paper Used in the Kirishitan Editions.) 503-510, TOMI

PAPER - Hist.

Labarre, E. J. The Sizes of Paper, Their Names, Origin and History. 35-54, BOCK
Renker, Armin. Die Forschungsstelle Papiergeschichte im Gutenberg-Museum zu Mainz. 80-89, BOCK

PAPER MAKING AND TRADE - Lucerne (Canton)

Blaser, Fritz. Eine Projektierte Papiermühle. 11-17, BOCK

PAPER MAKING AND TRADE - Mladziejowice, Poland - Hist.

Budka, Włodzimierz. Papiernia w Młodziejowicach. 199-210, PIEK

PAPER MAKING AND TRADE - Poczesna, Poland - Hist.

Budka, Włodzimierz. Papiernia w Poczesnej. 408-413, GRYC

PAPER SILHOUETTES
see Paper work

PAPER WORK

Rästner, Erhart. Scherenschnitt-Illustration. 196-219, BOLL

PAPERBACK BOOKS
see also Inexpensive editions

PAPERBACK BOOKS - Hist. - 15th cent.

Leuze, Otto. Mit Holzschnitten Verzierte Buchumschläge des 15. Jahrhunderts in der Württembergischen Landesbibliothek in Stuttgart. 165-169, LEID
Müller, Max. Der Älteste Bisher Bekannte Buchumschlag. 195-197, LEID

PAPERBACK BOOKS - U.S. - Hist.

Schick, Frank L. The Recurring Emergence of American Paperbacks. 195-202, GJEL

PAPYRUS

Debes, Dietmar. Zur Erwerbung des Papyrus Ebers. 139-141, BULL
Delisle, Léopold. Cujas Déchiffreur de Papyrus. 486-491, CHAT
Hartmann, Albert. Eine Federzeichnung auf einem Münchener Papyrus. 103-108, LEID
Kenyon, Sir Frederic George. Book Divisions in Greek and Latin Literature. 63-75, BISH

PAPYRUS COLLECTIONS - Giessen

Gundel, Hans Georg. Giessener Papyrus-Sammlungen im Neuen Raum. 51-55, GIES

PAPYRUS COLLECTIONS - Manchester, Eng.

Till, Walter. Die Nicht-Katalogisierten Coptica der John Rylands Library. 89-90, STUM

PAPYRUS COLLECTIONS - Vienna

Klos, Herbert. Papyrologen-Bibliothekare. 51-53, STUM
Till, Walter. Die Papyrussammlung. 149-164, BICK

PARGELLIS, STANLEY

PARG

Billington, Ray Allen. Stanley Pargellis: Newberry Librarian, 1942-1962. 3-18, PARG

PARGELLIS, STANLEY - Bibl.

Krummel, Donald W. The Writings of Stanley Pargellis. 221-231, PARG

PARIS - Antiquarians
see Antiquarians - Paris

PARIS - Architecture and building - National libraries
see Architecture and building - National libraries - Paris

PARIS - Architecture and building - Remodeled buildings and additions
see Architecture and buildings - Remodeled buildings and additions - Paris

PARIS - Art objects - Collections
see Art objects - Collections - Paris

PARIS. Bibliothèque de L'Arsenal

Kraemer, Erik von. En Bibliofiliens Storman. Antoine-René de Voyer d'Argenson, Markis av Paulmy. 182-196, DAHL
Le Gal, Simonne. La Bibliothèque des Dames au XVe Siècle, Vue par le Marquis de Paulmy. 55-63, CALO

PARIS. Bibliothèque de L'Arsenal. Mss.

Omont, Henry. Inventaire Sommaire des Manuscrits Grecs des Bibliothèques Mazarine, de L'Arsenal et Sainte-Geneviève, à Paris. 305-320, GRAU

PARIS. Bibliothèque de L'Arsenal. Mss. (599)

Boussard, Jacques. L'Évangéliaire d'Or, Manuscrit 599 de la Bibliothèque de L'Arsenal. 3-14, CALO

PARIS. Bibliothèque Mazarine. Mss.

Omont, Henry. Inventaire Sommaire des Manuscrits Grecs des Bibliothèques Mazarine, de L'Arsenal et Sainte-Geneviève, à Paris. 305-320, GRAU

PARIS. Bibliothèque Mazarine. Mss. (Breviary)

Battifol, Abbé Pierre. Note sur un Bréviaire Cassinésien du XIe Siècle. 201-209, HAVE

PARIS. Bibliothèque Nationale

CAIN

PARIS. Bibliothèque Nationale

Dormoy, Marie. Du Droit de Détruire. 489-492, BONN

Foncin, Myriem. L'Histoire d'une Collection de Cartes Réunies pour Louis XIV. 119-126, CALO

Lambert, Mayer. Die Hebräischen Erklärungen im Hebräisch-Französischen Glossar der Pariser Nationalbibliothek. 368-390, (Hebrew Section), HARK

Yamada, Tamaki. Furansu Kokuritsu Toshokan ni tsuite. (On the National Library of France.) 23-31, HAKO

PARIS. Bibliothèque Nationale. Cabinet d'Estampes

Fage, Jean. M. Julien Cain et la Photographie. 41-43, CAIN

PARIS. Bibliothèque Nationale. Département des Estampes

Adhémar, Jean. Julien Cain et le Cabinet des Estampes. 76-82, CAIN

Noailles, Duc de. Lecteur aux Estampes. 83, CAIN

Viellard, Roger. M. Julien Cain et les Estampes. 20-21, CAIN

PARIS. Bibliothèque Nationale. Département des Imprimés

Josserand, Pierre. L'Œuvre de Julien Cain au Département des Imprimés. 60-64, CAIN

Josserand, Pierre and Jean Bruno. Les Estampilles du Département des Imprimés de la Bibliothèque Nationale. 261-298, CALO

PARIS. Bibliothèque Nationale. Département des Manuscrits

Thomas, Marcel. L'Œuvre de Julien Cain au Cabinet des Manuscrits. 65-71, CAIN

PARIS. Bibliothèque Nationale. Département des Médailles et Antiques

Le Rider, Georges. Julien Cain et le Cabinet des Médailles. 72-75, CAIN

PARIS. Bibliothèque Nationale. Département de la Musique

Bridgman, Nanie. La Typographie Musicale Italienne (1475-1630) dans les Collections de la Bibliothèque Nationale de Paris. 24-27, FEDO

Lebeau, Elisabeth. Les Catalogues de Vente de Tableaux et d'Objets d'Art, Source de Documentation Musicale. 67-72, FEDO

PARIS. Bibliothèque Nationale - Hist.

Briet, Suzanne. Note sur Quelques Projets de Translation de la Bibliothèque Royale sous la Monarchie de Juillet. 22-23, STUM

Klaiber, Ludwig. Léopold Delisle und die Reform der Bibliothèque Nationale. 156-168, LEYH

PARIS. Bibliothèque Nationale. Mss.

Degering, Hermann. Handschriften aus Echternach und Orval in Paris. 48-85, MILF

Delaborde, Comte François. Note sur le Carolinus de Gilles de Paris. 195-203, CHAT

Jacob, Alfred. Notes sur les Manuscrits Grecs Palimpsestes de la Bibliothèque Nationale. 759-770, HAVE

PARIS. Bibliothèque Nationale. Mss. (8488a)

Lebègue, Henri. Le Waltharius du Parisinus 8488^{a}. 584-587, CHAT

PARIS. Bibliothèque Nationale. Mss. (24768)

Schulze, Alfred. Zu den Altfranzösischen Bernhardhandschriften. 389-404, WILM

PARIS. Bibliothèque Nationale. Mss. (Codex Trecensis)

Thewrewk de Ponor, Émile. Codex Festi Breviati Trecensis. 659-669, GRAU

PARIS. Bibliothèque Nationale. Mss. (Coll. Baluze, v. 270)

Poupardin, René. Un Fragment en Écriture Onciale de Julianus Antecessor. 221-223, CHAT

PARIS. Bibliothèque Nationale. Mss. (Fr. 67)

Barroux, Robert. Recueil Historique en Français Composé, Transcrit et Enluminé à Saint-Denis, vers 1280. 15-34, CALO

PARIS. Bibliothèque Nationale. Mss. (Fr. 147)

Bonnerot, Jean. En Marge du Manuscrit Français 147 de la B. N. 644-661, CHAT

PARIS. Bibliothèque Nationale. Mss. (Fr. 696)

Barroux, Robert. Recueil Historique en Français Composé, Transcrit et Enluminé à Saint-Denis, vers 1280. 15-34, CALO

PARIS. Bibliothèque Nationale. Mss. (Genesis-Codex)

Kemke, Johannes. Die Geschichte einer Handschriften-Versendung. 489-498, WILM

PARIS. Bibliothèque Nationale. Mss. (Gr. 1741)

Jacob, Alfred. La Miniscule Grecque Penchée et L'Âge du Parisinus Grec 1741. 52-56, CHAT

PARIS. Bibliothèque Nationale. Mss. (Lat. 653)

Souter, Alexander. A Fragment of an Unpublished Latin Text of the Epistle to the Hebrews, with a Brief Exposition. 39-49, EHRA

PARIS. Bibliothèque Nationale. Mss. (Lat. 2120 and Lat. 6496)

Nolhac, P. de. Vers Inédits de Pétrarque. 481-486, HAVE

PARIS. Bibliothèque Nationale. Mss. (Lat. 2589)

Billanovich, Giuseppe. Un Amico e un Libro del Petrarca. 99-104, FERR

PARIS. Bibliothèque Nationale. Mss. (Lat. 5784)

Sorbelli, Albano. Un Nuovo Codice della "Vita C. J. Caesaris" di Francesco Petrarca. II, 677-682, HORT

PARIS. Bibliothèque Nationale. Mss. (Lat. 8084)

Robert, Ulysse. Notice Paléographique sur le Manuscrit de Prudence, N° 8084 du Fonds Latin de la Bibliothèque Nationale. 405-413, GRAU

PARIS. Bibliothèque Nationale. Mss. (Lat. 10478)

Trudon des Ormes, A. Note sur un Fragment de la Règle Latine du Temple. 355-358, HAVE

PARIS. Bibliothèque Nationale. Mss. (Lat. 10756)

Schmitz, Wilhelm. Tironianum. 77-80, HAVE

PARIS. Bibliothèque Nationale. Mss. (Lat. 14643)

Ouy, Gilbert. Une Maquette de Manuscrit à Peintures. 43-51, CALO

PARIS. Bibliothèque Nationale. Mss. (Lat. Nouv. Acq. 1712)

Delisle, M. L. Un Nouveau Manuscrit des Livres des Miracles de Grégoire de Tours. 1-8, HAVE

PARIS. Bibliothèque Nationale. Mss. (Music)

Launay, Denise. À propos de Deux Manuscrits Musicaux aux Armes de Louis XIII. 63-67, FEDO

PARIS. Bibliothèque Sainte-Geneviève

Valous, Guy de. Une Exposition à la Bibliothèque Sainte-Geneviève: La Machine à Expliquer Le Déluge. 535-538, BONN

PARIS. Bibliothèque Sainte-Geneviève. Mss.

Omont, Henry. Inventaire Sommaire des Manuscrits Grecs des Bibliothèques Mazarine, de L'Arsenal et Sainte-Geneviève, à Paris. 305-320, GRAU

PARIS - Bookbinding - Fine bindings - Collections
see Bookbinding - Fine bindings - Collections - Paris

PARIS - Bookbinding - Hist.
see Bookbinding - Paris - Hist.

PARIS - Engravings - Collections
see Engravings - Collections - Paris

PARIS - Manuscripts - Collections
see Manuscripts - Collections - Paris

PARIS - Manuscripts (Palimpsests) Greek - Collections
see Manuscripts (Palimpsests) Greek - Collections - Paris

PARIS - Music libraries and collections
see Music libraries and collections - Paris

PARIS - Printing
see Printing - Paris

PARIS - Type and type-founding
see Type and type-founding - Paris

PARISH LIBRARIES - Denmark

Andersen, S. B. Centralbiblioteket—Set fra en Sognebibliotekars Side. 103-106, LASS

Ebstrup, E. Biblioteksmuligheder paa Landet. Forsøg paa en Nyorientering. 70-84, DØSS

Larsen, Hans Christian. Et År i et Sognebibliotek. 57-64, LASS

PARISH LIBRARIES - Malung, Sweden

MALU

PARISH LIBRARIES - Stockholm

Hornwall, Gert. Ett Föregångsbibliotek i Stockholm. Gustav Vasa Församlingsbibliotek 1909-1927. 127-135, HEIN

PARISH LIBRARIES - Sweden - Hist.

Hallvik, Bengt. Svensk Biblioteksdebatt Omkring År 1860. Ur en Tidningsläsares Citatsamling. 77-95, HEIN

PARISH LIBRARIES - Torslev, Denmark - Hist.

TORS

PARKER, JAMES, printer

Reid, Winnifred Reynolds. Beginnings of Printing in New Haven. From Letters of Benjamin Franklin and James Parker. 67-88, KEOG

Parkhi, G. R.
Symbiosis between Classification and Catalogue. 222-227, RANG
Colon Classification: The National Scheme of Classification for India. 94-98, RANG
Dr. Ranganathan's Plan for Library Development in Bombay. 397-400, RANG

Parthasarathy, K. S.
The Madras Library Association. 123-126, MADR

Parthasarathy, S.
Training of Library Personnel in India. 158-162, MADR

PARZIVAL
see Perceval (Romances, etc.)

PASCAL, BLAISE. Comparaison des Chrétiens

Lafuma, Louis. À propos d'un Petit Écrit de Pascal. 109-114, BONN

PASCHA
see De Pascha

Paschini, Pio.
Un Cardinale Editore: Marcello Cervini. 383-413, FERR

PASO HONROSO

Werner, Mulertt. Le Fecha del Manuscrito Escurialense del "Paso Honroso." II, 242-245, ARTI

PASSA, MARIO DE, monk
see Mario de Passa, monk

Passi, N. N.
Subject Indexing and Dr. Ranganathan. 228-238, RANG

PASSIONALS

Ranke, Friedrich. Eine Neue Handschrift des Gereimten Passionals. 301-316, KÖNI

PASSIONEI, DOMENICO, Cardinal - Library

Czumpelik, Rudolf. Kardinal Passionei und Seine Beziehungen zu Prinz Eugen. 23-24, STUM

Paszkowski, Wilhelm.
Goethes Verhältnis zum Bibliothekswesen. 159-172, WILM

Patil, G. M.
Dr. Ranganathan as I See Him. 685-689, RANG

Patrick, L. G., et al.
R. S. Hutton; on the Occasion of His Ninetieth Birthday. 277-286, HUTT

Patterson, M., jt. author

Bryant, Louise May and Mary Patterson. The List of Books Sent by Jeremiah Dummer. 423-492, KEOG

Patton, Mollie Marjorie, jt. author

Livingston, Dorothy Flower, Mollie Marjorie Patton, et al. Contribution to a Bibliography of Francis Bacon. Editions before 1700 in Yale Libraries. 95-143, KEOG

Pauer, Hans.
Grosser Entschluss. Ein Neues Ordnungssystem in der Porträtsammlung der Österreichischen Nationalbibliothek. 62-64, STUM
Die Porträtsammlung und das Bildarchiv. 165-179, BICK
Ein Staatsarchiv der Bildenden Künste. 516-522, BICK

Pauer, Max.
Anton Ruland und Karl Halm. Ein Bibliothekarischer Streit um Dublettenverkäufe vor Hundert Jahren. 121-135, REDE

PAUL, JEAN. Mss.

Berend, Eduard. Jean Pauls Handschriftlicher Nachlass. 336-346, HOFF

PAULINUS, SAINT, Bp. of Nola. Epistulae

Prete, Sesto. The Textual Tradition of the Correspondence between Ausonius and Paulinus. II, 309-330, ALBB

Paulli, R.
Bogfører-Dokumenter fra det 16. Aarhundrede. 215-223, COLL
Gregorius Middelthun. Bogbinder i Bergen, Stempelskærer på Kongsberg. 140-148, TVET

PAULMY D'ARGENSON, M. A. R., Marquis de
see Argenson, Marc Antoine René de Voyer, Marquis de Paulmy

Pauls, E.
Zur Geschichte des Archivs des Roerdepartements in Aachen. 72-92, (pt. 2), AACH

Paulsson, Egon.
Lånecentralen i Malmö. 548-551, HJEL

Paunel, Eugen.
Grillparzer als Bibliothekar. Meinungen, Hoffnungen, Enttäuschungen. 357-383, VORS

Paust, Albert.
Johann Heinrich Plath, ein Wegbereiter der Deutschen Bücherei. 64-67, STUM
——— Die Reichsbibliothek von 1848, ein Denkmal der Deutschen Einheit. 384-396, VORS
——— Sammelgebiet und Werbung. 58-74, LEIS
Paust, Albert, et al.
Bibliographie zur Geschichte der Deutschen Bücherei. 287-367, LEIZ

PAVIA - Printing
see Printing - Pavia

PAVIA. Universita. Biblioteca. Mss. (De Cod. Tic.)
Rasi, P. Nuove Osservazioni sul Carmen de Pascha. 577-604, CERI

Pavlov, Todor.
Slovo na Akad. Todor Pavlov, Presedatel na Bŭlgarskata Akademiia na Naukite, Proizneseno Pri Otkrivane na Tŭrzhestvenoto Sŭbranie. 7-8, TEOD

Pawlack, Erna.
Zur Frage der Ausbildung Nebenamtlicher Büchereileiter im Rahmen des Ländlichen Büchereiwesens. 124-134, LANF

PEDAGOGICAL LIBRARY, Kraków
see Kraków. Pedagogical Library

PEDERSEN, CHRISTIERN. Vocabularium ad Usum Dacorum. 1510
Larsen, Sofus. To Danske Palaeotyper Trykte i Paris. 183-197, COLL

Peebles, Bernard M.
The Bibliotheca Albana Urbinas as Represented in the Library of the Catholic University of America. 327-352, ALBA

PEIRESZ, NICOLAS CLAUDE FABRI DE
Kemke, Johannes. Die Geschichte einer Handschriften-Versendung. 489-498, WILM

Peitz, Wilhelm Maria, jt. author
Katterbach, Bruno and Wilhelm Maria Peitz, S. J. Die Unterschriften der Päpste und Kardinäle in den Bullae Maiores vom 11. bis 14. Jhdt. 177-274, EHRD

PELAYO, MARCELINO MENÉNDEZ Y
see Menéndez y Pelayo, Marcelino

Pélissier, Léon-J.
Un Collaborateur Provençal de Montfaucon. 429-439, CHAT

PELZER, AUGUSTE
PELZ

PELZER, AUGUSTE - Bibl.
Bibliographie de Monseigneur Pelzer. 17-21, PELZ

Pennink, R.
Petrarca, Teghen die Strael der Minnen. 71-85, HAGU

PENNSYLVANIA - Publishers and publishing
see Publishers and Publishing - Pennsylvania

PENNSYLVANIA. University. Library
PENN

PENNSYLVANIA. University. Library - Hist.
Hirsch, Rudolf and Margaret C. Nolan. The Peaceful Revolution. 25-34, DAVI

PENNSYLVANIA. University. Library. Mss. (Formularies)
Haskins, Charles Homer. Two Roman Formularies in Philadelphia. 275-286, EHRD

Pepino, Jan.
Aus der Täglichen Arbeit der Sächsischen Landesbibliothek. 86-91, DREL

PEPYS, SAMUEL - Library
Jackson, William A. Tunc et Nunc: or the Pepys and Taylor Collections of Early English Books on Navigation. 195-201, WROT

PERCEVAL (Romances, etc.) Mss.
Rosenfeld, Hans-Friedrich. Die Berliner Parzivalfragmente. 192-202, DEGE

PERERA, A. - Collections - Vienna
Gregor, Joseph. Die Handzeichnungen

der Sammlung Perera in der Wiener Nationalbibliothek. 407-420, VIEN

PERIODICALS
see also Serial publications

PERIODICALS

Miyanaka, Ichiko. Zasshi Towa Nani ka. (Definition of Periodicals.) 148-152, KYOT

PERIODICALS - Abbreviations of titles

Tamai, Tōkichi. Zenkoku Keizai Chōsa Kikan Rengōkai Seitei Gaikoku Zasshi-mei Ryakugo Shokitei ni tsuite. (On the Rules of Abbreviation of the Titles of Foreign Periodicals, Established by the National Federation of Economic Research Organizations.) 20-36, OTAT

PERIODICALS, American - Hist.

Lewis, Benjamin M. Engravings in Early American Magazines, 1741-1810. 203-218, GJEL

PERIODICALS, American - Michigan - Hist.

Bonk, W. J. Periodical Publishing in the Michigan Territory. 85-104, GJEL

PERIODICALS, Bulgarian - Bibl. - Hist.

Ivanchev, Dimitŭr and Stefan Stanchev. Bibliografiîa na Statiite v Bŭlgarskiîa Periodichen Pechat s Ogled na Praktikata na "Bulgarski Knigopis" za 1930 i 1931 g. 404-408, MIKN

PERIODICALS, Bulgarian - Hist.

Ivanchev, Dimitŭr. Pouki ot Stogodishninata na Bŭlgarskiîa Periodichen Pechat. 298-303, MIKN

PERIODICALS - Circulation procedures - Tokyo

Tsuda, Yoshinari. Kangai Kashidashi Yōkyu ni Ojirare Nakatta Zasshi oyobi Sono Riyū no Chōsa. (An Analysis of Dissatisfied Circulation Requests for Periodicals.) 297-313, HASH

PERIODICALS - Collections - Berlin

Laue, Max. Der Zeitschriftensaal. 14-20, HARN

PERIODICALS - Collections - Kraków

Marchut, Maria. Czasopisma. 21-24, KRAK

PERIODICALS - Collections - Uppsala

Samzelius, Jonas L:son. De Utländska Tidskrifterna vid Uppsala Universitet. Några Bidrag till Belysning av Förhallandet mellan Forskare och Bibliotek. 586-607, UPPS

PERIODICALS - Collections - Utrecht

Graafland, H. J. P. Hooft. De Tijdschriften en de Reekswerken der Universiteitsbibliotheek. 146-149, EVER

PERIODICALS - Curiosa

Laue, Max. Zeitschriftenkuriosa. 149-158, SCHW

PERIODICALS, European - Hist.

Widmann, Hans. Early History of European Periodicals. 515-522, RANG

PERIODICALS - Exchange
see Exchange of books, periodicals, etc.

PERIODICALS, German - Union lists

Jessen, Hans. Aus der Werkstatt des Gesamtkatalogs der Deutschen Presse. 363-368, JUCH

PERIODICALS - Illustrations
see Book illustration

PERIODICALS - Indexes and abstracts - Vienna

Kaliba, Hans. Gesellschaft und Kultur im Spiegel der Zeitung. Eine Dokumentationsstelle der Stadtbibliothek. 154-165, VIES

PERIODICALS, Juvenile
see Children's periodicals

PERIODICALS, Medical - German

Roth, Ernst. Die Speziell Medizinischen Deutschen Zeitschriften in den Jahren 1853, 1875 und 1901. 199-204, WILM

PERIODICALS, Netherlands - Hist. - 1897-1898

Ravesteyn, W. van. 'De Paradox': een Curiosum. 174-185, KOSS

PERIODICALS, Polish - Collections - Bydgoszcz

Nowakowska, Izabela. Czasopisma Rzadkie i Cenne. 89-96, BYDG

PERIODICALS - Printing

Rodenberg, Julius. Über Zeitungs- und Zeitschriftentypographie. 373-380, LEYG

PERIODICALS - Social science

Smith, Anne M. Social Sciences Journals Frequently Cited. 127-134, HASH

PERIODICALS - Statistics - U.S.

Eells, Walter Crosby. Periodicals Read by Junior College Students. 474-485, WILS

PERIODICALS, Theatrical - Bibl.

Hadamowsky, Franz. Wiener Theater-Periodica. 35-38, STUM

PERIODICALS, Theatrical - Collections - Vienna

Hadamowsky, Franz. Wiener Theater-Periodica. 35-38, STUM

PERIODICALS - Union lists

Gorter, A. Het Nut van Tijdschriften-lijsten. 436-440, BRUM

Perlbach, Max.
Die Berliner Doubletten von 1697 in Halle. 15-42, WILM

Perry, James Whiting.
The University Library as a Capital Assett. 46-53, COET

Perry, James Whiting, jt. author

Shera, Jesse H. and James W. Perry. Changing Concepts of Classification, Philosophical and Education Implications. 37-48, RANG

PERRY, JAMES WHITING. Encoded Telegraphic Abstracts

Melton, Jessica. Compatibility of Two Information Systems, Colon Classification and Western Reserve University. 49-62, RANG

PERSIA - Bookbinding
see Bookbinding - Persia

PERSON, NIKOLAUS - Bibl.

Häuser, Helmut. Zum Kartographischen Werk des Mainzer Kupferstechers und Ingenieurs Nikolaus Person. 170-186, BENZ

PERSONNEL
see also Certification of librarians; College and university librarians - Status; Ethics; Non-professional assistants; Volunteer assistants

PERSONNEL

Bowerman, George F. Some Library Personnel Problems. 103-112, PUTN
Kästner, Erhart. Über das Bibliothekarische Mißvergnügen und noch ein Zweiter Traktat. 295-302, WEHM

PERSONNEL - Aarhus, Denmark

Grundtvig, Vilh. Andre Forhold. 159-165, AARU

PERSONNEL - Administration

Möhlenbrock, Sigurd. Om Arbets- och Ansvarsfördelning. 203-214, HEIN

PERSONNEL - Administration - Stockholm

Kolmodin, Torsten. Om Personalredovisning. 257-261, GRAP

PERSONNEL - Bydgoszcz

Biernat, Barbara. Organizacja i Skład Osobowy. 63-68, BYDG

PERSONNEL - Copenhagen

Fabritius, Albert. 3-216, COPE

PERSONNEL - Examinations
see Personnel - Qualifications and selection

PERSONNEL - Frankfurt a.M.

Köster, Kurt. Die Deutsche Bibliothek 1945-1965. Weg und Auftrag. 21-77, EPPE

PERSONNEL - Hamburg

Breddin, Hans Harald. Die Bibliothekarische Arbeitsgemeinschaft der Hamburger Öffentlichen Bücherhallen. 110-114, HAMB

PERSONNEL - Mainz

Darapsky, Elisabeth. Bibliothekare der Stadtbibliothek Mainz. 17-30, MAIN

PERSONNEL - Medical Libraries
see Medical libraries

PERSONNEL - Oslo - Hist.

Prytz, Lizzie. Universitetsbibliotekets Personale 1813-1932. 258-276, OSLO

PERSONNEL - Qualifications and selection
see also Recruiting for librarianship

PERSONNEL - Qualifications and selection

Kammel, Karl. Die Prüfungen des Wissenschaftlichen Bibliotheksdienstes in Österreich. 423-428, BICK
Lohse, Gerhart. Gedanken zur Auswahl des Nachwuchses für die Wissenschaftliche Bibliothekarische Laufbahn. 73-84, JUCR
Wehmer, Carl. Eine Äusserung Jacob Willes über die Vorbildung der Bibliothekare aus dem Jahre 1921. 21-31, REDE

PERSONNEL - Qualifications and selection - Gt. Brit.

Minto, John. The Library Association Examinations. 285-295, HANS

PERSONNEL - Qualifications and selection - Norway
Andreassen, Anders. Hva Vil det Kreves av Fremtidens Folkebibliotekarer? 113-122, NORS

PERSONNEL - Qualifications and selection - Washington, D.C. - Hist.
Mearns, David C. Herbert Putnam and His Responsible Eye—A Memorial Tribute. 1-52, PUTP

PERSONNEL RECORDS - Stockholm
Kolmodin, Torsten. Om Personalredovisning. 257-261, GRAP

PERSONNEL-TRAINING
see In-service training

PERTZ, GEORG HEINRICH
Hortzschansky, Adalbert. Heinrich Pertz' Berufung zum Oberbibliothekar der Königlichen Bibliothek in Berlin. 115-126, SCHW

PERUGIA. San Domenico (Convent) Biblioteca
Cecchini, Giovanni. La Quattrocentesca Biblioteca del Convento di S. Domenico di Perugia. 249-254, GALL

Pescheck, Paul.
Die Entwicklung des Neueren Bibliotheksbaues. 264-280, MILF

Peterkin, Norman.
An American Composer: Carl Engel. 20-22, ENGE

Petersen, Carl S.
Dronning Sophie Amalies Bogsamling. 231-247, COLL

Petersen, Theodore.
The Paragraph Mark in Coptic Illuminated Ornament. 295-330, GREE

Peterson, John.
Kina i Göteborgs Stadsbibliotek. 1-21, (ninth paper), GÖTE

PETRARCA, FRANCESCO. Mss. <u>Bucolica Carmina</u>
Bertoni, Giulio. Sulla Composizione del Codice Estense 232 delle Egloghe del Petrarca e sull'Autenticità dei così Detti Argomenti. II, 719-725, HORT

PETRARCA, FRANCESCO. Mss. <u>De Vita Solitaria</u>
Rajna, P. Il Codice Vaticano 3357 del Trattato <u>De Vita Solitaria</u> di Francesco Petrarca. 641-686, CERI

PETRARCA, FRANCESCO. Mss. <u>Vers</u>
Nolhac, P. de. Vers Inédits de Pétrarque. 481-486, HAVE

PETRARCA, FRANCESCO. Mss. <u>Vita C. J. Caesaris</u>
Sorbelli, Albano. Un Nuovo Codice della "Vita C. J. Caesaris" di Francesco Petrarca. II, 677-682, HORT

PETRARCA, FRANCESCO. <u>Triumphi</u>
Wilkins, Ernst H. The Separate Fifteenth-Century Editions of the Triumphs of Petrarch. 748-751, WILS

PETRUS COMESTOR. Mss. <u>Sermones</u>
Hörmann, Wolfgang. Probleme einer Aldersbacher Handschrift (Clm. 2599). 335-389, HOFM

PETRUS, SAINT CANISIUS
see Canisius, Petrus, Saint

PETRUS VÉNÉRABLE
see Pierre le Vénérable

PETTERSEN, HJALMAR MARIUS
Amundsen, Leiv. Hjalmar Pettersen. 57-67, OSLN

Petz-Gebauer, Hannelore.
Bibliographie Fritz Redenbacher. 203-207, REDE
Zur Baugeschichte der Erlanger Universitätsbibliothek. 149-162, REDE

PETZET, ERICH
Petzet, Wolfgang. Leben und Werk des Literarhistorikers, Germanisten und Bibliothekars Dr. Erich Petzet. I, 160-162, GLAU

Petzet, Wolfgang.
Leben und Werk des Literarhistorikers, Germanisten und Bibliothekars Dr. Erich Petzet. I, 160-162, GLAU

PEUTINGER, KONRAD
Geissler, Paul. Zwei Unbekannte Holzschnittprobedrucke zum Theuerdank und Konrad Peutinger. 118-128, JUCH

Pfannmüller, Gustav.
Westfälische Schreiberverse aus dem Jahre 1238. 71-72, SCHR

Pfeifer, Hans.
Die Kartenabteilung. 147-155, DREL

Pfeifer, Hans, jt. author
Deckert, Helmut, Marita Kremer, Hans Pfeifer, and Liselotte Willi. Das

Neue Buchmuseum der Sächsischen Landesbibliothek. 175-205, DREL

Pfennig, Richard.
Unser Realkatalog. 109-113, HARN

Pfister, Arnold.
Vom Frühsten Musikdruck in der Schweiz. 160-178, BINZ

PFISTER, CONRAD

Roth, Carl. Conrad Pfister, Basilius Iselin und die Amerbachsche Bibliothek. 179-200, BINZ

Pfizer, Theodor, jt. ed.
HOFF

Pflaume, Heinz.
Zur Geschichte des Pflichtexemplars in Thüringen. 225-231, VORS

Pflug, Günther.
Der Einfluss der Elektronischen Datenverarbeitung auf die Katalogisierungspraxis. 111-124, FUCH

PHARMACEUTICAL LIBRARIES

Lage, Louise C., Lois B. Miller, and Donald Washburn. Dental, Nursing, and Pharmaceutical Libraries, 1947-1957. 371-377, DOEJ

PHARMACOPEIAS - Bibl.

Spencer, Marjory C. National and International Pharmacopeias: A Checklist. 410-420, DOEJ

PHILADELPHIA BIBLIOGRAPHICAL CENTER AND UNION LIBRARY CATALOGUE

Campion, Eleanor Este. The Union Library Catalogue. 19-24, DAVI
Clapp, Verner W. Bibliographical Vision. 35-41, DAVI

PHILADELPHIA, Pa. - Book industry and trade
see Book industry and trade - Philadelphia, Pa.

PHILADELPHIA, Pa. - Catalogs - Union
see Catalogs - Union - Philadelphia, Pa.

PHILODEMUS, of Gadara - Library

Comparetti, D. La Bibliothèque de Philodème. 118-129, CHAT

PHILODEMUS, of Gadara - Mss.

Comparetti, D. La Bibliothèque de Philodème. 118-129, CHAT

PHILOLOGY - Classification
see Classification - Special subjects - Philology

PHILOSOPHY LIBRARIES AND COLLECTIONS - Classification
see Classification - Special subjects - Philosophy

PHOTODUPLICATION
see Catalog cards - Reproduction; Copying methods; Duplicating processes; Photographic reproduction

PHOTOGRAPH COLLECTIONS - Paris

Fage, Jean. M. Julien Cain et la Photographie. 41-43, CAIN

PHOTOGRAPH COLLECTIONS - Uppsala

Taube, Gurli. Fotografen Osti och den Ostiska Plåtsamlingen på Carolina Rediviva. 280-292, GRAP

PHOTOGRAPH COLLECTIONS - Utrecht

Oppermann, O. De Verzameling Photo's van het Instituut voor Middeleeuwsche Geschiedenis. 242-243, EVER

PHOTOGRAPHIC REPRODUCTION
see also Catalog cards - Reproduction; Copying methods

PHOTOGRAPHIC REPRODUCTION

Longo, Luigi. Nuovo Materiale per la Produzione di Fotografie Inalterabili di Documenti: Vetro Fotosensibile. 535-537, GALL
Wilbur, James Benjamin. The Photostat. 520-527, PUTN

PHOTOGRAPHIC REPRODUCTION SERVICES - Bern

Meyer, Wilhelm Joseph. Der Photographische Dienst. 168, BERU

PHOTOGRAPHIC REPRODUCTION - Utrecht

Hulshof, A. De Handschriften en de Incunabelen der Utrechtsche Universiteitsbibliotheek en de Moderne Reproductietechniek. 150-159, EVER

PHOTOSTAT
see Photographic reproduction

Piccoli, Giuseppe.
Metodi Steganografici e Sistemi Crittografici Antichi. 597-605, GALL

Pichon, René.
Observations sur le Texte de la Consolatio ad Marciam de Sénèque. 230-231, CHAT

Pick, Hermann.
Der Unvollendet Gebliebene Bibliotheksbau des Großen Kurfürsten. 211-215, SCHW

PICTURE COLLECTIONS
 see also Photograph collections

PICTURE COLLECTIONS - Administration

 Björkbom, Carl. Om Ordnandet av
 Grafiska Porträttsamlingar. 20-22,
 MUNT

PICTURE COLLECTIONS - Berkeley, California

 Dakin, Susanna Bryant. "His Mild and
 Magnificent Eye." 55-61, HAMM

PICTURE COLLECTIONS - Bern

 Thormann, Anne-Marie. Die Bildersammlung. 96-107, BERU

PICTURE COLLECTIONS - Vienna

 Beetz, Wilhelm. Zur Geschichte der
 Porträtsammlung der Nationalbi-
 bliothek in Wien. 59-74, VIEN
 Pauer, Hans. Grosser Entschluss. Ein
 Neues Ordnungssystem in der
 Porträtsammlung der Österreichi-
 schen Nationalbibliothek. 62-64,
 STUM
 ————— Die Porträtsammlung und
 das Bildarchiv. 165-179, BICK
 ————— Ein Staatsarchiv der Bilden-
 den Künste. 516-522, BICK

PICTURE-WRITING, Moso

 Schubert, Johannes. Na-khi-Piktographie.
 Notizen über eine Wenig Beachtete
 Bilderschrift. 114-142, BOCK

Pieev, Aleksandr K.
 Nauchna Dešmost'. 30-34, DIAK
 Proslaven den' na Boris Diakovich. [5]-
 68, DIAK
 Reformirane na Plovdivskata Narodna
 Biblioteka. 26-29, DIAK

PIEKARSKI, KAZIMIERZ

 PIEK

PIEKARSKI, KAZIMIERZ

 Borowy, Wacław. Wspomnienie. 13-31,
 PIEK
 Gryczowa, Alodia. Dzieło Kazimierza
 Piekarskiego. 39-61, PIEK
 Nota Biograficzna. 11-12, PIEK
 Wegner, Jan. Wspomnienie o Pracy
 Naukowej Kazimierza Piekarskiego
 w Łowickim (1942-1944). 33-37,
 PIEK

PIEKARSKI, KAZIMIERZ - Bibl.

 Lipska, Helena. Bibliografia Prac
 Kazimierza Piekarskiego. 377-393,
 PIEK

PIERPONT MORGAN LIBRARY, New York
 (City)
 GREE

PIERPONT MORGAN LIBRARY, New York
 (City). Mss. (Gospels)

 Lowe, E. A. The Morgan Golden
 Gospels: The Date and Origin of the
 Manuscript. 266-279, GREE

PIERPONT MORGAN LIBRARY, New York
 (City). Mss. (No. 191)

 Rand, Edward Kennard. A Carolingian
 Gospel-Book in the Pierpont Morgan
 Library in New York. 89-104,
 EHRD

PIERPONT MORGAN LIBRARY, New York
 (City). Mss. (No. 500)

 Ettinghausen, Richard. The Covers of
 the Morgan Manâfi' Manuscript and
 Other Early Persian Bookbindings.
 459-473, GREE

PIERPONT MORGAN LIBRARY, New York
 (City). Mss. (M 555)

 Bühler, Curt F. Novello Cattanio: Un
 Viaggio Fatto alli Paesi del Continente Nuovo. 85-99, WROT

PIERPONT MORGAN LIBRARY, New York
 (City). Mss. (No. 564)

 Koehler, Wilhelm. The Fragments of
 an Eighth-Century Gospel Book in
 the Morgan Library (M 564): A Contribution to the History of the Vulgate. 238-265, GREE

PIERPONT MORGAN LIBRARY, New York
 (City). Mss. (No. 639)

 Weitzmann, Kurt. The Constantinopolitan Lectionary, Morgan 639.
 358-373, GREE

PIERPONT MORGAN LIBRARY, New York
 (City). Mss. (No. 803)

 Der Nersessian, Sirarpie. An Armenian
 Lectionary of the Fourteenth Century.
 231-237, GREE

PIERPONT MORGAN LIBRARY, New York
 (City). Mss. (No. 828)

 Skehan, Patrick W. An Illuminated
 Gospel Book in Ethiopic. 350-357,
 GREE

PIERPONT MORGAN LIBRARY, New York
 (City). Mss. (Piggott Obituary)

 Goldschmidt, E. P. An Obituary Rotulus from York, 1405. 379-383, GREE

PIERPONT MORGAN LIBRARY, New York
 (City). Mss. (Swift)

 Leslie, Sir Shane. The Swift Manuscripts
 in the Morgan Library. 445-448,
 GREE

POLAND - Education libraries
see Education libraries - Poland

POLAND - Libraries - Administration
see Libraries - Administration - Poland

POLAND - Monastic libraries
see Monastic libraries - Poland

POLAND - Oriental literature - Collections
see Oriental literature - Collections - Poland

POLAND - Printing
see Printing - Poland

POLAND - Private libraries
see Private libraries - Poland

POLAND - Scientific libraries
see Scientific libraries - Poland

Poli͡akov, A. S.
Epizod iz Istorii Gonenii͡a na Knigu. 306-345, MALE
Predislovie Redaktora. [xi]-xix, MALE

POLISH ACADEMY OF ART, Kraków. Mss. (Kazania Świętokrzyskie)

Krzyżanowski, Julian. O Artyźmie "Kazań Świętokrzyskich." 345-350, PIEK

POLISH PERIODICALS
see Periodicals, Polish

POLITICAL ECONOMY
see Economics

POLITICAL PARTIES - Finland - Collections

Schauman, Henrik. Monarkisternas och Republikanernas Arkiv. 97-100, NYBE

POLITICAL POETRY, English - 17th cent. - Collections - Vienna

Brotanek, Rudolf. Beschreibung der Handschrift 14090 (Suppl. 1776) der Nationalbibliothek in Wien. 145-162, VIEN

Pollard, Graham.
The Construction of English Twelfth-Century Bindings. 1-22, OLDH

POLSKA AKADEMIA UMIĘJETNOŚCI, Kraków
see Polish Academy of Art, Kraków

Polthier, Wilhelm.
Die Ehemalige Domstiftsbibliothek in Havelberg. 163-176, KUHN

POLYAENUS. Mss.

Mueller, Charles-Conrad. Sur les Manuscrits de Polyen. 723-729, GRAU

Pomassl, Gerhard.
Zehn Jahre Thüringer Zentralkatalog. 87-102, BULL

POMMERANIAN ALBUMS
see Albums, Pommeranian

POMPEIUS, SEXTUS FESTUS
see Festus, Sextus Pompeius

Ponińska, Irena.
Czytelnia. 24-29, KRAK

Pons, Abelardo Palanca.
Incunable Valenciano Poco Conocido. 589-596, GALL

Pons, Antoni.
Fra Mario de Passa, Lul-Lista i Bibliòfil. III, 317-337, RUBI

POOLE, WILLIAM FREDERICK

Roden, Carl B. The Boston Years of Dr. W. F. Poole. 388-394, PUTN

POPES - Libraries

Schunke, Ilse. Die Entwicklung der Päpstlichen Einbände vom 16. zum 17. Jahrhundert. II, 331-354, ALBB

Popiel, Jadwiga.
Dział Instrukcyjno-Metodyczny. 36-38, KRAK
Udział Pedagogicnej Biblioteki Wojewódzkiej w Realizacji Działu Programu Języka Polskiego: Podstawowe Wiadomości o Książce. 80-83, KRAK

Porcher, Jean.
Un Amateur de Peinture sous Charles VI: Jean Lebègue. 35-41, CALO

PORTOLAN ATLASES

Wagner, Henry R. The Portolan Atlases of American Interest in the Henry E. Huntington Library and Art Gallery. 498-509, PUTN

PORTRAIT COLLECTIONS
see Picture collections

POSEN. Biblioteca Raczyńskich

Collmann, O. Einige Mitteilungen über die Raczyńskische Bibliothek. 57-65, VERP

POSEN - Catalogs - Classed
see Catalogs - Classed - Posen

POSEN. Kaiser-Wilhelm-Bibliothek

Wenzel, B. Die Abteilung Bücherkunde im Realkatalog der Kaiser-Wilhelm-Bibliothek. 19-42, VERP

POSEN (Province) - Research libraries
see Research libraries - Posen (Province)

Posner, Ernst.
The College and University Archives in the United States. 363-374, MERC

Postell, William Dosite.
Research and Medical Librarianship. 399-403, DOEJ

Pou y Marti, José M.
Los Archivos de la Embajada de España cerca de la Santa Sede. 297-311, MERC

Poulsen, Chr.
Bibliotekets Udvikling 1912-37. 15-20, FRED

Poulton, R. K., jt. author

Farradane, J., R. K. Poulton, and Mrs. S. Datta. Problems in Analysis and Terminology for Information Retrieval. 287-290, KYLE

Poupardin, René.
Un Fragment en Écriture Onciale de Julianus Antecessor. 221-223, CHAT

Pousa, Ramón Fernández.
Menéndez Pelayo y el Códice Florentino de las Cantigas de Santa María de Alfonso X el Sabio. 235-255, MENE

Powell, Lawrence Clark, ed.
SAYE

Power, Leonore St. John.
Recollections of Anne Carroll Moore. 623-627, MOOR

Powers, Zara Jones.
A Yale Bibliophile in European Book Shops. 373-422, KEOG

POZNAŃ - Book illustration
see Book illustration - Poznań

Poznański, S.
Die Qirqisâni-Handschriften im British Museum. 195-218, STEI

Praesent, Hans.
Karten und Atlanten in den Bibliographien des Deutschen Buchhandels. 79-90, MIND
Die Kartensammlung. 148-164, LEIS

PRAGUE - Architecture and building - Remodeled buildings and additions
see Architecture and building - Remodeled buildings and additions - Prague

PRAGUE. Cathedral. Library. Mss. (B IV 1)

Collijn, Isak Gustaf Alfred. Kalendarium Munkalivense. Ein Schwedisch-Norwegisches Birgittinerkalendarium. 82-92, DEGE

PRAGUE - Classification - Systems - Dewey decimal
see Classification - Systems - Dewey decimal - Prague

PRAGUE. Czechoslovakian Academy of Sciences. Library
see Czechoslovakian Academy of Sciences. Library

PRAGUE - Exhibits and displays - Special subjects - Book illustration
see Exhibits and displays - Special subjects - Book illustration - Prague

PRAGUE - Incunabula, Czechoslovakian - Collections
see Incunabula, Czechoslovakian - Collections - Prague

PRAGUE. Metropolitanskapitel
see Prague. Cathedral. Library

PRAGUE. Národni a Universitni Knikovna
see Prague. National and University Library

PRAGUE. Národni Museum
see Prague. National Museum

PRAGUE. National and University Library

Adlerová, Eliška. Několik Umělecko-historických Poznámek k Výstavě Francouzské Ilustrované Knihy v Praž. Národnía a Universitné Knihovně. 80-83, EMLE
Hrozný, Jindřich. Povinné Výtisky. 64-68, EMLE
Slámová, Marie Olga. Kniha Návštev. 133-137, EMLE

PRAGUE. National and University Library - Hist.

Emler, Jan. Das Neue im Alten. 297-308, LEYG

PRAGUE. National and University Library - Mss. (Fol. 89)

Bartoš, F. M. Bible Kněze Jakuba, Faráře u. Sv. Mikuláše na Starém Městě v Praze. 83-86, EMLE

PRAGUE. National Museum. Library

Volf, Josef. Jak Získalo Národní Museum Své České Prvotisky. 148-152, EMLE

PRAGUE - Printing
see Printing - Prague

PRAGUE. Public Library

Thon, Jan. Emlerův Inspektorát Městské Knihovny Pražské. 73-79, EMLE

Prasad, Brij Nandan.
A Word of Tribute. 766, RANG

PRATO, Innocenzo a
see Innocenzo a Prato

Pratt, Anne Stokely.
The Books Sent from England by Jeremiah Dummer to Yale College. 7-44, KEOG

PRAYER-BOOKS
Ljunggren, Evald. Fragment av en Katolsk Andaktsbok på Svenska från 1525 (?). 265-267, COLL
Wegener Hans. Das Gebetbuch der Johanna von Bocholt. 228-232, BÖME

Predeek, Albert.
Antonio Panizzi und der Alphabetische Katalog des Britischen Museums. 257-282, LEYG
Die Bibliothekswissenschaft als Disziplin und Universitätslehrfach. 169-184, LEYH
Fortschritte im Katalogdruck nach dem Adrema-System. 197-210, MUNT
Rechtsstellung und Verwaltung der Amerikanischen Public Library. I, 163-175, GLAU

PREGLED NA DISERTATSII PO BIBLIOTEKOZNANIE I BIBLIOGRAFIIÂ V SSSR. 381-391, MIKN

Preisendanz, Karl.
Handschriftenausleihe in der Bibliotheca Palatina. 54-68, LEYG
Der Reichenauer Handschriftenkatalog von 1724. 199-206, LEID

Premerstein, Anton v.
Griechich-Heidnische Weissagungen über die Christliche Lehre in Handschriften und Kirchenmalereien. 647-666, VIEN

Presser, Helmut, jt. ed.
RUPP

PRESSES, University
Morpurgo, J. E. The Publishing Problem—a Kite for Policy Makers. 236-240, KYLE

PRESSES, University - Heidelberg - Hist.
Dyroff, Hans-Dieter. Die Bücherzensur der Universität Heidelberg 1652-1693. 98-119, BENZ

PRESSES, University - New Haven, Conn.
Rollins, Carl P. The Bibliographical Press at Yale University. 247-261, WROT

PRESSES, University - Uppsala - Hist.
Rudbeck, Gustaf. Bidrag till Uppsala Akademiska Boktryckeris Historia. 45-58, GRAP

Prete, Sesto, ed.
ALBA

Prete, Sesto.
The Textual Tradition of the Correspondence between Ausonius and Paulinus. II, 309-330, ALBB
The Vossianus Latinus III and the Arrangement of the Works of Ausonius. 353-366, ALBA

PRETORIA - Education for librarianship
see Education for librarianship - Pretoria

Pretzsch, Karl.
Die Kartensammlung. 232-239, HARN

PREUSSISCHER GESAMTKATALOG
see Deutscher Gesamtkatalog

PRICES, Book
see Books - Prices

Priest, Alan.
An Illuminated Buddhist Scroll in the Metropolitan Museum of Art. 122-128 GREE

PRIMER, ROYAL
see The Royal Primer

Prins, A. A.
De Behandeling der Postaanvragen. 250-253, EVER

PRINTED BOOK CATALOGS
see Catalogs - Printed book

PRINTERS, British
Mortimer, R. S. Biographical Notices of Printers and Publishers of Friends' Books up to 1750. 107-125, OFFO

PRINTERS - Cologne - 15th cent.
Juchhoff, Rudolf. Die Universität Köln und die Frühen Typographen. 233-243, BENZ

PRINTERS, Jewish
Marx, Alexander. Some Notes on the Use of Hebrew Type in Non-Hebrew Books, 1475-1520. 381-408, EAME

PRINTERS - Mainz
RUPP

PRINTERS' MARKS - Germany
Claus, Helmut. Migration von Bild-

stöcken bei den Leipziger Buchdruckern in der Frühen Reformationszeit. 63-81, LÜLF
Collijn, Isak Gustaf Alfred. Die Wanderung eines Druckerzeichens. Zu GfT 785-786. 74-79, HAEB

PRINTERS - New York (City)

Granniss, Ruth Shepard. The New York Printers and the Celebration of the French Revolution of 1830. 193-202, EAME

PRINTERS, Swedish

Waldén, Bertil. Verner von Heidenstam Som Målare. 71-106, ÖREB

PRINTING
see also Bookmaking; Music printing

PRINTING

Aliprandi, Giuseppe. Aspetti Particolari della Grafia. 39-46, GALL

PRINTING - Austria - Hist. - 16th cent

Wonisch, Othmar. Leonhard Höfler und Seine Stiftung zum Blutigen Kreuz in Leibnitz. 343-363, SCHT

PRINTING - Bamberg - Hist.

Müller, Max. *Casus Synodales*. Ein Bisher Unbekannter Bamberger Incunabeldruck. 40-44, VERZ
Wirth, Georg. Die Druckerei der Bamberger Fürstbischöfe—die Erste "Staatsdruckerei." 383-389, STOL

PRINTING - Basel - Hist.

Husner, Fritz. Die Editio Princeps des "Corpus Historiae Byzantinae." Johannes Oporin, Hieronymus Wolf und die Fugger. 143-162, SCHU
Rest, Josef. Das Basler Missale vom Jahre 1586. 207-212, LEID

PRINTING - Berlin - Hist.

Krause, Heinrich. Die Drucklegung der Andriaausgabe Joh. Agricolas. 131-136, SCHW

PRINTING - Bern - Hist.

Jacot, L. Réminiscences Typographiques. 152-155, LÜTH

PRINTING - Birmingham, Eng. - Hist.

Bockwitz, Hans H. Baskerville im Urteil Deutscher Zeitgenossen. III, 250-253, GLAU

PRINTING - Blind impressions - 15th cent.

Lydenberg, H. M. More Blind Impressions: With Light Therefrom? 601-613, WILS

PRINTING - Bulgaria - Hist.

T͡Sonchev, Petŭr T. Kŭm Istorii͡ata na Edna Bŭlgarska Pechatnit͡sa v T͡Sarigrad. 146-149, TEOB

PRINTING - Cagli, Italy - Hist.

Vichi Santovito, Nella. Una Correzione al Reichling ed Alcune Notizie sulla Stampa di Cagli. 215-220, ACCU

PRINTING - Cairo - Hist. - 1566

Cowley, A. E. Ein Soncino-Druck aus Kairo 1566. 89-90, FREN

PRINTING - California - Hist.

Cate, Chester March. The First California Laws Printed in English. 331-336, EAME

PRINTING - Cambridge, Mass. - Hist.

Wroth, Lawrence C. The Cambridge Press. 498-524, LYDE

PRINTING - Canada - Hist.

Tremaine, Marie. A Half-Century of Canadian Life and Print, 1751-1800. 371-390, WROT

PRINTING - Central Europe - Hist.

Gollub, H. Die Beiden Buchdrucker und Erzpriester Maletius. 159-180, KÖNI

PRINTING - Central Europe - Hist. - 15th cent.

Crous, Ernst. Die Anfänge des Antiquadrucks in Deutschland und Seinen Nachbarländern. 33-42, LOUB

PRINTING - China - Hist.

Iwamura, Shinobu. Tenri Toshokan Zō Shigen Tsukoho Sho. (On the Bank Note of the *Chin-yüan* Era in the *Yüan* Dynasty in the Tenri Central Library.) 339-343, TOMI
Kaneko, Kazumasa. *Kintei Bueiden Shuchin-ban Teishiki*. (Japanese Translation of: *Ching-tin Wu-ying-tien chü-ch'en-pan Ch'eng-shih*: "Brief Explanation of the Printing Process by Movable Types in the *Wu-ying-tien* Editions.") 409-434, TOMI

PRINTING - Cologne - Hist.

Schmidt, Adolf. Lippische Ablaßbriefe. 227-233, SCHW

PRINTING - Cologne - Hist. - 16th cent.

Corsten, Severin. Zur Person des Kölner Druckers Cornelius von Zierickzee. 9-17, JUCR

PRINTING - Czechoslovakia

Kabát, Karel. Typologické Badání. 115-117, EMLE

PRINTING - Czechoslovakia - Hist. - 16th cent.

Zuman, František. První Českobratrský Bělský Tisk. 212-218, ŽIVN

PRINTING - Erfurt - Hist.

Hase, Martin von. Zwei Drucke des Temporals des Johannes Regiomontanus von Wolfgang Stürmer in Erfurt. I, 61-66, GLAU

PRINTING - Erfurt - Hist. - 15th cent.

Voulliéme, Ernst. Zur Geschichte Einiger Erfurter Typen des XV. Jahrhunderts. 261-265, SCHW

PRINTING - Erfurt - Hist. - 16th cent.

Luther, Johannes. Ludwig Trutebul und die Druckerei "Zum Färbefaß" in Erfurt. 185-195, SCHW

PRINTING - Europe - Hist. - 16th cent.

Collijn, Isak Gustaf Alfred. Några Ord om Böcker Tryckta på Svenska i Utlandet under 1500-Talet. Med Anledning av ett till Universitetsbiblioteket i Oslo Gjort Nyförvärv. 23-29, MUNT

PRINTING - Europe - Hist. - 17th-19th cent.

Kawai, Tadanobu. Yoroppa ni okeru Printing Equipment ni tsuite. (On the Printing Equipment Used in Europe, 17th-19th Centuries.) 497-502, TOMI

PRINTING - Finland - Hist. - 1905

Donner, Kai. Tryckalster från Storstrejken. 164-169, HULA

PRINTING - France - Hist. - 15th-16th cent.

Beaulieux, Ch. Manuscrits et Imprimés en France XVe et XVIe Siècles. 417-428, CHAT
Högberg, Paul. Une Édition Rarissime du Roman de la Rose dans la Bibliothèque de L'Université Royale d'Uppsala. 268-291, UPPS

PRINTING - France - Hist. - 16th cent.

Seguin, Jean-Pierre. Faits Divers Sensationnels dans Seize Bulletins d'Information Imprimés en France, pendant le Règne de François Ier. 65-79, CALO

PRINTING - Friesland - Hist. - 15th cent.

Kruitwagen, B. De Freeska Landriucht-Drukkerij. 45-69, HAGU

PRINTING - Germany - Hist.

Luther, Arthur. Russische Dichter in Deutschen Künstlerischen Drucken. 75-79, BOCK

PRINTING - Germany - Hist. - 15th cent.

Badalić, Josip. Die Deutschen Offizinen in den Wiegendrucksammlungen Jugoslawiens. 31-37, SCHT
Crous, Ernst. Die Anfänge des Antiquadrucks in Deutschland und Seinen Nachbarländern. 33-42, LOUB
Molitor, Karl. Zur Druckergeschichte des XV. Jahrhunderts. 205-209, SCHW

PRINTING - Germany - Hist. - 15th-16th cent.

Wehmer, Carl. Mit Gemäl und Schrift. Kaiser Maximilian I. und der Buchdruck. 244-275, HOFF

PRINTING - Germany - Hist. - 16th-18th cent.

Crous, Ernst. Schrift und Satz im Berliner Buchdruck von der Mitte des 16. bis zur Mitte des 18. Jahrhunderts. Ein Beitrag zur Geschichte des Deutschen Buchstils in Wenig Bekannter Zeit. 37-45, LEID

PRINTING - Halifax, Nova Scotia - Hist.

Bishop, Olga Bernice. The First Printing Press in Canada, 1751-1800. 129-148, GJEL

PRINTING - Hamburg - Hist.

Braun, Hellmut. Der Hamburger Koran von 1694. 149-166, TIEM

PRINTING - Hist.
see also Printers' marks

PRINTING - Hist.

Braun, Hellmut. Der Hamburger Koran von 1694. 149-166, TIEM
Gardberg, Carl-Rudolf. Ur Paradsidornas Historia. Från Barock till Nyklassicism. 31-41, DAHA
Marx, Alexander. Some Notes on the Use of Hebrew Type in Non-Hebrew Books, 1475-1520. 381-408, EAME

PRINTING - Hist. - 15th cent.

Bühler, Curt F. Roman Types and Roman Printing in the Fifteenth Century. 101-110, WEHM

PRINTING - Hist. - 15th-17th cent.

Juchhoff, Rudolf. Aus der Werkstatt der Frühdruckforschung. 119-129, TIEM

PRINTING - Istanbul - Hist.
TSonchev, Petŭr T. Kŭm Istoriiata na Edna Bŭlgarska Pechatnitsa v TSarigrad. 146-149, TEOB

PRINTING - Italy - Hist.
Cutolo, Alessandro. Due Momenti Essenziali nella Storia del Libro in Italia. 311-323, GALL

PRINTING - Italy - Hist. - 16th cent.
Campana, Augusto. Osservazione sullo Stampatore Nicolò Brenta da Varenna. 57-64, GREG

PRINTING - Italy - Hist. - 18th cent.
Moneti, Elena Amico. L'Attività di una Tipografia Lucchese nel Settecento. 27-55, FERR

PRINTING - Japan - Hist.
Arai, Toshi. Kirishitan-ban no Shuppan to Sono Shūhen, I. (Publication of the Jesuit Printings in Japan and Related Problems, 16th-17th Centuries, Part I.) 45-59, TOMI
Araki, Toyosaburō. Ōsaka Hōmen no Fudazukai to Ginsatsu Hangi no Kosho. (Circulation of Bank Notes in the Osaka Area and the Wood-Blocks Used for Printing Them in the Edo Period.) 211-220, TOMI
Kabutogi, Shokyo. Heian Jidai no Kaihan. (Buddhist Sutras Printed during the Heian Period, 11th-13th Centuries.) 35-43, TOMI
Oda, Takeo. Tenri Toshokan Zō Vopell no Chikyugi ni tsuite. (Vopell's Terrestrial Globe, Printed with Wood-Blocks, Dated 1536.) 449-462, TOMI
Ouchida, Sadao. Tenri Toshokan Zō Moku-Katsuji Ban Shomoku Kō. (Check List of Japanese Printed Books in Movable Types of the Late Edo Period in the Tenri Central Library.) 295-305, TOMI
Tanaka, Kaido. Hyakumantō Darani Moji Kō. (Study of the Types Used in the Dharani in the Million Pagodas, 8th Century.) 25-34, TOMI

PRINTING - Jews - Hist.
Bamberger, S. Trennungsstrich, Fragezeichen und Ausrufungszeichen im Hebräischen Buchdruck. 109-110, FREN
——— Wandsbeker Druckperiode des Israel ben Abraham 1726 bis 1733. 101-108, FREN
Brilling, Bernhard. Die Jüdische Buchdruckerei in Auras (Niederschlesien). 97-100, FREN
M. C. Zur Geschichte des Hebräischen Buchdruckes in Russland und Polen. 91-96, FREN

PRINTING - Kentucky - Hist.
Thompson, Lawrence S. Printing and Collections of Printing in Kentucky. 508-514, RANG

PRINTING - Korea - Hist.
Nakamura, Hidetaka. Chosen-ban Kohan Insatsu ni tsuite. (On Early Korean Printed Books.) 375-386, TOMI

PRINTING - Legibility
see Legibility

PRINTING - Leipzig - Hist. - 18th cent.
Volkmann, Ludwig. Nachricht von dem Drucke einer Poetischen Bilderbibel. III, 235-242, GLAU

PRINTING - Lucca - Hist.
Moneti, Elena Amico. L'Attività di una Tipografia Lucchese nel Settecento. 27-55, FERR

PRINTING - Luxemburg - Hist.
Vekené, Emil van der. Die Anfänge der Buchdruckerkunst in Luxemburg. Mathias Birthon (1598-1604). 434-444, BENZ

PRINTING - Lyon - Hist. - 15th cent.
Rath, Erich von. Der Drucker von Buyers Ausgabe der Werke des Bartolus von 1482. Ein Beitrag zur Buchdruckergeschichte Lyons. 217-225, SCHW

PRINTING - Mainz - Hist.
RUPP
Schwenke, Paul. Die Mainzer Donatdrucke der Staatsbibliothek. 31-36, HARN

PRINTING - Maryland - Hist.
Wyllie, John Cook. The First Maryland Tract: A Reconsideration of the Date of Printing of the Maryland Charter. 475-483, WROT

PRINTING - Massachusetts - Hist.
Farrand, Max. William H. Whitmore and the Early Printed Laws of Massachusetts. 146-150, PUTN

PRINTING - Milan - Hist.
Santoro, Caterina. Due Contratti di Lavoro per L'Arte della Stampa a Milano. 185-192, ACCU

PRINTING - Mładziejowice, Poland - Hist.

Budka, Włodzimierz. Papiernia w Młodziejowicach. 199-210, PIEK

PRINTING - Moscow - Hist.

Horodisch, Abraham. Die Anfänge des Buchdrucks in Moskau. 208-225, BENZ

PRINTING - Münster - Hist.

Crous, Ernst. Münster i.W. und der Wiegendruck. 107-121, HAEB

PRINTING - Murcia - Hist.

Guarnaschelli, Teresa. Alfonso Fernandez da Cordova e la Prima Stampa di Murcia. 125-132, ACCU

PRINTING - Netherlands - Hist. - 15th cent.

Alblas, J. De Nederlandsche Incunabelen der Universiteitsbibliotheek. 33-36, SOME

PRINTING - New York (City) - Hist.

Hewlett, Leroy. James Rivington, Tory Printer. 165-194, GJEL

PRINTING - New York (State) - Hist.

Vail, R. W. G. A Patriotic Pair of Peripatetic Printers, the Up-State Imprints of John Holt and Samuel Loudon, 1776-1783. 391-422, WROT

PRINTING - Norway - Hist.

Sollied, P. R. Relationer fra Christiania, Bergen og Trondhjem om Smaae Piecers Censur. 91-105, OSLN

PRINTING - Nuremberg - Hist. - 16th cent.

Schottenloher, Karl. Hans Sachs und Hieronymus Höltzel. Ein Beitrag zur Geschichte der Nürnberger Flugschriften vom Jahre 1524. 235-255, SCHW

PRINTING - Padua - Hist.

Fantini, Bianca Saraceni. Prime Indagini sulla Stampa Padovana del Cinquecento. 415-485, FERR

PRINTING - Paris - Hist.

Colmi, Elsbet. Thomas Kees Wesaliensis. Aus der Werkstatt eines Weseler Druckers in Paris 1507-1515/16. 68-97, BENZ
Hofer, Philip. Adrian Le Roy and Robert Ballard: Printers of the Late Renaissance. 475-482, LYDE
Hunger, Herbert. Die Druckvorlage der Editio Princeps des Anonymus Neobarii. 46, STUM
Lerch, Alice H. Who Was the Printer of Jefferson's Notes? 44-56, LYDE
Wilmerding, Lucius. Le Prince, by Jean Louis Guez de Balzac: Note on a Paris Printing, 1631. 489-497, LYDE

PRINTING - Pavia - Hist.

Leporace, Tullia Gasparrini. Notizie e Documenti Inediti sul Tipografo Antonio Carcano (1475-1525). 327-356, FERR

PRINTING - Poland, Hist.

Jasińska, Stanisława. Czy Jan z Sącza Mógł Być Drukarzem Poznańskim? 341-353, GRYC
M. C. Zur Geschichte des Hebräischen Buchdruckes in Russland und Polen. 91-96, FREN

PRINTING - Prague - Hist.

Wharton, Leonard C. Brief Notes of Prague Printed Books in the British Museum. 42-45, EMLE

PRINTING - Presses - Hist.

Bengtsson, Bengt. Boktryckets "Gamla" och "Nya" Metoder på 1700-Talet. 33-44, GARD
Lodi, Teresa. La Vera Storia di un Presunto Cimelio Cinquecentesco (Il Cosiddetto Torchio della Biblioteca Medicea Orientale). 234-253, GREG
Morison, Stanley. The Learned Press as an Institution. 153-179, WEHM

PRINTING - Presses - New Haven, Conn.

Reid, Winnifred Reynolds. Beginnings of Printing in New Haven. From Letters of Benjamin Franklin and James Parker. 67-88, KEOG

PRINTING - Presses - Rouen

Verwey, H. de la Fontaine. Une Presse Secrète du XVIe Siècle: Abel Clémence, Imprimeur à Rouen. 81-89, CALO

PRINTING - Providence, R.I. - Hist.

Swan, Bradford F. The First Printing in Providence. 365-369, WROT

PRINTING - Rome (City) - Hist.

Barberi, Francesco. Le Edizioni Romane di Francesco Minizio Calvo. 57-98, FERR
Degering, Hermann. Wer War der Drucker der Erstausgabe des Vitruv? Ein Beitrag zur Geschichte des Römischen Buchdrucks. 175-202, HAEB

PRINTING - Russia - Hist.

M. C. Zur Geschichte des Hebräischen

Buchdruckes in Russland und Polen. 91-96, FREN

PRINTING - Specimens

RUPP

PRINTING - Specimens - Collections - Kentucky

Thompson, Lawrence S. Printing and Collections of Printing in Kentucky. 508-514, RANG

PRINTING - Stockholm - Hist.

Dahlberg, Ragnar. Bidrag till den Svenska Reformationstidens Bibliografi. 58-70, HULA

PRINTING - Strasbourg - Hist.

Baillet, Lina. Le Premier Manuel de Grec Paru à Strasbourg. 25-36, BENZ
Juchhoff, Rudolf. Johann und Konrad von Paderborn. Die Anfänge Ihrer Druckertätigkeit in Venedig und Strassburg. 211-227, BÖME
Voulliéme, Ernst. Peter Attendorn, ein Buchhändler und Drucker in Straβburg um 1490. 344-353, MILF

PRINTING - Sweden - Hist.

Ågren, Sven. Till Arkivleveransernas Historia. Några Anteckningar. 338-349, GRAP

PRINTING - Sweden - Hist. - 15th-16th cent.

Collijn, Isak Gustaf Alfred. Schwedische Donate. 47-52, SCHW

PRINTING - Switzerland - Hist.

Lange, Eugenie. Schweizer Drucke in Russischer Sprache. 68-76, BERU

PRINTING - U.S. - Hist.

EAME

Marino, Samuel J. French-Language Printing in the United States, 1711-1825. 43-62, GJEL

PRINTING - U.S. - Hist. - 18th cent.

Eames, Wilberforce. On the Use of Hebrew Types in English America before 1735. 481-502, FREI

PRINTING - U.S. - Hist. - 19th cent.

Keys, Thomas E. Some American Medical Imprints of the Nineteenth Century. 309-318, DOEJ

PRINTING - Uppsala - Hist.

Collijn, Isak Gustaf Alfred. Paul Grijs, Uppsalas Förste Boktryckare 1510-1519. 97-138, UPPS
Dahlberg, Ragnar. Helsingfors Universitetsbiblioteks Exemplar af Psalterium Dauidis 1510. 140-144, HULA

PRINTING - Uraz, Poland - Hist.

Brilling, Bernhard. Die Jüdische Buchdruckerei in Auras (Niederschlesien). 97-100, FREN

PRINTING - Valais (Canton) - Hist. - 15th cent.

Meyer, Wilhelm Joseph. Die Ersten für das Wallis Gedruckten Bücher im 15. Jahrhundert. 83-90, GODE

PRINTING - Venice - Hist.

Juchhoff, Rudolf. Johann und Konrad von Paderborn. Die Anfänge Ihrer Druckertätigkeit in Venedig und Strassburg. 211-227, BÖME
Leicht, Pier Silverio. L'Editore Veneziano Michele Tramezino ed i Suoi Privilegi. 357-367, FERR

PRINTING - Vermont - Hist.

Rugg, Harold Goddard. Isaac Eddy, Printer-Engraver. Bibliography of Eddy Publications. 313-329, EAME

PRINTING - Vianen, Netherlands - Hist. - 16th cent.

Verwey, H. de la Fontaine. Over Enige Boeken te Vianen Gedrukt Tijdens het 'Voorspel.' 20-34, KOSS

PRINTING - Vicenza - Hist.

Cristofari, Maria. La Tipografia Vicentina nel Secolo XVI. 191-214, FERR

PRINTING - Wandsbek, Ger. - Hist.

Bamberger, S. Wandsbeker Druckperiode des Israel ben Abraham 1726 bis 1733. 101-108, FREN

PRINTING - Wittenberg - Hist. - 16th cent.

Luther, Johannes. Drucker- und Verlegernöte in Wittenberg zur Zeit des Schmalkaldischen Krieges. 229-243, MILF

PRINTING - Yugoslavia - Hist. - 15th cent.

Badalič, Josip. Inkunabelforschungen in Jugoslawien. 13-15, STUM

Prinzhorn, Fritz.
Eigenart und Bedeutung der Parlaments- und Behördenbibliotheken. 293-307, JUCH
Rationalisierung im Bibliotheks-, Buch- und Zeitschriftenwesen. 327-332, KUHN

PRISMA - Lectuurvoorlichting

Nuiver, J. A. Centrale Boekbespreking voor de Openbare Bibliotheken. 552-558, BRUM

PRIVATE LIBRARIES
see also Book collecting

PRIVATE LIBRARIES

Blum, Rudolf. Bibliotheca Memmiana. Untersuchungen zu Gabriel Naudés "Advis pour Dresser une Bibliothèque." 209-232, WEHM
Lange, H. O. De Hollandske Bogauktioner i Deres Første Halve Aarhundrede. 179-194, ANNE
Nohrström, Holger. Några Krigsbytesböcker från Åbo Akademibiblioteks Grundläggningstid i Helsingfors Universitetsbibliotek. 69-81, HULT
Pötzl, Eduard. Der Bibliothekssport. 254-257, GLOS

PRIVATE LIBRARIES - Alsace

Knod, Gustav C. Aus der Bibliothek des Beatus Rhenanus. Second Book, 1-109, SCHL

PRIVATE LIBRARIES - Assyria

Meissner, Bruno. Wie Hat Assurbanipal Seine Bibliothek Zusammengebracht? 244-248, MILF

PRIVATE LIBRARIES - Austria

Adamovich, Ludwig. Zur Frage des Rechtsschutzes für Private Bibliotheken. 203-207, BICK
Ankwicz-Kleehoven, Hans. Die Bibliothek des Dr. Johann Cuspinian. 208-227, BICK
Berlstein, Alfred. Bibliotekarz i Pracownik Naukowy. 41-46, SZAC
Ecker, Karl. Die Sammlung Stefan Zweig. 321-330, BICK
Gerstinger, Hans. Johannes Sambucus als Handschriftensammler. 251-400, VIEN

PRIVATE LIBRARIES - Canada

FRAN

PRIVATE LIBRARIES - Catalogs - 1353

Molitor, Karl. Ein Westfälischer Bibliotheks-Katalog von 1353. 301-314, MÜNS

PRIVATE LIBRARIES - Catalogs - 15th cent.

Mercati, Angelo. La Biblioteca Privata e gli Arredi di Cappella di Gregorio XII. 128-165, EHRE
Ruf, Paul. Eine Altbayerische Gelehrtenbibliothek des 15. Jahrhunderts und Ihr Stifter Bernhard von Kraiburg. 219-239, STOL

PRIVATE LIBRARIES - Catalogs - 1501

Guidi, Pietro. Pietro Demetrio Guazzelli da Lucca il Primo Custode della Biblioteca Vaticana (1481-1511) e L'Inventario dei Suoi Libri. 192-218, EHRE

PRIVATE LIBRARIES - Catalogs - [16th cent.]

Knod, Gustav C. Aus der Bibliothek des Beatus Rhenanus. Second Book, 1-109, SCHL

PRIVATE LIBRARIES - Catalogs - 16th cent.

Schwarz, F. Analyse eines Kataloges. 326-338, KÖNI
Traut, Hermann. Dr. Adolf von Glauburg und Seine Bibliothek. 1-34, EBRA

PRIVATE LIBRARIES - Denmark

Dahl, Svend. Friedrich Münter und Seine Bibliothek. 291-305, BICK
Grundtvig, Vilh. Almindelig Historie. 11-51, AARU
Petersen, Carl S. Dronning Sophie Amalies Bogsamling. 231-247, COLL
Walde, O. Henrik Rantzaus Bibliotek och Dess Öden. 239-250, ANNE

PRIVATE LIBRARIES - Ermland

Brachvogel, Eugen, Monsignore. Die Bibliotheken der Geistlichen Residenzen des Ermlandes. 35-44, KÖNI

PRIVATE LIBRARIES - Europe

Czumpelik, Rudolf. Kardinal Passionei und Seine Beziehungen zu Prinz Eugen. 23-24, STUM
Mondolfo, Anita. La Biblioteca Landau-Finaly. 265-285, GREG

PRIVATE LIBRARIES - Finland

Carlsson, A. B. Rester av Michael Agricolas Boksamling i Svenska Bibliotek. 335-353, COLL
Dahlberg, Ragnar. En Volym ur Michael Agricolas Boksamling. 57-70, SCHA
Grönroos, Henrik. Då Böckerna Bytte Ägare. Bokauktioner i Åbo under "Hertiginnans av Finland" tid. 92-108, GÅRD
———— Om Böcker och Bokägare i Finland för 200 År Sedan. 1-15, NYBE
Lunelund-Grönroos, Birgit. Gymnasister och Böcker i det Gamla Borgå. 51-58, NYBE
Mickwitz, Ann-Mari. Kejsaren och den Gamla Kartan. 59-65, NYBE
Mustonen, Aarne. Kaukoidän Kirjatietoa. 66-77, NYBE

Nohrström, Holgar. Några Anteckningar Kring den s. k. Pälkäne-Abcboken. 341-354, HIRN
Nyberg, Paul. Dedikationerna i Zachris Topelii Bibliotek. 145-163, HULA
———— Några Anmärkningsvärda Böcker i Z. Topelius' Boksamling. 101-117, TUDE
Pipping, Hugo E. Två Bokägarmärken Anbragta Som Rygg- och Pärmstämpel. 1-11, DAHL

PRIVATE LIBRARIES - France

Arrighi, Marie. La Bibliothèque de L'Empereur Napoléon à Sainte-Hélène. 55-65, BONN
Bonnerot, Jean. Sainte-Beuve Bibliophile. 369-374, CALO
Collijn, Isak Gustaf Alfred. Journal de Voyage en Scandinavie d'un Bibliophile Français. 187-199, GODE
Coyecque, Ern. Guillaume Larcher, Bibliothécaire du Cabinet Henri IV. 129-132, GODE
Foncin, Myriem. L'Histoire d'une Collection de Cartes Réunies pour Louis XIV. 119-126, CALO
Jallut, Marguerite. Les Bibliothèques de Marie-Antoinette. 325-332, CALO
Kraemer, Erik von. En Bibliofiliens Storman. Antoine-René de Voyer d'Argenson, Markis av Paulmy. 182-196, DAHL
Lelièvre, Pierre. La Bibliothèque de Richard Mique, Architecte de la Reine Marie-Antoinette. 333-336, CALO
Piquard, Maurice. La Bibliothèque d'un Homme d'Etat au XVIe Siècle. 227-235, CALO
Wagner, Henry R. Hispanic Americana in the John Carter Brown Library. 423-455, WROT

PRIVATE LIBRARIES - Germany

Assmann, Karl. Die Anfänge der Sächsischen Landesbibliothek. 15-25, DREL
Balcke, Curt. Heinrich Friedrich von Diez und Sein Vermächtnis in der Preussischen Staatsbibliothek. 187-200, KUHN
Becker, Josef. Die Bibliothek des Zacharias Konrad von Uffenbach. 129-148, LEYG
Bogeng, G. A. E. Über Zacharias Conrad von Uffenbachs Erfahrungen und Erlebnisse bei der Benutzung Deutscher, Englischer, Holländischer Öffentlicher Büchersammlungen in den Jahren 1709-1711. 30-46, SCHW
Bollert, Martin. Johann Joachim Winckelmann als Bibliothekar des Grafen Bünau. 19-24, LEID
Dahlberg, Ragnar. Två Böcker med Märklig Proveniens i Helsingfors Universitetsbibliotek. 127-136, SCHA
Darmstaedter, Ludwig. Die Dokumentensammlung Darmstaedter und Ihr Übergang an die Preussische Staatsbibliothek. 167-169, HARN
Deetjen, Werner. Wielands Bibliothek. 1-10, WAHL
Degering, Hermann. Gottfried von Raesfeld. Sein Geschlecht, Sein Leben und Sein Testament. 137-250, MÜNS
Diesch, Carl. Fürst Boguslav Radziwill und Seine Bücherschenkung an die Königsberger Schlossbibliothek. 117-128, LEYG
———— Crotus Rubeanus im Dienste des Herzogs Albrecht. 45-61, KÖNI
Frey, Theophil. Nicolaus Ochsenbach, der Kunstliebende und -Sammelnde Schlosshauptmann auf Hohen-Tübingen (1562-1626). 407-427, LEYG
Fromm, Emil. Die Dante-Sammlung der Alfred von Reumont'schen Bibliothek. 94-141, (pt. 1), AACH
———— Geschichte der Stadtbibliothek. I. Die Rathshandbibliothek im 17. und 18. Jahrhundert. II. Die Dautzenbergsche Schenkung. III. Die Stadtbibliothek von Ihrer Eröffnung (1831) bis zum J. 1889. IV. Die Verwaltung der Stadtbibliothek seit dem J. 1889. 21-48, (pt. 1), AACH
Geissler, Paul. Zwei Unbekannte Holzschnittprobedrucke zum Theuerdank und Konrad Peutinger. 118-128, JUCH
Husung, Max Joseph. Joseph Niesert. Aus dem Leben eines Gelehrten Westfälischen Büchersammlers. 119-124, BÖME
Juchhoff, Rudolf. Die Büchersammlung des Generalpostmeisters von Nagler in der Preußischen Staatsbibliothek. 201-208, KUHN
Juntke, Fritz. Die Öffentlichen Bibliotheken in Königsberg in Preussen im 17. Jahrhundert. 288-293, KUHN
Kimmenauer, Alfred. Colmarer Beriana. Zu Ludwig Ber's Bibliothek und Papieren. 244-251, BENZ
Küster, A. Die Juristische Abteilung der Königlichen Universitäts-Bibliothek zu Münster. 268-300, MÜNS
Kuhnert, Ernst. Die Nova Bibliotheca des Herzogs Albrecht. 209-219, MILF
Kyriss, Ernst. Der Altdorfer Professor Georg Siegel als Büchersammler. 117-124, STOL
Lehmann, Paul. Aus der Bibliothek des Reformators Johannes Hessius. 101-124, LEYH
———— Aus einer Münchner Büchersammlung des Ausgehenden Mittelalters. 157-164, LEID
Leskien, Elfriede. Johann Gottlob Böhme, ein Leipziger Bücherfreund des 18. Jahrhunderts. 69-79, LEIP

Molitor, Karl. Ein Westfälischer Bibliotheks-Katalog von 1353. 301-314, MÜNS
Nidecker, Heinrich. Wilhelm Wackernagel. Bücher und Freunde. Ein Streifzug durch Seine Bibliothek. 177-191, SCHU
Reinhard, Ewald. I. H. von Wessenberg als Freund der Schönen Künste. 59-63, VERD
Rhodes, Dennis E. Konrad Stepeck of Nuremberg (c. 1424-c. 1495). 311-316, BENZ
Rohrbach, Peter P. Fachabteilungen und Sondersammlungen. 42-47, BERR
Ruf, Paul. Eine Altbayerische Gelehrtenbibliothek des 15. Jahrhunderts und Ihr Stifter Bernhard von Kraiburg. 219-239, STOL
Schmidt, Adolf. Baron Hüpsch in Köln als Inkunabelnsammler und Händler. 45-63, HAEB
——— Kölnische Einbände des Vierzehnten Jahrhunderts in der Amploniana zu Erfurt. 401-409, COLL
Schmidt, Christel. Aus der Sammlung Olga Hirsch: Ein Kreisrunder Einband von Caspar Meuser. 194-198, LOUB
Schmieder, Wolfgang. Johann Gottlob Immanuel Breitkopfs Privatbibliothek. Werden und Vergehen. II, 73-87, GLAU
Schreiber, Heinrich. Ein Erlanger Bibliothekenkenner des 18. Jahrhunderts: Friedrich Karl Gottlob Hirsching. 62-67, VERZ
Stoetzer, Walter. Die Kekulé-Bibliothek als Hilfsmittel der Dokumentation in der Chemischen Industrie. 130-135, LEUN
Traut, Hermann. Dr. Adolf von Glauburg und Seine Bibliothek. 1-34, EBRA
Tyszko, Oskar. Die Bestandsvermehrung der Hauptabteilung und Ihre Organisation. I, 89-129. BERS
Wand, Albert. Zur Geschichte der Dortmunder Bibliotheken. 29-58, VERD
Warda, Arthur. Die Exlibris des Herzogs Albrecht von Preussen. 349-354, KÖNI
Werhahn, Heinz Martin. Die Bücher des Dr. Peter Rinck. 181-188, JUCR
Wermke, Ernst. Friedrich August Gotthold und Seine Bibliothek. 354-373, KÖNI

PRIVATE LIBRARIES - Gt. Brit.

Granniss, Ruth Shepard. Thomas Britton. 196-202, LYDE
Hollaender, Albert E. J. Ein Unveröffentlichter Augenzeugenbericht über Napoleon I. an Bord des "Bellerophon" im Kriegshafen von Plymouth, Juli-August 1815. 44-45, STUM
Jackson, William A. Tunc et Nunc: or the Pepys and Taylor Collections of Early English Books on Navigation. 195-201, WROT
Roth, Cecil. Catalogue of Manuscripts in the Roth Collection. 503-535, MARX
Schunke, Ilse. Die Italienischen Einbände aus der Hamilton-Sammlung in Berlin. 17-32, LÜLF

PRIVATE LIBRARIES - Greece, Ancient

Comparetti, D. La Bibliothèque de Philodème. 118-129, CHAT

PRIVATE LIBRARIES - Hist. - Middle Ages

De Ghellinck, Joseph. En Marge des Catalogues des Bibliothèques Médiévales. 331-363, EHRE

PRIVATE LIBRARIES - Hungary

Scheiber, Alexander. Piyyutim from the Geniza Collection of David Kaufmann. 537-546, MARX

PRIVATE LIBRARIES - Italy

Guidi, Pietro. Pietro Demetrio Guazzelli da Lucca il Primo Custode della Biblioteca Vaticana (1481-1511) e L'Inventario dei Suoi Libri. 192-218, EHRE
Laurent, M.-H. Guillaume des Rosières et la Bibliothèque Pontificale à L'Époque de Clément VI. 579-603, PELZ
Leicht, P. S. La Biblioteca d'un Umanista. 77-81, GODE
Leyh, Georg. Die Camera della Segnatura—ein Bibliotheksraum? 171-177, LEID
Mariutti De Sánchez Rivero, Angela. Il Carteggio Inedito del Legato Araujo. 369-382, FERR
Mercati, Angelo. La Biblioteca Privata e gli Arredi di Cappella di Gregorio XII. 128-165, EHRE
Mercati, Giovanni, Cardinal. A Proposito dei Codici Naniani Greci 32 e 37. 280-285, GREE
Mondolfo, Anita. La Biblioteca Landau-Finaly. 265-285, GREG
Peebles, Bernard M. The Bibliotheca Albana Urbinas as Represented in the Library of the Catholic University of America. 327-352, ALBA
Roth, Cecil. A Seventeenth Century Library and Trousseau. 160-169, FREI
Ruysschaert, José. Recherche des Deux Bibliothèques Romaines Maffei des XVe et XVIe Siècles. 306-355, MERG
Schwarz, F. Analyse eines Kataloges. 326-338, KÖNI

PRIVATE LIBRARIES - Japan

Haenisch, Wolf. Die Kanazawa Bunko, eine Japanische Bibliotheksgründung des 13. Jahrhunderts. 271-280, JUCH
Ishii, Munetsugu. Ōhashi Toshokan ni

Kisō Seraretaru Nidai Seijika no Iaisho ni tsuite. (On the Collections Prized by the Late Two Statesmen which Were Donated to the Ōhashi Library.) 90-104, (part 1), OHAS
Miyake, Takashi, ed. Zaidan Hōjin Ōhashi Toshokan Nenpyō. (A Chronological Table of the Ōhashi Library, a Private Library.) 33-61, TSUB
Naito, Torajiro. Kansei Jidai no Zōshoka Ichihashi Shimosa no Kami. (On Lord Ichihashi Shimosa, a Book Collector of the Kansei Period.) 42-69, IMAI

PRIVATE LIBRARIES - Mohammedan countries

Grohmann, Adolf. Bibliotheken und Bibliophilen im Islamischen Orient. 431-442, VIEN

PRIVATE LIBRARIES - Netherlands

Alphen, G. van. Anthony Smets, Bibliothecaris van Drie Prinsen van Oranje (1636-1689). 119-160, HAGU
Brummel, Leendert. The Fagel Library in Trinity College, Dublin. 204-233, BRUE
Bussels, C. M. Over de Bibliotheek en de Kunstwerken van Charles Clement Roemers. 557-566, MAAS
Enelow, H. G. Isaac Belinfante, an Eighteenth Century Bibliophile. 5-30, FREI
Kernkamp, J. H. De Bibliotheek van den Koopman Daniel van der Meulen onder den Hamer. 187-203, EVER
Kronenberg, M. E. Erasmus-Uitgaven A°. 1531 in het Bezit van Kanunnik Mr. Jan Dircsz. van der Haer te Gorkum. 99-117, KOSS
Roelofs, Sjoerdtje. La "Collection Anny Antoine-Louis Koopman" à la Bibliothèque Royale de la Haye. 577-580, BRUM
Tans, J. A. G. Een Uitdagende Utrechtse Collectie: De Val des Pausdoms. 64-77, UTRE
Vermeeren, P. J. H. W. H. J. Baron van Westreenen van Tiellandt als Handschriftenverzamelaar. 603-609, BRUM

PRIVATE LIBRARIES - Norway

Christiansen, Reidar Th. Albrechtsons Visesamling. 106-130, OSLN
Munthe, W. Norske Boksamlere i Eldre Tid. 249-263, COLL
Nygård-Nilssen, Arne. J. B. Halvorsen. 33-56, OSLN
Schaanning, Maja. Litt om Professor Ludvig Daaes Boksamling. 214-225, MUNT
Tank, Roar. Peter Frederik Suhms Forhold til Thomas Angell. 37-41, KJAE
Wiesener, A. M. Bergenske Boksamlere. 254-286, MUNT

PRIVATE LIBRARIES - Poland

Brahmer, Mieczysław. O Bibliotece Pinoccich. 251-265, PIEK
Horodyski, Bogdan. Zarys Dziejów Biblioteki Ord. Zamojskiej. 295-341, PIEK
Lisowski, Stanisław. Do Dziejów Biblioteki Zygmunta Augusta. 241-249, PIEK
Mikulski, Tadeusz. Kniaźnin w Bibliotece Załuskich. 267-281, PIEK
Rudnicka, Jadwiga. Fragment Biblioteki Lompy. 281-306, GRYC

PRIVATE LIBRARIES - Russia

Bogdanovaía, Nadezhda G. Knizhnye Bogatstva Stroganovykh v 1578 g. 277-284, MALE
Il'inskiĭ, L. K. Biblioteka Iv. Mikh. Khvostova; k Istorii Bibliotek XVIII Veka. 346-374, MALE

PRIVATE LIBRARIES - Schleswig-Holstein

Klose, Olaf. Die Privatbibliotheken in Schleswig-Holstein. 256-262, JUCH

PRIVATE LIBRARIES - Silesia

Nentwig, Heinrich. Zwei Schlesische Majoratsbibliotheken. 129-138, WILM

PRIVATE LIBRARIES - South Africa - Hist.

Immelmann, R. F. M. A Contribution to the History of Scholarly Libraries in the Cape Province (before 1920). 25-44, COET

PRIVATE LIBRARIES - Spain

D'Alós, Ramon. Documenti per la Storia della Biblioteca di Alfonso il Magnanimo. 390-422, EHRE
Pons, Antoni. Fra Mario de Passa, Lul-Lista i Bibliòfil. III, 317-337, RUBI

PRIVATE LIBRARIES - Sweden

Ågren, Sven. Om Nordinska Handskriftssamlingen i Uppsala Universitetsbibliotek. Några Anteckningar. 468-497, UPPS
Berg, Gösta and Kurt Jonson. Bouppteckningar från Borgarhem i Stormaktstidens Örebro. 186-240, ÖREB
Dahlberg, Ragnar. Ätten Reuterholms Exlibris. 108-114, HULT
Gierow, Krister. Den Förste Universitetsbibliotekarien i Lund och "Bibliotheca Rostiana." 76-91, GARD
———— Henrik Reuterdahl Som Biblioteksman. 51-76, HEIN
Gobom, Nils. Gustaf Odencrants' E. T. A. Hoffmann-Samling i Linköpings Stifts- och Landsbibliotek. 262-279, GRAP
Gödel, Vilhelm. Erik Sparre. Till His-

torien om Hans Litterära Samlingar. 171-178, ANNE
Grape, Anders. Om Bröderna Salan och Deras Handskriftssamling. 139-170, ANNE
Gren, Erik. Bidrag till Michael Enemans Biografi. Studier och Bokförvärv. 445-494, GRAP
Hallberg, S. Göteborgs Stadsbibliotek. Det Första Halvseclet 1891-1940. 1-142, (first paper), GÖTE
Holmgren, Gustaf. Om Cronstedtska Samlingen i Uppsala Universitetsbibliotek och dess Tillkomst. Några Anteckningar. 519-560, GRAP
Hulth, J. M. Studenten Carolus Linnaeus' Bibliotek. 395-400, COLL
Kleberg, Tönnes. Zwei Stammbuchblätter von Grillparzer in der Universitätsbibliothek Uppsala. 51, STUM
Lagerborg, Rolf. Ur Hecatompolis Suionum. 112-125, HULA
Lundgren, Hjalmar. Carl Bernhard Wadströms Bibliotek. 95-106, GRAP
———— En Uppsala-Biblioteks Donator och dennes Biblioteksplaner. Några Randanmärkningar till ett par Ritningar. 461-467, UPPS
Nivanka, Eino. Amsterdamilainen Fr. Mullerin Antikvariaatti Nordenskiöldin Kirjakokoelman Päähankkijana. 122-133, DAHL
Odler, J. Bignami. Le Fonds de la Reine à la Bibliothèque Vaticane. I, 159-189, ALBB
Palmær, Margit. Mina Bibliotek. 63-70, ÖREB
Rickson, Levi. En Kvartett Bokvänner. 49-62, ÖREB
Uggla, Arvid HJ. Ett Läkarebibliotek från Början av 1700-Talet. 221-248, GRAP
Walde, O. En Svensk Boksamlare från Vasatiden. Hogenskild Bielke och Hans Bibliotek. 193-267, UPPS
———— Om Georg Stiernhielms Bibliotek. Några Anteckningar. 107-141, GRAP
Wistrand, Pär. Mina Bibliotek. 539-547, HJEL

PRIVATE LIBRARIES - Switzerland

Roth, Carl. Conrad Pfister, Basilius Iselin und die Amerbachsche Bibliothek. 179-200, BINZ

PRIVATE LIBRARIES - Turkey

Jacobs, Emil. Büchergeschenke für Sultan Mehemmed II. 20-26, LEYG

PRIVATE LIBRARIES - U.S.

Adams, Randolph G. A Goodly Company of American Book Collectors. 29-32, LYDE
Bay, J. Christian. Private Book Collectors of the Chicago Area: A Brief Review. 363-374, WILS
Jackson, William A. Tunc et Nunc: or the Pepys and Taylor Collections of Early English Books on Navigation. 195-201, WROT

PRIVATE MUSIC LIBRARIES
see Music libraries and collections

PRIVATELY PRINTED BOOKS

Ebert, Otto Erich. Die Privatdrucke und Ihre Pflege in der Deutschen Bücherei. 177-187, LEIS

PRIVATELY PRINTED BOOKS - Acquisitions

Semrau, Eberhard. Die Erwerbung Moderner Bibliophiler Werke. 43-52, REDE

PRIVATELY PRINTED BOOKS - Collections - Leipzig

Rodenberg, Julius. Die Sammlung der Künstlerischen Drucke. 165-176, LEIS

PRIVATELY PRINTED BOOKS - Germany - Bibl.

Ebert, Otto Erich. Aus der Werkstatt von Poeschel & Trepte. Ein Beitrag zur Bibliographie des Deutschen Privatdrucks. 7-37, MIND

PRIVETSTVIIA͡. 39-47, TEOD

PROCESSING
see Technical Services

Procházka, Jan Sv.
Jak Konservovat Kožené Vazby. 218-223, ŽIVN

Procksch, Otto.
Der Hebräische Schreiber und Sein Buch. 1-15, KUHN

PROFESSIONAL LIBRARIES - Norway

Schaanning, Hedvig. Litt om Fagbiblioteker i Norge. 109-118, NORN

PROFESSIONAL RESEARCH
see Research in librarianship

PROFESSIONAL SCHOOL LIBRARIES
see College and university libraries - Departmental and divisional libraries

PROFESSIONAL TRAINING
see Education for librarianship

PROHIBITED BOOKS AND PUBLICATIONS - Collections - Bern

Le Purgatoire. 119, BERU

Prokert, Heinz.
Fünf Briefe J. B. Alxingers an Ch. F. Blankenburg. 221-233, BULL

Propach, Elisabeth.
Die Ausbildung des Nachwuchses in Hamburg. 97-109, HAMB

PROPAGANDA AND THE LIBRARY
see also Library and the state

PROPAGANDA AND THE LIBRARY

Joerden, R. Gefährdetenpädagogik und Volksbücherei. 55-64, ACKE

PROPAGANDA AND THE LIBRARY - Berlin

Gittig, Heinz. Die Gesellschaftswissenschaftliche Beratungsstelle. I, 425-432, BERS

PROPRIETARY LIBRARIES - Basel

BASA

PROPRIETARY LIBRARIES - Gt. Brit. - Hist.

Beckwith, Frank. The Eighteenth-Century Proprietary Library in England. 81-98, OFFO

PROTEVANGELIUM JACOBI
see Bible. Mss. N.T. Apocryphal books. Protevangelium Jacobi

Prou, Maurice.
Supplique et Bulle du XIIIe Siècle. 614-621, CHAT

PROVERBS - Collections - Uppsala

Carlsson, A. B. Fragment av en Ordspråkssamling av Michael Agricola i Uppsala Universitetsbibliotek. 142-146, GRAP

PROVIDENCE, R. I. - Printing
see Printing - Providence, R.I.

PRUDENTIUS CLEMENS, Aurelius. Mss.

Robert, Ulysse. Notice Paléographique sur le Manuscrit de Prudence, N° 8084 du Fonds Latin de la Bibliothèque Nationale. 405-413, GRAU

PRÜM, Ger. (Benedictine abbey). Mss.

Degering, Hermann. Das Prümer Evangeliar (Ms. Lat. Theol. Fol. 733) in Berlin. 132-148, HARN

PRUSSIA. Auskunftsbureau der Deutschen Bibliotheken

Fick, Richard. Das Auskunftsbureau der Deutschen Bibliotheken. 272-277, HARN

PRUSSIA, East - National music
see National music - Prussia, East

Prytz, Johansen J.
Den Gamle Medicinske Katalog på Universitetsbiblioteket, København. 1-7, DAHA

Prytz, Lizzie.
Universitetsbibliotekets Personale 1813-1932. 258-276, OSLO

PSALTERIUM DAUIDIS. Uppsala, 1510

Dahlberg, Ragnar. Helsingsfors Universitetsbiblioteks Exemplar af Psalterium Dauidis 1510. 140-144, HULA

PSALTERIUM FLORIANESE

Birkenmajer, Aleksander. W Sprawie Rejestracji i Katalogowania Opraw Zabytkowych. 105-121, PIEK

PSALTERS

Birkenmajer, Aleksander. W Sprawie Rejestracji i Katalogowania Opraw Zabytkowych. 105-121, PIEK
Brom, A., Jr. Afbeeldingen van Orgels in het Utrechtsche Psalterium. 29-32, SOME
Collijn, Isak Gustaf Alfred. Kalendarium Munkalivense. Ein Schwedisch-Norwegisches Birgittiner-Kalendarium. 82-92, DEGE
Durrieu, Paul. L'Origine du Manuscrit Célèbre Dit le Psautier d'Utrecht. 639-657, HAVE
Hulshof, A. Het Utrechtsche Psalterium. 4-28, SOME

PSALTERS - Stockholm, 1630

Kilpi, Volter. Suomalainen Virsikirja [Manuale-nide] v:lta 1630 Teuvan Kirkonarkistossa. 122-126, SCHA

PSELLUS, MICHAEL, supposed author [Distici]

Festa, N. Nota sui Versiculi in Vitia et Virtutes. 568-576, CERI

Psichari, Jean.
L'Arbre Chantant. 628-633, CHAT

PSYCHIATRIC LIBRARIES
see Medical libraries

PUBBLICAZIONI DI ETTORE STAMPINI. xvii-xxvii, STAM

PUBBLICAZIONI DI LUIGI DE GREGORI. 32-39, GREG

PUBLIC AND THE LIBRARY
see Library and the public

PUBLIC LIBRARIANS

Möhring, Werner. Vom Volksbildneri-

schen Bemühen des Bibliothekars. 61-74, LANF
Schulz, Kurd. Zur Literaturpädagogischen Schulung der Nebenamtlichen Volksbibliothekare. 113-120, ACKE

PUBLIC LIBRARIANS - Bydgoszcz

Podgóreczny, Józef. Byli i Odeszli. 131-138, BYDG
———— Zasłużeni są Wśród Nas. 139-144, BYDG

PUBLIC LIBRARIANS - Germany

Bieber, Hedwig. Die Öffentliche Bücherei als Ausbildungsstätte. Erfahrungen und Anregungen. 75-87, LANF
Heinrich, Gisela. Heutige Probleme der Katalogarbeit und Annotierung in der Öffentlichen Bücherei und deren Bedeutung für die Ausbildung. 88-112, LANF
Hofmann, Gustav. Die Rolle des Gehobenen Mittleren Dienstes in den Deutschen Öffentlichen Wissenschaftlichen Bibliotheken. 43-54, STOL
Reuter, Rudolf. Berufsausbildung des Volksbibliothekars in Deutschland. II, 60-63, GLAU
Troost, Karl. Zur Volksbibliothekarischen Ausbildung an der Büchereischule. 135-156, LANF
Wallraf, Karlheinz. Zur Besprechungsarbeit mit Praktikanten. 113-123, LANF

PUBLIC LIBRARIANS - Gt. Brit.

Haugh, W. S. The Education of Librarians and Information Officers: Public Libraries. 287-290, HUTT

PUBLIC LIBRARIANS - Norway

Andreassen, Anders. Hva Vil det Kreves av Fremtidens Folkebibliotekarer? 113-122, NORS

PUBLIC LIBRARIES
see also Cooperative library systems; Research libraries; State and provincial library agencies - Public library services

PUBLIC LIBRARIES - Aachen

AACH

PUBLIC LIBRARIES - Aarhus, Denmark

Thomsen, Carl, AARH

PUBLIC LIBRARIES - Acquisitions - Germany

Rosin, Hans. Buchwirtschaftliche Konzentrationsbestrebungen im Volksbüchereiwesen. 93-102, ACKE

PUBLIC LIBRARIES - Acquisitions - Sheffield, Eng.

Simpson, E. The War Years. 19-20, LAMB

PUBLIC LIBRARIES - Administration - Germany

Hofmann, Walter. Die Leseordnung in der Volksbücherei. I, 71-79, GLAU

PUBLIC LIBRARIES - Administration - U.S.

Predeek, Albert. Rechtsstellung und Verwaltung der Amerikanischen Public Library. I, 163-175, GLAU

PUBLIC LIBRARIES - Aims and objectives

Joerden, R. Gefährdetenpädagogik und Volksbücherei. 55-64, ACKE
Khurshid, Anis. Public Library and the Development of Its Purpose. 434-440, RANG
Östling, Gösta. Stimulera Individens Strävan. Om Bibliotekens Uppgift i Samhället. 257-269, HEIN
Ranck, Samuel H. Social Service of the Public Library. 365-377, PUTN

PUBLIC LIBRARIES - Aims and objectives - Jena

Reiprich, Alfred. Arbeit und Aufgaben der Ernst-Abbe-Bücherei. 72-104, JENA

PUBLIC LIBRARIES - Aims and objectives - Norway

Kildal, Arne. Fremtidslinjer i Norsk Folkebibliotekvesen. 119-128, NORN

PUBLIC LIBRARIES - Aims and objectives - Sweden

Hjelmqvist, Bengt. Lika Möjligheter till Lån. Fragment av Liktal över Betänkende. 117-126, HEIN

PUBLIC LIBRARIES Architecture and building
see Architecture and building - Public libraries

PUBLIC LIBRARIES - Berlin

BERR

Woita, Irene. Abteilung Allgemeinbildende Bibliotheken. 48-51, BERR

PUBLIC LIBRARIES - Berlin - Hist. - Bibl.

Weser, Adolf. Bibliographie zur Geschichte des Deutschen Volksbüchereiwesens, mit einem Anhang: Die Entwicklung des Berliner Volksbüchereiwesens. 49-80, BERL

PUBLIC LIBRARIES - Berlin - Hist. - 1850-1945

Tyszko, Oskar. Die Entwicklung der Berliner Volksbüchereien von 1850 bis 1945. 7-25, BERL

PUBLIC LIBRARIES - Berlin - Hist. - 1945

Kreuziger, Max. Zur Neuorientierung Unserer Kulturarbeit. 5-6, BERL

PUBLIC LIBRARIES - Berlin - Hist. - 1945-1950

Hauke, Walter. Die Entwicklung der Berliner Volksbüchereien von 1945 bis 1950. 27-48, BERL

PUBLIC LIBRARIES - Berlin - Hist. - 1945-1955

Maurenbrecher, Rolf. Berliner Volksbüchereien 1945-1955. 119-130, SCHS

PUBLIC LIBRARIES - Berlin - Hist. - 1954-1956

Stremlau, Willi and Martin Thilo. Berliner Büchereigesetz und Büchereibau. 183-189, SCHS

PUBLIC LIBRARIES - Bern

BERT

PUBLIC LIBRARIES - Beroun, Czechoslovakia - Hist.

Poch, Josef. Z Dějin Veřejného Knihovnictví v Berouně. 128-133, EMLE

PUBLIC LIBRARIES - Book selection - Denmark

Thomsen, Svend. Folkebibliotekernes Bogbestand. Nogle Bemærkninger om Bibliotekernes Bogvalg og Opgaver. 1-16, DØSS

PUBLIC LIBRARIES - Book selection - Germany

Langfeldt, Johannes. Die Buchauswahl in Grossen Büchereien: Ein Beitrag zur Rationalisierung Unserer Arbeit. 27-38, ACKR

PUBLIC LIBRARIES - Book selection - U.S.

Swigchem, P. J. van. Boekselectieproblemen in de Amerikaanse Public Library. 226-236, KOSS

PUBLIC LIBRARIES - Bulgaria

Bozhinova-Troi͡anova, B. Chitalishtnite Biblioteki. 266-280, MIKN

PUBLIC LIBRARIES - Bydgoszcz

BYDG

PUBLIC LIBRARIES - Cataloging - Germany

Heinrich, Gisela. Heutige Probleme der Katalogarbeit und Annotierung in der Öffentlichen Bücherei und deren Bedeutung für die Ausbildung. 88-112, LANF

Schriewer, F. Die Zentralbücherei als Büchereityp. 103-111, ACKE

PUBLIC LIBRARIES - Centralization - Denmark

Andersen, S. B. Centralbiblioteket—Set fra en Sognebibliotekars Side. 103-106, LASS

Ebstrup, E. Biblioteksmuligheder paa Landet. Forsøg paa en Nyorientering. 70-84, DØSS

Hansen, Robert L. Centralbibliotekets Udvikling og Administration under Biblioteksloven. 17-36, LASS

Lassen, H. Hvenegaard. Centralbibliotekerne og deres Arbejdsvilkaar. 56-69, DØSS

Sejr, Emanuel. Statsbiblioteket og Centralbibliotekerne. 96-102, LASS

PUBLIC LIBRARIES - Centralization - France

Hansen, Robert L. Franske Centralbiblioteker. 97-107, HEIN

PUBLIC LIBRARIES - Centralization - Germany

Schriewer, F. Die Zentralbücherei als Büchereityp. 103-111, ACKE

PUBLIC LIBRARIES - Centralization - Hannover

Wilkens, Erik. Büchereien oder Büchereiwesen in einer Landschaft? 81-93, ACKR

PUBLIC LIBRARIES - Centralization - Holstebro, Denmark

Møballe, E. Maj 1920 til November 1926. 25-32, HOLS

PUBLIC LIBRARIES - Centralization - Horsens, Denmark

HORS

PUBLIC LIBRARIES - Centralization - Kalundborg, Denmark

Haugstrup, S. Kalundborg Bibliotek 1920-1926. 22-36, KALU

Møller, J. S. Kalundborg Folkebogsamling 1901-1920. 5-21, KALU

PUBLIC LIBRARIES - Centralization - Norway

Skancke, Mally. Norsk Oplandsarbejde. 107-116, LASS

PUBLIC LIBRARIES - Centralization - Sweden

Hjelmqvist, Bengt. Interessenkreise und Zentralmagazine: Über einen Neuen Schwedischen Organisationsplan. 15-18, ACKR
Wieslander, Henning. Svensk Oplandsarbejde. 117-122, LASS

PUBLIC LIBRARIES - Denmark

Gøtzsche, E. Folkebibliotekernes Laan fra de Videnskabelige og Faglige Biblioteker. 153-168, DØSS
Hansen, Robert L. H. O. Lange og Folkebibliotekerne. 341-355, LANE
Krogh-Jensen, G. Om Adgangen til Folkebibliotekerne Betragtninger over Bibliotekernes Reglementer. 105-131, DØSS

PUBLIC LIBRARIES - Denmark - Hist.

Thomsen, Svend. Folkebibliotekernes Bogbestand. Nogle Bemærkninger om Bibliotekernes Bogvalg og Opgaver. 1-16, DØSS

PUBLIC LIBRARIES - Dresden

Böhme, Rudolf. Volksbüchereiarbeit in Dresden. 31-40, DRES

PUBLIC LIBRARIES - Evaluation

Sealoff, Georgia. Anyone Can Make a Library Materials Center. It's What Happens There That Counts. 121-126, HASH

PUBLIC LIBRARIES - Finance
see also Budgets

PUBLIC LIBRARIES - Finance

Wijnstroom, Margreet. Het Uitleenrecht en de Openbare Bibliotheken. 626-639, BRUM

PUBLIC LIBRARIES - Finance - Germany

Rosin, Hans. Buchwirtschaftliche Konzentrationsbestrebungen im Volksbüchereiwesen. 93-102, ACKE

PUBLIC LIBRARIES - Finance - Kalundborg, Denmark

Haugstrup, S. Kalundborg Bibliotek 1920-1926. 22-36, KALU
Møller, J. S. Kalundborg Folkebogsamling 1901-1920. 5-21, KALU

PUBLIC LIBRARIES - Finance - Sweden

Hjelmqvist, Bengt. Lika Möjligheter till Lån. Fragment av Liktal över Betänkande. 117-126, HEIN

PUBLIC LIBRARIES - Finance - Viborg, Denmark

VIBO

PUBLIC LIBRARIES - Finland - Hist.

Kannila, Helle. Två Pionjärer för Folkbiblioteksidén i Finland. 137-147, HEIN

PUBLIC LIBRARIES - France - Hist.

Raux, Henri F. Un Initiateur de la Lecture Publique en France: Eugène Morel (1869-1934). 197-202, STOL

PUBLIC LIBRARIES - Frankfurt a.M.

FRAD

PUBLIC LIBRARIES - Frederikshavn, Denmark

FRED

PUBLIC LIBRARIES - Galicia - Hist.

Korpała, Józef. Z Dziejów Miejskich Bibliotek Publicznych w Galicji. 307-329, GRYC

PUBLIC LIBRARIES - Germany

LANJ

Briele, Wolfgang van der. Die Wissenschaftliche Stadtbibliothek—Heute. Probleme und Erfahrungen. 308-324, JUCH
Günnel, Peter. Walter Hofmann und das Deutsche Volksbüchereiwesen. 7-16, DRES
Hofmann, Walter. Die Behandlung der Organisation der Ausleihe in der Modernen Deutschen Bildungsbibliothek. 17-29, DRES
Pawlack, Erna. Zur Frage der Ausbildung Nebenamtlicher Büchereileiter im Rahmen des Ländlichen Büchereiwesens. 124-134, LANF

PUBLIC LIBRARIES - Germany - Hist.

Uhlendahl, Heinrich. Die Bibliothek der Deutschen Nationalversammlung von 1848/49. Eine Vorläuferin der Deutschen Bücherei. 147-155, LEYH

PUBLIC LIBRARIES - Germany - Hist. - Bibl.

Weser, Adolf. Bibliographie zur Geschichte des Deutschen Volksbüchereiwesens, mit einem Anhang: Die Entwicklung des Berliner Volksbüchereiwesens. 49-80, BERL

PUBLIC LIBRARIES - Gothenburg, Sweden

GÖTE

PUBLIC LIBRARIES - Güstrow (Stadt und Kreis) - Hist.

GÜST

PUBLIC LIBRARIES - Hamburg

HAMB

Breddin, Hans Harald. Die Bibliothekarische Arbeitsgemeinschaft der Hamburger Öffentlichen Bücherhallen. 110-114, HAMB
Zimmermann, Erich. Hinrich Murmester und die Älteste Hamburger Stadtbibliothek (1479/81). 40-49, TIEM

PUBLIC LIBRARIES - Hist.
see also Proprietary libraries

PUBLIC LIBRARIES - Hist.
Coetzee, P. C. Die Voorgeskiedenis van die Openbare Biblioteek. Kultuur-Historiese Beskouing. 221-233, VLEE

PUBLIC LIBRARIES - Hostebro, Denmark - Hist.
HOLS

PUBLIC LIBRARIES - Horsens, Denmark - Hist.
HORS

PUBLIC LIBRARIES - Jena
JENA

PUBLIC LIBRARIES - Kalundborg, Denmark - Hist.
Haugstrup, S. Kalundborg Bibliotek 1920-1926. 22-36, KALU
Møller, J. S. Kalundborg Folkebogsamling 1901-1920. 5-21, KALU

PUBLIC LIBRARIES - Königsberg - Hist. - 17th cent.
Juntke, Fritz. Die Öffentlichen Bibliotheken in Königsberg in Preussen im 17. Jahrhundert. 288-293, KUHN

PUBLIC LIBRARIES - Kristianstad, Norway
Edström, Wilhelm. Arvet från Bildningscirkeln. 7-136, KRIS

PUBLIC LIBRARIES - Legal aspects
see also Libraries - Legal aspects

PUBLIC LIBRARIES - Legal aspects - Germany
Hofmann, Walter. Die Leseordnung in der Volksbücherei. I, 71-79, GLAU

PUBLIC LIBRARIES - Legal aspects - U.S.
Predeek, Albert. Rechtsstellung und Verwaltung der Amerikanischen Public Library. I, 163-175, GLAU

PUBLIC LIBRARIES - Leipzig
Hofmann, Johannes. Die Leipziger Stadtbibliothek 1677-1927. 9-21, LEIP

PUBLIC LIBRARIES - Maastricht
Wouters, H. H. E. "Een Bibliotheque voor den Meesten Luyster van de Stadt." 9-28, MAAS

PUBLIC LIBRARIES - Mainz
MAIN

PUBLIC LIBRARIES - Mason City, Ia., region
Joeckel, Carleton B. Design for a Regional Library Service Unit. 571-582, WILS

PUBLIC LIBRARIES - Metropolitan areas
Joerden, Rudolf. Einige Richtlinien für die Aufbauplanung im Grossstädtischen Büchereiwesen. 19-25, ACKR

PUBLIC LIBRARIES - Netherlands
Gebhard, Annie C. Inlichtingendiensten in Openbare Bibliotheken. 431-435, BRUM
Nuiver, J. A. Centrale Boekbespreking voor de Openbare Bibliotheken. 552-558, BRUM
Riemsdijk, G. A. van. De Bibliotheek van Morgen. 569-576, BRUM
Zwier, Jac. Toezicht en Inspectie Openbare Bibliotheken. 640-644, BRUM

PUBLIC LIBRARIES - Norway
Høydal, Reinh. Folkebogsamlingane og Vår Tid. 89-97, NORS

PUBLIC LIBRARIES - Norway - Hist.
Arnesen, Arne. Våre Bybiblioteker 1913-1938. 39-52, NORN
Hagemann, Sonja. Det Var i Tredveårene. 74-85, NORS

PUBLIC LIBRARIES - Örebro, Sweden
Wieslander, Henning. Hundra Års Biblioteksrkönika från Örebro. 7-48, ÖREB

PUBLIC LIBRARIES - Písek
Lipš, František. První Soustavná Práce Knihovnická v Písku. 164-166, ŽIVN

PUBLIC LIBRARIES - Reference services
Gebhard, Annie C. Inlichtingendiensten in Openbare Bibliotheken. 431-435, BRUM

PUBLIC LIBRARIES - Reference services - Berlin
Fritzsche, Hans-Joachim. Erweiterter Benutzungsdienst und Beratungsstelle für Technische und Naturwissenschaftliche Literatur. 33-35, BERR

PUBLIC LIBRARIES - Reference services - Bydgoszcz

Makowski, Jerzy. Służba Informacyjno-bibliograficzna. 124-130, BYDG

PUBLIC LIBRARIES - Reference services - Frankfurt a.M.

Tiedemann, Eva. Die Auskunfts-Abteilung. 86-88, FRAD

PUBLIC LIBRARIES - Rotterdam

Kossmann, F. K. H. Rotterdam en de "Bijzondere" O.B. 496-500, BRUM

PUBLIC LIBRARIES - Services to business and industry
see also Industrial libraries

PUBLIC LIBRARIES - Services to business and industry - Sheffield, Eng.

Simons, Eric N. Service to Industry. 13-14, LAMB

PUBLIC LIBRARIES - Services to colleges and universities

Schmook, Ger. Dringende Bibliotheekproblemen te Antwerpen. 581-589, BRUM

PUBLIC LIBRARIES - Services to colleges and universities - Jena

Stössel, Waldemar. Ernst-Abbe-Bücherei und Universitätsbibliothek Jena. 118-119, JENA

PUBLIC LIBRARIES - Services to groups
see also Adult education - Library participation

PUBLIC LIBRARIES - Services to groups - Denmark

Gyde-Pedersen, Mette. Kulturelle og Sociale Særopgaver. 132-152, DØSS

PUBLIC LIBRARIES - Services to hospitals - Denmark

Gyde-Pedersen, Mette. Kulturelle og Sociale Særopgaver. 132-152, DØSS

PUBLIC LIBRARIES - Services to schools
see also School and public library relationship

PUBLIC LIBRARIES - Services to schools

Möhring, Werner. Volkshochschule und Volksbücherei. 95-124, ACKR

PUBLIC LIBRARIES - Services to students - Germany

Braun, W. Die Studienbücherei. 15-24, ACKE

Eggebrecht, W. Bücherei und Volkshochschule. 25-28, ACKE

PUBLIC LIBRARIES (Small) - Finance - Randers, Denmark

RAND

PUBLIC LIBRARIES (Small) - Germany

Kock, R. Zur Frage der Auswertung Statistischer Erhebungen Kleinstädtischer und Dörflicher Büchereien. 65-74, ACKE

PUBLIC LIBRARIES (Small) - Hamburg region

Struck, Christel. Die Volksbüchereien der Vororte und des Landgebietes. 68-74, HAMB

PUBLIC LIBRARIES (Small) - Norway

Bakken, Asbjørn. Små Bemerkninger om Store Saker. 177-186, NORS
Kjørvik, M. A. Folkebogsamlingane på Landsbygda og Vilkåra for Dei. 53-61, NORN
Kobro, Nancy. Nye Strømninger i Biblioteksarbeidet på Landsbygden. 62-65, NORN
Nyhuus, Haakon. De Norske Statsunderstøttede Folkebogsamlinger. 36-42, NORS
Rongen, Bjørn. Bøker Langs Landeveien. 120-130, KILD

PUBLIC LIBRARIES (Small) - Randers, Denmark - Hist.

RAND

PUBLIC LIBRARIES (Small) - Skagen, Denmark - Hist.

SKAG

PUBLIC LIBRARIES - South Africa

Levyns, J. E. P. Mr. D. H. Varley and the Institute of Citizenship. 25, VARL

PUBLIC LIBRARIES - Standards - Netherlands

Zwier, Jac. Toezicht en Inspectie Openbare Bibliotheken. 640-644, BRUM

PUBLIC LIBRARIES - State and regional development plans

Joeckel, Carleton B. Design for a Regional Library Service Unit. 571-582, WILS

PUBLIC LIBRARIES - State and regional development plans - Southern States

Wilson, Louis Round. Optima in Library Service for the South by 1950. 186-204, BISH

PUBLIC LIBRARIES - State and regional development plans - Switzerland

Escher, Hermann. Die Schweizerische Volksbibliothek (1922). 131-137, ESCH

PUBLIC LIBRARIES - State and regional development plans - Tennessee Valley

Rothrock, Mary U. Libraries and Regional Development. 666-674, WILS

PUBLIC LIBRARIES - State and regional development plans - U.S.

Kirkegaard, Preben. Amerikansk Oplandsarbejde. 135-146. LASS

PUBLIC LIBRARIES - Statistics - Berlin

Die Arbeit der Berliner Stadtbibliothek in Einigen Zahlen und Plänen. 56-59, BERR

Hauke, Walter. Die Entwicklung der Berliner Volksbüchereien von 1945 bis 1950. 27-48, BERL

PUBLIC LIBRARIES - Statistics - Frankfurt a.M.

Aus der Statistik der Deutschen Bibliothek. 92-99, FRAD

PUBLIC LIBRARIES - Statistics - Frederikshavn, Denmark

Poulsen, Chr. Bibliotekets Udvikling 1912-37. 15-20, FRED

PUBLIC LIBRARIES - Statistics - Gothenburg, Sweden

Hallberg, S. and O. von Feilitzen. Göteborgs Stadsbibliotek. Det Första Halvseklet 1891-1940. 1-142, (first paper), GÖTE

Molin, Nils. Från Låneexpeditionen. 11-20, (fourth paper), GÖTE

PUBLIC LIBRARIES - Statistics - Güstrow (Stadt und Kreis)

GÜST

PUBLIC LIBRARIES - Statistics - Hamburg

Chill, Gertrud. Ausgewählte Statistische Angaben. 133-139, HAMB

PUBLIC LIBRARIES - Statistics - Horsens, Denmark

HORS

PUBLIC LIBRARIES - Statistics - Jena

Reiprich, Alfred. Arbeit und Aufgaben der Ernst-Abbe-Bücherei. 72-104, JENA

PUBLIC LIBRARIES - Statistics - Skagen, Denmark

SKAG

PUBLIC LIBRARIES - Statistics - Visby, Sweden

Berättelse över Stadsbibliotekets Verksamhet 1965. 129-143, VISB

PUBLIC LIBRARIES - Sudetenland

Zifreund, Viktor. Wege und Ziele der Sudetendeutschen Volksbüchereiarbeit. 157-166, ACKE

PUBLIC LIBRARIES - Sweden

Wistrand, Pär. Mina Bibliotek. 539-547, HJEL

PUBLIC LIBRARIES - Sweden - Hist.

Hallvik, Bengt. Svensk Biblioteksdebatt Omkring År 1860. Ur en Tidningsläsares Citatsamling. 77-95, HEIN

Linder, Greta. När Vi Började. Minnen från Bibliotekskonsulenternas Tidiga År. 183-201, HEIN

PUBLIC LIBRARIES - Switzerland

Hirzel, B. Conrad Ferdinand Meyer und die Zürcher Stadtbibliothek. [45]-60, ESCK

Wild, Helen. Hermann Escher und die Schweizerischen Volksbibliotheken. 22-34, ESCK

——— Volksbücherei und Volksbücherei-Nachwuchs in der Schweiz. 145-155, ACKE

PUBLIC LIBRARIES - Technical services - Gothenburg, Sweden - Hist.

Broberg, Sven Grén. Några Minnen och Anteckningar. 1-10, (third paper), GÖTE

PUBLIC LIBRARIES - Use studies see Use studies - Public libraries

PUBLIC LIBRARIES - Viborg, Denmark

VIBO

PUBLIC LIBRARIES - Vienna

VIES

PUBLIC LIBRARIES - Visby, Sweden

Åberg, Åke. Visby Stadsbibliotek. Förhistoria och Begynnelseår. 5-30, VISB

PUBLIC LIBRARIES - Wuppertal

ELBE

PUBLIC LIBRARIES - Zürich

Wild, Helen. Volksbüchereiplanung in Gross-Zürich. 67-79, ACKR

Wyss, W. von. Erinnerungen an Alte Zeiten auf der Stadtbibliothek Zürich. 1-7, ESCK

PUBLIC RECORDS
see Archives, Government

PUBLIC RELATIONS OF LIBRARIES
see also Library and the public; Publicity

PUBLIC RELATIONS OF LIBRARIES - Sundbyberg, Sweden

Bianchini, Bianca. Muhammed och Berget. Redogörelse för en Experimentverksamhet i Sundbyberg. 33-50, HEIN

PUBLICACIONES DE MIGUEL ARTIGAS. I, xiii-xvi, ARTI

PUBLICHNAÏA BIBLIOTEKA, Leningrad
see Leningrad. Library

PUBLICITY
see also Exhibits and displays; Library publications

PUBLICITY - Bydgoszcz

Kochowa, Róża. Z Ksiąg Pamiątkowych Biblioteki i z Prasy Miejscowej—Uwagi, Opinie. 158-164, BYDG

PUBLICITY - Torslev, Denmark

TORS

PUBLISHERS AND LIBRARIES - Leipzig

Rötzsch, Helmut. Der Börsenverein der Deutschen Buchhändler zu Leipzig und die Deutsche Bücherei. 47-66, LEIZ

PUBLISHERS AND LIBRARIES - Norway

Butenschøn, Barthold A. Forleggeren og Biblioteket. 149-155, NORS

PUBLISHERS AND LIBRARIES - U.S.

Melcher, Frederic G. Working Together: Publisher, Bookseller, and Librarian. 619-621, MOOR

PUBLISHERS AND PUBLISHING
see also Presses, University

PUBLISHERS AND PUBLISHING

Morpurgo, J. E. The Publishing Problem—a Kite for Policy Makers. 236-240, KYLE

PUBLISHERS AND PUBLISHING - Directories - 16th cent.

Lutz, Hans. Konrad Gesners Beziehungen zu den Verlegern Seiner Zeit nach Seinen Pandekten von 1548. 109-117, GODE

PUBLISHERS AND PUBLISHING - Germany

Benton, Rita. Ignace Pleyel, Disputant. 21-24, FEDO

Schillmann, Fritz. Zur Geschichte des Bücherwesens des Deutschen Ritterordens. 278-282, KUHN

PUBLISHERS AND PUBLISHING - Germany - Hist. - 16th cent.

Scholderer, Victor. Georg Uebelin (Georgius Maxillus) and His Publications. 111-116, WEHM

PUBLISHERS AND PUBLISHING - Germany - Hist. - 20th cent.

Frels, Wilhelm. Das Deutsche Drama 1913-1920. Statistisches aus der Deutschen Bücherei. 38-50, MIND

PUBLISHERS AND PUBLISHING - Gt. Brit. - Hist.

Mortimer, R. S. Biographical Notices of Printers and Publishers of Friends' Books up to 1750. 107-125, OFFO

PUBLISHERS AND PUBLISHING - Japan

Yoshiike, Hiroshi. Shuppansha e no Chumon. (Book Publishing in Japan.) 227-229, KYOT

PUBLISHERS AND PUBLISHING - Japan - Hist.

Arai, Toshi. Kirishitan-ban no Shuppan to Sono Shūhen, I. (Publication of the Jesuit Printings in Japan and Related Problems, 16th-17th Centuries, Part I.) 45-59, TOMI
Kumura, Miyogo and Kazumasa Kaneko. Chokuhan Ko, 1, Kobun Kokyo 1. (Study of the Chokuhan, or the Imperial Editions, 16th Century, Part 1, Kobun Kokyo 1.) 61-86, TOMI
Nakamura, Yukihiko. Kogidō no Zōhan ni Kansuru Monjo ni tsuite. (Documents concerning the Arrangements for the Publication of Works of the Kogidō Masters of the Ito Family.) 113-151, TOMI
Shimasue, Kiyoshi. Hanpon ni Natta Yoshidake no Hon. (Works Published by the Sintoist Family of Yoshida.) 87-95, TOMI

PUBLISHERS AND PUBLISHING - Leipzig - Hist. - 16th cent.

Claus, Helmut. Migration von Bildstöcken bei den Leipziger Buchdruckern in der Frühen Reformationszeit. 63-81, LÜLF

PUBLISHERS AND PUBLISHING - Michigan - Hist.

Bonk, W. J. Periodical Publishing in the Michigan Territory. 85-104, GJEL
Kephart, John E. Antislavery Publishing in Michigan. 219-236, GJEL

PUBLISHERS AND PUBLISHING - Norway - Hist.

Tank, Roar. De Femti År. 9-32, OSLN

PUBLISHERS AND PUBLISHING - Padua - Hist.

Fantini, Bianca Saraceni. Prime Indagini sulla Stampa Padovana del Cinquecento. 415-485, FERR

PUBLISHERS AND PUBLISHING - Pennsylvania - Hist. - 1790-1800

Goff, Frederick R. The First Decade of the Federal Act for Copyright, 1790-1800. 101-128, WROT

PUBLISHERS AND PUBLISHING - Rome (City) - Hist.

Paschini, Pio. Un Cardinale Editore: Marcello Cervini. 383-413, FERR

PUBLISHERS AND PUBLISHING - Switzerland

Lange, Eugenie. Schweizer Drucke in Russischer Sprache. 68-76, BERU

PUBLISHERS AND PUBLISHING - Trent

Oberziner, Ludovico. La Libreria di un Patrizio Trentino del Secolo XVI. I, 371-412, HORT

PUBLISHERS AND PUBLISHING - U.S. - Hist.

Cunningham, Eileen-R. Some Items of Americana Medica Published Southwest of the Alleghenies and Their Authors. 25-26, STUM
Darling, Richard L. Children's Books Following the Civil War. 63-84, GJEL
Waters, Edward N. The Wa-Wan Press: An Adventure in Musical Idealism. 214-233, ENGE
Wegelin, Oscar. Mills Day's Proposed Hebrew Bible. 221-226, EAME

PUBLISHERS AND PUBLISHING - Venice - Hist.

Leicht, Pier Silverio. L'Editore Veneziano Michele Tramezino ed i Suoi Privilegi. 357-367, FERR

PUBLISHERS AND PUBLISHING - Wittenberg - Hist. - 16th cent.

Luther, Johannes. Drucker- und Verlegernöte in Wittenberg zur Zeit des Schmalkaldischen Krieges. 229-243, MILF

PUBLISHERS' CATALOGS - Europe - 16th cent. - Bibl.

Richter, Gunter. Die Sammlung von Drucker-, Verleger- und Buchführerkatalogen in den Akten der Kaiserlichen Bücherkommission. 317-372, BENZ

PUNCHED CARDS
see also Information retrieval - Systems

PUNJAB - Libraries and librarianship
see Libraries and librarianship - Punjab

PUPPET PLAYS - Collections - Tenri, Japan

Yuda, Yoshio, Hajime Uetani, and Minoru Imanishi. Tenri Toshokan Zō Jōruri Hangi Mokuroku. (Catalogue of the Wood-Blocks of Jōruri Texts in the Tenri Central Library.) 259-294, TOMI

Puranik, K. D.
Emergence of the Laws of Library Science. 145-149, MADR

Purdy, G. Flint.
The Evaluation of University Library Service. 638-644, WILS

LE PURGATOIRE. 119, BERU

Putnam, Herbert.
Congratulatory Message. 3, ENGE
Interpretive Service in a Library for Research. 211-213, MUNT
Letter to Mr. Hanson. 314, HANS
Reflections from Ingonish. 5-10, BISH

PUTNAM, HERBERT

PUTN

PUTP

Andrews, Charles McLean. The Story of the Transcripts. 47-56, PUTN
Belden, Charles F. D. The Library Service of Herbert Putnam in Boston. 10-14, PUTN
Bowker, Richard R. The Appointment of Herbert Putnam as Librarian of Congress. 15-21, PUTN
Burton, Theodore E. Herbert Putnam. 2-3, PUTN
Countryman, Gratia A. Mr. Putnam and the Minneapolis Public Library. 5-9, PUTN
Dewey, Melvil. Herbert Putnam. 22-23, PUTN
Gillett, Frederick H. Herbert Putnam. 4, PUTN
Keppel, Frederick P. Herbert Putnam. 255-256, PUTN
Roland-Marcel, Pierre R. Ma Visite à la Library of Congress. 395-398, PUTN
Utley, George B. The Library War Service and Its General Director. 474-491, PUTN

PUTNAM, HERBERT - Bibl.
Jones, Helen Dudenbostel. Writings and Addresses of Herbert Putnam and Books and Articles about Him. 53-80, PUTP

PYNNINEN, JUHO
Kannila, Helle. Två Pionjärer för Folkbiblioteksidén i Finland. 137-147, HEIN

QUALIFICATIONS OF PERSONNEL
see Personnel - Qualifications and selection

Quentin, Henri.
Une Correspondance Médicale de Pierre le Vénérable avec "Magister Bartholomaeus." 80-86, EHRA

Querol, Miguel.
Lista de los Catálogos Musicales Publicados en España. 103-105, FEDO

QUESNEL, PASQUIER - Library
Tans, J. A. G. Een Uitdagende Utrechtse Collectie: De Val des Pausdoms. 64-77, UTRE

QUESTIONNAIRES - Copenhagen
Birkelund, Palle. Det Kongelige Bibliotek og dets Publikum. 119-132, DAHA

Quevedo, Luis Torres.
El Número Poético. II, 219-228, ARTI

Qvigstad, J.
Bibliografiens Betydning for Forskninger 1-4, HALV

Racek, Fritz.
Von den Schuberthandschriften der Stadtbibliothek. 98-124, VIES

RACZYŃSKI, RACZYN
Warschauer, A. Über Einige Seltene Gelegenheitsdrucke aus der Provinz Posen. 67-74, VERP

RADIO LIBRARIES AND COLLECTIONS - Sweden
Lindberg, Folke. Broadcasting Libraries and Archives as Music Research Centres. 76-79, FEDO

RADIO - Library programs
Thorsen, Leif. Radio og Fjernsyn—Bog og Bibliotek. 65-76, THOM
Wieser, M. Buchwerbung durch den Rundfunk. 133-144, ACKE

RADZIWILL, PRINCE BOGUSLAV
see Boguslav Radziwill, Prince

RAESFELD, GOTTFRIED VON
Degering, Hermann. Gottfried von Raesfeld. Sein Geschlecht, Sein Leben und Sein Testament. 137-250, MÜNS

Rästner, Erhart.
Scherenschnitt-Illustration. 196-219, BOLL

RAETO-ROMANCE LITERATURE - Collections - Bern
Pieth, Friedrich. Die Rätoromanischen Bestände. 64-67, BERU

Räuber, Friedrich.
Der Begriff des Antiquariats nach der Verkaufsordnung. 286-299, MILF

Raff, Hermann.
Verzeichnis der Schriften von Georg Leyh. XIII-XXVI, LEYG

Rahman, Abdul.
Dr. Ranganathan: A Study of a Multifaceted Genius. 677-684, RANG

Rajagopalan, T. S.
India's Contribution to the International Federation for Documentation. 257-267, RANG

Rajamoni, A. N., jt. author
Muthiah, V. S. and A. N. Rajamoni. Dr. Ranganathan as a Public Speaker. 732-733, RANG

Rajbee, M.
Ranganathan: My Benefactor: A Book's Appreciation of Dr. Ranganathan. 305-311, RANG

Rajna, Pio.
Il Codice Vaticano 3357 del Trattato De Vita Solitaria di Francesco Petrarca. 641-686, CERI
Il Primo Capitolo del Trattato De Vulgari Eloquentia Tradotto e Commentato. 113-128, HORT

Ramabhadran, S.
Development of Library Administration. 155-157, MADR

RĀMĀYAṆA Mss.
Nobel, Johannes. Die Śārada-Handschrift des Rāmāyaṇa. 186-190, HARN

RAMPOLLA DEL TINDARO, MARIANO
Batllori, Miquel. El Pare Ehrle, Prefecte de la Vaticana, en la Seva Correspondència amb el Card. Rampolla. I, 75-117, ALBB

Ranck, Samuel H. Social Service of the Public Library. 365-377, PUTN

Rand, Edward Kennard.
A Carolingian Gospel-Book in the Pierpont Morgan Library in New York. 89-104, EHRD

Randall, William M.
Louis R. Wilson and the Graduate Library School. 645-650, WILS

Randé, Karel.
Osobní Vzpomínky. 68-73, EMLE

RANDERS, Denmark. Folkebibliotek

RAND

Raney, M. Llewellyn.
1909 and After. 651-658, WILS

Ranganathan, Shiyali Ramamrita.
Barbara Kyle and the Classification of Sociology. 271-274, KYLE
International Library Scene. 191-196, HOFM
Library Classification on the March. 72-95, SAYW
Telescoping of Facets and Mixed Notation. 154-156, DONK
Then, Now and Hereafter. 1-6, MADR

RANGANATHAN, SHIYALI RAMAMRITA

RANG

Donker Duyvis, Frits. On the Future Work for the Comparison of Classifications. 32-37, MADR
Mills, J. Dr. Ranganathan and the Study of Classification. 38-41, MADR
Puranik, K. D. Emergence of the Laws of Library Science. 145-149, MADR
Wells, A. J. Our Debt to India. 57-63, MADR

RANGANATHAN, SHIYALI RAMAMRITA.
Library Administration

Ramabhadran, S. Development of Library Administration. 155-157, MADR

Ranganathan, T.
The Ranganathan I Have Experienced. 696-699, RANG

Ranke, Friedrich.
Eine Neue Handschrift des Gereimten Passionals. 301-316, KÖNI

RANTZAU, HEINRICH

Schmidt-Herrling, Eleonore. Zwei Geschenkbände von Heinrich Rantzau in der Universitätsbibliothek Erlangen. 57-61, VERZ

RANTZAU, HEINRICH - Library

Walde, O. Henrik Rantzaus Bibliotek och Dess Öden. 239-250, ANNE

Rao, B. Sanjiva.
An Estimate of Dr. Ranganathan. 769-770, RANG

Rao, C. V. Subba.
Diary Leaves Afloat. 639-642, RANG

Rao, T. Gopalekrishna.
My Master. 715-719, RANG

RARE BOOK LIBRARIANS

Bishop, William Warner. Rare Book Rooms in Libraries. 375-385, WILS

RARE BOOK ROOMS

Bishop, William Warner. Rare Book Rooms in Libraries. 375-385, WILS

RARE BOOKS
see also Colophons; Illumination of books and manuscripts

RARE BOOKS

Cole, George Watson. Elizabethan Americana. 161-177, EAME
Collijn, Isak Gustaf Alfred. Some Rare Americana. 50-55, BISH

RARE BOOKS - Acquisitions - Hist. - 1859

Pauer, Max. Anton Ruland und Karl Halm. Ein Bibliothekarischer Streit um Dublettenverkäufe vor Hundert Jahren. 121-135, REDE

RARE BOOKS - Bibl.

VERE

Annan, Gertrude L. Outstanding Acquisitions of Rare Books in Medical Libraries of the United States in the Last Decade. 291-300, DOEJ
Deckert, Helmut, Marita Kremer, Hans Pfeifer, and Liselotte Willi. Das Neue Buchmuseum der Sächsischen Landesbibliothek. 175-205, DREL
Moricca Caputi, Ada. Di Alcuni Opuscoli Rari nella Biblioteca Casanatense. 153-165, ACCU

RARE BOOKS - Bibliography - Bibl.
see Bibliography - Bibl. - Rare books

RARE BOOKS - Binding - Fine bindings
see Bookbinding - Fine bindings

RARE BOOKS - Cataloging
see also Manuscripts - Cataloging

RARE BOOKS - Collections - Bern

Schazmann, Paul-Émile. Les Imprimés Anciens. 33-38, BERU

RARE BOOKS - Collections - Erlangen

Schmidt-Herrling, Eleonore. Zwei Geschenkbände von Heinrich Rantzau in der Universitätsbibliothek Erlangen. 57-61, VERZ

RARE BOOKS - Collections - Greifswald

Deutsch, Josef. Ebers Calendarium Historicum mit Handschriftlichen Eintragungen aus Wolgast. 71-78, KUHN

RARE BOOKS - Collections - Hague

Brummel, Leendert. De Boeken van Tongerloo in de Koninklijke Bibliotheek te 's-Gravenhage. 151-168, BRUE

RARE BOOKS - Collections - Kraków

Madrjas, Halina. Starodruki Pedagogicznej Biblioteki Wojewódzkiej w Krakowie. 50-55, KRAK

RARE BOOKS - Collections - Mainz

Benzing, Josef. Buchgeschichtliche Beiträge zu Einigen Frühdrucken der UB Mainz. 103-128, MAIZ

RARE BOOKS - Collections - Rome (City)

Moricca Caputi, Ada. Di Alcuni Opuscoli Rari nella Biblioteca Casanatense. 153-165, ACCU

RARE BOOKS - Collections - Uppsala

Kleberg, Tönnes. Ett Decennium av Gåvor. Kring en Utställning i Uppsala Universitetsbibliotek. 149-167, HEIN

RARE BOOKS - Collections - U.S.

Annan, Gertrude L. Outstanding Acquisitions of Rare Books in Medical Libraries of the United States in the Last Decade. 291-300, DOEJ

RARE BOOKS - Collections - Vatican

Vian, Nello. La Presentazione e gli Esemplari Vaticani della "Assertio Septem Sacramentorum" di Enrico VIII. II, 355-375, ALBB

RARE BOOKS - 16th cent.

Dahlberg, Ragnar. Helsingfors Universitetsbiblioteks Exemplar af Psalterium Dauidis 1510. 140-144, HULA
Tollenaere, F. de. Op het Spoor van een Onbekende Postincunabel? 246-249, KOSS
Widmann, Hans. Zu Reuchlins Rudimenta Hebraica. 492-498, BENZ

RARE BOOKS - 16th cent. - Bibl.

Barberi, Francesco. Le Edizioni Romane di Francesco Minizio Calvo. 57-98, FERR
Benzing, Josef. Buchgeschichtliche Beiträge zu Einigen Frühdrucken der UB Mainz. 103-128, MAIZ
Bömer, Aloys. Die Fünf Frühdrucke der Epistolae Obscurorum Virorum. 17-29, SCHW
Colmi, Elsbet. Thomas Kees Wesaliensis. Aus der Werkstatt eines Weseler Druckers in Paris 1507-1515/16. 68-97, BENZ
Dahlberg, Ragnar. Bidrag till den Svenska Reformationstidens Bibliografi. 58-70, HULA
Fantini, Bianca Saraceni. Prime Indagini sulla Stampa Padovana del Cinquecento. 415-485, FERR
Traut, Hermann. Dr. Adolf von Glauburg und Seine Bibliothek. 1-34, EBRA

RARE BOOKS - 16th cent. - Collections - Helsinki

Vallinkoski, J. Ett Danskt Bokfynd i Finland. 15-19, DAHA

RARE BOOKS - 16th-17th cent. - Bibl.

Cole, George Watson. Elizabethan Americana. 161-177, EAME
Stampe, Ernst. Komödien des Lebens aus Alten Drucken. 79-85, KUHN

RARE BOOKS - 17th cent. - Scandinavia

Kilpi, Volter. Suomalainen Virsikirja [Manuale-nide] v:lta 1630 Teuvan Kirkonarkistossa. 122-126, SCHA

RARE BOOKS - 17th-18th cent.

Warschauer, A. Über Einige Seltene Gelegenheitsdrucke aus der Provinz Posen. 67-74, VERP

RAS SHAMRA - Libraries
see Libraries - Ras Shamra

Rasi, P.
Nuove Osservazioni sul Carmen de Pascha. 577-604, CERI

Rasmussen, Detlef.
Andreas Schleiermacher und das Prinzip der Schlüsselung. 163-175, REDE

Rastogi, V. S.
Indian Librarianship and Dr. Ranganathan. 362-373, RANG

Rath, Erich von.
Der Drucker von Buyers Ausgabe der Werke des Bartolus von 1482. Ein Beitrag zur Buchdruckergeschichte Lyons. 217-225, SCHW
Karl Schaarschmidt. 283-296, LEYG
Die Kupferstichillustration im Wiegendruckzeitalter. 58-68, LEIP
Die Schriften Konrad Haeblers. 1-17, HAEB
Zur Biographie Ludwig Hains. 161-182, COLL

Rathe, Kurt.
Ein Architektur-Musterbuch der Spätgotik mit Graphischen Einklebungen. 667-692, VIEN

RATHSHANDBIBLIOTHEK, Aachen
see Aachen. Stadtbibliothek

RATISBON. Niedermünster (Abbey) Mss.
Boeckler, Albert. Das Erhardbild im Utacodex. 219-230, GREE

RATISBON. Saint Emmeram (Benedictine monastery). Biblioteca. Mss.
Grabmann, Martin. Mitteilungen aus Münchner Handschriften über Bisher Unbekannte Philosophen der Artisten-fakultät (Codd. Lat. 14246 und 14383). 73-83, LEID

RATJEN, HENNING
Kindervater, Josef. Nachrichten von einer Bibliotheksreise vor 100 Jahren. 230-244, LEYG

RATTI, ACHILLE
see also Pius XI, Pope

Ratti, Achille.
Manoscritti di Provenienza Francese nella Bibliotheca Ambrosiana di Milano. 588-597, CHAT
Reliquie di Antico Codice Bobbiese Ritrovate. 789-810, CERI

Rau, M. S. Ekambara.
A Unique Personality. 741-743, RANG

Raux, Henri F.
Un Initiateur de la Lecture Publique en France: Eugène Morel (1869-1934). 197-202, STOL

RAVELLO, Italy. Archivio. Mss.
Mazzoleni, Iole. Note Paleografiche e Diplomatiche su Alcune Carte Ravellesi dei Secc. XII-XIV. 539-547, GALL

RAVENNA. Biblioteca Comunale Classense. Mss.
Martin, Albert. Notice sur les Manuscrits Grecs de la Bibliothèque Classense, à Ravenne. 553-556, GRAU

RAVENNA - Manuscripts, Greek - Collections
see Manuscripts, Greek - Collections - Ravenna

Ravesteyn, W. van.
'De Paradox': een Curiosum. 174-185, KOSS

Raynaud, G.
Une Edition de Froissart Projetée par Christophe Plantin (1563-1565). 515-519, HAVE

Razzaque, M. A.
On First Seeing Dr. Ranganathan. 749-750, RANG

READER GUIDANCE
see also Books and reading

READER GUIDANCE
Wieselgren, O. Några Anteckningar om Våra Dagars Folklitteratur. 251-265, ANNE

READER GUIDANCE - Germany
Wallraf, Karlheinz. Zur Besprechungsarbeit mit Praktikanten. 113-123, LANF

READER GUIDANCE - Gt. Brit.
Wright, A. Shaw. The Series, "Readers' Guides." 73-79, MADR

READER GUIDANCE - U.S.
Milam, Carl H. Reading Courses: An Experiment in Adult Education. 356-364, PUTN

READER INTEREST CLASSIFICATION
see Shelf arrangement

READER SERVICES
see also Circulation procedures; Reference services

READER SERVICES - Berlin
Fritzsche, Hans-Joachim. Erweiterter Benutzungsdienst und Beratungsstelle für Technische und Naturwissenschaftliche Literatur. 33-35, BERR
Sabotke, Alice. Benutzungsabteilung—Ausleihe, Lesesäle, Freihandabteilung. 28-32, BERR

READER SERVICES - Bern
Meyer, Wilhelm Josef. Der Benützungsdienst. 163-168, BERU

READER SERVICES - Dresden
Pepino, Jan. Aus der Täglichen Arbeit der Sächsischen Landesbibliothek. 86-91, DREL

READER SERVICES - Leipzig
Schwidetzky, Georg. Der Benutzungsdienst. 137-147, LEIS

READERS' ADVISORY SERVICE
see Reader guidance

READERS' GUIDES
Wright, A. Shaw. The Series, "Readers' Guides." 73-79, MADR

READING

Waples, Douglas. On Developing Taste in Reading. 740-747, WILS

READING COURSES
see Reader guidance; Reading - Educational aspects

READING - Educational aspects

Busse, Gisela von. Vom Rechten Bücherlesen. Gedanken zur Herder-Interpretation. 244-257, TIEM
Frey, Jaroslav. Pozorování a Experiment v Pedagogice Čtenáře. 97-102, EMLE
Östling, Gösta. Stimulera Individens Strävan. Om Bibliotekens Uppgift i Samhället. 257-269, HEIN

READING - Educational aspects - Germany

Hofmann, Walter. Die Behandlung der Organisation der Ausleihe in der Modernen Deutschen Bildungsbibliothek. 17-29, DRES

READING GUIDANCE
see Reader guidance

READING INTERESTS
see also Circulation analysis

READING INTERESTS - U.S.

Eells, Walter Crosby. Periodicals Read by Junior College Students. 474-485, WILS

READING - Łodz, Poland

Nagórska, Izabela. Portrety Czytelników-Robotników w Łódzkiej Dzielnicy Chojny. 155-168, GRYC

READING ROOMS
see also Dormitory libraries

READING ROOMS

Munthe, Wilhelm. Vom Lesesaal ins Magazin Zurück. 350-357, LEYG

READING - Special groups of readers - Authors
see Authors and libraries

READING - Special groups of readers - Czechs in the U.S.

Malý, Jaromír. Pro Bibliografii Československo-amerického Tisku. 167-171, ŽIVN

READING - Special groups of readers - Journalists - Norway

Christensen, Chr. A. R. Presse og Bibliotek. 168-176, NORS

READING - Special groups of readers - Junior college students - U.S.

Eells, Walter Crosby. Periodicals Read by Junior College Students. 474-485, WILS

READING - Special groups of readers - Physicians - 18th cent.

Uggla, Arvid HJ. Ett Läkarebibliotek från Början av 1700-Talet. 221-248, GRAP

READING - Special groups of readers - Soldiers

Tveito, Dagfinn. Soldater og Kulturfront. 74-85, KILD

READING - Special groups of readers - Teachers - Poland

Misiewicz, Danuta. Zainteresowania Czytelnicze Nauczycieli. 107-109, KRAK

READING WITH A PURPOSE

Milam, Carl H. Reading Courses: An Experiment in Adult Education. 356-364, PUTN

RECATALOGING
see Cataloging - Recataloging

RECLASSIFICATION
see Classification - Reclassification

RECORDINGS - Administration

Očadlík, Mirko. Diskotéka. 124-128, EMLE

RECORDINGS - Care and preservation - Sweden

Lindberg, Folke. Broadcasting Libraries and Archives as Music Research Centres. 76-79, FEDO

RECORDINGS - Collections - Berlin

Doegen, Wilhelm. Die Lautabteilung. 253-258, HARN
———— Die Stimmensammlung zur Dokumentensammlung Darmstaedter. 258-259, HARN
Weise-Standfest, Hilde. Musikbibliothek und Diskothek, Kunstblätter-Sammlung, Musik- und Literaturveranstaltungen. 36-41, BERR

RECORDS MANAGEMENT
see Archives - Administration; Archives - Retention

RECRUITING FOR LIBRARIANSHIP - Denmark

Hansen, Robert L. Om Uddannelse af Bibliotekarer ved Folkebibliotekerne. 17-37, DØSS

Redenbacher, Fritz, ed.
STOL

Redenbacher, Fritz.
Adoratio Magorum. Die Heiligen Drei Könige in der Bibel von St. Gumbertus, Gesehen im Rahmen der Ikonographischen Überlieferung. 305-334, HOFM
Die Buchmalerei des Frühen Mittelalters im Urteil der Deutschen Romantik. 203-217, STOL
Einzelbild und Zyklus in der Bibelillustration des Frühen Mittelalters. 110-118, TIEM
Das Gebäude der Universitätsbibliothek Erlangen. 232-251, VORS

REDENBACHER, FRITZ
REDE

REDENBACHER, FRITZ - Bibl.
Petz-Gebauer, Hannelore. Bibliographie Fritz Redenbacher. 203-207, REDE

Redonet, Luis.
Un Valle Montañés en el Siglo XVI. II, 350-410, ARTI

Reedijk, C.
Stuivers en Centen of: Andermaal het Uitleenrecht. 559-568, BRUM

Reese, Gustave, ed.
ENGE

Refardt, Edgar.
Die Musiktexte J. V. Widmanns. 134-139, REFA
Vom Musikhändler Nägeli. 24-27, REFA

REFARDT, EDGAR
REFA

REFERENCE BOOKS
see also Bibliography; Encyclopedias and dictionaries; Research materials

REFERENCE BOOKS - Collections - Bern
Beck, Marcel. Die Handbibliothek im Lesesaal und der Bibliographische Apparat im Katalogsaal. 84-87, BERU

REFERENCE BOOKS - Prices
Raney, M. Llewellyn. 1909 and After. 651-658, WILS

REFERENCE BOOKS - Special subjects - Medicine - Bibl.
Jenkins, Frances B. Medical Reference Sources—A Backward Glance. 361-370, DOEJ

REFERENCE LIBRARIANS
Horner, G. W. The Answer?—That is the Question. 252-255, KYLE

REFERENCE LIBRARIES
see Research libraries

REFERENCE SERVICES
see also College and university libraries - Reference services; Public libraries - Reference services; Reader services; Research and the library

REFERENCE SERVICES
Below, Erich. Merkwürdige Bücherbestellungen. 316-321, KUHN
Bernhardt, Børge. Litt om Gjenfinning fra Brukersynspunkt. 174-182, TVET
Cheney, Frances Neel. Reference Service in English and American Literature. 41-47, HASH
Foskett, D. J. Technique of Reference Service. 68-72, MADR
Kolhatker, V. P. The Reference Librarian and His Tools. 80-84, MADR
Nagasawa, Masao. Daigaku Toshokan Kindaika no Kijiku toshite no Refarensu Wāku. (Reference Work as the Axis for the Modernization of the University Library.) 267-279, HASH
Nogami, Mamoru. Toshokan Kino no Bunseki to Ruien Kikan. Kokyo Toshokan no Refarensu Wāku no Tachiba Kara. (On the Function of the Library from the Standpoint of Reference Work.) 21-36, KYOT

REFERENCE SERVICES - Public libraries
see Public libraries - Reference services

REFORMATION - Bibliography - Bibl.
see Bibliography - Bibl. - Reformation

REFORMATION - L'vov
Schramm, Gottfried. Lemberg und die Reformation. 343-350, EPST

Regatillo, José Fernández.
Las Jornadas Montañesas del Emperador Carlos V en Su Primer Viaje a España (Fragmento de la Crónica de Laurent Vital). I, 119-131, ARTI

REGENSBURG
see Ratisbon

REGGIO EMILIA - Archives
see Archives - Reggio Emilia

REGGIO EMILIA. Archivio Capitolare
Tondelli, Leone. Cenni sull'Archivio Capitolare di Reggio Emilia. 263-267, MERC

REGIOMONTANUS, JOHANNES. Temporal
Hase, Martin von. Zwei Drucke des Temporals des Johannes Regio-

montanus von Wolfgang Stürmer in Erfurt. I, 61-66, GLAU

REGIONAL LIBRARIES
see also Cooperative library systems

REGIONAL LIBRARIES

Joeckel, Carleton B. Design for a Regional Library Service Unit. 571-582, WILS

REGIONAL LIBRARIES - Hannover

Wilkens, Erik. Büchereien oder Büchereiwesen in einer Landschaft? 81-93, ACKR

REGIONAL LIBRARIES - Tennessee Valley

Rothrock, Mary U. Libraries and Regional Development. 666-674, WILS

REGIONAL UNION CATALOGS
see Catalogs - Union

REGIS, JOHANN GOTTLOB. Mss. - Collections - Breslau

Schneider, Alfred. Aus Johann Gottlob Regis' Breslauer Tagen. 321-338, MILF

REGISTRATION OF BORROWERS - Netherlands

Reedijk, C. Stuivers en Centen of: Andermaal het Uitleenrecht. 559-568, BRUM
Wijnstroom, Margreet. Het Uitleenrecht en de Openbare Bibliotheken. 626-639, BRUM

Rehm, Wolfgang, jt. ed.
FEDO

Reichardt, Günther.
Die Bedeutung der Annotation für Bibliographie und Katalog. 86-109, VORS

REICHENAU, Ger. (Baden) (Benedictine abbey)

Preisendanz, Karl. Der Reichenauer Handschriftenkatalog von 1724. 199-206, LEID

REICHENAU, Ger. (Baden) (Benedictine abbey) Mss. (Evangelistar)

Schmidt, Adolf. Das Reichenauer Evangelistar. Handschrift CXC der Stadtbibliothek zu Leipzig. 22-41, LEIP

REICHERT, ARNO

Schnoor, Hans. Rechts und Links der Elbe. 88-91, BOLE

Reid, Winnifred Reynolds.
Beginnings of Printing in New Haven. From Letters of Benjamin Franklin and James Parker. 67-88, KEOG

Reider, Joseph.
The New Ornament of Jewish Books. 10-18, BLOC
Non-Jewish Motives in the Ornament of Early Hebrew Books. 150-159, FREI

Reifenberg, Hermann.
Die Liturgische Bedeutung der Mainzer Brevierhandschrift MS 4°33 des Jahres 1482. 90-102, MAIZ

REIN, Austria (Cistercian abbey) Buchbinderei

Laurin, Gertraut. Blindgedruckte Einzelstempelbände des XV. und XVI. Jahrhunderts im Zisterzienserstift Rein bei Graz. 10-30, SCHT

Reinhard, Ewald.
I. H. von Wessenberg als Freund der Schönen Künste. 59-63, VERD

REINOSO, FÉLIX JOSÉ. Examen de los "Delitos de Infidelidad a la Patria."

Santiago, Ignacio Aguilera. Notas sobre el Libro de Reinoso, "Delitos de Infidelidad a la Patria." I, 319-332, ARTI

Reiprich, Alfred.
Arbeit und Aufgaben der Ernst-Abbe-Bücherei. 72-104, JENA

Reisig, Otto.
Die Kartenrückseiten in Ihrer Bedeutung für die Zeitliche Festlegung der Spielkarten. 123-133, ALTE

Rekowa, Stanisława.
Formy Współpracy Pedagogicznej Biblioteki z Nauczycielem. 103-106, KRAK

RELIGIOUS ARCHIVES
see Archives, Church

RELIGIOUS LIBRARIES - Germany

Brachvogel, Eugen, Monsignore. Die Bibliotheken der Geistlichen Residenzen des Ermlandes. 35-44, KÖNI

RELIGIOUS LIBRARIES - Hist. - Ancient

Harnack, Adolf. Die Älteste Inschrift über einer Öffentlichen Kirchen-Bibliothek. 111-114, SCHW

RELIGIOUS LIBRARIES - Rotterdam

Kossmann, F. K. H. Rotterdam en de "Bijzondere" O.B. 496-500, BRUM

RELIGIOUS LITERATURE
see also Catholic literature

RELIGIOUS LITERATURE - Cataloging

Baader, Peter. Kirchen und Liturgien im Alphabetischen Katalog. Probleme Ihrer Einordnung. 24-40, FUCH

RELIGIOUS LITERATURE (Finnish) - Collections - Scandinavia

Kilpi, Volter. Suomalainen Virsikirja [Manuale-nide] v:lta 1630 Teuvan Kirkonarkistossa. 122-126, SCHA

RELIGIOUS PAINTING
see Christian art and symbolism

REMAINDERS
see Inexpensive editions

REMIGIUS, of Auxerre. Mss. <u>L'Expositio super Matheum</u>

Vilar, Joan. L'"Expositio Remigii Super Matheum" en el Còd. 548 de la Biblioteca de Catalunya. III, 263-281, RUBI

RENÉ I, D'ANJOU, King of Naples and Jerusalem. <u>Mss. Livre du Cuer d'Amours Espris</u>

Winkler, Emil. Die Textliche Stellung der Handschrift 2597 der Wiener Nationalbibliothek (René von Anjou, Livre du Cuer d'Amours Espris). 861-870, VIEN

Renker, Armin.
Die Forschungsstelle Papiergeschichte im Gutenberg-Museum zu Mainz. 80-89, BOCK

Renouard, Yves.
Intérêt et Importance des Archives Vaticanes pour L'Histoire Économique du Moyen Age Spécialement du XIVe Siècle. 21-41, MERC

RENTAL LIBRARIES - Japan - Hist.

Ishii, Atsushi. Shoki ni okeru Paionia no Katsuyaku—Wagakuni Junkai Bunko no Taihaika no Rekishi, I. (Activities of the Pioneers in the Early Period—a History of Circulating Libraries in Japan, I.) 34-49, TOKY

REPAIR OF BOOKS
see Books - Care and restoration

REPORTS
see Library publications

REPRINTS

Kaiser, Rudolf. Zur Unterscheidung Anscheinend Identischer Drucke. 127-129, SCHW

REPRINTS, Cheap
see Inexpensive editions

REPRINTS, Unauthorized - Hist.

Kliemann, Horst. Über Einige Versuche, sich gegen Nachdruck zu Wehren. 252-254, BENZ

REPRODUCTION OF CATALOG CARDS
see Catalog cards - Reproduction

REPROGRAPHY

Wolk, L. J. van der. De Reprografie en het Vermenigvuldigen van een Geschreven Tekst. 250-256, KOSS

REQUIRED READING
see College and university libraries - Required reading materials

<u>RERUM ITALICARUM SCRIPTORES</u>

Coen-Pirani, Emma. Il Contributo di Eruditi Veneti alla Pubblicazione dei "Rerum Italicarum Scriptores." 169-190, FERR

RESEARCH

Kirchner, Joachim. Gedanken zur Wissenschaftsgeschichtlichen Forschung. 325-332, JUCH

RESEARCH AND THE LIBRARY

Brinton, Crane. Patterns of Research and Changing Library Needs from the Viewpoint of the Humanities and Social Sciences. 7-12, PENN
Kaser, David. How Big Is a Research Library? 17-19, NASH
Kleve, Knut. Forskerens Ønskebibliotek. 138-140, NORS
Lydenberg, Harry M. Libraries and Scholarship: Should Libraries Be Passive Instruments of, or Active Participants in, Research? 90-98, PENN
Meyer-Abich, Adolf. Bibliotheken als Forschungsinstitute für Wissenschaftsgeschichte. 77-83, TIEM
Noé, A. C. The University Library and Research. 300-305, HANS
Zirkle, Conway. Patterns of Research and Changing Library Needs from the Viewpoint of the Natural Sciences. 12-18, PENN

RESEARCH AND THE LIBRARY - Uppsala

Lundberg, Oskar. Frågan om Forskarplatser och Forskarrum vid Uppsala Universitetsbibliotek. 59-76, GRAP

RESEARCH IN LIBRARIANSHIP
Krishna Rao, D. B. Research in Library Science. 150-154, MADR

RESEARCH LIBRARIANS
see College and university librarians; Documentalists; Librarians; Special librarians

RESEARCH LIBRARIES
see also College and university libraries; Special libraries

RESEARCH LIBRARIES
Golub, Ilja. Informačně-Bibliografické Funkce Vědecké Knihovny. 102-107, EMLE
Knorr, Friedrich. Der Beruf des Wissenschaftlichen Bibliothekars in Unserer Zeit. I, 112-118, GLAU
Liebaers, Herman. Des Expositions dans les Bibliothèques. 159-168, HOFM
Metcalf, Keyes DeWitt. Some Trends in Research Libraries. 145-166, BISH
Mumford, Quincy L. Automation in Research Libraries. 548-551, BRUM
Schmidt, Wieland. Offene Buchbestände in Universalbibliotheken. 125-142, FUCH
Usher, Robert James. The Place of the Endowed Reference Library in the Community. 467-473, PUTN

RESEARCH LIBRARIES - Acquisitions
Clapp, Verner W. The Balance of Conflicting Interests in the Building of Collections: Comprehensiveness Versus Selectivity. 65-72, PENN
Ellsworth, Ralph E. The Balance of Conflicting Interests in the Building of Collections: Comprehensiveness Versus Selectivity. 73-79, PENN

RESEARCH LIBRARIES - Aims and objectives - Norway
Tveterås, Harald L. Forskningsbibliotekene og Fremtiden. 131-137, NORS

RESEARCH LIBRARIES - Cape of Good Hope - Hist.
Immelmann, R. F. M. A Contribution to the History of Scholarly Libraries in the Cape Province (before 1920). 25-44, COET

RESEARCH LIBRARIES - Czechoslovakia
Žmavc, Ivan. O Vůdčích Funkcích Vědeckého Knihovnictví v Soustavě Národní Vzdělanosti. 157-158, EMLE

RESEARCH LIBRARIES - Finance
Gebhardt, Walther. Gedanken zum Personalbedarf einer Wissenschaftlichen Bibliothek. 55-65, HOFF

RESEARCH LIBRARIES - France
Metcalf, Keyes DeWitt. The Ever Expanding Demand for Materials and the Threatened Decline of Support: How Shall the Gap Be Filled? 27-36, PENN

RESEARCH LIBRARIES - Germany
Briele, Wolfgang van der. Die Wissenschaftliche Stadtbibliothek—Heute. Probleme und Erfahrungen. 308-324, JUCH
Kunze, Horst. Bemerkungen zum Thema "Wissenschaftliche Bibliotheken und Dokumentation." 203-213, VORS
Meyer, Herbert. Über die Namen Wissenschaftlicher Bibliotheken. 46-54, HOFF
Walter, Kurt. Zur Gegenwärtigen Lage des Auswärtigen Leihverkehrs der Wissenschaftlichen Bibliotheken. 143-157, JUCR

RESEARCH LIBRARIES - Germany - Hist.
Leyh, Georg. August Wilmanns und Emil Jacobs. 125-136, STOL

RESEARCH LIBRARIES - Norway - Hist.
Madshus, Sigrid. Fag- og Forskningsbibliotekene i Siste Decennium. 125-130, NORS

RESEARCH LIBRARIES - Posen (Province)
Jolowicz, J. Die Polnische Bibliographie in Ihrer Entwicklung und Ihrem Gegenwärtigen Stande. 75-88, VERP

RESEARCH LIBRARIES - Reference services
Putnam, Herbert. Interpretive Service in a Library for Research. 211-213, MUNT
Schneider, Georg. Die Bibliographie an den Wissenschaftlichen Bibliotheken. 322-326, KUHN

RESEARCH LIBRARIES - U.S.
Bishop, William Warner. Research Libraries in America. 13-19, MUNT
Kuhlman, A. F. Wanted: A New Policy for the Organization and Development of Library Resources for Research. 585-600, WILS
White, Carl M. The Research Library in Contemporary Society: A Problem of the Proper Recognition of Services Rendered. 43-54, PENN

RESEARCH LIBRARIES - U.S. - Hist.
Kaser, David. How Big Is a Research Library? 17-19, NASH

RESEARCH MATERIALS
see also Library resources; Special collections

RESEARCH MATERIALS
Kaser, David. How Big Is a Research Library? 17-19, NASH

RESEARCH MATERIALS - Collections - Basel
Roth, Paul. Ein Streifzug durch die Archivbestände. 45-67, BASL

RESEARCH MATERIALS - Collections - Nashville
Research Materials in Microform. 21, NASH

RESEARCH MATERIALS - Collections - New York (City)
Wroth, Lawrence C. The Pierpont Morgan Library and the Historian. 10-22, GREE

RESEARCH MATERIALS IN MICROFORM. 21, NASH

RESEARCH STUDIES BY LIBRARIANS
see Librarians as authors

RESERVED BOOKS
see College and university libraries - Required reading materials

RESIDENCE HALL LIBRARIES
see Dormitory libraries

Rest, Josef.
Das Basler Missale vom Jahre 1586. 207-212, LEID

REUCHLIN, JOHANN. Carmen Theologicum [1495/99?]
Geissler, Paul. Ein Unbekannter Reuchlin-Wiegendruck. 120-126, BENZ

REUCHLIN, JOHANN. De Rudimentis Hebraicis. 1506
Widmann, Hans. Zu Reuchlins Rudimenta Hebraica. 492-498, BENZ

REUCHLIN, JOHANN. Mss. Scenica Progymnasmata
Nelson, Axel. Zum Wimpfeling-Codex der Universitätsbibliothek zu Uppsala. 27-37, LEYG

REUMONT, ALFRED VON - Library
Fromm, Emil. Die Dante-Sammlung der Alfred von Reumont'schen Bibliothek. 94-141, (pt. 1), AACH

REUN (Cistercian abbey)
see Rein, Austria (Cistercian abbey)

Reuschel, Lieselotte, jt. author
Debes, Martha and Lieselotte Reuschel. Die Ehemalige Bibliothek des Börsenvereins der Deutschen Buchhändler zu Leipzig. 243-257, LEIZ

REUSS, JEREMIAS DAVID
Leyh, Georg. Bibliothekshistorisches aus dem J. D. Reuss-Briefwechsel. 1-9, SCHT

Reuter, Rudolf.
Berufsausbildung des Volksbibliothekars in Deutschland. II, 60-63, GLAU

REUTERDAHL, HENRIK
Gierow, Krister. Henrik Reuterdahl Som Biblioteksman. 51-76, HEIN

REUTERHOLM FAMILY (Nils Esbjörnsson Reuterholm) - Library
Dahlberg, Ragnar. Ätten Reuterholms Exlibris. 108-114, HULT

REVERDINO, GIORGIO
see Reverdy, Georges

REVERDY, GEORGES
Donati, Lamberto. Note Inedite di Alfred Cartier su Giorgio Reverdino, Illustratore di Libri. 379-401, GALL

REVIEWS
see Book reviews

Révillout, Eugène.
Une Thèse en Théologie du XVe Siècle. 243, CHAT

REVOLUTIONARY LITERATURE - Collections - Berlin
Gittig, Heinz. Die Gesellschaftswissenschaftliche Beratungsstelle. I, 425-432, BERS
Krabbe, Wilhelm. Die Revolutionssammlung. 90-91, HARN

Rey, Agapito.
A Pleasant Dialogue. 13-20, HAMM

Reychman, Jan.
Zbiory Orientaliów w Polsce XVIII w. 283-294, PIEK

Reyes, Enrique Sánchez.
Lenguas de Piedra: Sobre los Enigmas del Claustro Universitario Salmantino. I, 261-295, ARTI

Menéndez Pelayo, Director de la Biblioteca Nacional. 27-67, MENE

Reynvann, Marie J.
Lijst van de Geschriften van G. A. Evers 1907—1 Jan. 1940. 7-25, EVER

RHENANUS, BEATUS - Library

Knod, Gustav C. Aus der Bibliothek des Beatus Rhenanus. Second Book, 1-109, SCHL

Rhodes, Dennis E.
Konrad Stepeck of Nuremberg (c. 1424-c. 1495). 311-316, BENZ

RIANT, PAUL ÉDOUARD DIDIER, Comte

Collijn, Isak Gustaf Alfred. Journal de Voyage en Scandinavie d'un Bibliophile Français. 187-199, GODE

RIBE, Denmark. Katedralskolen. Bibliothek

Nielsen, L. Et Sjaeldent Danicum. 225-229, COLL

RICCARDO DI SAN VITTORE
see Richard, of Saint-Victor

Ricci, Seymour de.
Un Fragment en Onciale du "Pro Plancio" de Cicéron. 442-447, CHAT

RICHARD DE BURY
see Aungerville, Richard, known as Richard de Bury, Bp. of Durham (1287-1345)

RICHARD, OF SAINT-VICTOR. Ms. Beniamin Minor

Billanovich, Giuseppe. Un Amico e un Libro del Petrarca. 99-104, FERR

Richardson, Ernest Cushing.
Inspired Libraries. 378-387, PUTN

Richel, Arthur.
Astrologische Volksschriften der Aachener Stadtbibliothek. 49-93, (pt. 1), AACH
Ein Frankfurter Theater-Programm vom Jahre 1668. 117-127, EBRA

RICHEL, BERNHARD, music printer

Pfister, Arnold. Vom Frühsten Musikdruck in der Schweiz. 160-178, BINZ

RICHENBACH, JOHANN

Kyriss, Ernst. Nördlinger Bucheinbände eines Zeit- und Kunstgenossen Johann Richenbachs. I, 119-139, GLAU

RICHENBACH, JOHANN - Bibl.

Glauning, Otto. Ein Beitrag zur Kenntnis der Einbände Johann Richenbachs. 95-112, LEIP

Richer, Jean.
Le Manuscrit et Les Premières Éditions de "La Fée aux Miettes" de Charles Nodier. 365-371, BONN

Richnell, D. T.
The Education of Librarians and Information Officers: University Libraries. 291-300, HUTT

Richter, Gisela M. A.
The Morgan Eros. 143-147, GREE

Richter, Gunter.
Die Sammlung von Drucker-, Verleger- und Buchführerkatalogen in den Akten der Kaiserlichen Bücherkommission. 317-372, BENZ

Richter, Hubert.
Heinrich Geffcken und Seine Veröffentlichung des Tagebuchs Kaiser Friedrichs. 240-254, BOLL

Rickson, Levi.
En Kvartett Bokvänner. 49-62, ÖREB

Riedel, Friedrich W.
Die Libretto-Sammlung im Benediktinerstift Göttweig. 105-111, FEDO

RIEDEL, GEORG - Bibl.

Güttler, Hermann. Die Gelegenheitskompositionen Georg Riedels. 181-195, KÖNI

Riemsdijk, G. A. van.
De Bibliotheek van Morgen. 569-576, BRUM

RIES, Ger. Maria Maihingen (Birgittine monastery). Mss.

Collijn, Isak Gustaf Alfred. En Birgitta-Handskrift från Klostret Maria Maihingen. 8-14, GRAP

RIGA. Library. Mss.

Strauch, Philipp. Rigaer Handschriftenfragmente. 238-243, DEGE

RIGA, Stadtbibliothek
see Riga. Library

Riggs, John Beverley, ed.
DAVI

Rije, To van.
Statistische Gegevens van de Utrechtsche Universiteitsbibliotheek over de Laatste 25 Jaren. 70-75, SOME

Rijswijk, Willem van.
H. J. de Vleeschauwer—Exégète de la Pensée Kantienne. 49-57, VLEE

RINALDO RINALDINI

Bay, Jens Christian. Rinaldo Rinaldini (Capo Brigante) and George Washington. 18-33, BISH

RINCK, PETER - Library

Werhahn, Heinz Martin. Die Bücher des Dr. Peter Rinck. 181-188, JUCR

Ringdal, Johan R.
Vår Fremtid—Drøm og Virkelighet. Betraktninger over Science-Fiction-Litteraturen. 189-199, NORS

RINGER, HANS, of Wimbschpach, printer

Scholderer, Victor. Hans Ringer zu Wimbschpach. 417-420, BENZ

Risse, Joseph.
Ein Neuer Immermann-Fund, die Urhandschrift des "Alexis." 89-117, VERD

RITSCHL, FRIEDRICH WILHELM

RITS

Ritzler, Remigius.
Die Archivalischen Quellen der "Hierarchia Catholica." 51-74, MERC

Rius I Serra, Josep.
Un Full Visigòtic del Segle IX. II, 441-450, RUBI

RIVERO, ANGELA MARIUTTI DE SÁNCHEZ
see Mariutti de Sánchez Rivero, Angela

RIVINGTON, JAMES

Hewlett, Leroy. James Rivington, Tory Printer. 165-194, GJEL

Rivkind, Isaac.
Correspondence of Elijah Morpugo. 138-159, (Hebrew section), FREI

Robbins, Caroline.
The First Half Century. 10-18, DAVI

Robert, Pierre-Charles.
Inscriptions Laissées dans une Carrière de la Haute Moselle par des Légions Romaines. 329-340, GRAU

Robert, Ulysse.
Note sur l'Origine de L'Ę Cédillé dans les Manuscrits. 633-637, HAVE
Notice Paléographique sur le Manuscrit de Prudence, n° 8084 du Fonds Latin de la Bibliothèque Nationale. 405-413, GRAU

Robinson, A. M. L.
Mr. Varley's Contribution to Bibliography. 18-19, VARL

Robinson, Ida Marian.
Personnel Trends of a Decade in Medical Libraries. 386-388, DOEJ

Robinson, M. U.
School and College Libraries and the Teacher in Training. 147-150, OFFO

Robiou, Félix.
De Quelques Monuments Gréco-Égyptiens du Louvre. 601-609, GRAU

Robison, Dan M.
The Library Books of Nashville. 5-7, NASH

Rochlin, S. A.
Mr. D. H. Varley—A Researcher's Tribute 23, VARL

RODEMACHERN, MARGARETE VON

Schenk zu Schweinsberg, Eberhard, Frhr. Margarete von Rodemachern, eine Deutsche Bücherfreundin in Lothringen. 117-152, WEIM

Roden, Carl B.
The Boston Years of Dr. W. F. Poole. 388-394, PUTN
An Essay in Retrospection. 659-665, WILS

Rodenberg, Julius.
Die Sammlung der Künstlerischen Drucke. 165-176, LEIS
Über Zeitungs- und Zeitschriftentypographie. 373-380, LEYG
Zur Architektonik des Buches. 91-102, MIND

RÖDER (C. G.) firm, publishers, Leipzig

King, A. Hyatt. C. G. Röder's Music-Printing Business in 1885. 53-59, FEDO

Roelker, William Greene.
The Browns and Brown University. 235-246, WROT

Roelofs, Sjoerdtje.
La "Collection Anny Antoine - Louis Koopman" à la Bibliothèque Royale de la Haye. 577-580, BRUM

ROEMERS, CHARLES CLÉMENT - Library

Bussels, C. M. Over de Bibliotheek en de Kunstwerken van Charles Clément Roemers. 557-566, MAAS

Rötzsch, Helmut.
Der Börsenverein der Deutschen Buch-

händler zu Leipzig und die Deutsche Bücherei. 47-66, LEIZ
Die Deutsche Bücherei—die Deutsche Nationalbibliothek. 1-18, LEIZ

Rogers, Frank B.
Management Improvement in the Library. 404-409, DOEJ

Rohde, Fritz.
Verzeichnis der Bibliothekare an der Universitätsbibliothek in Marburg. 294-303, KUHN

Rohr, Christine.
Die Spanischen Bücherbestände der Österreichischen Nationalbibliothek. 534-537, BICK

Rohrbach, Peter P.
Fachabteilungen und Sondersammlungen. 42-47, BERR

Rohwer, Jürgen.
Die Bibliothek für Zeitgeschichte und Ihre Aufgabe in der Historischen Forschung. 112-138, HOFF

Rojnić, Matko.
Überblick über die Bibliographische Tätigkeit in Kroatien. 70-73, STUM

Roland-Marcel, Pierre R.
Ma Visite à la Library of Congress. 395-398, PUTN

ROLEVINCK, WERNER. Fasciculus Temporum
Stillwell, Margaret Bingham. The Fasciculus Temporum, a Genealogical Survey of Editions before 1480. 409-440, EAME

Rolla, P.
Saggio di Toponomastica Calabrese. 193-197, STAM

Rollins, Carl P.
The Bibliographical Press at Yale University. 247-261, WROT

Roloff, Heinrich, ed.
VORS

Roloff, Heinrich.
Aufstellung und Katalogisierung der Bestände. I, 131-174, BERS
Zur Theorie des Zentralkatalogs. 252-273, VORS

ROMAN CATHOLIC LIBRARIES
see Catholic libraries

ROMAN DE LA ROSE
Högberg, Paul. Une Édition Rarissime du Roman de la Rose dans la Bibliothèque de L'Université Royale d'Uppsala. 268-291, UPPS

ROMAN DE LA ROSE. Mss.
Söderhjelm, Werner. Un Manuscrit du Roman de la Rose à la Bibliothèque Royale de Stockholm. 75-90, COLL

ROMAN TYPE - Type and type-founding
see Type and type-founding— Roman type

ROME (City) - Antiquarians
see Antiquarians - Rome (City)

ROME (City) - Archives, Church - Inventories, calendars, etc.
see Archives, Church - Inventories, calendars, etc. - Rome (City)

ROME (City). Archivio di Stato, Laboratorio di Restauro
Lodolini, Armando. Origine e Attività del Laboratorio di Restauro Presso L'Archivio Centrale dello Stato. 519-534, GALL

ROME (City). Biblioteca Angelica
Gnoli, Tomaso. Giggi Zanazzo e le Sue Opere Edite ed Inedite alla Biblioteca Angelica. 183-191, GREG

ROME (City). Biblioteca Casanatense
Caputo, Ada Moricca. Frammenti dello "Speculum Perfectionis" (in un Manoscritto Casanatense). 549-558, GALL
Moricca, Luciano. Le Stampe del Goltzius nella Biblioteca Casanatense di Roma. 286-303, GREG
Moricca-Caputi, Ada. Di Alcuni Opuscoli Rari nella Biblioteca Casanatense. 153-165, ACCU
———— Appunti Su Alcuni Incunaboli Casanatensi. 304-316, GREG
Taurisano, Innocenzo, O. P. Il Padre Tommaso Masetti Ultimo Prefetto della Casanatense. 385-389, GREG

ROME (City). Biblioteca Casanatense. Mss. (378)
Muzzioli, Giovanni. Il Più Antico Codice della Biblioteca Casanatense. 323-332, GREG

ROME (City). Bibliotheca Hertziana
Harnack, Axel von. Einige Beobachtungen an den Deutschen Bibliotheken in Rom. 304-309, KUHN

ROME (City). Biblioteca Nazionale Centrale Vittorio Emanuele. Collezione Romana
Santovito-Vichi, Nella. La Collezione Romana della Biblioteca Nazionale Centrale di Roma. 353-377, GREG

ROME (City). Biblioteca Romana Sarti
Garinei-Canori, Costanza. La Col-

lezione Busuttil della Biblioteca Romana Sarti. 177-182, GREG

ROME (City). Biblioteca Vallicelliana. Mss. (C 82)

Martini, E. Una Lettera del Retore Teodulo (Thomas Magistros) al Monaco Ieroteo. 433-447, CERI

ROME (City) Biblioteca Vaticana
see Vatican. Biblioteca Vaticana

ROME (City) - Bookbinding
see Bookbinding - Rome (City)

ROME (City) Cappella Sistina
see Vatican. Cappella Sistina

ROME (City) - Catalogs
see Catalogs - Rome (City)

ROME (City). Deutsches Historisches Institut
see Deutsches Historisches Institut, Rome (City)

ROME (City) - Engravings - Collections
see Engravings - Collections - Rome (City)

ROME (City) - Hist. - Collections - Rome (City)

Santovito-Vichi, Nella. La Collezione Romana della Biblioteca Nazionale Centrale di Roma. 353-377, GREG

ROME (City) - Incunabula - Collections
see Incunabula - Collections - Rome (City)

ROME (City), International Institute of Agriculture
see International Institute of Agriculture, Rome (City)

ROME (City) Laboratorio di Restauro
see Rome (City) Archivio di Stato. Laboratorio di Restauro

ROME (City) - Librarians
see Librarians - Rome (City)

ROME (City) - Libraries
see Libraries - Rome (City)

ROME (City) - Manuscripts, Latin
see Manuscripts, Latin - Rome (City)

ROME (City) - Monastic libraries
see Monastic libraries - Rome (City)

ROME (City) - Music libraries and collections
see Music libraries and collections - Rome (City)

ROME (City) - Printing
see Printing - Rome (City)

ROME (City) - Publishers and publishing
see Publishers and publishing - Rome (City)

ROME (City). Santa Maria sopra Minerva (Church) Biblioteca

Meersseman, G. La Bibliothèque des Frères Prêcheurs de la Minerve à la Fin du XVe Siècle. 605-634, PELZ

ROME (City) - Second-hand books
see Second-hand books - Rome (City)

ROME (City) - Type and type-founding
see Type and type-founding - Rome (City)

Rongen, Bjørn.
Bøker Langs Landeveien. 120-130, KILD

Ronneberger, Werner.
Die Schlossbibliothek zu Jena. II, 64-72, GLAU

Roob, Helmut.
Schöne Breviere in der Gothaer Bibliothek. 55-61, LÜLF

Rooth, Erik.
Die Mittelalterlichen Deutschen Handschriften Einschliesslich der Lateinischen mit Deutschen Bestandteilen der Universitätsbibliothek zu Uppsala. 40-96, UPPS

ROSCHMANN, ANTON

Hochenegg, Hans. Die Roschmannsche Kupferstichsammlung. 400-414, BICK

ROSE, VALENTIN

Schmidt, Wieland. Erinnerungen. 9-16, SCHS

Rosen, David.
The Restoration of a Botticellesque Tondo in the Morgan Library. 129-131, GREE

Rosen, Edward.
Copernicus' Quotation from Sophocles. 367-379, ALBA

Rosenfeld, Hans-Friedrich.
Die Berliner Parzivalfragmente. 192-202, DEGE

Rosenfeld, Hellmut.
Die Titelholzschnitte der Bauernpraktik von 1508-1600 als Soziologische Selbstinterpretation. 373-389, BENZ

ROSENHANE FAMILY (Jöran Johansson) - Collections - Uppsala

Lewenhaupt, Eugène. Rosenhaneska Handskriftssamlingen i Uppsala Universitetsbiblioteket. 292-316, UPPS

ROSENKRANZ, KARL - Correspondence - Collections - Königsberg
Goldstein, Ludwig. Karl Rosenkranz und Alexander Jung. Mit vierzehn Unveröffentlichten Rosenkranz-Briefen. 132-158, KÖNI

Rosenthal, Erwin.
Eine Neuaufgefundene Arbeit Berthold Furtmeyrs. 213-217, LEID

Rosin, Hans, ed.
ACKE

Rosin, Hans.
Buchwirtschaftliche Konzentrationsbestrebungen im Volksbüchereiwesen. 93-102, ACKE

ROSSELLÒ, MONSERRATO
Lippi, Silvio. La Libreria di Monserrato Rosselò Giureconsulto e Bibliografo Sardo del Sec. XVI. II, 319-332, MANO

ROSSI, GIOVANNI VITTORIO. Epistolae ed Thyrrenum
Incisa della Rocchetta, Giovanni. Osservazioni sugli Autografi delle "Epistolae ed Thyrrenum" di Giano Nicio Eritreo. 215-226, GREG

Rost, Gottfried, jt. author
Krieger, Waldemar and Gottfried Rost. Das Gebäude der Deutschen Bücherei und Seine Technischen Einrichtungen. 259-270, LEIZ

ROSTIUS, CHRISTOFFER - Library
Gierow, Krister. Den Förste Universitetsbibliotekarien i Lund och "Bibliotheca Rostiana." 76-91, GARD

Roth, Carl.
Conrad Pfister, Basilius Iselin und die Amerbachische Bibliothek. 179-200, BINZ

Roth, Cecil.
Catalogue of Manuscripts in the Roth Collection. 503-535, MARX
A Seventeenth Century Library and Trousseau. 160-169, FREI

ROTH, CECIL - Library
Roth, Cecil. Catalogue of Manuscripts in the Roth Collection. 503-535, MARX

Roth, Ernst.
Die Speziell Medizinischen Deutschen Zeitschriften in den Jahren 1853, 1875 und 1901. 199-204, WILM

Roth, Paul.
Fünfzig Jahre Basler Staatsarchiv an der Martinsgasse. 9-28, BASL
Hundertfünfzig Jahre Allgemeine Lesegesellschaft in Basel. 7-46, BASA
Ein Streifzug durch die Archivbestände. 45-67, BASL

Rothe, Karl.
Geleitwort. 5, LEIP

Rother, Karl.
Die Philologie in den Realkatalogsystemen seit 1600 mit Besonderer Berücksichtigung der Klassischen Altertumswissenschaft. 300-320, MILF

Rothkrug, Michael.
An Apparently Unrecorded Appearance of Gray's Elegy, 1751: An Appendix to Stokes. 343-354, KEOG

Rothrock, Mary U.
Libraries and Regional Development. 666-674, WILS

Rottacker, Gustav.
Zur Büchereigesetzgebung in der Bundesrepublik. 39-47, ACKR

ROTTERDAM - Book industry and trade
see Book industry and trade - Rotterdam

ROTTERDAM - Public libraries
see Public libraries - Rotterdam

ROTTERDAM - Religious libraries
see Religious libraries - Rotterdam

IL ROTULO DI GIOSUE
Lietzmann, Hans. Zur Datierung der Josuarolle. 181-185, DEGE

ROUEN- Printing - Presses
see Printing - Presses - Rouen

Rouse, Roscoe.
The Libraries of Nineteenth-Century College Societies. 25-42, GJEL

ROYAL LIBRARIES
see Private libraries

ROYAL MALTA LIBRARY
see Valleta, Malta. Royal Public Library

THE ROYAL PRIMER
Merritt, Percival. The Royal Primer. Check List of Royal Primers. 35-60, EAME

RUBEANUS, JOHANNES CROTUS
see Crotus Rubeanus, Johannes

RUBIANUS, JOHANNES CROTUS
see Crotus Rubeanus, Johannes

RUBIÓ Y LLUCH, ANTONIO
RUBI

RUBIÓ Y LLUCH, ANTONIO - Bibl.
Bibliografia del Prof. Antoni Rubió i Lluch. I, ix-xv, RUBI

Ruckert, Ernest.
An Intermediate Form of Catalogue between the Classified and Subject Catalogue. 243-247, RANG

Rudbeck, Gustaf.
Bidrag till Uppsala Akademiska Boktryckeris Historia. 45-58, GRAP
Peter van Selow Stilgjutare och Boktryckare i Stockholm 1618-1648. 303-334, COLL
Uppsala Universitetsbiblioteks Exlibris. 391-397, UPPS

Rudbeck, Johannes.
Några Italianska Bokband från 1500-Talet. 411-420, COLL
Über die Herkunft der Grolier-Einbände. 183-190, LOUB

Rudnicka, Jadwiga.
Fragment Biblioteki Lompy. 281-306, GRYC

Rudnitzky, Günter.
Ein Sermon aus dem Schatzkästlein Unseres Vaters Apa Schenute. 12-18, WEHM

Rudomino, M.
Die Staatliche Allunionsbibliothek für Ausländische Literatur zu Moskau—Heute und Morgen. 175-181, HOFM

Rückert, Ernst.
Die Auskunftserteilung, eine der Hauptaufgaben der Deutschen Bücherei. 274-285, VORS
Bedeutende Deutsche Bibliothekare der Neueren Zeit. 73-76, STUM
Das Wachsen und Werden der Bestände. 75-90, LEIS

Rückert, Ernst and Rudi Franz.
Geschichte, Problematik und Gegenwärtiger Stand des Gruppenschlagwortkatalogs der Deutschen Bücherei. 175-196, LEIZ

Rückert, Friedrich, tr. Mss. Arabische Sprüche . . .
in: Kreyenborg, Hermann. Proben einer Ungedruckten Übertragung Arabischer Sprüche und Sinngedichte von Friedrich Rückert aus dem in der Universitätsbibliothek zu Münster i.W. Aufbewahrten Teilnachlasse des Dichters zum Erstenmal Mitgeteilt. 125-129, BÖME

Rühl, Franz.
Sur un Manuscrit Négligé de Justinus. 412-416, CHAT

Ruelle, Charles-Émile.
Notice du Codex Marcianus 246, Contenant le Traité du Philosophe Damascius sur les Premiers Principes. 547-552, GRAU

Ruf, Paul.
Eine Altbayerische Gelehrtenbibliothek des 15. Jahrhunderts und Ihr Stifter Bernhard von Kraiburg. 219-239, STOL
Ausgaben des Klosters Benediktbeuern für Bücher und Schreibzeug von 1495-1510. 219-227, LEID
Schmeller als Bibliothekar. 9-95, GRAT

Rugg, Harold Goddard.
Isaac Eddy, Printer-Engraver. Bibliography of Eddy Publications. 313-329, EAME

Ruhland, Wilhelm.
Kunz von Kauffungen als Vogt des Amtes Altenburg. Eine Amtsrechnung vom Jahre 1445/46. 9-30, ALTE

Ruin, Hans, jt. ed.
HIRN

RUIZ, LAVERDE GUMERSINDO
see Laverde Ruiz, Gumersindo

RULAND, ANTON
Pauer, Max. Anton Ruland und Karl Halm. Ein Bibliothekarischer Streit um Dublettenverkäufe vor Hundert Jahren. 121-135, REDE

RULES AND REGULATIONS - Denmark
Krogh-Jensen, G. Om Adgangen til Folkebibliotekerne Betragtninger over Bibliotekernes Reglementer. 105-131, DØSS

RULES AND REGULATIONS - Japan
Okuda, Katsumasa. Toshokan no Seisai Kitei no Iroiro. (On the Various Rules of Punishment in Libraries.) 63-74, TSUB

RULES, Cataloging
see Cataloging - Rules

RULES, Filing
see Filing

RUMANIA - Bibliography, National
see Bibliography, National - Rumania

RUMLER, GEORG
Juntke, Fritz. Georg Rumler, ein Hallischer Buchbinder aus der Zweiten Hälfte des 16. Jahrhunderts. 201-224, HAEK

Ruppel, Aloys.
Bemerkenswerte und Merkwürdige Mainzer Bibliothekare. 187-203, JUCH
Früheste Planung eines Gutenberg-denkmals. 241-246, STOL

RUPPEL, ALOYS
RUPP

Ruppert, Hans.
Der Alphabetische Katalog. 91-102, LEIS
Deutsche Bibliothekare in Selbstdarstellungen. 76-78, STUM

RURAL LIBRARIES
see also County libraries; Package libraries; Regional libraries; School libraries (Rural school)

RURAL LIBRARIES - Book selection - Denmark
Esben-Petersen, O. Bogvalget i Oplandsarbejdet. 87-95, LASS

RURAL LIBRARIES - Denmark
Ebstrup, E. Biblioteksmuligheder paa Landet. Forsøg paa en Nyorientering. 70-84, DØSS

RURAL LIBRARIES - Finance - Aarhus, Denmark
Bredsted, Åge. Oplandsarbejdets Okonomi. 37-47, LASS

RURAL LIBRARIES - Gt. Brit.
Jensen, E. Allerslev. Engelsk Oplandsarbejde. 123-134, LASS

RURAL LIBRARIES - Güstrow (Stadt und Kreis)
GÜST

RURAL LIBRARIES - Norway
Kjørvik, M. A. Folkebogsamlingane på Landsbygda og Vilkåra for Dei. 53-61, NORN
Kobro, Nancy. Nye Strømninger i Bibliotekarbeidet på Landsbygden. 62-65, NORN
Nyhuus, Haakon. De Norske Statsunderstøttede Folkebogsamlinger. 36-42, NORS
Skancke, Mally. Norsk Oplandsarbejde. 107-116, LASS

RURAL LIBRARIES - Sweden
Wieslander, Henning. Svensk Oplandsarbejde. 117-122, LASS

RURAL LIBRARIES - U.S.
Kirkegaard, Preben. Amerikansk Oplandsarbejde. 135-146, LASS

Rusenov, M. V.
D-r Nikola Mikhov v Svishchov. 243-246, MIKH

Rush, Charles Everett.
Another Pioneer Is Honored in His Own Country. 675-678, WILS
There is Honor in One's Own Country. 1-5, KEOG

Rusk, George Yeisley.
Techniques for the Resolution of Cultural Conflicts. 14-31, MADR

RUSSIA - Bibliography
see Bibliography - Russia

RUSSIA - Bibliography, National
see Bibliography, National - Russia

RUSSIA - Classification - Special subjects - Bibliography
see Classification - Special subjects - Bibliography - Russia

RUSSIA - Depository libraries
see Depository libraries - Russia

RUSSIA - Description and travel - 18th cent. - Collections - Finland
Grönroos, Henrik. Mitä Kirjat Kertoivat Saksasta ja Venäjästä 1700-Luvun Suomalaisille. 62-84, TUDE

RUSSIA - Legal deposit (of books, etc.)
see Legal deposit (of books, etc.) - Russia

RUSSIA - Libraries
see Libraries - Russia

RUSSIA - Library schools - Theses
see Library schools - Theses - Russia

RUSSIA - Library science
see Library science - Russia

RUSSIA - Printing
see Printing - Russia

RUSSIA - Private libraries
see Private libraries - Russia

RUSSIAN LITERATURE - Collections - Bern
Lange, Eugenie. Schweizer Drucke in Russischer Sprache. 68-76, BERU

RUSSIAN LITERATURE - Collections - Helsinki
Widnäs, Maria. Jacob Grot och Universitets Ryska Bibliotek. 144-163, DAHL

RUSSIAN TYPE - Type and type-founding
see Type and type-founding - Russian type

Ruysschaert, José.
Recherche des Deux Bibliothèques Ro-

maines Maffei des XVe et XVIe Siècles. 306-355, MERG

Rytz, Walter.
Bibliographie der Schweizerischen Naturwissenschaftlichen Literatur. 151-152, BERU

RZESZÓW, Poland. Synagogue. Mss. (Siddur)
Wischnitzer-Bernstein, Rahel. Der Siddur der Altstädtischen Synagoge in Rzeszów. 77-80, FREN

SBVV
see Schweizerischer Buchhändler und Verlegerverein

SVD
see Schweizerische Vereinigung für Dokumentation

Sabbadini, R.
Ciriaco d'Ancona e la Sua Descrizione Autografa del Peloponneso Trasmessa da Leonardo Botta. 181-247, CERI

SABIN, JOSEPH. Bibliotheca Americana
Adams, Randolph G. A Goodly Company of American Book Collectors. 29-32, LYDE

Sabotke, Alice.
Benutzungsabteilung—Ausleihe, Lesesäle, Freihandabteilung. 28-32, BERR

SACHS, HANS
Schottenloher, Karl. Hans Sachs und Hieronymus Höltzel. Ein Beitrag zur Geschichte der Nürnberger Flugschriften vom Jahre 1524. 235-255, SCHW

SACRAMENTARIES
Strittmatter, Anselm. The Pentecost Exultet of Reims and Besançon. 384-400, GREE

SACRAMENTARIUM GREGORIANUM. Mss.
Lietzmann, Hans. Handschriftliches zur Rekonstruktion des Sacramentarium Gregorianum. 141-158, EHRB

SACRED BOOKS
Richardson, Ernest Cushing. Inspired Libraries. 378-387, PUTN

SACRED LITERATURE
see Sacred books

SÄCHSISCHE LANDESBIBLIOTHEK, Dresden
see Dresden. Sächsische Landesbibliothek

ŠAFAŘIK, PAVEL JOSEF, 1795-1861
Bechyňová, Věnceslav. Bibliografická Spolupráce Ivana V. Sopova s P. J. Šafaříkem. 41-50, MIKH

SAGE, GEORGES LOUIS DE
see Le Sage, Georges Louis

Saha, J.
Professional Training in Documentation. 293-302, RANG

SAIKAKU. Okimiyage
Kanai, Toranosuke. Saikaku Okimiyage no Hanshita. (Study of the Calligraphy of the Wood-Blocks of Saikaku's Okimiyage.) 97-112, TOMI

ST. BENOÎT-SUR-LOIRE, France (Benedictine abbey). Mss. (Sallust's Historia)
Bloch, Herbert. The Structure of Sallust's Historiae: The Evidence of the Fleury Manuscript. 59-76, ALBA

SAINT CHARLES, LOUIS DE
see Jacob, Louis, in religion Louis de Saint-Charles

SAINT-DENIS, France (Benedictine abbey)
Barroux, Robert. Recueil Historique en Français Composé, Transcrit et Enluminé à Saint-Denis, vers 1280. 15-34, CALO

SAINT EMMERAM (Benedictine monastery) Ratisbon
see Ratisbon. Saint Emmeram (Benedictine monastery)

ST. GALL, Switzerland (Benedictine abbey). Mss.
Cagin, Paul. L'Observation Paléographique dans L'Étude du "Sacramentarium Triplex" de Saint-Gall. 92-112, CHAT

ST. GALL, Switzerland. Stiftsarchiv
Bruckner, Albert. Die Anfänge des St. Galler Stiftsarchivs. 119-131, BINZ

ST. GALL, Switzerland. Stiftsbibliothek. Mss.
Mocquereau, A. De la Clivis Épisématique dans les Manuscrits de Saint-Gall. 508-530, CHAT

ST. GALL, Switzerland. Stiftsbibliothek. Mss. (242)
Jammers, Ewald. Neumen im Lateinunterricht. 64-68, BOLE

ST. GALL, Switzerland. Stiftsbibliothek. Mss. (878)
Bischoff, Bernhard. Eine Sammelhand-

schrift Walahfrid Strabos (Cod. Sangall. 878). 30-48, LEYH

SAINT-MÉRY, MÉDÉRIC-LOUIS-ÉLIE MOREAU DE
see Moreau de Saint-Méry, Médéric-Louis-Elie

ST. PETERSBURG
see Leningrad

SAINT-SAËNS, CAMILLE. Correspondance

Boschot, Adolphe. Saint-Saëns et Sa "Correspondance Générale." 399-402, BONN

SAINT-VICTOR, RICHARD OF
see Richard, of Saint-Victor

SAINTE-BEUVE, CHARLES AUGUSTIN

Denkinger, Marc. Sainte-Beuve et L'Imprimeur Marc Ducloux. 209-219, BONN
Dormoy, Marie. Du Droit de Détruire. 489-492, BONN

SAINTE-BEUVE, CHARLES AUGUSTIN - Library

Bonnerot, Jean. Sainte-Beuve Bibliophile. 369-374, CALO

SAINTE-BEUVE, CHARLES AUGUSTIN. Pline-le-Jeune

Levaillant, Maurice. Le "Pline-le-Jeune" de Sainte-Beuve. 285-291, BONN

SAINTE-BEUVE, CHARLES AUGUSTIN. Volupté

Bruneau, Charles. Une Création de Sainte-Beuve: La Phrase "Molle" de Volupté. 189-196, BONN

Sakkers, J. C.
Wilt U even Uw Naam Zetten? 254-257, EVER

SALA, GUISEPPE

Sartori, Claudio. Un Catalogo di Guiseppe Sala del 1715. 112-116, FEDO

SALAMANCA - Inscriptions, Latin
see Inscriptions, Latin - Salamanca

SALAMANCA, Universidad

Reyes, Enrique Sánchez. Lenguas de Piedra: Sobre los Enigmas del Claustro Universitario Salmantino. I, 261-295, ARTI

SALAN FAMILY (Sweden) - Library

Grape, Anders. Om Bröderna Salan och Deras Handskriftssamling. 139-170, ANNE

SALARIES - Stockholm - Hist. - 1772

Carlsson, A. B. En Supplik af Gjörwell 1772. Ett Stycke Svensk Lärdomshistoria i Kanslikollegiet. 67-73, ANNE

SALEM (Cistercian abbey). Bibliotheca

Jammers, Ewald. Die Salemer Handschriftensammlung. 45-64, WEHM

SALERNO. Scuola Medica. Mss.

Schuster, Julius. Secreta Salernitana und Gart der Gesundheit. Eine Studie zur Geschichte der Naturwissenschaften und Medizin des Mittelalters. 203-237, DEGE

Salfinger, Theodor.
Zur Sprachkunst des Germanisten Andreas Heusler. 193-205, SCHU

SALICETO, BARTOLOMEO DA. Mss. Consilium pro Urbano VI.

Del Re, Niccolò. Il "Consilium pro Urbano VI" di Bartolomeo da Saliceto (Vat. Lat. 5608). I, 213-263, ALBB

SALISBURY, Rhodesia - Libraries
see Libraries - Salisbury, Rhodesia

Sallander, Hans.
Några Sällsynta, Delvis Okända Lågtyska, Danska och Svenska Upplagor av Johannes Avenarius' Christliche Gebete i Uppsala Universitetsbibliotek. 8-14, DAHA
Om Anders Anton von Stiernman Som Bibliografisk Författare. 561-576, GRAP

SALLUSTIUS CRISPUS, CAIUS. Mss. Historiae

Bloch, Herbert. The Structure of Sallust's Historiae: The Evidence of the Fleury Manuscript. 59-76, ALBA

SALOMONS-TEMPEL, LEYDEN
see Burgersdijk & Niermans, firm, booksellers, Leyden

SALVADORI, GIULIO. Mss.

Vian, Nello. I Manoscritti di Giulio Salvadori nella Biblioteca Vaticana. 505-519, FERR

SALZBURG - Bookbinding
see Bookbinding - Salzburg

SALZBURG. Bundesstaatliche Studienbibliothek. Mss. (V.1.H.162)

Frisch, Ernst von. Über die Salzburger Handschrift von Hugo von St. Victors Opusculum de Fructu Carnis et Spiritus. 67-71, LEID

Samaran, Charles.
Problèmes Archivistiques d'Aujourd'hui et de Demain. 1-13, MERC

SAMBUCUS, JOHANNES - Library

Gerstinger, Hans. Johannes Sambucus als Handschriftensammler. 251-400, VIEN

SAMBUCUS, JOHANNES. Mss.

Gerstinger, Hans. Aus dem "Tagebuche" des Kaiserl. Hofhistoriographen Johannes Sambucus (1531-1584). Cod. Vindob. Latin. 9039, Fol. 1 und 5. 373-383, BICK

SAMION-CONTET, J., jt. author

Hahn, André, Paule Dumaitre, and J. Samion-Contet. Le "De Humani Corporis Fabrica" d'André Vésale (1543). 91-97, CALO

SAMOSATA, Lucian of
see Lucianus Samosatensis

Samzelius, Jonas L:Son.
Om- och Tillbyggnaden av Carolina Rediviva Åren 1934-1945. 293-337, GRAP
De Utländska Tidskrifterna vid Uppsala Universitet. Några Bidrag till Belysning av Förhallandet mellan Forskare och Bibliotek. 586-607, UPPS

SAN DANIELE DEL FRIÙLI, Italy. Biblioteca Comunale Guarneriana

Leicht, P. S. La Biblioteca d'un Umanista. 77-81, GODE

SAN MARINO, Calif. Henry E. Huntington Library and Art Gallery
see Henry E. Huntington Library and Art Gallery, San Marino, Calif.

SAN MARINO, Calif. - Maps - Collections
see Maps - Collections - San Marino, Calif.

SAN VITTORE, RICCARDO DI
see Richard, of Saint-Victor

SÁNCHEZ RIVERO, ANGELA MARIUTTI DE
see Mariutti de Sánchez Rivero, Angela

SANCTO PARCIANO, DURANDUS DE
see Durandus de Sancto Parciano

SANDECKI, JAN

Jasińska, Stanisława. Czy Jan z Sącza Mógł Być Drukarzem Poznańskim? 341-353, GRYC

SANKT KATHARINENTHAL (Dominican monastery) Bibliothek. Mss. (Gradual)

Brenn, Franz. Die Sequenzen des Graduale von St. Katharinenthal. 23-42, OREL

SANKT PAUL (Benedictine abbey). Mss. (27.2.36)

Dold, Alban. Klassische Dichter-Bruchstücke nebst einem Bericht über die Palimpsestphotographische Aufnahme des Plinius-Codex von St. Paul in Kaernten. 369-377, GALL

SANT FELIN DE GIRONA. Mss.

Noguer i Mosqueras, Tomàs. Un Text Litúrgic en Català. II, 451-462, RUBI

SANTANDER. Catedral

Gallo, Gratiniano Nieto. El Monumento Funerario de Menéndez Pelayo, Obra de Victorio Macho. 257-261, MENE

Santiago, Ignacio Aguilera.
Notas sobre el Libro de Reinoso, "Delitos de Infidelidad a la Patria." I, 319-332, ARTI

Santifaller, Leo.
Die Älteste Originalurkunde des Österreichischen Staatsarchivs. 538-575, BICK
Das Oesterreichische Staatsarchiv. 313-336, MERC

SANTILLANA, Spain. Iglesia Colegial

Camino y Aguirre, Fernando González. Bibliotecas Medievales Montañesas. II, 14-50, ARTI

SANTINI, FORTUNATO - Library

Fédorov, Vladimir. V. V. Stasov chez L'Abb. F. Santini à Rome. 55-62, HOBO

Santoro, Caterina.
Due Contratti di Lavoro per L'Arte della Stampa a Milano. 185-192, ACCU

Santoro, Enza Fioroni.
Dell'Origine e degli Autori di Alcune Stampe Attribuite ad "Ignoto." 427-439, GALL

Santovito-Vichi, Nella.
La Collezione Romana della Biblioteca Nazionale Centrale di Roma. 353-377, GREG

SAPIDUS, JEAN, supposed author. Elementale Introductorium in Nominum & Verborum Declinatio nes Graecas. 1512

Baillet, Lina. Le Premier Manuel de Grec Paru à Strasbourg. 25-36, BENZ

SARDINI, GIACOMO
Moneti, Elena Amico. Giacomo Sardini, Patrizio Lucchese, Erudito e Bibliografo. 47-78, GALL

Sarnowska, Klara.
Bibliotheca Bernardina. 69-79, BYDG
Źródła i Opracowania Dotyczące Dziejów i Działalności Biblioteki Miejskiej w Bydgoszczy. 169-171, BYDG

Sartori, Claudio.
Un Catalogo di Guiseppe Sala del 1715. 112-116, FEDO

Sasaki, Kanzō.
Toshokan Rinri. (Ethical Standards for Library and Librarian.) 15-20, KYOT

Sastri, K. S. Ramaswamy.
The Genius of Dr. Ranganathan. 739-740, RANG

Sauer, August, ed.
"Ein Bruderzwist in Habsburg." Bruchstücke Früherer Fassungen. 321-342, GLOS

Sauer, Bruno.
Die Literarischen Sammlungen der Amerika-Gedenkbibliothek. 191-204, SCHS

Sauter, Hermann.
Ansprache. 29-35, MAIZ
Bibliographie der Holbach-Drucke in Deutschen und Österreichischen Bibliotheken. 390-416, BENZ

Sawamoto, Takahisa.
Agricultural Science Libraries in Japan. 107-119, HASH

Sawicka, Stanisława M.
Czeski Rękopis Iluminowany w Książnicy Miejskiej im. Kopernika w Toruniu. 28-34, EMLE

Sawyer, Ruth.
Storytelling Fifty Years A-growing. 593-598, MOOR

Saxena, R. S.
India's Contribution to Library Science. 625-631, RANG

SAXL, FRITZ
SAXL
Bing, Gertrud. Fritz Saxl (1890-1948): A Memoir. 1-46, SAXL

SAXOFFERATO, BARTOLUS DE
see Bartolus de Saxofferato

SAXONY - Bibliography - Bibl.
see Bibliography - Bibl. - Saxony

SAXONY - Libraries
see Libraries - Saxony

SAXONY, Lower - Catalogs - Union
see Catalogs - Union - Saxony,-Lower

SAXONY - Manuscripts, Greek - Collections
see Manuscripts, Greek - Collections - Saxony

SAXONY - Monastic libraries
see Monastic libraries - Saxony

Sayers, Frances Clarke.
Big Walking Day. 561-568, MOOR

SAYERS, FRANCES CLARKE
SAYE

SAYERS, WILLIAM CHARLES BERWICK
SAYW
Colwell, Eileen. W. C. Berwick Sayers and Children's Libraries. 18-21, SAYW
Filon, S. P. L. W. C. Berwick Sayers: His Connection with the National Central Library and His Contribution to Library Co-operation. 22-25, SAYW
Stewart, J. D. Sayers. 13-17, SAYW

Scaccia-Scarafoni, Camillo.
La Grammatica di Sulpizio Verolano in un Incunabulo Ignoto ai Bibliografi. 378-384, GREG
La Più Antica Edizione della Grammatica Latina di Aldo Manuzio Finora Sconosciuta ai Bibliografi. 193-203, ACCU

SCANDINAVIA - Associations
see Associations - Scandinavia

SCANDINAVIA - Bibliography
see Bibliography - Scandinavia

SCANDINAVIA - Cooperation
see Cooperation - Scandinavia

SCANDINAVIA - Depository libraries
see Depository libraries - Scandinavia

SCANDINAVIA - Government libraries
see Government libraries - Scandinavia

SCANDINAVIA - Interlibrary loans
see Interlibrary loans - Scandinavia

SCANDINAVIA - Libraries
see Libraries - Scandinavia

SCANDINAVIA - Scandinavian literature - Collections
see Scandinavian literature - Collections - Scandinavia

SCANDINAVIAN CORRESPONDENCE
see Correspondence, Scandinavian

SCANDINAVIAN LITERATURE - Collections - Germany

Jürgens, Adolf. Die Skandinavischen Studien und die Bibliotheken in Deutschland im Letzten Menschenalter. 97-127, MUNT

SCANDINAVIAN LITERATURE - Collections - Scandinavia

Munthe, Wilhelm. National Departments in Scandinavian Libraries. 296-299, HANS

SCANDINAVIANS IN GERMANY

Büscher, Alfred. Skandinavier, Dresden und die Landesbibliothek. 99-104, BOLL

SCANIA - Books - Prices
see Books - Prices - Scania

Schaaf, Fritz.
Zur Geschichte der Deutschen Bücherei nach 1945. 67-90, LEIZ

Schaanning, Hedvig.
Litt om Fagbiblioteker i Norge. 109-118, NORN

Schaanning, Maja.
Litt om Professor Ludvig Daaes Boksamling. 214-225, MUNT

SCHAARSCHMIDT, KARL

Rath, Erich von. Karl Schaarschmidt. 283-296, LEYG

Schäck, Ernst.
Ansprache. 14-25, MAIZ

Schäfer, Rosa Maria.
Das Deutsche Buch. 76-77, FRAD

SCHAFFGOTSCH, HANS ANTON, Graf - Library

Nentwig, Heinrich. Zwei Schlesische Majoratsbibliotheken. 129-138, WILM

SCHAFFGOTT'SCHE MAJORATSBIBLIOTHEK, Warmbrunn, Silesia
see Warmbrunn, Silesia. Schaffgott'sche Majoratsbibliothek

SCHAFFHAUSEN. Stadtbibliothek. Mss. (Generalia no. 1)

Frauenfelder, Reinhard. Die Älteste Handschrift in der Stadtbibliothek Schaffhausen. 155-160, LÜTH

Schaible, Eduard.
Abkürzung in Schrift und Sprache. 73-81, SCHR

Schapiro, Israel.
Bibliography of Hebrew Translations of English Works. 182-218, FREI

Schapiro, Meyer.
Two Romanesque Drawings in Auxerre and Some Iconographic Problems. 331-349, GREE

Scharoun, Hans.
[An Address.] 6-8, BERP

Schauer, Georg Kurt.
Die Sammlung Buchkunst. 149-161, EPPE

Schauman, Georg.
Biblioteksväsendets Organisation. 1-16, HULA

SCHAUMAN, GEORG

SCHA

Schauman, Henrik.
Festskrifter och Festnummer Tillägnade Lärare och Tjänstemän vid Universiteten i Helsingfors och Åbo. 319-350, DAHL
Monarkisternas och Republikanernas Arkiv. 97-100, NYBE
Samarbetet Mellan de Nordiska Parlamentsbiblioteken. 232-237, TVET

Schawe, Josef, ed.
GIES

Schawe, Josef.
D. Steuberi Catalogi und Nachrichten von der Marpurger und Giesser Bibliothec. Giessener Hs. 30. 204-214, JUCH
Die Früheren Unterkünfte der Universitätsbibliothek Giessen. 15-25, GIES

Schazmann, Paul-Emile.
La Bulle d'Excommunication de Georges de Supersaxo. Un Imprimé Officiel de 1519 Émanant de la Chancellerie Épiscopale de Bâle. 207-212, SCHU
Les Imprimés Anciens. 33-38, BERU
Marcel Godet et L'Histoire Moderne. 22-23, GODM
Les Périodiques Officiels. 48-50, BERU

SCHEDEL, HARTMANN

Jacobs, Emil. Ars Scripturarum. 177-186, MILF

SCHEDEL, HARTMANN. Liber Chronicarum. 1493

Bernoulli, Rudolf. Das Weltallbild in Hartmann Schedels Weltchronik. 48-58, LOUB

Scheiber, Alexander.
Medieval Hebrew Manuscripts as

Bindings in the Libraries and Archives of Hungary. 19-28, BLOC
Piyyutim from the Geniza Collection of David Kaufmann. 537-546, MARX

Scheidig, Walther.
Zur Baugeschichte der Weimarischen Bibliothek. 1-32, WEIM

Schenk, Erich.
Die Österreichische Musiküberlieferung der Züricher Zentralbibliothek. 576-581, BICK

Schenk zu Schweinsberg, Eberhard, Frhr.
Margarete von Rodemachern, eine Deutsche Bücherfreundin in Lothringen. 117-152, WEIM

Schenkl, Charles.
De Codicibus Quibus in Xenophontis Hierone Recensendo Utimur. 111-120, GRAU

SCHENUTE, SAINT
see Shanūdah, Anba, Saint

SCHERER, ALEXANDER NICOLAUS - Collections - Jena

Feyl, Othmar. Aus der Jenaer Aufklärung. 179-188, BULL

Schermall, Herbert.
Die Berliner Musikbibliotheken im Rückblick und in der Gegenwart. 99-117, SCHS

Scherrer, Paul.
Sub Aeternitatis Specie. 163-165, MADR
Die Zeit im Bibliothekarischen Beruf. 169-173, HOFM

SCHERTLIN VON BURTENBACH, SEBASTIAN, Ritter

Lutze, Eberhard. Eine Augsburger Bilderhandschrift aus dem Besitz des Sebastian Schertlin von Burtenbach (Ms. 1620 der UB Erlangen). 147-156, STOL

Schick, Frank L.
The Recurring Emergence of American Paperbacks. 195-202, GJEL

Schiller, Karl-Heinz.
Das Ludwigsburger Beispiel. 49-60, ACKR

Schilling, H.
Slavostní Večer. 5-6, ŽIVN

Schillmann, Fritz.
Zur Geschichte des Bücherwesens des Deutschen Ritterordens. 278-282, KUHN

Schirrmeister, Georg.
Über den Stand beim Bau Wissenschaftlicher Bibliotheken. 103-116, BULL

SCHLEIERMACHER, ANDREAS AUGUST

Rasmussen, Detlef. Andreas Schleiermacher und das Prinzip der Schlüsselung. 163-175, REDE

SCHLEIERMACHER, FRIEDRICH ERNST

Bauer, Johannes. Schleiermacherbildnisse. 86-96, KUHN

SCHLESWIG-HOLSTEIN - Private libraries
see Private libraries - Schleswig-Holstein

SCHLETTSTADT
see Sélestat, Alsace

SCHLOSS HOHENTÜBINGEN, Tübingen
see Tübingen. Schloss Hohentübingen

Schmekel, Ruth.
Der Bücherwurm. 14, ZIEG

SCHMELLER, JOHANN ANDREAS

Ruf, Paul. Schmeller als Bibliothekar. 9-95, GRAT

Schmid, Helmut H.
Ein Nürnberger Kalender von 1430 und Johann Blaubirer's Kalender von 1483. 247-253, STOL

SCHMID, KONRAD ARNOLD

Meyen, Fritz. Konrad Arnold Schmid (1716-1789), Professor am Collegium Carolinum zu Braunschweig. Ein Freund und Mitarbeiter Lessings. 333-354, JUCH

Schmid, Paul.
Verzeichnis der Schriften von Georg Leyh seit Juni 1937. 7-12, LEYH

Schmid, Wolfgang.
Urgentibus Imperii Fatis (Tac. Germ. 33). 381-392, ALBA

Schmidbauer, Richard.
"Nachlese": Ein Unbekannter Maioliband.—Eine Spielkarte und ein Kartenspiel. 255-259, STOL
Ein Unbekanntes Augsburger Pestblatt des 15. Jahrhunderts. 229-231, LEID

Schmidt, Adolf.
Baron Hüpsch in Köln als Inkunabelnsammler und Händler. 45-63, HAEB
Der Einband der Goldenen Bulle von 1356 in der Landesbibliothek zu Darmstadt. 105-117, LOUB
Kölnische Einbände des Vierzehnten Jahrhunderts in der Amploniana zu Erfurt. 401-409, COLL

Lippische Ablaßbriefe. 227-233, SCHW
Das Reichenauer Evangelistar. Handschrift CXC der Stadtbibliothek zu Leipzig. 22-41, LEIP
Zur Geschichte Deutscher Buchbinder im 16. Jahrhundert. 1-109, HAEK

Schmidt, Charles.
Des Vivres et des Livres. 41-44, GODE

Schmidt, Christel.
Aus der Sammlung Olga Hirsch: Ein Kreisrunder Einband von Caspar Meuser. 194-198, LOUB
Jakob Krause-Forschung: Ein Beitrag zur Methodik der Bucheinbandkunde. 191-193, LOUB

Schmidt, Erwin.
Giessener Bibliothekare. 26-50, GIES

Schmidt, Franz Paul, ed.
ALTE

Schmidt, Franz Paul.
Der Katalog der Klosterbibliothek Nienburg a.S. 31-79, ALTE

Schmidt, Ludwig.
Die Sächsischen Bibliotheken im Mittelalter. 105-115, BOLL

Schmidt, Philipp.
Die Bibelillustration als Laienexegese. 228-239, BINZ
Über die Sachliche Katalogisierung Umfassender Werke. 213-222, SCHU

Schmidt, Walter.
Das Wesen der Handbibliothek in Kirchlichen Archiven. 86-91, SCHV

Schmidt, Werner.
Die Verlagerung der Bestände im Zweiten Weltkrieg und Ihre Rückführung. I, 77-86, BERS

Schmidt, Wieland.
Bemerkungen zum Einband des Karlsruher Skizzenbuches von Hans Baldung Grien. 505-523, HOFM
Christus und die Sieben Laden. Betrachtungen zur Spätmittelalterlichen Deutschen Literaturgeschichte. 261-284, STOL
Erinnerungen. 9-16, SCHS
Hermann Degering, Erinnerungen aus der Staatsbibliothek. 126-129, LEUN
Hermann Neubert zum 60. Geburtstag am 9. Dezember 1952. 5-8, NEUB
In einem Kopert Gebunden. 59-82, REDE
Offene Buchbestände in Universalbibliotheken. 125-142, FUCH
Wissenschaft und Bibliographie. 127-129, FRAD
Zur Frage der Handschriftenkatalogisierung in Deutschland. 185-193, LEYH

Schmidt-Görg, Joseph ed.
HOBO

Schmidt-Görg, Joseph.
Anthony van Hoboken zum 75. Geburtstag. 7-9, HOBO

Schmidt-Herrling, Eleonore.
Einbände von Thomas Krüger in der Universitätsbibliothek Erlangen. 285-293, STOL
Zwei Geschenkbände von Heinrich Rantzau in der Universitätsbibliothek Erlangen. 57-61, VERZ

Schmidt-Künsemüller, Friedrich Adolf.
Ein Früher Typenmethodologischer Versuch in der Inkunabelkunde. 69-75, WEHM
Hermann Tiemann und das Deutsche Bibliothekswesen der Gegenwart. 11-22, TIEM
Der Streit um das Missale Speciale. 51-89, JUCH

Schmidt-Ott, Friedrich.
Persönliche Erinnerungen an Milkau. 22-24, MILK

Schmidt-Phiseldeck, Kay.
Musikalier, Kort og Billeder. 86-94, AARU
Notes sur les Buts du Catalogage des Livres et de la Musique. 117-121, FEDO

Schmieder, Wolfgang.
Ein Beitrag zur Verwaltung von Briefautographen. 133-140, BOLL
Johann Gottlob Immanuel Breitkopfs Privatbibliothek. Werden und Vergehen. II, 73-87, GLAU
Werkstatt-Erfahrungen beim Katalogisieren von Musikhandschriften. 121-125, FEDO

Schmitt, Franz Anselm.
Der Stand der Handschriften-Katalogisierung bei der Badischen Landesbibliothek in Karlsruhe. 216-231, HOFF
Stoff und Motiv in der Deutschen Literatur. Gedanken zu einer Neuen Bibliographie. 110-117, VORS

Schmitt, Jan.
Pokus o Českosl. Bibliografický Katalog 4. Třídy Desetinného Třídení. 171-173, ŽIVN

Schmitz, Wilhelm.
Tironianum. 77-80, HAVE

Schmitz-Kallenberg, Ludwig.
Ein in Vergessenheit Geratener Druck einer Papsturkundenlehre aus dem 18. Jahrhundert. 130-132, BÖME

Schmook, Ger.
Dringende Bibliotheekproblemen te Antwerpen. 581-589, BRUM
Wat met de Rug op de Plank, in het Rek? 29-50, JUCH

Schneider, Alfred.
Aus Johann Gottlob Regis' Breslauer Tagen. 321-338, MILF

Schneider, Georg.
Die Bibliographie an den Wissenschaftlichen Bibliotheken. 322-326, KUHN

Schneider, Heinrich
LÜBE

Schneider, Lambert.
Dank an Hanns W. Eppelsheimer. 165-166, FRAD

Schnellmann, Meinrad.
Die Innerschweizerischen Handschriften der Bürgerbibliothek Luzern. 223-232, SCHU

Schnoor, Hans.
Rechts und Links der Elbe. 88-91, BOLE

SCHNORR VON CAROLSFELD, HANS
Schnorr von Carolsfeld, Ludwig. Über den Bibliothekar, von dem Sohne eines Solchen. 295-299, STOL

Schnorr von Carolsfeld, Ludwig.
Über den Bibliothekar, von dem Sohne eines Solchen. 295-299, STOL

SCHNYDER, JOST L. B.
Blaser, Fritz. Eine Projektierte Papiermühle. 11-17, BOCK

SCHÖFFER, JOHANNES, printer
Grimm, Heinrich. Ulrichs von Hutten Persönliche Beziehungen zu den Druckern Johannes Schöffer in Mainz, Johannes Schott in Strassburg und Jakob Köbel zu Oppenheim. 140-156, BENZ

SCHÖFFER, PETER
Schmidt, Adolf. Lippische Ablaßbriefe. 227-233, SCHW

Schoene, Alfred.
De Isocratis Papyro Massiliensi (Iscor. or. II ad Nicoclem, paragr. 1-30). 481-504, GRAU

Schöne, Hermann.
Palimpsestblätter des Protevangelium Jacobi in Cesena. 263-276, BÖME

Schöne, Walter.
Zeitungswissenschaft und Deutsche Bibliotheken. Inkunabeln der Periodischen Presse. II, 36-39, GLAU

SCHÖNSPERGER, HANNS, printer
Wehmer, Carl. Mit Gemäl und Schrift. Kaiser Maximilian I. und der Buchdruck. 244-275, HOFF

SCHOLARLY LIBRARIES
see Research libraries

SCHOLARSHIP
see Learning and scholarship

Scholderer, Victor.
Georg Uebelin (Georgius Maxillus) and His Publications. 111-116, WEHM
Hans Ringer zu Wimbschpach. 417-420, BENZ

Scholem, Gerhard.
Einige Kabbalistische Handschriften im Britischen Museum. 51-69, FREN

Scholes, France V.
Remarks on the Occasion of the Serra Award. 69-75, HAMM

SCHOOL AND PUBLIC LIBRARY RELATIONSHIP
Möhring, Werner. Volkshochschule und Volksbücherei. 95-124, ACKR

SCHOOL AND PUBLIC LIBRARY RELATIONSHIP - Denmark
Thomsen, Carl. Bibliotekerne og det Øvrige Oplysningsarbejde. 85-93, DØSS

SCHOOL AND PUBLIC LIBRARY RELATIONSHIP - Germany
Jahrmann, Werner. Bücherei und Schule. Gedanken zur Jugendbüchereiarbeit. 215-231, SCHS

SCHOOL AND PUBLIC LIBRARY RELATIONSHIP - Norway
Deinboll, Rikka Bjølgerud. Samarbeide mellem Skole og Bibliotek. 73-82, NORN

SCHOOL LIBRARIANS
Robinson, M. U. School and College Libraries and the Teacher in Training. 147-150, OFFO

SCHOOL LIBRARIANSHIP - Certification
see Certification of librarians

SCHOOL LIBRARIES
see also Public libraries - Services to schools; School and public library relationship

SCHOOL LIBRARIES
Robinson, M. U. School and College Libraries and the Teacher in Training. 147-150, OFFO

SCHOOL LIBRARIES - Administration - Gothenburg, Sweden

Langfeldt, Johannes. Die Organisation des Schulbüchereiwesens in Gotenburg. 75-86, ACKE

SCHOOL LIBRARIES - Cataloging - Japan

Kamo, Hiroshi. Gakko Toshokan Yo Kemmei Hyomoku Hyo. (Subject Headings for School Library.) 206-217, KYOT

SCHOOL LIBRARIES - Denmark

Sørensen, Eleonora. Børne- og Skolebiblioteksarbejde. 94-104, DØSS
Thomsen, Carl. Die Zusammenarbeit zwischen Kinderbüchereien und Schülerbüchereien in Dänemark. 61-66, ACKR

SCHOOL LIBRARIES - Germany

LANJ

Joost, Siegfried. Bibliotheca Joachimica. Werden und Vergehen einer Deutschen Schulbibliothek. 233-256, WEHM

SCHOOL LIBRARIES - Gothenburg, Sweden

Langfeldt, Johannes. Die Organisation des Schulbüchereiwesens in Gotenburg. 75-86, ACKE

SCHOOL LIBRARIES (High school) - Guidance activities - Japan

Hashimoto, Tatsuki. Kōtogakko Toshokan ni okeru Dokusho Shidō. (A Guide for Reading in High School Library.) 177-191, KYOT

SCHOOL LIBRARIES - Japan

Shimizu, Masateru. Tenkai Suru Gakko Toshokan no Hitotsu no Arikata. (Program for a School Library.) 168-176, KYOT
Takahashi, Mamoru. Areya Koreya. (School Library.) 218-220, KYOT
Takebayashi, Kumahiko. Gakkō to Toshokan. (Schools and Libraries.) 1-8, HAKO

SCHOOL LIBRARIES - Kyoto - Hist.

Iuchi, Ryūzō. Kyoto no Gakko Toshokan Junen no Ayumi. (Ten Years of School Libraries in Kyoto.) 153-167, KYOT

SCHOOL LIBRARIES - Norway

Gjeldaker, Ivar. Folkeskolen Trenger Gode Skoleboksamlinger. 104-112, NORS

SCHOOL LIBRARIES (Rural schools) - Norway

Giœver, Hanna. Skoleboksamlinger på Landet. 83-96, NORN

Skancke, Mally. Norsk Oplandsarbejde. 107-116, LASS

SCHOOL LIBRARIES - Southern States

Wilson, Louis Round. Optima in Library Service for the South by 1950. 186-204, BISH

SCHOOL LIBRARIES - Standards - U.S.

Turner, Mabel. The Role of National Standards in the Development of the School Library in the United States. 143-150, HASH

SCHOOL LIBRARIES - U.S.

Lohrer, Alice. School libraries in the U.S. Meet the Challenges of Today. 81-90, HASH

SCHOTT, BERNHARD

Ziegler, Benno. Zur Geschichte des Privilegium Exclusivum des Mainzer Musikstechers Bernhard Schott. 293-305, LEID

SCHOTT, JOHANNES, printer

Grimm, Heinrich. Ulrichs von Hutten Persönliche Beziehungen zu den Druckern Johannes Schöffer in Mainz, Johannes Schott in Strassburg und Jakob Köbel zu Oppenheim. 140-156, BENZ
Scholderer, Victor. Georg Uebelin (Georgius Maxillus) and His Publications. 111-116, WEHM

Schottenloher, Karl.
Die Anfänge der Neueren Bibliographie. 233-239, LEID
Buchdrucker und Buchführer im Kampf der Schwärmer und Wiedertäufer, 1524-1568. 90-113, BOCK
Hans Sachs und Hieronymus Höltzel. Ein Beitrag zur Geschichte der Nürnberger Flugschriften vom Jahre 1524. 235-255, SCHW
Tagebuch-Aufzeichnungen in Immerwährenden Kalendern der Frühdruckzeit. II, 88-96, GLAU

SCHOTTENLOHER, KARL

SCHO

Hofmann, Gustav. Karl Schottenloher zum 75. Geburtstag. 1-6, SCHO

SCHOTTENLOHER, KARL - Bibl.

Schottenloher, Otto. Veröffentlichungen von Karl Schottenloher. 47-58, SCHO

Schottenloher, Otto.
Veröffentlichungen von Karl Schottenloher. 47-58, SCHO

Schrade, Hugo.
Zum Geleit. 5-6, JENA

SCHRAMM, ALBERT

SCHR

Stöwesand, Rudolf. Buch und Buchstabe. Prinzipielles und Persönliches als Einführung. 7-17, SCHR

SCHRAMM, ALBERT - Bibl.

Schramm, Hans Albert. Die Büchei und Schriften Albert Schramms. Eine Bibliographische Zusammenstellung. 116-120, SCHR

Schramm, Gottfried.
Lemburg und die Reformation. 343-350, EPST

Schramm, Hans Albert.
Die Bücher und Schriften Albert Schramms. Eine Bibliographische Zusammenstellung. 116-120, SCHR

Schreiber, Heinrich, ed.
GLAU

Schreiber, Heinrich.
Adolar Baldensheym, ein Leipziger Renaissancebuchbinder. 176-200, HAEK
Cavilla - ein Spätmittelalterliches Lesezeichen? II, 97-103, GLAU
Ein Erlanger Bibliothekenkenner des 18. Jahrhunderts: Friedrich Karl Gottlob Hirsching. 62-67, VERZ
Friedrich Adolf Ebert und die Monumenta Germaniae. 82-98, BOLL
Die Veröffentlichungen Otto Glaunings. I, 1-9, GLAU
Von der Goldschnittlyrik zum Schmetterlingsbuch. Orientalische Literatur in Deutscher Ausstattung. 82-92, SCHR

SCHRETTINGER, MARTIN WILLIBALD

Haeckel, Ilse. Schrettinger und die Säkularisation des Klosters Weiße-nohe. 117-120, REDE
Striedl, Hans. 150 Jahre Münchener Aufstellungsschema. 73-103, HOFM

Schriewer, F.
Die Zentralbücherei als Büchereityp. 103-111, ACKE

SCHRIFTENVERZEICHNIS JOHANNES LANGFELDT 1923-1957. 157-166, LANF

Schroers, Paul.
Antiquar und Bibliographie. 133-137, FRAD

SCHUBERT, FRANZ. Mss. - Collections - Vienna

Racek, Fritz. Von den Schuberthandschriften der Stadtbibliothek. 98-124, VIES

Schubert, Johannes.
Chinesische Bücherverzeichnisse. I, 176-184, GLAU
Na-khi-Piktographie. Notizen über eine Wenig Beachtete Bilderschrift. 114-142, BOCK

Schuder, Werner.
Der Bibliothekar und die Universitas Litterarum. 59-81, SCHS

SCHÜRER, MATHIAS, printer

Baillet, Lina. Le Premier Manuel de Grec Paru à Strasbourg. 25-36, BENZ

SCHÜTZ, JULIUS FRANZ

SCHT

Schuhmann, Ursula.
Aus der Arbeit der Kinder- und Jugendbibliothek Jena. 135-139, JENA

Schultheiss, Fr. G.
Zur Fortbildung des Halleschen Schemas. 43-56, VERP

Schultze, Walther [=Walter].
Die Kriegssammlung. 77-89, HARN
Die Schriften Paul Schwenkes. 1-16, SCHW
Die Zukunft Unserer Realkataloge. 224-237, KUHN

Schulz, Erich, ed.
VERD

Schulz, Erich.
Immermanns Briefe an Ferdinand Gessert. Ein Vorbericht. 119-133, VERD
Immermanns Übersetzung aus Dante. 297-301, BÖME

Schulz, Hans Ferdinand.
Buchhandel und Bibliographie. 130-132, FRAD

Schulz, Kurd.
Die Kirchliche Bibliothek in Ihrer Eigenständigkeit. 92-97, SCHV
Zur Literaturpädagogischen Schulung der Nebenamtlichen Volksbibliothekare. 113-120, ACKE

Schulz, Werner.
Die Amerikanischen Studentenbüchereien. 115-126, JUCR

Schulze, Alfred.
Zu den Altfranzösischen Bernhardhandschriften. 389-404, WILM

Schunke, Ilse, ed.
HAEK

Schunke, Ilse.
Beiträge zur Dresdner Bibliotheksgeschichte auf Grund von Einbandstudien. 397-414, VORS
Die Entwicklung der Päpstlichen Einbände vom 16. zum 17. Jahrhundert. II, 331-354, ALBB
Die Italienischen Einbände aus der Hamilton-Sammlung in Berlin. 17-32, LÜLF
Der Kölner Rollen- und Platteneinband im 16. Jahrhundert. 311-397, HAEK
Der Lederschnitt im Mittleren Deutschen Gebiet. 57-63, BOLE
Die Pariser Büchersendung des Hubert Languet an Kurfürst August von Sachsen 1566. 49-66, BOLL
Signet-Einbände. II, 104-112, GLAU

Schurig, Hans.
Zeittafel zur Geschichte der Deutschen Bücherei. 271-286, LEIZ

Schuster, Julius.
Secreta Salernitana und Gart der Gesundheit. Eine Studie zur Geschichte der Naturwissenschaften und Medizin des Mittelalters. 203-237, DEGE

Schuster, Wilhelm.
Die Frage nach der Autonomie der Pädagogik. 121-131, ACKE
Ein Studium Generale der Bibliothekare? 427-447, JUCH

SCHUSTER, WILHELM
SCHS
Schmidt, Wieland. Erinnerungen. 9-16, SCHS

SCHUTTERN (Benedictine monastery)
Kyriss, Ernst. Spätgotische Einbände des Benediktinerklosters Schuttern. 147-152, WEHM

SCHUTTERN (Benedictine monastery) Mss.
Dorez, Léon. Evangéliaire Exécuté à L'Abbaye de Schuttern (VIIIe-IXe Siècle). 293-299, CHAT

Schuurmans, J. J.
De Bibliotheken van de Veeartsenijkundige Faculteit en van het Instituut voor Muziekwetenschap Gevestigd in het Gebouw Bilstraat 172. 258-260, EVER

Schwabacher, Willy.
Ein Fränkischer Gnadenpfennig aus der Voit von Salzburg'schen Münzsammlung in der Erlanger Universitätsbibliothek. 68-74, VERZ

Schwarber, Karl.
Abschiedsansprache an Herrn Direktor Godet. 31-34, GODM
Das Basler Pflichtexemplar. 145-163, GODE
Marcel Godet und die Vereinigung Schweizerischer Bibliothekare. 3-8, GODM

SCHWARBER, KARL
SCHU

Schwartz, Benjamin.
A Judaeo-Greek Lament. 107-114, BLOC

Schwartz, Édouard.
De Quibusdam Scholiis in Euripidis Andromachen. 651-657, GRAU

Schwarz, Arthur Zacharias.
Nikolsburger Hebräische Handschriften. 170-181, FREI
Ein Vorschlag. 144, FREN

Schwarz, F.
Analyse eines Kataloges. 326-338, KÖNI

SCHWARZ, WALTER
SCHV
Lebenslauf D. Walter Schwarz. 98-101, SCHV

SCHWARZ, WALTER - Bibl.
Bibliographie D. Walter Schwarz. 102, SCHV

SCHWEIZERISCHE BIBLIOPHILEN GESELLSCHAFT. Bibliothek
Meyer, Wilhelm Josef. Die Bibliothek der Schweizer Bibliophilen Gesellschaft. 123-124, BERU

SCHWEIZERISCHE GESELLSCHAFT FÜR FAMILIENFORSCHUNG. Bibliothek
Meyer, Wilhelm Josef. Die Bibliothek der Schweizerischen Gesellschaft für Familienforschung. 124-125, BERU

SCHWEIZERISCHE KOMMISSION DER BÜCHERHILFE FÜR DAS KRIEGSGESCHÄDIGTE AUSLAND
Burckhardt, Felix. Die Schweizer Bücherhilfe für das Kriegsgeschädigte Ausland. 271-277, BICK

SCHWEIZERISCHE LANDESBIBLIOTHEK, Bern
see Bern. Schweizerische Landesbibliothek

SCHWEIZERISCHE VEREINIGUNG FÜR DOKUMENTATION
Merz, Otto. Die Schweizerische Vereinigung für Dokumentation Dankt. 180-181, BOUR

SCHWEIZERISCHE VOLKSBIBLIOTHEK, Bern
see Bern. Schweizerische Volksbibliothek

SCHWEIZERISCHER BUCHHÄNDLER- UND VERLEGERVEREIN
Mittler, Max. P. Bourgeois und der SBVV. 181-182, BOUR

SCHWEIZERISCHER GESAMTKATALOG
see Bern. Schweizerische Landesbibliothek. Schweizerischer Gesamtkatalog

SCHWEIZERISCHES GUTENBERGMUSEUM. Bern
see Bern. Schweizerisches Gutenbergmuseum

Schwenke, Paul.
Die Bibliothek als Ganzes. 1-10, HARN
Die Buchbinder mit dem Lautenspieler und dem Knoten. 122-144, HAEB
Die Mainzer Donatdrucke der Staatsbibliothek. 31-36, HARN
Zur Älteren Geschichte der Berliner Königlichen Bibliothek (1687-1698). 1-14, WILM

SCHWENKE, PAUL
SCHW
Schultze, Walther. Die Schriften Paul Schwenkes. 1-16, SCHW

Schwerz, F.
Karl J. Lüthi und das Buch. 150-152, LÜTH

Schwidetzky, Georg.
Der Benutzungsdienst. 137-147, LEIS
Die Unpersönlichen Drucksachen im Alphabetischen Katalog. 123-133, MIND

SCIENCE FICTION
Ringdal, Johan R. Vår Fremtid—Drøm og Virkelighet. Betraktninger over Science-Fiction-Litteraturen. 189-199, NORS

SCIENTIFIC LIBRARIES
see also Pharmaceutical libraries; Technical libraries

SCIENTIFIC LIBRARIES
Ammundsen, Vibeke. De Videnskabelige Biblioteker som Dokumentationscentraler. 159-173, TVET
Lancaster-Jones, Joyce. The UDC and the Science Museum Library. 163-164, DONK

SCIENTIFIC LIBRARIES - Bulgaria
Bozhinova-Troianova, B. Profilirane na Nauchnite Biblioteki u Nas. 61-72, MIKH

SCIENTIFIC LIBRARIES - Friesland, East
Möhlmann, Günther. Die Wissenschaftlichen Bibliotheken Ostfrieslands. 140-144, LEUN

SCIENTIFIC LIBRARIES - Poland
Baumgart, Jan. Struktura Organizacyjna Bibliotek Naukowych. 131-154, GRYC

SCIENTIFIC LITERATURE - Documentation
see Documentation - Special subjects - Science

SCORES
see Music literature and scores

Scott, E.
"There's Nothing Like a Good Book." 15-16, LAMB

Scott, J. W.
Richard Offor: A Bibliography of His Printed Works. 66-68, OFFO

SCOTT, MICHAEL. Mss. Liber Introductorius
Thorndike, Lynn. Manuscripts of Michael Scott's Liber Introductorius. 425-447, ALBA

SCRIBES (Judaism)
Freimann, Aaron. Jewish Scribes in Medieval Italy. 231-342, MARX

SCRITTI DI MONS. ANGELO MERCATI. IX-XXVII, MERC

SCUOLA DI BIBLIOTECONOMIA, Vatican. Biblioteca Vaticana
see Vatican. Biblioteca Vaticana. Scuola di Biblioteconomia

Sealoff, Georgia.
Anyone Can Make a Library Materials Center. It's What Happens There That Counts. 121-126, HASH

SEALS (Numismatics) - Collections - Basel
Galbreath, D. L. Ausgewählte Siegel des Basler Staatsarchivs. 90-94, BASL

SEALS (Numismatics) - Collections - Kraków
Ameisenowa, Zofia. Nieznany Wzór Złotniczy z XV w. w Bibliotece Jagiellońskiej. 365-369, PIEK

SECHARJAH, ISAAC BEN
see Isaac ben Secharjah

EL II CONGRESO DE COOPERACIÓN INTELECTUAL Y MENÉNDEZ PELAYO. 283-284, MENE

SECOND-HAND BOOKS - Rome (City)
Kleberg, Tönnes. Om Romersk Antikvariatbokhandel. 84-94, TVET

SECOND-HAND BOOKS - U.S.
Butler, Pierce. A Possible Field for Book Conservation. 399-403, WILS

SECULARIZATION
Haeckel, Ilse. Schrettinger und die Säkularisation des Klosters Weissenohe. 117-120, REDE

SECULARIZATION - Germany
Hilsenbeck, Adolf. Die Universitätsbibliothek Landshut-München und die Säkularisation (1803). 180-192, LEYG

Seeberg, Erich.
Ansprache bei der Trauerfeier am 29. Januar 1934 im Krematorium Wilmersdorf. 9-14, MILK

Seeger, Charles, ed.
KINK

Seemann, Artur.
Alere Flammam. 3-6, MIND

Seguin, Jean-Pierre.
Faits Divers Sensationnels dans Seize Bulletins d'Information Imprimés en France, pendant le Règne de François Ier. 65-79, CALO

Seif, Theodor.
Vom Alexanderroman. 745-770, VIEN

Sejr, Emanuel.
Benyttelse. 123-154, AARU
Statsbiblioteket og Centralbibliotekerne. 96-102, LASS
En Udlånsindskrænkning. Statsbibliotekets Krise 1912. 71-89, DAHA

Sekhon, S. S.
Dr. Ranganathan's Contribution to Social Education. 531-535, RANG

Sekino, Shinkichi.
Toshokan'in no Seikatsu Taido ni tsuite. (On the Attitude of Life of Librarians.) 37-40, OTAT

Selbmann, Ehrhard.
Zur Melanchthonbibliographie. Ein Werk Internationaler Bibliothekarischer Gemeinschaftsarbeit. 245-250, BULL

SELD, JÖRG
Waetzoldt, Stephan. Ein Silbereinband von Jörg Seld. 53-57, REDE

SELECTED LIST OF WORKS BY CARL ENGEL. 23-26, ENGE

SELECTION OF PERSONNEL
see Personnel - Qualifications and selection

SÉLESTAT, Alsace. Bibliothèque Municipale
SCHL

SÉLESTAT, Alsace. Bibliothèque Municipale. Collection Rhenanus
Knod, Gustav C. Aus der Bibliothek des Beatus Rhenanus. Second Book, 1-109, SCHL

SELESTAT, Alsace. Bibliothèque Municipale - Hist.
Gény, Joseph. Geschichte der Stadtbibliothek zu Schlettstadt. First Book, 1-75, SCHL

Selig, Karl-Ludwig.
Three Spanish Libraries of Emblem Books and Compendia. 81-90, PARG

SELOW, PETER VAN
Rudbeck, Gustaf. Peter van Selow Stilgjutare och Boktryckare i Stockholm 1618-1648. 303-334, COLL

Semrau, Eberhard.
Aufgaben und Probleme beim Aufbau eines Zentralkatalogs. 377-385, JUCH
Die Erwerbung Moderner Bibliophiler Werke. 43-52, REDE

SENCKENBERGISCHE BIBLIOTHEK, Frankfurt a.M.
see Frankfurt a.M. Senckenbergische Bibliothek

SENECA, LUCIUS ANNAEUS. Naturales Quaestiones
Gertz, Martin-Clarence. Emendationes Annaeanae. 353-379, GRAU

SENGING, MARTIN VON
see Martin von Senging

Seppälä, Arvo.
Eräitä Kansi- Ja Reunamerkintöjä Helsingin Yliopiston Kirjaston Kaksoiskappalekokoelmissa. 237-255, DAHL

SEQUENCES (Liturgy)
Brenn, Franz. Die Sequenzen des Graduale von St. Katharinenthal. 23-42, OREL

SERBO-CROATIAN CORRESPONDENCE
see Correspondence, Serbo-Croatian

SERIAL PUBLICATIONS
Bozhinova, Bozhana and Dimitŭr P. Ivanchev. Opit za Razgranichavane Poni͡atii͡ata "Spisanie" i "Vestnik"; Doklad. 411-417, MIKN

SERIAL PUBLICATIONS - Collections - Bern
Lüthi, Karl Jakob. Die Zeitschriften und Serienwerke. 51-55, BERU

SERIAL PUBLICATIONS - Collections - Uppsala
Samzelius, Jonas L:son. De Utländska Tidskrifterna vid Uppsala Universitet. Några Bidrag till Belysning av Förhellandet mellan Forskare och Bibliotek. 586-607, UPPS

SERIAL PUBLICATIONS - Collections - Utrecht
Graafland, H. J. P. Hooft. De Tijdschriften en de Reekswerken der Universiteitsbibliotheek. 146-149, EVER

SERIAL PUBLICATIONS - Exchange
see Exchange of books, periodicals, etc.

SERIAL PUBLICATIONS - Union lists
see Periodicals - Union lists

Serna, Gaspar Gómez de la.
El Centenario de Menéndez Pelayo en Italia. Dos Articulos del Padre Mondrone en "La Civiltá Cattolica." 263-270, MENE

Serruys, Daniel.
Contribution à L'Étude des "Canons" de L'Onciale Grecque. 492-499, CHAT

SERVASANCTUS, Frater
see Servasanto da Faenze, Frater

SERVASANTO DA FAENZE, Frater. Antidotarium Animae. 1485?
Kruitwagen, Bonaventura. Das Antidotarium Animae von Fr. Servasanctus O.F.M. (Lovanii, Joh. de Westfalia, c. 1485). 80-106, HAEB

Servolini, Luigi.
Le Carte Azzolini nella Biblioteca Comunale di Forlì. 615-701, GALL

Seshadri, T. R.
Dr. Ranganathan: A Karmayogin. 737-738, RANG

Sevensma, Tietse Pieter.
Bibliographie ou Documentation? 45-51, GODE
De Bibliotheca Neerlandica Manuscripta De Vreese in Leiden. 167-175, BISH
Eine Bibliothekarische Kriegserfahrung. 591-596, BICK
Le Dr. Jan Emler et la Collaboration Internationale des Bibliothèques. 34-37, EMLE
The Library of the League of Nations. 399-408, PUTN
Modern Librarianship. 235-240, MUNT
Der Salomons-Tempel in Leiden. 80-81, STUM

SEVERUS ALEXANDER, Emperor of Rome - Library
Harnack, Adolf von. Julius Afrikanus, der Bibliothekar des Kaisers Alexander Severus. 142-146, MILF

SEVILLE. Biblioteca Colombina. Mss. (7.2.23)
Weiss, Roberto. Humphrey Duke of Gloucester and Tito Livio Frulovisi. 218-227, SAXL

SEX BOOKS IN THE LIBRARY
see Censorship

Seyffert, Hans.
Über den Schlagwortkatalog der Universitätsbibliothek Kiel. 129-139, JUCR

Shafranovskij, K. I. and G. F. Podozerskaia.
Iz Istorii Organizatsii v XIX Veke Slavianskogo Otdeleniia Biblioteki Akademii Nauk v Peterburge. 351-362, MIKH

Shamurin, E. I.
Nekotorye Voprosy Bibliograficheskoj Terminologii. (V Sviazi s Razgranicheniem Otraslej i Vidov Bibliografii). 335-350, MIKH

SHANŪDAH, ANBA, SAINT. Mss.
Rudnitzky, Günter. Ein Sermon aus dem Schatzkästlein Unseres Vaters Apa Schenute. 12-18, WEHM

Sharma, H. D.
Dr. Ranganathan: The Man and His Works. 622-624, RANG

Sharma, Jagdish Saran.
My Invitation to Library Profession. 755-758, RANG

Sharma, Umesh Datta.
Nothing about Ranganathan. 636-638, RANG

Shastri, D. P.
Four Days with Dr. Ranganathan. 759-763, RANG

SHATSKY, JACOB
see Szocki, Jákob

Shaw, Ralph R.
Classification. 63-67, RANG
The Form and the Substance. 238-247, TVET

SHEFFIELD, Eng. - Archives
see Archives - Sheffield, Eng.

SHEFFIELD, Eng. - Branch libraries
see Branch libraries - Sheffield, Eng.

SHEFFIELD, Eng. Central Library
see Sheffield, Eng. Free Public Libraries and Museum

SHEFFIELD, Eng. - Children's library services
see Children's library services - Sheffield, Eng.

SHEFFIELD, Eng. City Libraries
see Sheffield, Eng. Free Public Libraries and Museum

SHEFFIELD, Eng. Free Public Libraries and Museum

LAMB

SHEFFIELD, Eng. Free Public Libraries and Museum. Mss. (Burke Papers)

Copeland, Thomas. The Opening of the Burke Papers. 24-25, LAMB

SHEFFIELD, Eng. - Librarians - Memoirs, reminiscences, etc.
see Librarians - Memoirs, reminiscences, etc. - Sheffield, Eng.

SHEFFIELD, Eng. - Public libraries - Acquisitions
see Public libraries - Acquisitions - Sheffield, Eng.

SHEFFIELD, Eng. - Public libraries - Services to business and industry
see Public libraries - Services to business and industry - Sheffield, Eng.

SHEFFIELD, Eng. Public Museum
see Sheffield, Eng. Free Public Libraries and Museum

SHEFFIELD, Eng. - War and the library
see War and the library - Sheffield, Eng.

SHELF ARRANGEMENT

Merrill, William Stetson. Order of Books by Date under Subjects. 282-284, HANS

SHELF ARRANGEMENT - Utrecht

Breuning, P. S. Over de Plaatsing der Boeken in de Universiteitsbibliotheek te Utrecht. 38-48, EVER

SHELF LISTS - Königsberg

Kuhnert, Ernst. Heinrich Zell. 137-147, SCHW

SHELVES, Access to
see Access to shelves

SHELVES AND SHELVING
see also Furniture; Shelf arrangement

SHELVES AND SHELVING

Van Hoesen, Henry B. and Norman Kilpatrick. Heights of Books in Relation to Height of Stack Tiers. 352-357, HANS

Shera, Jesse H.
Automation Without Fear. 168-181, SAYW
The Beginnings of Systematic Bibliography in America, 1642-1799. 263-278, WROT
The Changing Philosophy of Bibliographic Classification. 139-140, DONK
The Library as an Agency of Social Communication. 241-243, KYLE

Shera, Jesse H. and James W. Perry.
Changing Concepts of Classification, Philosophical and Education Implications. 37-48, RANG

SHERBORNE (Benedictine abbey) Mss.

Wormald, Francis. The Sherborne "Chartulary." 101-119, SAXL

Shigehiro, Torao.
Sho Wa Geijutsu Nariya. (Is Calligraphy A Fine Art?). 116-127, (pt. 1), OHAS

Shimasue, Kiyoshi.
Hanpon ni Natta Yoshidake no Hon. (Works Published by the Shintoist Family of Yoshida.) 87-95, TOMI

Shimizu, Masateru.
Tenkai Suru Gakko Toshokan no Hitotsu no Arikata. (Program for a School Library.) 168-176, KYOT

SHIP LIBRARIES, Norwegian

Kildal, Arni. Books for Norwegian Seamen. 401-407, RANG

SHOPOV, A. P. Smert' na Kniaza Potemkina

Berkov, P. N. Tragediia A. P. Shopova "Smŭrt'ta na Kniaza Potemkina" i ee Russkii Istochnik (Bibliograficheskoe Razyskanie). 19-30, MIKH

SHOPOV, I. V.

Bechyňová, Věnceslava. Bibliografická Spolupráce Ivana V. Šopova s P. J. Šafaříkem. 41-50, MIKH

Shores, Louis.
Encyclopedists Beware. 495-505, RANG

SHORTHAND, Greek

Mentz, Arthur. Römische und Griechische Stenographie. 67-70, SCHR

SHORTHAND, Italian - Liguria - 11th cent.

Cipolla, C. La Tachygraphie Ligurienne au XIe Siècle. 87-96, HAVE

SHORTHAND, Latin

Mentz, Arthur. Römische und Griechische Stenographie. 67-70, SCHR

Shukla, D. N.
Scientific Management of Libraries. 486-487, RANG

Shukla, L. S.
The Master-Educationist. 568-573, RANG

Sickel, Th. von.
Nouveaux Éclaircissements sur la Première Édition du Diurnus. 15-30, HAVE

Sickmann, Ludwig.
Der Katalogisierungsunterricht für Anfänger. Bericht über Erfahrungen im Bibliothekar-Lehrinstitut. 448-457, JUCH

SIDDUR, Mss.

Wischnitzer-Bernstein, Rahel. Der Siddur der Altstädtischen Synagoge in Rzeszów. 77-80, FREN

SIDOINE APOLLINAIRE
see Sidonius, C. Sollius Modestus Apollinaris. Ms.

SIDONIUS, C. Sollius Modestus Apollinaris. Ms.

Chatelain, Émile. Recherches sur un Manuscrit Célèbre de Sidoine Apollinaire. 321-327, GRAU

SIEGEL, GEORG - Library

Kyriss, Ernst. Der Altdorfer Professor Georg Siegel als Büchersammler. 117-124, STOL

Siegl, Jaromír.
Seznam Knih Městské Knihovny Kutnohorské z r. 1850. 199-207, ŽIVN

Sierks, Ruth.
Hilfe des Auslandes. 115-127, HAMB

SIGER DE BRABANT. Mss. Quaestiones

Grabmann, Martin. Neuaufgefundene "Quaestionen" Sigers von Brabant zu den Werken des Aristoteles (Clm. 9559). 103-147, EHRA

SIGFUSDATTER, BIRGITTA
see Birgitta Sigfusdatter

SIGISMUND II AUGUST, King of Poland - Library
see Zygmunt II August, King of Poland - Library

SILESIA - Private libraries
see Private libraries - Silesia

Silfverstolpe, C.
En Blick i Vadstena Klosters Arkiv och Bibliotek. [89]-[115], KLEM

SILHOUETTES, Paper
see Paper work

Sillib, Rudolf.
Ein Nachkömmling der Heidelberger Hofbuchbinderei des Kurfürsten Karl Ludwig von der Pfalz. 249-251, LEID

SILLIMAN, BENJAMIN

Keogh, Andrew. Benjamin Silliman's Trip to Europe in 1805. 416-422, LYDE

Sills, R. Malcolm and Eleanor Stuart Upton.
The "Trumbull Manuscript Collections" and Early Connecticut Libraries. 325-342, KEOG

Silow, Alvar.
Bibliotekens Samarbete. 214-220, GRAP

Silver, Rollo G.
The Boston Book Trade, 1790-1799. 279-303, WROT

Simon, K. R.
Rannie Bibliografii po Istorii. 247-255, MIKH

SIMON VON MELK

Leporini, Heinrich. Simon von Niederaltaich und Martin v. Senging. 575-590, VIEN

SIMON VON NIEDERALTAICH
see Simon von Melk

Simons, Eric N.
Change of Scene. 31, LAMB
Service to Industry. 13-14, LAMB

Simonsen, D.
Zur Bücherkunde. 164-168, STEI

SIMPLIFIED CATALOGING
see Cataloging, Simplified

Simpson, E.
The War Years. 19-20, LAMB

Singer, F. X.
Zum 100. Geburtstag von Karl August Barack. 1-16, BARA

Singh, Gurcharan, jt. author

Kaul, Jainath and Gurcharan Singh. Dr. Ranganathan and Standards for Documentation. 271-278, RANG

Singh, Hakam.
Dr. Ranganathan and Library Science. 614-621, RANG

Sinogowitz, Bernhard, ed.
REDE

Sinogowitz, Bernhard.
Gedanken zum Bayerischen Pflichtexemplarrecht. 195-202, REDE

SINT SERVAAS (Cathedral), Maastricht
see Maastricht. Sint Servaas (Cathedral)

SINUTHIUS, SAINT
see Shanūdah, Anba, Saint

Siropolko, Stepan.
L. J. Živný v Ukrajinské Knihovědné Literatuře. 22-23, ŽIVN

Sivaraman, K. M.
March of Library Legislation in Madras. 387-396, RANG
Team Work, Staff Council and Renaissance in Library Science. 475-485, RANG

SIZE OF LIBRARIES
see Libraries - Size

Sjögreen, Märta, jt. ed.
HEIN

SKAGEN, Denmark. Bibliotek
SKAG

Skancke, Mally.
Fra Arbeidet "Ute i Marken." 37-50, KILD
Norsk Oplandsarbejde. 107-116, LASS

SKARA, Sweden. Hägre Allmännaläroverket. Bibliotek
Collijn, Isak Gustaf Alfred. Zwei Widmungsexemplare eines Werkes des Valentinus Erythræus (1574). 111-116, LEYG

Skehan, Patrick W.
An Illuminated Gospel Book in Ethiopic. 350-357, GREE

SKENNINGE, Ingrid of
see Ingrid of Skenninge, Saint

SKINNER, MARK
Utley, George B. An Early "Friend" of Libraries. 725-730, WILS

Skovrøy, Peder Andersen.
Tredive Aar i Tønder. 15-77, TØND

SKOVRØY, PEDER ANDERSEN
Lausten-Thomsen, H. Inledning. 7-14, TØND

Skudlarska, Danuta.
Działalność Oświatowa i Kulturalna w Środowisku. 115-123, BYDG
Wrażenia z Wystaw. 165-167, BYDG

Skwarnicka, Zofia.
Jak Przygotować i Przeprowadzić Omówienie Nowości Pedagogicznych. 67-72, KRAK
Katalog Rzeczowy: Metodyka i Wykorzystanie. 56-61, KRAK

Skwarnicki, Marek.
Zarys Rozwoju Konceptcji i Organizacji Biblioteki Narodowej w Warszawie (1918-1954). 89-130, GRYC

Slade, William Adams.
The National Library: A Sonnet. 409, PUTN

Slámová, Marie Olga.
Kniha Návštěv. 133-137, EMLE

Ślusarczyk, Jadwiga.
Gromadzenie i Opracowanie Księgozbioru. 17-21, KRAK

SMÅLAND, Sweden - Views - Collections - Uppsala
Davidsson, Åke. Småländska Bilder i Uppsala Universitetsbibliotek. 75-85, OLSS

SMALL LIBRARIES
see Public libraries (Small)

Smend, Friedrich.
[An Address.] 12-24, BERP
Zur Kenntnis des Musikers Fortunato Santini. 90-98, BÖME

Smetana, Robert and Bedřich Václavek. Jak Katalogisovati Kramářské Písně. 137-143, EMLE

SMETS, ANTHONY
Alphen, G. van. Anthony Smets, Bibliothecaris van Drie Prinsen van Oranje (1636-1689). 119-160, HAGU

Smital, Ottokar. Miszellen zur Geschichte der Wiener Palatina. 771-794, VIEN

S[mith], A[nna] H[ester].
First in South Africa - as Far as We Know! 61-63, KENN

Smith, Anne M.
Social Sciences Journals Frequently Cited. 127-134, HASH

Smith, Carleton Sprague.
Otto Kinkeldey. 27-37, KINO

SNIMŠČIKOVA, FRAU Dr.
Fleischhack, Curt. Frau Dr. Snimščikova. 83-85, BULL

Snoek, Johs.
De Trefwoordencatalogus van de Bibliotheek der Psychiatrisch-Neurologische Kliniek. 261-277, EVER

SOCIAL SCIENCE LITERATURE - Collections - Berlin

Gittig, Heinz. Die Gesellschaftswissenschaftliche Beratungsstelle. I, 425-432, BERS

SOCIEDAD DE BIBLIÓFILOS CÁNTABROS

Solano, Tomás Maza. La Sociedad de Bibliófilos Cántabros que Intentó Formar Menéndez Pelayo. II, 147-188, ARTI

SOCIETY PUBLICATIONS - Collections - Bern

Lüthi, Karl Jakob. Die Abteilung V (Vereine, Gesellschaften und Anstalten). 45-47, BERU

SOCIOLOGICAL ASPECTS OF LIBRARIES
see Libraries - Sociological aspects

Söderhjelm, Werner.
Un Manuscrit du Roman de la Rose à la Bibliothèque Royale de Stockholm. 75-90, COLL

Sørensen, Eleonora.
Børne- og Skolebiblioteksarbejde. 94-104, DØSS

Soeters, P. C.
Hoe de Nederlandse Centrale Catalogus Begon. 590-593, BRUM

SOFIA. Bulgarian Bibliographical Institute

Borov, Todor. Die Primäre Nationalbibliographie Bulgariens. 20-44, VORS

SOFIA. Bŭlgarski Bibliografski Institut
see Sofia. Bulgarian Bibliographical Institute

SOFIA - Correspondence, Serbo-Croatian - Collections
see Correspondence, Serbo-Croatian - Collections - Sofia

SOFIA. Dŭrzhavan Biblioteka "Vasil Kolarov." Bŭlgarski Istoricheski Arkhiv
see Sofia. National Library. Bulgarian Historical Archive

SOFIA. Narodna Biblioteka
see Sofia. National Library

SOFIA - National libraries
see National libraries - Sofia

SOFIA. National Library

SOFI

Nedkov, Boris. Orientalistikata v Sofiiskata Narodna Biblioteka. 226-239, MIKN

SOFIA. National Library. Bulgarian Historical Archive

Bozhinov, Liuben Al. Dokumentite na Sŭrbokhŭrvatski Ezik v Bŭlgarskiia Istoricheski Arkhiv. 51-59, MIKH

SOFIA - Oriental literature - Collections
see Oriental literature - Collections - Sofia

SOFIA. Vasil Kolarov State Library
see Sofia. National Library

Sohla, Santosh M.
Dr. Ranganathan as I Understand Him. 585-587, RANG

Solana, Marcial.
Colaboración de Laverde en la Ciencia Española de Menéndez Pelayo. II, 51-104, ARTI

Solano, Tomás Maza.
La Sociedad de Bibliófilos Cántabros que Intentó Formar Menéndez Pelayo. II, 147-188, ARTI

Solar-Quintes, Nicolás A.
Las Ideas Musicales de Menéndez Pelayo. 159-167, MENE

Solberg, Thorvald.
Copyright and Librarians. 315-328, HANS
The United States and International Copyright. 410-422, PUTN

Sollied, P. R.
Relationer fra Christiania, Bergen og Trondhjem om Smaae Piecers Censur. 91-105, OSLN

Solomon, A. G.
What Is a Library? 333-340, RANG

SOLOTHURN (City) Zentralbibliothek. Mss. (S II 43)

Altermatt, Leo. Die von Staalsche Historienbibel der Zentralbibliothek Solothurn. 35-71, SCHU

SOMEREN, JAN FREDERIK VAN

SOME

Evers, Gerrit Albert. Jan Frederik van Someren. 5-6, EVER

Sommerfeld, Arnold.
Zu Pascual Jordans "Verdrängung und Komplementarität." 128, HELD

SOMMERFELDT, WILHELM PREUS

Haukaas, Kaare. Norsk Litterært Registreringsarbeid. 25-68, HALV

SOMOZA, JOSÉ. El Doctor Andrés Laguna
Lomba y Pedraja, José Ramón. Un Libro de Don José Somoza o si Se Quiere un Articulito. II, 229-241, ARTI

SONCINO, GERSON BEN ELIESER, printer
Cowley, A. E. Ein Soncino-Druck aus Kairo 1566. 89-90, FREN

SONCINO-GESELLSCHAFT DER FREUNDE DES JÜDISCHEN BUCHES, E.V., Berlin
Horodisch, Abraham. Ein Abenteuer im Geiste: Die Soncino-Gesellschaft der Freunde des Jüdischen Buches. 181-208, WEHM

SONGS - Collections - Erlangen
Weckerle, Ferdinand. Kulturgeschichtliches im Spiegel einer alten Erlanger Liedersammlung. 85-93, VERZ

SONGS (Folk-songs)
see Folk-songs

Sonnleithner, Rudolf.
Die Mondseer Bruchstücke der Ältesten Hochdeutschen Evangelienübersetzung. 795-804, VIEN

SOPHIE AMALIE, Consort of Frederik III, King of Denmark - Library
Petersen, Carl S. Dronning Sophie Amalies Bogsamling. 231-247, COLL

SOPHOCLES
Rosen, Edward. Copernicus' Quotation from Sophocles. 367-379, ALBA

SOPHOCLES. Fragmenta
Vitelli, Jérôme. Ad Euripide e Sofocle (Eur. Hipp. 115. 441 Soph. Frgm. 609 Dnd.). 97-102, GRAU

SOPHOCLES. Mss.
Wendel, Carl. Aus der Vorgeschichte des Laurentianus XXXII.9. 16-22, KUHN

Sorbelli, Albano.
Un Nuovo Codice della "Vita C. J. Caesaris" di Francesco Petrarca. II, 677-682, HORT
Lo "Specchio della Prudenza" di Frate Beltrame da Ferrara (GW 3807) Presunto Incunabulo. 205-213, ACCU

SORG, ANTON, printer
Voulliéme, Ernst. Eine Neue Bücheranzeige des Anton Sorg in Augsburg. 43-47, LOUB

SORORITY HOUSE LIBRARIES
see Dormitory libraries

SOURCE MATERIALS
see Research materials

Souter, Alexander.
A Fragment of an Unpublished Latin Text of the Epistle to the Hebrews, with a Brief Exposition. 39-49, EHRA

SOUTH AFRICA - Bibliography, National
see Bibliography, National - South Africa

SOUTH AFRICA - Libraries
see Libraries - South Africa

SOUTH AFRICA - Libraries and librarianship
see Libraries and librarianship - South Africa

SOUTH AFRICA - Private libraries
see Private libraries - South Africa

SOUTH AFRICA - Public libraries
see Public libraries - South Africa

SOUTH AFRICAN PUBLIC LIBRARY, Capetown
Bradlow, F. R. Douglas Varley and the Quarterly Bulletin, the Friends of the S. A. Library and Africana. 19-21, VARL
Bradshaw, S. D. H. Varley: a Tribute. 10-12, VARL
D. H. Varley. 5-7, VARL

SOUTHERN ASSOCIATION OF COLLEGES AND SCHOOLS
Lyle, Guy R. The University Library in the Self Survey Program of the Southern Association of Colleges and Secondary Schools, Inc. 91-96, HASH

SOUTHERN STATES - College and university libraries
see College and university libraries - Southern States

SOUTHERN STATES - Education for librarianship
see Education for librarianship - Southern States

SOUTHERN STATES - Libraries
see Libraries - Southern States

SOUTHERN STATES - Library resources
see Library resources - Southern States

SOUTHERN STATES - Library service
see Library service - Southern States

SOUTHERN STATES - Public libraries - State and regional development plans
see Public libraries - State and regional development plans - Southern States

SOUTHERN STATES - School libraries
see School libraries - Southern States

SOVIET UNION
see Russia

Spagnolo, D. Antonio.
Una Leggina di Giustiniano in un Miscellaneo Veronese del Secolo XI-XII. 193-194, CHAT

SPAIN - Archives
see Archives - Spain

SPAIN. Archivo General de la Corona de Aragón. Mss. (Cod. Ripoll 99)

Hämel, Adalbert. Arnaldus de Monte und der "Liber S. Jacobi." I, 147-159, RUBI

SPAIN. Cuerpo Facultativo de Archiveros, Bibliotecarios y Arqueólogos

Vega, Javier Lasso de la. El Cuerpo Facultativo de Archiveros, Bibliotecarios y Arqueólogos de España. 183-186, HOFM

SPAIN. Embajada. Catholic Church. Archivio.

Pou y Marti, José M. Los Archivos de la Embajada de España cerca de la Santa Sede. 297-311, MERC

Spain, Frances Lander, ed.
MOOR

Spain, Frances Lander, jt. author

Weeks, Elizabeth Harriet and Frances Lander Spain. Anne Carroll Moore—<u>A Contribution Toward a Bibliography</u>. 629-636, MOOR

SPAIN - Libraries
see Libraries - Spain

SPAIN - Manuscripts
see Manuscripts - Spain

SPAIN - Monastic libraries
see Monastic libraries - Spain

SPAIN - Music libraries and collections
see Music libraries and collections - Spain

SPAIN - Porticoes
see Porticoes - Spain

SPAIN - Private libraries
see Private libraries - Spain

SPAIN - Special libraries
see Special libraries - Spain

Spanier, Arthur.
Über Umfang und Herkunft der Sammlung Hebräischer Handschriften in der Kurfürstlichen Bibliothek zu Berlin. 245-253, KUHN

SPANISH AMERICA
see Latin America

SPANISH LITERATURE - Collections - Vienna

Rohr, Christine. Die Spanischen Bücherbestände der Österreichischen Nationalbibliothek. 534-537, BICK

SPARRE, ERIK - Library

Gödel, Vilhelm. Erik Sparre. Till Historien om Hans Litterära Samlingar. 171-178, ANNE

SPECIAL COLLECTIONS
see also Special subjects under the subject, e.g. Incunabula - Collections

SPECIAL COLLECTIONS - Aarhus, Denmark

Schmidt-Phiseldeck, Kay. Musikalier, Kort og Billeder. 86-94, AARU

SPECIAL COLLECTIONS - Berlin

BERR

BERS

SPECIAL COLLECTIONS - Bern

Wissler, Gustav. Marcel Godet als Direktor der Schweizerischen Landesbibliothek. 8-12, GODM

SPECIAL COLLECTIONS - Dresden

Deckert, Helmut. Die Übrigen Sondersammlungen. 166-171, DREL

SPECIAL COLLECTIONS - Frankfurt a.M.

Köster, Kurt. Die Deutsche Bibliothek 1945-1965. Weg und Auftrag. 21-77, EPPE

SPECIAL COLLECTIONS - Germany

Jürgens, Adolf. Die Skandinavischen Studien und die Bibliotheken in Deutschland im Letzten Menschenalter. 97-127, MUNT

SPECIAL COLLECTIONS - Halle

Gerhard, Karl. Die Ungarische Nationalbibliothek der Universität Halle-Wittenberg. 139-158, WILM

SPECIAL COLLECTIONS - Mainz

Nissen, Claus. Stiftungen und Nachlässe in der Stadtbibliothek. 35-38, MAIN

SPECIAL COLLECTIONS - Munich

Middendorf, Heinrich. Die Bayerische Staatsbibliothek 1945-1964. 7-61, HOFM

SPECIAL COLLECTIONS - Special subjects - Theatrical literature
see Theatrical libraries and collections

SPECIAL COLLECTIONS - Vienna

BICK

Doublier, Othmar. Ein Vierteljahrhundert aus der Geschichte der Hofbibliothek 1891-1916. 163-210, VIEN

SPECIAL COLLECTIONS - Weimar

Wahl, Hans. Die Weimarische Bibliothek als Erbin der Herzogin Anna Amalia. 158-167, WEIM

SPECIAL LIBRARIANS
see also Medical librarians; Rare book librarians

SPECIAL LIBRARIANS

Grunwald, Wilhelm. Der Spezialbibliothekar. Aufgaben, Auswahl, Ausbildungsvorschläge. 182-191, VORS

SPECIAL LIBRARIANS - Gt. Brit.

Bird, Jack. The Education of Librarians and Information Officers: General Review. 312-318, HUTT
Colinese, P. E. The Education of Librarians and Information Officers: Industrial Information Departments. 305-311, HUTT
Mallaber, K. A. The Education of Librarians and Information Officers: Government Libraries. 301-304, HUTT

SPECIAL LIBRARIES
see also Armed forces libraries; Art libraries and collections; Church libraries; Dental libraries; Education libraries; Genealogical libraries and collections; Geographical libraries and collections; Government libraries; Industrial libraries; Jewish libraries and collections; Law libraries; Medical libraries; Municipal reference libraries; Music libraries and collections; Newspaper libraries and collections; Nursing school libraries; Pharmaceutical libraries; Radio libraries and collections; Religious libraries; Research libraries; Scientific libraries; Ship libraries; State libraries; Sunday school libraries; Technical libraries; Theatrical libraries and collections

SPECIAL LIBRARIES - Berlin

Faden, Eberhard. Aus der Geschichte Gelehrter Gesellschaften und Ihrer Bibliotheken in Berlin. 17-40, SCHS

SPECIAL LIBRARIES - Denmark

Dahl, Svend. H. O. Lange og de Videnskabelige Biblioteker. 322-340, LANE

SPECIAL LIBRARIES - Norway

Bjørnstad, Per. Norsk Faglitteratur og Norsk Bibliotektjeneste i Vår Tekniske Tidsalder. 141-146, NORS
Madshus, Sigrid. Fag- og Forskningsbibliotekene i Siste Decennium. 125-130, NORS
Schaanning, Hedvig. Litt om Fagbiblioteker i Norge. 109-118, NORN

SPECIAL LIBRARIES - Spain - 17th cent.

Selig, Karl-Ludwig. Three Spanish Libraries of Emblem Books and Compendia. 81-90, PARG

<u>SPECULUM DOCTRINALE</u>

Polain, M.-Louis. Notes pour la Collation des Deux Tirages de L'Édition du Speculum Doctrinale, s. ind. typ. [Strasbourg, Adolphe Rusch]. 111-120, COLL

<u>SPECULUM HUMANE SALVATIONIS</u>. 1498.

Larsen, Sofus. To Danske Palaeotyper Trykte i Paris. 183-197, COLL

<u>SPECULUM PERFECTIONIS</u>. Ms. Francesco d'Assisi, Saint. Legend
see Francesco d'Assisi, Saint. Legend. <u>Speculum Perfectionis</u>. Ms.

Spencer, Marjory C.
National and International Pharmacopeias: A Checklist. 410-420, DOEJ

SPENSER, EDMUND. <u>The Faerie Queene</u>

Chew, Samuel C. Spencer's Pageant of the Seven Deadly Sins. 37-54, GREE

SPERATUS, PAULUS, Bp. - Library

Dahlberg, Ragnar. Två Böcker med Märklig Proveniens i Helsingfors Universitetsbibliotek. 127-136, SCHA

SPIELKARTENMUSEUM, Altenburg, Ger.
see Altenburg, Ger. Spielkartenmuseum

SPISOK TRUDOV PROFESSORS ALEKSANDRA IUSTINOVICHA MALEINA. [xx]-xxxii, MALE

Spivacke, Harold.
Carl Engel, Librarian. 13-19, ENGE

SPOKANE - Music libraries and collections
see Music libraries and collections - Spokane

SPOKANE - Music literature and scores - Manuscripts - Collections
see Music literature and scores - Manuscripts Collections - Spokane

Springer, Hermann.
Zur Musiktypographie in der Inkunabelzeit. 173-180, WILM

Springmann, Wolfgang.
W. van der Briele und die Geschichtliche Entwicklung der Wuppertaler Bibliotheken. 7-40, BRIE

Srinivasan, G. A.
Ranganathan as Known to Me. 700-710, RANG

Srivastava, Anand Prakash.
What Matters with Dr. Ranganathan. 720-722, RANG

STACKS
see Shelves and shelving

Stählin, Agnes.
Kleine Sprachlehre des Schlagwortkatalogs. 333-345, STOL
Zur Geschichte der Systematischen Kataloge der Universitätsbibliothek Erlangen. 137-147, REDE

STAHL, JANUARIUS
Preisendanz, Karl. Der Reichenauer Handschriftenkatalog von 1724. 199-206, LEID

Stampe, Ernst.
Komödien des Lebens aus Alten Drucken. 79-85, KUHN

STAMPINI, ETTORE
STAM
Moricca, Umberto. Cenni Biografici. ix-xvi, STAM

STAMPINI, ETTORE - Bibl.
Pubblicazioni di Ettore Stampini. xvii-xxvii, STAM

Stanchev, Stefan, jt. author
Ivanchev, Dimitur and Stefan Stanchev. Bibliografiia na Statiite v Bŭlgarskiia Periodichen Pechat s Ogled na Praktikata na "Bŭlgarski Knigopis" za 1930 i 1931 g. 404-408, MIKN

STANDARDIZATION
Verman, Lal C. Dr. Ranganathan and Standardization. 268-270, RANG
Voorhoeve, N. A. J. F. Donker Duyvis and Standardization. 39-50, DONR

STANDARDS OF LIBRARY SERVICE
see Public libraries - Standards; School libraries - Standards

STANDARDS OF PUBLIC LIBRARIES
see Public libraries - Standards

Stange, Alfred.
Beiträge zur Kaisheimer Buchmalerei. 277-281, LEID

Stapfer, Albert d'.
Lettres in: Huri, Nelly. Quatre Lettres d'Albert Stapfer. 499-507, BONN

Starr, Helen K.
Mr. Hanson and His Friends. 329-333, HANS

STATE AND PROVINCIAL LIBRARY AGENCIES - Public library services - Aarhus, Denmark
Sejr, Emanuel. Benyttelse. 123-154, AARU

STATE LIBRARIES - Aarhus, Denmark
AARU

STATE LIBRARIES - Acquisitions - Aarhus, Denmark
Haugsted, Ejler. Ordning, Opstilling, Bogbestand. 53-80, AARU

STATE LIBRARIES - Acquisitions - Aarhus, Denmark - Hist.
Grundtvig, Vilh. Almindelig Historie. 11-51, AARU

STATE LIBRARIES - Administration - Weimar - Hist.
Blumenthal, Hermann. Älteste Verwaltungsgeschichte der Landesbibliothek Weimar (1691-1750). 46-86, WEIM

STATE LIBRARIES - Bavaria
Böck, Karl. Zum Geleit. xxiii-xxvi, HOFM

STATE LIBRARIES - Dresden
DREL

STATE LIBRARIES - Finance - Aarhus, Denmark
Grundtvig, Vilh. Andre Forhold. 159-165, AARU

STATE LIBRARIES - Germany
Kunze, Horst. Die Landesbibliotheken Gestern, Heute und Morgen. 1-14, DREL
Leppla, Rupprecht. Die Landesbibliotheken als Gattung. 116-125, BOLL

STATE LIBRARIES - Germany - Hist.
Ihme, Heinrich. Landesbibliothek und Landesgeschichte. 94-111, HOFF

STATE LIBRARIES - Hamburg
Voigt, Christian. Die Staats- und Universitäts-Bibliothek Hamburg. Ihr

Weg von der Gelehrtenbibliothek zur Wissenschaftlichen Gebrauchsbibliothek. 23-39, TIEM

STATE LIBRARIES - Kassel

KASS

STATE LIBRARIES - Königsberg

KÖNI

STATE LIBRARIES - Reference services - Dresden

Hofmann, Hans. Auskunft. 97-104, BOLE

STATE LIBRARIES - Statistics - Dresden

Assmann, Karl. Die Sächsische Landesbibliothek von 1945 bis 1955. Zerstörung, Wiederaufbau und Gegenwärtiger Stand der Arbeit. 29-85, DREL

STATE LIBRARIES - Statistics - Munich

Middendorf, Heinrich. Die Bayerische Staatsbibliothek 1945-1964. 7-61, HOFM

STATE LIBRARIES - Weimar

WEIM

STATE PUBLICATIONS
see Government publications

STATE PUBLICATIONS - Cataloging
see Documents - Cataloging

STATISTICAL RESEARCH - Frankfurt a.M.

Busch, August. Statistische Forschung in Frankfurt a.M. 161-168, EBRA

STATISTICS
see also Circulation - Statistics

STATISTICS

Okuda, Katsumasa. Toshokan Tōkei Omoumama. (Occasional Thoughts on Library Statistics.) 79-89, (pt. 1), OHAS

STATISTICS - College and university libraries
see College and university libraries - Statistics

STATISTICS - National libraries
see National libraries - Statistics

STATISTICS - Public libraries
see Public libraries - Statistics

STATIUS, Achilles
see Estaço, Aquiles

STATSBIBLIOTEK, Aarhus, Denmark
see Aarhus, Denmark. Statsbibliotek

STATUS OF LIBRARIANS
see Librarians - Status

STATUTES, Italian - Collections - Berlin

Paalzow, Hans. Einiges über die Italienischen Stadtrechte. 371-388, WILM

Staveley, Ronald.
Student and Tutor. 56-71, SAYW

STAVELOT, Belgium (Benedictine abbey) Mss.

Kirchner, Joachim. Das Staveloter Evangeliar der Preussischen Staatsbibliothek. 160-171, DEGE

Steenberghen, F. van.
L'Œuvre Scientifique de Monseigneur Pelzer. 7-16, PELZ

Steffens, Franz.
Über die Abkürzungsmethoden der Schreibschule von Bobbio. 244-254, CHAT

Stefl, Max.
Von Büchern und Büchermenschen. 20-23, HELD

STEIERMARK
see Styria

Stein, Ernst.
Die Herstellung von Fachbibliographien, Dargestellt an einem Beispiel aus der Arbeit der Technisch-Wissenschaftlichen Auskunftsstelle der Universitätsbibliothek Jena an der Bibliographischen Erfassung der Internationalen Laser-Literatur. 117-129, BULL

Steinacker, Harold.
Zum Liber Diurnus und zur Frage nach dem Ursprung der Frühminuskel. 105-176, EHRD

Steinberg, Heinz.
Die Zukunft der Preussischen Staatsbibliothek. 34-40, BERP

Steiner, Herbert.
Zur Hofmannsthal-Ausgabe. 347-348, HOFF

Steinglass, Dora.
A Bibliography of the Writings of Joshua Bloch. 180-219, BLOC

STEINSCHNEIDER, MORITZ

STEI

Baron, Salo W. Moritz Steinschneider's Contribution to Jewish Historiography. 83-148, MARX

Kohut, George Alexander. Steinschneideriana. 65-127, FREI

STEINSCHNEIDER, MORITZ - Bibl.

Kohut, George Alexander. Bibliography of the Writings of Prof. Dr. M. Steinschneider. V-XXXIX, STEI

Steinschneider, Moritz.
Briefe in: Kohut, George Alexander. Steinschneideriana. 65-127, FREI

STENDHAL, pseud.
see Beyle, Marie Henri

Stensgård, Erling.
Katalogiseringen. 95-114, AARU

STEPECK, KONRAD

Rhodes, Dennis E. Konrad Stepeck of Nuremberg (c. 1424—c. 1495). 311-316, BENZ

Stern, Ludwig.
Mitteilungen aus der Lübener Kirchenbibliothek. 67-96, WILM

STEUBER, JOHANN. Mss. Bibliotheca Marpurgensis. 1631

Schawe, Josef. D. Steuberi Catalogi und Nachrichten von der Marpurger und Giesser Bibliothec. Giessener Hs. 30. 204-214, JUCH

Stevens, David H.
Islands of Influence. 679-684, WILS

Stevens, Henry Newton.
The DeBry Collector's Painefull Peregrination along the Pleasant Pathway to Perfection. 269-276, EAME

Stevens, Henry Newton and Roland Tree.
Comparative Cartography Exemplified in an Analytical & Bibliographical Description of Nearly One Hundred Maps and Charts of the American Continent Published in Great Britain during the Years 1600-1850. 305-363, WROT

Stevenson, L. G., ed.
FRAN

Stewart, J. D.
Sayers. 13-17, SAYW

Stickler, Michael, jt. ed.
STUM

Stickler, Michael.
Dr. Alois Kisser, Generaldirektor-Stellvertreter der Österreichischen Nationalbibliothek. 9-10, STUM

Stiennon, J.
Un Fragment Inédit d'un Obituaire de Saint-Servais de Maestricht (XIVe et XVe Siècles). 131-167, MAAS

Stier, Friedrich.
Geschichte der Ernst-Abbe-Bücherei und Lesehalle zu Jena. 18-45, JENA

STIERNHIELM, GEORG - Library

Walde, O. Om Georg Stiernhielms Bibliotek. Några Anteckningar. 107-141, GRAP

STIERNMAN, ANDERS ANTON VON

Sallander, Hans. Om Anders Anton von Stiernman Som Bibliografisk Författare. 561-576, GRAP

STILES, EZRA. MSS. CORRESPONDENCE - COLLECTIONS - YALE

Bridgwater, Dorothy Wildes. President Stiles's Letter to Ebeling. 307-316, KEOG

Stilwell, Margaret Bingham.
The Fasciculus Temporum, a Genealogical Survey of Editions before 1480. 409-440, EAME

Stjernberg, C. W.
Domkapitelsavhandlingar efter 1890. Jämte Tillägg och Rättelser till Aks. Josephson, Avhandlingar ock Program (1855-1890). Bibliografi. 608-620, UPPS

STOBAEUS, JOANNES. Mss. Florilegium

Gebhardt, Oskar von. Eine Verlorene und eine Wiedergefundene Stobaeus-Handschrift. 243-264, WILM

Stock, Hildegard.
Dank und Erinnerung. 15-18, ZIEG

STOCKHOLM. Collegium Societatis Jesu in Suetia. Bibliotheca

Collijn, Isak Gustaf Alfred. Bibliotheca "Collegii Societatis Jesu in Suetia." Några Bidrag till Kännedomen om Jesuiternas Boksamling på Gråmunkeholmen. 75-91, ANNE

STOCKHOLM - Foreign language books - Collections
see Foreign language books - Collections - Stockholm

STOCKHOLM. Gustav Vasa Församlingsbibliotek

Hornwall, Gert. Ett Föregångsbibliotek i Stockholm. Gustav Vasa Församlingsbibliotek 1909-1927. 127-135, HEIN

STOCKHOLM. Kungliga Biblioteket

Adde, Gustaf. Äldre Finskspråkiga

Skrifter i Svenska Bibliotek. 269-294, COLL
Carlsson, A. B. En Supplik af Gjörwell 1772. Ett Stycke Svensk Lärdomshistoria i Kanslikollegiet. 67-73, ANNE
Dahlgren, E. W. Gamla Tyska Kartor i Kungl. Biblioteket. 93-123, ANNE

STOCKHOLM. Kungliga Biblioteket - Hist.
Sundström, Einar. Om Tillkomsten av Kungl. Bibliotekets Svenska Tryckavdelning. 507-516, COLL

STOCKHOLM. Kungliga Biblioteket. Mss. (Cod. Holm. A 227 and A 228)
Wieselgren, O. Två i Kungl. Biblioteket Befintliga Miniatyrhandskrifter ur den Gent-Brüggeska Skolan. 91-101, COLL

STOCKHOLM. Kungliga Biblioteket. Mss. (Roman de la Rose)
Söderhjelm, Werner. Un Manuscrit du Roman de la Rose à la Bibliothèque Royale de Stockholm. 75-90, COLL

STOCKHOLM - Maps, German - Collections
see Maps, German - Collections - Stockholm

STOCKHOLM - Parish libraries
see Parish libraries - Stockholm

STOCKHOLM - Personnel - Administration
see Personnel - Administration - Stockholm

STOCKHOLM - Personnel records
see Personnel records - Stockholm

STOCKHOLM - Printing
see Printing - Stockholm

STOCKHOLM. Riksarkivet
see Sweden. Riksarkivet

STOCKHOLM. Royal Institute of Technology
see Stockholm. Tekniska Högskolan. Bibliotek

STOCKHOLM. Stadsbibliotek
Hjelmqvist, Fredrik. Die Stockholmer Stadtbücherei als Einheitsbücherei. 43-46, ACKE
———— Utlandets Författere och Allmänheten i Stockholm. Några Siffror ur Stockholms Stadsbiblioteks Utlåning. 88-96, MUNT
Kolmodin, Torsten. Om Personalredovisning. 257-261, GRAP

STOCKHOLM - Technical libraries - Book selection
see Technical libraries - Book selection - Stockholm

STOCKHOLM. Tekniska Högskolan. Bibliotek
Björkbom, Carl. Bokvalsproblem vid ett Tekniskt Centralbibliotek. 51-61, DAHA

STOCKHOLM - Use Studies - Technical libraries
see Use studies - Technical libraries - Stockholm

Stössel, Waldemar.
Ernst-Abbe-Bücherei und Universitätsbibliothek Jena. 118-119, JENA

Stoetzer, Walter.
Die Kekulé-Bibliothek als Hilfsmittel der Dokumentation in der Chemischen Industrie. 130-135, LEUN

Stöwesand, Rudolf, ed.
SCHR

Stöwesand, Rudolf.
Buch und Buchstabe. Prinzipielles und Persönliches als Einführung. 7-17, SCHR
Der Schreibgriffel der Babylonier. Ein Bericht, Abgestattet vor der Internationalen Gesellschaft für Schrift- und Buchkunde Anläßlich Ihrer Jahresversammlung am 1. Dezember 1929 in der Universität Frankfurt a.M. 105-115, SCHR

Stoianov, Man'o.
Knigi ot Bŭlgari na Chuzhdi Ezitsi do Osvobozhdenieto. Bibliografski Pregled. 283-291, MIKH

Stoĭkov, Stoĭko.
Akademik Aleksandŭr Teodorov-Balan i Bŭlgarskiīat Ezik. 9-30, TEOD

Stoilov, Vasil.
Spomeni za D-r Nikola V. Mikhov. 273-281, MIKH

Stois, Max.
Bibliothek und Editio Princeps. 283-288, LEID

Stokes, Roy.
"... Not for Trafficking Alone ..." 48-55, SAYW

Stollreither, Eugen.
Die Auflösung der Heilsbronner Universitätsbibliothek. 75-84, VERZ
Die Universitätsbibliothek Erlangen zur Zeit der Praktikantentätigkeit August von Platens. 216-229, LEYG

STOLLREITHER, EUGEN
STOL

Stoltz, G.
Arne Kildals Første Bedrift som Biblioteksmann. 18-22, KILD

Stopp, Klaus.
Die Schreibweisen von Mainz auf Alten Karten. 421-433, BENZ

STORAGE AND DEPOSIT LIBRARIES
Bostwick, Arthur Elmore. Nomads. 97-102, PUTN

STORY HOUR AND STORY TELLING
Baker, Augusta. Once upon a Time. 9-14, SAYE
Sawyer, Ruth. Storytelling Fifty Years A-growing. 593-598, MOOR

STRABO, WALAHFRID
see Walahfrid Strabo

Strang, Mary.
Good Labour of Old Days. 537-550, MOOR

STRASBOURG - Book industry and trade
see Book industry and trade - Strasbourg

STRASBOURG - Incunabula
see Incunabula - Strasbourg

STRASBOURG - Manuscripts - Collections
see Manuscripts - Collections - Strasbourg

STRASBOURG - Printing
see Printing - Strasbourg

STRASBOURG. Universitäts- und Landesbibliothek - Hist.
BARA
Ficker, Johannes. Ein Straßburger Akademisches Gedenkbuch aus dem Reformationszeitalter. 211-229, WOLF

STRASBOURG. Universitäts- und Landesbibliothek. Mss.
Ficker, Johannes. Handschriftliches der Alten Strassburger Universitätsbibliothek. 44-65, ESCZ

STRASSBURG
see Strasbourg

Straub, Hans.
Christoph Martin Wieland an Johann III Bernoulli. Ein Unveröffentlichter Brief aus der "Gothaer Sammlung" der Basler Universitätsbibliothek. 233-245, SCHU

Strauch, Philipp.
Rigaer Handschriftenfragmente. 238-243, DEGE

Strebl, Laurenz, jt. author
Stummvoll, Josef and Laurenz Strebl. Copying of the Old Catalogue of the Austrian National Library. 175-178, RANG

STREITBERGER, AURELIUS
Dumrath, Karlheinrich. "Gott zu Ehren und Unsern Nachkommen zum Besten." 2-15, SCHV

Stremlau, Willi and Martin Thilo.
Berliner Büchereigesetz und Büchereibau. 183-189, SCHS

Striedl, Hans, jt. ed.
HOFM

Striedl, Hans.
150 Jahre Münchener Aufstellungsschema. 73-103, HOFM
Der Humanist Johann Albrecht Widmanstetter (1506-57) als Klassischer Philologe. 96-120, GRAT

STRIKE LITERATURE - Finland, 1905 - Collections - Helsinki
Donner, Kai. Tryckalster från Storstrejken. 164-169, HULA

Strittmatter, Anselm.
The Pentecost Exultet of Reims and Besançon. 384-400, GREE

STROGANOV FAMILY - Library
Bogdanovaîa, Nadezhda G. Knizhnye Bogatstva Stroganovykh v 1578 g. 277-284, MALE

Strohm, Adam.
Louis Round Wilson. 685, WILS

Strout, Ruth French.
An Enquiry into the Role of the Cataloger. 135-141, HASH

Struck, Christel.
Die Volksbüchereien der Vororte und des Landgebietes. 68-74, HAMB

Struck, Gustav.
Handschriftenschätze der Landesbibliothek Kassel. 1-127, (part 2), KASS

Strübing, Eduard.
Zwei Einbände Jakob Krauses in der Weimarer Landesbibliothek. 153-157, WEIM

STUDENTS, Junior College - Reading - Special groups of readers
see Reading - Special groups of readers - Junior college students

STUDENTS' LIBRARIES
see Private libraries

STUDENTS' SOCIETIES - Libraries
Rouse, Roscoe. The Libraries of Nineteenth-Century College Societies. 25-42, GJEL

STUDIENBIBLIOTHEK. Salzburg. Bundesstaatliche
see Salzburg. Bundesstaatliche Studienbibliothek

STUDY CUBICLES
see Carrels

STUDY LIBRARIES
see College and university libraries - Technical services; College and university libraries - Undergraduate libraries and collections

STÜRMER, WOLFGANG
Hase, Martin von. Zwei Drucke des Temporals des Johannes Regiomontanus von Wolfgang Stürmer in Erfurt. I, 61-66, GLAU

Stummvoll, Josef, ed.
BICK

Stummvoll, Josef.
Die Abschreibung des Alphabetischen Kataloges der Österreichischen Nationalbibliothek. 594-600, BRUM
Die Druckschriftenbestände der Österreichischen Nationalbibliothek und die Abschreibung des Alphabetischen Kataloges 1501 bis 1929. 105-118, HOFM
Die Präfekten der Bibliotheca Palatina Vindobonensis, der Früheren Kaiserl. Königl. Hof- und Jetzigen Österreichischen Nationalbibliothek bis zur Gegenwart. 3-21, BICK

Stummvoll, Josef and Laurenz Strebl.
Copying of the Old Catalogue of the Austrian National Library. 175-178, RANG

STUMMVOLL, JOSEF
STUM
Zimmel, Bruno. DDr. Josef Stummvoll, Generaldirektor der Österreichischen Nationalbibliothek. 5-8, STUM

Sturel, René.
À Propos d'un Manuscrit du Musée Condé. 575-583, CHAT

STUTTGART. Bibliothek für Zeitgeschichte
Rohwer, Jürgen. Die Bibliothek für Zeitgeschichte und Ihre Aufgabe in der Historischen Forschung. 112-138, HOFF

STUTTGART - Hölderlin, Friedrich - Collections
see Hölderlin, Friedrich - Collections - Stuttgart

STUTTGART - Incunabula - Collections
see Incunabula - Collections - Stuttgart

STUTTGART. Landesbibliothek
Autenrieth, Johanne. Ältere und Neuere Handschriftenkataloge aus dem Umkreis der Stuttgarter Handschriftensammlung. 165-188, HOFF
Kyriss, Ernst. Einbände mit Hoheitszeichen Herzog Carl Eugens. 232-243, HOFF
Leuze, Otto. Mit Holzschnitten Verzierte Buchumschläge des 15. Jahrhunderts in der Württembergischen Landesbibliothek in Stuttgart. 165-169, LEID

STUTTGART. Landesbibliothek. Hölderlin-Archiv
Lohrer, Liselotte. Hölderlin-Ausgabe und Hölderlin-Archiv. Entstehung und Geschichte. 289-314, HOFF

STUTTGART. Landesbibliothek. Mss. (Cod. Brev. 4°, Nr. 1)
Irtenkauf, Wolfgang. Zur Liturgischen Seite des Eberhardgebetbuches. 189-203, HOFF

STUTTGART. Landesbibliothek. Mss. (Cod. Hist. Q 102)
Oehme, Ruthardt. Der Ämteratlas des Herzogtums Württemberg 1575 (WLB Cod. Hist. Q 102). 204-215, HOFF

STUTTGART - War records - Collections
see War records - Collections - Stuttgart

STUTTGART. Weltkriegsbücherei
see Stuttgart. Bibliothek für Zeitgeschichte

STUTTGART. Württembergische Bibliotheksgesellschaft
see Württembergische Bibliotheksgesellschaft, Stuttgart

STUTTGART. Württembergische Landesbibliothek
see Stuttgart. Landesbibliothek

STUTTGART. Zentralkatalog der Wissenschaftlichen Bibliotheken des Landes Baden-Württemberg
Zunker, Ernst. Die Bedeutung Regionaler Zentralkataloge für das Erfassungsgebiet. 151-164, HOFF

STYLUS - Babylonia

Stöwesand, Rudolf. Der Schreibgriffel der Babylonier. Ein Bericht, Abgestattet vor der Internationalen Gesellschaft für Schrift- und Buchkunde Anläßlich Ihrer Jahresversammlung am 1. Dezember 1929 in der Universität Frankfurt a.M. 105-115, SCHR

STYRIA - Bookbinding
see Bookbinding - Styria

SUBJECT BIBLIOGRAPHY
see Bibliography

SUBJECT CATALOGING
see Classification; Subject headings

SUBJECT CATALOGS
see Catalogs - Subject

SUBJECT DEPARTMENTS IN LIBRARIES
see College and university libraries - Departmental and divisional libraries

SUBJECT HEADINGS

Hamada, Toshio. Kenmei Kosei no Ichishian; Senpaku no Shuruimei o to Chūsin to shite. (A Trial Method of Constructing a Subject Index Using Names Indicating Kinds of Ships.) 221-227, HASH
Lasso de la Vega, Javier. La CDU como Medio para Hacer Sistemáticas las Listas de Epigrafes de los Catálogos de Asuntos. 169-170, DONK
Schmidt, Philipp. Über die Sachliche Katalogisierung Umfassender Werke. 213-222, SCHU
Schwidetzky, Georg. Die Unpersönlichen Drucksachen im Alphabetischen Katalog. 123-133, MIND
Wright, Wyllis E. Subject Headings in the Reference Department of the New York Public Library. 431-436, LYDE
Zastrau, H. O. Gedanken zur Sachkatalogisierung. Über die Normung und Bildung von Schlagwörtern. 54-69, COET

SUBJECT HEADINGS - Germany

Stählin, Agnes. Kleine Sprachlehre des Schlagwortkatalogs. 333-345, STOL

SUBJECT HEADINGS - Special subjects - Biography - Dresden

Boden, Charlotte. Der Biographische Katalog und das Personalrepertorium der Sächsischen Landesbibliothek. 21-37, BOLL

SUBJECT HEADINGS - Special subjects - Chemistry

Grunwald, Wilhelm. Zur Sacherschliessung im Bereiche der Chemie. 393-403, JUCH

SUBJECT HEADINGS - Special subjects - Music

Bush, Helen E. and David Judson Haykin. Music Subject Headings. 39-45, KINO

SUBJECT HEADINGS - Special subjects - Patent literature

Masuyama, Takehiko. Tokkyo Bunken to Yunitāmu no Riyō. (Patent Literature and the Feasibility of Employing Uniterm System.) 239-266, HASH

SUBJECT HEADINGS - Special subjects - Ships

Hamada, Toshio. Kenmei Kosei no Ichishian; Senpaku no Shuruimei o to Chūsin to shite. (A Trial Method of Constructing a Subject Index Using Names Indicating Kinds of Ships.) 221-227, HASH

SUBJECT HEADINGS - Special subjects - Vatican

Fraschetti-Santinelli, Italia. L'Ordinamento della Voce "Roma" nel Catalogo per Soggetti. 151-163, GREG

SUBJECT HEADINGS - Special subjects - Vienna

Alker, Hugo. Geschichte der Sachkatalogisierung an der Universitätsbibliothek Wien 1774-1954. 118-132, VORS

SUBJECT INTERESTS IN READING
see Reading interests

SUBPROFESSIONAL ASSISTANTS
see Non-professional assistants

Subramanyam, D. [=Subramaniam].
Ideal of University Education. 443-450, RANG
A Tribute of Reverence. 744-746, RANG

SUDETENLAND - Public libraries
see Public libraries - Sudetenland

SUHM, PETER FREDERIK - Library

Tank, Roar. Peter Frederik Suhms Forhold til Thomas Angell. 37-41, KJAE

SULPITIUS, JOANNES. De Octo Partibus Orationis Libellus. 1500

Scaccia-Scarafoni, Camillo. La Grammatica di Sulpizio Verolano in un Incunabulo Ignoto ai Bibliografi. 378-384, GREG

SULPIZIO VEROLANO
see Sulpitius, Joannes

Sulz, Eugen.
Die Büchereischule der Stadt Essen 1921-1933. 13-16, LANF

SUNDAY SCHOOL LIBRARIES
Walter, Frank Keller. A Poor but Respectable Relation—The Sunday School Library. 731-739, WILS

SUNDBYBERG, Sweden - Public relations of libraries
see Public relations of libraries - Sundbyberg, Sweden

SUNDBYBERG, Sweden. Stadsbiblioteket
Bianchini, Bianca. Muhammed och Berget. Redogörelse för en Experimentverksamhet i Sundbyberg. 33-50, HEIN

Sundström, Einar.
Om Tillkomsten av Kungl. Bibliotekets Svenska Tryckavdelning. 507-516, COLL

SURVEYS
see also Use studies

SURVEYS - College and university libraries - U.S.
Thompson, Lawrence S. The University Library Survey in America. 347-353, STOL

Susemihl, François.
De Rhetoricorum Aristoteleorum Libro Primo Quaestiones Criticae. 87-96, GRAU

Sustrac, Charles.
Quelques Observations sur la Classification Décimale. 37-38, EMLE

SŪTRA, VIMALAKĪRTI
see Vimalakīrtinirdeśa-sūtra

Sutter, Berthold, ed.
SCHT

Suzuka, Osamu.
Kinyū ni okeru Hompō Kosho no Toriatsukai ni tsuite. (A Guide for Cataloging Old Japanese Books.) 115-130, KYOT

Suzuki, Ryūichi.
Ryūkō Fushi no Gakujutsu Mokuroku. (On the First Chinese Book Catalog by Ryūkō [father and son].) 104-114, KYOT

SVENSKA OSTINDISKA COMPANIET
Lunelund-Grönroos, Birgit. Peter Johan Bladhs "Räkning öfwer Böcker til 1771. Års Slut." 85-100, TUDE

SVERDRUP, GEORG
Daae, Ludvig. Professor Georg Sverdrup. 1-42, (pt. 2), OSLU

SWABIA - Archives, Literary
see Archives, Literary - Swabia

SWAINE, CHARLES
Adams, Percy G. The Case of Swaine Versus Drage: An Eighteenth-Century Publishing Mystery Solved. 157-168, PARG

Swaminathan, S.
Libraries in India: Yesterday and Today. 353-361, RANG

Swan, Bradford F.
The First Printing in Providence. 365-369, WROT

Swarzenski, Hanns.
The Kneeling "Acolyte" in the Morgan Library. 179-183, GREE

SWEDEN - Authors and libraries
see Authors and libraries - Sweden

SWEDEN - Bibliography, National
see Bibliography, National - Sweden

SWEDEN - Bookmobile services - Public Libraries
see Bookmobile services - Public libraries - Sweden

SWEDEN - Books - Owners' marks
see Books - Owners' marks - Sweden

SWEDEN - Catholic libraries
see Catholic libraries - Sweden

SWEDEN - College and university librarians - Education
see College and university librarians - Education - Sweden

SWEDEN - College and university libraries - Administration
see College and university libraries - Administration - Sweden

SWEDEN - College and university libraries - Departmental and divisional libraries
see College and university libraries - Departmental and divisional libraries - Sweden

SWEDEN - Cooperation
see Cooperation - Sweden

SWEDEN - Depository libraries
see Depository libraries - Sweden

SWEDEN - Dissertations, Academic
see Dissertations, Academic - Sweden

SWEDEN - Finnish literature collections
see Finnish literature collections - Sweden

SWEDEN - Kings and rulers - Libraries

Dahlberg, Ragnar. Några Okända Svenska Kungliga Pärmstämplar. 42-50, TUDE

SWEDEN - Libraries
see Libraries - Sweden

SWEDEN - Manuscripts - Collections
see Manuscripts - Collections - Sweden

SWEDEN - Monastic libraries
see Monastic libraries - Sweden

SWEDEN - Music libraries and collections
see Music libraries and collections - Sweden

SWEDEN. National Archives
see Sweden. Riksarkivet

SWEDEN - Parish libraries
see Parish libraries - Sweden

SWEDEN - Printing
see Printing - Sweden

SWEDEN - Private libraries
see Private libraries - Sweden

SWEDEN - Public libraries
see Public libraries - Sweden

SWEDEN - Public libraries - Aims and objectives
see Public libraries - Aims and objectives - Sweden

SWEDEN - Public libraries - Centralization
see Public libraries - Centralization - Sweden

SWEDEN - Public libraries - Finance
see Public libraries - Finance - Sweden

SWEDEN - Radio libraries and collections
see Radio libraries and collections - Sweden

SWEDEN - Recordings - Care and preservation
see Recordings - Care and preservation - Sweden

SWEDEN. Riksarkivet

Ågren, Sven. Till Arkivleveransernas Historia. Några Anteckningar. 338-349, GRAP

Grill, Erik. The Barrow Method in Sweden. 489-492, GALL

SWEDEN. Riksarkivet. Erik Sparres Samling

Gödel, Vilhelm. Erik Sparre. Till Historien om Hans Litteräre Samlingar. 171-178, ANNE

SWEDEN - Rural libraries
see Rural libraries - Sweden

SWEDENBORG, EMANUEL. Mss. Kort Relation om Smälte-Wärket vid Store Kopparberget

Jörgensen, Arne. Ett Bidrag till Swedenborgs Bibliografi. 105-107, SCHA

SWEDISH AUTHORS
see Authors, Swedish

SWEDISH CORRESPONDENCE
see Correspondence, Swedish

SWEDISH LIBRARIANS
see Librarians, Swedish

SWEDISH LITERATURE - Collections - Gothenburg, Sweden

Marklund, E. "Svenstrycket." 21-34, (fifth paper), GÖTE

SWIFT, JONATHAN. Mss.

Leslie, Sir Shane. The Swift Manuscripts in the Morgan Library. 445-448, GREE

SWIFT, JONATHAN. Mss. Directions to Servants

Davis, Herbert. The Manuscripts of Swift's "Directions to Servants." 433-444, GREE

Swigchem, P. J. van.
Boekselectieprobelemen in de Amerikaanse Public Library. 226-236, KOSS

SWINESHEAD, RICHARD

Kibre, Pearl. Cardinal Domenico Grimani, Questio de Intensione et Remissione Qualitatis: A Commentary on the Tractate of that Title by Richard Suiseth (Calculator). 147-203, ALBA

Swingle, Walter T.
Chinese Books: Their Character and Value and Their Place in the Western Library. 429-444, PUTN

SWISS MANUSCRIPTS
see Manuscripts, Swiss

SWISS NATIONAL UNION CATALOG
see Bern. Schweizerische Landesbibliothek. Schweizerischer Gesamtkatalog

SWITZERLAND - Armed forces libraries
see Armed forces libraries - Switzerland

SWITZERLAND - Associations
see Associations - Switzerland

SWITZERLAND - Book industry and trade
see Book industry and trade - Switzerland

SWITZERLAND - Bookmobile services - Regional libraries
see Bookmobile services - Regional libraries - Switzerland

SWITZERLAND - Catalogs - Union
see Catalogs - Union - Switzerland

SWITZERLAND - Classification - Systems - Universal decimal
see Classification - Systems - Universal decimal - Switzerland

SWITZERLAND - Cooperation
see Cooperation - Switzerland

SWITZERLAND - Education for librarianship
see Education for librarianship - Switzerland

SWITZERLAND - Libraries
see Libraries - Switzerland

SWITZERLAND - Package libraries
see Package libraries - Switzerland

SWITZERLAND - Planning, Library
see Planning, Library - Switzerland

SWITZERLAND - Printing
see Printing - Switzerland

SWITZERLAND - Private libraries
see Private libraries - Switzerland

SWITZERLAND - Public libraries
see Public libraries - Switzerland

SWITZERLAND - Public libraries - State and regional development plans
see Public libraries - State and regional development plans - Switzerland

SWITZERLAND - Publishers and publishing
see Publishers and publishing - Switzerland

SWITZERLAND. Schweizerische Kommission der Bücherhilfe an das Kriegsgeschädigte Ausland
see Schweizerische Kommission der Bücherhilfe an das Kriegsgeschädigte Ausland

Symons, Harry C.
The Academic Advisor. 54-60, DAVI

SZACKI, JÁKOB

SZAC

Szmańda, Edward.
Dyrektor i Działacz Oświatowy Józef Podgóreczny. 145-148, BYDG
Początki i Rozwój Działalności. 9-62, BYDG

Taam, Cheuk-Woon.
The Discovery of the Tun-Huang Library and Its Effect on Chinese Studies. 686-705, WILS

TABLETS (Paleography)

Haebler, Konrad. Zwei Nürnberger Tonformen. 103-110, COLL
Kapelrud, Arvid S. Et Fønikisk Bibliotek fra det 14. Århundre før Kr. 77-83, TVET
Zeretelli, G. Zwei Unedierte Griechische Schultafeln. 113-117, CHAT

TACITUS, CORNELIUS. Germania

Schmid, Wolfgang. Urgentibus Imperii Fatis (Tac. Germ. 33). 381-392, ALBA

Taira, Shunsei.
Meiji no Ichi Zasshi ni Arawareta Bukkyo Toshokan Kensetsuron. (A Proposal for Establishing a Buddhist Library in Japan.) 95-98, KYOT

Takada, Sadakichi.
Sakuin no Kōsatsu. (Consideration on Indexing.) 14-19, OTAT

Takahashi, Mamoru.
Areya Koreya. (School Library.) 218-220, KYOT

Takebayashi, Kumahiko.
Gakkō to Toshokan. (Schools and Libraries.) 1-8, HAKO
Kansai Bunko Kyōkai, Sono Rehishiteki Igi. (Kansai Bunko Kyōkai, Its Historical Significance.) 37-52, KYOT

Takeda, Goichi.
Tosho no Hozon ni tsuite. (On the Conservation of Books.) 16-28, IMAI

Takeuchi, Zensaku.
Genkō no Nihon Chosha Kigo no Shujuso. (Various Aspects of Author Marks Used in Japan at Present.) 3-21, TSUB
Tosho Bunrui to Tosho Kigo ni Kansuru Ichi Kosatsu. (An Observation Relating to Classification of Books and Numbers.) 1-24, (pt. 1), OHAS

TALMUD TORAH. Library. Leghorn
see Leghorn. Talmud Torah. Biblioteca

Tamai, Tōkichi.
Zenkoku Keizai Chōsa Kikan Rengōkai Seitei Gaikoku Zasshi-mei Ryakugo

Shokitei ni tsuite. (On the Rules of Abbreviation of the Titles of Foreign Periodicals, Established by the National Federation of Economic Research Organizations.) 20-36, OTAT

Tanaka, Kaido.
Hyakumantō Darani Moji Kō. (Study of the Types Used in the Dharani in the Million Pagodas, 8th Century.) 25-34, TOMI

Tanaka, Takashi.
Tosho no Chikara. (The Utility of Books.) 13-21, HAKO

TANDHEELKUNDIG INSTITUUT. Bibliotheek - Utrecht
see Utrecht. Tandheelkundig Instituut. Bibliotheek

Taniguchi, Kan'ichirō.
Tosho Seiri no Kaiko. (Book Processing.) 221-223, KYOT

Tank, Roar, jt. ed.
OSLN

Tank, Roar.
De Femti År. 9-32, OSLN
Peter Frederik Suhms Forhold til Thomas Angell. 37-41, KJAE

Tans, J. A. G.
Een Uitdagende Utrechtse Collectie: De Val des Pausdoms. 64-77, UTRE

Taracena, Blas.
Notas de Arquitectura Románica. Las Galerías Porticadas. II, 411-428, ARTI

TARANTO - Inscriptions, Latin
see Inscriptions, Latin - Taranto

TARENTUM
see Taranto

TASSARA, GABRIEL GARCÍA Y
see García y Tassara, Gabriel

Tatzer, Leopold.
Seltene Viennensia der Stadtbibliothek. 46-69, VIES

Taube, Gurli.
Fotografen Osti och den Ostiska Plåtsamlingen på Carolina Rediviva. 280-292, GRAP

Taube, N. E.
Några Ord om Utländska Kartor i Uppsala Universitetsbibliotek. 526-536, UPPS

Tauber, Maurice F.
Classification of Books in College and University Libraries: Historical Aspects. 706-724, WILS
Dr. Ranganathan and Proposals for Cooperative Cataloguing. 171-174, RANG

Taurisano, Innocenzo, O.P.
Il Padre Tommaso Masetti Ultimo Prefetto della Casanatense. 385-389, GREG

Tautz, Kurt.
Die Turnbull Library in Wellington - ein Spiegel des Pazifischen Raumes. 263-270, JUCH

TAX CAMPAIGNS
see Public libraries - Finance

Taylor, Archer.
The History of Bibliography. 193-199, PARG

TAYLOR, HENRY CALHOUN

Jackson, William A. Tunc et Nunc: or the Pepys and Taylor Collections of Early English Books on Navigation. 195-201, WROT

Tazawa, Kyōji.
Toshokan Wa Doko e Ikuka. (Future of the Library.) 7-14, KYOT

TEACHERS - Instruction in library use
see Instruction in library use - Teachers and administrators

TEACHING

Krishnan, A. Dr. Ranganathan's Humanisation of Teaching Technique. 558-567, RANG
Mittal, R. L. Study of Dr. Ranganathan as an Author and a Teacher. 574-577, RANG
Shukla, L. S. The Master-Educationist. 568-573, RANG

TEACHING WITH THE JOINT UNIVERSITY LIBRARIES (Symposium). 7-9, NASH

TECHNICAL LIBRARIES - Book selection - Stockholm

Björkbom, Carl. Bokvalsproblem vid ett Tekniskt Centralbibliotek. 51-61, DAHA

TECHNICAL LIBRARIES - Germany

Meyen, Fritz. Die Technisch-wissenschaftlichen Bibliotheken, Ihre Entwicklung und Ihre Stellung im Rahmen des Deutschen Bibliothekswesens. 102-125, LEUN
Trommsdorff, Paul. Technische Literatur in Deutschen Bibliotheken. 344-351, HANS

TECHNICAL LIBRARIES - Norway

Bjørnstad, Per. Norsk Faglitteratur og

Norsk Bibliotektjeneste i Vår Tekniske Tidsalder. 141-146, NORS
Munthe, Wilhelm. De Videnskapelige Biblioteker. 97-108, NORN

TECHNICAL LITERATURE - Collections - Berlin
Fritzsche, Hans-Joachim. Erweiterter Benutzungsdienst und Beratungsstelle für Technische und Naturwissenschaftliche Literatur. 33-35, BERR

TECHNICAL LITERATURE - Collections - Germany
Trommsdorff, Paul. Technische Literatur in Deutschen Bibliotheken. 344-351, HANS

TECHNICAL LITERATURE - Collections - Jena
Meinhardt, Walter. Betriebsbücherei des VEB Carl Zeiss, Jena. 128-134, JENA

TECHNICAL LITERATURE - Collections - Sheffield, Eng.
Simons, Eric N. Service to Industry. 13-14, LAMB

TECHNICAL LITERATURE - Germany
Konrad, Joachim. Das Fachbuch im Buchhandel und in den Bibliotheken. 120-126, JENA

TECHNICAL PROCESSES
see Technical services

TECHNICAL SERVICES
see also Access to shelves; Acquisitions; Bookbinding; Cataloging; Classification; Public libraries - Technical services; Reader services

TECHNICAL SERVICES, Cooperative
see Cataloging, Cooperative

TECHNICAL SERVICES - Cost and economies
Bauhuis, Walter. Vereinfachungen beim Gang des Buches durch die Bibliothek. 133-142, VORS

TECHNICAL SERVICES - Japan
Taniguchi, Kan'ichirō. Tosho Seiri no Kaiko. (Book Processing.) 221-223, KYOT

TECHNICAL SERVICES - Teaching - Germany
Bieber, Hedwig. Die Öffentliche Bücherei als Ausbildungsstätte. Erfahrungen und Anregungen. 75-87, LANF

Teichl, Robert.
Bibliotheksinschriften. 81-83, STUM
Ein Europäischer Bibliothekenführer um das Jahr 1780. Die Handschrift des Pfarrverwalters von Maria-Taferl Adalbert Blumenschein. 172-179, LEYG
Die Rettung des Prunksaales der Wiener Hofbibliothek durch Nicolas v. Paccassi (1760-1769). 615-626, BICK
Der Wiegendruck im Kartenbild. 805-806, VIEN

TELEVISION AND READING
Thorsen, Leif. Radio og Fjernsyn—Bog og Bibliotek. 65-76, THOM

TELEVISION - Library programs
Thorsen, Leif. Radio og Fjernsyn—Bog og Bibliotek. 65-76, THOM

Tellefsen, Th.
Fra det Gamle Bibliotek. 423-448, MUNT

TEMPLARS. Mss. Regula
Trudon des Ormes, A. Note sur un Fragment de la Règle Latine du Temple. 355-358, HAVE

TEMPLIN, Ger. Joachimsthalisches Gymnasium
Joost, Siegfried. Bibliotheca Joachimica. Werden und Vergehen einer Deutschen Schulbibliothek. 233-256, WEHM

TEMPLUM SALOMONIS, Leyden
see Burgersdijk & Niermans, firm, booksellers, Leyden

TENGNAGEL, SEBASTIAN
Lhotsky, Alphons. Die Wiener Palatina und die Geschichtsforschung unter Sebastian Tengnagel. 450-462, BICK

TENNESSEE VALLEY - Public libraries - State and regional development plans
see Public libraries - State and regional development plans - Tennessee Valley

TENNESSEE VALLEY - Regional libraries
see Regional libraries - Tennessee Valley

TENRI, Japan - Bank-notes - Collections
see Bank-notes - Collections - Tenri, Japan

TENRI, Japan. Central Library
Ishizu, Teruzi. Tenri Toshokan Zō Kierukegoru Zenchosaku no Shohanbon. (The First Editions of All Kierkegaard's Works in the Tenri Central Library.) 477-484, TOMI
Nishida, Tatsuo. Tenri Toshokan Zō Seikabun Muryojushu Yokyo ni tsuite. (The Hsi-hsia Version of Wu-liang-shou-tsung yao-ching in the Tenri Central Library.) 357-366, TOMI

Ouchida, Sadao. Tenri Toshokan Zō Moku-Katsuji Ban Shomoku Kō. (Check List of Japanese Printed Books in Movable Types of the Late Edo Period in the Tenri Central Library.) 295-305, TOMI
Yuda, Yoshio, Hajime Uetani, and Minoru Imanishi. Tenri Toshokan Zō Jōruri Hangi Makuroku. (Catalogue of the Wood-Blocks of Jōruri Texts in the Tenri Central Library.) 259-294, TOMI

TENRI, Japan - Jōruri texts - Collections
see Jōruri texts - Collections - Tenri, Japan

TENRI, Japan - Kierkegaard, Søren Aabye - Collections
see Kierkegaard, Søren Aabye - Collections - Tenri, Japan

Teodorov-Balan, Aleksandŭr.
Komu Shto e Knigata? 7-8, TEOB
Rozhdenie i Otrechenie na Edin Stoletnik. 9-15, MIKN

TEODOROV-BALAN, ALEKSANDŬR

TEOB

TEOD

Dinekov, Petŭr. Akademik Aleksandŭr Teodorov-Balan i Bŭlgarskata Literatura. 31-37, TEOD
Pavlov, Todor. Slovo na Akad. Todor Pavlov, Predsedatel na Bŭlgarskata Akademiia na Naukite, Proizneseno Pri Otkrivane na Tŭrzhestvenoto Sŭbranie. 7-8, TEOD
Stoĭkov, Stoĭko. Akademik Aleksandŭr Teodorov-Balan i Bŭlgarskiiat Ezik. 9-30, TEOD
Vŭlchev, Velichko. Tvorchestvoto na Vazov v Otsenkata na Aleksandŭr Teodorov-Balan. 187-197, TEOD

TEODOROV-BALAN, ALEKSANDŬR. Bulgarski Knigopis za Sto Godine, 1806-1905

Teodorov-Balan, A. Rozhdenie i Otrechenie na Edin Stoletnik. 9-15, MIKN

TEODULO, MONK
see Thomas Magister

TERGESTE
see Trieste

TERMINOLOGY
see Bibliography - Terminology; Documentation - Terminology

TERMITE DAMAGE - Italy

Bonaventura, Gustavo. La Minaccia delle Termiti e di Altri Insetti al Nostro Patrimonio Artistico e Culturale. 205-234, GALL

TERNAUX-COMPANS, HENRI - Library

Wagner, Henry R. Hispanic Americana in the John Carter Brown Library. 423-455, WROT

TERNAUX, HENRI
see Ternaux-Compans, Henri

TEUVA, Finland. Kirkko. Arkisto

Kilip, Volter. Suomalainen Virsikirja [Manuale-nide] v:lta 1630 Teuvan Kirkonarkistossa. 122-126, SCHA

Thakore, Aroon V.
Ranganathan: The Magic Man. 764-765, RANG

THEATRICAL LIBRARIES AND COLLECTIONS - Bern

Kachler, Karl G. Die Schweizerische Theatersammlung. 125, BERU

THEATRICAL LIBRARIES AND COLLECTIONS - Vienna

Gregor, Joseph and Karl Ecker. Die Theatersammlung. 180-199, BICK
Hadamowsky, Franz. Das Hoftheater Leopolds I. und das Kostümwerk des L. O. Burnacini. 384-398, BICK

THEATRICAL PERIODICALS
see Periodicals, Theatrical

Thédenat, Henri.
Sur une Inscription Inédite Conservée au Municipe de Tarente. 515-524, GRAU

Theele, Joseph, ed.
FULD

Theele, Joseph.
Aus der Bibliothek des Kölner Kreuzbrüderklosters. 253-263, DEGE
Aus der Geschichte der Landesbibliothek Fulda. 289-292, LEID
Beiträge zur Geschichte der Landesbibliothek Fulda. 89-96, FULD
Bibliothekskundliche Nachrichten aus dem 18. Jahrhundert. II, 144-149, GLAU
Fuldaer Bucheinbände des 16. Jahrhunderts. 165-175, HAEK

THEODORICUS BRITO. Apuleii Rhetorica

Thomas, Paul. Un Commentaire du Moyen Âge sur la Rhétorique de Cicéron. 41-45, GRAU

THEODULUS, Monk
see Thomas Magister

THEOLOGICAL LIBRARIES
see Religious libraries

THEOLOGICAL SEMINARY LIBRARIES
see Religious libraries

THEUERDANK

Geissler, Paul. Zwei Unbekannte Holzschnittprobedrucke zum Theuerdank und Konrad Peutinger. 118-128, JUCH

Thewrewk de Ponor, Émile.
Codex Festi Breviati Trecensis. 659-669, GRAU

Thillainayagam, V.
The Madras State Bibliography. 506-507, RANG

Thilo, Martin, jt. author

Stremlau, Willi and Martin Thilo. Berliner Büchereigesetz und Büchereibau. 183-189, SCHS

Thirumalaimuthuswamy, A.
Five Laws of Library Science. 321-325, RANG

Thomas, Émile.
Note sur un Gemblacensis Aujourd'hui à Bruxelles, nº 5348-5352, XIIe Siècle. 47-48, GRAU

Thomas, Henry.
Diego Hurtado de Mendoza and His Plaquette Bindings. 474-480, GREE

THOMAS MAGISTER. Mss. Lettera

Martini, E. Una Lettera del Retore Teodulo (Thomas Magistros) al Monaco Ieroteo. 433-447, CERI

Thomas, Marcel.
L'Œuvre de Julien Cain au Cabinet des Manuscrits. 65-71, CAIN

Thomas, Paul.
Un Commentaire du Moyen Âge sur la Rhétorique de Cicéron. 41-45, GRAU
Sur Quelques Passages de Lucain. 271-274, CHAT

THOMASKLOSTER, Leipzig
see Leipzig. Sankt Thomas (Abbey) Bibliotheca

Thommessen, Olaf.
Bibliotek og Bokhandel. 156-160, NORS

Thompson, Anthony.
Verden er Én (The World is One). 248-254, TVET

Thompson, Lawrence S.
The Libraries of Colonial Spanish America. 257-266, WEHM
Das Moderne Türkische Bibliothekswesen. 86-89, STUM
Printing and Collections of Printing in Kentucky. 508-514, RANG
The University Library Survey in America. 347-353, STOL

Thomsen, Carl
AARH

Thomsen, Carl.
Bibliotekerne og det Øvrige Oplysningsarbejde. 85-93, DØSS
Bygherren, Bygmesteren og Bibliotekaren. 237-247, HEIN
Harald Hvenegaard Lassen. 9-16, LASS
Die Zusammenarbeit Zwischen Kinderbüchereien und Schülerbüchereien in Dänemark. 61-66, ACKR

THOMSEN, CARL

THOM

Lassen, H. Hvenegaard. Carl Thomsen. 27-33, THOM

THOMSEN, CARL - Bibl.

Fortegnelse over Artikler og Bøger af Carl Thomsen. 105-112, THOM

Thomsen, Niels P.
Et Par Ord til Afslutning. 38-39, HOLS

Thomsen, Peter.
Die Erste Ausgabe von Johann Friedrich Naumanns Naturgeschichte der Vögel Deutschlands. 220-239, BOLL

Thomsen, Svend.
Folkebibliotekernes Bogbestand. Nogle Bemærkninger om Bibliotekernes Bogvalg og Opgaver. 1-16, DØSS

Thon, Jan, jt. ed.
EMLE

Thon, Jan.
Emlerův Inspektorát Městské Knihovny Pražské. 73-79, EMLE

THORBECKE, JAN RUDOLF

Groot, J. R. de. Thorbecke en de Leidse Bibliothecaris Van Voorst. 450-455, BRUM

THOREAU, HENRY DAVID. Plan . . . of Brooks Farm

Hatch, Benton L. Thoreau's Plan of a Farm. 317-324, KEOG

Thorin, Ernest, ed.
GRAU

Thormann, Anne-Marie.
Die Bildersammlung. 96-107, BERU

Thorndike, Lynn.
Manuscripts of Michael Scott's Liber Introductorius. 425-447, ALBA

Thornton, Mary Lindsay.
Bibliography of Louis Round Wilson. 339-352, WILS

Thorsen, Leif.
Radio og Fjernsyn—Bog og Bibliotek. 65-76, THOM

THÜRINGEN
see Thuringia

THÜRINGER ZENTRALKATALOG
see Jena. Thüringer Zentralkatalog

THÜRINGISCHE LANDESBIBLIOTHEK, Altenburg, Ger.
see Altenburg, Ger. Thüringische Landesbibliothek

THURINGIA - Catalogs - Union
see Catalogs - Union - Thuringia

THURINGIA - Legal deposit (of books, etc.)
see Legal deposit (of books, etc.) - Thuringia

TIBULLUS, ALBIUS. Mss. - Bibl.
Ullman, B. L. Achilles Statius' Manuscripts of Tibullus. 449-468, ALBA

Tiedemann, Eva.
Die Auskunfts-Abteilung. 86-88, FRAD
Hanns Wilhelm Eppelsheimer, Curriculum Vitae und Bibliographischer Bericht. 9-19, EPPE

TIELLANDT, WILLEM H. J. WESTREENEN VAN
see Westreenen van Tiellandt, Willem Hendrik Jacob, Baron van

Tiemann, Hermann.
Materialien zur Bedarfsberechnung für ein Etatmodell. 9-20, REDE
Wort und Bild in der Fabeltradition bis zu La Fontaine. 237-260, HOFM

TIEMANN, HERMANN
TIEM
Schmidt-Künsemüller, Friedrich Adolf. Hermann Tiemann und das Deutsche Bibliothekswesen der Gegenwart. 11-22, TIEM

TIEMANN, HERMANN - Bibl.
Kayser, Werner. Verzeichnis der Veröffentlichungen, Vorlesungen, Vorträge und Referate Hermann Tiemanns, 1923-1959. 350-360, TIEM

Till, Walter.
Die Koptischen Eheverträge. 627-638, BICK
Die Nicht-Katalogisierten Coptica der John Rylands Library. 89-90, STUM
Die Papyrussammlung. 149-164, BICK

Timmer, E. M. A.
Pamfletten en Perikelen. 199-218, HAGU

TIPOGRAFIA MEDICEA ORIENTALE, Rome (City) - Hist.
Lodi, Teresa. La Vera Storia di un Presunto Cimelio Cinquecentesco (Il Cosiddetto Torchio della Biblioteca Medicea Orientale). 234-253, GREG

TIRONIAN NOTES
Chatelain, Émile. Notes Tironiennes d'un Manuscrit de Genève. 81-86, HAVE
Legendre, Paul. Notes Tironiennes du Vatic. Lat. Reg. 846. 312-331, CHAT
Mentz, Arthur. Die Anfügung in den Tironischen Noten. 501-507, CHAT
Schmitz, Wilhelm. Tironianum. 77-80, HAVE

Tisserand, Roger.
L'Académie de Dijon et Denis Diderot. 152-162, OURS

Tisserant, Eugène, Cardinal.
Inventaire Sommaire des Manuscrits Arabes du Fonds Borgia à la Bibliothèque Vaticane. 1-34, EHRE
Notes et Impressions sur les Bibliothèques d'Amerique. 445-457, PUTN
On the Use of Ultraviolet Rays for Detecting Repairs in Printed Books, Especially Incunabula. 341-343, HANS
The Preparation of a Main Index for the Vatican Library Manuscripts. 176-185, BISH

DIE TITELDRUCKE DER DEUTSCHEN BÜCHEREI
Franz, Rudi. Die Titeldrucke der Deutschen Bücherei. 157-173, LEIZ

TITELDRUCKE, LEIPZIGER
see Leipziger Titeldrucke

TITUREL. Mss.
Kroker, Ernst. Bruchstücke einer Handschrift des Jüngeren Titurel in der Leipziger Stadtbibliothek. 42-48, LEIP

Tobolka, Zdeněk V.
De Quelques Problèmes Relatifs aux Bibliothèques Parlementaires. 144-148, EMLE

Tocci, Luigi Michelini.
Agapito, Bibliotecario "Docto, Acorto et Diligente" della Biblioteca Urbinate alle Fine del Quattrocento. II, 245-280, ALBB

TØNDER, Denmark. Bibliotek
TØND
Skovrøy, P. Tredive Aar i Tønder. 15-77, TØND

Togashi, Shigehiro.
Toshokanjin no Negoto. (Function of the Library.) 223-227, KYOT

Tokarz-Wisłocka, Stanisława, ed.
KRAK

TOKYO. Gojunen Kai
TOKY

TOKYO. Keio University. Japan Library School - Hist.
Hashimoto, Takashi. Toshokangakka no Jittai to Sono Tembō. Japan Library School, Yesterday, Today, and Tomorrow. (In both English and Japanese.) 1-11, (3rd section), HASH

TOKYO. Keio University. Kitasato Memorial Medical Library
Tsuda, Yoshinari. Kangai Kashidashi Yōkyu ni Ōjirare Nakatta Zasshi oyobi Sono Riyū no Chōsa. (An Analysis of Dissatisfied Circulation Requests for Periodicals.) 297-313, HASH

TOKYO. Library Staff Training Institute. Students
TOKY

TOKYO. Ōhashi Library
Ishii, Munetsugu. Ōhashi Toshokan ni Kisō Seraretaru Nidai Seijika no Iaisho ni tsuite. (On the Collections Prized by the Late Two Statesmen Which Were Donated to the Ōhashi Library.) 90-104, (pt. 1), OHAS
Kotani, Genzo. Ōhashi Toshokan Shozō Hakubunkan Hakkō Tosho Mokuroku. (A Catalogue of the Books Published by Hakubunkan in the Collections of the Ōhashi Library.) 105-132, TSUB
———— Ōhashi Toshokan Shozō Hakubunkan Hakkō Tosho Mokuroku—Showa Juyonen Gogatsu Matsujitsu Genzai. (The List of Books Published by Hakubunkan Which Are in the Collections of the Ōhashi Library—as of the End of March, 1939.) 1-157, (pt. 2), OHAS
Miyake, Takashi, ed. Zaidan Hōjin Ōhashi Toshokan Nenpyō. (A Chronological Table of the Ōhashi Library, a Private Library.) 33-61, TSUB

TOKYO - Periodicals - Circulation procedures
see Periodicals - Circulation procedures - Tokyo

TOKYO - Use studies - Medical libraries
see Use studies - Medical libraries - Tokyo

Tollenaere, F. de.
Op het Spoor van een Onbekende Postincunabel? 246-249, KOSS

Tomescu, Mircea.
Sur L'Évolution de la Bibliographie dans la République Populaire Roumaine. 293-306, MIKH

Tominaga, Makita.
Inkyunabura—Insatsu Moji o Meguru Kaisetsu to Shōkai. (Incunabula—an Introduction Centering on the Problem of the Types.) 1-23, TOMI

TOMINAGA, MAKITA
TOMI

Tondelli, Leone.
Cenni sull'Archivio Capitolare di Reggio Emilia. 263-267, MERC

TONGERLOO, Belgium (Premonstratensian abbey)
Brummel, Leendert. De Boeken van Tongerloo in de Koninklijke Bibliotheek te 's-Gravenhage. 151-168, BRUE

TOPELIUS, ZAKARIAS - Library
Nyberg, Paul. Dedikationerna i Zachris Topelii Bibliotek. 145-163, HULA
———— Några Anmärkningsvärda Böcker i Z. Topelius' Boksamling. 101-117, TUDE

Topsøe-Jensen, H.
Om et Eksemplar af H. Steffens: "Was Ich Erlebte" i Universitetsbibliotekets 1. Afd., København. 95-100, DAHA

Toropov, A. D.
Moskovskiĭ Bibliograficheskiĭ Kruzhov; Stranichka Vospominaniĭ. 275-276, MALE

TORQUEMADA, JUAN DE, Cardinal. Meditationes
Donati, Lamberto. Meditationes Johannis de Turrecremata. 99-128, GREG

Torre, Elías Ortiz de la.
Pedro González de Agüero y Su Estatua Funeraria en Agüero (Santander). I, 70-92, ARTI

TORSLEV, Denmark - Parish libraries
see Parish libraries - Torslev, Denmark

TORSLEV, Denmark - Publicity
see Publicity - Torslev, Denmark

TORSLEV, Denmark (Sogn) Bibliotek
TORS

TORUN, Poland. Copernicus City Library
Sawicka, Stanisława M. Czeski Rękopis Iluminowany w Książnicy Miejskiej im. Kopernika w Toruniu. 28-34, EMLE

Toschi, Antonio.
Elenco delle Pubblicazioni del Prof. Domenico Fava. 41-62, FAVA

Totok, Wilhelm.
Die Nationalbibliographien. Versuch einer Analyse. 107-123, FRAD

TOULET, PAUL JEAN. Mariage de Don Quichotte
Martineau, Henri. La Publication du "Mariage de Don Quichotte" de Paul-Jean Toulet. 457-460, BONN

TOURS - Manuscripts
see Manuscripts - Tours

TOURS. Saint Martin (Abbey) Mss.
Köhler, Wilhelm. Turonische Handschriften aus der Zeit Alkuins. 172-180, DEGE

Towne, Jackson E.
University Library Building Planning. 461-471, RANG

Townsend, Rebecca Dutton, Margaret Currier, et al.
A Selection of Baskerville Imprints in the Yale University Library. 285-297, KEOG

Traĭkov, Nikola.
Khŭrvatska Bibliografiia na Bŭlgarskata Knizhnina. 189-204, MIKN

Traĭkov, Veselin N.
Bulgarica; Literatura na Chuzhdi Ezitsi Vŭrkhu Bŭlgariia i Bŭlgarskiia Narod. 43-66, TEOB
Nesamostoiatelnite Bibliografii i Vkliuchvaneto im v Tekushchata Bibliografiia na Bibliografiite. 307-311, MIKH

Traĭkov, Veselin N. and Bozhana Troianova.
Literaturna i Nauchna Dejnost Bibliografiia na Po-Znachitelnite Publikatsii 1920-1960. 20-43, BORO

TRAINEES IN LIBRARY SERVICE
see Education for librarianship

TRAMEZINO, MICHELE, publisher
Leicht, Pier Silverio. L'Editore Veneziano Michele Tramezino ed i Suoi Privilegi. 357-367, FERR

Transfeldt, Walter.
Preussische Staatsbibliothek und Familienforschung. 261-270, KUHN

TRANSLATIO S. ALEXANDRI. Mss.
Lehmann, Paul. Eine Fuldaer Handschrift. I, 140-144, GLAU

Traut, Hermann.
Dr. Adolf von Glauburg und Seine Bibliothek. 1-34, EBRA

TRE VENEZIE
see Trentino-Alto Adige, Italy

Tree, Roland, jt. author
Stevens, Henry and Roland Tree. Comparative Cartography Exemplified in an Analytical & Bibliographical Description of Nearly One Hundred Maps and Charts of the American Continent Published in Great Britain during the Years 1600-1850. 305-363, WROT

Tremaine, Marie.
A Half-Century of Canadian Life and Print, 1751-1800. 371-390, WROT

Trenkler, Ernst.
Die Kartensammlung. 139-148, BICK
Ein Unbekanntes "Livre d'Heures" der Österreichischen Nationalbibliothek. 639-645, BICK

TRENKLER, ERNST
STUM
Kammel, Karl. Dr. Ernst Trenkler, Oberstaatsbibliothekar, Direktor der Druckschriftensammlung der Österreichischen Nationalbibliothek. 11-12, STUM

Trenkov, Khristo.
Svobodata na Pechata; Sushtina i Ogranichena. 255-265, MIKN
Za Bibliografskata Profesiia. 313-321, MIKH
Za Otboro na Materiala v Obshtata Tekushta Registratsionna Bibliografiia. 375-379, TEOD

TRENT - Publishers and publishing
see Publishers and publishing - Trent

TRENTINO-ALTO ADIGE, Italy - Aristoteles - Collections
see Aristoteles - Collections - Trentino-Alto Adige, Italy

TRENTINO-ALTO ADIGE, Italy - Libraries
see Libraries - Trentino-Alto Adige, Italy

Trepte, Heinz.
Die Richtlinien für den Schlagwortkatalog

der Sächsischen Landesbibliothek. 117-135, DREL

TRIESTE. Biblioteca Civica

Brumati, Antonio. L'"Atlas Mayor" della Biblioteca Civica di Trieste. II, 665-675, HORT

TRISTAN. Mss.

Gichtel, Paul. Die Bilder der Münchener Tristan-Handschrift (Cod. Germ. 51). 391-457, HOFM

Trivedi, B. I.
Dr. S. R. Ranganathan. 609-613, RANG

Troi͡anova, Bozhana, jt. author

Traĭkov, Veselin and Bozhana Troi͡anova. Literaturna i Nauchna Dejnost Bibliografii͡a na Po-Znachitelnite Publikatsii 1920-1960. 20-43, BORO

Trommsdorff, Paul.
Technische Literatur in Deutschen Bibliotheken. 344-351, HANS

TRONDHEIM - Architecture and building - Research libraries
see Architecture and building - Research libraries - Trondheim

TRONDHEIM - Librarians
see Librarians - Trondheim

TRONDHEIM. Norske Videnskabers Selskab
see Norske Videnskabers Selskab, Trondheim

Troost, Karl.
Zur Volksbibliothekarischen Ausbildung an der Büchereischule. 135-156, LANF

TROSS, LUDWIG

Brummel, Leendert. Dr. Ludwig Tross en de Koninklijke Bibliotheek. 169-177, BRUE

Troxel, Wilma.
The Medical Library Association, 1947-1957. 378-385, DOEJ

Troxell, Gilbert McCoy.
Bookplates of the Yale Libraries, 1780-1846. 145-156, KEOG

TROYES, France. Bibliothèque Municipale. Mss. (no. 504)

Ernout, A. Codex Trecensis, n° 504. 83-91, CHAT

Trudon des Ormes, A.
Note sur un Fragment de la Règle Latine du Temple. 355-358, HAVE

TRUEBA Y COSÍO, JOAQUÍN TELESFORO

Barreda, Fernando. Aportaciones a la Biografía de d. Telesforo Trueba y Cosío. I, 32-55, ARTI

TRUEBA Y COSÍO, JOAQUÍN TELESFORO. Carta

Arenas, Manuel Núñez de. Páginas Románticas: Una Carta Inédita de Trueba y Cosío. I, 56-61, ARTI

TRUMBULL, BENJAMIN. Mss. - Collections - Yale

Sills, R. Malcolm and Eleanor Stuart Upton. The "Trumbull Manuscript Collections" and Early Connecticut Libraries. 325-342, KEOG

TRUSTEES AND BOARDS
see also
Governing authorities of libraries

TRUSTEES AND BOARDS - Frankfurt a.M.

Kuratorium und Beirat der Deutschen Bibliothek. 162-164, EPPE

TRUTEBUL, LUDWIG, printer

Luther, Johannes. Ludwig Trutebul und die Druckerei "Zum Färbefaß" in Erfurt. 185-195, SCHW

T͡Sonchev, Petŭr T.
Kŭm Istorii͡ata na Ědna Bŭlgarska Pechatnit͡sa v T͡Sarigrad. 146-149, TEOB

Tsuboya, Zenshirō.
Jushi. (Words of Congratulation.) [prelim.], OHAS

TSUBOYA, ZENSHIRŌ

TSUB

Ishii, Munetsugu. Tsuboya Sensei to Toshokan Jigyō. (Mr. Tsuboya and His Library Activities.) 73-82, TSUB

Tsuda, Yoshinari.
Kangai Kashidashi Yōkyu ni Ōjirare Nakatta Zasshi oyobi Sono Riyū no Chōsa. (An Analysis of Dissatisfied Circulation Requests for Periodicals.) 297-313, HASH

Tudeer, Lauri O. Th., ed.
DAHL

Tudeer, Lauri O. Th.
Bibliotheca Nationis Viburgensis 1797-1827. 98-111, HULA
En Mainzer Gratulation från 1604-1605. 250-253, MUNT

TUDEER, LAURI O. Th.

TUDE

TÜBINGEN - College and university libraries - Hist.
see College and university libraries - Hist. - Tübingen

TÜBINGEN. Max-Planck-Institut für Ausländisches und Internationales Privatrecht. Bibliothek
see Hamburg. Max-Planck-Institut für Ausländisches und Internationales Privatrecht. Bibliothek

TÜBINGEN. Schloss Hohentübingen

Frey, Teophil. Nicolaus Ochsenbach, der Kunstliebende und -Sammelnde Schlosshauptmann auf Hohen-Tübingen (1562-1626). 407-427, LEYG

TÜBINGEN. Universität. Bibliothek - Hist.

Widmann, Hans. Die Zugänglichkeit der Universitätsbibliothek Tübingen (bis zur Mitte des 19. Jahrhunderts). 215-229, JUCH

TÜRLIN, HEINRICH VON DEM
see Heinrich, von dem Türlin

Tukalevskij, Vladimír.
K Ohlasu L. J. Živného v Cizině. 64-66, ŽIVN

"TUN-HUANG LIBRARY"

Taam, Cheuk-Woon. The Discovery of the Tun-Huang Library and Its Effect on Chinese Studies. 686-705, WILS

TUNKELO, EEMIL AUKUSTI

TUNK

TURIN. Università. Biblioteca. Mss. (I. VI.2 [K I 7])

Keller, Otto. Über einen Verbrannten Codex des Horaz. 531-534, CHAT

TURKEY - Libraries
see Libraries - Turkey

TURKEY - Private libraries
see Private libraries - Turkey

TURKU, Finland. Akademi. Bibliotek

Nohrström, Holger. Några Krigsbytesböcker från Åbo Akademibiblioteks Grundläggningstid i Helsingfors Universitetsbibliotek. 69-81, HULT

TURKU, Finland. Akademi. (1640-1827) Bibliotek

Jörgensen, Arne. Anteckningar om Universitetsbiblioteket under Första Året efter Åbo Brand. 17-42, HULA
Vallinkoski, J. Ett Bortglömt Handskriftslån från Akademibiblioteket i Åbo på 1740-Talet. 197-201, GARD

TURKU, Finland. Akademi. (1918-) Bibliotek

Vallinkoski, J. Ett Bortglömt Handskriftslån från Akademibiblioteket i Åbo på 1740-Talet. 197-201, GARD

TURKU, Finland. Akademi. (1640-1827) Bibliotek. Mss.

Vallinkoski, J. Ett Bortglömt Handskriftslån från Akademibiblioteket i Åbo på 1740-Talet. 197-201, GARD

TURKU, Finland. Akademi. (1640-1827) Viborg Nation. Biblioteket - Hist.

Tudeer, Lauri O. Th. Bibliotheca Nationis Viburgensis 1797-1827. 98-111, HULA

TURKU, Finland. Akademi. Employees

Schauman, Henrik. Festskrifter och Festnummer Tillägnäde Lärare och Tjänstemän vid Universiteten i Helsingfors och Åbo. 319-350, DAHL

TURKU, Finland - Auction sales
see Auction sales - Turku, Finland

TURKU, Finland - Bookbinders
see Bookbinders - Turku, Finland

TURNBULL LIBRARY, Wellington, N.Z.
see Alexander Turnbull Library, Wellington, N.Z.

Turner, C. H.
The Nomina Sacra in Early Latin Christian Mss. 62-74, EHRD

Turner, Mabel.
The Role of National Standards in the Development of the School Library in the United States. 143-150, HASH

TURRECREMATA, JOANNES DE
see Torquemada, Juan de, Cardinal

Tveito, Dagfinn.
Soldater og Kulturfront. 74-85, KILD

Tveterås, Harald L.
A Federation for Library Co-operation across the Frontiers: Nordisk Vitenskapelig Bibliotekarforbund. 601-602, BRUM
Forskningsbibliotekene og Fremtiden. 131-137, NORS

TVETERÅS, HARALD L.

TVET

TVETERÅS, HARALD L. - Bibl.

Collin, Torborg. Bibliografi over Harald L. Tveterås' Trykte Arbeider. 255-263, TVET

Twemlow, J. A.
John de Nigravalle, a Fictitious Librarian of the Vatican. 219-226, EHRE

Tyaganatarajan, T.
Universal Cataloguing Code: Ifla's Initiative. 141-146, RANG

Tyler, Alice S.
Library-Extension: A Basic Factor in Adequate Book Service. 458-466, PUTN

TYPE AND TYPE-FOUNDING - Erfurt - Hist. - 15th cent.

Voullième, Ernst. Zur Geschichte Einiger Erfurter Typen des XV. Jahrhunderts. 261-265, SCHW

TYPE AND TYPE-FOUNDING - Friesland - Hist. - 15th cent.

Kruitwagen, B. De Freeska Landriucht-Drukkerij. 45-69, HAGU

TYPE AND TYPE-FOUNDING - Germany - Hist.

Johnson, Alfred F. Notes on Some German Types Used in the Reformation Period. 226-232, BENZ

TYPE AND TYPE-FOUNDING - Gothic type - Germany - Hist.

Zeitler, Julius. Moderne Frakturschriften. 69-76, LOUB

TYPE AND TYPE-FOUNDING - Hebrew type

Bamberger, S. Trennungsstrich, Fragezeichen und Ausrufungszeichen im Hebräischen Buchdruck. 109-110, FREN
Cowley, A. E. Ein Soncino-Druck aus Kairo 1566. 89-90, FREN
Eames, Wilberforce. On the Use of Hebrew Types in English America before 1735. 481-502, FREI
Marx, Alexander. Some Notes on the Use of Hebrew Type in Non-Hebrew Books, 1475-1520. 381-408, EAME
Zafran, Herbert C. Elias Hutter's Hebrew Bible. 29-39, BLOC

TYPE AND TYPE-FOUNDING - Hebrew type - Hist.

Marx, Moses. On the Date of Appearance of the First Printed Hebrew Books. 481-501, MARX

TYPE AND TYPE-FOUNDING - Hist.

Freys, Ernst. Johann Baptist Bernharts "Gesammelte Schriften." Ein Vorläufer von Haeblers Typenrepertorium. 145-174, HAEB
Schmidt-Künsemüller, Friedrich Adolf. Ein Früher Typenmethodologischer Versuch in der Inkunabelkunde. 69-75, WEHM

TYPE AND TYPE-FOUNDING - Music
see Music printing

TYPE AND TYPE-FOUNDING - Paris

Veyrin-Forrer, Jeanne. Les Premiers Caractères de François-Ambroise Didot (1781-1785). 159-173, CALO

TYPE AND TYPE-FOUNDING - Roman type - Hist. - 15th cent.

Bühler, Curt F. Roman Types and Roman Printing in the Fifteenth Century. 101-110, WEHM

TYPE AND TYPE-FOUNDING - Rome (City) - Hist.

Degering, Hermann. Wer War der Drucker der Erstausgabe des Vitruv? Ein Beitrag zur Geschichte des Römischen Buchdrucks. 175-202, HAEB

TYPE AND TYPE-FOUNDING - Russian type

Horodisch, Abraham. Die Anfänge des Buchdrucks in Moskau. 208-225, BENZ

TYPE AND TYPE-FOUNDING - U.S. - Hist.

Wroth, Lawrence C. The First Work with American Types. 129-142, EAME

TYPEWRITING

Aliprandi, Giuseppe. Aspetti Particolari della Grafia. 39-46, GALL

TYPOGRAPHERS
see Printers

TYPOGRAPHY
see Bookmaking; Printing

Tyszko, Oskar.
Die Bestandsvermehrung der Hauptabteilung und Ihre Organisation. I, 89-129, BERS
Die Entwicklung der Berliner Volksbüchereien von 1850 bis 1945. 7-25, BERL

UDC
see Classification - Systems - Universal decimal

UEBELIN, GEORG, publisher, 16th cent.

Scholderer, Victor. Georg Uebelin (Georgius Maxillus) and His Publications. 111-116, WEHM

Uematsu, Yasushi.
Beikoku Giin Toshokan no Kanseki ni tsuite. (On the Chinese Collections in the Library of Congress, U.S.A.) 9-12, HAKO

Uematsu, Yasushi, jt. author
Meier, Franz Joseph, [trans.] Der Artikel Tosho ("Buch") im Nihon-Bungaku-Daijiten. [Translation of a Japanese Article by Shinkichi Hashimoto and Yasushi Uematsu.] 205-216, LEYH

Uemura, Chōzaburō.
Sangyō Toshokan. (Industrial Libraries.) 1-13, OTAT

Uetani, Hajime, jt. author
Yuda, Yoshio, Hajime Uetani, and Minoru Imanishi. Tenri Toshokan Zō Jōruri Hangi Mokuroku. (Catalogue of the Wood-Blocks of Jōruri Texts in the Tenri Central Library.) 259-294, TOMI

UFFENBACH, ZACHARIAS KONRAD VON
Bogeng, Gustav Adolf Erich. Über Zacharias Conrad von Uffenbachs Erfahrungen und Erlebnisse bei der Benutzung Deutscher, Englischer, Holländischer Öffentlicher Büchersammlungen in den Jahren 1709-1711. 30-46, SCHW

UFFENBACH, ZACHARIAS KONRAD VON - Library
Becker, Josef. Die Bibliothek des Zacharias Konrad von Uffenbach. 129-148, LEYG

UGARIT
see Ras Shamra

Uggla, Arvid HJ.
Ett Läkarebibliotek från Början av 1700-Talet. 221-248, GRAP
Uppsala Universitetsbiblioteks Samling av Nyisländsk Litteratur. Några Meddelanden. 537-574, UPPS

Uhde-Bernays, Hermann.
Eine Deutsche Akademie. 24-25, HELD

Uhlendahl, Heinrich.
Die Bibliothek der Deutschen Nationalversammlung von 1848/49. Eine Vorläuferin der Deutschen Bücherei. 147-155, LEYH
Die Deutsche Bücherei im Rahmen der Deutschen Bibliotheken. 1-35, LEIS
Erinnerungen an die Zweihundertjahrfeier der Nationalbibliothek Wien. 646-652, BICK
Ernstes und Heiteres aus der Auskunftsstelle der Deutschen Bücherei. 90-91, STUM
Leipziger Zetteldruck. 53-61, GODE

Ulbricht, Walter.
Vorsitzender des Staatsrates der Deutschen Demokratischen Republik. XI-XII, LEIZ

ULEĬ
Zamkov, Nikolaĭ K. "Uleĭ," Zhurnal V. G. Anastasevicha (1811-1812 g.g.); Bibliograficheskoe Opisanie. 39-57, MALE

Ullman, B. L.
Achilles Statius' Manuscripts of Tibullus. 449-468, ALBA

Ullmann, Regina.
Ein Sich in der Erinnerung Spiegelndes Bild. 13-14, HELD

ULTRAVIOLET RAYS
Tisserant, Eugène. On the Use of Ultraviolet Rays for Detecting Repairs in Printed Books, Especially Incunabula. 341-343, HANS

UNDERGRADUATE LIBRARIES AND COLLECTIONS - College and university libraries
see College and university libraries - Undergraduate libraries and collections

UNESCO
see United Nations. Educational, Scientific and Cultural Organization

Unger, Willy.
Benutzungseinrichtungen, Benutzungspolitik und Gebrauchsöffentlichkeit. I, 175-221, BERS

UNION CATALOGS
see Catalogs - Union

UNION LIBRARY CATALOG OF THE PHILADELPHIA METROPOLITAN AREA
see Philadelphia Bibliographical Center and Union Library Catalog

UNION LISTS
see Periodicals - Union lists

UNION OF SOUTH AFRICA
see South Africa

UNITED NATIONS
Breycha-Vauthier, Arthur C. de. Role of the United Nations Libraries in the World of Librarianship. 488-491, RANG

UNITED NATIONS. Dag Hammarskjöld Library
Breycha-Vauthier, Arthur C. de. Internationale Bibliotheken und Ihre Probleme. 20-21, STUM
Willers, Uno. Dag Hammarskjöld Som Bibliofil. Föredrag vid Invigningen av Dag Hammerskjöld Memorial Library den 17 November 1961. 249-256, HEIN

UNITED NATIONS. Educational, Scientific and Cultural Organization

Boerlin, E. Dr. Pierre Bourgeois und die UNESCO. 186-188, BOUR
Brummel, Leendert. National and International Organization of Bibliography. 17-19, STUM

UNITED NATIONS. Educational, Scientific and Cultural Organization. Division of Libraries, Documentation and Archives

Carter, Edward. The Birth of Unesco's Library Programmes. 183-196, TVET

UNITED NATIONS. Library

Landheer, B. De Bibliotheek van de Verenigde Naties en Andere Internationale Bibliotheken. 505-513, BRUM

UNITED NATIONS. Library - Geneva

Bresha-Botie, A. S. Biblioteka Obŭedinennykh Natsij v Zheneve i Mezhdunarodnoe Mezhbibliotechnoe Sotrudnichestvo. 121-126, MIKH

U. S. - Archives, College and university
see Archives, College and university - U. S.

U. S. Archives, Government
see Archives, Government - U. S.

U. S. - Bibliography
see Bibliography - U. S.

U. S. - Bibliography, National
see Bibliography, National - U. S.

U. S. - Biography - Collections - Washington, D.C.

Johnson, Allen. The Library of Congress: A Depository of American Biography. 224-225, PUTN

U. S. - Book collecting
see Book collecting - U. S.

U. S. - Book fairs
see Book fairs - U. S.

U. S. - Book illustration - Hist.
see Book illustration - Hist. U. S.

U. S. - Book industry and trade
see Book industry and trade - U. S.

U. S. - Cataloging, Cooperative
see Cataloging, Cooperative - U. S.

U. S. - Catalogs - Printed book
see Catalogs - Printed book - U. S.

U. S. College and university libraries
see College and university libraries - U. S.

U. S. - College and university libraries - Acquisitions
see College and university libraries - Acquisitions - U. S.

U. S. - College and university libraries - Administration
see College and university libraries - Administration - U. S.

U. S. - College and university libraries - Undergraduate libraries and collections
see College and university libraries - Undergraduate libraries and collections - U. S.

U. S. - Computers
see Computers - U. S.

U. S. - Copyright
see Copyright - U. S.

U. S. - Dormitory libraries
see Dormitory libraries - U. S.

U. S. - Education for librarianship
see Education for librarianship - U. S.

U. S. - Hist. - Sources - Collections - Washington, D.C.

Andrews, Charles McLean. The Story of the Transcripts. 47-56, PUTN

U. S. - Instruction in library use - Teachers and administrators
see Instruction in library use - Teachers and administrators - U. S.

U. S. - Librarianship
see Librarianship - U. S.

U. S. - Libraries
see Libraries - U. S.

U. S. - Libraries and librarianship
see Libraries and librarianship - U. S.

U. S. - Library extension
see Library extension - U. S.

U. S. Library of Congress

Andrews, Charles McLean. The Story of the Transcripts. 47-56, PUTN
Bishop, William Warner. Thirty Years of the Library of Congress, 1899 to 1929. 24-34, PUTN
Bowker, Richard R. The Appointment of Herbert Putnam as Librarian of Congress. 15-21, PUTN
Fess, Simeon D. The Library of Congress. 1, PUTN
Johnson, Allen. The Library of Congress: A Depository of American Biography. 224-225, PUTN
Roland-Marcel, Pierre R. Ma Visite à la Library of Congress. 395-398, PUTN

Swingle, Walter T. Chinese Books: Their Character and Value and Their Place in the Western Library. 429-444, PUTN

U. S. Library of Congress. Card Division

Hastings, Charles Harris. Reminiscences and Observations on the Card Distribution Work of the Library of Congress. 195-206, PUTN

U. S. Library of Congress. Card Division. L.C. Printed Cards, How to Order and Use Them (1928 ed.) by C. H. Hastings (Japanese transl.)

Aizawa, Toyokatsu. Beikoku Giin Toshokan Insatsu Kādo ni tsuite. (On the Printed Cards of the Library of Congress.) 83-104, TSUB

U. S. Library of Congress. Catalog Division

Starr, Helen K. Mr. Hanson and His Friends. 329-333, HANS

U. S. Library of Congress - Catalogs

Hanson, James Christian Meinrich. The Library of Congress and Its New Catalogue: Some Unwritten History. 178-194, PUTN

U. S. Library of Congress. Folklore Section

Emrich, Duncan B. Folklore Section of the Library of Congress. 331-334, BICK

U. S. Library of Congress - Hist.

Ashley, Frederick W. Three Eras in the Library of Congress. 57-67, PUTN
Hanson, James Christian Meinrich. Organization and Reorganization of Libraries. 519-532, WILS
Mearns, David C. Herbert Putnam and His Responsible Eye—A Memorial Tribute. 1-52, PUTP

U. S. Library of Congress. Law Library

Borchard, Edwin Montefiore. The Law Division of the Library of Congress. 89-96, PUTN

U. S. Library of Congress. Library of Congress Catalog: Books Represented by Library of Congress Printed Cards

Dewton, Johannes L. Die Kataloge der Kongressbibliothek in Buchform. 27-28, STUM

U. S. Library of Congress. Map Division

Hicks, Frederick G. Thirty Years Ago. 207-210, PUTN

U. S. Library of Congress - [Microfilm Projects]

Evans, Luther H. Current Microfilm Projects at the Library of Congress. 31, STUM

U. S. Library of Congress. Music Division

Spivacke, Harold. Carl Engel, Librarian. 13-19, ENGE

U. S. Library of Congress - National Union Catalog

Mumford, L. Quincy. The National Union Catalog of the Library of Congress—Its Past and Its Prospects. 209-215, TVET

U. S. Library of Congress. Orientalia Division

Uematsu, Yasushi. Beikoku Giin Toshokan no Kanseki ni tsuite. (On the Chinese Collections in the Library of Congress, U.S.A.) 9-12, HAKO

U. S. Library of Congress. Rare Books Division

Goff, Frederick R. Early Music Books in the Rare Books Division of the Library of Congress. 58-74, KINO

U. S. - Library schools - Accreditation and standards
see Library schools - Accreditation and standards - U. S.

U. S. - Library schools - Theses
see Library schools - Theses - U. S.

U. S. - Medical libraries
see Medical libraries - U. S.

U. S. Naval Postgraduate School, Monterey, Calif. Library

Larson, Edgar R. Technical Reports Retrieval by Computer at the U.S. Naval Postgraduate School Library. 71-80, HASH

U. S. - Negro librarians - Education
see Negro librarians - Education - U. S.

U. S. - Paperback books
see Paperback books - U. S.

U. S. - Planning, Library
see Planning, Library - U. S.

U. S. - Private libraries
see Private libraries - U. S.

U. S. - Public libraries - Administration
see Public libraries - Administration - U. S.

U. S. - Public libraries - Book selection
see Public libraries - Book selection - U. S.

U. S. - Public libraries - Legal aspects
see Public libraries - Legal aspects - U. S.

U. S. - Public libraries - State and regional development plans
see Public libraries - State and regional development plans - U.S.

U. S. - Reader guidance
see Reader guidance - U. S.

U. S. - Reading - Special groups of readers - Junior college students
see Reading - Special groups of readers - Junior college students - U. S.

U. S. - Research libraries
see Research libraries - U. S.

U. S. - Rural libraries
see Rural libraries - U. S.

U. S. - School libraries
see School libraries - U. S.

U. S. - School libraries - Standards
see School libraries - Standards - U. S.

U. S. - Second-hand books
see Second-hand books - U. S.

U. S. - Type and type-founding
see Type and type-founding - U. S.

U. S. Veterans Administration. Library Service

Gartland, Henry J. The Veteran Administration Library Program, 1946-1956. 389-398, DOEJ

U. S. Veterans Administration. Medical and General Reference Library

Gartland, Henry J. The Veterans Administration Library Program, 1946-1956. 389-398, DOEJ

UNIVERSITY LIBRARIANS
see College and university librarians

UNIVERSITY LIBRARIES
see College and university libraries

UNIVERSITY PRESSES
see Presses, University

UNPUBLISHED WORKS
see Manuscripts

Unterkircher, Franz.
Aus dem Matrikelbuch der Burgpfarre. 91-94, STUM
"De Arte Venandi cum Avibus." 653-661, BICK

Updike, Daniel Berkeley.
Amicus Amico. 525, LYDE

UPPSALA AKADEMISKA BOKTRYCKERIET - Hist.

Rudbeck, Gustaf. Bidrag till Uppsala Akademiska Boktryckeris Historia. 45-58, GRAP

UPPSALA (Archdiocese) Synodalcirculär, 1513-1535

Lundström, Herman. Det Äldsta Tryckta Svenska Synodalcirkuläret. Ett Nyupptäckt Upsalatryck från 1513. 215-225, ANNE

UPPSALA - Architecture and building - College and university libraries
see Architecture and building - College and university libraries - Uppsala

UPPSALA - Architecture and building - Remodeled buildings and additions
see Architecture and building - Remodeled buildings and additions - Uppsala

UPPSALA - Art libraries and collections
see Art libraries and collections - Uppsala

UPPSALA - Bookplates
see Bookplates - Uppsala

UPPSALA - Carrels
see Carrels - Uppsala

UPPSALA - Children's library service
see Children's library service - Uppsala

UPPSALA - College and university libraries - Acquisitions
see College and university libraries - Acquisitions - Uppsala

UPPSALA - Correspondence - Collections
see Correspondence - Collections - Uppsala

UPPSALA - Drawings - Collections
see Drawings - Collections - Uppsala

UPPSALA - Exchange of books, periodicals, etc.
see Exchange of books, periodicals, etc. - Uppsala

UPPSALA - Gifts, contributions, etc.
see Gifts, contributions, etc. - Uppsala

UPPSALA - Habermann, Johann - Collections
see Habermann, Johann - Collections - Uppsala

UPPSALA - Icelandic literature (Modern) - Collections
see Icelandic literature (Modern) - Collections - Uppsala

UPPSALA - Librarians
see Librarians - Uppsala

UPPSALA - Manuscripts - Collections
see Manuscripts - Collections - Uppsala

UPPSALA - Maps - Collections
see Maps - Collections - Uppsala

UPPSALA - Periodicals - Collections
see Periodicals - Collections - Uppsala

UPPSALA - Photograph collections
see Photograph collections - Uppsala

UPPSALA - Presses, university
see Presses, university - Uppsala

UPPSALA - Printing
see Printing - Uppsala

UPPSALA - Proverbs - Collections
see Proverbs - Collections - Uppsala

UPPSALA - Rare books - Collections
see Rare books - Collections - Uppsala

UPPSALA - Research and the library
see Research and the library - Uppsala

UPPSALA - Serial publications - Collections
see Serial publications - Collections - Uppsala

UPPSALA - Småland, Sweden - Views - Collections
see Småland, Sweden - Views - Collections - Uppsala

UPPSALA. Universitet. Bibliotek

UPPS

Adde, Gustaf. Äldre Finskspråkiga Skrifter i Svenska Bibliotek. 269-294, COLL
Bring, Samuel E. Från Tempeltornet till Carolina? 199-213, GRAP
Carlsson, A. B. Fragment av en Ordspråkssamling av Michael Agricola i Uppsala Universitetsbibliotek. 142-146, GRAP
Colliander, Elof. Die Niederdeutschen Drucke der Universitätsbibliothek zu Uppsala aus dem 16., 17. und 18. Jahrhundert. 147-170, GRAP
Collijn, Isak Gustaf Alfred. Bibliotheca "Collegii Societatis Jesu in Suetia." Några Bidrag till Kännedomen om Jesuiternas Boksamling på Gråmunkeholmen. 75-91, ANNE
Davidsson, Åke. Småländska Bilder i Uppsala Universitetsbibliotek. 75-85, OLSS
Ekholm, Gunnar. Upsala Universitetsbiblioteks Gravyrsamling. 125-138, ANNE
Henriksson, Karl-Erik. Notes on the Acquisition Work in the Uppsala University Library. 228-236, DAHL
Kleberg, Tönnes. Das Bibliothekssystem einer Universität als Einheit. Reflexionen über einen Organisationsvorschlag an der Universität Uppsala. 119-124, HOFM
———— Ett Decennium av Gåvor. Kring en Utställning i Uppsala Universitetsbibliotek. 149-167, HEIN
———— Gli Scambi Internazionali della Reale Biblioteca Universitaria di Upsala. 505-510, GALL
———— Some Facts about the International Exchange Relations of the Uppsala University Library. 98-101, MADR
———— Zwei Stammbuchblätter von Grillparzer in der Universitätsbibliothek Uppsala. 51, STUM
Lewin, Bernhard. Uppsala Universitetsbiblioteks Samling av Arabiska 1500- och 1600-Talstryck. 577-604, GRAP
Lundberg, Oskar. Frågan om Forskarplatser och Forskarrum vid Uppsala Universitetsbibliotek. 59-76, GRAP
Sallander, Hans. Några Sällsynta, Delvis Okända Lågtyska, Danska och Svenska Upplagor av Johannes Avenarius' Christliche Gebete i Uppsala Universitetsbibliotek. 8-14, DAHA
Samzelius, Jonas L:Son. Om- och Tillbyggnaden av Carolina Rediviva Åren 1934-1945. 293-337, GRAP
Taube, Gurli. Fotografen Osti och den Ostiska Plåtsamlingen på Carolina Rediviva. 280-292, GRAP

UPPSALA. Universitet. Bibliotek. Cronstedska Samlingen

Holmgren, Gustaf. Om Cronstedtska Samlingen i Uppsala Universitetsbibliotek och dess Tillkomst. Några Anteckningar. 519-560, GRAP

UPPSALA. Universitet. Bibliotek. Mss. (Correspondence)

Lewenhaupt, Eugène. Upsala Universitetsbiblioteks Brefsamlingar. Försök till Historik. 195-207, ANNE

UPPSALA. Universitet. Bibliotek. Mss. (Döbeln papers)

Döbeln, Ernst von. Björkholms-Samlingen i Uppsala Universitetsbibliotek. Några ord om vor. Döbelnska Släktarkivet. 398-406, UPPS

UPPSALA. Universitet. Bibliotek. Mss. (Drake papers)

Heyman, Harold J. Något om Drakeska Arkivet i Uppsala Universitetsbibliotek. 249-256, GRAP

UPPSALA. Universitet. Bibliotek. Mss. (Hallenberg papers)

Carlsson, A. B. Jonas Hallenbergs Anteckningar och Samlingar till Gustaf II Adolfs Historia i Uppsala Universitetsbibliotek. 498-525, UPPS

UPPSALA. Universitet. Bibliotek. Mss. (Linné)

Hulth, J. M. Uppsala Universitetsbiblioteks Förvärv av Linneanska Originalmanuskript. 407-424, UPPS

UPPSALA. Universitet. Bibliotek. Mss. (Nordin Collection)

Ågren, Sven. Om Nordinska Handskriftssamlingen i Uppsala Universitetsbibliotek. Några Anteckningar. 468-497, UPPS

UPPSALA. Universitet. Bibliotek. Mss. (Rosenhane Papers)

Lewenhaupt, Eugène. Rosenhaneska Handskriftssamlingen i Uppsala Universitetsbibliotek. 292-316, UPPS

UPPSALA. Universitet. Bibliotek. Mss. (C 687)

Nelson, Axel. Zum Wimpfeling-Codex der Universitätsbibliothek zu Uppsala. 27-37, LEYG

UPPSALA. Universitet. Bibliotek. Mss. (K 8)

Carlquist, Gunnar. Skåneprästen Albert Raffn och Finansieringen av Hans Bok "Den Himmelske Herredag" (1633). 42-50, DAHA

UPPSALA. Universitet. Bibliotek. Mss. (X 396-399)

Nelson, Axel. Aus J. H. Lidéns Tagebuch über Seinen Aufenthalt in Göttingen in den Jahren 1768-1769. 255-263, MILF

Upton, Eleanor Stuart, jt. author

Sills, R. Malcolm and Eleanor Stuart Upton. The "Trumbull Manuscript Collections" and Early Connecticut Libraries. 325-342, KEOG

URAZ, Poland - Printing
see Printing - Uraz, Poland

<u>URGENTIBUS IMPERII FATIS</u> (Tac. Germ. 33)

Schmid, Wolfgang. <u>Urgentibus Imperii Fatis</u> (Tac. Germ. 33). 381-392, ALBA

URIOT, JOSEPH

Kyriss, Ernst. Einbände mit Hoheitszeichen Herzog Carl Eugens. 232-243, HOFF

USE STUDIES

Sakkers, J. C. Wilt U even Uw Naam Zetten? 254-257, EVER

USE STUDIES - Archives

Holtzmann, Walt[h]er. Paolo Kehr e le Ricerche Archivistiche per <u>L'Italia Pontificia</u>. 43-49, MERC

Ritzler, Remigius. Die Archivalischen Quellen der "Hierarchia Catholica." 51-74, MERC

USE STUDIES - Archives - Basel

Burckhardt, August. Feststellungen und Gedanken über die Benützung des Archivs. 29-33, BASL

USE STUDIES - Catalogs

Miller, Robert A. On the Use of the Card Catalog. 629-637, WILS

USE STUDIES - College and university libraries - British Columbia

Smith, Anne M. Social Sciences Journals Frequently Cited. 127-134, HASH

USE STUDIES - Medical libraries - Tokyo

Tsuda, Yoshinari. Kangai Kashidashi Yōkyu ni Ōjirare Nakatta Zasschi oyobi Sono Riyū no Chōsa. (An Analysis of Dissatisfied Circulation Requests for Periodicals.) 297-313, HASH

USE STUDIES - National libraries - Berlin

Krause, Heinrich. Die Bibliotheksbenutzung von 1905-1920. 119-125, HARN

USE STUDIES - National libraries - Berlin - Hist.

Unger, Willy. Benutzungseinrichtungen, Benutzungspolitik und Gebrauchsöffentlichkeit. I, 175-221, BERS

USE STUDIES - Public libraries

Laursen, Johs. Lehm. Biblioteksbenyttelsens Intensivering og dens Følger. 169-182, HEIN

USE STUDIES - Public libraries - Frederiksberg, Denmark

Laursen, Johs. Lehm. Biblioteksbenyttelsens Intensivering og dens Følger. 169-182, HEIN

USE STUDIES - Public libraries - Gliwice (City) Upper Silesia

Horstmann, H. Altersaufbau und

Lesestetigkeit in einer Volksbücherei. 47-54, ACKE

USE STUDIES - Public libraries - Hamburg

Fenske, Herbert. Soziologische Zusammensetzung der Leserschaft. 75-82, HAMB

USE STUDIES - Public libraries - Łódź, Poland

Nagórska, Izabela. Portrety Cyztelników-Robotników w Łódzkiej Dzielnicy Chojny. 155-168, GRYC

USE STUDIES - State libraries - Aarhus, Denmark

Sejr, Emanuel. Benyttelse. 123-154, AARU

USE STUDIES - State libraries - Dresden

Assmann, Karl. Die Sächsische Landesbibliothek von 1945 bis 1955. Zerstörung, Wiederaufbau und Gegenwärtiger Stand der Arbeit. 29-85, DREL

USE STUDIES - Technical libraries - Stockholm

Björkbom, Carl. Bokvalsproblem vid ett Tekniskt Centralbibliotek. 51-61, DAHA

Usher, Robert James.
The Place of the Endowed Reference Library in the Community. 467-473, PUTN

Ussani, V.
Quisquilie Onomastiche. 105-110, STAM

UTACODEX

Boeckler, Albert. Das Erhardbild im Utacodex. 219-230, GREE

Utley, George B.
An Early "Friend" of Libraries. 725-730, WILS
The Library War Service and Its General Director. 474-491, PUTN

UTRECHT. Akademieboekerij
see Utrecht. Rijksuniversiteit. Bibliotheek

UTRECHT - Catalogs - Classed
see Catalogs - Classed - Utrecht

UTRECHT - Catalogs - Subject
see Catalogs - Subject - Utrecht

UTRECHT. Centrale Oud-Katholieke Bibliotheek

Tans, J. A. G. Een Uitdagende Utrechtse Collectie: De Val des Pausdoms. 64-77, UTRE

UTRECHT - College and university libraries
see College and university libraries - Utrecht

UTRECHT - College and university libraries - Administration
see College and university libraries - Administration - Utrecht

UTRECHT - College and university libraries - Reference services
see College and university libraries - Reference services - Utrecht

UTRECHT - College and university libraries - Statistics
see College and university libraries - Statistics - Utrecht

UTRECHT - College and university libraries - Technical services
see College and university libraries - Technical services - Utrecht

UTRECHT - Dental libraries
see Dental libraries - Utrecht

UTRECHT - Duties of librarians
see Duties of librarians - Utrecht

UTRECHT - French literature - Collections
see French literature - Collections - Utrecht

UTRECHT - German literature - Collections
see German literature - Collections - Utrecht

UTRECHT - Incunabula - Collections
see Incunabula - Collections - Utrecht

UTRECHT - Manuscripts - Collections
see Manuscripts - Collections - Utrecht

UTRECHT. Nieuwlicht (Carthusian monastery)
see Bloemendaal, Netherlands. Nova Lux (Carthusian monastery)

UTRECHT. Nova Lux (Carthusian monastery)
see Bloemendaal, Netherlands. Nova Lux (Carthusian monastery)

UTRECHT. Paleis van Lodewijk Napoleon

Evers, Gerrit Albert. Het Paleis van Koning Lodewijk Napoleon te Utrecht en Zijne Inrichting tot Universiteitsbibliotheek. 42-62, SOME

UTRECHT - Periodicals - Collections
see Periodicals - Collections - Utrecht

UTRECHT - Photograph collections
see Photograph collections - Utrecht

UTRECHT PSALTER

Brom, A., Jr. Afbeeldingen van Orgels

in het Utrechtsche Psalterium. 29-32, SOME
Durrieu, Paul. L'Origine du Manuscrit Célèbre, Dit le Psautier d'Utrecht. 639-657, HAVE
Hulshof, Abraham. Het Utrechtsche Psalterium. 4-28, SOME

UTRECHT. Rijksuniversiteit. Anglistische Bibliotheek Anglia

Draat, P. Fijn van. Anglia. 69-73, EVER

UTRECHT. Rijksuniversiteit. Bibliotheek

EVER

SOME

UTRECHT. Rijksuniversiteit. Bibliotheek

UTRE

Tans, J. A. G. Een Uitdagende Utrechtse Collectie: De Val des Pausdoms. 64-77, UTRE
Veenendaal, T. De Vierdaagsche en de Utrechtsche Universiteitsbibliotheek. 282-283, EVER

UTRECHT. Rijksuniversiteit. Bibliotheek. Archief

Kohlbrugge, J. H. F. Dr. H. F. Kohlbrugge en Zijn Archief in de Universiteitsbibliotheek. 217-236, EVER

UTRECHT. Rijksuniversiteit. Bibliotheek. Catalogs

Gras, Elisabeth J. De Systematische Catalogus der Utrechtse Universiteitsbibliotheek. 107-115, EVER

UTRECHT. Rijksuniversiteit. Bibliotheek. Centrale Duitsche Bibliotheek

Bongertman, W. De Centrale Duitsche Bibliotheek. 33-37, EVER

UTRECHT. Rijksuniversiteit. Bibliotheek - Hist.

Bongertman, W. Hoe de Utrechtsche Akademie-Boekerij in de St. Janskerk Gehuisvest Was. 37-41, SOME
Evers, Gerrit Albert. Het Paleis van Koning Lodewijk Napoleon te Utrecht en Zijne Inrichting tot Universiteitsbibliotheek. 42-62, SOME
Oudendijk, Johanna K. De Universiteitsbibliotheek te Utrecht als Koninklijk Paleis en als Voorwerp van Koninklijke Belangstelling. 244-249, EVER

UTRECHT. Rijksuniversiteit. Bibliotheek. Mss. (Psalter)

Brom, A., Jr. Afbeeldingen van Orgels in het Utrechtsche Psalterium. 29-32, SOME
Durrieu, Paul. L'Origine du Manuscrit Célèbre, Dit le Psautier d'Utrecht. 639-657, HAVE
Hulshof, Abraham. Het Utrechtsche Psalterium. 4-28, SOME

UTRECHT. Rijksuniversiteit. Ethnologisch Instituut. Bibliotheek - Catalogs

Grolman, Hermina C. A. Hoe de Centrale Systematische Catalogus aan het Volkenkundig Instituut te Utrecht tot Stand Kwam. 116-122, EVER

UTRECHT. Rijksuniversiteit. Fonds ten Behoeve van Indologische Studiën. Bibliotheek

Fischer, H. Th. De Bibliotheek van het Fonds ten Behoeve van Indologische Studiën aan de Rijksuniversiteit te Utrecht. 64-68, EVER

UTRECHT. Rijksuniversiteit. Instituut voor Middeleeuwsche Geschiedenis

Oppermann, O. De Verzameling Photo's van het Instituut voor Middeleeuwsche Geschiedenis. 242-243, EVER

UTRECHT. Rijksuniversiteit. Instituut voor Muziekwetenschap. Bibliotheek

Schuurmans, J. J. De Bibliotheken van de Veeartsenijkundige Faculteit en van het Instituut voor Muziekwetenschap Gevestigd in het Gebouw Bilstraat 172. 258-260, EVER

UTRECHT. Rijksuniversiteit. Leeszaal. Drift 31

Danner, H. W. Het Gebouw Drift 31. 60-63, EVER

UTRECHT. Rijksuniversiteit. Veeartsenijkundige Faculteit. Bibliotheek

Schuurmans, J. J. De Bibliotheken van de Veeartsenijkundige Faculteit en van het Instituut voor Muziekwetenschap Gevestigd in het Gebouw Bilstraat 172. 258-260, EVER

UTRECHT. Rijksuniversiteit. Volkenkundig Instituut. Bibliotheek - Catalogs

Grolman, Hermina C. A. Hoe de Centrale Systematische Catalogus aan het Volkenkundig Instituut te Utrecht tot Stand Kwam. 116-122, EVER

UTRECHT - Serial publications - Collections
see Serial publications - Collections - Utrecht

UTRECHT - Shelf arrangement
see Shelf arrangement - Utrecht

UTRECHT. Sint Janskerk. Akademieboekerij
see Utrecht. Rijksuniversiteit. Bibliotheek

UTRECHT. Tandheelkundig Instituut. Bibliotheek

Hulshoff, Margaretha H. De Bibliotheek

van het Tandheelkundig Instituut. 160-163, EVER

Václavek, Bedřich, jt. author
Smetana, Robert and Bedřich Václavek. Jak Katalogisovati Kramářské Písně. 137-143, EMLE

VADSTENA, Sweden (Birgittine monastery) Biblioteca
Silfverstolpe, C. En Blick i Vadstena Klosters Arkiv och Bibliotek. [89]-[115], KLEM

VÄXJÖ, Sweden (Diocese) - Church libraries
see Church libraries - Växjö, Sweden (Diocese)

Vail, R. W. G.
A Patriotic Pair of Peripatetic Printers, the Up-State Imprints of John Holt and Samuel Loudon, 1776-1783. 391-422, WROT

Vajpayee, S. B.
Ranganathan: The Teacher. 593, RANG

VALAIS (Canton) - Printing
see Printing - Valais (Canton)

VALENCIA. Biblioteca Universitaria Provincial
Pons, Abelardo Palanca. Incunable Valenciano Poco Conocido. 589-596, GALL

VALERIO MASSIMO
see Valerius Maximus

VALERIUS MAXIMUS. Factorum et Dictorum Memorabilium Libri
Dahlberg, Ragnar. En Volym ur Michael Agricolas Boksamling. 57-70, SCHA

Valkhoff, P.
Het Franse Boek in de Utrechtse Universiteitsbibliotheek. 278-281, EVER

VALLETTA, Malta. Royal Public Library
Inguanez, Mauro. A Hand-List of the Incunabula of the Royal Malta Library. 407-411, GREE

Vallinkoski, J.
Ett Bortglömt Handskriftslån från Akademibiblioteket i Åbo på 1740-Talet. 197-201, GARD
Ett Danskt Bogfynd in Finland. 15-19, DAHA
F. W. Pippingin Väitöskirjasarjan De Bibliothecariis Academiae Aboënsis Julkaisematon XXI Osa. 108-124, NYBE
Poimintoja Kirjojen Kansimerkinnöistä Helsingin Yliopiston Kirjastossa. 9-23, TUDE
Turun Kirjansitojat Vapauden ajan Alkupuoliskolla. 197-227, DAHL

VĀLMĪKI. Mss. Rāmāyaṇa
Nobel, Johannes. Die Śārada-Handschrift des Rāmāyaṇa. 186-190, HARN

Valous, Guy de.
Une Exposition à la Bibliothèque Sainte-Geneviève: La Machine à Expliquer Le Déluge. 535-538, BONN

Van Den Gheyn, J., S.J.
Rectifications Paléographiques. 163-168, CHAT

Van Der Briele, Wolfgang.
Eine Bibelhandschrift des 13. Jahrhunderts in der Dortmunder Stadtbibliothek. 7-11, VERD

VAN DER HAER, Jan - Library
Kronenberg, M. E. Erasmus-Uitgaven A°. 1531 in het Bezit van Kanunnik Mr. Jan Dircsz van der Haer te Gorkum. 99-117, KOSS

VAN DER MEULEN, DANIEL
see Meulen, Daniel van der

Van Hoesen, Henry B. and Norman Kilpatrick.
Heights of Books in Relation to Height of Stack Tiers. 352-357, HANS

Van Toch, Jeannie.
Styky L. J. Živného s Knihovnictvím Anglickým a Americkým. 25-64, ZIVN

VAN VOORST, JOHANNES
Groot, J. R. de. Thorbecke en de Leidse Bibliothecaris Van Voorst. 450-455, BRUM

Vander Linden, Albert, jt. ed.
BORR
BORV

VANDERBILT UNIVERSITY, Nashville. School of Medicine. Library
Cunningham, Eileen-R. Some Items of Americana Medica Published Southwest of the Alleghenies and Their Authors. 25-26, STUM

Vanselow, Otto.
Veraltete Literatur. 339-348, KÖNI

Varley, Douglas H.
Varley Valedictory. 32-34, VARL

VARLEY, DOUGLAS H.
VARL

VARLEY, DOUGLAS H. - Bibl.

Bibliography of the Writings of D. H. Varley. 59-66, VARL

Vartdal, Hroar.
Über Kartenkatalogisierung. Die Kartensammlung der Universitätsbibliothek zu Oslo. 481-492, MUNT

VATICAN - Acquisitions
see Acquisitions - Vatican

VATICAN. Appartamento Borgia. Camera della Segnatura

Leyh, Georg. Die Camera della Segnatura—ein Bibliotheksraum? 171-177, LEID

VATICAN - Archives
see Archives - Vatican

VATICAN. Archivio Vaticano

Dahl, Svend. P. A. Munch i Vatikanets Arkiv. 30-48, MUNT
Renouard, Yves. Intérêt et Importance des Archives Vaticanes pour L'Histoire Économique du Moyen Âge Spécialement du XIVe Siècle. 21-41, MERC
Ritzler, Remigius. Die Archivalischen Quellen der "Hierarchia Catholica." 51-74, MERC

VATICAN. Archivio Vaticano. Hist. - 13th cent.

Ehrle, Francesco, Cardinal. Die Frangipani und der Untergang des Archivs und der Bibliothek der Päpste am Anfang des 13. Jahrhunderts. 448-485, CHAT

VATICAN. Archivio Vaticano. Mss. (AA. Arm. E. 123)

Michelini, Tocci Luigi. I Due Manoscritti Urbinati dei Privilegi dei Montefeltro. 206-257, MERC

VATICAN. Biblioteca Vaticana

ALBB

Auvray, Lucien. Notices sur Quelques Cartulaires et Obituaires Français Conservés à la Bibliothèque du Vatican. 381-409, HAVE
Mercati, Giovanni, Cardinal. I. Uno Scambio Strano di Qualche Interesse per Tre Grandi Biblioteche. II. Amici Innominati del Savile in Roma? 17-26, FERR
Sorbelli, Albano. Lo "Specchio della Prudenza" di Frate Beltrame da Ferrara (GW 3807) Presunto Incunabulo. 205-213, ACCU

VATICAN. Biblioteca Vaticana. Biblioteca Urbinate

Tocci, Luigi Michelini. Agapito, Bibliotecario "Docto, Acorto et Diligente" della Biblioteca Urbinate alla Fine del Quattrocento. II, 245-280, ALBB

VATICAN. Biblioteca Vaticana - Catalogs

Fraschetti-Santinelli, Italia. L'Ordinamento della Voce "Roma" nel Catalogo per Soggetti. 151-163, GREG

VATICAN. Biblioteca Vaticana - Hist.

Albareda, Anselmo M. Il Vescovo di Barcellona Pietro Garsias Bibliotecario della Vaticana sotto Alessandro VI. 1-18, MERG
Batllori, Miquel. El Pare Ehrle, Prefecte de la Vaticana, en la Seva Correspondència amb el Card. Rampolla. I, 75-117, ALBB
Berra, Luigi. Due Listi di Libri per la Biblioteca Vaticana. 19-27, MERG
Ciceri, Angelo. Un Precursore ed un Amico di Alfonso Gallo: Mons. Achille Ratti (Papa Pio XI). 279-294, GALL
Guidi, Pietro. Pietro Demetrio Guazzelli da Lucca il Primo Custode della Biblioteca Vaticana (1481-1511) e L'Inventario dei Suoi Libri. 192-218, EHRE
Hanson, James Christian Meinrich. Organization and Reorganization of Libraries. 519-532, WILS
Laurent, M.-H. Guillaume des Rosières et la Bibliothèque Pontificale à L'Époque de Clément VI. 579-603, PELZ
Mercati, Giovanni, Cardinal. Cenni di A. del Monte e G. Lascaris sulle Perdite della Biblioteca Vaticana nel Sacco del 1527. 605-632, CERI
Müntz, Eugène. La Bibliothèque du Vatican pendant la Révolution Française. 579-591, HAVE
Wieland, Franz. Früheste Vorläufer der Vaticana. 159-168, LEYG

VATICAN. Biblioteca Vaticana - Hist. - 13th cent.

Ehrle, Francesco, Cardinal. Die Frangipani und der Untergang des Archivs und der Bibliothek der Päpste am Anfang des 13. Jahrhunderts. 448-485, CHAT

VATICAN. Biblioteca Vaticana - Hist. - 1555-1565

De Maio, Romeo. La Biblioteca Apostolica Vaticana sotto Paolo IV e Pio IV (1555-1565). I, 265-313, ALBB

VATICAN. Biblioteca Vaticana. Mss.

Donati, Lamberto. Le Fonti Iconografiche di Alcuni Manoscritti Urbinati della Biblioteca Vaticana—Osservazioni Intorno ai Cosiddetti "Tarocchi del Mantegna." 48-129, MERG
Gerstinger, Hans. Ein Bisher Unbeachtetes Verzeichnis Griechischer

Handschriften der Vaticana aus dem Jahre 1553. 11-19, LEYG
Hebbelynck, Ad. Inventaire Sommaire des Manuscrits Coptes de la Bibliothèque Vaticane. 35-82, EHRE
Mercati, Giovanni, Cardinal. Codici del Convento di S. Francesco in Assisi nella Biblioteca Vaticana. 83-127, EHRE
Nogara, B. Di Alcune Vite e Commenti Medioevali di Ovidio. 413-431, CERI
Tisserant, Eugène. Inventaire Sommaire des Manuscrits Arabes du Fonds Borgia à la Bibliothèque Vaticane. 1-34, EHRE

VATICAN. Biblioteca Vaticana. Mss. (3357)

Rajna, P. Il Codice Vaticano 3357 del Trattato De Vita Solitaria di Francesco Petrarca. 641-686, CERI

VATICAN. Biblioteca Vaticana. Mss. (3421)

Chatelain, Émile. Recherches sur un Manuscrit Célèbre de Sidoine Apollinaire. 321-327, GRAU

VATICAN. Biblioteca Vaticana. Mss. (Cod. 5318)

Wolf, Johannes. Ein Brief Pietro Arons an Giovanni dal Lago. 65-70, KUHN

VATICAN. Biblioteca Vaticana. Mss. (Cod. Lat. 3864)

Bloch, Herbert. The Structure of Sallust's Historiae: The Evidence of the Fleury Manuscript. 59-76, ALBA

VATICAN. Biblioteca Vaticana. Mss. (Etiop.: Zēnā Mārqos)

Cerulli, Enrico. Gli Atti di Zēnā Mārqos, Monaco Etiope del Sec. XIV. I, 191-212, ALBB

VATICAN. Biblioteca Vaticana. Mss. (Greek 2137 R.)

Santoro, Enza Fioroni. Dell'Origine e degli Autori di Alcune Stampe Attribuite ad "Ignoto." 427-439, GALL

VATICAN. Biblioteca Vaticana. Mss. (Hebrew 356, 372, 400)

Millàs i Vallicrosa, Josep M.ª. Manuscrits Hebraics d'Origen Català a la Biblioteca Vaticana. I, 97-109, RUBI

VATICAN. Biblioteca Vaticana. Mss. Indexes

Tisserant, Eugène, Cardinal. The Preparation of a Main Index for the Vatican Library Manuscripts. 176-185, BISH

VATICAN. Biblioteca Vaticana. Mss. (Lat. 3958)

Meersseman, G. La Bibliothèque des Frères Prêcheurs de la Minerve à la Fin du XVe Siècle. 605-634, PELZ

VATICAN. Biblioteca Vaticana. Mss. (Lat. Reg. 846)

Legendre, Paul. Notes Tironiennes du Vatic. Lat. Reg. 846. 312-331, CHAT

VATICAN. Biblioteca Vaticana. Mss. (Molza)

Vattasso, M. I Codici Molziani della Biblioteca Vaticana con un'Appendice di Carmi Inediti o Rari. 531-555, CERI

VATICAN. Biblioteca Vaticana. Mss. (Ottobon. 356)

Andrieu, Michel. Le Missel de la Chapelle Papale à la Fin du XIIIe Siècle. 348-376, EHRB

VATICAN. Biblioteca Vaticana. Mss. (Ottobon. Lat. 74)

Campana, Augusto. Per il "Textus Evangelii" Donato da Enrico II a Montecassino (Vat. Ottobon. Lat. 74). 34-47, MERG

VATICAN. Biblioteca Vaticana. Mss. (Ottobon. Lat. 3027)

Holtzmann, Walther. Über die Vatikanische Handschrift der "Collectio Brugensis" (Ottobon. Lat. 3027). I, 391-414, ALBB

VATICAN. Biblioteca Vaticana. Mss. (Pal. Graec. 431)

Lietzmann, Hans. Zur Datierung der Josuarolle. 181-185, DEGE

VATICAN. Biblioteca Vaticana. Mss. (Reg. 886)

Lindsay, W.-M. The Notae Iuris of Vat. Reg. 886. 155-162, CHAT

VATICAN. Biblioteca Vaticana. Mss. (Salvadori)

Vian, Nello. I Manoscritti di Giulio Salvadori nella Biblioteca Vaticana. 505-519, FERR

VATICAN. Biblioteca Vaticana. Mss. (Stobaeus)

Gebhardt, Oskar von. Eine Verlorene und Wiedergefundene Stobaeus-Handschrift. 243-264, WILM

VATICAN. Biblioteca Vaticana. Mss. (Vat. Etiop. 251-299)

Lantschoot, Arnold van. Inventaire Sommaire des Manuscrits Vaticans Éthiopiens. I, 453-[514], ALBB

VATICAN. Biblioteca Vaticana. Mss. (Vat. Gr.: Vita Procli)

Mogenet, Joseph. Holstenius et L'Horoscope de Proclus. II, 281-308, ALBB

VATICAN. Biblioteca Vaticana. Mss. (Vat. Gr. 2008)
Follieri, Enrica. Un Canone Inedito di S. Andrea di Creta per L'Annunciazione (Vat. Gr. 2008 e Crypt. Δ . a. VII). I, 337-357, ALBB

VATICAN. Biblioteca Vaticana. Mss. (Vat. Lat. 2343)
Kuttner, Stephan. Analecta Iuridica Vaticana (Vat. Lat. 2343). I, 415-452, ALBB

VATICAN. Biblioteca Vaticana. Mss. (Vat. Lat. 4770)
Balboni, Dante. Il Rito della Benedizione delle Palme (Vat. Lat. 4770). I, 55-74, ALBB

VATICAN. Biblioteca Vaticana. Mss. (Vat. Lat. 4939)
Bertolini, Ottorino. La Collezione Canonica Beneventana del Vat. Lat. 4939. I, 119-137, ALBB

VATICAN. Biblioteca Vaticana. Mss. (Vat. Lat. 5608)
Del Re, Niccolò. Il "Consilium pro Urbano VI" di Bartolomeo da Saliceto (Vat. Lat. 5608). I, 213-263, ALBB

VATICAN. Biblioteca Vaticana. Mss. (Vat. Lat. 10726)
Bevilacqua, Mario. Una "Quaestio" di Niccolò Matarelli (Vat. Lat. 10726). I, 139-157, ALBB

VATICAN. Biblioteca Vaticana. Scuola di Biblioteconomia
Giordani, Igino. La Scuola Vaticana di Biblioteconomia. 495-503, WILS

VATICAN - Bookbinding - Fine bindings - Collections
see Bookbinding - Fine bindings - Collections - Vatican

VATICAN - Canon law - Collections
see Canon law - Collections - Vatican

VATICAN. Cappella Sistina. Mss.
Llorens, José Maria. Los Codices Musicales de la "Capella Sixtina" en la Historia del Arte. II, 191-209, ALBB

VATICAN - Catalogs - Subject
see Catalogs - Subject - Vatican

VATICAN - Illumination of books and manuscripts
see Illumination of books and manuscripts - Vatican

VATICAN - Liturgies - Collections
see Liturgies - Collections - Vatican

VATICAN - Manuscripts, Arabic - Collections
see Manuscripts, Arabic - Collections - Vatican

VATICAN - Manuscripts - Collections
see Manuscripts - Collections - Vatican

VATICAN - Manuscripts, Coptic - Collections
see Manuscripts, Coptic - Collections - Vatican

VATICAN - Manuscripts, Ethiopian - Collections
see Manuscripts, Ethiopian - Collections - Vatican

VATICAN - Manuscripts, Greek - Collections
see Manuscripts, Greek - Collections - Vatican

VATICAN - Maps - Collections
see Maps - Collections - Vatican

VATICAN - Music libraries and collections
see Music libraries and collections - Vatican

VATICAN - Rare books - Collections
see Rare books - Collections - Vatican

VATICAN. Scuola di Biblioteconomia
see Vatican. Biblioteca Vaticana. Scuola di Biblioteconomia

VATICAN - Subject headings - Special subjects
see Subject headings - Special subjects - Vatican

VATOPEDI (Monastery) Mt. Athos
see Athos (Monasteries) Vatopedi

Vattasso, M.
I Codici Molziani della Biblioteca Vaticana con un'Appendice di Carmi Inediti o Rari. 531-555, CERI

Veenendaal, T.
De Vierdaagsche en de Utrechtsche Universiteitsbibliotheek. 282-283, EVER

Vega, Javier Lasso de la.
El Cuerpo Facultativo de Archiveros, Bibliotecarios y Arqueólogos de España. 183-186, HOFM

VEILLOT, JEAN. Mss. [Motet]
Launay, Denise. À Propos de Deux Manuscrits Musicaux aux Armes de Louis XIII. 63-67, FEDO

Vekené, Emil van der.
Die Anfänge der Buchdruckerkunst in Luxemburg. Mathias Birthon (1598-1604). 434-444, BENZ

VELDEKE, HEINRICH VON
see Heinrich von Veldeke

Velemínský, Karel.
L. J. Živný a Jeho Účast na Vzniku Našeho Zákona o Veřejných Knihovnách Obecních. 144-146, ŽIVN

VELUM PRINTED BOOKS
Madsen, Victor. Pergamenttryk i det Kongelige Bibliotek i København. Et Supplement. 199-214, COLL

Vendryes, J.
Réflexions sur les Éditions de Textes. 539-547, BONN

VENEZIA TRIDENTIA
see Trentino-Alto Adige, Italy

VENICE - Araujo, Joaquim de. Mss. - Collections
see Araujo, Joaquim de. Mss. - Collections - Venice

VENICE. Biblioteca Nazionale Marciana. Mss. (Araujo)
Mariutti De Sánchez Rivero, Angela. Il Carteggio Inedito del Legato Araujo. 369-382, FERR

VENICE. Biblioteca Nazionale Marciana. Mss. (Cod. Mar. 246)
Ruelle, Charles-Émile. Notice du Codex Marcianus 246, Contenant le Traité du Philosophe Damascius sur les Premiers Principes. 547-552, GRAU

VENICE. Biblioteca Nazionale Marciana. Mss. (Ital. Cl. V. 26 [5714])
Laurent, M. H. Les Sources Hagiographiques de S. Catherine de Sienne et le Ms. Marciano Ital. Cl. V. 26. 521-531, FERR

VENICE. Biblioteca Nazionale Marciana. Mss. (Naniani)
Mercati, Giovanni, Cardinal. A Proposito dei Codici Naniani Greci 32 e 37. 280-285, GREE

VENICE. Bibliothèque de Saint-Marc
see Venice. Biblioteca Nazionale Marciana

VENICE. Marciano
see Venice. Biblioteca Nazionale Marciana

VENICE - Printing
see Printing - Venice

VENICE - Publishers and publishing
see Publishers and publishing - Venice

Vengerov, S. A.
Nasha Zadacha. 1-4, MALE

VEREENIGING VAN LETTERKUNDIGEN
Reedijk, C. Stuivers en Centen of: Andermaal het Uitleenrecht. 559-568, BRUM

VEREIN DEUTSCHER BIBLIOTHEKARE
VERD
VERP
VERZ

VEREIN DEUTSCHER PHILOLOGEN UND SCHULMÄNNER. SEKTION FÜR BIBLIOTHEKSWESEN
VERE

VEREINIGUNG BERLINER BIBLIOTHEKARE
MILK

VEREINIGUNG SCHWEIZERISCHER BIBLIOTHEKARE
Borgeaud, Marc-Auguste. Le Rôle de M. Pierre Bourgeois à L'ABS. 177-180, BOUR
Schwarber, Karl. Marcel Godet und die Vereinigung Schweizerischer Bibliothekare. 3-8, GODM

VEREINIGUNG SCHWEIZERISCHER BIBLIOTHEKARE - Hist.
Godet, Marcel. Hermann Escher et les Bibliothèques Suisses. 8-19, ESCK

VERGILIUS MARO, PUBLIUS. Appendix Vergiliana. Mss. Copa
Lenchantin de Gubernatis, M. De Codice Bononiensi quo Copa et Moretum Continentur. 199-201, STAM

VERGILIUS MARO, PUBLIUS. Appendix Vergiliana. Mss. Moretum
Lenchantin de Gubernatis, M. De Codice Bononiensi quo Copa et Moretum Continentur. 199-201, STAM

Verman, Lal C.
Dr. Ranganathan and Standardization. 268-270, RANG

Vermeeren, P. J. H.
Handschriften van het Kapittel van Sint Servaas ter Koninklijke Bibliotheek in 's-Gravenhage. 179-193, MAAS
W. H. J. Baron van Mestreenen van Tiellandt als Handschriftenverzamelaar. 603-609, BRUM

VERMERCKT DŸE GROSSENN WUNDER ZAICHEN... 1491-1494
Geissler, Paul. Ein Seltener Augsburger Wiegendruck. Das Älteste Gedruckte Buch über Altötting. 316-322, VORS

DIE VERÖFFENTLICHUNGEN DER DEUTSCHEN BIBLIOTHEK. 165-171, EPPE

VERÖFFENTLICHUNGEN DER UNIVERSITÄTSBIBLIOTHEK ERLANGEN. 115-118, VERZ

VERÖFFENTLICHUNGEN ÜBER DIE DEUTSCHE BIBLIOTHEK. 172-174, EPPE

VERÖFFENTLICHUNGEN VON HANS LÜLFING. 7-8, LÜLF

VERÖFFENTLICHUNGEN VON PROF. DR. KARL BULLING. 9-11, BULL

VERONA. Biblioteca Capitolare. Mss. (LXIV [62])

Spagnolo, D. Antonio. Una Leggina di Giustiniano in un Miscellaneo Veronese del Secolo XI-XII. 193-194, CHAT

VERSOR, JOHANNES

Birkenmajer, Alexander. Die Wiegendrucke der Physischen Werke Johannes Versors. 121-135, COLL

VERTICAL FILES
see Ephemeral materials; Pamphlets; Picture collections

Verwey, H. de la Fontaine.
Bij het Afscheid van Prof. Dr. L. Brummel als Bibliothecaris van de Koninklijke Bibliotheek. 379-386, BRUM
Boekbanden uit de Oranje Nassau-Bibliotheek. 161-179, HAGU
Jacob Geel en de Koninklijke Bibliotheek. 414-426, BRUM
Over Enige Boeken te Vianen Gedrukt Tijdens het 'Voorspel.' 20-34, KOSS
Une Presse Secrète du XVIe Siècle: Abel Clémence, Imprimeur à Rouen. 81-89, CALO

Vesaas, Halldis Moren.
Bøkenes Rike. 7-8, NORS

VESALIUS, ANDREAS. De Humani Corporis Fabrica

Hahn, André, Paule Dumaitre, and J. Samion-Contet. Le "De Humani Corporis Fabrica" d'André Vésale (1543). 91-97, CALO

VETERANS ADMINISTRATION. Library service, U. S.
see U.S. Veterans Administration. Library service

Veyrin-Forrer, Jeanne.
Les Premiers Caractères de François-Ambroise Didot (1781-1785). 159-173, CALO

Vian, Nello.
I Manoscritti di Giulio Salvadori nella Biblioteca Vaticana. 505-519, FERR
La Presentazione e gli Esemplari Vaticani della "Assertio Septem Sacramentorum" di Enrico VIII. II, 355-375, ALBB

VIANEN, Netherlands - Printing
see Printing - Vianen, Netherlands

VIBORG, Denmark. Centralbibliotek

VIBO

VIBORG, Denmark (Diocese) Bibliotek

VIBO

VIBORG, Denmark - Public libraries - Finances
see Public libraries - Finances - Viborg, Denmark

VIBORG, Denmark. Stifts Bibliotek

VIBO

VIBORG NATION, Turku, Finland
see Turku, Finland. Akademi (1640-1827) Viborg Nation. Bibliotek

VICENZA - Printing
see Printing - Vicenza

Vichi Santovito, Nella.
Una Correzione al Reichling ed Alcune Notizie sulla Stampa di Cagli. 215-220, ACCU

Vickery, B. C.
The Classification of Chemical Substances: An Historical Survey. 151-167, SAYW
Ranganathan's Work on Classification. 108-110, RANG

VIDENSKABSSELSKABET I TRONDHEIM
see Norske Videnskabers Selskab, Trondheim

Vieillard, Roger.
M. Julien Cain et les Estampes. 20-21, CAIN

VIENNA. Akademie der Bildenden Künste. Bibliothek

Freiberg, Siegfried. Die Bibliothek der Akademie der Bildenden Künste in Wien. 32-33, STUM

VIENNA - Anonyms and pseudonyms - Collections
see Anonyms and pseudonyms - Collections - Vienna

VIENNA - Architecture and building - National libraries
see Architecture and building - National libraries - Vienna

VIENNA - Archives
see Archives - Vienna

VIENNA - Art libraries and collections
see Art libraries and collections - Vienna

VIENNA - Biography - Collections - Vienna

Wernigg, Ferdinand. Quellen zur Wiener Biographie. Versuch einer Praktischen Anleitung. 125-153, VIES

VIENNA - Catalogs
see Catalogs - Vienna

VIENNA - Catalogs - Author
see Catalogs - Author - Vienna

VIENNA - Catalogs - Subject
see Catalogs - Subject - Vienna

VIENNA - Documentation - Indexes and abstracts
see Documentation - Indexes and abstracts - Vienna

VIENNA - Drawings - Collections
see Drawings - Collections - Vienna

VIENNA - Hist. - Collections - Vienna

Tatzer, Leopold. Seltene Viennensia der Stadtbibliothek. 46-49, VIES

VIENNA - Hunting diaries - Collections
see Hunting diaries - Collections - Vienna

VIENNA. KK. Hofbibliothek
see Vienna. Nationalbibliothek

VIENNA - Librarians
see Librarians - Vienna

VIENNA - Library resources
see Library resources - Vienna

VIENNA - Manuscripts - Collections
see Manuscripts - Collections - Vienna

VIENNA - Manuscripts, German - Old High German - Collections
see Manuscripts, German - Old High German - Collections - Vienna

VIENNA - Maps - Collections
see Maps - Collections - Vienna

VIENNA - Music libraries and collections
see Music libraries and collections - Vienna

VIENNA - Music literature and scores - Manuscripts - Collections
see Music literature and scores - Manuscripts - Collections - Vienna

VIENNA - National libraries
see National libraries - Vienna

VIENNA - National libraries - Acquisitions
see National libraries - Acquisitions - Vienna

VIENNA. Nationalbibliothek [honoree]

VIEN

VIENNA. Nationalbibliothek [subject]

BICK

Beetz, Wilhelm. Zur Geschichte der Porträtsammlung der Nationalbibliothek in Wien. 59-74, VIEN
Frieberger, Kurt. Habent Sua Fata Libelli. 34, STUM
Hadamowsky, Franz. Wiener Theater-Periodica. 35-38, STUM
Haiböck, Lambert. Nationalbibliothek und Staatsdruckerei. 39, STUM
Stummvoll, Josef. Die Abschreibung des Alphabetischen Kataloges der Österreichischen Nationalbibliothek. 594-600, BRUM
———— Die Druckschriftenbestände der Österreichischen Nationalbibliothek und die Abschreibung des Alphabetischen Kataloges 1501 bis 1929. 105-118, HOFM
Stummvoll, Josef and Laurenz Strebl. Copying of the Old Catalogue of the Austrian National Library. 175-178, RANG

VIENNA. Nationalbibliothek - Hist.

Bick, Josef. Der Unveröffentlichte Zweite Teil der Dilucida Repraesentatio Bibliothecae Caesareae des S. Kleiner und J. J. Sedelmayr. 75-86, VIEN
Groag, Edmund. Zur Geschichte des Bücherankaufes in der Hofbibliothek. 421-430, VIEN
Kammel, Karl. Dr. Ernst Trenkler, Oberstaatsbibliothekar, Direktor der Druckschriftensammlung der Österreichischen Nationalbibliothek. 11-12, STUM
Smital, Ottokar. Miszellen zur Geschichte der Wiener Palatina. 771-794, VIEN
Stickler, Michael. Dr. Alois Kisser, Generaldirektor-Stellvertreter der Österreichischen Nationalbibliothek. 9-10, STUM
Zimmel, Bruno. DDr. Josef Stummvoll, Generaldirektor der Österreichischen Nationalbibliothek. 5-8, STUM

VIENNA. Nationalbibliothek - Hist. - 1891-1916

Doublier, Othmar. Ein Vierteljahrhundert aus der Geschichte der Hofbibliothek 1891-1916. 163-210, VIEN

VIENNA. Nationalbibliothek. Kupferstichsammlung

Rathe, Kurt. Ein Architektur-Musterbuch

der Spätgotik mit Graphischen Einklebungen. 667-692, VIEN

VIENNA. Nationalbibliothek. Mss.

Ausserer, Karl. Die Heraldischen Handschriften der Wiener Nationalbibliothek. 7-36, VIEN
Gerstinger, Hans. Johannes Sambucus als Handschriftensammler. 251-400, VIEN
Lach, Robert. Aus dem Handschriftenschatze der Musikaliensammlung der Wiener Nationalbibliothek. 553-574, VIEN
Leporini, Heinrich. Simon von Niederaltaich und Martin v. Senging. 575-590, VIEN
Seif, Theodor. Vom Alexanderroman. 745-770, VIEN

VIENNA. Nationalbibliothek. Mss. (Ambraser Sammlung)

Menhardt, Hermann. Die Altdeutschen Ambrasiani der Österreichischen Nationalbibliothek. 56-57, STUM

VIENNA. Nationalbibliothek. Mss. (Bach)

Nowak, Leopold. Ein Bach-Fund. 95-98, FEDO

VIENNA. Nationalbibliothek. Mss. (Cod. Phil. Gr. 261)

Hunger, Herbert. Die Druckvorlage der Editio Princeps des Anonymus Neobarii. 46, STUM

VIENNA. Nationalbibliothek. Mss. (Cod. Ser. Nov. 13241)

Trenkler, Ernst. Ein Unbekanntes "Livre d'Heures" der Österreichischen Nationalbibliothek. 639-645, BICK

VIENNA. Nationalbibliothek. Mss. (Cod. Vindob. 14105)

Collijn, Isak Gustaf Alfred. Über den Verfasser des Cod. Vindob. 14105. 286-290, BICK

VIENNA. Nationalbibliothek. Mss. (Cod. Vindob. Lat. 9039)

Gerstinger, Hans. Aus dem "Tagebuche" des Kaiserl. Hofhistoriographen Johannes Sambucus (1531-1584). Cod. Vindob. Latin. 9039, Fol. 1 und 5. 373-383, BICK

VIENNA. Nationalbibliothek. Mss. (Lat. 9699)

Gerstinger, Hans. Ein Bisher Unbeachtetes Verzeichnis Griechischer Handschriften der Vaticana aus dem Jahre 1553. 11-19, LEYG

VIENNA. Nationalbibliothek. Mss. (Papyrus)

Klos, Herbert. Papyrologen-Bibliothekare. 51-53, STUM

VIENNA. Nationalbibliothek. Mss. (Ser. n. 2765)

Unterkircher, Franz. Aus dem Matrikelbuch der Burgpfarre. 91-94, STUM

VIENNA. Nationalbibliothek. Mss. (2597)

Winkler, Emil. Die Textliche Stellung der Handschrift 2597 der Wiener Nationalbibliothek (René von Anjou, Livre du Cuer d'Amours Espris). 861-870, VIEN

VIENNA. Nationalbibliothek. Mss. (3093)

Sonnleithner, Rudolf. Die Mondseer Bruchstücke der Ältesten Hochdeutschen Evangelienübersetzung. 795-804, VIEN

VIENNA. Nationalbibliothek. Mss. (14090, Suppl. 1776)

Brotanek, Rudolf. Beschreibung der Handschrift 14090 (Suppl. 1776) der Nationalbibliothek in Wien. 145-162, VIEN

VIENNA. Nationalbibliothek. Musikaliensammlung

Lach, Robert. Aus dem Handschriftenschatze der Musikaliensammlung der Wiener Nationalbibliothek. 553-574, VIEN

VIENNA. Nationalbibliothek. Musiksammlung

Nowak, Leopold. Ein Druck mit Melodien für Theophilanthropen. 61, STUM

VIENNA. Nationalbibliothek. Porträtsammlung

Pauer, Hans. Grosser Entschluss. Ein Neues Ordnungssystem in der Porträtsammlung der Österreichischen Nationalbibliothek. 62-64, STUM

VIENNA. Nationalbibliothek. Sammlung A. Perera

Gregor, Joseph. Die Handzeichnungen der Sammlung Perera in der Wiener Nationalbibliothek. 407-420, VIEN

VIENNA. Österreichische Nationalbibliothek
see Vienna. Nationalbibliothek

VIENNA. Palatina. Bibliothek
see Vienna. Nationalbibliothek

VIENNA - Papyrus collections
see Papyrus collections - Vienna

VIENNA - Periodicals - Indexes and abstracts
see Periodicals - Indexes and abstracts - Vienna

VIENNA - Periodicals, Theatrical - Collections
see Periodicals, Theatrical - Collections - Vienna

VIENNA - Picture collections
see Picture collections - Vienna

VIENNA - Public libraries
see Public libraries - Vienna

VIENNA - Schubert, Franz. Mss. - Collections
see Schubert, Franz. Mss. - Collections - Vienna

VIENNA - Spanish literature - Collections
see Spanish literature - Collections - Vienna

VIENNA - Special collections
see Special collections - Vienna

VIENNA. Staatsarchiv
see Austria. Staatsarchiv

VIENNA. Stadtbibliothek

VIES

VIENNA - Subject headings
see Subject headings - Vienna

VIENNA - Theatrical libraries and collections
see Theatrical libraries and collections - Vienna

VIENNA. Universität. Bibliothek

Gans, Johann. Die Universitätsbibliothek in Wien im und nach dem Kriege. 358-367, BICK

VIENNA. Universität. Bibliothek - Catalogs

Alker, Hugo. Geschichte der Sachkatalogisierung an der Universitätsbibliothek Wien 1774-1954. 118-132, VORS

Vigilucci, P. D.
Alfonso Gallo e Camaldoli. 703-706, GALL

Viguers, Ruth Hill.
To Catch the Nightingale. 29-40, SAYE

Vilar, Joan.
L'"Expositio Remigii Super Matheum" en el Còd. 548 de la Biblioteca de Catalunya. III, 263-281, RUBI

VILLEDIEU, ALEXANDRE DE
see Alexandre de Villedieu

VIMALAKĪRTINIRDEŚA-SŪTRA. Mss.

Priest, Alan. An Illuminated Buddhist Scroll in the Metropolitan Museum of Art. 122-128, GREE

Vincent, Auguste.
Les Premières Éditions de L'Institutio Principis Christiani d'Érasme. 91-96, GODE

VINCENT DE BEAUVAIS. Speculum Doctrinale

Polain, M.-Louis. Notes pour la Collation des Deux Tirages de L'Édition du Speculum Doctrinale, s. ind. typ. [Strasbourg, Adolphe Rusch]. 111-120, COLL

VINCENTIUS BELLAVACENSIS
see Vincent de Beauvais

VINCI, LEONARDO DA
see Leonardo da Vinci

VISBY, Sweden - Book selection
see Book selection - Visby, Sweden

VISBY, Sweden. Länsbibliotek

Berättelse över Stadsbibliotekets Verksamhet 1965. 129-143, VISB

VISBY, Sweden - Public libraries
see Public libraries - Visby, Sweden

VISBY, Sweden - Public libraries - Statistics
see Public libraries - Statistics - Visby, Sweden

VISBY, Sweden. Stadsbibliotek

VISB

Berättelse över Stadsbibliotekets Verksamhet 1965. 129-143, VISB

VISBY, Sweden. Stadsbibliotek - Hist.

Åberg, Åke. Visby Stadsbibliotek. Förhistoria och Begynnelseår. 5-30, VISB

Vischer, Christoph.
Die Stammbücher der Universitätsbibliothek Basel. Ein Beschreibendes Verzeichnis. 247-264, SCHU

VITAL, LAURENT. Relation du Premier Voyage de Charles-Quint en Espagne

Regatillo, José Fernández. Las Jornadas Montañesas del Emperador Carlos V en su Primer Viaje a España (Fragmento de la Crónica de Laurent Vital). I, 119-131, ARTI

Vitelli, G.
Un Papiro del Museo Graeco-Romano di Alessandria. 288-292, CHAT

Vitelli, Jérôme.
Ad Euripide e Sofocle (Eur. Hipp. 115. 441 Soph. Frgm. 609 Dnd.). 97-102, GRAU

VITRUVIUS POLLIO. De Architectura Libri Decem. 1486

Degering, Hermann. Wer War der Drucker der Erstausgabe des Vitruv? Ein Beitrag zur Geschichte des Römischen Buchdrucks. 175-202, HAEB

VITRUVIUS POLLIO. [Opera] 1487

Degering, Hermann. Nachträgliches zur Vitruvausgabe vom Jahre 1487 in der Leipziger Stadtbibliothek. 54-57, LEIP

VIVARIUM (Monastery) Biblioteca. Mss.

Weinburger, Wilhelm. Handschriften von Vivarium. 75-88, EHRD

Vleeschauwer, H. J. de.
Le Libre Accès aux Livres dans la Bibliothèque Universitaire. 70-87, COET

VLEESCHAUWER, H. J. de

VLEE

Rijswijk, Willem van. H. J. de Vleeschauwer—Exégète de la Pensée Kantienne. 49-57, VLEE

Vogel, Paul Heinz.
Ein "Kuriosum" des 18. Jahrhunderts. Die Biblia Pentapla. 445-455, BENZ

Voigt, Christian.
Die Staats- und Universitäts-Bibliothek Hamburg. Ihr Weg von der Gelehrtenbibliothek zur Wissenschaftlichen Gebrauchsbibliothek. 23-39, TIEM

Volbehr, Lilli.
Geschichte der Hamburger Öffentlichen Bücherhallen. 25-62, HAMB
Eine Tagesausleihe in der Bücherhalle Mönckebergstrasse. 83-96, HAMB

Volf, Josef.
Jak Získalo Národní Museum Své České Prvotisky. 148-152, EMLE
Z Životních cest Lad. J. Živného. 14-18, ŽIVN

Volkmann, Ludwig.
Nachricht von dem Drucke einer Poetischen Bilderbibel. 235-242, GLAU

VOLUNTEER ASSISTANTS - Hamburg

Propach, Elisabeth. Die Ausbildung des Nachwuchses in Hamburg. 97-109, HAMB

VON HOCHBERG FAMILY (Fürstenstein) - Library

Nentwig, Heinrich. Zwei Schlesische Majoratsbibliotheken. 129-138, WILM

VON MÜLINEN FAMILY - Library

Haeberli, Hans. Die Handschriftensammlungen Gottlieb Emanuel von Hallers und der Familie von Mülinen. 51-78, BERT

VON STAAL FAMILY (Hans von Staal) - Library

Altermatt, Leo. Die von Staalsche Historienbibel in der Zentralbibliothek Solothurn. 35-71, SCHU

Vontobel, Willy.
Bibliographie der Schweizergeschichte. 153-154, BERU
Dr. Pierre Bourgeois als Direktor der Schweizerischen Landesbibliothek. 168-177, BOUR

Voorhoeve, N. A. J.
F. Donker Duyvis and Standardization. 39-50, DONR

VOORST, JOHANNES VAN
see Van Voorst, Johannes

Vooys, C. G. N. de.
Heeft de Utrechtse Kunstenaar Erhard Reeuwich ook Letterkundige Verdiensten? 284-288, EVER

VOPELL, CASPAR

Oda, Takeo. Tenri Toshokan Zō Vopell no Chikyugi ni tsuite. (Vopell's Terrestrial Globe, Printed with Wood-Blocks, Dated 1536.) 449-462, TOMI

Vorstius, Joris.
Vergangenheit, Gegenwart und Zukunft des Deutschen Gesamtkatalogs. 312-328, LEYG

VORSTIUS, JORIS

VORS

VORSTIUS, JORIS - Bibl.

Kaegbein, Paul. Veröffentlichungen von Joris Vorstius 1917-1953. 1-16, VORS

VOSSIANUS LATINUS III. Ms.

Prete, Sesto. The Vossianus Latinus III and the Arrangement of the Works of Ausonius. 353-366, ALBA

Vossnack, Lieselotte, jt. ed.
LEUN

Vossnack, Lieselotte.
Ein Vorentwurf zu Berninis Johannes-predigt (Bibliothek der Techn. Hochschule Hannover, Sammlung Haupt XX e 1). 55-65, LEUN

Voulliéme, Ernst.
Die Inkunabelsammlung. 22-31, HARN
Nachträge zu den Buchhändleranzeigen des 15. Jahrhunderts in Getreuen Nachbildungen Herausg. von K. Burger. 18-44, HAEB
Eine Neue Bücheranzeige des Anton Sorg in Augsburg. 43-47, LOUB
Peter Attendorn, ein Buchhändler und Drucker in Straßburg um 1490. 344-353, MILF
Zur Bibliographie Heinrich Knoblochtzers in Heidelberg. Der Totentanz. 137-151, COLL
Zur Geschichte Einiger Erfurter Typen des XV. Jahrhunderts. 261-265, SCHW

Vreese, Willem de.
Briefwisseling van Jan Frans Willems en Jakob Grimm. 264-295, DEGE

VREESE, WILLEM DE
Sevensma, Tietse Pieter. De Bibliotheca Neerlandica Manuscripta De Vreese in Leiden. 167-175, BISH

Vŭlchev, Veličko.
Tvorchestvoto na Vazov v Otsenkata na Aleksandŭr Teodorov-Balan. 187-197, TEOD

VULPIUS, CHRISTIAN AUGUST
Bulling, Karl. Zur Jenaer Tätigkeit des Weimarer Bibliothekars Christian August Vulpius während der Jahre 1802-1817. 102-116, WEIM

VULPIUS, CHRISTIAN AUGUST. Rinaldo Rinaldini
Bay, Jens Christian. Rinaldo Rinaldini (Capo Brigante) and George Washington. 18-33, BISH

Vŭzharova, M.
Aleksandŭr Teodorov-Balan kato Bibliograf. 9-41, TEOB

Vyas, H. K.
Pioneer Trustee of Library Movement in India. 729-731, RANG

Vykoukal, F. V.
L. J. Živný a Knihopisný Ústav. 66-69, ŽIVN

WA-WAN PRESS - Bibl.
Waters, Edward N. The Wa-Wan Press: An Adventure in Musical Idealism. 214-233, ENGE

WÅHLIN, LARS PETER OLAF, Librarian
Hallberg, S. Göteborgs Stadsbibliotek. Det Första Halvseklet 1891-1940. 1-142, (first paper), GÖTE

Waal, Anna de.
De Opleiding. 610-617, BRUM

WACKERNAGEL, WILHELM - Library
Nidecker, Heinrich. Wilhelm Wackernagel. Bücher und Freunde. Ein Streifzug durch Seine Bibliothek. 177-191, SCHU

WADSTRÖM, CARL BERNHARD - Library
Lundgren, Hjalmar. Carl Bernhard Wadströms Bibliotek. 95-106, GRAP

WAESBERGHE, JANSONIUS VAN, firm. Catalogus Librorum Novissime Impressorum
Grosheide, D. Aankondiging van Nieuwe Uitgaven in de Zeventiende Eeuw. 456-462, BRUM

Waetzoldt, Stephan.
Ein Silbereinband von Jörg Seld. 53-57, REDE

Wagner, Ewald, ed.
FUCH

Wagner, Ewald.
Grusswort. 5-8, FUCH

Wagner, Henry R.
Hispanic Americana in the John Carter Brown Library. 423-455, WROT
The Portolan Atlases of American Interest in the Henry E. Huntington Library and Art Gallery. 498-509, PUTN
Sixteenth-Century Mexican Imprints. Location Table of Mexican Sixteenth-Century Books. 249-268, EAME

Wagner, R. L.
Les Valeurs de L'Italique. Notes de Lecture sur Lucien Leurven de Stendhal. 381-390, BONN

Wahl, Gustav.
Statistisches über Bibliotheksaustellungen. 141-145, BOLL

Wahl, Hans.
Die Weimarische Bibliothek als Erbin der Herzogin Anna Amalia. 158-167, WEIM

WAHLE, JULIUS
WAHL

WALAHFRID STRABO. Mss.
Bischoff, Bernhard. Eine Sammelhandschrift Walahfrid Strabos (Cod. Sangall. 878). 30-48, LEYH

Walde, O.
Henrik Rantzaus Bibliotek och Dess Öden 239-250, ANNE
Om Georg Stiernhielms Bibliotek. Några Anteckningar. 107-141, GRAP
En Svensk Boksamlare från Vasatiden. Hogenskild Bielke och Hans Bibliotek. 193-267, UPPS

Waldén, Bertil.
Verner von Heidenstam Som Målare. 71-106, ÖREB

WALDMANN, HANS. Mss. - Collections - Zürich
Forrer, L., ed. Die Sog. Waldmannschen Spruchbriefe. [61]-[112], ESCK

Waldmann, Hans.
Spruchbriefe in: Forrer, L., ed. Die Sog. Waldmannschen Spruchbriefe. [61]-[112], ESCK

Walford, A. J.
Documentation Services and Library Co-operation in the Social Sciences. 256-260, KYLE

Walker, J. M.
The Branches—Some Recollections. 21-23, LAMB

Wall, Alexander J.
Books on Architecture Printed in America, 1775-1830. 299-311, EAME
Ephemeral Library Material, Its Preservation, Care and Value. 423-430, LYDE

Wallach, Luitpold.
The Unknown Author of the Libri Carolini: Patristic Exegesis, Mozarabic Antiphons, and the Vetus Latina. 469-515, ALBA

WALLIS
see Valais

WALL-PAPER, Newspapers on
see Newspapers on wall-paper

Wallraf, Karlheinz.
Zur Besprechungsarbeit mit Praktikanten. 113-123, LANF

Walter, Frank Keller.
Notes on the Beginning of a Mid-West University Library. 510-519, PUTN
A Poor but Respectable Relation—The Sunday School Library. 731-739, WILS

Walter, Kurt.
Zur Gegenwärtigen Lage des Auswärtigen Leihverkehrs der Wissenschaftlichen Bibliotheken. 143-157, JUCR

WALTER MUIR WHITEHILL: A RECORD. PUBLICATIONS. 17-74, WHIT

WALTERS ART GALLERY, Baltimore. Mss. (no. 28)
Strittmatter, Anselm. The Pentecost Exultet of Reims and Besançon. 384-400, GREE

Walther, Carl and Karl Fill.
Die Deutsche Gesamtausgabe der Dezimalklassifikation. 167-168, DONK

Walther, Hans.
Kleine Mittellateinische Dichtungen aus Zwei Erfurter Handschriften. 296-315, DEGE

Walton, Clarence E.
HARV

Walton, Mary.
J. P. Lamb and the Archives. 17-18, LAMB

Wand, Albert.
Zur Geschichte der Dortmunder Bibliotheken. 29-58, VERD

WANDSBEK, Ger. - Printing
see Printing - Wandsbek, Ger.

WANG AN-SHI. [Poem]
Meier, Franz Joseph. Ein Bibliophiles Gedicht von Wang An-Shi (1019-86). 121-123, GRAT

Wangermée, R.
Les Œuvres de Charles van den Borren. 19-53, BORR

Waples, Douglas.
On Developing Taste in Reading. 740-747, WILS

WAPOWSKI, BERNARD
Olszewicz, Bolesław. Wzmianki o Mapach Bernarda Wapowskiego w Listach z r. 1529. 371-376, PIEK

WAR AND THE LIBRARY
Hoffmann, Wilhelm. Einige Gedanken zum Wiederaufbau Kriegsgeschädigter Bibliotheken. 39-41, STUM

WAR AND THE LIBRARY - Berlin
Kunze, Horst. Demokratisierung und Sozialistische Umgestaltung. I, 49-76, BERS
Schmidt, Werner. Die Verlagerung der Bestände im Zweiten Weltkrieg und Ihre Rückführung. I, 77-86, BERS

WAR AND THE LIBRARY - Berlin - 1914-1918
Paalzow, Hans. Die Kriegsbücherei. 285, HARN

WAR AND THE LIBRARY - Dresden

Assmann, Karl. Die Sächsische Landesbibliothek von 1945 bis 1955. Zerstörung, Wiederaufbau und Gegenwärtiger Stand der Arbeit. 29-85, DREL

WAR AND THE LIBRARY - Hamburg

Sierks, Ruth. Hilfe des Auslandes. 115-127, HAMB

WAR AND THE LIBRARY - Holland

Sevensma, Tietse Pieter. Eine Bibliothekarische Kriegserfahrung. 591-596, BICK

WAR AND THE LIBRARY - Italy

Apollonj, Ettore. Problemi Estetici nella Ricostruzione di Biblioteche Sinistrate dalla Guerra. 79-85, GALL
Fischer, Anton. Ersatzmöglichkeiten für Verlorene und Nicht Mehr Restaurable Einbände. 441-453, GALL

WAR AND THE LIBRARY - Jena

Burr, Viktor. Aus dem Ersten Jahr nach der Zerstörung der Universitätsbibliothek Jena (1945/46). 63-81, BULL

WAR AND THE LIBRARY - Norway

Andreassen, Anders. Fragmenter av Min Svenske Dagbok. 23-31, HEIN

WAR AND THE LIBRARY - Sheffield, Eng.

Simpson, E. The War Years. 19-20, LAMB

WAR RECORDS - Collections - Berlin

Schultze, Walter. Die Kriegssammlung. 77-89, HARN

WAR RECORDS - Collections - Stuttgart

Rohwer, Jürgen. Die Bibliothek für Zeitgeschichte und Ihre Aufgabe in der Historischen Forschung. 112-138, HOFF

WAR RECORDS - (1870-71 War) - Collections - Berlin

Hirsch. Paul. Die "Kriegssammlung" der Königlichen Bibliothek zu Berlin. 97-106, WILM

Ward, John.
The Lute Music of MS Royal Appendix 58. 117-125, KINK

Warda, Arthur.
Die Exlibris des Herzogs Albrecht von Preussen. 349-354, KÖNI

<u>WARHAFFTE VND ERSCHROECKLICHE NEWE ZEITTUNG.</u> 1582

Scholderer, Victor. Hans Ringer zu Wimbschpach. 417-420, BENZ

WARMBRUNN, Silesia. Schaffgott'sche Majoratsbibliothek

Nentwig, Heinrich. Zwei Schlesische Majoratsbibliotheken. 129-138, WILM

WARSAW. Biblioteka Narodowa
see Warsaw. National Library

WARSAW - Libraries - Administration
see Libraries - Administration - Warsaw

WARSAW. National Library

Skwarnicki, Marek. Zarys Rozwoju Koncepcji i Organizacji Biblioteki Narodowej w Warszawie (1918-1954). 89-130, GRYC

Warschauer, A.
Über Einige Seltene Gelegenheitsdrucke aus der Provinz Posen. 67-74, VERP

Wasberg, Gunnar Christie, ed.
NORS

Washburn, Donald, jt. author

Lage, Louise C., Lois B. Miller, and Donald Washburn. Dental, Nursing, and Pharmaceutical Libraries, 1947-1957. 371-377, DOEJ

WASHINGTON, D.C. - Cataloging - Recataloging
see Cataloging - Recataloging - Washington, D.C.

WASHINGTON, D.C. - Catalogs - Printed book
see Catalogs - Printed book - Washington, D.C.

WASHINGTON, D.C. - Chinese literature - Collections
see Chinese literature - Collections - Washington, D.C.

WASHINGTON, D.C. - Classification - Reclassification
see Classification - Reclassification - Washington, D.C.

WASHINGTON, D.C. - Documents - Collections
see Documents - Collections - Washington, D.C.

WASHINGTON, D.C. - Folklore - Collections
see Folklore - Collections - Washington, D.C.

WASHINGTON, D.C. - Microfilms - Collections
see Microfilms - Collections - Washing ton, D.C.

WASHINGTON, D.C. - Music libraries and collections
see Music libraries and collections - Washington, D.C.

WASHINGTON, D.C. - U.S. - Biography - Collections
see U.S. - Biography - Collections - Washington, D.C.

WASSENBERGISCHE STADTBIBLIOTHEK, Constance von
see Constance. Von Wassenbergische Stadtbibliothek

Watanabe, Shigeo.
Post-war Children's Literature in Japan. 151-158, HASH

WATERMARKS
see also Paper

WATERMARKS

La Rue, Jan. Classification of Watermarks for Musicological Purposes. 59-63, FEDO

Waters, Edward N.
The Wa-Wan Press: An Adventure in Musical Idealism. 214-233, ENGE

WATER-SOAKED BOOKS
see Books - Care and restoration

WAXEN TABLETS
see Tablets (Paleography)

Weber, Christoph.
Der Gesamtkatalog der Preussischen Wissenschaftlichen Bibliotheken. 259-272, HARN

Weber, Hans-Oskar.
Die Beanspruchung der Staats- und Universitätsbibliothek Göttingen durch den Deutschen Leihverkehr. 161-168, JUCR
Bibliographisch Selbständig / Bibliographisch Unselbständig. Ein Diskussionsbeitrag. 143-151, FUCH

Weber, Ulrich.
Vier Unveröffentlichte Briefe Wilhelm Brambachs an Carl Dziatzko aus dem Besitz der Universitätsbibliothek Göttingen oder: Scherz- und Schimpf-spiel zwischen Gelehrten. 171-178, JUCR

WECHTLIN, JOHANN

Oldenbourg, M. Consuelo. Die Holzschnitte des Vrs Graf zur Passion und die des Johann Wechtlin zum Leben Jesu. Ein Bibliographisches Verzeichnis Ihrer Verwendungen. 291-310, BENZ

Weckerle, Ferdinand.
Kulturgeschichtliches im Spiegel einer Alten Erlanger Liedersammlung. 85-93, VERZ

Weeks, Elizabeth Harriet and Frances Lander Spain. Anne Carroll Moore—<u>A Contribution Toward a Bibliography</u>. 629-636, MOOR

Weelderen, C. P. A. A. Buyen van.
Statistische Gegevens van de Bibliotheek der Rijksuniversiteit te Utrecht over 1914-1939. 55-59, EVER

Wegelin, Oscar.
Mills Day's Proposed Hebrew Bible. 221-226, EAME

WEGENER, CASPAR FREDERICK - Library

Grundtvig, Vilh. Almindelig Historie. 11-51, AARU

Wegener, Hans.
Die Deutschen Volkshandschriften des Späten Mittelalters. 316-324, DEGE
Das Gebetbuch der Johanna von Bocholt. 228-232, BÖME
Eine Hamburger Großgärtnerei des 18. Jahrhunderts und Ihr Katalog. 177-181, TIEM

Wegner, Jan.
Wspomnienie o Pracy Naukowej Kazimierza Piekarskiego w Łowickim (1942-1944). 33-37, PIEK

Wehmer, Carl.
Eine Äußerung Jacob Willes über die Vorbildung der Bibliothekare aus dem Jahre 1921. 21-31, REDE
Mit Gemäl und Schrift. Kaiser Maximilian I. und der Buchdruck. 244-275, HOFF
Zur Echtheitskritik der Metallschnittplatten Schreiber 2746a und Schreiber 2865. 143-157, BOCK

WEHMER, CARL

WEHM

Weiher, Anton.
Von Platen, Stifter und Fontane. 153-159, HELD

Weil, Gotthold.
Goethes Brief an H. F. von Diez vom 15. November 1815. 182-186, KUHN
Die Orientalische Abteilung. 180-186, HARN

Weil, Henri.
Horatiana. 57-58, CHAT
D'un Signe Critique dans le Meilleur Manuscrit de Démosthène. 13-20, GRAU

WEIMAR - Architecture and building - State libraries
see Architecture and building - State libraries - Weimar

WEIMAR - Catalogs - Union
see Catalogs - Union - Weimar

WEIMAR - Gifts, contributions, etc.
see Gifts, contributions, etc. - Weimar

WEIMAR. Grossherzogliche Bibliothek
see Weimar. Landesbibliothek

WEIMAR. Landesbibliothek

WEIM

Paszkowski, Wilhelm. Goethes Verhältnis zum Bibliothekswesen. 159-172, WILM

WEIMAR. Landesbibliothek. Mss.

Hecker, Max, ed. Ein "Weimarischer Kunstfreund" in der Gemäldesammlung der Brüder Boisserée. Zwei Briefe Heinrich Meyers an die Erbgrossherzogin Maria Paulowna. 185-200, WEIM

WEIMAR. Landesbibliothek. Mss. (Q 59)

Schenk zu Schweinsberg, Eberhard, Frhr. Margarete von Rodemachern, eine Deutsche Bücherfreundin in Lothringen. 117-152, WEIM

WEIMAR. Landesbibliothek. Musikaliensammlung

Münnich, Richard. Aus der Musikaliensammlung der Weimarer Landesbibliothek, Besonders dem Nachlass der Anna Amalia. 168-184, WEIM

WEIMAR - Librarians
see Librarians - Weimar

WEIMAR - Library and the state
see Library and the state - Weimar

WEIMAR - Music libraries and collections
see Music libraries and collections - Weimar

WEIMAR - Special collections
see Special collections - Weimar

Weinacht, Paul.
Johann Christoph Döll als Vorstand der Karlsruher Hofbibliothek 1843-1872. II, 150-157, GLAU

Weinburger, Wilhelm.
Handschriften von Vivarium. 75-88, EHRD

Weinhold, Liesbeth.
Musiktitel und Datierung. 136-140, FEDO

Weise-Standfest, Hilde, jt. ed.
BERR

Weise-Standfest, Hilde.
Musikbibliothek und Diskothek, Kunstblätter-Sammlung, Musik- und Literaturveranstaltungen. 36-41, BERR

Weiss, Roberto.
Humphrey Duke of Gloucester and Tito Livio Frulovisi. 218-227, SAXL

WEISSENAU (Benedictine abbey)

Haeckel, Ilse. Schrettinger und die Säkularisation des Klosters Weißenohe. 117-120, REDE

WEISSENOHE
see Weissenau (Benedictine abbey)

Weitenkampf, Frank.
Influences and Trends in Nineteenth-Century Illustration. 345-350, LYDE

Weitzmann, Kurt.
The Constantinopolitan Lectionary, Morgan 639. 358-373, GREE

WELLINGTON, N.Z. - National libraries
see National libraries - Wellington, N.Z.

WELLINGTON, N.Z. - Turnbull Library
see Alexander Turnbull Library, Wellington, N.Z.

Wellisch, H.
New Publication Methods for the UDC, a Proposal. 145-148, DONK

Wells, A. J.
Our Debt to India. 57-63, MADR

Wendel, Carl.
Aus der Vorgeschichte des Laurentianus XXXII.9. 16-22, KUHN
Die Griechischen Handschriften der Provinz Sachsen. 354-378, MILF

Wendling, Willi
MANN

Wendt, Bernhard.
Antiquariatskataloge als Bibliographische Hilfsmittel für Reformationsdrucke. 476-491, BENZ

Wenig, Otto, ed.
BURR

Wenzel, B.
Die Abteilung Bücherkunde im Realkatalog der Kaiser-Wilhelm-Bibliothek. 19-42, VERP

Werhahn, Heinz Martin.
Die Bücher des Dr. Peter Rinck. 181-188, JUCR

WERLAUFF, ERICH C.
Nissen, Kristian. Den Werlauffske Gave. En Innholdsrik Kartbunke i Universitetsbibliotekets Kartsamling. 150-167, OSLN

WERLAUFF, ERICH C. Historiske Efterretninger om det Store Kongelige Bibliotek. 1844. Supplement
Madsen, Victor. Pergamenttryk i det Kongelige Bibliotek i København. Et Supplement. 199-214, COLL

Wermke, Ernst.
Friedrich August Gotthold und Seine Bibliothek. 354-373, KÖNI

Wermter, Ernst Manfred.
Die Raumverteilung im Gebäude der Stadtbibliothek seit 1912. 31-34, MAIN
Studien und Quellen zur Geschichte der Jesuitenbibliotheken in Mainz 1561-1773. 51-70, MAIN

Werner, Heinz.
Rückschau und Ausblick. 5-21, BERR

Werner, Mulertt.
La Fecha del Manuscrito Escurialense del "Paso Honroso." II, 242-245, ARTI

Wernigg, Ferdinand.
Quellen zur Wiener Biographie. Versuch einer Praktischen Anleitung. 125-153, VIES

Wernly, Julia.
Bibliographie der Schweizerischen Landeskunde. 149-150, BERU

Weser, Adolf, jt. ed.
BERR

Weser, Adolf.
Bibliographie zur Geschichte des Deutschen Volksbüchereiwesens, mit einem Anhang: Die Entwicklung des Berliner Volksbüchereiwesens. 49-80, BERL
Erschliessung der Bestände durch Kataloge und Bibliographien. 22-27, BERR

Wesseling, J. C. G.
La CDU et les Sciences Sociales. 157-159, DONK

Wessely, Charles.
Un Nouveau Fragment de la Version Grecque du Vieux Testament par Aquila. 224-229, CHAT

WESSENBERG, IGNAZ HEINRICH KARL, Freiherr von - Library
Reinhard, Ewald. I. H. von Wessenberg als Freund der Schönen Künste. 59-63, VERD

WESTERN RESERVE UNIVERSITY
Focke, Helen M. Education in Documentation at Western Reserve University: Yesterday, Today, and (Tomorrow?). 49-57, HASH

WESTPHALIA - Copyists
see Copyists - Westphalia

WESTPHALIA, Johannes of
see Johann von Paderborn

WESTPHALIA, Konrad of
see Konrad von Paderborn

WESTPHALIA - Monastic libraries
see Monastic libraries - Westphalia

WESTPHALIA. Staatsarchiv
Molitor, Karl. Ein Westfälischer Bibliotheks-Katalog von 1353. 301-314, MÜNS

WESTPHALIA. Staatsarchiv. Mss. (I, 261)
Ohly, Kurt. Das Inkunabelverzeichnis Bernhards von Mallinckrodt. (Handschrift des Staatsarchivs Münster I 261). 37-62, BÖME

WESTREENEN VAN TIELLANDT, WILLEM HENDRIK JACOB, Baron van - Library
Vermeeren, P. J. H. W. H. J. Baron van Westreenen van Tiellandt als Handschriftenverzamelaar. 603-609, BRUM

Wharton, Leonard C.
Brief Notes of Prague Printed Books in the British Museum. 42-45, EMLE
My Relations with Mr. Živný. Mé Styky s Živným. [In both English and Polish.] 23-25, ŽIVN

White, Carl M.
The Research Library in Contemporary Society: A Problem of the Proper Recognition of Services Rendered. 43-54, PENN

WHITEHILL, WALTER MUIR
WHIT

WHITEHILL, WALTER MUIR - Bibl.
Walter Muir Whitehill: A Record. Publications. 17-74, WHIT

Whitrow, Magda.
Some Aspects of Descriptive Cataloguing in International Bibliography. 291-295, KYLE

WIBALD, Abbot of Stavelot and Corvey
Boeckler, Albert. Corveyer Buchmalerei unter Einwirkung Wibalds von Stablo. 133-147, BÖME

Widmann, Hans.
Early History of European Periodicals. 515-522, RANG
Johann Jakob Moser und die Bibliotheken. Zugleich ein Beitrag zur Geschichte des Verhältnisses zwischen Zentralbibliothek und Institutsbibliotheken. 125-146, LEYH
Zu Reuchlins Rudimenta Hebraica. 492-498, BENZ
Die Zugänglichkeit der Universitätsbibliothek Tübingen (bis zur Mitte des 19. Jahrhunderts). 215-229, JUCH

WIDMANN, J. V. - Collections - Bern
Refardt, Edgar. Die Musiktexte J. V. Widmanns. 134-139, REFA

Widnäs, Maria.
Jacob Grot och Universitetets Ryska Bibliotek. 144-163, DAHL

Wieder, Joachim, jt. ed.
HOFM

Wieder, Joachim.
Bickham's "Musical Entertainer" in der Englischen Buchkunst des 18. Jahrhunderts. 147-158, JUCH

WIELAND, CHRISTOPH MARTIN - Library
Deetjen, Werner. Wielands Bibliothek. 1-10, WAHL

Wieland, Franz.
Früheste Vorläufer der Vaticana. 159-168, LEYG

Wiernik, Peter.
Abraham Solomon Freidus (1867-1923). XXIII-XXX, FREI

WIESBADEN. Königliche Landesbibliothek
see Wiesbaden. Nassauische Landesbibliothek

WIESBADEN. Nassauische Landesbibliothek
WIES

WIESBADEN. Öffentliche Bibliothek
see Wiesbaden. Nassauische Landesbibliothek

WIESBADEN. Regierungsbibliothek
see Wiesbaden. Nassauische Landesbibliothek

Wiese, Berthold.
Zu einer Kritischen Ausgabe des "Ninfale Fiesolano" Boccaccios. 347-361, HORT

Wieselgren, O.
Några Anteckningar om Våra Dagars Folklitteratur. 251-265, ANNE
Två i Kungl. Biblioteket Befintliga Miniatyrhandskrifter ur den Gent-Brüggeska Skolan. 91-101, COLL

WIESELGREN, PETER
Gierow, Krister. Biblioteksmannen Peter Wieselgren. 127-155, OLSS

Wiesener, A. M.
Bergenske Boksamlere. 254-286, MUNT

Wieser, Hans.
Ein Tiroler Lederschnittband. 662-665, BICK

Wieser, M.
Buchwerbung durch den Rundfunk. 133-144, ACKE

Wieslander, Henning, ed.
ÖREB

Wieslander, Henning.
Hundra Års Bibliotekskrönika från Örebro. 7-48, ÖREB
Svensk Oplandsarbejde. 117-122, LASS

Wiig, Hanna.
Barnearbeide i Norske Byer og Ladesteder. 66-72, NORN

Wijk, Louise E. van.
Het Album Amicorum van Bernardus Paludanus (Berend ten Broeke). 97-118, HAGU

Wijnstroom, Margreet.
Het Uitleenrecht en de Openbare Bibliotheken. 626-639, BRUM

Wilbur, James Benjamin.
The Photostat. 520-527, PUTN

Wild, Helen.
Hermann Escher und der Zwingli-Verein; mit Liste der Historischen Publikationen Hermann Eschers. 1-5, ESCZ
Hermann Escher und die Schweizerischen Volksbibliotheken. 22-34, ESCK
Volksbücherei und Volksbücherei-Nachwuchs in der Schweiz. 145-155, ACKE
Volksbüchereiplanung in Gross-Zürich. 67-79, ACKR

Wilhelm, Adolf.
Inscriptiones Graecae I^2 945. 666-672, BICK

Wilkens, Erik.
Büchereien oder Büchereiwesen in einer Landschaft? 81-93, ACKR

Wilkins, Ernest H.
The Separate Fifteenth-Century Editions of the Triumphs of Petrarch. 748-751, WILS

Will, Edmund.
Zur Geschichte der Braunsberger Bibliotheken bis zum Beginn des Neunzehnten Jahrhunderts. 374-388, KÖNI

Will, Erich.
Die Wiegendrucke des Gratianischen Dekretes und Ihr Bestand in der Universitätsbibliothek Freiburg i.Br. 191-217, JUCR

Wille, Hans.
Dürer-Erinnerungen in Josef Führichs Illustrationen zu "Der Wilde Jäger" von G. A. Bürger. 60-74, BRIE

WILLEMS, JAN FRANS - Correspondence - Collections - Berlin

Vreese, Willem de. Briefwisseling van Jan Frans Willem en Jakob Grimm. 264-295, DEGE

Willers, Uno.
Dag Hammarskjöld Som Bibliofil. Föredrag vid Invigningen av Dag Hammarskjöld Memorial Library den 17 November 1961. 249-256, HEIN

WILLES, JACOB

Wehmer, Carl. Eine Äußerung Jacob Willes über die Vorbildung der Bibliothekare aus dem Jahre 1921. 21-31, REDE

Willi, Liselotte.
Die Musikabteilung. 156-165, DREL

Willi, Liselotte, jt. author

Deckert, Helmut, Marita Kremer, Hans Pfeifer, and Liselotte Willi. Das Neue Buchmuseum der Sächsischen Landesbibliothek. 175-205, DREL

Williams, Richmond D.
The Longwood Achievement. 46-53, DAVI

WILMANNS, AUGUST

WILM

Leyh, Georg. August Wilmanns und Emil Jacobs. 125-136, STOL

Wilmerding, Lucius.
Le Prince, by Jean Louis Guez de Balzac: Note on a Paris Printing, 1631. 489-497, LYDE

WILSON, H. W., firm, publishers

Raney, M. Llewellyn. 1909 and After. 651-658, WILS

Wilson, Leslie.
Barbara Kyle. 227-228, KYLE

Wilson, Louis Round.
Library Conditions and Objectives in the South. 528-538, PUTN
Optima in Library Service for the South by 1950. 186-204, BISH
What Type Research Librarian? 112-122, PENN

WILSON, LOUIS ROUND

WILS

Keppel, Frederick P. Louis Round Wilson, 583-584, WILS
Randall, William M. Louis R. Wilson and the Graduate Library School. 645-650, WILS
Rush, Charles E. Another Pioneer Is Honored in His Own Country. 675-678, WILS
Strohm, Adam. Louis Round Wilson. 685, WILS

WILSON, LOUIS ROUND - Bibl.

Thornton, Mary Lindsay. Bibliography of Louis Round Wilson. 339-352, WILS

WIMPHELING, JAKOB

Nelson, Axel. Zum Wimpfeling-Codex der Universitätsbibliothek zu Uppsala. 27-37, LEYG

WINCHESTER COLLEGE, Winchester, Eng. Library - Hist.

Blakiston, J. M. G. Winchester College Library in the Eighteenth and Early Nineteenth Centuries. 23-45, OLDH

WINCKELMANN, JOHANN JOACHIM

Bollert, Martin. Johann Joachim Winckelmann als Bibliothekar des Grafen Bünau. 19-24, LEID
——— Joh. Joach. Winckelmann und Joh. Mich. Francke. I, 11-17, GLAU

Wind, Edgar.
The Revival of Origen. 412-424, GREE

WINDING, JENS CHRISTIAN, printer

Sollied, P. R. Relationer fra Christiania, Bergen og Trondhjem om Smaae Piecers Censur. 91-105, OSLN

Winkler, Emil.
Die Textliche Stellung der Handschrift 2597 der Wiener Nationalbibliothek (René von Anjou, Livre du Cuer d'Amours Espris). 861-870, VIEN

Winship, George Parker.
The Eliot Indian Tracts. 179-192, EAME
Lydenberg in Cambridge and New York. 269-272, LYDE

Winter, Arno.
Die Neugründung und Entwicklung der Gesellschaft in den Jahren 1948 bis 1958. 10-15, DEUD

Winterfeld, Luise von.
Vier Leibrentenquittungen von 1456-1478 aus dem Dortmunder Stadtarchiv. 27-28, VERD

Wirth, Georg.
Die Druckerei der Bamberger Fürstbischöfe—die Erste "Staatsdruckerei." 383-389, STOL

Wischnitzer-Bernstein, Rahel.
Der Siddur der Altstädtischen Synagoge in Rzeszów. 77-80, FREN

WISCONSIN. University. Library
Lamb, Eliza. The Expansive Classification in Use. 265-269, HANS

WISCONSIN. University. Library - Hist.
Hanson, James Christian Meinrich. Organization and Reorganization of Libraries. 519-532, WILS

WISE, THOMAS J.
Juchhoff, Rudolf. Die Literarische Fälschung des Thomas J. Wise. 41-48, BRIE

Wisłocka, Stanisława.
Pedagogiczna Biblioteka Wojewódzka w Krakowie. Rys Historyczny. 7-13, KRAK
Szkolenie Zawodowe. 83-88, KRAK

Wiśniowski, Jerzy, ed.
BYDG

Wissler, Gustav.
Die Kataloge. 133-139, BERU
Marcel Godet als Direktor der Schweizerischen Landesbibliothek. 8-12, GODM
Die Musikalien. 87-94, BERU
Pubblicazioni in Lingua Italiana. 59-64, BERU
Der Sachkatalog. 139-143, BERU
Das Systematische Verzeichnis. 148-149, BERU

Wistrand, Pär.
Mina Bibliotek. 539-547, HJEL

WITELO, supposed author, Liber de Intelligentiis
Baeumker, Clemens. Zur Frage nach Abfassungszeit und Verfasser des Irrtümlich Witelo Zugeschriebenen Liber de Intelligentiis. 87-102, EHRA

Withington, Mary C., ed.
KEOG

WITTENBERG - Printing
see Printing - Wittenberg

WITTENBERG - Publishers and publishing
see Publishers and publishing - Wittenberg

WITTENBERG. Universität. Bibliothek - Hist.
Gerhard, Karl. Die Ungarische Nationalbibliothek der Universität Halle-Wittenberg. 139-158, WILM

Witty, Francis J.
Four Music Books at Washington from the Pontificate of Benedict XIII. 517-[533], ALBA

WITZ, JEAN
see Sapidus, Jean

DAS WÖCHENTLICHE VERZEICHNIS
see Frankfurt a.M. Deutsche Bibliothek. Deutsche Bibliographie; Wöchentliches Verzeichnis

Woita, Irene.
Abteilung Allgemeinbildende Bibliotheken. 48-51, BERR

Woledge, G.
Richard Offor. 63-65, OFFO

WOLF, HIERONYMUS, 1516-1580
Husner, Fritz. Die Editio Princeps des "Corpus Historiae Byzantinae." Johannes Oporin, Hieronymus Wolf und die Fugger. 143-162, SCHU

Wolf, Johannes.
Ein Brief Pietro Arons an Giovanni dal Lago. 65-70, KUHN
Zwei Tagelieder des 14. Jahrhunderts. 325-327, DEGE

WOLF, JOHANNES
WOLJ

WOLF, JOHANNES - Bibl.
Bibliographie der Gedruckten Arbeiten von Johannes Wolf. 1-5, WOLJ

WOLFENBÜTTEL. Bibliotheca Augusta
see Wolfenbüttel. Herzog-August-Bibliothek

WOLFENBÜTTEL. Herzog-August-Bibliothek

Busch, Friedrich. Alltagssorgen, die Immer Zeitgemäss Bleiben (aus Friedrich Adolf Eberts Freundeskreis). 136-139, LEUN
Collijn, Isak Gustaf Alfred. Zwei Widmungsexemplare eines Werkes des Valentinus Erythræus. 111-116, LEYG

WOLFENBÜTTEL. Herzog-August-Bibliothek. Mss. (Codex Carolinus)

Dold, Alban. Die Provenienz der Altlateinischen Römerbrieftexte in den Gotisch-Lateinischen Fragmenten des Codex Carolinus von Wolfenbüttel. 13-29, LEYH

Wolff, Hans J.
Grundsätze des Bibliotheksverwaltungsrechts. 279-286, WEHM

Wolff, Herbert
GÜST

Wolffheim, Werner, jt. ed.
WOLJ

WOLFRAM, GEORG

WOLF

WOLFRAM, GEORG - Bibl.

Bibliographie der Werke Georg Wolframs. IX-XVI, WOLF

WOLFRAM VON ESCHENBACH, 12th cent. Mss. Titurel

Kroker, Ernst. Bruchstücke einer Handschrift des Jüngeren Titurel in der Leipziger Stadtbibliothek. 42-48, LEIP

WOLGAST. Sankt Petrikirche. Bibliothek

Deutsch, Josef. Ebers Calendarium Historicum mit Handschriftlichen Eintragungen aus Wolgast. 71-78, KUHN

Wolk, L. J. van der.
De Reprografie en het Vermenigvuldigen van een Geschreven Tekst. 250-256, KOSS

Wonisch, Othmar.
Leonhard Höfler und Seine Stiftung zum Blutigen Kreuz in Leibnitz. 343-363, SCHT

WOOD-CUTS
see Wood-engravings

WOOD-ENGRAVINGS - Collections - Breslau

Molsdorf, Wilhelm. Zwei Unbekannte Holzschnitte des Formschneiders Casper in der Breslauer Staats- und Universitäts-Bibliothek. 249-254, MILF

WOOD-ENGRAVINGS - Collections - Erlangen

Zimmermann, Hildegard. Hans Sebald Beham und Sein Werkanteil an der Holzschnittsammlung der Erlanger Universitätsbibliothek. 105-114, VERZ

WOOD-ENGRAVINGS - 16th cent.

Geissler, Paul. Zwei Unbekannte Holzschnittprobedrucke zum Theuerdank und Konrad Peutinger. 118-128, JUCH

WOOD-PULP

Bishop, William Warner. One Problem for 1950—Woodpulp Paper in Books. 407-415, LYDE

Wormald, Francis.
The Sherborne "Chartulary." 101-119, SAXL

Wormann, C.
The Jewish National and University Library in Jerusalem Since the Establishment of the State of Israel. 116-117, MADR

Woude, S. van der, ed.
VERW

Woude, S. van der.
Uit de Prille Jeugd van de Nederlandse Stads-Universiteitsbibliotheken. 618-625, BRUM

Wouters, H. H. E.
"Een Bibliotheque voor den Meesten Luyster van de Stadt." 9-28, MAAS

WREDE, FERDINAND

WRED

WREDE, RABBE GOTTLIEB

Kannila, Helle. Två Pionjärer för Folkbiblioteksidén i Finland. 137-147, HEIN

Wright, A. Shaw.
The Series, "Readers' Guides." 73-79, MADR

Wright, Wyllis E.
Subject Headings in the Reference Department of The New York Public Library. 431-436, LYDE

WRITERS
see Authors

WRITERS' ASSOCIATION, Netherlands
see Vereeniging van Letterkundigen

WRITING - Hist.
see also Paleography

WRITING - Hist.

Cipolla, C. La Tachygraphie Ligurienne au XIe Siècle. 87-96, HAVE
Kinkeldey, Otto. Palm Leaf Books. 88-115, BISH
Löffler, Karl. Zur Geschichte der Abendländischen Schreibformen. Eine Würdigung des Gleichbetitelten Buches von Hermann Delitsch. 61-66, SCHR
Procksch, Otto. Der Hebräische Schreiber und Sein Buch. 1-15, KUHN

WRITING (in religion, folklore, etc.)

Augapfel, Julius. Das ب وّ im Qurân. 384-393, KARA

WRITING - Norway - Hist.

Omang, Reidar. Overgangen fra Gotisk til Latinsk Skrift. 239-254, OSLO

WRITING TABLETS
see Tablets (Paleography)

Wroth, Lawrence C.
The Cambridge Press. 498-524, LYDE
The First Work with American Types. 129-142, EAME
The Pierpont Morgan Library and the Historian. 10-22, GREE

WROTH, LAWRENCE C.

WROT

Adams, Marion W. and Jeannette D. Black. A List of Published Writings of Lawrence C. Wroth to December 31, 1950. 485-504, WROT
Lewis, Wilmarth S. Introduction. xix-xxi, WROT
Wagner, Henry R. Hispanic Americana in the John Carter Brown Library. 423-455, WROT

WU-LIANG-SHOU-TSUNG YAO-CHING (Si-hia version)

Nishida, Tatsuo. Tenri Toshokan Zō Seikabun Muryojushu Yokyo ni tsuite. (The Hsi-hsia Version of Wu-liang-shou-tsung yao-ching in the Tenri Central Library.) 357-366, TOMI

WU-YING-TIEN EDITIONS (Japanese transl.)

Kaneko, Kazumasa. Kintei Bueiden Shuchin-ban Teishiki. (Japanese Translation of: Ching-tin Wu-ying-tien chü-ch'en-pan Ch'eng-shih: "Brief Explanation of the Printing Process by Movable Types in the Wu-ying-tien Editions.") 409-434, TOMI

WÜRTTEMBERG - Associations
see Associations - Württemberg

WÜRTTEMBERGISCHE BIBLIOTHEKS-GESELLSCHAFT, Stuttgart

Maier, Walter. Anfänge, Werden und Wirken der Württembergischen Bibliotheksgesellschaft. 276-288, HOFF

WÜRTTEMBERGISCHE LANDESBIBLIOTHEK, Stuttgart
see Stuttgart. Landesbibliothek

WÜRZBURG. Universität. Bibliothek

Handwerker, Otto. Bibliothekare und Universitäten, mit Belegen aus der Geschichte der Würzburger Universitätsbibliothek. 85-94, LEID

WÜRZBURG. Universität. Bibliothek - Hist. - 1859

Pauer, Max. Anton Ruland und Karl Halm. Ein Bibliothekarischer Streit um Dublettenverkäufe vor Hundert Jahren. 121-135, REDE

Wulf, Ursel.
Die Jugendbüchereien der Hamburger Öffentlichen Bücherhallen. 63-67, HAMB

WULFILA, Bp. of the Goths. Mss.

Dold, Alban. Die Provenienz der Altlateinischen Römerbrieftexte in den Gotisch-Lateinischen Fragmenten des Codex Carolinus von Wolfenbüttel. 13-29, LEYH

WUPPERTAL - Public libraries
see Public libraries - Wuppertal

WUPPERTAL. Stadtbibliothek

ELBE

Springmann, Wolfgang. W. van der Briele und die Geschichtliche Entwicklung der Wuppertaler Bibliotheken. 7-40, BRIE

WUPPERTAL. Stadtbücherei
see Wuppertal. Stadtbibliothek

Wustmann, Felix.
Drei Unbekannte Briefe Alexander v. Humboldts in der Universitätsbibliothek Leipzig. 265-269, BULL

Wyllie, John Cook.
The First Maryland Tract: A Reconsideration of the Date of Printing of the Maryland Charter. 475-483, WROT

WYMPFELING, JACOB
see Wimpheling, Jacob

Wyss, W. von.
Erinnerungen an Alte Zeiten auf der Stadtbibliothek Zürich. 1-7, ESCK

XENOPHON. Mss. Hiero
Schenkl, Charles. De Codicibus Quibus in Xenophontis Hierone Recensendo Utimur. 111-120, GRAU

YALE - Gifts, contributions, etc.
see Gifts, contributions, etc. - Yale

YALE UNIVERSITY. Bibliographical Press - Bibl.
Rollins, Carl P. The Bibliographical Press at Yale University. 247-261, WROT

YALE UNIVERSITY. Library
KEOG

YALE UNIVERSITY. Library
Keogh, Andrew. Benjamin Silliman's Trip to Europe in 1805. 416-422, LYDE
——— Bishop Berkeley's Gift of Books to Yale in 1733. 128-147, MUNT
——— The Yale Library of 1742. 76-87, BISH

YALE UNIVERSITY. Library. Mss.
Nemoy, Leon. Notes on Some Arabic Manuscripts on Curious Subjects in the Yale University Library. 45-66, KEOG

YALE UNIVERSITY. Library. Mss. (Stiles)
Bridgwater, Dorothy Wildes. President Stiles's Letter to Ebeling. 307-316, KEOG

YALE UNIVERSITY. Library. Mss. (Trumbull)
Sills, R. Malcolm and Eleanor Stuart Upton. The "Trumbull Manuscript Collections" and Early Connecticut Libraries. 325-342, KEOG

Yamada, Tamaki.
Furansu Kokuritsu Toshokan ni tsuite. (On the National Library of France.) 23-31, HAKO

Yarmolinsky, Avrahm.
A Seventeenth-Century Russian Manuscript in the New York Public Library. 323-334, LYDE

Yayoshi, Mitsunaga.
Kokusho Mokuroku ni okeru Bunrui Shisō no Hattatsu. (Progress of the Idea of Classification in the Catalogues of Japanese Books.) 66-83, OTAT

YORK, Eng. St. Mary's (Benedictine monastery) Mss.
Goldschmidt, E. P. An Obituary Rotulus from York, 1405. 379-383, GREE

Yoshiike, Hiroshi.
Shuppansha e no Chumon. (Book Publishing in Japan.) 227-229, KYOT

YOUNG ADULTS' LIBRARY SERVICES
see also Public libraries - Services to schools; School libraries

YOUNG ADULTS' LIBRARY SERVICES
Hunt, Hannah. Young Adults and Libraries: Crisis or Challenge? 59-69, HASH

YOUNG ADULTS' LIBRARY SERVICES - Berlin
Meyer, Hanna. Die Kinder- und Jugendbuchabteilung. I, 433-441, BERS

YOUNG ADULTS' LIBRARY SERVICES - Germany
Jahrmann, Werner. Bücherei und Schule. Gedanken zur Jugendbüchereiarbeit. 215-231, SCHS

YOUNG ADULTS' LIBRARY SERVICES - Hamburg
Wulf, Ursel. Die Jugendbüchereien der Hamburger Öffentlichen Bücherhallen. 63-67, HAMB

YOUNG ADULTS' LIBRARY SERVICES - Jena
Schuhmann, Ursula. Aus der Arbeit der Kinder- und Jugendbibliothek Jena. 135-139, JENA

YOUNG ADULTS' LITERATURE
see also Children's literature

YOUNG ADULTS' LITERATURE - Germany (Democratic Republic, 1949-)
Kunze, Horst. Books for Children and Youth. 523-527, RANG

Yuda, Yoshio, Hajime Uetani, and Minoru Imanishi.
Tenri Toshokan Zō Jōruri Hangi Mokuroku. (Catalogue of the Wood-Blocks of Jōruri Texts in the Tenri Central Library.) 259-294, TOMI

YUGOSLAVIA - Incunabula - Collections
see Incunabula - Collections - Yugoslavia

YUGOSLAVIA - Printing
see Printing - Yugoslavia

ZKA
see Zentralkatalog der Ausländischen Literatur

Z KRONIKI ŻAŁOBNEJ. 123-124, KRAK

Zachariassen, Aksel.
Bibliotekene og Opplysningsorganisasjonene. 161-167, NORS

Zachrisson, Bror.
Probleme des Studiums der Lesbarkeit von Gedrucktem Text. 158-164, BOCK

Zafren, Herbert C.
Elias Hutter's Hebrew Bible. 29-39, BLOC

ZAINER, GÜNTHER
Dold, Alban. Ein Unbekanntes Spezimen einer "Günther-Zainer"-Bibel. 105-110, LEYG
Geldner, Ferdinand. Der Verkaufspreis des Günther Zainer'schen Catholicon von 1469 (GW 3183). 37-42, STOL

ZAŁUSKI FAMILY (Warsaw) - Library
Mikulski, Tadeusz. Kniaźnin w Bibliotece Załuskich. 267-281, PIEK

Zambaur, Eduard von.
Die Orientalischen Münzen der Sammlung Will in der Universitätsbibliothek Erlangen. 94-104, VERZ

Zamkov, Nikolaĭ K.
"Uleĭ," Zhurnal V. G. Anastasevicha (1811-1812 g.g.); Bibliograficheskoe Opisanie. 39-57, MALE

ZAMOJSKI, JAN
Horodyski, Bogdan. Zarys Dziejów Biblioteki Ord. Zamojskiej. 295-341, PIEK

ZANAZZO, GIGGI - Collections - Rome (City)
Gnoli, Tomaso. Giggi Zanazzo e le Sue Opere Edite ed Inedite alla Biblioteca Angelica. 183-191, GREG

Zastrau, H. O.
Gedanken zur Sachkatalogisierung. Über die Normung und Bildung von Schlagwörtern. 54-69, COET

Zaunick, Rudolph.
Erinnerungen und Glückwunsch. 84-87, BOLE

Zedler, Gottfried.
Über die Preise und Auflagenhöhe Unserer Ältesten Drucke. 267-288, SCHW

Zehntner, Hans.
Die Handschriftlichen Nachlässe von Schweizer Komponisten in der Universitätsbibliothek Basel. 297-315, SCHU
Musikerbriefe in der Universitätsbibliothek Basel. 140-149, FEDO

Zeidler, Jakob.
Ein Censurexemplar von Grillparzer's: "König Ottokar's Glück und Ende." 287-311, GLOS

ZEISS (CARL) JENA, VEB. Betriebsbücherei
Meinhardt, Walter. Betriebsbücherei des VEB Carl Zeiss, Jena. 128-134, JENA

ZEISSBERG, HEINRICH VON
Doublier, Othmar. Ein Vierteljahrhundert aus der Geschichte der Hofbibliothek 1891-1916. 163-210, VIEN

Zeitler, Julius.
Moderne Frakturschriften. 69-76, LOUB

ZEITSCHRIFTENVERZEICHNISSE
see Frankfurt a.M. Deutsche Bibliothek. Zeitschriftenverzeichnisse

Zelenka, Ignác.
Edizioni Liturgiche della Pečerskaja Lavra di Kiev nella Biblioteca Vaticana. II, 377-414, ALBB

ZELL, HEINRICH
Kuhnert, Ernst. Heinrich Zell. 137-147, SCHW

Zeller, Bernhard, jt. ed.
HOFF

Zeller, Bernhard.
Fünf Jahre Deutsches Literaturarchiv in Marbach. Ergebnisse, Erfahrungen, Planungen. 349-384, HOFF

Zeltner, Hermann.
Philosophie als Bibliographischer Begriff. 177-194, REDE

ZĒNĀ MĀRQOS. Mss. - Collections - Rome (City)
Cerulli, Enrico. Gli Atti di Zēnā Mārqos, Monaco Etiope del Sec. XIV. I, 191-212, ALBB

ZENKOKU KEIZAI CHOSA KIKAN RENGOKAI
see National Federation of Economic Research Organizations, Japan

ZENTRALBIBLIOTHEK, Zürich
see Zürich. Zentralbibliothek

ZENTRALKATALOG DER AUSLÄNDISCHEN LITERATUR
Iwand, Käthe. Der Zentralkatalog der Ausländischen Literatur. 369-376, JUCH

ZENTRALKATALOG DER WISSENSCHAFTLICHEN BIBLIOTHEKEN DES LANDES NORDRHEIN-WESTFALEN. Cologne
see Cologne. Zentralkatalog der Wissenschaftlichen Bibliotheken des Landes Nordrhein-Westfalen

Zeretelli, G.
Zwei Unedierte Griechische Schultafeln. 113-117, CHAT

Ziegler, Benno.
Zur Geschichte des Privilegium Exclusivum des Mainzer Musikstechers Bernhard Schott. 293-305, LEID

Ziegler, Hans.
Pommersche Stammbücher. 19-30, ZIEG

ZIEGLER, HANS
ZIEG
Stock, Hildegard. Dank und Erinnerung. 15-18, ZIEG
Zunker, Ernst. Das Leben und Wirken Hans Zieglers. 7-11, ZIEG

ZIEGLER, HANS - Bibl.
Zunker, Ernst. Das Leben und Wirken Hans Zieglers. 7-11, ZIEG

ZIERICKZEE, CORNELIUS VAN
see Cornelius van Zierickzee

Ziesemer, Walther.
Zur Kenntnis des Bibliothekswesens Preussens im 15. Jahrhundert. 393-400, KÖNI

Zifreund, Viktor, ed.
LANF

Zifreund, Viktor.
Wege und Ziele der Sudetendeutschen Volksbüchereiarbeit. 157-166, ACKE

Zimmel, Bruno, jt. ed.
STUM

Zimmel, Bruno.
DDr. Josef Stummvoll, Generaldirektor der Österreichischen Nationalbibliothek. 5-8, STUM

Zimmermann, Erich.
Hinrich Murmester und die Älteste Hamburger Stadtbibliothek (1479/81). 40-49, TIEM

Zimmermann, Hildegard.
Hans Sebald Beham und Sein Werkanteil an der Holzschnittsammlung der Erlanger Universitätsbibliothek. 105-114, VERZ
Luther-Bibeln des 16. Jahrhunderts in der Universitätsbibliothek zu Münster i.W. 153-159, BÖME

ZIMOROWICZ, BARTŁOMEJ
Badecki, Karol. Bartłomieja Zimorowicza "Żywot Kozaków Lisowskich." 351-364, PIEK

Zingarelli, N.
La Processione nell'Eden Dantesco. 363-369, HORT

Zirkle, Conway.
Patterns of Research and Changing Library Needs from the Viewpoint of the Natural Sciences. 12-18, PENN

Živný, Ladislav Jan.
Bibliografie prací L. J. Živného. 224-233, ŽIVN
Znaky Literárních a Grafických Dokumentů a Jejich Funkce v Soupisné Praxi. 152-157, EMLE

ŽIVNÝ, LADISLAV JAN
ŽIVN

ŽIVNÝ, LADISLAV JAN - Bibl.
Živný, Ladislav Jan. Bibliografie prací L. J. Živného. 224-233, ŽIVN

Žmavc, Ivan.
O Vůdčích Funkcích Vědeckého Knihovnictví v Soustavě Národní Vzdělanosti. 157-158, EMLE

ZOLL, JOHANNES.
Kyriss, Ernst. Johannes Zoll, ein Tübinger Buchbinder des 15. Jahrhunderts. 84-93, LEYH

ZÜRICH - Authors and libraries
see Authors and libraries - Zürich

ZÜRICH (Canton) Staatsarchiv
Forrer, L., ed. Die Sog. Waldmannschen Spruchbriefe. [61]-[112], ESCK
Muralt, Leonhard von. Jörg Berger. 98-126, ESCZ

ZÜRICH - Catalogs
see Catalogs - Zürich

ZÜRICH - Catalogs - Subject
see Catalogs - Subject - Zürich

ZÜRICH. Centralbibliothek
see Zürich. Zentralbibliothek

ZÜRICH - Literary museums
see Literary museums - Zürich

ZÜRICH - Müller, Jörg - Mss. Correspondence - Collections
see Müller, Jörg - Mss. Correspondence - Collections - Zürich

ZÜRICH - Music libraries and collections
see Music libraries and collections - Zürich

ZÜRICH. Pestalozzianum

Escher, Hermann. Das Neue Pestalozzihaus in Zürich (1933). 138-142, ESCH

ZÜRICH. Pestalozzianum. Bibliothek

Wild, Helen. Hermann Escher und die Schweizerischen Volksbibliotheken. 22-34, ESCK

ZÜRICH - Public libraries
see Public libraries - Zürich

ZÜRICH. Stadtbibliothek

Escher, Hermann. Der Schlagwortkatalog der Stadtbibliothek Zürich (1890-1897). 59-70, ESCH
Hirzel, B. Conrad Ferdinand Meyer und die Zürcher Stadtbibliothek. [45]-60, ESCK

ZÜRICH. Stadtbibliothek - Hist.

Berchem, V. van. Hermann Escher Historien. 35-43, ESCK
Wyss, W. von. Erinnerungen an Alte Zeiten auf der Stadtbibliothek Zürich. 1-7, ESCK

ZÜRICH. Stadtbibliothek. Mss. (Codex C. 43)

Cagin, Paul. L'Observation Paléographique dans L'Étude du "Sacramentarium Triplex" de Saint-Gall. 92-112, CHAT

ZÜRICH. Zentralbibliothek

Escher, Hermann. Moderne Bibliotheksbestrebungen und Bibliotheksaufgaben mit Besonderer Rücksicht auf die Geplante Zürcherische Zentralbibliothek (1912). 71-85, ESCH
Schenk, Erich. Die Österreichische Musiküberlieferung der Züricher Zentralbibliothek. 576-581, BICK

ZÜRICH. Zentralbibliothek - Hist.

Berchem, V. van. Hermann Escher Historien. 35-43, ESCK
Escher, Hermann. Die Errichtung der Zentralbibliothek in Zürich (1915). 86-104, ESCH

ZÜRICH. Zentralbibliothek. Mss. (Jörg Müller)

Corrodi-Sulzer, A. Neues aus dem Leben des Bürgermeisters Jörg Müller. 212-238, ESCZ

ZÜRICH. Zentralbibliothek. Zwingli-Museum

Wild, Helen. Hermann Escher und der Zwingli-Verein; mit Liste der Historischen Publikationen Hermann Eschers. 1-5, ESCZ

Zuman, František.
První Českobratrský Bělský Tisk. 212-218, ŽIVN

"ZUM FÄRBEFASS," Druckerei, Erfurt
see Druckerei "Zum Färbefass," Erfurt

Zunker, Ernst, ed.
ZIEG

Zunker, Ernst.
Die Bedeutung Regionaler Zentralkataloge für das Erfassungsgebiet. 151-164, HOFF
Der Greifswalder "Medizinische Lesezirkel" vom Jahre 1802. Ein Randkapitel der Greifswalder Bibliotheksgeschichte. 415-431, VORS
Das Leben und Wirken Hans Zieglers. 7-11, ZIEG

Zuuren, P. van.
Donker Duyvis and the NIVE. 51-64, DONR

Zweig, Arnold.
Pforten der Zukunft. 7-9, JENA

ZWEIG, STEFAN - Library

Ecker, Karl. Die Sammlung Stefan Zweig. 321-330, BICK

ZWIAZEK BIBLIOTEKARZY POLSKICH

Grycz, Józef. Po Czwartym Zjeździe Bibliotekarzy Polskich w Warszawie 30. Maja—2. Czerwca 1936 r. 24-28, EMLE

Zwier, Jac.
Toezicht en Inspectie Openbare Bibliotheken. 640-644, BRUM

ZWINGLI-MUSEUM, Zürich
see Zürich. Zentralbibliothek. Zwingli-Museum

ZYGMUNT II AUGUST, King of Poland - Library

Lisowski, Stanisław. Do Dziejów Biblioteki Zygmunta Augusta. 241-249, PIEK

ZYRICKSEN, CORNELIUS VON, printer

Juchhoff, Rudolf. Verwertung einer Restauflage um 1500. 478-481, BRUM

ŻYWIEC, Poland - Education libraries see Education libraries - Żywiec, Poland

ŻYWIEC, Poland. Pedagogical Library

Dyczkowska, Ludwika. Współpraca Pedagogicznej Biblioteki Powiatowyej w Żywcu z Ośrodkami Metodycznymi. 99-103, KRAK